Colt Model 1911 Semi-Automatic Pistol

Adopted by the U.S. Ordnance Department in 1911, the Colt semi-automatic pistol was originally manufactured by Colt and the government's Springfield Armory. In 1917, with the US entry into World War I, the government contracted with Colt for one million pistols and contracts were signed for the production of a total of two million more pistols with Remington-UMC, North American Arms, Savage, Winchester, National Cash Register Co., Burroughs Adding Machine, Lamston Monotype, and Caron Bros. A total of 629,000 pistols were completed by the war's end in 1918. Production was resumed in 1924 with a series of design modifications introduced during the inter-war period resulting in the Model 1911 A1. From the onset of World War II until its end in 1945 Colt, Remington UMC, Remington-Rand, Ithaca, Singer, and Union Switch and Signal Company manufactured nearly 2 million M1911A1s.

NRA Perfect Condition is 100 percent original condition. This Colt 1911 has all original parts and commands the same price with or without the box. The frame and receiver are in perfect condition with no wear or damage. The checkering on the grip is in "as new" condition and the wood shows no wear, scratches, or stains.

NRA Good Condition ranges from 60 to 80 percent original condition. There are no replacement parts. This 1911 has worn, rounded edges on the frame with slight pitting and scratches. The bluing is thinning on the working surfaces and stampings show minor wear in areas. The checkering on the grips is slightly rounded with minor nicks. The wood is in good condition, not cracked or stained. A good condition pistol must be in safe working condition.

NRA Fair Condition ranges from 20 to 60 percent original condition. This Model 1911 is in well-worn condition with the frame retaining only 40 percent of its original finish. Some major and minor parts have been replaced and scratches and pitting from rust and corrosion are evident on the frame and slide. Serial numbers and other markings are shallow and difficult to identify. While the grips on this pistol are not badly scratched or soiled, they show worn checkering and several large and small dents. The gun must function and shoot properly.

Winchester Model 94

Winchester produced approximately 2,550,000 Model 94 lever action rifles between 1894 and 1962. The Model 94 was manufactured in both rifle and carbine versions with several configurations that included pistol- and straight-grip stocks, various grades of wood, and several different barrel lengths and magazine capacities. Crescent and shotgun style buttstocks and takedown barrels were also offered. The Model 94 was produced in 25-35, 30, 30-30, 32-40 and 38-55 calibers.

NRA Perfect Condition ranges from 95 to 100 percent original condition. This Model 94 shows very little use and looks in new condition with 96 percent of its original finish remaining. All parts are original and in excellent condition. There is no noticeable wear with the wood and metal showing no stains, scratches or nicks. The bluing is in near-perfect condition. The action functions smoothly and the rifle is in perfect working condition.

NRA Good Condition ranges from 60 to 80 percent original condition. There are no replacement parts. The gun has all original parts and shows no corrosive rusting or pitting. The edges of the action are slightly rounded and the bluing is beginning to wear thin on the working surfaces. The stampings show minor wear in areas. There are no broken parts and the stock fits smoothly to the metal with only minor nicking. The gun must be in safe working condition.

NRA Fair Condition ranges from 20 to 60 percent original condition. This Model 94 is in well-worn condition with some minor parts replaced or requiring restoration or adjustment. The serial numbers and descriptive stampings are shallow and hard to read. The wood is badly scratched and dented with evident repairs. There is corrosive pitting and scratches but the gun remains in safe firing condition.

Winchester Model 12

When introduced in 1912, the hammerless Model 12 slide-action shotgun was offered only in 20-guage with a 2½-inch chamber. In 1914 12- and 16-guage versions were introduced followed by a 28-guage in 1937. The Model 12 was available with various chokes and with walnut, straight or pistol grip stock and forearm. Winchester sold more than 1,900,000 Model 1912s during the shotgun's 51-year history.

NRA Perfect Condition is 100 percent original condition. This Model 12 is in NIB condition and has not been previously sold at retail. The shotgun shows no signs of use and retains 100 percent of its original finish. All parts are original and in new condition.

NRA Good Condition ranges from 60 to 80 percent original condition. This gun has all original parts in good condition. There is no corrosive pitting or rusting and the action displays only slightly rounded edges. The gun retains 70 percent of its original finish with bluing beginning to wear on the working surfaces. The stock fits smoothly to the metal and has only minor nicking. The shotgun must be in good working order.

NRA Fair Condition ranges from 20 to 60 percent original condition. Showing a well-worn condition, this gun may require minor parts to be replaced or adjusted. The serial numbers and descriptive stamping are shallow and difficult to read. The wood is badly scratched and dented with evident repairs. Corrosive pitting and scratches in the metal, while considerable, do not render the gun unsafe.

Twenty-Seventh Edition
Completely Revised And Updated

Gun Trader's Guide

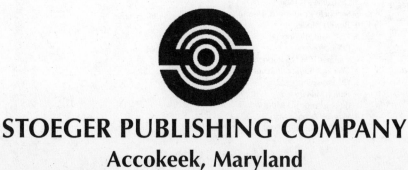

STOEGER PUBLISHING COMPANY
Accokeek, Maryland

Stoeger Publishing®
Great Outdoor Books & More Since 1924

STOEGER PUBLISHING COMPANY
is a division of Benelli U.S.A.

Benelli U.S.A.
Vice President and General Manager: Stephen Otway
Vice President of Marketing and Communications:
  Stephen McKelvain

Stoeger Publishing Company
President: Jeffrey K. Reh
Publisher: Jay Langston
Managing Editor: Harris J. Andrews
Design and Production Director: Cynthia T. Richardson
Photography Director: Alex Bowers
Imaging Specialist: William Graves
National Sales Manager: Jennifer Thomas
Special Accounts Manager: Julie Brownlee
Editorial Assistant: Christine Lawton
Administrative Assistant: Shannon McWilliams
Editor / Gun Trader's Guide: Stephen D. Carpenteri

ISBN:0-88317-287-9   BK0402
Library of Congress Control number: 2003116081

Manufactured in the United States of America

*Distributed to the book trade and
to the sporting goods trade by:*
Stoeger Industries, Stoeger Publishing Company
17603 Indian Head Highway, Suite 200
Accokeek, Maryland 20607-2501

OTHER PUBLICATIONS:

Shooter's Bible
  The World's Standard Firearms
  Reference Book
Gun Trader's Guide
  Complete Fully Illustrated
  Guide to Modern Firearms with
  Current Market Values

Hunting & Shooting
Advanced Black Powder Hunting
Archer's Bible
Complete Book of Whitetail Hunting
Elk Hunter's Bible
Great Shooters of the World
Hunt Club Management Guide
Hunting America's Wild Turkey
Hunting and Shooting with the Modern Bow
Hunting Whitetails East & West
Shotgunning for Deer
Trailing the Hunter's Moon
The Turkey Hunter's Tool Kit: Shooting Savvy
Taxidermy Guide
Tennessee Whitetails
The Ultimate in Rifle Accuracy
Cowboy Action Shooting

Collecting Books
Sporting Collectibles
The Working Folding Knife
The Lore of Spices

Firearms
Antique Guns
P-38 Automatic Pistol
Complete Guide to Compact Handguns
Complete Guide to Service Handguns
America's Great Gunmakers
Firearms Disassembly with Exploded Views
Rifle Guide
Gunsmithing at Home
The Book of the Twenty-Two
Complete Guide to Modern Rifles
Complete Guide to Classic Rifles
FN Browning Armorer to the World
Heckler & Koch: Armorers of the Free World
How to Buy & Sell Used Guns
Legendary Sporting Rifles
Modern Beretta Firearms
Spanish Handguns
The Walther Handgun Story

Reloading
Complete Reloading Guide
The Handloader's Manual of
  Cartridge Conversions
Modern Sporting Rifle Cartridges

Fishing
Bassing Bible
Flyfishing for Trout - A to Z
Fishing Online: 1,000 Best Web Sites
Fishing Made Easy
Ultimate Bass Boats
The Flytier's Companion
Deceiving Trout
Peter Dean's Guide to Fly-Tying
The Flytier's Manual
Flytier's Master Class
Handbook of Fly Tying
The Fly Fisherman's
  Entomological Pattern Book
Fiberglass Rod Making
To Rise a Trout

Motorcycles & Trucks
The Legend of Harley-Davidson
The Legend of the Indian
Best of Harley-Davidson
Classic Bikes
Great Trucks
4X4 Vehicles

Cooking game
Fish & Shellfish Care & Cookery
Game Cookbook
Dress 'Em Out
Wild About Venison
Wild About Game Birds
Wild About Waterfowl
Wild About Freshwater Fish
Wild About Seafood
World's Best Catfish Bookbook

Front Cover: The twenty-seventh edition's cover features a table-full of commercial and military firearms honoring an American tradition — the gun show.

1. Beretta Model 92 Compact
2. Walther Model PP DA
   Automatic Pistol Commercial
   Model (Post-War)
3. Colt 1917 Army DA Revolver
4. Stoeger Standard Luger
5. Winchester Model 70
   Featherweight (Pre 1964)
6. Winchester Model 61
   Hammerless Slide-action
   Repeater
7. Colt Government
   Model 1911(Springfield)
8. Navy Arms Model 1875
   Deluxe Wells Fargo
   Schofield Revolver (A. Uberti)
9. Beretta Model 92F
10. Colt Banker's Special
    DA Revolver
11. Walther TPH DA Pocket Pistol
12. Colt Frontier Scout Revolver
13. FN Browning 1922
    Police/Military
    (w/Nazi proofs 1940-44)
14. Webley & Scott Mark 1,
    No. 2 Automatic Pistol

Introduction

Welcome to the 27th edition of Stoeger's Gun Trader's Guide. This 2004 issue provides the gun enthusiast, collectors and dealers with more specifications and photographs of collectible firearms than ever before. In the past 50 years, the Gun Trader's Guide has grown tremendously, and now lists more than 6,000 firearms and variations.

The first edition of the Gun Trader's Guide contained some 1,360 listings accompanied by 100 illustrations. Now, after 26 revisions, the book as evolved into a comprehensive catalog of the modern rifles, shotguns and handguns dating back to the 1800s.

The current edition of the Gun Trader's Guide has been expanded to include more listings than ever before, with nearly 2,750 illustrations. Hundreds of thousands of gun buffs have made the Gun Trader's Guide their primary reference for identification and comparison of sporting, military and law enforcement firearms, including rare and unusual collectibles and commemoratives.

NEW, SIMPLIFIED STRUCTURE

Production data for each firearm includes:
- *Specifications*
- *Variations of different models*
- *Dates of manufacture*
- *Current values*
- *Tabbed sections for user-friendly reference*
- *A complete index of all firearms included in the text*

The format of the Gun Trader's Guide is simple and straightforward, listing thousands of firearms manufactured since the late 1800s in the United States and abroad. Most entries include complete specifications including model number and name, caliber/gauge, barrel length, overall length, weight, distinguishing features, model variations and the dates of manufacture (when they can be accurately determined). Illustrative photos accompany the text to help the reader with identifications and comparisons.

The Gun Trader's Guide is revised annually to ensure that its wealth of information is both current and detailed. The principal features that contribute to the unique nature of this comprehensive firearms reference guide include the extensive pictorial format and accompanying detailed specifications lists. It provides a convenient procedure for identifying vintage firearms while simultaneously determining and verifying their current values.

Values shown are based on national averages obtained by conferring with gun dealers, collectors and auctioneers around the country, not by applying an arbitrary mathematical formula that could produce unrealistic figures. The values listed herein accurately reflect the prices being negotiated nationwide at the time of publication.

In some rare cases, however, such as with the Winchester Model 1873 " One of One Thousand" rifle or the Parker AA1 Special shotgun in 28 gauge, where very little (if any) trading took place, knowledgeable, active gun collectors were consulted to obtain current market values.

ORGANIZATION OF LISTINGS

In earlier editions of the Gun Trader's Guide, firearms were frequently organized chronologically by date of production with manufacturers' listings. This is because firearms experts know that many gun companies used the date that a particular model was introduced as the model number. For example, the Colt U. S. Model 1911 semi-automatic pistol was introduced in 1911; the French Model 1936 military rifle was introduced in 1936; and the Remington Model 32 shotgun debuted in 1932. However, during the first quarter of the 20th century, gun makers began assigning model names and numbers that did not relate to the year that the gun was introduced. As these recent models and their variations multiplied through the years, it because increasingly difficult to track them by date, especially for the less-experienced collectors.

Some Winchester and Remington firearms are grouped differently in this edition. For example, the Winchester model 1894, in its many variations, has been produced since 1894 and is still being manufactured as the "Model 94" by the U. S. Repeating Arms Co. (now owned by Browning). In general, Winchester used the year of introduction to name its firearms, i.e., Model 1890, 1892, 1894, 1895, etc. Shortly after World War I, Winchester dropped the first two digits and listed the modes as 90, 92, 94, 95, etc. Later, guns were given model numbers that had no relation to the date of manufacture. Marlin and several other manufacturers used a similar approach in handling model designations.

Consequently, Winchester rifles are grouped alphanumerically in two different groups: Early Winchesters, manufactured before 1920 under the four-digit model/date designations; and guns manufactured after 1920 with their revised model format designations. If any difficulty is encountered in locating a particular model, the different models and their variations are cross-referenced in the index.

Past readers had reported difficulty in finding certain Remington rifles. In this edition, Remington rifles have been grouped according to action type, that is, single-shot rifles, slide actions, autoloaders, etc. Our surveys revealed this to be the easiest way to locate a particular firearm. Again, use the index if difficulty in finding a specific model is encountered.

In researching data for this edition, we found that not all manufacturers' records were available and some information was unattainable. For example, many early firearms production records were destroyed in a fire that ravaged the Winchester plant. Some manufacturers' records have simply been lost, or were not maintained accurately. These circumstances resulted in some minor deviations in the presentation format of certain model listings. For example, production dates may not be listed when manufacturing records are unavailable. As an alternative, approximate dates of manufacture may be listed to reflect the "availability" of guns from the manufacturer or distributor. These figures may represent disposition dates indicating when that particular model was shipped to a distributor or importer. Frequently, especially with foreign manufacturers, production records are unavailable. Therefore, availability information is often based on importation records that reflect domestic distribution only.

This information is included simply to advise the reader of the procedure and policy used regarding these published dates and further establish the distinction between "production dates," which are based on manufacturers' records, and "availability dates," which are based on distribution records in the absence of reliable production data.

To further ensure that we have the most accurate information available, we encourage and solicit the users of the Gun Trader's Guide to communicate with our research staff at the Stoeger offices and forward any verifiable information they may have, especially in relation to older, out-of-production models.

CAUTION TO READERS

To comply with Federal regulations, all gun manufacturers who produce or import firearms intended for disposition to the general public and designed to accept large capacity ammunition feeding devices are required to redesign those models to limit their capacities to 10 rounds or less or discontinue production or importation of that model. This amendment to the Gun Control Act of 1968 prohibits the manufacture, transfer or possession of all such devices manufactured after Oct. 13, 1994. The grandfather clause of this amendment exempts all such devices lawfully possessed at the time the legislation became law. These pre-ban arms (manufactured before Oct. 13, 1994) may therefore be bought, sold or trade without any additional restrictions imposed by this law.

All post-ban feeding devices must meet the new requirements. For the purposes of this book, models previously designed to accept high capacity feeding devices will be listed at their original specifications if only the feeding device was modified to reduce that capacity.

Regarding shotguns, the reader should be aware that shotgun barrels must be 18 inches or longer except when used by military or law enforcement personnel. A special permit from the Bureau of Alcohol, Tobacco and Firearms is required to possess all others.

ACKNOWLEDGEMENTS

The publisher wishes to express special thanks to the many collectors, dealers manufacturers, shooting editors and other industry professionals who provided product information and willingly shared their knowledge in making this the best Gun Trader's Guide ever.

Also, our appreciation is extended to the firearms manufacturers' and distributors' public relations, production and research personnel who we work with throughout the year. We are especially grateful to everyone for their assistance and cooperation in compiling information for the Gun Trader's Guide and for allowing us to reproduce photographs and illustrations of their products.

Finally, our thanks to all the dedicated readers who take the time to write us with comments, suggestions and queries about various collectible firearms. We appreciate your input and encourage you to continue.

Send your comments or suggestions to:

Editor,
Gun Trader's Guide,
Stoeger Publishing Co.,
17603 Indian Head Hwy,
Suite 200,
Accokeek, MD 20607-2501

Great Outdoor Books Since 1925

How To Use This Guide

Are you buying or selling a used gun? Perhaps you want to establish the value of a favorite gun in your collection. Most gun enthusiasts inevitably turn to the Gun Trader's Guide to determine specifications, date of manufacture and the value of a specific collectible firearm. Opening the book, he silently asks two questions: "How much will I be able to get (or expect to pay) for this gun?" and, "How was that price determined?"

Prices contained in this book are retail, meaning the price the consumer may expect to pay for a gun in similar condition. However, many variables must be considered when buying or selling any used gun. Scarcity, demand, geographical location, the buyer's position and the gun's condition are all factors in determining the selling price of a particular gun. Sentiment affects the value on an individual's gun, but can be neither logically catalogued nor, in most cases, effectively marketed (unless you are in possession of a gun owned by Jack O'Connor, Ernest Hemingway or the like).

To illustrate how the price of a particular gun may fluctuate, let us consider the popular Winchester Model 94 and see what its value might be.

The Model 1894 (called a Model 94 in most circles) is a lever-action, solid-frame repeater. Round or octagon barrels of 26 inches were standard when the rifle was first introduced in 1894. However, half-octagon barrels were available for a slight increase in price. Various magazine lengths were also produced.

Fancy-grade versions in all Model 94 calibers were available with 26-inch round, octagon or half-octagon nickel steel barrels. This grade used a checkered, fancy walnut pistol grip stock and forearm and were available with either shotgun or rifle-type butt plates.

In addition, Winchester produced this model in a carbine-style configuration with a saddle ring on the left side of the receiver. The carbine had a 20-inch round barrel and full or half magazine. Some carbines were supplied with standard grade barrels while others were made of nickel steel. Trapper models were also available with shortened 14-, 16- and 18-inch barrels.

In later years, the Rifle and Trapper models were discontinued and only the carbine remained. Eventually, the saddle ring was eliminated from this model and the carbine butt stock was replaced with a shotgun-type butt stock and shortened forend.

After World War II, the finish on Winchester Model 94 carbines changed to strictly hot caustic bluing, thus, pre-war models usually demand a premium price over post-war models.

Then, in 1964, beginning with serial number 2,700,000, the action on the Winchester Model 94 was redesigned for easier manufacturing. Many collectors and enthusiasts considered this design change to be inferior to former designs and the value for later models reflects this. Whether this evaluation was correct or not is not the issue because a stronger justification for a price increase for pre-1964 models was that there were no longer available. This diminished availability placed them immediately in the "scarce" class and made them increasingly desirable to collectors.

Shortly after the 1964 transition, Winchester began producing Model 94 commemoratives in a variety of configurations, further adding to the confusion with the concept of "limited production." Increased availability adversely affected the annual appreciation and price stability of these commemorative models, and the negative response generated by this marketing practice was further stimulated when the Winchester Company was sold in the 1980s and the long-established name of this firearms manufacturer was changed to U. S. Repeating Arms Company. This firm still manufactured the Model 94 in both standard Carbine and Big Bore models, and later introduced its Angle-Eject models, which allowed for the mounting of telescopic sights direction over, instead of in front of, the action.

With the above facts in mind, let's explore the Gun Trader's Guide and try to establish the value of your Winchester Model 94. We will assume that you recently inherited a rifle that has the inscription Winchester Model 94 on the barrel. Turn to the Rifle section in the book and look under the Ws until you find the Winchester entries. The Contents section will also indicate where the Winchester Rifle Section begins, and the Index (in the back of the book) is another possible means of locating the listing we are looking for.

The listings in the Gun Trader's Guide are arranged within each manufacturer's entry, first my model number in consecutive numerical order followed by model names in alphabetical order. At first glance, you realize that there are two model designations that may apply to your gun – the original designation (Model 1894) or the revised, shorter designation (Model 94). Which of these applies to your recently acquired Winchester?

The first step is to try to match the appearance of your gun with an illustration in the book. The guns may all look similar at first glance, but close evaluation and careful attention to detail will enable you to eliminate the models that do not apply. Further examination of your gun might reveal a curved or crescent-shaped butt plate, for example. By careful observation of your gun's characteristics and close visual comparison of the photo-

graphic examples shown in the book, you may logically conclude that your gun is the Winchester Model 94 Lever Action Rifle.

You have now tentatively determined your model, but to be sure, you should read through the specifications and further establish that the barrel on the pictured rifle is 26 inches long and round, octagonal or half-octagonal. Upon measuring, you find that your rifle barrel is approximately 26 inches long, per-

---

When the dealer offers you about half of what you expected, you are shocked!

---

haps a trifle under, and it is obviously not round. (Keep in mind that the guns shown in the Gun Trader's Guide are not always shown in proportion to one another. For example, a carbine barrel might not appear to be shorter than a standard rifle barrel.)

Additionally, your rifle is marked .38-55 (it's caliber designation). The caliber offerings in the specifications list include .38-55, so you are further convinced that this is your gun. You may read on to determine that this rifles was manufactured from 1894 to 1937. After that date, only the shorter-barreled carbine was offered by Winchester, and then only in calibers .25-35, .30-30 and .32 Special.

At this point, you know you have a Winchester Model 94 rifle manufactured before World War II. You read the value as $1,596 and decide to take the rifle to a dealer to initiate a sale.

Here are some of the scenarios that you may encounter:

SCENARIO I

If the rifle is truly in excellent condition, that is, if it retains at least 95 percent of its original finish on both the metal and wood and has a perfect bore; the gun does have a full retail value of $1,596. However, remember that the dealer is in business and must make some profit. If he pays you the full value of the gun, he will be forced to charge more than the retail value when he sells it in order to make a reasonable profit. If more than the fair market value is charged, either the gun will not sell or someone will pay more than the gun is worth. Therefore, expect a reputable dealer to offer you less than the published price of the gun. However, the exact amount you receive will vary. For example, if this dealer already has a dozen or so of this item on his shelf and they do not sell well; his offer will probably be considerably under the fair market value. But, if the dealer does not have any of this model in stock and knows several collectors who need it to complete their collections, chances are his offer will be considerably higher.

SCENARIO II

Perhaps you overlooked the true state of the rifle's condition. Suppose the gun apparently functions flawlessly but not much of its original bluing remains. There are several shiny, bare metal spots mixed with a brown patina over the remaining metal. Also, much of the original varnish on the wood has been worn off from extended use. Consequently, your rifle is not truly in "excellent" condition and you must settle for a lesser value for it than is shown in this book.

While any gun's exterior condition is a big factor in determining its value, internal parts also play an important role in pricing. Photograph courtesy of Browning Firearms, 2004

SCENARIO III

Suppose your Winchester Model 94 rifles looks nearly new, as if it were just out of the box, and the action functions perfectly. You are convinced that the dealer is going to pay you full value for the gun (less a reasonable margin of profit that may be as high as 35 percent). When the dealer offers you about half of what you expected, you are shocked!

Although the rifle looks new to you, the experienced dealer detects that the gun has been refinished. Perhaps you did not notice the rounding of the formerly sharp edges on the receiver, or the slight funneling of some of the screw holes, all signs that the rifles has been refinished. A knowledgeable gun dealer will examine the rifle closely to determine that it functions properly. The condition of interior parts may also be a factor in determining the value of a particular firearm.

If your rifle is not truly in Excellent condition as you had originally assumed, it is, therefore, worth much less than "book" value.

Now, if you know for certain that your rifle has never been refinished or otherwise repaired, there is still at least 95 percent of its original finish left and you believe you have a firearm that is worth full book value, understand that a dealer will still offer you anywhere from 25 to 50 percent less than book value, especially if he is overstocked with this model.

One alternative to working with a dealer is to advertise your gun in a local newspaper or arrange a sale directly to a private individual. However, this approach often proves both frustrating and expensive unless you are not in a hurry to sell the gun. In addition, there may be federal and local restrictions on the sale of firearms in your state.

If you experience such complications, chances are the next time you have a firearms to sell you will be more than happy to take it to a dealer, fully aware that he will want to make his fair share of profit.

CONDITION

The condition of a firearm is an important factor in determining its value. In some rare and unusual models, a variation in condition from "Excellent" to "Very Good" can reduce the gun's value by several thousand dollars. Therefore, the collector must be able to determine the gun's conditions before he can accurately estimate the current market value of the firearm.

Several sets of standards of gun value are available, but the National Rifle Association Standards of Condition of Modern Firearms are probably the most common. In recent years, condition has been established by the percentage of original finish remaining on the wood and metal of the firearm. Let's examine how these standards are applied.

EXCELLENT

Keep in mind that a firearm's condition is evaluated based on natural aging of the original, unretouched firearm. When a collectible firearm has been expertly refinished to "Excellent" condition, a rule of thumb is to deduct 50 percent of its value as indicated in this book. If the finishing job was poorly executed, deduct 80 percent.

For the purpose of assigning comparative values as a basis for trading, firearms listed in this book are assumed to be in "Excellent" condition if they have 95 percent or more remaining original finish, no noticeable marring of the bore, wood or metal and no pitting or rust spots.

To the novice, this means a practically new gun, almost as though you had just removed it from the factory carton. The trained eye, however, will easily see the difference between "New" or "Mint" condition and "Excellent."

VERY GOOD

Any defects, no matter how minor, will lower the value of the subject firearms below those listed in this book. For example, if more than 5 percent of the original finish is gone and there are minor surface dents or scratches – regardless of how small – the gun is no longer in "Excellent" condition. Rather, it is now considered to be in "Very Good" condition, provided the gun is in perfect working order with all original parts. In this state, and despite the minor defects, the gun will still look relatively new to the uninitiated gun buyer.

GOOD

If the gun is in perfect working condition and functions properly but has minor wear on working surfaces (perhaps some bad scratches on the wood or metal, etc.) the gun is considered to be in "Good" condition, one grade below "Very Good," according to the NRA standards. Again, the price in this book for that particular firearm must be reduced to reflect its true at-condition value.

The two remaining NRA conditions, "Fair" and "Poor," mean the gun has little or no value to a collector in normal situations. Of course, an exceedingly rare gun in poor condition might be extremely valuable compared to a standard production gun, so never discount a collectible firearm until you have done your homework!

Previous editions of the Gun Trader's Guide gave multiplication factors to use for firearms in other than "Excellent" condition. These factors are listed below, but please

be aware that they are simply a rough means of establishing the value of a gun in other than "Excellent" condition. To find the value of your gun, simply multiply the price listed in this book by the appropriate factor:

Multiplication Factors For Guns Not In Excellent Condition

Condition	X Factor
Mint or New (NiB)	1.25
Excellent (Ex)	1.00
Very Good	.85
Good (Gd)	.68
Fair	.35
Poor	.15

CAUTION!

Remember, the word "guide" in Gun Trader's Guide should be taken literally. This book is meant to be a reference only and is not the gospel of the collectible gun trade. We sincerely hope, however, that you find this publication helpful when you decide to buy or sell a used or collectible firearm.

Also, keep in mind that gun values vary from region to region. For this reason, we recommend that you attend gun shows and actions near you to develop a better understanding of gun values and pricing in your part of the country

NATIONAL RIFLE ASSOCIATION STANDARDS OF CONDITION

- **New:** *Not previously sold at retail. In same condition as current factory production.*

- **New, discontinued:** *Same as New, but a discontinued model.*

- **Perfect:** *In new condition in every respect, sometimes referred to as mint.*

- **Excellent:** *New condition. Used very little, no noticeable marring of wood or metal, bluing perfect (except at muzzle or sharp edges).*

- **Very Good:** *In perfect working condition, no appreciable wear on working surfaces, no corrosion or pitting, only minor surface dents or scratches.*

- **Good:** *In safe working condition, minor wear on working surfaces. No broken parts, no corrosion or pitting that will interfere with proper functioning.*

- **Fair:** *In safe working condition but well worn, perhaps requiring replacement of minor parts or other adjustments that should be reported by the seller. No rust, but may have corrosion pits that do not render the gun unsafe or inoperable.*

- **Poor:** *Badly worn, rusty and battered, perhaps requiring major adjustment or repairs to return to operating condition.*

Contents

Winchester Model 94 Traditional

Winchester Model 12 Standard

Mossberg Model 500 Persuader Law Enforcement

Stoeger Publishing.
Great Outdoor Books Since 1925

Twenty-Seventh Edition
GUN TRADER'S GUIDE

Handguns

NOTE: *The following abbreviations are used throughout the Handgun section: DA = Double Action; SA = Single Action; LR = LR; WMR = Winchester Magnum Rimfire; adj. = Adjustable; avail. = Available; bbl., = Barrel; disc. = Discontinued; TT = Target Trigger; TH = Target Hammer*

Accu-Tek Model AT-.380

Accu-Tek Model BL-9

Accu-Tek HC-380SS

AA ARMS — Monroe, North Carolina

AP-9 SERIES
Semiautomatic recoil-operated pistol w/polymer integral grip/frame design. Fires from a closed bolt. Caliber: 9mm Parabellum. 10- or 20*-shot magazine, 3-, 5- or 11-inch bbl., 11.8 inches overall w/5-inch bbl., Weight: 3.5 lbs. Fixed blade, protected post front sight adjustable for elevation, winged square notched rear. Matte phosphate/blue or nickel finish. Checkered polymer grip/frame. Made 1988 to date.

AP9 model
(pre-94 w/ventilated bbl., shroud . . NiB $438 Ex $335 Gd $216
AP9 Mini model
(post-94 w/o bbl., shroud) . . . . NiB $227 Ex $206 Gd $129
AP9 Target model
(pre-94 w/11-inch bbl.) . . . . NiB $433 Ex $360 Gd $247
Nickel finish, add. $25

ACCU-TEK — Chino, California

MODEL AT-9 AUTO PISTOL
Caliber: 9mm Para. 8-shot magazine, Double action only. 3.2-inch bbl., 6.25 inches overall. Weight: 28 oz. Fixed blade front sight, adj. rear w/3-dot system. Firing pin block with no external safety. Stainless or black over stainless finish. Checkered black nylon grips. Announced 1992, but made1995 to date.
Satin stainless model . . . . NiB $268 Ex $206 Gd $129
Matte black stainless . . . . NiB $238 Ex $190 Gd $130

MODEL AT-25 AUTO PISTOL
Similar to Model AT380 except chambered .25 ACP w/7-shot magazine, Made 1992-96.
Lightweight w/aluminum frame. . . . . NiB $154 Ex $129 Gd $77
Bright stainless (disc. 1991) . . . . NiB $168 Ex $135 Gd $92
Satin stainless model . . . . NiB $162 Ex $130 Gd $89
Matte black stainless . . . . NiB $155 Ex $124 Gd $83

MODEL AT-32 AUTO PISTOL
Similar to Model AT-.380 except chambered .32 ACP. Made 1990 to date.
Lightweight w/aluminum
Frame (disc. 1991). . . . . NiB $129 Ex $103 Gd $70
Satin stainless model . . . . NiB $180 Ex $154 Gd $103
Matte black stainless . . . . NiB $180 Ex $154 Gd $103

MODEL AT-40 DA AUTO PISTOL
Caliber: .40 S&W. Seven-shot magazine, 3.2-inch bbl., 6.25 inches overall. Weight: 28 oz. Fixed blade front sight, adj. rear w/3-dot system. Firing pin block with no external safety. Stainless or black over stainless finish. Checkered black nylon grips. Announced 1992, but made 1995-96.
Satin stainless model . . . . NiB $268 Ex $201 Gd $139
Matte black stainless . . . . NiB $268 Ex $201 Gd $139

MODEL AT-380 AUTO PISTOL
Caliber: .380 ACP. Five-shot magazine, 2.75-inch bbl., 5.6 inches overall. Weight: 20 oz. External hammer w/slide safety. Grooved black composition grips. Alloy or stainless frame w/steel slide. Black, satin aluminum or stainless finish. Made 1992 to date.
Standard alloy frame (disc. 1992) . . . NiB $161 Ex $129 Gd $88
Satin stainless model . . . . NiB $256 Ex $206 Gd $144
Matte black stainless . . . . NiB $256 Ex $206 Gd $144

MODELS BL-9, BL 380 . . . . NiB $180 Ex $144 Gd $98
Ultra compact DAO semiautomatic pistols. Calibers: .380 ACP, 9mm Para. 5-shot magazine, 3-inch bbl., 5.6 inches overall. Weight: 24 oz. Fixed sights. Carbon steel frame and slide w/black finish. Polymer grips. Made 1997 to date.

MODELS CP-9, CP-40, CP-45
Compact, double action only, semiautomatic pistols. Calibers: 9mm Parabellum, .40 S&W, .45 ACP, 8-, 7- or 6-shot magazine, 3.2-inch bbl., 6.25 inches overall. Weight: 28 oz. Fixed blade front sight, adj. rear w/3-dot system. Firing-pin block with no external safety. Stainless or black over stainless finish. Checkered black nylon grips. Made1997 to date.
Black stainless model. . . . . NiB $227 Ex $170 Gd $118
Satin stainless model . . . . NiB $227 Ex $170 Gd $118

MODEL HC-380SS AUTO PISTOL . . . . NiB $257 Ex $206 Gd $154
Caliber: .380 ACP. 13-shot magazine, 2.75-inch bbl., 6 inches overall. Weight: 28 oz. External hammer w/slide safety. Checkered black composition grips. Stainless finish. Made 1993 to date.

ACTION ARMS — Philadelphia, Pennsylvania
See also listings under CZ pistols. Action Arms stopped importing firearms in 1994.

AT-84 DA AUTOMATIC PISTOL . . . NiB $561 Ex $489 Gd $438
Caliber: 9mm Para. 15-shot magazine, 4.75-inch bbl., 8 inches overall. Weight: 35 oz. Fixed front sight, drift-adj. rear. Checkered walnut grips. Blued finish. Made in Switzerland 1987-89.

AT-84P DA AUTO PISTOL . . . . (SRP) NiB $680 Ex $541 Gd $350
Compact version of the Model AT-84. Only a few prototypes were manufactured in 1985. No resale value established.

AT-88P DA AUTO PISTOL . . . . (SRP) NiB $642 Ex $513 Gd $349
Compact version of the AT-88S w/3.7-inch bbl. Only a few prototypes of this model were manufactured in 1985. No resale value established. Note: The AT-88 pistol series was later manufactured by Sphinx-Muller as the AT-2000 series.

AT-88S DA AUTOMATIC PISTOL. . . NiB $566 Ex $463 Gd $304
Calibers: 9mm Para. or .41 Action Express, 10-shot magazine, 4.6-inch bbl., 8.1 inches overall. Weight: 35.3 oz. Fixed blade front sight, adj. rear. Checkered walnut grips. Imported 1989-91.

ADVANTAGE ARMS — St. Paul, Minnesota

MODEL 422 . . . . NiB $175 Ex $134 Gd $82
Hammerless, top-break, 4-bbl., derringer w/rotating firing pin. Calibers: .22 LR and .22 Mag., 4-cartridge capacity, 2.5 inch bbl., 4.5 inches overall. Weight: 15 oz. Fixed sights. Walnut grips. Blued, nickel or PDQ matte black finish. Made 1985-87.

S. A. ALKARTASUNA FABRICA DE ARMAS — Guernica, Spain

"RUBY" AUTOMATIC PISTOL. . . . . NiB $278 Ex $258 Gd $154
Caliber: .32 Automatic (7.65mm). Nine-shot magazine, 3.63-inch bbl., 6.38 inches overall. Weight: About 34 oz. Fixed sights. Blued finish. Checkered wood or hard rubber grips. Made 1917-22. Note: Mfd. by a number of Spanish firms, the Ruby was a secondary standard service pistol of the French Army in World Wars I and II. Specimens made by Alkartasuna bear the "Alkar" trademark.

Action Arms AT-84 with Prototype of Model AT-84P in background

AMERICAN ARMS — Kansas City, Missouri

BISLEY SA REVOLVER . . . . NiB $438 Ex $350 Gd $258
Umberti reproduction of Colt's Bisley. Caliber: .45 LC. Six-shot cylinder, 4.75-, 5.5- or 7.7-inch bbl., Case-hardened steel frame. Fixed blade front sight, grooved top strap rear. Hammer block safety. Imported 1997 to date.

CX-22 DA AUTOMATIC PISTOL
Similar to Model PX-.22 except w/8-shot magazine, 3.33-inch bbl., 6.5 inches overall. Weight: 22 oz. Made 1990 to 1995.
Standard w/chrome
Slide (disc. 1990). . . . . NiB $206 Ex $160 Gd $103
Classic model . . . . NiB $186 Ex $149 Gd $102

EP-380 DA AUTOMATIC PISTOL . . . . NiB $463 Ex $434 Gd $402
Caliber: .380 Automatic. Seven-shot magazine, 3.5-inch bbl., 6.5 inches overall. Weight: 25 oz. Fixed front sight, square notch adj. rear. Stainless finish. Checkered wood grips. Made 1989-91.

ESCORT DA AUTO PISTOL . . . . NiB $278 Ex $206 Gd $113
Caliber: .380 ACP. 7-shot magazine, 3.38-inch bbl., 6.13 inches overall. Weight: 19 ounces. Fixed, low-profile sights. Stainless steel frame, slide, and trigger. Nickel-steel bbl., Soft polymer grips. Loaded chamber indicator. Made 1995-97 .

MATEBA AUTO REVOLVER
Unique combination action design allows both slide and cylinder to recoil together causing cylinder to rotate. Single or double action. Caliber: .357 Mag. Six-shot cylinder, 4- or 6-inch bbl., 8.77 inches overall w/4-inch bbl., Weight: 2.75 lbs. Steel/alloy frame. Ramped blade front sight, adjustable rear. Blue finish. Smooth walnut grips. Imported 1997 to date.
Mateba model (w/4-inch bbl.) . . . . NiB $1062 Ex $849 Gd $578
Mateba model (w/6-inch bbl.) . . . . NiB $1127 Ex $901 Gd $613

P-98 DA AUTOMATIC PISTOL . . . . NiB $175 Ex $144 Gd $103
Caliber: .22 LR. Eight-shot magazine, 5-inch bbl., 8.25 inches overall. Weight: 25 oz. Fixed front sight, square notch adj. rear. Blued finish. Serrated black polymer grips. Made 1989-96.

**American Arms
Regulator Deluxe Model**

**American Derringer
Model 1**

**American Derringer
Model 3**

PK-22 DA AUTOMATIC PISTOL . . . NiB $170 Ex $144 Gd $118
Caliber: .22 LR. Eight-shot magazine, 3.33-inch bbl., 6.33 inches overall. Weight: 22 oz. Fixed front sight, V-notch rear. Blued finish. Checkered black polymer grips. Made 1989-96.

PX-22 DA AUTOMATIC PISTOL . . . NiB $170 Ex $144 Gd $118
Caliber: .22 LR. Seven-shot magazine, 2.75-inch bbl., 5.33 inches overall. Weight: 15 oz. Fixed front sight, V-notch rear. Blued finish. Checkered black polymer grips. Made 1989-96.

PX-25 DA AUTOMATIC PISTOL . . . NiB $180 Ex $144 Gd $129
Same general specifications as the Model PX-22 except chambered for .25 ACP. Made 1991-92.

REGULATOR SA REVOLVER
Similar in appearance to the Colt Single-Action Army. Calibers: .357 Mag., .44-.40, .45 Long Colt. Six-shot cylinder, 4.75- or 7.5-inch bbl., blade front sight, fixed rear. Brass trigger guard/backstrap on Standard model. Casehardened steel on Deluxe model. Made 1992 to date.
Standard model . . . . NiB $330 Ex $257 Gd $160
Standard combo set

(cont'd.) REGULATOR SA REVOLVER
(45 LC/.45 ACP & .44-.40/.44 Spec.). . . . NiB $355 Ex $278 Gd $196
Deluxe model . . . . .NiB $322 Ex $257 Gd $175
Deluxe combo set (.45 LC/.45
ACP & .44-40/.44 Spec.) . . . . NiB $376 Ex $324 Gd $180
Stainless steel . . . . NiB $354 Ex $283 Gd $193

BUCKHORN SA REVOLVER
Similar to Regulator model except chambered .44 Mag. w/4.75-, 6- or 7.7-inch bbl., Fixed or adjustable sights. Hammer block safety. Imported 1993-96.
Buckhorn model (standard sights) . . NiB $335 Ex $263 Gd $180
W/adjustable sights, add $15

SABRE DA AUTOMATIC PISTOL
Calibers: 9mm Para., .40 S&W. Eight-shot magazine (9mm), 9-shot (.40 S&W), 3.75-inch bbl., 6.9 inches overall. Weight: 26 oz. Fixed blade front sight, square, notch adj. rear. Black polymer grips. Blued or stainless finish. Advertised 1991 but not imported.
Blued finish . . . . NiB $398 Ex $318 Gd $216
Stainless steel . . . . NiB $437 Ex $339 Gd $238

SPECTRE DA AUTO PISTOL
Blowback action, fires closed bolt. Calibers: 9mm Para., .40 S&W, .45 ACP. 30-shot magazine, 6-inch bbl., 13.75 inches overall. Weight: 4 lbs. 8 oz. Adj. post front sight, fixed U-notch rear. Black nylon grips. Matte black finish. Imported 1990-94.
9mm Para. NiB $515 Ex $438 Gd $391
.40 S&W (disc. 1991) . . . . NiB $412 Ex $330 Gd $225
.45 ACP . . . . NiB $470 Ex $381 Gd $268

WOODMASTER SA AUTO PISTOL . . . . NiB $225 Ex $180 Gd $123
Caliber: .22 LR. 10-shot magazine, 5.88-inch bbl., 10.5 inches overall. Weight: 31 oz. Fixed front sight, square-notch adj. rear. Blued finish. Checkered wood grips. Disc. 1989.

454 SSA REVOLVER . . . . NiB $901 Ex $711 Gd $515
Umberti SSA chambered 454. Six-shot cylinder, 6-inch solid raised rib or 7.7-inch top-ported bbl., satin nickel finish. Hammer block safety. Imported 1996-97.

AMERICAN DERRINGER CORPORATION — Waco, Texas

MODEL 1, STAINLESS
Single-action pocket pistol similar to the Remington O/U derringer. Two-shot capacity. More than 60 calibers from .22 LR to .45-70. Three- inch bbl., 4.82 inches overall, weight: 15 oz. Automatic bbl., selection. Satin or high-polished stainless steel. Rosewood grips. Made 1980 to date.
.45 Colt, .44-40 Win., .44
Special, .410 . . . . NiB $393 Ex $348 Gd $280
.45-70, .44 Mag., 41 Mag.,
.30-30 Win., .223 Rem. . . . . NiB $479 Ex $463 Gd $357
.357 Max., .357 Mag., .45 Win.
Mag., 9mm Para. . . . . NiB $342 Ex $318 Gd $230
.38 Special, .38 Super, .32 Mag.,
.22 LR, .22 WRM. . . . . NiB $326 Ex $299 Gd $178

MODEL 2 STEEL "PEN" PISTOL
Calibers: .22 LR, .25 Auto, .32 Auto (7.65mm). single-shot. Two-inch bbl., 5.6 inches overall (4.2 inches in pistol format). Weight: 5 oz. Stainless finish. Made 1993-94.
.22 LR . . . . NiB $173 Ex $138 Gd $97
.25 Auto. NiB $178 Ex $143 Gd $102
.32 Auto. NiB $204 Ex $153 Gd $112

MODEL 3 STAINLESS STEEL . . . . NiB $97 Ex $77 Gd $51
Single-shot. Calibers: .32 Mag. or .38 Special. 2.5-inch bbl., 4.9 inches overall. Weight: 8.5 oz. Rosewood grips. Made 1984-95.

MODEL 4 DOUBLE DERRINGER
Calibers: .357 Mag., .357 Max., .44 Mag., .45 LC, .45 ACP (upper bbl., and 3-inch .410 shotshell (lower bbl.). 4.1-inch bbl, 6 inches overall. Weight: 16.5 oz. Stainless steel. Staghorn grips. Made 1984 to date.
.357 Mag., .357 Max . . . . NiB $433 Ex $377 Gd $255
.44 Mag., .45 LC, .45 ACP . . . . NiB $525 Ex $466 Gd $306
Engraved, add $1125

MODEL 6
Caliber: .22 Mag., .357 Mag., .45 LC, .45 ACP or .45 LC/.410 or .45 Colt. Bbl.: 6 inches, 8.2 inches overall. Weight: .22 oz. Satin or high-polished stainless steel w/rosewood grips. Made 1986 to date.
.22 Magnum . . . . NiB $449 Ex $342 Gd $275
.357, .45 ACP, .45 LC . . . . NiB $449 Ex $342 Gd $286
.45/LC/.410 O/U . . . . NiB $459 Ex $347 Gd $306
Engraved, add $1295

MODEL 7
Same general specifications as the Model 1 except high-strength aircraft aluminum is used to replace some of the stainless steel parts, which reduces its weight to 7.5 oz. Made 1986 to date.
.22 LR, .22 WMR. . . . . NiB $296 Ex $153 Gd $102
Calibers .32, .38 and .44 . . . . NiB $510 Ex $459 Gd $398

MODEL 10
Same general specifications as the Model 7 except chambered for .38 Special, .45 ACP or .45 Long Colt.
.38 Special or .45 ACP . . . . NiB $337 Ex $280 Gd $229
.45 Long Colt . . . . NiB $388 Ex $280 Gd $229
Model 11 . . . . NiB $198 Ex $158 Gd $107
Same general specifications as Model 7 except with a matte gray finish only, weight: 11 oz. Made 1980 to date.

25 AUTOMATIC PISTOL
Calibers: .25 ACP or .250 Mag. Bbl.: 2.1 inches, 4.4 inches overall. Weight: 15.5 oz. Smooth rosewood grips. Limited production.
.25 ACP blued
(est. production 50) . . . . NiB $561 Ex $408 Gd $306
.25 ACP stainless
(est. production 400) . . . . NiB $408 Ex $306 Gd $255
.250 Mag. stainless
(est. production 100) . . . . NiB $571 Ex $510 Gd $393

MODEL 38 DA DERRINGER
Hammerless, double action, double bbl (o/u). Calibers: .22 LR, .38 Special, 9mm Para., .357 Mag., .40 S&W. Three-inch bbl., weight: 14.5 oz. Made 1990 to date.
.22 LR or .38 Special . . . . NiB $444 Ex $407 Gd $357
9mm Para. . . . . NiB $241 Ex $194 Gd $131
.357 Mag. . . . . NiB $484 Ex $444 Gd $388
.40 S&W . . . . NiB $287 Ex $230 Gd $156

ALASKAN SURVIVAL MODEL . . . . . NiB $484 Ex $443 Gd $306
Same general specifications as the Model 4 except upper bbl., chambered for .45-70 or 3-inch .410 and .45 Colt lower bbl. Also available in .45 Auto, .45 Colt, .44 Special, .357 Mag. and .357 Max. Made 1985 to date.

COP DA DERRINGER . . . . NiB $255 Ex $224 Gd $194
Hammerless, double-action, four-bbl., derringer. Caliber: .357 Mag. 3.15-inch bbl., 5.5 inches overall. Weight: 16 oz. Blade front sight,

American Derringer
Model .38 DA

American Derringer
Lady Derringer

open notched rear. Rosewood grips. Intro. 1990 but only limited production. No resale value established.

LADY DERRINGER
Same general specifications as Model 1 except w/custom-tuned action fitted w/scrimshawed synthetic ivory grips. Calibers: .32 H&R Mag., .32 Special, .38 Special (additional calibers on request). Deluxe Grade engraved and highly polished w/French fitted jewelry box. Made 1991 to date.
Lady Derringer . . . . NiB $367 Ex $337 Gd $296
Deluxe . . . . NiB $382 Ex $352 Gd $311
Engraved . . . . NiB $938 Ex $867 Gd $816

MINI-COP DA DERRINGER . . . . . . NiB $265 Ex $204 Gd $143
Same general specifications as the American Derringer Cop except chambered for .22 Magnum. Made 1990-95.

SEMMERLING LM-4
Manually operated repeater. Calibers: .45 ACP or 9mm. Five-shot (.45 ACP) or 7-shot magazine (9mm)., 3.6-inch bbl., 5.2 inches overall. Weight: 24 oz. Made 1997 to date. Limited availability.
Blued finish . . . . NiB $2544 Ex $2035 Gd $1384
Stainless steel . . . . (SRP) NiB $3379 Ex $2703 Gd $1838

TEXAS COMMEMORATIVE
Same general specifications as Model 1 except w/solid brass frame, stainless bbls. and rosewood grips. Calibers: .22 LR, .32 Mag., .38 Special, .44-40 Win. or .45 Colt. Made 1991 to date.
.38 Special . . . . NiB $372 Ex $331 Gd $255
.44-40 or .45 Colt . . . . NiB $459 Ex $408 Gd $382

AMT
.45 ACP Backup

AMT
.45 ACP Hardballer

AMT
.45 ACP Hardballer Long Slide

AMERICAN FIREARMS MFG. CO., INC. — San Antonio, Texas

25 AUTO PISTOL
Caliber: .25 Auto. 8-shot magazine, 2.1-inch bbl., 4.4 inches overall. Weight: 14.5 oz. Fixed sights. Stainless or blued ordnance steel. Smooth walnut grips. Made 1966-74.
Stainless steel model . . . . NiB $226 Ex $184 Gd $129
Blued steel model . . . . NiB $170 Ex $144 Gd $108

380 AUTO PISTOL. . . . . NiB $721 Ex $669 Gd $592
Caliber: .380 Auto. 8-shot magazine, 3.5-inch bbl., 5.5 inches overall. Weight: 20 oz. Stainless steel. Smooth walnut grips. Made 1972-74.

AMT (ARCADIA MACHINE & TOOL) — Irwindale, California (Previously Irwindale Arms, Inc.)

NOTE: *The AMT Backup II automatic pistol was introduced in 1993 as a continuation of the original .380 backup with the traditional double action function and a redesigned double safety.*

45 ACP HARDBALLER
Caliber: .45 ACP. Seven-shot magazine, 5-inch bbl., 8.5 inches overall. Weight: 39 oz. Adj. or fixed sights. Serrated matte slide rib w/loaded chamber indicator. Extended combat safety, adj. trigger and long grip safety. Wraparound Neoprene grips. Stainless steel. Made 1978 to date.
.45 ACP Hardballer . . . . NiB $463 Ex $309 Gd $185
Long slide conversion kit
(disc. 1997), add $300

45 ACP HARDBALLER LONG SLIDE
Similar to the standard AMT Hardballer except w/2-inch-longer bbl. and slide. Also chambered for .400 Cor-Bon. Made 1980 to date.
.45 ACP long slide . . . . NiB $438 Ex $360 Gd $232
.400 Cor-Bon long slide
(Intro.1998). . . . . NiB $418 Ex $335 Gd $228
5-inch conversion kit
(disc. 1997), add $300

1911 GOVERNMENT MODEL
AUTO PISTOL . . . . NiB $335 Ex $283 Gd $206
Caliber: .45 ACP. Seven-shot magazine, 5-inch bbl., 8.5 inches overall. Weight: 38 ounces. Fixed sights. Wraparound Neoprene grip. Made 1979 to date.

AUTOMAG II
AUTOMATIC PISTOL . . . . NiB $412 Ex $288 Gd $175
Caliber: .22 Mag. Seven- or 9-shot magazine, bbl., lengths: 3.38-4.5-, 6-inch. Weight: 32 oz. Fully adj. Millett sights. Stainless finish. Smooth black composition grips. Made 1986 to date.

AUTOMAG III
AUTOMATIC PISTOL . . . . NiB $541 Ex $463 Gd $360
Calibers: .30 M1 and 9mm Win. Mag. Eight-shot magazine., 6.38-inch bbl., 10.5 inches overall. Weight: 43 ounces. Millet adj. sights. Stainless finish. Carbon fiber grips. Made 1989 to date.

AUTOMAG IV
AUTOMATIC PISTOL . . . . NiB $545 Ex $458 Gd $360
Calibers: 10mm Mag., .45 Win. Mag. 8- or 7-shot magazine, 6.5- or 8.63-inch bbl., 10.5 inches overall. Weight: 46 oz. Millet adj. sights. Stainless finish. Carbon fiber grips. Made 1990 to date.

AUTOMAG V
AUTOMATIC PISTOL . . . . NiB $876 Ex $747 Gd $669
Caliber: .50 A.E. Five-shot magazine, 7-inch bbl., 10.5 inches overall. Weight: 46 oz. Custom adj. sights. Stainless finish. Carbon fiber grips. Made 1994-95.

BACKUP AUTOMATIC PISTOL
Caliber: .22LR, .380 ACP. Eight-shot (.22LR) or 5-shot (.380 ACP) magazine, 2.5-inch bbl., 5 inches overall. Weight: 18 oz. Open sights. Carbon fiber or walnut grips. Stainless steel finish. Made 1990 to date.
.22 LR (disc. 1987) . . . . NiB $309 Ex $191 Gd $134
.380 ACP (disc. 1993) . . . . NiB $257 Ex $180 Gd $124

BACKUP II
AUTOMATIC PISTOL . . . . **NiB $268 Ex $196 Gd $154**
Caliber: .380 ACP, 5-shot magazine, 2.5-inch bbl., 5 inches overall. Weight: 18 oz. Open sights. Stainless steel finish. Carbon-fiber grips. Made 1993 to date.

BACKUP DAO AUTO PISTOL
Calibers: .380 ACP, .38 Super, 9mm Para., .40 Cor-Bon, .40 S&W, .45 ACP. Six-shot (.380, .38 Super 9mm) or 5-shot (.40 Cor-Bon, .40 S&W, .45 ACP) magazine, 2.5-inch bbl., 5.75-inches overall. Weight: 18 oz. (.380 ACP) or 23 oz. Open fixed sights. Stainless steel finish. Carbon fiber grips. Made 1992 to date.
.380 ACP . . . . **NiB $232 Ex $180 Gd $139**
.38 Super, 9mm . . . . **NiB $257 Ex $196 Gd $124**
.40 Cor-Bon, .40 S&W,
.45 ACP . . . . **NiB $251 Ex $201 Gd $137**

BULL'S EYE
TARGET MODEL . . . . **NiB $412 Ex $350 Gd $304**
Caliber: .40 S&W. Eight-shot magazine, 5-inch bbl., 8.5 inches overall. Weight: 38 oz. Millet adjustable sights. Wide adj. trigger. Wraparound Neoprene grips. Made 1990-92.

JAVELINA
JAVELINA . . . . **NiB $577 Ex $474 Gd $360**
Caliber: 10mm. Eight-shot magazine, 7-inch bbl., 10.5 inches overall. Weight: 48 oz. Long grip safety, beveled magazine well, wide adj. trigger. Millet adj. sights. Wraparound Neoprene grips. Stainless finish. Made 1991-93.

LIGHTNING AUTO PISTOL
Caliber: .22 LR. 10-shot magazine, 5-, 6.5-, 8.5-, 10-inch bbl., 10.75 inches overall (6.5-inch bbl.). Weight: 45 oz. (6.5-inch bbl.). Millett adj. sights. Checkered rubber grips. Stainless finish. Made 1984-87.
Standard model . . . . **NiB $360 Ex $206 Gd $154**
Bull's-Eye model . . . . **NiB $430 Ex $360 Gd $294**

ON DUTY DA PISTOL
Calibers: .40 S&W, 9mm Para., .45 ACP. 15-shot (9mm), 13-shot (.40 S&W) or 9-shot (.45 ACP) magazine, 4.5-inch bbl., 7.75 inches overall. Weight: 32 oz. Hard anodized aluminum frame. Stainless steel slide and bbl., Carbon fiber grips. Made 1991-94.
9mm or .40 S&W . . . . **NiB $397 Ex $304 Gd $257**
.45 ACP . . . . **NiB $438 Ex $360 Gd $206**

SKIPPER AUTO PISTOL
SKIPPER AUTO PISTOL . . . . **NiB $386 Ex $288 Gd $257**
Calibers: .40 S&W and .45 ACP. Seven-shot magazine, 4.25-inch bbl., 7.5 inches overall. Weight: 33 oz. Millet adj. sights. Walnut grips. Matte finish stainless steel. Made 1990-92.

ANSCHUTZ PISTOLS — Ulm, Germany
Mfd. by J.G. Anschutz GmbH Jagd und Sportwaffenfabrik

Currently imported by Accuracy International, Boseman, MT and AcuSport Corporation, Bellefontaine, OH

MODEL 64P
Calibers: .22 LR or .22 Magnum. Five- or 4-shot magazine, 10-inch bbl., 64MS action w/two-stage trigger. Target sights optional. Rynite black synthetic stock. Imported 1998 to date.
.22 LR . . . . **NiB $482 Ex $370 Gd $312**
.22 Mag. . . . . **NiB $514 Ex $499 Gd $442**
W/tangent
sights, add **$80**

AMT Backup

AMT Backup DAO

AMT Bull's Eye Target

AMT Skipper

GRADING: **NiB** = New in Box   **Ex** = Excellent or NRA 95%   **Gd** = Good or NRA 68%

Anschutz Exemplar

Anschutz Exemplar Hornet

Anschutz Exemplar XIV

Astra Model .44 DA

EXEMPLAR (1416P/1451P) BOLT-ACTION PISTOL
Caliber: .22 LR, single-shot or 5-shot clip. Seven- or 10-inch bbl., 19 inches overall (10-inch bbl.). Weight: 3.33 lbs. Match 64 action. Slide safety. Hooded ramp post front sight, adjustable open notched rear. European walnut contoured grip. Exemplar made 1987-95 and 1400 series made 1997 to date. Note: The .22 WMR chambering was also advertised but never manufactured.
Exemplar w/7- or 10-inch bbl. . . . . NiB $411 Ex $359 Gd $302
Left-hand model (disc. 1997). . . . . . NiB $520 Ex $468 Gd $385
Model 1451P (single-shot). . . . . NiB $422 Ex $338 Gd $230
Model 1416P (5-shot repeater) . . . . NiB $410 Ex $328 Gd $223

EXEMPLAR HORNET. . . . . NiB $868 Ex $6712 Gd $572
Based on the Anschutz Match 54 action, tapped and grooved for scope mounting with no open sights. Caliber: .22 Hornet, 5-shot magazine, 10-inch bbl., 20 inches overall. Weight: 4.35 lbs. Checkered European walnut grip. Winged safety. Made 1990 to 1995.

EXEMPLAR XIV . . . . NiB $520 Ex $468 Gd $385
Same general specifications as the standard Exemplar bolt-action pistol except w/14-inch bbl., weight: 4.15 lbs. Made 1989-95.

ARMSCOR (Arms Corp.) — Manila, Philippines
Currently imported by K.B.I., Harrisburg, PA. (Imported 1991-95 by Ruko Products, Inc., Buffalo NY. Previously by Armscor Precision, San Mateo, CA.)

MODEL M1911-A1
AUTOMATIC PISTOL . . . . NiB $398 Ex $357 Gd $214
Caliber: .45 ACP. Eight-shot magazine, 5-inch bbl., 8.75 inches overall. Weight: 38 oz. Blade front sight, drift adjustable rear w/3-dot system. Skeletonized tactical hammer and trigger. Extended slide release and beavertail grip safety. Parker-ized finish. Checkered composition or wood stocks. Imported 1996-97.

MODEL 200DC/TC
DA REVOLVER . . . . NiB $168 Ex $148 Gd $122
Caliber: .38 Special. Six-shot cylinder, 2.5-, 4-, or 6-inch bbl.; 7.3, 8.8, or 11.3 inches overall. Weight: 22, 28, or 34 oz. Ramp front and fixed rear sights. Checkered mahogany or rubber grips. Imported 1996 to date.

ASAI AG — Advanced Small Arms Industries Solothurn, Switzerland
Currently imported by Magnum Research Inc., Minneapolis, MN.

See listings under Magnum Research Pistols

ASTRA PISTOLS — Guernica, Spain Manufactured by Unceta y Compania
Currently imported by E.A.A. Corporation, Sharpes, FL.

MODEL 357 DA REVOLVER . . . . . . NiB $255 Ex $219 Gd $184
Caliber: .357 Magnum. Six-shot cylinder. 3-, 4-, 6-, 8.5-inch bbl., 11.25 inches overall (with 6-inch bbl.). Weight: 42 oz. (with 6-inch bbl.). Ramp front sight, adj. rear sight. Blued finish. Checkered wood grips. Imported 1972-88.

MODEL 44 DA REVOLVER
Similar to Astra ..357 except chambered for .44 Magnum. Six- or 8.5-inch bbl., 11.5 inches overall (6-inch bbl.). Weight: 44 oz. (6-inch bbl.). Imported 1980-93.
Blued finish (disc. 1987) . . . . NiB $286 Ex $240 Gd $214
Stainless finish (disc. 1993) . . . . NiB $291 Ex $240 Gd $214

MODEL 41 DA REVOLVER . . . . . . .NiB $286 Ex $245 Gd $163
Same general specifications as Model 44 except in .41 Mag. Imported 1980-85.

MODEL 45
DA REVOLVER. . . . . NiB $291 Ex $240 Gd $214
Similar to Astra .357 except chambered for .45 Colt or .45 ACP. Six- or 8.5-inch bbl., 11.5 inches overall (with 6-inch bbl.). Weight: 44 oz. (6-inch bbl.). Imported 1980-87.

MODEL 200 FIRECAT
VEST POCKET AUTO PISTOL . . . . . **NiB $255 Ex $204 Gd $189**
Caliber: .25 Automatic (6.35mm). Six-shot magazine, 2.25-inch bbl., 4.38 inches overall. Weight: 11.75 oz. Fixed sights. Blued finish. Plastic grips. Made 1920 to date. U.S. importation disc. in 1968.

MODEL 202 FIRECAT
VEST POCKET AUTO PISTOL . . . . . **NiB $484 Ex $408 Gd $357**
Same general specifications as the Model 200 except chromed and engraved w/pearl grips. U.S. importation disc. 1968.

MODEL 400 AUTO PISTOL . . . . . . **NiB $408 Ex $367 Gd $153**
Caliber: 9mm Bayard Long (.38 ACP, 9mm Browning Long, 9mm Glisenti, 9mm Para. and 9mm Steyr cartridges may be used interchangeably in this pistol because of its chamber design). Nine-shot magazine., 6-inch bbl., 10 inches overall. Weight: 35 oz. Fixed sights. Blued finish. Plastic grips. Made 1922-45. Note: This pistol, as well as Astra Models 600 and 3000, is a modification of the Browning Model 1912.

MODEL 600 MIL./POLICE-TYPE
AUTO PISTOL . . . . **NiB $403 Ex $326 Gd $194**
Calibers: .32 Automatic (7.65mm), 9mm Para. Magazine: 10-shot (.32 cal.) or 8-shot (9mm)., 5.25-inch bbl., 8 inches overall. Weight: About 33 oz. Fixed sights. Blued finish. Checkered wood or plastic grips. Made 1944-.45.

MODEL 800 CONDOR
MILITARY AUTO PISTOL . . . . . . **NiB $1504 Ex $1122 Gd $739**
Similar to Models 400 and 600 except has an external hammer. Caliber: 9mm Para. Eight-shot magazine, 5.25-inch bbl., 8.25 inches overall. Weight: 32.5 oz. Fixed sights. Blued finish. Plastic grips. Imported 1958-65.

MODEL 2000 CAMPER
AUTOMATIC PISTOL . . . . **NiB $377 Ex $265 Gd $173**
Same as Model 2000 Cub except chambered for .22 Short only, has 4-inch bbl., overall length, 6.25 inches, weight: 11.5 oz. Imported 1955-60.

MODEL 2000 CUB
POCKET AUTO PISTOL . . . . **NiB $255 Ex $194 Gd $122**
Calibers: .22 Short, .25 Auto. Six-shot magazine, 2.25-inch bbl., 4.5 inches overall. Weight: About 11 oz. Fixed sights. Blued or chromed finish. Plastic grips. Made 1954 to date. U.S. importation disc. 1968.

MODEL 3000
POCKET AUTO PISTOL . . . . **NiB $510 Ex $490 Gd $229**
Calibers: .22 LR, .32 Automatic (7.65mm), .380 Auto (9mm Short). Ten-shot magazine (.22 cal.), 7-shot (.32 cal.), 6-shot (.380 cal.). Four-inch bbl., 6.38 inches overall. Weight: About 22 oz. Fixed sights. Blued finish. Plastic grips. Made 1947-56.

MODEL 3003
POCKET AUTO PISTOL . . . . **NiB $1020 Ex $663 Gd $490**
Same general specifications as the Model 3000 except chromed and engraved w/pearl grips. Disc. 1956.

MODEL 4000
ALCON AUTO PISTOL . . . . **NiB $510 Ex $408 Gd $245**
Similar to Model 3000 except has an external hammer. Calibers: .22 LR, .32 Automatic (7.65mm), .380 Auto (9mm Short). Ten-shot magazine (.22 LR), 8-shot (.32 Auto), 7-shot (.380 Auto), 3.66-inch bbl., 6.5-inches overall. Weight: 20 oz. (.22 cal.) or 24.75 oz. (.32 and .380). Fixed sights. Blued finish. Plastic grips. Made 1956-71.

MODEL A-60 DA
AUTOMATIC PISTOL . . . . **NiB $408 Ex $357 Gd $224**
Similar to the Constable except in .380 only, w/13-shot magazine and slide-mounted ambidextrous safety. Blued finish only. Imported 1980-91.

**Astra Model
3003 Pocket**

**Astra Model
4000 Falcon**

**Astra
Model A-80**

MODEL A-70 COMPACT AUTO PISTOL
Calibers: 9mm Para., .40 S&W. Eight-shot (9mm) or 7-shot (.40 S&W) magazine., 3.5-inch bbl., 6.5 inches overall. Blued, nickel or stainless finish. Weight: 29.3 oz. Imported 1992-96.
Blued finish . . . . **NiB $280 Ex $255 Gd $173**
Nickel finish . . . . **NiB $311 Ex $286 Gd $204**
Stainless finish . . . . **NiB $372 Ex $332 Gd $280**

MODEL A-75 DECOCKER AUTO PISTOL
Similar to the Model 70 except in 9mm, .40 S&W and .45 ACP w/decocking system and contoured pebble-textured grips. Imported 1993-97.
Blued finish, 9mm or .40 S&W . . . . **NiB $286 Ex $255 Gd $189**
Nickel finish, 9mm or .40 S&W . . . . **NiB $301 Ex $255 Gd $173**
Stainless, 9mm or .40 S&W . . . . **NiB $291 Ex $255 Gd $184**
Blued finish, .45 ACP . . . . **NiB $316 Ex $255 Gd $163**
Nickel finish, .45 ACP . . . . **NiB $340 Ex $275 Gd $163**
Stainless, .45 ACP . . . . **NiB $382 Ex $331 Gd $229**

Astra Cadix DA

Astra Constable DA

Auto-Ordnance 1927
A-5 w/drum magazine

MODEL A-75 ULTRALIGHT . . . . . . NiB $306 Ex $260 Gd $173
Similar to the standard Model 75 except 9mm only w/24-oz. alloy frame. Imported 1994-97.

MODEL A-80 AUTO PISTOL . . . . . . NiB $377 Ex $326 Gd $214
Calibers: 9mm Para., .38 Super, .45 ACP. 15-shot magazine or 9-shot (.45 ACP). Bbl.: 3.75 inches., 7 inches overall. Weight: 36 oz. Imported 1982-89. See illustration previous page.

MODEL A-90 DA
AUTOMATIC PISTOL . . . . NiB $408 Ex $331 Gd $224
Calibers: 9mm Para., .45 ACP. 15-shot (9mm) or 9-shot (.45 ACP) magazine, 3.75-inch bbl., 7 inches overall. Weight: about 40 oz. Fixed sights. Blued finish. Checkered plastic grips. Imported 1985-90.

MODEL A-100 DA AUTO PISTOL
Same general specifications as the Model A-90 except selective double action chambered for 9mm Para., .40 S&W or .45 ACP. Imported 1991-97.

(cont'd) **MODEL A-100 DA AUTO PISTOL**
Blued finish . . . . NiB $382 Ex $331 Gd $229
Nickel finish . . . . NiB $48 Ex $354 Gd $224
For night sights, add $85

CADIX DA REVOLVER
Calibers: .22 LR, .38 Special. Nine-shot (.22 LR) or 5-shot (.38 cal.) cylinder. Four- or 6-inch bbl., Weight: About 27 oz. (6-inch bbl.). Ramp front sight, adj. rear sight. Blued finish. Plastic grips. Imported 1960-68.
Standard model . . . . NiB $199 Ex $168 Gd $102
Lightly engraved model . . . . NiB $319 Ex $255 Gd $173
Heavily engraved model (shown) . . . . . NiB $631 Ex $505 Gd $344

CONSTABLE DA AUTO PISTOL
Calibers: .22 LR, .32 Automatic (7.65mm), .380 Auto (9mm Short). Magazine capacity: 10-shot (.22 LR), 8-shot (.32), 7-shot (.380). 3.5-inch bbl., 6.5 inches overall. Weight: about 24 oz. Blade front sight, windage adj. rear. Blued or chromed finish. Imported 1965-92.
Stainless finish . . . . NiB $351 Ex $280 Gd $191
Blued finish . . . . NiB $300 Ex $240 Gd $163
Chrome finish (disc. 1990) . . . . NiB $319 Ex $255 Gd $173

AUTAUGA ARMS — Prattville, Alabama

MODEL 32 (MK II)
DAO AUTOMATIC PISTOL . . . . NiB $331 Ex $229 Gd $173
Caliber: .32 ACP. Six-shot magazine, 2-inch bbl., weight: 11.36 oz.. Double action only. Stainless steel. Black polymer grips. Made 1997 to date.

AUTO-ORDNANCE CORPORATION — West Hurley, New York

1911 A1 GOVERNMENT AUTO PISTOL
Copy of Colt 1911 A1 semiautomatic pistol. Calibers: 9mm Para., .38 Super, 10mm, .45 ACP. 9-shot (9mm, .38 Super) or 7-shot 10mm, .45 ACP) magazine. Five-inch bbl., 8.5 inches overall. Weight: 39 oz. Fixed blade front sight, rear adj. Blued, satin nickel or Duo-Tone finish. Checkered plastic grips. Made 1983-99.
.45 ACP caliber . . . . NiB $367 Ex $301 Gd $219
9mm, 10mm, .38 Super . . . . NiB $376 Ex $301 Gd $205

1911A1 .40 S&W PISTOL . . . . NiB $367 Ex $301 Gd $219
Similar to the Model 1911 A1 except has 4.5-inch bbl., w/7.75-inch overall length. Eight-shot magazine, weight: 37 oz. Blade front and adj. rear sights w/3-dot system. Checkered black rubber wraparound grips. Made 1991-99.

1911 "THE GENERAL" . . . . NiB $388 Ex $326 Gd $204
Caliber: .45 ACP. Seven-shot magazine, 4.5-inch bbl., 7.75 inches overall. Weight: 37 oz. Blued nonglare finish. Made 1992-99.

1927 A-5 SEMIAUTOMATIC PISTOL
Similar to Thompson Model 1928A submachine gun except has no provision for automatic firing and does not have detachable buttstock. Caliber: .45 ACP, 5-, 15-, 20- and 30-shot detachable box magazines. 30-shot drum also available. 13-inch finned bbl., 26 inches overall. Weight: About 6.75 lbs. Adj. rear sight, blade front. Blued finish. Walnut grips. Made 1977-94.
W/box magazine . . . . NiB $886 Ex $709 Gd $482
W/drum magazine (illustrated) . . . . NiB $1212 Ex $969 Gd $659

ZG-51 PIT BULL
AUTOMATIC PISTOL . . . . NiB $393 Ex $316 Gd $219
Caliber: .45 ACP. Seven-shot magazine, 3.5-inch bbl., 7 inches overall. Weight: 32 oz. Fixed front sight, square-notch rear. Blued finish. Checkered plastic grips. Made 1991-99.

LES BAER — Hillsdale, Illinois

1911 CONCEPT SERIES AUTOMATIC PISTOL
Similar to Government 1911 built on steel or alloy full-size or compact frame. Caliber: .45 ACP. Seven-shot magazine, 4.25- or 5-inch bbl. Weight: 34 to 37 oz. Adjustable low mount combat or BoMar target sights. Blued, matte black, Two-Tone or stainless finish. Checkered wood grips. Made 1996 to date.

Concept models I & II.......... NiB $1141	Ex $913	Gd $621
Concept models III, IV & VII.... NiB $1256	Ex $1005	Gd $683
Concept models V, VI & VIII .... NiB $1307	Ex $1045	Gd $711
Concept models IX & X........ NiB $1320	Ex $1056	Gd $718

1911 PREMIER SERIES AUTOMATIC PISTOL
Similar to the Concept series except also chambered for .38 Super, 9x23 Win., .400 Cor-Bon and .45 ACP. 5- or 6-inch bbl. Weight: 37 to .40 oz. Made 1996 to date.

Premier II
(9x23 w/5-inch bbl.) .... NiB $1396 Ex $1117 Gd $760
Premier II (.400
Cor-Bon w/5-inch bbl.) .... NiB $1269 Ex $1015 Gd $691
Premier II (.45 ACP
w/5-inch bbl.) .... NiB $1179 Ex $943 Gd $642
Premier II (.45 ACP
S/S w/5-inch bbl.) .... NiB $1307 Ex $1045 Gd $711
Premier II (.45/.400
combo w/5-inch bbl.) .... NiB $1467 Ex $1173 Gd $798
Premier II (.38
Super w/6-inch bbl.) .... NiB $1651 Ex $1321 Gd $899
Premier II (.400
Cor-Bon w/6-inch bbl.) ...... NiB $1485 Ex $1188 Gd $808
Premier II (.45 ACP
w/6-inch bbl.) .... NiB $1396 Ex $1117 Gd $760

S.R.P. AUTOMATIC PISTOL
Similar to F.B.I. Contract "Swift Response Pistol" built on a (customer-supplied) Para-Ordance over-sized frame or a 1911 full-size or compact frame. Caliber: .45 ACP. Seven-shot magazine, 5-inch bbl., weight: 37 oz. Ramp front and fixed rear sights, w/Tritium Sight insert.

SRP 1911Government
or Commanche model........ NiB $2034 Ex $1627 Gd $1107
SRP P-12 model............ NiB $2327 Ex $1861 Gd $1266
SRP P-13 model............ NiB $2104 Ex $1683 Gd $1144
SRP P-14 model............ NiB $1977 Ex $1581 Gd $1075

1911 ULTIMATE MASTER COMBAT SERIES AUTOMATIC PISTOL
Model 1911 in Combat Competition configuration. Calibers: .38 Super, 9x23 Win., .400 Cor-Bon and .45 ACP. Five- or 6-inch NM bbl., weight: 37 to 40 oz. Made 1996 to date.

Ultimate MC (.38 or 9x23
w/5-inch bbl.) .... NiB $2104 Ex $1683 Gd $1144
Ultimate MC (.400 Cor-Bon
w/5-inch bbl.) .... NiB $1944 Ex $1555 Gd $1058
Ultimate MC (.45 ACP
w/5-inch bbl.) .... NiB $1849 Ex $1479 Gd $1006
Ultimate MC (.38 or 9x23
w/6-inch bbl.) .... NiB $2161 Ex $1729 Gd $1176
Ultimate MC (.400 Cor-Bon
w/6-inch bbl.) .... NiB $2008 Ex $1606 Gd $1092
Ultimate MC (.45 ACP
w/6-inch bbl.) .... NiB $1906 Ex $1525 Gd $1037
Ultimate "Steel Special"
(.38 Super Bianchi SPS)....... NiB $2416 Ex $1933 Gd $1315
Ultimate "PARA" (.38, 9x23
or .45 IPSC comp).......... NiB $2454 Ex $1963 Gd $1335
W/Triple-Port Compensator, add....................... $95

**Auto-Ordnance
ZG-51 Pit Bull**

1911 CUSTOM CARRY SERIES AUTOMATIC PISTOL
Model 1911 in Combat Carry configuration built on steel or alloy full-size or compact frame. 4.5- or 5-inch NM bbl., chambered for .45 ACP. Weight: 34 to 37 oz.
Custom carry (steel frame
w/4.24- or 5-inch bbl.) .... NiB $1339 Ex $1071 Gd $728
Custom carry (alloy frame
w/4.24-inch bbl.)............. NiB $1562 Ex $1250 Gd $850

BAUER FIREARMS CORPORATION — Fraser, MI

.25 AUTOMATIC PISTOL......... NiB $153 Ex $133 Gd $92
Stainless steel. Caliber: .25 Automatic. Six-shot magazine, 2.13-inch bbl., 4 inches overall. Weight: 10 oz. Fixed sights. Checkered walnut or simulated pearl grips. Made 1972-84.

BAYARD PISTOLS — Herstal, Belgium
Mfd. by Anciens Etablissements Pieper

MODEL 1908
POCKET AUTOMATIC PISTOL .... NiB $357 Ex $255 Gd $127
Calibers: .25 Automatic (6.35mm). .32 Automatic (7.65mm), .380 Automatic (9mm Short). Six-shot magazine, 2.25-inch bbl., 4.88 inches overall. Weight: About 16 oz. Fixed sights. Blued finish. Hard rubber grips. Intro. 1908. Disc. 1923.

MODEL 1923 POCKET
.25 AUTOMATIC PISTOL......... NiB $357 Ex $296 Gd $153
Caliber: .25 Automatic (6.35mm). 2.13-inch bbl., 4.31 inches overall. Weight: 12 oz. Fixed sights. Blued finish. Checkered hard-rubber grips. Intro. 1923. Disc. 1930.

MODEL 1923 POCKET
AUTOMATIC PISTOL .... NiB $365 Ex $296 Gd $153
Calibers: .32 Automatic (7.65mm), .380 Automatic (9mm Short). Six-shot magazine, 3.31-inch bbl., 5.5 inches overall. Weight: About 19 oz. Fixed sights. Blued finish. Checkered hard-rubber grips. Intro. 1923. Disc. 1940.

MODEL 1930 POCKET
.25 AUTOMATIC PISTOL......... NiB $357 Ex $255 Gd $122
This is a modification of the Model 1923, which it closely resembles.

BEEMAN PRECISION ARMS, INC. — Santa Rosa, CA

P08 AUTOMATIC PISTOL .... NiB $403 Ex $337 Gd $173
Caliber: .22 LR. 10-shot magazine, 3.8-inch bbl., 7.8 inches overall. Weight: 25 oz. Fixed sights. Blued finish. Checkered hardwood grips. Imported 1969-91.

Benelli MP90S

Benelli MP95E

Beretta Model 21

MINI P08 AUTOMATIC PISTOL . . . NiB $376 Ex $301 Gd $205
Caliber: Same general specifications as P08 except shorter 3.5-inch bbl., 7.4 inches overall. Weight: 20 oz. Imported 1986-91.

SP METALLIC SILHOUETTE PISTOLS
Caliber: .22 LR. Single-shot. Bbl. lengths: 6-, 8-, 10- or 15-inches. Adj. rear sight. Receiver contoured for scope mount. Walnut target grips w/adj. palm rest. Models SP made 1985-86 and SPX 1993-94.

SP Standard W/8-or 10-inch bbl.. . . NiB $249	Ex $199	Gd $136
SP Standard W/12-inch bbl. . . . . . . NiB $294	Ex $235	Gd $159
SP Standard W/15-inch bbl. . . . . . . NiB $312	Ex $250	Gd $170
SP Deluxe W/8-or 10-inch bbl. . . . NiB $300	Ex $240	Gd $163
SP Deluxe W/12-inch bbl.. . . . . NiB $319	Ex $255	Gd $173
SP Deluxe W/15-inch bbl.. . . . . NiB $338	Ex $270	Gd $184
SPX Standard W/10-inch bbl. . . . . . NiB $631	Ex $505	Gd $344
SPX Deluxe W/10-inch bbl.. . . . . . . NiB $861	Ex $688	Gd $468

BEHOLLA PISTOL — Suhl, Germany
Mfd. by both Becker and Holländer and
Stenda-Werke GmbH

POCKET AUTOMATIC PISTOL . . . . NiB $229 Ex $184 Gd $112
Caliber: .32 Automatic (7.65mm). Seven-shot magazine, 2.9-inch bbl., 5.5 inches overall. Weight: 22 oz. Fixed sights. Blued finish. Serrated wood or hard rubber grips. Made by Becker and Hollander 1915-1920, by Stenda-Werke circa 1920-25. Note: Essentially the same pistol was manufactured concurrently w/the Stenda version as the "Leonhardt" by H. M. Gering and as the "Menta" by August Menz.

BENELLI PISTOLS — Urbino, Italy
Imported by Benelli USA

MP90S WORLD CUP TARGET PISTOL
Semiautomatic blowback action. Calibers: .22 Short, .22LR, .32 W.C. Five-shot magazine, 4.33-inch fixed bbl. 6.75 inches overall. Weight: 36 oz. Post front sight, adjustable rear. Blue finish. Anatomic shelf-style grip. Imported 1992 to 2001.

MP90S (.22 LR) . . . . NiB $1270	Ex $1081	Gd $566
MP90S (.22 Short, disc. 1995). . . . NiB $1062	Ex $850	Gd $578
MP90S (.32 WC) . . . . NiB $1319	Ex $1056	Gd $718
W/conversion kit, add. $550

MP95E SPORT TARGET PISTOL
Similar to the MP90S except with 5- or 9-shot magazine, 4.25- inch bbl., Blue or chrome finish. Checkered target grip. Imported 1994 to date.

Blue MP95 (.22 LR) . . . . NiB $721	Ex $592	Gd $360
Blue MP95 (.32 WC) . . . . NiB $709	Ex $566	Gd $385
Chrome, add $85

BERETTA USA CORP. — Accokeek, Maryland

Beretta firearms are manufactured by Fabbrica D'Armi Pietro Beretta S. p. A. in the Gardone Val Trompia (Brescia), Italy. This prestigious firm has been in business since 1526. In 1977, Beretta U.S.A. Corp., a manufacturing and importing facility, opened in Accokeek, MD. (Previously imported by Garcia Corp., J.L. Galef & Son, Inc. and Berben Corporation.) Note: Beretta also owns additional firearms manufacturing companies including: Benelli, Franchi, Sako, Stoeger, Tikka and Uberti.

MODEL 20 DOUBLE-
ACTION AUTO PISTOL. . . . . NiB $165 Ex $144 Gd $93
Caliber: .25 ACP. Eight-shot magazine, 2.5-inch bbl., 4.9 inches overall. Weight: 10.9 oz. Plastic or walnut grips. Fixed sights. Made 1984-85.

MODEL 21 DOUBLE-ACTION AUTO PISTOL
Calibers: .22 LR and .25 ACP. Seven-shot (.22 LR) or 8-shot (..25 ACP) magazine, 2.5-inch bbl., 4.9 inches overall. Weight: About 12 oz. Blade front sight, V-notch rear. Walnut grips. Made 1985 to date.

Blued finish . . . . NiB $200	Ex $160	Gd $108
Nickel finish (.22 LR only). . . . . NiB $238	Ex $191	Gd $130
Model 21EL engraved model . . . . . . NiB $315	Ex $252	Gd $172

MODEL 70 AUTOMATIC PISTOL . . NiB $232 Ex $185 Gd $126
Improved version of Model 1935. Steel or lightweight alloy. Calibers: .32 Auto (7.65mm), .380 Auto (9mm Short). Eight-shot (.32) or 7-shot (.380) magazine, 3.5-inch bbl., 6.5 inches overall. Weight: Steel, 22.25 oz.; alloy, 16 oz. Fixed sights. Blued finish. Checkered plastic grips. Made 1959-85. Note: Formerly marketed in U.S. as "Puma" (alloy model in .32) and "Cougar" (steel model in .380). Disc.

HANDGUNS

MODEL 70S . . . . **NiB $247 Ex $216 Gd $134**
Similar to Model 70T except chambered for .22 Auto and .380 Auto.
Longer bbl. guide and safety lever blocking hammer. Front blade and
rear sight fixed on breechblock. Weight: 1 lb., 7 oz. Made 1977-85.

MODEL 70T
AUTOMATIC PISTOL . . . . **NiB $283 Ex $257 Gd $154**
Similar to Model 70. Caliber: .32 Automatic (7.65mm). Nine-shot
magazine, 6-inch bbl., 9.5 inches overall. Weight: 19 oz. adj. rear
sight, blade front sight. Blued finish. Checkered plastic grips. Intro.
in 1959. disc.

MODEL 71
AUTOMATIC PISTOL . . . . **NiB $227 Ex $201 Gd $129**
Same general specifications as alloy Model 70. Caliber: .22 LR. Six-
inch bbl., 8-round magazine, Adj. rear sight frame. Single action.
Made 1959-89. Note: Formerly marketed in U.S. as the "Jaguar
Plinker."

Beretta Model 71

MODEL 72 . . . . **NiB $227 Ex $201 Gd $124**
Same as Model 71 except has 6-inch bbl., weight: 18 oz. Intro. in
1959. Disc. Note: Formerly marketed in U.S as "Jaguar Plinker."

MODEL 76 AUTO TARGET PISTOL
Caliber: .22 LR. 10-shot magazine, 6-inch bbl., 8.8 inches overall.
Weight: 33 oz. adj. rear sight, front sight w/interchangeable blades.
Blued finish. Checkered plastic or wood grips. Made 1966-85.
Note: Formerly marketed in the U.S. as the "Sable."
Model 76 w/plastic grips . . . . **NiB $380 Ex $304 Gd $207**
Model 76W w/wood grips . . . . **NiB $444 Ex $355 Gd $242**

MODEL 81 DOUBLE-
ACTION AUTO PISTOL . . . . **NiB $319 Ex $257 Gd $165**
Caliber: .32 Automatic (7.65mm). 12-shot magazine, 3.8-inch bbl.,
6.8 inches overall. Weight: 23.5 oz. Fixed sights. Blued finish.
Plastic grips. Made principally for the European market 1975-84,
w/similar variations as implemented on the Model 84.

Beretta Model 72

MODEL 82 DOUBLE-
ACTION AUTO PISTOL . . . . **NiB $303 Ex $242 Gd $165**
Caliber: .32 ACP. Similar to the Model 81 except with a slimmer-
profile frame designed to accept a single column 9-shot magazine.
Matte black finish. Importation disc. 1984.

MODEL 84 DOUBLE-
ACTION AUTO PISTOL . . . . **NiB $304 Ex $258 Gd $154**
Same as Model 81 except made in caliber .380 Automatic w/13-
shot magazine, 3.82-inch bbl., 6.8 inches overall. Weight: 23 oz.
Fixed front and rear sights. Made 1975-82.

Beretta Model 84

MODEL 84B DA AUTO PISTOL . . . **NiB $304 Ex $257 Gd $175**
Improved version of Model 84 w/strengthened frame and slide, and
firing-pin block safety added. Ambidextrous reversible magazine
release. Blued or nickel finish. Checkered black plastic or wood
grips. Other specifications same. Made c. 1982-84.

MODEL 84(BB) DOUBLE-ACTION AUTO PISTOL
Improved version of Model 84B w/further-strengthened slide, frame
and recoil spring. Caliber: .380 ACP. 13-shot magazine, 3.82-inch
bbl., 6.8 inches overall. Weight: 23 oz. Checkered black plastic or
wood grips. Blued or nickel finish. Notched rear and blade front
sight. Made c. 1984-94.
Blued w/plastic grips . . . . **NiB $438 Ex $350 Gd $238**
Blued w/wood grips . . . . **NiB $457 Ex $366 Gd $248**
Nickel finish w/wood grips . . . . **NiB $503 Ex $402 Gd $273**

MODEL 84 CHEETAH SEMI-AUTO PISTOL
Similar to the Model 84 BB except with required design changes as
mandated by regulation, including reduced magazine capacity (10-
shot magazine) and marked as 9mm short (.380) as a marketing
strategy to counter increased availability of 9mm chamberings from
other manufacturers. Made 1994 to date. See illustration next page.
Blued w/plastic grips . . . . **NiB $418 Ex $335 Gd $228**
Blued w/wood grips . . . . **NiB $457 Ex $366 Gd $248**
Nickel finish w/wood grips . . . . **NiB $495 Ex $397 Gd $270**

MODEL 85 DOUBLE-
ACTION AUTO PISTOL . . . . **NiB $448 Ex $350 Gd $196**
Similar to the Model 84 except designed with a slimmer-profile
frame to accept a single column 8-shot magazine, no ambidextrous
magazine release. Matte black finish. Weight: 21.8 oz. Introduced
in 1977 following the Model 84. See illustration next page.

MODEL 85B DA AUTO PISTOL . . . **NiB $453 Ex $360 Gd $227**
Improved version of the Model 85. Imported 1982-85.

GRADING: **NiB** = New in Box   **Ex** = Excellent or NRA 95%   **Gd** = Good or NRA 68%

Beretta Model 84 Cheetah (Nickel finish)

Beretta Model 85

Beretta Model 85BB

Beretta Model 86 Cheetah

MODEL 85BB DOUBLE-ACTION PISTOL
Improved version of the Model 85B w/strengthened frame and slide. Caliber: .380 ACP. Eight-shot magazine, 3.82 inch bbl., 6.8 inches overall. Weight: 21.8 oz. Blued or nickel finish. Checkered black plastic or wood grips. Imported 1985-94.
Blued finish
w/plastic grips . . . . NiB $386 Ex $309 Gd $210
Blued finish
w/wood grips . . . . NiB $432 Ex $345 Gd $235
Nickel finish
w/wood grips . . . . NiB $483 Ex $386 Gd $263

MODEL 85 CHEETAH SEMI-AUTO PISTOL
Similar to the Model 85 BB except with required design changes as mandated by regulation and marked as 9mm short (.380) as a marketing strategy to counter increased availability of 9mm chamberings from other manufacturers. Made 1994 to date.
Blued w/plastic grips . . . . NiB $386 Ex $309 Gd $198
Blued w/wood grips . . . . NiB $439 Ex $355 Gd $248
Nickel w/wood grips . . . . NiB $483 Ex $397 Gd $279

MODEL 85F DOUBLE-ACTION PISTOL
Similar to the Model 85BB except has re-contoured trigger guard and manual ambidextrous safety w/decocking device. Bruniton finish. Imported in 1990.
Matte black Bruniton
finish w/plastic grips . . . . NiB $386 Ex $309 Gd $196
Matte black Bruniton
finish w/wood grips . . . . NiB $452 Ex $366 Gd $255

MODEL 86 CHEETAH
DA AUTO PISTOL . . . . NiB $500 Ex $391 Gd $196
Caliber: .380 auto. Eight-shot magazine, 4.4- inch bbl., 7.3 inches overall. Weight: 23.3 oz. Bruniton finish w/wood grips. Made 1986-89. (Reintroduced 1990 in the Cheetah series.)

MODEL 87 CHEETAH AUTO PISTOL
Similar to the Model 85 except in .22 LR w/8- or 10- shot magazine (Target) and optional extended 6-inch bbl. (Target in single action). Overall length: 6.8 to 8.8 inches. Weight: 20.1 oz. to 29.4 oz (Target). Checkered wood grips. Made 1987 to date.
Blued finish
(double-action) . . . . NiB $500 Ex $391 Gd $196
Target model
(single action) . . . . NiB $454 Ex $366 Gd $252

MODEL 89
GOLD STANDARD TARGET
AUTOMATIC PISTOL . . . . NiB $649 Ex $525 Gd $335
Caliber: .22 LR. Eight-shot magazine, 6-inch bbl., 9.5 inches overall. Weight: 41 oz. Adj. target sights. Blued finish. Target-style walnut grips. Made 1988 to date.

MODEL 90
DA AUTO PISTOL . . . . NiB $283 Ex $204 Gd $134
Caliber: .32 Auto (7.65mm). Eight-shot magazine, 3.63-inch bbl., 6.63 inches overall. Weight: 19.5 oz. Fixed sights. Blued finish. Checkered plastic grips. Made 1969-83.

MODEL 92 DA AUTO
PISTOL (1ST SERIES) . . . . NiB $669 Ex $566 Gd $283
Caliber: 9mm Para. 15-shot magazine, 4.9-inch bbl., 8.5 inches overall. Weight: 33.5 oz. Fixed sights. Blued finish. Plastic grips. Initial production of 5,000 made in 1976.

MODEL 92D DA AUTO PISTOL

Same general specifications as Model 92F except DA only w/bobbed hammer and 3-dot sight. Made 1992 to date.
Model 92D . . . . **NiB $474 Ex $371 Gd $283**
With Tritium
sight system add **$80**

MODEL 92F COMPACT

DA AUTOMATIC PISTOL . . . . **NiB $587 Ex $474 Gd $196**
Caliber: 9mm Para. 12-shot magazine, 4.3-inch bbl., 7.8 inches overall. Weight: 31.5 oz. Wood grips. Square-notched rear sight, blade front integral w/slide. Made 1986-93.

MODEL 92F COMPACT L TYPE M DA AUTOMATIC PISTOL

Same general specifications as the original 92F Compact except 8-shot magazine, Weight: 30.9 oz. Bruniton matte finish. Made 1998 to date.
Model 92F
Compact L Type M . . . . **NiB $587 Ex $474 Gd $196**
Model 92F
Compact L Type M Inox . . . . **NiB $587 Ex $474 Gd $196**
W/Tritium
sight system, add **$80**

MODEL 92F DA AUTOMATIC PISTOL

Same general specifications as Model 92 except w/slide-mounted safety and repositioned magazine release. Replaced Model 92SB. Blued or stainless finish. Made 1985 to date.
Blued finish . . . . **NiB $587 Ex $474 Gd $206**
Stainless finish . . . . **NiB $587 Ex $474 Gd $206**
Model 92F-EL gold. . . . . **NiB $720 Ex $592 Gd $430**

MODEL 92FS DA AUTOMATIC PISTOL

Calibers: 9mm, 9mmx19 and .40 S&W. 15- shot magazine, 4.9- inch bbl., 8.5 inches overall. Weight: 34.4 to 35.3 oz. Ambidextrous safety/decock lever. Chrome-lined bore w/combat trigger guard. Bruniton finish w/plastic grips or Inox finish w/rubber grips. Made 1991 to date.
Model 92FS . . . . **NiB $639 Ex $505 Gd $283**
Model 92FS, Inox . . . . **NiB $664 Ex $561 Gd $283**
Model 92FS — Brigadier
(Made 1999 to date) . . . . **NiB $547 Ex $438 Gd $298**
Model 92FS —
Brigadier Inox . . . . **NiB $664 Ex $561 Gd $288**
Model 92FS — Centurion
(Made 1992 to date) . . . . **NiB $664 Ex $561 Gd $288**
Model 92FS — 470th Anniver.
(Made 1999) . . . . **NiB $2153 Ex $1905 Gd $1107**

MODEL 92S DA AUTO

PISTOL (2ND SERIES) . . . . **NiB $669 Ex $566 Gd $257**
Revised version of Model 92 w/ambidextrous slide-mounted safety modification intended for both commercial and military production. Evolved to Model 92S-1 for U.S. Military trials. Made 1980-85.

MODEL 92SB DA

AUTO PISTOL (3RD SERIES) . . . . . . **NiB $690 Ex $597 Gd $299**
Same general specifications as standard Model 92 except has slide-mounted safety and repositioned magazine release. Made 1981-85.

MODEL 92 SB-F

DA AUTO PISTOL . . . . **NiB $669 Ex $566 Gd $257**
Caliber: 9mm Para. 15-shot magazine, bbl.: 4.9 inches, 8.5 inches overall. Weight: 34 oz. Plastic or Beretta Model 92 SB-F DA Auto Pistol wood grips. Square-notched rear sight, blade front sight integral w/slide. This model, also called Model 92S-1, is the standard-issue sidearm for the U.S. Armed Forces. Made 1985 to date.

Beretta Model 90

Beretta Model 92F

**Beretta Model 92
Compact L Type M**

**Beretta Model 92FS
Brigadier Inox**

Beretta Model 96

Beretta Model 949
Olimpionico

Beretta Model 950BS
Jetfire

MODEL 96 DOUBLE-ACTION AUTO PISTOL

Same general specifications as Model 92F except in .40 S&W. 10-shot magazine (9-shot in Compact model). Made 1992 to date.

Model 96 D (DA only)	NiB $425	Ex $340	Gd $231
Model 96 Centurion (compact)	NiB $4674	Ex $371	Gd $232
W/Tritium sights, add			$80
W/Tritium sights system, add			$95

MODEL 101 . . . . NiB $257 Ex $227 Gd $129
Same as Model 70T except caliber .22 LR, has 10-shot magazine, Intro. in 1959. Disc.

MODEL 318

(1934) AUTO PISTOL . . . . NiB $283 Ex $247 Gd $134
Caliber: .25 Automatic (6.35mm). Eight-shot magazine, 2.5-inch bbl., 4.5 inches overall. Weight: 14 oz. Fixed sights. Blued finish. Plastic grips. Made 1934 to c. 1939.

MODEL 949

OLIMPIONICO AUTO PISTOL . . . . NiB $680 Ex $566 Gd $206
Calibers: .22 Short, .22 LR. Five-shot magazine, 8.75-inch bbl., 12.5 inches overall. Weight: 38 oz. Target sights. Adj. bbl., weight. Muzzle brake. Checkered walnut grips w/thumbrest. Made 1959-64.

MODEL 950B AUTO PISTOL. . . . . . NiB $163 Ex $124 Gd $72
Same general specifications as Model 950CC except caliber .25 Auto, has 7-shot magazine, Made 1959 to date. Note: Formerly marketed in the U.S. as "Jetfire."

MODEL 950BS JETFIRE SA PISTOL

Calibers: .25 ACP or .22 Short (disc.1992). Seven- or 8- shot magazine, 2.4- or 4- inch bbl., 4.5 to 4.7 inches overall. Weight: 9.9 oz. Fixed blade front and V-notch rear sights. Matte Blue or Inox (Stainless) finish. Checkered black plastic grips. Made 1987 to date.

Blued finish	NiB $161	Ex $129	Gd $88
Nickel finish	NiB $212	Ex $170	Gd $115
Inox finish	NiB $186	Ex $149	Gd $102
W/4-inch bbl.,			
(.22 Short)	NiB $194	Ex $154	Gd $105

MODEL 950CC

AUTO PISTOL . . . . NiB $139 Ex $118 Gd $72
Caliber: .22 Short. Six-shot magazine, hinged 2.38-inch bbl., 4.75 inches overall. Weight: 11 oz. Fixed sights. Blued finish. Plastic grips. Made 1959 to date. Note: Formerly marketed in the U.S. as "Minx M2."

MODEL 950CC

SPECIAL AUTO PISTOL. . . . . NiB $139 Ex $118 Gd $72
Same general specifications as Model 950CC Auto except has 4-inch bbl. Made 1959 to date. Note: Formerly marketed in the U.S. as "Minx M4."

MODEL 951 (1951)

MILITARY AUTO PISTOL . . . . NiB $294 Ex $242 Gd $165
Caliber: 9mm Para. Eight-shot magazine, 4.5-inch bbl., 8 inches overall. Weight: 31 oz. Fixed sights. Blued finish. Plastic grips. Made 1952 to date. Note: This is the standard pistol of the Italian Armed Forces, also used by Egyptian and Israeli armies and by the police in Nigeria. Egyptian and Israeli models usually command a premium. Formerly marketed in the U.S. as the "Brigadier."

MODEL 1915

AUTO PISTOL . . . . NiB $978 Ex $721 Gd $309
Calibers: 9mm Glisenti and .32 ACP (7.65mm). Eight-shot magazine, 4-inch bbl., 6.7 inches overall (9mm), 5.7 inches (.32 ACP). Weight: 30 oz. (9mm), 20 oz. (.32 ACP). Fixed sights. Blued finish. Wood grips. Made 1915-1922. An improved postwar 1915/1919 version in caliber .32 ACP was later offered for sale in 1922 as the Model 1922.

MODEL 1923

AUTO PISTOL . . . . NiB $1030 Ex $875 Gd $257
Caliber: 9mm Glisenti (Luger). Eight-shot magazine, 4-inch bbl., 6.5 inches overall. Weight: 30 oz. Fixed sights. Blued finish. Plastic grips. Made c. 1923-36.

MODEL 1934 AUTO PISTOL

Caliber: .380 Automatic (9mm Short). Seven-shot magazine, 3.38-inch bbl., 5.88 inches overall. Weight: 24 oz. Fixed sights. Blued finish. Plastic grips. Official pistol of the Italian Armed Forces. Wartime pieces not as well made and finished as commercial models. Made 1934-59.

Commercial model	NiB $386	Ex $335	Gd $196
War model	NiB $360	Ex $330	Gd $185

MODEL 1935 AUTO PISTOL

Caliber: .32 ACP (7.65mm). Eight-shot magazine, 3.5-inch bbl., 5.75 inches overall. Weight: 24 oz. Fixed sights. Blued finish. Plastic grips. A roughly-finished version of this pistol was produced during WW II. Made 1935-1959.

Commercial model . . . . NiB $360 Ex $324 Gd $180
War model . . . . NiB $309 Ex $257 Gd $154

MODEL 3032 DA SEMIAUTOMATIC TOMCAT

Caliber: .32 ACP. Seven-shot magazine, 2.45-inch bbl., 5 inches overall. Weight: 14.5 oz. Fixed sights. Blued or stainless finish. Made 1996 to date.

Matte blue . . . . NiB $273 Ex $206 Gd $124
Polished blue . . . . NiB $318 Ex $263 Gd $192
Stainless . . . . NiB $343 Ex $278 Gd $196

**Beretta
Model 3032 Tomcat**

MODEL 8000/8040/8045 COUGAR DA PISTOL

Calibers: 9mm, .40 S&W and .45 Auto. Eight- or 10- shot magazine, 3.6 to 3.7- inch bbl., 7- to 7.2 inches overall. Weight: 32 to 32.6 oz. Short recoil action w/rotating barrel. Fixed sights w/3-dot Tritium system. Textured black composition grips. Matte black Bruniton finish w/alloy frame. Made 1994 to date.

**8000 Cougar D
(9mm DAO)** . . . . NiB $618 Ex $561 Gd $309
**8000 Cougar F
(9mm DA)** . . . . NiB $618 Ex $561 Gd $309
**8040 Cougar D
(.40 S&W DAO)** . . . . NiB $618 Ex $561 Gd $309
**8040 Cougar F
(.40 S&W DA)** . . . . NiB $618 Ex $561 Gd $309
**8045 Cougar D
(.45 Auto DAO)** . . . . NiB $639 Ex $566 Gd $319
**8045 Cougar F
(.45 Auto DA)** . . . . NiB $639 Ex $566 Gd $319

**Beretta
Model 8000 Cougar D**

MODEL 8000/8040/8045 MINI COUGAR DA PISTOL

Calibers: 9mm, .40 S&W and .45 Auto. Six- 8- or 10-shot magazine, 3.6- to 3.7- inch bbl., 7 inches overall. Weight: 27.4 to 30.4 oz. Fixed sights w/3-dot Tritium system. Ambidextrous safety/decocker lever. Matte black Bruniton finish w/anodized aluminum alloy frame. Made 1998 to date.

**8000 Mini
Cougar D (9mm DAO)** . . . . NiB $639 Ex $505 Gd $247
**8000 Mini
Cougar F (9mm DA)** . . . . NiB $659 Ex $525 Gd $257
**8040 Mini
Cougar D (.40 S&W DAO)** . . . . NiB $659 Ex $525 Gd $257
**8040 Mini
Cougar F (.40 S&W DA)** . . . . NiB $659 Ex $525 Gd $257
**8045 Mini
Cougar D (.45 Auto DAO)** . . . . NiB $649 Ex $515 Gd $232
**8045 Mini
Cougar F (.45 Auto DA)** . . . . NiB $659 Ex $525 Gd $257

**Beretta
Model 8000 Cougar F**

MODEL 9000S SUBCOMPACT PISTOL SERIES

Calibers: 9mm, .40 S&W. 10-shot magazine, 3.5- inch bbl., 6.6 inches overall. Weight: 25.7 to 27.5 oz. Single/double and double-action only. Front and rear dovetail sights w/3- dot system. Chrome-plated barrel w/Techno-polymer frame. Geometric locking system w/tilt barrel. Made 1999 to date. See illustration next page.

Type D (9mm) . . . . NiB $496 Ex $417 Gd $256
Type D (.40 S&W) . . . . NiB $510 Ex $407 Gd $257
Type F (9mm) . . . . NiB $536 Ex $437 Gd $263
Type F (.40 S&W) . . . . NiB $546 Ex $452 Gd $272

**Beretta
Model 8040 Mini Cougar D**

**Beretta
Model 9000 Type F**

**Bernardelli
Model 60 Pocket**

**Bernardelli
Model 80 Pocket**

VINCENZO BERNARDELLI, S.P.A.
Gardone V. T. (Brescia), Italy

Currently imported by Armsport, Inc., Miami, FL

MODEL 60 POCKET
AUTOMATIC PISTOL . . . . NiB $227 Ex $201 Gd $134
Calibers: .22 LR, .32 Auto (7.65mm), .380 Auto (9mm Short). Eight-shot magazine (.22 and .32), 7-shot (.380). 3.5-inch bbl., 6.5

(cont'd) **MODEL 60**
inches ovr-all. Weight: About 25 oz. Fixed sights. Blued finish. Bakelite grips. Made 1959-90.

MODEL 68 AUTOMATIC PISTOL . . . NiB $144 Ex $124 Gd $82
Caliber: 6.35. Five- and 8-shot magazine, 2.13-inch bbl., 4.13 inches overall. Weight: 10 oz. Fixed sights. Blued or chrome finish. Bakelite or pearl grips. This model, like its .22-caliber counterpart, was known as the "Baby" Bernardelli. Disc. 1970.

**MODEL 69 AUTOMATIC
TARGET PISTOL . . . . NiB $592 Ex $489 Gd $309**
Caliber: .22 LR. 10-shot magazine, 5.9-inch bbl., 9 inches overall. Weight: 2.2 lbs. Fully adj. target sights. Blued finish. Stippled right- or left-hand wraparound walnut grips. Made 1987 to date. Note: This was previously Model 100.

**MODEL 80
AUTOMATIC PISTOL . . . . NiB $191 Ex $165 Gd $103**
Calibers: .22 LR, .32 ACP (7.65mm), .380 Auto (9mm Short). Magazine capacity: 10-shot (.22), 8-shot (.32), 7-shot (.380). 3.5-inch bbl., 6.5 inches overall. Weight: 25.6 oz. adj. rear sight, white dot front sight. Blued finish. Plastic thumbrest grips. Note: Model 80 is a modification of Model 60 designed to conform w/U.S. import regulations. Made 1968-88.

**MODEL 90
SPORT TARGET . . . . NiB $216 Ex $191 Gd $113**
Same as Model 80 except has 6-inch bbl., 9 inches overall, weight: 26.8 oz. Made 1968-90.

**MODEL 100 TARGET
AUTOMATIC PISTOL . . . . NiB $407 Ex $335 Gd $216**
Caliber: .22 LR. 10-shot magazine, 5.9-inch bbl., 9 inches overall. Weight: 37.75 oz. Adj. rear sight, interchangeable front sights. Blued finish. Checkered walnut thumbrest grips. Made 1969-86. Note: Formerly Model 69.

MODEL AMR AUTO PISTOL . . . . . . NiB $407 Ex $335 Gd $206
Simlar to Model USA except with 6-inch bbl. and target sights. Imported 1992-94.

"BABY" AUTOMATIC PISTOL . . . . . NiB $257 Ex $180 Gd $103
Calibers: .22 Short, .22 Long. Five-shot magazine, 2.13-inch bbl., 4.13 inches overall. Weight: 9 oz. Fixed sights. Blued finish. Bakelite grips. Made 1949-68.

**MODEL P010
AUTOMATIC PISTOL . . . . NiB $695 Ex $592 Gd $360**
Caliber: .22 LR. Five- and 10-shot magazine, 5.9-inch bbl. w/7.5-inch sight radius. Weight: 40 oz. Interchangeable front sight, adj. rear. Blued finish. Textured walnut grips. Made 1988-92 and 1995-97.

P018 COMPACT MODEL . . . . NiB $500 Ex $474 Gd $232
Slightly smaller version of the Model P018 standard DA automatic except has 14-shot magazine and 4-inch bbl., 7.68 inches overall. Weight: 33 oz. Walnut grips only. Imported 1987-96.

P018 DOUBLE-ACTION AUTOMATIC PISTOL
Caliber: 9mm Para. 16-shot magazine, 4.75-inch bbl., 8.5 inches overall. Weight: 36 oz. Fixed combat sights. Blued finish. Checkered plastic or walnut grips. Imported 1987-96.
W/plastic grips . . . . NiB $500 Ex $412 Gd $237
W/walnut grips . . . . NiB $529 Ex $427 Gd $298

P. ONE DA AUTO PISTOL

Caliber: 9mm Parabellum or .40 S&W. 10- or 16-shot magazine, 4.8-inch bbl., 8.35 inches overall. Weight: 34 oz. Blade front sight, adjustable rear w/3-dot system. Matte black or chrome finish. Checkered walnut or black plastic grips. Imported 1993-97.

Model P One blue finish . . . . NiB $597 Ex $500 Gd $288
Model P One chrome finish. . . . . . NiB $629 Ex $510 Gd $356
W/walnut grips, add 35

P. ONE PRACTICAL VB AUTO PISTOL

Similar to Model P One except chambered for 9x21mm w/2-, 4- or 6-port compensating system for IPSC competition. Imported 1993-97.
Model P One
Practical (2 port) . . . . NiB $1030 Ex $953 Gd $680
Model P One
Practical (4 port) . . . . NiB $1157 Ex $937 Gd $657
Model P One
Practical (6 port) . . . . NiB $1553 Ex $1257 Gd $878
W/chrome finish, add $60

SPORTER AUTOMATIC PISTOL . . . . . NiB $314 Ex $283 Gd $180
Caliber .22 LR. Eight-shot magazine, bbl., lengths: 6-, 8- and 10-inch, 13 inches overall (10-inch bbl.). weight: About 30 oz. (10-inch bbl.) Target sights. Blued finish. Walnut grips. Made 1949-68.

MODEL USA AUTO PISTOL

Single-action, blowback. Calibers: .22 LR, .32 ACP, .380 ACP. Seven-shot magazine or 10-shot magazine (.22 LR). 3.5-inch bbl., 6.5 inches overall. Weight: 26.5 oz. Ramped front sight, adjustable rear. Blue or chrome finish. Checkered black bakelite grips w/thumbrest. Imported 1991-97.

Model USA blue finish . . . . NiB $391 Ex $304 Gd $15
Model USA chrome finish . . . . NiB $480 Ex $397 Gd $289

VEST POCKET

AUTOMATIC PISTOL . . . . NiB $257 Ex $201 Gd $129
Caliber: .25 Auto (6.35mm). Five- or 8-shot magazine, 2.13-inch bbl., 4.13 inches overall. Weight: 9 oz. Fixed sights. Blued finish. Bakelite grips. Made 1945-68.

Bernardelli P010

Bernardelli "Baby"

BERSA PISTOLS — Argentina

Currently imported by Eagle Imports, Wanamassa, NJ (Previously by Interarms & Outdoor Sports)

MODEL 83 DOUBLE-ACTION AUTO PISTOL

Similar to the Model 23 except for the following specifications: Caliber: .380 ACP. Seven-shot magazine, 3.5-inch bbl., Front blade sight integral on slide, square-notch rear adj. for windage. Blued or satin nickel finish. Custom wood grips. Imported 1988-94.

Blued finish . . . . NiB $240 Ex $184 Gd $153
Satin nickel . . . . NiB $300 Ex $250 Gd $187

MODEL 85 DOUBLE-ACTION AUTO PISTOL

Same general specifications as Model 83 except 13-shot magazine, Imported 1988-94. See illustration next page.

Blued finish . . . . NiB $291 Ex $250 Gd $143
Satin nickel . . . . NiB $389 Ex $321 Gd $235

MODEL 86 DOUBLE-ACTION AUTO PISTOL

Same general specifications as Model 85 except available in matte blued finish and w/Neoprene grips. Imported 1992-94.

Matte blued finish . . . . NiB $321 Ex $270 Gd $163
Nickel finish . . . . NiB $381 Ex $311 Gd $221

Bernardelli P018

MODEL 95 DA AUTOMATIC PISTOL

Caliber: .380 ACP. Seven-shot magazine, 3.5-inch bbl., weight: 23 oz. Wraparound rubber grips. Blade front and rear notch sights. Imported 1995 to date.

Blued finish . . . . NiB $234 Ex $168 Gd $112
Nickel finish . . . . NiB $257 Ex $191 Gd $135

Bersa Model 85

Bersa Model 383

Bersa Thunder .380

Bersa Thunder .380 Deluxe

MODEL 97
AUTO PISTOL . . . . NiB $331 Ex $286 Gd $173
Caliber: .380 ACP. Seven-shot magazine, 3.3-inch bbl., 6.5 inches overall. Weight: 28 oz. Intro. 1982. Disc.

MODEL 223
Same general specifications as Model 383 except in .22 LR w/10-round magazine capacity. Disc. 1987.
Double action . . . . NiB $204 Ex $173 Gd $112
Single action . . . . NiB $194 Ex $163 Gd $109

MODEL 224
Caliber: .22 LR. 10-shot magazine, 4-inch bbl., weight: 26 oz. Front blade sight, square-notched rear adj. for windage. Blued finish. Checkered nylon or custom wood grips. Made 1984. SA. disc. 1986.
Double-action . . . . NiB $204 Ex $173 Gd $112
Single action . . . . NiB $199 Ex $172 Gd $106

MODEL 226
Same general specifications as Model 224 but w/6-inch bbl. Disc. 1987.
Double action . . . . NiB $204 Ex $173 Gd $112
Single action . . . . NiB $194 Ex $163 Gd $109

MODEL 383 AUTO PISTOL
Caliber: .380 Auto. Seven-shot magazine, 3.5-inch bbl. Front blade sight integral on slide, square-notched rear sight adj. for windage. Custom wood grips on double-action, nylon grips on single action. Blued or satin nickel finish. Made 1984. SA. disc. 1989.
Double action . . . . NiB $122 Ex $97 Gd $51
Single action . . . . NiB $163 Ex $123 Gd $76
Satin nickel . . . . NiB $205 Ex $163 Gd $89

MODEL 622
AUTO PISTOL . . . . NiB $159 Ex $127 Gd $87
Caliber: .22 LR. Seven-shot magazine, 4- or 6-inch bbl., 7 or 9 inches overall. Weight: 2.25 lbs. Blade front sight, square-notch rear adj. for windage. Blued finish. Nylon grips. Made 1982-87.

MODEL 644
AUTO PISTOL . . . . NiB $234 Ex $199 Gd $122
Caliber: .22 LR. 10-shot magazine, 3.5-inch bbl., weight: 26.5 oz. 6.5 inches overall. Adj. rear sight, blade front. Contoured black nylon grips. Made 1980-88.

THUNDER 9
AUTO PISTOL . . . . NiB $240 Ex $199 Gd $122
Caliber: 9mm Para. 15-shot magazine, 4-inch bbl., 7.38 inches overall. Weight: 30 oz. Blade front sight, adj. rear w/3-dot system. Ambidextrous safety and decocking device. Matte blued finish. Checkered black polymer grips. Made 1993-96.

THUNDER .22
AUTO PISTOL (MODEL 23)
Caliber: .22 LR, 10-shot magazine, 3.5-inch bbl., 6.63 inches overall. Weight: 24.5 oz. Notched-bar dovetailed rear, blade integral w/slide front. Black polymer grips. Made 1989 to date.
Blued finish . . . . NiB $234 Ex $199 Gd $112
Nickel finish . . . . NiB $247 Ex $199 Gd $134

THUNDER .380 AUTO PISTOL

Caliber: .380 ACP. Seven-shot magazine, 3.5-inch bbl., 6.63 inches overall. Weight: 25.75 oz. Notched-bar dovetailed rear, blade integral w/slide front. Blued, satin nickel, or Duo-Tone finish. Made 1995 to date.

Blued finish	NiB $229	Ex $245	Gd $117
Satin nickel finish	NiB $269	Ex $219	Gd $156
Duo-Tone finish	NiB $256	Ex $209	Gd $149

THUNDER .380 PLUS AUTO PISTOL

Same general specifications as standard Thunder .380 except has 10-shot magazine and weight: 26 oz. Made 1995-97.

Matte finish	NiB $236	Ex $189	Gd $129
Satin nickel finish	NiB $287	Ex $229	Gd $156
Duo-Tone finish	NiB $268	Ex $214	Gd $146

BROLIN ARMS — La Verne, California

"LEGEND SERIES" SA AUTOMATIC PISTOL

Caliber: .45 ACP. Seven-shot magazine, 4- or 5-inch bbl., weight: 32-36 oz. Walnut grips. Single action, full size, compact, or full size frame compact slide. Matte blued finish. Lowered and flared ejection port. Made 1995 to date.

Model L45	NiB $433	Ex $372	Gd $229
Model L45C	NiB $449	Ex $388	Gd $255
Model L45T	NiB $459	Ex $399	Gd $265

"PATRIOT SERIES" SA AUTOMATIC PISTOL

Caliber: .45 ACP. Seven-shot magazine, 3.25- and 4-inch bbl., weight: 33-37 oz. Wood grips. Fixed rear sights. Made 1996 to date.

Model P45	NiB $597	Ex $484	Gd $306
Model P45C (disc. 1997)	NiB $622	Ex $632	Gd $561
Model P45T (disc. 1997)	NiB $632	Ex $510	Gd $286

"PRO-STOCK AND PRO-COMP" SA PISTOL

Caliber: .45 ACP. Eight-shot magazine, 4- or 5-inch bbl., weight: 37 oz. Single action, blued or two-tone finish. Wood grips. Bomar adjustable sights. Made 1996-97.

Model Pro comp	NiB $699	Ex $561	Gd $381
Model Pro stock	NiB $632	Ex $510	Gd $337

TAC SERIES

Caliber: .45 ACP. Eight-shot magazine, 5-inch bbl., 8.5 inches overall. Weight: 37 oz. Low profile combat or Tritium sights. Beavertail grip safety. Matte blue, chrome or two-tone finish. Checkered wood or contoured black rubber grips. Made 1997 to date.

Model TAC 11 service	NiB $622	Ex $505	Gd $306
Model TAC 11 compact	NiB $632	Ex $510	Gd $306
W/Tritium sights, add			$95

BRONCO PISTOL — Eibar, Spain
Manufactured by Echave y Arizmendi

MODEL 1918 POCKET

AUTOMATIC PISTOL . . . . NiB $178 Ex $153 Gd $76
Caliber: .32 ACP (7.65mm). Six-shot magazine 2.5-inch bbl., 5 inches overall. Weight: 20 oz. Fixed sights. Blued finish. Hard rubber grips. Made c.1918-.25.

SEMIAUTOMATIC PISTOL . . . . NiB $163 Ex $127 Gd $90
Caliber: .25 ACP, 6-shot magazine, 2.13-inch bbl., 4.13 inches overall. Weight: 11 oz. Fixed sights. Blued finish. Hard rubber grips. Made 1919-35.

**Browning
Model 25 Automatic**

BROWNING PISTOLS — Morgan, Utah

The following Browning pistols have been manufactured by Fabrique Nationale d'Armes de Guerre (now Fabrique Nationale Herstal) of Herstal, Belgium, by Arms Technology Inc. of Salt Lake City and by J. P. Sauer & Sohn of Eckernforde, W. Germany. (See also FN Browning and J.P. Sauer & Sohn listings.)

.25 AUTOMATIC PISTOL

Same general specifications as FN Browning Baby (see separate listing). Standard Model, blued finish, hard rubber grips. Light Model, nickel-plated, Nacrolac pearl grips. Renaissance Engraved Model, nickel-plated, Nacrolac pearl grips. Made by FN 1955-69.

Standard model	NiB $515	Ex $453	Gd $206
Lightweight model	NiB $515	Ex $453	Gd $206
Renaissance model	NiB $1004	Ex $772	Gd $412

.32 AND .380 AUTOMATIC PISTOL, 1955 TYPE

Same general specifications as FN Browning .32 (7.65mm) and .380 Pocket Auto. Standard Model, Renaissance Engraved Model as furnished in .25 Automatic. Made by FN 1955-69.

Standard model (.32 ACP)	NiB $446	Ex $360	Gd $237
Standard model (.380 ACP)	NiB $376	Ex $309	Gd $206
Renaissance model	NiB $978	Ex $824	Gd $592

.380 AUTOMATIC PISTOL, 1971 TYPE

Same as .380 Automatic, 1955 Type except has longer slide, 4.44-inch bbl., is 7.06 inches overall, weight: 23 oz. Rear sight adj. for windage and elevation, plastic thumbrest grips. Made 1971-75.

Standard model	NiB $407	Ex $309	Gd $206
Renaissance model	NiB $1004	Ex $798	Gd $515

BDA DA AUTOMATIC PISTOL

Similar to SIG-Sauer P220. Calibers: 9mm Para., .38 Super Auto, .45 Auto. Nine-shot magazine (9mm and .38), 7-shot (.45 cal), 4.4-inch bbl., 7.8 inches overall. Weight: 29.3 oz. Fixed sights. Blued finish. Plastic grips. Made 1977-79 by J. P. Sauer.

BDA model, 9mm, .45 ACP	NiB $479	Ex $407	Gd $257
BDA model, .38 Super	NiB $489	Ex $391	Gd $299

BDA-.380 DA AUTOMATIC PISTOL

Caliber: .380 Auto. 10- or 13-shot magazine, bbl. length: 3.81 inches., 6.75 inches overall. Weight: 23 oz. Fixed blade front sight, square-notch drift-adj. rear sight. Blued or nickel finish. Smooth walnut grips. Made 1982-97 by Beretta. See illustration next page.

Blued finish	NiB $463	Ex $355	Gd $206
Nickel finish	NiB $449	Ex $366	Gd $258

Browning
BDA .380 Nickel finish

Browning
BDM 9mm DA

Browning
Buck Mark 22 Field (5.5)

Browning
Buck Mark 22 Bullseye

Browning
Buck Mark 22 Plus

BDM SERIES AUTOMATIC PISTOLS

Calibers: 9mm Para., 10-shot magazine, 4.73-inch bbl., 7.85 inches overall. Weight: 31 oz., windage adjustable sights w/3-dot system. Low profile removable blade front sights. Matte blued, Bi-Tone or silver chrome finish. Selectable shooting mode and decocking safety lever. Made 1991 to date.

BDM Standard................ NiB $495 Ex $397 Gd $270
BDM Practical................ NiB $503 Ex $402 Gd $273
BDM-D Silver Chrome .... NiB $509 Ex $407 Gd $277

BUCK MARK .22 AUTOMATIC PISTOL

Caliber: .22 LR. 10-shot magazine, 5.5- inch bbl., 9.5 inches overall. Weight: 32 oz. Black molded grips. Adj. rear sight. Blued or nickel finish. Made 1985 to date.

Blued finish .... NiB $221 Ex $180 Gd $103
Nickel finish .... NiB $282 Ex $232 Gd $168

BUCK MARK .22 BULLSEYE PISTOL

Same general specifications as the standard Buck Mark 22 except w/7.25-inch fluted barrel, 11.83 inches overall. Weight: 36 oz. Adjustable target trigger. Undercut post front sight, click-adjustable Pro-Target rear. Laminated, Rosewood, black rubber or composite grips. Made 1996 to date.

Standard model
(composite grips)............... NiB $335 Ex $273 Gd $185
Target model .... NiB $412 Ex $309 Gd $185

BUCK MARK .22

BULLSEYE TARGET .... NiB $412 Ex $309 Gd $185
Caliber: .22 LR. 10-shot magazine, 7.25- inch fluted bbl., 11.83 inches overall. Weight: 31 oz. Rosewood wrap-around finger groove grips w/matte blued finish. Made 1996 to date.

BUCK MARK .22 FIELD

(5.5) AUTO PISTOL............. NiB $335 Ex $247 Gd $154
Calibers: .22 LR. 10-shot magazine, 5.5- inch bbl., 9.58 inches overall. Weight: 35.5 oz. Standard sights. Matte Blue finish. Made 1991 to date.

BUCK MARK .22 MICRO AUTOMATIC PISTOL

Same general specifications as standard Buck Mark .22 except w/4-inch bbl., 8 inches overall. Weight: 32 oz. Molded composite grips. Ramp front sight, Pro Target rear sight. Made 1992 to date.

Blued finish .... NiB $273 Ex $216 Gd $111
Nickel finish .... NiB $293 Ex $245 Gd $184

**Browning
Buck Mark .22 Silhouette**

**Browning
Buck Mark .22 Target (5.5)**

BUCK MARK .22 MICRO PLUS AUTO PISTOL
Same specifications as the Buck Mark .22 Micro except ambidextrous, laminated wood grips. Made 1996 to date.
Blued finish . . . . NiB $273 Ex $216 Gd $113
Nickel finish . . . . NiB $306 Ex $255 Gd $192

BUCK MARK .22 PLUS AUTOMATIC PISTOL
Same general specifications as standard Buck Mark .22 except for black molded, impregnated hardwood grips. Made 1987 to date.
Blued finish . . . . NiB $273 Ex $216 Gd $103
Nickel finish . . . . NiB $312 Ex $261 Gd $195

BUCK MARK .22 TARGET (5.5) AUTO PISTOL
Caliber: .22 LR. 10-shot magazine, 5.5- inch bbl., 9.6 inches overall. Weight: 35.5 oz. Pro target sights. Wrap-around walnut or contoured finger groove grips. Made 1990 to date.
Matte blue finish . . . . NiB $360 Ex $288 Gd $154
Nickel finish (1994 to date) . . . . NiB $43 Ex $358 Gd $262
Gold finish (1991-99) . . . . NiB $477 Ex $397 Gd $295

BUCK MARK .22 SILHOUETTE . . . . NiB $371 Ex $294 Gd $154
Same general specifications as standard Buck Mark .22 except for 9.88-inch bbl. Weight: 53 oz. Target sights mounted on full-length scope base, and laminated hardwood grips and forend. Made 1987 to date.

BUCK MARK .22
UNLIMITED SILHOUETTE . . . . NiB $438 Ex $340 Gd $206
Same general specifications as standard Buck Mark .22 Silhouette except w/14-inch bbl., 18.69 inches overall. Weight: 64 oz. Interchangeable post front sight and Pro Target rear. Nickel finish. Made 1992 to date.

**Browning
Buck Mark .22 Micro Plus**

BUCK MARK .22
VARMINT AUTO PISTOL. . . . . NiB $324 Ex $263 Gd $165
Same general specifications as standard Buck Mark .22 except for 9.88-inch bbl. Weight: 48 oz. No sights, full-length scope base, and laminated hardwood grips. Made 1987 to date.

CHALLENGER AUTOMATIC PISTOL
Caliber: .22 LR. 10-shot magazine, bbl. lengths: 4.5 and 6.75-inches. 11.44 inches overall (with 6.75-inch bbl.). Weight: 38 oz. (6.75-inch bbl.). Removable blade front sight, screw adj. rear. Standard finish, blued, also furnished gold inlaid (Gold model) and engraved and chrome-plated (Renaissance model). Checkered walnut grips. Finely figured and carved grips on Gold and Renaissance models. Standard made by FN 1962-75, higher grades. Intro. 1971. Disc.
Standard model . . . . NiB $386 Ex $324 Gd $206
Gold model . . . . NiB $1493 Ex $1287 Gd $575
Renaissance model . . . . NiB $1493 Ex $1287 Gd $575

CHALLENGER II
AUTOMATIC PISTOL . . . . NiB $227 Ex $196 Gd $113
Same general specifications as Challenger Standard model w/6.75-inch bbl. except changed grip angle and impregnated hardwood grips. Original Challenger design modified for lower production costs. Made by ATI 1976-83.

**Browning Challenger
Standard Model**

**Browning Challenger
Renaissance Model**

**Browning
Challenger III Sporter .22**

**Browning
9mm Hi-Power w/Molded Grips**

**Browning
9mm Hi-Power Ambidextrous Safety**

**Browning
Hi-Power Captain**

**Browning
Hi-Power Mark III**

CHALLENGER III
AUTOMATIC PISTOL . . . . **NiB $227   Ex $196   Gd $113**
Same general description as Challenger II except has 5.5 inch bull bbl., alloy frame and new sight system. Weight: 35 oz. Made 1982-84. Sporter Model w/6.75-inch bbl.. Made 1984-86.

HI-POWER AUTOMATIC PISTOL
Same general specifications as FN Browning Model 1935 except chambered for 9mm Para., .30 Luger and .40 S&W. 10- or 13-shot magazine, 4.63-inch bbl., 7.75 inches overall. Weight: 32 oz. (9mm) or 35 oz. (.40 S&W). Fixed sights, also available w/rear sight adj. for windage and elevation, and ramp front sight. Ambidextrous safety added after 1989. Standard model blued, chrome-plated or Bi-Tone finish. Checkered walnut, contour-molded Polyamide or wraparound rubber grips. Renaissance Engraved model chrome-plated, w/Nacrolac pearl grips. Made by FN from1955 to date.
**Standard model,
fixed sights, 9mm** . . . . **NiB $711   Ex $577   Gd $412**
**Standard model, fixed sights,
.40 S&W (intro. 1986)** . . . . **NiB $721   Ex $695   Gd $515**
**Standard model, .30
Luger (1986-89)** . . . . **NiB $695   Ex $592   Gd $386**
**Renaissance model,
fixed sights.** . . . . **NiB $1390   Ex $1329   Gd $515**
**W/adjustable
rear sight, add** **$50**
**W/ambidextrous
safety, add** **$95**
**W/moulded grips,
deduct** **$40**
**W/tangent rear sight
(1965-78), add*** **$295**
**W/T-Slot grip &
tangent sight
(1965-78), add*** **$595**
*Check FN agent to certify value

HI-POWER
CAPITAN AUTOMATIC . . . . **NiB $628   Ex $515   Gd $335**
Similar to the standard Hi-Power except fitted w/adj. 500-meter tangent rear sight and rounded serrated hammer. Made 1993 to date.

HI-POWER MARK
III AUTOMATIC PISTOL . . . . **NiB $556   Ex $407   Gd $309**
Calibers: 9mm and .40 S&W. 10-shot magazine, 4.75-inch bbl., 7.75 inches overall. Weight: 32 oz. Fixed sights with molded grips. Durable non-glare matte blue finish. Made 1985 to date.

**Browning
Hi-Power Practical**

**Browning
Hi-Power Silver Chrome**

HI-POWER PRACTICAL AUTOMATIC PISTOL
Similar to the standard Hi-Power except has silver-chromed frame and blued slide w/Commander-style hammer. Made 1991 to date.
W/fixed sights . . . . NiB $587 Ex $448 Gd $309
W/adj. sights . . . . NiB $620 Ex $508 Gd $365

HI-POWER SILVER CHROME
AUTOMATIC PISTOL . . . . NiB $716 Ex $566 Gd $324
Calibers: 9mm and .40 S&W. 10-shot magazine, 4.75-inch bbl., 7.75 inches overall. Weight: 36 oz. Adjustable sights with Pachmayer grips. Silver-chromed finish. Made 1991 to date.

HI-POWER 9MM CLASSIC
Limited Edition 9mm Hi-Power, w/silver-gray finish, high-grade engraving and finely-checkered walnut grips w/double border. Proposed production of the Classic was 5000 w/less than half that number produced. Gold Classic limited to 500 w/two-thirds proposed production in circulation. Made 1985-86.
Gold classic. . . . . NiB $2569 Ex $2055 Gd $1398
Standard classic. . . . . NiB $1281 Ex $1025 Gd $697

INTERNATIONAL
MEDALIST AUTOMATIC
TARGET PISTOL . . . . NiB $876 Ex $721 Gd $412
Modification of Medalist to conform w/International Shooting Union rules. 5.9-inch bbl., Smaller grip with no forearm. Weight: 42 oz. Made 1970-73.

MEDALIST AUTOMATIC TARGET PISTOL
Caliber: .22 LR. 10-shot magazine, 6.75-inch bbl. w/vent rib, 11.94 inches overall. Weight: 46 oz. Removable blade front sight, click-adj. micrometer rear. Standard finish, blued also furnished gold-inlaid (Gold Model) and engraved and chrome-plated (Renaissance Model). Checkered walnut grips w/thumbrest (for right- or left-handed shooter). Finely figured and carved grips on Gold and Renaissance Models. Made by FN 1962-75. Higher grades. Intro. 1971.
Standard model . . . . NiB $876 Ex $721 Gd $463
Gold model . . . . NiB $2008 Ex $1699 Gd 907
Renaissance model . . . . NiB $2450 Ex $2008 Gd $1258

NOMAD
AUTOMATIC PISTOL . . . . NiB $309 Ex $257 Gd $154
Caliber: .22 LR. 10-shot magazine, bbl. lengths: 4.5 and 6.75-inches, 8.94 inches overall (4.5-inch bbl.). Weight: 34 oz. (with 4.5-inch bbl.). Removable blade front sight, screw adj. rear. Blued finish. Plastic grips. Made by FN 1962-74.

**Browning
Hi-Power 9mm Classic**

**Browning
Medalist International**

**Browning
Medalist Automatic Target Pistol**

Browning
Renaissance

Charter Arms
Bonnie

Charter Arms
Clyde

**RENAISSANCE 9MM, .25 AUTO
AND .380 AUTO (1955) ENGRAVED
MODELS, CASED SET** .... **NiB $4629 Ex $3703 Gd $2518**
One pistol of each of the three models in a special walnut carrying case, all chrome-plated w/Nacrolac pearl grips. Made by FN 1955-69.

BRYCO ARMS INC. — Irvine, California Distributed by Jennings Firearms. Inc. Carson City, NV

MODELS J22, J25 AUTO PISTOL
Calibers: .22 LR, .25 ACP. Six-shot magazine, 2.5-inch bbl., about 5 inches overall. Weight: 13 oz. Fixed sights. Chrome, satin nickel or black Teflon finish. Walnut, grooved black Cycolac or resin-impregnated wood grips. Made from 1981 to date.
Model J-22 .... **NiB $83 Ex $66 Gd $45**
Model J-25 (disc. 1995)............. **NiB $66 Ex $56 Gd $41**

MODELS M25, M32, M38 AUTO PISTOL
Calibers: .25 ACP, .32 ACP, .380 ACP. Six-shot magazine, 2.81-inch bbl., 5.31 inches overall. Weight: 11oz. to 15 oz. Fixed sights. Chrome, satin nickel or black Teflon finish. Walnut, grooved, black Cycolac or resin-impregnated wood grips. Made from 1988 to date.
Model M25 (disc.) .... **NiB $66 Ex $51 Gd $41**
Model M32 .... **NiB $96 Ex $76 Gd $52**
Model M38 .... **NiB $108 Ex $87 Gd $59**

MODEL M48
AUTO PISTOL .... **NiB $87 Ex $76 Gd $51**
Calibers: .22 LR, .32 ACP, .380 ACP. Seven-shot magazine, 4-inch bbl., 6.69 inches overall. Weight: 20 oz. Fixed sights. Chrome, satin nickel or black Teflon finish. Smooth wood or black Teflon grips. Made from 1989-95.

MODEL M58
AUTO PISTOL .... **NiB $87 Ex $76 Gd $51**
Caliber: .380 ACP. 10-shot magazine, 3.75-inch bbl., 5.5 inches overall. Weight: 30 oz. Fixed sights. Chrome, satin nickel, blued or black Teflon finish. Smooth wood or black Teflon grips. Made 1993-95.

MODEL M59
AUTO PISTOL .... **NiB $97 Ex $87 Gd $51**
Caliber: 9mm Para. 10-shot magazine, 4-inch bbl., 6.5 inches overall. Weight: 33 oz. Fixed sights. Chrome, satin nickel, blued or black Teflon finish. Smooth wood or black Teflon grips. Made 1994-96.

MODEL NINE SA
AUTO PISTOL .... **NiB $122 Ex $102 Gd $61**
Similar to Bryco/Jennings Model M59 except w/redesigned slide w/loaded chamber indicator and frame mounted ejector. Weight: 30 oz. Made 1997 to date.

MODEL T-.22
TARGET PISTOL .... **NiB $115 Ex $92 Gd $62**
Similar to Bryco/Jennings Model M48 except chambered for .22 LR only, w/target configuration sights and redesigned slide w/loaded chamber indicator and hold open. Made 1997 to date.

BUDISCHOWSKY PISTOL — Mt. Clemens, Michigan, Mfd. by Norton Armament Corporation

TP-70 DA AUTOMATIC PISTOL
Calibers: .22 LR, .25 Auto. Six-shot magazine, 2.6-inch bbl., 4.65 inches overall. Weight: 12.3 oz. Fixed sights. Stainless steel. Plastic grips. Made 1973-77.
.22 LR .... **NiB $337 Ex $280 Gd $204**
.25 Auto...................... **NiB $326 Ex $255 Gd $173**

CALICO LIGHT WEAPONS SYSTEMS — Bakersfield, California

MODEL 110 AUTO PISTOL....... **NiB $637 Ex $569 Gd $408**
Caliber: .22 LR. 100-shot magazine, 6-inch bbl., 17.9 inches overall. Weight: 3.75 lbs. Adj. post front sight, fixed U-notch rear. Black finish aluminum frame. Molded composition grip. Made 1986-94.

MODEL M-950 AUTO PISTOL .... **NiB $459 Ex $382 Gd $263**
Caliber 9mm Para. 50- or 100-shot magazine, 7.5-inch bbl., 14 inches overall. Weight: 2.25 lbs. Adj. post front sight, fixed U-notch rear. Glass-filled polymer grip. Made 1989-94.

CHARTER ARMS CORPORATION — Stratford, Connecticut

MODEL 40 AUTOMATIC PISTOL..... NiB $270 Ex $245 Gd $127
Caliber: .22 RF. Eight-shot magazine, 3.3-inch bbl., 6.3 inches over-all. Weight: 21.5 oz. Fixed sights. Checkered walnut grips. Stainless steel finish. Made 1985-86.

MODEL 79K
DA AUTOMATIC PISTOL .... NiB $331 Ex $306 Gd $194
Calibers: .380 or .32 Auto. Seven-shot magazine, 3.6-inch bbl., 6.5 inches overall. Weight: 24.5 oz. Fixed sights. Checkered walnut grips. Stainless steel finish. Made 1985-86.

BONNIE AND CLYDE SET........ NiB $433 Ex $372 Gd $240
Matching pair of shrouded 2.5-inch bbl., revolvers chambered for .32 Magnum and .38 Special. Blued finish w/scrolled name on bbls.. Made 1989-90.

BULLDOG .44 DA REVOLVER
Caliber: .44 Special. Five-shot cylinder, 2.5- or 3-inch bbl., 7 or 7.5 inches over-all. Weight: 19 or 19.5 oz. Fixed sights. Blued, nickel-plated or stainless finish. Checkered walnut Bulldog or square buttgrips. Made from 1973-96.
Blued finish/
Pocket Hammer (2.5-inch) .... NiB $229 Ex $199 Gd $92
Blued finish/
Bulldog grips (3-inch disc. 1988) .... NiB $209 Ex $165 Gd $112
Electroless nickel............... NiB $236 Ex $189 Gd $129
Stainless steel/
Bulldog grips (disc. 1992) .... NiB $199 Ex $158 Gd $102
Neoprene grips/
Pocket Hammer............... NiB $204 Ex $163 Gd $111

BULLDOG .357 DA REVOLVER .... NiB $189 Ex $153 Gd $92
Caliber: .357 Magnum. Five-shot cylinder, 6-inch bbl., 11 inches overall. Weight: 25 oz. Fixed sights. Blued finish. Square, checkered walnut grips. Intro. 1977-96.

BULLDOG NEW POLICE DA REVOLVER
Same general specifications as Bulldog Police except chambered for .44 Special. Five-shot cylinder, 2.5- or 3.5-inch bbl. Made 1990-92.
Blued finish .... NiB $236 Ex $175 Gd $123
Stainless finish (2.5-inch bbl. only)........ NiB $178 Ex $143 Gd $92

BULLDOG POLICE DA REVOLVER
Caliber: .38 Special or .32 H&R Magnum. Six-shot cylinder, 4-inch bbl., 8.5 inches overall. Weight: 20.5 oz. Adj. rear sight, ramp front. Blued or stainless finish. Square checkered walnut grips. Made 1976-93. Shroud dropped on new model.
Blued finish .... NiB $209 Ex $165 Gd $112
Stainless finish.................. NiB $199 Ex $160 Gd $101
.32 H&R Magnum (disc.1992)..... NiB $214 Ex $168 Gd $112

BULLDOG PUG DA REVOLVER
Caliber: .44 Special. Five-shot cylinder, 2.5 inch bbl., 7.25 inches overall. Weight: 20 oz. Blued or stainless finish. Fixed ramp front sight, fixed square-notch rear. Checkered Neoprene or walnut grips. Made 1988-93.
Blued finish .... NiB $229 Ex $199 Gd $128
Stainless finish .... NiB $229 Ex $199 Gd $128

BULLDOG TARGET DA REVOLVER
Calibers: .357 Magnum, .44 Special (latter intro. in 1977). Four-inch bbl., 8.5 inches overall. Weight: 20.5 oz. in .357. Adj. rear sight, ramp front. Blued finish. Square checkered walnut grips. Made 1976-92.
Blued finish (disc.1989)......... NiB $194 Ex $152 Gd $103
Stainless steel .... NiB $229 Ex $153 Gd $87

**Charter Arms
Bulldog Police**

**Charter Arms
Bulldog Police**

**Charter Arms
Bulldog Target**

**Charter Arms
Bulldog Tracker**

**Charter Arms
Explorer II**

**Charter Arms
Pathfinder**

**Charter Arms Explorer II
Silvertone w/optional barrels**

**Charter Arms Police Undercover
.32 H&R Magnum**

**Charter Arms Undercover
.32 S&W Long**

**Charter Arms
Undercover Stainless**

BULLDOG TRACKER
DA REVOLVER. . . . . **NiB $189 Ex $153 Gd $92**
Caliber: .357 Mag. Five-shot cylinder, 2.5-, 4- or 6-inch bbl., 11 inches overall (6-inch bbl.). Weight: 21 oz. (2.5-inch bbl.). Adj. rear sight, ramp front. Checkered walnut grips. Blued finish. 4- or 6-inch bbl., Disc.1986. Reintroduced 1989-92. See illustration previous page.

EXPLORER II SEMIAUTO SURVIVAL PISTOL
Caliber: .22 RF. Eight-shot magazine, 6-, 8- or 10-inch bbl., 13.5 inches overall (6-inch bbl.). Weight: 28 oz. finishes: Black, heat cured, semigloss textured enamel or silvertone anticorrosion. Disc.1987.
Standard model . . . . **NiB $92 Ex $82 Gd $51**
Silvertone (w/optional
6- or 10-inch bbl.) . . . . **NiB $114 Ex $101 Gd $61**

OFF-DUTY DA REVOLVER
Calibers: .22 LR or .38 Special. Six-shot (.22 LR) or 5-shot (.38 Spec.) cylinder. Two-inch bbl., 6.25 inches overall. Weight: 16 oz. Fixed rear sight, Partridge-type front sight. Plain walnut grips. Matte black, nickel or stainless steel finish. Made 1992-96.
Matte black finish . . . . **NiB $173 Ex $148 Gd $87**
Nickel finish . . . . **NiB $204 Ex $154 Gd $102**
Stainless steel . . . . **NiB $193 Ex $156 Gd $102**

PATHFINDER DA REVOLVER
Calibers: .22 LR, .22 WMR. Six-shot cylinder, bbl. lengths: 2-, 3-, 6-inches, 7.13 inches overall (in 3-inch bbl.), and regular grips. Weight: 18.5 oz. (3-inch bbl.). Adj. rear sight, ramp front. Blued or stainless finish. Plain walnut regular, checkered Bulldog or square buttgrips. Made 1970 to date. Note: Originally designated "Pocket Target," name was changed in 1971 to "Pathfinder." Grips changed in 1984. Disc.1993.
Blued finish . . . . **NiB $189 Ex $153 Gd $92**
Stainless finish . . . . **NiB $189 Ex $153 Gd $92**

CHARTER ARMS PIT BULL DA REVOLVER
Calibers: 9mm, .357 Magnum, .38 Special. Five-shot cylinder, 2.5-, 3.5- or 4-inch bbl., 7 inches overall (2.5-inch bbl.). Weight: 21.5 to 25 oz. All stainless steel frame. Fixed ramp front sight, fixed square-notch rear. Checkered Neoprene grips. Blued or stainless finish. Made 1989-93.
Blued finish . . . . NiB $235 Ex $184 Gd $102
Stainless finish . . . . NiB $245 Ex $194 Gd $102

CHARTER ARMS UNDERCOVER DA REVOLVER
Caliber: .38 Special. Five-shot cylinder,. bbl., lengths: 2-, 3-, 4-inches, 6.25 inches overall (2-inch bbl.), and regular grips. Weight: 16 oz. (2-inch bbl.). Fixed sights. Plain walnut, checkered Bulldog or square buttgrips. Made 1965-96.
Blued or nickel-plated finish . . . . NiB $178 Ex $148 Gd $87
Stainless finish . . . . NiB $265 Ex $199 Gd $112

CHARTER ARMS UNDERCOVER
Same general specifications as standard Undercover except chambered for .32 H&R Magnum or .32 S&W Long, has 6-shot cylinder and 2.5-inch bbl.
.32 H&R Magnum (blued) . . . . NiB $178 Ex $148 Gd $87
.32 H&R Magnum
nickel. . . . . NiB $178 Ex $148 Gd $87
.32 H&R Magnum (stainless) . . . . . . NiB $265 Ex $199 Gd $153
.32 S&W Long (blued) disc. 1989. . . NiB $265 Ex $199 Gd $153

CHARTER ARMS UNDERCOVER POCKET POLICE DA REVOLVER
Same general specifications as standard Undercover except has 6-shot cylinder and pocket-type hammer. Blued or stainless steel finish. Made 1969-81.
Blued finish . . . . NiB $158 Ex $143 Gd $92
Stainless steel . . . . NiB $214 Ex $175 Gd $126

CHARTER ARMS UNDERCOVER POLICE DA REVOLVER
Same general specifications as standard Undercover except has 6-shot cylinder. Made 1984-89. Reintroduced 1993.
Blued, .38 Special . . . . NiB $209 Ex $178 Gd $102
Stainless, .38 Special . . . . NiB $208 Ex $168 Gd $117
.32 H&R Magnum . . . . NiB $189 Ex $153 Gd $107

CHARTER ARMS UNDER-
COVERETTE DA REVOLVER . . . . . . NiB $158 Ex $143 Gd $92
Same as Undercover model w/2-inch bbl. except caliber .32 S&W Long, 6-shot cylinder, blued finish only. Weight: 16.5 oz. Made 1972-83.

CIMARRON F.A. CO. — Fredricksburg, Texas

CIMARRON EL PISTOLERO
SINGLE-ACTION REVOLVER. . . . . . NiB $403 Ex $306 Gd $178
Calibers: .357 Mag., .45 Colt. Six-shot cylinder, 4.75- 5.5- or 7.5-inch bbl., polished brass backstrap and triggerguard. Otherwise, same as Colt Single-Action Army revolver w/parts being interchangeable. Made 1997-98.

COLT MANUFACTURING CO., INC. — Hartford, Connecticut

Previously Colt Industries, Firearms Division. Production of some Colt handguns spans the period before World War II to the postwar years. Values shown for these models are for earlier production. Those manufactured c. 1946 and later generally are less desirable to collectors and values are approximately 30 percent lower.

**Cimarron
El Pistolero**

NOTE: *For ease in finding a particular firearm, Colt handguns are grouped into three sections: Automatic Pistols, Single-Shot Pistols, Derringers and Revolvers. For a complete listing, please refer to the Index.*

AUTOMATIC PISTOLS

COLT MODEL 1900 .38 AUTOMATIC PISTOL
Caliber: .38 ACP (modern high-velocity cartridges should not be used in this pistol). Seven-shot magazine, 6-inch bbl., 9 inches overall. Weight: 35 oz. Fixed sights. Blued finish. Hard rubber and plain or checkered walnut grips. Sharp-spur hammer. Combination rear sight and safety unique to the Model 1900 (early production). In mid-1901 a solid rear sight was dovetailed into the slide. (SN range 1-4274) Made 1900-03. Note: 250 models were sold to the military (50 Navy and 200 Army).
Early commercial model
(w/sight/safety) . . . . NiB $6760 Ex $4836 Gd $1768
Late commercial model
(W/dovetailed sight) . . . . NiB $4857 Ex $3832 Gd $2605
Army Model w/U.S. inspector
marks (1st Series - SN 90-150
w/inspector mark J.T.T). . . . . NiB $15,600 Ex $10,400 Gd $8304
(2nd Series - SN 1600-1750
w/inspector mark R.A.C.) . . . . NiB $9750 Ex $7800 Gd $5304
Navy model (Also marked
w/USN-I.D. number) . . . . NiB $17,160 Ex $11,384 Gd $8554

COLT MODEL 1902 MILITARY .38 AUTOMATIC PISTOL
Caliber: .38 ACP (modern high-velocity cartridges should not be used in this pistol). Eight-shot magazine, 6-inch bbl., 9 inches overall. Weight: 37 oz. Fixed sights w/blade front and V-notch rear. Blued finish. Checkered hard rubber grips. Round back hammer, changed to spur type in 1908. No safety but fitted w/standard military swivel. About 18,000 produced with split SN ranges. The government contract series (15,001-15,200) and the commercial sales series (15,000 receding to 11,000) and (30,200-47,266). Made 1902-29.
Early military model (w/front
slide serrations) . . . . NiB $3588 Ex $3328 Gd $3120
Late military model (w/rear
slide serrations) . . . . NiB $2827 Ex $2288 Gd $2080
Marked "U.S. Army" (SN 15,001-
15,200) . . . . NiB $8840 Ex $6760 Gd $4420

COLT MODEL 1902 SPORTING
.38 AUTOMATIC PISTOL. . . . . . . NiB $3640 Ex $2340 Gd $936
Caliber: .38 ACP (modern high-velocity cartridges should not be used in this pistol). Seven-shot magazine, 6-inch bbl., 9 inches overall. Weight: 35 oz. Fixed sights w/blade front and V-notch rear. Blued finish. Checkered hard rubber grips. Round back hammer was standard but some spur hammers were installed during late production. No safety and w/o swivel as found on military model. Total production about 7,500 w/split SN ranges (4275-10,999) and (30,000-30,190) Made 1902-08.

Colt
Model 1902 Military

Colt
Model 1903 Pocket Hammer

Colt
Model 1903 Pocket Hammerless

MODEL 1903 POCKET .32 AUTOMATIC PISTOL
FIRST ISSUE - COMMERCIAL SERIES

Caliber: .32 Auto. Eight-shot magazine, 4-inch bbl., 7 inches overall. Weight: 23 oz. Fixed sights. Blued or nickel finish. Checkered hard rubber grips. Hammerless (concealed hammer). Slide lock and grip safeties. Fitted w/barrel bushing but early models have no magazine safety. Total production of the Model 1903 reached 572,215. The First Issue production occurred 1903-08 (SN range 1-72,000).

Blued finish . . . . NiB $879 Ex $572 Gd $406
Nickel finish . . . . NiB $972 Ex $593 Gd $421

MODEL 1903 POCKET .32 AUTOMATIC PISTOL
SECOND ISSUE - COMMERCIAL SERIES

Same as First Issue but with 3.75-inch bbl. and small extractor. Production occurred 1908-10 (SN range 72,001 -105,050).

Blued finish . . . . NiB $650 Ex $478 Gd $338
Nickel finish . . . . NiB $673 Ex $536 Gd $369

MODEL 1903 POCKET .32 AUTOMATIC PISTOL,
THIRD ISSUE - COMMERCIAL SERIES

Caliber: .32 Auto. Similar to Second Issue w/3.75-inch bbl. except with integral barrel bushing and locking lug at muzzle end of bbl. Production occurred 1910-26 (SN range 105,051-468,096).

Blued finish . . . . NiB $560 Ex $425 Gd $275
Nickel finish . . . . NiB $600 Ex $450 Gd $250

MODEL 1903 POCKET .32 AUTOMATIC PISTOL
FOURTH ISSUE - COMMERCIAL SERIES

Caliber: .32 Auto. Similar to Third Issue except a slide lock safety change was made when a Tansley-style disconnector was added on all pistols above SN 468,097, which prevents firing of cartridge in chamber when the magazine is removed. Blued or nickel finish. Checkered walnut grips. These design changes were initiated 1926-.45 (SN range 105,051-554,446)

Blued finish . . . . NiB $556 Ex $445 Gd $303
Nickel finish . . . . NiB $619 Ex $495 Gd $337

MODEL 1903 POCKET (HAMMER) .38 AUTOMATIC PISTOL

Caliber: .38 ACP (modern high-velocity cartridges should not be used in this pistol). Similar to Model 1902 Sporting .38 but w/shorter frame, slide and 4.5-inch bbl. Overall dimension reduced to 7.5 inches. Weight: 31 oz. Fixed sights w/blade front and V-notch rear. Blued finish. Checkered hard rubber grips. Round back hammer, changed to spur type in 1908. No safety. (SN range 16,001-47,226 with some numbers above 30,200 assigned to 1902 Military). Made 1903-1929.

Early model
(round hammer) . . . . NiB $2175 Ex $1885 Gd $900
Late model
(spur hammer) . . . . NiB $1740 Ex $1150 Gd $650

MODEL 1903 POCKET HAMMERLESS (CONCEALED HAMMER) .32 AUTOMATIC PISTOL - MILITARY

Caliber: .32 ACP. Eight-shot magazine, Similar to Model 1903 Pocket .32 except concealed hammer and equipped w/magazine safety. Parkerized or blued finish. (SN range with "M" prefix M1-M200,000) Made 1941-.45.

Blued service model (marked
"U.S. Property") . . . . NiB $1435 Ex $950 Gd $650
Parkerized service model (marked
"U.S. Property") . . . . NiB $1425 Ex $460 Gd $600
Blued documented
Officer's model . . . . NiB $3375 Ex $3600 Gd $1500
Parkerized documented
Officer's model . . . . NiB $2325 Ex $2000 Gd $1400

MODEL 1905 .45 AUTOMATIC PISTOL

Caliber: .45 (Rimless) Automatic. Seven-shot magazine, 5-inch bbl., 8 inches overall. Weight: 32.5 oz. Fixed sights w/blade front and V-notch rear. Blued finish. Checkered walnut, hard rubber or pearl grips. Predecessor to Model 1911 Auto Pistol and contributory to the development of the .45 ACP cartridge. (SN range 1-6100) Made 1905-11.

Commercial model . . . . NiB $5500 Ex $3250 Gd $1500
W/slotted backstrap
(500 produced) . . . . NiB $8250 Ex $7500 Gd $6000
W/shoulder stock/holster . . . . $7500 to $10,000

MODEL 1905 .45 (1907)
CONTRACT PISTOL . . . . NiB $12,000 Ex $9500 Gd $6250

Variation of the Model 1905 produced to U.S. Military specifications, including loaded chamber indicator, grip safety and lanyard loop. Only 201 were produced, but 200 were delivered and may be identified by the chief inspector's initials "K.M." (SN range 1-201) Made 1907-08.

MODEL 1908 POCKET .25 HAMMERLESS AUTO PISTOL

Caliber: .25 Auto. Six-shot magazine, 2-inch bbl., 4.5 inches overall. Weight: 13 oz. Flat-top front, square-notch rear sight in groove. Blued, nickel or Parkerized finish. Checkered hard rubber grips on early models, checkered walnut on later type, special pearl grips illustrated. Both a grip safety and slide lock safety are included on all models. The Tansley-style safety disconnector was added in 1916 at pistol No. 141000. (SN range 1-409,061) Made 1908-41.

Blued finish . . . . NiB $884	Ex $676	Gd $520
Nickel finish . . . . NiB $936	Ex $780	Gd $624
Marked "U.S. Property" (w/blued finish) . . . . NiB $3219	Ex $1633	Gd $1247
Marked "U.S. Property" (w/parkerized finish) . . . . NiB $2590	Ex $2080	Gd $1404

Colt
Model 1905 Military

MODEL 1908 POCKET .380 AUTOMATIC PISTOL

Similar to Pocket .32 Auto w/3.75-inch bbl. except chambered for .380 Auto w/seven-shot magazine. Weight: 23 oz. Blue, nickel or Parkerized finish. (SN range 1-138,009) Made 1908-45.

First Issue (made 1908-11, w/bbl., lock and bushing, w/SN 1-6,250) . . . . . NiB $884	Ex $676	Gd $312
Second Issue (made 1911-28, w/o bbl., lock and bushing, w/SN 6,251-92,893) . . . . NiB $832	Ex $520	Gd $260
Third Issue (made 1928-45, w/safety disconnector, w/SN 92,894-138,009) . . . . NiB $552	Ex $442	Gd $301
Parkerized service model (Marked "U.S. Property" made 1942-45, w/SN "M" prefix.) . . . . . NiB $2340	Ex $1716	Gd $1456
Documented officer's model (service model w/military assignment papers) . . . . NiB $2796	Ex $2236	Gd $1520

Colt
Model 1908 Pocket 25

NOTE: *During both World Wars, Colt licensed other firms to make these pistols under government contract, including Ithaca Gun Co., North American Arms Co., Ltd. (Canada), Remington-Rand Co., Remington-UMC, Singer Sewing Machine Co., and Union Switch & Signal Co. M1911 also produced at Springfield Armory.*

MODEL 1911 AUTOMATIC PISTOL

Caliber: .45 Auto. Seven-shot magazine, 5-inch bbl., 8.5 inches overall. Weight: 39 oz. Fixed sights. Blued finish on Commercial model. Parkerized or similar finish on most military pistols. Checkered walnut grips (early production), plastic grips (later production). Checkered, arched mainspring housing and longer grip safety spur adopted in 1923 (on M1911A1).

Model 1911 commercial (C-series) . . . . NiB $1756	Ex $1404	Gd $955
Model 1911A1 commercial (Pre-WWII) . . . . NiB $3634	Ex $2907	Gd $1977

Colt
Model 1911

U.S. GOVERNMENT MODEL 1911

Colt manufacture. . . . . NiB $1347	Ex $1139	Gd $811
North American manufacture . . . . NiB $24,636	Ex $19,708	Gd $13,401
Remington-UMC manufacture. . . . . NiB $2242	Ex $1794	Gd $1220
Springfield manufacture . . . . . . NiB $2204	Ex $1763	Gd $1200
Navy Model M1911 type. . . . . . NiB $2926	Ex $2340	Gd $1591

U.S. GOVERNMENT MODEL 1911A1

Singer manufacture . . . . . NiB $25,936	Ex $20,748	Gd $14,109
Colt, Ithaca, Remington- Rand manufacture. . . . . NiB $942	Ex $754	Gd $513
Union Switch & Signal manufacture . . . . NiB $1424	Ex $1139	Gd $775

Colt
1991 A1

Colt Cadet .22

Colt All American
Model 2000

MODEL M1991 A1 SEMIAUTO PISTOL
Reissue of Model 1911A1 (see above) w/a continuation of the original serial number range 1945. Caliber: .45 ACP. Seven-shot magazine, 5-inch bbl., 8.5 inches overall. Weight: 39 oz. Fixed blade front sight, square notch rear. Parkerized finish. Black composition grips. Made 1991 to date. (Commander and Compact variations intro. 1993).

Standard model	NiB $884	Ex $827	Gd $624
Commander w/4.5-inch bbl.,	NiB $624	Ex $562	Gd $312
Compact w/3.5-inch bbl., (six-shot)	NiB $728	Ex $624	Gd $468

.22 CADET AUTOMATIC PISTOL . . . . . NiB $240 Ex $192 Gd $131
Caliber: 22 LR. 10-shot magazine, 4.5-inch vent rib bbl., 8.63 inches overall. Weight: 33.5 oz. Blade front sight, dovetailed rear. Stainless finish. Textured black polymer grips w/Colt medallion. Made 1993-95. Note: The Cadet Model name was disc. under litigation but the manufacturer continued to produce this pistol configuration as the Model "Colt 22". For this reason the "Cadet" model will command slight premiums.

.22 SPORT AUTOMATIC PISTOL . . . . . NiB $411 Ex $307 Gd $156
Same specifications as Cadet Model except renamed Colt .22 w/composition monogrip or wraparound black rubber grip. Made 1995-98.

.22 TARGET PISTOL. . . . . NiB $307 Ex $260 Gd $130
Similar to Colt 22 Sport Model except w/6-inch vent rib bbl., 10.12 inches overall. Weight: 40.5 oz. Partridge style front sight, adjustable white outline rear on full length grooved rib. Made 1995 to date.

ACE AUTOMATIC PISTOL
Caliber: .22 LR (regular or high speed). 10-shot magazine. Built on the same frame as the Government Model .45 Auto w/same safety features, etc. Hand-honed action, target bbl., adj. rear sight. 4.75-inch bbl., 8.25. inches overall. Weight: 38 oz. Made 1930-.40.

Commercial model	NiB $2016	Ex $1612	Gd $1096
Service model (1938-42)	NiB $2854	Ex $2283	Gd $1553

ALL AMERICAN
MODEL 2000 DA PISTOL . . . . NiB $780 Ex $676 Gd $416
Hammerless semiautomatic w/blued slide and polymer or alloy receiver fitted w/roller-bearing trigger. Caliber: 9mm Para. 15-shot magazine, 4.5-inch bbl., 7.5 inches overall. Weight: 29 oz. (Polymer) or 33 oz (Alloy). Fixed blade front sight, square-notch rear w/3-dot system. Matte blued slide w/black polymer or anodized aluminum receiver. Made 1992-94.

AUTOMATIC .25 PISTOL
As a result of the 1968 Firearms Act restricting the importation of the Colt Pocket Junior that was produced in Spain, Firearms International was contracted by Colt to manufacture a similar blowback action with the same exposed hammer configuration. Both the U.S. and Spanish-made .25 automatics were recalled to correct an action malfunction. Returned firearms were fitted with a rebounding firing pin to prevent accidental discharges. Caliber: .25 ACP. Six-shot magazine, 2.25-inch bbl., 4.5 inches overall. Weight: 12.5 oz. Integral blade front, square-notch rear sight groove. Blued finish. Checkered wood grips w/Colt medallion. Made 1970-75.

Model as issued	NiB $312	Ex $260	Gd $104
Model recalled & refitted	NiB $312	Ex $260	Gd $104

CHALLENGER
AUTOMATIC PISTOL . . . . NiB $515 Ex $411 Gd $208
Same basic design as Woodsman Target, Third Issue but lacks some of the refinements. Fixed sights. Magazine catch on butt as in old Woodsman. Does not stay open on last shot. Lacks magazine safety. 4.5- or 6-inch bbl., 9 to 10.5 inches overall. Weight: 30 oz. (4.5-inch bbl.) or 31.5 oz. (6-inch bbl.) Blued finish. Checkered plastic grips. Made 1950-55.

COMBAT COMMANDER AUTOMATIC PISTOL
Same as Lightweight Commander except has steel frame w/blued or nickel-plated finish. Weight: 36 oz. Made 1950-76.

9mm Para.	NiB $644	Ex $515	Gd $350
.38 Super, .45 ACP.	NiB $748	Ex $598	Gd $407

COMMANDER LIGHTWEIGHT AUTOMATIC PISTOL
Same basic design as Government Model except w/shorter 4.25-inch bbl., and a special lightweight "Coltalloy" receiver and mainspring housing. Calibers: .45 Auto, .38 Super Auto, 9mm Para. Seven-shot magazine (.45 cal.), nine-shot (.38 Auto and 9mm), 8 inches overall. Weight: 26.5 oz. Fixed sights. Round spur hammer. Improved safety lock. Blued finish. Checkered plastic or walnut grips. Made 1950-76.

9mm Para.	NiB $630	Ex $504	Gd $343
.38 Super, .45 ACP.	NiB $682	Ex $546	Gd $371

CONVERSION
UNIT—.22-.45. . . . . NiB $2796 Ex $2236 Gd $1520
Converts Service Ace .22 to National Match .45 Auto. Unit consists of match-grade slide assembly and bbl., bushing, recoil spring, recoil spring guide and plug, magazine and slide stop. Made 1938-42.

CONVERSION
UNIT — .45-.22 . . . . NiB $488 Ex $390 Gd $265
Converts Government Model .45 Auto to a .22 LR target pistol. Unit consists of slide assembly, bbl., floating chamber (as in Service Ace), bushing, ejector, recoil spring, recoil spring guide and plug, magazine and slide stop. The component parts differ and are not interchangable between post war, series 70, series 80, ACE I and ACE II units. Made 1938 to date.

DELTA ELITE SEMIAUTO PISTOL
Caliber: 10 mm. Five-inch bbl., 8.5 inches overall. Eight-round magazine, Weight: 38 oz. Checkered Neoprene combat grips w/Delta medallion. Three-dot, high-profile front and rear combat sights. Blued or stainless finish. Made 1987-96.
First Edition
(500 Ltd. edition) . . . . **NiB $1164 Ex $971 Gd $63**
Blued finish . . . . **NiB $618 Ex $494 Gd $336**
Matte stainless finish . . . . **NiB $644 Ex $515 Gd $350**
Ultra stainless finish . . . . **NiB $748 Ex $598 Gd $407**

DELTA GOLD CUP SEMIAUTO PISTOL
Same general specifications as Delta Elite except in match configuration w/Accro adjustable rear sight. Made 1989-93 and 1995-96.
Blued finish (disc. 1991) . . . . **NiB $716 Ex $572 Gd $389**
Stainless steel finish . . . . **NiB $931 Ex $780 Gd $624**

GOLD CUP MARK III
NATIONAL MATCH . . . . **NiB $1092 Ex $879 Gd $593**
Similar to Gold Cup National Match .45 Auto except chambered for .38 Special Mid Range. Five-shot magazine, Made 1961-74.

GOLD CUP NATIONAL
MATCH .45 AUTO. . . . . **NiB $988 Ex $832 Gd $476**
Match version of Government Model .45 Auto w/same general specifications except: match grade bbl., w/new design bushing, flat mainspring housing, long wide trigger w/adj. stop, hand-fitted slide w/improved ejection port, adj. rear sight, target front sight, checkered walnut grips w/gold medallions. Weight: 37 oz. Made 1957-70.

GOVERNMENT MODEL 1911/1911A1
See Colt Model 1911.

HUNTSMAN . . . . **NiB $468 Ex $364 Gd $260**
Same specifications as the Challenger. Made 1955-76.

MK I & IL/SERIES '90 DOUBLE
EAGLE COMBAT COMMANDER . . . . . **NiB $592 Ex $473 Gd $321**
Calibers: .40 S&W, .45 ACP. Seven-shot magazine, 4.25-inch bbl., 7.75 inches overall. Weight: 36 oz. Fixed blade front sight, square-notch rear. Checkered Xenoy grips. Stainless finish. Made 1992-96.

MK IL/SERIES '90 DOUBLE EAGLE DA SEMIAUTO PISTOL
Calibers: .38 Super, 9mm, .40 S&W, 10mm, .45 ACP. Seven-shot magazine. Five-inch bbl., 8.5 inches overall. Weight: 39 oz. Fixed or Accro adj. sights. Matte stainless finish. Checkered Xenoy grips. Made 1991-96.
.38 Super, 9mm, .40
S&W (fixed sights) . . . . **NiB $622 Ex $496 Gd $334**
.45 ACP (adjustable sights) . . . . **NiB $618 Ex $494 Gd $336**
.45 ACP (fixed sights) . . . . **NiB $592 Ex $4573 Gd $321**
10mm (adjustable sights) . . . . **NiB $612 Ex $489 Gd $333**
10mm (fixed sights) . . . . **NiB $586 Ex $468 Gd $318**

MK IL/SERIES '90 DOUBLE
EAGLE OFFICER'S ACP . . . . **NiB $618 Ex $496 Gd $336**
Same general specifications as Double Eagle Combat Commander except chambered for .45 ACP only, 3.5-inch bbl., 7.25 inches overall. Weight: 35 oz. Also available in lightweight (25 oz.) w/blued finish (same price). Made 1990-93.

MK IV/SERIES '70 COMBAT COMMANDER
Same general specifications as the Lightweight Commander except made 1970-83.
Blued finish . . . . **NiB $595 Ex $473 Gd $312**
Nickel finish . . . . **NiB $662 Ex $438 Gd $342**

**Colt Delta
Gold Cup**

**Colt Gold Cup
National Match**

**Colt MK II/Series '90
Double Eagle Officer's ACP**

MK IV/SERIES '70 GOLD CUP
NATIONAL MATCH .45 AUTO . . . . **NiB $988 Ex $811 Gd $624**
Match version of MK IV/Series '70 Government Model. Caliber: .45 Auto only. Flat mainspring housing. Accurizor bbl., and bushing. Solid rib, Colt-Elliason adj. rear sight undercut front sight. Adj. trigger, target hammer. 8.75 inches overall. Weight: 38.5 oz. Blued finish. Checkered walnut grips. Made 1970-84.

MK IV/SERIES '70 GOV'T.
AUTO PISTOL . . . . **NiB $832 Ex $624 Gd $364**
Calibers: .45 Auto, .38 Super Auto, 9mm Para. Seven-shot magazine in .45, 9-shot in .38 and 9mm. Five-inch bbl., 8.38 inches overall. Weight: 38 oz., (.45); 39 oz. in .38 and 9mm. Fixed rear sight and ramp front sight. Blued or nickel-plated finish. Checkered walnut grips. Made 1970-84.

Colt MK IV/ Series '80 .380

Colt MK IV/Series '80 Combat Commander

Colt MK IV/Series '80 Gold Cup National Match

Colt MK IV/Series '80 Government Model

MK IV/SERIES '80 .380 AUTOMATIC PISTOL

Caliber: .380 ACP, 3.29-inch bbl., 6.15 inches overall. Weight: 21.8 oz. Composition grips. Fixed sights. Made since 1984 to date.
Blued finish
(disc.1997)...................... NiB $442 Ex $307 Gd $203
Bright nickel
(disc.1995)...................... NiB $515 Ex $374 Gd $224
Satin nickel
Coltguard (disc.1989) .... NiB $494 Ex $338 Gd $218
Stainless finish................. NiB $499 Ex $348 Gd $234

MK IV/SERIES '80 COMBAT COMMANDER

Updated version of the MK IV/Series '70 w/same general specifications. Blued, two-tone or stainless steel w/"pebbled" black Neoprene wraparound grips. Made since 1979.
Blued finish
(disc.1996)...................... NiB $588 Ex $489 Gd $312
Satin nickel
(disc.1987)...................... NiB $619 Ex $504 Gd $327
Stainless finish................. NiB $640 Ex $494 Gd $350
Two-tone finish .... NiB $665 Ex $515 Gd $354

MK IV/SERIES '80 COMBAT ELITE

Same general specifications as MK IV/Series '80 Combat Commander except w/Elite enhancements. Calibers: .38 Super, .40 S&W, .45 ACP. Stainless frame w/blued steel slide. Accro adj. sights and beavertail grip safety. Made 1992-96.
.38 Super,
.45 ACP .... NiB $759 Ex $645 Gd $343
.40 S&W .... NiB $728 Ex $624 Gd $312

MK IV/SERIES '80 GOLD CUP NATIONAL MATCH

Same general specifications as Match '70 version except w/additional finishes and "pebbled" wraparound Neoprene grips. Made 1983-96.
Blued finish .... NiB $910 Ex $728 Gd $364
Bright blued
finish .... NiB $951 Ex $662 Gd $437
Stainless finish................. NiB $749 Ex $603 Gd $374

MK IV/SERIES '80 GOVERNMENT MODEL

Same general specifications as Government Model Series '70 except also chambered in .40 S&W, w/"pebbled" wraparound Neoprene grips, blued or stainless finish. Made since 1983.
Blued finish .... NiB $725 Ex $515 Gd $317
Bright blued
finish .... NiB $806 Ex $551 Gd $446
Bright stainless
finish .... NiB $728 Ex $624 Gd $312
Matte stainless finish............ NiB $725 Ex $519 Gd $322

MK IV/SERIES '80 LIGHT-

WEIGHT COMMANDER .... NiB $619 Ex $484 Gd $312
Updated version of the MK IV/Series '70 w/same general specifications.

MK IV/SERIES '80 MUSTANG .380 AUTOMATIC

Caliber: .380 ACP. Five- or 6-shot magazine, 2.75-inch bbl., 5.5 inches overall. Weight: 18.5 oz. Blued, nickel or stainless finish. Black composition grips. Made 1986-97.
Blued finish .... NiB $432 Ex $333 Gd $234
Nickel finish
(disc.1994)..................... NiB $488 Ex $332 Gd $241
Satin nickel
Coltguard (disc.1988) .... NiB $468 Ex $312 Gd $232
Stainless finish................. NiB $488 Ex $332 Gd $241

MK IV/SERIES '80 MUSTANG PLUS II

Caliber: .380 ACP, 7-round magazine, 2.75-inch bbl., 5.5 inches overall. Weight: 20 oz. Blued or stainless finish w/checkered black composition grips. Made 1988-96.

Blued finish . . . . NiB $432 Ex $333 Gd $237
Stainless finish . . . . NiB $488 Ex $332 Gd $242

MK IV/SERIES '80 MUSTANG POCKETLITE

Same general specifications as the Mustang 30 except weight: 12.5 oz. w/aluminum alloy receiver. Blued, chrome or stainless finish. Optional wood grain grips. Made since 1988.

Blued finish . . . . NiB $432 Ex $333 Gd $234
Lady Elite
(two-tone) finish . . . . NiB $457 Ex $411 Gd $270
Stainless finish . . . . NiB $488 Ex $332 Gd $242
Teflon/stainless finish . . . . NiB $515 Ex $328 Gd $229

MK IV/SERIES '80 OFFICER'S ACP AUTOMATIC PISTOL

Calibers: .40 S&W and .45 ACP, 3.63-inch bbl., 7.25 inches overall. Weight: 34 oz. Made 1984-97. .40 S&W, disc.1992.

Blued finish
(disc.1996). . . . . NiB $541 Ex $438 Gd $298
Matte finish . . . . NiB $518 Ex $413 Gd $290
Satin nickel finish . . . . NiB $604 Ex $481 Gd $319
Stainless steel . . . . NiB $566 Ex $452 Gd $308

MK IV/SERIES '80
SA LIGHTWEIGHT CONCEALED
CARRY OFFICER . . . . NiB $613 Ex $491 Gd $327

Caliber: .45 ACP. Seven-shot magazine, 4.25-inch bbl., 7.75 inches overall. Weight: 35 oz. Aluminum alloy receiver w/stainless slide. Dovetailed low-profile sights w/3-dot system. Matte stainless finish w/blued receiver. Wraparound black rubber grip w/finger grooves. Made since 1998.

MK IV/SERIES '90 DEFENDER
SA LIGHTWEIGHT . . . . NiB $603 Ex $479 Gd $311

Caliber: .45 ACP. Seven-shot magazine, 3-inch bbl., 6.75 inches over-all. Weight: 22.5 oz. Aluminum alloy receiver w/stainless slide. Dovetailed low-profile sights w/3-dot system. Matte stainless finish w/Nickel-Teflon receiver. Wraparound black rubber grip w/finger grooves. Made since 1998.

MK IV/SERIES 90
PONY DAO PISTOL . . . . NiB $498 Ex $406 Gd $267

Caliber: .380 ACP. Six-shot magazine, 2.75-inch bbl., 5.5 inches overall. Weight: 19 oz. Ramp front sight, dovetailed rear. Stainless finish. Checkered black composition grips. Made since 1997.

MK IV/SERIES 90
PONY POCKETLITE . . . . NiB $478 Ex $390 Gd $253

Similar to standard weight Pony Model except w/aluminum frame. Brushed stainless and Teflon finish. Made 1997 to date.

NATIONAL MATCH AUTOMATIC PISTOL

Identical to the Government Model .45 Auto but w/hand-honed action, match-grade bbl., adj. rear and ramp front sights or fixed sights. Made 1932-40.

W/adjustable
sights . . . . NiB $2796 Ex $2236 Gd $1520
W/fixed sights . . . . NiB $1944 Ex $1555 Gd $1058

NRA CENTENNIAL
.45 GOLD CUP
NATIONAL MATCH . . . . NiB $1410 Ex $1144 Gd $770

Only 2500 produced in 1971.

Colt MK IV/Series
'80 Mustang Plus II

Colt MK IV/Series '80
Mustang Pocketlite

Colt MK IV/Series
'80 Officer's ACP

POCKET JUNIOR MODEL
AUTOMATIC PISTOL . . . . NiB $364 Ex $270 Gd $156

Made in Spain by Unceta y Cia (Astra). Calibers: .22 Short, .25 Auto. Six-shot magazine, 2.25 inch bbl., 4.75 inches overall. Weight: 12 oz. Fixed sights. Checkered walnut grips. Note: In 1980, this model was subject to recall to correct an action malfunction. Returned firearms were fitted with a rebounding firing pin to prevent accidental discharges. Made 1958-68. See illustration next page.

Colt Pocket Junior

Colt Woodsman
Match Target Second Issue

Colt Super Match .38

SUPER .38 AUTOMATIC PISTOL
Identical to Government Model .45 Auto except for caliber and magazine capacity. Caliber: .38 Automatic. Nine-shot magazine, Made 1928-70.
Pre-war . . . . NiB $2762 Ex $2204 Gd $1602
Post-war. NiB $1025 Ex $812 Gd $564

SUPER MATCH .38 AUTOMATIC PISTOL
Identical to Super .38 Auto but w/hand-honed action, match grade bbl., adjustable rear sight and ramp front sight or fixed sights. Made 1933-46.
W/adjustable sights . . . . NiB $6884 Ex $5507 Gd $3745
W/fixed sights . . . . NiB $4616 Ex $3692 Gd $2511

TARGETSMAN. . . . . NiB $624 Ex $562 Gd $208
Similar to Woodsman Target but has "economy" adj. rear sight, lacks automatic slide stop. Made 1959-76.

WOODSMAN MATCH TARGET AUTOMATIC PISTOL
FIRST ISSUE. . . . . NiB $1456 Ex $1404 Gd $780
Same basic design as other Woodsman models. Caliber: .22 LR. 10-shot magazine, 6.5-inch bbl., slightly tapered w/flat sides, 11 inches overall. Weight: 36 oz. Adjustable rear sight. Blued finish. Checkered walnut one-piece grip w/extended sides. Made 1938-42.

Colt Targetsman

WOODSMAN MATCH TARGET AUTO PISTOL,
SECOND ISSUE. . . . . NiB $884 Ex $707 Gd $437
Same basic design as Woodsman Target Third Issue. Caliber: .22 LR (reg. or high speed). 10-shot magazine, Six-inch flat-sided heavy bbl., 10.5 inches overall. Weight: 40 oz. Click adj. rear sight, ramp front. Blued finish. Checkered plastic or walnut grips. Made 1948-76.

WOODSMAN MATCH TARGET "4 1/2" AUTO-
MATIC PISTOL . . . . NiB $832 Ex $510 Gd $364
Same as Match Target second issue except w/4.5-inch bbl., 9 inches overall. Weight: 36 oz. Made 1950-76.

WOODSMAN SPORT MODEL AUTOMATIC PISTOL,
FIRST ISSUE. . . . . NiB $910 Ex $728 Gd $468
Caliber: .22 LR (reg. or high speed). Same as Woodsman Target second issue except has 4.5-inch bbl., adjustable rear sight w/fixed or adjustable front sight. Weight: 27 oz., 8.5 inches overall. Made 1933-48.

Colt Woodsman
Match Target First Issue

WOODSMAN SPORT MODEL AUTOMATIC
PISTOL, SECOND ISSUE. . . . . NiB $910 Ex $728 Gd $468
Same as Woodsman Target third Issue but w/4.5-inch bbl., 9 inches overall. Weight: 30 oz. Made 1948-76.

WOODSMAN TARGET MODEL
AUTOMATIC, FIRST ISSUE . . . . **NiB $728 Ex $676 Gd $312**
Caliber: .22 LR (reg. velocity). 10-shot magazine, 6.5-inch bbl., 10.5 inches overall. Weight: 28 oz. Adjustable sights. Blued finish. Checkered walnut grips. Made 1915-.32. Note: The mainspring housing of this model is not strong enough to permit safe use of high-speed cartridges. Change to a new heat-treated mainspring housing was made at pistol No. 83,790. Many of the old models were converted by installation of new housings. The new housing may be distinguished from the earlier type by the checkering in the curve under the breech. The new housing is grooved straight across, while the old type bears a diagonally-checkered oval.

WOODSMAN TARGET MODEL
AUTOMATIC, SECOND ISSUE . . . . **NiB $676 Ex $520 Gd $312**
Caliber: .22 LR (reg. or high speed). Same as original model except has heavier bbl., and high-speed mainspring housing. (See note under Woodsman, First Issue). Weight: 29 oz. Made 1932-48.

WOODSMAN TARGET MODEL
AUTOMATIC, THIRD ISSUE . . . . . . **NiB $541 Ex $416 Gd $234**
Same basic design as previous Woodsman pistols but w/longer grip, magazine catch on left side, larger thumb safety, slide stop, slide stays open on last shot, magazine disconnector thumbrest grips. Caliber: .22 LR (reg. or high speed). 10-shot magazine, 6-inch bbl., 10.5 inches overall. Weight: 32 oz. Click adjustable rear sight, ramp front sight. Blued finish. Checkered plastic or walnut grips. Made 1948-76.

WORLD WAR I 50TH ANNIVERSARY
COMMEMORATIVE SERIES
Limited production replica of Model 1911 .45 Auto engraved w/battle scenes, commemorating Battles at Chateau Thierry, Belleau Wood Second Battle of the Marne, Meuse Argonne. In special presentation display cases. Production: 7,400 Standard model, 75 Deluxe, 25 Special Deluxe grade. Match numbered sets offered. Made in 1967, 68, 69. Values indicated are for commemoratives in new condition.
Standard grade . . . . **NiB $942 Ex $754 Gd $513**
Deluxe grade . . . . **NiB $1944 Ex $1555 Gd $1058**
Special Deluxe grade . . . . **NiB $3836 Ex $3068 Gd $2086**

WORLD WAR II
COMMEMORATIVE
.45 AUTO . . . . **NiB $962 Ex $806 Gd $614**
Limited production replica of Model 1911A1 .45 Auto engraved w/respective names of locations where historic engagements occurred during WW II, as well as specific issue and theater identification. European model has oak leaf motif on slide, palm leaf design frames the Pacific issue. Cased. 11,500 of each model were produced. Made in 1970. Value listed is for gun in new condition.

WORLD WAR II
50TH ANNIVERSARY
COMMEMORATIVE . . . . **NiB $2231 Ex $1867 Gd $1374**
Same general specifications as the Colt World War II Commemorative .45 Auto except slightly different scroll engraving, 24-karat gold-plate trigger, hammer, slide stop, magazine catch, magazine catch lock, safety lock and four grip screws. Made in 1995 only.

WORLD WAR II
D-DAY
INVASION COMMEMORATIVE . . . . **NiB $1316 Ex $1243 Gd $862**
High-luster and highly decorated version of the Colt Model 1911A1. Caliber: .45 ACP. Same general specifications as the Colt Model 1911 except for 24-karat gold-plated hammer, trigger, slide stop, magazine catch, magazine catch screw, safety lock and four grip screws. Also has scrolls and inscription on slide. Made in 1991 only.

**Colt Woodsman
Sport Model First Issue**

**Colt Woodsman
Sport Model Second Issue**

**Colt Woodsman
Target Model First Issue**

**Colt Woodsman
Target Model Second Issue**

**Colt Woodsman
Target Model Third Issue**

Colt
World War II D-Day Invasion Commemorative

Colt
Camp Perry First Issue

Colt
Camp Perry Second Issue

Colt
Woodsman Match Target First Issue

Colt World War II
50th Anniversary Commemorative

WORLD WAR II GOLDEN ANNIVER-SARY V-J DAY TRIBUTE .45 AUTO . . . . NiB $2392 Ex $1966 Gd $1394
Basic Colt Model 1911A1 design w/highly-polished bluing and decorated w/specialized tributes to honor V-J Day. Two 24-karat gold scenes highlight the slide. 24-karat gold-plated hammer. Checkered wood grips w/gold medallion on each side. Made 1995.

NOTE: *For ease in finding a particular firearm, Colt handguns are grouped into three sections: Automatic Pistols (which precedes this one), this section, and Revolvers, which follows. For a complete listing, please refer to the index.*

SINGLE-SHOT PISTOLS & DERRINGERS

CAMP PERRY MODEL SINGLE-
SHOT PISTOL, FIRST ISSUE . . . . NiB $1684 Ex $1347 Gd $916
Built on Officers' Model frame. Caliber: .22 LR (embedded head chamber for high-speed cartridges after 1930). 10 inch bbl., 13.75 inches overall. Weight: 34.5 oz. Adj. target sights. Hand-finished action. Blued finish. Checkered walnut grips. Made 1926-34.

CAMP PERRY MODEL
SECOND ISSUE. . . . . NiB $1456 Ex $1196 Gd $832
Same general specifications as First Issue except has shorter hammer fall and 8-inch bbl., 12 inches overall. Weight: 34 oz. Made 1934-41 (about 440 produced).

CIVIL WAR CENTENNIAL MODEL PISTOL
Single-shot replica of Colt Model 1860 Army Revolver. Caliber: .22 Short. Six-inch bbl., weight: 22 oz. Blued finish w/gold-plated frame, grip frame, and trigger guard, walnut grips. Cased. 24,114 were produced. Made in 1961.
Single pistol. . . . . NiB $254 Ex $203 Gd $138
Pair w/consecutive serial numbers . . . . NiB $586 Ex $468 Gd $318

DERRINGER NO. 4
Replica of derringer No. 3 (1872 Thuer Model). Single-shot w/side-swing bbl., Caliber: .22 Short, 2.5-inch bbl., 4.9 inches overall. Weight: 7.75 oz. Fixed sights. Gold-plated frame w/blued bbl., and walnut grips or completely nickel- or gold-plated w/simulated ivory or pearl grips. Made 1959-63. 112,000 total production. (SN w/D or N suffix)
Single pistol (gun only) . . . . NiB $130 Ex $104 Gd $71
Single pistol (cased w/accessories) . . . . NiB $390 Ex $286 Gd $156

DERRINGER NO. 4 COMMEMORATIVE MODELS
Limited production version of .22 derringers issued, w/appropriate inscription, to commemorate historical events. Additionally, non-firing models (w/unnotched bbls.) were furnished in books, picture frames and encased in plexiglass as singles or in cased pairs..
No. 4 Presentation Derringers
(Non-firing w/accessories) . . . . NiB $390
Ltd. Ed. Book Series
(W/nickel-plated derringers) . . . . NiB $364
1st Presentation Series
(Leatherette covered metal case) . . . . NiB $338
2nd Presentation Series
(Single wooden case) . . . . NiB $234
2nd Presentation Series
(Paired wooden case) . . . . NiB $364
1961 Issue Geneseo, Illinois,
125th Anniversary (104 produced). . . . . NiB $723
1962 Issue Fort McPherson,
Nebraska, Centennial (300 produced) . . . . NiB $442

LORD AND LADY DERRINGERS (NO. 5)
Same as Derringer No. 4. Lord model with blued bbl., w/gold-plated frame and walnut grips. Lady model is gold-plated w/simulated pearl grips. Furnished in cased pairs. Made 1970-72. (SN w/Der sufix)
Lord derringer, pair in case . . . . NiB $456 Ex $364 Gd $248
Lady derringer, pair in case . . . . NiB $468 Ex $374 Gd $255
Lord and Lady derringers,
one each, in case. . . . . NiB $487 Ex $390 Gd $265

ROCK ISLAND ARSENAL
CENTENNIAL PISTOL . . . . NiB $416 Ex $411 Gd $224
Limited production (550 pieces) version of Civil War Centennial Model single-shot .22 pistol, made exclusively for Cherry's Sporting Goods, Geneseo, Illinois, to commemorate the centennial of the Rock Island Arsenal in Illinois. Cased. Made in 1962.

Colt Agent
First Issue

Colt Anaconda

NOTE: *This section of Colt handguns contains only revolvers. For automatic pistols or single-shot pistols and derringers, please see the two sections that precede this. For a complete listing, please refer to the Index.*

REVOLVERS

.38 DS II REVOLVER . . . . NiB $436 Ex $341 Gd $228
Caliber: .38 Special. Six-shot cylinder, 2-inch bbl., 7 inches overall. Weight: 21 oz. Ramp front sight, fixed notch rear. Satin stainless finish. Black rubber combat grip w/finger grooves. Made 1997 to date.

AGENT DA REVOLVER,
FIRST ISSUE. . . . . NiB $442 Ex $390 Gd $239
Same as Cobra, first issue except has short-grip frame .38 Special only, weight: 14 oz. Made 1955-72.

AGENT (LW) DA REVOLVER,
SECOND ISSUE. . . . . NiB $411 Ex $380 Gd $208
Same as Colt Agent, first issue except has shrouded ejector rod and alloy frame. Made 1973-86.

ANACONDA DA REVOLVER
Calibers: .44 Mag., .45 Colt., bbl. lengths: 4, 6 or 8 inches; 11.63 inches overall (with 6-inch bbl.). Weight: 53 oz. (6-inch bbl.). Adj. white outline rear sight, red insert ramp-style front. Matte stainless or Realtree gray camo finish. Black Neoprene combat grips w/finger grooves. Made since 1990.
Matte stainless . . . . NiB $676 Ex $515 Gd $312
Realtree gray camo
finish (disc. 1996) . . . . NiB $728 Ex $546 Gd $338
Custom model
(.44 Mag. w/ported bbl.) . . . . NiB $910 Ex $624 Gd $312
First Edition model
(Ltd. Edition 1000). . . . . NiB $988 Ex $780 Gd $416
Hunter model
(.44 Mag. w/2x scope). . . . . NiB $1139 Ex $931 Gd $546

Colt Banker's Special

Colt Bisley

Colt Buntline Special .45

Colt Commando Special

ANACONDA TITANIUM DA REVOLVER
Same general specifications as the standard Anaconda except chambered .44 Mag. only w/titanium-plated finish, gold-plated trigger, hammer and cylinder release. Limited edition of 1,000 distributed by American Historical Foundation w/personalized inscription. Made 1996.
One of 1000 . . . . NiB $2464 Ex $1971 Gd $1341
Presentation case, add $200

ARMY SPECIAL DA REVOLVER . . . . . . NiB $754 Ex $676 Gd $416
.41-caliber frame. Calibers: .32-20, .38 Special (.41 Colt). Six-shot cylinder, right revolution. Bbl., lengths: 4-, 4.5, 5-, and 6-inches, 9.25 inches overall (4-inch bbl.). Weight: 32 oz. (4-inch bbl.). Fixed sights. Blued or nickel-plated finish. Hard rubber grips. Made 1908-27. Note: This model has a somewhat heavier frame than the New Navy, which it replaced. Serial numbers begin w/300,000. The heavy .38 Special High Velocity loads should not be used in .38 Special arms of this model.

BANKER'S SPECIAL DA REVOLVER
This is the Police Positive w/a 2-inch bbl., otherwise specifications same as that model, rounded butt intro. in 1933. Calibers: .22 LR (embedded head-cylinder for high speed cartridges intro. 1933), .38 New Police. 6.5 inches overall. Weight: 23 oz. (.22 LR), 19 oz. (.38). Made 1926-.40.
.38 caliber . . . . NiB $1056 Ex $845 Gd $60
.22 caliber . . . . NiB $2083 Ex $1676 Gd $1160

BISLEY MODEL SA REVOLVER
Variation of the Single-Action Army, developed for target shooting w/modified grips, trigger and hammer. Calibers: General specifications same as SA Army. Target Model made w/flat-topped frame and target sights. Made 1894-1915.
Standard model . . . . NiB $8184 Ex $6547 Gd $4452
Target model (flat-top) . . . . . . NiB $12,026 Ex $9620 Gd $6542

BUNTLINE SPECIAL .45 . . . . NiB $1202 Ex $962 Gd $654
Same as standard SA Army except has 12-inch bbl., caliber .45 Long Colt. Made 1957-75.

COBRA DA REVOLVER,
ROUND BUTT, FIRST ISSUE . . . . . . NiB $468 Ex $374 Gd $255
Lightweight Detective Special w/same general specifications as that model except w/Colt-alloy frame. Two-inch bbl., calibers: .38 Special, .38 New Police, .32 New Police. Weight: 15 oz., (.38 cal.). Blued finish. Checkered plastic or walnut grips. Made 1951-73.

COBRA DA REVOLVER,
SECOND ISSUE . . . . NiB $468 Ex $364 Gd $208
Lightweight version of Detective Special, Second Issue has aluminum alloy frame. 16.5 oz. Made 1973-81.

COBRA DA REVOLVER
SQUARE BUTT . . . . NiB $442 Ex $338 Gd $208
Lightweight Police Positive Special w/same general specifications except has Colt-alloy frame, 4-inch bbl., Calibers: .38 Special, .38 New Police, .32 New Police. Weight: 17 oz. in .38 caliber. Blued finish. Checkered plastic or walnut grips. Made 1951-73.

COMMANDO SPECIAL
DA REVOLVER . . . . NiB $442 Ex $338 Gd $234
Caliber: .38 Special. Six-shot cylinder, 2-inch bbl., 6.88 inches overall. Weight: 21.5 oz. Fixed sights. Low-luster blued finish. Made 1982-86.

DETECTIVE SPECIAL DA REVOLVER, FIRST ISSUE
Similar to Police Positive Special w/2-inch bbl., otherwise specifications same as that model, rounded butt intro. 1933. .38 Special only in pre-war issue. Blued or nickel-plated finish. Weight: 17 oz. 6.75 inches overall. Made 1926-46.
Blued finish . . . . NiB $468 Ex $364 Gd $260
Nickel finish . . . . NiB $853 Ex $692 Gd $510

**Colt Cobra
Round Butt First Issue**

**Colt
Detective Special First Issue**

DETECTIVE SPECIAL DA REVOLVER, 2ND ISSUE
Similar to Detective special first issue except w/2- or 3-inch bbl., and also chambered .32 New Police, .38 New Police. Wood, plastic or over-sized grips. Made 1947-72.

Blued finish . . . . NiB $456 Ex $364 Gd $248
Nickel finish . . . . NiB $514 Ex $411 Gd $2680
W/three-inch bbl., add $95

DETECTIVE SPECIAL DA REVOLVER, 3RD ISSUE
"D" frame, shrouded ejector rod. Caliber: .38 Special. Six-shot cylinder, 2-inch bbl., 6.88 inches overall. Weight: 21.5 oz. Fixed rear sight, ramp front. Blued or nickel-plated finish. Checkered walnut wraparound grips. Made 1973-84.

Blued finish . . . . NiB $468 Ex $364 Gd $260
Nickel finish . . . . NiB $478 Ex $385 Gd $265
W/three-inch bbl., add $75

**Colt
Detective Special Second Issue**

DETECTIVE SPECIAL DA REVOLVER, 4TH ISSUE
Similar to Detective Special, Third Issue except w/alloy frame. Blued or chrome finish. Wraparound black neoprene grips w/Colt medallion. Made 1993-95.

Blued finish . . . . NiB $442 Ex $411 Gd $260
Chrome finish . . . . NiB $447 Ex $364 Gd $237
DAO model (bobbed hammer) . . . . NiB $478 Ex $385 Gd $265

DIAMONDBACK DA REVOLVER
"D" frame, shrouded ejector rod. Calibers: .22 LR, .22 WRF, .38 Special. Six-shot cylinder, 2.5-, 4- or 6-inch bbl., w/vent rib, 9 inches overall (with 4-inch bbl). Weight: 31.75 oz. (.22 cal., 4-inch bbl.), 28.5 oz. (.38 cal.). Ramp front sight, adj. rear. Blued or nickel finish. Checkered walnut grips. Made 1966-84.

Blued finish . . . . NiB $676 Ex $572 Gd $260
Nickel finish . . . . NiB $607 Ex $463 Gd $307
.22 Mag. model . . . . NiB $640 Ex $494 Gd $321
W/2.5-inch bbl., add $75

DA ARMY (1878) REVOLVER . . . . NiB $5460 Ex $4940 Gd $2600
Also called DA Frontier. Similar in appearance to the smaller Lightning Model but has heavier frame of different shape, round disc on left side of frame, lanyard loop in butt. Calibers: .38-40, .44-40, .45 Colt. Six-shot cylinder, bbl. lengths: 3.5- and 4-inches (w/o ejector), 4.75-, 5.5- and 7.5-inches w/ejector. 12.5 inches overall (7.5-inch bbl.). Weight: 39 oz. (.45 cal., 7.5-inch bbl.). Fixed sights. Hard rubber bird's-head grips. Blued or nickel finish. Made 1878-1905.

**Colt
Diamondback**

**Colt Lightning/Thunderer
1877-1912**

**Idaho Territorial
Centennial 1963 Issue**

New Jersey Tercentenary — 1964 issue

**General Hood Centennial
1964 issue**

FRONTIER SCOUT REVOLVER

SA Army replica, scale. Calibers: .22 Short, Long, LR or .22 WMR (interchangeable cylinder available). Six-shot cylinder, 4.75-inch bbl., 9.9 inches overall. Weight: 24 oz. Fixed sights. Plastic grips. Originally made w/bright alloy frame. Since 1959 w/steel frame and blued finish or all-nickel finish w/composition, wood or Staglite grips. Made 1958-71.

Blued finish, plastic grips. . . . . NiB $394 Ex $317 Gd $213
Nickel finish, wood grips. . . . . NiB $442 Ex $364 Gd $244
Buntline model, add $60
Extra interchangeable
cylinder, add $75

FRONTIER SCOUT REVOLVER COMMEMORATIVE MODELS

Limited production versions of Frontier Scout issued, w/appropriate inscription, to commemorate historical events. Cased. Note: Values indicated are for commemoratives in new condition.

1961 ISSUES
Kansas Statehood Centennial
(6201 produced) . . . . NiB $452
Pony Express Centennial
(1007 produced) . . . . NiB $494
1962 ISSUES
Columbus, Ohio, Sesquicentennial
(200 produced) . . . . NiB $619
Fort Findlay, Ohio, Sesqui-
centennial (130 produced) . . . . NiB $759
Fort Findlay Cased Pair, .22 Long
Rifle and .22 Magnum (20 produced) . . . . NiB $3068
New Mexico Golden Anniversary . . . . NiB $463
West Virginia Statehood
Centennial (3452 produced) . . . . NiB $452

1963 ISSUES
Arizona Territorial Centennial
(5355 produced) . . . . NiB $442
Battle of Gettysburg Centennial
(1019 produced) . . . . NiB $452
Carolina Charter Tercentenary
(300 produced) . . . . NiB $442
Fort Stephenson, Ohio, Sesquicentennial
(200 produced) . . . . NiB $619
General John Hunt Morgan Indiana Raid . . . . NiB $702
Idaho Territorial Centennial (902 produced) . . . . NiB $442

1964 ISSUES
California Gold Rush
(500 produced) . . . . NiB $463
Chamizal Treaty (450 produced) . . . . NiB $468
General Hood Centennial
(1503 produced) . . . . NiB $452
Montana Territorial Centennial
(2300 produced) . . . . NiB $442
Nevada "Battle Born"
(981 produced) . . . . NiB $452
Nevada Statehood Centennial
(3984 produced) . . . . NiB $437
New Jersey Tercentenary
(1001 produced) . . . . NiB $432
St. Louis Bicentennial
(802 produced) . . . . NiB $452
Wyoming Diamond Jubilee
(2357 produced) . . . . NiB $442

1965 ISSUES
Appomattox Centennial
(1001 produced) . . . . NiB $442
Forty-Niner Miner
(500 produced) . . . . NiB $452
General Meade Campaign
(1197 produced) . . . . NiB $452
Kansas Cowtown Series—Wichita
500 produced) . . . . NiB $442
Old Fort Des Moines Reconstruction
(700 produced) . . . . NiB $463
Oregon Trail (1995 produced) . . . . NiB $452
St. Augustine Quadricentennial
(500 produced) . . . . NiB $463

1966 ISSUES
Colorado Gold Rush
(1350 produced) .... NiB $463
Dakota Territory (1000 produced) .... NiB $442
Indiana Sesquicentennial
(1500 produced) .... NiB $437
Kansas Cowtown Series—Abilene
(500 produced) .... NiB $442
Kansas Cowtown Series—Dodge City
(500 produced) .... NiB $452
Oklahoma Territory (1343 produced) .... NiB $442

1967 ISSUES
Alamo (4500 produced) .... NiB $452
Kansas Cowtown Series—Coffeyville
(500 produced)..................................... NiB $442
Kansas Trail Series—Chisholm
Trail (500 produced)............................... NiB $452
Lawman Series—
Bat Masterson (3000 produced) .... NiB $463

1968 ISSUES
Kansas Trail Series—Santa Fe Trail
(501 produced)..................................... NiB $442
Kansas Trail Series—Pawnee Trail
(501 produced)..................................... NiB $432
Lawman Series—Pat Garrett
(3000 produced).................................... NiB $473
Nebraska Centennial
(7001 produced).................................... NiB $437

1969 ISSUES
Alabama Sesquicentennial
(3001 produced) .... NiB $437
Arkansas Territory Sesquicentennial
(3500 produced) .... NiB $432
California Bicentennial (5000 produced)................. NiB $416
General Nathan Bedford Forrest
(3000 produced) .... NiB $442
Golden Spike (11,000 produced) .... NiB $463
Kansas Trail Series—Shawnee Trail
(501 produced) .... NiB $437
Lawman Series—Wild Bill Hickock
(3000 produced) .... NiB $473

1970 ISSUES
Kansas Fort Series—Fort Larned
(500 produced) .... NiB $442
Kansas Fort Series—Fort Hays
(500 produced) .... NiB $442
Kansas Fort Series—Fort Riley
(500 produced)..................................... NiB $442
Lawman Series—Wyatt Earp
(3000 produced) .... NiB $546
Maine Sesquicentennial
(3000 produced) .... NiB $432
Missouri Sesquicentennial (3000 produced) .... NiB $437

1971 ISSUES
Kansas Fort Series—Fort Scott (500 produced) .... NiB $442

1972 ISSUES
Florida Territory Sesquicentennial (2001 produced) ... NiB $437

1973 ISSUES Azizona ranger
(3001 produced) .... NiB $633 Ex $546 Gd $328

Indiana Sesquicentennial
1966 Issue

Golden Spike
Centennial 1969 Issue

Colt King Cobra

COLT KING COBRA REVOLVER
Caliber: .357 Mag., bbl. lengths: 2.5-, 4-, 6- or 8-inches, 9 inches overall (with 4-inch bbl.). Weight: 42 oz., average. Matte stainless steel finish. Black Neoprene combat grips. Made 1986 to date. 2.5-inch bbl. and "Ultimate" bright or blued finish. Made 1988-92.
Matte stainless.................. NiB $436 Ex $342 Gd $229
Ultimate bright stainless .... NiB $478 Ex $369 Gd $252
Blued.......................... NiB $416 Ex $364 Gd $208

**LAWMAN MK III
DA REVOLVER**
"J" frame, shrouded ejector rod on 2-inch bbl., only. Caliber: .357 Magnum. Six-shot cylinder, bbl. lengths: 2-, 4-inch. 9.38 inches overall (w/4-inch bbl.), Weight: (with 4-inch bbl.), 35 oz. Fixed rear sight, ramp front. Service trigger and hammer or target trigger and wide-spur hammer. Blued or nickel-plated finish. Checkered walnut service or target grips. Made 1969-1982.
Blued finish .... NiB $390 Ex $286 Gd $156
Nickel finish .... NiB $411 Ex $312 Gd $172

Colt Lawman
MK V

Colt New Central
Fire Lightning

Colt New Navy

LAWMAN MK V DA REVOLVER
Similar to Trooper MK V. Caliber: .357 Mag. Six-shot cylinder, 2- or 4-inch bbl., 9.38 inches overall (4-inch bbl.). Weight: 35 oz. (4-inch bbl.). Fixed sights. Checkered walnut grips. Made 1983-85.
Blued finish . . . . NiB $286 Ex $238 Gd $156
Nickel finish . . . . NiB $317 Ex $251 Gd $168

MAGNUM CARRY DA REVOLVER . . . . NiB $416 Ex $333 Gd $234
Similar to Model DS II except chambered for .357 Magnum. Made 1998 to date.

MARINE CORPS MODEL (1905) DA REVOLVER
General specifications same as New Navy Second Issue except has round butt, was supplied only in .38 caliber (.38 Short & Long Colt, .38 Special) w/6-inch bbl. (SN range 10,001-10,926) Made 1905-09.
Marine Corps model . . . . NiB $2912 Ex $2340 Gd $1586
Marked "USMC" . . . . NiB $3848 Ex $3224 Gd $2210

METROPOLITAN MK
III DA REVOLVER . . . . NiB $442 Ex $343 Gd $238
Same as Official Police MK III except has 4-inch bbl. w/service or target grips. Weight: 36 oz. Made 1969-72.

NEW DA CENTRAL
FIRE REVOLVER . . . . NiB $1814 Ex $1451 Gd $987
Also called Lightning Model. Calibers: .38 and .41 centerfire. Six-shot cylinder, bbl. lengths: 2.5-, 3.5-, 4.5- and 6-inch without ejector, 4.5- and 6-inch w/ejector, 8.5 inches overall (3.5-inch bbl.). Weight: 23 oz. (.38 cal., with 3.5-inch bbl.) Fixed sights. Blued or nickel finish. Hard rubber bird's-head grips. Made 1877-09.

NEW FRONTIER BUNTLINE SPECIAL
Same as New Frontier SA Army except has 12-inch bbl.,
Second generation (1962-75) . . . NiB $1294 Ex $1035 Gd $704
Third generation (1976-92) . . . . . . NiB $1072 Ex $858 Gd $583

NEW FRONTIER SA ARMY REVOLVER
Same as SA Army except has flat-top frame, adj. target rear sight, ramp front sight, smooth walnut grips. 5.5- or 7.5-inch bbl., Calibers: .357 Magnum, .44 Special, .45 Colt. Made 1961-92.
Second generation (1961-75) . . . . NiB $1248 Ex $988 Gd $624
Third generation (1976-92) . . . . . . NiB $1040 Ex $832 Gd $572

NEW FRONTIER SA .22 REVOLVER . . . . . NiB $364 Ex $260 Gd $146
Same as Peacemaker .22 except has flat-top frame, adj. rear sight, ramp front sight. Made 1971-76; reintro. 1982-86.

NEW NAVY (1889) DA, FIRST ISSUE
Also called New Army. Calibers: .38 Short & Long Colt, .41 Short & Long Colt. Six-shot cylinder, left revolution. Bbl. lengths: 3-, 4.5- and 6-inches, 11.25 inches overall (with 6-inch bbl.). Weight: 32 oz. with 6-inch bbl. Fixed sights, knife-blade and V-notch. Blued or nickel-plated finish. Walnut or hard rubber grips. Made 1889-94. Note: This model, which was adopted by both the Army and Navy, was Colt's first revolver of the solid frame, swing-out cylinder type. It lacks the cylinder-locking notches found on later models made on this .41 frame; ratchet on the back of the cylinder is held in place by a double projection on the hand.
First issue. . . . . NiB $1814 Ex $1451 Gd $987
First issue w/3-inch bbl. . . . . . . NiB $2536 Ex $2028 Gd $1379
Navy contract, marked
"U.S.N.(SN 1-1500) . . . . NiB $3374 Ex $2699 Gd $1836

NEW NAVY (1892) DA, SECOND ISSUE
Also called New Army. General specifications same as First Issue except has double cylinder notches and double locking bolt. Calibers: .38 Special added in 1904 and .32-20 in 1905. Made 1892-07. Note: The heavy .38 Special High Velocity loads should not be used in .38 Special arms of this model.
Second issue . . . . NiB $1554 Ex $1243 Gd $846
Second issue w/3-inch bbl. . . . . NiB $2276 Ex $1820 Gd $1238
Navy contract, marked "U.S.N". . . . . . NiB $2594 Ex $2075 Gd $1411

NEW POCKET DA REVOLVER . . . . NiB $644 Ex $515 Gd $350
Caliber: .32 Short & Long Colt. Six-shot cylinder. bbl. lengths: 2.5, 3.5- and 6-inches. 7.5 inches overall w/3.5-inch bbl., Weight: 16 oz., with 3.5-inch bbl. Fixed sights, knife-blade and V-notch. Blued or nickel finish. Rubber grips. Made 1893-05.

NEW POLICE DA REVOLVER . . . . . NiB $546 Ex $484 Gd $312
Built on New Pocket frame but w/larger grip. Calibers: .32 Colt New Police, .32 Short & Long Colt. Bbl. lengths: 2.5-, 4- and 6-inches, 8.5 inches overall (with 4-inch bbl.). Weight: 17 oz., with 4-inch bbl. Fixed knife-blade front sight, V-notch rear. Blued or nickel finish. Rubber grips. Made 1896-05.

NEW POLICE TARGET DA REVOLVER . . . . . NiB $1404 Ex $1248 Gd $728
Target version of the New Police w/same general specifications. Target sights. Six-inch bbl., blued finish only. Made 1896-05.

NEW SERVICE DA REVOLVER

Calibers: .38 Special, .357 Magnum (intro. 1936), .38-40, .44-40, .44 Russian, .44 Special, .45 Auto, .45 Colt, .450 Eley, .455 Eley, .476 Eley. Six-shot cylinder, bbl. lengths: 4-, 5- and 6-inch in .38 Special and .357 Magnum, 4.5-, 5.5- and 7.5 inches in other calibers; 9.75 inches overall (with 4.5-inch bbl.). Weight: 39 oz. (.45 cal. with 4.5-inch bbl.). Fixed sights. Blued or nickel finish. Checkered walnut grips. Made 1898-42. Note: More than 500,000 of this model in caliber .45 Auto (designated "Model 1917 Revolver") were purchased by the U.S. Gov't. during WW I. These arms were later sold as surplus to National Rifle Association members through the Director of Civilian Marksmanship. Price was $16.15 plus packing charge. Supply exhausted during the early 1930s.

Commercial model . . . . NiB $1684 Ex $1347 Gd $916
Magnum . . . . NiB $1072 Ex $858 Gd $583
1917 Army. . . . . NiB $1034 Ex $827 Gd $563

NEW SERVICE TARGET . . . . NiB $1175 Ex $1035 Gd $624

Target version of the New Service. Calibers: Originally chambered for .44 Russian, .450 Eley, .455 Eley and .476 Eley, later models in .44 Special, .45 Colt and .45 Auto. Six- or 7.5-inch bbl., 12.75 inches overall (7.5-inch bbl.). Adj. target sights. Hand-finished action. With blued finish. Checkered walnut grips. Made 1900-40.

OFFICERS' MODEL MATCH . . . . . . NiB $728 Ex $598 Gd $312

Same general design as Officers' Model revolvers. Has tapered heavy bbl., wide hammer spur, Adjustable rear sight ramp front sight, large target grips of checkered walnut. Calibers: .22 LR, .38 Special. Six-inch bbl., 11.25 inches overall. Weight: 43 oz. (in .22 cal.), 39 oz. (.38 cal.). Blued finish. Made 1953-70.

OFFICERS' MODEL SPECIAL. . . . . . NiB $780 Ex $520 Gd $312

Target version of Officers' Model Second Issue w/similar characters except w/heavier, nontapered bbl. redesigned hammer. Ramp front sight, Colt Officers' Model Special "Coltmaster" rear sight adj. for windage and elevation. Calibers: .22 LR, .38 Special. Six-inch bbl. 11.25 inches overall. Weight: 39 oz. (in .38 cal.), 43 oz., (.22 cal.). Blued finish. Checkered plastic grips. Made 1949-53.

OFFICERS' MODEL TARGET DA
REVOLVER, FIRST ISSUE . . . . NiB $1202 Ex $962 Gd $654

Caliber: .38 Special. Six-inch bbl., hand-finished action, adj. target sights. Checkered with walnut grips. General specifications same as New Navy, Second Issue. Made 1904-08.

OFFICERS' MODEL TARGET, SECOND ISSUE

Calibers: .22 LR (intro. 1930, embedded head-cylinder for high-speed cartridges after 1932), .32 Police Positive (made 1932-1942), .38 Special. Six-shot cylinder, bbl. lengths: 4-, 4.5-, 5-, 6- and 7.5-inch (in .38 Special) or 6-inch only (.22 LR and .32 PP), 11.25 inches overall (6-inch bbl. in .38 Special). Adj. target sights. Blued finish. Checkered walnut grips. Hand-finished action. General features same as Army Special and Official Police of same date. Made 1908-49 (w/exceptions noted).

Second issue (.38 caliber) . . . . NiB $994 Ex $796 Gd $541
Second issue (.32 caliber) . . . . . . NiB $1592 Ex $1274 Gd $866
Second issue (.22 caliber) . . . . NiB $1106 Ex $884 Gd $601
W/shorter bbls. (4-, 4.5- or 5-inches), add 40%

OFFICIAL POLICE DA REVOLVER

Calibers: .22 LR (intro. 1930, embedded head-cylinder for high-speed cartridges after 1932), .32-20 (disc. 1942), .38 Special, .41 Long Colt (disc. 1930). Six-shot cylinder, bbl. lengths: 4-, 5-, and 6-inch or 2-inch and 6-inch heavy bbl. in .38 Special only; .22 LR w/4- and 6-inch bbls. only; 11.25 inches overall. Weight: 36

Colt New Service

Colt New Service Target

Colt Officer's Match

**Colt
Officers' Target Second Issue**

(cont'd) OFFICIAL POLICE DA REVOLVER

oz. (standard 6-inch bbl.) in .38 Special. Fixed sights. Blued or nickel-plated finish. Checkered walnut grips on all revolvers of this model except some of postwar production had checkered plastic grips. Made 1927-69. Note: This model is a refined version of the Army Special, which it replaced in 1928 at about serial number 520,000. The Commando .38 Special was a wartime adaptation of the Official Police made to government specifications. Commando can be identified by its sandblasted blued finish. Serial numbers start w/number 1-50,000 (1942-45). See illustration next page.

Commercial model (pre-war) . . . . . NiB $520 Ex $416 Gd $283
Commercial model (post-war) . . . . . NiB $456 Ex $364 Gd $248
Commando model . . . . NiB $552 Ex $442 Gd $301

Colt Official Police

Colt
Peacekeeper

Colt
Pocket Positive

Colt
Police Positive First Issue

OFFICIAL POLICE MK
III DA REVOLVER . . . . **NiB $260 Ex $208 Gd $140**
"J" frame, without shrouded ejector rod. Caliber: .38 Special. Six-shot cylinder. bbl., lengths: 4-, 5-, 6-inches, 9.25 inches overall w/4-inch bbl., weight: 34 oz. (4-inch bbl.). Fixed rear sight, ramp front. Service trigger and hammer or target trigger and wide-spur hammer. Blued or nickel-plated finish. Checkered walnut service grips. Made 1969-75.

PEACEKEEPER DA REVOLVER . . . . . **NiB $411 Ex $338 Gd $146**
Caliber: .357 Mag. Six-shot cylinder, 4- or 6-inch bbl., 11.25 inches overall (6-inch bbl.). Weight: 46 oz. (with 6-inch bbl.). Adj. white outline rear sight, red insert ramp-style front. Non-reflective matte blued finish. Made 1985-89.

PEACEMAKER .22 SECOND AMENDMENT
COMMEMORATIVE. . . . . **NiB $572 Ex $468 Gd $208**
Caliber: .22, revolver w/7.5-inch bbl., nickel-plated frame, bbl. ejector rod assembly, hammer and trigger, blued cylinder, backstrap and trigger guard. Black pearlite grips. bbl., inscribed "The Right to Keep and Bear Arms." Presentation case. Limited edition of 3000 issued in 1977. Top value is for revolver in new condition.

PEACEMAKER .22 SA REVOLVER . . **NiB $364 Ex $260 Gd $208**
Calibers: .22 LR and .22 WMR. Furnished w/cylinder for each caliber, 6-shot. Bbl.: 4.38-, 6- or 7.5-inches, 11.25 inches overall (with 6-inch bbl.). Weight: 30.5 oz. (with 6-inch bbl.). Fixed sights. Black composite grips. Made 1971-76.

POCKET POSITIVE
DA REVOLVER. . . . . **NiB $546 Ex $484 Gd $312**
General specifications same as New Pocket except this model has positive lock feature (see Police Positive). Calibers: .32 Short & Long Colt (disc. 1914), .32 Colt New Police (.32 S&W Short & Long). Fixed sights, flat top and square notch. Blue or nickel finish. Made 1905-40.
Blue finish . . . . **NiB $514 Ex $411 Gd $280**
Nickel finish . . . . **NiB $618 Ex $494 Gd $336**

POLICE POSITIVE DA, FIRST ISSUE
Improved version of the New Police w/the "Positive Lock," which prevents the firing pin coming in contact w/the cartridge except when the trigger is pulled. Calibers: .32 Short & Long Colt (disc. 1915), .32 Colt New Police (.32 S&W Short & Long), .38 New Police (.38 S&W). Six-shot cylinder, bbl. lengths: 2.5- (.32 cal. only), 4- 5- and 6-inches; 8.5 inches overall (with 4-inch bbl.). Weight 20 oz. (with 4-inch bbl.). Fixed sights. Blued or nickel finish. Rubber or checkered walnut grips. Made 1905-47.
Blue finish . . . . **NiB $456 Ex $364 Gd $248**
Nickel finish . . . . **NiB $520 Ex $416 Gd $283**

POLICE POSITIVE DA, SECOND ISSUE
Same as Detective Special second issue except has 4-inch bbl., 9 inches overall, weight: 26.5 oz. Intro. in 1977. Note: Original Police Positive (First Issue) has a shorter frame, is not chambered for .38 Special.
Blue finish . . . . **NiB $442 Ex $354 Gd $240**
Nickel finish . . . . **NiB $514 Ex $411 Gd $280**

POLICE POSITIVE
SPECIAL DA REVOLVER . . . . **NiB $514 Ex $411 Gd $280**
Based on the Police Positive w/frame lengthened to permit longer cylinder. Calibers: .32-20 (disc. 1942), .38 Special, .32 New Police and .38 New Police (intro. 1946). Six-shot cylinder; bbl. lengths: 4-(only length in current production), 5- and 6-inch; 8.75 inches overall (with 4-inch bbl.). Weight: 23 oz. (with 4-inch bbl. in .38 Special). Fixed sights. Checkered grips of hard rubber, plastic or walnut. Made 1907-73.

COLT POLICE POSITIVE
TARGET DA REVOLVER. . . . . **NiB $774 Ex $619 Gd $421**
Target version of the Police Positive. Calibers: .22 LR (intro. 1910, embedded-head cylinder for high-speed cartridges after 1932), .22 WRF (1910-35), .32 Short & Long Colt, (1915), .32 New Police (.32 S&W Short & Long). Six-inch bbl., blued finish only, 10.5 inches overall. Weight: 26 oz. in .22 cal. Adj. target sights. Checkered walnut grips. Made 1905-40.

PYTHON DA REVOLVER

"I" frame, shrouded ejector rod. Calibers: .357 Magnum, .38 Special. Six-shot cylinder, 2.5-, 4-, 6- or 8-inch vent rib bbl., 11.25 inches overall (with 6-inch bbl.). Weight: 44 oz. (6-inch bbl.). Adj. rear sight, ramp front. Blued, nickel or stainless finish. Checkered walnut target grips. Made 1955 to date. Ultimate stainless finish made 1985 to date.

Blued finish . . . . NiB $931 Ex $806 Gd $312
Royal blued
finish . . . . NiB $635 Ex $520 Gd $372
Nickel finish. . . . . NiB $623 Ex $510 Gd $365
Stainless finish . . . . NiB $701 Ex $572 Gd $408
Ultimate stainless
finish . . . . NiB $962 Ex $806 Gd $364
Hunter model
(w/2x scope) . . . . NiB $1451 Ex $1274 Gd $728
Silhouette model
(w/2x scope) . . . . NiB $1509 Ex $1325 Gd $676

SHOOTING MASTER DA REVOLVER

Deluxe target arm based on the New Service model. Calibers: Originally made only in .38 Special, .44 Special, .45 Auto and .45 Colt added in 1933, .357 Magnum in 1936. Six-inch bbl., 11.25 inches overall. Weight: 44 oz., in (.38 cal.), adj. target sights. Hand-finished action. Blued finish. Checkered walnut grips. Rounded butt. Made 1932-41.

Shooting Master
.38 Special . . . . NiB $1300 Ex $1144 Gd $728
Shooting Master
.357 Mag. . . . . NiB $1347 Ex $1071 Gd $717
Shooting Master
.44 Special,
.45 ACP, .45LC . . . . NiB $3744 Ex $3432 Gd $1976

SA ARMY REVOLVER

Also called Frontier Six-Shooter and Peacemaker. Available in more than 30 calibers including: .22 Rimfire (Short, Long, LR), .22 WRF, .32 Rimfire, .32 Colt, .32 S&W, .32-20, .38 Colt, .38 S&W, .38 Special, .357 Magnum, .38-40, .41 Colt, .44 Rimfire, .44 Russian, .44 Special, .44-40, .45 Colt, .45 Auto, .450 Boxer, 450 Eley, .455 Eley, .476 Eley. Six-shot cylinder. Bbl. lengths: 4.75, 5 .5 and 7.5 inches w/ejector or 3 and 4 inches w/o ejector. 10.25 inches overall (with 4.75-inch bbl.). Weight: 36 oz. (.45 cal. w/4.75-inch bbl.). Fixed sights. Also made in Target Model w/flat top-strap and target sights. Blued finish w/casehardened frame or nickel-plated. One-piece smooth walnut or checkered black rubber grips. Note: S.A. Army Revolvers w/serial numbers above 165,000 (circa 1896) are adapted to smokeless powder and cylinder pin screw was changed to spring catch at about the same time. The "First Generation" of SA Colts included both blackpowder and smokeless configurations and were manufactured from 1873 to 1940. Production resumed in 1955 w/serial number 1001SA and continued through 1975 to complete the second series, which is referred to as the "Second Generation." In 1976, the "Third Generation" of production began and continues to to date. However, several serial number rollovers occurred at 99,999. For example, in 1978 the "SA" suffix became an "SA" prefix and again in 1993, when the serial number SA99,999 was reached, the serialization format was changed again to include both an "S" prefix and an "A" suffix. Although the term "Fourth Generation" is frequently associated with this rollover, no series change actually occurred, therefore, the current production is still a "Third Generation" series. Current calibers: .357 Magnum, .44 Special, .45 Long Colt.

Pinched frame
(1873 only) . . . . NiB $79,438 Ex $63,550 Gd $43,214

Colt SA Army

**Colt
Police Positive Target**

Colt Python

(cont'd.) SA ARMY REVOLVER

Early commercial
(1873-77) . . . . NiB $40,938 Ex $32,750 Gd $22,270
Early military
(1873-77) . . . . NiB $46,875 Ex $37,500 Gd $25,500
Large bore
rimfire
(1875-80) . . . . NiB $38,125 Ex $30,500 Gd $20,740
Small bore
rimfire (1875-80) . . . . NiB $29,375 Ex $23,500 Gd $15,980
Frontier
six-shooter,
.44-40
(1878-82) . . . . NiB $44,438 Ex $35,550 Gd $24,174
Storekeeper's
model, no ejector
(1883-98) . . . . NiB $46,875 Ex $37,500 Gd $25,500
Sheriff's model
(1883-98) . . . . NiB $44,375 Ex $35,500 Gd $24,140
Target model,
flat top strap,
target sights . . . . NiB $24,375 Ex $19,500 Gd $13,260
U.S. Cavalry
model, .45
(1873-92) . . . . NiB $43,125 Ex $34,500 Gd $23,460

Colt SA Army — 125th Anniversary

Colt 150th Anniversary Deluxe

Colt 150th Anniversary Engraving Sampler

In the previous section the GTG deviates from the observed practice of listing only the value of firearms produced after 1900. This deliberate departure from the standard format is intended to provide a general reference and establish proper orientation for the reader, because the Colt SSA had its origins in the last quarter of the 19th century. Consequently, antique firearms produced prior to 1898 have been listed as a preface and introduction to the first series of production (what is now recognized as "1st Generation") in order to systematically demonstrate the progressive and sequential development of the multi-generation Colt SAA. Therefore, the previous general values have been provided to establish a point of reference to allow a more comprehensive examination of the evolution of the Colt SAA. However, please note that the following values apply only to original models, not to similar S.A.A. revolvers of more recent manufacture.

Standard model, pre-war
(1st generation) . . . . $12,750 to 65,000
Standard model
(1955-75)
(2nd generation) . . . . NiB $2244 Ex $1795 Gd $1221
Standard model
(1976 to date) . . . . NiB $1063 Ex $850 Gd $578

SA ARMY — 125TH ANNIVERSARY . . . . . NiB $1744 Ex $1395 Gd $949
Limited production deluxe version of SA Army issued in commemoration of Colt's 125th Anniversary. Caliber: .45 Long Colt., 7.5-inch bbl., cold-plated frame trigger, hammer, cylinder pin, ejector rod tip, and grip medallion. Presentation case w/anniversary medallion. Serial numbers "50AM." 7368 were made in 1961. See illustration previous page.

SA ARMY COMMEMORATIVE MODELS
Limited production versions of SA Army .45 issued, w/appropriate inscription to commemorate historical events. Cased. Note: Values indicated are for commemorative revolvers in new condition.

1963 ISSUES
Arizona Territorial Centennial
(1280 produced) . . . . NiB $1468
West Virginia Statehood
Centennial (600 produced) . . . . NiB $1390

1964 ISSUES
Chamizal Treaty (50 produced) . . . . NiB $1493
Colonel Sam Colt Sesquicentennial
Presentation (4750 produced) . . . . NiB $1468
Deluxe Presentation
(200 produced) . . . . NiB $2729
Special Deluxe Presentation
(50 produced) . . . . NiB $4337
Montana Territorial Centennial
(851 produced) . . . . NiB $1468
Nevada "Battle Born"
(100 produced) . . . . NiB $1540
Nevada Statehood Centennial
(1877 produced) . . . . NiB $1437
New Jersey Tercentenary
(250 produced) . . . . NiB $1425
Pony Express Presentation
(1004 produced) . . . . NiB $1540
St. Louis Bicentennial
(450 produced) . . . . NiB $1468
Wyatt Earp Buntline
(150 produced) . . . . NiB $2673

1965 ISSUES
Appomattox Centennial
(500 produced) . . . . NiB $1468
Old Fort Des Moines Recon-
struction (200 produced) . . . . NiB $1390

1966 ISSUES
Abercrombie & Fitch Trailblazer
—Chicago (100 produced) . . . . NiB $1287
Abercrombie & Fitch Trailblazer
—New York (200 produced) . . . . NiB $1262
Abercrombie & Fitch Trailblazer
—San Francisco (100 produced) . . . . NiB $1287
California Gold Rush
(130 produced) . . . . NiB $1468
General Meade (200 produced) . . . . NiB $1468
Pony Express Four Square (4 guns) . . . . NiB $6437

1967 ISSUES
Alamo (1000 produced) . . . . NiB $1468
Lawman Series—Bat Masterson
(500 produced) . . . . NiB $1643

1968 ISSUES
Lawman Series—Pat Garrett (500 produced) . . . . NiB $1468

Colt SA Army Flat Top

1969 ISSUES
Lawman Series—Wild Bill Hickok
(500 produced) . . . . NiB $1468

1970 ISSUES
Lawman Series—Wyatt Earp
(501 produced) . . . . NiB $2673
Missouri Sesquicentennial (501 produced) . . . . NiB $1468
Texas Ranger (1000 produced) . . . . NiB $2367

1971 ISSUES
NRA Centennial, .357 or .45 (5001 produced) . . . . . . NiB $1468

1975 ISSUES
Peacemaker Centennial .45
(1501 produced) . . . . NiB $1493
Peacemaker Centennial .44-40
(1501 produced) . . . . NiB $1596
Peacemaker Centennial Cased
Pair (501 produced) . . . . NiB $3085

1979 ISSUES
Ned Buntline .45 (3000 produced) . . . . NiB $1056

1986 ISSUES
Colt 150th Anniversary (standard) . . . . NiB $1746
Colt 150th Anniversay (engraved) . . . . NiB$2776

COLT SA COWBOY REVOLVER . . . . NiB $458
SSA variant designed for "Cowboy Action Shooting." Caliber: .45 Colt. Six-shot cylinder, 5.5-inch bbl., 11 inches overall. Weight: 42 oz. Blade front sight, fixed V-notch rear. Blued finish w/color case-hardened frame. Smooth walnut grips. Made 1999 to date.

SA SHERIFF'S MODEL .45
Limited edition replica of Storekeeper's Model in caliber .45 Colt, made exclusively for Centennial Arms Corp. Chicago, Illinois. Numbered "1SM." Blued finish w/casehardened frame or nickel-plated. Walnut grips. Made in 1961.
Blued finish (478 produced) . . . . NiB $2697 Ex $2158 Gd $1468
Nickel finish (25 produced) . . . . . NiB $6560 Ex $5248 Gd $3569

THREE-FIFTY-SEVEN DA REVOLVER
Heavy frame. Caliber: .357 Magnum. Six-shot cylinder, 4 or 6-inch bbl. Quickdraw ramp front sight, Accro rear sight. Blued finish. Checkered walnut grips. 9.25 or 11.25 inches overall. Weight: 36 oz. (4-inch bbl.), 39 oz. (6 inch bbl.). Made 1953-61.
W/standard hammer and service grips . . . . . NiB $560 Ex $448 Gd $305
W/wide-spur hammer and target grips . . . . . NiB $598 Ex $479 Gd $325

TROOPER DA REVOLVER
Same specifications as Officers' Model Match except has 4-inch bbl. w/quick-draw ramp front sight, weight: 34 oz. in .38 caliber. Made 1953-69.
W/standard hammer and service grips . . . . . NiB $432 Ex $345 Gd $235
W/wide-spur hammer and target grips . . . . . NiB $495 Ex $397 Gd $270

Colt Trooper

Colt Trooper MK V

Colt U.S. Bicentennial Commemorative Set

TROOPER MK III DA REVOLVER

"J"frame, shrouded ejector rod. Calibers: .22 LR, .22 Magnum, .38 Special, .357 Magnum. Six-shot cylinder. bbl. lengths: 4-, 6-inches. 9.5 inches overall (with 4-inch bbl.). Weight: 39 oz. (4-inch bbl.). Adj. rear sight, ramp front. Target trigger and hammer. Blued or nickel-plated finish. Checkered walnut target grips. Made 1969-78.

Blued finish . . . . NiB $407 Ex $335 Gd $129
Nickel finish. NiB $453 Ex $360 Gd $129

TROOPER MK V REVOLVER

Re-engineered Mark III for smoother, faster action. Caliber: .357 Magnum. Six-shot cylinder, bbl. lengths: 4-, 6-, 8-inch w/vent rib. Adj. rear sight, ramp front, red insert. Checkered walnut grips. Made 1982-86.

Blued finish . . . . NiB $438 Ex $360 Gd $257
Nickel finish. NiB $489 Ex $412 Gd $232

VIPER DA REVOLVER . . . . NiB $438 Ex $386 Gd $257

Same as Cobra, Second Issue except has 4-inch bbl., 9 inches overall, weight: 20 oz. Made 1977-84.

U.S. BICENTENNIAL
COMMEMORATIVE SET. . . . . NiB $2317

Replica Colt 3rd Model Dragoon revolver w/accessories, Colt SA Army revolver, and Colt Python revolver. Matching roll-engraved unfluted cylinders, blued finish and rosewood grips w/Great Seal of the United States silver medallion. Dragoon revolver has silver grip frame. Serial numbers 0001 to 1776. All revolvers in set have same number. Deluxe drawer-style presentation case of walnut w/book compartment containing a reproduction of "Armsmear." Issued in 1976. Value is for revolvers in new condition.

COONAN ARMS, INC. — Maplewood, Minnesota (formerly St. Paul, Minnesota)

MODEL .357 MAGNUM AUTO PISTOL

Caliber: .357 Mag. Seven-shot magazine, 5- or 6-inch bbl., 8.3 inches overall (with 5-inch bbl.). Weight: 42 oz. Front ramp interchangeable sight, fixed rear sight, adj. for windage. Black walnut grips. Made 1983-99.

Model A Std. grade w/o grip
safety (disc. 1991). . . . . NiB $804 Ex $644 Gd $438
Model B Std. grade w/5-inch bbl., ... NiB $580 Ex $463 Gd $315
Model B Std. grade w/6-inch bbl., ... NiB $612 Ex $489 Gd $333
Model B w/5-inch
compensated bbl., (Classic). . . . . NiB $1095 Ex $875 Gd $595
Model B w/6-inch
compensated bbl.. NiB $869 Ex $695 Gd $472

.357 MAGNUM CADET COMPACT

Similar to the standard .357 Magnum model except w/3.9-inch bbl., on compact frame. Six-shot (Cadet), 7- or 8-shot magazine (Cadet II). Weight: 39 oz., 7.8 inches overall. Made 1993-99.

Cadet model . . . . NiB $689 Ex $551 Gd $375
Cadet II model. . . . . NiB $809 Ex $649 Gd $360

CZ PISTOLS — Uhersky Brod (formerly Strakonice), Czechoslovakia Mfd. by Ceska Zbrojovka-Nardoni Podnik (formerly Bohmische Waffenfabrik A. G.)

Currently imported by CZ USA, Kansas City, KS. Previously by Magnum Research and Action Arms. Vintage importation is by Century International Arms.

MODEL 27 AUTO PISTOL . . . . NiB $566 Ex $463 Gd $268
Caliber: .32 Automatic (7.65mm). Eight-shot magazine, 4-inch bbl., 6 inches overall. Weight: 23.5 oz. Fixed sights. Blued finish. Plastic grips. Made 1927-51. Note: After the German occupation. (March 1939), Models 27 and .38 were marked w/manufacturer code "fnh." Designation of Model .38 was changed to "Pistole 39(t)."

MODEL .38 AUTO PISTOL (VZ SERIES)
Caliber: .380 Automatic (9mm). Nine-shot magazine, 3.75-inch bbl., 7 inches overall. Weight: 26 oz. Fixed sights. Blued finish. Plastic grips. After 1939 designated as T39. Made 1938-.45.
CZ DAO model . . . . NiB $399 Ex $321 Gd $221
CZ SA/DA model . . . . NiB $1274 Ex $984 Gd $659

MODEL 50 DA AUTO PISTOL . . . . . . NiB $174 Ex $139 Gd $95
Similar to Walther Model PP except w/frame-mounted safety and trigger guard not hinged. Caliber: .32 ACP (7.65mm), 8-round magazine, 3.13-inch bbl., 6.5 inches overall. Weight: 24.5 oz. Fixed sights. Blued finished. Intro. in 1950. disc. Note: "VZ50" is the official designation of this pistol used by the Czech National Police ("New Model .006" was the export designation but very few were released).

MODEL 52 SA AUTO PISTOL
Roller-locking breech system. Calibers: 7.62mm or 9mm Para. Eight-shot magazine, 4.7-inch bbl., 8.1 inches overall. Weight: 31 oz. Fixed sights. Blued finish. Grooved composition grips. Made 1952-56.
7.62mm model . . . . NiB $185 Ex $154 Gd $88
9mm model . . . . NiB $185 Ex $154 Gd $88

MODEL 70 DA AUTO PISTOL . . . . . . NiB $418 Ex $335 Gd $228
Similar to Model 50 but redesigned to improve function and dependability. Made 1962-83.

MODEL 75 DA/DAO AUTOMATIC PISTOL
Calibers: 9mm Para. or .40 S&W w/selective action mode. 10-, 13- or 15-shot magazine, 3.9-inch bbl., (Compact) or 4.75-inch bbl., (Standard), 8 inches overall (Standard). Weight: 35 oz. Fixed sights. Blued, nickel, Two-Tone or black polymer finish. Checkered wood or high-impact plastic grips. Made 1994 to date.
Black polymer finish . . . . NiB $380 Ex $304 Gd $207
High-polish blued finish . . . . NiB $444 Ex $355 Gd $242
Matte blued finish . . . . NiB $406 Ex $324 Gd $220
Nickel finish . . . . NiB $432 Ex $345 Gd $235
Two-tone finish . . . . NiB $418 Ex $335 Gd $228
W/.22 Kadet conversion, add $250
Compact model, add $35

82 DA AUTO PISTOL . . . . NiB $309 Ex $283 Gd $160
Similar to the standard CZ 83 model except chambered in 9x18 Makarov. This model currently is the Czech military sidearm.

83 DA AUTOMATIC PISTOL
Calibers: .32 ACP, .380 ACP. 15-shot (.32 ACP) or 13-shot (.380 ACP) magazine, 3.75-inch bbl., 6.75 inches overall. Weight: 26.5 oz. Fixed sights. Blued (standard); chrome and nickel (optional special edition) w/brushed, matte or polished finish. Checkered black plastic grips. Made 1985 to date.
Standard finish . . . . NiB $340 Ex $268 Gd $154
Special edition . . . . NiB $480 Ex $383 Gd $257
Engraved . . . . NiB $1075 Ex $850 Gd $577

85 AUTOMATIC DA PISTOL
Same as CZ 75 except w/ambidextrous slide release and safety. Calibers: 9mm Para., 7.65mm. Made 1986 to date.
Black polymer finish . . . . NiB $439 Ex $350 Gd $239
High-polish blued finish . . . . NiB $546 Ex $438 Gd $283
Matte blued finish . . . . NiB $489 Ex $335 Gd $232

CZ Model 75 Compact

CZ Model 75 Kadet

CZ Model 83

CZ Model 85 Combat

CZ Model 97B

CZ Model 100

Daewoo DH40

85 COMBAT DA AUTOMATIC PISTOL
Similar to the standard CZ 85 model except w/13-shot magazine, combat-style hammer, fully adj. rear sight and walnut grips. Made 1986 to date.

Black polymer
finish . . . . NiB $469 Ex $407 Gd $232
High-polished
blued finish . . . . NiB $509 Ex $407 Gd $277
Matte blued
finish . . . . NiB $509 Ex $407 Gd $277

MODEL 97B DA
AUTOLOADING PISTOL . . . . NiB $541 Ex $474 Gd $283
Similar to the CZ Model 75 except chambered for the .45 ACP cartridge. 10-shot magazine, Frame-mounted thumb safety that allows single-action, cocked-and-locked carry. Made 1997 to date.

MODEL 100 DA
AUTOMATIC PISTOL . . . . NiB $376 Ex $319 Gd $185
Caliber: 9mm, .40 S&W. 10-shot magazine, 3.8-inch bbl., Weight: 25 oz. Polymer grips w/fixed low-profile sights. Made 1996 to date.

MODEL 1945 DA
POCKET AUTO PISTOL . . . . NiB $238 Ex $191 Gd $130
Caliber: .25 Auto (6.35mm). Eight-shot magazine, 2.5-inch bbl., 5 inches overall. Weight: 15 oz. Fixed sights. Blued finish. Plastic grips. Intro. 1945. disc.

DUO POCKET
AUTO PISTOL . . . . NiB $232 Ex $201 Gd $124
Caliber: .25 Automatic (6.35mm). Six-shot magazine, 2.13 inch bbl., 4.5 inches overall. Weight: 14-.5 oz. Fixed sights. Blued or nickel finish. Plastic grips. Made c.1926-60.

DAEWOO PISTOLS — Seoul, Korea
Mfd. by Daewoo Precision Industries Ltd.

Imported by Daewoo Precision Industries, Southhampton, PA, Previously by Nationwide Sports Distributors and KBI, Inc.

DH40 AUTO PISTOL . . . . NiB $393 Ex $335 Gd $204
Caliber: .40 S&W. 12-shot magazine, 4.25-inch bbl., 7 inches overall. Weight: 28 oz. Blade front sight, dovetailed rear w/3-dot system. Blued finish. Checkered composition grips. DH/DP series feature a patented "fastfire" action w/5-6 lb. trigger pull. Made 1994-96.

DH45 AUTO PISTOL . . . . NiB $632 Ex $510 Gd $344
Caliber: .45 ACP. 13-shot magazine, 5-inch bbl., 8.1 inches overall. Weight: 35 oz. Blade front sight, dovetailed rear w/3-dot system. Blued finish. Checkered composition grips. Announced 1994, but not imported.

DP51 AUTO PISTOL . . . . NiB $367 Ex $291 Gd $194
Caliber: 9mm Para. 13-shot magazine, 4.1-inch bbl., 7.5 inches overall. Weight: 28 oz. Blade front and square-notch rear sights. Matte black finish. Checkered composition grips. Made 1991-96.

DP52 AUTO PISTOL . . . . NiB $326 Ex $280 Gd $163
Caliber: .22 LR. 10-shot magazine, 3.8-inch bbl., 6.7 inches overall. Weight: 23 oz. Blade front sight, dovetailed rear w/3-dot system. Blued finish. Checkered wood grips. Made 1994-96.

DAKOTA/E.M.F. CO. — Santa Ana, California

MODEL 1873 SA REVOLVER
Calibers: .22 LR, .22 Mag., .357 Mag., .45 Long Colt, .30 M1 carbine, .38-40, .32-20, .44-40. Bbl. lengths: 3.5, 4.75, 5.5, 7.5 inches. Blued or nickel finish. Engraved models avail.
Standard model . . . . NiB $331 Ex $255 Gd $204
W/extra cylinder . . . . NiB $679 Ex $566 Gd $421

MODEL 1875 OUTLAW
SA REVOLVER . . . . NiB $427 Ex $342 Gd $233
Calibers: .45 Long Colt, .357 Mag., .44-40. 7.5-inch bbl. Casehardened frame, blued finish. Walnut grips. This is an exact replica of the Remington Number 3 revolver produced 1875-89.

MODEL 1890 REMINGTON POLICE
Calibers: .357 Mag., .44-40, .45 Long Colt, 5.75-inch bbl., blued or nickel finish. Similar to Outlaw w/lanyard ring and no bbl. web .
Standard model . . . . NiB $453 Ex $362 Gd $246
Nickel model . . . . NiB $542 Ex $433 Gd $295
Engraved model . . . . NiB $631 Ex $505 Gd $344

BISLEY SA REVOLVER
Calibers: .44-40, .45 Long Colt, .357 Mag, 5.5- or 7.5-inch bbl., disc. 1992. Reintroduced 1994.
Standard model . . . . NiB $357 Ex $291 Gd $199
Target model . . . . NiB $403 Ex $321 Gd $204

HARTFORD SA REVOLVER
Calibers: .22 LR, .32-20, .357 Mag., .38-40, .44-40, .44 Special, .45 Long Colt. These are exact replicas of the original Colts w/steel backstraps, trigger guards and forged frames. Blued or nickel finish. Imported 1990 to date.
Standard model . . . . NiB $357 Ex $280 Gd $184
Engraved model . . . . NiB $631 Ex $505 Gd $344
Hartford Artillery,
U.S. Cavalry models . . . . NiB $403 Ex $331 Gd $204

SHERIFF'S MODEL
SA REVOLVER . . . . NiB $393 Ex $306 Gd $204
Calibers: .32-20, .357 Mag., .38-40, .44 Special, .44-40, .45 LC. 3.5-inch bbl. Reintroduced 1994.

TARGET SA REVOLVER . . . . NiB $393 Ex $270 Gd $189
Calibers: .45 Long Colt, .357 Mag., .22 LR; 5.5- or 7.5-inch bbl. Polished, blued finish, casehardened frame. Walnut grips. Ramp front, blade target sight, adj. rear sight.

CHARLES DALY HANGUNS — Manila, Philippines. Currently imported by K.B.I., Harrisburg, PA.

MODEL M1911-A1 FIELD FS AUTOMATIC PISTOL
Caliber: .45 ACP. Eight- or 10-shot magazine (Hi-Cap), 5-inch bbl., 8.75 inches overall. Weight: 38 oz. Blade front sight, drift adjustable rear w/3-dot system. Skeletonized tactical hammer and trigger. Extended slide release and beavertail grip safety. Matte blue, stainless or Duo finish. Checkered composition or wood stocks. Imported 1996 to date.
Matte blue (Field FS) . . . . NiB $444 Ex $382 Gd $229
Stainless (Empire FS) . . . . NiB $607 Ex $484 Gd $306
Duo (Superior FS) . . . . NiB $478 Ex $382 Gd $260
W/.22 conversion kit, add $200

Dakota Hartford

DAVIS INDUSTRIES, INC. — Chino, California

MODEL D DERRINGER
Single-action double derringer. Calibers: .22 LR, .22 Mag., .25 ACP, .32 Auto, .32 H&R Mag., 9mm, .38 Special. Two-shot capacity, 2.4-inch or 2.75-inch bbl., 4 inches overall (2.4-inch bbl.). Weight: 9 to 11.5 oz. Laminated wood grips. Black Teflon or chrome finish. Made 1987 to date.
.22 LR or .25 ACP . . . . NiB $76 Ex $61 Gd $42
.22 Mag., .32 H&R Mag., .38 Spec. . . . . . NiB $96 Ex $76 Gd $52
.32 Auto. . . . . NiB $90 Ex $71 Gd $49
9mm Para. NiB $108 Ex $87 Gd $59

LONG BORE DERRINGER. . . . . NiB $96 Ex $76 Gd $52
Similar to Model D except in calibers .22 Mag., .32 H&R Mag., .38 Special, 9mm Para. 3.75-inch bbl., weight: 16 oz. Made 1995 to date.

MODEL P-.32 . . . . NiB $83 Ex $66 Gd $45
Caliber: .32 Auto. Six-round magazine, 2.8-inch bbl., 5.4 inches overall. Weight: 22 oz. Black Teflon or chrome finish. Laminated wood grips. Made 1987 to date.

MODEL P-.380 . . . . NiB $87 Ex $76 Gd $51
Caliber: .380 Auto. Five-shot magazine, 2.8-inch bbl., 5.4 inches overall. Weight: 22 oz. Black Teflon or chrome finish. Made 1990 to date.

DESERT INDUSTRIES, INC. — Las Vegas, Nevada (Previously Steel City Arms, Inc.)

DOUBLE DEUCE DA PISTOL . . . . . NiB $357 Ex $301 Gd $204
Caliber: .22 LR. Six-shot magazine, 2.5-inch bbl., 5.5 inches overall. Weight: 15 oz. Matte-finish stainless steel. Rosewood grips.

TWO-BIT SPECIAL PISTOL . . . . NiB $357 Ex $301 Gd $194
Similar to the Double Deuce model except chambered in .25 ACP w/5-shot magazine,

(NEW) DETONICS MFG. CORP — Phoenix, Arizona (Previously Detonics Firearms Industries, Bellevue, WA)

COMBAT MASTER
Calibers: .45 ACP, .451 Detonics Mag. Six-round magazine, 3.5-inch bbl., 6.75 inches overall. Combat-type w/fixed or adjustable sights. Checkered walnut grip. Stainless steel construction. Disc. 1992.
MK I matte stainless,
fixed sights, (disc. 1981) . . . . NiB $541 Ex $459 Gd $306
MK II stainless steel
finish, (disc. 1979) . . . . NiB $541 Ex $459 Gd $306

Detonics Combat Master

Detonics Scoremaster

Dreyse Model 1907

(cont'd) COMBAT MASTER
MK III chrome,
(disc. 1980) . . . . NiB $478 Ex $382 Gd $260
MK IV polished blued,
adj. sights, (disc. 1981) . . . . NiB $529 Ex $423 Gd $288
MK V matte stainless,
fixed sights, (disc. 1985) . . . . NiB $676 Ex $541 Gd $367
MK VI polished ptainless, adj.
sights, (disc. 1989). . . . . NiB $733 Ex $586 Gd $399
MK VI in .451 Magnum,
(disc. 1986) . . . . NiB $1084 Ex $867 Gd $590
MK VII matte stainless steel,
no sights, (disc. 1985) . . . . NiB $957 Ex $765 Gd $520
MK VII in .451 Magnum,
(disc. 1980) . . . . NiB $1269 Ex $1015 Gd $691

POCKET 9 . . . . NiB $586 Ex $459 Gd $357
Calibers: 9mm Para., .380. Six-round magazine, three-inch bbl., 5.88 inches overall. Fixed sights. Double- and single-action trigger mechanism. Disc. 1986.

SCOREMASTER . . . . NiB $1025 Ex $867 Gd $714
Calibers: .45 ACP, .451 Detonics Mag. Seven-round magazine. Five- or 6-inch heavyweight match bbl., 8.75 inches overall. Weight: 47 oz. Stainless steel construction, self-centering bbl., system. Disc. 1992.

SERVICE MASTER . . . . NiB $841 Ex $688 Gd $433
Caliber: .45 ACP. Seven-round magazine, 4.25-inch bbl., weight: 39 oz. Interchangeable front sight, Millett rear sight. Disc. 1986.

SERVICE MASTER II. . . . . NiB $943 Ex $765 Gd $484
Same general specifications as standard Service Master except comes in polished stainless steel w/self-centering bbl., system. Disc. 1992.

DOWNSIZER CORPORATION — Santee, California

MODEL WSP
DAO PISTOL . . . . NiB $423 Ex $306 Gd $204
Single-shot, tip-up pistol. Calibers: .22 Mag., .32 Mag., .380 ACP. 9mm Parabellum, .357 Mag., .40 S&W, .45 ACP. Six-shot cylinder, 2.10-inch bbl. w/o extractor, 3.25 inches overall. Weight: 11 oz. No sights. Stainless finish. Synthetic grips. Made 1994 to date.

DREYSE PISTOLS — Sommerda, Germany
Mfd. by Rheinische Metallwaren und Maschinenfabrik ("Rheinmetall")

MODEL 1907
AUTOMATIC PISTOL . . . . NiB $255 Ex $189 Gd $127
Caliber: .32 Auto (7.65mm). Eight-shot magazine, 3.5-inch bbl., 6.25 inches overall. Weight: About 24 oz. Fixed sights. Blued finish. Hard rubber grips. Made c. 1907-14.

VEST POCKET
AUTOMATIC PISTOL . . . . NiB $331 Ex $240 Gd $153
Conventional Browning type. Caliber: .25 Auto (6.35mm). Six-shot magazine, 2-inch bbl., 4.5 inches overall. Weight: About 14 oz. Fixed sights. Blued finish. Hard rubber grips. Made c. 1909-14.

DWM PISTOL — Berlin, Germany
Mfd. by Deutsche Waffen-und-Munitionsfabriken

POCKET AUTOMATIC PISTOL . . . . NiB $766 Ex $613 Gd $417
Similar to the FN Browning Model 1910. Caliber: .32 Automatic (7.65mm). 3.5-inch bbl., 6 inches overall. Weight: About 21 oz. Blued finish. Hard rubber grips. Made c. 1921-31.

ED BROWN — Perry, Montana

"CLASS A LTD" SA
AUTOMATIC PISTOL . . . . NiB $2317 Ex $1957 Gd $875
Caliber: .38 Super, 9mm, 9x23, .45 ACP. Seven-shot magazine, 4.25- or 5-inch bbl., weight: 34-39 oz. Rubber checkered or optional Hogue exotic wood grip. M1911 style single action pistol. Fixed front and rear Novak Lo-mount or fully adjustable sights.

"CLASSIC CUSTOM" SA
AUTOMATIC PISTOL . . . . NiB $2832 Ex $2317 Gd $1133
Caliber: .45 ACP. Seven-shot magazine, 4.25- or 5-inch bbl.,
weight: 39 oz. Exotic Hogue wood grip w/modified ramp or post
front and rear adjustable sights.

"SPECIAL FORCES" SA
AUTOMATIC PISTOL . . . . NiB $1236 Ex $1045 Gd $695
Caliber: .45 ACP. Seven-shot magazine, 4.25- or 5-inch bbl.,
weight: 34-39 oz. Rubber checkered, optional exotic wood grips.
Single action M1911 style pistol.

ENFIELD REVOLVER — Enfield Lock, Middlesex, England
Manufactured by Royal Small Arms Factory

(BRITISH SERVICE) NO. 2
MK 1 REVOLVER . . . . NiB $242 Ex $201 Gd $139
Webley pattern. Hinged frame. Double action. Caliber: .380 British
Service (.38 S&W w/200-grain bullet). Six-shot cylinder, 5-inch bbl.,
10.5 inches overall. Weight: About 27.5 oz. Fixed sights. Blued finish.
Vulcanite grips. First issued in 1932, this was the standard revolver of
the British Army in WW II. Now obsolete. Note: This model also pro-
duced w/spurless hammer as No. 2 Mk 1* and Mk 1**.

ENTREPRISE ARMS — Irwindale, California

"ELITE" SA AUTO-
MATIC PISTOL . . . . NiB $644 Ex $582 Gd $515
Single action M1911 style pistol. Caliber: .45 ACP. 10-shot magazine, 3.25-, 4.25-, 5-inch bbl., (models P325, P425, P500). Weight:
36-40 oz. Ultraslim checkered grips, Tactical 2 high profile sights
w/3-dot system. Lightweight adjustable trigger. Blued or matte black
oxide finish. Made 1997 to date.

"MEDALIST" SA AUTOMATIC PISTOL
Similar to Elite model except machined to match tolerances and target configuration. Caliber: .45 ACP, .40 S&W. 10-shot magazine, 5-
inch compensated bbl. w/dovetail front and fully adjustable rear Bo-
Mar sights. Weight: 40 oz. Made 1997 to date.
.40 S&W model . . . . NiB $1024 Ex $819 Gd $557
.45 ACP model . . . . NiB $895 Ex $716 Gd $487

"TACTICAL" SA AUTOMATIC PISTOL
Similar to Elite model except in combat carry configuration. De-
horned frame and slide w/ambidextrous safety. Caliber: .45 ACP. 10-
shot magazine, 3.25-, 4.25-, 5-inch bbl., weight: 36-40 oz. Tactical
2 Ghost Ring or Novak Lo-mount sights.
Tactical 2 ghost
ring sights . . . . NiB $953 Ex $850 Gd $515
Novak Lo-Mount . . . . NiB $818 Ex $654 Gd $445
Tactical plus model . . . . NiB $886 Ex $711 Gd $484

BOXER SA AUTO-
MATIC PISTOL . . . . NiB $1236 Ex $1025 Gd $669
Similar to Medalist model except w/profiled slide configuration and
fully adjustable target sights. weight: 42 oz. Made 1997 to date.

"TSM" SA AUTOMATIC PISTOL
Similar to Elite model except in IPSC configuration. Caliber: .45
ACP, .40 S&W. 10-shot magazine, 5-inch compensated bbl.,
w/dovetail front and fully adjustable rear Bo-Mar sights. Weight: 40
oz. Made 1997 to date.

Enfield
(British Service)No. 2 MK 1 Revolver

Erma
Model ER-772 Match Revolver

(cont'd) **"TSM" SA AUTOMATIC PISTOL**
TSM I model . . . . NiB $2060 Ex $1854 Gd $978
TSM II model . . . . NiB $2157 Ex $1725 Gd $1173
TSM III model . . . . NiB $2382 Ex $1905 Gd $1296

ERMA-WERKE — Dachau, Germany

MODEL ER-772
MATCH REVOLVER . . . . NiB $1133 Ex $901 Gd $510
Caliber: .22 LR. Six-shot cylinder, 6-inch bbl., 12 inches overall.
Weight: 47.25 oz. Adjustable micrometer rear sight and front sight
blade. Adjustable trigger. Interchangeable walnut sporter or match
grips. Polished blued finish. Made 1991-94.

MODEL ER-773
MATCH REVOLVER . . . . NiB $953 Ex $850 Gd $463
Same general specifications as Model 772 except chambered for .32
S&W. Made 1991-95.

MODEL ER-777
MATCH REVOLVER . . . . NiB $901 Ex $798 Gd $463
Caliber: .357 Magnum. Six-shot cylinder. 4- or 5.5-inch bbl., 9.7 to
11.3 inches overall. Weight: 43.7 oz. (with 5.5-inch bbl.).
Micrometer adj. rear sight. Checkered walnut sporter or match-style
grip (interchangeable). Made 1991-95.

MODEL ESP-85A COMPETITION PISTOL
Calibers: .22 LR and .32 S&W Wadcutter. Eight- or 5-shot maga-
zine, 6-inch bbl., 10 inches overall. Weight: 40 oz. Adj. rear
sight, blade front sight. Checkered walnut grip w/thumbrest.
Made 1991-97.
Match model . . . . NiB $1262 Ex $953 Gd $566
Chrome match . . . . NiB $1374 Ex $1143 Gd $849
Sporting model . . . . NiB $1088 Ex $870 Gd $592
Conversion unit .22 LR . . . . NiB $998 Ex $798 Gd $543
Conversion unit .32 S&W . . . . . . NiB $1095 Ex $875 Gd $595

European American Armory
Big Bore Bounty Hunter

MODEL KGP68
AUTOMATIC PISTOL . . . . NiB $463 Ex $412 Gd $257
Luger type. Calibers: .32 Auto (7.65mm), .380 Auto (9mm Short). Six-shot magazine (.32 Auto), 5-shot (.380 Auto), 4-inch bbl., 7.38 inches overall. Weight: 22.5 oz. Fixed sights. Blued finish. Checkered walnut grips. Made 1968-93.

MODEL KGP69
AUTOMATIC PISTOL . . . . NiB $463 Ex $412 Gd $191
Luger type. Caliber: .22 LR. Eight-shot magazine, 4-inch bbl., 7.75 inches overall. Weight: 29 oz. fixed sights. Blued finish. Checkered walnut grips. Imported 1969-93.

Erma-Werke
Model KGP69

EUROPEAN AMERICAN ARMORY — Hialeah, Florida
See also listings under Astra Pistols.

EUROPEAN MODEL AUTO PISTOL
Calibers: .32 ACP (SA only), .380 ACP (SA or DA), 3.85-inch bbl., 7.38 overall, 7-shot magazine, Weight: 26 oz. Blade front sight, drift-adj. rear. Blued, chrome, blue/chrome, blue/gold, Duo-Tone or Wonder finish. Imported 1991 to date.

Blued .32 caliber (disc. 1995)	NiB $159	Ex $127	Gd $87
Blue/chrome .32 caliber			
(disc. 1995)	NiB $185	Ex $148	Gd $101
Chrome .32 caliber			
(Disc. 1995).	NiB $192	Ex $153	Gd $104
Blued .380 caliber	NiB $166	Ex $133	Gd $90
Blue/chrome .380 caliber			
(disc. 1993)	NiB $185	Ex $148	Gd $101
DA .380 caliber (disc. 1994)	NiB $204	Ex $163	Gd $111
Lady .380 caliber (disc. 1995)	NiB $249	Ex $199	Gd $136
Wonder finish .380 caliber	NiB $166	Ex $133	Gd $90

BIG BORE BOUNTY HUNTER SA REVOLVER
Calibers: .357 Mag., .41 Mag., .44-40, .44 Mag., .45 Colt. Bbl. lengths: 4.63, 5.5, 7.5 inches. Blade front and grooved topstrap rear sights. Blued or chrome finish w/color casehardened or gold-plated frame. Smooth walnut grips. Imported 1992 to date.

Blued finish	NiB $249	Ex $199	Gd $136
Blued w/color-			
casehardened frame	NiB $321	Ex $260	Gd $153
Blued w/gold-plated frame	NiB $300	Ex $240	Gd $163
Chrome finish	NiB $337	Ex $275	Gd $197
Gold-plated frame, add			$100

Erma Model ESP-85A
Competition Pistol

BOUNTY HUNTER SA REVOLVER
Calibers: .22 LR, .22 Mag. Bbl. lengths: 4.75, 6 or 9 inches. Blade front and dovetailed rear sights. Blued finish or blued w/gold-plated frame. European hardwood grips. Imported 1991 to date.
Blued finish (4.75-inch bbl.) . . . . NiB $83 Ex $66 Gd $45
Blued .22 LR/.22 WRF combo
(4.75-inch bbl.) . . . . NiB $102 Ex $82 Gd $55
Blued .22 LR/.22 WRF combo
(6-inch bbl.). . . . . NiB $108 Ex $87 Gd $59
Blued .22 LR/.22 WRF combo
(9-inch bbl.). . . . . NiB $115 Ex $92 Gd $62

EA22 TARGET . . . . NiB $363 Ex $291 Gd $198
Caliber: .22 LR. 12-shot magazine, 6-inch bbl., 9.10 inches overall. Weight: 40 oz. Ramp front sight, fully adj. rear. Blued finish. Checkered walnut grips w/thumbrest. Made 1991-94.

FAB 92 AUTO PISTOL
Similar to the Witness model except chambered in 9mm only w/slide-mounted safety and no cock-and-lock provision. Imported 1992-95.
FAB 92 standard . . . . NiB $342 Ex $286 Gd $178
FAB 92 compact . . . . NiB $342 Ex $286 Gd $178

STANDARD GRADE REVOLVER
Calibers: .22 LR, .22 WRF, .32 H&R Mag., .38 Special. Two-, 4- or 6-inch bbl., blade front sight, fixed or adj. rear. Blued finish. European hardwood grips w/finger grooves. Imported 1991 to date.
.22 LR (4-inch bbl.) . . . . NiB $172 Ex $138 Gd $94
.22 LR (6-inch bbl.) . . . . NiB $185 Ex $148 Gd $101
.22 LR combo (4-inch bbl.) . . . . NiB $249 Ex $199 Gd $136
.22 LR combo (6-inch bbl.) . . . . NiB $287 Ex $229 Gd $156
.32 H&R, .38 Special (2-inch bbl.) . . NiB $178 Ex $143 Gd $97
.38 Special (4-inch bbl.) . . . . NiB $192 Ex $153 Gd $104
.357 Mag. NiB $209 Ex $173 Gd $102

TACTICAL GRADE REVOLVER
Similar to the Standard model except chambered in .38 Special only. Two- or 4-inch bbl., fixed sights. Available w/compensator. Imported 1991-93.
Tactical revolver . . . . NiB $224 Ex $194 Gd $122
Tactical revolver w/compensator . . . . . NiB $325 Ex $260 Gd $176

WINDICATOR TARGET REVOLVER . . . . . . NiB $433 Ex $331 Gd $204
Calibers: .22 LR, .38 Special, .357 Magnum. Eight-shot cylinder in .22 LR, 6-shot in .38 Special and .357 Magnum. Six-inch bbl. w/bbl. weights. 11.8 inches overall. Weight: 50.2 oz. Interchangeable blade front sight, fully adj. rear. Walnut competition-style grips. Imported 1991-93.

WITNESS DA AUTO PISTOL
Similar to the Brno CZ-75 w/a cocked-and-locked system. Double or single action. Calibers: 9mm Para. .38 Super, .40 S&W, 10mm; .41 AE and .45 ACP. 16-shot magazine (9mm), 12 shot (.38 Super/.40 S&W), or 10-shot (10mm/.45 ACP), 4.75-inch bbl., 8.10 inches overall. Weight: 35.33 oz. Blade front sight, rear sight adj. for windage w/3-dot sighting system. Steel or polymer frame. Blued, satin chrome, blue/chrome, stainless or Wonder finish. Checkered rubber grips. EA Series imported 1991 to date.
9mm blue . . . . NiB $357 Ex $286 Gd $194
9mm chrome or blue/chrome. . . . . NiB $370 Ex $296 Gd $201
9mm stainless . . . . NiB $427 Ex $342 Gd $233
9mm Wonder finish. . . . . NiB $382 Ex $306 Gd $208
.38 Super and .40 S&W blued. . . . . NiB $376 Ex $301 Gd $205
.38 Super and .40 S&W chrome
or blue/chrome. . . . . NiB $414 Ex $331 Gd $225
.38 Super and .40 S&W stainless . . . . . . NiB $440 Ex $352 Gd $239
.38 Super and .40 S&W Wonder finish . . . NiB $402 Ex $321 Gd $218
10mm, .41 AE and .45 ACP blued. . . . . . NiB $465 Ex $372 Gd $253

European American Armory
Windicator Target

European American Armory Witness

(cont'd) WITNESS DA AUTO PISTOL
10mm, .41 AE and .45 ACP
chrome or blue/chrome . . . . NiB $484 Ex $388 Gd $263
10mm, .41 AE and .45 ACP stainless. . . . . . NiB $542 Ex $433 Gd $295
10mm, .41 AE and
.45 ACP Wonder finish . . . . NiB $491 Ex $393 Gd $267

COMPACT WITNESS DA AUTO PISTOL (L SERIES)
Similar to the standard Witness series except more compact w/ 3.625-inch bbl., and polymer or steel frame. Weight: 30 oz. Matte blued or Wonder finish. EA Compact series imported 1999 to date.
9mm blue . . . . NiB $367 Ex $306 Gd $204
9mm Wonder finish. . . . . NiB $388 Ex $331 Gd $214
.38 Super and .40 S&W blued. . . . . NiB $376 Ex $301 Gd $205
.38 Super and .40 S&W Wonder finish . . . . NiB $402 Ex $321 Gd $218
10mm, .41 AE and .45 ACP blued. . . . . NiB $465 Ex $372 Gd $253
10mm, .41 AE and .45 ACP Wonder fin. . . . NiB $491 Ex $393 Gd $267
W/ported bbl., add $30

WITNESS CARRY COMP
Double/Single action. Calibers: .38 Super, 9mm Parabellum, .40 S&W, 10mm, .45 ACP. 10-, 12- or 16-shot magazine, 4.25-inch bbl., w/1-inch compensator. Weight: 33 oz., 8.10 inches overall. Black rubber grips. Post front sight, drift adjustable rear w/3-dot system. Matte blue, Duo-Tone or Wonder finish. Imported 1992 to date.
9mm, .40 S&W . . . . NiB $433 Ex $367 Gd $204
.38 Super, 10mm, .45 ACP. . . . . NiB $376 Ex $301 Gd $205
W/Duo-Tone finish (disc.), add $25
W/Wonder finish, add $10

Feather Guardian Angel Derringer

FEG Mark II AP-.22

WITNESS LIMITED
CLASS AUTO PISTOL . . . . NiB $872 Ex $729 Gd $408
Single action. Calibers: .38 Super, 9mm Parabellum, .40 S&W, .45 ACP. 10-shot magazine, 4.75-inch bbl., Weight: 37 oz. Checkered competition-style walnut grips. Long slide w/post front sight, fully adj. rear. Matte blue finish. Imported 1994 to date.

WITNESS SUBCOMPACT DA AUTO PISTOL
Calibers: 9mm Para., .40 S&W, 41 AK, .45 ACP. 13-shot magazine in 9mm, 9-shot in .40 S&W, 3.66-inch bbl., 7.25 inches overall. Weight: 30 oz. Blade front sight, rear sight adj. for windage. Blued, satin chrome or blue/chrome finish. Imported 1995-97.
9mm blue . . . . NiB $331 Ex $306 Gd $280
9mm chrome or blue/chrome . . . . . NiB $376 Ex $301 Gd $205
.40 S&W blue . . . . NiB $376 Ex $301 Gd $205
.40 S&W chrome or blue/chrome . . NiB $414 Ex $331 Gd $225
.41 AE blue . . . . NiB $447 Ex $357 Gd $243
.41 AE chrome or blue/chrome . . . . NiB $478 Ex $382 Gd $260
.45 ACP blued . . . . NiB $459 Ex $367 Gd $250
.45 ACP chrome or blue/chrome . . . NiB $433 Ex $367 Gd $255

WITNESS TARGET PISTOLS
Similar to standard Witness model except fitted w/2- or 3-port compensator, competition frame and S/A target trigger. Calibers: 9mm Para., 9x21, .40 S&W, 10mm and .45 ACP, 5.25-inch match bbl., 10.5 inches overall. Weight: 38 oz. Square post front sight, fully adj. rear or drilled and tapped for scope. Blued or hard chrome finish. Low-profile competition grips. Imported 1992 to date.
**Silver Team (blued w/2-port
compensator)** . . . . NiB $876 Ex $699 Gd $469
**Gold Team (chrome
w/3-port compensator)** . . . . NiB $1817 Ex $1423 Gd $1001

FAS PISTOLS — Malino, Italy
Currently imported by Nygord Precision
Products (Previously by Beeman Precision
Arms and Osborne's, Cheboygan, MI)

601 SEMIAUTOMATIC MATCH TARGET PISTOL
Caliber: .22 Short. Five-shot top-loading magazine, 5.6-inch ported and ventilated bbl., 11 inches overall. Weight: 41.5 oz. Removable, adj. trigger group. Blade front sight, open-notch fully adj. rear. Stippled walnut wrapaound or adj.target grips.
Right-hand model . . . . NiB $924 Ex $739 Gd $503
Left-hand model . . . . NiB $1045 Ex $892 Gd $510

602 SEMIAUTOMATIC MATCH TARGET PISTOL
Similar to Model FAS 601 except chambered for .22 LR. Weight: 37 oz.
Right-hand model . . . . NiB $892 Ex $612 Gd $459
Left-hand model . . . . NiB $913 Ex $612 Gd $484

603 SEMIAUTOMATIC
MATCH TARGET PISTOL . . . . NiB $994 Ex $892 Gd $510
Similar to Model FAS 601 except chambered for .32 S&W (wadcutter).

607 SEMIAUTOMATIC
MATCH TARGET PISTOL . . . . NiB $994 Ex $892 Gd $459
Similar to Model FAS 601 except chambered for .22 LR, w/removable bbl. weights. Imported 1995 to date.

FEATHER INDUSTRIES, INC. — Boulder, Colorado

GUARDIAN ANGEL DERRINGER
Double-action over/under derringer w/interchangeable drop-in loading blocks. Calibers: .22 LR, .22 WMR, 9mm, .38 Spec. Two-shot capacity, 2-inch bbl., 5 inches overall. weight: 12 oz. Stainless steel. Checkered black grip. Made 1988-95.
.22 LR, .22 WMR . . . . NiB $184 Ex $82 Gd $51
9mm, .38 Special (disc. 1989) . . . . NiB $122 Ex $87 Gd $56

FEG (FEGYVERGYAN) PISTOLS — Budapest,
Soroksariut, Hungary (Currently imported by
KBI, Inc. and Century International Arms
(Previously by Interarms)

MARK II AP-.22 DA AUTOMATIC PISTOL . . . . NiB $240 Ex $204 Gd $122
Caliber: .22 LR. Eight-shot magazine, 3.4-inch bbl., Weight: 23 oz. Drift-adj. sights. Double action, all-steel pistol. Imported 1997 to date.

MARK II AP-.380 DA AUTOMATIC PISTOL . . . NiB $240 Ex $204 Gd $133
Caliber: .380. Seven-shot magazine, 3.9-inch bbl., weight 27 oz. Drift-adj. sights. Double action, all-steel pistol. Imported 1997 to date.

**MARK II APK-.380 DA
AUTOMATIC PISTOL.** . . . . NiB $240 Ex $204 Gd $133
Caliber: .380. Seven-shot magazine, 3.4-inch bbl., weight: 25 oz. Drift-adj. sights. Double action, all-steel pistol. Imported 1997 to date.

MODEL GKK-9 (92C) AUTO PISTOL . . . . NiB $321 Ex $286 Gd $163
Improved version of the double-action FEG Model MBK. Caliber: 9mm Para. 14-shot magazine, 4-inch bbl., 7.4 inches overall. Weight: 34 oz. Blade front sight, rear sight adj. for windage. Checkered wood grips. Blued finish. Imported 1992-93.

HANDGUNS

MODEL GKK-.45 AUTO PISTOL
Improved version of the double-action FEG Model MBK. Caliber: .45 ACP. Eight-shot magazine, 4.1-inch bbl., 7.75 inches overall. Weight: 36 oz. Blade front sight, rear sight adj. for windage w/3-dot system. Checkered walnut grips. Blued or chrome finish. Imported 1993-96.
Blued model (disc. 1994) ....NiB $312 Ex $250 Gd $170
Chrome model.................NiB $306 Ex $270 Gd $163

MODEL MBK-9HP
AUTO PISTOL ....NiB $255 Ex $229 Gd $102
Similar to the double-action Browning Hi-Power. Caliber: 9mm Para. 14-shot magazine, 4.6-inch bbl., 8 inches overall. Weight: 36 oz. Blade front sight, rear sight adj. for windage. Checkered wood grips. Blued finish. Imported 1992-93.

MODEL PJK-9HP AUTO PISTOL
Similar to the single-action Browning Hi-Power. Caliber: 9mm Para. 13-shot magazine, 4.75-inch bbl., 8 inches overall. Weight: 21 oz. Blade front sight, rear sight adj. for windage w/3-dot system. Checkered walnut or rubber grips. Blued or chrome finish. Imported 1992 to date.
Blued model ....NiB $249 Ex $199 Gd $136
Chrome model.................NiB $255 Ex $229 Gd $153

MODEL PSP-.25 AUTO PISTOL
Similar to the Browning .25. Caliber: .25 ACP. Six-shot magazine, 2.1-inch bbl., 4.1 inches overall. Weight: 9.5 oz. Fixed sights. Checkered composition grips. Blued or chrome finish.
Blued model ....NiB $255 Ex $178 Gd $133
Chrome model.................NiB $255 Ex $178 Gd $133

MODEL SMC-.22 AUTO PISTOL ... NiB $243 Ex $194 Gd $132
Same general specifications as FEG Model SMC-.380 except in .22 LR. Eight-shot magazine, 3.5-inch bbl., 6.1 inches overall. Weight: 18.5 oz. Blade front sight, rear sight adj. for windage. Checkered composition grips w/thumbrest. Blued finish.

MODEL SMC-.380 AUTO PISTOL ... NiB $209 Ex $184 Gd $117
Similar to the Walther DA PPK w/alloy frame. Caliber: .380 ACP. Six-shot magazine, 3.5-inch bbl., 6.1 inches overall. Weight: 18.5 oz. Blade front sight, rear sight adj. for windage. Checkered composition grips w/ thumbrest. Blued finish. Imported 1993 to date.

MODEL SMC-918 AUTO PISTOL.... NiB $214 Ex $184 Gd $127
Same general specifications as FEG Model SMC-.380 except chambered in 9x18mm Makarov. Imported 1994-97.

FIALA OUTFITTERS, INC. — New York

REPEATING PISTOL.............NiB $484 Ex $408 Gd $204
Despite its appearance, which closely resembles that of the early Colt Woodsman and High-Standard, this arm is not an automatic pistol. It is hand-operated by moving the slide to eject, cock and load. Caliber: .22 LR. 10-shot magazine, bbl. lengths: 3-, 7.5- and 20-inch. 11.25 inches overall (with 7.5-inch bbl.). Weight: 31 oz. (with 7.5-inch bbl.). Target sights. Blued finish. Plain wood grips. Shoulder stock was originally supplied for use w/20-inch bbl. Made 1920-23. Value shown is for pistol w/one bbl. and no shoulder stock.

F.I.E. CORPORATION — Hialeah, Florida
The F.I.E Corporation became QFI (Quality Firearms Corp.) of Opa Locka, Fl., about 1990, when most of F.I.E's models were disc.

FEG Model PJK-9HP

F.I.E. Model A27BW

MODEL A27BW "THE
BEST" SEMIAUTO ....NiB $127 Ex $107 Gd $71
Caliber: .25 ACP. Six-round magazine, 2.5-inch bbl., 6.75 inches overall. Weight: 13 oz. Fixed sights. Checkered walnut grip. Disc. 1990.

ARMINIUS DA STANDARD REVOLVER
Calibers: .22 LR, .22 combo w/interchangeable cylinder, .32 S&W, .38 Special, .357 Magnum. Six, 7 or 8 rounds depending on caliber. Swing out cylinder. bbl. lengths: 2-, 3-, 4, 6-inch. Vent rib on calibers other than .22, 11 inches overall (with 6-inch bbl.). Weight: 26 to 30 oz. Fixed or micro-adj. sights. Checkered plastic or walnut grips. Blued finish. Made in Germany. disc. See illustration next page.
.22 LR ....NiB $82 Ex $71 Gd $51
.22 Combo......................NiB $153 Ex $127 Gd $76
.32 S&W ....NiB $163 Ex $121 Gd $80
.38 Special......................NiB $114 Ex $136 Gd $91
.357 Magnum ....NiB $193 Ex $158 Gd $112

BUFFALO SCOUT SA REVOLVER
Calibers: .22 LR, .22 WRF, .22 combo w/interchangeable cylinder. 4.75-inch bbl., 10 inches overall. Weight: 32 oz. Adjustable sights. Blued or chrome finish. Smooth walnut or black checkered nylon grips. Made in Italy. disc.
Blued standard..................NiB $76 Ex $56 Gd $36
Blued convertible ....NiB $96 Ex $76 Gd $52
Chrome standard................NiB $83 Ex $66 Gd $45
Chrome convertible.............NiB $117 Ex $96 Gd $68

F.I.E. Arminius

F.I.E. Titan Tiger

F.I.E. Titan II

F.I.E. Model TZ75

HOMBRE SA REVOLVER . . . . **NiB $224 Ex $184 Gd $112**
Calibers: .357 Magnum, .44 Magnum, .45 Colt. Six-shot cylinder. bbl. lengths: 6 or 7.5 inches, 11 inches overall (with 6-inch bbl.). Weight: 45 oz. (6-inch bbl.). Fixed sights. Blued bbl., w/color-casehardened receiver. Smooth walnut grips. Made 1979-90.

SUPER TITAN II
Caliber: .32 ACP or .380 ACP, 3.25-inch bbl., weight: 28 oz. Blued or chrome finish. Disc. 1990.
.32 ACP in blue . . . . **NiB $219 Ex $189 Gd $102**
.32 ACP in chrome . . . . **NiB $198 Ex $158 Gd $107**
.380 ACP in blue . . . . **NiB $204 Ex $163 Gd $111**
.380 ACP in chrome . . . . **NiB $223 Ex $178 Gd $121**

TEXAS RANGER
SINGLE-ACTION REVOLVER
Calibers: .22 LR, .22 WRF, .22 combo w/interchangeable cylinder. bbl., lengths: 4.75-, 6.5-, 9-inch. 10 inches overall (with 4.75-inch bbl.). Weight: 32 oz. (with 4.75-inch bbl.). Fixed sights. Blued finish. Smooth walnut grips. Made 1983-90.
Standard . . . . **NiB $82 Ex $71 Gd $41**
Convertible . . . . **NiB $139 Ex $115 Gd $86**

LITTLE RANGER SA REVOLVER
Same as the Texas Ranger except w/3.25-inch bbl. and bird's-head grips. Made 1986-90.
Standard . . . . **NiB $82 Ex $71 Gd $51**
Convertible . . . . **NiB $145 Ex $120 Gd $90**

TITAN TIGER DOUBLE-
ACTION REVOLVER . . . . **NiB $133 Ex $112 Gd $71**
Caliber: .38 Special. Six-shot cylinder, 2- or 4-inch bbl., 8.25 inches overall (with 4-inch bbl.). Weight: 30 oz. (4-inch bbl.). Fixed sights. Blued finish. Checkered plastic or walnut grips. Made in the U.S. Disc. 1990.

TITAN II SEMIAUTOMATIC
Caiibers: .22 LR, .32 ACP, .380 ACP. 10-round magazine, integral tapered post front sight, windage-adjustable rear sight. European walnut grips. Blued or chrome finish. Disc. 1990.
.22 LR in blue . . . . **NiB $133 Ex $107 Gd $56**
.32 ACP in blued . . . . **NiB $172 Ex $138 Gd $94**
.32 ACP in
chrome . . . . **NiB $217 Ex $177 Gd $126**
.380 ACP in blue . . . . **NiB $198 Ex $158 Gd $107**
.380 ACP in
chrome . . . . **NiB $223 Ex $178 Gd $121**

MODEL TZ75 DA SEMIAUTOMATIC
Double action. Caliber: 9mm. 15-round magazine, 4.5-inch bbl., 8.25 inches overall. Weight: 35 oz. Ramp front sight, windage-adjustable rear sight. European walnut or black rubber grips. Imported 1988-90.
Blued finish . . . . **NiB $382 Ex $331 Gd $224**
Satin chrome . . . . **NiB $453 Ex $362 Gd $246**

YELLOW ROSE SA REVOLVER
Same general specifications as the Buffalo Scout except in .22 combo w/interchangeable cylinder and plated in 24-karat gold. Limited Edition w/scrimshawed ivory polymer grips and American walnut presentation case. Made 1987-90.
Yellow Rose
.22 combo . . . . **NiB $133 Ex $112 Gd $97**
Yellow Rose
Limited Edition . . . . **NiB $255 Ex $214 Gd $153**

FIREARMS INTERNATIONAL CORP. — Washington, D.C.

MODEL D
AUTOMATIC PISTOL . . . . **NiB $236 Ex $189 Gd $129**
Caliber: .380 Automatic. Six-shot magazine, 3.3-inch bbl., 6.13 inches overall. Weight: 19.5 oz. Blade front sight, windage-adjustable rear sight. Blued, chromed, or military finish. Checkered walnut grips. Made 1974-77.

REGENT DA
REVOLVER. . . . . **NiB $115 Ex $92 Gd $62**
Calibers: .22 LR, .32 S&W Long. Eight-shot cylinder (.22 LR), or 7-shot (.32 S&W). Bbl. lengths: 3-, 4-, 6-inches (.22 LR) or 2.5-, 4-inches (.32 S&W). Weight: 28 oz.(with 4-inch bbl.). Fixed sights. Blued finish. Plastic grips. Made 1966-72.

**Firearms International
Model D**

**Firearms
International Regent**

FN BROWNING PISTOLS — Liege, Belgium
Mfd. by Fabrique Nationale Herstal

See also Browning Pistols.

6.35MM POCKET AUTO PISTOL
(See FN Browning Baby Auto Pistol)

MODEL 1900 POCKET
AUTO PISTOL . . . . **NiB $515 Ex $417 Gd $206**
Caliber: .32 Automatic (7.65mm). Seven-shot magazine, 4-inch bbl., 6.75 inches overall. Weight: 22 oz. Fixed sights. Blued finish. Hard rubber grips. Made 1899-10.

MODEL 1903 MILITARY AUTO PISTOL
Caliber: 9mm Browning Long. Seven-shot magazine, 5-inch bbl., 8 inches overall. Weight: 32 oz. Fixed sights. Blued finish. Hard rubber grips. Note: Aside from size, this pistol is of the same basic design as the Colt Pocket .32 and .380 Automatic pistols. Made 1903-39.
Model 190
Standard . . . . **NiB $509 Ex $407 Gd $277**
Model 1903
(w/slotted backstrap). . . . . **NiB $766 Ex $613 Gd $417**
Model 1903 (w/slotted
backstrap, shoulder stock
and extended magazine) . . . . . . **NiB $3124 Ex $2523 Gd $1716**

MODEL 1910
POCKET AUTO PISTOL . . . . **NiB $360 Ex $335 Gd $216**
Calibers: .32 Auto (7.65mm), .380 Auto (9mm). Seven-shot magazine (.32 cal.), or 6-shot (.380 cal.), 3.5-inch bbl., 6 inches overall. Weight: 20.5 oz. Fixed sights. Blued finish. Hard rubber grips. Made 1910-54.

MODEL 1922 (10/.22)
POLICE/MILITARY AUTO
Calibers: .32 Auto (7.65mm), .380 Auto (9mm). Nine-shot magazine (.32 cal.), or 8-shot (.380 cal.), 4.5-inch bbl., 7 inches overall. Weight: 25 oz. Fixed sights. Blued finish. Hard rubber grips. Made 1922-59.
Model 1910
commercial . . . . **NiB $412 Ex $335 Gd $206**
Model 191
Military contract . . . . **NiB $509 Ex $407 Gd $277**
Model 1910 (w/Nazi
proofs 1940-44), add **$25%**

**FN Browning
6.35mm Pocket**

**FN Browning
1900 Pocket**

**FN Browning 1910
Pocket**

**FN Browning 1922
Police/Military**

**FN Browning 1935
Military Hi-Power**

**FN Browning
Baby**

MODEL 1935 MILITARY HI-POWER PISTOL

Variation of the Browning-Colt .45 Auto design. Caliber: 9mm Para.13-shot magazine, 4.63-inch bbl., 7.75 inches overall. Weight: About 35 oz. Adjustable rear sight and fixed front, or both fixed. Blued finish (Canadian manufacture Parkerized). Checkered walnut or plastic grips. Note: Above specifications in general apply to both the original FN production and the pistols made by John Inglis Company of Canada for the Chinese government. A smaller version, w/shorter bbl. and slide and 10-shot magazine, was made by FN for the Belgian and Rumanian Governments about 1937-1940. Both types were made at the FN plant during the German occupation of Belgium.

Pre-war commercial (w/fixed sights)..... NiB $1030 Ex $824 Gd $618
Pre-war commercial
(w/tangent sight only).............. NiB $1931 Ex $1236 Gd $618
Pre-war commercial
(w/tangent sight, slotted backstrap) ... NiB $2832 Ex $2472 Gd $1287
Pre-war Belgian military contract....... NiB $1095 Ex $875 Gd $595
Pre-war Foreign military contract..... NiB $2054 Ex $1643 Gd $1118
War production (w/fixed sights) .... NiB $766 Ex $613 Gd $417
War production (w/tangent sight only).. NiB $1281 Ex $1025 Gd $697
War production
(w/tangent sight and slotted backstrap) ... NiB $3284 Ex $2626 Gd $1786
Post-war/pre-BAC (w/fixed sights) .... NiB $638 Ex $510 Gd $347
Post-war/pre-BAC (w/tangent sight only) .. NiB $709 Ex $566 Gd $385
Post-war/pre-BAC
(w/tangent sight, slotted backstrap) .... NiB $1281 Ex $1025 Gd $697
Inglis manufacture
Canadian military (w/fixed sights) .... NiB $927 Ex $695 Gd $412
Canadian military
(w/fixed sight, slotted) .... NiB $1739 Ex $1390 Gd $946
Canadian military
(w/tangent sight, slotted) .... NiB $1410 Ex $1128 Gd $767
Canadian military
(marked w/Inglis logo) .... NiB $2478 Ex $1983 Gd $1348
Chinese military contract
(w/tangent sight, slotted) .... NiB $3219 Ex $2575 Gd $1751
Canadian military
(w/fixed sight, slotted backstrap) ...... NiB $1739 Ex $1390 Gd $946
Canadian military
(marked w/Inglis logo) .... NiB $2478 Ex $1983 Gd $1348
W/issue wooden holster, add $400

BABY AUTO PISTOL .... NiB $515 Ex $453 Gd $309
Caliber: .25 Automatic (6.35mm). Six-shot magazine, 2.13-inch bbl., 4 inches overall. Weight: 10 oz. Fixed sights. Blued finish. Hard rubber grips. Made 1931-83.

FOREHAND & WADSWORTH — Worcester, Massachusetts

REVOLVERS
See listings of comparable Harrington & Richardson and Iver Johnson revolvers for values.

FORT WORTH FIREARMS — Fort Worth, TX

MATCH MASTER STANDARD........... NiB $335 Ex $210 Gd $185
Semi-automatic. Caliber: .22LR. Equipped with 3 7/8-, 4 1/2-, 5 1/2-, 7 1/2- or 10-inch bull bbl., double extractors, includes upper push button and standard magazine release, angled grip, low profile frame. Mfg. 1995-2000.

MATCH MASTER DOVETAIL . . . . . . NiB $410 Ex $335 Gd$245
Similar to Match Master except has 3 7/8-, 4 1/2-, or 5 1/2-inch bbl. with dovetail rib.

MATCH MASTER DELUXE . . . . NiB $470 Ex $365 Gd $270
Similar to Match master Standard except has Weaver rib on bbl.
W/10-inch bbl.. . . . . Add $100

SPORT KING . . . . NiB $470 Ex $220 Gd $195
Semi-automatic. Caliber: .22 LR. Equipped with 4 1/2- or 5 1/2-inch bbl., blued finish, military grips, drift sights, 10 shot magazine. Mfg 1995-2000.

CITATION . . . . NiB $335 Ex $240 Gd $195
Semi-automatic. Caliber: .22 LR. Equipped with 5 1/2-inch bull bbl. or 7 1/2-inch fluted bbl., military grips, 10-shot magazine.

TROPHY . . . . NiB $355 Ex $270 Gd $205
Semi-automatic. Caliber: .22 LR. Equipped with 5 1/2- or 7 1/2-inch bull bbl. blued finish, military grips, 10-shot magazine.
W/LH action (5 1/2-inch bbl. only) . . . . Add $50

VICTOR . . . . NiB $415 Ex $325 Gd $235
Semi-automatic. Caliber: .22LR. Equipped with 3 7/8-, 4 1/2- (VR or Weaver rib), 8- (Weaver rib) or 10-inch (Weaver rib) bbls.; blued finish, military grips, 10-shot magazine.
W/4 1/2- or 4 1/2-inch Weaver rib bbls.. . . . . Add $80
W/8- or 10-inch Weaver rib bbls. . . . . Add $175

OLYMPIC. . . . . NiB $545 Ex $430 Gd $320
Semi-automatic. Caliber: .22 LR or Short. Equipped with 6 1/2-inch fluted bbl., blued finish, military grips, 10-shot magazine.

SHARPSHOOTER . . . . NiB $325 Ex $265 Gd $190
Semi-automatic. Caliber: .22 LR. Equipped with 5 1/2-inch bull bbl.,blued finish, military grips, 10-shot magazine.

LE FRANCAIS PISTOLS — St. Etienne, France
Produced by Manufacture Francaise d'Armes et Cycles

ARMY MODEL AUTOMATIC PISTOL . . . NiB $1561 Ex $1144 Gd $728
Similar in operation to the Le Francais .25 Automatics. Caliber: 9mm Browning Long. Eight-shot magazine, 5-inch bbl., 7.75 inches overall. Weight: About 34 oz. Fixed sights. Blued finish. Checkered walnut grips. Made from 1928-.38.

POLICEMAN MODEL
AUTOMATIC PISTOL . . . . NiB $867 Ex $816 Gd $306
DA. Hinged bbl., Caliber: .25 Automatic (6.35mm). Seven-shot magazine, 3.5-inch bbl., 6 inches overall. Weight: About 12 oz. Fixed sights. Blued finish. Hard rubber grips. Intro. 1914. disc.

STAFF OFFICER MODEL
AUTOMATIC PISTOL . . . . NiB $280 Ex $235 Gd $153
Caliber: .25 Automatic. Similar to the "Policeman" model except does not have cocking-piece head, barrel, is about an inch shorter and weight is an ounce. less. Introduced in 1914. disc.

FREEDOM ARMS — Freedom, Wyoming

MODEL 1997
PREMIER GRADE SA REVOLVER
Calibers: .357 Mag., .41 Mag. or .45 LC. Five- or 6-shot cylinder, 4.25-, 5-, 5.5-, 6- or 7.5- inch bbl., removable front blade with adjustable or fixed rear sight. Hardwood or black micarta grips. Satin stainless finish. Made 1997 to date.
Premier grade 97 . . . . NiB $1699 Ex $1262 Gd $721
For extra cylinder, add. $200
For fixed sights, deduct $75

MODEL FA-.44 (83-44) SA REVOLVER
Similar to Model 454 Casull except chambered in .44 Mag. Made from 1988 to date.
Field grade. . . . . NiB $1365 Ex $1025 Gd $772
Premier grade . . . . NiB $1699 Ex $1236 Gd $721
Silhouette class (w/10-inch bbl.) . NiB $1370 Ex $1030 Gd $783
Silhouette pac
(10-inch bbl., access.) . . . . NiB $1365 Ex $1025 Gd $772
For fixed sights, deduct $95

MODEL FA-.45 (83-45) SA REVOLVER
Similar to Model 454 Casull except chambered in .45 Long Colt. Made 1988-90.
Field grade . . . . NiB $1236 Ex $927 Gd $566
Premier grade . . . . NiB $1101 Ex $881 Gd $598
For fixed sights, deduct $95

MODEL FA-252 (83-22) SA REVOLVER
Calibers: .22 LR w/optional .22 Mag. cylinder. Bbl. lengths: 5.13 and 7.5 (Varmint Class), 10 inches (Silhouette Class). Adjustable express or competition silhouette sights. Brushed or matte stainless finish. Black Micarta (Silhouette) or black and green laminated hardwood grips (Varmint). Made 1991 to date.
Silhouette class . . . . NiB $1883 Ex $1571 Gd $618
Silhouette class
w/extra .22 Mag. cyl . . . . NiB $1448 Ex $1159 Gd $788
Varmint class . . . . NiB $1095 Ex $875 Gd $595
Varmint class
w/extra .22 Mag. cyl . . . . NiB $1384 Ex $1107 Gd $753

MODEL FA-353 (83-357) SA REVOLVER
Caliber: .357 Mag., bbl. lengths: 4.75, 6, 7.5 or 9 inches. Removable blade front sight, adjustable rear. Brushed or matte stainless finish. Pachmayr Presentation or impregnated hardwood grips.
Field grade. . . . . NiB $966 Ex $772 Gd $525
Premier grade . . . . NiB $1574 Ex $1468 Gd $618
Silhouette class
(w/9-inch bbl.) . . . . NiB $985 Ex $788 Gd $536

MODEL FA-454AS (83-454) REVOLVER
Caliber: .454 Casull (w/optional .45 ACP, .45 LC, .45 Win. Mag. cylinders). Five-shot cylinder, bbl. lengths: 4.75, 6, 7.5 or 10 inches. Adjustable express or competition silhouette sights. Pachmayr presentation or impregnated hardwood grips. Brushed or matte stainless steel finish.
Field grade. . . . . NiB $1573 Ex $1159 Gd $515
Premier grade . . . . NiB $2035 Ex $1699 Gd $618
Silhouette class (w/10-inch bbl.) . . . NiB $998 Ex $798 Gd $543
For extra cylinder, add. $250

MODEL FA-454FS REVOLVER
Same general specifications as Model FA-454AS except w/fixed sight.
Field grade. . . . . NiB $1603 Ex $1390 Gd $824
Premier grade . . . . NiB $1639 Ex $1416 Gd $824

GRADING: NiB = New in Box   Ex = Excellent or NRA 95%   Gd = Good or NRA 68%

**Freedom Arms
FA-252**

**Freedom Arms
FA-454AS**

MODEL FA-454 GAS REVOLVER ...... **NiB $1603 Ex $1390 Gd $824**
Field Grade version of Model FA-454AS except not made w/12-inch bbl., Matte stainless finish, Pachmayr presentation grips. Adj. Sights or fixed sight on 4.75-inch bbl.,

MODEL FA-555 REVOLVER
Similar to Model .454 Casull except chambered in .50 AK. Made 1994 to date.
Field grade .... **NiB $1416 Ex $1025 Gd $772**
Premier grade .... **NiB $1777 Ex $1287 Gd $927**

**MODEL FA-BG-22LR
MINI-REVOLVER** .... **NiB $180 Ex $139 Gd $103**
Caliber: .22 LR. Three-inch tapered bbl., partial high-gloss stainless steel finish. Disc. 1987.

**MODEL FA-BG-22M
MINI-REVOLVER** .... **NiB $206 Ex $154 Gd $113**
Same general specifications as model FA-BG-22LR except in caliber .22 WMR. Disc. 1987.

**MODEL FA-BG-22P
MINI-REVOLVER** .... **NiB $206 Ex $165 Gd $103**
Same general specifications as Model FA-BG-22LR except in .22 percussion. Disc. 1987.

MODEL FA-L-22LR MINI-REVOLVER ... **NiB $165 Ex $154 Gd $77**
Caliber: .22 LR, 1.75-inch contoured bbl., partial high-gloss stainless steel finish. Bird's-head-type grips. Disc. 1987.

**MODEL FA-L-22M
MINI-REVOLVER** .... **NiB $175 Ex $144 Gd $103**
Same general specifications as Model FA-L-22LR except in caliber .22 WMR. Disc. 1987.

MODEL FA-L-22P MINI-REVOLVER .... **NiB $190 Ex $129 Gd $93**
Same general specifications as Model FA-L-22LR except in .22 percussion. Disc. 1987.

MODEL FA-S-22LR MINI-REVOLVER ... **NiB $165 Ex $154 Gd $77**
Caliber: .22 LR. One-inch contoured bbl., partial high-gloss stainless steel finish. Disc. 1988.

MODEL FA-S-22M MINI-REVOLVER... **NiB $165 Ex $144 Gd $103**
Same general specifications as Model FA-S-22LR except in caliber .22 WMR. Disc. 1988.
MODEL FA-S-22P MINI-REVOLVER .... **NiB $165 Ex $144 Gd $77**
Same general specifications as Model FA-S-22LR except in .22 percussion. Disc. 1988.

FRENCH MILITARY PISTOLS — Cholet, France
Mfd. originally by Société Alsacienne de Constructions Mécaniques (S.A.C.M.). Currently made by Manufacture d'Armes Automatiques, Lotissement Industriel des Pontots, Bayonne

MODEL 1935A AUTOMATIC PISTOL...... **NiB $280 Ex $229 Gd $102**
Caliber: 7.65mm Long. Eight-shot magazine, 4.3-inch bbl., 7.6 inches overall. Weight: 26 oz. Two-lug locking system similar to the Colt U.S. M1911A1. Fixed sights. Blued finish. Checkered grips. Made 1935-45. Note: This pistol was used by French troops during WW II and in Indo-China 1945-54.

MODEL 1935S AUTOMATIC PISTOL ...... **NiB $331 Ex $301 Gd $153**
Similar to Model 1935A except shorter (4.1-inch bbl., and 7.4 inches overall) and heavier (28 oz.). Single-step lug locking system.

MODEL 1950 AUTOMATIC PISTOL .... **NiB $414 Ex $331 Gd $225**
Caliber: 9mm Para. Nine-shot magazine, 4.4-inch bbl., 7.6 inches overall. Weight: 30 oz. Fixed sights, tapered post front and U-notched rear. Similar in design and function to the U.S. .45 service automatic except no bbl., bushing.

MODEL MAB F1 AUTOMATIC PISTOL...... **NiB $561 Ex $510 Gd $204**
Similar to Model MAB P-15 except w/6-inch bbl. and 9.6 inches overall. Adjustable target-style sights. Parkerized finish.

MODEL MAB P-8 AUTOMATIC PISTOL ..... **NiB $491 Ex $393 Gd $267**
Similar to Model MAB P-15 except w/8-shot magazine,

MODEL MAB P-15 AUTOMATIC PISTOL .... **NiB $561 Ex $510 Gd $306**
Caliber: 9mm Para. 15-shot magazine, 4.5-inch bbl., 7.9 inches overall. Weight: 38 oz. Fixed sights, tapered post front and U-notched rear.

FROMMER PISTOLS — Budapest, Hungary
Mfd. by Fémáru-Fegyver-és Gépgyár R.T.

**LILLIPUT POCKET
AUTOMATIC PISTOL** .... **NiB $408 Ex $306 Gd $153**
Caliber: .25 Automatic (6.35mm). Six-shot magazine, 2.14-inch bbl., 4.33 inches overall. Weight: 10.13 oz. Fixed sights. Blued finish. Hard rubber grips. Made during early 1920s. Note: Although similar in appearance to the Stop and Baby, this pistol is blowback operated.

STOP POCKET AUTOMATIC PISTOL .. **NiB $306 Ex $255 Gd $102**
Locked-breech action, outside hammer. Calibers: .32 Automatic (7.65mm), .380 Auto (9mm short). Seven-shot (.32 cal.) or 6-shot (.380 cal.) magazine, 3.88-inch bbl., 6.5 inches overall. Weight: About 21 oz. Fixed sights. Blued finish. Hard rubber grips. Made 1912-20.

BABY POCKET AUTOMATIC PISTOL .. **NiB $255 Ex $219 Gd $102**
Similar to Stop model except has 2-inch bbl., 4.75 inches overall. Weight 17.5 oz. Magazine capacity is one round less than Stop Model. Intro. shortly after WW I.

Galena Industries Inc., — Sturgis, South Dakota

Galena Industries purchased the rights to use the AMT trademark in 1998. Many, but not all, original AMT designs were included in the transaction.

AMT BACKUP . . . . **NiB $320 Ex $225 Gd $180**
Caliber: .380 (small frame, 2.5-inch bbl. only), .38 Super, .357 Sig, .40 S&W, .400 CorBon, .45 ACP, 9mm; magazine capacity: 5 or 6 rounds. Double action, 3-inch bbl., weight: 18 oz. (in .380), or 23 oz.
.38 Super, .357 Sig, .400 CorBon. . . . . **Add $50**

AUTOMAG II SEMI AUTO . . . . **NiB $438 Ex $309 Gd $232**
Caliber: .22 WMR, 9-shot magazine (except 7-shot in 3.38-inch bbl.); 3.38- 4.5- or 6-inch bbls.; weight: About 32 oz.

AUTOMAG III . . . . **NiB $541 Ex $412 Gd $309**
Similar to Automag II except chambered for the .30 Carbine cartridge, 6.38-inch bbl., stainless steel finish, weight: About 43 oz.

AUTOMAG IV . . . . **NiB $618 Ex $463 Gd $360**
Caliber: .45 Winchester Magnum; 7-round magazine, 6.5-inch bbl., weight: 46 oz.

AUTOMAG .440 CORBON . . . . **NiB $927 Ex $772 Gd $515** Semiautomatic, 7.5-inch bbl., 5-round magazine, checkered walnut grips, matte black finish, weight: 46 oz. Intro. 2000.

GALENA HARDBALLER . . . . **NiB $458 Ex $335 Gd $257**
Based on the Colt Model 1911 frame. Caliber: .45 ACP, .40 S&W, .400 CorBon, 7-round magazine capacity, 5-inch bbl., weight: About 38 oz.

GALENA LONGSLIDE . . . . **NiB $541 Ex $412 Gd $309**
Similar to Hardballer model except caliber: .45 ACP, 7-inch bbl., 7-round magazine capacity, stainless steel finish, weight: About 46 ounces.

GALENA ACCELERATOR . . . . **NiB $566 Ex $438 Gd $309**
Similar to Hardballer model except caliber: .400 CorBon, 7-inch bbl., 7-round magazine capacity, stainless steel finish, weight: About 46 ounces.

GALENA COMMANDO . . . . **NiB $438 Ex $309 Gd $232**
Similar to Hardballer model except caliber: .40 S&W, 4-inch bbl., 8-round magazine capacity, stainless steel finish, weight: About 38 ounces.

GALESI PISTOLS — Collebeato (Brescia), Italy Mfd. by Industria Armi Galesi

MODEL 6
POCKET AUTOMATIC PISTOL . . . . . **NiB $163 Ex $122 Gd $82**
Calibers: .22 Long, .25 Automatic (6.35mm). Six-shot magazine, 2.25-inch bbl., 4.38 inches overall. Weight: About 11 oz. Fixed sights. Blued finish. Plastic grips. Made from 1930 to date.

MODEL 9 POCKET
AUTOMATIC PISTOL
Calibers: .22 LR, .32 Auto (7.65mm), .380 Auto (9mm Short). Eight-shot magazine, 3.25-inch bbl., 5.88 inches overall. Weight: About 21 oz. Fixed sights. Blued finish. Plastic grips. Made from 1930 to date.

**Galesi
Model 6 Pocket**

(cont'd) **MODEL 9 POCKET
AUTOMATIC PISTOL**
Note: Specifications vary, but those shown for .32 Automatic are commom.
**.22 LR or
.380 Auto.** . . . . **NiB $194 Ex $153 Gd $102**
.32 Auto. . . . . **NiB $163 Ex $143 Gd $92**

GLISENTI PISTOL — Carcina (Brescia), Italy Mfd. by Societa Siderurgica Glisenti

MODEL 1910 ITALIAN
SERVICE AUTOMATIC. . . . . **NiB $816 Ex $688 Gd $357**
Caliber: 9mm Glisenti. Seven-shot magazine, 4-inch bbl., 8.5 inches overall. Weight: About 32 oz. Fixed sights. Blued finish. Hard rubber or plastic grips. Adopted 1910 and used through WWII.

GLOCK, INC. — Smyrna, Georgia

NOTE: *Models: 17, 19, 20, 21, 22, 23, 24, 31, 32, 33, 34 and 35 were fitted with a redesigned grip-frame in 1998. Models: 26, 27, 29, 30 and all "C" guns (compensated models) retained the original frame design.*

MODEL 17 DA AUTOMATIC PISTOL
Caliber: 9mm Parabellum. 10-, 17- or 19-shot magazine, 4.5-inch bbl., 7.2 inches overall. Weight: 22 oz. w/o magazine, Polymer frame, steel bbl., slide and springs. Fixed or adj. rear sights. Matte, nonglare finish. Made of only 35 components, including three internal safety devices. Imported 1983 to date.
Model 17 (w/fixed sights) . . . . **NiB $505 Ex $433 Gd $255**
Model 17C (compensated bbl.) . . . . **NiB $663 Ex $556 Gd $280**
W/adjustable sights, add **$30**
W/Meprolight sights, add **$80**
W/Trijicon sights, add **$105**

MODEL 17L COMPETITION
Same general specifications as Model 17 except weight: 23.35 oz. with 6-inch bbl. 8.85 inches overall. Imported 1988 to date. Imported1983 to date.
Model 1 L7 (w/fixed sights) . . . . **NiB $663 Ex $556 Gd $306**
W/ported bbl., (early production), add **$35**
W/adjustable sights, add **$30**

Glock Model 19 Compact

Glock Model 30

MODEL 19 COMPACT

Same general specifications as Model 17 except smaller version with 4-inch bbl., 6.85 inches overall and weight: 21 oz. Imported 1988 to date.

Model 19 (w/fixed sights) . . . . NiB $505 Ex $433 Gd $255
Model 19C (compensated bbl.) . . . . NiB $516 Ex $413 Gd $280
W/adjustable sights, add $30
W/Meprolight sights, add $80
W/Trijicon sights, add $105

MODEL 20 DA AUTO PISTOL

Caliber: 10mm. 15-shot, hammerless, 4.6-inch bbl., 7.59 inches overall. Weight: 26.3 oz. Fixed or adj. sights. Matte, nonglare finish. Made from 1991 to date.

Model 20 (w/fixed sights) . . . . NiB $714 Ex $612 Gd $255
Model 19C (compensated bbl.) . . . . NiB $679 Ex $544 Gd $370
W/adjustable sights, add $30
W/Meprolight sights, add $80
W/Trijicon sights, add $105

MODEL 21 AUTOMATIC PISTOL

Same general specifications as Model 17 except chambered in .45 ACP. 13-shot magazine, 7.59 inches overall. Weight: 25.2 oz. Imported 1991 to date.

Model 21 (w/fixed sights) . . . . NiB $620 Ex $495 Gd $306
Model 21C (compensated bbl.) . . . . NiB $673 Ex $539 Gd $365
W/adjustable sights, add $30
W/Meprolight sights, add $80
W/Trijicon sights, add $105

MODEL .22 AUTOMATIC PISTOL

Same general specifications as Model 17 except chambered for .40 S&W. 15-shot magazine, 7.4 inches overall. Imported 1992 to date.

Model .22 (w/fixed sights) . . . . NiB $654 Ex $505 Gd $301
Model 22C
(compensated bbl.) . . . . NiB $603 Ex $482 Gd $327
W/adjustable sights, add $30
W/Meprolight sights, add $80
W/Trijicon sights, add $105

MODEL 23 AUTOMATIC PISTOL

Same general specifications as Model 19 except chambered for .40 S&W. 13-shot magazine, 6.97 inches overall. Imported 1992 to date.

Model 23 (w/fixed sights) . . . . NiB $505 Ex $433 Gd $280
Model 23C (compensated bbl.) . . . . NiB $542 Ex $433 Gd $295
W/adjustable sights, add $30
W/Meprolight sights, add $80
W/Trijicon sights, add $105

MODEL 24 AUTOMATIC PISTOL

Caliber: .40 S&W, 10- and 15-shot magazines (the latter for law enforcement and military use only), 8.85 inches overall. Weight: 26.5 oz. Manual trigger safety; passive firing block and drop safety. Made 1995 to date.

Model 24 (w/fixed sights) . . . . NiB $678 Ex $535 Gd $306
Model 24C (compensated bbl.) . . . . NiB $666 Ex $532 Gd $362
W/adjustable sights, add $30

MODEL 26 DA AUTOMATIC PISTOL

Caliber: 9mm, 10-round magazine, 3.47-inch bbl., 6.3 inches overall. Weight: 19.77 oz. Imported 1995 to date.

Model 26 (w/fixed sights) . . . . NiB $505 Ex $433 Gd $306
Model 26C (compensated bbl.) . . . . NiB $549 Ex $439 Gd $298
W/adjustable sights, add $30

MODEL 27 DA AUTO PISTOL

Similar to the Glock Model .22 except subcompact. Caliber: .40 S&W, 10-shot magazine, 3.5-inch bbl., Weight: 21.7 oz. Polymer stocks, fixed or fully adjustable sights. Imported 1995 to date.

Model 27 (w/fixed sights) . . . . NiB $505 Ex $433 Gd $306
W/adjustable sights, add $30
W/Meprolight sights, add $80
W/Trijicon sights, add $105

MODEL 28 COMPACT (LAW ENFORCEMENT ONLY)

Same general specifications as Model .25 except smaller version. .380 ACP with 3.5-inch bbl., weight: 20 oz. Imported 1999 to date.

MODEL 29 DA AUTO PISTOL

Similar to the Glock Model 20 except subcompact. Caliber: 10mm. 10-shot magazine, 3.8-inch bbl., weight: 27.1 oz. Polymer stocks, fixed or fully adjustable sights. Imported 1997 to date.

Model 29 (w/fixed sights) . . . . NiB $597 Ex $500 Gd $306
W/adjustable sights, add $30
W/Meprolight sights, add $80
W/Trijicon sights, add $100

MODEL 30 DA AUTO PISTOL

Similar to the Glock Model 21 except subcompact. Caliber: .45 ACP. 10-shot magazine, 3.8-inch bbl., weight: 26.5 oz. Polymer stocks, fixed or fully adjustable sights. Imported 1997 to date.

Model 27 (w/fixed sights) . . . . NiB $597 Ex $500 Gd $306
W/adjustable sights, add $30
W/Meprolight sights, add $80
W/Trijicon sights, add $105

MODEL 31 DA AUTOMATIC PISTOL
Caliber: .357 Sig., safe action system. 10- 15- or 17-shot magazine, 4.49-inch bbl., weight: 23.28 oz. Safe Action trigger system w/3 safeties. Imported 1998 to date.
Model 31
(w/fixed sights) . . . . NiB $505 Ex $433 Gd $306
Model 31C
(compensated bbl.) . . . . NiB $564 Ex $458 Gd $322
W/adjustable sights, add $30
W/Meprolight sights, add $80
W/Trijicon sights, add $105

MODEL .32 DA AUTOMATIC PISTOL
Caliber: .357 Sig., safe action system. 10- 13- or 15-shot magazine, 4.02-inch bbl., weight: 21.52 oz. Imported 1998 to date.
Model .32
(w/fixed sights) . . . . NiB $505 Ex $433 Gd $306
Model 32C . . . . NiB $523 Ex $418 Gd $285
W/adjustable sights, add $30
W/Meprolight sights, add $80
W/Trijicon Sights, add $105

MODEL 33 DA AUTOMATIC PISTOL
Caliber: .357 Sig., safe action system. Nine- or 11-shot magazine, 3.46-inch bbl. Weight: 19.75 oz. Imported 1998 to date.
Model 33
(w/fixed sights) . . . . NiB $505 Ex $433 Gd $306
W/adjustable sights, add $30
W/Meprolight sights, add $80
W/Trijicon sights, add $105

MODEL 34 AUTO PISTOL . . . . NiB $668 Ex $566 Gd $331
Similar to Model 17 except w/redesigned grip-frame and extended slide-stop lever and magazine release. 10-, 17- or 19-shot magazine, 5.32- inch bbl. Weight: 22.9 oz. Fixed or adjustable sights. Imported 1998 to date.

MODEL 35 AUTO PISTOL . . . . NiB $668 Ex $597 Gd $331
Similar to Model 34 except .40 S&W. Imported 1998 to date.

MODEL 36 DA AUTOMATIC PISTOL
Caliber: .45 ACP., safe action system. Six-shot magazine, 3.78-inch bbl., weight: 20.11 oz. Safe Action trigger system w/3 safeties. Imported 1999 to date.
Model 36
(w/fixed sights) . . . . NiB $597 Ex $500 Gd $306
W/adjustable sights, add $30
W/Meprolight sights, add $80
W/Trijicon sights, add $105

DESERT STORM
COMMEMORATIVE. . . . . NiB $1015 Ex $841 Gd $510
Same specifications as Model 17 except "Operation Desert Storm, January 16-February 27, 1991" engraved on side of slide w/list of coalition forces. Limited issue of 1,000 guns. Made in 1991.

GREAT WESTERN ARMS CO. — North Hollywood, California

NOTE: *Values shown are for improved late model revolvers early Great Westerns are variable in quality and should be evaluated accordingly. It should also be noted that, beginning about July 1956, these revolvers were offered in kit form. Values of guns assembled from these kits will, in general, be of less value than factory-completed weapons.*

Grendel Model P-12

DOUBLE BARREL DERRINGER . . . . NiB $306 Ex $280 Gd $153
Replica of Remington Double Derringer. Caliber: .38 S&W. Double bbls. (superposed), 3-inch bbl. Overall length: 5 inches. Fixed sights. Blued finish. Checkered black plastic grips. Made 1953-62.

SA FRONTIER REVOLVER . . . . NiB $510 Ex $459 Gd $255
Replica of the Colt Single Action Army Revolver. Calibers: .22 LR, .357 Magnum, .38 Special, .44 Special, .44 Magnum .45 Colt. Six-shot cylinder, bbl. lengths: 4.75-, 5.5 and 7.5-inches. Weight: 40 oz. in .22 cal. w/5.5-inch bbl. Overall length: 11.13 inches w/5.5-inch bbl. Fixed sights. Blued finish. Imitation stag grips. Made 1951-1962.

GRENDEL, INC. — Rockledge, Florida

MODEL P-10 AUTOMATIC PISTOL
Hammerless, blow-back action. DAO with no external safety. Caliber: .380 ACP. 10-shot box magazine integrated in grip. Three-inch bbl., 5.3 inches overall. Weight: 15 oz. Matte blue, nickel or green Teflon finish. Made 1988-91.
Blued finish . . . . NiB $143 Ex $127 Gd $87
Nickel finish . . . . NiB $1848 Ex $153 Gd $109
Teflon finish . . . . NiB $194 Ex $158 Gd $112
W/compensated bbl., add $45

MODEL P-12 DA AUTOMATIC PISTOL
Caliber: .380 ACP. 11-shot Zytel magazine, 3-inch bbl., 5.3 inches overall. Weight: 13 oz. Fixed sights. Polymer DuPont ST-800 grip. Made 1991-95.
Standard model . . . . NiB $158 Ex $133 Gd $87
Electroless nickel . . . . NiB $205 Ex $168 Gd $121

MODEL P-30 AUTOMATIC PISTOL
Caliber: .22 WMR. 30-shot magazine, 5-or 8-inch bbl., 8.5 inches overall w/5-inch bbl., weight: 21 oz. Blade front sight, fixed rear sight. Made 1991-95.
W/5-inch bbl., ... NiB $245 Ex $204 Gd $178
W/8-inch bbl., ... NiB $245 Ex $204 Gd $178

MODEL P-31
AUTOMATIC PISTOL . . . . NiB $357 Ex $321 Gd $194
Caliber: .22 WMR. 30-shot Zytel magazine, 11-inch bbl., 17.3 inches overall. Weight: 48 oz. Adj. blade front sight, fixed rear. Checkered black polymer DuPont ST-800 grip and forend. Made 1991-95.

Hammerli Model
33MP Free Pistol

Hammerli
Model 101

Hammerli
Model 102 Deluxe

Hammerli
Model 105

GUNSITE — Paulden, Arizona

"ADVANCED TACTICAL" SA AUTO PISTOL
Manufactured w/Colt 1991 or Springfield 1991 parts. Caliber: .45 ACP. Eight-shot magazine, 3.5-, 4.25-, 5-inch bbl. Weight: 32-38 oz. Checkered or laser-engraved walnut grips. Fixed or Novak Lo-mount sights.
Stainless finish . . . . NiB $1014 Ex $811 Gd $552
Blued finish . . . . NiB $886 Ex $709 Gd $482

"CUSTOM CARRY" SA AUTO PISTOL
Caliber: .45 ACP. Eight-shot magazine, 3.5-, 4.25-, 5-inch bbl., Weight: 32-38 oz. Checkered or laser-engraved walnut grips. Fixed Novak Lo-mount sights. Single action, manufactured based on enhanced colt models.
Stainless finish . . . . NiB $1052 Ex $841 Gd $572
Blued finish . . . . NiB $1014 Ex $811 Gd $552

H&R 1871, INC. — Gardner, Massachusetts

NOTE: *In 1991, H&R 1871, Inc. was formed from the residual of the parent company, Harrington & Richardson, and then took over the New England Firearms facility. H&R 1871 produced firearms under both their logo and the NEF brand name until 1999, when the Marlin Firearms Company acquired the assets of H&R 1871. See listings under Harrington & Richardson, Inc.*

HÄMMERLI AG JAGD-UND SPORTWAFFE FABRIK — Lenzburg, Switzerland

Currently imported by Sigarms, Inc., Exeter, NH. Previously by Hammerli, USA; Beeman Precision Arms & Mandall Shooting Supplies.

MODEL 33MP FREE PISTOL . . . . . . NiB $953 Ex $747 Gd $463
System Martini single-shot action, set trigger. Caliber: .22 LR. 11.5-inch octagon bbl., 16.5 inches overall. Weight: 46 oz. Micrometer rear sight, interchangeable front sights. Blued finish. Walnut grips, forearm. Imported 1933-49.

MODEL 100 FREE PISTOL
Same general specifications as Model 33MP. Improved action and sights, redesigned stock. Standard model has plain grips and forearm, deluxe model has carved grips and forearm. Imported 1950-56.
Standard model . . . . NiB $824 Ex $680 Gd $463
Deluxe model . . . . NiB $1020 Ex $793 Gd $515

MODEL 101 . . . . NiB $906 Ex $680 Gd $515
Similar to Model 100 except has heavy round bbl. w/matte finish, improved action and sights, adj. grips. Weight: About 49 oz. Imported 1956-60.

MODEL 102
Same as Model 101 except bbl., has highly polished blued finish. Deluxe model (illustrated) has carved grips and forearm. Made 1956-60.
Standard model . . . . NiB $906 Ex $680 Gd $515
Deluxe model . . . . NiB $1020 Ex $793 Gd $515

MODEL 103 . . . . NiB $935 Ex $775 Gd $450
Same as Model 101 except has lighter octagon bbl. (as in Model 100) w/highly polished blued finish, grips and forearm of select French walnut. Weight: About 46 oz. Imported 1956-60.

MODEL 104 . . . . NiB $783 Ex $680 Gd $360
Similar to Model 102 except has lighter round bbl., improved action redesigned grips and forearm. Weight: 46 oz. Imported 1961-65.

MODEL 105 . . . . NiB $963 Ex $736 Gd $412
Similar to Model 103 except has improved action, redesigned grips and forearm. Imported 1961-65.

MODEL 106 . . . . NiB $937 Ex $711 Gd $391
Similar to Model 104 except has improved trigger and grips. Made 1966-71.

MODEL 107
Similar to Model 105 except has improved trigger and stock. Deluxe model (illustrated) has engraved receiver and bbl., carved grips and forearm. Imported 1966-71.
Standard model . . . . NiB $1020 Ex $793 Gd $391
Deluxe model . . . . NiB $1360 Ex $1020 Gd $463

Hammerli
Model 106

Hammerli
Model 107 Deluxe

Hammerli
Model 120 Heavy Barrel

Hammerli
Model 120-1

Hammerli
Model 150

Hammerli
Model 160

MODEL 120 HEAVY BARREL

Same as Models 120-1 and 120-2 except has 5.7-inch heavy bbl., weight: 41 oz. Available w/standard or adj. grips. Imported 1972 to date.

W/standard grips . . . . NiB $618 Ex $556 Gd $309
W/adj. grips . . . . NiB $669 Ex $515 Gd $309

MODEL 120-1 SINGLE-
SHOT FREE PISTOL . . . . NiB $618 Ex $556 Gd $309

Side lever-operated bolt action. Adj. single-stage or two-stage trigger. Caliber: .22 LR, 9.9-inch bbl., 14.75 inches overall. Weight: 44 oz. Micrometer rear sight, front sight on high ramp. Blued finish bbl., and receiver, lever and grip frame anodized aluminum. Checkered walnut thumbrest grips. Imported 1972 to date.

MODEL 120-2 . . . . NiB $618 Ex $556 Gd $309

Same as Model 120-1 except has hand-contoured grips w/adj. palm rest (available for right or left hand). Imported 1972 to date.

MODELS 150/151 FREE PISTOLS

Improved Martini-type action w/lateral-action cocking lever. Set trigger adj. for weight, length and angle of pull. Caliber: .22 LR, 11.3-inch round free-floating bbl., 15.4 inches overall. Weight: 43 oz. (w/extra weights, 49.5 oz.). Micrometer rear sight, front sight on high ramp. Blued finish. Select walnut forearm and grips w/adj. palm shelf. Imported 1972-93.

Model 150 (disc. 1989) . . . . NiB $1905 Ex $1540 Gd $875
Model 151 (disc. 1993) . . . . NiB $1905 Ex $1540 Gd $875

MODEL 152 ELECTRONIC PISTOL

Same general specifications as Model 150 except w/electronic trigger. Made 1990-92

Right hand . . . . NiB $2055 Ex $1648 Gd $1020
Left hand . . . . NiB $1926 Ex $1552 Gd $1074

MODELS 160/162 FREE PISTOLS

Caliber: .22 LR. Single-shot. 11.31-inch bbl., 17.5 inches overall. Weight: 46.9 oz. Interchangeable front sight blades, fully adj. match rear. Match-style stippled walnut grips w/adj. palm shelf and polycarbon fiber forend. Imported 1993 to date.

Model 160 w/mechanical
Set trigger . . . . NiB $177 Ex $1519 Gd $824
Model 162 w/ electronic trigger . . . . NiB $1834 Ex $1468 Gd $998

MODEL 208 STANDARD
AUTO PISTOL . . . . NiB $1648 Ex $1339 Gd $824

Caliber: .22 LR. Eight-shot magazine, 5.9-inch bbl., 10 inches overall. Weight: 35 oz. (bbl. weight adds 3 oz.). Micrometer rear sight, ramp front. Blued finish. Checkered walnut grips w/adj. heel plate. Imported 1966-88.

MODEL 208S TARGET PISTOL . . . . . NiB $1802 Ex $1339 Gd $695

Caliber: .22 LR. Eight-shot magazine, 6-inch bbl., 10.2 inches overall. Weight: 37.3 oz. Micrometer rear sight, ramp front sight. Blued finish. Stippled walnut grips w/adj. heel plate. Imported 1990 to date.

MODEL 211 . . . . NiB $1596 Ex $1313 Gd $711

Same as Model 208 except has standard thumbrest grips. Imported 1966-91.

**Hammerli
Model 208**

**Hammerli
Model 215**

**Hammerli
Model 206 International**

**Hammerli
Model 207 International**

**Hammerli
International Model 210**

**Hammerli
Model 232 Rapid Fire**

MODEL 212
HUNTER'S PISTOL . . . . **NiB $1287 Ex $1112 Gd $669**
Caliber: .22 LR, 4.88-inch bbl., 8.5 inches overall. Weight: 31 oz. Blade front sight, square-notched fully adj. rear. Blued finish. Checkered walnut grips. Imported 1984-93.

MODEL 215 . . . . **NiB $1437 Ex $1081 Gd $592**
Similar to the Model 208 except w/heavier bbl. and fewer deluxe features. Imported 1990-93.

MODEL 230-1 RAPID
FIRE AUTO PISTOL . . . . **NiB $1437 Ex $1159 Gd $669**
Caliber: .22 Short. Five-shot magazine, 6.3-inch bbl., 11.6 inches overall. Weight: 44 oz. Micrometer rear sight, post front. Blued finish. Smooth walnut thumbrest grips. Imported 1970-83.

MODEL 230-2 . . . . **NiB $757 Ex $675 Gd $664**
Same as Model 230-1 except has checkered walnut grips w/adj. heel plate. Imported 1970-83.

MODEL 232 RAPID FIRE
AUTO PISTOL . . . . **NiB $1437 Ex $1159 Gd $669**
Caliber: .22 Short. Six-shot magazine, 5.1-inch ported bbl., 10.5 inches overall. Weight: 44 oz. Fully adj. target sights. Blued finish. Stippled walnut wraparound target grips. Imported 1984-93.

INTERNATIONAL MODEL
206 AUTO PISTOL. . . . . **NiB $695 Ex $644 Gd $340**
Calibers: .22 Short, .22 LR. Six-shot (.22 Short) or 8-shot (.22 LR) magazine, 7.1-inch bbl. w/muzzle brake, 12.5 inches overall. Weight: 33 oz. (.22 Short), 39 oz. (.22 LR) (supplementary weights add 5 and 8 oz.). Micrometer rear sight, ramp front. Blued finish. Standard thumbrest grips. Imported 1962-69.

INTERNATIONAL
MODEL 207 . . . . **NiB $747 Ex $669 Gd $386**
Same as Model 206 except has grips w/adj. heel plate, weight: 2 oz. more. Made 1962-69.

INTERNATIONAL
MODEL 209
AUTO PISTOL . . . . **NiB $824 Ex $711 Gd $500**
Caliber: .22 Short. Five-shot mag., 4.75-inch bbl., w/muzzle brake and gas-escape holes, 11 inches overall. Weight: 39 oz. (interchangeable front weight adds 4 oz.). Micrometer rear sight, post front. Blued finish. Standard thumbrest grips of checkered walnut. Imported 1966-70.

INTERNATIONAL
MODEL 210 . . . . **NiB $824 Ex $736 Gd $541**
Same as Model 209 except has grips w/adj. heel plate, is 0.8-inch longer and weight: 1 ounce more. Made 1966-70.

MODEL 280 TARGET PISTOL

Carbon-reinforced synthetic frame and bbl., housing. Calibers: .22 LR, .32 S&W Long WC. Six-shot (.22 LR) or 5-shot (.32 S&W) magazine, 4.5-inch bbl. w/interchangeable metal or carbon fiber counterweights. 11.88 inches overall. Weight: 39 oz. Micro-adj. match sights w/interchangeable elements. Imported 1988 to date.

.22 LR . . . . NiB $1493 Ex $1159 Gd $592
.32 S&W
Long WC . . . . NiB $1652 Ex $1344 Gd $951
.22/.32
Conversion
kit, add $800

VIRGINIAN SA REVOLVER . . . . NiB $541 Ex $505 Gd $257
Similar to Colt Single-Action Army except has base pin safety system (SWISSAFE). Calibers: .357 Magnum, .45 Colt. Six-shot cylinder. 4.63-, 5.5- or 7.5-inch bbl., 11 inches overall (with 5.5-inch bbl.). Weight: 40 oz. (with 5.5-inch bbl.). Fixed sights. Blued bbl. and cylinder, casehardened frame, chrome-plated grip frame and trigger guard. One-piece smooth walnut stock. Imported 1973-76 by Interarms, Alexandria, Va.

WALTHER
OLYMPIA MODEL 200
AUTOMATIC PISTOL, 1952-TYPE. . . . NiB $680 Ex $623 Gd $397
Similar to 1936 Walther Olympia Funfkampf model. Calibers: .22 Short, .22 LR. Six-shot (.22 Short) or 10-shot (.22 LR) magazine, 7.5-inch bbl., 10.7 inches overall. Weight: 27.7 oz. (.22 Short, light alloy breechblock), 30.3 oz. (.22 LR). Supplementary weights provided. Adj. target sights. Blued finish. Checkered walnut thumbrest grips. Imported 1952-58.

WALTHER
OLYMPIA MODEL 200,1958-TYPE . . . NiB $736 Ex $623 Gd $427
Same as Model 200 1952 type except has muzzle brake, 8-shot magazine (.22 LR). 11.6 inches overall. Weight: 30 oz. (.22 Short), 33 oz. (.22 LR). Imported 1958-63.

WALTHER
OLYMPIA MODEL 201 . . . . NiB $680 Ex $623 Gd $397
Same as Model 200,1952 Type except has 9.5-inch bbl. Imported 1955-57.

WALTHER
OLYMPIA MODEL 202 . . . . NiB $736 Ex $623 Gd $463
Same as Model 201 except has grips w/adj. heel plate. Imported 1955-57.

WALTHER
OLYMPIA MODEL 203
Same as corresponding Model 200 (1955 type lacks muzzle brake) except has grips w/adj. heel plate. Imported1955-63.
1955 type . . . . NiB $736 Ex $623 Gd $463
1958 type . . . . NiB $793 Ex $680 Gd $484

WALTHER
OLYMPIA MODEL 204
American model. Same as corresponding Model 200 (1956-Type lacks muzzle brake) except in .22 LR only, has slide stop and micrometer rear sight. Imported 1956-63.
1956-type . . . . NiB $767 Ex $654 Gd $505
1958-type . . . . NiB $824 Ex $711 Gd $510

WALTHER
OLYMPIA MODEL 205
American model. Same as Model 204 except has grips w/adj. heel plate. Imported 1956-63.
1956-type . . . . NiB $824 Ex $711 Gd $510
1958-type . . . . NiB $881 Ex $767 Gd $541

Hammerli-Walther
Olympia Model 203 1958-Type

Hammerli-Walther
Olympia Model 205

SIG-Hammerli
Model P240 Target

MODEL P240 TARGET AUTO PISTOL

Calibers: .32 S&W Long (wadcutter), .38 Special (wadcutter). Five-shot magazine, 5.9-inch bbl., 10 inches overall. Weight: 41 oz. Micrometer rear sight, post front. Blued finish/smooth walnut thumbrest grips. Accessory .22 LR conversion unit available. Imported 1975-86.

.32 S&W Long . . . . NiB $1519 Ex $1262 Gd $7021
.38 Special . . . . NiB $2183 Ex $1746 Gd $1188
.22 LR conversion
unit, add . . . . NiB $566 Ex $510 Gd $340

Harrington & Richardson SL .32

Harrington & Richardson USRA
Model Single-Shot Target Pistol

Harrington & Richardson Model 4

Harrington & Richardson Model 5

HARRINGTON & RICHARDSON, INC. —
Gardner, Massachusetts
Now H&R 1871, Inc., Gardner, Mass.

Formerly Harrington & Richardson Arms Co. of Worcester, Mass. One of the oldest and most distinguished manufacturers of handguns, rifles and shotguns, H&R suspended operations on January 24, 1986. In 1987, New England Firearms was established as an independent company producing selected H&R models under the NEF logo. In 1991, H&R 1871, Inc., was formed from the residual of the parent company and then took over the New England Firearms facility. H&R 1871 produced firearms under both its logo and the NEF brand name until 1999, when the Marlin Firearms Company acquired the assets of H&R 1871.

NOTE: *For ease in finding a particular firearm, H&R handguns are grouped into Automatic/Single-Shot Pistols, followed by Revolvers. For a complete listing, please refer to the index.*

AUTOMATIC/SINGLE-SHOT PISTOLS

SL .25 PISTOL . . . . **NiB $382 Ex $337 Gd $168**
Modified Webley & Scott design. Caliber: .25 Auto. Six-shot magazine, 2-inch bbl., 4.5 inches overall. Weight: 12 oz. Fixed sights. Blued finish. Black hard rubber grips. Made 1912-16.

SL .32 PISTOL . . . . **NiB $337 Ex $311 Gd $153**
Modified Webley & Scott design. Caliber: .32 Auto. Eight-shot magazine, 3.5-inch bbl., 6.5 inches overall. Weight: About 20 oz. Fixed sights. Blued finish. Black hard rubber grips. Made 1916-24.

**USRA MODEL SINGLE-
SHOT TARGET PISTOL** . . . . **NiB $459 Ex $433 Gd $229**
Hinged frame. Caliber: .22 LR, bbl. lengths: 7-, 8- and 10-inch. Weight: 31 oz. w/10-inch bbl., Adj. target sights. Blued finish. Checkered walnut grips. Made 1928-41.

REVOLVERS

**MODEL 4
(1904) DA** . . . . **NiB $97 Ex $87 Gd $36**
Solid frame. Calibers: .32 S&W Long, .38 S&W. Six-shot cylinder (.32 cal.), or 5-shot (.38 cal.), bbl. Lengths: 2.5-, 4.5- and 6-inch. Weight: About 16 oz. (in .32 cal.) Fixed sights. Blued or nickel finish. Hard rubber grips. Disc. prior to 1942.

MODEL 5 (1905) DA . . . . **NiB $97 Ex $87 Gd $41**
Solid frame. Caliber: .32 S&W. Five-shot cylinder, bbl., lengths: 2.5-, 4.5- and 6-inch. Weight: About 11 oz. Fixed sights. Blued or nickel finish. Hard rubber grips. Disc. prior to 1942.

MODEL 6 (1906) DA . . . . **NiB $97 Ex $87 Gd $41**
Solid frame. Caliber: .22 LR. Seven-shot cylinder, bbl. lengths: 2.5, 4.5- and 6-inches. Weight: About 10 oz. Fixed sights. Blued or nickel finish. Hard rubber grips. Disc. prior to 1942.

.22 SPECIAL DA. . . . . **NiB $168 Ex $143 Gd $71**
Heavy hinged frame. Calibers: .22 LR, .22 Mag. Nine-shot cylinder, 6-inch bbl., weight: 23 oz. Fixed sights, front gold-plated. Blued finish. Checkered walnut grips. Recessed safety cylinder on later models for high-speed ammunition. Disc. prior to 1942.

MODEL 199 SPORTSMAN
SA REVOLVER . . . . **NiB $280 Ex $240 Gd $112**
Hinged frame. Caliber: .22 LR. Nine-shot cylinder, 6-inch bbl., 11 inches overall. Weight: 30 oz. Adj. target sights. Blued finish. Checkered walnut grips. Disc. 1951.

MODEL 504 DA . . . . **NiB $168 Ex $148 Gd $102**
Caliber: .32 H&R Magnum. Five-shot cylinder, 4- or 6-inch bbl., (square butt), 3- or 4-inch bbl., round butt. Made 1984-86.

MODEL 532 DA . . . . **NiB $102 Ex $92 Gd $51**
Caliber: .32 H&R Magnum. Five-shot cylinder, 2.5- or 4-inch bbl., weight: Approx. 20 and 25 oz. respectively. Fixed sights. American walnut grips. Lustre blued finish. Made 1984-86.

MODEL 586 DA . . . . **NiB $178 Ex $158 Gd $102**
Caliber: .32 H&R Magnum. Five-shot cylinder. bbl. lengths: 4.5, 5.5, 7.5, 10 inches. Weight: 30 oz. average. Adj. rear sight, blade front. Walnut finished hardwood grips. Made 1984-86.

MODEL 603 TARGET . . . . **NiB $168 Ex $122 Gd $82**
Similar to Model 903 except in .22 WMR. Six-shot capacity w/unfluted cylinder. Made 1980-83.

MODEL 604 TARGET . . . . **NiB $173 Ex $133 Gd $82**
Similar to Model 603 except w/6-inch bull bbl., weight: 38 oz. Made 1980-83.

MODEL 622/623 DA . . . . **NiB $117 Ex $97 Gd $51**
Solid frame. Caliber: .22 Short, Long, LR, 6-shot cylinder. bbl., lengths: 2.5-, 4-, 6-inches. Weight: 26 oz. (with 4-inch bbl.). Fixed sights. Blued finish. Plastic grips. Made 1957-86. Note: Model 623 is same except chrome or nickel finish.

MODEL 632/633
GUARDSMAN DA REVOLVER . . . . . **NiB $106 Ex $82 Gd $46**
Solid Frame. Caliber: .32 S&W Long. Six-shot cylinder, bbl., lengths: 2.5- or 4-inch. Weight: 19 oz. (with 2.5-inch bbl.). Fixed sights. Blued or chrome finish. Checkered Tenite grips (round butt on 2.5-inch, square butt on 4-inch). Made 1953-86. Note: Model 633 is the same except for chrome or nickel finish.

MODEL 649/650 DA . . . . **NiB $143 Ex $122 Gd $82**
Solid frame. Side loading and ejection. Convertible model w/two 6-shot cylinders. Calibers: .22 LR, .22 WMR. 5.5-inch bbl., Weight: 32 oz. Adj. rear sight, blade front. Blued finish. One-piece, Western-style walnut grip. Made 1976-86. Note: Model 650 is same except nickel finish.

MODEL 666 DA . . . . **NiB $102 Ex $92 Gd $36**
Solid frame. Convertible model w/two 6-shot cylinders. Calibers: .22 LR, .22 WMR. Six-inch bbl., weight: 28 oz. Fixed sights. Blued finish. Plastic grips. Made 1976-78.

MODEL 676 DA . . . . **NiB $143 Ex $122 Gd $46**
Solid frame. Side loading and ejection. Convertible model w/two 6-shot cylinders. Calibers: .22 LR, .22 WMR, bbl. lengths: 4.5-, 5.5-, 7.5-, 12-inches. Weight: 32 oz. (with 5.5-inch bbl.). Adj. rear sight, blade front. Blued finish, color-casehardened frame. One-piece, Western-style walnut grip. Made 1976-1980.

Harrington & Richardson
Model 6

Harrington & Richardson
.22 Special

Harrington & Richardson
Model 199 Sportsman

Harrington & Richardson
Model 632

Harrington & Richardson
Model 622

GRADING: NiB = New in Box   **Ex** = Excellent or NRA 95%   **Gd** = Good or NRA 68%

Harrington & Richardson
Model 649

Harrington & Richardson
Model 650

Harrington & Richardson
Model 666

Harrington & Richardson
Model 686

Harrington & Richardson
Model 830

Harrington & Richardson
Model 676

Harrington & Richardson
Model 830

MODEL 686 DA . . . . NiB $189 Ex $163 Gd $92
Caliber: .22 LR and .22 WMR. Six-shot magazine, 4.5-, 5.5-, 7.5-,
10- or 12-inch bbl. Adj. rear sight, ramp and blade front. Blued,
color-casehardened frame. Weight: 31 oz. (with 4.5-inch bbl.).
Made 1980-86.

MODEL 732/733 DA . . . . NiB $130 Ex $102 Gd $56
Solid frame, swing-out 6-shot cylinder. Calibers: .32 S&W, .32 S&W
Long. bbl., lengths: 2.5-, 4-inch. Weight: 26 oz. (with 4-inch bbl.).
Fixed sights (windage adj. rear on 4-inch bbl. model). Blued finish.
Plastic grips. Made 1958-86. Note: Model 733 is the same except
with nickel finish.

MODEL 826 DA . . . . NiB $133 Ex $107 Gd $61
Caliber: .22 WMR. Six-shot magazine, 3-inch bull bbl., ramp and
blade front sight, adj. rear. American walnut grips. Weight: 28 oz.
Made 1981-83.

MODEL 829/830 DA
Same as Model 826 except in .22 LR caliber. Nine-shot capacity.
Made 1981-83.
Model 829, blued . . . . NiB $133 Ex $112 Gd $66
Model 830, nickel . . . . NiB $138 Ex $117 Gd $71

MODEL 832,1833 DA
Same as Model 826 except in .32 SW Long. Blued or nickel finish.
Made 1981-83.
Model 832, blued . . . . NiB $151 Ex $127 Gd $71
Model 833, nickel . . . . NiB $148 Ex $132 Gd $76

MODEL 900/901 DA . . . . NiB $92 Ex $87 Gd $46
Solid frame, snap-out cylinder. Calibers: .22 Short, Long, LR. Nine-
shot cylinder, bbl. lengths: 2.5-, 4-, 6-inches. Weight: 26 oz. (with
6-inch bbl.). Fixed sights. Blued finish. Cycolac grips. Made 1962-
73. Note: Model 901 (disc. in 1963) is the same except has chrome
finish and white Tenite grips.

MODEL 903 TARGET . . . . NiB $153 Ex $138 Gd $82
Caliber: .22 LR. Nine-shot capacity. SA/DA, 6-inch target-weight
flat-side bbl., swing-out cylinder. Weight: 35 oz. Blade front sight,
adj. rear. American walnut grips. Made 1980-83.

MODEL 904 TARGET . . . . NiB $153 Ex $235 Gd $82
Similar to Model 903 except 4- or 6-inch bull bbl. Weight: 32 oz.

Harrington & Richardson Model 900

Harrington & Richardson Model 925

Harrington & Richardson Model 903

Harrington & Richardson Model 905

Harrington & Richardson Model 922, First Issue

Harrington & Richardson Model 922, Second Issue

Harrington & Richardson Model 926

MODEL 905
TARGET . . . . **NiB $183 Ex $143 Gd $100**
Same as Model 904 except w/4-inch bbl. only. Nickel finish. Made 1981-83.

MODEL 922
DA REVOLVER
FIRST ISSUE . . . . **NiB $211 Ex $163 Gd $112**
Solid frame. Caliber: .22 LR. Nine-shot cylinder, 10-inch octagon bbl., (early model) or 6-inches, round bbl. (later production). Weight: 26 oz. (with 6-inch bbl.). Fixed sights. Blued finish. Checkered walnut grips. Safety cylinder on later models. Disc. prior to 1942.

MODEL 922/923
DA REVOLVER,
SECOND ISSUE . . . . **NiB $96 Ex $76 Gd $52**
Solid frame. Caliber: .22 LR. Nine-shot cylinder, bbl. lengths: 2.5-, 4-, 6-inches. Weight: 24 oz. (with 4-inch bbl.). Fixed sights. Blued finish. Plastic grips. Made 1950-86. Note: Second Issue Model 922 has a different frame from that of the First Issue. Model 923 is same as Model 922, Second Issue except for nickel finish.

MODEL 925
DEFENDER . . . . **NiB $140 Ex $112 Gd $77**
DA. Hinged frame. Caliber: .38 S&W. Five-shot cylinder, 2.5-inch bbl., weight: 22 oz. Adj. rear sight, fixed front. Blued finish. One-piece wraparound grip. Made 1964-78.

MODEL 926 DA . . . . **NiB $140 Ex $112 Gd $77**
Hinged frame. Calibers: .22 LR, .38 S&W. Nine-shot (.22 LR) or 5-shot (.38) cylinder, 4-inch bbl., weight: 31 oz. Adj. rear sight, fixed front. Blued finish. Checkered walnut grips. Made 1968-78.

Harrington & Richardson
Model 939

Harrington & Richardson
Model 949

Harrington & Richardson
Model 950

Harrington & Richardson
Model 999, First Issue

Harrington & Richardson
Model 999, Second Issue

Harrington & Richardson
Model 929

MODEL 929/930
SIDEKICK DA REVOLVER . . . . NiB $114 Ex $92 Gd $63
Caliber: .22 LR. Solid frame, swing-out 9-shot cylinder, bbl. lengths: 2.5-, 4-, 6-inches. Weight: 24 oz. (with 4-inch bbl.). Fixed sights. Blued finish. Checkered plastic grips. Made 1956-86. Note: Model 930 is same except with nickel finish.

MODEL 939/940
ULTRA SIDEKICK
DA REVOLVER . . . . NiB $151 Ex $117 Gd $82
Solid frame, swing-out 9-shot cylinder. Safety lock. Calibers: .22 Short, Long, LR. Flat-side 6-inch bbl. w/vent rib. Weight: 33 oz. Adj. rear sight, ramp front. Blued finish. Checkered walnut grips. Made 1958-86, reintroduced by H&R 1871 in 1992. Note: Model 940 is same except has round bbl.

MODEL 949/950
FORTY-NINER
DA REVOLVER . . . . NiB $138 Ex $107 Gd $71
Solid frame. Side loading and ejection. Calibers: .22 Short, Long, LR. Nine-shot cylinder, 5.5- or 7.5 inch bbl., weight: 31 to 38 oz. Adj. rear sight, blade front. Blued or nickel finish. One-piece, Western-style walnut grip. Made 1960-86, reintroduced by H&R 1871 in 1992-99. Note: Model 950 is same except has nickel finish.

MODEL 976 DA . . . . NiB $112 Ex $87 Gd $61
Same as Model 949 except has color-casehardened frame, 7.5-inch bbl. Weight: 36 oz. Intro. 1977. disc.

HARRINGTON & RICHARDSON
MODEL 999 SPORTSMAN
DA REVOLVER, FIRST ISSUE . . . . NiB $204 Ex $163 Gd $97
Hinged frame. Calibers: .22 LR, .22 Mag. Same specifications as Model 199 Sportsman Single Action. Disc. before 1942.

MODEL 999 SPORTSMAN
DA REVOLVER
SECOND ISSUE . . . . NiB $219 Ex $173 Gd $102
Hinged frame. Caliber: .22 LR. Nine-shot cylinder, 6-inch bbl. w/vent rib. Weight: 30 oz. Adj. sights. Blued finish. Checkered walnut grips. Made 1950-86.

(NEW) MODEL 999
SPORTSMAN
DA REVOLVER . . . . NiB $217 Ex $173 Gd $118
Hinged frame. Caliber: .22 Short, Long, LR. Nine-shot cylinder. Six-inch bbl. w/vent rib. Weight: 30 oz. Blade front sight adj. for elevation, square-notched rear adj. for windage. Blued finish. Checkered hardwood grips. Reintroduced by H&R 1871 in 1992.

AMERICAN DA . . . . **NiB $96 Ex $76 Gd $52**
Solid frame. Calibers: .32 S&W Long, .38 S&W. Six-shot (.32 cal.) or 5-shot (.38 cal.) cylinder, bbl. lengths: 2.5-,4.5- and 6-inches. Weight: About 16 oz. Fixed sights. Blued or nickel finish. Hard rubber grips. Disc. prior to 1942.

AUTOMATIC EJECTING DA REVOLVER . . . . . . **NiB $173 Ex $138 Gd $92**
Hinged frame. Calibers: .32 S&W Long, .38 S&W. Six-shot (.32 cal.) or 5-shot (.38 cal.) cylinder, bbl. lengths: 3.25-, 4-, 5- and 6-inches. Weight: 16 oz. (.32 cal.), 15 oz. (.38 cal.). Fixed sights. Blued or nickel finish. Black hard rubber grips. Disc. prior to 1942.

BOBBY DA . . . . **NiB $306 Ex $250 Gd $158**
Hinged frame. Calibers: .32 S&W, .38 S&W. Six-shot cylinder (.32 cal.) or 5-shot (.38 cal.). Four-inch bbl., 9 inches overall. Weight: 23 oz. Fixed sights. Blued finish. Checkered walnut grips. Disc. 1946. Note: Originally designed and produced for use by London's bobbies.

DEFENDER .38 DA . . . . **NiB $148 Ex $117 Gd $76**
Hinged frame. Based on the Sportsman design. Caliber: .38 S&W. Bbl. lengths: 4- and 6-inches, 9 inches overall (with 4-inch bbl.). Weight: 25 oz. with 4-inch bbl. Fixed sights. Blued finish. Black plastic grips. Disc. 1946. Note: This model was manufactured during WW II as an arm for plant guards, auxiliary police, etc.

EXPERT MODEL DA . . . . **NiB $192 Ex $153 Gd $104**
Same specifications as .22 Special except has 10-inch bbl., weight: 28 oz. Disc. prior to 1942.

HAMMERLESS DA, LARGE FRAME . . . . **NiB $127 Ex $102 Gd $66**
Hinged frame. Calibers: .32 S&W Long 38 S&W. Six-shot (.32 cal.), or 5-shot (.38 cal.) cylinder, bbl. lengths: 3.25-, 4-, and 6-inches. Weight: About 17 oz. Fixed sights. Blued or nickel finish. Hard rubber grips. Disc. prior to 1942.

HAMMERLESS DA, SMALL FRAME . . . . **NiB $127 Ex $102 Gd $69**
Hinged frame. Calibers: .22 LR, .32 S&W. Seven-shot (.22 cal.) or 5-shot (.32 cal.) cylinder, bbl. lengths: 2-, 3-, 4-, 5- and 6-inches. Weight: About 13 oz. Fixed sights. Blued or nickel finish. Hard rubber grips. Disc. prior to 1942.

HUNTER MODEL DA . . . . **NiB $143 Ex $113 Gd $71**
Solid frame. Caliber: .22 LR. Nine-shot cylinder, 10-inch octagon bbl., weight: 26 oz. Fixed sights. Blued finish. Checkered walnut grips. Safety cylinder on later models. Note: An earlier Hunter Model was built on the smaller 7-shot frame. Disc. prior to 1942.

NEW DEFENDER DA . . . . **NiB $260 Ex $204 Gd $143**
Hinged frame. Caliber: .22 LR. Nine-shot cylinder, 2-inch bbl., 6.25 inches overall. Weight: 23 oz. Adj. sights. Blued finish. Checkered walnut grips, round butt. Note: Basically, this is the Sportsman DA w/a short bbl., Disc. prior to 1942.

PREMIER DA . . . . **NiB $107 Ex $92 Gd $61**
Small hinged frame. Calibers: .22 LR, .32 S&W. Seven-shot (.22 LR) or 5-shot (.32) cylinder. Bbl. Lengths: 2-, 3-, 4-, 5 and 6-inches. Weight: 13 oz. (in .22 LR), 12 oz. (in .32 S&W). Fixed sights. Blued or nickel finish. Black hard rubber grips. Disc. prior to 1942. (See illustration next page.)

MODEL STR 022 BLANK REVOLVER . . . . **NiB $82 Ex $66 Gd $45**
Caliber: .22 RF blanks. Nine-shot cylinder, 2.5-inch bbl. Weight: 19 oz. Satin blued finish.

MODEL STR 032 BLANK REVOLVER . . . . **NiB $96 Ex $76 Gd $52**
Same general specifications as STR 022 except chambered for .32 S&W blank cartridges.

**Harrington & Richardson
Automatic Ejecting**

Harrington & Richardson Bobby

**Harrington & Richardson
Defender .38**

**Harrington & Richardson
Hammerless, Small Frame**

**Harrington & Richardson
Premier**

**Harrington & Richardson
Target**

**Harrington & Richardson
Trapper**

**Harrington & Richardson
Ultra Sportsmen**

**Harrington & Richardson
Vest Pocket**

**Harrington & Richardson
Young American**

TARGET MODEL DA . . . . **NiB $166 Ex $133 Gd $90**
Small hinged frame. Calibers: .22 LR, .22 W.R.F. Seven-shot cylinder, 6-inch bbl., weight: 16 oz. Fixed sights. Blued finish. Checkered walnut grips. Disc. prior to 1942.

TRAPPER MODEL DA . . . . **NiB $153 Ex $122 Gd $82**
Solid frame. Caliber: .22 LR. Seven-shot cylinder, 6-inch octagon bbl., weight: 12.5 oz. Fixed sights. Blued finish. Checkered walnut grips. Safety cylinder on later models. Disc. prior to 1942.

ULTRA SPORTSMAN . . . . **NiB $227 Ex $178 Gd $127**
SA. Hinged frame. Caliber: .22 LR. Nine-shot cylinder, 6-inch bbl., weight: 30 oz. Adj. target sights. Blued finish. Checkered walnut grips. This model has short action, wide hammer spur, cylinder is length of a .22 LR cartridge. Disc. prior to 1942.

VEST POCKET DA . . . . **NiB $96 Ex $76 Gd $52**
Solid frame. Spurless hammer. Calibers: .22 Rimfire, .32 S&W. Seven-shot (.22 cal.) or 5-shot (.32 cal.) cylinder, 1.13-inch bbl., weight: About 9 oz. Blued or nickel finish. Hard rubber grips. Disc. prior to 1942.

YOUNG AMERICA DA . . . . **NiB $96 Ex $76 Gd $52**
Solid frame. Calibers: .22 Long, .32 S&W. Seven-shot (.22 cal.) or 5-shot (.32 cal.) cylinder. Bbl. lengths: 2-, 4.5- and 6-inches. Weight: About 9 oz. Fixed sights. Blued or nickel finish. Hard rubber grips. Disc. prior to 1942.

HARTFORD ARMS & EQUIPMENT CO. — Hartford, Connecticut

Hartford pistols were the forebearer of the original High Standard line. High Standard Mfg. Corp. acquired Hartford Arms & Equipment Co. in 1932. The High Standard Model B is essentially the same as the Hartford Automatic.

AUTOMATIC TARGET PISTOL. . . . . NiB $661 Ex $535 Gd $357
Caliber: .22 LR. 10-shot magazine, 6.75-inch bbl., 10.75 inches overall. Weight: 31 oz. Target sights. Blued finish. Black rubber grips. This gun closely resembles the early Colt Woodsman and High Standard pistols. Made 1929-30.

REPEATING PISTOL. . . . . NiB $504 Ex $403 Gd $274
Same general design as the automatic pistol of this manufacture, but this model is a hand-operated repeating pistol on the order of the Fiala. Made 1929-30.

SINGLE-SHOT TARGET PISTOL. . . . NiB $496 Ex $393 Gd $255
Similar in appearance to the Hartford Automatic. Caliber: .22 LR, 6.75-inch bbl., 10.75 inches overall. Weight: 38 oz. Target sights. Mottled frame and slide, blued bbl., Black rubber or walnut grips. Made 1929-30.

HASKELL MANUFACTURING — Lima, Ohio
See listings under Hi-Point.

HAWES FIREARMS — Van Nuys, California

DEPUTY MARSHAL SA REVOLVER
Calibers: .22 LR, also .22 WMR in two-cylinder combination. Six-shot cylinder, 5.5-inch bbl., 11 inches overall. Weight: 34 oz. Adj. rear sight, blade front. Blued finish. Plastic or walnut grips. Imported from 1973-81.
.22 LR (plastic grips) . . . . NiB $90 Ex $71 Gd $49
Combination, .22 LR/.22 WMR (plastic) . . . . . . NiB $96 Ex $76 Gd $52
Walnut grips, add $10

DEPUTY DENVER MARSHAL
Same as Deputy Marshal SA except has brass frame. Imported from 1973-81.
.22 LR (plastic grips) . . . . NiB $96 Ex $76 Gd $52
Combination, .22 LR/.22 WMR (plastic) . . . . . . NiB $96 Ex $76 Gd $52
Walnut grips add $10

DEPUTY MONTANA MARSHAL
Same as Deputy Marshal except has brass grip frame. Walnut grips only. Imported from 1973-81.
.22 LR . . . . NiB $127 Ex $102 Gd $71
Combination, .22 LR/.22 WMR . . . . . NiB $153 Ex $122 Gd $84

DEPUTY SILVER CITY MARSHAL
Same as Deputy Marshal except has chrome-plated frame, brass grip frame, blued cylinder and bbl., Imported from 1973-81.
.22 LR (plastic grips) . . . . NiB $102 Ex $82 Gd $51
Combination, .22 LR/.22 WMR (plastic) . . . . NiB $122 Ex $102 Gd $71
Walnut grips add $10

DEPUTY TEXAS MARSHAL
Same as Deputy Marshal except has chrome finish. Imported from 1973-81.
.22 LR (plastic grips) . . . . NiB $107 Ex $92 Gd $61
Combination, .22 LR/.22 WMR (plastic) . . . . NiB $138 Ex $117 Gd $76
Walnut grips add. $10

FAVORITE SINGLE-SHOT TARGET PISTOL $150
Replica of Stevens No. 35. Tip-up action. Caliber: .22 LR. Eight-inch bbl., 12 inches overall. Weight: 24 oz. Target sights. Chrome-plated frame. Blued bbl., Plastic or rosewood grips (add $5). Imported 1972-76.

Hawes
Deputy Denver Marshal

Hawes
Deputy Marshall

Hawes
Deputy Montana Marshal

Hawes
Deputy Silver City

Hawes
Deputy Texas Marshal

Hawes Sauer
Chief Marshal

Hawes Sauer
Federal Marshal

Hawes Sauer
Montana Marshal

Hawes Sauer
Montana Marshal .22

Hawes Sauer
Silver City Marshal

Hawes Sauer
Texas Marshal

SAUER CHIEF MARSHAL SA TARGET REVOLVER

Same as Western Marshal except has adj. rear sight and front sight, oversized rosewood grips. Not made in .22 caliber. Imported from 1973-81.

.357 Magnum or .45 Colt . . . . NiB $255 Ex $204 Gd $139
.44 Magnum . . . . NiB $287 Ex $229 Gd $156
Combination .357 Magnum
and 9mm Para.
.45 Colt and .45 Auto . . . . NiB $286 Ex $240 Gd $127
Combination
.44 Magnum and .44-40 . . . . NiB $280 Ex $229 Gd $153

SAUER FEDERAL MARSHAL

Same as Western Marshal except has color-casehardened frame, brass grip frame, one-piece walnut grip. Not made in .22 caliber. Imported from 1973-81.

.357 Magnum or .45 Colt . . . . NiB $240 Ex $189 Gd $127
.44 Magnum . . . . NiB $275 Ex $209 Gd $138
Combination
.357 Magnum and 9mm Para.,
.45 Colt and .45 Auto . . . . NiB $286 Ex $240 Gd $127
Combination .44 Magnum and .44-40 . . . . NiB $280 Ex $229 Gd $153

SAUER MONTANA MARSHAL

Same as Western Marshal except has brass grip frame. Imported from 1973-81.

.357 Magnum or .45 Colt . . . . NiB $255 Ex $204 Gd $139
.44 Magnum . . . . NiB $287 Ex $229 Gd $156
Combination .357 Magnum and 9mm Para.,
.45 Colt and .45 Auto . . . . NiB $306 Ex $245 Gd $166
Combination .44 Magnum and .44-40 . . . . NiB $319 Ex $255 Gd $173
.22 LR . . . . NiB $249 Ex $199 Gd $136
Combination .22 LR and .22 WMR . . . . NiB $268 Ex $214 Gd $146

SAUER SILVER CITY MARSHAL

Same as Western Marshal except has nickel plated frame, brass grip frame, blued cylinder and bbl., pearlite grips. Imported from 1973-81.

.44 Magnum . . . . NiB $306 Ex $245 Gd $166
Combination .357 Magnum and 9mm Para.
.45 Colt and .45 Auto . . . . NiB $280 Ex $209 Gd $127
Combination .44 Magnum and .44-40 . . . . NiB $306 Ex $219 Gd $153

SAUER TEXAS MARSHAL

Same as Western Marshal except nickel plated, has pearlite grips. Imported from 1973-81.

.357 Magnum or .45 Colt . . . . NiB $287 Ex $229 Gd $156
.44 Magnum . . . . NiB $306 Ex $245 Gd $166
Combination .357 Magnum and 9mm Para.,
.45 Colt and .45 Auto . . . . NiB $331 Ex $265 Gd $181
Combination .44 Magnum and .44-40 . . . . NiB $351 Ex $280 Gd $191
.22 LR . . . . NiB $249 Ex $199 Gd $136
Combination .22 LR and .22 WMR . . . . NiB $275 Ex $209 Gd $138

SAUER WESTERN MARSHAL SA REVOLVER
Calibers: .22 LR (disc.), .357 Magnum, .44 Magnum, .45 Auto. Also in two-cylinder combinations: .22 WMR (disc.), 9mm Para., .44-40, .45 Auto. Six-shot cylinder, bbl. lengths: 5.5-inch (disc.), 6-inch, 11.75 inches overall (with 6-inch bbl.). Weight: 46 oz. Fixed sights. Blued finish. Originally furnished w/simulated stag plastic grips. Recent production has smooth rosewood grips. Made from 1968 by J. P. Sauer & Sohn, Eckernforde, Germany. Imported from 1973-81.

.357 Magnum or .45 Colt	NiB $255	Ex $204	Gd $139
.44 Magnum	NiB $294	Ex $235	Gd $159
Combination .357 Magnum and 9mm Para.,			
.45 Colt and .45 Auto	NiB $275	Ex $219	Gd $143
Combination .44 Magnum			
and .44-40	NiB $306	Ex $245	Gd $166
.22 LR	NiB $204	Ex $153	Gd $113
Combination .22 LR			
and .22 WMR	NiB $224	Ex $189	Gd $133

Hawes Sauer
Western Marshal

HECKLER & KOCH — Oberndorf/Neckar, West Germany, and Chantilly, Virginia

MODEL HK4 DA AUTO PISTOL
Calibers: .380 Automatic (9mm Short), .22 LR, .25 Automatic (6.35mm), .32 Automatic (7.65mm) w/conversion kits. Seven-shot magazine (.380 Auto), 8-shot in other calibers, 3.4-inch bbl., 6.19 inches overall. Weight: 18 oz. Fixed sights. Blued finish. Plastic grip. Disc. 1984.

.22 LR or .380 Automatic	NiB $397	Ex $304	Gd $196
.25 ACP or .32 ACP Automatic	NiB $397	Ex $304	Gd $196
.380 Automatic w/.22			
conversion unit	NiB $509	Ex $407	Gd $277
.380 Automatic w/.22, .25, .32			
conversion units	NiB $701	Ex $561	Gd $382

Heckler & Koch
Model HK4

MODEL MARK 23
DA AUTO PISTOL . . . . NiB $2169 Ex $1643 Gd $1112
Short-recoil semiautomatic pistol w/polymer frame and steel slide. Caliber: .45 ACP. 10-shot magazine, 5.87-inch bbl., 9.65 inches overall. Weight: 43 oz. Seven interchangeable rear sight adjustment units w/3-dot system. Developed primarily in response to specifications by the Special Operations Command (SOCOM) for a Special Operations Forces Offensive Handgun Weapon System. Imported 1996 to date.

MODEL P7K3 DA
AUTO PISTOL
Caliber: .380 ACP. Eight-round magazine, 3.8 inch-bbl., 6.3 inches overall. Weight: About 26 oz. Adj. rear sight. Imported 1988-94.

P7K3 in .380 Cal.	NiB $850	Ex $680	Gd $463
.22 LR conversion kit	NiB $618	Ex $525	Gd $350
.32 ACP conversion kit	NiB $309	Ex $257	Gd $165

Heckler &Koch
Model P7K3

MODEL P7M8 . . . . NiB $882 Ex $706 Gd $480
Squeeze-cock SA semiautomatic pistol. Caliber: 9mm Para. Eight-shot magazine, 4.13-inch bbl., 6.73 inches overall. Weight: 29.9 oz. Matte black or nickel finish. Adj. rear sight. Imported 1985 to date. See illustration next page.

MODEL P7M10
Caliber: .40 S&W. Nine-shot magazine, 4.2-inch bbl., 6.9 inches overall. Weight: 43 oz. Fixed front sight blade, adj. rear w/3-dot system. Imported 1992-94.

Blued finish	NiB $1035	Ex $783	Gd $541
Nickel finish	NiB $1045	Ex $793	Gd $551

Heckler & Koch
Mark 23

Heckler & Koch
Model P7M8

Heckler & Koch
Model P7M13

Heckler & Koch
Model P7 (PSP)

Heckler & Koch
Model P9S DA

Heckler & Koch USP45

MODEL P7M13 . . . . **NiB $927   Ex $726   Gd $505**
Caliber: 9mm. 13-shot magazine, 4.13-inch bbl., 6.65 inches over-all. Weight: 34.42 oz. Matte black finish. Adj. rear sight. Imported 1985-94.

MODEL P7(PSP)
AUTO PISTOL . . . . **NiB $766   Ex $613   Gd $417**
Caliber: 9mm Para. Eight-shot magazine, 4.13-inch bbl., 6.54 inches overall. DA. Weight: About 33.5 oz. Blued finish. Imported 1983-85 and again in 1990 with limited availability.

MODEL P9S
DA AUTOMATIC PISTOL
Calibers: 9mm Para., .45 Automatic. Nine-shot (9mm) or 7-shot (.45 Auto) magazine. Four-inch bbl., 7.63 inches overall. Weight: 32 ounces. Fixed sights. Blued finish. Contoured plastic grips. Disc. 1986.
9mm . . . . **NiB $747   Ex $561   Gd $391**
.45 Automatic . . . . **NiB $762   Ex $618   Gd $407**

MODEL P9S TARGET
COMPETITION KIT
Same as Model P9S Target except comes w/extra 5.5-inch bbl. and bbl. weights. Also available w/walnut competition grip.
W/standard grip . . . . **NiB $1153   Ex $922   Gd $627**
W/competition grip . . . . **NiB $1224   Ex $978   Gd $665**

MODEL SP89 . . . . **NiB $3811   Ex $3038   Gd $2060**
Semiautomatic, recoil-operated, delayed roller-locked bolt system. Caliber: 9mm Para. 15-shot magazine, 4.5-inch bbl., 13 inches overall. Weight: 68 oz. Hooded front sight, adj. rotary-aperture rear. Imported 1989-93.

MODEL USP
AUTO PISTOL
Polymer integral grip/frame design w/recoil reduction system. Calibers: 9mm Para., .40 S&W or .45 ACP. 15-shot (9mm) or 13-shot (.40 S&W and .45ACP) magazine, 4.13- or 4.25-inch bbl., 6.88 to 7.87 inches overall. Weight: 26.5-30.4 oz. Blade front sight, adj. rear w/3-dot system. Matte black or stainless finish. Stippled black polymer grip. Available in SA/DA or DAO. Imported 1993 to date.
Matte
Black finish . . . . **NiB $669   Ex $505   Gd $350**
Stainless . . . . **NiB $612   Ex $489   Gd $333**
W/Tritium sights, add **$95**
W/ambidextrous decocking lever, add **$20**

**Heckler & Koch Model USP45
Compact 50th Anniversary**

**Heckler & Koch
Model USP9 Compact (Stainless)**

**Heckler & Koch
Model USP357 Compact**

**Heckler & Koch
Model USP Expert**

**Heckler & Koch
Model USP Tactical**

MODEL USP9 COMPACT
Caliber: 9mm. 10- shot magazine, 4.25- inch bbl., 7.64 inches over-all. Weight: 25.5 oz. Short recoil w/modified Browning action. 3-dot sighting system. Polymer frame w/integral grips. Imported 1997 to date.

Blued finish . . . . **NiB $618 Ex $505 Gd $340**
Stainless finish . . . . **NiB $654 Ex $530 Gd $360**
**W/ambidextrous
decocking lever, add** **$15**

MODEL USP40 COMPACT
Caliber: .40 S&W. 10-shot magazine, 3.58- inch bbl., 6.81 inches overall. Weight: 27 oz. Short recoil w/modified Browning action. 3-dot sighting system. Polymer frame w/integral grips. Imported 1997 to date.

Blued finish . . . . **NiB $669 Ex $541 Gd $345**
Stainless finish . . . . **NiB $716 Ex $566 Gd $360**
**W/ambidextrous
decocking lever, add** **$15**

MODEL USP45 COMPACT
Caliber: .45 ACP. Eight-shot magazine, 3.8- inch bbl., 7.09 inches overall. Weight: 28 oz. Short recoil w/modified Browning action. 3-dot sighting system. Polymer frame w/integral grips. Imported 1998 to date.

Blued finish . . . . **NiB $669 Ex $541 Gd $345**
Stainless finish . . . . **NiB $716 Ex $566 Gd $360**
**W/ambidextrous
decocking lever, add** **$15**
**50th Anniversary
(1 of 1,000)** . . . . **NiB $1281 Ex $1025 Gd $697**

MODEL
USP EXPERT . . . . **NiB $1365 Ex $1025 Gd $747**
Caliber: .45 ACP. 10-shot magazine, 6.2- inch bbl., 9.65 inches overall. Weight: 30 oz. Adjustable 3-dot target sights. Short recoil modified Browning action w/recoil reduction system. Reinforced polymer frame w/integral grips and match-grade slide. Imported 1999 to date.

MODEL USP
TACTICAL . . . . **NiB $1066 Ex $824 Gd $541**
SOCOM Enhanced version of the USP Standard Model, w/4.92-inch threaded bbl. Chambered for .45 ACP only. Imported 1998 to date.

**Heckler & Koch
Model VP'7OZ**

**Heritage
Rough Rider**

**Heritage
Sentry**

MODEL VP 70Z AUTO PISTOL . . . . NiB $566 Ex $438 Gd $309
Caliber: 9mm Para. 18-shot magazine, 4.5-inch bbl., 8 inches overall. Weight: 32.5 oz. DA Fixed sights. Blued slide, plastic receiver and grip. Disc. 1986.

HELWAN PISTOLS
See listings under Interarms.

HERITAGE MANUFACTURING — Opa Locka, Florida

MODEL HA25 AUTO PISTOL
Caliber: .25 ACP. Six-shot magazine, 2.5-inch bbl., 4.63 inches overall. Weight: 12 oz. Fixed sights. Blued or chrome finish. Made 1993 to date.
Blued . . . . NiB $124 Ex $98 Gd $67
Chrome . . . . NiB $129 Ex $103 Gd $72

ROUGH RIDER SA REVOLVER
Calibers: .22 LR, .22 Mag. Six-shot cylinder. bbl. lengths: 2.75, 3.75, 4.75, 6.5 or 9 inches. Weight: 31-38 oz. Blade front sight, fixed rear. High-polished blued finish w/gold accents. Smooth walnut grips. Made 1993 to date.
.22 LR . . . . NiB $113 Ex $88 Gd $67
.22 LR/.22 WRF combo . . . . NiB $144 Ex $113 Gd $82

SENTRY DA REVOLVER
Calibers: .22 LR, .22 Mag., .32 Mag., 9mm or .38 Special. Six- or 8-shot (rimfire) cylinder, 2- or 4-inch bbl., 6.25 inches overall (2-inch bbl.). Ramp front sight, fixed rear. Blued or nickel finish. Checkered polymer grips. Made from 1993-97.
Blued . . . . NiB $115 Ex $93 Gd $64
Nickel . . . . NiB $128 Ex $103 Gd $72

STEALTH DA AUTO PISTOL . . . . . . NiB $263 Ex $211 Gd $145
Calibers: 9mm, .40 S&W. 10-shot magazine, 3.9-inch bbl., weight: 20.2 oz. Gas-delayed blowback, double action only. Ambidextrous trigger safety. Blade front sight, drift-adj. rear. Black chrome or stainless slide. Black polymer grip frame. Made from 1996 to date.

HI-POINT FIREARMS — Mansfield, Ohio

MODEL JS-9MM
AUTO PISTOL . . . . NiB $122 Ex $97 Gd $61
Caliber: 9mm Para. Eight-shot magazine, 4.5-inch bbl., 7.75 inches overall. Weight: 39 oz. Fixed low-profile sights w/3-dot system. Matte blue, matte black or chrome finish. Checkered synthetic grips. Made from 1990-98.

MODEL JS-
**9MM COMPETITION PISTOL
(STALLARD) . . . . NiB $112 Ex $92 Gd $61**
Similar to standard JS-9 except w/4-inch compensated bbl. w/ shortened slide and adj. sights. 10-shot magazine, 7.25 inches overall. Weight: 30 oz. Made from 1998 to date.

MODEL JS-9MM/
**C-9MM COMPACT PISTOL
(BEEMILLER) . . . . NiB $113 Ex $92 Gd $60**
Similar to standard JS-9 except w/3.5-inch bbl. and shortened slide w/alloy or polymer frame. 6.72 inches overall. Weight: 29 oz. or 32 oz. Three-dot-style sights. Made from 1993 to date.

MODEL CF-.380
POLYMER . . . . NiB $76 Ex $56 Gd $36
Caliber: .380 ACP. Eight-shot magazine, 3.5-inch bbl., 6.72 inches overall. Weight: 32 oz. Three-dot sights. Made from 1994 to date.

MODEL JS-.40/J
**C-.40 AUTO PISTOL
(IBERIA) . . . . NiB $141 Ex $112 Gd $76**
Similar to Model JS-9mm except in caliber .40 S&W.

MODEL JS-.45/JH-.45
**AUTO PISTOL
(HASKELL) . . . . NiB $158 Ex $122 Gd $82**
Similar to Model JS-9mm except in caliber .45 ACP w/7-shot magazine and two-tone Polymer finish.

J. C. HIGGINS

See Sears, Roebuck & Company

HIGH STANDARD SPORTING FIREARMS — East Hartford, Connecticut Formerly High Standard Mfg. Co., Hamden, Connecticut

A long-standing producer of sporting arms, High Standard disc. its operations in 1984. See new High Standard models under separate entry, HIGH STANDARD MFG. CO., INC.

NOTE: *For ease in finding a particular firearm, High Standard handguns are grouped into three sections: Automatic pistols (below), derringers and revolvers. For a complete listing, please refer to the Index.*

AUTOMATIC PISTOLS

MODEL A
HAMMERLESS . . . . **NiB $765 Ex $607 Gd $413**
Caliber: .22 LR. 10-shot magazine, bbl. lengths: 4.5-, 6.75-inch. 11.5 inches overall (6.75-inch bbl.). Weight: 36 oz. (in 6.75-inch bbl.). Adj. target sights. Blued finish. Checkered walnut grips. Made 1938-42.

High Standard
Model A

MODEL B
AUTOMATIC PISTOL . . . . **NiB $449 Ex $362 Gd $286**
Original Standard pistol. Hammerless. Caliber: .22 LR. 10-shot magazine, bbl. lengths: 4.5-, 6.75-inch, 10.75 inches overall (with 6.75-inch bbl.). Weight: 33 oz. (6.75-inch bbl.). Fixed sights. Blued finish. Hard rubber grips. Made 1932-42.

High Standard
Model B

MODEL C
AUTOMATIC PISTOL . . . . **NiB $918 Ex $719 Gd $464**
Same as Model B except in .22 Short. Made 1935-42.

MODEL D
AUTOMATIC PISTOL . . . . **NiB $829 Ex $663 Gd $451**
Same general specifications as Model A but heavier bbl., weight: 40 oz. (6.75-inch bbl.). Made 1937-42.

High Standard
Model D

DURA-MATIC
AUTOMATIC PISTOL . . . . **NiB $312 Ex $250 Gd $170**
Takedown. Caliber: .22 LR. 10-shot magazine, 4.5 or 6.5 inch interchangeable bbl., 10.88 inches overall (6.5-inch bbl.). Weight: 35 oz. (in 6.5-inch bbl.). Fixed sights. Blued finish. Checkered grips. Made 1952-70.

High Standard
Dura-Matic

MODEL E
AUTOMATIC PISTOL . . . . **NiB $1713 Ex $1316 Gd $1015**
Same general specifications as Model A but w/extra heavy bbl. and thumbrest grips. Weight: 42 oz. (6.75-inch bbl.). Made 1937-42.

FIELD-KING
AUTOMATIC PISTOL
FIRST MODEL
Same general specifications as Sport-King but w/heavier bbl. and target sights. Late model 6.75-inch bbls. have recoil stabilizer and lever take-down feature. Weight: 43 oz. (6.75-inch bbl.). Made 1951-58.
W/one bbl. . . . . **NiB $653 Ex $551 Gd $337**
W/both bbls. . . . . **NiB $721 Ex $624 Gd $447**

FIELD-KING AUTOMATIC PISTOL
SECOND MODEL
Same general specifications as First Model Field-King but w/button take-down and marked FK 100 or FK 101.
W/one bbl. . . . . **NiB $637 Ex $510 Gd $229**
W/both bbls. . . . . **NiB $771 Ex $637 Gd $413**

High Standard
Model E

High Standard
G-.380

High Standard
Model G-B

High Standard
Model G-E

High Standard
Model H-A

High Standard
Model H-B

FLITE-KING AUTOMATIC PISTOL — FIRST MODEL
Same general specifications as Sport-King except in .22. Short w/aluminum alloy frame and slide and marked FK 100 or FK 101. Weight: 26 oz. (6.5-inch bbl.). Made 1953-58.
W/one bbl. . . . . NiB $504 Ex $403 Gd $274
W/both bbls. . . . . NiB $606 Ex $485 Gd $329

FLITE-KING AUTOMATIC PISTOL — SECOND MODEL
Same as Flite-King—First Model except w/steel frame and marked in the 102 or 103 series. Made 1958-66.
Model 102 . . . . NiB $589 Ex $423 Gd $301
Model 103 . . . . NiB $544 Ex $403 Gd $280

MODEL G-.380
AUTOMATIC PISTOL . . . . NiB $580 Ex $500 Gd $336
Lever takedown. Visible hammer. Thumb safety. Caliber: .380 Automatic. Six-shot magazine, 5-inch bbl., weight: 40 oz. Fixed sights. Blued finish. Checkered plastic grips. Made 1943-50.

MODEL G-B AUTOMATIC PISTOL
Lever takedown. Hammerless. Interchangeable bbls. Caliber: .22 LR. 10-shot magazine, bbl. lengths: 4.5, 6.75 inches, 10.75 inches overall (with 6.75-inch bbl.). Weight: 36 oz. (with 6.75-inch bbl.). Fixed sights. Blued finish. Checkered plastic grips. Made 1948-51.
W/one bbl. . . . . NiB $561 Ex $423 Gd $301
W/both bbls. . . . . NiB $580 Ex $500 Gd $337

MODEL G-D AUTOMATIC PISTOL
Lever takedown. Hammerless. Interchangeable bbls. Caliber: .22 LR. 10-shot magazine, bbl. lengths: 4.5, 6.75 inches. 11.5 inches overall (with 6.75-inch bbl.). Weight: 41 oz. (6.75-inch bbl.). Target sights. Blued finish. Checkered walnut grips. Made 1948-51.
W/one bbl. . . . . NiB $932 Ex $711 Gd $510
W/both bbls. . . . . NiB $1069 Ex $839 Gd $592

MODEL G-E AUTOMATIC PISTOL
Same general specifications as Model G-D but w/extra heavy bbl. and thumbrest grips. Weight: 44 oz. (with 6.75-inch bbl.). Made 1949-51.
W/one bbl. . . . . NiB $1369 Ex $1159 Gd $886
W/both bbls. . . . . NiB $1643 Ex $1303 Gd $1025

MODEL H-A
AUTOMATIC PISTOL . . . . NiB $1279 Ex $1133 Gd $767
Same as Model A but w/visible hammer, no thumb safety. Made 1939-42.

MODEL H-B
AUTOMATIC PISTOL . . . . NiB $666 Ex $520 Gd $364
Same as Model B but w/visible hammer, no thumb safety. Made 1940-42.

MODEL H-D
AUTOMATIC PISTOL . . . . NiB $1199 Ex $1009 Gd $690
Same as Model D but w/visible hammer, no thumb safety. Made 1939-42.

MODEL H-DM
AUTOMATIC PISTOL . . . . NiB $683 Ex $566 Gd $418
Also called H-D Military. Same as Model H-D but w/thumb safety. Made 1941-51.

MODEL H-E
AUTOMATIC PISTOL . . . . NiB $2502 Ex $1952 Gd $1030
Same as Model E but w/visible hammer, no thumb safety. Made 1939-42.

High Standard Olympic Military

High Standard Model H-E

High Standard Olympic Automatic – First Model

High Standard Olympic Automatic – Second Model

High Standard Olympic I.S.U.

High Standard Olympic I.S.U. Military

OLYMPIC AUTOMATIC PISTOL FIRST MODEL (G-O)
Same general specifications as Model G-E but in .22 Short w/light alloy slide. Made 1950-51.
W/one bbl. . . . . NiB $1155 Ex $1020 Gd $515
W/both bbls. . . . . NiB $1739 Ex $1390 Gd $946

OLYMPIC AUTOMATIC SECOND MODEL
Same general specifications as Supermatic but in .22 Short w/light alloy slide. Weight: 39 oz. (6.75-inch bbl.). Made 1951-58.
W/one bbl. . . . . NiB $1075 Ex $948 Gd $623
W/both bbls. . . . . NiB $1369 Ex $1107 Gd $798

OLYMPIC AUTOMATIC PISTOL
THIRD MODEL . . . . NiB $1073 Ex $860 Gd $613
Same as Supermatic Trophy w/bull bbl. except in .22 Short. Made 1963-66.

OLYMPIC COMMEMORATIVE
Limited edition of Supermatic Trophy Military issued to commemorate the only American-made rimfire target pistol ever to win an Olympic gold medal. Highly engraved w/Olympic rings inlaid in gold. Deluxe presentation case. Two versions issued: In 1972 (.22 LR) and 1980 (.22 Short).
1972 issue . . . . NiB $6175 Ex $5145 Gd $3348
1980 issue . . . . NiB $2048 Ex $1699 Gd $1154

OLYMPIC I.S.U . . . . NiB $895 Ex $716 Gd $487
Same as Supermatic Citation except caliber .22 Short, 6.75- or 8-inch tapered bbl. w/stabilizer, detachable weights. Made from 1958-77. Eight-inch bbl. disc. in 1966.

OLYMPIC I.S.U. MILITARY . . . . . NiB $2075 Ex $1025 Gd $576
Same as Olympic I.S.U. except has military grip and bracket rear sight. Intro. in 1965. disc.

OLYMPIC MILITARY . . . . NiB $1045 Ex $850 Gd $644
Same as Olympic — Third Model except has military grip and bracket rear sight. Made in 1965.

PLINKER . . . . NiB $322 Ex $257 Gd $175
Similar to Dura-Matic w/same general specifications. Made 1971-73. See illustration next page.

SHARPSHOOTER
AUTOMATIC PISTOL . . . . NiB $724 Ex $592 Gd $407
Takedown. Hammerless. Caliber: .22 LR. 10-shot magazine, 5.5-inch bull bbl., 9 inches overall. Weight: 42 oz. Micrometer rear sight, blade front sight. Blued finish. Plastic grips. Made 1971-83. See illustration next page.

High Standard Plinker

High Standard — Sharpshooter

High Standard Sport-King
Automatic — First Model

High Standard Sport-King
Automatic — Second Model

High Standard Sport-King
Automatic — Third Model

High Standard Supermatic

SPORT-KING AUTOMATIC
FIRST MODEL
Takedown. Hammerless. Interchangeable bbls. Caliber: .22 LR. 10-shot magazine, bbl. lengths: 4.5-, 6.75-inches. 11.5 inches overall (with 6.75-inch bbl.). Weight: 39 oz. (with 6.75-inch bbl.). Fixed sights. Blued finish. Checkered plastic thumbrest grips. Made 1951-58. Note: 1951-54 production has lever takedown as in "G" series. Later version (illustrated) has push-button takedown.

W/one bbl. . . . . NiB $354 Ex $284 Gd $194
W/both bbls. . . . . NiB $437 Ex $350 Gd $238

SPORT-KING AUTOMATIC PISTOL
SECOND MODEL . . . . NiB $380 Ex $304 Gd $207
Caliber: .22 LR. 10-shot magazine, 4.5- or 6.75 inch interchangeable bbl. 11.25 inches overall (with 6.75-inch bbl.). Weight: 42 oz. (with 6.75-inch bbl.). Fixed sights. Blued finish. Checkered grips. Made 1958-70.

SPORT-KING AUTOMATIC PISTOL
THIRD MODEL . . . . NiB $341 Ex $273 Gd $185
Similar to Sport-King — Second Model w/same general specifications. Blued or nickel finish. Intro. in 1974. disc.

SPORT-KING LIGHTWEIGHT
Same as standard Sport-King except has forged aluminum alloy frame. Weight: 30 oz. w/6.75-inch bbl. Made 1954-65.

W/one bbl. . . . . NiB $362 Ex $256 Gd $165
W/both bbls. . . . . NiB $438 Ex $360 Gd $193

SUPERMATIC
AUTOMATIC PISTOL
Takedown. Hammerless. Interchangeable bbls. Caliber: .22 LR. 10-shot magazine, bbl. lengths: 4.5-, 6.75-inches. Late model 6.75-inch bbls. have recoil stabilizer feature. Weight: 43 oz. (with 6.75-inch bbl.) 11.5 inches overall (with 6.75-inch bbl.). Target sights. Elevated serrated rib between sights. Adj. bbl. weights add 2 or 3 oz. Blued finish. Checkered plastic thumbrest grips. Made 1951-58.

W/one bbl. . . . . NiB $709 Ex $566 Gd $385
W/both bbls. . . . . NiB $869 Ex $695 Gd $473

SUPERMATIC CITATION
Same as Supermatic Tournament except 6.75-, 8- or 10-inch tapered bbl. w/stabilizer and two removable weights. Also furnished w/Tournament's 5.5-inch bull bbl., adj. trigger pull, recoil-proof click-adj. rear sight (bbl.-mounted on 8- and 10-inch bbls.), checkered walnut thumbrest grips on bull bbl. model. Currently mfd. w/only bull bbl. Made 1958-66.

W/5.5-inch bull bbl. . . . . NiB $669 Ex $515 Gd $257
W/6.75-inch
tapered bbl. NiB $669 Ex $515 Gd $257
W/8-inch tapered bbl. . . . . NiB $906 Ex $716 Gd $505
W/10-inch tapered bbl. . . . . NiB $1101 Ex $922 Gd $690

**High Standard Victor
Solid Rib Barrel**

**High Standard
Supermatic Citation Bull Barrel**

**High Standard
Supermatic Citation Military Fluted Barrel**

**High Standard
Supermatic Tournament Bull Barrel**

**High Standard
Supermatic Tournament Military Tapered Barrel**

**High Standard
Supermatic Trophy Bull Barrel**

SUPERMATIC CITATION MILITARY

Same as Supermatic Citation except has military grip and bracket rear sight as in Supermatic Trophy. Made from 1965-73.

W/bull bbl. . . . . **NiB $609 Ex $487 Gd $335**
W/fluted bbl. . . . . **NiB $844 Ex $695 Gd $505**

SUPERMATIC
TOURNAMENT . . . . **NiB $618 Ex $541 Gd $252**

Takedown. Caliber: .22 LR. 10-shot magazine, interchangeable 5.5-inch bull or 6.75-inch heavy tapered bbl., notched and drilled for stabilizer and weights. 10 inches overall (with 5.5-inch bbl.). Weight: 44 oz. (5.5-inch bbl.). Click adj. rear sight, undercut ramp front. Blued finish. Checkered grips. Made 1958-66.

SUPERMATIC
TOURNAMENT
MILITARY . . . . **NiB $608 Ex $484 Gd $324**

Same as Supermatic Tournament except has military grip. Made 1965-71.

SUPERMATIC TROPHY

Same as Supermatic Citation except with 5.5-inch bull bbl., or 7.25-inch fluted bbl., w/detachable stabilizer and weights, extra magazine, High-luster blued finish, checkered walnut thumbrest grips. Made 1963-66.

W/bull bbl. . . . . **NiB $1128 Ex $922 Gd $463**
W/fluted bbl. . . . . **NiB $1159 Ex $937 Gd $489**

SUPERMATIC
TROPHY MILITARY

Same as Supermatic Trophy except has military grip and bracket rear sight. Made 1965-84.

W/bull bbl. . . . . **NiB $952 Ex $850 Gd $443**
W/fluted bbl. . . . . **NiB $448 Ex $855 Gd $469**

VICTOR
AUTOMATIC . . . . **NiB $819 Ex $644 Gd $412**

Takedown. Caliber: .22 LR. 10-shot magazine, 4.5-inch solid or vent rib and 5.5-inch vent rib, interchangeable bbl., 9.75 inches overall (with 5.5-inch bbl.). Weight: 52 oz. (with 5.5-inch bbl.). Rib mounted target sights. Blued finish. Checkered walnut thumbrest grips. Standard or military grip configuration. Made from 1972-84 (standard-grip model, 1974-75).

**High Standard
Derringer**

**High Standard Double-
Nine — Steel Frame**

**High Standard
Durango**

**High Standard
Sierra**

NOTE: *High Standard automatic pistols can be found in the preceding section, while revolvers immediately follow this derringer listing.*

DERRINGERS

DERRINGER
Hammerless, double action, two-shot, double bbl. (over/under). Calibers: .22 Short, Long, LR or .22 Magnum Rimfire, 3.5-inch bbls., 5 inches overall. Weight: 11 oz. Standard model has blued or nickel finish w/plastic grips. Presentation model is goldplated in walnut case. Standard model made from 1963 (.22 S-L-LR) and 1964 (.22 MRF) to 1984. Gold model, 1965-83.

(cont'd) **DERRINGER**
Gold Presentation One
Derringer..................... NiB $709 Ex $566 Gd $385
Silver Presentation One
Derringer..................... NiB $676 Ex $541 Gd $368
Presentation Set, matched
pair, consecutive numbers
(1965 only) .... NiB $1281 Ex $1025 Gd $697
Standard model (blue).......... NiB $251 Ex $201 Gd $137
Standard model (nickel) .... NiB $277 Ex $221 Gd $150
Standard model
(Electroless nickel)............. NiB $289 Ex $232 Gd $158
Standard model (blue).......... NiB $251 Ex $201 Gd $137

REVOLVERS

NOTE: *Only High Standard revolvers can be found in this section. See the preceding sections for automatic pistols and derringers. For a complete listing of High Standard handguns, please refer to the Index.*

CAMP GUN. .... NiB $257 Ex $206 Gd $140
Same as Sentinel Mark I/Mark IV except has 6-inch bbl., adj. rear sight, target-style checkered walnut grips. Caliber: .22 LR or .22 WMR. Made 1976-83.

DOUBLE-NINE DA REVOLVER —ALUMINUM FRAME
Western-style version of Sentinel. Blued or nickel finish w/simulated ivory, ebony or stag grips, 5.5-inch bbl., 11 inches overall. Weight: 27.25 oz. Made 1959-71.
Blue model .... NiB $216 Ex $170 Gd $98
Nickel model.................... NiB $227 Ex $180 Gd $106

DOUBLE-NINE—STEEL FRAME
Similar to Double-Nine—Aluminum Frame, w/same general specifications except w/steel frame and has extra cylinder for .22 WMR, walnut grips. Intro. in 1971. disc.
Blue model .... NiB $275 Ex $219 Gd $149
Nickel model.................... NiB $288 Ex $228 Gd $155

DOUBLE-NINE DELUXE .... NiB $284 Ex $228 Gd $154
Same as Double-Nine — Steel Frame except has adj. target rear sight. Intro. in 1971. disc.

DURANGO
Similar to Double-Nine—Steel Frame except .22 LR only, available w/4.5- or 5.5-inch bbl. Made 1971-73.
Blue model .... NiB $177 Ex $140 Gd $93
Nickel model.................... NiB $190 Ex $149 Gd $98

HIGH SIERRA DA REVOLVER
Similar to Double-Nine—Steel Frame except has 7-inch octagon bbl., w/gold-plated grip frame, fixed or adj. sights. Made 1973-1983.
W/fixed sights .... NiB $345 Ex $276 Gd $187
W/adj. sights .... NiB $365 Ex $294 Gd $203

HOMBRE
Similar to Double-Nine—Steel Frame except .22 LR only, lacks single-action type ejector rod and tube, has 4.5-inch bbl. Made 1971-73.
Blue model .... NiB $171 Ex $137 Gd $91
Nickel model.................... NiB $190 Ex $149 Gd $101

KIT GUN DA REVOLVER .... NiB $203 Ex $161 Gd $102
Solid frame, swing-out cylinder. Caliber: .22 LR. Nine-shot cylinder, 4-inch bbl., 9 inches overall. Weight: 19 oz. Adj. rear sight, ramp front. Blued finish. Checkered walnut grips. Made 1970-73.

High Standard Longhorn
Steel Frame

High Standard
Kit Gun

High Standard
Sentinel

High Standard
Longhorn Aluminum Frame

LONGHORN
ALUMINUM FRAME
Similar to Double-Nine—Aluminum Frame except has Longhorn hammer spur, 4.5-, 5.5- or 9.5-inch bbl., Walnut, simulated pearl or simulated stag grips. Blued finish. Made 1960-1971.
W/4.5- or 5.5-inch bbl. . . . . **NiB $237 Ex $190 Gd $129**
W/9.5-inch bbl . . . . **NiB $261 Ex $206 Gd $137**

LONGHORN
STEEL FRAME
Similar to Double-Nine — Steel Frame except has 9.5-inch bbl. w/fixed or adj. sights. Made 1971-1983
W/fixed sights . . . . **NiB $256 Ex $206 Gd $142**
W/adj. sights . . . . **NiB $392 Ex $324 Gd $227**

NATCHEZ . . . . **NiB $247 Ex $201 Gd $142**
Similar to Double-Nine — Aluminum Frame except 4.5-inch bbl., 10 inches overall, weight: 25.25 oz., blued finish, simulated ivory bird's-head grips. Made 1961-66.

High Standard
Natchez

POSSE . . . . **NiB $174 Ex $139 Gd $95**
Similar to Double-Nine — Aluminum Frame except 3.5-inch bbl., 9 inches overall, weight: 23.25 oz. Blued finish, brass-grip frame and trigger guard, walnut grips. Made 1961-66.

SENTINEL DA REVOLVER
Solid frame, swing-out cylinder. Caliber: .22 LR. Nine-shot cylinder, 3- 4- or 6-inch bbl. Nine inches overall (with 4-inch-bbl.). Weight: 19 oz. (with 4-inch bbl.). Fixed sights. Aluminum frame. Blued or nickel finish. Checkered grips. Made 1955-56.
Blue model . . . . **NiB $145 Ex $116 Gd $79**
Blue/green model . . . . **NiB $139 Ex $129 Gd $101**
Gold model . . . . **NiB $319 Ex $288 Gd $165**
Nickel model . . . . **NiB $154 Ex $139 Gd $88**
Pink model . . . . **NiB $335 Ex $299 Gd $165**

SENTINEL DELUXE
Same as Sentinel except w/4- or 6-inch bbl., wide trigger, drift-adj. rear sight, two-piece square-butt grips. Made 1957-74. Note: Designated Sentinel after 1971.
Blue model . . . . **NiB $144 Ex $129 Gd $93**
Nickel model . . . . **NiB $170 Ex $154 Gd $103**

High Standard
Posse

**High Standard
Sentinel I**

**High Standard
Sentinel Mark II**

**High Standard
Sentinel Mark III**

**High Standard
Sentinel Snub**

SENTINEL IMPERIAL

Same as Sentinel except has onyx-black or nickel finish, two-piece checkered walnut grips, ramp front sight. Made 1962-65.

Blue model . . . . NiB $144 Ex $129 Gd $83
Nickel model . . . . NiB $154 Ex $144 Gd $93

SENTINEL 1 DA REVOLVER

Steel frame. Caliber: .22 LR. Nine-shot cylinder, bbl. lengths: 2-, 3-, 4-inch, 6.88 inches overall (with 2-inch bbl.). Weight: 21.5 oz. (2-inch bbl.). Ramp front sight, fixed or adj. rear. Blued or nickel finish. Smooth walnut grips. Made 1974-83.

Blue model . . . . NiB $238 Ex $191 Gd $130
Nickel model . . . . NiB $303 Ex $242 Gd $165
W/adj. sights . . . . NiB $329 Ex $263 Gd $178

SENTINEL MARK II

DA REVOLVER. . . . . NiB $283 Ex $257 Gd $144
Caliber: .357 Magnum. Six-shot cylinder, bbl. lengths: 2.5-, 4-, 6-inch, 9 inches overall w/4-inch bbl., weight: 38 oz. (with 4-inch bbl.). Fixed sights. Blued finish. Walnut service or combat-style grips. Made 1974-76.

SENTINEL MARK III . . . . NiB $315 Ex $252 Gd $172

Same as Sentinel Mark II except has ramp front and adj. rear sights. Weight: 40 oz. (with 4-inch bbl.). Blued finish. Made 1974-76.

SENTINEL MARK IV

Same as Sentinel Mark I except in .22 WMR. Made 1974-83.

Blue model . . . . NiB $289 Ex $232 Gd $158
Nickel model . . . . NiB $315 Ex $252 Gd $172
W/adj. sights . . . . NiB $348 Ex $278 Gd $190

SENTINEL SNUB

Same as Sentinel Deluxe except w/2.75-inch bbl., (7.25 inches overall, weight: 15 oz.), checkered bird's head-type grips. Made 1957-74.

Blued finish . . . . NiB $149 Ex $144 Gd $93
Nickel finish . . . . NiB $160 Ex $154 Gd $103

HIGH STANDARD MFG. CO., INC. —
Houston, Texas
Distributed from Hartford, Connecticut

10X AUTOMATIC PISTOL . . . . NiB $953 Ex $747 Gd $438

Caliber: .22 LR. 10-shot magazine, 5.5-inch bbl., 9.5 inches overall. Weight: 45 oz. Checkered walnut grips. Blued finish. Made from 1994 to date.

OLYMPIC I.S.U. AUTOMATIC PISTOL

Same specifications as the 1958 I.S.U. issue. See listing under previous High Standard Section.

Olympic I.S.U. model . . . . NiB $566 Ex $463 Gd $206
Olympic I.S.U. military model. . . . . NiB $510 Ex $412 Gd $206
Military model. . . . . NiB $432 Ex $345 Gd $235

SPORT KING AUTO PISTOL . . . . NiB $335 Ex $268 Gd $182

Caliber: .22 LR. 10-shot magazine, 4.5- or 6.75-inch bbl., 8.5 or 10.75 inches overall. Weight: 44 oz. (with 4.5-inch bbl.), 46 oz. (with 6.75-inch bbl.). Fixed sights, slide mounted. Checkered walnut grips. Parkerized finish. Advertised in 1996 to date. No resale value established.

SUPERMATIC CITATION AUTO PISTOL

Caliber: .22 LR. 10-shot magazine, 5.5- or 7.75-inch bbl., 9.5 or 11.75 inches overall. Weight: 44 oz. (with 5.5-inch bbl.), 46 oz. (with 7.75-inch bbl.). Frame-mounted, micro-adj. rear sight, undercut ramp

(cont'd) SUPERMATIC CITATION AUTO PISTOL
front sight. Blued or Parkerized finish. Made 1994 to date.
Supermatic Citation model . . . . NiB $427 Ex $335 Gd $191
.22 Short conversion . . . . NiB $330 Ex $268 Gd $180

CITATION MS AUTO PISTOL . . . . . NiB $647 Ex $566 Gd $309
Similar to the Supermatic Citation except has 10-inch bbl., 14 inches overall. Weight: 49 oz. Made 1994 to date.

SUPERMATIC TOURNAMENT . . . . . NiB $380 Ex $304 Gd $207
Caliber: .22 LR. 10-shot magazine, bbl. lengths: 4.5, 5.5, or 6.75 inches, overall length: 8.5, 9.5 or 10.75 inches. Weight: 43, 44 or 45 oz.
depending on bbl. length. Micro-adj. rear sight, undercut ramp front
sight. Checkered walnut grips. Parkerized finish. Made 1994 to date.

SUPERMATIC TROPHY
Caliber: .22 LR. 10-shot magazine, 5.5 or 7.25-inch bbl., 9.5 or
11.25 inches overall. Weight: 44 oz. (with 5.5-inch bbl.). Micro-adj.
rear sight, undercut ramp front sight. Checkered walnut grips
w/thumbrest. Blued or Parkerized finish. Made 1994 to date.
Supermatic Trophy . . . . NiB $444 Ex $355 Gd $242
.22 Short Conversion . . . . NiB $330 Ex $268 Gd $180

VICTOR AUTOMATIC
Caliber: .22 LR.10-shot magazine, 4.5- or 5.5-inch ribbed bbl., 8.5
or 9.5 inches overall. Weight: 45 oz. (with 4.5-inch bbl.), 46 oz.
(with 5.5-inch bbl.). Micro-adj. rear sight, post front. Checkered
walnut grips. Blued or Parkerized finish. Made 1994 to date.
Victor Model . . . . NiB $510 Ex $412 Gd $206
.22 Short conversion . . . . NiB $330 Ex $268 Gd $180

HOPKINS & ALLEN ARMS CO. — Norwich, Connecticut

HOPKINS & ALLEN REVOLVERS
*See listings of comparable Harrington & Richardson and Iver
Johnson models for values.*

INGRAM — Mfd. by Military Armament Corp.

See listings under M.A.C. (Military Armament Corp.)

Note: *Military Armament Corp. ceased production of the select-fire
automatic, M10 (9mm & .45 ACP) and M11 (.380 ACP) in 1977.
Commercial production resumed on semiautomatic versions under
the M.A.C. banner until 1982.*

INTERARMS — Alexandria, Virginia

See also Bersa Pistol.

**HELWAN BRIGADIER
AUTO PISTOL . . . . NiB $201 Ex $154 Gd $93**
Caliber: 9mm Para. Eight-shot magazine, 4.25-inch bbl., 8 inches
overall. Weight: 32 oz. Blade front sight, dovetailed rear. Blued finish. Grooved plastic grips. Imported 1987-95.

VIRGINIAN DRAGOON SA REVOLVER
Calibers: .357 Magnum, .44 Magnum, .45 Colt. Six-shot cylinder.
Bbls.: 5- (not available in .44 Magnum), 6-, 7.5-, 8.38-inch (latter
only in .44 Magnum w/adj. sights), 11.88 inches overall with (6-
inch bbl.). Weight: 48 oz. (with 6-inch bbl.). Fixed sights or micrometer rear and ramp front sights. Blued finish w/color-casetreated
frame. Smooth walnut grips. SWISSAFE base pin safety system.

Interarms/Helwan
Brigadier

Interarms Virginian
SA Revolver

(cont'd) VIRGINIAN DRAGOON SA REVOLVER
Manufactured by Interarms Industries Inc., Midland, VA. 1977-84.
Standard Dragoon . . . . NiB $263 Ex $232 Gd $165
Engraved Dragoon . . . . NiB $561 Ex $484 Gd $330
Deputy model . . . . NiB $257 Ex $221 Gd $160
Stainless. . . . . NiB $263 Ex $232 Gd $206

**VIRGINIAN REVOLVER
SILHOUETTE MODEL . . . . NiB $376 Ex $227 Gd $221**
Same general specifications as regular model except designed in
stainless steel w/untapered bull bbl., lengths of 7.5, 8.38 and 10.5
inches. Made 1985-86.

VIRGINIAN SA REVOLVER . . . . . . NiB $509 Ex $407 Gd $277
Similar to Colt Single-Action Army except has base pin safety system. Imported 1973-76. (See also listing under Hämmerli.)

INTRATEC U.S.A., INC. — Miami, Florida

**CATEGORY 9 DAO
SEMIAUTOMATIC . . . . NiB $221 Ex $185 Gd $103**
Blowback action w/polymer frame. Caliber: 9mm Para. Eight-shot
magazine, 3-inch bbl., 7.7 inches overall. Weight: 18 oz. Textured
black polymer grips. Matte black finish. Made 1993 to date.

**CATEGORY 40
DAO SEMIAUTOMATIC . . . . NiB $219 Ex $175 Gd $119**
Locking-breech action w/polymer frame. Caliber: .40 S&W. Seven-
shot magazine, 3.25-inch bbl., 8 inches overall. Weight: 21 oz.
Textured black polymer grips. Matte black finish. Made 1994 to date.

**CATEGORY 45
DAO SEMIAUTOMATIC . . . . NiB $237 Ex $196 Gd $133**
Locking-breech action w/polymer frame. Caliber: .45 ACP. Six-shot
magazine, 3.25-inch bbl., 8 inches overall. Weight: 21 oz. Textured
black polymer grips. Matte black finish. Made 1994 to date.

Japanese
Model 14 (1925)

Japanese
Model 26 DAO Revolver

MODEL PROTEC .22 DA SEMIAUTOMATIC
Caliber: .25 ACP. 10-shot magazine, 2.5-inch bbl., 5 inches overall. Weight: 14 oz. Wraparound composition grips. Black Teflon, satin grey or Tec-Kote finish. Advertised in 1992.
ProTec .22 standard . . . . NiB $113 Ex $82 Gd $31
ProTec .22 w/satin or Tec-Kote . . . . NiB $118 Ex $87 Gd $36

MODEL PROTEC .25 DA SEMIAUTOMATIC
Caliber: .25 ACP. Eight-shot magazine, 2.5-inch bbl., 5 inches overall. Weight: 14 oz. Fixed sights. Wraparound composition grips. Black Teflon, satin grey or Tec-Kote finish. Made 1991 to date. Note: Formerly Model Tec-.25.
ProTec .25 standard . . . . NiB $91 Ex $71 Gd $49
ProTec .25 w/satin or Tec-Kote . . . . NiB $97 Ex $77 Gd $52

MODEL TEC-9 SEMIAUTOMATIC
Caliber: 9mm Para. 20- or 36-round magazine, 5-inch bbl., weight: 50-51 oz. Open fixed front sight, adj. rear. Military nonglare blued or stainless finish.
Tec-9 w/blued finish . . . . NiB $252 Ex $201 Gd $136
Tec-9 w/nickel finish . . . . NiB $251 Ex 201 Gd $137
Tec 9S w/stainless finish . . . . NiB $335 Ex $268 Gd $180

MODEL TEC-9M SEMIAUTOMATIC
Same specifications as Model Tec-9 except has 3-inch bbl. without shroud and 20-round magazine, blued or stainless finish.
Tec-9M w/blued finish . . . . NiB $226 Ex $180 Gd $123
Tec-9MS w/stainless finish . . . . NiB $303 Ex $242 Gd $165

MODEL TEC-22T SEMIAUTOMATIC
Caliber: .22 LR. 10/.22-type 30-shot magazine, 4-inch bbl., 11.19 inches overall. Weight: 30 oz. Protected post front sight, adj. rear sight. Matte black or Tec-Kote finish. Made 1989 to date.

(cont'd) MODEL TEC-22T SEMIAUTOMATIC
Tec-22T standard . . . . NiB $165 Ex $134 Gd $93
Tec-22TK Tec-Kote . . . . NiB $200 Ex $160 Gd $108

MODEL TEC
DOUBLE DERRINGER . . . . NiB $116 Ex $93 Gd $62
Calibers: .22 WRF, .32 H&R Mag., .38 Special. Two-shot capacity, 3-inch bbl., 4.63 inches overall. Weight: 13 oz. Fixed sights. Matte black finish. Made 1986-88.

ISRAEL ARMS — Kfar Sabs, Israel
Imported by Israel Arms International, Houston TX

MODEL BUL-M5 LOCKED
BREECH (2000) AUTO PISTOL . . . . NiB $407 Ex $273 Gd $237
Similar to the M1911 U.S. Government model. Caliber: .45 ACP. Seven-shot magazine, 5-inch bbl., 8.5 inches overall. Weight: 38 oz. Blade front and fixed, low-profile rear sights.

KAREEN MK II (1500) AUTO PISTOL
Single-action only. Caliber: 9mm Para. 10-shot magazine, 4.75-inch bbl., 8 inches overall. Weight: 33.6 oz. Blade front sight, rear adjustable for windage. Textured black composition or rubberized grips. Blued, two-tone, matte black finish. Imported 1996 to date.
Blued or matte black finish . . . . NiB $407 Ex $314 Gd $221
Two-tone finish . . . . NiB $613 Ex $474 Gd $341
Meprolite sights, add $40

KAREEN MK II COMPACT
(1501) AUTO PISTOL . . . . NiB $397 Ex $330 Gd $232
Similar to standard Kareen MKII except w/3.85-inch bbl., 7.1 inches overall. Weight: 32 oz. Imported 1997 to date.

GOLAN MODEL (2500) AUTO PISTOL
Single or double action. Caliber: 9mm Para., .40 S&W. 10-shot magazine, 3.85-inch bbl., 7.1 inches overall. Weight: 34 oz. Steel slide and alloy frame w/ambidextrous safety and decocking lever. Matte black finish. Imported 1997 to date.
9mm Para. NiB $837 Ex $669 Gd $455
.40 S&W . . . . NiB $676 Ex $541 Gd $368

GAL MODEL
(5000) AUTO PISTOL . . . . NiB $354 Ex $283 Gd $193
Caliber: .45 ACP. Eight-shot magazine, 4.25-inch bbl., 7.25 inches overall. Weight: 42 oz. Low profile 3-dot sights. Combat-style black rubber grips. Imported 1997 to date.

JAPANESE MILITARY PISTOLS — Tokyo, Japan Manufactured by Government Plant

MODEL 14 (1925)
AUTOMATIC PISTOL . . . . NiB $638 Ex $510 Gd $347
Modification of the Nambu Model 1914, changes chiefly intended to simplify mass production. Standard round trigger guard or over-sized guard for use w/gloves. Caliber: 8mm Nambu. Eight-shot magazine, 4.75-inch bbl., 9 inches overall. Weight: About 29 oz. Fixed sights. Blued finish. Grooved wood grips. Intro. 1925 and mfd. through WW II.

MODEL 26 DAO REVOLVER . . . . . . NiB $566 Ex $381 Gd $248
Top-break frame. Caliber: 9mm. Six-shot cylinder w/automatic extractor/ejector, 4.7-inch bbl., adopted by the Japanese Army from 1893 to 1914, replaced by the Model 14 Automatic Pistol but remained in service through World War II.

MODEL 94 (1934)
AUTOMATIC PISTOL . . . . **NiB $278 Ex $206 Gd $129**
Poorly designed and constructed, this pistol is unsafe and can be fired merely by applying pressure on the sear, which is exposed on the left side. Caliber: 8mm Nambu. Six-shot magazine, 3.13-inch bbl., 7.13 inches overall. Weight: About 27 oz. Fixed sights. Blued finish. Hard rubber or wood grips. Intro. in 1934, principally for export to Latin American countries, production continued thru WW II.

NAMBU MODEL
1914 AUTOMATIC PISTOL . . . . . **NiB $1648 Ex $1442 Gd $700**
Original Japanese service pistol, resembles Luger in appearance and Glisenti in operation. Caliber: 8mm Nambu. Seven-shot magazine, 4.5-inch bbl., 9 inches overall. Weight: About 30 oz. Fixed front sight, adj. rear sight. Blued finish. Checkered wood grips. Made 1914-1925.

Japanese Model 94 (1934)

JENNINGS FIREARMS INC. — Currently Mfd. by Bryco Arms, Irvine, California Previously by Calwestco, Inc. & B.L. Jennings

See additional listings under Bryco Arms.

MODEL J AUTO PISTOL
Calibers: .22 LR, .25 ACP. Six-shot magazine, 2.5-inch bbl., about 5 inches overall. Weight: 13 oz. Fixed sights. Chrome, satin nickel or black Teflon finish. Walnut, grooved black Cycolac or resin-impregnated wood grips. Made from 1981-85 under Jennings and Calwestco logos; from 1985 to date by Bryco Arms.
Model J-22. . . . . **NiB $72 Ex $57 Gd $36**
Model J-25. . . . . **NiB $67 Ex $51 Gd $31**

Jennings Model J Auto Pistol

IVER JOHNSON ARMS, INC. — Jacksonville, Arkansas

Operation of this company dates back to 1871, when Iver Johnson and Martin Bye partnered to manufacture metallic cartridge revolvers. Johnson became the sole owner and changed the name to Iver Johnson's Arms & Cycle Works, which it was known as for almost 100 years. Modern management shortened the name, and after several owner changes the firm was moved from Massachusetts, its original base, to Jacksonville, Arkansas. In 1987, the American Military Arms Corporation (AMAC) acquired the operation, which subsequently ceased in 1993.

NOTE: *For ease in finding a particular firearm, Iver Johnson handguns are divided into two sections: Automatic Pistols (below) and Revolvers, which follow. For the complete handgun listing, please refer to the Index.*

AUTOMATIC PISTOLS

9MM DA AUTOMATIC . . . . **NiB $380 Ex $304 Gd $207**
Caliber: 9mm. Six-round magazine, 3-inch bbl., 6.5 inches overall. Weight: 26 oz. Blade front sight, adj. rear. Smooth hardwood grip. Blued or matte blued finish. Intro. 1986.

COMPACT .25 ACP . . . . **NiB $170 Ex $139 Gd $87**
Bernardelli V/P design. Caliber: .25 ACP. Five-shot magazine, 2.13-inch bbl., 4.13 inches overall. Weight: 9.3 oz. Fixed sights. Checkered composition grips. Blued slide, matte blued frame and color-casehardened trigger. Made 1991 to 93.

Iver Johnson Enforcer

ENFORCER . . . . **NiB $463 Ex $355 Gd $246**
Semiautomatic. Caliber: .30 U.S. Carbine. Five-, 15-, or 30-round magazine, 9.5-inch bbl., weight: 5.5 lbs. Adj. sights. Walnut stock. Made mid-1980s to 1993.

PP30 SUPER
ENFORCER AUTOMATIC . . . . **NiB $433 Ex $340 Gd $206**
Caliber: .30 U.S. Carbine. Fifteen- or 30-shot magazine, 9.5-inch bbl., 17 inches overall. Weight: 4 pounds. Adj. peep rear sight, blade front. American walnut stock. Made 1984-86.

PONY AUTOMATIC PISTOL
Caliber: .380 Auto. Six-shot magazine, 3.1-inch bbl., 6.1 inches overall. Blue, matte blue, nickel finish or stainless. Weight: 20 oz. Wooden grips. Smallest of the locked breech automatics. Made 1982-88. Reintroduced 1990-93.
Blue or matte
blue model . . . . **NiB $309 Ex $257 Gd $174**
Nickel model. . . . . **NiB $360 Ex $268 Gd $175**
Deluxe model . . . . **NiB $386 Ex $309 Gd $216**

Iver Johnson
Model TP

Iver Johnson
Model 55 Target

Iver Johnson
Model 55-S

Iver Johnson
Model 56 Blank Revolver

Iver Johnson
Model 57A Target

MODEL TP-22 DA
AUTOMATIC . . . . NiB $144 Ex $103 Gd $62
Calibers: .22 LR, Seven-shot magazine, 2.85-inch bbl., 5.39 inches overall. Blued finish. Weight: 14.46 oz. Made 1982-93.

MODEL TP25 DA
POCKET PISTOL . . . . NiB $180 Ex $144 Gd $98
Double-action automatic. Caliber: .25 ACP. Seven-shot magazine, 3-inch bbl., 5.5 inches overall. Weight: 12 oz. Black plastic grips and blued finish. Made 1982-93.

TRAILSMAN
AUTOMATIC PISTOL
Caliber: .22 LR. 10-shot magazine, 4.5 or 6-inch bbl., 8.75 inches overall (with 4.5-inch bbl.). Weight: 46 oz. Fixed target-type sights. Checkered composition grips. Made 1984-90.
Standard model . . . . NiB $212 Ex $170 Gd $115
Deluxe model . . . . NiB $251 Ex $201 Gd $137

REVOLVERS

MODEL 55 TARGET DA REVOLVER . . . . NiB $134 Ex $103 Gd $62
Solid frame. Caliber: .22 LR. Eight-shot cylinder, bbl. lengths: 4.5-, 6-inches. 10.75 inches overall (with 6-inch bbl.). Weight: 30.5 oz. (with 6-inch bbl.). Fixed sights. Blued finish. Walnut grips. Note: Original model designation was 55; changed to 55A when loading gate was added in 1961. Made 1955-77.

MODEL 55-S REVOLVER . . . . NiB $144 Ex $103 Gd $62
Same general specifications as the Model 55 except for 2.5-inch bbl. and small, molded pocket-size grip.

MODEL 56
BLANK REVOLVER . . . . NiB $83 Ex $67 Gd $45
Solid frame. Caliber: .22 blanks only. Eight-shot cylinder, 2.5-inch solid bbl., 6.75 inches overall. Weight: 10 oz.

MODEL 57A
TARGET DA REVOLVER . . . . NiB $113 Ex $98 Gd $62
Solid frame. Caliber: .22 LR. Eight-shot cylinder, bbl. lengths: 4.5-, and 6-inches. 10.75 inches overall. Weight: 30.5 oz. with 6-inch bbl. Adj. sights. Blued finish. Walnut grips. Note: Original model designation was 57, changed to 57A when loading gate was added in 1961. Made 1956-75.

MODEL 66 TRAILSMAN
DA REVOLVER . . . . NiB $103 Ex $72 Gd $51
Hinged frame. Rebounding hammer. Caliber: .22 LR. Eight-shot cylinder, 6-inch bbl., 11 inches overall. Weight: 34 oz. Adj. sights. Blued finish. Walnut grips. Made 1958-75.

**Iver Johnson
Model 66 Trailsman**

**Iver Johnson
Model 67 Viking**

MODEL 67 VIKING DA REVOLVER . . . . NiB $142 Ex $113 Gd $77
Hinged frame. Caliber: .22 LR. Eight-shot cylinder, bbl. lengths: 4.5-
and 6-inches, 11 inches overall (with 6-inch bbl.). Weight: 34 oz.
(with 6-inch bbl.). Adj. sights. Walnut grips w/thumbrest. Made
1964-75.

**MODEL 67S VIKING
SNUB REVOLVER** . . . . NiB $144 Ex $103 Gd $62
DA. Hinged frame. Calibers: .22 LR, .32 S&W Short and Long, .38
S&W. Eight-shot cylinder in .22, 5-shot in .32 and .38 calibers; 2.75-
inch bbl. Weight: 25 oz. Adj. sights. Tenite grips. Made 1964-75.

MODEL 1900 DA REVOLVER . . . . . . NiB $124 Ex $103 Gd $57
Solid frame. Calibers: .22 LR, .32 S&W, .32 S&W Long, .38 S&W.
Seven-shot cylinder (.22 cal.), 6-shot (.32 S&W), 5-shot (.32 S&W
Long, .38 S&W); bbl. lengths: 2.5-, 4.5- and 6-inches. Weight: 12
oz. (in .32 S&W w/2.5-inch bbl.). Fixed sights. Blued or nickel fin-
ish. Hard rubber grips. Made 1900-47.

**Iver Johnson
Model 67S Viking Snub**

**MODEL 1900
TARGET DA REVOLVER** . . . . NiB $175 Ex $139 Gd $93
Solid frame. Caliber: .22 LR. Seven-shot cylinder, bbl. lengths: 6-
and 9.5-inches. Fixed sights. Blued finish. Checkered walnut grips.
(This earlier model does not have counterbored chambers as in the
Target Sealed 8. Made 1925-42.)

AMERICAN BULLDOG DA REVOLVER
Solid frame. Calibers: .22 LR, .22 WMR, .38 Special. Six-shot cylinder in .22, 5-shot in .38. Bbl. lengths: 2.5-, 4-inch. 9 inches overall
(with 4-inch bbl.). Weight: 30 oz. (with 4-inch bbl.). Adj. sights.
Blued or nickel finish. Plastic grips. Made 1974-76.
.38 Special . . . . NiB $165 Ex $134 Gd $82
Other calibers . . . . NiB $144 Ex $103 Gd $62

**Iver Johnson
Model 1900 Target**

ARMSWORTH MODEL 855 SA . . . . NiB $232 Ex $165 Gd $118
Hinged frame. Caliber: .22 LR. Eight-shot cylinder, 6-inch bbl.,
10.75 inches overall. Weight: 30 oz. Adj. sights. Blued finish.
Checkered walnut one-piece grip. Adj. finger rest. Made 1955-57.

CADET DA REVOLVER . . . . NiB $142 Ex $118 Gd $67
Solid frame. Calibers: .22 LR, .22 WMR, .32 S&W Long, .38 S&W, .38
Special. Six- or 8-shot cylinder in .22, 5-shot in other calibers, 2.5-inch
bbl., 7 inches overall. Weight: 22 oz. Fixed sights. Blued finish or nickel finish. Plastic grips. Note: Loading gate added in 1961, .22 cylinder
capacity changed from 8 to 6 rounds in 1975. Made 1955-77.

CATTLEMAN SA REVOLVER
Patterned after the Colt Army SA revolver. Calibers: .357 Magnum, .44
Magnum, .45 Colt. Six-shot cylinder. Bbl. lengths: 4.75-, 5.5- (not avail-
able in .44), 6- (.44 only), 7.25-inch. Weight: About 41 oz. Fixed sights.
Blued bbl., and cylinder color-casehardened frame, brass grip frame.
One-piece walnut grip. Made by Aldo Uberti, Brescia, Italy, 1973-78.
.44 Magnum . . . . NiB $257 Ex $206 Gd $129
Other calibers . . . . NiB $227 Ex $184 Gd $113

**Iver Johnson
Cadet**

Iver Johnson
Cattleman

Iver Johnson
Champion .22 Target

Iver Johnson
Sealed 8

Iver Johnson
Rookie

Iver Johnson
Safety Hammer

CATTLEMAN BUCKHORN
SA REVOLVER
Same as standard Cattleman except has adj. rear and ramp front sights. Bbl. lengths: 4.75- (.44 only), 5.75- (not available in .44), 6- (.44 only), 7.5- or 12-inches bbl., weight: About 44 oz. Made 1973-78.

.357 Magnum or .45
Colt w/12-inch bbl. . . . . NiB $309 Ex $227 Gd $154
.357 Magnum or .45
Colt w/5.75- or 7.5-inch bbl. . . . . . NiB $257 Ex $201 Gd $134
.44 Magnum, w/12-inch bbl. . . . . . . NiB $386 Ex $309 Gd $210
.44 Magnum, other bbls. . . . . NiB $309 Ex $257 Gd $165

CATTLEMAN BUNTLINE SA REVOLVER
Same as Cattleman Buckhorn except has 18-inch bbl., walnut shoulder stock w/brass fittings. Weight: About 56 oz. Made 1973-78.
.44 Magnum . . . . NiB $495 Ex $397 Gd $270
Other calibers . . . . NiB $444 Ex $355 Gd $242

CATTLEMAN TRAIL BLAZER . . . . . . NiB $196 Ex $154 Gd $103
Similar to Cattleman Buckhorn except .22 caliber has interchangeable .22 LR and .22 WMR cylinders, 5.5- or 6.5-inch bbl., weight: About 40 oz. Made 1973-78.

CHAMPION
.22 TARGET SA . . . . NiB $238 Ex $191 Gd $130
Hinged frame. Caliber: .22 LR. Eight-shot cylinder. Single action. Counterbored chambers as in Sealed 8 model, 6-inch bbl., 10.75 inches overall. Weight: 28 oz. Adj. target sights. Blued finish. Checkered walnut grips, adj. finger rest. Made 1938-48.

DELUXE TARGET . . . . NiB $237 Ex $191 Gd $139
Same as Sportsman except has adj. sights. Made 1975-76.

PROTECTOR SEALED
8 DA REVOLVER . . . . NiB $180 Ex $129 Gd $92
Hinged frame. Caliber: .22 LR. Eight-shot cylinder, 2.5-inch bbl., 7.25 inches overall. Weight: 20 oz. Fixed sights. Blued finish. Checkered walnut grips. Made 1933-49.

ROOKIE
DA REVOLVER. . . . . NiB $103 Ex $82 Gd $62
Solid frame. Caliber: .38 Special. Five-shot cylinder, 4-inch bbl., 9-inches overall. Weight: 30 oz. Fixed sights. Blued or nickel finish. Plastic grips. Made 1975-77.

SAFETY HAMMER
DA REVOLVER. . . . . NiB $144 Ex $113 Gd $72
Hinged frame. Calibers: .22 LR, .32 S&W, .32 S&W Long, .38 S&W. Seven-shot cylinder (.22 cal.), 6-shot (.32 S&W Long), 5-shot (.32 S&W, .38 S&W). bbl. lengths: 2, 3, 3.25, 4, 5 or 6 inches. Weight w/4-inch bbl.: 15 oz. (.22, .32 S&W), 19.5 oz. (.32 S&W Long) or 19 oz. (.38 S&W). Fixed sights. Blued or nickel finish. Hard rubber, round butt grips or square butt, rubber or walnut grips available. Note: .32 S&W Long and .38 S&W models built on heavy frame. Made 1892-1950.

SAFETY HAMMERLESS
DA REVOLVER. . . . . NiB $154 Ex $124 Gd $77
Similar to the Safety Hammer Model except w/shrouded hammerless frame. Made 1895-1950.

SIDEWINDER
DA REVOLVER . . . . **NiB $144 Ex $129 Gd $72**
Solid frame. Caliber: .22 LR. Six- or 8-shot cylinder, bbl. lengths: 4.75, 6 inches; 11.25 inches overall (with 6-inch bbl.). Weight: 31 oz. (with 6-inch bbl.). Fixed sights. Blued or nickel finish w/plastic staghorn grips or color-casehardened frame w/walnut grips. Note: Cylinder capacity changed from 8 to 6 rounds in 1975. Intro. 1961. disc.

SIDEWINDER "S" . . . . **NiB $154 Ex $129 Gd $87**
Same as Sidewinder except has interchangeable cylinders in .22 LR and .22 WMR, adj. sights. Intro. 1974. disc.

SPORTSMAN
DA REVOLVER . . . . **NiB $133 Ex $103 Gd $72**
Solid frame. Caliber: .22 LR. Six-shot cylinder. Bbl. lengths: 4.75-, 6-inches, 10.75 inches overall (with 6-inch bbl.). Weight: 30.5 oz. (with 6-inch bbl.). Fixed sights. Blued finish. Plastic grips. Made 1974-76.

SUPERSHOT 9-SHOT
DA REVOLVER . . . . **NiB $149 Ex $124 Gd $67**
Same as Supershot Sealed 8 except has nine non-counterbored chambers. Made 1929-49.

SUPERSHOT .22 DA REVOLVER . . . . . **NiB $102 Ex $82 Gd $51**
Hinged frame. Caliber: .22 LR. Seven-shot cylinder, 6-inch bbl. Fixed sights. Blued finish. Checkered walnut grips. This earlier model does not have counterbored chambers as in the Supershot Sealed 8. Made 1929-49.

SUPERSHOT MODEL 844 DA . . . . . . **NiB $180 Ex $139 Gd $92**
Hinged frame. Caliber: .22 LR. Eight-shot cylinder, bbl. lengths: 4.5- or 6-inch, 9.25 inches overall (with 4.5-inch bbl.). Weight: 27 oz. (4.5-inch bbl.). Adj. sights. Blued finish. Checkered walnut one-piece grip. Made 1955-56.

SUPERSHOT SEALED
8 DA REVOLVER . . . . **NiB $180 Ex $139 Gd $93**
Hinged frame. Caliber: .22 LR. Eight-shot cylinder, 6-inch bbl., 10.75 inches overall. Weight: 24 oz. Adj. target sights. Blued finish. Checkered walnut grips. Postwar model does not have adj. finger rest as earlier version. Made 1931-57.

SWING-OUT DA REVOLVER
Calibers: .22 LR, .22 WMR, .32 S&W Long, .38 Special. Six-shot cylinder in .22, 5-shot in .32 and .38, 2-, 3-, 4-inch plain bbl., or 4-6-inch vent rib bbl., 8.75 inches overall (with 4-inch bbl.). Fixed or adj. sights. Blued or nickel finish. Walnut grips. Made in 1977.
W/plain barrel, fixed sights . . . . **NiB $154 Ex $124 Gd $82**
W/vent rib, adj. sights . . . . **NiB $144 Ex $175 Gd $103**

TARGET 9-SHOT DA REVOLVER . . . . **NiB $186 Ex $149 Gd $102**
Same as Target Sealed 8 except has nine non-counterbored chambers. Made 1929-46.

TARGET SEALED 8 DA REVOLVER . . . . **NiB $175 Ex $134 Gd $98**
Solid frame. Caliber: .22 LR. Eight-shot cylinder, bbl. lengths: 6- and 10-inches. 10.75 inches overall (with 6-inch bbl.). Weight: 24 oz. (with 6-inch bbl.). Fixed sights. Blued finish. Checkered walnut grips. Made 1931-57.

TRIGGER-COCKING SA TARGET . . . . **NiB $242 Ex $191 Gd $134**
Hinged frame. First pull on trigger cocks hammer, second pull releases hammer. Caliber: .22 LR. Eight-shot cylinder, counterbored chambers, 6-inch bbl., 10.75 inches overall. Weight: 24 oz. Adj. target sights. Blued finish. Checkered walnut grips. Made 1940-47.

Iver Johnson Sidewinder

Iver Johnson Supershot Sealed 8

Iver Johnson Target Sealed 8

Kahr Model K9

KAHR ARMS — Blauvelt, New York
MODEL K9
DAO AUTO PISTOL
Caliber: 9mm Para. Seven-shot magazine, 3.5-inch bbl., 6 inches overall. Weight: 24 oz. Fixed sights. Matte black, electroless nickel, Birdsong Black-T or matte stainless finish. Wraparound textured polymer or hardwood grips. Made 1994 to date.
Duo-Tone finish . . . . **NiB $689 Ex $551 Gd $375**
Matte black finish . . . . **NiB $566 Ex $438 Gd $299**
Electroless nickel finish . . . . **NiB $592 Ex $474 Gd $322**
Black-T finish . . . . **NiB $809 Ex $592 Gd $433**
Matte stainless finish . . . . **NiB $547 Ex $438 Gd $298**
Lady K9 model . . . . **NiB $528 Ex $422 Gd $287**
Elite model . . . . **NiB $560 Ex $448 Gd $305**
Tritium Night Sights, add **$90**

Kel-Tec Model P-11

Kimber Model Classic .45

MODEL K40 DAO AUTO PISTOL
Similar to Model K9 except chambered .40 S&W w/5- or 6-shot magazine, Weight: 26 oz. Made 1997 to date.

Matte black finish	NiB $521	Ex $417	Gd $283
Electroless nickel finish	NiB $622	Ex $500	Gd $343
Black-T finish	NiB $658	Ex $520	Gd $344
Matte stainless finish	NiB $547	Ex $433	Gd $286
Covert model (shorter grip-frame)	NiB $516	Ex $407	Gd $267
Elite model	NiB $591	Ex $479	Gd $336
Tritium Night Sights, add			$90

MODEL MK9 DAO AUTO PISTOL
Similar to Model K9 except w/Micro-Compact frame. Six- or 7- shot magazine, 3- inch bbl., 5.5 inches overall. Weight: 22 oz. Stainless or Duo-Tone finish. Made 1998 to date.

Duo-Tone finish	NiB $710	Ex $572	Gd $396
Matte stainless finish	NiB $591	Ex $479	Gd $325
Elite model	NiB $593	Ex $479	Gd $325
Tritium Night Sights, add			$90

KBI, INC — Harrisburg, Pennsylvania

MODEL PSP-.25 AUTO PISTOL.... NiB $237 Ex $180 Gd $113
Caliber: .25 ACP. Six-shot magazine, 2.13-inch bbl., 4.13 inches overall. Weight: 9.5 oz. All-steel construction w/dual safety system. Made 1994 to date.

KEL-TEC CNC INDUSTRIES, INC. — Cocoa, Florida

MODEL P-11 DAO PISTOL
Caliber: 9mm Parabellum or .40 S&W. 10-shot magazine, 3.1- inch bbl., 5.6 inches overall. Weight: 14 oz. Blade front sight, drift adjustable rear. Aluminum frame w/steel slide. Checkered black, gray, or green polymer grips. Matte blue, nickel, stainless steel or Parkerized finish. Made 1995 to date.

9mm	NiB $272	Ex $221	Gd $158
.40 S&W	NiB $274	Ex $216	Gd $142
Parkerized finish, add			$40
Nickel finish, add (disc. 1995)			$30
Stainless finish, add (1996 to date)			$55
Tritium Night Sights, add			$80
.40 cal. conversion kit, add			$175

KIMBER MANUFACTURING, INC. — Yonkers, New York (Formerly Kimber of America, Inc.)

MODEL CLASSIC .45
Similar to Government 1911 built on steel, polymer or alloy full-size or compact frame. Caliber: .45 ACP. Seven-, 8-, 10- or 14-shot magazine, 4- or 5-inch bbl., 7.7 or 8.75 inches overall. Weight: 28 oz. (Compact LW), 34 oz. (Compact or Polymer) or .38 oz. (Custom FS). McCormick low-profile combat or Kimber adj. target sights. Blued, matte black oxide or stainless finish. Checkered custom wood or black synthetic grips. Made from 1994 to date.

Custom (matte black)	NiB $618	Ex $515	Gd $324
Custom Royal (polished blue)	NiB $676	Ex $541	Gd $368
Custom stainless (satin stainless)	NiB $638	Ex $510	Gd $347
Custom Target (matte black)	NiB $650	Ex $520	Gd $353
Target Gold Match (polished blue)	NiB $895	Ex $6716	Gd $487
Target stainless Match (polished stainless)	NiB $717	Ex $819	Gd $556
Polymer (matte black)	NiB $727	Ex $582	Gd $396
Polymer Stainless (satin stainless slide)	NiB $876	Ex $695	Gd $476
Polymer Target (matte black slide)	NiB $818	Ex $654	Gd $445
Compact (matte black)	NiB $573	Ex $458	Gd $312
Compact stainless (satin stainless)	NiB $638	Ex $510	Gd $347
Compact LW (matte black w/alloy frame)	NiB $658	Ex $494	Gd $340

KORTH PISTOLS — Ratzeburg, Germany

Currently imported by Keng's Firearms Specialty, Inc. Previously by Beeman Precision Arms; Osborne's and Mandall Shooting Supply

REVOLVERS COMBAT, SPORT, TARGET
Calibers: .357 Mag. and .22 LR w/interchangeable combination cylinders of .357 Mag./9mm Para. or .22 LR/.22 WMR also .22 Jet, .32 S&W and .32 H&R Mag. Bbls: 2.5-, 3-, 4-inch (combat) and 5.25- or 6-inch (target). Weight: 33 to 42 oz. Blued, stainless, matte silver or polished silver finish. Checkered walnut grips. Imported 1967 to date.

Standard rimfire model	NiB $3244	Ex $2565	Gd $1700
Standard centerfire model	NiB $3291	Ex $2570	Gd $1741
ISU Match Target model	NiB $4017	Ex $3255	Gd $2153
Custom stainless finish, add			$450
Matte silver finish, add			$650
Polished silver finish, add			$950

SEMIAUTOMATIC PISTOL
Calibers: 30 Luger, 9mm Para., .357 SIG, .40 S&W, 9x21mm. 10- or 14-shot magazine, 4- or 5-inch bbl., all-steel construction, recoil-operated. Ramp front sight, adj. rear. Blued, stainless, matte silver or polished silver finish. Checkered walnut grips. Imported 1988 to date.
Standard model . . . . NiB $4886 Ex $3909 Gd $2658
Matte silver finish, add $650
Polished silver finish, add $950

Lahti Automatic Pistol

LAHTI PISTOLS — Mfd. by Husqvarna Vapenfabriks A. B. Huskvarna, Sweden, and Valtion Kivaar Tedhas ("VKT") Jyväskyla, Finland

AUTOMATIC PISTOL
Caliber: 9mm Para. Eight-shot magazine, 4.75-inch bbl., weight: About 46 oz. Fixed sights. Blued finish. Plastic grips. Specifications given are those of the Swedish Model 40 but also apply in general to the Finnish Model L-35, which differs only slightly. A considerable number of Swedish Lahti pistols were imported and sold in the U.S. The Finnish model, somewhat better made, is rare. Finnish Model L-35 adopted 1935. Swedish Model 40 adopted 1940 and mfd. through 1944.
Finnish L-35 model . . . . NiB $2369 Ex $1844 Gd $1221
Swedish 40 model . . . . NiB $474 Ex $350 Gd $206

L.A.R. MANUFACTURING, INC. — West Jordan, Utah

MARK I GRIZZLY WIN. MAG. AUTOMATIC PISTOL
Calibers: .357 Mag., .45 ACP, .45 Win. Mag. Seven-shot magazine, 6.5-inch bbl., 10.5 inches overall. Weight: 48 oz. Fully adj. sights. Checkered rubber combat-style grips. Blued finish. Made from 1983 to date. 8- or 10-inch bbl., Made 1987-99.
.357 Mag. (6.5 inch barrel) . . . . . NiB $1105 Ex $8465 Gd $628
.45 Win. Mag.(6.5 inch barrel) . . . NiB $953 Ex $773 Gd $515
8-inch barrel . . . . NiB $1236 Ex $1030 Gd $747
10-inch barrel . . . . NiB $1313 Ex $1056 Gd $726

MARK IV GRIZZLY
AUTOMATIC PISTOL . . . . NiB $1035 Ex $850 Gd $566
Same general specifications as the L.A.R. Mark I except chambered for .44 Magnum, has 5.5- or 6.5-inch bbl., beavertail grip safety, matte blued finish. Made 1991-99.

MARK V AUTO PISTOL . . . . NiB $927 Ex $721 Gd $515
Similar to the Mark I except chambered in 50 Action Express. Six-shot magazine, 5.4- or 6.5-inch bbl., 10.6 inches overall (with 5.4-inch bbl.). Weight: 56 oz. Checkered walnut grips. Made 1993-99.

L.A.R. Mark I Grizzly

Laseraim Series I

LASERAIM TECHNOLOGIES INC. Little Rock, Arkansas

SERIES I SA AUTO PISTOL
Calibers: .40 S&W, .45 ACP, 10mm. Seven or 8- shot magazine, 3.875- or 5.5-inch dual-port compensated bbl., 8.75 or 10.5 inches overall. Weight: 46 or 52 oz. Fixed sights w/Laseraim or adjustable Millet sights. Textured black composition grips. Extended slide release, ambidextrous safety and beveled magazine well. Stainless or matte black Teflon finish. Made 1993 to date.
Series I w/adjustable sights . . . . NiB $408 Ex $306 Gd $204
Series I w/fixed sights . . . . NiB $357 Ex $275 Gd $194
Series I w/fixed sights (HotDot) . . . NiB $510 Ex $408 Gd $275
Series I Dream Team (RedDot) . . . . NiB $755 Ex $602 Gd $398
Series I Illusion (Laseraim) . . . . NiB $816 Ex $622 Gd $408

**Laseraim
Velocity 400 Series w/Laser Sight**

**Laseraim Series III
w/LA93 Illusion III Scope**

**Llama Model IIIA
Deluxe Chrome Engraved First Issue**

**Llama Model IIIA
Deluxe Blue Engraved Second Issue**

SERIES II SA AUTO PISTOL
Similar to Series I except w/stainless finish and no bbl., compensator. Made 1993-96.

Series II w/adjustable sights . . . . . . NiB $345	Ex $283	Gd $191
Series II w/fixed sights. . . . . NiB $322	Ex $255	Gd $173
Series II Dream Team. . . . . NiB $638	Ex $505	Gd $344
Series II Illusion. . . . . NiB $676	Ex $535	Gd $364

SERIES III SA AUTO PISTOL
Similar to Series II except w/serrated slide and 5-inch compensated bbl., only. Made 1994 to date.

Series III w/
adjustable sights . . . . NiB $555	Ex $444	Gd $302
Series III w/fixed sights . . . . NiB $504	Ex $403	Gd $274

VELOCITY SERIES SA AUTO PISTOL
Similar to Series I except chambered for .357 Sig. or .400 Cor-Bon, 3.875-inch unported bbl., (compact) or 5.5-inch dual-port compensated bbl. Made 1997 to date. See illustration previous page.

Compact model (unported) . . . . NiB $351	Ex $283	Gd $191
Government model (ported) . . . . . . NiB $414	Ex $331	Gd $225
W/wireless laser
(HotDot), add $150		

LIGNOSE PISTOLS — Suhl, Germany
Aktien-Gesellschaft "Lignose" Abteilung

The following Lignose pistols were manufactured from 1920 to the mid-1930s. They were also marketed under the Bergmann name.

EINHAND MODEL 2A
POCKET AUTO PISTOL . . . . NiB $306 Ex $275 Gd $102
As the name implies, this pistol is designed for one-hand operation, pressure on a "trigger" at the front of the guard retracts the slide. Caliber: .25 Auto. (6.35 mm). Six-shot magazine, 2-inch bbl., 4.75 inches overall. Weight: About 14 oz. Blued finish. Hard rubber grips.

MODEL 2 POCKET
AUTO PISTOL . . . . NiB $337 Ex $255 Gd $184
Conventional Browning type. Same general specifications as Einhand Model 2A but lacks the one-hand operation.

EINHAND MODEL
3A POCKET AUTO PISTOL . . . . NiB $398 Ex $306 Gd $209
Same as the Model 2A except has longer grip, 9-shot magazine, weight: About 16 oz.

LLAMA HANDGUNS — Mfd. by Gabilondo y Cia, Vitoria, Spain (Imported by S.G.S., Wanamassa, New Jersey)

NOTE: *For ease in finding a particular Llama handgun, the listings are divided into two groupings: Automatic Pistols (below) and Revolvers, which follow. For a complete listing of Llama handguns, please refer to the index.*

AUTOMATIC PISTOLS

MODEL IIIA
AUTOMATIC PISTOL . . . . NiB $214 Ex $189 Gd $133
Caliber: .380 Auto. Seven-shot magazine, 3.69-inch bbl., 6.5 inches overall. Weight: 23 oz. Adj. target sights. Blued finish. Plastic grips. Intro. 1951. disc.

MODELS IIIA, XA, XV DELUXE
Same as standard Model IIIA, XA and XV except engraved w/blued or chrome finish and simulated pearl grips. Disc. 1984.
Chrome-engraved finish. . . . . NiB $319 Ex $255 Gd $173
Blue-engraved finish . . . . NiB $287 Ex $229 Gd $156

MODEL VIII
AUTOMATIC PISTOL . . . . NiB $362 Ex $245 Gd $183
Caliber: .38 Super. Nine-shot magazine, 5-inch bbl., 8.5 inches overall. Weight: 40 oz. Fixed sights. Blued finish. Wood grips. Intro. in 1952. Disc.

MODELS VIII, IXA, XI DELUXE
Same as standard Models VIII, IXA and XI except finish (chrome engraved or blued engraved) and simulated pearl grips. Disc. 1984.
Chrome-engraved finish. . . . . NiB $414 Ex $331 Gd $225
Blue-engraved finish . . . . NiB $447 Ex $357 Gd $243

MODEL IXA AUTOMATIC PISTOL . . . . NiB $306 Ex $229 Gd $143
Same as model VIII except .45 Auto, 7-shot magazine,

MODEL XA AUTOMATIC PISTOL. . . . . NiB $214 Ex $184 Gd $103
Same as model IIIA except .32 Auto, 8-shot magazine,

MODEL XI AUTOMATIC PISTOL . . . . . NiB $312 Ex $250 Gd $170
Same as model VIII except 9mm Para.

MODEL XV AUTOMATIC PISTOL. . . . . NiB $255 Ex $204 Gd $127
Same as model XA except .22 LR.

MODELS BE-IIIA, BE-XA, BE-XV . . . . . . NiB $347 Ex $275 Gd $184
Same as models IIIA, XA and XV except w/blued-engraved finish. Made 1977-84.

MODELS BE-VIII,
BE-IXA, BE-XI DELUXE . . . . NiB $408 Ex $326 Gd $222
Same as models VIII, IXA and XI except w/blued-engraved finish. Made 1977-84.

MODELS C-IIIA, C-XA, C-XV . . . . . NiB $393 Ex $306 Gd $199
Same as models IIIA, XA and XV except in satin chrome.

MODELS C-VIII, C-IXA, C-XI . . . . . NiB $393 Ex $306 Gd $199
Same as models VIII, IXA and XI except in satin chrome.

MODELS CE-IIIA,
CE-XA, CE-XV . . . . NiB $433 Ex $367 Gd $245
Same as models IIIA, XA and XV except w/chrome engraved finish. Made 1977-84.

MODELS CE-VIII,
CE-IXA, CE-XI . . . . NiB $403 Ex $306 Gd $240
Same as models VIII, IXA and XI, w/except chrome engraved finish. Made 1977-84.

COMPACT FRAME
AUTO PISTOL . . . . NiB $408 Ex $311 Gd $204
Calibers: 9mm Para., .38 Super, .45 Auto. Seven-, 8- or 9-shot magazine, 5-inch bbl., 7.88 inches overall. Weight: 34 oz. Blued, satin-chrome or Duo-Tone finishes. Made 1990 to date. Duo-Tone disc. 1993.

DUO-TONE LARGE
FRAME AUTO PISTOL . . . . NiB $382 Ex $316 Gd $209
Caliber: .45 ACP. Seven-shot magazine, 5-inch bbl., 8.5 inches overall. Weight: 36 oz. Adj. rear sight. Blued finished w/satin chrome. Polymer black grips. Made 1990-93.

Llama Model XA First Issue

Llama Model C-XI

Llama Model CE-IIIA

Llama Model Compact

**Llama Duo-Tone
Large Frame**

**Llama M-82
DA Auto**

Llama MINI-MAX II

Llama MAX-I

DUO-TONE SMALL
FRAME AUTO PISTOL . . . . **NiB $347 Ex $255 Gd $163**
Calibers: .22 LR, .32 and .380 Auto. Seven- or 8-shot magazine, 3.69 inch bbl., 6.5 inches overall. Weight: 23 oz. Square-notch rear sight, Partridge-type front. Blued finish w/chrome. Made 1990-93.

MODEL G-IIIA DELUXE . . . . **NiB $1084 Ex $867 Gd $590**
Same as Model IIIA except gold damascened w/simulated pearl grips. Disc. 1982.

LARGE-FRAME AUTOMATIC PISTOL (IXA)
Caliber: .45 Auto. Seven-shot magazine, 5-inch bbl., weight: 2 lbs., 8 oz. Adj. rear sight, Partridge-type front. Walnut grips or teakwood on satin chrome model. Later models w/polymer grips. Made from 1984 to date.
Blued finish . . . . **NiB $342 Ex $235 Gd $153**
Satin chrome finish . . . . **NiB $388 Ex $306 Gd $204**

M-82 DA AUTOMATIC PISTOL. . . . . **NiB $714 Ex $561 Gd $352**
Caliber: 9mm Para. 15-shot magazine, 4.25-inch bbl., 8 inches overall. Weight: 39 oz. Drift-adj. rear sight. Matte blued finish. Matte black polymer grips. Made from 1988-93.

M-87 COMPETITION PISTOL . . . . **NiB $1061 Ex $848 Gd $576**
Caliber: 9mm Para. 15-shot magazine, 5.5-inch bbl., 9.5 inches overall. Weight: 40 oz. Low-profile combat sights. Satin nickel finish. Matte black grip panels. Built-in ported compensator to minimize recoil and muzzle rise. Made 1989-93.

MICRO-MAX SA AUTOMATIC PISTOL
Caliber: .380 ACP. Seven-shot magazine, 3.125-inch bbl., weight: 23 oz. Blade front sight, drift adjustable rear w/3-dot system. Matte blue or satin chrome finish. Checkered polymer grips. Imported 1997 to date.
Matte blue finish . . . . **NiB $265 Ex $214 Gd $149**
Satin chrome finish . . . . **NiB $301 Ex $240 Gd $169**

MINI-MAX SA AUTOMATIC PISTOL
Calibers: 9mm, .40 S&W or .45 ACP. Six- or 8-shot magazine, 3.5-inch bbl., 8.3 inches overall. Weight: 35 oz. Blade front sight, drift adjustable rear w/3-dot system. Matte blue, Duo-Tone or satin chrome finish. Checkered polymer grips. Imported 1996 to date.
Duo-Tone finish. . . . . **NiB $306 Ex $255 Gd $163**
Matte blue finish . . . . **NiB $269 Ex $229 Gd $143**
Satin chrome finish . . . . **NiB $331 Ex $255 Gd $173**
Stainless (disc.) . . . . **NiB $351 Ex $280 Gd $194**

MINI-MAX II SA AUTOMATIC PISTOL
Cal: .45 ACP only. 10-shot mag., 3.625 inch bbl., 7.375 inch overall. Wt: 37 oz. Blade front sight, drift adj. rear w/3-dot system. Shortened barrel and grip. Matte and Satin Chrome finish. Imp. 1998.
Matte blue finish . . . . **NiB $420 Ex $337 Gd $229**
Satin chrome finish . . . . **NiB $455 Ex $362 Gd $250**

MAX-I SA AUTOMATIC PISTOL
Calibers: 9mm or .45 ACP. 7- or 9-shot magazine, 4.25- to 5.125 inch bbl., weight: 34 or 36 oz. Blade front sight, drift adj. rear w/3-dot system. Matte blue, Duo-Tone or satin chrome finish. Checkered black rubber grips. Imported 1995 to date.
Duo-Tone finish. . . . . **NiB $265 Ex $214 Gd $138**
Matte blue finish . . . . **NiB $265 Ex $214 Gd $133**
Satin chrome finish . . . . **NiB $301 Ex $235 Gd $143**

MAX-II SA AUTOMATIC PISTOL
Same as the MAX-I with 4.25 bbl. except w/10-shot mag. Weight: 39 oz. Matte blue or satin chrome finish. Imp. 1996 to date.
Matte blue finish . . . . **NiB $255 Ex $204 Gd $140**
Satin Chrome finish. . . . . **NiB $291 Ex $235 Gd $148**

OMNI 45
DOUBLE-ACTION
AUTOMATIC PISTOL . . . . **NiB $408 Ex $326 Gd $214**
Caliber: .45 Auto. Seven-shot magazine, 4.25-inch bbl., 7.75 inches overall. Weight: 40 oz. Adj. rear sight, ramp front. Highly polished deep blued finish. Made 1984-86.

OMNI 9MM
DOUBLE-ACTION
AUTOMATIC . . . . **NiB $447 Ex $357 Gd $243**
Same general specifications as .45 Omni except chambered for 9mm w/13-shot magazine. Made 1983-86.

SINGLE-ACTION
AUTOMATIC PISTOL . . . . **NiB $418 Ex $326 Gd $212**
Calibers: .38 Super, 9mm, .45 Auto. Nine-shot magazine (7-shot for .45 Auto), 5-inch bbl., 8.5 inches overall. Weight: 2 lbs., 8 oz. Intro. in 1981.

SMALL-FRAME
AUTOMATIC PISTOL
Calibers: .380 Auto (7-shot magazine), .22 RF (8 shot magazine), 3.69-inch bbl., weight: 23 oz. Partridge-blade front sight, adj. rear. Blued or satin-chrome finish.
Blued finish . . . . **NiB $331 Ex $255 Gd $163**
Satin-chrome finish . . . . **NiB $393 Ex $306 Gd $204**

REVOLVERS

MARTIAL DOUBLE-
ACTION REVOLVER . . . . **NiB $250 Ex $204 Gd $133**
Calibers: .22 LR, .38 Special. Six-shot cylinder, bbl. lengths: 4-inch (.38 Special only) or 6-inch; 11.25 inches overall (w/6-inch bbl.). Weight: About 36 oz. w/6-inch bbl. Target sights. Blued finish. Checkered walnut grips. Made 1969-76.

MARTIAL
DOUBLE-ACTION DELUXE
Same as standard Martial except w/satin chrome, chrome-engraved, blued engraved or gold damascened finish. Simulated pearl grips. Made 1969-78.
Satin-chrome finish . . . . **NiB $311 Ex $255 Gd $153**
Chrome-engraved finish. . . . . **NiB $367 Ex $296 Gd $194**
Blue-engraved finish . . . . **NiB $357 Ex $286 Gd $194**
Gold-damascened finish . . . . **NiB $1525 Ex $1236 Gd $918**

COMANCHE I
DOUBLE-ACTION
REVOLVER. . . . . **NiB $265 Ex $214 Gd $153**
Same general specifications as Martial .22. Made 1977-83.

COMANCHE II . . . . **NiB $250 Ex $204 Gd $133**
Same general specifications as Martial .38. Made 1977-83.

COMANCHE III
DOUBLE-ACTION
REVOLVER. . . . . **NiB $265 Ex $214 Gd $138**
Caliber: .357 Magnum. Six-shot cylinder, 4-inch bbl., 9.25 inches overall. Weight: 36 oz. Adj. rear sight, ramp front. Blued finish. Checkered walnut grips. Made from 1975-95. Note: Prior to 1977, this model was designated "Comanche."

COMANCHE III
CHROME. . . . . **NiB $345 Ex $260 Gd $180**
Same gen. specifications as Comanche III except has satin chrome finish, 4- or 6-inch bbl. Made 1979-92.

Llama
Comanche I

Llama
Comanche III Chrome

Llama
Martial Double-Action Revolver

Llama
Martial Deluxe Gold-Damascened

Llama
Super Comanche IV

**Luger 1900
American Eagle**

SUPER COMANCHE IV DA REVOLVER . . . NiB $347 Ex $280 Gd $189
Caliber: .44 Magnum. Six-shot cylinder, 6-inch bbl., 11.75 inches overall. Weight: 50 oz. Adj. rear sight, ramp front. Polished deep blued finish. Checkered walnut grips. Made from 1980-93.

SUPER COMANCHE V DA REVOLVER . . . . NiB $331 Ex $260 Gd $181
Caliber: .357 Mag. Six-shot cylinder, 4-, 6- or 8.5-inch bbl., weight: 48 ozs. Ramped front blade sight, click-adj. Rear. Made from 1980-89.

LORCIN Engineering Co., Inc. — Mira Loma, California

MODEL L-22 SEMIAUTOMATIC PISTOL . . . . . NiB $76 Ex $61 Gd $42
Caliber: 22 LR. Nine-shot magazine, 2.5-inch bbl., 5.25 inches overall. Weight: 16 oz. Blade front sight, fixed notch rear w/3-dot system. Black Teflon or chrome finish. Black, pink or pearl composition grips. Made 1990 to date.

MODEL L-25, LT-.25 SEMIAUTOMATIC PISTOL
Caliber: 25 ACP. Seven-shot magazine, 2.4-inch bbl., 4.8 inches overall. Weight: 12 oz. (LT-25) or 14.5 oz. (L-25). Blade front sight, fixed rear. Black Teflon or chrome finish. Black, pink or pearl composition grips. Made 1989 to date.
Model L-25 . . . . NiB $64 Ex $51 Gd $35
Model LT-25. . . . . NiB $76 Ex $61 Gd $42
Model Lady Lorcin. . . . . NiB $83 Ex $66 Gd $45

MODEL L-32 SEMIAUTOMATIC PISTOL . . . . . NiB $83 Ex $66 Gd $45
Caliber: 32 ACP. Seven-shot magazine, 3.5-inch bbl., 6.6 inches overall. Weight: 27 oz. Blade front sight, fixed notch rear. Black Teflon or chrome finish. Black composition grips. Made 1992 to date.

MODEL L-380 SEMIAUTOMATIC PISTOL
Caliber: .380 ACP. Seven- or 10-shot magazine, 3.5-inch bbl., 6.6 inches overall. Weight: 23 oz. Blade front sight, fixed notch rear. Matte Black finish. Grooved black composition grips. Made 1994 to date.
Model L9MM (7-shot) . . . . NiB $90 Ex $71 Gd $49
Model L9MM (10-shot) . . . . NiB $121 Ex $97 Gd $66

MODEL L9MM SEMIAUTOMATIC PISTOL
Caliber: 9mm Parabellum. 10- or 13-shot magazine, 4.5-inch bbl., 7.5 inches overall. Weight: 31 oz. Blade front sight, fixed notch rear w/3-dot system. Black Teflon or chrome finish. Black composition grips. Made 1992 to date.
Model L-380 (10-shot) . . . . NiB $133 Ex $107 Gd $71
Model L-380 (13-shot) . . . . NiB $163 Ex $133 Gd $82

O/U DERRINGER . . . . NiB $96 Ex $76 Gd $52
Caliber: .38 Special/.357 Mag., .45LC. Two-shot derringer. 3.5-inch bbls.

(cont'd) O/U DERRINGER
6.5 inches overall. Weight: 12 oz. Blade front sight, fixed notch rear. Stainless finish. Black composition grips. Made 1996 to date.

LUGER PISTOLS

Mfd. by Deutsche Waffen und Munitionsfabriken (DWM), Berlin, Germany. Previously by Koniglich Gewehrfabrik Erfurt, Heinrich Krieghoff Waffenfabrik, Mauser-Werke, Simson & Co., Vickers Ltd., Waffenfabrik, Bern.

1900 AMERICAN EAGLE . . . . . . NiB $3068 Ex $1716 Gd $884
Caliber: 7.65 mm. Eight-shot magazine; thin, 4.75-inch; tapered bbl.; 9.5 inches overall. Weight: 32 oz. Fixed rear sight, dovetailed front sight. Grip safety. Checkered walnut grips. Early-style toggle, narrow trigger, wide guard, no stock lug. American Eagle over chamber. Estimated 8000 production.

1900 COMMERCIAL . . . . NiB $3120 Ex $2600 Gd $1378
Same specifications as Luger 1900 American Eagle except DWM on early-style toggle, no chamber markings. Estimated 8000 production.

1900 SWISS . . . . NiB $3900 Ex $3120 Gd $1404
Same specifications as Luger 1900 American Eagle except Swiss cross in sunburst over chamber. Estimated 9000 production.

1902 AMERICAN EAGLE . . . . . . NiB $8840 Ex $6760 Gd $3640
Caliber: 9mm Para. Eight-shot magazine, 4-inch heavy tapered bbl., 8.75 inches overall. Weight: 30 oz. Fixed rear sight, dovetailed front sight. Grip safety. Checkered walnut grips. American Eagle over chamber, DWM on early-style toggle, narrow trigger, wide guard, no stock lug. Estimated 700 production.

1902 CARBINE . . . . NiB $12,350 Ex $9880 Gd $6718
Caliber: 7.65mm. Eight-shot magazine, 11.75-inch tapered bbl., 16.5 inches overall. Weight: 46 oz. Adj. 4-position rear sight, long ramp front sight. Grip safety. Checkered walnut grips and forearm. DWM on early-style toggle, narrow trigger, wide guard, no chamber markings, stock lug. Estimated 3200 production.
Model 1902 carbine (gun only). . . . . NiB $7864 Ex $6292 Gd $4279
Model 1902 carbine
(gun only, American Eagle) . . . . NiB $11,043 Ex $8835 Gd $6007
W/issued stock and matching numbers, add $4550
W/original stock and non-matching numbers, add $2550

1902 CARTRIDGE COUNTER . . . . . . NiB $27,040 Ex $17,160 Gd $8996
Caliber: 9mm Para. Eight-shot magazine, Heavy, tapered 4-inch bbl., 8.75 inches overall. Weight: 30 oz. Fixed rear sight, dovetailed front sight. Grip safety. Checkered walnut grips. DWM on dished toggle w/lock, American Eagle over chamber when marked. No stock lug. Estimated production unknown.

1902 COMMERCIAL . . . . NiB $8320 Ex $6760 Gd $3484
Same basic specifications as Luger 1902 Cartridge Counter except DWM on early-style toggle, narrow trigger, wide guard, no chamber markings, no stock lug. Estimated 400 production.

1902 AMERICAN EAGLE . . . . . . NiB $8840 Ex $6760 Gd $3640
Same basic specifications as Luger 1902 Commercial except American Eagle over chamber, DWM on early-style toggle, narrow trigger, wide guard, no stock lug. Estimated 700 production.

**1902 AMERICAN EAGLE
CARTRIDGE COUNTER** . . . . NiB $26,936 Ex $17,160 Gd $9048
Same basic specifications as Luger 1902 Cartridge Counter except American Eagle over chamber, DWM on early-style toggle, narrow trigger, wide guard, no stock lug. Estimated 700 production.

1904 GL "BABY" . . . . **Nib $195,000 Ex $156,000 Gd $106,080**
Caliber: 9mm Para. Seven-shot magazine, 3.25-inch bbl., 7.75 inches overall. Weight: Approx. 20 oz. Serial number 10077B. "GL" marked on rear of toggle. Georg Luger's personal sidearm. Only one made in 1904.

1904 NAVAL (REWORKED) . . . . . . **Nib $12,676 Ex $10,140 Gd $6895**
Caliber: 9mm Para. Eight-shot magazine, bbl., length altered to 4 inches., 8.75 inches overall. Weight: 30 oz. Adj. two-position rear sight, dovetailed front sight. Thumb lever safety. Checkered walnut grips. Heavy tapered bbl., DWM on new-style toggle w/lock, 1902 over chamber. W/or without grip safety and stock lug. Estimated 800 production.

1906 (11.35) . . . . **Nib $117,000 Ex $93,600 Gd $63,648**
Caliber: .45 ACP. Six-shot magazine, 5-inch bbl., 9.75 inches overall. Weight: 36 oz. Fixed rear sight, dovetailed front sight. Grip safety. Checkered walnut grips. GL monogram on rear toggle link, larger frame w/altered trigger guard and trigger, no proofs, no markings over chamber. No stock lug. Estimated production is 2. Note: This version of the Luger pistol is the most valuable next to the "GL" Baby Luger.

1906 AMERICAN EAGLE
(7.65) . . . . **Nib $2912 Ex $2080 Gd $988**
Caliber: 7.65mm. Eight-shot magazine, thin 4.75-inch tapered bbl., 9.5 inches overall. Weight: 32 oz. Fixed rear sight, dovetailed front sight. Grip safety. Checkered walnut grips. DWM on new-style toggle, American Eagle over chamber. No stock lug. Estimated 8000 production.

1906 AMERICAN EAGLE (9MM) . . . . . . **Nib $2787 Ex $2236 Gd $1248**
Same basic specifications as the 7.65mm 1906 except in 9mm Para. w/4-inch barrel, 8.75 inches overall, weight: 30 ounces. Estimated 3500 production.

1906 BERN (7.65MM) . . . . **Nib $2496 Ex $2184 Gd $1362**
Same basic specifications as the 7.65mm 1906 American Eagle except checkered walnut grips w/.38-inch borders, Swiss Cross on new-style toggle, Swiss proofs, no markings over chamber, no stock lug. Estimated 17,874 production.

1906 BRAZILIAN (7.65MM) . . . . **Nib $2600 Ex $1872 Gd $728**
Same general specifications as the 7.65mm 1906 American Eagle except w/Brazilian proofs, no markings over chamber, no stock lug. Estimated 4500 produced.

1906 BRAZILIAN (9MM) . . . . . . **Nib $2536 Ex $2028 Gd $1379**
Same basic specifications as the 9mm 1906 American Eagle except w/Brazilian proofs, no markings over chamber, no stock lug. Production unknown, but less than 4000 is estimated by collectors.

1906 COMMERCIAL
Calibers: 7.65mm, 9mm. Same specifications as the 1906 American Eagle versions (above) except no chamber markings and no stock lug. Estimated production: 6000 (7.65mm) and 3500 (9mm).
7.65mm . . . . **Nib $2912 Ex $1924 Gd $1248**
9mm . . . . **Nib $2912 Ex $1924 Gd $1248**

1906 DUTCH . . . . **Nib $1886 Ex $1508 Gd $1025**
Caliber: 9mm Para. Same specifications as the 9mm 1906 American Eagle except tapered bbl., w/proofs, no markings over chamber, no stock lug. Estimated 3000 production.

1906 LOEWE AND COMPANY . . . . . . **Nib $4616 Ex $3692 Gd $2511**
Caliber: 7.65mm. Eight-shot magazine, 6-inch tapered bbl., 10.75 inches overall. Weight: 35 oz. Adj. two-position rear sight, dovetailed front sight. Grip safety. Checkered walnut grips. Loewe & Company over chamber, Naval proofs, DWM on new-style toggle, no stock lug. Estimated production unknown.

1906 NAVAL
Caliber: 9mm Para. Eight-shot magazine, 6-inch tapered bbl., 10.75 inches overall. Weight: 35 oz. Adj. two-position rear sight, dovetailed front sight. Grip safety and thumb safety w/lower marking (1st issue), higher marking (2nd issue). Checkered walnut grips. No chamber markings, DWM on new-style toggle w/o lock, but w/stock lug. Est. production: 9000 (1st issue); 2,000 (2nd issue).
First issue . . . . **Nib $3800 Ex $3000 Gd $1200**
Second issue . . . . **Nib $4000 Ex $3400 Gd $1200**

1906 NAVAL COMMERCIAL . . . . **Nib $3800 Ex $3000 Gd $1200**
Same as the 1906 Naval except lower marking on thumb safety, no chamber markings. DWM on new-style toggle, w/stock lug and commercial proofs. Estimated 3000 production.

1906 PORTUGUESE
ARMY . . . . **Nib $1800 Ex $1400 Gd $500**
Same specifications as the 7.65mm 1906 American Eagle except w/Portuguese proofs, crown and crest over chamber. No stock lug. Estimated 3500 production.

1906 PORTUGUESE NAVAL . . . . **Nib $9500 Ex $6000 Gd $2000**
Same as the 9mm 1906 American Eagle except w/Portuguese proofs, crown and anchor over chamber, no stock lug.

1906 RUSSIAN . . . . **Nib $15,000 Ex $9950 Gd $5500**
Same general specifications as the 9mm 1906 American Eagle except thumb safety has markings concealed in up position, DWM on new-style toggle, DWM bbl., proofs, crossed rifles over chamber. Estimated production unknown.

1906 SWISS . . . . **Nib $2400 Ex $1750 Gd $1200**
Same general specifications as the 7.65mm 1906 American Eagle Luger except Swiss Cross in sunburst over chamber, no stock lug. Estimated 10,300 production.

1906 SWISS (REWORK) . . . . **Nib $2400 Ex $1750 Gd $1200**
Same basic specifications as the 7.65mm 1906 Swiss except in bbl. lengths of 3.63, 4 and 4.75 inches, overall length 8.38 inches (with 4-inch bbl.). Weight 32 oz. (with 4-inch bbl.). DWM on new-style toggle, bbl., w/serial number and proof marks, Swiss Cross in sunburst or shield over chamber, no stock lug. Estimated production unknown.

1906 SWISS POLICE . . . . **Nib $2400 Ex $1750 Gd $1200**
Same general specifications as the 7.65mm 1906 Swiss except DWM on new-style toggle, Swiss Cross in matted field over chamber, no stock lug. Estimated 10,300 production.

1908 BULGARIAN . . . . **Nib $2500 Ex $1800 Gd $750**
Caliber: 9mm Para. Eight-shot magazine, 4-inch tapered bbl., 8.75 inches overall. Weight: 30 oz. Fixed rear sight dovetailed front sight. Thumb safety w/lower marking concealed. Checkered walnut grips. DWM chamber marking, no proofs, crown over shield on new-style toggle lanyard loop, no stock lug. Estimated production unknown.

1908 COMMERCIAL . . . . **Nib $1200 Ex $800 Gd $500**
Same basic specifications as the 1908 Bulgarian except higher marking on thumb safety. No chamber markings, commercial proofs, DWM on new-style toggle, no stock lug. Estimated 4000 production.

1908 ERFURT MILITARY . . . . **Nib $1219 Ex $995 Gd $709**
Caliber: 9mm Para. Eight-shot magazine, 4-inch tapered bbl., 8.75 inches overall. Weight: 30 oz. Fixed rear sight dovetailed front sight. Thumb safety w/higher marking concealed. Checkered walnut grips. Serial number and proof marks on barrel, crown and Erfurt on new-style toggle, dated chamber, but no stock lug. Estimated production unknown.

Luger 1923 Stoeger

1908 MILITARY

Same general specifications as the 9mm 1908 Erfurt Military Luger except first and second issue have thumb safety w/higher marking concealed, serial number on bbl., no chamber markings, proofs on frame, DWM on new-style toggle but no stock lug. Estimated production: 10,000 (first issue) and 5000 (second issue). Third issue has serial number and proof marks on barrel, dates over chamber, DWM on new-style toggle but no stock lug. Estimated 3000 production.

First issue. . . . . **Nib $1248 Ex $832 Gd $520**
Second issue . . . . **Nib $1248 Ex $780 Gd $416**
Third issue . . . . **Nib $1560 Ex $988 Gd $624**

1908 NAVAL . . . . Nib $4096 Ex $3276 Gd $2228

Same basic specifications as the 9mm 1908 military Lugers except w/6-inch bbl, adj. two-position rear sight, no chamber markings, DWM on new-style toggle, w/stock lug. Estimated 26,000 production.

1908 NAVAL
(COMMERCIAL) . . . . Nib $4680 Ex $3120 Gd $1560

Same specifications as the 1908 Naval Luger except no chamber markings or date. Commercial proofs, DWM on new-style toggle, w/stock lug. Estimated 1900 produced.

1914 ERFURT ARTILLERY . . . . . . Nib $2600 Ex $1820 Gd $858

Caliber: 9mm Para. Eight-shot magazine, 8-inch tapered bbl., 12.75 inches overall. Weight: 40 oz. Artillery rear sight, Dovetailed front sight. Thumb safety w/higher marking concealed. Checkered walnut grips. Serial number and proof marks on barrel, crown and Erfurt on new-style toggle, dated chamber, w/stock lug. Estimated production unknown.

1914 ERFURT MILITARY . . . . Nib $1248 Ex $832 Gd $520

Same specifications as the 1914 Erfurt Artillery except w/4-inch bbl., and corresponding length, weight, etc.; fixed rear sight. Estimated 3000 production.

1914 NAVAL . . . . Nib $3380 Ex $2340 Gd $1040

Same specifications as 9mm 1914 Lugers except has 6-inch bbl. w/corresponding length and weight, adj. two-position rear sight. Dated chamber, DWM on new-style toggle, w/stock lug. Estimated 40,000 produced.

1914-1918 DWM ARTILLERY . . . . . . Nib $2288 Ex $1872 Gd $910

Caliber: 9mm Para. Eight-shot magazine, 8-inch tapered bbl., 12.75 inches overall. Weight: 40 oz. Artillery rear sight, dovetailed front sight. Thumb safety w/higher marking concealed. Checkered walnut grips. Serial number and proof marks on barrel, DWM on new-style toggle, dated chamber, w/stock lug. Estimated 3000 production.

1914-1918 DWM MILITARY . . . . . Nib $1144 Ex $832 Gd $520

Same specifications as the 9mm 1914-1918 DWM Artillery except w/4-inch tapered bbl., and corresponding length, weight, etc., and fixed rear sight. Production unknown.

1920 CARBINE

Caliber: 7.65mm. Eight-shot magazine, 11.75-inch tapered bbl., 15.75 inches overall. Weight: 44 oz. Four-position rear sight, long ramp front sight. Grip (or thumb) safety. Checkered walnut grips and forearm. Serial numbers and proof marks on barrel, no chamber markings, various proofs, DWM on new-style toggle, w/stock lug. Estimated production unknown.

Model 1920 Carbine
(gun only) . . . . **Nib $5616 Ex $4888 Gd $2600**
Model 1920 Carbine
(W/shoulder stock), add **$2500**

1920 NAVY CARBINE . . . . Nib $3706 Ex $2964 Gd $2016

Caliber: 7.65mm. Eight-shot magazine, 11.75-inch tapered bbl., 15.75 inches overall. Two-position sliding rear sight. Naval military proofs and no forearm. Production unknown.

1920 COMMERCIAL . . . . Nib $858 Ex $650 Gd $364

Calibers: 7.65mm, 9mm Para. Eight-shot magazine, 3.63-, 3.75-, 4-, 4.75-, 6-, 8-, 10-, 12-, 16-, 18- or 20-inch tapered bbl., overall length: 8.375 to 24.75 inches. Weight: 30 oz. (with 3.63-inch bbl.). Varying rear sight configurations, dovetailed front sight. Thumb safety. Checkered walnut grips. Serial numbers and proof marks on barrel, no chamber markings, various proofs, DWM or crown over Erfurt on new-style toggle, w/stock lug. Production not documented.

1920 DWM OR ERFURT MILITARY . . . . . . Nib $936 Ex $728 Gd $494

Caliber: 9mm Para. Eight-shot magazine, 4-inch tapered barrel, 8.75 inches overall. Weight: 30 oz. Fixed rear sight dovetailed front sight. Thumb safety. Checkered walnut grips. Serial numbers and proof marks on barrel, dated chamber, various proofs, DWM or crown over Erfurt on new-style toggle, w/stock lug. Esimated 3000 production.

1920 POLICE. . . . . Nib $1227 Ex $952 Gd $645

Same specifications as 9mm 1920 DWM w/some dated chambers, various proofs, DWM or crown over Erfurt on new-style toggle, identifying marks on grip frame, w/stock lug. Estimated 3000 production.

1923 COMMERICAL . . . . Nib $858 Ex $546 Gd $296

Calibers: 7.65mm and 9mm Para. Eight-shot magazine, 3.63-, 3.75-, 4-, 6-, 8-, 12- or 16-inch tapered bbl., overall length: 8.38 inches (with 3.63-inch bbl.). Weight: 30 oz. (with 3.63-inch bbl.). Various rear sight configurations, dovetailed front sight. Thumb lever safety. Checkered walnut grips. DWM on new-style toggle, serial number and proofs on barrel, no chamber markings, w/stock lug. Estimated 15,000 production.

1923 DUTCH COMMERICAL . . . . Nib $1664 Ex $1456 Gd $624

Same basic specifications as 1923 Commercial Luger w/same caliber offerings, but only 3.63- or 4-inch bbl. Fixed rear sight, thumb lever safety w/arrow markings. Production unknown.

1923 KRIEGHOFF COMMERCIAL . . . . . Nib $1716 Ex $1352 Gd $801

Same specifications as 1923 Commercial Luger, w/same caliber offerings but bbl., lengths of 3.63, 4, 6, and 8 inches. "K" marked on new-style toggle. Serial number, proofs and Germany on barrel. No chamber markings, but w/ stock lug. Production unknown.

1923 SAFE AND LOADED . . . . . . Nib $1508 Ex $1040 Gd $520

Same caliber offerings, bbl., lengths and specifications as the 1923 Commercial except thumb lever safety, safe markings, w/stock lug. Estimated 10,000 production.

1923 STOEGER

Same general specifications as the 1923 Commercial Luger with the same caliber offerings and bbl., lengths of 3.75, 4, 6, 8 and up to 24 inches. Thumb lever safety. DWM on new-style toggle, serial number and/or proof marks on barrel. American Eagle over chamber but no stock lug. Estimated production less than 1000 (also see Stoeger listings). Note: Qualified appraisals should be obtained on all Stoeger Lugers with bbl. lengths over 8 inches to ensure accurate values.

3.75-, 4-, or 6-inch bbl. . . . . **Nib $2854 Ex $2283 Gd $1553**
8-inch bbl. . . . . **Nib $3836 Ex $3068 Gd $2086**

1926 "BABY" PROTOTYPE . . **Nib $110,500 Ex $88,400 Gd $60,112**
Calibers: 7.65mm Browning and 9mm Browning (short). Five-shot magazine, 2.31-inch bbl., about 6.25 inches overall. Small-sized-frame and toggle assembly. Prototype for a Luger "pocket pistol," but never manufactured commercially. Checkered walnut grips, slotted for safety. Only four known to exist, but as many as a dozen could have been made.

1929 SWISS . . . . **Nib $1820 Ex $1144 Gd $650**
Caliber: 7.65mm. Eight-shot magazine, 4.75-inch tapered bbl., 9.5 inches overall. Weight: 32 oz. Fixed rear sight, dovetailed front sight. Long grip safety and thumb lever w/S markings. Stepped receiver and straight grip frame. Checkered plastic grips. Swiss Cross in shield on new-style toggle. Serial numbers and proofs on barrel, no markings over chamber and no stock lug. Estimated 1900 produuction.

1934 KRIEGHOFF
COMMERCIAL (SIDE FRAME) . . . . **Nib $2860 Ex $2184 Gd $832**
Caliber: 7.65mm or 9mm Para. Eight-shot magazine, bbl. lengths: 4, 6, and 8 inches, overall length: 8.75 (with 4-inch bbl.). Weight: 30 oz. (with 4-inch bbl.). Various rear sight configurations w/dovetailed front sight. Thumb lever safety. Checkered brown plastic grips. Anchor w/H K Krieghoff Suhl on new-style toggle, but no chamber markings. Tapered bbl., w/serial number and proofs; w/stock lug. Estimated 1700 production.

1934 KRIEGHOFF S
Caliber: 9mm Para. Eight-shot magazine, 4-inch tapered bbl., 8.75 inches overall. Weight: 30 oz. Fixed rear sight, dovetailed front sight. Thumb lever safety. Anchor w/H K Krieghoff Suhl on new-style toggle, S dated chamber, bbl., proofs and stock lug. Early model: Checkered walnut or plastic grips. Estimated 2500 production. Late model: Checkered brown plastic grips. Est. 1200 production.
Early model . . . . **Nib $3504 Ex $2803 Gd $1906**
Late model . . . . **Nib $2536 Ex $2028 Gd $1379**

1934 BYF . . . . **Nib $1248 Ex $936 Gd $520**
Caliber: 9mm Para. Eight-shot magazine, 4-inch tapered bbl., 8.75 inches overall. Weight: 30 oz. Fixed rear sight, dovetailed front sight. Thumb lever safety. Checkered walnut or plastic grips. byf on new-style toggle, serial number and proofs on bbl., 41-42 dated chamber and w/stock lug. Estimated 3000 productlon.

1934 MAUSER S/42 K . . . . **Nib $4680 Ex $3952 Gd $1560**
Caliber: 9mm Para. Eight-shot magazine, 4-inch tapered bbl., 8.75 inches overall. Weight: 30 oz. Fixed rear sight dovetailed front sight. Thumb lever safety. Checkered walnut or plastic grips. 42 on new-style toggle, serial number and proofs on barrel, 1939-.40 dated chamber markings and w/stock lug. Estimated 10,000 production.

1934 MAUSER S/42 (DATED) . . . . . **Nib $1040 Ex $806 Gd $416**
Same specifications as Luger 1934 Mauser 42 except 41 dated chamber markings and w/stock lug. Production unknown.

Luger S42

1934 MAUSER BANNER (MILITARY) . . . . . . **Nib $2704 Ex $1872 Gd $988**
Same specifications as Luger 1934 Mauser 42 except Mauser in banner on new-style toggle, tapered bbl., w/serial number and proofs usually, dated chamber markings and w/stock lug. Production unknown.

1934 MAUSER COMMERCIAL . . . . **Nib $1560 Ex $1092 Gd $624**
Same specifications as Luger 1934 Mauser 42 except checkered walnut grips. Mauser in banner on new-style toggle, tapered bbl., usually w/serial number and proofs, no chamber markings, but w/ stock lug. Production unknown.

1934 MAUSER DUTCH . . . . **Nib $2912 Ex $1768 Gd $520**
Same specifications as Luger 1934 Mauser 42 except checkered walnut grips. Mauser in banner on new-style toggle, tapered bbl., w/caliber, 1940 dated chamber markings and w/stock lug. Production unknown.

1934 MAUSER LATVIAN . . . . . . **Nib $2965 Ex $2018 Gd $1768**
Caliber: 7.65mm. Eight-shot magazine, 4-inch tapered bbl., 8.75 inches overall. Weight: 30 oz. Fixed square-notched rear sight, dovetailed Partridge front sight. Thumb lever safety. Checkered walnut stocks. Mauser in banner on new-style toggle,1937 dated chamber markings and w/stock lug. Production unknown.

1934 MAUSER (OBERNDORF) . . . . **Nib $2926 Ex $2340 Gd $1591**
Same as 1934 Mauser 42 except checkered walnut grips. Oberndorf 1934 on new-style toggle, tapered bbl., w/proofs and caliber, Mauser banner over chamber and w/stock lug (also see Mauser).

1934 SIMSON-S TOGGLE . . . . . . **Nib $1924 Ex $1352 Gd $572**
Same as 1934 Mauser 42 except checkered walnut grips, S on new-style toggle, tapered bbl., w/serial number and proofs, no chamber markings; w/stock lug. Estimated 10,000 production.

42 MAUSER BANNER (BYF) . . . . . **Nib $1248 Ex $936 Gd $520**
Same specifications as Luger 1934 Mauser 42 except weight: 32 oz. Mauser in banner on new-style toggle, w/serial number and proofs usually, dated chamber markings and w/stock lug. Estimated 3,500 production.

ABERCROMBIE AND FITCH . . . . **Nib $5980 Ex $4524 Gd $988**
Calibers: 7.65mm and 9mm Para. Eight-shot magazine, 4.75-inch tapered bbl., 9.5 inches overall. Weight: 32 oz. Fixed rear sight, dovetailed front sight. Grip safety. Checkered walnut grips. DWM on new-style toggle Abercrombie & Fitch markings on barrel, Swiss Cross in sunburst over chamber, no stock lug. Est. 100 production.

**Luna Model 200
Free Pistol**

DUTCH ROYAL AIR FORCE . . . . **Nib $2912 Ex $1768 Gd $520**
Caliber: 9mm Para. Eight-shot magazine, 4-inch tapered bbl., 8.75 inches overall. Weight: 30 oz. Fixed rear sight dovetailed front sight. Grip safety and thumb safety w/markings and arrow. Checkered walnut grips. DWM on new-style toggle, bbl., dated w/serial number and proofs, no markings over chamber, no stock lug. Estimated 4000 production.

DWM (G DATE) . . . . **Nib $1378 Ex $936 Gd $468**
Caliber: 9mm Para. Eight-shot magazine, 4-inch tapered bbl., 8.75 inches overall. Weight: 30 oz. Fixed rear sight, dovetailed front sight. Thumb lever safety. Checkered walnut grips. DWM on new-style toggle, serial number and proofs on barrel, G (1935 date) over chamber and w/stock lug. Production unknown.

DWM AND ERFURT . . . . **Nib $1164 Ex $931 Gd $633**
Caliber: 9mm Para. Eight-shot magazine, 4- or 6-inch tapered bbl., overall length: 8.75 or 10.75 inches. Weight: 30 or 38 oz. Fixed rear sight, dovetailed front sight. Thumb safety. Checkered walnut grips. Serial numbers and proof marks on barrel, double dated chamber, various proofs, DWM or crown over Erfurt on new-style toggle and w/stock lug. Production unknown.

KRIEGHOFF 36 . . . . **Nib $3114 Ex $2491 Gd $1694**
Caliber: 9mm Para. Eight-shot magazine, 4-inch tapered bbl., 8.75 inches overall. Weight: 30 oz. Fixed rear sight, dovetailed front sight. Thumb lever safety. Checkered brown plastic grips. Anchor w/H K Krieghoff Suhl on new-style toggle, 36 dated chamber, serial number and proofs on barrel and w/stock lug. Estimated 700 production.

**KRIEGHOFF-DATED
1936-1945** . . . . **Nib $3182 Ex $2600 Gd $1040**
Same specifications as Luger Krieghoff 36 except 1936-45 dated chamber, bbl. proofs. Est. 8600 production.

KRIEGHOFF (GRIP SAFETY) . . . **Nib $4738 Ex $3791 Gd $2578**
Same specifications as Luger Krieghoff 36 except grip safety and thumb lever safety. No chamber markings, tapered bbl., w/serial number, proofs and caliber, no stock lug. Production unknown.

**MAUSER BANNER
(GRIP SAFETY)** . . . . **Nib $2704 Ex $1872 Gd $988**
Caliber: 7.65mm. Eight-shot magazine, 4.75-inch tapered bbl., 9.5 inches overall. Weight: 30 oz. Fixed rear sight, dovetailed front sight. Grip safety and thumb lever safety. Checkered walnut grips. Mauser in banner on new-style toggle, serial number and proofs on barrel, 1939 dated chamber markings, but no stock lug. Production unknown.

MAUSER BANNER 42 (DATED) . . . . **Nib $1560 Ex $1092 Gd $624**
Caliber: 9mm Para. Eight-shot magazine, 4-inch tapered bbl., 8.75 inches overall. Weight: 30 oz. Fixed rear sight, dovetailed front sight. Thumb lever safety. Checkered walnut or plastic grips. Mauser in banner on new-style toggle serial number and proofs on bbl., (usually) 1942 dated chamber markings and stock lug. Production unknown.

**MAUSER BANNER
(SWISS PROOF)** . . . . **Nib $3276 Ex $2548 Gd $1300**
Same specifications as Luger Mauser Banner 42 above except checkered walnut grips and 1939 dated chamber.

MAUSER FREISE . . . . **Nib $4616 Ex $3692 Gd $2511**
Same specifications as Mauser Banner 42 except checkered walnut grips, tapered bbl. w/proofs on sight block and Freise above chamber. Production unknown.

S/42
Caliber: 9mm Para. Eight-shot magazine, 4-inch tapered barrel. 8.75 inches overall. Weight: 30 oz. Fixed rear sight, dovetailed front sight. Thumb lever safety. Checkered walnut grips. S/42 on new-style toggle, serial number and proofs on barrel and w/stock lug. Dated Model: Has dated chamber; estimated 3000 production. G Date: Has G (1935 date) over chamber; estimated 3000 production. K Date: Has K (1934 date) over chamber; prod. figures unknown.

Dated model	Nib $1040	Ex $806	Gd $416
G date model	Nib $1138	Ex $910	Gd $619
K date model	Nib $2464	Ex $1971	Gd $1341

**RUSSIAN
COMMERCIAL** . . . . **Nib $2796 Ex $2236 Gd $1520**
Caliber: 7.65mm. Eight-shot magazine, 3.63-inch tapered bbl., 8.38 inches overall. Weight: 30 oz. Fixed rear sight, dovetailed front sight. Thumb lever safety. Checkered walnut grips. DWM on new-style toggle, Russian proofs on barrel, no chamber markings but w/stock lug. Production unknown.

SIMSON AND COMPANY
Calibers: 7.65mm and 9mm Para. Eight-shot magazine, Weight: 32 oz. Fixed rear sight, dovetailed front sight. Thumb lever safety. Checkered walnut grips. Simson & Company Suhl on new-style toggle, serial number and proofs on barrel, date over chamber and w/stock lug. Estimated 10,000 production.

**Simson and
Company
(9mm w/1925 date)** . . . . **Nib $2600 Ex $2080 Gd $702**
**Simson and
Company
(undated)** . . . . **Nib $1508 Ex $832 Gd $468**
**Simson and
Company
(S code)** . . . . **Nib $1924 Ex $1352 Gd $572**

VICKERS-DUTCH . . . . **Nib $2912 Ex $2080 Gd $832**
Caliber: 9mm Para. Eight-shot magazine, 4-inch tapered bbl., 8.75 inches overall. Weight: 30 oz. Fixed rear sight, dovetailed front sight. Grip safety and thumb lever w/arrow markings. Checkered walnut grips (coarse). Vickers LTD on new-style toggle, no chamber markings, dated barrel but no stock lug. Estimated 10,000 production.

LUNA FREE PISTOL — Zella-Mehlis, Germany
Originally mfd. by Ernst Friedr. Buchel and later by Udo Anschutz

MODEL 200 FREE PISTOL . . . . **Nib $1144 Ex $1030 Gd $624**
Single-shot. System Aydt action. Set trigger. Caliber: .22 LR. Eleven-inch bbl., weight: 40 oz. Target sights. Blued finish. Checkered and carved walnut grip and forearm; improved design w/adj. hand base on later models of Udo Anschutz manufacture. Made prior to WWII.

M.A.C. (Military Armament Corp.) — Stephensville, Texas, Dist. by Defense Systems International, Marietta, Georgia. Previously by Cobray, SWD and RPB Industries

INGRAM MODEL 10 AUTO PISTOL
Select fire (NFA-Title II-Class III) SMG based on Ingram M10 blowback system using an open bolt design with or without telescoping stock. Calibers: 9mm or .45 ACP. Cyclic rate: 750 RPM (9mm) or 900 RPM (.45 ACP). 32- or 30-round magazine, 5.75-inch threaded bbl. (to accept muzzle brake) bbl. extension or suppressor, 10.5 inches overall w/o stock or 10.6 (w/telescoped stock) and 21.5 (w/extended stock). Weight: 6.25 pounds. Front protected post sight, fixed aperture rear sight. Garand-style safety in trigger guard.

9mm model . . . . Nib $884 Ex $806 Gd $572
.45 ACP model. . . . . Nib $8584 Ex $806 Gd $572
W/bbl. extension, add $195
W/suppressor, add. $495

INGRAM MODEL 10A1S SEMIAUTOMATIC
Similar to the Model 10 except (Class I) semiautomatic w/closed bolt design to implement an interchangable component system to easily convert to fire 9mm and .45 ACP.

9mm model . . . . Nib $307 Ex $286 Gd $208
.45 ACP model . . . . Nib $317 Ex $291 Gd $208
W/bbl. extension, add $150
W/fake suppressor, add $195

INGRAM MODEL 11 SEMIAUTOMATIC
Similar to the Model 10A1 except (Class I) semiautomatic chambered .380 ACP.

.380 ACP model. . . . . Nib $676 Ex $619 Gd $499
W/bbl. extension, add $150
W/fake suppressor, add $195

MAGNUM RESEARCH INC. — Minneapolis, Minnesota

BABY EAGLE SEMIAUTOMATIC . . . . Nib $432 Ex $364 Gd $218
DA. Calibers: 9mm, .40 S&W, .41 AE. 15-shot magazine (9mm), 9-shot magazine (.40 S&W), 10-shot magazine (.41 AE), 4.75-inch bbl., 8.15 inches overall. Weight: 35.4 oz. Combat sights. Matte blued finish. Imported 1991-96 and 1999 to date.

DESERT EAGLE MK VII SEMIAUTOMATIC
Gas-operated. Calibers: .357 Mag., .41 Mag., .44 Mag., .50 Action Express (AE). Eight- or 9-shot magazine, 6-inch w/standard bbl., or 10- and 14-inch w/polygonal bbl., 10.6 inches overall (with 6-inch bbl.). Weight: 52 oz. (w/alum. alloy frame) to 67 oz. (w/steel frame). Fixed or adj. combat sights. Combat-type trigger guard. finish: Military black oxide, nickel, chrome, stainless or blued. Wraparound rubber grips. Made by Israel Military Industries 1984-95.

.357 standard (steel) or alloy (6-inch bbl.) . . . Nib $884 Ex $676 Gd $411
.357 stainless steel (6-inch bbl.) . . . . . Nib $942 Ex $754 Gd $513
.41 Mag. standard (steel) or alloy
6-inch bbl.) . . . . Nib $878 Ex $702 Gd $477
.41 Mag. stainless steel (6-inch bbl.). . . Nib $846 Ex $676 Gd $460
.44 Mag. standard (steel) or alloy
(6-inch bbl.) . . . . Nib $826 Ex $660 Gd $449
.44 Mag. stainless steel (6-inch bbl.). . . Nib $904 Ex $723 Gd $492
.50 AE Magnum standard . . . . Nib $976 Ex $780 Gd $530
Add for 10-inch bbl. . . . . Nib $125 Ex $100 Gd $68
Add for 14-inch bbl. . . . . Nib $156 Ex $125 Gd $85

Magnum Research Model Desert Eagle Mark XIX (Shown w/Optional Leupold Scope

Magnum Research Model One Pro .45

MODEL DESERT EAGLE MARK XIX SEMI-AUTOMATIC PISTOL
Interchangeable component system based on .50-caliber frame. Calibers: .357 Mag., .44 Mag., .50 AE. Nine-, 8-, 7-shot magazine, 6- or 10-inch bbl. w/dovetail design and cross slots to accept scope rings. Weight: 70.5 oz. (6-inch bbl.) or 79 oz. 10.75 or 14.75 inches overall. Sights: Post front and adjustable rear. Blue, chrome or nickel finish; available brushed, matte or polished. Hogue soft rubber grips. Made 1995 to date.

.357 Mag. (W/6-inch bbl.). . . . . Nib $1066 Ex $910 Gd $416
.44 Mag. (W/6-inch bbl.) . . . . Nib $994 Ex $796 Gd $541
.50 AE (W/6-inch bbl.) . . . . Nib $1034 Ex $827 Gd $562
W/10-inch bbl., add $50
Two caliber conversion (bbl., bolt & mag.), add $395
XIX Platform System
3 caliber-conversion w/6 bbls.) . . . . Nib $2854 Ex $2283 Gd $1553
XIX6 System (two caliber-conversion
w/2 6-inch bbls.) . . . . Nib $1886 Ex $1508 Gd $1025
XIX10 System
(two cal.-conv. w/ two 10 inch bbls.) . . . . . . Nib $2048 Ex $1638 Gd $1114
Custom shop finish, add $15%
24K gold finish, add. $35%

(ASAI) MODEL ONE PRO .45 PISTOL
Calibers: .45 ACP or .400 COR-BON, 3.75- inch bbl., 7.04 or 7.83 (IPSC Model) inches overall. Weight: 23.5 (alloy frame) or 31.1 oz. 10-shot magazine. Short recoil action. SA or DA mode w/de-cocking lever. Steel or alloy grip-frame. Textured black polymer grips. Imported 1998 to date.
Model 1P45 . . . . Nib $578 Ex $463 Gd $315
Model 1C45/400 (compensator kit), add $175
Model 1C400NC (400 conversion kit), add $125

Magnum Research SSP-91 Lone Eagle Pistol
(w/Optional Leupold Scope)

Mauser
Model 80-SA

Mauser
Model 90-DA

MOUNTAIN EAGLE SEMIAUTOMATIC

Caliber: .22 LR. 15-shot polycarbonate resin magazine, 6.5-inch injection-molded polymer and steel bbl., 10.6 inches overall. Weight: 21 oz. Ramp blade front sight, adj. rear. Injection-molded, checkered and textured grip. Matte black finish. Made 1992-96.

Mountain Eagle (standard, 6.5-inch bbl.) . . . NiB $188 Ex $151 Gd 103
Mountain Eagle (compact 4.5-inch bbl.) . . . . NiB $176 Ex $140 Gd $96

SSP-91 LONE EAGLE PISTOL

Single-shot action w/interchangeable rotating breech bbl., assembly. Calibers: .22 LR, .22 Mag., .22 Hornet, .22-250, .223 Rem., .243 Win., 6mm BR, 7mm-08, 7mm BR, .30-06, .30-30, .308 Win., .35 Rem., .357 Mag., .44 Mag., .444 Marlin. 14-inch interchangeable bbl. assembly, 15 inches overall. Weight: 4.5 lbs. Black or chrome finish. Made 1991 to date.

SSP-91 S/S pistol (complete gun w/black finish) . . . . . . NiB $395 Ex $328 Gd $192
SSP-91 S/S pistol (complete gun w/chrome finish) . . . NiB $581 Ex $494 Gd $383
Extra 14-inch bbl., action w/black finish. . . . . . NiB $650 Ex $587 Gd $505
Extra 14-inch bbl., action w/chrome finish. . . . NiB $744 Ex $670 Gd $575
Ambidextrous stock assembly . . . . NiB $98 Ex $78 Gd $53
W/muzzle brake, add $65
W/open sights, add $30

MAUSER PISTOLS — Oberndorf, Germany
Waffenfabrik Mauser of Mauser-Werke A.G.

MODEL 80-SA AUTOMATIC . . . . . NiB $468 Ex $338 Gd $198
Caliber: 9mm Para. 13-shot magazine, 4.66-inch bbl., 8 inches overall. Weight: 31.5 oz. Blued finish. Hardwood grips. Made 1991-94.

MODEL 90 DA AUTOMATIC . . . . . NiB $463 Ex $338 Gd $198
Caliber: 9mm Para. 14-shot magazine, 4.66-inch bbl., 8 inches overall. Weight: 35 oz. Blued finish. Hardwood grips. Made 1991-94.

MODEL 90 DAC COMPACT . . . . . . NiB $468 Ex $338 Gd $198
Caliber: 9mm Para. 14-shot magazine, 4.13-inch bbl., 7.4 inches overall. Weight: 33.25 oz. Blued finish. Hardwood grips. Made 1991-94.

MODEL 1898 (1896) MILITARY AUTO PISTOL
Caliber: 7.63mm Mauser, but also chambered for 9mm Mauser and 9mm Para. w/the latter being identified by a large red "9" in the grips. 10-shot box magazine, 5.25-inch bbl., 12 inches overall. Weight: 45 oz. Adj. rear sight. Blued finish. Walnut grips. Made 1897-1939. Note: Specialist collectors recognize a number of variations at significantly higher values. Price here is for more common commercial and military types with original finish.

Commercial model (pre-war) . . . . NiB $3380 Ex $2600 Gd $962
Commercial model (wartime) . . . . NiB $1872 Ex $1404 Gd $520
Red 9 Commercial model (fixed sight) . . . . . . NiB $1144 Ex $884 Gd $416
Red 9 WWI Contract (tangent sight) . . . . NiB $2028 Ex $1456 Gd $676
W/stock sssembly (matching SN), add $550

MODEL HSC DA AUTO PISTOL
Calibers: .32 Auto (7.65mm), .380 Auto (9mm Short). Eight-shot (.32) or 7-shot (.380) magazine, 3.4-inch bbl., 6.4 inches overall. Weight: 23.6 oz. Fixed sights. Blued or nickel finish. Checkered walnut grips. Made 1938-.45 and from 1968-96.

Commercial model (low grip screw) . . . . . . NiB $4160 Ex $3120 Gd $1924
Commercial model (wartime) . . . . NiB $416 Ex $338 Gd $187
Nazi military model (pre-war) . . . . NiB $780 Ex $572 Gd $208
Nazi military model (wartime) . . . . NiB $468 Ex $364 Gd $187
French production (postwar) . . . . NiB $390 Ex $312 Gd $182
Mauser production (postwar) . . . . NiB $364 Ex $307 Gd $156
Recent importation (Armes De Chasse) . . . . . . NiB $494 Ex $442 Gd $250
Recent importation (Interarms) . . . . NiB $338 Ex $286 Gd $156
Recent importation (European Amer. Arms) . . . NiB $276 Ex $234 Gd $130
Recent importation (Gamga, USA) . . . . NiB $411 Ex $343 Gd $229
American Eagle model (1 of 5000) . . . . NiB $456 Ex $364 Gd $248

LUGER LANGE PISTOL 08
Caliber: 9mm Para. Eight-inch bbl., Checkered grips. Blued finish. Accessorized w/walnut shoulder stock, front sight tool, spare magazine, leather case. Currently in production. Commemorative version made in limited quantities w/ivory grips and 14-carat gold monogram plate.

HANDGUNS

Mauser Model 1898 (1896) Military

Mauser Parabellum Luger

(cont'd) **LUGER LANGE PISTOL 08**
Commemorative model (100 produced) . . . NiB $2594 Ex $2075 Gd $1411
Commemorative matched pair . . . . NiB $5194 Ex $4155 Gd $2826
Cartridge counter model. . . . . NiB $3374 Ex $2699 Gd $1836
Carbine model (w/matching buttstock) . NiB $6306 Ex $5044 Gd $3430

PARABELLUM LUGER AUTO PISTOL
Current commercial model. Swiss pattern with grip safety. Calibers: 7.65mm Luger, 9mm Para. Eight-shot magazine, bbl. lengths: 4-, 6-inch, 8.75 inches overall (with 4-inch bbl.). Weight: 30 oz. (with 4-inch bbl.). Fixed sights. Blued finish. Checkered walnut grips. Made from 1970 to date. Note: Pistols of this model sold in the U.S. have the American Eagle stamped on the receiver.
Standard model (blue) . . . . NiB $1066 Ex $811 Gd $596

POCKET MODEL 1910 AUTO PISTOL
Caliber: .25 Auto (6.35mm). Nine-shot magazine, 3.1-inch bbl., 5.4 inches overall. Weight: 15 oz. Fixed sights. Blued finish. Checkered walnut or hard rubber grips. Made 1910-34.
Model 1910 (standard) . . . . NiB $442 Ex $312 Gd $146
Model 1910 (w/side latch) . . . . NiB $462 Ex $369 Gd $251

POCKET MODEL 1914 AUTOMATIC . . . . NiB $442 Ex $312 Gd $151
Similar to Pocket Model 1910. Caliber: .32 Auto (7.65mm). Eight-shot magazine, 3.4-inch bbl., 6 inches overall. Weight: 21 oz. Fixed sights. Blued finish. Checkered walnut or hard rubber grips. Made 1914-34

POCKET MODEL 1934 . . . . NiB $468 Ex $338 Gd $156
Similar to Pocket Models 1910 and 1914 in the respective calibers. Chief difference is in the more streamlined, one-piece grips. Made 1934-39.

WTP MODEL I AUTO PISTOL . . . . . NiB $515 Ex $338 Gd $146
"Westentaschen-Pistole" (Vest Pocket Pistol). Caliber: .25 Automatic (6.35mm). Six-shot magazine, 2.5-inch bbl., 4 inches overall. Weight: 11.5 oz. Blued finish. Hard rubber grips. Made 1922-37.

WTP MODEL II AUTO PISTOL . . . . NiB $676 Ex $546 Gd $208
Similar to Model I but smaller and lighter. Caliber: .25 Automatic (6.35mm). Six-shot magazine, 2-inch bbl., 4 inches overall. Weight: 9.5 oz. Blued finish. Hard rubber grips. Made 1938-40.

MERWIN HULBERT & CO., — New York, NY

FIRST MODEL
FRONTIER ARMY . . . . NiB $3640 Ex $1872 Gd $780
Single action, .44 caliber, 7.5-inch bbl. Square butt, open top, scoop flutes on cylinder, two screws above trigger guard

SECOND MODEL
FRONTIER ARMY . . . . NiB $5200 Ex $1768 Gd $936
Similar to First Model except has only one screw above trigger guard.

SECOND MODEL
POCKET ARMY . . . . NiB $5200 Ex $1300 Gd $832
Similar to Second Model except has bird's-head butt instead of square butt, 3.5- or 7-inch (scarce) bbl. May be marked "Pocket Army."

THIRD MODEL
FRONTIER ARMY . . . . NiB $5200 Ex $1300 Gd $832
Caliber: .44, 7-inch round bbl. with no rib, single action. Square butt, top strap, usually has conventional fluting on cylinder but some have scoop flutes.

THIRD MODEL
FRONTIER ARMY . . . . NiB $4940 Ex $1144 Gd $780
Similar to Third Model Frontier Army SA except is double action.

THIRD MODEL
POCKET ARMY . . . . NiB $4940 Ex $1144 Gd $780
Caliber: .44, 3.5- or 7.5-inch bbl. with no rib. Single action, bird's-head butt, top strap.

THIRD MODEL
POCKET ARMY . . . . NiB $4680 Ex $1040 Gd $728
Similar to Third Model Pocket Army SA except is double action.

FOURTH MODEL
FRONTIER ARMY . . . . NiB $6760 Ex $3640 Gd $1820
Caliber: .44, 3.5- 5- or 7-inch unique ribbed bbl. Single action, square butt, top strap, conventional flutes on cylinder.

FOURTH MODEL
FRONTIER ARMY
Similar to Fourth Model Frontier Army SA except is double action.
. . . . NiB $6240 Ex $3120 Gd $1716

(The following handguns are foreign copies of Merwin Hulbert Co. guns and may be marked as such, or as "Sistema Merwin Hulbert," but rarely with the original Hopkins & Allen markings. These guns will usually bring half or less of a comparable genuine Merwin Hulbert product.)

FIRST POCKET MODEL . . . . NiB $1560 Ex $468 Gd $234
Caliber: .38 Special, 5-shot cylinder (w/cylinder pin exposed at front of frame), single action. Spur trigger; round loading hole in recoil shield, no loading gate.

SECOND POCKET MODEL . . . . . NiB $1404 Ex. $390 Gd $208
Similar to First Pocket Model except has sliding loading gate.

THIRD POCKET MODEL . . . . NiB $1300 Ex $364 Gd $192
Similar to First Pocket Model except has enclosed cylinder pin.

THIRD POCKET
MODEL W/TRIGGER GUARD . . . . NiB $1300 Ex $390 Gd $218
Similar to First Pocket Model except w/conventional trigger guard.

Mauser WTP Model I

**Mitchell Arms
Citation II**

**Mitchell Arms
Sharpshooter II**

**MEDIUM FRAME
POCKET MODEL . . . . NiB $988 Ex $322 Gd $182**
Caliber: .38 Spec., 5-shot cylinder, DA, may have hammer spur.

**MEDIUM FRAME
POCKET MODEL 32 . . . . NiB $1144 Ex $364 Gd $208**
Similar to Medium Frame Pocket Model except .32 caliber, 7-shot cylinder, double action. . . . .

TIP-UP MODEL 22 . . . . NiB $1144 Ex $520 Gd $260
Similar to S&W Model One except .22 caliber, 7-shot cylinder, spur trigger. Scarce. . . . .

MITCHELL ARMS, INC. — Santa Ana, California
MODEL 1911 GOLD SIGNATURE
Caliber: .45 ACP. Eight-shot magazine, 5-inch bbl., 8.75 inches overall. Weight: 39 oz. Interchangeable blade front sight, drift-adj. combat or fully adj. rear. Smooth or checkered walnut grips. Blued or stainless finish. Made 1994-96.
Blued model w/fixed sights . . . . . . NiB $607 Ex $535 Gd $342
Blued model w/adj. sights . . . . NiB $627 Ex $546 Gd $352
Stainless model w/fixed sights . . . . NiB $780 Ex $663 Gd $561
Stainless model w/adj. sights . . . . . NiB $811 Ex $688 Gd $586

ALPHA MODEL AUTO PISTOL
Dual action w/interchangeable trigger modules. Caliber: .45 ACP. Eight-shot magazine, 5-inch bbl., 8.75 inches overall. Weight: 39 oz. Interchangeable blade front sight, drift-adj. rear. Smooth or checkered walnut grips. Blued or stainless finish. Made from 1994 to date. Advertised 1995, but not manufactured.
Blued model w/fixed sights . . . . NiB $890 Ex $712 Gd $484
Blued model w/adj. sights . . . . NiB $924 Ex $739 Gd $503
Stainless model w/fixed sights . . . . NiB $924 Ex $739 Gd $503
Stainless model w/adj. sights . . . . NiB $955 Ex $764 Gd $519

AMERICAN EAGLE PISTOL . . . . NiB $593 Ex $474 Gd $322
Stainless-steel re-creation of the American Eagle Parabellum auto pistol. Caliber: 9mm Para. Seven-shot magazine, 4-inch bbl., 9.6 inches overall. Weight: 26.6 oz. Blade front sight, fixed rear. Stainless finish. Checkered walnut grips. Made 1993-94.

CITATION II AUTO PISTOL . . . . . . NiB $403 Ex $301 Gd $173
Re-creation of the High Standard Supermatic Citation Military. Caliber: .22 LR. 10-shot magazine, 5.5-inch bull bbl. or 7.25 fluted bbl., 9.75 inches overall (5.5-inch bbl.). Weight: 44.5 oz. Ramp front sight, slide-mounted micro-adj. rear. Satin blued or stainless finish. Checkered walnut grips w/thumbrest. Made 1992-96.

OLYMPIC L.S.U. AUTO PISTOL. . . . NiB $841 Ex $561 Gd $281
Similar to the Citation II model except chambered in .22 Short, 6.75-inch round tapered bbl. w/stabilizer and removable counterweights. Made 1992-96.

SHARPSHOOTER II AUTO PISTOL. . . . . . . NiB $326 Ex $286 Gd $173
Re-creation of the High Standard Sharpshooter. Caliber: .22 LR. 10-shot magazine, 5-inch bull bbl., 10.25 inches overall. Weight: 42 oz. Ramp front sight, slide-mounted micro-adj. rear. Satin blued or stainless finish. Checkered walnut grips w/thumbrest. Made 1992-96.

MODEL SA SPORT KING II. . . . . . . NiB $274 Ex $219 Gd $149
Caliber: .22 LR. 10-shot magazine, 4.5- or 6.75-inch bbl., 9 or 11.25 inches overall. Weight: 39 or 42 oz. Checkered walnut or black plastic grips. Blade front sight and drift adjustable rear. Made 1993-94.

SA ARMY REVOLVER
Calibers: .357 Mag., .44 Mag., .45 Colt/.45 ACP. Six-shot cylinder. bbl., lengths: 4.75, 5.5, 7.5 inches; weight: 40-43 oz. Blade front sight, grooved top strap or adj. rear. Blued or nickel finish w/color-casehardened frame. Brass or steel backstrap/trigger guard. Smooth one-piece walnut grips. Imported 1987-94 and 1997 to date.
Standard model w/blued finish . . . . NiB $376 Ex $301 Gd $205
Standard model w/nickel finish. . . . . NiB $414 Ex $332 Gd $225
Standard model w/stainless backstrap . . . . . NiB $447 Ex $357 Gd $243
.45 Combo w/blued finish . . . . NiB $504 Ex $403 Gd $274
.45 Combo w/nickel finish . . . . NiB $542 Ex $433 Gd $295

TROPHY II AUTO PISTOL. . . . . NiB $433 Ex $357 Gd $173
Similar to the Citation II model except w/gold-plated trigger and gold-filled markings. Made 1992-96.

VICTOR II AUTO PISTOL . . . . **NiB $504 Ex $403 Gd $274**
Re-creation of the High Standard Victor w/full-length vent rib. Caliber: .22 LR. 10-shot magazine, 4.5- or 5.5-inch bbl., 9.75 inches overall (with 5.5-inch bbl.). Weight: 52 oz. (with 5.5-inch bbl.). Rib-mounted target sights. Satin blued or stainless finish. Checkered walnut grips w/thumbrest. Made 1992-96.

GUARDIAN ANGEL
DERRINGER . . . . **NiB $127 Ex $102 Gd $69**
Hammerless, double-action O/U derringer w/interchangeable drop-in breech block. Calibers: .22 LR, .22 WRM. Two-shot capacity. Two-inch bbl., 5 inches overall. Weight: 12 oz. Blue, nickel or gold finish. Blade front and fixed rear sights. Checkered black grips. Made 1996-97.

GUARDIAN II . . . . **NiB $243 Ex $194 Gd $132**
Caliber: .38 Special, Six-shot cylinder, 2-, 4- or 6-inch bbl., 8.5 inches overall (with 4-inch bbl.). Weight: 32 oz (with 4-inch bbl.). Blade ramp front and fixed rear sights. Checkered combat or target grips. Blued finish. Made 1995.

GUARDIAN III . . . . **NiB $280 Ex $229 Gd $143**
Same specifications as Guardian II model except w/adjustable rear sights. Made 1995.

TITAN II DA . . . . **NiB $311 Ex $245 Gd $168**
Caliber: .357 Mag. Six-shot cylinder. 2-, 4- or 6-inch bbl., 7.75 inches overall (with 4-inch bbl.). Weight: 38 oz (with 4-inch bbl.). Blade front and fixed rear sights. Crane mounted cylinder release. Blued or stainless finish. Made 1995.

TITAN III DA. . . . . **NiB $352 Ex $275 Gd $184**
Same specification as the Titan II except w/adjustable rear sight. Made 1995.

Mitchell Arms SA
Army Revolver

Mitchell Arms
Victor II

MKE PISTOL — Ankara, Turkey
Mfd. by Makina ve Kimya Endüstrisi Kurumu

KIRIKKALE DA
AUTOMATIC PISTOL . . . . **NiB $372 Ex $301 Gd $173**
Similar to Walther PP. Calibers: .32 Auto (7.65mm), .380 Auto (9mm Short). Seven-shot magazine, 3.9-inch bbl., 6.7 inches overall. Weight: 24 oz. Fixed sights. Blued finish. Checkered plastic grips. Made 1948-88. Note: This is a Turkish Army standard service pistol.

MOA CORPORATION — Dayton, Ohio

MAXIMUM SINGLE-SHOT PISTOL
Calibers: .22 Hornet to .454 Casull Mag. Armoloy, Chromoloy or stainless falling block action fitted w/blued or stainless 8.75-, 10- or 14-inch Douglas bbl., weight: 60-68 oz. Smooth walnut grips. Made 1986 to date.
Chromoloy receiver
(blued bbl.) . . . . **NiB $815 Ex $709 Gd $357**
Armoloy receiver (blued bbl.) . . . . . **NiB $826 Ex $729 Gd $377**
Stainless receiver (blued bbl.) . . . . . **NiB $923 Ex $826 Gd $581**
W/stainless bbl., add $95
W/extra bbl., add $250

MAXIMUM CARBINE PISTOL
Similar to Maximum Pistol except w/18-inch bbl. Made 1986-88 and 1994 to date.
MOA Maximum (blued bbl.) . . . . . . **NiB $841 Ex $663 Gd $439**
MOA Maximum (stainless bbl.) . . . . **NiB $913 Ex $739 Gd $495**

MKE Kirikkale

MOA Maximum
Carbine Pistol

Mossberg Brownie
"Pepperbox" Pistol

Navy Arms
Model 1875 Schofield

Navy Arms
Model 1875 SA Revolver

Navy Arms
Frontier Standard

Navy Arms
Frontier Target Model

O.F. MOSSBERG & SONS, INC. — North Haven, Connecticut

BROWNIE "PEPPERBOX" PISTOL . . . . **NiB $357 Ex $306 Gd $173**
Hammerless, top-break, double-action, four bbls. w/revolving firing pin. Caliber: .22 LR, 2.5-inch bbls., weight: 14 oz. Blued finish. Serated grips. Approximately 37,000 made 1919-.32.

NAMBU PISTOLS
See Listings under Japanese Military Pistols.

NAVY ARMS COMPANY — Martinsburg, West Virginia

MODEL 1873 SA REVOLVER
Calibers: .44-40, .45 Colt. Six-shot cylinder, bbl. lengths: 3, 4.75, 5.5, 7.5 inches, 10.75 inches overall (with 5.5-inch bbl.). Weight: 36 oz. Blade front sight, grooved topstrap rear. Blued w/color-case-hardened frame or nickel finish. Smooth walnut grips. Made 1991 to date.
Blued finish w/brass backstrap . . . . **NiB $355 Ex $288 Gd $154**
U.S. Artillery model w/5-inch bbl. . . . . **NiB $386 Ex $309 Gd $210**
U.S. Cavalry model w/7-inch bbl. . . . **NiB $418 Ex $335 Gd $228**
Bisley model . . . . **NiB $355 Ex $304 Gd $154**
Sheriff's model (disc. 1998) . . . . **NiB $350 Ex $278 Gd $154**

MODEL 1875 SCHOFIELD REVOLVER
Replica of S&W Model 3, top-break single-action w/auto ejector. Calibers: .44-40 or .45 LC. Six-shot cylinder, 5- or 7-inch bbl., 10.75 or 12.75 inches overall. Weight: 39 oz. Blade front sight, square-notched rear. Polished blued finish. Smooth walnut grips. Made 1994 to date.
Cavalry model (7-inch bbl.) . . . . **NiB $618 Ex $541 Gd $257**
**Deluxe Cavalry model
(engraved)** . . . . **NiB $1481 Ex $1184 Gd $788**
Wells Fargo model (5-inch bbl.) . . . **NiB $638 Ex $510 Gd $347**
**Deluxe Wells Fargo
model (engraved)** . . . . **NiB $1448 Ex $1159 Gd $788**
Hideout model (3.5-inch bbl.) . . . . . **NiB $612 Ex $489 Gd $333**

MODEL 1875 SA REVOLVER . . . . . . **NiB $380 Ex $304 Gd $207**
Replica of Remington Model 1875. Calibers: .357 Magnum, .44-40, .45 Colt. Six-shot cylinder, 7.5-inch bbl., 13.5 inches overall. Weight: About 48 oz. Fixed sights. Blued or nickel finish. Smooth walnut grips. Made in Italy c.1955-1980. Note: Originally marketed in the U.S. as Replica Arms Model 1875 (that firm was acquired by Navy Arms Co).

FRONTIER SA REVOLVER . . . . **NiB $297 Ex $237 Gd $161**
Calibers: .22 LR, .22 WMR, .357 Mag., .45 Colt. Six-shot cylinder, bbl. lengths: 4.5-, 5.5-, 7.5-inches, 10.25 inches overall (with 4.5-inch bbl.). Weight: About 36 oz. (with 4.5-inch bbl.). Fixed sights. Blued bbl., and cylinder, color-casehardened frame, brass grip frame. One-piece smooth walnut grip. Imported 1975-79.

FRONTIER TARGET MODEL . . . . . . **NiB $322 Ex $257 Gd $175**
Same as standard Frontier except has adj. rear sight and ramp front sight. Imported 1975-79.

BUNTLINE FRONTIER. . . . . **NiB $483 Ex $386 Gd $263**
Same as Target Frontier except has detachable shoulder stock and 16.5-inch bbl. Calibers: .357 Magnum and .45 Colt only. Made 1975-79.

LUGER (STANDARD) AUTOMATIC . . . . NiB $161 Ex $129 Gd $88
Caliber: .22 LR, standard or high velocity. 10-shot magazine, bbl. length: 4.5 inches, 8.9 inches overall. Weight: 1 lb., 13.5 oz. Square blade front sight w/square notch, stationary rear sight. Walnut checkered grips. Non-reflecting black finish. Made 1986-88.

**ROLLING BLOCK
SINGLE-SHOT PISTOL** . . . . NiB $350 Ex $294 Gd $175
Calibers: .22 LR, .22 Hornet, .357 Magnum. Eight-inch bbl., 12 inches overall. Weight: About 40 oz. Adjustable sights. Blued bbl., color-casehardened frame, brass trigger guard. Smooth walnut grip and forearm. Imported 1965-80.

TT-OLYMPIA PISTOL . . . . NiB $257 Ex $232 Gd $154
Reproduction of the Walther Olympia Target Pistol. Caliber: .22 LR. Eight inches overall 4.6-inch bbl., weight: 28 oz. Blade front sight, adj. rear. Blued finish. Checkered hardwood grips. Imported 1992-94.

NEW ENGLAND FIREARMS — Gardner, Massachusetts

In 1987, New England Firearms was established as an independent company producing select H&R models under the NEF logo. In 1991, H&R 1871, Inc. was formed from the residual of the parent company and took over the New England Firearms facility. H&R 1871 produced firearms under both their logo and the NEF brand name until 1999, when the Marlin Firearms Company acquired the assets of H&R 1871.

MODEL R73 REVOLVER . . . . NiB $129 Ex $98 Gd $62
Caliber: .32 H&R Mag. Five-shot cylinder, 2.5- or 4-inch bbl., 8.5 inches overall (with 4-inch bbl.). Weight: 26 oz. (with 4 inch bbl.). Fixed or adjustable sights. Blued or nickel finish. Walnut-finish hardwood grips. Made from 1988-99.

MODEL R92 REVOLVER . . . . NiB $129 Ex $98 Gd $62
Same general specifications as Model R73 except chambered for .22 LR. Nine-shot cylinder. Weight: 28 oz. w/4 inch bbl., Made 1988-99.

MODEL 832 STARTER PISTOL . . . . NiB $92 Ex $73 Gd $49
Calibers: .22 Blank, .32 Blank. Nine- and 5-shot cylinders, respectively. Push-pin swing-out cylinder. Solid wood grips w/NEF medallion insert.

ULTRA REVOLVER . . . . NiB $161 Ex $129 Gd $88
Calibers: .22 LR, .22 Mag. Nine-shot cylinder in .22 LR, 6-shot cylinder in .22 Mag., 4- or 6-inch ribbed bull bbl., 10.75 inches overall (with 6-inch bbl.). Weight: 36 oz. (with 6-inch bbl.). Blade front sight, adj. square-notched rear. Blued or nickel finish. Walnut-finish hardwood grips. Made from 1989-99.

LADY ULTRA REVOLVER . . . . NiB $154 Ex $118 Gd $72
Same basic specifications as the Ultra except in .32 H&R Mag. w/5-shot cylinder and 3-inch ribbed bull bbl., 7.5 inches overall. Weight: 31 oz. Made 1992 -99.

NORTH AMERICAN ARMS — Provo, Utah

MODEL 22LR . . . . NiB $159 Ex $127 Gd $87
Same as Model 22S except chambered for .22 LR., is 3.88-inches overall, weight: 4.5 oz. Made 1976 to date.

MODEL 22S MINI REVOLVER . . . . . NiB $172 Ex $138 Gd $94
Single-Action. Caliber: .22 Short. Five-shot cylinder, 1.13-inch bbl., 3.5-inches overall. Weight: 4 oz. Fixed sights. Stainless steel. Plastic grips. Made from 1975 to date.

Navy Arms
Rolling Block Single-Shot

Navy Arms
TT-Olympia Pistol

New England Firearms
Model R73 Revolver

New England Firearms
Model 832 Starter Pistol

MODEL 450 MAGNUM EXPRESS
Single-Action. Calibers: .450 Magnum Express, .45 Win. Mag. Five-shot cylinder, 7.5- or 10.5-inch bbl., matte or polished stainless steel finish. Walnut grips. Presentation case. Disc. 1986.
Matte stainless model . . . . NiB $1224 Ex $969 Gd $714
Polished stainless model . . . . NiB $1428 Ex $1122 Gd $867
W/10-inch bbl., add $250
W/combo cylinder, add $225

Ortgies
Pocket Automatic Pistol

BLACK WIDOW REVOLVER
SA. Calibers: .22 LR., .22 WMR. Five-shot cylinder, 2-inch heavy vent bbl., 5.88-inches overall. Weight: 8.8 oz. Fixed or adj. sights. Full-size black rubber grips. Stainless steel brush finish. Made from 1990 to date.
Adj. sight model . . . . NiB $261 Ex $219 Gd $127
Adj. sight combo model . . . . NiB $301 Ex $245 Gd $173
Fixed sight model . . . . NiB $210 Ex $168 Gd $114
Fixed sight combo model. . . . . NiB $290 Ex $240 Gd $176

GUARDIAN DAO PISTOL . . . . NiB $362 Ex $291 Gd $296
Caliber: .32 ACP. Six-shot magazine, 2-inch bbl., 4.4 inches overall. Weight: 13.5 oz. Fixed sights. Black synthetic grips. Stainless steel. Made 1997 to date.

MINI-MASTER TARGET REVOLVER
SA. Calibers: .22 LR., .22 WMR. Five-shot cylinder, 4-inch heavy vent rib bbl., 7.75-inches overall. Weight: 10.75 oz. Fixed or adj. sights. Black rubber grips. Stainless steel brush finish. Made from 1990 to date.
Adj. sight model . . . . NiB $250 Ex $204 Gd $173
Adj. sight combo model . . . . NiB $358 Ex $294 Gd $212
Fixed sight model . . . . NiB $249 Ex $199 Gd $136
Fixed sight combo model. . . . . NiB $325 Ex $268 Gd $195

NORWEGIAN MILITARY PISTOLS
Mfd. by Kongsberg Vaapenfabrikk, Government Arsenal at Kongsberg, Norway

MODEL 1914
AUTOMATIC PISTOL . . . . NiB $414 Ex $331 Gd $225
Similar to Colt Model 1911 .45 Automatic w/same general specifications except has lengthened slide stop. Made 1919-46.

NORWEGIAN
MODEL 1912 . . . . NiB $2677 Ex $2142 Gd $1457
Same as the model 1914 except has conventional slide stop. Only 500 were made.

OLYMPIC ARMS, INC.
Olympia Washington

OA-93 AR SEMIAUTOMATIC PISTOL
AR-15 style receiver with no buffer tube or charging handle. Caliber: .223 Rem. or 7.62x39mm. Five-, 20- or 30-shot detachable

(cont'd) OA-93 AR SEMIAUTOMATIC PISTOL
magazine, 6-, 9- or 14-inch stainless steel bbl., 15.75 inches overall w/6-inch bbl., weight: 4 lbs., 3 oz. Flattop upper with no open sights. Vortex flash suppressor. A2 stowaway pistol grip and forward pistol grip. Made 1993-94. Note: All post-ban versions of OA-93 style weapons are classified by BATF as "Any Other Weapon" and must be transferred by a Class III dealer. Values listed here are for limited-production, pre-ban guns.
Model OA-93
(.223 Rem.) . . . . NiB $3570 Ex $2856 Gd $2601
Model OA-93
(7.62x39mm) . . . . NiB $4386 Ex $4182 Gd $3876

OA-96 AR SEMI-
AUTOMATIC PISTOL . . . . NiB $882 Ex $790 Gd $704
Similar to Model OA-93 AR except w/6.5-inch bbl. only chambered for .223 Rem. Additional compliance modifications include a fixed (nonremovable) well-style magazine and no forward pistol grip. Made 1996 to date.

ORTGIES PISTOLS — Erfurt, Germany
Manufactured by Deutsche Werke A.G.

POCKET AUTO-
MATIC PISTOL . . . . NiB $306 Ex $255 Gd $184
Calibers: .32 Auto (7.65mm), .380 Auto (9mm). Seven-shot magazine (.380 cal.), 8-shot (.32 cal.), 3.25-inch bbl., 6.5-inches overall. Weight: 22 oz. Fixed sights. Blued finish. Plain walnut grips. Made in 1920's.

VEST POCKET
AUTOMATIC PISTOL . . . . NiB $280 Ex $224 Gd $153
Caliber: .25 Auto (6.35mm). Six-shot magazine, 2.75-inch bbl., 5.19 inches overall. Weight: 13.5 oz. Fixed sights. Blued finish. Plain walnut grips. Made in 1920's.

PHOENIX ARMS — Ontario, California

MODEL HP22/HP25
SA AUTO PISTOLS. . . . . NiB $121 Ex $69 Gd $41
Caliber: .22 LR, .25 ACP. 10-shot magazine, 3-inch bbl., 5.5 inches overall. Weight: 20 oz. Checkered synthetic grips. Blade front sight, adjustable rear. Blue, chrome or nickel finish. Made 1994 to date.

MODEL HP
RANGE-MASTER TARGET SA
AUTO PISTOL . . . . NiB $131 Ex $102 Gd $71
Similar to Model HP .22 except w/5.5-inch target bbl. and extended magazine, Ramp front sight, adjustable notch rear on vent rib. Checkered synthetic grips. Blue or satin nickel finish. Made 1998 to date.

MODEL HP
RANGE-MASTER DELUXE TARGET
SA AUTO PISTOL . . . . NiB $229 Ex $133 Gd $92
Similar to Model HP Rangemaster Target model except w/dual-2000 laser sight and custom wood grips. Made 1998 to date.

"RAVEN" SA
AUTO PISTOL . . . . NiB $70 Ex $51 Gd $36
Caliber: .25 ACP. Six-shot magazine, 2.5 inch bbl., 4.75 inches overall. Weight: 15 oz. Ivory, pink pearl, or black slotted stocks. Fixed sights. Blue, chrome or nickel finish. Made 1993 to date.

PARA-ORDNANCE MFG. INC. — Scarborough, Ontario, Canada

LIMITED EDITION SERIES

Custom-tuned and fully accessorized "Limited Edition" versions of standard "P" Models. Enhanced-grip frame and serrated slide fitted w/match-grade bbl., and full-length recoil spring guide system. Beavertail grip safety and skeletonized hammer. Ambidextrous safety and trigger-stop adjustment. Fully adjustable or contoured low-mount sights. For pricing see individual models.

MODEL P-10 SA AUTO PISTOL

Super compact. Calibers: .40 S&W, .45 ACP. 10-shot magazine, 3-inch bbl., weight: 24 oz. (alloy frame) or 31 oz. (steel frame). Ramp front sight and drift adjustable rear w/3-dot system. Steel or alloy frame. Matte black, Duo-Tone or stainless finish. Made 1997 to date.

Alloy model	NiB $644	Ex $515	Gd $335
Duo-Tone model	NiB $638	Ex $510	Gd $347
Stainless steel model	NiB $727	Ex $592	Gd $419
Steel model	NiB $622	Ex $500	Gd $343
Limited model (tuned & accessorized), add			$125

P-12 COMPACT AUTO PISTOL

Calibers: .45 ACP. 11-shot magazine, 3.5-inch bbl., 7-inches overall. Weight: 24 oz. (alloy frame). Blade front sight, adj. rear w/3-dot system. Textured composition grips. Matte black alloy or steel finish. Made 1990 to date.

Model P1245 (alloy)	NiB $658	Ex $526	Gd $357
Model P1245C (steel)	NiB $786	Ex $628	Gd $426
Limited model (tuned & accessorized), add			$125

P-13 AUTO PISTOL

Same general specifications as Model P-12 except w/12-shot magazine, 4.5-inch bbl., 8-inches overall. Weight: 25 oz. (alloy frame). Blade front sight, adj. rear w/3-dot system. Textured composition grips. Matte black alloy or steel finish. Made 1990 to date.

Model P1345 (alloy)	NiB $788	Ex $566	Gd $360
Model P1345C (steel)	NiB $799	Ex $640	Gd $435
Limited model (tuned & accessorized), add			$125

P-14 AUTO PISTOL

Caliber: .45 ACP. 13-shot magazine, 5-inch bbl., 8.5 inches overall. Weight: 28 oz. Alloy frame. Blade front sight, adj. rear w/3-dot system. Textured composition grips. Matte black alloy or steel finish. Made from 1990 to date.

Model P1445 (alloy)	NiB $644	Ex $515	Gd $335
Model P1445C (steel)	NiB $712	Ex $572	Gd $392
Limited model (tuned & accessorized), add			$125

MODEL P-15 AUTO PISTOL

Caliber: .40 S&W. 10-shot magazine, 4.25-inch bbl., 7.75 inches overall. Weight: 28 to 36 oz. Steel, alloy or stainless receiver. Matte black, Duotone or stainless finish. Made 1996-99.

Model P1540 (alloy)	NiB $644	Ex $515	Gd $448
Model P1540C (steel)	NiB $609	Ex $489	Gd $336
Duotone stainless model	NiB $684	Ex $556	Gd $393
Stainless model	NiB $725	Ex $592	Gd $422

MODEL P-16 SA AUTO PISTOL

Caliber: .40 S&W. 10- or 16-shot magazine, 5-inch bbl., 8.5 inches overall. Weight: 40 oz. Ramp front sight and drift adjustable rear w/3-dot system. Carbon steel or stainless frame. Matte black, Duotone or stainless finish. Made 1997 to date.

Blue steel model	NiB $659	Ex $530	Gd $360
Duotone model	NiB $680	Ex $551	Gd $386

Para-Ordnance
P-12 Compact

Para-Ordnance
P-14 Auto Pistol

Plainfield
Model 71

(cont'd) **MODEL P-16 SA AUTO PISTOL**

Stainless model	NiB $798	Ex $680	Gd $366
Limited model (tuned & accessorized), add			$125

MODEL P-18 SA AUTO PISTOL

Caliber: 9mm Parabellum. 10- or 18-shot magazine, 5-inch bbl., 8.5 inches overall. Weight: 40 oz. Dovetailed front sight and fully adjustable rear. Bright stainless finish. Made 1998 to date.

Stainless model	NiB $747	Ex $592	Gd $463
Limited model (tuned & accessorized), add			$125

Plainfield Model 72

Radom P-35

Record-Match
Model 200 Free Pistol

PLAINFIELD MACHINE COMPANY — Dunellen, New Jersey

This firm disc. operation about 1982.

MODEL 71 AUTOMATIC PISTOL
Calibers: .22 LR, .25 Automatic w/conversion kit available. 10-shot magazine (.22 LR) or 8-shot (.25 Auto), 2.5-inch bbl., 5.13 inches overall. Weight: 25 oz. Fixed sights. Stainless steel frame/slide. Checkered walnut grips. Made 1970-82. See illustration previous page.
.22 LR or .25 Auto only . . . . NiB $153 Ex $132 Gd $87
W/conversion kit . . . . NiB $184 Ex $153 Gd $92

MODEL 72 AUTOMATIC PISTOL
Same as Model 71 except has aluminum slide, 3.5-inch bbl., 6 inches overall. Made 1970-82
.22 LR or .25 Auto only . . . . NiB $163 Ex $138 Gd $71
W/conversion kit . . . . NiB $178 Ex $143 Gd $97

PROFESSIONAL ORDNANCE, INC. — Lake Havasu City, Arizona

MODEL CARBON-15 TYPE 20
SEMIAUTOMATIC PISTOL . . . . NiB $824 Ex $747 Gd $489
Similar to Carbon-15 Type 97 except w/unfluted barrel. Weight: 40 oz. Matte black finish. Made 1999 to date.

MODEL CARBON-15 TYPE 97
SEMIAUTOMATIC PISTOL . . . . NiB $901 Ex $850 Gd $515
AR-15 operating system w/recoil reduction system. Caliber: .223 Rem. 10-shot magazine, 7.25-inch fluted bbl., 20 inches overall. Weight: 46 oz. Ghost ring sights. Carbon-fiber upper and lower receivers w/Chromoly bolt carrier. Matte black finish. Checkered composition grip. Made 1996 to date.

RADOM PISTOL — Radom, Poland Manufactured by the Polish Arsenal

P-35 AUTOMATIC PISTOL
Variation of the Colt Government Model .45 Auto. Caliber: 9mm Para. Eight-shot magazine, 4.75-inch bbl., 7.75 inches overall. Weight: 29 oz. Fixed sights. Blued finish. Plastic grips. Made 1935 thru WWII.
Commercial model
(Polish Eagle) . . . . NiB $2350 Ex $1600 Gd $463
Nazi military model
(W/slotted backstrap) . . . . NiB $900 Ex $700 Gd $196
Nazi military model
(W/takedown lever) . . . . NiB $550 Ex $375 Gd $191
Nazi military model
(No takedown lever or slot) . . . . . . NiB $386 Ex $306 Gd $185
Nazi military model (Parkerized) . . . . NiB $1030 Ex $824 Gd $206

RECORD-MATCH PISTOLS — Zella-Mehlis, Germany, Manufactured by Udo Anschütz

MODEL 200 FREE PISTOL . . . . NiB $1020 Ex $963 Gd $721
Basically the same as Model 210 except w/different stock design and conventional set trigger, spur trigger guard. Made prior to WW II.

MODEL 210 FREE PISTOL . . . . . . NiB $1360 Ex $1298 Gd $722
System Martini action, set trigger w/button release. Caliber: .22 LR. Single-shot, 11-inch bbl., weight: 46 oz. Target sights micrometer rear. Blued finish. Carved and checkered walnut forearm and stock w/adj. hand base. Also made w/dual action (Model 210A); weight 35 oz. Made prior to WWII.

REISING ARMS CO. — Hartford, Connecticut

TARGET AUTOMATIC PISTOL . . . . . NiB $489 Ex $360 Gd $180
Hinged frame. Outside hammer. Caliber: .22 LR. 12-shot magazine, 6.5-inch bbl., fixed sights. Blued finish. Hard rubber grips. Made 1921-24.

REMINGTON ARMS COMPANY — Ilion, New York

MODEL 51 AUTOMATIC PISTOL
Calibers: .32 Auto, .380 Auto. Seven-shot magazine, 3.5-inch bbl., 6.63 inches overall. Weight: 21 oz. Fixed sights. Blued finish. Hard rubber grips. Made 1918-34.
.32 ACP . . . . NiB $772 Ex $644 Gd $335
.380 ACP . . . . NiB $669 Ex $541 Gd $283

Remington Model 51

**Remington
95 Double Derringer**

MODEL 95 DOUBLE DERRINGER

SA. Caliber: 41 Short Rimfire. Three-inch double bbls. (superposed), 4.88 inches overall. Early models have long hammer spur and two-armed extractor, but later guns have short hammer spur and sliding extractor (a few have no extractor). Fixed blade front sight and grooved rear. finish: Blued, blued w/nickel-plated frame or fully nickel-plated; also w/factory engraving. Grips: Walnut, checkered hard rubber, pearl, ivory. Weight: 11 oz. Made 1866-1935. Approximately 150,000 were manufactured. Note: During the 70 years of its production, serial numbering of this model was repeated two or three times. Therefore, aside from hammer and extractor differences between the earlier and later models, the best clue to the age of a Double Derringer is the stamping of the company's name on the top of the bbl., or side rib. Prior to 1888, derringers were stamped "E. Remington & Sons, Ilion, N.Y." on one side rib and "Elliot's Patent Dec. 12, 1865" on the other (Type I-early & mid-production) and on the top rib (Type I-late production). In 1888-1911, "Remington Arms Co., Ilion, N.Y." and patent date were stamped on the top rib (Type II) and from 1912-35 "Remington Arms - U.M.C. Co., Ilion, N.Y." and patent date were stamped on the top rib.

**Model 95 (Early Type I,
w/o extractor)** . . . . NiB $2060 Ex $2008 Gd $721
**Model 95 (Mid Type I,
w/extractor)** . . . . NiB $2214 Ex $2060 Gd $819
**Model 95 (Late Type I,
w/extractor)** . . . . NiB $2266 Ex $2060 Gd $824
**Model 95 (Type II
produced 1988-11)** . . . . NiB $1854 Ex $1442 Gd $618
**Model 95 (Type III,
produced 1912-35)** . . . . NiB $895 Ex $716 Gd $487
**Factory-engraved model w/ivory
or pearl grips, add** $35%

**Remington
XP-100 Custom**

NEW MODEL SINGLE-SHOT TARGET PISTOL

Also called Model 1901 Target. Rolling-block action. Calibers: .22 Short & Long, .25 Stevens, .32 S&W, .44 S&W Russian. 10-inch half-octagon bbl., 14 inches overall. Weight: 45 oz. (.22 cal.). Target sights. Blued finish. Checkered walnut grips and forearm. Made 1901-09.
Model 1901 (.22 caliber). . . . . . NiB $2575 Ex $2280 Gd $980
**Model 1901
(.25 Stevens, .32 S&W)** . . . . NiB $2254 Ex $1802 Gd $1226
Model 1901 (.44 Russian) . . . . . NiB $2781 Ex $2523 Gd $1081

**Remington
XP-100 Custom Heavy Barrel**

MODEL XP-100 CUSTOM PISTOL . . . . NiB $510 Ex $407 Gd $216

Bolt-action, single-shot, long-range pistol. Calibers: .223 Rem., 7mm-08 or .35 Rem. 14.5-inch bbl., standard contour or heavy. Weight: About 4.25 lbs. Currently in production.

MODEL XP-100 SILHOUETTE. . . . . NiB $560 Ex $448 Gd $305

Same general specifications as Model XP-100 except chambered for 7mm BR Rem. and 35 Rem. 14.75-inch bbl., weight: 4.13 lbs. Made 1987-92.

**Remington
XP-100 Silhouette**

**Remington
XP-100 Single-Shot**

**Remington
XP-100 Varmint Special**

**Rossi Model 88
DA Revolver**

**Rossi Model 851
DA revolver**

Rossi DA Revolver

MODEL XP-100 SINGLE-SHOT PISTOL ... NiB $432 Ex $345 Gd $235
Bolt action. Caliber: 221 Rem. Fireball. 10.5-inch vent rib bbl., 16.75 inches overall. Weight: 3.75 lbs. Adj. rear sight, blade front, receiver drilled and tapped for scope mounts. Blued finish. One-piece brown nylon stock. Made 1963-88.

MODEL XP-100 VARMINT SPECIAL ..... NiB $510 Ex $407 Gd $216
Bolt-action, single-shot, long-range pistol. Calibers: .223 Rem., 7mm BR. 14.5-inch bbl., 21.25 inches overall. Weight: About 4.25 lbs. One-piece Du Pont nylon stock w/universal grips. Made 1986-92.

MODEL XP-100R CUSTOM REPEATER
Same general specifications as Model XP-100 Custom except 4- or 5-shot repeater chambered for .22-250, .223 Rem., .250 Savage, 7mm-08 Rem., .308 Win., .35 Rem. and .350 Rem. Mag. Kevlar-reinforced synthetic or fiberglass stock w/blind magazine and sling swivel studs. Made 1992-94 and 1998 to date.
Model XP-100R (fiberglass stock) .... NiB $676 Ex $541 Gd $368
Model XP-100R KS (kevlar stock) .... NiB $613 Ex $566 Gd $360

XP-22R
RIMFIRE REPEATER .... NiB $544 Ex $435 Gd $296
Bolt-action clip repeater built on Model 541-style action. Calibers: .22 Short, Long, LR. Five-shot magazine, 14.5-inch bbl., weight: 4.25 lbs. Rem. synthetic stock. Announced 1991 but not produced.

RG REVOLVERS — Mfg. By Rohm Gmbh, Germany *(Imported by R.G. Industries, Miami, Florida)*

MODEL 23
SA/DA. 6-shot magazine, swing-out cylinder. Caliber: .22 LR. 1.75- or 3.38-inch bbl., Overall length: 5.13 and 7.5 inches. Weight: 16-17 oz. Fixed sights. Blued or nickel finish. Disc. 1986.
Blued finish .... NiB $95 Ex $80 Gd $50
Nickel finish .... NiB $95 Ex $80 Gd $50

MODEL 38S
SA/DA. Caliber: .38 Special. Six-shot magazine, swing-out cylinder. Three- or 4-inch bbl., overall length: 8.25 and 9.25 inches. Weight: 32-34 oz. Windage-adj. rear sight. Blued finish. Disc. 1986.
W/plastic grips .... NiB $131 Ex $105 Gd $71
W/wood grips .... NiB $150 Ex $120 Gd $82

ROSSI REVOLVERS — Sáo Leopoldo, Brazil Manufactured by Amadeo Rossi S.A. *(Imported by Interarms, Alexanderia, Virginia)*

MODEL 31 DA REVOLVER .... NiB $120 Ex $105 Gd $70
Caliber: .38 Special. Five-shot cylinder, 4-inch bbl., weight: 20 oz. Blued or nickel finish. Disc. 1985.

MODEL 51 DA REVOLVER .... NiB $125 Ex $110 Gd $80
Caliber: .22 LR. Six-shot cylinder, 6-inch bbl., weight: 28 oz. Blued finish. Disc. 1985.

MODEL 68 .... NiB $165 Ex $135 Gd $70
Caliber: .38 Special. Five-round magazine, 2- or 3-inch bbl., overall length: 6.5 and 7.5 inches. Weight: 21-23 oz. Blued finish. Nickel finish available w/3-inch bbl. Disc. 1998.

MODEL 84 DA REVOLVER .... NiB $190 Ex $155 Gd $125
Caliber: .38 Special. Six-shot cylinder, 3-inch bbl., 8 inches overall. Weight: 27.5 oz. Stainless steel finish. Imported 1984-86.

MODEL 85 DA REVOLVER .... NiB $206 Ex $165 Gd $112
Same as Model 84 except has vent rib. Imported 1985-86.

MODEL 88 DA REVOLVER
Caliber: .38 Special. Five-shot cylinder, 2- or 3-inch bbl., weight: 21 oz. Stainless steel finish. Imported 1988-98.
Model 88 (disc.) .... NiB $195 Ex $145 Gd $110
**Model 88 Lady Rossi
(round butt) .... NiB $219 Ex $175 Gd $119**

MODEL 88/2 DA REVOLVER. ...... NiB $181 Ex $145 Gd $99
Caliber: .38 Special. Five-shot cylinder, 2- or 3-inch bbl., 6.5 inches overall. Weight: 21 oz. Stainless steel finish. Imported 1985-87.

MODEL 89 DA REVOLVER .... NiB $175 Ex $135 Gd $115
Caliber: .32 S&W. Six-shot cylinder, 3-inch bbl., 7.5 inches overall. Weight: 17 oz. Stainless steel finish. Imported 1989-90.

MODEL 94 DA REVOLVER . . . . **NiB $163 Ex $143 Gd $97**
Caliber: .38 Special. Six-shot cylinder, 3-inch bbl., 8 inches overall.
Weight: 29 oz. Imported 1985-88.

MODEL 95 (951) REVOLVER . . . . . **NiB $192 Ex $153 Gd $104**
Caliber: .38 Special. Six-round magazine, 3-inch bbl., 8 inches
overall. Weight: 27.5 oz. Vent rib. Blued finish. Imported 1985-90.

MODEL 351/352 REVOLVERS
Caliber: .38 Special. Five-shot cylinder, 2-inch bbl., 6.87 inches
overall. Weight: 22 oz. Ramp front and rear adjustable sights.
Stainless or matte blued finish. Imported 1999 to date.
Model 351 (matte blue finish) . . . . . **NiB $255 Ex $204 Gd $133**
Model 352 (stainless finish) . . . . **NiB $204 Ex $163 Gd $111**

MODEL 461/462 REVOLVERS
Caliber: .357 Magnum. Six-shot cylinder, 2-inch heavy bbl., 6.87
inches overall. Weight: 26 oz. Rubber grips w/ serrated ramp front
sight. Stainless or matte blued finish. Imported 1999 to date.
Model 461
(Matte blue finish) . . . . **NiB $255 Ex $204 Gd $133**
Model 462
(stainless finish) . . . . **NiB $280 Ex $235 Gd $168**

MODEL 511 DA REVOLVER . . . . . **NiB $194 Ex $163 Gd $127**
Similar to the Model 51 except in stainless steel. Imported 1986-
1990.

MODEL 515 DA REVOLVER . . . . . . **NiB $210 Ex $168 Gd $114**
Calibers: .22 LR, .22 Mag. Six-shot cylinder, 4-inch bbl., 9 inches
overall. Weight: 30 oz. Red ramp front sight, adj. square-notched
rear. Stainless finish. Checkered hardwood grips. Imported from
1992 to date.

MODEL 518 DA REVOLVER . . . . . . **NiB $198 Ex $158 Gd $108**
Similar to the Model 515 except in caliber .22 LR. Imported 1993
to date.

MODEL 677 DA REVOLVER . . . . . **NiB $220 Ex $178 Gd $124**
Caliber: .357 Mag. Six-shot cylinder, 2-inch bbl., 6.87 inches overall. Weight: 26 oz. Serrated front ramp sight, channel rear. Matte
blue finish. Contoured rubber grips. Imported 1997 to date.

MODEL 720 DA REVOLVER . . . . . **NiB $223 Ex $178 Gd $121**
Caliber: .44 Special. Five-shot cylinder, 3-inch bbl., 8 inches overall. Weight: 27.5 oz. Red ramp front sight, adj. square-notched rear.
Stainless finish. Checkered Neoprene combat-style grips. Imported
from 1992 to date.

MODEL 841 DA REVOLVER . . . . . . **NiB $210 Ex $168 Gd $114**
Same general specifications as Model 84 except has 4-inch bbl., (9
inches overall), weight: 30 oz. Imported 1985-86.

MODEL 851 DA REVOLVER . . . . . . **NiB $208 Ex $178 Gd $117**
Same general specifications as Model 85 except w/3-or 4-inch bbl.,
8 inches overall (with 3-inch bbl.). Weight: 27.5 oz. (with 3-inch
bbl.). Red ramp front sight, adj. square-notched rear. Stainless finish.
Checkered hardwood grips. Imported 1991 to date.

MODEL 877 DA REVOLVER . . . . . **NiB $231 Ex $189 Gd $135**
Same general specifications as Model 677 except stainless steel.
Made 1996 to date.

MODEL 941 DA REVOLVER . . . . . . **NiB $192 Ex $153 Gd $104**
Caliber: .38 Special. Six-shot cylinder, 4-inch bbl., 9 inches overall.
Weight: 30 oz. Blued finish. Imported 1985-86.

Rossi Model 971
DA Revolver

MODEL 951 DA REVOLVER . . . . . . **NiB $214 Ex $173 Gd $121**
Previous designation M95 w/same general specifications.

MODEL 971 DA REVOLVER
Caliber: .357 Magnum. Six-shot cylinder, 2.5-, 4- or 6-inch bbl., 9
inches overall (with 4-inch bbl.). Weight: 36 oz. (with 4-inch bbl.).
Blade front sight, adj. square-notched rear. Blued or stainless finish.
Checkered hardwood grips. Imported 1990 to date.
Blued finish . . . . **NiB $198 Ex $158 Gd $107**
Stainless finish . . . . **NiB $210 Ex $168 Gd $114**
W/compensated
bbl., add **$15**

MODEL 971 VRC
DA REVOLVER . . . . **NiB $272 Ex $219 Gd $133**
Same general specifications as Model 971 stainless except w/venti-
lated rib and compensated bbl. Made 1996 to date.

CYCLOPS DA REVOLVER . . . . **NiB $393 Ex $309 Gd $235**
Caliber: .357 Mag. Six-shot cylinder, 6- or 8-inch compensated
slab-sided bbl., 11.75 or 13.75 inches overall. Weight: 44 oz. or 51
oz. Undercut blade front sight, fully adjustable rear. B-Square scope
mount and rings. Stainless steel finish. Checkered rubber grips.
Made 1997 to date.

DA REVOLVER. . . . . **NiB $159 Ex $127 Gd $87**
Calibers: .22 LR, .32 S&W Long, .38 Special. Five-shot (.38) or 6-
shot cylinder (other calibers), bbl. lengths: 3-, 6-inches. Weight: 22
oz. (3-inch bbl.). Adj. Rear sight, ramp front. Blued or nickel finish.
Wood or plastic grips. Imported 1965-91.

SPORTSMAN'S .22 . . . . **NiB $223 Ex $178 Gd $121**
Caliber: .22 LR. Six-round magazine, 4-inch bbl., 9 inches overall.
Weight: 30 oz. Stainless steel finish. Disc. 1991.

RUBY PISTOL
Manufactured by Gabilondo y Urresti, Eibar, Spain, and others

7.65MM
AUTOMATIC PISTOL . . . . **NiB $270 Ex $204 Gd $71**
Secondary standard service pistol of the French Army in world wars
I and II. Essentially the same as the Alkartasuna (see separate listing).
Other manufacturers: Armenia Elgoibarresa y Cia., Eceolaza y
Vicinai y Cia., Hijos de Angel Echeverria y Cia., Bruno Salaverria y
Cia., Zulaika y Cia., all of Eibar, Spain-Gabilondo y Cia., Elgoibar
Spain; Ruby Arms Company, Guernica, Spain. Made 1914-.22.

Ruger Mark I Target W/5.5-inch Untapered Bull Barrel

Ruger Mark II

Ruger Mark II .22/.45 KP4

Ruger Mark II Stainless W/10-inch Bull Barrel

RUGER HANDGUNS — Southport, Connecticut Manufactured by Sturm, Ruger & Co.

Rugers made in 1976 are designated "Liberty" in honor of the U.S. Bicentennial and bring a premium of approximately 25 percent in value over regular models.

NOTE: *For ease in finding a particular Ruger handgun, the listings are divided into two groups: Automatic/Single-Shot Pistols (below) and Revolvers, which follow. For a complete listing, please refer to the index.*

AUTOMATIC/SINGLE-SHOT PISTOLS

HAWKEYE SINGLE-SHOT PISTOL . . . . . NiB $1339 Ex $1133 Gd $618
Built on a SA revolver frame w/cylinder replaced by a swing-out breechblock and fitted w/a bbl., w/integral chamber. Caliber: .256 Magnum. 8.5-inch bbl., 14.5 inches overall. Weight: 45 oz. Blued finish. Ramp front sight, click adj. rear. Smooth walnut grips. Made 1963-65 (3300 produced).

MARK I TARGET MODEL AUTOMATIC PISTOL
Caliber: .22 LR. 10-shot magazine, 5.25- and 6.88-inch heavy tapered or 5.5-inch untapered bull bbl., 10.88 inches overall (with 6.88-inch bbl.). Weight: 42 oz. (in 5.5- or 6.88-inch bbl.). Undercut target front sight, adj. rear. Blued finish. Hard rubber grips or checkered walnut thumbrest grips. Made 1951-81.
Standard . . . . NiB $257 Ex $206 Gd $134
W/red medallion . . . . NiB $515 Ex $438 Gd $283
Walnut grips, add $15

MARK II AUTOMATIC PISTOL
Caliber: .22 LR, standard or high velocity 10-shot magazine, 4.75- or 6-inch tapered bbl., 8.31 inches overall (with 4.75-inch bbl.). Weight: 36 oz. Fixed front sight, square notch rear. Blued or stainless finish. Made 1982 to date.
Blued. . . . . NiB $283 Ex $247 Gd $124
Stainless . . . . NiB $330 Ex $278 Gd $108
Bright stainless (ltd.
prod. 5,000 in 1982). . . . . NiB $509 Ex $407 Gd $277

MARK II .22/.45 AUTOMATIC PISTOL
Same general specifications as Ruger Mark II .22 LR except w/blued or stainless receiver and bbl., in four lengths: 4-inch tapered w/adj. sights (P4), 4.75-inch tapered w/fixed sights (KP4), 5.25-inch tapered w/adj. sights (KP 514) and 5.5-inch bull (KP 512). Fitted w/Zytel grip frame of the same design as the Model 1911 45 ACP. Made 1993 to date.
Model KP4 (4.75-inch bbl.). . . . . NiB $221 Ex $194 Gd $118
Model KP512, KP514
(w/5.5- or 5.25-inch bbl.) . . . . NiB $274 Ex $243 Gd $185
Model P4, P512
(Blued w/4- or 5.5-inch bbl.) . . . . NiB $212 Ex $170 Gd $115

MARK II BULL BARREL MODEL
Same as standard Mark II except for bull bbl. (5.5- or 10-inch). Weight: About 2.75 lbs.
Blued finish . . . . NiB $238 Ex $191 Gd $130
Stainless finish (intro. 1985) . . . . . . NiB $322 Ex $257 Gd $175

MARK II GOVERNMENT MODEL AUTO PISTOL
Civilian version of the Mark II used by U.S. Armed Forces. Caliber: .22 LR. 10-shot magazine, 6.88-inch bull bbl., 11.13 inches overall. Weight: 44 oz. Blued or stainless finish. Made from 1986 to date.
Blued model (MK687G commercial) . . . . . NiB $345 Ex $278 Gd $144
Stainless steel model
(KMK678G commercial) . . . . NiB $335 Ex $268 Gd $182
W/U.S. markings (military model) . . . . NiB $566 Ex $515 Gd $340

MARK II TARGET MODEL
Caliber: .22 LR. 10-shot magazine, 4-, 5.5- and 10-inch bull bbl. or 5.25- and 6.88-inch heavy tappered bbl., weight: 38 oz. to 52 oz. 11.13 inches overall (with 6.88-inch bbl.). Made from 1982 to date.
Blued . . . . NiB $283 Ex $247 Gd $129
Stainless steel . . . . NiB $350 Ex $278 Gd $108

**Ruger Mark II
Target Model**

**Ruger P-89
DAC/DAO**

Ruger P-90

**Ruger P-93
Compact**

MODEL P-85 AUTOMATIC PISTOL

Caliber: 9mm. DA, recoil-operated. 15-shot capacity, 4.5 inch bbl., 7.84 inches overall. Weight: 32 oz. Fixed rear sight, square-post front. Available w/decocking levers, ambidextrous safety or in DA only. Blued or stainless finish. Made 1987-92.

Blued finish	NiB $345	Ex $304	Gd $206
Stainless steel finish	NiB $360	Ex $324	Gd $288

MODEL P-89 AUTOMATIC PISTOL

Caliber: 9mm. DA w/slide-mounted safety levers. 15-shot magazine, 4.5-inch bbl., 7.84 inches overall. Weight: 32 oz. Square-post front sight, adj. rear w/3-dot system. Blued or stainless steel finish. Grooved black Xenoy grips. Made from 1992 to date.

P-89 blued	NiB $391	Ex $340	Gd $206
P-89 stainless	NiB $438	Ex $371	Gd $309

MODEL P-89 DAC/DAO AUTO PISTOLS

Similar to the standard Model P-89 except the P-89 DAC has ambidextrous decocking levers. The P-89 DAO operates in double-action-only mode. Made 1991 to date.

P-89 DAC blued	NiB $391	Ex $335	Gd $206
P-89 DAC stainless	NiB $438	Ex $360	Gd $257
P-89 DAO stainless	NiB $438	Ex $360	Gd $257

MODEL P-90, KP90 DA AUTOMATIC PISTOL

Caliber: .45 ACP. Seven-shot magazine, 4.5-inch bbl., 7.88 inches overall. Weight: 33.5 oz. Square-post front sight adj. square-notched rear w/3-dot system. Grooved black Xenoy composition grips. Blued or stainless finish. DAC model has ambidextrous decocking levers. Made 1991 to date.

Model P-90 blued	NiB $438	Ex $360	Gd $206
Model P-90 DAC (decockers)	NiB $448	Ex $371	Gd $216
Model KP-90 DAC stainless	NiB $448	Ex $376	Gd $319
Model KP-90 DAC (decockers)	NiB $453	Ex $381	Gd $324

MODEL P-91 DA AUTOMATIC PISTOL

Same general specifications as the Model P-90 except chambered for .40 S&W w/12-shot double-column magazine, Made 1992-94.

Model P-91 Standard	NiB $397	Ex $345	Gd $288
Model P-91 DAC (decockers)	NiB $412	Ex $330	Gd $268
Model P-91 DAO (DA only)	NiB $418	Ex $335	Gd $268

MODEL P-93 COMPACT AUTO PISTOL

Similar to the standard Model P-89 except w/3.9-inch bbl., (7.3 inches overall) and weight: 31 oz. Stainless steel finish. Made 1993 to date.

Model P-93 DAC (decocker) (disc. 1994)	NiB $463	Ex $381	Gd $252
Model P-93 DAO (DA only)	NiB $443	Ex $350	Gd $242

MODEL P-94 AUTOMATIC PISTOL

Similar to the Model P-91 except w/4.25-inch bbl., Calibers: 9mm or .40 S&W. Blued or stainless steel finish. Made 1994 to date.

Model KP-94 DAC (S/S decocker)	NiB $463	Ex $3676	Gd $330
Model KP-94 DAO (S/S dble. action only)	NiB $438	Ex $371	Gd $325
Model P-94 DAC (Blued decocker)	NiB $412	Ex $324	Gd $288
Model P-94 DAO (blued dble. action only)	NiB $402	Ex $308	Gd $268

Ruger Bearcat SA
(Old Model)

Ruger Bisley
Colt .45 Long (New Model)

Ruger Bisley
Single-Six Small Frame

Ruger Blackhawk

Ruger Blackhawk
SA .44

Ruger P-97

MODEL P-95 AUTOMATIC PISTOL
Caliber: 9mm Parabellum. 10-shot magazine, 3.9-inch bbl., 7.3 inches overall. Weight: 27 oz. Square-post front sight, drift adjustable rear w/3-dot system. Molded polymer grip-frame fitted w/stainless or chrome-moly slide. Ambidextrous decocking levers (P-95D) or double action only (DAO). Matte black or stainless finish. Made 1997 to date.

P-95 blued . . . . NiB $355 Ex $288 Gd $165
P-95 stainless . . . . NiB $391 Ex $314 Gd $170

MODEL P-97 AUTOMATIC PISTOL
Caliber: .45 ACP. Eight-shot magazine, 4.5- inch bbl., 7.25 inches overall. Weight: 30.5 oz. Square-post front sight adj. square-notched rear w/3-dot system. Grooved black Xenoy composition grips. Blued or stainless finish. DAC model has ambidextrous decocking levers. Made 1999 to date.
Model KP-97
DAO stainless . . . . NiB $407 Ex $324 Gd $206
Model KP-97
DAC (decockers) . . . . NiB $407 Ex $324 Gd $206

STANDARD MODEL AUTOMATIC PISTOL
Caliber: .22 LR. Nine-shot magazine, 4.75- or 6-inch bbl., 8.75 inches overall (with 4.75-inch bbl.). Weight: 36 oz. (with 4.75 inch bbl.). Fixed sights. Blued finish. Hard rubber or checkered walnut grips. Made from 1949 to date. Note: After the death of Alexander Sturm in 1951, the color of the eagle on the grip medallion was changed from red to black as a memorial. Known as the "Red Eagle Automatic," this early type is now a collector's item. Made 1951-81.
W/red eagle medallion . . . . NiB $541 Ex $438 Gd $237
W/black eagle medallion . . . . NiB $201 Ex $180 Gd $103
Walnut grips, add $15

NOTE: *This section contains only Ruger Revolvers. Automatic and Single-Shot Pistols may be found on the preceding pages. For a complete listing of Ruger handguns, please refer to the index.*

REVOLVERS

BEARCAT SA (OLD MODEL)
Aluminum frame. Caliber: .22 LR. Six-shot cylinder, 4-inch bbl., 8.88 inches overall. Weight: 17 oz. Fixed sights. Blued finish. Smooth walnut grips. Made 1958-73.
W/brass trigger guard . . . . NiB $360 Ex $309 Gd $206
W/aniodized
aluminum trigger . . . . NiB $618 Ex $597 Gd $309

BEARCAT, SUPER (OLD MODEL) . . . . NiB $360 Ex $299 Gd $196
Same general specifications as Bearcat except has steel frame. Weight: 25 oz. Made 1971-73.

NEW MODEL BEARCAT REVOLVER
Same general specifications as Super Bearcat except all steel frame and trigger guard. Interlocked mechanism and transfer bar. Calibers: .22 LR and .22WMR. Interchangeable 6-shot cylinders (disc. 1996). Smooth walnut stocks w/Ruger medallion. Made 1994 to date.
Convertible model (disc.
1996 after factory recall) . . . . NiB $360 Ex $283 Gd $206
Standard model (.22 LR only) . . . . NiB $319 Ex $257 Gd $154

BISLEY SA REVOLVER, LARGE FRAME
Calibers: .357 Mag., .41 Mag. .44 Mag., .45 Long Colt. 7.5-inch bbl., 13 inches overall. Weight: 48 oz. Non-fluted or fluted cylinder, no engraving. Ramp front sight, adj. rear. Satin blued or stainless. Made 1986 to date.
Blued finish . . . . NiB $433 Ex $345 Gd $185
Vaquero/Bisley (blued w/case colored fr.) . . . . NiB $433 Ex $345 Gd $185
Vaquero/Bisley (stainless steel) . . . NiB $425 Ex $330 Gd $196
W/ivory grips, add $35

BISLEY SINGLE-SIX REVOLVER, SMALL FRAME
Calibers: .22 LR and .32 Mag. Six-shot cylinder, 6.5-inch bbl., 11.5 inches overall. Weight: 41 oz. Fixed rear sight, blade front. Blue finish. Goncalo Alves grips. Made 1986 to date.
.22 caliber . . . . NiB $345 Ex $257 Gd $154
.32 H&R Mag. . . . . NiB $397 Ex $309 Gd $268

BLACKHAWK SA CONVERTIBLE (OLD MODEL)
Same as Blackhawk except has extra cylinder. Caliber combinations: .357 Magnum and 9mm Para., .45 Colt and .45 Automatic. Made 1967-72.
.357/9mm combo (early w/o prefix SN) . . . NiB $412 Ex $360 Gd $201
.357/9mm combo (late w/prefix SN) . . . . . NiB $406 Ex $324 Gd $220
.45 LC/.45 ACP combo
(1967-85 & 1999 to date) . . . . NiB $515 Ex $463 Gd $299

BLACKHAWK SA REVOLVER (OLD MODEL)
Calibers: .30 Carbine, .357 Magnum, .41 Magnum, .45 Colt. Six-shot cylinder, bbl. lengths: 4.63-inch (.357, .41, .45 caliber), 6.5-inch (.357, .41 caliber), 7.5-inch (.30, .45 caliber). 10.13 inches overall (.357 Mag. w/4.63-inch bbl.). Weight: 38 oz. (.357 w/4.63-inch bbl.). Ramp front sight, adj. rear. Blued finish. Checkered hard rubber or smooth walnut grips. Made 1956-73.
.30 Carbine, .357 Mag. . . . . NiB $412 Ex $360 Gd $201
.41 Mag. . . . . NiB $412 Ex $309 Gd $201
.45 Colt . . . . NiB $433 Ex $371 Gd $206

BLACKHAWK SA "FLAT-TOP" REVOLVER (OLD MODEL)
Similar to standard Blackhawk except w/"Flat Top" cylinder strap. Calibers: .357 or .44 Magnum. Six-shot fluted cylinder, 4.625-, 6.5-, 7.5- or 10-inch bbl., adj. rear sight, ramp front. Blued finish. Black rubber or smooth walnut grips. Made 1956-63.
.357 Mag. (w/4.625-inch bbl.) . . . . NiB $515 Ex $463 Gd $232
.357 Mag. (w/6.5-inch bbl.) . . . . NiB $721 Ex $567 Gd $309
.357 Mag. (w/10-inch bbl.) . . . . NiB $1236 Ex $1082 Gd $618
.44 Mag. (w/fluted cylinder/ 4.625-inch bbl.) . . NiB $721 Ex $567 Gd $309
.44 Mag. (w/fluted cylinder/ 6.5-inch bbl.) . . . . NiB $773 Ex $618 Gd $360
.44 Mag. (w/fluted cylinder/ 10-inch bbl.) . . NiB $1236 Ex $1082 Gd $618

GP-100 DA REVOLVER
Caliber: .357 Magnum. Three- to 4-inch heavy bbl., or 6-inch standard or heavy bbl., Overall length: 9.38 or 11.38 inches. Cushioned grip panels. Made from 1986 to date.
Blued finish . . . . NiB $412 Ex $324 Gd $191
Stainless steel finish . . . . NiB $438 Ex $335 Gd $232

Ruger GP-100
DA Revolver

Ruger New Model Blackhawk Convertible

Ruger Blackhawk High-Gloss Stainless
(New Model) .357 Magnum

NEW MODEL BLACKHAWK CONVERTIBLE
Same as New Model Blackhawk except has extra cylinder. Blued finish only. Caliber combinations: .357 Magnum/9mm Para., .44 Magnum/.44-40, .45 Colt/.45 ACP. (Limited Edition Buckeye Special .32-20/.32 H&R Mag. or .38-40/10mm). Made 1973 to date.
.32-20/.32 H&R Mag. (1989-90) . . . . NiB $381 Ex $304 Gd $165
.38-40/10mm (1990-91) . . . . NiB $354 Ex $283 Gd $193
.357/9mm combo . . . . NiB $381 Ex $304 Gd $165
.44/.44-40 combo (disc.1982) . . . . NiB $418 Ex $335 Gd $228
.45 LC/.45 ACP combo (disc. 1985) . . . . . NiB $386 Ex $309 Gd $210

NEW MODEL BLACKHAWK SA REVOLVER
Interlocked mechanism. Calibers: .30 Carbine, .357 Magnum, .357 Maximum, .41 Magnum, .44 Magnum, .44 Special, .45 Colt. Six-shot cylinder, bbl. lengths: 4.63-inch (.357, .41, .45 Colt); 5.5 inch (.44 Mag., .44 Spec.); 6.5-inch (.357, .41, .45 Long Colt); 7.5-inch (.30, .45, .44 Special, .44 Mag.); 10.5-inch in .44 Mag; 10.38 inches overall (.357 Mag. w/4.63-inch bbl.). Weight: 40 oz. (.357 w/4.63-inch bbl.). Adj. rear sight, ramp front. Blued finish or stainless steel; latter only in .357 or .45 LC. Smooth walnut grips. Made 1973 to date.
Blued finish . . . . NiB $360 Ex $252 Gd $139
High-gloss stainless (.357 Mag., .45 LC) . . . NiB $354 Ex $283 Gd $193
Satin stainless (.357 Mag., .45 LC) . . . . . . NiB $341 Ex $273 Gd $185
.357 Maximum SRM (1984-85) . . . . NiB $381 Ex $304 Gd $180

Ruger Blackhawk Blued finish (New Model

Ruger Single-Six SSM (New Model)

Ruger Super Blackhawk (New Model)

Ruger Super Single-Six Convertible (New Model)

Ruger Police Service-Six Stainless Steel

Ruger Redhawk

Ruger Super Redhawk Stainless DA Scope-Ring

NEW MODEL SINGLE-SIX SSM REVOLVER . . . . NiB $309 Ex $283 Gd $154
Same general specifications as standard Single-Six except chambered for .32 H&R Magnum cartridge. Bbl. lengths: 4.63, 5.5, 6.5 or 9.5 inches.

NEW MODEL SUPER BLACKHAWK SA REVOLVER
Interlocked mechanism. Caliber: .44 Magnum. Six-shot cylinder, 5.5-inch, 7.5-inch and 10.5-inch bull bbl. 13.38 inches overall. Weight: 48 oz. Adj. rear sight, ramp front. Blued and stainless steel finish. Smooth walnut grips. Made 1973 to date, 5.5-inch bbl. made 1987 to date.
Blued finish . . . . NiB $386 Ex $309 Gd $196
**High-gloss stainless
(1994-96)** . . . . NiB $380 Ex $304 Gd $207
Satin stainless steel . . . . NiB $367 Ex $293 Gd $200

NEW MODEL SUPER SINGLE-SIX CONVERTIBLE REVOLVER
SA w/interlocked mechanism. Calibers: .22 LR and .22 WMR. Interchangeable 6-shot cylinders. Bbl. lengths: 4.63, 5.5, 6.5, 9.5 inches. 10.81 inches overall (with 4.63 inch bbl.). Weight: 33 oz. (with 4.63-inch bbl.). Adj. rear sight, ramp front. Blued finish or stainless steel; latter only w/5.5- or 6.5-inch bbl., smooth walnut grips. Made 1972 to date.
Blued finish . . . . NiB $299 Ex $227 Gd $113
High-gloss stainless (1994-96) . . . . . NiB $238 Ex $191 Gd $130
Stainless steel . . . . NiB $335 Ex $263 Gd $206

POLICE SERVICE-SIX
Same general specifications as Speed-Six except has square butt. Stainless steel models and 9mm Para. caliber available w/only 4-inch bbl., Made 1971-88.
.38 Special, blued finish . . . . NiB $257 Ex $227 Gd $175
.38 Special, stainless steel . . . . NiB $278 Ex $242 Gd $216
**.357 Magnum or 9mm Para.,
blued finish** . . . . NiB $257 Ex $227 Gd $175
.357 Magnum, stainless steel . . . . . . NiB $283 Ex $247 Gd $216

REDHAWK DA REVOLVER
Calibers: .357 Mag., .41 Mag., .45 LC, .44 Mag. Six-shot cylinder, 5.5- and 7.5-inch bbl., 11 and 13 inches overall, respectively. Weight: About 52 oz. Adj. rear sight, interchangeable front sights. Stainless finish. Made 1979 to date; .357 Mag. disc. 1986. Alloy steel model w/blued finish intro. in 1986 in .41 Mag. and .44 Mag. calibers.
Blued finish . . . . **NiB $494 Ex $330 Gd $185**
Stainless steel . . . . **NiB $530 Ex $417 Gd $335**

**Ruger
Super Redhawk Stainless**

SUPER REDHAWK STAINLESS DA SCOPE-RING REVOLVER
Calibers: .44 Mag., .454 Casull and .45 LC. Six-shot cylinder, 7.5- to 9.5- inch bbl., 13 to 15 inches overall. Weight: 53 to 58 oz. Integral scope mounting system w/stainless rings. Adjustable rear sight. Cushioned grip panels. Made 1987 to date.
**Model .44 Mag. 7.5- inch
bbl., stainless** . . . . **NiB $566 Ex $463 Gd $335**
**Model .44 Mag. 9.5- inch
bbl., stainless** . . . . **NiB $566 Ex $463 Gd $335**
**Model .454 Casull & 45 LC
Stainless/target gray stainless** . . . . . **NiB $659 Ex $536 Gd $407**

SECURITY-SIX DA REVOLVER
Caliber: .357 Magnum, handles .38 Special. Six-shot cylinder, bbl. lengths: 2.25-, 4-, 6-inch, 9.25 inches overall (with 4-inch bbl.). Weight: 33.5 oz. (with 4-inch bbl.). Adj. rear sight, ramp front. Blued finish or stainless steel. Square butt. Checkered walnut grips. Made 1971-85.
Blued finish . . . . **NiB $257 Ex $206 Gd $140**
Stainless steel . . . . **NiB $303 Ex $242 Gd $165**

**Ruger
Single-Six**

SINGLE-SIX SA REVOLVER (OLD MODEL)
Calibers: .22 LR, .22 WMR. Six-shot cylinder. bbl., lengths: 4.63, 5.5, 6.5, 9.5 inches, 10.88 inches overall (with 5.5-inch bbl.). Weight: About 35 oz. Fixed sights. Blued finish. Checkered hard rubber or smooth walnut grips. Made 1953-73. Note: Pre-1956 model w/flat loading gate is worth about twice as much as later version.
Standard . . . . **NiB $309 Ex $232 Gd $118**
**Convertible (w/two cylinders,
.22 LR/.22 WMR)** . . . . **NiB $463 Ex $412 Gd $206**

SINGLE-SIX — LIGHTWEIGHT . . . . **NiB $515 Ex $412 Gd $180**
Same general specifications as Single-Six except has 4.75-inch bbl., lightweight alloy cylinder and frame, 10 inches overall length, weight: 23 oz. Made in 1956.

**Ruger
Single-Six Lightweight**

SP101 DA REVOLVER
Calibers: .22 LR, .32 Mag., 9mm, .38 Special+P, .357 Mag. Five- or 6-shot cylinder, 2.25-, 3.06- or 4-inch bbl., weight: 25-34 oz. Stainless steel finish. Cushioned grips. Made 1988 to date. See illustration next page.
Standard model . . . . **NiB $397 Ex $252 Gd $247**
**DAO model (DA only,
spurless hammer)** . . . . **NiB $376 Ex $288 Gd $247**

**Ruger
Super Single-Six Convertible**

SPEED-SIX DA REVOLVER
Calibers: .38 Special, .357 Magnum, 9mm Para. Six-shot cylinder, 2.75-, 4-inch bbl., (9mm available only w/2.75-inch bbl.). 7.75 inches overall (2.75-inch bbl.). Weight: 31 oz. (with 2.75-inch bbl.). Fixed sights. Blued or stainless steel finish; latter available in .38 Special (with 2.75 inch bbl.), .357 Magnum and 9mm w/either bbl., Round butt. Checkered walnut grips. Made 1973-87.
.38 Special, blued finish . . . . **NiB $237 Ex $211 Gd $161**
.38 Special, stainless steel . . . . **NiB $288 Ex $252 Gd $124**
**.357 Magnum or 9mm Para.,
blued finish** . . . . **NiB $309 Ex $257 Gd $185**
**.357 Magnum or 9mm Para.,
stainless steel** . . . . **NiB $309 Ex $257 Gd $185**

Ruger Single-Six Fixed Sight

Ruger Vaquero Stainless Steel

Ruger Vaquero Blued

Ruger SP101

SUPER BLACKHAWK
SA .44 MAGNUM REVOLVER (OLD MODEL)
SA w/heavy frame and unfluted cylinder. Caliber: .44 Magnum. Six-shot cylinder. 6.5- or 7.5-inch bbl., Adj. rear sight, ramp front. Steel or brass grip frame w/square-back trigger guard. Smooth walnut grips. Blued finish. Made 1956-73.

W/6.5-inch bbl., ... NiB $397 Ex $304 Gd $175
W/7.5-inch bbl., ... NiB $397 Ex $304 Gd $175
W/brass gripframe .... NiB $895 Ex $716 Gd $487

VAQUERO SA REVOLVER
Calibers: .357 Mag., .44-40, .44 Magnum, .45 Colt. Six-shot cylinder. Bbl. lengths: 4.625, 5.5, 7.5 inches, 13.63 inches overall (with 7.5-inch bbl.). Weight: 41 oz. (with 7.5-inch bbl.). Blade front sight, grooved topstrap rear. Blued w/color casehardened frame or polished stainless finish. Smooth rosewood grips w/Ruger medallion. Made 1993 to date.
Blued w/color-case
hardened frame............... NiB $433 Ex $330 Gd $278
Stainless finish................. NiB $433 Ex $330 Gd $278
W/ivory grips, add................................... $41

RUSSIAN SERVICE PISTOLS Mfd. by Government plants at Tula and elsewhere

Tokarev-type pistols have also been made in Hungary, Poland, Yugoslavia, People's Republic of China, N. Korea.

MODEL 30 TOKAREV SERVICE AUTOMATIC
Modified Colt-Browning type. Caliber: 7.62mm Russian Auto (also uses 7.63mm Mauser Auto cartridge). Eight-shot magazine, 4.5-inch bbl., 7.75 inches overall. Weight: About 29 oz. Fixed sights. Made 1930 mid-1950s. Note: A slightly modified version w/improved locking system and different disconnector was adopted in 1933.
Standard Service Model TT30 ..... NiB $331 Ex $296 Gd $168
Standard Service Model TT33 ..... NiB $331 Ex $296 Gd $168
Recent imports (distinguished
by importer marks) .... NiB $143 Ex $112 Gd $61

MODEL PM
MAKAROV AUTO PISTOL........ NiB $459 Ex $408 Gd $194
Double-action, blowback design. Caliber: 9mm Makarov. Eight-shot magazine, 3.8-inch bbl., 6.4 inches overall. Weight: 26 oz. Blade front sight, square-notched rear. Checkered composition grips.
Standard Service Model PM
(Pistole Makarov)............... NiB $478 Ex $382 Gd $260
Recent imports (distinguished
by importer marks) .... NiB $192 Ex $153 Gd $104

SAKO HANDGUNS — Riihimaki, Finland Manufactured by Oy Sako Ab

.22-.32 OLYMPIC PISTOL (TRIACE)
Calibers: .22 LR, .22 Short, .32 S&W Long. Five-round magazine, 6- or 8.85- (.22 Short) inch bbl., weight: About 46 oz. (.22 LR); 44 oz. (.22 Short); 48 oz. (.32). Steel frame. ABS plastic, anatomically designed grip. Non-reflecting matte black upper surface and chromium-plated slide. Equipped w/carrying case and tool set. Limited importation 1983-89.
Sako .22 or .32
Single pistol................. NiB $1326 Ex $1173 Gd $663
Sako Triace, triple-barrel set
w/wooden grip .... NiB $2550 Ex $2244 Gd $1224

SAUER HANDGUNS
Mfd. through WW II by J. P. Sauer & Sohn, Suhl, Germany. Now mfd. by J. P. Sauer & Sohn, GmbH, Eckernförde, West Germany

See also listings under Sig Sauer.

MODEL 1913 POCKET
AUTOMATIC PISTOL . . . . **NiB $301 Ex $230 Gd $148**
Caliber: .32 Automatic (7.65mm). Seven-shot magazine, 3-inch bbl., 5.88 inches overall. Weight: 22 oz. Fixed sights. Blued finish. Black hard rubber grips. Made 1913-30.

MODEL 1930 POCKET AUTOMATIC PISTOL
Authority Model (Behorden Model). Successor to Model 1913, has improved grip and safety. Caliber: .32 Auto (7.65mm). Seven-shot magazine, 3-inch bbl., 5.75 inches overall. Weight: 22 oz. Fixed sights. Blued finish. Black hard rubber grips. Made 1930-38. Note: Some pistols made w/indicator pin showing when cocked. Also mfd. w/dual slide and receiver; this type weight: about 7 oz. less than the standard model.
Steel model . . . . **NiB $332 Ex $235 Gd $148**
Dural (alloy) model . . . . **NiB $1563 Ex $1250 Gd $867**

MODEL 38H DA AUTOMATIC PISTOL
Calibers: .25 Auto (6.35mm), .32 Auto (7.65mm), .380 Auto (9mm). Specifications shown are for .32 Auto model. Seven-shot magazine, 3.25-inch bbl., 6.25 inches overall. Weight: 20 oz. Fixed sights. Blued finish. Black plastic grips. Also made in dual model weighing about 6 oz. less. Made 1938-1945. Note: This pistol, designated Model .38, was mfd. during WW II for military use. Wartime models are inferior in design to earlier production, as some lack safety lever.
.22 caliber . . . . **NiB $4080 Ex $3060 Gd $1275**
.32 ACP . . . . **NiB $403 Ex $331 Gd $189**
.32 ACP (w/Nazi proofs) . . . . **NiB $504 Ex $403 Gd $274**
.380 ACP . . . . **NiB $3507 Ex $2754 Gd $1275**

POCKET .25 (1913)
AUTOMATIC PISTOL . . . . **NiB $306 Ex $245 Gd $148**
Smaller version of Model 1913, issued about same time as .32 caliber model. Caliber: .25 Auto (6.35mm). Seven-shot magazine, 2.5-inch bbl., 4.25 inches overall. Weight: 14.5 oz. Fixed sights. Blued finish. Black hard rubber grips. Made 1913-30.

SINGLE-ACTION REVOLVERS
See listings under Hawes.

Sako Model .22-.32 Olympic

Sauer 1930 Pocket

Savage Model 101

SAVAGE ARMS CO. — Utica, New York

MODEL 101 SA
SINGLE-SHOT PISTOL . . . . **NiB $153 Ex $122 Gd $61**
Barrel integral w/swing-out cylinder. Calibers: .22 Short, Long, LR. 5.5-inch bbl. Weight: 20 oz. Blade front sight, slotted rear, adj. for windage. Blued finish. Grips of compressed, impregnated wood. Made 1960-68.

MODEL 501/502F "STRIKER" SERIES PISTOLS
Calibers: .22 LR., and .22 WMR. 5- or 10- shot magazine, 10-inch bbl., 19 inches overall. Weight: 4 lbs. Drilled and tapped sights for scope mount (installed). Ambidextrous rear grip. Made 2000 to date.
Model 501F, .22 LR . . . . **NiB $189 Ex $168 Gd $128**
Model 502F, .22 WMR . . . . **NiB $209 Ex $184 Gd $133**

MODEL 510/516 "STRIKER" SERIES PISTOLS
Calibers: 223 Rem., .22-250 Rem., .243 Win., 7mm-08 Rem., .260 Rem., and .308 Win. Three-shot magazine, 14-inch bbl., .22.5 inches overall. Drilled and tapped for scope mounts. Left hand bolt with right hand ejection. Stainless steel finish. Made 1998 to date.

(cont'd.) **MODEL 510/516 "STRIKER" SERIES PISTOLS**
Model 510F . . . . **NiB $393 Ex $342 Gd $184**
Model 516FSAK . . . . **NiB $484 Ex $398 Gd $342**
Model 516FSS . . . . **NiB $388 Ex $342 Gd $326**
Model 516BSAK . . . . **NiB $484 Ex $398 Gd $342**
Model 516BSS . . . . **NiB $546 Ex $439 Gd $357**

MODEL 1907 AUTOMATIC PISTOL
Caliber: .32 ACP, 10-shot magazine, 3.25-inch bbl., 6.5 inches overall. Weight: 19 oz. Checkered hard rubber or steel grips marked "Savage Quality," circling an Indian-head logo. Optional pearl grips. Blue, nickel, silver or gold finish. Made 1908-20.
Blued model (.32 ACP) . . . . **NiB $433 Ex $306 Gd $117**
Blued model (.380 ACP) . . . . **NiB $561 Ex $459 Gd $204**
W/ optional nickel,
silver or gold finish, add . . . . **$750-$1200**
W/optional pearl grips, add . . . . **$225-$950**

Sears/J.C. Higgins Model 88 DA Revolver

Security Model PM 357

Security Model PPM 357

Security Model PSS38

MODEL 1910 AUTOMATIC PISTOL
Calibers: .32 Auto, .380 Auto. 10-shot magazine (.32 cal.), 9-shot (.380 cal.). 3.75-inch bbl., (.32 cal.), 4.25-inch (.380 cal.). 6.5 inches overall (.32 cal.), 7 inches (.380 cal.). Weight: About 23 oz. Fixed sights. Blued finish. Hard rubber grips. Made in hammerless type w/grip safety or w/exposed hammer spur. Made 1910-17.
.32 ACP . . . . NiB $306 Ex $255 Gd $163
.380 ACP . . . . NiB $479 Ex $388 Gd $255

MODEL 1915 AUTOMATIC PISTOL
Same general specifications as the Savage Model 1907 except the Model 1915 is hammerless and has a grip safety. It is also chambered for both the .32 and .380 ACP. Made 1915-17.
.32 ACP . . . . NiB $535 Ex $459 Gd $229
.380 ACP . . . . NiB $669 Ex $536 Gd $364

U.S. ARMY TEST MODEL 1910 . NiB $7650 Ex $5610 Gd $2550
Caliber: .45 ACP, Seven-shot magazine w/exposed hammer. An enlarged version of the Model 1910 manufactured for military trials between 1907 and 1911. Note: Most "Trial Pistols" were refurbished and resold as commercial models. Values are for original Government Test Issues Models.

MODEL 1917 AUTOMATIC PISTOL
Same specifications as 1910 Model except has spur-type hammer and redesigned, heavier grip. Made 1917-28.
.32 ACP . . . . NiB $306 Ex $255 Gd $112
.380 ACP . . . . NiB $663 Ex $586 Gd $255

SEARS, ROEBUCK & COMPANY — Chicago, Illinois

J.C. HIGGINS MODEL 80
AUTO PISTOL . . . . NiB $178 Ex $127 Gd $97
Caliber: .22 LR. 10-shot magazine, 4.5- or 6.5-inch interchangeable bbl., 10.88 inches overall (with 6.5-inch bbl.). Weight: 41 oz. (with 6.5-inch bbl.). Fixed Partridge sights. Blued finish. Checkered grips w/thumbrest.

J.C. HIGGINS MODEL 88
DA REVOLVER . . . . NiB $117 Ex $92 Gd $61
Caliber: .22 LR. Nine-shot cylinder, 4- or 6-inch bbl., 9.5 inches (with 4-inch bbl.). Weight: 23 oz. (with 4-inch bbl.). Fixed sights. Blued or nickel finish. Checkered plastic grips.

J.C. HIGGINS RANGER
DA REVOLVER . . . . NiB $143 Ex $112 Gd $71
Caliber: .22 LR. Nine-shot cylinder, 5.5-inch bbl., 10.75 inches overall. Weight: 28 oz. Fixed sights. Blued or chrome finish. Checkered plastic grips.

SECURITY INDUSTRIES OF AMERICA — Little Ferry, New Jersey

MODEL PM 357 DA REVOLVER . . . . . NiB $229 Ex $178 Gd $127
Caliber: .357 Magnum. Five-shot cylinder, 2.5-inch bbl., 7.5 inches overall. Weight: 21 oz. Fixed sights. Stainless steel. Walnut grips. Made 1975-78.

MODEL PPM357 DA REVOLVER . . . . . NiB $229 Ex $178 Gd $127
Caliber: .357 Magnum. Five-shot cylinder, 2-inch bbl., 6.13 inches overall. Weight: 18 oz. Fixed sights. Stainless steel. Walnut grips. Made from 1976-78. Note: Spurless hammer (illustrated) was disc. in 1977; this model has the same conventional hammer as other Security revolvers.

MODEL PSS 38
DA REVOLVER . . . . **NiB $178 Ex $153 Gd $112**
Caliber: .38 Special. Five-shot cylinder, 2-inch bbl., 6.5 inches over-all. Weight: 18 oz. Fixed sights. Stainless steel. Walnut grips. Intro. 1973. disc.

R. F. SEDGLEY. INC. — Philadelphia, Pennsylvania

BABY HAMMERLESS
EJECTOR REVOLVER . . . . **NiB $561 Ex $459 Gd $204**
DA. Solid frame. Folding trigger. Caliber: .22 Long. Six-shot cylin-der, 4 inches overall. Weight: 6 oz. Fixed sights. Blued or nickel fin-ish. Rubber grips. Made c. 1930-39.

L. W. SEECAMP, INC. — Milford, Connecticut

MODEL LWS .25
DAO PISTOL . . . . **NiB $408 Ex $331 Gd $224**
Caliber: .25 ACP. Seven-shot magazine, 2-inch bbl., 4.125 inches overall. Weight: 12 oz. Checkered black polycarbonate grips. Matte stainless finish. No sights. Made 1981-85.

MODEL LWS .32 DAO PISTOL
Caliber: .32 ACP. Six-shot magazine, 2-inch bbl., 4.25 inches over-all. Weight: 12.9 oz. Ribbed sighting plane with no sights. Checkered black Lexon grips. Stainless steel. Made 1985 to date. Limited production results in inflated resale values.
Matte stainless finish . . . . **NiB $586 Ex $535 Gd $403**
Polished stainless finish . . . . **NiB $612 Ex $546 Gd $408**

SHERIDAN PRODUCTS, INC. — Racine, Wisconsin

KNOCKABOUT
SINGLE-SHOT PISTOL . . . . **NiB $102 Ex $92 Gd $40**
Tip-up type. Caliber: .22 LR, Long, Short; 5-inch bbl., 6.75 inches overall. Weight: 24 oz. Fixed sights. Checkered plastic grips. Blued finish. Made 1953-60.

SIG PISTOLS — Neuhausen am Rheinfall, Switzerland, Mfd. by SIG Schweizerische Industrie-Gesellschaft

See also listings under SIG-Sauer.

MODEL P210-1
AUTOMATIC PISTOL . . . . **NiB $2060 Ex $1725 Gd $1009**
Calibers: .22 LR, 7.65mm Luger, 9mm Para. Eight-shot magazine, 4.75-inch bbl., 8.5 inches overall. Weight: 33 oz. (.22 cal.) or 35 oz. (7.65mm, 9mm). Fixed sights. Polished blued finish. Checkered wood grips. Made 1949-86.

MODEL P210-2 . . . . **NiB $1545 Ex $1313 Gd $772**
Same as Model P210-1 except has sandblasted finish, plastic grips. Not avail. in .22 LR. Disc. 1987.

MODEL P210-5
TARGET PISTOL . . . . **NiB $2055 Ex $1802 Gd $1004**
Same as Model P210-2 except has 6-inch bbl., micrometer adj. rear sight, target front sight, adj. trigger stop, 9.7 inches overall. Weight: About 38.3 oz. Disc. 1997.

SIG
Model P210-1

SIG
Model P210-6 Target Pistol

MODEL P210-6 TARGET PISTOL . . . . . . **NiB $1931 Ex $1545 Gd $901**
Same as Model P210-2 except has micrometer adj. rear sight, target front sight, adj. trigger stop. Weight: About 37 oz. Disc. 1987.

P210 .22 CONVERSION UNIT . . . . **NiB $766 Ex $613 Gd $417**
Converts P210 pistol to .22 LR. Consists of bbl., w/recoil spring, slide and magazine,

SIG SAUER HANDGUNS
Mfd. by J. P. Sauer & Sohn of West Germany, SIG of Switzerland, and other manufacturers

MODEL P220 DA/DAO AUTOMATIC PISTOL
Calibers: 22LR, 7.65mm, 9mm Para., .38 Super, .45 Automatic. Seven-shot in .45, 9-shot in other calibers, 4.4-inch bbl., 8 inches overall. Weight: 26.5 oz.(9mm). Fixed sights. Blue, electroless nick-el, K-Kote, Duo/nickel or Ilaflon finish. Alloy frame. Checkered plas-tic grips. Imported 1976 to date. Note: Also sold in U.S. as Browning BDA. See illustration next page.
Blue finish . . . . **NiB $690 Ex $597 Gd $360**
Duo/nickel finish . . . . **NiB $731 Ex $592 Gd $406**
Nickel finish . . . . **NiB $762 Ex $669 Gd $433**
K-Kote finish . . . . **NiB $731 Ex $592 Gd $354**
Ilaflon finish . . . . **NiB $731 Ex $592 Gd $406**
.22 conversion kit, add **$680**
W/Siglite sights, add **$92**

MODEL P220 SPORT AUTOMATIC . . . . . **NiB $1210 Ex $978 Gd $772**
Similar to Model P220 except .45 ACP only w/4.5-inch compensat-ed bbl., 10-shot magazine, adj. target sights. Weight: 46.1 oz. Stainless finish. Made 1999 to date.

**SIG Sauer
P220**

**SIG Sauer
P225**

**SIG Sauer
P230**

MODEL P225 DA AUTOMATIC

Caliber: 9mm Para. Eight-shot magazine, 3.85-inch bbl., 7 inches overall. Weight: 26.1 oz. Blue, nickel, K-Kote, Duo/nickel or Ilaflon finish.

Blued finish . . . . NiB $541 Ex $463 Gd $360
Duo/nickel finish. . . . . NiB $587 Ex $510 Gd $407
Nickel finish . . . . NiB $613 Ex $536 Gd $433
K-Kote finish . . . . NiB $613 Ex $536 Gd $433
W/Siglite sights, add $105

MODEL P226 DA/DAO AUTOMATIC

Caliber: .357 SIG, 9mm Para., .40 S&W, 10- or 15-shot magazine, 4.4-inch bbl., 7.75 inches overall. Weight: 29.5 oz. Alloy frame. Blue, electroless nickel, K-Kote, Duo/nickel or Nitron finish. Imported 1983 to date.

Blued finish . . . . NiB $762 Ex $628 Gd $360
Duo/nickel finish. . . . . NiB $803 Ex $711 Gd $386
Nickel finish . . . . NiB $709 Ex $566 Gd $385
K-Kote finish . . . . NiB $676 Ex $541 Gd $368
Nitron finish
(Blacken stainless) . . . . NiB $683 Ex $546 Gd $371
W/Siglite sights, add $85

MODEL P228 DA AUTOMATIC

Same general specifications as Model P226 except w/3.86-inch bbl., 7.13 inches overall. 10- or 13-shot magazine, Imported 1990-97.

Blued finish . . . . NiB $695 Ex $592 Gd $360
Duo/nickel finish. . . . . NiB $737 Ex $634 Gd $403
Electroless nickel finish . . . . NiB $767 Ex $664 Gd $433
K-Kote finish . . . . NiB $742 Ex $639 Gd $407
For Siglite nite sights, add $102

MODEL P229 DA/DAO AUTOMATIC

Same general specifications as Model P228 except w/3.86-inch bbl., 10- or 12-shot magazine, weight: 32.5 oz. Nitron or Satin Nickel finish. Imported 1991 to date.

Nitron finish
(Blackened stainless) . . . . NiB $747 Ex $644 Gd $360
Satin nickel finish . . . . NiB $788 Ex $685 Gd $402
For Siglite nite sights, add $100

MODEL P229

SPORT AUTOMATIC . . . . NiB $1210 Ex $953 Gd $772
Similar to Model P229 except .357 SIG only w/4.5-inch compensated bbl., adj. target sights. Weight: 43.6 oz. Stainless finish. Made 1998 to date.

MODEL P230 DA AUTOMATIC PISTOL

Calibers: .22 LR, .32 Auto (7.65mm), .380 Auto (9mm Short), 9mm Ultra. 10-shot magazine in .22, 8-shot in .32, 7-shot in 9mm; 3.6-inch bbl., 6.6 inches overall. Weight: 18.2 oz. or 22.4 oz. (steel frame). Fixed sights. Blued or stainless finish. Plastic grips. Imported 1976-96.

Blued finish . . . . NiB $438 Ex $335 Gd $221
Stainless finish (P230SL) . . . . NiB $494 Ex $412 Gd $391

MODEL P232 DA/DAO AUTOMATIC PISTOL

Caliber: .380 ACP. Seven-shot magazine, 3.6-inch bbl., 6.6 inches overall. Weight: 16.2 oz. or 22.4 oz. (steel frame). Double/single action or double action only. Blade front and notch rear drift adjustable sights. Alloy or steel frame. Automatic firing pin lock and heelmounted magazine release. Blue, Duo or stainless finish. Stippled black composite stocks. Imported 1997 to date.

Blued finish . . . . NiB $463 Ex $402 Gd $224
Duo finish . . . . NiB $484 Ex $422 Gd $244
Stainless finish . . . . NiB $500 Ex $443 Gd $371
For Siglite nite sights, add $40

MODEL P239 DA/DAO AUTOMATIC PISTOL

Caliber: .357 SIG, 9mm Parabellum or .40 S&W. Seven- or 8-shot magazine, 3.6-inch bbl., 6.6 inches overall. Weight: 28.2 oz. Double/single action or double action only. Blade front and notch rear adjustable sights. Alloy frame w/stainless slide. Ambidextrous frame- mounted magazine release. Matte black or Duo finish. Stippled black composite stocks. Made 1996 to date.

Matte black finish . . . . NiB $515 Ex $453 Gd $227
DAO finish. NiB $554 Ex $443 Gd $301
For Siglite nite sights, add $100

SMITH & WESSON, INC. — Springfield, Massachusetts

NOTE: *For ease in locating a particular S&W handgun, the listings are divided into two groupings: Automatic/Single-Shot Pistols (below) and Revolvers (page 153). For a complete handgun listing, please refer to the index.*

AUTOMATIC/SINGLE-SHOT PISTOLS

.32 AUTOMATIC PISTOL. . . . . NiB $2884 Ex $2163 Gd $1545
Caliber: .32 Automatic. Same general specifications as .35 caliber model, but barrel is fastened to the receiver instead of hinged. Made 1924-37.

MODEL .22 SPORT SERIES
Caliber: .22 LR. 10-shot magazine, 4-, 5.5- or 7-inch standard (A-series) or bull bbl., (S-series). Single action. Eight, 9.5 or 11 inches overall. Weight: 28 oz. to 33 oz. Partridge front sight, fully adjustable rear. Alloy frame w/stainless slide. Blued finish. Black polymer or Dymondwood grips. Made 1997 to date.
Model 22A (w/4-inch bbl.)	NiB $216	Ex $191	Gd $113
Model 22A (w/5.5-inch bbl.)	NiB $246	Ex $220	Gd $142
Model 22A (w/7-inch bbl.)	NiB $285	Ex $260	Gd $182
Model 22S (w/5.5-inch bbl.)	NiB $319	Ex $294	Gd $216
Model 22S (w/7-inch bbl.)	NiB $251	Ex $201	Gd $137
W/bull bbl., add $40			
W/Dymondwood grips, add $75			

35 (1913) AUTOMATIC PISTOL . . . NiB $798 Ex $669 Gd $386
Caliber: 35 S&W Auto. Seven-shot magazine, 3.5-inch bbl., (hinged to frame). 6.5 inches overall. Weight: 25 oz. Fixed sights. Blued or nickel finish. Plain walnut grips. Made 1913-21.

MODEL 39 9MM DA AUTO PISTOL
Calibers: 9mm Para. Eight-shot magazine, 4-inch barrel. Overall length: 7.44-inches. Steel or alloy frames. Weight: 26.5 oz. (w/alloy frame). Click adjustable rear sight, ramp front. Blued or nickel finish. Checkered walnut grips. Made 1954-82. Note: Between 1954 and 1966, 927 pistols were produced w/steel instead of alloy. In 1970, Model 39-1 w/alloy frame and steel slide. In 1971, Model 39-2 was introduced as an improved version of the original Model 39 w/modified extractor.
Model 39 (early production) 1954-70
First series (SN range 1000-2600)	NiB $1493	Ex $1287	Gd $644
9mm blue(w/steel frame & slide, produced 1966)	NiB $1236	Ex $1004	Gd $597
9mm blue (w/alloy frame)	NiB $418	Ex $335	Gd $228
Nickel finish, add $35			
Models 39-1, 39-2 (late production)			
1970-82 9mm blue (w/alloy frame)	NiB $371	Ex $257	Gd $206
Nickel finish, add $35			

MODEL 41 .22 AUTOMATIC PISTOL
Caliber: .22 LR, .22 Short (not interchangeably). 10-shot magazine, bbl. lengths: 5-, 5.5-, 7.75-inches; latter has detachable muzzle brake, 12 inches overall (with 7.75-inch bbl.). Weight: 43.5 oz. (with 7.75-inch bbl.). Click adj. rear sight, undercut Partridge front. Blued finish. Checkered walnut grips w/thumbrest. 1957 to date.
.22 LR model	NiB $695	Ex $551	Gd $257
.22 Short model (w/counter-weights & muzzle brake)	NiB $1127	Ex $901	Gd $613
W/extended sight, add $95			
W/muzzle brake, add $45			

**Smith & Wesson
Model 22A Sport Series**

**Smith & Wesson
Model 22S Sport Series w/Dymondwood Grips**

**Smith & Wesson
Model 41 .22**

MODEL 46 .22 AUTO PISTOL. . . . . NiB $463 Ex $345 Gd $206
Caliber: .22 LR. 10-shot magazine, bbl. lengths: 5-, 5.5-, 7-inches. 10.56 inches overall (with 7-inch bbl.). Weight: 42 oz. (with 7-inch bbl.). Click adj. rear sight, undercut Partridge front. Blued finish. Molded nylon grips w/thumbrest. Only 4,000 produced. Made 1959-68. See illustration next page.

MODEL 52 .38 MASTER AUTO
Caliber: .38 Special (midrange wadcutter only). Five-shot magazine, 5-inch bbl., overall length: 8.63 inches. Weight: 41 oz. Micrometer click rear sight, Partridge front on ramp base. Blued finish. Checkered walnut grips. Made 1961-94. See illustration next page.
Model 52 (1961-63)	NiB $901	Ex $798	Gd $407
Model 52-1 (1963-71)	NiB $695	Ex $566	Gd $304
Model 52-2 (1971-93)	NiB $695	Ex $566	Gd $304
Model 52-A USA Marksman (fewer than 100 mfg.)	NiB $3090	Ex $2626	Gd $1751

Smith & Wesson
Model 46

Smith & Wesson
Model 52

Smith & Wesson
Model 59

Smith & Wesson
Model 422

Smith & Wesson
Model 439

MODEL 59
9MM DA AUTO
Similar specifications as Model 39 except has 14-shot staggered column magazine, checkered nylon grips. Made 1971-82.
Model 59, blue . . . . NiB $397 Ex $350 Gd $221
Model 59, nickel . . . . NiB $434 Ex $381 Gd $232
Model 59
(early production
w/smooth grip frame) . . . . NiB $580 Ex $463 Gd $315

MODEL 61
ESCORT POCKET AUTOMATIC PISTOL
Caliber: .22 LR. Five-shot magazine, 2.13-inch bbl., 4.69 inches overall. Weight: 14 oz. Fixed sights. Blued or nickel finish. Checkered plastic grips. Made 1970-73.
Model 61, blue . . . . NiB $257 Ex $216 Gd $113
Model 61, nickel . . . . NiB $283 Ex $237 Gd $113

MODEL 410
AUTO PISTOL . . . . NiB $474 Ex $340 Gd $180
Caliber: .40 S&W. Double action. 10-shot magazine, 4-inch bbl., 7.5 inches overall. Weight: 28.5 oz. Alloy frame w/steel slide. Post front sight, fixed rear w/3-dot system. Matte blue finish. Checkered synthetic grips w/straight backstrap. Made 1996 to date.

MODEL 411
AUTO PISTOL . . . . NiB $453 Ex $386 Gd $283
Similar to S&W Model 915 except in caliber .40 S&W. 11-shot magazine, made 1994-96.

MODEL 422 SA
AUTO PISTOL
Caliber: .22 LR. 10-shot magazine, 4.5- or 6-inch bbl., 7.5 inches overall (with 4.5-inch bbl.). Weight: 22-23.5 oz. Fixed or adjustable sights. Checkered plastic or walnut grips. Blued finish. Made from 1987-96.
Standard model . . . . NiB $191 Ex $154 Gd $103
Target model . . . . NiB $232 Ex $180 Gd $108

MODEL 439
9MM AUTOMATIC
DA. Caliber: 9mm Para. Two 8-round magazines, 4-inch bbl., 7.44 inches overall. Alloy frame. Weight: 30 oz. Serrated ramp square front sight, square notch rear. Checkered walnut grips. Blued or nickel finish. Made 1979-88.
Model 439, blue . . . . NiB $397 Ex $324 Gd $216
Model 439, nickel . . . . NiB $432 Ex $359 Gd $299
W/adjustable sights, add $24

Smith & Wesson
Model 645

Smith & Wesson
Model 459

MODEL 457
COMPACT AUTO PISTOL . . . . **NiB $480 Ex $345 Gd $185**
Caliber: .45 ACP. Double action. Seven-shot magazine, 3.75-inch bbl., 7.25 inches overall. Weight: 29 oz. Alloy frame w/steel slide. Post front sight, fixed rear w/3-dot system. Bobbed hammer. Matte blue finish. Wraparound synthetic grip w/straight backstrap. Made 1996 to date.

MODEL 459 DA AUTOMATIC
Caliber: 9mm Para. Two 14-round magazines, 4-inch bbl., 7.44 inches overall. Alloy frame. Weight: 28 oz. Blued or nickel finish. Made 1979-87.
Model 459, blue . . . . NiB $422 Ex $355 Gd $247
Model 459, nickel . . . . NiB $468 Ex $402 Gd $278
FBI Model (brushed finish) . . . . NiB $669 Ex $618 Gd $340

MODEL 469
(MINI) AUTOMATIC . . . . **NiB $382 Ex $330 Gd $227**
DA. Caliber: 9mm Para. Two 12-round magazines, 3.5-inch bbl., 6.88 inches overall. Weight: 26 oz. Yellow ramp front sight, dovetail mounted square-notch rear. Sandblasted blued finish. Optional ambidextrous safety. Made 1982-88.

Smith & Wesson
Model 469

MODEL 539 DA AUTOMATIC
Similar to Model 439 except w/steel frame. Caliber: 9mm Para. Two 8-round magazines, 4-inch bbl., 7.44 inches overall. Weight: 36 oz. Blued or nickel finish. Made 1980-83.
Model 539, blue . . . . NiB $463 Ex $407 Gd $309
Model 539, nickel . . . . NiB $500 Ex $443 Gd $335
W/adjustable sights, add $30

MODEL 559 DA AUTOMATIC
Similar to Model 459 except w/steel frame. Caliber: 9mm Para. Two 14-round magazines, 4-inch bbl., 7.44 inches overall. Weight: 39.5 oz. Blued or nickel finish. (3750 produced) Made 1980-83.
Model 559, blue . . . . NiB $500 Ex $448 Gd $257
Model 559, nickel . . . . NiB $530 Ex $484 Gd $288
W/adjustable sights, add $30

MODEL 622 SA AUTO PISTOL
Same general specifications as Model 422 except w/stainless finish. Made from 1989-96.
Standard model . . . . NiB $227 Ex $180 Gd $165
Target model . . . . NiB $283 Ex $232 Gd $180

Smith & Wesson
Model 639

MODEL 639 AUTOMATIC . . . . NiB $433 Ex $309 Gd $283
Caliber: 9mm Para. Two 12-round magazines, 3.5-inch bbl., 6.9 inches overall. Weight: 36 oz. Stainless. Made 1982-88.

Smith & Wesson
Model 659

Smith & Wesson
Model 745

Smith & Wesson
Model 1026

MODEL 645 DA AUTOMATIC
Caliber: .45 ACP. Eight-shot. 5-inch bbl., overall length: 8.5 inches. Weight: Approx. 38 oz. Red ramp front, fixed rear sights. Stainless. Made 1986-88. See illustration previous page.
Model 645 (w/fixed sights) . . . . **NiB $489 Ex $376 Gd $309**
Model 645 (w/adjustable sights) . . . **NiB $515 Ex $402 Gd $335**

MODEL 659 9MM AUTOMATIC
DA. Similar to S&W Model 459 except weight: 39.5 oz. and finish is satin stainless steel finish. Made 1983-88.
Model 659 (w/fixed sights) . . . . **NiB $458 Ex $345 Gd $309**
Model 659 (w/adjustable sights) . . . . **NiB $484 Ex $371 Gd $335**

MODEL 669 AUTOMATIC. . . . . . . NiB $438 Ex $314 Gd $213
Caliber: 9mm. 12-shot magazine, 3.5 inch bbl., 6.9 inches overall. Weight: 26 oz. Serrated ramp front sight w/red bar, fixed rear. Nonglare stainless steel finish. Made 1986-88.

MODEL 745 AUTOMATIC PISTOL
Caliber: .45 ACP. Eight-shot magazine, 5-inch bbl., 8.63 inches overall. Weight: 38.75 oz. Fixed sights. Blued slide, stainless frame. Checkered walnut grips. Similar to the model 645, but w/o DA capability. Made 1987-90.
W/standard competition features . . . . **NiB $592 Ex $453 Gd $345**
IPSC Commemorative (first 5,000) . . . . . . **NiB $701 Ex $561 Gd $382**

MODEL 908/909/910 AUTO PISTOLS
Caliber: 9mm Parabellum. Double action. Eight-shot (Model 908), 9-shot (Model 909) or 10-shot (Model 910) magazine; 3.5- or 4-inch bbl.; 6.83 or 7.38 inches overall. Weight: 26 oz. to 28.5 oz. Post front sight, fixed rear w/3-dot system. Matte blue steel slide w/alloy frame. Delrin synthetic wrap-around grip w/straight backstrap. Made 1994 to date.
Model 908 . . . . **NiB $437 Ex $319 Gd $180**
Model 909 (disc 1996) . . . . **NiB $371 Ex $283 Gd $180**
Model 910 . . . . **NiB $437 Ex $319 Gd $180**

MODEL 915 AUTO PISTOL . . . . . . NiB $360 Ex $263 Gd $180
DA. Caliber: 9mm Para. 15-shot magazine, 4-inch bbl., 7.5 inches overall. Weight: 28.5 oz. Post front sight, fixed square-notched rear w/3-dot system. Xenoy wraparound grip. Blued steel slide and alloy frame. Made 1992-94.

MODEL 1000 SERIES DA AUTO
Caliber: 10mm. Nine-shot magazine, 4.25- or 5-inch bbl., 7.88 or 8.63 inches overall. Weight: About 38 oz. Post front sight, adj. or fixed square-notched rear w/3-dot system. One-piece Xenoy wrap-around grips. Stainless slide and frame. Made 1990-94.
Model 1006 (fixed sights, 5 inch bbl.) . . . . **NiB $654 Ex $541 Gd $412**
Model 1006 (Adj. sights, 5 inch bbl.) . . . . . **NiB $682 Ex $569 Gd $440**
Model 1026 (fixed sights, 5 inch bbl., decocking lever) . . . . **NiB $649 Ex $541 Gd $412**
Model 1066 (fixed sights, 4.25 inch bbl.) . . . . **NiB $628 Ex $530 Gd $407**
Model 1076 (fixed sights, 4.25 inch bbl., frame-mounted decocking lever, straight backstrap) . . . . **NiB $664 Ex $546 Gd $412**
Model 1076 (same as above w/Tritium night sight) . . . . **NiB $706 Ex $587 Gd $453**
Model 1086 (same as model 1076 in DA only) . . . . **NiB $731 Ex $530 Gd $407**

MODEL 2206 SA AUTOMATIC PISTOL
Similar to Model 422 except w/stainless-steel slide and frame, weight: 35-39 oz. Partridge front sight on adj. sight model; post w/white dot on fixed sight model. Plastic grips. Made 1990-96.
Standard model . . . . **NiB $299 Ex $232 Gd $180**
Target model . . . . **NiB $371 Ex $283 Gd $237**

MODEL 2213
SPORTSMAN AUTO . . . . **NiB $263 Ex $206 Gd $165**
Caliber: .22 LR. Eight-shot magazine, 3-inch bbl., 6.13 inches overall. Weight: 18 oz. Partridge front sight, fixed square-notched rear w/3-dot system. Black synthetic molded grips. Stainless steel slide w/alloy frame. Made 1992-99.

MODEL 2214
SPORTSMAN AUTO . . . . **NiB $237 Ex $191 Gd $134**
Same general specifications as Model 2214 except w/blued slide and matte black alloy frame. Made from 1990-99.

MODEL 3904/3906 DA AUTO PISTOL
Caliber: 9mm. Eight-shot magazine, 4-inch bbl., 7.5 inches overall. Weight: 25.5 oz. (Model 3904) or 34 oz. (Model 3906). Fixed or adj. sights. Delrin one-piece wraparound, checkered grips. Alloy frame w/blued carbon steel slide (Model 3904) or satin stainless (Model 3906). Made 1989-91.

Model 3904 w/adjustable sights . . . . NiB $484 Ex $417 Gd $335
Model 3904 w/fixed sights . . . . NiB $463 Ex $397 Gd $288
Model 3904 w/Novak LC sight . . . . NiB $489 Ex $381 Gd $257
Model 3906 w/adjustable sights . . . . NiB $554 Ex $477 Gd $405
Model 3906 w/Novak LC sight . . . . NiB $525 Ex $448 Gd $376

Smith & Wesson
Model 3906

MODEL 3913/3914 DA AUTOMATIC
Caliber: 9mm Parabellum (Luger). Eight-shot magazine, 3.5-inch bbl., 6.88 inches overall. Weight: 25 oz. Post front sight, fixed or adj. square-notched rear. One-piece Xenoy wraparound grips w/straight backstrap. Alloy frame w/stainless or blued slide. Made 1990 to date.

Model 3913 stainless . . . . NiB $633 Ex $489 Gd $391
Model 3913LS Lady Smith stainless
w/contoured trigger guard . . . . NiB $649 Ex $494 Gd $391
Model 3913TSW (intro. 1998) . . . . NiB $633 Ex $489 Gd $391
Model 3914 blued compact
(disc 1995) . . . . NiB $479 Ex $385 Gd $280

MODEL 3953/3954 DA AUTO PISTOL
Same general specifications as Model 3913/3914 except double action only. Made from 1991 to date.

Model 3953 stainless,
double action only . . . . NiB $633 Ex $489 Gd $391
Model 3954 blued, double
action only (disc. 1992) . . . . NiB $458 Ex $391 Gd $288

Smith & Wesson
Model 3953

MODEL 4000 SERIES DA AUTO
Caliber: .40 S&W. 11-shot magazine, 4-inch bbl., 7.88 inches overall. Weight: 28-30 oz. w/alloy frame or 36 oz. w/stainless frame. Post front sight, adj. or fixed square-notched rear w/2 white dots. Straight backstrap. One-piece Xenoy wraparound grips. Blued or stainless finish. Made between 1990-93.

Model 4003 stainless w/alloy frame . . . . . . NiB $603 Ex $510 Gd $407
Model 4003 TSW w/
S&W Tactical options . . . . NiB $762 Ex $665 Gd $371
Model 4004 blued w/alloy frame . . . . NiB $547 Ex $438 Gd $298
Model 4006 stainless
frame, fixed sights . . . . NiB $556 Ex $474 Gd $288
Model 4006 stainless
frame, Adj. sights . . . . NiB $675 Ex $561 Gd $412
Model 4006 TSW w/
S&W Tactical options . . . . NiB $767 Ex $664 Gd $371
Model 4013 stainless frame,
fixed sights . . . . NiB $613 Ex $5000 Gd $294
Model 4013 TSW w/
S&W Tactical options . . . . NiB $752 Ex $597 Gd $433
Model 4014 blued, fixed sights
(disc. 1993) . . . . NiB $525 Ex $438 Gd $283
Model 4026 w/decocking
Lever (disc. 1994) . . . . NiB $639 Ex $536 Gd $412
Model 4043 DA only, stainless
w/alloy frame . . . . NiB $762 Ex $659 Gd $371
Model 4044 DA only,
blued w/alloy frame . . . . NiB $556 Ex $474 Gd $304
Model 4046 DA only, stainless
frame, fixed sights . . . . NiB $675 Ex $556 Gd $412
Model 4046 TSW w/
S&W Tactical options . . . . NiB $778 Ex $669 Gd $360
Model 4046 DA only, stainless
frame, Tritium night sight . . . . NiB $915 Ex $807 Gd $533

Smith & Wesson
Model 4013

Smith & Wesson
Model 4046

**Smith & Wesson
Model 4053**

**Smith & Wesson
Model 4586**

**Smith & Wesson Model 5904
w/Adjustable Sights**

MODEL 4013/4014 DA AUTOMATIC

Caliber: .40 S&W. Eight-shot capacity, 3.5-inch bbl., 7 inches overall. Weight: 26 oz. Post front sight, fixed Novak LC rear w/3-dot system. One-piece Xenoy wraparound grips. Stainless or blued slide w/alloy frame. Made 1991 to date.

Model 4013 w/stainless slide (disc. 1996) .... NiB $613 Ex $494 Gd $288
Model 4013 Tactical w/stainless slide .... NiB $752 Ex $597 Gd $433
Model 4014 w/blued slide (disc. 1993) ...... NiB $525 Ex $438 Gd $242

MODEL 4053/4054 DA AUTO PISTOL

Same general specifications as Model 4013/4014 except double action only. Alloy frame fitted w/blued steel slide. Made 1991-97.

(cont'd) MODEL 4053/4054 DA AUTO PISTOL

Model 4053 DA only w/stainless slide .... NiB $525 Ex $438 Gd $386
Model 4053 TSW w/ S&W Tactical options ... NiB $752 Ex $597 Gd $427
Model 4054 DA only w/blued slide
(disc. 1992)............................ NiB $525 Ex $438 Gd $386

MODEL 4500 SERIES DA AUTOMATIC

Caliber: .45 ACP. Six-, 7- or 8-shot magazine, bbl. lengths: 3.75, 4.25 or 5 inches; 7.13 to 8.63 inches overall. Weight: 34.5 to 38.5 oz. Post front sight, fixed Novak LC rear w/3-dot system or adj. One-piece Xenoy wraparound grips. Satin stainless finish. Made 1990 to date.

Model 4505 w/fixed sights, 5-inch bbl........ NiB $592 Ex $515 Gd $309
Model 4505 w/Novak LC sight, 5-inch bbl. ... NiB $620 Ex $543 Gd $337
Model 4506 w/fixed sights, 5-inch bbl........ NiB $700 Ex $566 Gd $422
Model 4506 w/Novak LC sight, 5-inch bbl. ... NiB $734 Ex $600 Gd $453
Model 4513T (TSW) w/3.75-inch bbl.
Tactical Combat .... NiB $675 Ex $551 Gd $412
Model 4516 w/3.75-inch bbl............... NiB $675 Ex $546 Gd $360
Model 4526 w/5-inch bbl., alloy frame,
decocking lever, fixed sights .... NiB $654 Ex $546 Gd $412
Model 4536, decocking lever .... NiB $659 Ex $556 Gd $422
Model 4546, w/3.75-inch bbl., DA only ..... NiB $659 Ex $556 Gd $422
Model 4553T (TSW) w/3.75-inch bbl.
Tactical Combat .... NiB $620 Ex $543 Gd $332
Model 4556, w/3.75-inch bbl., DA only ..... NiB $592 Ex $515 Gd $309
Model 4563 TSW w/4.25-inch bbl.
Tactical Combat .... NiB $675 Ex $551 Gd $412
Model 4566 w/4.25-inch bbl.,
ambidextrous safety, fixed sights .... NiB $644 Ex $541 Gd $360
Model 4566 TSW w/4.25-inch bbl.
Tactical Combat .... NiB $675 Ex $551 Gd $412
Model 4576 w/4.25-inch bbl.,
decocking lever .... NiB $654 Ex $546 Gd $360
Model 4583T TSW w/4.25-inch bbl.
Tactical Combat .... NiB $620 Ex $543 Gd $422
Model 4586 w/4.25-inch bbl., DA only ...... NiB $700 Ex $566 Gd $412
Model 4586 TSW w/4.25-inch bbl.
Tactical Combat .... NiB $675 Ex $551 Gd $350

MODEL 5900 SERIES DA AUTOMATIC

Caliber: 9mm. 15-shot magazine, 4-inch bbl., 7.5 inches overall. Weight: 26-38 oz. Fixed or adj. sights. One-piece Xenoy wraparound grips. Alloy frame w/stainless-steel slide (Model 5903) or blued slide (Model 5904) stainless-steel frame and slide (Model 5906). Made 1989/90 to date.

Model 5903 w/adjustable sights .... NiB $716 Ex $577 Gd $283
Model 5903 w/Novak LC rear sight .... NiB $716 Ex $577 Gd $283
Model 5903 TSW w/4-inch bbl.,
Tactical Combat .... NiB $716 Ex $577 Gd $283
Model 5904 w/adjustable sights .... NiB $554 Ex $443 Gd $301
Model 5904 w/Novak LC rear sight .... NiB $546 Ex $427 Gd $288
Model 5905 w/Adjustable Sights .... NiB $566 Ex $448 Gd $335
Model 5905 w/Novak LC rear sight .... NiB $654 Ex $546 Gd $360
Model 5906 w/adjustable sights .... NiB $649 Ex $541 Gd $335
Model 5906 w/Novak LC rear sight .... NiB $628 Ex $438 Gd $309
Model 5906 w/Tritium night sight........... NiB $752 Ex $633 Gd $489
Model 5906 TSW w/4-inch bbl.,
Tactical Combat .... NiB $747 Ex $649 Gd $469
Model 5924 anodized frame, blued slide ..... NiB $587 Ex $438 Gd $242
Model 5926 Stain. frame, decocking lever .... NiB $675 Ex $546 Gd $412
Model 5943 alloy frame/
stainless slide, DA only .... NiB $649 Ex $541 Gd $330
Model 5943 TSW w/4-inch bbl., DA only .... NiB $618 Ex $494 Gd $336
Model 5944 alloy frame/
blued slide, DA only .... NiB $556 Ex $453 Gd $319
Model 5946 stainless frame/slide, DA only ... NiB $613 Ex $412 Gd $288
Model 5946 TSW w/4-inch bbl., DA only..... NiB $620 Ex $543 Gd $144

MODEL 6900 COMPACT SERIES

Double action. Caliber: 9mm. 12-shot magazine, 3.5-inch bbl., 6.88 inches overall. Weight: 26.5 oz. Ambidextrous safety. Post front sight, fixed Novak LC rear w/3-dot system. Alloy frame w/blued carbon steel slide (Model 6904) or stainless steel slide (Model 6906). Made 1989 to date.

Model 6904	NiB $587	Ex $422	Gd $288
Model 6906 w/fixed sights	NiB $603	Ex $484	Gd $391
Model 6906 w/Tritium night sight	NiB $726	Ex $526	Gd $453
Model 6926 same as model 6906 w/decocking lever	NiB $613	Ex $494	Gd $288
Model 6944 same as model 6904 in DA only	NiB $525	Ex $438	Gd $242
Model 6946 same as model 6906 in DA only ,fixed sights	NiB $613	Ex $494	Gd $288
Model 6946 w/Tritium night sight	NiB $675	Ex $551	Gd $350

SIGMA SW380 AUTOMATIC PISTOL . . . . . NiB $294 Ex $252 Gd $175
Caliber: .380 ACP. Double-action only. Six-shot magazine, 3-inch bbl., weight: 14 oz. Black integral polymer gripframe w/checkered back and front straps. Fixed channel sights. Polymer frame w/hammerless steel slide. Made 1996 to date.

SIGMA SW9 SERIES AUTOMATIC PISTOL
Caliber: 9mm Parabellum. Double action only. 10-shot magazine, 3.25-, 4- or 4.5-inch bbl., weight: 17.9 oz. to 24.7 oz. Polymer frame w/hammerless steel slide. Post front sight and drift adjustable rear w/3-dot system. Gray or black integral polymer gripframe w/checkered back and front straps. Made 1994 to date.

Model SW9C (compact w/3.25-inch bbl.)	NiB $463	Ex $366	Gd $273
Model SW9F (blue slide w/4.5-inch bbl.)	NiB $500	Ex $402	Gd $288
Model SW9M (compact w/3.25-inch bbl.)	NiB $309	Ex $278	Gd $180
Model SW9V (stainless slide w/4-inch bbl.)	NiB $371	Ex $309	Gd $257
Tritium night sight, add			$210

SW40 SERIES AUTOMATIC PISTOL
Same general specifications as SW9 series except chambered for .40 S&W w/4- or 4.5-inch bbl., weight: 24.4 to 26 oz. Made 1994 to date.

Model SW40C (compact w/4inch bbl.)	NiB $463	Ex $366	Gd $273
Model SW40F (blue slide w/4.5inch bbl.)	NiB $463	Ex $366	Gd $273
Model SW40V (stainless slide w/4inch bbl.)	NiB $371	Ex $309	Gd $257
Tritium night sight, add			$210

MODEL 1891 SINGLE-SHOT TARGET PISTOL, FIRST MODEL
Hinged frame. Calibers: .22 LR, .32 S&W, .38 S&W. Bbl. lengths: 6-, 8- and 10-inches, approx. 13.5 inches overall (with 10-inch bbl.). Weight: About 25 oz. Target sights, barrel catch rear adj. for windage and elevation. Blued finish. Square butt, hard rubber grips. Made 1893-1905. Note: This model was available also as a combination arm w/accessory .38 revolver bbl. and cylinder enabling conversion to a pocket revolver. It has the frame of the .38 SA revolver Model 1891 w/side flanges, hand and cylinder stop slots.

Single-shot pistol, .22 LR	NiB $824	Ex $669	Gd $335
Single-shot pistol, .32 S&W or .38 S&W	NiB $1153	Ex $922	Gd $627
Combination set, revolver and single-shot barrel	NiB $1281	Ex $1025	Gd $697

MODEL 1891 SINGLE-SHOT TARGET PISTOL, SECOND MODEL . . . . NiB $1133 Ex $772 Gd $386
Similar to the First Model except side flanges, hand and stop slots eliminated, cannot be converted to revolver, redesigned rear sight. Caliber: .22 LR only, 10-inch bbl. only. Made 1905-09.

PERFECTED SINGLE-SHOT TARGET PISTOL
Similar to Second Model except has double-action lockwork. Caliber: .22 LR only, 10-inch bbl. Checkered walnut grips, extended

Smith & Wesson
Model 1

(cont'd) PERFECTED SINGLE-SHOT TARGET PISTOL
square-butt target type. Made 1909-23. Note: In 1920 and thereafter, this model was made w/barrels having bore diameter of .223 instead of .226 and tight, short chambering. The first group of these pistols was produced for the U.S. Olympic Team of 1920, thus the designation Olympic Model.

Pre-1920 type	NiB $1751	Ex $772	Gd $309
Olympic model	NiB $1442	Ex $1025	Gd $613

STRAIGHT LINE SINGLE-SHOT
TARGET PISTOL . . . . NiB $1802 Ex $1236 Gd $566
Frame shaped like that of an automatic pistol, barrel swings to the left on pivot for extracting and loading, straight-line trigger and hammer movement. Caliber: .22 LR. 10-inch bbl., 11.25 inches overall. Weight: 34 oz. Target sights. Blued finish. Smooth walnut grips. Supplied in metal case w/screwdriver and cleaning rod. Made 1925-36.

NOTE: *The following section contains only S&W Revolvers. For a complete listing of S&W handguns, please refer to the index.*

REVOLVERS

MODEL 1 HAND EJECTOR
DA REVOLVER. . . . . NiB $721 Ex $618 Gd $397
First Model. Forerunner of the .32 Hand Ejector and Regulation Police models, this was the first S&W revolver of the solid-frame, swing-out cylinder type. Top strap of this model is longer than those of later models, and it lacks the usual S&W cylinder latch. Caliber: .32 S&W Long. Bbl. lengths: 3.25-, 4.25-, and 6-inches. Fixed sights. Blued or nickel finish. Round butt, hard rubber stocks. Made 1896-1903.

NO. 3 SA FRONTIER. . . . . NiB $9332 Ex $6180 Gd $1957
Caliber: .44-40 WCF. Bbl. lengths: 4-, 5- and 6.5-inch. Fixed or target sights. Blued or nickel finish. Round, hard rubber or checkered walnut grips. Made 1885-1908.

NO. 3 SA (NEW MODEL) . . . . . NiB $3856 Ex $3085 Gd $2098
Hinged frame. Six-shot cylinder. Caliber: .44 S&W Russian. Bbl. lengths: 4-, 5-, 6-, 6.5-, 7.5- and 8-inches. Fixed or target sights. Blued or nickel finish. Round, hard rubber or checkered walnut grips. Made 1878-1908. Note: Value shown is for standard model. Specialist collectors recognize numerous variations w/a range of higher values.

NO. 3 SA TARGET . . . . NiB $6695 Ex $3347 Gd $1226
Hinged frame. Six-shot cylinder. Calibers: .32/.44 S&W, .38/.44 S&W Gallery & Target. 6.5-inch bbl. only. Fixed or target sights. Blued or nickel finish. Round, hard rubber or checkered walnut grips. Made 1887-1910.

Smith & Wesson
Model 10 (Two-inch Barrel)

Smith & Wesson
Model 12 (Two-inch Barrel

Smith & Wesson Model 13
(Heavy Barrel)

Smith & Wesson
Model 14

MODEL 10 .38 MILITARY & POLICE DA

Also called Hand Ejector Model of 1902, Hand Ejector Model of 1905, Model K. Manufactured substantially in its present form since 1902, this model has undergone numerous changes, most of them minor. Round- or square-butt models, the latter intro. in 1904. Caliber: .38 Special. Six-shot cylinder, bbl. lengths: 2-(intro. 1933), 4-, 5-, 6- and 6.5-inch (latter disc. 1915) also 4-inch heavy bbl., (intro. 1957); 11.13 inches overall (square-butt model w/6-inch bbl.). Round-butt model is 1/4-inch shorter, weight: About 1/2 oz. less. Fixed sights. Blued or nickel finish. Checkered walnut grips, hard rubber available in round-butt style. Current Model 10 has short action. Made 1902 to date. Note: S&W Victory Model, wartime version of the M & P .38, was produced for the U.S. Government from 1940 to the end of the war. A similar revolver, designated .38/200 British Service Revolver, was produced for the British Government during the same period. These arms have either brush-polish or sandblast blued finish, and most of them have plain, smooth walnut grips, lanyard swivels.

Model of 1902 (1902-05)	NiB $618	Ex $484	Gd $206
Model of 1905 (1905-40)	NiB $515	Ex $397	Gd $206
.38/200 British Service (1940-45) . . .	NiB $360	Ex $263	Gd $113
Victory Model (1942-45)	NiB $367	Ex $294	Gd $200
Model of 1944 (1945-48)	NiB $226	Ex $180	Gd $123
Model 10 (1948 - date)	NiB $360	Ex $263	Gd $113

MODEL 10 .38 MILITARY
& POLICE HEAVY BARREL . . . . NiB $360 Ex $263 Gd $113
Same as standard Model 10 except has heavy 4-inch bbl., weight: 34 oz. Made 1957 to date.

MODEL 12 .38 M
& PAIRWEIGHT . . . . NiB $376 Ex $268 Gd $144
Same as standard Military & Police except has light alloy frame, furnished w/2- or 4-inch bbl. only, weight: 18 oz. (w/2-inch bbl.). Made 1952-86.

MODEL 12/13 (AIR FORCE MODEL)
DA REVOLVER . . . . NiB $824 Ex $747 Gd $489
Special "Air Force" Model designed with alloy cylinder and frame to be used as a "Survival Weapon" for air crews. Athough this weapon was actually a first-series Model 12, the Air Force stamped "M13" on the top strap. Issued 1953 but recalled for function problems in 1954.

MODEL 13 .357
MILITARY/POLICE. . . . . NiB $319 Ex $237 Gd $129
Same as Model 10 .38 Military & Police Heavy Barrel except chambered for .357 Magnum and .38 Special w/3- or 4-inch bbl. Round or square butt configuration. Made 1974-98.

MODELS 14 (K38) AND 16 (K32) MASTERPIECE REVOLVERS
Calibers: .22 LR, .22 Magnum Rimfire, .32 S&W Long, .38 Special. Six-shot cylinder. DA/SA. Bbl. lengths: 4- (.22 WMR only), 6-, 8.38-inch (latter not available in K32), 11.13 inches overall (with 6-inch bbl.). Weight: 38.5 oz. (with 6-inch bbl.). Click adj. rear sight, Partridge front. Blued finish. Checkered walnut grips. Made 1947 to date. (Model 16 disc. 1974, w/only 3,630 produced; reissued 1990-93.)

Model 14 (K-38 double-action)	NiB $309	Ex $257	Gd $154
Model 14 (K-38 single action, 6-inch bbl.)	NiB $335	Ex $268	Gd $165
Model 14 (K-38 single action, 8.38-inch bbl.)	NiB $367	Ex $294	Gd $200
Model 16 (K-32 double-action) 1st Issue	NiB $1390	Ex $1185	Gd $772
Model 16 (K-32 double-action)	NiB $438	Ex $283	Gd $196

MODELS 15 (.38) AND 18 (.22) COMBAT MASTERPIECE DA REVOLVERS
Same as K-.22 and K-.38 Masterpiece but w/2- (.38) or 4-inch bbl., and Baughman quick-draw front sight. 9.13 inches overall w/4-inch bbl., Weight: 34 oz. (.38 cal.). Made 1950 to date.
Model 15 . . . . NiB $350 Ex $206 Gd $185
Model 18 (disc. 1985) . . . . NiB $360 Ex $283 Gd $196
W/target options TH & TT, add $35

MODEL 17 K-.22 MASTERPIECE DA REVOLVER
Caliber: 22LR. Six-shot cylinder, Bbl lengths: 4, 6 or 8.38 inches. 11.13 inches overall (with 6-inch bbl.). Weight: 38 oz. (with 6-inch bbl.). Partridge-type front sight, S&W micrometer click rear. Checkered walnut Service grips with S&W monogram. S&W blued finish. Made 1947-93 and 1996-98.
Model 17 (4-inch bbl.) . . . . NiB $592 Ex $515 Gd $309
Model 17 (6-inch bbl.) . . . . NiB $592 Ex $515 Gd $309
Model 17 (8.38-inch bbl.) . . . . NiB $618 Ex $566 Gd $391
W/target options TH & TT, add $35

MODEL 19 .357 COMBAT MAGNUM DA REVOLVER
Caliber: .357 Magnum. Six-shot cylinder, bbl. lengths: 2.5 (round butt), 4, or 6 inches, 9.5 inches overall (with 4-inch bbl.). Weight: 35 oz. (with 4-inch bbl.). Click adj. rear sight, ramp front. Blued or nickel finish. Target grips of checkered Goncalo Alves. Made 1956 to date (2.5- and 6-inch bbls. were disc. in 1991).
Model 19 (2.5-inch bbl.) . . . . NiB $355 Ex $273 Gd $175
Model 19 (4-inch bbl.) . . . . NiB $365 Ex $283 Gd $184
Model 19 (6-inch bbl.) . . . . NiB $371 Ex $288 Gd $190
Model 19 (8.38-inch bbl.) . . . . NiB $354 Ex $283 Gd $193
W/target options TH & TT, add $60

MODEL 20 .38/.44 HEAVY DUTY DA
Caliber: .38 Special. Six-shot cylinder, bbl. lengths: 4, 5 and 6.5 inches;10.38 inches overall (with 5-inch bbl.). Weight: 40 oz. (with 5-inch bbl.). Fixed sights. Blued or nickel finish. Checkered walnut grips. Short action after 1948. Made 1930-56 and 1957-67.
Pre-World War II . . . . NiB $613 Ex $505 Gd $350
Postwar . . . . NiB $360 Ex $294 Gd $154

MODEL 21 1950 .44 MILITARY DA REVOLVER
Postwar version of the 1926 Model 44 Military. Caliber: .44 Special, 6-shot cylinder. Bbl. lengths: 4-, 5- and 6.5-inches. 11.75 inches overall (w/6.5-inch bbl.) Weight: 39.5 oz. (w/6.5-inch bbl.). Fixed front sight w/square-notch rear sight; target model has micrometer click rear sight adj. for windage and elevation. Checkered walnut grips w/S&W monogram. Blued or nickel finish. Made 1950-67.
Model 21 (4- or 5-inch bbl.) . . . . NiB $1802 Ex $1622 Gd $669
Model 21 (6.5-inch bbl.) . . . . NiB $2704 Ex $2433 Gd $1004

MODEL .22 1950 ARMY DA . . . . . . NiB $1802 Ex $1622 Gd $669
Postwar version of the 1917 Army w/same general specifications except redesigned hammer. Made 1950-67.

.22/.32 TARGET DA REVOLVER
Also known as the "Bekeart Model." Design based upon ".32 Hand Ejector." Caliber: .22 LR (recessed head cylinder for high-speed cartridges intro. 1935). Six-shot cylinder, 6-inch bbl., 10.5 inches overall. Weight: 23 oz. Adj. target sights. Blued finish. Checkered walnut grips. Made 1911-53. Note: In 1911, San Francisco gun dealer Phil Bekeart, who suggested this model, received 292 pieces. These are the true "Bekeart Model" revolvers and are marked with separate identification numbers on the base of the wooden grip.
.22/.32 Target model . . . . NiB $309 Ex $257 Gd $134
.22/.32 Target model (early prod. 1-3000) . . . . NiB $438 Ex $309 Gd $185
.22/.32 Target model (Bekeart model) . . . . NiB $1107 Ex $901 Gd $206

.22/.32 KIT GUN . . . . NiB $309 Ex $242 Gd $180
Same as .22/.32 Target except has 2- or 4-inch bbl., round grips, 6 or 8 inches overall, weight: 19-21oz. Made 1935-53.

Smith & Wesson
Model 15

Smith & Wesson
Model 17 K-22

Smith & Wesson
Model 18 (See Model 15 for description)

Smith & Wesson
Model 19 (Round Butt)

Smith & Wesson
Model 19 (Square Butt)

Smith & Wesson
Model 22/32 Kit Gun

Smith & Wesson
Model 20

Smith & Wesson
Model 22/32 Target Revolver

Smith & Wesson
Model 21

Smith & Wesson
Model 23

Smith & Wesson
Model 22

MODEL 24 1950 .44 TARGET DA REVOLVER
Postwar version of the 1921 Model .44 with 4-, 5- or 6.5-inch
ribbed bbl., redesigned hammer, micrometer click rear sight. Matte
or polished blue finish. Made 1950-67. Model 24 reintroduced
1983 only.
Model 24 (1950)
w/4-inch bbl. . . . . NiB $989 Ex $814 Gd $525
Model 24 (1950)
w/5-inch bbl. . . . . NiB $1002 Ex $829 Gd $541
Model 24 (1950)
w/6.5-inch bbl. . . . . NiB $716 Ex $592 Gd $386
Model 24 (1950) w/polished
blue finish, add 20%
Model 24 (1950)
w/nickel finish, add 50%
Model 24
.44 Target reintroduced
(7,500 produced in 1983-84)
Model 24 (w/4-inch bbl.) . . . . NiB $463 Ex $438 Gd $335
Model 24 (w/6.5-inch bbl.) . . . . NiB $412 Ex $386 Gd $283
Model 24-3 .44
Lew Horton Special (produced in 1983)
Model 24-3 (w/3-inch bbl.) . . . . NiB $391 Ex $335 Gd $257

MODEL 23 .38/.44 OUTDOORSMAN DA REVOLVER
Target version of the .38/44 Heavy Duty. 6.5- or 8.75-inch bbl.,
weight: 41.75 oz. Target sights, micrometer-click rear on postwar
models. Blued or nickel finish. 1950 transition model has ribbed
barrel, redesigned hammer. Made 1930-67.
Prewar model (plain bbl.) . . . . NiB $669 Ex $566 Gd $288
Postwar (ribbed bbl.) . . . . NiB $803 Ex $680 Gd $346

MODEL .25 1955 .45 TARGET DA REVOLVER

Same as 1950 Model .44 Target, but chambered for .45 ACP, .45 Auto Rim or .45 LC w/4-, 6- or 6.5-inch bbl. Made 1955 to 1991 in several variations. Note: In 1961, the .45 ACP was designated Model .25-2, and in 1978 the .45 LC was designated Model .25-5.

Model 25 1955 .45 Target

Model 25 (.45 ACP w/4- or 6-inch bbl.)	NiB $463	Ex $412	Gd $206
Model 25 (.45 ACP w/6.5-inch pinned bbl.)	NiB $669	Ex $566	Gd $360
Model 25 (.45 LC early production)	NiB $1390	Ex $1236	Gd $618

Model 25-2 .45 ACP

Model 25 (w/3-inch bbl., Lew Horton Special)	NiB $515	Ex $463	Gd $386
Model 25 (w/4-inch bbl.)	NiB $470	Ex $376	Gd $255
Model 24-3 (w/6.5-inch bbl.)	NiB $483	Ex $386	Gd $263

Model 25-5 .45 LC

Model 25 (w/4-inch bbl.)	NiB $470	Ex $376	Gd $255
Model 24-3 (w/6.5-inch bbl.)	NiB $509	Ex $407	Gd $277

Smith & Wesson
Model 24 Target

Smith & Wesson
Model 25 Target

MODEL 26 1950 .45 LIGHT TARGET DA REVOLVER

Similar to 1950 Model Target except w/lighter bbl. Note: Lighter profile was not well received. (Only 2768 produced)

Model 26 (.45 ACP or .45 Auto Rim

w/6.5-inch bbl.)	NiB $793	Ex $680	Gd $283
Model 26 (.45 LC, < 200 produced)	NiB $2379	Ex $2039	Gd $850
W/4- or 5-inch bbl., add			25%

MODEL 27 .357 MAGNUM DA

Caliber: .357 Magnum. Six-shot cylinder, bbl. lengths: 3.5-, 4-, 5-, 6-, 6.5-and 8.38-inches, 11.38 inches overall (with 6-inch bbl.). Weight: 44 oz. (with 6-inch bbl.). Adj. target sights, Baughman quick-draw ramp front sight on 3.5-inch bbl., Blued or nickel finish. Checkered walnut grips. Made 1935-94. Note: Until 1938, the .357 Magnum was custom made in any barrel length from 3.5-inch to 8.75-inch. Each of these revolvers was accompanied by a registration certificate and has its registration number stamped on the inside of the yoke. Postwar magnums have a redesigned hammer w/shortened fall and the new S&W micrometer click rear sight.

Prewar registered model

(Reg number on yoke)	NiB $1281	Ex $1025	Gd $697
Prewar model without registration number	NiB $391	Ex $309	Gd $211
Early model w/pinned bbl., recessed cyl.	NiB $431	Ex $340	Gd $232
Late model w/8.38-inch bbl.	NiB $400	Ex $317	Gd $219
Late model, w/3.5-5-inch bbl.	NiB $438	Ex $376	Gd $247
Late model, other bbl. lengths	NiB $438	Ex $376	Gd $247

Smith & Wesson
Model 27

MODEL 28 HIGHWAY PATROLMAN

Caliber: .357 Magnum. Six-shot cylinder, bbl. lengths: 4- or 6-inches, 11.25 inches overall (with 6-inch bbl.). Weight: 44 oz. (with 6-inch bbl.). Adj.rear sight, ramp front. Blued finish. Checkered walnut grips, Magna or target type. Made 1954-86.

Prewar registered model

(reg number on yoke)	NiB $1281	Ex $1025	Gd $697
Prewar model without registration number	NiB $895	Ex $716	Gd $487
Early model w/pinned bbl., recessed cylinder, 5-screws	NiB $362	Ex $314	Gd $254
Late model, all bbl. lengths	NiB $278	Ex $242	Gd $196

Smith & Wesson
Model 28

MODEL 29 .44 MAGNUM DA REVOLVER

Caliber: .44 Magnum. Six-shot cylinder. bbl., lengths: 4-, 5-, 6.5-, 8.38-inches. 11.88 inches overall (with 6.5-inch bbl.). Weight: 47 oz. (with 6.5-inch bbl.). Click adj. rear sight, ramp front. Blued or nickel finish. Checkered Goncalo Alves target grips. Made 1956-98.

Early Production Standard Series (disc. 1983)

3-Screw model (1962-83)	NiB $669	Ex $566	Gd $309
4-Screw model (1957-61)	NiB $716	Ex $669	Gd $438
5-Screw model (1956-57)	NiB $933	Ex $747	Gd $508
W/5-inch bbl., 3- or 4-screw models, add			95%

(cont'd) **MODEL 29 .44 MAGNUM DA REVOLVER**
Late Production standard series (disc. 1998)

Model 29 (w/4- or 6.5-inch bbl.)	NiB $444	Ex $355	Gd $242
Model 29 (w/3-inch bbl., Lew Horton Special)	NiB $438	Ex $360	Gd $304
Model 29 (w/8.38-inch bbl.)	NiB $497	Ex $394	Gd $307
Model 29 Classic (w/5- or 6.5-inch bbl.)	NiB $489	Ex $386	Gd $278
Model 29 Classic (w/8.38-inch bbl.)	NiB $497	Ex $400	Gd $307
Model 29 Classic DX (w/6.5-inch bbl.)	NiB $644	Ex $541	Gd $309
Model 29 Classic DX (w/8.38-inch bbl.)	NiB $652	Ex $549	Gd $317
Model 29 Magna Classic (w/7.5-inch ported bbl.)	NiB $875	Ex $747	Gd $407
Model 29 Silhouette (w/10.63-inch bbl.)	NiB $566	Ex $489	Gd $307

**Smith & Wesson
Model 29**

**Smith & Wesson
Model 31**

**Smith & Wesson
Model 32**

**Smith & Wesson
Model 34**

MODEL 30 .32 HAND
EJECTOR DA REVOLVER . . . . NiB $309 Ex $268 Gd $180
Caliber: .32 S&W Long. Six-shot cylinder, bbl. lengths: 2-(intro. 1949), 3-, 4- and 6-inches, 8 inches overall (with 4-inch bbl.). Weight: 18 oz. (with 4-inch bbl.). Fixed sights. Blued or nickel finish. Round, checkered walnut or hard rubber grips. Made 1903-76.

MODELS 31 & 33 REGULATION POLICE DA REVOLVER
Same basic type as .32 Hand Ejector except has square buttgrips. Calibers: .32 S&W Long (Model 31) .38 S&W (Model 33). Six-shot cylinder in .32 cal., 5-shot in .38 caliber. Bbl., lengths: 2- (intro. 1949), 3-, 4- and 6-inches in .32 cal., 4-inch only in .38 cal., 8.5 inches overall (with 4-inch bbl.). Weight: 18 oz. (.38 cal. w/4-inch bbl.), 18.75 oz. (.32 cal. w/4-inch bbl.). Fixed sights. Blued or nickel finish. Checkered walnut grips. Made from 1917. Model 33 disc. in 1974; Model 31 disc. in 1992.
Model 31 . . . . NiB $299 Ex $242 Gd $180
Model 33 . . . . NiB $335 Ex $283 Gd $180

.32 DOUBLE-ACTION
REVOLVER . . . . NiB $438 Ex $391 Gd $149
Hinged frame. Caliber: .32 S&W. Five-shot cylinder, bbl. lengths: 3-, 3.5- and 6-inches. Fixed sights. Blued or nickel finish. Hard rubber grips. Made from 1880-1919. Note: Value shown applies generally to the several varieties. Exception is the rare first issue of 1880 (identified by squared sideplate and serial no. 1 to 30) valued up to $2,500.

MODEL .32 TERRIER DA . . . . NiB $340 Ex $227 Gd $129
Caliber: .38 S&W. Five-shot cylinder, 2-inch bbl., 6.25 inches overall. Weight: 17 oz. Fixed sights. Blued or nickel finish. Checkered walnut or hard rubber grips. Built on .32 Hand Ejector frame. Made 1936-74.

.32-20 MILITARY & POLICE DA . . . NiB $402 Ex $273 Gd $206
Same as M & P 38 except chambered for .32-20 Winchester cartridge. First intro. in the 1899 model, M & P revolvers were produced in this caliber until about 1940. Values same as M & P .38 models.

MODEL 34 1953
.22/.32 KIT GUN. . . . . NiB $309 Ex $242 Gd $180
Same general specifications as previous .22/.32 Kit Gun except w/2-inch or 4-inch bbl. and round or square grips, blued or nickel finish. Made 1936-91.

MODEL 35 1953
.22/.32 TARGET . . . . NiB $438 Ex $309 Gd $206
Same general specifications as previous model .22/.32 Target except has micrometer-click rear sight. Magna type target grips. Weight: 25 oz. Made 1953-74.

MODEL 36 CHIEFS SPECIAL DA
Based on .32 Hand Ejector w/frame lengthened to permit longer cylinder for .38 Special cartridge. Caliber: .38 Special. Five-shot cylinder, bbl. lengths: 2- or 3-inches, 6.5 inches overall (with 2-inch bbl.). Weight: 19 oz. Fixed sights. Blued or nickel finish. Checkered walnut grips, round or square butt. Made 1952 to date.
Blued model . . . . NiB $304 Ex $237 Gd $160
Nickel model . . . . NiB $3126 Ex $249 Gd $172
**Early model (5-screw,
small trigger guard,
SN 1-2500) . . . . NiB $380 Ex $304 Gd $200**

SUPER BLACK EAGLE II

Beyond Perfection

Benelli.
Performance Worth the Price

17603 Indian Head Highway
Accokeek, MD 20607
Tel: 301-283-6981
Fax: 301-283-6988
www.benelliusa.com

For more information on the Super Black Eagle II visit our website at www.benelliusa.com.

MODEL 37 AIRWEIGHT
CHIEFS SPECIAL .... NiB $422 Ex $294 Gd $191
Same general specifications as standard Chiefs Special except has light alloy frame, weight: 12.5 oz. w/2-inch bbl., blued finish only. Made 1954 to date.

MODEL 38 BODYGUARD AIRWEIGHT DA REVOLVER
Shrouded hammer. Light alloy frame. Caliber: .38 Special. Five-shot cylinder, 2- or 3-inch bbl., 6.38 inches overall (w/2-inch bbl). Weight: 14.5 oz. Fixed sights. Blued or nickel finish. Checkered walnut grips. Made 1955-98.
Blued model .... NiB $360 Ex $268 Gd $175
Nickel model .... NiB $376 Ex $283 Gd $191
Early model (pinned &
recessed, pre-1981) .... NiB $322 Ex $257 Gd $175

.38 DA REVOLVER. .... NiB $515 Ex $360 Gd $201
Hinged frame. Caliber: .38 S&W. Five-shot cylinder, bbl. lengths: 4-, 4.25-, 5-, 6-, 8- and 10-inch. Fixed sights. Blued or nickel finish. Hard rubber grips. Made 1880-1911. Note: Value shown applies generally to the several varieties. Exceptions are the first issue of 1880 (identified by squared sideplate and serial no. 1 to 4,000) and the 8- and 10-inch bbl. models of the third issue (1884-95).

MODEL .38 HAND EJECTOR DA
Military & Police — First Model. Resembles Colt New Navy in general appearance, lacks bbl., lug and locking bolt common to all later S&W hand ejector models. Caliber: .38 Long Colt. Six-shot cylinder, bbl. lengths: 4-, 5-, 6- and 6.5-inch, 11.5 inches overall (with 6.5-inch bbl.). Fixed sights. Blued or nickel finish. Round, checkered walnut or hard rubber grips. Made 1899-1902.
Standard model
(civilian issue) .... NiB $669 Ex $566 Gd $211
Army Model (marked U.S.
Army Model, 1000 issued) ..... NiB $1957 Ex $1648 Gd $644
Navy Model (marked USN,
1000 issued) .... NiB $1442 Ex $1648 Gd $644

.38 MILITARY &
POLICE TARGET DA .... NiB $618 Ex $463 Gd $216
Target version of the Military & Police w/standard features of that model. Caliber: .38 Special, six-inch bbl. Weight: 32.25 oz. Adj. target sights. Blued finish. Checkered walnut grips. Made 1899-1940. For values, add $175 for corresponding M&P 38 models.

MODEL .38 PERFECTED DA ...... NiB $824 Ex $515 Gd $206
Hinged frame. Similar to earlier .38 DA Model but heavier frame, side latch as in solid-frame models, improved lockwork. Caliber: .38 S&W. Five-shot cylinder, bbl. lengths: 3.25, 4, 5 and 6 inches. Fixed sights. Blued or nickel finish. Hard rubber grips. Made 1909-20.

MODEL .40 CENTENNIAL
DA HAMMERLESS REVOLVER ..... NiB $489 Ex $438 Gd $268
Similar to Chiefs Special but has Safety Hammerless-type mechanism w/grip safety. Two-inch bbl. Weight: 19 oz. Made 1953-74.

MODEL 42 CENTENNIAL AIRWEIGHT
Same as standard Centennial model except has light alloy frame, weight: 13 oz. Made 1954-74.
Blued model .... NiB $489 Ex $438 Gd $268
Nickel model .... NiB $1030 Ex $978 Gd $566

MODEL 43 1955 .22/.32
KIT GUN AIRWEIGHT .... NiB $438 Ex $360 Gd $191
Same as Model 34 Kit Gun except has light alloy frame, square grip. Furnished w/3.5-inch bbl., weight: 14.25 oz. Made 1954-74.

Smith & Wesson
Model 36

Smith & Wesson
Model 37

Smith & Wesson
Model 38 Bodyguard Airweight

MODEL 44 1926 MILITARY DA REVOLVER
Basically the same as the early New Century model with extractor rod casing but lacking the "Triple Lock" feature. Caliber: .44 S&W Special. Six-shot cylinder, bbl. lengths: 4, 5 and 6.5 inches, 11.75 inches overall (with 6.5-inch bbl.). Weight: 39.5 oz. (with 6.5-inch bbl.). Fixed sights. Blued or nickel finish. Checkered walnut grips. Made 1926-41.
Standard model .... NiB $895 Ex $716 Gd $487
Target model w/6.5-inch bbl.,
target sights, blued .... NiB $3798 Ex $3038 Gd $2066

.44 AND .38 DA REVOLVERS
Also called Wesson Favorite (lightweight model), Frontier (caliber .44-40). Hinged frame. Six-shot cylinder. Calibers: .44 S&W Russian, .38-40, .44-40. Bbl. lengths: 4-, 5-, 6- and 6.5-inch. Weight: 37.5 oz. (with 6.5-inch bbl.). Fixed sights. Blued or nickel finish. Hard rubber grips. Made 1881-1913, Frontier disc. 1910.
Standard model, .44 Russian ... NiB $4635 Ex $1957 Gd $700
Standard model, .38-40 .... NiB $4635 Ex $1957 Gd $700
Frontier model .... NiB $4635 Ex $1957 Gd $700
Favorite model .... NiB $10,300 Ex $8240 Gd $2884

**Smith & Wesson
Model 48**

**Smith & Wesson
Model 49 Bodyguard**

**Smith & Wesson
Model 57**

**Smith & Wesson
Model 60**

**Smith & Wesson
Model 63**

**Smith & Wesson
Model 64**

.44 HAND EJECTOR MODEL DA REVOLVER

First Model, New Century, also called "Triple Lock" because of its third cylinder lock at the crane. Six-shot cylinder. Calibers: .44 S&W Special, .450 Eley, .455 Mark II. Bbl. lengths: 4-, 5-, 6.5- and 7.5-inch. Weight: 39 oz. (with 6.5-inch bbl.). Fixed sights. Blued or nickel finish. Checkered walnut grips. Made 1907-66.

Second Model is basically the same as New Century except crane lock ("Triple Lock" feature) and extractor rod casing eliminated. Calibers: .44 S&W Special .44-40 Win. .45 Colt. Bbl. lengths: 4-, 5-, 6.5- and 7.5-inch; 11.75 inches overall (with 6.5-inch bbl.). Weight: 38 oz. (with 6.5-inch bbl.). Fixed sights. Blued or nickel finish. Checkered walnut grips. Made 1915-37.

First Model series w/triple lock (1907-15)
Standard model,
.44 S&W Special . . . . NiB $2343 Ex $1931 Gd $865
Standard model w/
special calibers . . . . NiB $2343 Ex $1931 Gd $875
British 455
Target model . . . . NiB $3296 Ex $3038 Gd $659
Second Model series w/o triple lock (1915-37)
Standard model,
.44 S&W Special . . . . NiB $1751 Ex $1571 Gd $736
Standard model
w/special calibers . . . . NiB $2343 Ex $1931 Gd $865
Third Model series (see S&W Model .44/1926)
Fourth Model series (see S&W Model .44/1950)

.44 HAND EJECTOR,
SECOND MODEL
DA REVOLVER. . . . . NiB $695 Ex $613 Gd $299
Basically the same as New Century except crane lock ("Triple Lock" feature) and extractor rod casing eliminated. Calibers: .44 S&W Special .44-40 Win. .45 Colt. Bbl. lengths: 4-, 5-, 6.5- and 7.5-inches, 11.75 inches overall (with 6.5-inch bbl.). Weight: .38 oz. (with 6.5-inch bbl.). Fixed sights. Blued or nickel finish. Checkered walnut grips. Made 1915-37.

MODEL 48 (K-.22) MASTERPIECE M.R.F. DA REVOLVER
Caliber: .22 Mag. and .22 RF. Six-shot cylinder, bbl. lengths: 4, 6 and 8.38 inches, 11.13 inches overall (w/ 6-inch bbl.). Weight: 39 oz. Adj. rear sight, ramp front. Made 1959-86.

Model 48 (4- or 6-inch bbl.) ...... NiB $283 Ex $252 Gd $180
Model 48 (8.38-inch bbl.) .... NiB $319 Ex $299 Gd $196
W/target options TH & TT, add $50

MODEL 49 BODYGUARD
Same as Model 38 Bodyguard Airweight except has steel frame, weight: 20.5 oz. Made 1959-96.

Blued model .... NiB $309 Ex $268 Gd $165
Nickel model .... NiB $335 Ex $294 Gd $191

MODEL 51 1960 .22/.32 KIT GUN ...... NiB $412 Ex $360 Gd $232
Same as Model 34 Kit Gun except chambered for .22 WMR 3.5-inch bbl., weight: 24 oz. Made 1960-74.

MODEL 53 .22 MAGNUM DA
Caliber: .22 Rem. Jet C.F. Magnum. Six-shot cylinder (inserts permit use of .22 Short, Long, or LR cartridges). Bbl. lengths: 4, 6, 8.38 inches, 11.25 inches overall (with 6-inch bbl.). Weight: 40 oz. (with 6-inch bbl.). Micrometer-click rear sight ramp front. Checkered walnut grips. Made 1960-74.

Model 53 (4- or 6-inch bbl.) ...... NiB $757 Ex $669 Gd $407
Model 53 (8.38-inch bbl.) .... NiB $778 Ex $700 Gd $417
W/target options TH & TT, add $35

MODEL 57 41 MAGNUM DA REVOLVER
Caliber: 41 Magnum. Six-shot cylinder, bbl. lengths: 4-, 6-, 8.38-inch. Weight: 40 oz. (with 6-inch bbl.). Micrometer click rear sight, ramp front. Target grips of checkered Goncalo Alves. Made 1964-93.

Model 57 (w/4- or 6-inch bbl.) ..... NiB $360 Ex $263 Gd $180
Model 57 (w/8.63-inch bbl.) .... NiB $381 Ex $283 Gd $201
Model 57 (w/pinned bbl., recessed cylinder), add 10%

MODEL 58 41 MILITARY
& POLICE DA REVOLVER .... NiB $510 Ex $463 Gd $304
Caliber: 41 Magnum. Six-shot cylinder, 4-inch bbl. 9.25 inches overall. Weight: 41 oz. Fixed sights. Checkered walnut grips. Made 1964-82.

MODEL 60 STAINLESS DA
Caliber: .38 Special or .357 Magnum. Five-shot cylinder, bbl. lengths: 2, 2.1 or 3 inches, 6.5 or 7.5 inches overall. Weight: 19 to 23 oz. Square-notch rear sight, ramp front. Satin finish stainless steel. Made 1965-96 (.38 Special) and 1996 to date .357/.38).

.38 Special (disc. 1996) .... NiB $360 Ex $257 Gd $196
.357 Mag. .... NiB $412 Ex $304 Gd $216
Lady Smith (W/smaller grip) ...... NiB $443 Ex $294 Gd $221

MODEL 63 (1977) KIT GUN DA .... NiB $376 Ex $252 Gd $201
Caliber: .22 LR. Six-shot cylinder, 2- or 4-inch bbl., 6.5 or 8.5 inches overall. Weight: 19 to 24.5 oz. Adj. rear sight, ramp front. Stainless steel. Checkered walnut or synthetic grips.

MODEL 64 .38 M&P STAINLESS .... NiB $402 Ex $273 Gd $206
Same as standard Model 10 except satin-finished stainless steel, square butt w/4-inch heavy bbl., or round butt w/2-inch bbl. Made 1970 to date.

MODEL 65 .357 MILITARY/POLICE STAINLESS
Same as Model 13 except satin-finished stainless steel. Made 1974 to date.

Model 65 M&P .... NiB $407 Ex $270 Gd $211
Model 65 Lady Smith (W/smaller grip) ...... NiB $443 Ex $309 Gd $232

**Smith & Wesson
Model 66 Combat Magnum**

**Smith & Wesson
Model 67 Combat Masterpiece**

MODEL 66 .357 COMBAT MAGNUM STAINLESS
Same as Model 19 except satin-finished stainless steel. Made 1971 to date.

Model 66 (2.5-inch bbl.) .... NiB $475 Ex $331 Gd $243
Model 66 (3-inch bbl.) .... NiB $463 Ex $319 Gd $232
Model 66 (4-inch bbl.) .... NiB $463 Ex $319 Gd $232
Model 66 (6-inch bbl.) .... NiB $484 Ex $411 Gd $262
W/target options TH & TT, add $48

MODEL 67 .38 COMBAT
MASTERPIECE STAINLESS .... NiB $469 Ex $319 Gd $232
Same as Model 15 except satin-finished stainless steel available only w/4-inch bbl. Made 1972-88 and 1991 to date.

MODEL 68 .38 COMBAT
MASTERPIECE STAINLESS .... NiB $772 Ex $644 Gd $510
Same as Model 66 except w/4- or 6-inch bbl., chambered for .38 Special. Made to accommodate CA Highway Patrol because they were not authorized to carry .357 magnums. Made 1976-83. (7500 produced)

125th Anniversary Commemorative
Issued to celebrate the 125th anniversary of the 1852 partnership of Horace Smith and Daniel Baird Wesson. Standard Edition is Model 25 revolver in .45 Colt w/6.5-inch bbl., bright blued finish, gold-filled bbl., roll mark "Smith & Wesson 125th Anniversary," sideplate marked w/gold-filled Anniversary seal, smooth Goncalo Alves grips, in presentation case w/nickel silver Anniversary medallion and book, "125 Years w/Smith & Wesson," by Roy Jinks. Deluxe Edition is same except revolver is Class A engraved w/gold-filled seal on sideplate, ivory grips, Anniversary medallion is sterling silver and book is leather bound. Limited to 50 units. Total issue is 10,000 units, of which 50 are Deluxe Edition and two are a Custom Deluxe Edition and not for sale. Made in 1977.

Standard edition .... NiB $766 Ex $613 Gd $417
Deluxe edition .... NiB $2183 Ex $1746 Gd $1188

**Smith & Wesson
125th Commemorative Deluxe Edition**

**Smith & Wesson
Model 586 Distinguished Combat Magnum**

**Smith & Wesson
Model 625**

**Smith & Wesson
Model 629**

**Smith & Wesson
Model 629 Classic**

317 AIRLITE DA REVOLVER

Caliber: .22 LR. Eight-shot cylinder, 1.88- or 3-inch bbl., 6.3 or 7.2 inches overall. Weight: 9.9 oz. or 11 oz. Ramp front sight, notched frame rear. Aluminum, carbon fiber, stainless and titanium construction. Brushed aluminum finish. Synthetic or Dymondwood grips. Made 1997 to date.

**Model 317
(w/1.88-inch bbl.)** . . . . NiB $438 Ex $309 Gd $227
**Model 317
(w/3-inch bbl.)** . . . . NiB $438 Ex $309 Gd $227
**Model 317
(w/Dymondwood grips), add.** $68

MODEL 520

DA REVOLVER. . . . . NiB $335 Ex $283 Gd $129
Caliber: .357 Mag. Six-shot cylinder. N-Frame w/4-inch bbl. Weight: 40 oz. Fixed sights. In 1980, 3000 were made for the N.Y. State Police, but that agency did not purchase those firearms. (Sold commercially).

MODEL 547

DA REVOLVER. . . . . NiB $304 Ex $273 Gd $191
Caliber: 9mm. Six-shot cylinder, bbl. length: 3 or 4 inches, 7.31 inches overall. Weight: 32 oz. Square-notch rear sight, ramp front. Disc. 1986.

MODEL 581 REVOLVER

Caliber: .357 Magnum. Bbl. lengths: 4 inches, weight: 34 oz. Serrated ramp front sight, square notch rear. Checkered walnut grips. Made 1985-92.
Blued finish . . . . NiB $283 Ex $232 Gd $165
Nickel finish . . . . NiB $304 Ex $252 Gd $185

MODEL 586 DISTINGUISHED COMBAT MAGNUM

Caliber: .357 Magnum. Six-shot cylinder, bbl. lengths: 4, 6 and 8.38 inches, overall length: 9.75 inches (with 4-inch bbl.). Weight: 42, 46, 53 oz., respectively. Red ramp front sight, micrometer-click adj. rear. Checkered grip. Blued or nickel finish. Made 1980-99.
**Model 586
(w/4- or 6-inch bbl.)** . . . . NiB $381 Ex $294 Gd $191
**Model 586
(w/8.63-inch bbl.)** . . . . NiB $404 Ex $316 Gd $213
**Model 586 (w/adjustable
front sight), add.** $35
**Model 586
(w/nickel finish), add.** $45

MODEL 610 DA REVOLVER

. . . . . . NiB $659 Ex $515 Gd $407
Similar to Model 625 except in caliber 10mm. Magna classic grips. Made 1990-91 and 1998 to date.

MODEL 617 DA REVOLVER
Similar to Model 17 except in stainless. Made 1990 to date.
Semi-target model w/4- or 6-inch bbl. . . . . NiB $484 Ex $330 Gd $232
Target model w/6-inch bbl. . . . . NiB $484 Ex $330 Gd $232
Target model w/8.38-inch bbl. . . . . NiB $484 Ex $330 Gd $232
W/10-shot cylinder, add $94

MODEL 624 DOUBLE-ACTION REVOLVER
Same general specifications as Model 24 except satin finished stainless steel. Limited production of 10,000. Made 1985-86.
Model 624 w/4-inch bbl. . . . . NiB $350 Ex $257 Gd $232
Model 624 w/6.5-inch bbl. . . . . NiB $375 Ex $272 Gd $246
Model 624 w/3-inch bbl., round
butt (Lew Horton spec.) . . . . NiB $407 Ex $360 Gd $407

MODEL 625 DA REVOLVER . . . . . . NiB $494 Ex $350 Gd $242
Same general specifications as Model 25 except 3-, 4- or 5-inch bbl., round-butt Pachmayr grips and satin stainless steel finish. Made 1989 to date.

MODEL 627 DA REVOLVER . . . . . . NiB $494 Ex $350 Gd $242
Same general specifications as Model 27 except satin stainless steel finish. Made 1989-91.

MODEL 629 DA REVOLVER
Same as Model 29 in .44 Magnum except in stainless steel. Classic made 1990 to date.
Model 629 (3-inch bbl., Backpacker) . . . . NiB $592 Ex $458 Gd $335
Model 629 (4- and 6-inch bbl.) . . . . NiB $615 Ex $481 Gd $355
Model 629 (8.38-inch bbl.) . . . . NiB $631 Ex $477 Gd $374
Model 629 Classic (5- and 6.5-inch bbl.) . . . . . NiB $618 Ex $469 Gd $355
Model 629 Classic (8.38-inch bbl.) . . . . NiB $644 Ex $494 Gd $381
Model 629 Classic DX (6.5-inch bbl.) . . . . NiB $819 Ex $654 Gd $525
Model 629 Classic DX (8.38-inch bbl.) . . . . . . NiB $852 Ex $687 Gd $558
Model 629 Magna Classic (w/7.5-inch
ported bbl.) . . . . NiB $998 Ex $798 Gd $543

MODEL 631 DA REVOLVER
Similar to Model 31 except chambered for .32 H&R Mag. Goncalo Alves combat grips. Made 1991-92.
Fixed sights, 2-inch bbl. . . . . NiB $350 Ex $283 Gd $206
Adjustable sights, 4-inch bbl. . . . . NiB $354 Ex $283 Gd $193
Lady Smith, 2-inch bbl. . . . . NiB $376 Ex $304 Gd $232
Lady Smith, 2-inch bbl. (black stainless). . . . . NiB $380 Ex $304 Gd $207

MODEL 632 CENTENNIAL DA
Same general specifications as Model 640 except chambered for .32 H&R Mag. 2- or 3-inch bbl., weight: 15.5 oz. Stainless slide w/alloy frame. Fixed sights. Santoprene combat grips. Made in 1991-92.
Model 632 w/2-inch bbl. . . . . NiB $324 Ex $247 Gd $201
Model 632 w/3-inch bbl. . . . . NiB $324 Ex $247 Gd $201

MODEL 637 CHIEFS
SPECIAL AIRWEIGHT DA . . . . NiB $417 Ex $283 Gd $216
Same general specifications as Model 37 except w/clear anodized fuse alloy frame and stainless cylinder. 560 made in 1991 and reintroduced in 1996.

MODEL 638 BODYGUARD
AIRWEIGHT DA . . . . NiB $433 Ex $309 Gd $237
Same general specifications as Model .38 except w/clear anodized fuse alloy frame and stainless cylinder. 1200 made in 1989 and reintroduced in 1998.

MODEL 640 CENTENNIAL DA . . . . NiB $433 Ex $309 Gd $237
Caliber: .38 Special. Five-shot cylinder, 2, 2.1 or 3-inch bbl., 6.31 inches overall. Weight: 20-22 oz. Fixed sights. Stainless finish. Smooth hardwood service grips. Made 1990 to date.

**Smith & Wesson
Model 640**

**Smith & Wesson
Model 642 Centennial Airweight**

MODEL 642 CENTENNIAL AIRWEIGHT DA REVOLVER
Same general specifications as Model 640 except w/stainless steel/aluminum alloy frame and finish. Weight 15.8 oz. Santoprene combat grips. Made 1990-93 and reintroduced 1996.
Model 642
Centennial . . . . NiB $433 Ex $309 Gd $227
Model 642 Lady Smith
(W/smaller grip) . . . . NiB $433 Ex $309 Gd $227

MODEL 648
DA REVOLVER. . . . . NiB $360 Ex $257 Gd $201
Same general specifications as Models 17/617 except in stainless and chambered for .22 Mag. Made 1990-93.

MODEL 649
BODYGUARD DA. . . . . NiB $458 Ex $309 Gd $227
Caliber: .38 Special. Five-shot cylinder, bbl. length: 2 inches, 6.25 inches overall. Weight: 20 oz. Square-notch rear sight ramp front. Stainless frame and finish. Made 1986 to date.

MODEL 650
REVOLVER. . . . . NiB $257 Ex $206 Gd $196
Caliber: .22 Mag. Six-shot cylinder, 3-inch bbl., 7 inches overall. Weight: 23.5 oz. Serrated ramp front sight, fixed square-notch rear. Round butt, checkered walnut monogrammed grips. Stainless steel finish. Made 1983-86.

Smith & Wesson
Model 696

Smith & Wesson
Model K-22 Outdoorsman

Smith & Wesson
Lady Smith First Model

Smith & Wesson
Lady Smith Second Model

MODEL 651 STAINLESS DA

Caliber: .22 Mag. Rimfire. Six-shot cylinder, bbl. length: 3 and 4 inches, 7 and 8.63 inches, respectively, overall. Weight: 24.5 oz. Adj. rear sight, ramp front. Made 1983-87 and 1990-98. Note: Optional .22 LR cylinder available during early production.

Model 651 w/3- or 4-inch bbl. . . . . NiB $366 Ex $257 Gd $196
Model 651 w/extra cylinder . . . . . . NiB $572 Ex $489 Gd $386

MODEL 657 REVOLVER

Caliber: 41 Mag. Six-shot cylinder. Bbl. lengths: 4, 6 or 8.4 inches; 9.6, 11.4, and 13.9 inches overall. Weight: 44.2, 48 and 52.5 oz. Serrated black ramp front sight on ramp base click rear, adj. for windage and elevation. Satin finished stainless steel. Made 1986 to date.

W/4- or 6-inch bbl. . . . . NiB $551 Ex $386 Gd $299
W/8.4-inch bbl. . . . . NiB $568 Ex $404 Gd $316

MODEL 681 . . . . NiB $330 Ex $238 Gd $201
Same as S&W Model 581 except in stainless finish only. Made 1991-93.

MODEL 686

Same as S&W Model 586 Distinguished Combat Magnum except in stainless finish w/additional 2.5-inch bbl. Made 1991 to date.

Model 686 (w/2.5-inch bbl.) . . . . NiB $489 Ex $360 Gd $330
Model 686 (w/4- or 6-inch bbl.) . . . . NiB $515 Ex $386 Gd $355
Model 686 (w/8.63-inch bbl.) . . . . NiB $546 Ex $417 Gd $407
Model 686 (w/adjustable
front sight), add. $35

MODEL 686 PLUS

Same as standard Model 686 Magnum except w/7-shot cylinder and 2.5-, 4- or 6-inch bbl. Made 1996 to date.

Model 686 Plus (w/2.5-inch bbl.) . . . . NiB $505 Ex $340 Gd $257
Model 686 Plus (w/4-inch bbl.) . . . . NiB $527 Ex $363 Gd $278
Model 686 Plus (w/6-inch bbl.) . . . . NiB $418 Ex $335 Gd $228

MODEL 696 . . . . NiB $500 Ex $324 Gd $257
Caliber: .44 S&W Special. L-Frame w/five-shot cylinder, 3-inch shrouded bbl., 8.38 inches overall. Weight: 48 oz. Red ramp front sight, micrometer-click adj. rear. Checkered synthetic grip. Satin stainless steel. Made 1997 to date.

MODEL 940 CENTENNIAL DA . . . . NiB $402 Ex $273 Gd $227
Same general specifications as Model 640 except chambered for 9mm. Two- or 3-inch bbl., Weight: 23-25 oz. Santoprene combat grips. Made 1991 to date.

MODEL 1891 SA REVOLVER

Hinged frame. Caliber: .38 S&W. Five-shot cylinder, bbl. lengths: 3.25, 4, 5 and 6-inches. Fixed sights. Blued or nickel finish. Hard rubber grips. Made 1891-1911. Note: Until 1906, an accessory single-shot target bbl. (see Model 1891 Single-Shot Target Pistol) was available for this revolver.

Revolver only. . . . . NiB $2369 Ex $1700 Gd $803
Set w/.22 single-shot bbl. . . . . . NiB $3090 Ex $2060 Gd $1545

1917 ARMY DA REVOLVER

Caliber: .45 Automatic, using 3-cartridge half-moon clip or .45 Auto Rim, without clip. Six-shot cylinder, 5.5-inch bbl., 10.75 inches overall. Weight: 36.25 oz. Fixed sights. Blued finish (blue-black finish on commercial model, brush polish on military). Checkered walnut grips (commercial model, smooth on military). Made under U.S. Government contract 1917-19 and produced commercially 1919-1941. Note: About 175,000 of these revolvers were produced during WW I. The DCM sold these to NRA members during the 1930s at $16.15 each.

Commercial model . . . . NiB $669 Ex $515 Gd $294
Military model. . . . . NiB $824 Ex $618 Gd $227

K-22 MASTERPIECE DA . . . . **NiB $1236 Ex $1081 Gd $618**
Improved version of K-22 Outdoorsman w/same specifications but w/micrometer-click rear sight, short action and antibacklash trigger. Fewer than 1100 manufactured in 1940.

K-22 OUTDOORSMAN DA . . . . . . **NiB $592 Ex $515 Gd $294**
Design based on the .38 Military & Police Target. Caliber: .22 LR. Six-shot cylinder, 11.13 inches overall. Weight: 35 oz. Adj. target sights. Blued finish. Checkered walnut grip. Made 1931-40.

K32 AND K38 HEAVY MASTERPIECES
Same as K32 and K38 Masterpiece but w/heavy bbl. Weight: 38.5 oz. Made 1950-53. Note: All K32 and K38 revolvers made after September 1953 have heavy bbls. and the "Heavy Masterpiece" designation was disc. Values for Heavy Masterpiece models are the same as shown for Models 14 and 16. (See separate listing).

K-32 TARGET DA REVOLVER . . . . **NiB $1390 Ex $1123 Gd $772**
Same as .38 Military & Police Target except chambered for .32 S&W Long cartridge, slightly heavier bbl., weight: 34 oz. Only 98 produced. Made 1938-.40.

LADY SMITH (MODEL M HAND EJECTOR) DA REVOLVER
Caliber: .22 LR. Seven-shot cylinder, bbl. length: 2.25-, 3-, 3.5- and 6-inch (Third Model only), approximately 7 inches overall w/3.5-inch bbl., weight: About 9.5 oz. Fixed sights, adj. target sights available on Third Model. Blued or nickel finish. Round butt, hard rubber grips on First and Second models; checkered walnut or hard rubber square buttgrips on Third Model. First Model —1902-06: Cylinder locking bolt operated by button on left side of frame, no bbl., lug and front locking bolt. Second Model —1906-11: Rear cylinder latch eliminated, has bbl. lug, forward cylinder lock w/draw-bolt fastening. Third Model —1911-21: Same as Second Model except has square grips, target sights and 6-inch bbl. available. Note: Legend has it that a straight-laced D.B. Wesson ordered discontinuance of the Lady Smith when he learned of the little revolver's reputed popularity w/ladies of the evening. The story, which undoubtedly has enhanced the appeal of this model to collectors, is not true: The Lady Smith was disc. because of difficulty of manufacture and high frequency of repairs.
First model . . . . **NiB $2884 Ex $1854 Gd $448**
Second model . . . . **NiB $2060 Ex $1545 Gd $438**
Third model, w/fixed sights,
2.25- or 3.5-inch bbl. . . . . **NiB $2060 Ex $1545 Gd $448**
Third model, w/fixed sights,
6-inch bbl. . . . . **NiB $2060 Ex $1519 Gd $438**
Third model, w/adj. sights,
6-inch bbl. . . . . **NiB $4017 Ex $1638 Gd $716**

REGULATION POLICE
DA (I FRAME) . . . . **NiB $612 Ex $489 Gd $333**
Calibers: .32 S&W (6-shot) or .38 S&W (5-shot) built on .32 Hand Ejector frames. Two-, 3-, 3.25-, 4-, 4.25- or 6-inch bbl., weight: 20-24 oz. Fixed sights. Blue or nickel finish. Checkered walnut grips. Made 1917-57. Note: After 1957 "J" Frames replaced the older "I" Frames and designations changed to Model 31 and 33 respectively.
Regulation Police, .32 S&W . . . . **NiB $335 Ex $283 Gd $129**
Regulation Police, .38 S&W . . . . **NiB $335 Ex $283 Gd $129**

REGULATION POLICE TARGET DA
Target version of the Regulation Police w/standard features of that model. Calibers: .32 S&W Long or .38 S&W. 6-inch bbl., 10.25 inches overall. Weight: 20 oz. Adjustable target sights. Blue or nickel finish. Checkered walnut grips. Made about 1917-57.
Regulation Police Target, .32 S&W . . . . **NiB $669 Ex $566 Gd $257**
Regulation Police Target, .38 S&W . . . . **NiB $669 Ex $566 Gd $257**

Smith & Wesson
Regulation Police Target

Smith & Wesson
Safety Hammerless

SAFETY HAMMERLESS
REVOLVER . . . . **NiB $1236 Ex $824 Gd $335**
Also called New Departure Double Action. Hinged frame. Calibers: .32 S&W, .38 S&W. Five-shot cylinder, bbl. lengths: 2, 3- and 3.5-inch (.32 cal.) or 2-, 3.25-, 4-, 5- and 6-inch (.38 cal.); 6.75 inches overall (.32 cal. w/3-inch bbl.) or 7.5 inches (.38 cal. w/3.25-inch bbl.). Weight: 14.25 oz. (.32 cal. w/3-inch bbl.) or 18.25 oz. (.38 cal. 2.5-inch bbl.). Fixed sights. Blued or nickel finish. Hard rubber grips. Made 1888-1937 (.32 cal.); 1887-1941 (.38 cal. w/various minor changes.)

TEXAS RANGER
COMMEMORATIVE. . . . . **NiB $1236 Ex $942 Gd $669**
Issued to honor the 150th anniversary of the Texas Rangers. Model 19 .357 Combat Magnum w/4-inch bbl., sideplate stamped w/Texas Ranger Commemorative Seal, smooth Goncalo Alves grips. Special Bowie knife in presentation case. 8,000 sets made in 1973. Top value is for set in new condition.

SPHINX ENGINEERING SA. — Porrentruy, Switzerland

MODEL AT-380 DA PISTOL
Caliber: .380 ACP. 10-shot magazine, 3.27- inch bbl., 6.03 inches overall. Weight: 25 oz. Stainless steel frame w/blued slide or Palladium finish. Slide latch w/ambidextrous magazine release. Imported 1993-96.
Model AT-380 two-tone
(w/blued slide) . . . . **NiB $444 Ex $382 Gd $280**
Model AT-380 N/pall
(w/Palladium finish) . . . . **NiB $516 Ex $455 Gd $353**

NOTE: *The AT-88 pistol series was previously manufactured by ITM in Switzerland and imported by Action Arms before Sphinx-Muller resumed production of these firearms, now designated as the AT-2000 series.*

**Springfield Armory
1911-A1 Post '90 Series Trophy Model**

**Springfield Armory
1911-A1 PDP Series Defender**

**Springfield Armory
1911-A1 Champion**

**Springfield Armory
1911-A1 Compact**

**Sphinx
Model AT2000S Scope Optional**

MODEL AT2000S DA AUTOMATIC PISTOL

Calibers: 9mm Parabellum, .40 S&W. 15- or 11-shot magazine respectively, 4.53-inch bbl., (S-standard), 3.66-inch bbl., (P-compact), 3.34-inch bbl., (H-subcompact), 8.25 inches overall. Weight: 36.5 oz. Fixed sights w/3-dot system. Stainless frame w/blued slide or Palladium finish. Ambidextrous safety. Checkered walnut or neoprene grips. Imported 1993-96.

Model AT2000S (standard) . . . . NiB $984 Ex $765 Gd $459
Model AT2000P (compact) . . . . NiB $867 Ex $637 Gd $418
Model AT2000H (subcompact) . . . . NiB $867 Ex $637 Gd $418
.40 S&W, add $90
For Palladium finish (disc. 1994). . . . . . NiB $204 Ex $181 Gd $151

MODEL AT2000C/2000CS COMPETITOR

Similar to the Model AT2000S except also chambered for 9x21mm. 10-shot magazine, 5.31-inch compensated bbl., 9.84 inches overall. Weight: 40.56 oz. Fully adjustable BoMar or ProPoint sights. Made 1993-96.

Model 2000C (w/BoMar sight) . . . . NiB $1759 Ex $1300 Gd $867
Model 2000CS (w/ProPoint sight). . . . . . NiB $1759 Ex $1300 Gd $867

MODEL AT2000GM/GMS GRAND MASTER

Similar to the AT2000C except single action only w/square trigger guard and extended beavertail grip. Imported 1993-96.

Model 2000GM (w/BoMar sight) . . . . NiB $2289 Ex $1831 Gd $1245
Model 2000GMS (w/ProPoint sight). . . . . . NiB $2416 Ex $1933 Gd $1315

SPRINGFIELD, INC. — Geneseo, Illinois (Formerly Springfield Armory)

MODEL M1911 SERIES AUTO PISTOL

Springfield builds the "PDP" (Personal Defense Pistol) Series based on the self-loading M 1911-A1 pistol (military specifications model) as adopted for a standard service weapon by the U.S. Army. With enhancements and modifications they produce a full line of firearms including Ultra-Compacts, Lightweights, Match Grade and Competition Models. For values see specific models.

MODEL 1911-A1 GOVERNMENT

Calibers: 9mm Para., .38 Super, .40 S&W, 10mm or .45 ACP., 7-, 8-, 9- or 10-shot magazine, 4- or 5-inch bbl., 8.5 inches overall. Weight: 36 oz. Fixed combat sights. Blued, Parkerized or Duo-Tone finish. Checkered walnut grips. Note: This is an exact duplicate of the Colt M1911-A1 that was used by the U.S. Armed Forces as a service weapon.

Blued finish . . . . NiB $408 Ex $367 Gd $286
Parkerized finish . . . . NiB $408 Ex $367 Gd $286

MODEL 1911-A1 (PRE '90 SERIES)
Calibers: 9mm Parabellum, .38 Super, 10mm, .45 ACP. Seven-, 8-, 9- or 10-shot magazine, bbl. length: 3.63, 4, 4.25 or 5 inches, 8.5 inches overall. Weight: 36 oz. Fixed combat sights. Blued, Duo-Tone or Parkerized finish. Checkered walnut stocks. Made 1985-90.

Government model (blued)	NiB $408	Ex $367	Gd $286
Government model (Parkerized)	NiB $408	Ex $367	Gd $286
Bullseye model (wadcutter)	NiB $1443	Ex $1224	Gd $765
Combat Commander model (blued)	NiB $444	Ex $393	Gd $280
Combat Commander model (Parkerized)	NiB $444	Ex $393	Gd $280
Commander model (blued)	NiB $459	Ex $423	Gd $291
Commander model (Duo-Tone)	NiB $459	Ex $454	Gd $321
Commander model (Parkerized)	NiB $459	Ex $423	Gd $291
Compact model (blued)	NiB $490	Ex $454	Gd $286
Compact model (Duo-Tone)	NiB $541	Ex $505	Gd $337
Compact model (Parkerized)	NiB $459	Ex $423	Gd $255
Defender model (blued)	NiB $525	Ex $479	Gd $321
Defender model (Parkerized)	NiB $495	Ex $445	Gd $286
Defender model (Custom Carry)	NiB $816	Ex $739	Gd $469
National Match model (Hardball)	NiB $796	Ex $663	Gd $469
Trophy Master (Competition)	NiB $1326	Ex $1122	Gd $765
Trophy Master (Distinguished)	NiB $2040	Ex $1708	Gd $1045
Trophy Master (Competition)	NiB $1697	Ex $1479	Gd $908

MODEL 1911-A1 (POST '90 SERIES)
SA linkless operating system w/steel or alloy frame. Calibers: 9mm Parabellum, .38 Super, .40 S&W, 10mm, .45 ACP. Seven-, 8-, 9- or 10-shot magazine, bbl. length: 3.63, 4, 4.25 or 5 inches; 8.5 inches overall. Weight: 28 oz. to 36 oz. Fixed combat sights. Blued, Duo-Tone, Parkerized or stainless finish. Checkered composition or walnut stocks. Made 1990 to date.

Mil-Spec model (blued)	NiB $474	Ex $382	Gd $286
Mil-Spec model (Parkerized)	NiB $474	Ex $382	Gd $286
Standard model (blued)	NiB $465	Ex $372	Gd $253
Standard model (Parkerized)	NiB $663	Ex $510	Gd $357
Standard model (stainless)	NiB $688	Ex $535	Gd $408
Trophy model (blued)	NiB $989	Ex $790	Gd $433
Trophy model (Duo-Tone)	NiB $969	Ex $801	Gd $444
Trophy model (stainless)	NiB $1031	Ex $863	Gd $506

MODEL 1911-A1 PDP SERIES
PDP Series (Personal Defense Pistol). Calibers: .38 Super, .40 S&W, .45 ACP. Seven-, 8-, 9-, 10-, 13- or 17-shot magazine, bbl. length: 4, 5, 5.5 or 5.63 inches, 9 to 11 inches overall w/compensated bbl. Weight: 34.5 oz. to 42.8 oz. Post front sight, adjustable rear w/3-dot system. Blued, Duo-Tone, Parkerized or stainless finish. Checkered composition or walnut stocks. Made 1991 to date.

Defender model (blued)	NiB $867	Ex $750	Gd $459
Defender model (Duo-Tone)	NiB $867	Ex $750	Gd $459
Defender model (Parkerized)	NiB $867	Ex $750	Gd $459
.45 ACP Champion Comp model (blued)	NiB $709	Ex $510	Gd $331
.45 ACP Compact Comp HC model (blued)	NiB $795	Ex $704	Gd $490
.38 Sup Factory Comp model (blued)	NiB $795	Ex $704	Gd $459
.45 ACP Factory Comp model (blued)	NiB $795	Ex $704	Gd $459
.38 Sup Factory Comp HC model (blued)	NiB $795	Ex $704	Gd $459
.45 ACP Factory Comp HC model (blued)	NiB $795	Ex $704	Gd $459

MODEL M1911-A1 CHAMPION
Calibers: .38 ACP, .45 ACP. Six- or 7-shot magazine, 4-inch bbl.

**Springfield Armory
M1911-A1 Ultra Compact Parkerized**

(cont'd) MODEL M1911-A1 CHAMPION
Weight: 26.5 to 33.4 oz. Low profile post front sight and drift adjustable rear w/3-dot sighting system. Commander-style hammer and slide. Checkered walnut grips. Blue, Bi-Tone, Parkerized or stainless finish. Made 1992 to date.

.380 ACP standard (disc. 1995)	NiB $382	Ex $306	Gd $204
.45 ACP Parkerized	NiB $459	Ex $357	Gd $204
.45 ACP blued	NiB $459	Ex $367	Gd $229
.45 ACP Bi-Tone (B/H Model)	NiB $709	Ex $510	Gd $301
.45 ACP stainless	NiB $714	Ex $505	Gd $403
.45 super tuned	NiB $892	Ex $561	Gd $459

MODEL M1911-A1 COMPACT
Similar to the standard M1911 w/champion length slide on a steel or alloy frame w/a shortened grip. Caliber: .45 ACP. Six- or 7-shot magazine (10+ law enforcement only), 4-inch bbl. weight: 26.5 to 32 oz. Low profile sights w/3-dot system. Checkered walnut grips. Matte blue, Duo-Tone or Parkerized finish. Made 1991-96.

Compact Parkerized	NiB $423	Ex $362	Gd $229
Compact blued	NiB $491	Ex $429	Gd $297
Compact Duo-Tone	NiB $423	Ex $362	Gd $229
Compact stainless	NiB $739	Ex $561	Gd $484
Compact comp (ported)	NiB $847	Ex $739	Gd $459
High capacity blue	NiB $551	Ex $413	Gd $337
High capacity stainless	NiB $591	Ex $514	Gd $376

MODEL M1911-A1 ULTRA COMPACT
Similar to M1911 Compact except chambered for .380 ACP or .45 ACP. 6- or 7-shot magazine, 3.5-inch bbl., weight: 22 oz. to 30 oz. Matte Blue, Bi-Tone, Parkerized (military specifiactions) or stainless finish. Made 1995 to date. See illustration next page.

.380 ACP Ultra (disc. 1996)	NiB $678	Ex $484	Gd $270
.45 ACP Ultra Parkerized	NiB $678	Ex $484	Gd $270
.45 ACP Ultra blued	NiB $678	Ex $484	Gd $270
.45 ACP Ultra Bi-Tone	NiB $790	Ex $597	Gd $382
.45 ACP Ultra stainless	NiB $760	Ex $535	Gd $433
.45 ACP ultra high capacity Parkerized	NiB $750	Ex $535	Gd $306
.45 ACP ultra high capacity blue	NiB $750	Ex $535	Gd $306
.45 ACP ultra high capacity stainless	NiB $760	Ex $535	Gd $433
.45 ACP V10 ultra comp Parkerized	NiB $704	Ex $495	Gd $280
.45 ACP V10 ultra comp blue	NiB $704	Ex $495	Gd $280
.45 ACP V10 ultra comp stainless	NiB $760	Ex $535	Gd $433
.45 ACP V10 ultra super tuned	NiB $943	Ex $790	Gd $433

**Springfield Armory
M1911-A1 Ultra Compact Bi-Tone**

**Springfield Armory
P9 Combat**

**Springfield Armory
M1911-A1 Ultra Compact Stainless**

Springfield Armory Panther

**Springfield Armory
M1911-A1 Ultra Compact Super Tuned**

FIRECAT
AUTOMATIC PISTOL
Calibers: 9mm, .40 S&W. Eight-shot magazine (9mm) or 7-shot magazine (.40 S&W), 3.5-inch bbl., 6.5 inches overall. Weight: 25.75 oz. Fixed sights w/3-dot system. Checkered walnut grip. Matte blued finish. Made 1991-93.
9mm . . . . **NiB $505 Ex $433 Gd $280**
.40 S&W . . . . **NiB $505 Ex $433 Gd $280**

PANTHER
AUTO PISTOL . . . . **NiB $546 Ex $459 Gd $280**
Calibers: 9mm, .40 S&W. 15-shot magazine (9mm) or 11-shot magazine (.40 S&W), 3.8-inch bbl., 7.5 inches overall. Weight: 28.95 oz. Blade front sight, rear adj. for windage w/3-dot system. Checkered walnut grip. Matte blued finish. Made 1991-93.

MODEL P9 DA COMBAT SERIES
Calibers: 9mm, .40 S&W, .45 ACP. Magazine capacity: 15-shot (9mm), 11-shot (.40 S&W) or 10-shot (.45 ACP), 3.66-inch bbl., (Compact and Sub-Compact), or 4.75-inch bbl., (Standard), 7.25 or 8.1 inches overall. Weight: 32 to 35 oz. Fixed sights w/3-dot system. Checkered walnut grip. Matte blued, Parkerized, stainless or Duo-Tone finish. Made 1990-94.
**Compact model (9mm,
Parkerized)** . . . . **NiB $439 Ex $382 Gd $245**
**Sub-Compact model (9mm,
Parkerized)** . . . . **NiB $479 Ex $423 Gd $286**
**Standard model (9mm,
Parkerized)** . . . . **NiB $459 Ex $382 Gd $245**
W/blued finish, add. $25
W/Duo-Tone finish, add $235
W/stainless finish, add. $20
.40 S&W, add. $35
.45 ACP add. $95

MODEL P9 COMPETITION SERIES

Same general specifications as Model P9 except in target configuration w/5-inch bbl., (LSP Ultra) or 5.25-inch bbl. Factory Comp model w/dual port compensator system, extended safety and magazine release.

Factory Comp model
(9mm Bi-Tone) . . . . NiB $606 Ex $484 Gd $329
Factory Comp model
(9mm stainless) . . . . NiB $720 Ex $576 Gd $392
LSP Ultra model
(9mm Bi-Tone) . . . . NiB $555 Ex $444 Gd $302
LSP Ultra model
(9mm stainless) . . . . NiB $593 Ex $474 Gd $322
.40 S&W, .45 ACP: add $90

STALLARD ARMS — Mansfield, Ohio
See listings under Hi-Point.

STAR PISTOLS — Eibar, Spain
Star, Bonifacio Echeverria, S.A.

MODEL 30M DA AUTO PISTOL . . . NiB $357 Ex $301 Gd $219
Caliber: 9mm Para. 15-shot magazine, 4.38-inch bbl., 8 inches overall. Weight: 40 oz. Steel frame w/combat features. Adj. sights. Checkered composition grips. Blued finish. Made 1984-91.

MODEL 30PK DA AUTO PISTOL . . . . NiB $357 Ex $301 Gd $219
Same gen. specifications as Star Model 30M except 3.8-inch bbl., weight: 30 oz. Alloy frame. Made 1984-89.

MODEL 31P DA AUTO PISTOL
Same general specifications as Model 30M except removable backstrap houses complete firing mechanism. Weight: 39.4 oz. Made 1990-94.
Blued finish . . . . NiB $357 Ex $301 Gd $214
Starvel finish . . . . NiB $388 Ex $331 Gd $245

MODEL 31 PK DA AUTO PISTOL . . . . NiB $357 Ex $301 Gd $214
Same general specifications as Model 31P except w/alloy frame. Weight: 30 oz. Made 1990-97.

MODEL A AUTOMATIC PISTOL . . . NiB $331 Ex $280 Gd $154
Modification of the Colt Government Model .45 Auto, which it closely resembles, but lacks grip safety. Caliber: .38 Super. Eight-shot magazine, 5-inch bbl., 8 inches overall. Weight: 35 oz. Fixed sights. Blued finish. Checkered grips. Made 1934-97. (No longer imported.)

MODELS AS, BS, PS. . . . . NiB $337 Ex $306 Gd $214
Same as Models A, B and P except have magazine safety. Made in 1975.

MODEL B . . . . NiB $331 Ex $255 Gd $143
Same as Model A except in 9mm Para. Made 1934-75.

MODEL BKM. . . . . NiB $316 Ex $275 Gd $173
Similar to Model BM except has aluminum frame weight: 25.6 oz. Made 1976-92.

MODEL BKS STARLIGHT
AUTOMATIC PISTOL . . . . NiB $270 Ex $133 Gd $148
Light alloy frame. Caliber: 9mm Para. Eight-shot magazine, 4.25-inch bbl., 7 inches overall. Weight: 25 oz. Fixed sights. Blued or chrome finish. Plastic grips. Made 1970-81.

Star Model 30M

Star Model 30PK

Star Model AS

Star Model BKS

MODEL BM AUTOMATIC PISTOL
Caliber: 9mm. Eight-shot magazine, 3.9-inch bbl., 6.95 inches over-all. Weight: 34.5 oz. Fixed sights. Checkered walnut grips. Blued or Starvel finish. Made 1976-92.
Blued finish . . . . **NiB $291 Ex $250 Gd $158**
Starvel finish . . . . **NiB $321 Ex $280 Gd $189**

MODEL CO POCKET
AUTOMATIC PISTOL . . . . **NiB $255 Ex $194 Gd $112**
Caliber: .25 Automatic (6.35mm), 2.75-inch bbl., 4.5 inches over-all. Weight: 13 oz. Fixed sights. Blued finish. Plastic grips. Made 1941-57.

MODEL CU STARLET
POCKET PISTOL . . . . **NiB $240 Ex $204 Gd $112**
Light alloy frame. Caliber: .25 Auto (6.35mm). Eight-shot magazine, 2.38-inch bbl., 4.75 inches overall. Weight: 10.5 oz. Fixed sights. Blued or chrome-plated slide w/frame anodized in black, blue, green, gray or gold. Plastic grips. Made 1957-97. (U.S. importation disc. 1968.)

MODEL F
AUTOMATIC PISTOL . . . . **NiB $331 Ex $229 Gd $102**
Caliber: .22 LR. 10-shot magazine, 4.5-inch bbl., 7.5 inches over-all. Weight: 25 oz. Fixed sights. Blued finish. Plastic grips. Made 1942-67.

MODEL F
OLYMPIC RAPID-FIRE . . . . **NiB $459 Ex $331 Gd $122**
Caliber: .22 Short. Nine-shot magazine, 7-inch bbl., 11.06 inches overall. Weight: 52 oz. w/weights. Adj. target sight. Adj. 3-piece bbl. weight. Aluminum alloy slide. Muzzle brake. Plastic grips. Made 1942-67.

MODEL FM
. . . . **NiB $306 Ex $229 Gd $92**
Similar to Model FR except has heavier frame w/web in front of trig-ger guard, 4.25-inch heavy bbl., Weight: 32 oz. Made 1972-91.

MODEL FR
. . . . **NiB $331 Ex $229 Gd $92**
Similar to Model F w/same general specifications but restyled, has slide stop and adj. rear sight. Made 1967-72.

MODEL FRS
. . . . **NiB $357 Ex $255 Gd $92**
Same as Model FR except has 6-inch bbl., weight: 28 oz. Also avail. in chrome finish. Made 1967-91.

MODEL FS
. . . . **NiB $331 Ex $229 Gd $92**
Same as regular Model F but w/6-inch bbl. and adj. sights. Weight: 27 oz. Made 1942-67.

MODEL H
. . . . **NiB $357 Ex $255 Gd $92**
Same as Model HN except .32 Auto (7.65mm), 7-shot magazine, weight: 20 oz. Made 1934-41.

MODEL HK LANCER
AUTOMATIC PISTOL . . . . **NiB $250 Ex $219 Gd $122**
Similar to Starfire w/same general specifications except .22 LR. Made 1955-68.

MODEL HN
AUTOMATIC PISTOL . . . . **NiB $382 Ex $270 Gd $102**
Caliber: .380 Auto (9mm Short). Six-shot magazine, 2.75-inch bbl., 5.56 inches overall. Weight: 20 oz. Fixed sights. Blued finish. Plastic grips. Made 1934-41.

Star Model F

Star Model F
Olympic Rapid-Fire

Star Model FS

MODEL I
AUTOMATIC PISTOL . . . . **NiB $357 Ex $255 Gd $97**
Caliber: .32 Auto (7.65mm). Nine-shot magazine, 4.81-inch bbl., 7.5 inches overall. Weight: 24 oz. Fixed sights. Blued finish. Plastic grips. Made 1934-36.

MODEL IN
. . . . **NiB $403 Ex $270 Gd $97**
Same as Model I except caliber .380 Auto (9mm Short), 8-shot mag-azine, weight: 24.5 oz. Made 1934-36.

MODEL M MILITARY
AUTOMATIC PISTOL . . . . **NiB $331 Ex $280 Gd $163**
Modification of the Colt Government Model .45 Auto, which it closely resembles, but without grip safety. Calibers: 9mm Bergmann (Largo), .45 ACP, 9mm Para. Eight-shot magazine except 7-shot in .45 caliber, 5-inch bbl., 8.5 inches overall. Weight: 36 oz. Fixed sights. Blued finish. Checkered grips. Made 1934-39.

MODELS M40, M43, M45 FIRESTAR AUTO PISTOLS

Calibers: 9mm, .40 S&W, .45 ACP. Seven-shot magazine (9mm) or 6-shot (other calibers). 3.4-inch bbl., 6.5 inches overall. Weight: 30.35 oz. Blade front sight, adj. rear w/3-dot system. Checkered rubber grips. Blued or Starvel finish. Made 1990-97.

M40 blued (.40 S&W)	NiB $301	Ex $255	Gd $153
M40 Starvel (.40 S&W)	NiB $321	Ex $275	Gd $173
M43 blued (9mm)	NiB $301	Ex $260	Gd $173
M43 Starvel (9mm)	NiB $321	Ex $275	Gd $173
M45 blued (.45 ACP)	NiB $331	Ex $301	Gd $173
M45 Starvel (.45 ACP)	NiB $352	Ex $321	Gd $194

MEGASTAR AUTOMATIC PISTOL

Calibers: 10mm, .45 ACP. 12-shot magazine, 4.6-inch bbl., 8.44 inches overall. Weight: 47.6 oz. Blade front sight, adj. rear. Checkered composition grip. finishes: Blued or Starvel. Made from 1992-97.

Blued finish, 10mm or .45 ACP	NiB $459	Ex $382	Gd $280
Starvel finish, 10mm or .45 ACP	NiB $489	Ex $412	Gd $310

MODEL P . . . . **NiB $357 Ex $291 Gd $163**
Same as Model A except caliber .45 Auto, has 7-shot magazine. Made 1934-75.

MODEL PD AUTOMATIC PISTOL

Caliber: .45 Auto. Six-shot magazine, 3.75-inch bbl., 7 inches overall. Weight: 25 oz. Adj. rear sight, ramp front. Blued or Starvel finish. Checkered walnut grips. Made 1975-92.

Blued finish	NiB $352	Ex $296	Gd $173
Starvel finish	NiB $372	Ex $316	Gd $194

MODEL S . . . . **NiB $239 Ex $204 Gd $102**
Same as Model SI except caliber .380 Auto (9mm), 7-shot magazine, weight: 19 oz. Made 1941-65.

MODEL SL AUTOMATIC PISTOL . . . . **NiB $280 Ex $239 Gd $153**
Reduced-size modification of the Colt Government Model .45 Auto, lacks grip safety. Caliber: .32 Auto (7.65mm). Eight-shot magazine, 4-inch bbl., 6.5 inches overall. Weight: 20 oz. Fixed sights. Blued finish. Plastic grips. Made 1941-65.

STARFIRE DK AUTOMATIC PISTOL . . . . . **NiB $469 Ex $357 Gd $184**
Light alloy frame. Caliber: .380 Automatic (9mm Short). Seven-shot magazine, 3.13-inch bbl.. 5.5 inches overall. Weight: 14.5 oz. Fixed sights. Blued or chrome-plated slide w/frame anodized in black, blue, green, gray or gold. Plastic grips. Made 1957-97. U.S. importation disc. 1968.

MODEL SUPER A AUTOMATIC PISTOL . . . **NiB $403 Ex $331 Gd $153**
Caliber: .38 Super. Improved version of Model A but has disarming bolt permitting easier takedown, cartridge indicator, magazine safety, take-down magazine, improved sights w/luminous spots for aiming in darkness. This is the standard service pistol of the Spanish Armed Forces, adopted 1946.

MODEL SUPER B AUTOMATIC PISTOL

Caliber: 9mm Para. Similar to Model B except w/improvements described under Model Super A. Made c. 1946-89/90.

Super blued finish	NiB $331	Ex $255	Gd $143
Starvel finish	NiB $362	Ex $286	Gd $173

MODELS SUPER M, SUPER P . . . . . **NiB $806 Ex $663 Gd $296**
Calibers: .45 ACP, 9mm Parabellum or 9mm Largo, (Super M) and 9mm Parabellum (Super P). Improved versions of the Models M & P w/same general specifications, but has disarming bolt permitting easier takedown, cartridge indicator, magazine safety, take-down magazine, improved sights w/luminous spots for aiming in darkness.

MODELS SUPER SL, SUPER S . . . . . **NiB $280 Ex $240 Gd $153**
Same general specifications as the regular Model SI and S except w/improvements described under Super Star. Made c. 1946-72.

Star
Model M Military

Star
Model PD

MODEL SUPER SM . . . . **NiB $280 Ex $240 Gd $178**
Similar to Model Super S except has adj. rear sight, wood grips. Made 1973-81.

SUPER TARGET MODEL . . . . **NiB $1275 Ex $969 Gd $510**
Same as Super Star model except w/adj. target rear sight. (Disc.)

ULTRASTAR DA AUTOMATIC PISTOL . . . . **NiB $301 Ex $255 Gd $168**
Calibers: 9mm Parabellum or .40 S&W. Nine-shot magazine, 3.57-inch bbl., 7 inches overall. Weight: 26 oz. Blade front, adjustable rear w/3-dot system. Polymer frame. Blue metal finish. Checkered black polymer grips. Imported 1994-97.

STENDA-WERKE PISTOL — Suhl, Germany

POCKET AUTOMATIC PISTOL . . . . **NiB $229 Ex $173 Gd $102**
Essentially the same as the Beholla (see listing of that pistol for specifications). Made c. 1920-.25. Note: This pistol may be marked "Beholla" along w/the Stenda name and address.

STERLING ARMS CORPORATION — Gasport, New York

MODEL 283 TARGET 300
AUTO PISTOL . . . . **NiB $158 Ex $102 Gd $87**
Caliber: .22 LR. 10-shot magazine, bbl. lengths: 4.5-, 6- 8-inch. 9 inches overall w/4.5-inch bbl., Weight: 36 oz. w/4.52-inch bbl. Adj. sights. Blued finish. Plastic grips. Made 1970-71.

Sterling
Model 283 Target 300

Sterling
Model 284 Target 300L

Sterling
Model 285 Husky

Sterling
Model 286 Trapper

Sterling
Model 300

Sterling
Model 400

MODEL 284 TARGET 300L . . . . NiB $178 Ex $127 Gd $92
Same as Model 283 except has 4.5- or 6-inch Luger-type bbl. Made 1970-71.

MODEL 285 HUSKY . . . . NiB $178 Ex $127 Gd $92
Same as Model 283 except has fixed sights, 4.5-inch bbl only. Made 1970-71.

MODEL 286 TRAPPER . . . . NiB $178 Ex $127 Gd $92
Same as Model 284 except w/fixed sights. Made 1970-71.

MODEL 287 PPL-.380
AUTOMATIC PISTOL . . . . NiB $127 Ex $102 Gd $69
Caliber: .380 Auto. Six-shot magazine, 1-inch bbl., 5.38 inches overall. Weight: 22.5 oz. Fixed sights. Blued finish. Plastic grips. Made 1971-72.

MODEL 300
AUTOMATIC PISTOL . . . . NiB $127 Ex $97 Gd $51
Caliber: .25 Auto. Six-shot magazine, 2.33-inch bbl., 4.5 inches overall. Weight: 13 oz. Fixed sights. Blued or nickel finish. Plastic grips. Made 1972-83.

MODEL 300S. . . . . NiB $138 Ex $102 Gd $61
Same as Model 300 except in stainless steel. Made 1976-83.

MODEL 302 . . . . NiB $127 Ex $97 Gd $51
Same as Model 300 except in .22 LR. Made 1973-83.

MODEL 302S. . . . . NiB $127 Ex $97 Gd $51
Same as Model 302 except in stainless steel. Made 1976-83.

MODEL 400 DA
AUTOMATIC PISTOL . . . . NiB $173 Ex $143 Gd $112
Caliber: .380 Auto. Seven-shot magazine, 3.5-inch bbl., 6.5 inches overall. Weight: 24 oz. Adj. rear sight. Blued or nickel finish. Checkered walnut grips. Made 1975-83.

MODEL 400S. . . . . NiB $199 Ex $153 Gd $112
Same as Model 400 except stainless steel. Made 1977-83.

MODEL 450 DA
AUTO PISTOL . . . . NiB $229 Ex $199 Gd $153
Caliber: .45 Auto. Eight-shot magazine, 4-inch bbl., 7.5 inches overall. Weight: 36 oz. Adj. rear sight. Blued finish. Smooth walnut
grips. Made 1977-83.

MODEL PPL-22
AUTOMATIC PISTOL . . . . NiB $178 Ex $127 Gd $92
Caliber: .22 LR. 10-shot magazine, 1-inch bbl., 5.5 inches overall.
Weight: About 24 oz. Fixed sights. Blued finish. Wood grips. Only
382 made 1970-71.

Stevens No. 10

Stevens No. 35

Stevens No. 38

J. STEVENS ARMS & TOOL CO. — Chicopee Falls, Mass.

This firm was established in Civil War era by Joshua Stevens, for
whom the company was named. In 1936 it became a subsidiary of
Savage Arms.

NO. 10
SINGLE-SHOT
TARGET PISTOL . . . . NiB $224 Ex $204 Gd $122
Caliber: .22 LR. 8-inch bbl., 11.5 inches overall. Weight: 37 oz.
Target sights. Blued finish. Hard rubber grips. In external appear-
ance this arm resembles an automatic pistol but it has a tip-up
action. Made 1919-39.

NO. 35
OFFHAND MODEL SINGLE-SHOT
TARGET PISTOL . . . . NiB $357 Ex $306 Gd $189
Tip-up action. Caliber: .22 LR. Bbl. lengths: 6, 8, 10, 12.25 inches.
Weight: 24 oz. w/6-inch bbl. Target sights. Blued finish. Walnut
grips. Note: This pistol is similar to the earlier "Gould" model. Made
1907-39.

OFFHAND NO. 35 SINGLE-SHOT
PISTOL/SHOTGUN. . . . . NiB $357 Ex $306 Gd $153
Same general specifications as the standard No. 35 pistol except
chambered for the .410 shotshell. Six-, 8-, 10-, or 12-inch half-
ocatagonal bbl., iron frame either blued, nickel plated, or casehardened. BATF Class 3 license required to purchase. Made
1923-42.

NO. 36
SINGLE-SHOT PISTOL . . . . NiB $734 Ex $561 Gd $357
Tip-up action. Calibers: .22 Short and LR, .22 WRF, .25 Stevens, .32
Short Colt, .38 Long Colt, .44 Russian. 10- or 12-inch half-octago-
nal bbl., iron or brass frame w/nickel plated finish. Blued bbl.
Checkered walnut grips. Made 1880-1911.

NO. 37
SINGLE-SHOT PISTOL . . . . NiB $918 Ex $739 Gd $459
Similar specifications to the No. 38 except the finger spur on the
trigger guard has been omitted. Made 1889-1903.

NO. 38
SINGLE-SHOT PISTOL . . . . NiB $433 Ex $398 Gd $280
Tip-up action. Calibers: .22 Short and LR, .22 WRF, .25 Stevens, .32
Stevens, .32 Short Colt. Iron or brass frame. Checkered grips. Made
1884-1903.

NO. 41
TIP-UP SINGLE-SHOT PISTOL . . . . NiB $280 Ex $229 Gd $148
Tip-up action. Caliber: .22 Short, 3.5-inch half-octagonal bbl. Blued
metal parts w/optional nickel frame. Made 1896-1915.

STEYR PISTOLS — Steyr, Austria

GB SEMIAUTOMATIC PISTOL
Caliber: 9mm Para. 18-round magazine, 5.4-inch bbl., 8.9 inches
overall. Weight: 2.9 lbs. Post front sight, fixed, notched rear.
Double, gas-delayed, blow-back action. Made 1981-88.
Commercial model . . . . NiB $618 Ex $541 Gd $345
Military model
(Less than 1000 imported). . . . . . . NiB $566 Ex $463 Gd $391

M12 AUTOMATIC PISTOL
Caliber: 9mm Steyr. Eight-shot fixed magazine, charger loaded; 5.1-
inch bbl., 8.5 inches overall. Weight: 35 oz. Fixed sights. Blued fin-
ish. Checkered wood grips. Made 1911-19. Adopted by the Austro-
Hungarian Army in 1912. Note: Confiscated by the Germans in
1938, an estimated 250,000 of these pistols were converted to 9mm
Para. and stamped w/an identifying "08" on the left side of the slide.
Mfd. by Osterreichische Waffenfabrik-Gesellschaft.
Commercial model (9mm Steyr) . . . NiB $463 Ex $386 Gd $304
Military model (9mm Steyr-
Austro-Hungarian Army) . . . . NiB $469 Ex $391 Gd $149
Military model (9mm Parabellum
Conversion marked "08") . . . . NiB $927 Ex $772 Gd $402

**Stoeger
American Eagle Luger P08 Stainless**

**Stoeger
American Eagle Luger Navy Model**

**Stoeger
Standard Luger**

**Targa
Model GT380XE**

STOEGER LUGERS
Formerly mfd. by Stoeger Industries, So. Hackensack, N.J.; later by Classic Arms, Union City, N.J.

AMERICAN EAGLE LUGER
Caliber: 9mm Para. Seven-shot magazine, 4- or 6-inch bbl., 8.25 inches overall (with 4-inch bbl). or 10.25 inches (with 6-inch bbl.). Weight: 30 or 32 oz. Checkered walnut grips. Stainless steel w/brushed or matte black finish. Made from 1994 to date.
**Model P-08
stainless
(4-inch bbl.)**..................NiB $653 Ex $357 Gd $286
**Navy model
(6-inch bbl.)**..................NiB $653 Ex $357 Gd $286
**W/matte black
finish, add**......................................$50

**STANDARD LUGER .22
AUTOMATIC PISTOL**............NiB $148 Ex $122 Gd $71
Caliber: .22 LR. 10-shot magazine, 4.5- or 5.5-inch bbl., 8.88 inches overall (with 4.5-inch bbl.). Weight: 29.5 oz. (with 4.5-inch bbl.). Fixed sights. Black finish. Smooth wood grips. Made 1969-86.

**STEEL FRAME LUGER
.22 AUTO PISTOL**..............NiB $153 Ex $127 Gd $87
Caliber: .22 LR. 10-shot magazine, 4.5-inch bbl., 8.88 inches overall. Blued finish. Checkered wood grips. Features one piece forged and machined steel frame. Made 1980-86.

**TARGET LUGER
.22 AUTO PISTOL**............NiB $184 Ex $178 Gd $136
Same as Standard Luger .22 except has target sights 9.38 inches overall w/4.5-inch bbl., Checkered wood grips. Made 1975-86.

TARGA PISTOLS — Italy
Manufactured by Armi Tanfoglio Guiseppe

**MODEL GT26S
AUTO PISTOL**....................NiB $96 Ex $76 Gd $52
Caliber: .25 ACP. Six-shot magazine, 2.5-inch bbl., 4.63 inches overall. Weight: 15 oz. fixed sights. Checkered composition grips. Blued or chrome finish. Disc. 1990.

**MODEL GT32
AUTO PISTOL**
Caliber: .32 ACP. Six-shot magazine, 4.88-inch bbl., 7.38 inches overall. Weight: 26 oz. fixed sights. Checkered composition or walnut grips. Blued or chrome finish.
Blued finished..................NiB $127 Ex $102 Gd $71
Chrome finish..................NiB $143 Ex $107 Gd $82

**MODEL GT380
AUTOMATIC PISTOL**
Same as the Targa GT32 except chambered for .380 ACP.
Blued finish....................NiB $147 Ex $117 Gd $80
Chrome finish..................NiB $159 Ex $127 Gd $87

**MODEL GT380XE
AUTOMATIC PISTOL**............NiB $178 Ex $138 Gd $97
Caliber: .380 ACP. 11-shot magazine, 3.75-inch bbl., 7.38 inches overall. Weight: 28 oz. Fixed sights. Blued or satin nickel finish. Smooth wooden grips. Made 1980-90.

Taurus Model .44

Taurus Model 66

FORJAS TAURUS S.A. — Porto Alegre, Brazil

MODEL 44 DA REVOLVER
Caliber: .44 Mag. Six-shot cylinder, 4-, 6.5-, or 8.38-inch bbl.
Weight: 44.75 oz., 52.5 or 57.25 oz. Brazilian hardwood grips.
Blued or stainless steel finish. Made 1994 to date.
Blued finish . . . . **NiB $408 Ex $331 Gd $163**
Stainless . . . . **NiB $464 Ex $372 Gd $301**

MODEL 65 DA REVOLVER
Caliber: .357 Magnum. 6-shot cylinder, 3- or 4-inch bbl., weight: 32
oz. Front ramp sight, square notch rear. Checkered walnut target grip.
Royal blued or satin nickel finish. Imported 1992-97 and 1999 to date.
Blue . . . . **NiB $352 Ex $265 Gd $102**
Stainless . . . . **NiB $357 Ex $270 Gd $112**

MODEL 66 DA REVOLVER
Calibers: .357 Magnum, .38 Special. Six-shot cylinder, 3-, 4- and 6-inch bbl.,
weight: 35 oz. Serrated ramp front sight, rear click adj. Checkered walnut
grips. Royal blued or nickel finish. Imported 1992-97 and 1999 to date.
Blue . . . . **NiB $311 Ex $240 Gd $143**
Stainless . . . . **NiB $372 Ex $250 Gd $199**

MODEL 73 DA REVOLVER . . . . **NiB $178 Ex $153 Gd $102**
Caliber: .32 Long. Six-shot cylinder, 3-inch heavy bbl., weight: 20
oz. Checkered grips. Blued or satin nickel finish. Disc. 1993.

Taurus
Model 74 Target Grade

MODEL 74 TARGET
GRADE DA REVOLVER . . . . **NiB $189 Ex $178 Gd $112**
Caliber: .32 S&W Long. Six-shot cylinder, 3-inch bbl., 8.25 inches
overall. Weight: 20 oz. Adj. rear sight, ramp front. Blued or nickel
finish. Checkered walnut grips. Made 1971-90.

MODEL 80 DA REVOLVER
Caliber: .38 Special. Six-shot cylinder, bbl. lengths: 3, 4 inches, 9.25
inches overall (with 4-inch bbl.). Weight: 30 oz. (with 4-inch bbl.) Fixed
sights. Blued or nickel finish. Checkered walnut grips. Made 1996-97.
Blued . . . . **NiB $194 Ex $148 Gd $87**
Stainless . . . . **NiB $250 Ex $184 Gd $133**

Taurus Model 80

MODEL 82 HEAVY BARREL
Same as Model 80 except has heavy bbl., weight: 33 oz. w/4-inch
bbl., Made 1971 to date.
Blued . . . . **NiB $199 Ex $153 Gd $92**
Stainless . . . . **NiB $204 Ex $163 Gd $102**

MODEL 83 HEAVY BARREL TARGET GRADE
Same as Model 84 except has heavy bbl., weight: 34.5 oz. Made
1977 to date. See illustration next page.
Blued . . . . **NiB $219 Ex $158 Gd $97**
Stainless . . . . **NiB $255 Ex $189 Gd $138**

Taurus Model 82

Taurus Model 83

Taurus Model 84

Taurus
Model 85 Concealed Hammer

Taurus Model 86

Taurus
Model 85 w/Spur Hammer

MODEL 84 TARGET
GRADE REVOLVER . . . . **NiB $255 Ex $199 Gd $133**
Caliber: .38 Special. Six-shot cylinder, 4-inch bbl., 9.25 inches over-all. Weight: 31 oz. Adj. rear sight, ramp front. Blued or nickel finish. Checkered walnut grips. Made 1971-89.

MODEL 85 DA REVOLVER
Caliber: .38 Special. Five-shot cylinder, 2- or 3-inch. bbl., weight: 21 oz. Fixed sights. Checkered walnut grips. Blued, satin nickel or stainless-steel finish. Currently in production. Model 85CH is the same as the standard version except for concealed hammer.
Blued or satin nickel . . . . **NiB $270 Ex $204 Gd $97**
Stainless steel . . . . **NiB $331 Ex $240 Gd $178**

MODEL 86 TARGET
MASTER DA REVOLVER . . . . **NiB $275 Ex $204 Gd $133**
Caliber: .38 Special. Six-shot cylinder, 6-inch bbl., 11.25 inches overall. Weight: 34 oz. Adj. rear sight, Partridge-type front. Blued finish. Checkered walnut grips. Made 1971-94.

MODEL 94 TARGET GRADE
Same as Model 74 except .22 LR. w/9-shot cylinder, 3- or 4-inch bbl., weight: 25 oz. Blued or stainless finish. Made 1971 to date.
Blued finish . . . . **NiB $250 Ex $184 Gd $97**
Stainless finish . . . . **NiB $296 Ex $214 Gd $153**

MODEL 96 TARGET MASTER . . . . . **NiB $280 Ex $204 Gd $133**
Same as Model 86 except in .22 LR. Made 1971 to date.

MODEL 431 DA REVOLVER
Caliber: .44 Spec. Five-shot cylinder, 3- or 4-inch solid-rib bbl. w/ejector shroud. Weight: 35 oz. w/4-inch bbl., Serrated ramp front sight, notched topstrap rear. Blued or stainless finish. Made 1992-97.
Blued finish . . . . **NiB $224 Ex $173 Gd $102**
Stainless finish . . . . **NiB $291 Ex $219 Gd $173**

MODEL 441 DA REVOLVER
Similar to the Model 431 except w/6-inch bbl. and fully adj. target sights. Weight: 40 oz. Made 1991-97.
Blued finish . . . . **NiB $245 Ex $184 Gd $102**
Stainless finish . . . . **NiB $362 Ex $255 Gd $194**

MODEL 445 DA REVOLVER
Caliber: .44 Special. Five-shot cylinder, 2-inch bbl., 6.75 inches overall. Weight: 28.25 oz. Serrated ramp front sight, notched frame rear. Standard or concealed hammer. Santoprene I grips. Blue or stainless finish. Imported 1997 to date.
Blue model . . . . **NiB $275 Ex $209 Gd $102**
Stainless model . . . . **NiB $367 Ex $229 Gd $158**

MODEL .454 DA RAGING BULL REVOLVER
Caliber: .454 Casull. Five-shot cylinder, ported 6.5- or 8.4-inch vent rib bbl., 12 inches overall (w/6.5-inch bbl.). Weight: 53 or 63 oz. Partridge front sight, micrometer adj. rear. Santoprene I or walnut grips. Blue or stainless finish. Imported 1997 to date.
Blue model . . . . NiB $811 Ex $658 Gd $484
Stainless model . . . . NiB $796 Ex $724 Gd $648

MODEL 669/669VR DA REVOLVER
Caliber: .357 Mag. Six-shot cylinder, 4- or 6-inch solid-rib bbl. w/ejector shroud Model 669VR has vent rib bbl., weight: 37 oz. w/4-inch bbl., Serrated ramp front sight, micro-adj. rear. Royal blued or stainless finish. Checkered Brazilian hardwood grips. Made 1989 to date.
Model 669 blued . . . . NiB $265 Ex $194 Gd $117
Model 669 stainless . . . . NiB $331 Ex $250 Gd $194
Model 669VR blued . . . . NiB $275 Ex $204 Gd $127
Model 669VR stainless . . . . NiB $342 Ex $260 Gd $204

**Taurus
Model 669**

MODEL 741/761 DA REVOLVER
Caliber: .32 H&R Mag. Six-shot cylinder, 3- or 4-inch solid-rib bbl. w/ejector shroud. Weight: 20 oz. w/3-inch bbl., Serrated ramp front sight, micro-adj. rear. Blued or stainless finish. Checkered Brazilian hardwood grips. Made 1991-97.
Model 741
blued. . . . . NiB $209 Ex $158 Gd $97
Model 741
stainless . . . . NiB $280 Ex $219 Gd $153
Model 761
(6-inch bbl.,
blued, 34 oz.) . . . . NiB $255 Ex $189 Gd $102

MODEL 941 TARGET REVOLVER
Caliber: .22 Magnum. Eight-shot cylinder. Solid-rib bbl. w/ejector shroud. Micro-adj. rear sight. Brazilian hardwood grips. Blued or stainless finish.
Blued finish . . . . NiB $265 Ex $194 Gd $97
Stainless finish . . . . NiB $301 Ex $235 Gd $153

**Taurus
Model PT-.22**

MODEL PT .22 DA
AUTOMATIC PISTOL . . . . NiB $178 Ex $138 Gd $71
Caliber: .22 LR. Nine-shot magazine, 2.75-inch bbl., weight: 12.3 oz. Fixed open sights. Brazilian hardwood grips. Blued finish. Made 1991 to date.

MODEL PT .25 DA
AUTOMATIC PISTOL . . . . NiB $178 Ex $138 Gd $71
Same general specifications as Model PT 22 except in .25 ACP w/eight-shot magazine, Made from 1992 to date.

**Taurus
Model PT-58**

MODEL PT-58 SEMI-
AUTOMATIC PISTOL . . . . NiB $331 Ex $280 Gd $194
Caliber: .380 ACP. Twelve-shot magazine, 4-inch bbl., 7.2 inches overall. Weight: 30 oz. Blade front sight, rear adj. for windage w/3-dot sighting system. Blued, satin nickel or stainless finish. Made 1988-96.

MODEL PT 92AF SEMIAUTOMATIC PISTOL
Double action. Caliber: 9mm Para. Fifteen-round magazine, 5-inch bbl., 8.5 inches overall. Weight: 24 oz. Blade front sight, notched bar rear. Smooth Brazilian walnut grips. Blued, satin nickel or stainless finish. Made 1991 to date.
Blued finish . . . . NiB $439 Ex $347 Gd $199
Satin nickel finish . . . . NiB $479 Ex $388 Gd $240
Stainless finish . . . . NiB $449 Ex $357 Gd $286

**Taurus
Model PT92**

**Taurus
Model PT-99AF**

**Taurus
Model PT-908**

**Texas Arms
Defender Derringer**

MODEL PT-92AFC COMPACT PISTOL
Same general specifications as Model PT-92AF except w/13-shot magazine, 4.25-inch bbl., 7.5 inches overall. Weight: 31 oz. Made 1991-96.
Blued finish . . . . NiB $342 Ex $291 Gd $194
Satin nickel finish . . . . NiB $379 Ex $329 Gd $233
Stainless finish . . . . NiB $408 Ex $316 Gd $255

MODEL PT 99AF SEMI-
AUTOMATIC PISTOL . . . . NiB $474 Ex $362 Gd $204
Same general specifications as Model PT-92AF except rear sight is adj. for elevation and windage, and finish is blued or satin nickel.

MODEL PT 100 DA AUTOMATIC PISTOL
Caliber: .40 S&W. Eleven-shot magazine, 5-inch bbl., weight: 34 oz. Fixed front sight, adj. rear w/3-dot system. Smooth hardwood grip. Blued, satin nickel or stainless finish. Made 1991-97.
Blued finish . . . . NiB $459 Ex $352 Gd $204
Satin finish . . . . NiB $449 Ex $393 Gd $245
Stainless finish . . . . NiB $413 Ex $362 Gd $229

MODEL PT 101 DA AUTOMATIC PISTOL
Same general specifications as Model 100 except w/micrometer click adj. sights. Made 1992-96.
Blued finish . . . . NiB $474 Ex $362 Gd $204
Satin nickel finish . . . . NiB $520 Ex $408 Gd $250
Stainless finish . . . . NiB $479 Ex $403 Gd $280

MODEL PT 111 MILLENNIUM DAO PISTOL
Caliber: 9mm Parabellum. 10-shot magazine, 3.12-inch bbl., 6 inches overall. Weight: 19.1 oz. Fixed low-profile sights w/3-dot system. Black polymer grip/frame. Blue or stainless slide. Imported 1998 to date.
Blue model . . . . NiB $362 Ex $194 Gd $138
Stainless model . . . . NiB $362 Ex $296 Gd $138

MODEL PT 908 SEMIAUTOMATIC PISTOL
Caliber: 9mm Para. Eight-shot magazine, 3.8-inch bbl., 7 inches overall. Weight: 30 oz. Post front sight, drift-adj. combat rear w/3-dot system. Blued, satin nickel or stainless finish. Made 1993-97.
Blued finish . . . . NiB $337 Ex $291 Gd $194
Satin nickel finish . . . . NiB $337 Ex $301 Gd $194
Stainless finish . . . . NiB $546 Ex $428 Gd $280

MODEL PT 911 COMPACT SEMIAUTOMATIC PISTOL
Caliber: 9mm Parabellum. 10-shot magazine, 3.75-inch bbl., 7.05 inches overall. Weight: 28.2 oz. Fixed low-profile sights w/3-dot system. Santoprene II grips. Blue or stainless finish. Imported 1997 to date.
Blue model . . . . NiB $423 Ex $342 Gd $189
Stainless model . . . . NiB $546 Ex $428 Gd $280

MODEL PT 938 COMPACT SEMIAUTOMATIC PISTOL
Caliber: 380 ACP. 10-shot magazine, 3.72-inch bbl., 6.75 inches overall. Weight: 27 oz. Fixed low-profile sights w/3-dot system. Santoprene II grips. Blue or stainless finish. Imported 1997 to date.
Blue model . . . . NiB $408 Ex $342 Gd $184
Stainless model . . . . NiB $363 Ex $291 Gd $198

MODEL PT 940 COMPACT SEMIAUTOMATIC PISTOL
Caliber: .40 S&W. 10-shot magazine, 3.75-inch bbl., 7.05 inches overall. Weight: 28.2 oz. Fixed low-profile sights w/3-dot system. Santoprene II grips. Blue or stainless finish. Imported 1997 to date.
Blue model . . . . NiB $433 Ex $362 Gd $194
Stainless model . . . . NiB $444 Ex $367 Gd $296

MODEL PT 945 COMPACT SEMIAUTOMATIC PISTOL
Caliber: .45 ACP. Eight-shot magazine, 4.25-inch bbl., 7.48 inches overall. Weight: 29.5 oz. Fixed low-profile sights w/3-dot system. Santoprene II grips. Blue or stainless finish. Imported 1995 to date.
Blue model . . . . NiB $459 Ex $372 Gd $214
Stainless model . . . . NiB $484 Ex $393 Gd $316

TEXAS ARMS — Waco, Texas

DEFENDER DERRINGER . . . . NiB $280 Ex $240 Gd $143
Calibers: 9mm, .357 Mag., .44 Mag., .45 ACP, .45 Colt/.410. Three-inch bbl., 5 inches overall. Weight: 21 oz. Blade front sight, fixed rear. Matte gun-metal gray finish. Smooth grips. Made 1993 to date.

TEXAS LONGHORN ARMS — Richmond, Texas

"THE JEZEBEL" PISTOL . . . . NiB $268 Ex $214 Gd $146
Top-break, single-shot. Caliber: .22 Short, Long or LR. Six-inch half-round bbl., 8 inches overall. Weight: 15 oz. Bead front sight, adj. rear. One-piece walnut grip. Stainless finish. Intro. in 1987.

SA REVOLVER CASED SET
Set contains one each of the Texas Longhorn Single Actions. Each chambered in the same caliber and w/the same serial number. Intro. in 1984.
Standard set. . . . . NiB $5610 Ex $4488 Gd $3052
Engraved set . . . . NiB $7332 Ex $5865 Gd $3988

**SOUTH TEXAS ARMY LIMITED
EDITION SA REVOLVER** . . . . NiB $1729 Ex $1275 Gd $994
Calibers: All popular centerfire pistol calibers. Six-shot cylinder, 4.75-inch bbl.,10.25 inches overall. Weight: 40 oz. Fixed sights. Color casehardened frame. One-piece deluxe walnut grips. Blued bbl., Intro. in 1984.

SESQUICENTENNIAL SA REVOLVER . . . . . NiB $2416 Ex $1933 Gd $1315
Same as South Texas Army Limited Edition except engraved and nickel-plated w/one-piece ivory grip. Intro. in 1986.

**TEXAS BORDER SPECIAL
SA REVOLVER** . . . . NiB $1524 Ex $1219 Gd $829
Same as South Texas Army Limited Edition except w/3.5-inch bbl. and bird's-head grips. Intro. in 1984.

**WEST TEXAS FLAT TOP
TARGET SA REVOLVER** . . . . NiB $1525 Ex $1275 Gd $992
Same as South Texas Army Limited Edition except w/choice of bbl. lengths from 7 .5 to 15 inches. Same special features w/flat-top style frame and adj. rear sight. Intro. in 1984.

THOMPSON PISTOL — West Hurley, New York
Mfd. by Auto-Ordnance Corporation

MODEL 27A-5 SEMIAUTOMATIC PISTOL
Similar to Thompson Model 1928A submachine gun except has no provision for automatic firing, does not have detachable buttstock. Caliber: .45 Auto, 20-shot detachable box magazine (5-, 15- and 30-shot box magazines, 39-shot drum also available), 13-inch finned bbl., overall length: 26 inches. Weight: About 6.75 lbs. Adj. rear sight, blade front. Blued finish. Walnut grips. Intro. 1977. See Auto-Ordnance in Handgun Section.

THOMPSON/CENTER ARMS — Rochester, New Hampshire

CONTENDER SINGLE-SHOT PISTOL
Break frame, underlever action. Calibers: (rimfire) .22 LR. .22 WMR, 5mm RRM; (standard centerfire), .218 Bee, .22 Hornet, .22 Rem. Jet, .221 Fireball, .222 Rem., .25-35, .256 Win. Mag., .30 M1 Carbine, .30-30, .38 Auto, .38 Special .357 Mag./Hot Shot, 9mm Para., .45 Auto, .45 Colt, .44 Magnum/Hot Shot; (wildcat centerfire) .17 Ackley Bee, .17 Bumblebee, .17 Hornet, .17 K Hornet, .17 Mach IV, .17-.222, .17-.223, .22 K Hornet, .30 Herrett, .357 Herrett, .357-4 B&D. Interchangeable bbls.: 8.75- or 10-inch standard octagon (.357 Mag., .44 Mag. and .45 Colt available w/detachable choke for use w/Hot Shot cartridges); 10-inch w/vent rib and detachable internal choke tube for Hot Shots, .357 and .44 Magnum only; 10-inch

Thompson
Contender Single-Shot Pistol

Thompson
Center Contender Bull Barrel

(cont'd) CONTENDER SINGLE-SHOT PISTOL
bull bbl., .30 or .357 Herrett only. 13.5 inches overall w/10-inch bbl., Weight: 43 oz. (w/standard 10-inch bbl.). Adj. rear sight, ramp front; vent rib model has folding rear sight, adj. front; bull bbl., available w/or w/o sights. Lobo 1.5/ scope and mount (add $40 to value). Blued finish. Receiver photoengraved. Checkered walnut thumbrest grip and forearm (pre-1972 model has different grip w/silver grip cap). Made 1967 to date, w/the following revisions and variations.
Standard model. . . . . NiB $306 Ex $255 Gd $143
Vent rib model . . . . NiB $408 Ex $306 Gd $168
Bull bbl. model, w/sights . . . . NiB $388 Ex $301 Gd $163
Bull bbl. model, without sights . . . . NiB $377 Ex $286 Gd $148
Extra standard bbl. . . . . NiB $229 Ex $178 Gd $76
Extra vent rib or bull bbl. . . . . NiB $275 Ex $189 Gd $92

CONTENDER BULL BARREL . . . . . . NiB $388 Ex $301 Gd $163
Caliber offerings of the bull bbl. version expanded in 1973 and 1978, making it the Contender model w/the widest range of caliber options: .22 LR, .22 Win. Mag., .22 Hornet, .223 Rem., 7mm T.C.U., 7x30 Waters, .30 M1 Carbine, .30-30 Win., .32 H&R Mag., .32-20 Win., .357 Rem. Max., .357 Mag., 10mm Auto, .44 Magnum, .445 Super Magnum. 10-inch heavy bbl., Partridge-style iron sights. Contoured Competitor grip. Blued finish.

CONTENDER INTERNAL CHOKE MODEL
Originally made in 1968-69 w/octagonal bbl., this Internal Choke version in .45 Colt/.410 caliber only was reintroduced in 1986 w/10-inch bull bbl. Vent rib also available. Fixed iron rear sight, bead front. Detachable choke screws into muzzle. Blued finish. Contoured American black walnut Competitor grip, also since 1986, has nonslip rubber insert permanently bonded to back of grip.
W/bull bbl. . . . . NiB $408 Ex $321 Gd $184
W/vent rib . . . . NiB $433 Ex $347 Gd $236

CONTENDER OCTAGON BARREL . . . . . . NiB $355 Ex $260 Gd $173
The original Contender design, this octagonal bbl., version began to see the discontinuance of caliber offerings in 1980. Now it is available in .22 LR only, 10-inch octagonal bbl., Partridge-style iron sights. Contoured Competitor grip. Blued finish.

**Uberti
Rolling Block Target**

**Uberti
Cattleman Sabre**

**Uberti
Cattleman Buntline Target**

CONTENDER STAINLESS
Similar to the standard Contender models except stainless steel w/blued sights. Black Rynite forearm and ambidextrous finger-groove grip. Made from 1993 to date.

Standard SS model (10-inch bbl.)	NiB $444 Ex $321 Gd $224
SS Super 14	NiB $454 Ex $331 Gd $235
SS Super 16	NiB $459 Ex $337 Gd $240

CONTENDER SUPER 14/16
Calibers: .22 LR, .222 Rem., .223 Rem., 6mm T.C.U., 6.5mm T.C.U., 7mm T.C.U., 7x30 Waters, .30 Herrett, .30-30 Win., .357 Herrett, .357 Rem. Max., .35 Rem., 10mm Auto, .44 Mag., .445 Super Mag. 14- or 16.25-inch bull bbl., 18 or 20.25 inches overall. Weight: 43-65 oz. Partridge-style ramp front sight, adj. target rear. Blued finish. Made 1978 to date.

Super 14	NiB $367 Ex $260 Gd $173
Super 16	NiB $372 Ex $265 Gd $178

CONTENDER TC ALLOY II
Calibers: .22 LR, .223 Rem., .357 Magnum, .357 Rem. Max., .44 Magnum, 7mm T.C.U., .30-30 Win., .45 Colt/.410 (w/internal choke), .35 Rem. and 7-30 Waters (14-inch bbl.). 10- or 14-inch bull bbl. or 10-inch vent rib bbl. (w/internal choke). All metal parts permanently electroplated w/T/C Alloy II, which is harder than stainless steel, ensuring smoother action, 30 percent longer bbl. life. Other design specifications the same as late model Contenders. Made 1986-89.

T/C Alloy II 10-inch bull bbl.	NiB $362 Ex $301 Gd $245
T/C Alloy II vent rib bbl. w/choke	NiB $414 Ex $331 Gd $225
T/C Alloy II Super 14	NiB $447 Ex $357 Gd $243

ENCORE SINGLE-SHOT PISTOL
Similar to the standard Contender models except w/10-, 12- or 15-inch bbl., Calibers: .22-250 Rem., .223 Rem., .243 Win., .260 Rem., .270 Win., 7mm BR Rem., 7mm-08 Rem., 7.62x39mm, .308 Win., .30-06 Spfd., .44 Rem. Mag., .444 Marlin, .45-70 Govt., .45 LC/410. Blue or stainless finish. Walnut or composition, ambidextrous finger-groove grip. Hunter Model w/2.5-7x pistol scope. Note: Encore bbls. are not interchangeable with Contenter models. Made from 1998 to date.

Encore model w/10-inch bbl. (blue, disc.)	NiB $439 Ex $372 Gd $199
Encore model w/12-inch bbl. (blue)	NiB $439 Ex $372 Gd $199
Encore model w/15-inch bbl. (blue)	NiB $447 Ex $482 Gd $207
Hunter model w/2.5-7x scope	NiB $714 Ex $612 Gd $367
Encore model (stainless), add	$55

UBERTI HANDGUNS — Mfd. by Aldo Uberti, Ponte Zanano, Italy
(Imported by Uberti USA, Inc.)

MODEL 1871 ROLLING BLOCK
TARGET PISTOL . . . . NiB $342 Ex $280 Gd $168
Single shot. Calibers: .22 LR, .22 Magnum, .22 Hornet and .357 Magnum; 9.5-inch bbl., 14 inches overall. Weight: 44 oz. Ramp front sight, fully adjustable rear. Smooth walnut grip and forearm. Color casehardened frame w/brass trigger guard. Blued half-octagon or full round barrel.

MODEL 1873 CATTLEMAN SA REVOLVER
Calibers: .357 Magnum, .38-40, .44-40, .44 Special, .45 Long Colt, .45 ACP. Six-shot cylinder, Bbl length: 3.5, 4.5, 4.75, 5.5, 7.5 or 18 inches; 10.75 inches overall (5.5-inch bbl.). Weight: 38 oz. (5.5-inch bbl.). Color casehardened steel frame w/steel or brass back strap and trigger guard. Nickel-plated or blued barrel and cylinder. Imported 1997 to date.

First issue	NiB $372 Ex $316 Gd $173
Bisley	NiB $372 Ex $316 Gd $178
Bisley (flattop)	NiB $372 Ex $316 Gd $178
Buntline (reintroduced 1992)	NiB $372 Ex $316 Gd $178
Quick Draw	NiB $372 Ex $316 Gd $178
Sabre (bird head)	NiB $372 Ex $316 Gd $178
Sheriff's model	NiB $372 Ex $316 Gd $178
Convertible cylinder, add	$51
Stainless steel, add	$125
Steel backstrap and trigger guard, add	$55
Target sights, add	$60

MODEL 1875 REMINGTON OUTLAW
Replica of Model 1875 Remington. Calibers: .357 Mag., .44-40, .45 ACP, .45 Long Colt. Six-shot cylinder, 5.5- to 7.5-inch bbl., 11.75 to 13.75 inches overall. Weight: 44 oz. (with 7.5 inch bbl). Color casehardened steel frame w/steel or brass back strap and trigger guard. Blue or nickel finish.

Blue model	NiB $403 Ex $301 Gd $153
Nickel model (disc. 1995)	NiB $510 Ex $423 Gd $265
Convertible cylinder (.45 LC/.45 ACP), add	$92

MODEL 1890 REMINGTON POLICE
Similar to Model 1875 Remington except without the web under the ejector housing.

Blue Model	NiB $403 Ex $301 Gd $153
Nickel Model (disc. 1995)	NiB $510 Ex $423 Gd $265
Convertible Cylinder (.45 LC/.45 ACP), add	$92

ULTRA LIGHT ARMS, INC — Granville, WV.

MODEL 20 SERIES PISTOLS
Calibers: .22-250 thru .308 Win. Five-shot magazine, 14-inch bbl., weight: 4 lbs. Composite Kevlar, graphite reinforced stock. Benchrest grade action available in right- or left-hand models. Timney adjustable trigger w/three function safety. Bright or matte finish. Made 1987-99.
Model 20 Hunter's Pistol (disc. 1989). . . NiB $1321 Ex $1173 Gd $663
Model 20 Reb Pistol (disc. 1999) . . . . . . NiB $1504 Ex $1224 Gd $688

UNIQUE PISTOLS — Hendaye, France
Mfd. by Manufacture d'Armes des Pyrénées
Currently imported by Nygord Precision Products(Previously by Beeman Precision Arms)

MODEL B/CF AUTOMATIC PISTOL . . . . . . NiB $211 Ex $201 Gd $133
Calibers: .32 ACP, .380 ACP. Nine-shot (.32) or 8-shot (.38) magazine, 4-inch bbl., 6.6 inches overall. Weight: 24.3 oz. Blued finish. Plain or thumbrest plastic grips. Intro. 1954. Disc.

MODEL D2 . . . . NiB $309 Ex $257 Gd $201
Same as Model D6 except has 4.5-inch bbl., 7.5 inches overall, weight: 24.5 oz. Made 1954 to date.

MODEL D6 AUTOMATIC PISTOL . . . . NiB $309 Ex $257 Gd $144
Caliber: .22 LR. 10-shot magazine, 6-inch bbl., 9.25 inches overall. Weight: About 26 oz. Adj. sights. Blued finish. Plain or thumbrest plastic grips. Intro. in 1954. Disc.

MODEL DES/32U RAPID FIRE PISTOL
Caliber: .32 S&W Long (wadcutter). Five- or 6-shot magazine, 5.9-inch bbl., weight: .40.2 oz. Blade front sight, micro-adj. rear. Trigger adj. for weight and position. Blued finish. Stippled handrest grips. Imported 1990 to date.
Right-hand model . . . . NiB $1397 Ex $1262 Gd $644
Left-hand model . . . . NiB $1454 Ex $1326 Gd $708

MODEL DES/69-U TARGET PISTOL
Caliber: .22 LR. Five-shot magazine, 5.9-inch bbl., w/250 gm counterweight. 10.6 inches overall. Trigger adjusts for position and pull. Weight: 35.3 oz. Blade front sight, micro-adj. rear. Checkered walnut thumbrest grips w/adj. handrest. Blued finish. Imported 1969 to date.
Right-hand model . . . . NiB $1185 Ex $1025 Gd $515
Left-hand model . . . . NiB $1215 Ex $1056 Gd $546

MODEL DES/VO RAPID FIRE
MATCH AUTOMATIC PISTOL . . . . NiB $1030 Ex $793 Gd $541
Caliber: .22 Short. Five-shot magazine, 5.9-inch bbl., 10.4 inches overall. Weight: 43 oz. Click adj. rear sight blade front. Checkered walnut thumbrest grips w/adj. handrest. Trigger adj. for length of pull. Made 1974 to date.

KRIEGS MODELL L AUTOMATIC PISTOL . . . . NiB $335 Ex $257 Gd $165
Caliber: .32 Auto (7.65mm). Nine-shot magazine, 3.2-inch bbl., 5.8 inches overall. Weight: 26.5 oz. Fixed sights. Blued finish. Plastic grips. Mfd. during German occupation of France 1940-45. Note: Bears the German military acceptance marks and may have grips marked "7.65m/m 9 SCHUSS."

MODEL L AUTOMATIC PISTOL . . . . NiB $257 Ex $206 Gd $103
Calibers: .22 LR, .32 Auto (7.65mm), .380 Auto (9mm Short). 10-shot magazine in .22, 7 in .32, 6 in .380; 3.3-inch bbl.; 5.8 inches overall. Weight: 16.5 oz. (.380 Auto w/light alloy frame), 23 oz. (w/steel frame). Fixed sights. Blued finish. Plastic grips. Intro. 1955. Disc.

Unique D6

Unique
DES/69 Standard Match

Unique
Model DES/VO Rapid Fire Match

MODEL MIKROS POCKET
AUTOMATIC PISTOL . . . . NiB $206 Ex $160 Gd $103
Calibers: .22 Short, .25 Auto (6.35mm). Six-shot magazine, 2.25-inch bbl., 4.44 inches overall. Weight: 9.5 oz. (light alloy frame), 12.5 oz. (steel frame.). Fixed sights. Blued finish. Plastic grips. Intro. 1957. Disc. See illustration next page.

MODEL RR
AUTOMATIC PISTOL . . . . NiB $185 Ex $175 Gd $113
Postwar commercial version of WWII Kriegsmodell w/same general specifications. Intro. 1951. Disc.

MODEL 2000-U MATCH PISTOL
Caliber: .22 Short. Designed for U.I.T. rapid fire competitution. Five-shot top-inserted magazine, 5.5-inch bbl., w/five vents for recoil reduction. 11.4 inches overall. Weight: 43.4 oz. Special light alloy frame, solid steel slide and shock absorber. Stippled French walnut w/adj. handrest. Imported 1990-96.
Right-hand model . . . . NiB $1339 Ex $1081 Gd $575
Left-hand model . . . . NiB $1370 Ex $1112 Gd $546

GRADING: **NiB** = New in Box   **Ex** = Excellent or NRA 95%   **Gd** = Good or NRA 68%

**Unique
Mikros Pocket**

U.S. Arms Abilene

Universal Enforcer (3000)

**Uzi
Semi-automatic Pistol**

UNITED STATES ARMS CORPORATION — Riverhead, New York

ABILENE SA REVOLVER
Safety Bar action. Calibers: .357 Mag., .41 Mag., .44 Mag., .45 Colt and .357/9mm convertible model w/two cylinders. Six-shot cylinder, bbl. lengths: 4.63-, 5.5-, 6.5-inch, 7.5- and 8.5-inches in .44

(cont'd) **ABILENE SA REVOLVER**
Mag. only. Weight: About 48 oz. Adj. rear sight, ramp front. Blued finish or stainless steel. Smooth walnut grips. Made 1976-83.
.44 Magnum, blued finish . . . . NiB $306 Ex $255 Gd $168
.44 Magnum, stainless steel . . . . NiB $357 Ex $296 Gd $204
Other calibers, blued finish. . . . . . . NiB $287 Ex $229 Gd $156
.357 Magnum, stainless steel. . . . . . NiB $351 Ex $280 Gd $191
Convertible, .357 Mag./9mm
Para., blued finish . . . . NiB $306 Ex $255 Gd $168

UNIVERSAL FIREARMS CORPORATION — Hialeah, Florida

This company was purchased by Iver Johnson Arms in the mid-1980s, when the Enforcer listed below was disc.. An improved version was issued under the Iver Johnson name (see separate listing).

ENFORCER (3000)
SEMIAUTOMATIC PISTOL . . . . NiB $280 Ex $229 Gd $163
M-1 Carbine-type action. Caliber: 30 Carbine. Five-, 15- or 30-shot clip magazine, 10.25-inch bbl., 17.75 inches overall. Weight: 4.5 lbs. (with 30-shot magazine). Adj. rear sight, blade front. Blued finish. Walnut stock w/pistol grip and handguard. Made 1964-83.

UZI PISTOLS — Mfd. by Israel Military Industries, Israel
(Currently imported by UZI America)

SEMIAUTOMATIC PISTOL . . . . NiB $994 Ex $867 Gd $663
Caliber: 9mm Para. 20-round magazine, 4.5-inch bbl., about 9.5 inches overall. Weight: 3.8 lbs. Front post-type sight, rear open-type, both adj. Disc. 1993.

"EAGLE" SERIES
SEMIAUTOMATIC DA PISTOL
Caliber: 9mm Parabellum, .40 S&W, .45 ACP (Short Slide). 10-shot magazine, 3.5-, 3.7- and 4.4-inch bbl., weight: 32 oz. to 35 oz. Blade front sight, drift adjustable tritium rear. Matte blue finish. Black synthetic grips. Imported 1997 to date.
Compact model
(DA or DAO) . . . . NiB $495 Ex $449 Gd $337
Polymer compact model . . . . NiB $455 Ex $449 Gd $337
Full-size model . . . . NiB $455 Ex $449 Gd $337
Short slide model. . . . . NiB $495 Ex $449 Gd $337

WALTHER PISTOLS — Manufactured by German, French and Swiss firms
The following Walther pistols were made before and during World War II by Waffenfabrik Walther, Zella-Mehlis (Thür.), Germany.

MODEL 1
AUTOMATIC PISTOL . . . . NiB $669 Ex $541 Gd $232
Caliber: .25 Auto (6.35mm). Six-shot. 2.1-inch bbl., 4.4 inches overall. Weight: 12.8 oz. Fixed sights. Blued finish. Checkered hard rubber grips. Intro. 1908.

MODEL 2
AUTOMATIC PISTOL
Caliber: .25 Auto (6.35mm). Six-shot magazine, 2.1-inch bbl., 4.2 inches overall. Weight: 9.8 oz. Fixed sights. Blued finish. Checkered hard rubber grips. Intro. 1909.
Standard model . . . . NiB $463 Ex $438 Gd $139
Pop-up sight model . . . . NiB $1437 Ex $1025 Gd $566

MODEL 3 AUTOMATIC PISTOL . . . . **NiB $1545 Ex $1287 Gd $566**
Caliber: .32 Auto (7.65mm). Six-shot magazine, 2.6-inch bbl., 5 inches overall. Weight: 16.6 oz. Fixed sights. Blued finish. Checkered hard rubber grips. Intro. 1910.

MODEL 4 AUTOMATIC PISTOL . . . . **NiB $412 Ex $335 Gd $153**
Caliber: .32 Auto (7.65mm). Eight-shot magazine, 3.5-inch bbl., 5.9 inches overall. Weight: 18.6 oz. Fixed sights. Blued finish. Checkered hard rubber grips. Made 1910-18.

MODEL 5 AUTOMATIC PISTOL . . . . **NiB $500 Ex $438 Gd $139**
Improved version of Model 2 w/same general specifications, distinguished chiefly by better workmanship and appearance. Intro. in 1913.

MODEL 6 AUTOMATIC PISTOL . . . . . . **NiB $6180 Ex $4635 Gd $1081**
Caliber: 9mm Para. Eight-shot magazine, 4.75-inch bbl., 8.25 inches overall. Weight: 34 oz. Fixed sights. Blued finish. Checkered hard rubber grips. Made 1915-17. Note: The powerful 9mm Para. cartridge is too much for the simple blow-back system of this pistol, so firing is not recommended.

MODEL 7 AUTOMATIC PISTOL . . . . **NiB $669 Ex $515 Gd $206**
Caliber: .25 Auto. (6.35mm). Eight-shot magazine, 3-inch bbl., 5.3 inches overall. Weight: 11.8 oz. Fixed sights. Blued finish. Checkered hard rubber grips. Made 1917-18.

MODEL 8 AUTOMATIC PISTOL . . . . **NiB $510 Ex $463 Gd $153**
Caliber: .25 Auto. (6.35mm). Eight-shot magazine, 2.88-inch bbl., 5.13 inches overall. Weight: 12.38 oz. Fixed sights. Blued finish. Checkered plastic grips. Made 1920-45.

**MODEL 8 LIGHTWEIGHT
AUTOMATIC PISTOL** . . . . **NiB $509 Ex $407 Gd $277**
Same as standard Model Eight except about 25 percent lighter due to use of aluminum alloys.

**MODEL 9 VEST POCKET
AUTOMATIC PISTOL** . . . . **NiB $618 Ex $541 Gd $165**
Caliber: .25 Auto (6.35mm). Six-shot magazine, 2-inch bbl., 3.94 inches overall. Weight: 9 oz. Fixed sights. Blued finish. Checkered plastic grips. Made 1921-45.

MODEL HP DOUBLE-ACTION AUTOMATIC
Prewar commercial version of the P38 marked with an "N" proof over an "Eagle" or "Crown." The "HP" is an abbreviation of "Heeres Pistole" (Army Pistol). Caliber: 9mm Para. 8-shot magazine, 5-inch bbl., 8.38 inches overall. Weight: About 34.5 oz. Fixed sights. Blued finish. Checkered wood or plastic grips. The Model HP is distinguished by its notably fine material and workmanship. Made 1937-44. (SN range 1000-25900)
**First production (Swedish Trials
model H1000-H2000)** . . . . **NiB $3026 Ex $2420 Gd $1646**
**Standard commercial production
(2000-24,000)** . . . . **NiB $1545 Ex $1339 Gd $819**
**War production - marked "P38"
(24,000-26,000)** . . . . **NiB $1236 Ex $1025 Gd $669**
W/Nazi proof "Eagle/359," add **$240**

**OLYMPIA FUNFKAMPF
MODEL AUTOMATIC** . . . . **NiB $1777 Ex $1442 Gd $566**
Caliber: .22 LR. 10-shot magazine, 9.6-inch bbl., 13 inches overall. Weight: 33 oz., less weight. Set of 4 detachable weights. Adj. target sights. Blued finish. Checkered grips. Intro. 1936.

**OLYMPIA HUNTING
MODEL AUTOMATIC** . . . . **NiB $1648 Ex $1236 Gd $453**
Same general specifications as Olympia Sport Model but w/4-inch bbl., Weight: 28.5 oz.

Walther Model 5

Walther Model 8

Walther Model 9

**OLYMPIA RAPID FIRE
MODEL AUTOMATIC** . . . . **NiB $1648 Ex $1236 Gd $556**
Caliber: .22 Short. Six-shot magazine, 7.4-inch bbl., 10.7 inches overall. Weight: (without 12.38 oz. detachable muzzle weight,) 27.5 oz. Adj. target sights. Blued finish. Checkered grips. Made about 1936-40.

**OLYMPIA SPORT
MODEL AUTOMATIC** . . . . **NiB $1004 Ex $850 Gd $433**
Caliber: .22 LR. 10-shot magazine, 7.4-inch bbl., 10.7 inches overall. Weight: 30.5 oz., less weight. Adj. target sights. Blued finish. Checkered grips. Set of four detachable weights was supplied at extra cost. Made about 1936-40.

Walther PP
(Prewar)

P38 MILITARY DA AUTOMATIC
Modification of the Model HP adopted as an official German Service arm in 1938 and produced throughout WW II by Walther (code "ac"), Mauser (code "byf") and a few other manufacturers. General specifications and appearance same as Model HP, but w/a vast difference in quality, the P38 being a mass-produced military pistol. Some of the late wartime models were very roughly finished and tolerances were quite loose.

War Production w/Walther banner (1940)
Zero Ser. 1st Iss. (SN 01-01,000) . . . . NiB $7725 Ex $5871 Gd $2060
Zero Ser. 2nd Iss. (SN 01,000-03,500) . . . . . . NiB $6180 Ex $4789 Gd $1957
Zero Ser. 3rd Iss. (SN 03,500-013,000) . . . . . . NiB $2832 Ex $2060 Gd $824

WALTHER CONTRACT PISTOLS (LATE 1940-44)
"480" code Series (SN 1-7,600) . . . . NiB $5407 Ex $3605 Gd $1236
"ac" code Ser. w/no date (SN 7,350-9,700)... NiB $5665 Ex $4326 Gd $1854
"ac" code Ser. w/.40 below
code (SN 9,700-9,900A) . . . . NiB $4120 Ex $3605 Gd $1545
"ac40" code inline Ser. (SN 1-9,900B) . . . . NiB $2060 Ex $1648 Gd $618
"ac" code Ser. w/41 below code (SN 1-4,5001) . . . . . NiB $1545 Ex $1390 Gd $721
"ac" code Ser. w/42 below code
(SN 4,500I-9,300K) . . . . NiB $1287 Ex $1133 Gd $515
"ac" code Ser. w/43 date (inline or below) . . . . . . NiB $618 Ex $463 Gd $309
"ac" code Ser. w/45 (inline or below) . . . . NiB $566 Ex $463 Gd $283

MAUSER CONTRACT PISTOLS (LATE 1942-44)
"byf" code Ser. w/42 date (19,000 prod.) . . . . . NiB $1133 Ex $1030 Gd $618
"bcf" code Ser. w/43, 44 or 45 date
(inline or below) . . . . NiB $721 Ex $618 Gd $463
"svw" code Ser. (French prod. w/Nazi proofs)... NiB $1133 Ex $953 Gd $463
"svw" code Ser. (French prod. w/star proof) . . . . . NiB $463 Ex $376 Gd $257

SPREEWERKE CONTRACT PISTOLS (LATE 1942-45)
"cyq" code 1st Ser. w/Eagle over
359 (500 prod.) . . . . NiB $1668 Ex $1334 Gd $907
"cyq" code Standard Ser. (300,000 prod.) . . . . NiB $798 Ex $412 Gd $309
"cyq" code "0" Ser. (5,000 prod.) . . . . NiB $1030 Ex $1025 Gd $438

MODEL PP DA AUTOMATIC PISTOL
Polizeipistole (Police Pistol). Calibers: .22 LR (5.6mm), .25 Auto (6.35mm), .32 Auto (7.65mm), .380 Auto (9mm). Eight-shot magazine, (7-shot in .380), 3.88-inch bbl., 6.94 inches overall. Weight: 23 oz. Fixed sights. Blued finish. Checkered plastic grips. 1929-45. Post-War production and importation 1952 to present.

NOTE: Wartime models are inferior in quality to prewar commercial pistols.

COMMERCIAL MODEL W/CROWN "N" PROOF
.22 cal. (w/comm. Crown "N" proof) . . . . NiB $1025 Ex $875 Gd $557
.25 cal. (w/comm. Crown "N" proof) . . . . NiB $3557 Ex $3193 Gd $1545
.32 cal. (w/comm. Crown "N" proof) . . . . NiB $510 Ex $438 Gd $257
.32 cal. (w/Dural (alloy) frame) . . . . NiB $586 Ex $504 Gd $296

(cont'd) **Commercial Model w/Crown "N" Proof**
.32 cal. (w/Verchromt Fin., pre-war) . . . . NiB $1030 Ex $1442 Gd $500
.32 cal. (A.F.Stoeger Contract, pre-war) . . . . . . NiB $1699 Ex $1236 Gd $438
.32 cal. (Allemagne French contract,
pre-war) . . . . NiB $1236 Ex $1030 Gd $438
.380 cal. (w/Comm. Crown "N" proof) . . . . . . NiB $1287 Ex $1025 Gd $541
.380 cal. (w/Verchromt Fin., pre-war) . . . . NiB $2472 Ex $2163 Gd $749

WARTIME MODEL WITH EAGLE "N" PROOF
.32 cal. (w/Waffenampt proofs) . . . . NiB $566 Ex $479 Gd $538
.32 cal. (w/Eagle "C" Nazi Police markings) . . . . . NiB $850 Ex $716 Gd $391
.32 cal. (w/Eagle "F" Nazi Police markings) . . . . . NiB $850 Ex $716 Gd $391
.32 cal. (w/NSKK markings) . . . . NiB $2961 Ex $2111 Gd $721
.32 cal. (w/NSDAP Gruppe markings) . . . . NiB $2343 Ex $1983 Gd $669
.380 cal. (w/Waffenampt proofs) . . . . NiB $1287 Ex $1025 Gd $665

COMMERCIAL MODEL (POST-WAR)
.22 cal. (German manufacture) . . . . NiB $953 Ex $824 Gd $412
.32 cal. (German manufacture) . . . . NiB $850 Ex $489 Gd $357
.380 cal. (German manufacture) . . . . NiB $978 Ex $824 Gd $283
.22 cal. (French manufacture) . . . . NiB $463 Ex $407 Gd $170
.32 cal. (French manufacture) . . . . NiB $463 Ex $407 Gd $170
.380 cal. (French manufacture) . . . . NiB $510 Ex $447 Gd $186
.22, .32 or .380 Cal. (other foreign manuf.) . . . . . NiB $309 Ex $242 Gd $154

MODEL PP SPORT DA AUTOMATIC PISTOL
Target version of the Model PP. Caliber: .22 LR. Eight-shot magazine, 5.75- to 7.75 inch bbl. w/adjustable sights. Blue or nickel finish. Checkered plastic grips w/thumbrest. Made 1953-70.
PP Sport (Walther manufacture) . . . . NiB $901 Ex $798 Gd $541
PP Sport (Manurhin manufacture) . . . . NiB $721 Ex $669 Gd $443
PP Sport C model (comp./single act.) . . . . NiB $922 Ex $839 Gd $541
W/nickel finish, add $170
W/matched bbl., weights, add $75

MODEL PP DELUXE ENGRAVED
These elaborately engraved models are available in blued finish, silver- or gold-plated.
Blued finish . . . . NiB $1421 Ex $1236 Gd $1030
Silver-plated . . . . NiB $1751 Ex $1329 Gd $1133
Gold-plated . . . . NiB $1957 Ex $1638 Gd $1236
W/ivory grips, add $250
W/presentation case, add $700
.22 caliber, add $50
.380 caliber, add 95%

MODEL PP LIGHTWEIGHT
Same as standard Model PP except about 25 percent lighter due to use of aluminum alloys (Dural). Values 40 percent higher. (See individual listings).

WALTHER MODEL PP
SUPER DA PISTOL . . . . NiB $837 Ex $669 Gd $455
Caliber: 9x18mm. Seven-shot magazine, 3.6-inch bbl., 6.9 inches overall. Weight: 30 oz. Fixed sights. Blued finish. Checkered plastic grips. Made 1974-81.

MODEL PP 7.65MM
PRESENTATION . . . . NiB $1867 Ex $1493 Gd $1016
Made of soft aluminum alloy in green-gold color, these pistols were not intended to be fired.

MODEL PPK DOUBLE-ACTION AUTOMATIC PISTOL
Polizeipistole Kriminal (Detective Pistol). Calibers: .22 LR (5.6mm), .25 Auto (6.35mm), .32 Auto (7.65mm), .380 Auto (9mm). Seven-shot magazine, (6-shot in .380), 3.25-inch bbl., 5.88 inches overall. Weight: 19 oz. Fixed sights. Blued finish. Checkered plastic grips. *Note: Wartime models are inferior in workmanship to prewar commercial pistols. Made 1931-45.*

NOTE: *After both World Wars, the Walther manufacturing facility was required to cease the production of "restricted" firearms as part of the armistice agreements. Following WW II, Walther moved its manufacturing facility from the original location in Zella/Mehilis, Germany to Ulm/Donau. In 1950, the firm Manufacture de Machines du Haut Rhine at Mulhouse, France was licensed by Walther and started production of PP and PPK models at the Manurhin facility in 1952. The MK II Walthers as produced at Manurhin were imported into the U.S. until 1968 when CGA importation requirements restricted the PPK firearm configuration from further importation. As a result, Walther developed the PPK/S to conform to the new regulations and licensed Interarms to produce the firearm in the U.S. from 1986-99. From 1984-86, Manurhin imported PP and PPK/S type firearms under the Manurhin logo. Additional manufacturing facilities (both licensed & unlicensed) that produced PP and PPK type firearms were established after WW II in various locations and other countries including: China, France, Hungary, Korea, Romania and Turkey. In 1996, Walther was sold to Umarex Sportwaffen GmbH and manufacturing facilities were relocated in Arnsberg, Germany. In 1999, Walther formed a partnership with Smith and Wesson and selected Walther firearms are licensed for production in the U.S.*

Walther PPK
(WW II)

Walther PPK
Silver-Plated

COMMERCIAL MODEL W/EAGLE "N" PROOF (PREWAR)
.22 cal. (w/Comm. Eagle "N" proof)...... NiB $1287 Ex $1133 Gd $484
.25 cal. (w/Comm. Eagle "N" proof)...... NiB $5150 Ex $3090 Gd $2678
.32 cal. (w/Comm. Eagle "N" proof)......... NiB $669 Ex $463 Gd $360
.380 cal. (w/Comm. Eagle "N" proof)...... NiB $2575 Ex $2060 Gd $824

WARTIME MODEL W/EAGLE "N" PROOF
.22 cal. (w/Comm. Eagle "N" proof)...... NiB $1281 Ex $1025 Gd $697
.22 cal. (w/Dural frame) .... NiB $1545 Ex $1236 Gd $1133
.32 cal. (w/Comm. Eagle "N" proof)......... NiB $566 Ex $463 Gd $257
.32 cal. (w/Dural frame) .... NiB $804 Ex $644 Gd $438
.32 cal. (w/Verchromt Fin., Pre-War) ... NiB $2163 Ex $1648 Gd $669
.380 cal. (w/Comm. Eagle "N" proof)...... NiB $2678 Ex $2060 Gd $721
.380 cal. (w/Dural frame) .... NiB $2884 Ex $2163 Gd $772
.380 cal. (w/Verchromt Fin., Pre-War) ... NiB $3244 Ex $2472 Gd $1777
.22 cal. (w/Comm. Eagle "N" proof)......... NiB $721 Ex $711 Gd $489
.32 cal. (w/Waffenampt proofs)............. NiB $953 Ex $669 Gd $309
.32 cal. (w/Eagle "C" Nazi Police markings) ... NiB $953 Ex $669 Gd $268
.32 cal. (w/Eagle "F" Nazi Police markings)...... NiB $1287 Ex $927 Gd $386
.32 cal. (w/NSKK markings)............... NiB $2054 Ex $1643 Gd $1118
.32 cal. (w/NSDAP Gruppe markings) .... NiB $1957 Ex $1442 Gd $1004
.380 cal. (w/Waffenampt proofs) .... NiB $1236 Ex $927 Gd $669

COMMERCIAL MODEL (POST-WAR)
.22 cal. (German manufacture).............. NiB $953 Ex $824 Gd $309
.32 cal. (German manufacture).............. NiB $850 Ex $489 Gd $283
.380 cal. (German manufacture)............. NiB $978 Ex $489 Gd $386
.22 cal. (French manufacture) .... NiB $2060 Ex $772 Gd $386
.32 cal. (French manufacture) .... NiB $772 Ex $566 Gd $335
.380 cal. (French manufacture) .... NiB $1081 Ex $747 Gd $360
.22, .32 or .380 cal. (other foreign manuf.) ... NiB $289 Ex $232 Gd $158

COMMERCIAL MODEL (U.S. PRODUCTION)
.380 cal. (w/blue finish).................... NiB $489 Ex $376 Gd $330
.380 cal. (w/nickel finish) .... NiB $489 Ex $376 Gd $330
.32 or .380 Cal. (stainless steel)............. NiB $489 Ex $376 Gd $330

MODEL PPK DELUXE ENGRAVED
These elaborately engraved models are available in blued finish, chrome-, silver- or gold-plated.
Blued finish .... NiB $1699 Ex $1339 Gd $1004
Chrome-plated .... NiB $2781 Ex $1390 Gd $1025
Silver-plated .... NiB $1983 Ex $1442 Gd $2378

(cont'd) MODEL PPK DELUXE ENGRAVED
Gold-plated .... NiB $2317 Ex $1725 Gd $1236
W/ivory grips, add $250
W/Presentation case, add $700
.22 cal, add $50
.25 cal, add $100
.380 cal, add $95

MODEL PPK LIGHTWEIGHT
Same as standard Model PPK except about 25 percent lighter due to aluminum alloys. Values 50 percent higher.

MODEL PPK 7.65MM
PRESENTATION.............. NiB $1622 Ex $1164 Gd $669
Made of soft aluminum alloy in green-gold color, these pistols were not intended to be fired.

MODEL PPK/S DA AUTOMATIC PISTOL
Designed to meet the requirements of the U.S. Gun Control Act of 1968, this model has the frame of the PP and the shorter slide and bbl., of the PPK. Overall length: 6.1 inches. Weight: 23 oz. Other specifications are the same as those of standard PPK except steel frame only. German, French and U.S. production 1971 to date. U.S. version made by Interarms 1978-99.
.22 cal. (German manufacture) ... NiB $1081 Ex $772 Gd $386
.32 cal. (German manufacture) .... NiB $772 Ex $566 Gd $304
.380 cal. (German manufacture) .. NiB $1081 Ex $747 Gd $309
.22 cal. (French manufacture) ..... NiB $747 Ex $515 Gd $360
.32 cal. (French manufacture) ..... NiB $752 Ex $438 Gd $298
.380 cal. (French manufacture) .... NiB $798 Ex $489 Gd $345
.22, .32 or .380 cal., blue
(U.S. manufacture) .... NiB $489 Ex $376 Gd $257
.22, .32 or .380 cal., stainless
(U.S. manuf.) .... NiB $489 Ex $376 Gd $335

NOTE: *Interarms (Interarmco) acquired a license from Walther in 1978 to manufacturer PP and PPK models at the Ranger Manufacturing Co., Inc. in Gadsden, Alabama. In 1988 the Ranger facility was licensed as EMCO and continued to produce Walther firearms for Interarms until 1996. From 1996-99, Black Creek in Gadsden, Alabama produced Walther pistols for Interarms. In 1999, Smith & Wesson acquired manufacturing rights for Walther firearms at the Black Creek facility.*

Walther Free Pistol

MODELS PPK/S DELUXE ENGRAVED

These elaborately engraved models are available in blued finish, chrome-, silver- or gold-plated.

Blued finish . . . . NiB $1442 Ex $1030 Gd $978
Chrome-plated. . . . . NiB $1329 Ex $1030 Gd $721
Silver-plated. . . . . NiB $1493 Ex $1081 Gd $989
Gold-plated . . . . NiB $1668 Ex $1334 Gd $907

NOTE: *The following Walther pistols are now manufactured by Carl Walther, Waffenfabrik, Ulm/Donau, Germany.*

Walther GSP

SELF-LOADING

SPORT PISTOL . . . . NiB $721 Ex $669 Gd $438
Caliber: .22 LR. 10-shot magazine, bbl. lengths: 6- and 9-inch, 9.88 inches overall w/6-inch bbl. Target sights. Blued finish. One-piece, wood or plastic grips, checkered. Intro. in 1932.

MODEL FREE PISTOL . . . . NiB $1802 Ex $1365 Gd $711
Single-Shot. Caliber: .22 LR. 11.7-inch heavy bbl., Weight: 48 oz. Adj. grips and target sights w/electronic trigger. Importation disc. 1991.

MODEL GSP TARGET AUTOMATIC PISTOL

Calibers: .22 LR, .32 S&W Long Wadcutter. Five-shot magazine, 4.5-inch bbl., 11.8 inches overall. Weights: 44.8 oz. (.22 cal.) or 49.4 oz. (.32 cal.). Adj. target sights. Black finish. Walnut thumbrest grips w/adj. handrest. Made 1969-94.
.22 LR . . . . NiB $1437 Ex $1236 Gd $489
.32 S&W Long
Wadcutter . . . . NiB $1643 Ex $1133 Gd $510
Conversion unit.
.22 Short
or .22 LR add. . . . . NiB $922 Ex $803 Gd $824

MODEL OSP RAPID

FIRE TARGET PISTOL. . . . . NiB $1519 Ex $1056 Gd $489
Caliber: .22 Short. Five-shot magazine, 4.5-inch bbl., 11.8 inches overall. Weight: 42.3 oz. Adj. target sights. Black finish. Walnut thumbrest grips w/adj. handrest. .22 LR conversion unit available (add $275). Made 1968-94.

MODEL P4 (P38-LV)

DA PISTOL . . . . NiB $716 Ex $613 Gd $299
Similar to P38 except has an uncocking device instead of a manual safety. Caliber: 9mm Para. 4.3-inch bbl., 7.9 inches overall. Other general specifications same as for current model P38. Made 1974-82.

MODEL P5 DA PISTOL

MODEL P5 DA PISTOL . . . . NiB $798 Ex $669 Gd $438
Alloy frame w/frame-mounted decocking levers. Caliber: 9mm Para. Eight-shot magazine, 3.5-inch bbl., 7 inches overall. Weight: 28 oz. blued finish. Checkered walnut or synthetic grips. Made 1988 to date.

MODEL P5

COMPACT PISTOL . . . . NiB $978 Ex $850 Gd $412
Similar to model P5 except w/3.1-inch bbl. and weight: 26 oz. Made 1988-96.

Walther P5

MODEL P38 (P1) DA AUTOMATIC

Postwar commercial version of the P38, has light alloy frame. Calibers: .22 LR, 7.65mm Luger, 9mm Para. Eight-shot magazine, bbl., lengths: 5.1-inch in .22 caliber, 4.9- inch in 7.65mm and 9mm, 8.5 inches overall. Weight: 28.2 oz. Fixed sights. Nonreflective black finish. Checkered plastic grips. Made 1957-89. Note: The "P1" is W. German Armed Forces official pistol.
.22 LR . . . . NiB $721 Ex $608 Gd $360
Other calibers . . . . NiB $669 Ex $566 Gd $304

MODEL P38 DELUXE ENGRAVED PISTOL

Elaborately engraved, available in blued or chrome-, silver- or gold-plated finish.
Blued finish . . . . NiB $1854 Ex $1365 Gd $772
Chrome-plated. . . . . NiB $1519 Ex $1184 Gd $747
Silver-plated. . . . . NiB $1493 Ex $1184 Gd $792
Gold-plated . . . . NiB $1854 Ex $1545 Gd $1030

MODEL P38K . . . . **NiB $716 Ex $618 Gd $283**
Short-barreled version of current P38, the "K" standing for "kurz" (meaning short). Same general specifications as standard model except 2.8-inch bbl., 6.3 inches overall, weight: 27.2 oz. Front sight is slide mounted. Caliber: 9mm Para. Made 1974-80.

MODEL P 88
DA AUTOMATIC
PISTOL . . . . **NiB $1365 Ex $1210 Gd $474**
Caliber: 9mm Para. 15-shot magazine, 4-inch bbl., 7.38 inches overall. Weight: 31.5 oz. Blade front sight, adj. rear. Checkered black synthetic grips. External hammer w/ambidextrous decocking levers. Alloy frame w/matte blued steel slide. Made 1987-93.

MODEL P 88 DA COMPACT
Similar to the standard P 88 Model except w/10- or 13-shot magazine, 3.8-inch bbl., 7.1 inches overall. Weight: 29 oz. Imported 1993 to date.
Model P88
(early importation) . . . . **NiB $875 Ex $747 Gd $489**
Model P88
(post 94 importation) . . . . **NiB $772 Ex $644 Gd $412**

MODEL P99 DA
AUTOMATIC PISTOL . . . . **NiB $566 Ex $489 Gd $335**
Calibers: 9mm Para., .40 S&W or 9x21mm. 10-shot magazine, 4-inch bbl., 7.2 inches overall. Weight: 22-25 oz. Ambidextrous magazine release, decocking lever and 3-function safety. Interchangeable front post sight, micro-adj. rear. Polymer gripframe w/blued slide. Imported 1997 to date.

MODEL TPH DA POCKET PISTOL
Light alloy frame. Calibers: .22 LR, .25 ACP (6.35mm). Six-shot magazine, 2.25-inch bbl., 5.38 inches overall. Weight: 14 oz. Fixed sights. Blued finish. Checkered plastic grips. Made 1968 to date. Note: Few Walther-made models reached the U.S. because of import restrictions. A U.S.-made version was mfd. by Interarms from 1986-99.
German model . . . . **NiB $798 Ex $644 Gd $278**
U.S. model . . . . **NiB $376 Ex $340 Gd $206**

NOTE: The Walther Olympia Model pistols were manufactured 1952-1963 by Hämmerli AG Jagd-und Sportwaffenfabrik, Lenzburg, Switzerland, and marketed as "Hämmerli-Walther." See Hämmerli listings for specific data.

OLYMPIA MODEL
200 AUTO PISTOL,
1952 TYPE . . . . **NiB $680 Ex $618 Gd $397**
Similar to 1936 Walther Olympia Funfkampf Model.

For the following Hammerli-Walther Models
(200, 201, 202, 203, 204, and 205)
See listings under Hammerli Section.

WARNER PISTOL — Norwich, Connecticut
Warner Arms Corp. (or Davis-Warner Arms Co.)

INFALLIBLE POCKET
AUTOMATIC PISTOL . . . . **NiB $463 Ex $360 Gd $103**
Caliber: .32 Auto. Seven-shot magazine, 3-inch bbl., 6.5 inches overall. Weight: About 24 oz. Fixed sights. Blued finish. Hard rubber grips. Made 1917-19.

Walther P38

Walther P38K

Walther P88

Walther TPH (Current)

**Hamerelli-Walther
Model 200, 1952 Type**

**Webley Mark III
38 Military & Police Revolver**

WEBLEY & SCOTT LTD. — London and Birmingham, England

**MODEL 9MM MILITARY
& POLICE AUTOMATIC** . . . . **NiB $978 Ex $875 Gd $489**
Caliber: 9mm Browning Long. Eight-shot magazine, 8 inches overall. Weight: 32 oz. Fixed sights. Blued finish. Checkered Vulcanite grips. Made 1909-30.

**MODEL 25
HAMMER AUTOMATIC** . . . . **NiB $335 Ex $257 Gd $129**
Caliber: .25 Automatic. Six-shot magazine, overall length: 4.75 inches. Weight: 11.75 oz. No sights. Blued finish. Checkered Vulcanite grips. Made 1906-40.

**MODEL 25 HAMMERLESS
AUTOMATIC** . . . . **NiB $386 Ex $232 Gd $129**
Caliber: .25 Automatic. Six-shot magazine, overall length: 4.25 inches, weight: 9.75 oz. Fixed sights. Blued finish. Checkered Vulcanite grips. Made 1909-.40.

**MARK I 455
AUTOMATIC PISTOL** . . . . **NiB $1802 Ex $1339 Gd $566**
Caliber: .455 Webley Auto. Seven-shot magazine, 5-inch bbl., 8.5 inches overall. Weight: About 39 oz. Fixed sights. Blued finish. Checkered Vulcanite grips. Made 1913-31. Reissued during WWII. Total production about 9,300. Note: Mark I No. 2 is same pistol w/adj. rear sight and modified manual safety.

**MARK III 38 MILITARY
& POLICE REVOLVER** . . . . **NiB $360 Ex $304 Gd $144**
Hinged frame. DA. Caliber: .38 S&W. Six-shot cylinder, bbl. lengths: 3- and 4-inches. 9.5 inches overall (with 4-inch bbl.). Weight: 21 oz. (with 4-inch bbl.). Fixed sights. Blued finish. Checkered walnut or Vulcanite grips. Made 1897-45.

**MARK IV 22 CALIBER
TARGET REVOLVER** . . . . **NiB $695 Ex $566 Gd $206**
Same frame and general appearance as Mark IV .38. Caliber: .22 LR. Six-shot cylinder, 6-inch bbl., 10.13 inches overall. Weight: 34 oz. Target sights. Blued finish. Checkered grips. Disc. 1945.

**MARK IV 38 MILITARY
& POLICE REVOLVER** . . . . **NiB $463 Ex $386 Gd $193**
Identical in appearance to the double-action Mark IV .22 w/hinged frame except chambered for .38 S&W. Six-shot cylinder, bbl. length: 3-, 4- and 5-inches; 9.13 inches overall (with 5-inch bbl.). Weight: 27 oz. (with 5-inch bbl.). Fixed sights. Blued finish. Checkered grips. Made 1929-c. 1957.

**MARK VI NO. 1 BRITISH
SERVICE REVOLVER** . . . . **NiB $309 Ex $257 Gd $165**
DA. Hinged frame. Caliber: 455 Webley. Six-shot cylinder, bbl. lengths: 4-, 6- and 7.5-inches; 11.25 inches overall (with 6-inch bbl.). Weight: 38 oz. (with 6-inch bbl.). Fixed sights. Blued finish. Checkered walnut or Vulcanite grips. Made 1915-1947.

**MARK VI 22
TARGET REVOLVER** . . . . **NiB $463 Ex $386 Gd $185**
Same frame and general appearance as the Mark VI 455. Caliber: .22 LR. Six-shot cylinder, 6-inch bbl., 11.25 inches overall. Weight: 40 oz. Target sights. Blued finish. Checkered walnut or Vulcanite grips. Disc. 1945.

**METROPOLITAN POLICE
AUTOMATIC PISTOL** . . . . **NiB $463 Ex $309 Gd $170**
Calibers: .32 Auto, .380 Auto. Eight-shot (.32) or 7-shot (.380) magazine, 3.5-inch bbl., 6.25 inches overall. weight: 20 oz. Fixed sights. Blued finish. Checkered Vulcanite grips. Made 1906-40 (.32) and 1908-20 (.380).

RIC MODEL DA REVOLVER . . . . . . **NiB $304 Ex $257 Gd $113**
Royal Irish Constabulary or Bulldog Model. Solid frame. Caliber: .455 Webley. Five-shot cylinder, 2.25-inch bbl., weight: 21 oz. Fixed sights. Blued finish. Checkered walnut or vulcanite grips. Disc.

**SEMIAUTOMATIC
SINGLE-SHOT PISTOL** . . . . **NiB $978 Ex $772 Gd $489**
Similar in appearance to the Webley Metropolitan Police Automatic, this pistol is "semiautomatic" in the sense that the fired case is extracted and ejected and the hammer cocked as in a blow-back automatic pistol; it is loaded singly and the slide manually operated in loading. Caliber: .22 Long, 4.5- or 9-inch bbl., 10.75 inches overall (with 9-inch bbl.). Weight: 24 oz. (with 9-inch bbl.). Adj. sights. Blued finish. Checkered Vulcanite grips. Made 1911-27.

SINGLE-SHOT TARGET PISTOL . . . . . . **NiB $386 Ex $257 Gd $103**
Hinge frame. Caliber: .22 LR. 10-inch bbl., 15 inches overall. Weight: 37 oz. Fixed sights on earlier models, current production has adj. rear sight. Blued finish. Checkered walnut or Vulcanite grips. Made 1909 to date.

FOSBERY AUTOMATIC REVOLVER
Hinged frame. Recoil action revolves cylinder and cocks hammer. Caliber: 455 Webley. Six-shot cylinder, 6-inch bbl., 12 inches overall. Weight: 42 oz. Fixed or adjustable sights. Blued finish. Checkered walnut grips. Made 1901-1939. Note: A few were produced in caliber .38 Colt Auto w/an 8-shot cylinder (very rare).
1901 model . . . . **NiB $6180 Ex $5665 Gd $3090**
1902 model . . . . **NiB $5665 Ex $4120 Gd $1545**
1904 model . . . . **NiB $5665 Ex $4120 Gd $1545**
.38 Colt (8-shot), add **100%**
Target model w/adjustable

WESSON FIREARMS CO., INC. — Palmer, Massachusetts
Formerly Dan Wesson Arms, Inc.

MODEL 8 SERVICE
Same general specifications as Model 14 except caliber .38 Special. Made 1971-75. Values same as for Model 14.

MODEL 8-2 SERVICE
Same general specifications as Model 14-2 except caliber .38 Special. Made 1975 to date. Values same as for Model 14-2.

MODEL 9 TARGET
Same as Model 15 except caliber .38 Special. Made 1971-75. Values same as for Model 15.

MODEL 9-2 TARGET
Same as Model 15-2 except caliber .38 Special. Made 1975 to date. Values same as for Model 15-2.

MODEL 9-2H HEAVY BARREL
Same general specifications as Model 15-2H except caliber .38 Special. Made 1975 to date. Values same as for Model 15-2H. Disc. 1983.

MODEL 9-2HV VENT RIB HEAVY BARREL
Same as Model 15-2HV except caliber .38 Special. Made 1975 to date. Values same as for Model 15-2HV.

MODEL 9-2V VENT RIB
Same as Model 15-2V except caliber .38 Special. Made 1975 to date. Values same as for Model 15-2H.

MODEL 11 SERVICE DA REVOLVER
Caliber: .357 Magnum. Six-shot cylinder. bbl. lengths: 2.5-, 4-, 6-inches interchangeable bbl. assemblies, 9 inches overall (with 4-inch bbl.). Weight: 38 oz. (with 4-inch bbl.). Fixed sights. Blued finish. Interchangeable grips. Made 1970-71. Note: The Model 11 has an external bbl., nut.

W/one bbl. assembly and grip..... NiB $206 Ex $178 Gd $133
Extra bbl. assembly, add $60
Extra grip, add....................................$45

MODEL 12 TARGET
Same general specifications as Model 11 except has adj. sights. Made 1970-71.

W/one-bbl. assembly and grip..... NiB $250 Ex $206 Gd $143
Extra bbl. assembly, add $60
Extra grip, add....................................$25

MODEL 14 SERVICE DA REVOLVER
Caliber: .357 Magnum. Six-shot cylinder, bbl. length: 2.25-, 3.75, 5.75-inches; interchangeable bbl. assemblies, 9 inches overall (with 3.75-inch bbl.). Weight: 36 oz. (with 3.75-inch bbl.). Fixed sights. Blued or nickel finish. Interchangeable grips. Made 1971-75. Note: Model 14 has recessed bbl., nut.

W/one-bbl. assembly and grip..... NiB $229 Ex $191 Gd $143
Extra bbl. assembly, add $60
Extra grip, add....................................$25

MODEL 14-2 SERVICE DA REVOLVER
Caliber: .357 Magnum. Six-shot cylinder, bbl. lengths: 2.5-, 4-, 6-, 8-inch; interchangeable bbl. assemblies, 9.25 inches overall (with 4-inch bbl.) Weight: 34 oz. (with 4-inch bbl.). Fixed sights. Blued finish. Interchangeable grips. Made 1975 to date. Note: Model 14-2 has recessed bbl. nut.

**Dan Wesson
Model 14-2 Service**

(cont'd) MODEL 14-2 SERVICE DA REVOLVER
W/one bbl. assembly
(8 inch) and grip .... NiB $219 Ex $173 Gd $122
W/one bbl. assembly
(other lengths) and grip.......... NiB $219 Ex $173 Gd $122
Extra bbl. assembly, 8 inch, add $65
Extra bbl. assembly,
other lengths, add $50
Extra grip, add..$25

MODEL 15 TARGET
Same general specifications as Model 14 except has adj. sights. Made 1971-75.

W/one bbl. assembly
and grip...................... NiB $275 Ex $224 Gd $127
Extra bbl. assembly, add $60
Extra grip, add..$25

MODEL 15-2 TARGET
Same general specifications as Model 14-2 except has adj. rear sight and interchangeable blade front; also avail. w/10-, 12- or 15-inch bbl., Made 1975 to date.

W/one bbl. assembly (8 inch) and grip. NiB $286 Ex $235 Gd $127
W/one bbl. assembly (10 inch) and grip.. NiB $286 Ex $235 Gd $127
W/one bbl. assembly
(12 inch)/grip. Disc................ NiB $286 Ex $235 Gd $127
W/one bbl. assembly
(15 inch)/grip. Disc................ NiB $286 Ex $235 Gd $127
W/one-bbl. assembly
(other lengths)/grip................ NiB $178 Ex $143 Gd $97
Extra bbl. assembly (8 inch), add $65
Extra bbl. assembly (10 inch), add $65
Extra bbl. assembly (12 inch). Disc., add $65
Extra bbl. assembly (15 inch). Disc., add $65
Extra bbl. assembly (other lengths), add $65
Extra grip, add..$25

MODEL 15-2H HEAVY BARREL
Same as Model 15-2 except has heavy bbl., assembly weight: with 4-inch bbl., 38 oz. Made 1975-83.

W/one bbl. assembly (8 inch) and grip ...... NiB $204 Ex $168 Gd $112
W/one bbl. assembly (10 inch) and grip ..... NiB $204 Ex $168 Gd $112
W/one bbl. assembly (12 inch) and grip ..... NiB $204 Ex $168 Gd $112
W/one bbl. assembly (15 inch) and grip ..... NiB $204 Ex $168 Gd $112
W/one bbl. assembly
(other lengths)/grip .... NiB $204 Ex $168 Gd $112
Extra bbl. assembly (8 inch), add...........................$65
Extra bbl. assembly (10 inch), add..........................$65
Extra bbl. assembly (12 inch), add..........................$65
Extra bbl. assembly (15 inch), add $65
Extra bbl. assembly
(other lengths), add...................................$65
Extra grip, add..$25

Dan Wesson
Model 15-2H Interchangeable Heavy

MODEL 15-2HV VENT RIB HEAVY BARREL

Same as Model 15-2 except has vent rib heavy bbl. assembly; weight: (w/4-inch bbl.) 37 oz. Made 1975 to date.

W/one bbl. assembly (8 inch) and grip	NiB $240	Ex $204	Gd $127
W/one bbl. assembly (10 inch) and grip	NiB $240	Ex $204	Gd $127
W/one bbl. assembly (12 inch) and grip	NiB $240	Ex $204	Gd $127
W/one bbl. assembly (15 inch) and grip	NiB $255	Ex $240	Gd $163
W/one bbl. assembly (other lengths) and grip	NiB $219	Ex $173	Gd $118
Extra bbl. assembly (8 inch), add			$65
Extra bbl. assembly (10 inch), add			$65
Extra bbl. assembly (12 inch), add			$65
Extra bbl. assembly (15 inch), add			$65
Extra bbl. assembly (other lengths), add			$65
Extra grip, add			$25

MODEL 15-2V VENT RIB

Same as Model 15-2 except has vent rib bbl. assembly, weight: 35 oz. (with 4-inch bbl.). Made 1975 to date. Values same as for 15-2H.

HUNTER PACS

Dan Wesson Hunter Pacs are offered in all Magnum calibers and include heavy vent rib 8-inch shrouded bbl., Burris scope mounts, bbl. changing tool in a case.

HP22M-V	NiB $765	Ex $586	Gd $367
HP22M-2	NiB $618	Ex $495	Gd $337
HP722M-V	NiB $720	Ex $576	Gd $392
HP722M-2	NiB $695	Ex $555	Gd $378
HP32-V	NiB $669	Ex $535	Gd $364
HP32-2	NiB $580	Ex $464	Gd $315
HP732-V	NiB $702	Ex $561	Gd $381
HP732-2	NiB $657	Ex $525	Gd $357
HP15-V	NiB $657	Ex $525	Gd $357
HP15-2	NiB $606	Ex $484	Gd $329
HP715-V	NiB $708	Ex $566	Gd $385
HP715-2	NiB $657	Ex $525	Gd $357
HP41-V	NiB $574	Ex $459	Gd $312
HP741-V	NiB $759	Ex $607	Gd $413
HP741-2	NiB $657	Ex $525	Gd $357
HP44-V	NiB $746	Ex $597	Gd $406
HP44-2	NiB $657	Ex $525	Gd $357
HP744-V	NiB $822	Ex $658	Gd $448
HP744-2	NiB $797	Ex $637	Gd $433
HP40-V	NiB $504	Ex $403	Gd $274
HP40-2	NiB $720	Ex $576	Gd $392
HP740-V	NiB $861	Ex $688	Gd $468
HP740-2	NiB $797	Ex $637	Gd $433
HP375-V	NiB $491	Ex $393	Gd $267
HP375-2	NiB $836	Ex $669	Gd $455
HP45-V	NiB $631	Ex $505	Gd $344

WHITNEY FIREARMS COMPANY — Hartford, Connecticut

WOLVERINE AUTOMATIC PISTOL

Dural frame/shell contains all operating components. Caliber: .22 LR. 10-shot magazine, 4.63-inch bbl., 9 inches overall. Weight: 23 oz. Partridge-type sights. Blued or nickel finish. Plastic grips. Made 1955-62.

Wolverine model, blue	NiB $438	Ex $360	Gd $206
Wolverine model, nickel	NiB $618	Ex $489	Gd $237

WICHITA ARMS — Wichita, Kansas

CLASSIC PISTOL

Caliber: Chambered to order. Bolt-action, single-shot. 11.25-inch octagonal bbl., 18 inches overall. Weight: 78 oz. Open micro sights. Custom-grade checkered walnut stock. Blued finish. Made 1980-97.

Standard	NiB $3378	Ex $2317	Gd $2060
Presentation grade (engraved)	NiB $5407	Ex $3656	Gd $2832

HUNTER PISTOL . . . . NiB $1287 Ex $901 Gd $721
Bolt-action, single-shot. Calibers: .22 LR, .22 WRF, 7mm Super Mag., 7-30 Waters, .30-30 Win., .32 H&R Mag., .357 Mag., .357 Super Mag. 10.5-inch bbl., 16.5 inches overall, weight: 60 oz. No sights (scope mount only). Stainless steel finish. Walnut stock. Made 1983-94.

INTERNATIONAL PISTOL . . . . NiB $700 Ex $479 Gd $360
Top-break, single-shot. SA. Calibers: 7-30 Waters, 7mm Super Mag., 7R (.30-30 Win. necked to 7mm), .30-30 Win. .357 Mag., .357 Super Mag., .32 H&R Mag., .22 Mag., .22 LR. 10- and 14-inch bbl. (10.5 inch for centerfire calibers). Weight: 50-71 oz. Partridge front sight, adj. rear. Walnut forend and grips.

MK-40

SILHOUETTE PISTOL . . . . NiB $1566 Ex $1081 Gd $875
Calibers: .22-250, 7mm IHMSA, .308 Win. Bolt-action, single-shot. 13-inch bbl., 19.5 inches overall. Weight: 72 oz. Wichita Multi-Range sight system. Aluminum receiver w/blued bbl., gray Fiberthane glass stock. Made 1981 to date.

SILHOUETTE

PISTOL (WSP) . . . . NiB $1931 Ex $1550 Gd $1236
Calibers: .22-250, 7mm IHMSA 308 Win. Bolt-action, single-shot. 14.94-inch bbl., 21.38 inches overall. Weight: 72 oz. Wichita Multi-Range sight system. Blued finish. Walnut or gray Fiberthane glass stock. Walnut center or rear grip. Made 1979 to date.

WILKINSON ARMS — Parma, Idaho

"LINDA" SEMI-

AUTOMATIC PISTOL . . . . NiB $695 Ex $644 Gd $360
Caliber: 9mm Para. Luger. 31-shot magazine, 8.25-inch bbl., 12.25 inches overall. Weight: 77 oz. Rear peep sight w/blade front. Blued finish. Checkered composition grips.

"SHERRY" SEMI-

AUTOMATIC PISTOL . . . . NiB $255 Ex $206 Gd $113
Caliber: .22 LR. Eight-shot magazine, 2.13-inch bbl., 4.38 inches overall. Weight: 9.25 oz. Crossbolt safety. Fixed sights. Blued or blue-gold finish. Checkered composition grips.

Twenty-Seventh Edition
GUN TRADER'S GUIDE

Rifles

Action Arms Timber Wolfe

Alpha Arms Custom

Alpha Arms Alaskan

Alpha Arms Jaguar

AA ARMS — Monroe, North Carolina

AR-9 SEMIAUTOMATIC CARBINE . . . . . . NiB $765 Ex $637 Gd $357
Semiautomatic recoil-operated rifle w/side-folding metal stock design. Fires from a closed bolt. Caliber: 9mm Parabellum. 20-shot magazine. 16.25-inch bbl., 33 inches overall. Weight: 6.5 lbs. Fixed blade, protected postfront sight adjustable for elevation, winged square notched rear. Matte phosphate/blue or nickel finish. Checkered polymer grip/frame. Made 1991-94.

ACTION ARMS — Philadelphia, Pennsylvania

MODEL B SPORTER
SEMI-AUTOMATIC CARBINE . . . . . NiB $556 Ex $484 Gd $306
Similar to Uzi Carbine (see separate listing) except w/thumbhole stock. Caliber: 9mm Parabellum, 10-shot magazine. 16-inch bbl. Weight: 8.75 lbs. Post front sight; adj. rear. Imported 1993-94.

TIMBER WOLFE REPEATING RIFLE
Calibers: .357 Mag./.38 Special and .44 Mag. slide-action. Tubular magazine holds 10 and 8 rounds, respectively. 18.5-inch bbl. 36.5 inches overall. Weight: 5.5 lbs. Fixed blade front sight; adj. rear. Receiver w/integral scope mounts. Checkered walnut stock. Imported 1989-94.

(cont'd.) TIMBER WOLFE REPEATING RIFLE
Blued model . . . . NiB $286 Ex $229 Gd $153
Chrome model, add. $50
.44 Mag., add $100

ALPHA ARMS, INC. — Dallas, Texas

CUSTOM BOLT-ACTION RIFLE . . . . NiB $1555 Ex $1224 Gd $765
Calibers: .17 Rem. thru .338 Win. Mag. Right or left-hand action in three action lengths w/three-lug locking system and 60-degree bolt rotation. 20- to 24-inch round or octagonal bbl. Weight: 6 to 7 lbs. No sights. Presentation-grade California Claro walnut stock w/hand-rubbed oil finish, custom inletted sling swivels and ebony forend tip. Made 1984-89.

ALASKAN BOLT-ACTION RIFLE . . . . . . NiB $1555 Ex $1224 Gd $765
Similar to Custom model except w/stainless-steel bbl. and receiver w/all other parts coated w/Nitex. Weight: 6.75 to 7.25 lbs. Open sights w/bbl.-band sling swivel. Classic-style Alpha wood stock w/Niedner-style steel grip cap and solid recoil pad. Made 1984-89.

GRAND SLAM
BOLT-ACTION RIFLE . . . . NiB $1224 Ex $969 Gd $663
Same as Custom model except w/Alphawood (fiberglass and wood) classic-style stock featuring Niedner-style grip cap. Weight: 6.5 lbs. Left-hand models. Made 1984-89.

JAGUAR BOLT-ACTION RIFLE
Same as Custom Rifle except designed on Mauser-style action w/claw extractor drilled and tapped for scope. Originally designated Alpha Model 1. Calibers: .243, 7mm-08, .308 original chambering (1984-85) up to .338 Win. Mag. in standard model; .338 thru .458 Win. Mag. in Big Five model (1984-85). Teflon-coated trigger guard/floorplate assembly. Made 1984-88.

Jaguar Grade I	NiB $969	Ex $765	Gd $551
Jaguar Grade II	NiB $1173	Ex $561	Gd $510
Jaguar Grade III	NiB $1224	Ex $969	Gd $663
Jaguar Grade IV	NiB $1326	Ex $969	Gd $663
Big Five model	NiB $1581	Ex $1122	Gd $867

AMERICAN ARMS — N. Kansas City, Missouri

1860 HENRY . . . . NiB $852 Ex $637 Gd $357
Replica of 1860 Henry rifle. Calibers: .44-40 or .45 LC. 24.25-inch half-octagonal bbl. 43.75 inches overall. Weight: 9.25 lbs. Brass frame and appointments. Straight-grip walnut buttstock.

1866 WINCHESTER
Replica of 1866 Winchester. Calibers: .44-40 or .45 LC. 19-inch round tapered bbl. (carbine) or 24.25-inch tapered octagonal bbl. (rifle). 38 to 43.25 inches overall. Weight: 7.75 or 8.15 lbs. Brass frame, elevator and buttplate. Walnut buttstock and forend.

Carbine	NiB $663	Ex $561	Gd $342
Rifle	NiB $663	Ex $561	Gd $342

1873 WINCHESTER
Replica of 1873 Winchester rifle. Calibers: .44-40 or .45 LC. 24.25-inch tapered octagonal bbl. w/tubular magazine. Color casehardened steel frame w/brass elevator and ejection port cover. Walnut buttstock w/steel buttplate.

Standard model	NiB $790	Ex $637	Gd $357
Deluxe model	NiB $1032	Ex $826	Gd $561

AMERICAN SPIRIT ARMS CORP.— Scottsdale, Arizona

ASA BULL BARREL FLATTOP RIFLE . . . NiB $950 Ex $625 Gd $450
Semi-automatic. Caliber: ..223 Rem. Patterned after AR-15. Forged steel lower receiver, aluminum flattop upper receiver, 24-inch stainless bull barrel, free-floating aluminum hand guard, includes Harris bipod.

ASA BULL BARREL A2 RIFLE . . . . NiB $875 Ex $650 Gd $450
Similar to Flattop Rifle except has A2 upper receiver with carrying handle and sights. Introduced 1999.

OPEN MATCH RIFLE . . . . NiB $1350 Ex $950 Gd $650
Caliber: .223 Rem. Bbl.: 16-inch fluted and ported stainless steel match with round shroud. Flattop without sights, forged upper and lower receiver, match trigger. Introduced 2001.

LIMITED MATCH RIFLE . . . . NiB $1300 Ex $825 Gd $525
Caliber: .223 Rem. Bbl.: 16-inch fluted stainless steel match with round shroud. National Match front and rear sights; match trigger.

DCM SERVICE RIFLE . . . . NiB $1300 Ex $975 Gd $525
Caliber: .223 Rem. Bbl.: 20-inch stainless steel match type with free-floating shroud. National Match front and rear sights; match trigger; pistol grip.

ASA M4 RIFLE . . . . NiB $850 Ex $595 Gd $400
Caliber: .223 Rem. Non-collapsible stock, M4 hand guard, 16-inch bbl. w/muzzle brake; aluminum flattop upper receiver.

ASA A2 RIFLE . . . . NiB $820 Ex $550 Gd $425
Caliber: .223 Rem. A2 receiver; 20-inch National Match barrel. Introduced 1999.

ASA CARBINE . . . . NiB $970 Ex $625 Gd $525
Caliber: .223 Rem. or Short. Side-charging, flattop receiver; M4 hand guard; 16-inch National Match bbl. w/slotted muzzle brake.

POST-BAN CARBINE . . . . NiB $830 Ex $580 Gd $425
Caliber: .223 Rem. Wilson 16-inch National Match bbl.; non-collapsible stock. Introduced 1999.

BULL BARREL A2 INVADER . . . . NiB $955 Ex $645 Gd $465
Caliber: .223 Rem. Similar to ASA 24-inch bull bbl. rifle except has 16-inch stainless steel bbl.. Introduced 1999.

A2 CAR CARBINE . . . . NiB $950 Ex $645 Gd $475
Caliber: 9mm Parabellum. Forged receiver, non-collapsible stock. Bbl.: 16-inch Wilson w/o muzzle brake, bird cage flash hider (pre-ban) or muzzle brake (post-ban).

FLATTOP CAR RIFLE . . . . NiB $950 Ex $725 Gd $525
Caliber: 9mm Parabellum. Similar to A2 CAR Rifle except flattop design w/o sights. Introduced 2002.

ASA TACTICAL RIFLE . . . . NiB $1675 Ex $995 Gd $675
Caliber: .308 Win. Bbl.: 16-inch stainless steel regular or match; side-charging handle; pistol grip.
Match model (w/fluted bbl. match trigger, chrome finish) . Add $525

ASA 24-INCH MATCH RIFLE . . . . NiB $1675 Ex $995 Gd $675
Caliber: .308 Win. Bbl.: 24-inch stainless steel match with or w/o fluting/porting. Side-charging handle; pistol grip. Introduced 2002.

AMT (ARCADIA MACHINE & TOOL) — Irwindale, California

BOLT-ACTION REPEATING RIFLE
Winchester-type push-feed or Mauser-type controlled-feed short-, medium- or long-action. Calibers: .223 Remington, .22-250 Remington, .243 A, .243 Winchester, 6mm PPC, .25-06 Remington, 6.5x08, .270 Winchester, 7x57 Mauser, 7mm-08 Remington, 7mm Remington Mag., 7.62x39mm, .308 Winchester, .30-06, .300 Winchester Mag., .338 Winchester Mag., .375 H&H, .416 Remington, .416 Rigby, .458 Winchester Mag. 22- to 28-inch number 3 contour bbl. Weight: 7.75 to 8.5 lbs. Sights: None furnished; drilled and tapped for scope mounts. Classic composite or Kevlar stock. Made 1996-97.

Standard model	NiB $816	Ex $637	Gd $459
Deluxe model	NiB $1020	Ex $816	Gd $510

BOLT-ACTION SINGLE-SHOT RIFLE
Winchester-type cone breech push-feed or Mauser-type controlled-feed action. Calibers: .22 Hornet, .22 PPC, .222 Remington, .223 Remington, .22-250 Remington, .243 A, .243 Winchester, 6mm PPC, 6.5x08, .270 Win., 7mm-08 Remington, .308 Winchester 22- to 28-inch #3 contour bbl. Weight: 7.75 to 8.5 lbs. Sights: None furnished; drilled and tapped for scope mounts. Classic composite or Kevlar stock. Made 1996-97.

Standard model	NiB $841	Ex $663	Gd $510
Deluxe model	NiB $1015	Ex $816	Gd $612

RIFLES

GRADING: **NiB** = New in Box   **Ex** = Excellent or NRA 95%   **Gd** = Good or NRA 68%   **195**

Anschutz Model 54.18MS-REP

CHALLENGER AUTOLOADING TARGET RIFLE SERIES I, II & III

Similar to Small Game Hunter except w/McMillan target fiberglass stock. Caliber: .22 LR. 10-shot magazine. 16.5-, 18-, 20- or 22-inch bull bbl. Drilled and tapped for scope mount; no sights. Stainless steel finish. Made 1994-98.

Challenger I Standard . . . . NiB $714 Ex $510 Gd $331
Challenger II w/muzzle brake . . . . . NiB $848 Ex $688 Gd $484
Challenger III w/bbl extension . . . . NiB $753 Ex $612 Gd $432
W/jewelled trigger, add $200

LIGHTNING 25/22
AUTOLOADING RIFLE . . . . NiB $224 Ex $178 Gd $112
Caliber: .22 LR. 25-shot magazine. 18-inch tapered or bull bbl. Weight: 6 lbs. 37 inches overall. Sights: Adj. rear; ramp front. Folding stainless-steel stock w/matte finish. Made 1984-94.

LIGHTNING SMALL GAME HUNTER SERIES
Similar to AMT 25/22 except w/conventional matte black fiberglass/nylon stock. 10-shot rotary magazine. 22-inch bbl. 40.5 inches overall. Weight: 6 lbs. Grooved for scope; no sights. Made 1987-94 (Series I), 1992-93 (Series II).

Hunter I . . . . NiB $212 Ex $173 Gd $112
Hunter II (w/22-inch
heavy target bbl.) . . . . NiB $229 Ex $184 Gd $122

MAGNUM HUNTER AUTO RIFLE . . . . NiB $376 Ex $301 Gd $205
Similar to Lightning Small Game Hunter II model except chambered in .22 WRF w/22-inch match-grade bbl. Made 1993 to date.

ANSCHUTZ RIFLES — Ulm, Germany
Mfd. by J.G. Anschutz GmbH Jagd und
Sportwaffenfabrik

Currently imported by AcuSport Corp.; Accuracy International; Champion's Choice; Champion Shooter's Supply, Go Sportsmen's Supply, Inc.; Gunsmithing Inc. (Previously by Precision Sales Int'l., Inc.)

Anschutz models 1407 ISU, 1408-ED, 1411, 1413, 1418, 1432, 1433, 1518 and 1533 were marketed in the U.S by Savage Arms. Further, Anschutz models 1403, 1416, 1422D, 1441, 1516 and 1522D were sold as Savage/Anschutz with Savage model designations (see also listings under Savage Arms

MODEL 54 18MS . . . . NiB $1236 Ex $978 Gd $669
Bolt-action, single-shot, Caliber: .22 LR. 22-inch bbl. European hardwood stock w/cheekpiece. Stipple-checkered forend and Wundhammer swell pistol-grip. Receiver grooved, drilled and tapped for scope blocks. Weight: 8.4 lbs. Imported 1982-97.

MODEL 54.18MS-REP REPEATING RIFLE
Same as model 54.18MS except w/repeating action and 5-shot magazine. 22- to 30-inch bbl. 41-49 inches overall. Avg. weight: 7 lbs., 12 oz. Hardwood or synthetic gray thumbhole stock. Imported 1989-97.

(cont'd.) **MODEL 54.18MS-REP REPEATING RIFLE**
Standard MS-REP model . . NiB $1390 Ex $1133 Gd $721
MS-REP Deluxe w/Fibergrain stock. . NiB $1262 Ex $1030 Gd $669

MODEL 64S BOLT-ACTION SINGLE-SHOT RIFLE
Bolt-action, single-shot. Caliber: .22 LR. 26-inch bbl. Checkered European hardwood stock w/Wundhammer swell pistol-grip and adj. buttplate. Single-stage trigger. Aperture sights. Weight: 8.25 lbs. Imported 1963-82.
Standard . . . . NiB $515 Ex $361 Gd $257
Left-hand model . . . . NiB $515 Ex $361 Gd $283

MODEL 64MS BOLT-ACTION SINGLE-SHOT RIFLE
Bolt-action, single-shot. Caliber: .22 LR. 21.25-inch bbl. European hardwood silhouette-style stock w/cheekpiece. Forend base and Wundhammer swell pistol-grip, stipple-checkered. Adj. two-stage trigger. Receiver grooved, drilled and tapped for scope blocks. Weight: 8 lbs. Imported 1982-96.
Standard or Featherweight
(disc. 1988) . . . . NiB $798 Ex $695 Gd $334
Left-hand model . . . . NiB $824 Ex $700 Gd $453

MODEL 64MSR BOLT-ACTION REPEATER
Similar to Anschutz Model 64MS except repeater w/5-shot magazine. Imported 1996 to date.
Standard model . . . . NiB $798 Ex $695 Gd $412
Left-hand model . . . . NiB $824 Ex $695 Gd $412

MODEL 520/61 SEMIAUTOMATIC. . . . . . NiB $406 Ex $257 Gd $103
Caliber: .22 LR. 10-shot magazine. 24-inch bbl. Sights: Folding leaf rear, hooded ramp front. Receiver grooved for scope mounting. Rotary-style safety. Monte Carlo stock and beavertail forend, checkered. Weight: 6.5 lbs. Imported 1982-83.

MODEL 525 AUTOLOADER
Caliber: .22 LR. 10-shot magazine. 20- or 24-inch bbl. 39 to 43 inches overall. Weight: 6.1 to 6.5 lbs. Adj. folding rear sight; hooded ramp front. Checkered European hardwood Monte Carlo style buttstock and beavertail forend. Sling swivel studs. Imported since 1982.
Carbine model
(disc. 1986) . . . . NiB $391 Ex $257 Gd $154
Rifle model (24-inch bbl.) . . . . NiB $483 Ex $386 Gd $263

MODEL 1403B . . . . NiB $875 Ex $669 Gd $360
A lighter-weight model designed for Biathlon competition. Caliber: .22 LR. 21.5-inch bbl. Adj. two-stage trigger. Adj. grooved wood buttplate, stipple-checkered deep thumb-rest flute and straight pistol-grip. Weight: 9 lbs. w/sights. Imported 1982-1992.

MODEL 1403D MATCH SINGLE-SHOT TARGET RIFLE
Caliber: .22 LR. 25-inch bbl. 43 inches overall. Weight: 8.6 lbs. No sights, receiver grooved for Anschutz target sights. Walnut-finished hardwood target stock w/adj. buttplate. Importation disc. 1992.
Standard model . . . . NiB $638 Ex $510 Gd $347
W/match sights . . . . NiB $895 Ex $716 Gd $487

Anschutz Model 1416D

Anschutz Model 1418

Anschutz Model 1422D

RIFLES

MODEL 1407 ISU MATCH 54 RIFLE
Bolt-action, single-shot, caliber: .22 LR. 26.88-inch bbl. Scope bases. Receiver grooved for Anschutz sights. Single-stage adj. trigger. Select walnut target stock w/deep forearm for position shooting, adj. buttplate, hand stop and swivel. Weight: 10 lbs. Imported 1970-81.
Standard model . . . . NiB $566 Ex $489 Gd $232
Left-hand model . . . . NiB $566 Ex $489 Gd $232
W/international sights, add $65

MODEL 1408-ED
SUPER RUNNING BOAR . . . . NiB $412 Ex $360 Gd $309
Bolt-action, single-shot, caliber: .22 LR. 23.5-inch bbl. w/sliding weights. No metallic sights. Receiver drilled and tapped for scope-sight bases. Single-stage adj. trigger. Oversize bolt knob. Select walnut stock w/thumbhole, adj. comb and buttplate. Weight: 9.5 lbs. Intro. 1976. Disc.

MODEL 1411 MATCH 54 RIFLE
Bolt-action, single-shot. Caliber: .22 LR. 27.5-inch extra heavy bbl. w/mounted scope bases. Receiver grooved for Anschutz sights. Single-stage adj. trigger. Select walnut target stock w/cheekpiece (adj. in 1973 and later production), full pistol-grip, beavertail forearm, adj. buttplate, hand stop and swivel. Model 1411-L has left-hand stock. Weight: 11 lbs. Disc.
W/Non-adj. cheekpiece . . . . NiB $412 Ex $360 Gd $206
W/adj. cheekpiece . . . . NiB $580 Ex $463 Gd $315
with Anschutz
International Sight set . . . . NiB $315 Ex $129 Gd $88

MODEL 1413 SUPER MATCH 54 RIFLE
Freestyle international target rifle w/specifications similar to those of Model 1411, except w/special stock w/thumbhole, adj. pistol grip, adj. cheekpiece in 1973 and later production, adj. hook buttplate, adj. palmrest. Model 1413-L has left-hand stock. Weight: 15.5 lbs. Disc.
W/Non-adj. cheekpiece . . . . NiB $747 Ex $669 Gd $340
W/Adj. cheekpiece . . . . NiB $624 Ex $500 Gd $309
With Anschutz
International Sight set $275

MODEL 1416D . . . . NiB $534 Ex $515 Gd $309
Bolt-action sporter. Caliber: .22 LR. 22.5-inch bbl. Sights: Folding leaf rear; hooded ramp front. Receiver grooved for scope mounting. Select European stock w/cheekpiece, skip-checkered pistol grip and forearm. Weight: 6 lbs. Imported 1982 to date.

MODEL 1416D CLASSIC/CUSTOM SPORTERS
Same as Model 1416D except w/American classic-style stock (Classic) or modified European-style stock w/Monte Carlo roll-over cheekpiece and Schnabel forend (Custom). Weight: 5.5 lbs. (Classic); 6 lbs. (Custom). Imported 1986 to date.
Model 1416D Classic . . . . NiB $592 Ex $474 Gd $322
Model 1416D Classic,
"True" left-hand . . . . NiB $638 Ex $510 Gd $347
Model 1416D Custom . . . . NiB $573 Ex $458 Gd $303
Model 1416D fiberglass (1991-92) . . . . NiB $701 Ex $561 Gd $382

MODEL 1418 BOLT-ACTION
SPORTER . . . . NiB $360 Ex $283 Gd $154
Caliber: .22 LR. 5- or 10-shot magazine. 19.75-inch bbl. Sights: Folding leaf rear; hooded ramp front. Receiver grooved for scope mounting. Select walnut stock, Mannlicher type w/cheekpiece, pistol-grip and forearm skip checkered. Weight: 5.5 lbs. Intro. 1976. Disc.

MODEL 1418D BOLT-ACTION
SPORTER . . . . NiB $922 Ex $809 Gd $463
Caliber: .22 LR. 5- or 10-shot magazine. 19.75-inch bbl. European walnut Monte Carlo stock, Mannlicher type w/cheekpiece, pistol-grip and forend skip-line checkered, buffalo horn Schnabel tip. Weight: 5.5 lbs. Imported from 1982-95 and 1998 to date.

MODEL 1422D CLASSIC/CUSTOM RIFLE
Bolt-action sporter. Caliber: .22 LR. 5-shot removable straight-feed clip magazine. 24-inch bbl. Sights: Folding leaf rear; hooded ramp front. Select European walnut stock, classic type (Classic); Monte Carlo w/hand-carved rollover cheekpiece (Custom). Weight: 7.25 lbs. (Classic) 6.5 lbs. (Custom). Imported 1982-89.
Model 1422D Classic . . . . NiB $747 Ex $592 Gd $360
Model 1422D Custom . . . . NiB $824 Ex $747 Gd $412

Anschutz Model 1427B

Anschutz Model 1432

Anschutz Model 1432D

MODEL 1427B BIATHLON RIFLE
Bolt-action clip repeater. Caliber: .22 LR. 21.5-inch bbl. Two-stage trigger w/wing-type safety. Hardwood stock w/deep fluting, pistol grip and deep forestock with adj. hand stop rail. Target sights w/adjustable weights. Advertised in 1981 but imported from 1982 to date as Model 1827B. (See that model designation for current values)

MODEL 1430D MATCH . . . . NiB $695 Ex $566 Gd $340
Improved version of Model 64S. Bolt-action, single-shot. Caliber: .22 LR. 26-inch medium-heavy bbl. Walnut Monte Carlo stock w/cheekpiece, adj. buttplate, deep midstock tapered to forend. Pistol-grip and contoured thumb groove w/stipple checkering. Single-stage adj. trigger. Target sights. Weight: 8.38 lbs. Imported 1982-83.

MODEL 1432 BOLT-ACTION SPORTER
Caliber: .22 Hornet. 5-shot box magazine. 24-inch bbl. Sights: Folding leaf rear, hooded ramp front. Receiver grooved for scope mounting. Select walnut stock w/Monte Carlo comb and cheekpiece, pistol-grip and forearm skip-checkered. Weight: 6.75 lbs. Imported 1974-87. (Reintroduced as 1700/1730 series)
Early model
(1974-85). . . . . NiB $1226 Ex $875 Gd $618
Late model
(1985-87). . . . . NiB $1056 Ex $824 Gd $541

MODEL 1432D CLASSIC/CUSTOM RIFLE
Bolt-action sporter similar to Model 1422D except chambered for Caliber: .22 Hornet. 4-shot magazine. 23.5-inch bbl. Weight: 7.75 lbs. (Classic); 6.5 lbs. (Custom). Classic stock on Classic model; fancy-grade Monte Carlo w/hand-carved rollover cheekpiece (Custom). Imported 1982-87. (Reintroduced as 1700/1730 series)
Model 1432D Classic . . . . NiB $1226 Ex $875 Gd $618
Model 1432D Custom . . . . NiB $1055 Ex $824 Gd $541

MODEL 1433 BOLT-ACTION SPORTER . . . . . NiB $1035 Ex $824 Gd $566
Caliber: .22 Hornet. 5-shot box magazine. 19.75-inch bbl. Sights: Folding leaf rear, hooded ramp front. Receiver grooved for scope mounting. Single-stage or double-set trigger. Select walnut Mannlicher stock; cheekpiece, pistol-grip and forearm skip-checkered. Weight: 6.5 lbs. Imported 1976-86.

MODEL 1448D CLAY BIRD. . . . . . . NiB $304 Ex $273 Gd $185
Similar to Model 1449 except chambered for Caliber: .22 LR. w/22.5-inch smooth bore bbl. and no sights. Walnut-finished hardwood stock. Imported 1999 to date.

MODEL 1449 YOUTH SPORTER . . . . NiB $237 Ex $191 Gd $129
Bolt-action sporter version of Model 2000. Caliber: .22 LR. 5-shot box magazine. 16.25-inch bbl. Weight: 3.5 lbs. Hooded ramp front sight, addition. Walnut-finished hardwood stock. Imported 1989-92.

MODEL 1450B TARGET RIFLE . . . . NiB $644 Ex $463 Gd $309
Biathlon rifle developed on 2000 Series action. 19.5-inch bbl. Weight: 5.5 lbs. Adj. buttplate. Target sights. Imported 1993-94.

MODEL 1451 E/R SPORTER/TARGET
Bolt-action, single-shot (1451E) or repeater (1451R). Caliber: .22 LR. 22- or 22.75-inch bbl. w/o sights. Select hardwood stock w/stippled pistolgrip and vented forearm. beavertail forend, adj. cheekpiece, and deep thumb flute. Weight: 6.5 lbs. Imported 1996 to date.
Model 1451E (disc. 1997) . . . . NiB $412 Ex $309 Gd $206
Model 1451R . . . . NiB $448 Ex $395 Gd $2407
MODEL 1451D CLASSIC/CUSTOM RIFLE
Same as Model 1451R except w/walnut-finished hardwood stock (Classic) or modified European-style walnut stock w/Monte Carlo rollover cheekpiece and Schnabel forend (Custom). Weight: 5 lbs. Imported 1996 to date.
Model 1451D Classic (Super) . . . . . NiB $309 Ex $232 Gd $154
Model 1451D Custom . . . . NiB $448 Ex $407 Gd $268

Anschutz Model 1700

Anschutz Model 1803D

Anschutz Model 1907

MODEL 1451 ST- R RIFLE . . . . NiB $435 Ex $395 Gd $280
Same as Model 1451R except w/two-stage trigger and walnut-finished hardwood uncheckered stock. Imported 1999 to date.

MODEL 1516D CLASSIC/CUSTOM RIFLE
Same as Model 1416D except chambered for Caliber: .22 Magnum RF, with American classic-style stock (Classic) or modified European-style stock w/Monte Carlo rollover cheekpiece and Schnabel forend (Custom). Weight: 5.5 lbs. (Classic), 6 lbs. (Custom). Imported 1986 to date.
Model 1516D Classic . . . . NiB $650 Ex $500 Gd $325
Model 1516D Custom . . . . NiB $675 Ex $550 Gd $350

MODELS 1516D/1518D LUXUS RIFLES
The alpha designation for these models was changed from Custom to Luxus in 1996-98. (See current Custom listings for Luxus values.)

MODELS 1518/1518D SPORTING RIFLES
Same as Model 1418 except chambered for .22 Magnum RF, 4-shot box magazine. Model 1518 intro. 1976. Disc. Model 1518D has full Mannlicher-type stock. Imported 1982 to date.
Model 1518. . . . . NiB $700 Ex $580 Gd $350
Model 1518D . . . . NiB $895 Ex $700 Gd $475
W/set trigger, add $125

MODEL 1522D CLASSIC/CUSTOM RIFLE
Same as Model 1422D except chambered for .22 Magnum RF, 4-shot magazine. Weight: 6.5 lbs. (Custom). Fancy-grade Classic or Monte Carlo stock w/hand-carved rollover cheekpiece. Imported 1982-89. (Reintroduced as 1700D/1730D series)
Model 1522D Classic . . . . NiB $1000 Ex $800 Gd $550
Model 1522D Custom . . . . NiB $1000 Ex $800 Gd $550

MODEL 1532D CLASSIC/CUSTOM RIFLE
Same as Model 1432D except chambered for .222 Rem. Three-shot mag. Weight: 6.5 lbs. (Custom). Classic stock on Classic Model; fancy-grade Monte Carlo stock w/handcarved rollover cheekpiece (Custom). Imported 1982-89. (Reintroduced as 1700D/174 D0 series)
Model 1532D Classic . . . . NiB $895 Ex $700 Gd $350
Model 1532D Custom . . . . NiB $1190 Ex $900 Gd $600

MODEL 1533 . . . . NiB $1000 Ex $750 Gd $500
Same as Model 1433 except chambered for .222 Rem. Three-shot box magazine. Imported 1976-94.

MODEL 1700 SERIES BOLT-ACTION REPEATER
Match 54 Sporter. Calibers: .22 LR., .22 Magnum, .22 Hornet, .222 Rem. Five-shot removable magazine 24-inch bbl. 43 inches overall. Weight: 7.5 lbs. Folding leaf rear sight, hooded ramp front. Select European walnut stock w/cheekpiece and Schnabel forend tip. Imported 1989 to date.
Standard Model 1700
Bavarian — rimfire cal. NiB $915 Ex $835 Gd $475
Standard Model 1700
Bavarian — centerfire cal. . . . . NiB $1225 Ex $950 Gd $600
Model 1700 Classic (Classic
stock, 6.75 lbs.) rimfire cal. . . . . NiB $1075 Ex $895 Gd $600
Model 1700D Classic — centerfire cal. . . . . NiB $1188 Ex $950 Gd $646
Model 1700D Custom — rimfire cal. . . . . NiB $994 Ex $795 Gd $541
Model 1700D Custom — centerfire cal. . . . . . NiB $1219 Ex $975 Gd $663
Model 1700D Graphite Cust. (McMillian graphite
reinforced stock, 22 inch bbl., intro. 1991) . . NiB $1050 Ex $875 Gd $550
Select walnut and gold trigger . . . . .add $181
Model 1700 FWT Feather-
weight (6.5 lbs.) rimfire calibers . . . . NiB $1031 Ex $825 Gd $561
Model 1700 FWT — centerfire cal. . . . . NiB $1200 Ex $1050 Gd $650

Anschutz Model 2013

MODEL 1733D MANNLICHER....... NiB $1293 Ex $1081 Gd $772
Same as Model 1700D except w/19-inch bbl. and Mannlicher-style stock. 39 inches overall. Weight: 6.25 lbs. Imported 1993-96 (Reintroduced in 1998).

MODEL 1740 MONTE CARLO SPORTER
Caliber: .22 Hornet or .222 Rem. Three and 5-shot magazines respectively. 24-inch bbl. 43.25 inches overall. Weight: 6.5 lbs. Hooded ramp front, folding leaf rear. Drilled and tapped for scope mounts. Select European walnut stock w/roll-over cheekpiece, checkered grip and forend. Imported 1997 to date.
Model 1740 Custom .... NiB $1244 Ex $978 Gd $618
Model 1740 Classic
(Meistergrade).............. NiB $1410 Ex $1128 Gd $767

MODEL 1743 MONTE CARLO
SPORTER................... NiB $1262 Ex $1030 Gd $669
Similar to Model 1740 except w/Mannlicher full stock. Imported 1997 to date.

MODEL 1803D MATCH SINGLE-SHOT TARGET RIFLE
Caliber: .22 LR. 25.5-inch bbl. 43.75 inches overall. Weight: 8.5 lbs. No sights; receiver grooved, drilled and tapped for scope mounts. Blonde or walnut-finished hardwood stock w/adj. cheekpiece, stippled grip and forend. Left-hand version. Imported 1987-92.
Right-hand model
(Reintroduced as 1903D) .... NiB $927 Ex $772 Gd $463
Left-hand model .... NiB $998 Ex $798 Gd $543

MODEL 1807 ISU
STANDARD MATCH .... NiB $1262 Ex $978 Gd $618
Bolt-action single-shot. Caliber: 22 LR. 26-inch bbl. Improved Super Match 54 action. Two-stage match trigger. Removable cheekpiece, adj. buttplate, thumbpiece and forestock w/stipple-checkered. Weight: 10 lbs. Imported 1982-88. (Reintroduced as 1907 ISU)

MODEL 1808ED SUPER RUNNING TARGET
Bolt-action single-shot. Caliber: .22 LR. 23.5-inch bbl. w/sliding weights. Improved Super Match 54 action. Heavy beavertail forend w/adj.cheekpiece and buttplate. Adj. single-stage trigger. Weight: 9.5 lbs. Imported from 1982-96.
Right-hand model .... NiB $1535 Ex $1236 Gd $772
Left-hand model .... NiB $1577 Ex $1262 Gd $858

MODEL 1808MS-R
METALLIC SILHOUETTE .... NiB $1905 Ex $1442 Gd $824
Bolt-action repeater. Caliber: .22 LR. 19.2-inch bbl. w/o sights. Thumbhole Monte Carlo stock w/grooved forearm enhanced w/ "Anschutz" logo. Weight: 8.2 lbs. Imported from 1998 to date.

MODEL 1810 SUPER MATCH II....... NiB $1880 Ex $1339 Gd $824
A less detailed version of the Super Match 1813 model. Tapered forend w/deep receiver area. Select European hardwood stock. Weight: 13.5 lbs. Imported 1982-88 (reintroduced as 1910 series).

MODEL 1811 PRONE MATCH........ NiB $1730 Ex $1519 Gd $762
Bolt-action single-shot. Caliber: .22 LR. 27.5-inch bbl. Improved Super Match 54 action. Select European hardwood stock w/beavertail forend, adj. cheekpiece, and deep thumb flute. Thumb groove and pistol grip w/stipple checkering. Adj. buttplate. Weight: 11.5 lbs. Imported 1982-88. (Reintroduced as 1911Prone Match)

MODEL 1813 SUPER MATCH......... NiB $2184 Ex $1854 Gd $772
Bolt-action single-shot. Caliber: .22 LR. 27.5-inch bbl. Improved Super Match 54 action w/light firing pin, one-point adj. trigger. European walnut thumbhole stock, adj. palm rest, forend and pistol grip stipple checkered. Adj. cheekpiece and hook buttplate. Weight: 15.5 lbs. Imported 1982-88. (Reintroduced as 1913 Super Match)

MODEL 1827 BIATHLON RIFLE
Bolt-action clip repeater. Caliber: .22 LR. 21.5-inch bbl. 42.5 inches overall. Weight: 8.5 to 9 lbs. Slide safety. Adj. target sight set w/snow caps. European walnut stock w/cheekpiece, stippled pistol grip and forearm w/adj. weights. Fortner straight pull bolt option offered in 1986. Imported 1982 to date.
Mdl. 1827B w/Sup. Mat. 54 action .... NiB $2266 Ex $2060 Gd $927
Model 1827B, left-hand .... NiB $2012 Ex $1627 Gd $1135
Model 1827BT w/Fortner
Option, right-hand .... NiB $2369 Ex $2163 Gd $927
Model 1827BT, left-hand .... NiB $2528 Ex $2039 Gd $1415
Model 1827BT w/laminated stock, add $175
W/stainless steel bbl., add $205

MODEL 1907 ISU INTERNATIONAL MATCH RIFLE
Updated version of Model 1807 w/same general specifications as Model 1913 except w/26-inch bbl. 44.5 inches overall. Weight: 11 lbs. Designed for ISU 3-position competition. Fitted w/vented beechwood or walnut, blonde or color-laminated stock. Imported 1989 to date.
Right-hand model .... NiB $1478 Ex $1287 Gd $772
Left-hand model .... NiB $1664 Ex $1349 Gd $946
W/laminated stock, add $135
W/walnut stock, add $100
W/stainless steel bbl., add $130

MODEL 1910 INTERNATIONAL SUPER MATCH RIFLE
Updated version of Model 1810 w/same general specifications Model 1913 except w/less-detailed hardwood stock w/tapered forend. Weight: 13.5 lbs. Imported 1989 to date.
Right-hand model .... NiB $2472 Ex $1983 Gd $1009
Left-hand model .... NiB $2466 Ex $2003 Gd $1412

MODEL 1911 PRONE MATCH RIFLE
Updated version of Model 1811 w/same general specifications Model 1913 except w/specialized prone match hardwood stock w/beavertail forend. Weight: 11.5 lbs. Imported 1989 to date.
Right-hand model .... NiB $2266 Ex $2060 Gd $927
Left-hand model .... NiB $18,064 Ex $14,471 Gd $9874

Anschutz Achiever

MODEL 1912
LADIES' SPORT RIFLE . . . . NiB $1740 Ex $1524 Gd $772
Similar to the Model 1907 designed for ISU 3-position competition
w/same general U.I.T. specifications except w/shorter dimensions to
accomodate smaller competitors. Weight: 11.4 lbs. Imported 1999
to date.

MODEL 1913 STANDARD RIFLE . . . . . . NiB $1502 Ex $1133 Gd $772
Similar to 1913 Super Match w/economized appointments.
Imported 1997 to date.

MODEL 1913 SUPER MATCH RIFLE
Bolt-action single-shot Super Match (updated version of Model 1813).
Caliber: .22 LR. 27.5-inch bbl. Weight: 14.2 lbs. Adj. two-stage trig-
ger. Vented International thumbhole stock w/adj. cheekpiece, hand
and palm rest, fitted w/10-way butthook. Imported 1989 to date.
Right-hand model . . . . NiB $2183 Ex $1854 Gd $772
Left-hand model . . . . NiB $2254 Ex $1802 Gd $1226
W/laminated stock, add $130
**W/stainless
steel bbl., add** $140

MODEL 2007 ISU STANDARD RIFLE
Bolt-action single-shot. Caliber: .22 LR. 19.75-inch bbl. 43.5 to
44.5 inches overall. Weight: 10.8 lbs. Two-stage trigger. Standard
ISU stock w/adj. cheekpiece. Imported 1992 to date.
Right-hand model . . . . NiB $1880 Ex $1416 Gd $803
Left-hand model . . . . NiB $1987 Ex $1607 Gd $1121
W/stainless steel bbl., add $140

MODEL 2013
LADIES' SPORT RIFLE . . . . NiB $2086 Ex $1905 Gd $814
Similar to the Model 2007 designed for ISU 3-position competition
w/same general U.I.T. specifications except w/shorter dimensions to accomodate smaller competitors. Weight: 11.4 lbs. Imported 1999 to date.

MODEL 2013
BENCHREST RIFLE (BR-50) . . . . . NiB $1684 Ex $1519 Gd $772
Bolt-action single-shot. Caliber: .22 LR. 19.6-inch bbl. 43 inches
overall. Weight: 10.3 lbs. Adjustable trigger for single or two-stage
function. Benchrest-configuration stock. Imported 1999 to date.
MODEL 2013 SILHOUETTE RIFLE . . . . NiB $2070 Ex $1545 Gd $824
Bolt-action single-shot. Caliber: .22 LR. 20-inch bbl. 45.5 inches overall.
Weight: 11.5 lbs. Two-stage trigger. Thumbhole black synthetic or laminat-
ed stock w/adj. cheekpiece, hand and palm rest. Imported 1994 to date.

MODEL 2013 SUPER MATCH RIFLE
Bolt-action single-shot. Caliber: .22 LR. 19.75- or 27.1-inch bbl. 43 to
50.1 inches overall. Weight: 15.5 lbs. Two-stage trigger. International
thumbhole, black synthetic or laminated stock w/adj. cheekpiece, hand
and palm rest; fitted w/10-way butthook. Imported 1992 to date.
Right-hand model . . . . NiB $2420 Ex $2184 Gd $1030

Left-hand model . . . . NiB $2399 Ex $1936 Gd $1345
W/laminated stock, add $180

ACHIEVER BOLT-ACTION RIFLE. . . . . NiB $360 Ex $283 Gd $154
Caliber: .22 LR. 5-shot magazine. Mark 2000-type repeating action.
19.5-inch bbl. 36.5 inches overall. Weight: 5 lbs. Adj. open rear
sight; hooded ramp front. Plain European hardwood target-style
stock w/vented forend and adj. buttplate. Imported since 1987.

ACHIEVER ST-SUPER TARGET . . . . . NiB $489 Ex $360 Gd $206
Same as Achiever except single-shot w/22-inch bbl. and adj. stock.
38.75 inches overall. Weight: 6.5 lbs. Target sights. Imported since 1994.

BR-50 BENCH REST RIFLE. . . . . . . NiB $2008 Ex $1571 Gd $927
Single-shot. Caliber: .22 LR. 19.75-inch bbl. (23 inches w/muzzle
weight). 37.75-42.5 inches overall. Weight: 11 lbs. Grooved receiver, no
sights. Walnut-finished hardwood or synthetic benchrest stock w/adj.
cheekpiece. Imported 1994-97. (Reintroduced as Model 2013 BR-50)

**KADETT BOLT-ACTION
REPEATING RIFLE** . . . . NiB $309 Ex $206 Gd $129
Caliber: .22 LR. 5-shot detachable box magazine. 22-inch bbl. 40 inches
overall. Weight: 5.5 lbs. Adj. folding leaf rear sight; hooded ramp front.
Checkered European hardwood stock w/walnut-finish. Imported 1987-88.

MARK 2000 MATCH . . . . NiB $407 Ex $299 Gd $180
Takedown, bolt-action single-shot. Caliber: .22 LR. 26-inch heavy
bbl. Walnut stock w/deep-fluted thumb-groove, Wundhammer
swell pistol grip, beavertail forend. Adj. buttplate, single-stage adj.
trigger. Weight: 8 lbs. Imported 1982-89.

ARMALITE, INC. — Geneseo, Illinois
(Formerly Costa Mesa, California)

*Armalite was in Costa Mesa, California from 1959-73. Following
the acquisition by Eagle Arms in 1995, production resumed under
the Armalite, Inc. Logo in Geneseo, Illinois.*
Production by ARMALITE

AR-7 EXPLORER SURVIVAL RIFLE. . . NiB $139 Ex $113 Gd $62
Takedown. Semiautomatic. Caliber: .22 LR. Eight-shot box magazine. 16-inch cast aluminum bbl. w/steel liner. Sights: Peep rear;
blade front. Brown plastic stock, recessed to stow barrel, action, and
magazine. Weight: 2.75 lbs. Will float stowed or assembled. Made
1959-1973 by Armalite; 1974-90 by Charter Arms; 1990-97 by
Survival Arms, Cocoa, FL.; 1997 to date by Henry Repeating Arms
Co., Brooklyn, NY.

AR-7 EXPLORER CUSTOM RIFLE . . . NiB $191 Ex $154 Gd $77
Same as AR-7 Survival Rifle except w/deluxe walnut stock w/cheek-
piece and pistol grip. Weight: 3.5 lbs. Made 1964-70.

Armalite AR-10

Armalite AR-10 (T) Target Carbine

Armalite M-15A2 National Match

Armalite M-15A2 HBAR

AR-180 SEMIAUTOMATIC RIFLE
Commercial version of full automatic AR-18 Combat Rifle. Gas-operated semiautomatic. Caliber: .223 Rem. (5.56mm). Five, 20-, 30-round magazines. 18.25-inch bbl. w/flash hider/muzzle brake. Sights: Flip-up "L" type rear, adj. for windage; post front, adj. for elevation. Accessory: 3x scope and mount (add $60 to value). Folding buttstock of black nylon, rubber buttplate and pistol grip, heat dissipating fiberglass forend (hand guard), swivels, sling. 38 inches overall, 28.75 inches folded. Weight: 6.5 lbs. Note: Made by Armalite Inc. 1969-72, manufactured for Armalite by Howa Machinery Ltd., Nagoya, Japan, 1972-73; by Sterling Armament Co. Ltd., Dagenham, Essex, England, 1976 to 94. Importation disc.
**Armalite AR-180 (Mfg. by
Armalite-Costa Mesa)** . . . . NiB $1236 Ex $1030 Gd $721
Armalite AR-180 (Mfg. by Howa) . . . . . . NiB $1410 Ex $1127 Gd $767

(cont'd.) **AR-180 SEMIAUTOMATIC RIFLE**
Armalite AR-180 (Mfg. by Sterling) . . . . . . NiB $1024 Ex $819 Gd $557
W/3x scope and mount, add $225

Production by ARMALITE, Inc.

AR-10 (A) SEMIAUTOMATIC SERIES
Gas-operated semiautomatic action. Calibers: .243 Win. or .308 Win. (7.62 x 51mm). 10-shot magazine. 16- or 20-inch bbl. 35.5 or 39.5 inches overall. Weight: 9 to 9.75 lbs. Post front sight, adj. aperture rear. Black or green composition stock. Made 1995 to date.
AR-10 A2 (Std. carbine) . . . . NiB $1880 Ex $1571 Gd $618
AR-10 A2 (Std. rifle) . . . . NiB $1210 Ex $1025 Gd $592
AR-10 A4 (S.P. carbine) . . . . NiB $1262 Ex $1025 Gd $592
AR-10 A4 (S.P. rifle) . . . . NiB $1262 Ex $1025 Gd $592
W/stainless steel bbl., add $120

Armi Jager AP-74 Wood Stock

AR-10 (T) TARGET
Similar to Armalite Model AR-10A except in National Match configuration w/three-slot short Picatinny rail system and case deflector. 16- or 24-inch bbl. Weight: 8.25 to 10.4 lbs. Composite stock and handguard. No sights. Optional National Match carry handle and detachable front sight. Made 1995 to date.
AR-10 T (Rifle) . . . . NiB $1880 Ex $1571 Gd $927
AR-10 T (Carbine) . . . . NiB $1880 Ex $1571 Gd $927

MODEL AR-50 SS BOLT-ACTION
RIFLE . . . . NiB $2369 Ex $2008 Gd $1236
Caliber: .50 BMG. 31-inch bbl. w/muzzle brake. 59 inches overall. Weight: 41 lbs. Modified octagonal-form receiver, drilled and slotted for scope rail. Single-stage trigger. Triple front-locking bolt lug w/spring-loaded plunger for automatic ejection. Magnesium phosphate steel, hard-anodized aluminum finish. Made 1999 to date.

M15 SERIES
Gas-operated semiautomatic w/A2-style forward-assist mechanism and push-type pivot pin for easy takedown. Caliber: .223. 7-shot magazine. 16-, 20- or 24-inch bbl. Weight: 7-9.2 lbs. Composite or retractable stock. Fully adj. sights. Black anodized finish. Made 1995 to date.
M-15A2 (Carbine) . . . . NiB $850 Ex $721 Gd $566
M-15A2 (Service Rifle) . . . . NiB $901 Ex $772 Gd $577
M-15A2 (National Match) . . . . NiB $1262 Ex $1025 Gd $669
M-15A2
(Golden Eagle heavy bbl.) . . . . NiB $1236 Ex $1004 Gd $644
M-15A2 M4C
(retractable stock, disc. 1997) . . . . NiB $1184 Ex $917 Gd $592
M-15A4 (Action Master, disc. 1997) . . . . . NiB $1062 Ex $850 Gd $578
M-15A4 (Predator) . . . . NiB $901 Ex $772 Gd $577
M-15A4 (S.P. Rifle) . . . . NiB $875 Ex $721 Gd $463
M-15A4 (S.P. Carbine) . . . . NiB $824 Ex $669 Gd $412
M-15A4T (Eagle Eye Carbine) . . . . NiB $1236 Ex $978 Gd $669
M-15A4T (Eagle Eye Rifle) . . . . NiB $1287 Ex $953 Gd $669

ARMI JAGER — Turin, Italy

AP-74 COMMANDO . . . . NiB $257 Ex $196 Gd $124
Similar to standard AP-74 but styled to resemble original version of Uzi 9mm submachine gun w/wood buttstock. Lacks carrying handle and flash suppressor. Has different type front sight mount and guards, wood stock, pistol grip and forearm. Intro. 1976. Disc.

AP-74 SEMIAUTOMATIC RIFLE
Styled after U.S. M16 military rifle. Caliber: .22 LR, .32 Auto (pistol cartridge). Detachable clip magazine; capacity: 14 rounds caliber .22 LR, 9 rounds .32 ACP. 20-inch bbl. w/flash suppressor. Weight: 6.5 lbs. M16 type sights. Stock, pistol-grip and forearm of black plastic, swivels and sling. Intro. 1974. Disc.
.22 LR . . . . NiB $309 Ex $257 Gd $154
.32 Auto . . . . NiB $335 Ex $283 Gd $165

AP-74 WOOD STOCK MODEL
Same as standard AP-74 except w/wood stock, pistol-grip and forearm weight: 7 lbs. Disc.
.22 LR . . . . NiB $386 Ex $309 Gd $196
.32 Auto . . . . NiB $412 Ex $309 Gd $196

ARMSCOR (Arms Corp.) — Manila, Philippines (Imported until 1991 by Armscor Precision, San Mateo, CA; 1991-95 by Ruko Products, Inc., Buffalo NY: Currently imported by K.B.I., Harrisburg, PA)

MODEL 20 AUTO RIFLE
Caliber: .22 LR. 15-shot magazine. 21-inch bbl. 39.75 inches overall. Weight: 6.5 lbs. Sights: Hooded front; adj. rear. Checkered or plain walnut finished mahogany stock. Blued finish. Imported 1990-91. (Reinstated by Ruko in the M series.)
Model 20 (checkered stock) . . . . NiB $121 Ex $97 Gd $66
Model 20C (carbine-style stock) . . . . . NiB $108 Ex $87 Gd $59
Model 20P (plain stock) . . . . NiB $96 Ex $76 Gd $52

MODEL 1600 AUTO RIFLE
Caliber: .22 LR. 15-shot magazine. 19.5-inch bbl. 38 inches overall. Weight: 6 lbs. Sights: Post front; aperture rear. Plain mahogany stock. Matte black finish. Imported 1987-91. (Reinstated by Ruko in the M series.)
Standard model . . . . NiB $143 Ex $102 Gd $71
Retractable stock model . . . . NiB $153 Ex $117 Gd $76

MODEL AK22 AUTO RIFLE
Caliber: .22 LR. 15- or 30-shot magazine. 18.5-inch bbl. 36 inches overall. Weight: 7 lbs. Sights: Post front; adj. rear. Plain mahogany stock. Matte black finish. Imported 1987-91.
Standard model . . . . NiB $189 Ex $168 Gd $102
Folding stock model . . . . NiB $204 Ex $173 Gd $127

MODEL M14 SERIES BOLT-ACTION RIFLE
Caliber: .22 LR. 10-shot magazine. 23-inch bbl. Weight: 6.25 lbs. Open sights. Walnut or walnut finished mahogany stock. Imported 1991-97.
M14P Standard model . . . . NiB $97 Ex $71 Gd $46
M14D Deluxe model
(checkered stock, disc. 1995) . . . . NiB $83 Ex $66 Gd $45

MODEL M20 SERIES SEMIAUTOMATIC RIFLE
Caliber: .22 LR. 10- or 15-shot magazine. 18.25- or 20.75-inch bbl. Weight:5.5 to 6.5 lbs. 38 to 40.5 inches overall. Hooded front sight w/windage adj. rear. Walnut finished mahogany stock. Imported 1990-97.
M20C carbine model . . . . NiB $102 Ex $82 Gd $51
M20P standard model . . . . NiB $92 Ex $71 Gd $51
M20S Sporter Deluxe (checkered
mahogany stock) . . . . NiB $127 Ex $112 Gd $61
M20SC Super Classic (checkered
walnut stock) . . . . NiB $255 Ex $199 Gd $82

A-Square — Hannibal

MODEL M1400 BOLT-ACTION RIFLE

Similar to Model 14P except w/checkered stock w/Schnabel forend. Weight: 6 lbs. Imported 1990-97.

M1400LW (Lightweight, disc. 1992) . . . . . . NiB $194 Ex $163 Gd $102
M1400S (Sporter) . . . . NiB $127 Ex $102 Gd $71
M1400SC (Super Classic) . . . . NiB $249 Ex $199 Gd $136

MODEL M1500 BOLT-ACTION RIFLE

Caliber: .22 Mag. 5-shot magazine. 21.5-inch bbl. Weight: 6.5 lbs. Open sights. Checkered mahogany stock. Imported 1991-97.

M1500 (standard) . . . . NiB $127 Ex $127 Gd $71
M1500LW (Euro-style walnut
stock, disc. 1992) . . . . NiB $178 Ex $153 Gd $102
M1500SC (Monte Carlo stock) . . . . NiB $184 Ex $153 Gd $112

MODEL M1600 AUTO RIFLE

Rimfire replica of Armalite Model AR 180 (M16) except chambered for Caliber .22 LR. 15-shot magazine. 18-inch bbl. Weight: 5.25 lbs. Composite or retractable buttstock w/composite handguard and pistol grip. Carrying handle w/adj. aperture rear sight and protected post front. Black anodized finish. Imported 1991-97.

M-1600 (standard w/fixed stock) . . . . . . NiB $147 Ex $117 Gd $80
M-1600R (retractable stock) . . . . NiB $159 Ex $127 Gd $87

MODEL M1800 BOLT-ACTION RIFLE

Caliber: .22 Hornet. 5-shot magazine. 22-inch bbl. Weight: 6.6 lbs. Checkered hardwood or walnut stock. Sights: Post front; adj. rear. Imported 1995 to date.

M-1800 (standard) . . . . NiB $255 Ex $184 Gd $127
M-1800SC (checkered walnut stock) . . . . . NiB $357 Ex $286 Gd $204

MODEL M2000 AUTO RIFLE

Similar to Model 20P except w/checkered mahogany stock and adj. sights. Imported 1991 to date.

M2000S (standard) . . . . NiB $127 Ex $102 Gd $69
M2000SC (checkered walnut stock) . . . . . . NiB $236 Ex $189 Gd $129

ARNOLD ARMS — Arlington, Washington

AFRICAN SAFARI

Calibers: .243 to .458 Win. Magnum. 22- to 26-inch bbl. Weight: 7-9 lbs. Scope mount standard or w/optional M70 Express sights. Chrome-moly in four finishes. "A" and "AA" Fancy Grade English walnut stock with number 5 standard wraparound checkering pattern. Ebony forend tip. Made 1996 to date.

With "A" Grade English
walnut: matte blue . . . . NiB $4456 Ex $3565 Gd $2425
Std. polish . . . . NiB $4711 Ex $3769 Gd $2563
Hi-Luster . . . . NiB $4909 Ex $3927 Gd $2670
Stainless steel matte . . . . NiB $4456 Ex $3565 Gd $2424
With "AA" Grade English
Walnut: C-M matte blue . . . . NiB $4431 Ex $3544 Gd $2410
Std. polish . . . . NiB $4711 Ex $3769 Gd $2563
Hi-Luster . . . . NiB $4909 Ex $3927 Gd $2670
Stainless steel matte . . . . NiB $4456 Ex $3564 Gd $2425

ALASKAN TROPHY

Calibers: .300 Magnum to .458 Win. Magnum. 24- to 26-inch bbl. Weight: 7-9 lbs. Scope mount w/Express sights standard. Stainless steel or chrome-moly Apollo action w/fibergrain or black synthetic stock. Barrel band on 357 H&H and larger magnums. Made 1996 to date.

Matte finish . . . . NiB $3053 Ex $2443 Gd $1662
Std. polish . . . . NiB $3309 Ex $2646 Gd $1800
Stainless steel . . . . NiB $3124 Ex $2499 Gd $1699

A-SQUARE COMPANY INC. — Louisville, Kentucky (Formerly Bedford, KY)

CAESAR BOLT-ACTION RIFLE

Custom rifle built on Remington's 700 receiver. Calibers: Same as Hannibal, Groups I, II and III. 20- to 26-inch bbl. Weight: 8.5 to 11 lbs. Express 3-leaf rear sight, ramp front. Synthetic or classic Claro oil-finished walnut stock w/flush detachable swivels and Coil-Chek recoil system. Three-way adj. target trigger; 3-position safety. Right- or left-hand. Made 1984 to date.

Synthetic stock model . . . . NiB $3193 Ex $2575 Gd $1751
Walnut stock model . . . . NiB $2832 Ex $2163 Gd $1545

GENGHIS KHAN BOLT-ACTION RIFLE

Custom varmint rifle developed on Winchester's M70 receiver; fitted w/heavy tapered bbl. and Coil-Chek stock. Calibers: .22-250 Rem., .243 Win., .25-06 Rem., 6mm Rem. Weight: 8-8.5 lbs. Made 1994 to date.

Synthetic stock model . . . . NiB $3914 Ex $3080 Gd $2111
Walnut stock model . . . . NiB $3244 Ex $2626 Gd $1802

HAMILCAR BOLT-ACTION RIFLE

Similar to Hannibal Model except lighter. Calibers: .25-06, .257 Wby., 6.5x55 Swedish, .270 Wby., 7x57, 7mm Rem., 7mm STW, 7mm Wby., .280 Rem., .30-06, .300 Win., .300 Wby., .338-06, 9.3x62. Weight: 8-8.5 lbs. Made 1994 to date.

Synthetic stock model . . . . NiB $3728 Ex $2982 Gd $2028
Walnut stock model . . . . NiB $3284 Ex $2626 Gd $1786

HANNIBAL BOLT-ACTION RIFLE

Custom rifle built on reinforced P-17 Enfield receiver. Calibers: Group I: 30-06; Group II: 7mm Rem. Mag., .300 Win. Mag., .416 Taylor, .425 Express, .458 Win. Mag.; Group III: .300 H&H, .300 Wby. Mag., 8mm Rem. Mag., .340 Wby. Mag., .375 H&H, .375 Wby. Mag., .404 Jeffery, .416 Hoffman, .416 Rem. Mag., .450 Ackley, .458 Lott; Group IV: .338 A-Square Mag., .375 A-Square Mag., .378 Wby. Mag., .416 Rigby, .416 Wby. Mag., .460 Short Square Mag., .500 A-Square Mag. 20- to 26-inch bbl. Weight: 9 to 11.75 lbs. Express 3-leaf rear sight, ramp front. Classic Claro oil-finished walnut stock or synthetic stock w/flush detachable swivels and Coil-Chek recoil system. Adj. trigger w/2-position safety. Made 1983 to date.

Synthetic stock model . . . . NiB $3669 Ex $2935 Gd $1996
Walnut stock model . . . . NiB $3470 Ex $2776 Gd $1888

Auto-Ordnance
Thompson Model 27A-1
Deluxe

Auto-Ordnance
Thompson Model 27A-1
Standard Carbine

Auto-Ordnance
Thompson M1 Carbine

RIFLES

AUSTRIAN MILITARY RIFLES — Steyr, Austria Manufactured at Steyr Armory

MODEL 90
STEYR-MANNLICHER RIFLE . . . . . . NiB $280 Ex $153 Gd $102
Straight-pull bolt action. Caliber: 8mm. 5-shot magazine. Open sights. 10-inch bayonet. Cartridge clip forms part of the magazine mechanism. Some of these rifles were provided with a laced canvas hand guard, others were of wood.

MODEL 90
STEYR-MANNLICHER CARBINE . . . NiB $280 Ex $184 Gd $102
Same general specifications as Model 90 rifle except w/19.5-inch bbl., weight 7 lbs. No bayonet stud or supplemental forend grip.

MODEL 95
STEYR-MANNLICHER CARBINE . . . NiB $280 Ex $184 Gd $102
Same general specifications as Model 95 rifle except w/19.5-inch bbl., weight 7 lbs. Post front sight; adj. rear carbine sight.

MODEL 95
STEYR-MANNLICHER
SERVICE RIFLE. . . . . NiB $255 Ex $133 Gd $97
Straight-pull bolt action. Caliber: 8x50R Mannlicher (many of these rifles were altered during World War II to use the 7.9mm German service ammunition). 5-shot Mannlicher-type box magazine. 30-inch bbl. Weight: 8.5 lbs. Sights: Blade front; rear adj. for elevation. Military-type full stock.

AUTO-ORDNANCE CORPORATION — West Hurley, New York (Manufacturing rights acquired by Kahr Arms 1999)

THOMPSON MODEL 22-27A-3 . . . NiB $716 Ex $592 Gd $412
Same-bore version of Deluxe Model 27A-1. Same general specifications except 22 LR w/lightweight alloy receiver, weight 6.5 lbs. Magazines include 5-, 20-, 30- and 50-shot box types, 80-shot drum. Made 1977-94.

THOMPSON MODEL 27A-1 DELUXE
Same as Standard Model 27A-1 except w/finned bbl. w/compensator, adj. rear sight, pistol-grip forestock. Caliber: .22 LR, l0mm (1991-93) or 45 ACP. Weight: 11.5 lbs. Made 1976-99.
.22 LR (Limited production) . . . . NiB $1281 Ex $1025 Gd $697
10mm or 45 ACP . . . . NiB $715 Ex $592 Gd $463
50-round drum magazine, add $250
100-round drum magazine, add $450
Violin carrying case, add. $100

THOMPSON MODEL 27A-1
STANDARD SEMIAUTO CARBINE. . . . . . . NiB $618 Ex $566 Gd $360
Similar to Thompson submachine gun ("Tommy Gun") except has no provision for automatic firing. Caliber: .45 Auto. 20-shot detachable box magazine (5-,15- and 30-shot box magazines, 39-shot drum also available). 16-inch plain bbl. Weight: 14 lbs. Sights: Aperture rear; blade front. Walnut buttstock, pistol grip and grooved forearm, sling swivels. Made 1976-86.

GUN TRADER'S GUIDE

THOMPSON 27A-1C
LIGHTWEIGHT CARBINE . . . . **NiB $741 Ex $592 Gd $403**
Similar to Model 27A-1 except w/lightweight alloy receiver. Weight: 9.25 lbs. Made 1984 to date.

THOMPSON M1
SEMI-AUTOMATIC CARBINE . . . . . **NiB $715 Ex $592 Gd $412**
Similar to Model 27A-1 except in M-1 configuration w/side cocking lever and horizontal forearm. Weight: 11.5 lbs. Made 1986 to date.

BARRETT FIREARMS MFG., INC. — Murfreesboro, Tennessee

MODEL 82 A-1
SEMI-AUTOMATIC RIFLE . . . . . **NiB $6952 Ex $5356 Gd $3296**
Caliber: .50 BMG. 10-shot detachable box magazine. 29-inch recoiling bbl. w/muzzle brake. 57 inches overall. Weight: 28.5 lbs. Open iron sights and 10x scope. Composit stock w/Sorbothance recoil pad and self-leveling bipod. Blued finish. Made 1985 to date.

MODEL 90
BOLT-ACTION RIFLE . . . . **NiB $3553 Ex $3038 Gd $1854**
Caliber: .50 BMG. Five shot magazine. 29-inch match bbl. 45 inches overall. Weight: 22 lbs. Composite stock w/retractable bipod. Made 1990-95.

MODEL 95 BOLT-ACTION . . . . **NiB $4609 Ex $3553 Gd $2626**
Similar to Model 90 bullpup design chambered for .50 BMG except w/improved muzzle brake and extendable bipod. Made 1995 to date.

BEEMAN PRECISION ARMS INC. — Santa Rosa, California

Since 1993 all European firearms imported by Beeman have been distributed by Beeman Outdoor Sports, Div., Roberts Precision Arms, Inc., Santa Rosa, CA.

WEIHRAUCH HW MODELS 60J AND 60J-ST
BOLT-ACTION RIFLES
Calibers: .22 LR (60J-ST), .222 Rem. (60J). 22.8-inch bbl. 41.7 inches overall. Weight: 6.5 lbs. Sights: Hooded blade front; open adj. rear. Blued finish. Checkered walnut stock w/cheekpiece. Made 1988-94.
Model 60J . . . . **NiB $463 Ex $700 Gd $566**
Model 60J-ST . . . . **NiB $580 Ex $463 Gd $315**

WEIHRAUCH HW MODEL 60M
SMALL BORE RIFLE . . . . **NiB $618 Ex $515 Gd $330**
Caliber: .22 LR. Single-shot. 26.8-inch bbl. 45.7 inches overall. Weight: 10.8 lbs. Adj. trigger w/push-button safety. Sights: Hooded blade front on ramp, precision aperture rear. Target-style stock w/stippled forearm and pistol grip. Blued finish. Made 1988-94.

WEIHRAUCH HW
MODEL 660 MATCH RIFLE . . . . **NiB $875 Ex $747 Gd $360**
Caliber: .22 LR. 26-inch bbl. 45.3 inches overall. Weight: 10.7 lbs. Adj. match trigger. Sights: globe front, precision aperture rear. Match-style walnut stock w/adj. cheekpiece and buttplate. Made 1988-94.

FEINWERKBAU MODEL 2600 SERIES TARGET RIFLE
Caliber: .22 LR. Single-shot. 26.3-inch bbl. 43.7 inches overall.

(cont'd) **FEINWERKBAU MODEL 2600 SERIES TARGET RIFLE**
Weight: 10.6 lbs. Match trigger w/fingertip weight adjustment dial. Sights: Globe front; micrometer match aperture rear. Laminated hardwood stock w/adj. cheekpiece. Made 1988-94.
Standard Model 2600
(left-hand) . . . . **NiB $1617 Ex $1236 Gd $824**
Standard Model 2600
(right-hand) . . . . **NiB $1442 Ex $1133 Gd $721**
Free Rifle Model 2602
(left-hand) . . . . **NiB $2060 Ex $1648 Gd $927**
Free Rifle Model 2602
(right-hand) . . . . **NiB $2060 Ex $1648 Gd $927**

BELGIAN MILITARY RIFLES
Mfd. by Fabrique Nationale D'Armes de Guerre, Herstal, Belgium; Fabrique D'Armes de L'Etat, Lunich, Belgium

Hopkins & Allen Arms Co. of Norwich, Conn., as well as contractors in Birmingham, England, also produced these guns during World War I.

MODEL 1889 MAUSER
MILITARY RIFLE . . . . **NiB $204 Ex $133 Gd $82**
Caliber: 7.65mm Belgian Service (7.65mm Mauser). 5-shot projecting box magazine. 30.75-inch bbl. w/jacket. Weight: 8.5 lbs. Adj. rear sight, blade front. Straight-grip military stock. This, and the carbine version, was the principal weapon of the Belgian Army at the start of WWII. Made 1889 to c.1935.

MODEL 1916
MAUSER CARBINE . . . . **NiB $229 Ex $178 Gd $92**
Same as Model 1889 Rifle except w/20.75-inch bbl. Weighs 8 lbs. and has minor differences in the rear sight graduations, lower band closer to the muzzle and swivel plate on side of buttstock.

MODEL 1935 MAUSER
MILITARY RIFLE . . . . **NiB $306 Ex $229 Gd $127**
Same general specifications as F.N. Model 1924; minor differences. Caliber: 7.65mm Belgian Service. Mfd. by Fabrique Nationale D'Armes de Guerre.

MODEL 1936 MAUSER
MILITARY RIFLE . . . . **NiB $229 Ex $184 Gd $124**
An adaptation of Model 1889 w/German M/98-type bolt, Belgian M/89 protruding box magazine. Caliber: 7.65mm Belgian Service. Mfd. by Fabrique Nationale D'Armes de Guerre.

BENTON & BROWN FIREARMS, INC. — Fort Worth, Texas

MODEL 93 BOLT-ACTION RIFLE
Similar to Blaser Model R84 (the B&B rifle is built on the Blaser action, see separate listing) with an interchangeable bbl. system. Calibers: .243 Win., 6mm Rem., .25-06, .257 Wby., .264 Win., .270 Win., .280 Rem., 7mm Rem Mag., .30-06, .308, .300 Wby., .300 Win. Mag., .338 Win., .375 H&H. 22- or 24-inch bbl. 41 or 43 inches overall. Bbl.-mounted scope rings and one-piece base; no sights. Two-piece walnut or fiberglass stock. Made 1993 to date.
Walnut stock model . . . . **NiB $1802 Ex $1648 Gd $917**
Fiberglass stock model . . . . **NiB $1596 Ex $1236 Gd $875**
Extra bbl. assembly, add **$475**
Extra bolt assembly, add **$425**

Beretta 501
Bolt-Action Sporter

Beretta AR-70

BERETTA U.S.A. CORP. — Accokeek, Maryland, Manufactured by Fabbrica D'Armi Pietro Beretta, S.p.A., Gardone Val Trompia (Brescia), Italy

455 SxS EXPRESS DOUBLE RIFLE
Sidelock action w/removable sideplates. Calibers: .375 H&H, .458 Win. Mag., .470 NE, .500 NE (3 inches), .416 Rigby. Bbls.: 23.5 or 25.5-inch. Weight: 11 lbs. Double triggers. Sights: Blade front; V-notch folding leaf rear. Checkered European walnut forearm and buttstock w/recoil pad. Color casehardened receiver w/blued bbls. Made 1990 to date.
Model 455 . . . . NiB $40,938 Ex $32,750 Gd $22,270
Model 455EELL. . . . . NiB $51,875 Ex $41,500 Gd $28,220

500 BOLT-ACTION SPORTER
Centerfire bolt-action rifle w/Sako A I short action. Calibers: .222 Rem., .223 Rem. Five shot magazine. 23.63-inch bbl. Weight: 6.5 lbs. Available w/ or w/o iron sights. Tapered dovetailed receiver. European walnut stock. Disc. 1986.
Standard . . . . NiB $613 Ex $515 Gd $360
DL Model . . . . NiB $1481 Ex $1184 Gd $805
500 EELL
Engraved . . . . NiB $1545 Ex $1339 Gd $876
W/iron sights, add 10%

501 BOLT-ACTION SPORTER
Same as Model 500 except w/Sako A II medium action. Calibers: .243 Win., .308 Win. Weight: 7.5 lbs. Disc. 1986.
Standard . . . . NiB $638 Ex $510 Gd $347
Standard
w/iron sights . . . . NiB $613 Ex $566 Gd $360
DL model. . . . . NiB $1463 Ex $1184 Gd $824
501 EELL (engraved) . . . . NiB $1596 Ex $1339 Gd $875
W/iron sights, add 10%

502 BOLT-ACTION SPORTER
Same as Model 500 except w/Sako A III long action. Calibers: .270 Win., 7mm Rem. Mag., .30/06, 375 H&H. Weight: 8.5 lbs. Disc. 1986.
Standard model . . . . NiB $701 Ex $561 Gd $382
DL model. . . . . NiB $1648 Ex $1287 Gd $875
502 EELL (engraved) . . . . NiB $1796 Ex $1437 Gd $977
W/iron sights, add 10%

AR-70 SEMIAUTOMATIC RIFLE . . . . NiB $1905 Ex $1674 Gd $978
Caliber: .223 Rem. (5.56mm). 30-shot magazine. 17.75-inch bbl. Weight: 8.25 lbs. Sights: Rear peep adj. for windage and elevation; blade front. High-impact synthetic buttstock. Imported 1984-89.

EXPRESS S686/S689 SABLE O/U RIFLE
Calibers: .30-06 Spfld., 9.3x74R, and .444 Marlin. 24-inch bbl. Weight: 7.7 lbs. Drilled and tapped for scope mount. European-style cheek rest and ventilated rubber recoil pad. Imported 1995 to date.
Model S686/S689 Silver Sable II. . . . . NiB $45635 Ex $3605 Gd $2060
Model S689 Gold Sable . . . . NiB $6180 Ex $5150 Gd $2987
Model S686/S689 EELL
Diamond Sable. . . . . NiB $12,875 Ex $9270 Gd $6180
W/extra bbl. set, add $325
W/detachable claw mounts, add $595

EXPRESS SSO O/U EXPRESS DOUBLE RIFLE
Sidelock. Calibers: .375 H&H Mag., .458 Win. Mag., 9.3 x 74R. 23-24- or 25.5-inch blued bbls. Weight: 11 lbs. Double triggers. Express sights w/blade front and V-notch folding leaf rear. Optional Zeiss scope w/claw mounts. Color casehardened receiver w/scroll engraving, game scenes and gold inlays on higher grades. Checkered European walnut forearm and buttstock w/cheekpiece and recoil pad. Imported 1985 to date.
Model SS0 (disc. 1989) . . . . NiB $9270 Ex $8137 Gd $5150
Model SS05 (disc. 1990) . . . . NiB $10,300 Ex $8755 Gd $6180
Model SS06 Custom . . . . NiB $26,265 Ex $20,085 Gd $12,360
Model SS06 EELL Gold Custom . . . . NiB $29,767 Ex $26,265 Gd $14,935
Extra bbl. assembly, add $6250
Claw mounts, add $550

Beretta Mato Deluxe

Beretta Mato Synthetic

Blaser Model R84

MATO
Calibers: .270 Win., .280 Rem., 7mm Rem. Mag, .300 Win. Mag., .338 Win. Mag., .375 H&H. 23.6-inch bbl. Weight: 8 lbs. Adjustable trigger. Drop-out box magazine. Drilled and tapped for scope w/ or w/o adj. sights. Walnut or synthetic stock. Manufactured based on Mauser 98 action. Made in 1997 to date.
Standard model . . . . NiB $1236 Ex $927 Gd $618
Deluxe model . . . . NiB $1905 Ex $1545 Gd $824
.375 H&H w/iron sights, add. $300

SMALL BORE SPORTING CARBINE/TARGET RIFLE
Semiautomatic w/bolt handle in raised or conventional single-shot bolt-action w/handle in lowered position. Caliber: .22 LR. Four, 5-, 8-, 10- or 20-shot magazines. 20.5-inch standard or heavy bbl. Sights: 3-leaf folding rear, partridge front. Target or sporting stock w/checkered pistol grip and forend and sling swivels. Weight: 5.5 to 6 lbs.
Sporter model (Super Sport X) . . . . NiB $386 Ex $309 Gd $201
Target model (Olympia X) . . . . NiB $260 Ex $438 Gd $283

BLASER USA, INC. — Fort Worth, Texas
Mfd. by Blaser Jagdwaffen GmbH, Germany *(Imported by Sigarms, Exeter, NH; Autumn Sales, Inc., Fort Worth, TX)*

MODEL R84 BOLT-ACTION RIFLE
Calibers: .22-250, .243, 6mm Rem., .25-06, .270, .280 Rem., .30-06- .257 Wby. Mag., .264 Win. Mag., 7mm Rem Mag., .300 Win. Mag., .300 Wby. Mag., .338 Win. Mag., .375 H&H. Interchangeable bbls. w/standard or Magnum bolt assemblies. Bbl. length: 23 inches (standard); 24 inches (Magnum). 41 to 42 inches overall. Weight: 7 to 7.25 lbs. No sights. Bbl.-mounted scope system. Two-piece Turkish walnut stock w/solid black recoil pad. Imported 1989-94.

(cont'd.) **MODEL R84 BOLT-ACTION RIFLE**
Model R84 Standard . . . . NiB $2163 Ex $1648 Gd $1025
Model R84 Deluxe
(game scene) . . . . NiB $2987 Ex $1957 Gd $1226
Model R84 Super Deluxe
(Gold and silver inlays) . . . . NiB $3605 Ex $1957 Gd $1339
Left-hand model, add $125
Extra bbl. assembly, add $650

MODEL R93 SAFARI SERIES BOLT-ACTION REPEATER
Similar to Model R84 except restyled action w/straight-pull bolt, unique safety and searless trigger mechanism. Additional chamberings: 6.5x55, 7x57, .308, .416 Rem. Optional open sights. Imported 1994-98.
Model R93 Safari . . . . NiB $3682 Ex $3090 Gd $1957
Model R93 Safari Deluxe . . . . NiB $4120 Ex $3914 Gd $3090
Model R84 Safari
Super Deluxe . . . . NiB $4635 Ex $4120 Gd $3244
Extra bbl. assembly, add $525

MODEL R93 CLASSIC SERIES BOLT-ACTION REPEATER
Similar to Model R93 Safari except w/expanded model variations. Imported 1998 to date.
Model R93 Attache
(Premium wood, fluted bbl.) . . . . NiB $4326 Ex $3656 Gd $2884
Model R93 Classic
(.22-250 to .375 H&H) . . . . NiB $3341 Ex $2673 Gd $1818
Model R93 Classic Safari (.416 Rem.) . . . . . NiB $3728 Ex $2982 Gd $2028
Model R93 LX (.22-250 to .416 Rem.) . . . . . NiB $1668 Ex $1334 Gd $907
Model R93 Synthetic (.22-250
to .375 H&H) . . . . NiB $1281 Ex $1025 Gd $697
Extra bbl. assembly, add $550

Brno Model II

Brno Model 21H
Bolt-Action Sporting Rifle

Brno Model 22F

Brno Hornet
Bolt-Action Sporting Rifle

RIFLES

BRITISH MILITARY RIFLES
Mfd. at Royal Small Arms Factory, Enfield Lock, Middlesex, England, as well as private contractors

RIFLE NO. 1 MARK III . . . . **NiB $255 Ex $153 Gd $102**
Short magazine Lee-Enfield (S.M.L.E.). Bolt action. Caliber: .303 British. 10-shot box magazine. 25.25-inch bbl. Weight: 8.75 lbs. Sights: Adj. rear; blade front w/guards. Two-piece, full-length military stock. Note: The earlier Mark III (approved 1907) is virtually the same as Mark III (adopted 1918) except for sights and different magazine cut-off that was eliminated on the latter.

RIFLE NO. 3 MARK I (PATTERN 14) . . . . . . **NiB $280 Ex $204 Gd $102**
Modified Mauser-type bolt action. Except for caliber .303 British and long-range sight, this rifle is the same as U.S. Model 1917 Enfield. See listing of the latter for general specifications.

RIFLE NO. 4 MARK I . . . . **NiB $229 Ex $178 Gd $102**
Post-World War I modification of the S.M.L.E. intended to simplify mass production. General specifications same as Rifle No. 1 Mark III except w/aperture rear sight and minor differences in construction and weighs 9.25 lbs.

LIGHT RIFLE NO. 4 MARK I . . . . . . **NiB $178 Ex $127 Gd $92**
Modification of the S.M.L.E. Caliber: .303 British. 10-shot box magazine. 23-inch bbl. Weight: 6.75 lbs. Sights: Micrometer click rear peep; blade front. One-piece military-type stock w/recoil pad. Made during WWII.

RIFLE NO. 5 MARK I . . . . **NiB $306 Ex $204 Gd $127**
Jungle Carbine. Modification of the S.M.L.E. similar to Light Rifle No. 4 Mark I except w/20.5-inch bbl. w/flash hider, carbine-type stock. Made during WWII, originally designed for use in the Pacific Theater.

BRNO SPORTING RIFLES — Brno, Czech Republic, Manufactured by Ceska Zbrojovka *Imported by Euro-Imports, El Cajon, CA (Previously by Bohemia Arms & Magnum Research)*

See also CZ rifles.

MODEL I BOLT-ACTION
SPORTING RIFLE . . . . **NiB $618 Ex $541 Gd $360**
Caliber: .22 LR. Five shot detachable magazine. 22.75-inch bbl. Weight: 6 lbs. Sights: three-leaf open rear; hooded ramp front. Sporting stock w/checkered pistol grip, swivels. Made 1946-73.

MODEL II BOLT-ACTION
SPORTING RIFLE . . . . **NiB $669 Ex $566 Gd $360**
Same as Model I except w/deluxe grade stock. Made 1949-57.

MODEL III BOLT-ACTION
TARGET RIFLE . . . . **NiB $721 Ex $669 Gd $412**
Same as Model I except w/heavy bbl. and target stock. Made 1948-56.

MODEL IV BOLT-ACTION
TARGET RIFLE . . . . **NiB $772 Ex $607 Gd $412**
Same as Model III except w/improved target trigger mechanism. Made 1956-62.

MODEL V BOLT-ACTION
SPORTING RIFLE . . . . **NiB $721 Ex $546 Gd $360**
Same as Model I except w/improved trigger mechanism. Made 1956-73.

Brno Model-ZKM 611

Brown Precision High Country Youth Rifle

MODEL 21H BOLT-ACTION
SPORTING RIFLE. . . . . NiB $772 Ex $618 Gd $412
Mauser-type action. Calibers: 6.5x57mm, 7x57mm 8x57mm. Five shot box magazine. 20.5-inch bbl. Double set trigger. Weight: 6.75 lbs. Sights: Two-leaf open rear-hooded ramp front. Half-length sporting stock w/cheekpiece, checkered pistol-grip and forearm, swivels. Made 1946-55.

MODEL 22F. . . . . NiB 1024 Ex $819 Gd $557
Same as Model 21H except w/full-length Mannlicher-type stock, weight: 6 lbs., 14 oz. Disc.

MODEL 98 STANDARD
Calibers: .243 Win., .270 Win., .30-06, .308 Win., .300 Win. Mag., 7x57mm, 7x64mm, or 9.3x62mm. 23.8-inch bbl. Overall 34.5 inches. Weight: 7.25 lbs. Checkered walnut stock w/Bavarian cheekpiece. Imported 1998 to date.
Standard calibers . . . . NiB $444 Ex $355 Gd $242
Calibers .300 Win., Mag., 9.3x62mm . . . . . NiB $495 Ex $397 Gd $270
W/single set trigger, add. $100

MODEL 98 MANNLICHER
Similar to Model 98 Standard except full length stock and set triggers. Imported 1998 to date.
Standard calibers . . . . NiB $612 Ex $489 Gd $333
Calibers .300 Win. Mag., 9.3x62mm. . . . . . NiB $676 Ex $541 Gd $368

ZBK-110 SINGLE-SHOT
Calibers: .22 Hornet, .222 Rem., 5.6x52R, 5.6x50 Mag., 6.5x57R, 7x57R, and 8x57JRS. 23.8-inch bbl. Weight: 6.1 lbs. Walnut checkered buttstock and forearm w/Bavarian cheekpiece. Imported 1998 to date.
Standard model. NiB $232 Ex $175 Gd $124
Lux model. . . . . NiB $386 Ex $257 Gd $180
Calibers 7x57R and 8x57 JRS, add $25
W/interchangeable 12 ga.
shotgun bbl., add $132

HORNET BOLT-ACTION
SPORTING RIFLE. . . . . NiB $978 Ex $850 Gd $463
Miniature Mauser action. Caliber: .22 Hornet. Five-shot detachable box magazine. 23-inch bbl. Double set trigger. Weight: 6.25 lbs.

(cont'd.) **HORNET BOLT-ACTION SPORTING RIFLE**
Sights: Three-leaf open rear hooded ramp front. Sporting stock w/checkered pistol grip and forearm, swivels. Made 1949-74. Note: This rifle was also marketed in U.S. as "Z-B Mauser Varmint Rifle." (Reintroduced as Model ZKB 680)

MODEL ZKB 680
BOLT-ACTION RIFLE. . . . . NiB $483 Ex $386 Gd $263
Calibers: .22 Hornet, .222 Rem. 5-shot detachable box magazine. 23.5-inch bbl. Weight: 5.75 lbs. Double-set triggers. Adj. open rear sight, hooded ramp front. Walnut stock. Imported 1985-92.

MODEL ZKM 611 SEMIAUTOMATIC RIFLE
Caliber: .22 WMR. Six-round magazine. 20-inch bbl. 37 inches overall. Weight: 6.2 lbs. Hooded front sight; mid-mounted rear sight. Checkered walnut or beechwood stock. Single thumb-screw takedown. Grooved receiver for scope mounting. Imported 1992 to date.
Standard beechwood model . . . . . . NiB $418 Ex $335 Gd $228
Deluxe walnut model . . . . NiB $520 Ex $412 Gd $257

BROWN PRECISION COMPANY — Los Molinos, California

MODEL 7 SUPER LIGHT SPORTER . . . . . NiB $1025 Ex $927 Gd $669
Lightweight sporter built on a Remington Model 7 barreled action w/18-inch factory bbl. Weight: 5.25 lbs. Kevlar stock. Made 1984-92.

HIGH COUNTRY BOLT-ACTION SPORTER
Custom sporting rifles built on Blaser, Remington 700, Ruger 77 and Winchester 70 actions. Calibers: .243 Win., .25-06, .270 Win., 7mm Rem. Mag., .308 Win., .30-06. Five-shot magazine (4-shot in 7mm Mag.). 22- or 24-inch bbl. Weight: 6.5 lbs. Fiberglass stock w/recoil pad, sling swivels. No sights. Made 1975 to date.
Standard High Country . . . . NiB $1133 Ex $978 Gd $721
Custom High Country . . . . NiB $2060 Ex $1638 Gd $927
Left-hand action, add. $200
Stainless bbl., add $200
70, 77 or Blaser actions, add. $125
70 SG action, add $350

Brown Precision Pro-Hunter

Brown Precision Tactical Elite

HIGH COUNTRY YOUTH RIFLE . . . . NiB $1236 Ex $927 Gd $618
Similar to standard Model 7 Super Light except w/Kevlar or graphite stock, scaled-down to youth dimensions. Calibers: .223, .243, 6mm, 7mm-08, .308. Made 1992 to date.

PRO-HUNTER BOLT-ACTION RIFLE
Custom sporting rifle built on Remington 700 or Winchester 70 SG action fitted w/match-grade Shilen bbl. chambered in customer's choice of caliber. Matte blued, nickel or Teflon finish. Express-style rear sight hooded ramp front. Synthetic stock. Made 1989 to date
Standard Pro-Hunter . . . . NiB $2420 Ex $2008 Gd $1133
Pro-Hunter Elite (1993 to date) . . . . . . NiB $3450 Ex $2678 Gd $1802

PRO-VARMINTER BOLT-ACTION RIFLE
Custom varminter built on a Remington 700 or 40X action fitted w/Shilen stainless steel benchrest bbl. Varmint or benchrest-style stock. Made 1993 to date.
Standard Pro-Varminter . . . . NiB $1844 Ex $1390 Gd $927
Pro-Hunter w/Rem 40X action . . . . . . NiB $2420 Ex $1844 Gd $1226

SELECTIVE TARGET MODEL . . . . . NiB $1226 Ex $927 Gd $592
Tactical law-enforcement rifle built on a Remington 700V action. Caliber: .308 Win. 20-, 22- or 24-inch bbl. Synthetic stock. Made 1989-92.

TACTICAL ELITE RIFLE . . . . NiB $2575 Ex $2266 Gd $1236
Similar to Selective Target Model except fitted w/select match-grade Shilen benchrest heavy stainless bbl. Calibers: .223, .308, .300 Win. Mag. Black or camo Kevlar/graphite composite fiberglass stock w/adj. buttplate. Non-reflective black Teflon metal finish. Made 1993 to date.

BROWNING RIFLES — Morgan, Utah
Mfd. for Browning by Fabrique Nationale d'Armes de Guerre (now Fabrique Nationale Herstal), Herstal, Belgium; Miroku Firearms Mfg. Co., Tokyo, Japan; A.T.I., Salt Lake City, Ut; Oy Sako Ab, Riihimaki, Finland.

.22 AUTOMATIC RIFLE, GRADE I
Similar to discontinued Remington Model 241A. Autoloading. Take-down. Calibers: .22 LR. .22 Short (not interchangeably). Tubular magazine in butt-stock holds 11 LR. 16 Short. Bbl. lengths: 19.25 inches (.22 LR), 22.25 inches (.22 Short). Weight: 4.75 lbs. (.22 LR); 5 lbs. (.22 Short). Receiver scroll engraved. Open rear sight, bead front. Checkered pistol-grip butt-stock, semibeavertail forearm. Made 1965-72 by FN; 1972 to date by Miroku. Note: Illustrations are of rifles manufactured by FN.
FN manufacture. . . . . NiB $592 Ex $412 Gd $206
Miroku manufacture . . . . NiB $309 Ex $206 Gd $154

.22 AUTOMATIC RIFLE, GRADE II
Same as Grade I except satin chrome-plated receiver engraved w/small game animal scenes, gold-plated trigger select walnut stock and forearm. .22 LR only. Made 1972-84.
FN manufacture. . . . . NiB $1004 Ex $664 Gd $463
Miroku manufacture . . . . NiB $412 Ex $335 Gd $206

.22 AUTOMATIC RIFLE, GRADE III
Same as Grade I except satin chrome-plated receiver elaborately hand-carved and engraved w/dog and game-bird scenes, scrolls and leaf clusters: gold-plated trigger, extra-fancy walnut stock and forearm, skip-checkered. .22 LR only. Made 1972-84.
FN manufacture. . . . . NiB $2060 Ex $1648 Gd $1024
Miroku manufacture . . . . NiB $824 Ex $505 Gd $407

.22 AUTOMATIC, GRADE VI . . . . . . NiB $721 Ex $515 Gd $335
Same general specifications as standard .22 Automatic except for engraving, high-grade stock w/checkering and glossy finish. Made by Miroku 1986 to date.

MODEL 52 BOLT-ACTION RIFLE . . . . NiB $721 Ex $566 Gd $360
Limited edition of Winchester Model 52C Sporter. Caliber: .22 LR. 5-shot magazine. 24-inch bbl. Weight: 7 lbs. Micro-Motion trigger. No sights. Checkered select walnut stock w/rosewood forend and metal grip cap. Blued finish. Only 5000 made in 1991-92.

MODEL 53 LEVER-ACTION RIFLE . . . . NiB $746 Ex $618 Gd $402
Limited edition of Winchester Model 53. Caliber: .32-20. 7-shot tubular half-magazine. 22-inch bbl. Weight: 6.5 lbs. Adj. rear sight, bead front. Select walnut checkered pistol-grip stock w/high-gloss finish. Classic-style forearm. Blued finish. Only 5000 made in 1990. See illustration next page.

Browning Model 53
Lever-Action Limited Edition

Browning Model 71
Grade I Lever-Action

Browning Model 71
High-Grade Carbine

Browning Model 71
High-Grade

Browning Model 78
Single-Shot .45-70

MODEL 65 GRADE I
LEVER-ACTION RIFLE . . . . NiB $721 Ex $463 Gd $360
Caliber: .218 Bee. 7-shot tubular half-magazine. 24-inch bbl. Weight: 6.75 lbs. Sights: Adj. buckhorn-style rear, hooded bead front. Select walnut pistol-grip stock w/high-gloss finish. Semibeavertail forearm. Limited edition of 3500 made in 1989.

MODEL 65 HIGH GRADE RIFLE . . . . NiB $1802 Ex $927 Gd $618
Same general specifications as Model 65 Grade I except w/engraving and gold-plated animals on grayed receiver. Cut checkering on pistol grip and forearm. Limited edition of 1500 made in 1989.

MODEL 71 GRADE I CARBINE . . . . NiB $721 Ex $541 Gd $360
Same general specifications as Model 71 Grade I Rifle except carbine w/20-inch round bbl. and weighs 8 lbs. Limited edition of 4000 made in 1986-87.

MODEL 71 GRADE I
LEVER-ACTION RIFLE . . . . NiB $814 Ex $618 Gd $412
Caliber: .348 Win. 4-shot magazine. 24-inch round bbl. Weight: 8 lbs., 2 oz. Open buckhorn sights. Select walnut straight grip stock w/satin finish. Classic-style forearm, flat metal buttplate. Limited edition of 3000 made in 1986-87.

MODEL 71 HIGH-GRADE CARBINE . . . . . NiB $1184 Ex $1004 Gd $566
Same general specifications as Model 71 High Grade Rifle, except carbine w/20-inch round bbl. Limited edition of 3000 made in 1986-88.

MODEL 71 HIGH-GRADE RIFLE . . . . NiB $1262 Ex $978 Gd $695
Caliber: .348 Win. Four shot magazine. 24-inch round bbl. Weight: 8 lbs., 2 oz. Engraved receiver. Open buckhorn sights. Select walnut checkered pistol-grip stock w/high-gloss finish. Classic-style forearm, flat metal buttplate. Limited edition of 3000 made in 1987.

78 BICENTENNIAL SET . . . . NiB $3605 Ex $2961 Gd $1957
Special Model 78 .45-70 w/same specifications as standard type, except sides of receiver engraved w/bison and eagle, scroll engraving on top of receiver, lever, both ends of bbl. and buttplate; high-grade walnut stock and forearm. Accompanied by an engraved hunting knife and stainless steel commemorative medallion, all in an alder wood presentation case. Each item in set has matching serial number beginning with "1776" and ending with numbers 1 to 1,000. Edition limited to 1,000 sets. Made in 1976.

78 SINGLE-SHOT RIFLE
Falling-block lever-action similar to Winchester 1885 High Wall single-shot rifle. Calibers: .22-250, 6mm Rem., .243 Win., .25-06, 7mm Rem. Mag., .30-06, .45-70 Govt. 26-inch octagon or heavy round bbl.; 24-inch octagon bull bbl. on .45-70 model. Weight: 7.75 lbs. w/octagon bbl.; w/round bbl., 8.5 lbs.; .45-70, 8.75 lbs. Furnished w/o sights except .45-70 model w/open rear sight, blade front. Checkered fancy walnut stock and forearm. .45-70 model w/straight-grip stock and curved buttplate; others have Monte Carlo comb and cheekpiece, pistol-grip w/cap, recoil pad. Made 1973-83 by Miroku. Reintroduced in 1985 as Model 1885.
All calibers except .45-70 . . . . NiB $772 Ex $644 Gd $402
.45-70 . . . . NiB $850 Ex $669 Gd $412

Browning Model 1885
High-Wall Single-Shot

Browning Model 1885
High-Wall Traditional Hunter

Browning Model 1885
Low-Wall Single-Shot

Browning Model 1885
BPCR Single-Shot

RIFLES

MODEL 1885 SINGLE-SHOT RIFLE
Calibers: .22 Hornet, .223, .243, (Low Wall); .357 Mag., .44 Mag., .45 LC (L/W Traditional Hunter); .22-250, .223 Rem., .270 Win., 7mm Rem. Mag., .30-06, .454 Casull Mag., .45.70 (High Wall); .30.30 Win., .38-55 WCF, .45 Govt. (H/W Traditional Hunter); .40-65, .45 Govt. and .45.90 (BPCR). 24-, 28-, 30 or 34-inch round, octagonal or octagonal and round bbl. 39.5, 43.5, 44.25 or 46.125 inches overall. Weight: 6.25, 8.75, 9, 11, or 11.75 lbs. respectively. Blued or color casehardened receiver. Gold-colored adj. trigger. Drilled and tapped for scope mounts w/no sights or vernier tang rear sight w/globe front and open sights on .45-70 Govt. Walnut straight-grip stock and Schnabel forearm w/cut checkering and high-gloss or oil finish. Made 1985 to date.
Low Wall model w/o sights (Intro. 1995) . . NiB $772 Ex $669 Gd $438
Traditional Hunter model (Intro. 1998) . . . NiB $927 Ex $875 Gd $489
High Wall model w/o sights (Intro. 1985) . . . . NiB $721 Ex $566 Gd $412
Traditional Hunter model (Intro. 1997) . . NiB $1004 Ex $798 Gd $463
BPCR model w/no
ejector (Intro. 1996) . . . . NiB $1596 Ex $1287 Gd $922
BPCR Creedmoor Model .45-90
(Intro. 1998) . . . . NiB $1596 Ex $1236 Gd $875

MODEL 1886 MONTANA
CENTENNIAL RIFLE . . . . NiB $1905 Ex $1535 Gd $953
Same general specifications as Model 1886 High Grade lever-action except w/specially engraved receiver designating Montana Centennial; also different stock design. Made in 1986 in limited issue by Miroku.

MODEL 1886 GRADE I
LEVER-ACTION RIFLE . . . . NiB $1226 Ex $901 Gd $669
Caliber: .45-70 Govt., 8-round magazine. 26-inch octagonal bbl. 45 inches overall. Weight: 9 lbs., 5 oz. Deep blued finish on receiver. Open buckhorn sights. Straight-grip walnut stock. Classic-style forearm. Metal buttplate. Satin finish. Made in 1986 in limited issue 7,000 by Miroku.

MODEL 1886 HIGH-
GRADE LA RIFLE . . . . NiB $1493 Ex $1133 Gd $819
Same general specifications as the Model 1886 Grade I except receiver is grayed, steel embellished w/scroll; elk and American bison engraving. High-gloss stock. Made in 1986 in limited issue of 3,000 by Miroku.

MODEL 1895 GRADE I LA RIFLE . . . . NiB $772 Ex $721 Gd $669
Caliber: .30-06, .30-40 Krag. Four shot magazine. 24-inch round bbl. 42 inches overall. Weight: 8 lbs. French walnut stock and Schnabel forend. Sights: Rear buckhorn; gold bead on elevated ramp front. Made in 1984 in limited issue of 8,000 (2,000 chambered for .30-40 Krag and 6,000 chambered for .30-06). Mfd. by Miroku.

MODEL 1895 HIGH-
GRADE LA RIFLE. . . . . NiB $1390 Ex $1236 Gd $875
Same general specifications as Model 1895 Grade I except engraved receiver and Grade III French walnut stock and forend w/fine checkering. Made in 1985 in limited issue of 1000 in each caliber by

Browning Model 1886
Grade I

Browning Model 1886
High-Grade

Browning Model 1895
Grade I

Browning
A-Bolt Eclipse

MODEL A-BOLT .22 RIFLE
Calibers: .22 LR. .22 Magnum. 5- and 15-shot magazines. 22-inch round bbl. 40.25 inches overall. Weight: 5 lbs., 9 oz. Gold-colored adj. trigger. Laminated walnut stock w/checkering. Rosewood forend grip cap; pistol grip. With or w/o sights. Ramp front and adj. folding leaf rear on open sight model. 22 LR made 1985-96; 22 Magnum, 1990-96.

Grade I .22 LR . . . . NiB $360 Ex $275 Gd $191
Grade I .22 Magnum . . . . NiB $438 Ex $355 Gd $206
Deluxe Grade
Gold Medallion . . . . NiB $541 Ex $412 Gd $299

MODEL A-BOLT ECLIPSE BOLT RIFLE
Same general specifications as Hunter Grade except fitted w/gray and black laminated thumbhole stock. Available in both short and long action w/two bbl. configurations w/BOSS. Mfd. by Miroku 1996 to date.

Eclipse w/standard bbl. . . . . NiB $875 Ex $747 Gd $608
Eclipse Varmint w/heavy bbl. . . . . NiB $1025 Ex $875 Gd $747
Eclipse M-1000
(Target .300 Win. Mag.) . . . . NiB $1184 Ex $917 Gd $669

MODEL A-BOLT EURO-BOLT RIFLE
Same general specifications as Hunter Grade except w/checkered satin-finished walnut stock. W/continental-style cheekpiece, palm-swell grip and Schnabel forend. Mannlicher-style spoon bolt handle and contoured bolt shroud. 22- or 26-inch bbl. w/satin blued finish. Weight: 6.8 to 7.4 lbs. Calibers: .22-250 Rem., .243 Win., .270 Win., .30.06, .308 Win., 7mm Rem. Mag. Mfd. by Miroku 1993-94; 1994-96 (Euro-Bolt II).

Euro-Bolt . . . . NiB $608 Ex $463 Gd $304
Euro-Bolt II . . . . NiB $644 Ex $566 Gd $407
BOSS option, add $90

MODEL A-BOLT HUNTER GRADE RIFLE
Calibers: .22 Hornet, .223 Rem., .22-250 Rem., .243 Win., .257 Roberts, 7mm-08 Rem., .308 Win., (short action) .25-06 Rem., .270 Win., .280 Rem., .284 Win., .30-06, 7mm Rem. Mag., .300 Win. Mag., .338 Win. Mag. Four-shot magazine (standard), 3-shot (magnum). 22-inch bbl. (standard), 24-inch (magnum). Weight: 7.5 lbs. (standard), 8.5 lbs. (magnum). With or w/o sights. Classic-style walnut stock. Produced in two action lengths w/nine locking lugs, fluted bolt w/60 degree rotation. Mfd. by Miroku 1985-93; 1994 to date (Hunter II).

Hunter . . . . NiB $618 Ex $566 Gd $402
Hunter II . . . . NiB $716 Ex $515 Gd $438
Hunter Micro . . . . NiB $721 Ex $566 Gd $463
BOSS option, add $90
Open sights, add $50

MODEL A-BOLT MEDALLION GRADE RIFLE
Same as Hunter Grade except w/high-gloss deluxe stock rosewood grip cap and forend; high-luster blued finish. Also in .375 H&H w/open sights. Left-hand models available in long action only. Mfd. by Miroku 1988-93; 1994 to date (Medallion II). Bighorn Sheep Ltd. Ed.

(600 made 1986, .270 Win.) . . . . NiB $1287 Ex $978 Gd $669
Gold Medallion Deluxe Grade . . . . NiB $676 Ex $541 Gd $368
Gold Medallion II Deluxe Grade . . . . NiB $701 Ex $561 Gd $382
Medallion, Standard Grade . . . . NiB $541 Ex $463 Gd $283
Medallion II, Standard Grade . . . . NiB $547 Ex $438 Gd $298
Medallion, .375 H&H . . . . NiB $917 Ex $695 Gd $412
Medallion II, .375 H&H . . . . NiB $927 Ex $669 Gd $463
Micro Medallion . . . . NiB $592 Ex $463 Gd $309
Micro Medallion II . . . . NiB $618 Ex $489 Gd $335
Pronghorn Antelope Ltd. Ed.
(500 made 1987, .243 Win.) . . . . NiB $1126 Ex $978 Gd $798
BOSS option, add $90

Browning A-Bolt .22

Browning A-Bolt
Euro-Bolt

Browning A-Bolt
Hunter

Browning A-Bolt
Hunter with BOSS

Browning A-Bolt
Medallion Custom Trophy

Browning A-Bolt
Medallion White Gold

Browning A-Bolt
Medallion

Browning A-Bolt
Medallion (Left-Handed)

RIFLES

Browning A-Bolt Composite Stalker

Browning A-Bolt Stainless Stalker

Browning BAR, Grade IV

Browning BAR, Grade V

MODEL A-BOLT STALKER RIFLE
Same general specifications as Model A-Bolt Hunter Rifle except w/checkered graphite-fiberglass composite stock and matte blued or stainless metal. Non-glare matte finish of all exposed metal surfaces. 3 models: Camo Stalker orig. w/multi-colored laminated wood stock, matte blued metal; Composite Stalker w/graphite-fiberglass stock, matte blued metal; w/composite stock, stainless metal. Mfd. by Miroku 1987-93; 1994 to date. (Stalker II).

Camo Stalker (orig. laminated stock)	NiB $566	Ex $407	Gd $232
Composite Stalker	NiB $608	Ex $463	Gd $335
Composite Stalker II	NiB $608	Ex $463	Gd $335
Stainless Stalker	NiB $644	Ex $541	Gd $438
Stainless Stalker II	NiB $669	Ex $566	Gd $463
Stainless Stalker, .375 H&H	NiB $818	Ex $695	Gd $566
BOSS option, add			$90
Left-hand model, add			$90

MODEL A-BOLT
VARMINT II RIFLE . . . . NiB $721 Ex $669 Gd $510
Same general specifications as Stalker model except w/22-inch heavy bbl. w/BOSS system and varmint-style black laminated wood stock. Calibers: .22-250, .223 or .308. No sights. Bright blue or satin finish. Mfd. by Miroku 1994 to date.

MODEL B-92 LEVER-ACTION RIFLE . . . . . NiB $463 Ex $402 Gd $206
Calibers: .357 Mag. and .44 Rem. Mag. 11-shot magazine. 20-inch round bbl. 37.5 inches overall. Weight: 5.5 to 6.4 lbs. Seasoned French walnut stock w/high gloss finish. Cloverleaf rear sight; steel post front. Made 1979-89 by Miroku.

BAR AUTOMATIC RIFLE,
GRADE I, STANDARD CALIBERS . . . . . NiB $711 Ex $541 Gd $386
Gas-operated semiautomatic. Calibers: .243 Win., .270 Win., .280 Rem., .308 Win., .30-06. Four-round box magazine. 22-inch bbl. Weight: 7.5 lbs. Folding leaf rear sight, hooded ramp front. French walnut stock and forearm checkered, QD swivels. Made 1967-92 by FN.

BAR, GRADE I, MAGNUM CALIBERS . . . . NiB $721 Ex $669 Gd $505
Same as BAR in standard calibers, except w/24-inch bbl.chambered 7mm Rem. Mag. or .300 Win. Mag. .338 Win. Mag. w/3-round box magazine and recoil pad. Weight: 8.5 lbs. Made 1969-92 by FN.

BAR, GRADE II
Same as Grade I except receiver engraved w/big-game heads (deer and antelope on standard-caliber rifles, ram and grizzly on Magnum-caliber) and scrollwork, higher grade wood. Made 1967-74 by FN.

Standard calibers	NiB $917	Ex $772	Gd $566
Magnum calibers	NiB $1025	Ex $747	Gd $510

BAR, GRADE III
Same as Grade I except receiver of grayed steel engraved w/big-game heads (deer and antelope on standard-caliber rifles, moose and elk on Magnum-caliber) framed in fine-line scrollwork, gold-plated trigger, stock and forearm of highly figured French walnut, hand-checkered and carved. Made 1971-74 by FN.

Standard calibers	NiB $978	Ex $917	Gd $515
Magnum calibers	NiB $1236	Ex $1159	Gd $644

BAR, GRADE IV
Same as Grade I except receiver of grayed steel engraved w/full detailed rendition of running deer and antelope on standard-caliber rifles, moose and elk on Magnum-caliber gold-plated trigger, stock and forearm of highly figured French walnut, hand checkered and carved. Made 1971-86 by FN.

Standard calibers	NiB $1610	Ex $1287	Gd $875
Magnum calibers	NiB $1867	Ex $1493	Gd $1016

BAR, GRADE V
Same as Grade I except receiver w/complete big-game scenes executed by a master engraver and inlaid w/18K gold (deer and antelope on standard-caliber rifles, moose and elk on Magnum caliber), gold-plated trigger, stock and forearm of finest French walnut, intricately hand-checkered and carved. Made 1971-74 by FN.

Standard calibers	NiB $3155	Ex $2523	Gd $1716
Magnum calibers	NiB $3605	Ex $2935	Gd $2008

Browning BAR
Mark II Safari

Browning BAR
Mark II Safari

Browning BAR .22

Browning BAR .22
('82 Model)

MODEL BAR MARK II SAFARI AUTOMATIC RIFLE
Same general specifications as standard BAR semiautomatic rifle, except w/redesigned gas and buffer systems, new bolt release lever, and engraved receiver. Made 1993 to date.

Standard calibers . . . . NiB $669 Ex $608 Gd $412
Magnum calibers. NiB $747 Ex $644 Gd $438
Lightweight (Alloy receiver
w/20-inch bbl.) . . . . NiB $592 Ex $505 Gd $309
BAR Mk II Grade III (intro. 1996). . . . . NiB $2163 Ex $1983 Gd $1133
BAR Mk II Grade IV (intro. 1996). . . . . NiB $2364 Ex $1725 Gd $1287
W/BOSS option, add $60
W/open sights, add $15

BAR .22 AUTOMATIC RIFLE
Semiautomatic. Caliber: .22 LR. Tubular magazine holds 15 rounds. 20.25-inch bbl. Weight: 6.25 lbs. Sights: Folding-leaf rear, gold bead front on ramp. Receiver grooved for scope mounting. French walnut pistol-grip stock and forearm checkered. Made 1977-85.

Grade I . . . . NiB $360 Ex $299 Gd $165
Grade II. . . . . NiB $438 Ex $402 Gd $206

BBR LIGHTNING BOLT-ACTION RIFLE . . . NiB $541 Ex $438 Gd $324
Bolt-action rifle w/short bolt throw of 60 degrees. Calibers: .25-06 Rem., .270 Win., .30-06, 7mm Rem. Mag., .300 Win. Mag. 24-inch bbl. Weight: 8 lbs. Made 1979-84.

BL-.22 LEVER-ACTION REPEATING RIFLE
Short-throw lever-action. Caliber: .22 LR, Long, Short. Tubular magazine holds 15 LR, 17 Long 22 Short. 20-inch bbl. Weight: 5 lbs. Sights: Folding leaf rear; bead front. Receiver grooved for scope

(cont'd.) BL .22 LEVER-ACTION REPEATING RIFLE
mounting. Walnut straight-grip stock and forearm, bbl. band. Made 1970 to date by Miroku.

Grade I . . . . NiB $335 Ex $201 Gd $134
Grade II
w/scroll engraving. . . . . NiB $360 Ex $232 Gd $165

BLR LEVER-ACTION REPEATING RIFLE
Calibers: (short action only) .243 Win., .308 Win., .358 Win. Four round detachable box magazine. 20-inch bbl. Weight: 7 lbs. Sights: Windage and elevation adj. open rear; hooded ramp front. Walnut straight-grip stock and forearm, checkered, bbl. band, recoil pad. Made 1966 by BAC/USA; 1969-73 by FN; 1974-80 by Miroku. Note: USA manufacture of this model was limited to prototypes and pre-production guns only and may be identified the "MADE IN USA" roll stamp on the bbl.

FN model. . . . . NiB $716 Ex $489 Gd $335
Miroku model . . . . NiB $438 Ex $309 Gd $206
USA model . . . . NiB $1133 Ex $978 Gd $566

BLR LIGHTNING MODEL
Lightweight version of the Browning BLR '81 w/forged alloy receiver and redesigned trigger group. Calibers: Short Action— .22-250 Rem., .223 Rem., .243 Win., 7mm-08 Rem., .308 Win.; Long Action— .270 Win., 7mm Rem. Mag., .30-06, .300 Win. Mag. Three or 4-round detachable box magazine. 20-, 22- or 24-inch bbl. Weight: 6.5 to 7.75 lbs. Pistol-grip style walnut stock and forearm, cut checkering and recoil pad. Made by Miroku 1995 to date.

BLR Lightning model short action. . . . . . . NiB $463 Ex $402 Gd $206
BLR Lightning model long action . . . . NiB $489 Ex $438 Gd $283

Browning BBR Lightning

Browning BL-.22, Grade I

Browning BPR Pump Rifle

BLR MODEL '81

Redesigned version of the Browning BLR. Calibers: .222-50 Rem., .243 Win., .308 Win., .358 Win; Long Action— .270 Win., 7mm Rem. Mag., .30-06. Fourround detachable box magazine. 20-inch bbl. Weight: 7 lbs. Walnut straight-grip stock and forearm, cut checkering, recoil pad. Made by Miroku 1981-95; Long Action intro. 1991.

BLR Model '81 short action	NiB $566	Ex $407	Gd $257
BLR Model '81 long action	NiB $608	Ex $412	Gd $299

BPR-22 PUMP RIFLE

Hammerless slide-action repeater. Specifications same as for BAR-.22, except also available chambered for .22 Magnum RF; magazine capacity, 11 rounds. Made 1977-82 by Miroku.

Model I	NiB $257	Ex $206	Gd $144
Model II	NiB $463	Ex $407	Gd $232

BPR PUMP RIFLE

Slide-action repeater based on proven BAR designs w/forged alloy receiver and slide that cams down to clear bbl. and receiver. Calibers: .243 Win., .308 Win., .270 Win., .30-06, 7mm Rem. Mag. .300 Win. Mag. Three or 4-round detachable box magazine. 22- or 24-inch bbl. w/ramped front sight and open adj. rear. Weight: 7.2 to 7.4 lbs. Made 1997 to date by Miroku.

BPR Model standard calibers	NiB $818	Ex $644	Gd $407
BPR Model magnum calibers	NiB $901	Ex $669	Gd $438

HIGH-POWER BOLT-ACTION
RIFLE, MEDALLION GRADE .... NiB $1699 Ex $1540 Gd $922
Same as Safari Grade except receiver and bbl. scroll engraved, ram's head engraved on floorplate; select walnut stock w/rosewood forearm tip, grip cap. Made 1961-74.

HIGH-POWER BOLT-ACTION
RIFLE, OLYMPIAN GRADE .... NiB $3708 Ex $3322 Gd $1802
Same as Safari Grade except bbl. engraved; receiver, trigger guard and floorplate satin chrome-plated and engraved w/game scenes appropriate to caliber; finest figured walnut stock w/rosewood forearm tip and grip cap, latter w/18K-gold medallion. Made 1961-74.

HIGH-POWER BOLT-ACTION RIFLE,
SAFARI GRADE, MEDIUM ACTION ..... NiB 1025$ Ex $772 Gd $541
Same as Standard except medium action. Calibers: .22-250, .243 Win., .264 Win. Mag., .284 Win. Mag., .308 Win. Bbl.: 22-inch lightweight bbl.; .22-250 and .243 also available w/24-inch heavy bbl. Weight: 6 lbs., 12 oz. w/lightweight bbl.; 7 lbs. 13 oz. w/heavy bbl. Made 1963-74 by Sako.

HIGH-POWER BOLT-ACTION RIFLE,
SAFARI GRADE, SHORT ACTION .... NiB $1025 Ex $772 Gd $541
Same as Standard except short action. Calibers: .222 Rem., .222 Rem. Mag. 22-inch lightweight or 24-inch heavy bbl. No sights. Weight: 6 lbs., 2 oz. w/lightweight bbl.; 7.5 lbs. w/heavy bbl. Made 1963-74 by Sako.

HIGH-POWER BOLT-ACTION RIFLE,
SAFARI GRADE, STANDARD ACTION .. NiB $1313 Ex $1025 Gd $819
Mauser-type action. Calibers: .270 Win., .30-06, 7mm Rem. Mag., .300 H&H Mag., .300 Win. Mag., .308 Norma Mag. .338 Win. Mag., .375 H&H Mag., .458 Win. Mag. Cartridge capacity: 6 rounds in .270, .30-06; 4 in Magnum calibers. Bbl. length: 22 in., in .270, .30-06; 24 in., in Magnum calibers. Weight: 7 lbs., 2 oz., in .270, .30-06; 8.25 lbs. in Mag. calibers. Folding leaf rear sight, hooded ramp front. Checkered stock w/pistol grip, Monte Carlo cheekpiece, QD swivels; recoil pad on Magnum models. Made 1959-74 by FN.

"T-BOLT" T-1 .22 REPEATING RIFLE

Straight-pull bolt action. Caliber: .22 LR. Five shot clip magazine. 24-inch bbl. Peep rear sight w/ramped blade front. Plain walnut stock w/pistol grip and laquered finish. Weight: 6 lbs. Also left-hand model. Made 1965-74 by FN.

Right-hand model	NiB $463	Ex $402	Gd $232
Left-hand model	NiB $489	Ex $407	Gd $232

"T-BOLT" T-2

Same as T-1 Model except w/checkered fancy figured walnut stock. Made 1966-74 by FN. (Reintroduced briefly during the late 1980's with oil-finished stock)

Original model	NiB $489	Ex $407	Gd $232
Reintroduced model	NiB $438	Ex $360	Gd $206

Browning
BL-22 II

Browning
BLR Model '81

Browning High-Power
Bolt-Action Rifle, Medallion Grade

Browning High-Power
Safari Grade Medium Action, Heavy Barrel

Browning High-Power
Safari Grade Short Action, Heavy Barrel

Browning High-Power
Safari Grade Standard Action

F.N. BROWNING FAL SEMIAUTOMATIC RIFLE

Same as F.N. FAL Semiautomatic Rifle. See F.N. listing for specifications. Sold by Browning for a brief period c. 1960.

F.N. FAL standard
model (G-series)..................... NiB $3862 Ex $2729 Gd $1931
F.N. FAL lightweight
model (G-series)..................... NiB $4661 Ex $4115 Gd $2575
F.N. FAL heavy bbl..
model (G-series)..................... NiB $7236 Ex $5948 Gd $4586
BAC FAL model...................... NiB $2961 Ex $2626 Gd $1638

BSA GUNS LTD. — Birmingham, England (Previously Imported by Samco Global Arms, BSA Guns Ltd and Precision Sports)

NO. 12 MARTINI SINGLE-SHOT
TARGET RIFLE................. NiB $592 Ex $463 Gd $335
Caliber .22 LR. 29-inch bbl. Weight: 8.75 lbs. Parker-Hale Model 7 rear sight and Model 2 front sight. Straight-grip stock, checkered forearm. Note: This model was also available w/open sights or w/BSA No. 20 and 30 sights. Made before WWII.

Browning "T-Bolt" T-1

Browning "T-Bolt" T-2

MODEL 12/15 MARTINI HEAVY .... NiB $613 Ex $463 Gd $299
Same as Standard Model 12/15 except w/extra heavy bbl., weighs 11 lbs.

MODEL 12/15 MARTINI
SINGLE-SHOT TARGET RIFLE ..... NiB $541 Ex $407 Gd $283
Caliber: .22 LR. 29-inch bbl. Weight: 9 lbs. Parker-Hale No. PH-7A rear sight and No. FS-22 front sight. Target stock w/high comb and cheekpiece, beavertail forearm. Note: This is a post-WWII model; however, a similar rifle, the BSA-Parker Model 12/15, was produced c. 1938.

NO. 13 MARTINI SINGLE-SHOT
TARGET RIFLE .... NiB $515 Ex $407 Gd $257
Caliber: .22 LR. Lighter version of the No.12 w/same general specifications except w/25-inch bbl., weighs 6.5lbs. Made before WWII.

NO. 13 SPORTING RIFLE
Same as No. 13 Target except fitted w/Parker-Hale "Sportarget" rear sight and bead front sight. Also available in .22 Hornet. Made before WWII.
.22 Long Rifle .... NiB $566 Ex $407 Gd $268
.22 Hornet .... NiB $772 Ex $613 Gd $407

MODEL 15 MARTINI
SINGLE-SHOT TARGET RIFLE .... NiB $541 Ex $407 Gd $257
Caliber: .22 LR. 29-inch bbl. Weight: 9.5 lbs. BSA No. 30 rear sight and No. 20 front sight. Target stock w/cheekpiece and pistol-grip, long, semi-beavertail forearm. Made before WWII.

CENTURION MODEL
MATCH RIFLE .... NiB $510 Ex $360 Gd $257
Same general specifications as Model 15 except w/"Centurion" match bbl. Made before WWII.

CF-2 BOLT-ACTION
HUNTING RIFLE .... NiB $412 Ex $335 Gd $201
Mauser-type action. Calibers: 7mm Rem. Mag., .300 Win. Mag. 3-shot magazine. 23.6-inch bbl. Weight: 8 lbs. Sights: Adj. rear; hooded ramp front. Checkered walnut stock w/Monte Carlo comb, rollover cheekpiece, rosewood forend tip, recoil pad, sling swivels. Made 1975-87. See Ithaca-BSA CF-2.

CF-2 STUTZEN RIFLE .... NiB $510 Ex $360 Gd $257
Calibers: .222 Rem., .22-250, .243 Win., .270 Win., .308 Win. .30-06. Four round capacity (5 in 222 Rem.). 20.6-inch bbl. 41.5 inches (approx.) overall length. Weight: 7.5 to 8 lbs. Williams front and rear sights. Hand-finished European walnut stock. Monte Carlo cheekpiece and Wundhammer palm swell. Double-set triggers. Importation disc. 1987.

CFT TARGET RIFLE .... NiB $818 Ex $613 Gd $438
Single-shot bolt action. Caliber: 7.62mm. 26.5-inch bbl. About 47.5 inches overall. Weight: 11 lbs., incl. accessories. Bbl. and action weight: 6 lbs., 12 oz. Importation disc. 1987.

MAJESTIC DELUXE FEATHERWEIGHT BOLT-ACTION HUNTING RIFLE
Mauser-type action. Calibers: .243 Win., .270 Win., .308 Win., .30-06, .458 Win. Mag. Four shot magazine. 22-inch bbl. w/BESA recoil re-ducer. Weight: 6.25 lbs.; 8.75 lbs. in 458. Folding leaf rear sight, hooded ramp front. Checkered European-style walnut stock w/cheekpiece, pistol-grip, Schnabel forend, swivels, recoil pad. Made 1959-65.
.458 Win. Mag. caliber .... NiB $566 Ex $438 Gd $283
Other calibers .... NiB $463 Ex $407 Gd $232

BSA MAJESTIC DELUXE
STANDARD WEIGHT .... NiB $438 Ex $257 Gd $175
Same as Featherweight model except heavier bbl. w/o recoil reducer. Calibers: .22 Hornet, .222 Rem., .243 Win., 7x57mm, .308 Win., .30-06. Weight: 7.25 to 7.75 lbs. Disc.

MARTINI-INTERNATIONAL
ISU MATCH RIFLE .... NiB $953 Ex $721 Gd $479
Similar to MK III, but modified to meet International Shooting Union "Standard Rifle" specifications. 28-inch standard weight bbl. Weight: 10.75 lbs. Redesigned stock and forearm, latter attached to bbl. w/"V" section alloy strut. Intro. 1968. Disc.

MARTINI-INTERNATIONAL
MARK V MATCH RIFLE .... NiB $978 Ex $747 Gd $510
Same as ISU model except w/heavier bbl. Weight: 12.25 lbs. Intro. 1976. Disc.

MARTINI-INTERNATIONAL
MATCH RIFLE SINGLE-SHOT
HEAVY PATTERN .... NiB $695 Ex $541 Gd $438
Caliber: .22 LR. 29-inch heavy bbl. Weight: 14 lbs. Parker-Hale "International" front and rear sights. Target stock w/full cheekpiece and pistol-grip, broad beavertail forearm, handstop, swivels. Right- or left-hand models. Mfd. 1950-53.

MARTINI-INTERNATIONAL
MATCH RIFLE — LIGHT PATTERN .... NiB $669 Ex $541 Gd $412
Same general specifications as Heavy Pattern except w/26-inch lighter weight bbl. Weight: 11 lbs. Disc.

MARTINI-INTERNATIONAL
MK II MATCH RIFLE .... NiB $875 Ex $566 Gd $438
Same general specifications as original model. Heavy and Light Pattern. Improved trigger mechanism and ejection system. Redesigned stock and forearm. Made 1953-59.

MARTINI-INTERNATIONAL
MK III MATCH RIFLE .... NiB $978 Ex $747 Gd $509
Same general specifications as MK II Heavy Pattern. Longer action frame w/I-section alloy strut to which forearm is attached; bbl. is fully floating. Redesigned stock and forearm. Made 1959-67.

BSA
Model 12/15 Martini

BSA
Model 15 Martini

BSA CFT Target

BSA
Martini-International ISU Match

BSA
Martini-International Mark V Match

BSA
Martini-International MK III Match

RIFLES

MONARCH DELUXE BOLT-ACTION
HUNTING RIFLE . . . . **NiB $335 Ex $299 Gd $201**
Same as Majestic Deluxe Standard Weight model except w/redesigned
stock of U.S. style w/contrasting hardwood forend tip and grip cap.
Calibers: .222 Rem., .243 Win., .270 Win., 7mm Rem. Mag., .308
Win., .30-06. 22-inch bbl. Weight: 7 to 7.25 lbs. Made 1965-74.

MONARCH DELUXE
VARMINT RIFLE . . . . **NiB $438 Ex $360 Gd $232**
Same as Monarch Deluxe except w/24-inch heavy bbl. and weighs
9 lbs. Calibers: .222 Rem., .243 Win. See illustration next page.

BUSHMASTER FIREARMS —
(Quality Parts Company), Windham, Maine

M17S BULLPUP . . . . **NiB $850 Ex $716 Gd $489**
Caliber: .223. 21.5-inch bbl. Weight: 8.2 lbs. Polymer stocks.
Handle w/fixed open sights w/Weaver-type rail for any optics.
Semi-auto, self-compensating short stroke gas piston. Forward trig-
ger/grip w/rear chamber. Bullpup style. Alloy receiver. Synthetic
lower receiver is hinged to upper w/hinged takedown system.
Accepts M-16 type magazines. Made 1992 to date.

BSA Monarch Deluxe Varmint

MODEL XM15 E2S SERIES
Caliber: .223. 16-, 20-, 24- or 26-inch bbl. Weight: 7 to 8.6 lbs. Polymer stocks. Adjustable sights w/dual flip-up aperture; optional flattop rail accepts scope. Direct gas-operated w/rotating bolt. Forged alloy receiver. All steel-coated w/manganese phosphate. Accepts M-16 type magazines. Made 1989 to date.
XM15 E2S Carbine. . . . . NiB $1081 Ex $901 Gd $644
XM15 E2S Target Rifle . . . . NiB $1133 Ex $850 Gd $592

CALICO LIGHT WEAPONS SYSTEMS — Bakersville, California

LIBERTY 50/100 SEMIAUTOMATIC RIFLE
Retarded blowback action. Caliber: 9mm. 50- or 100-shot helical-feed magazine. 16.1-inch bbl. 34.5 inches overall. Weight: 7 lbs. Adjustable post front sight and aperture rear. Ambidextrous rotating safety. Glass-filled polymer or thumbhole-style wood stock. Made 1995 to date.
Model Liberty 50. . . . . NiB $739 Ex $586 Gd $331
Model Liberty 100. . . . . NiB $816 Ex $790 Gd $408

MODEL M-100 SEMIAUTOMATIC SERIES
Similar to the Liberty 100 Model except chambered for .22 LR. Weight: 5 lbs. 34.5 inches overall. Folding or glass-filled polymer stock and forearm. Made 1986 to date.
Model M-100 w/folding
stock (disc. 1994). . . . . NiB $433 Ex $296 Gd $153
Model M-100 FS w/fixed
stock (1996) . . . . NiB $607 Ex $408 Gd $280

MODEL M-105
SEMI-AUTOMATIC SPORTER . . . . . NiB $301 Ex $229 Gd $153
Similar to the Liberty 100 Model except fitted w/walnut buttstock and forearm. Made 1986 to date.

MODEL M-900 SEMIAUTOMATIC CARBINE
Caliber: 9mm Parabellum. 50- or 100-shot magazine. 16.1-inch bbl. 28.5 inches overall. Weight: 3.7 lbs. Post front sight adj. for windage and elevation, fixed notch rear. Collapsible steel buttstock and glass-filled polymer grip. Matte black finish. Made 1989-94.
Model M-100 w/folding
stock (disc. 1994) . . . . NiB $535 Ex $408 Gd $255
Model M-100 FS w/fixed
stock (Intro. 1996) . . . . NiB $505 Ex $357 Gd $229

MODEL M-951 TACTICAL CARBINE
Similar to Model 900 except w/long compensator and adj. forward grip. Made 1990-94.
Model 951. . . . . NiB $505 Ex $357 Gd $260
Model 951-S . . . . NiB $535 Ex $301 Gd $280

CANADIAN MILITARY RIFLES — Quebec, Canada, Manufactured by Ross Rifle Co.

MODEL 1907 MARK II
ROSS MILITARY RIFLE . . . . NiB $331 Ex $229 Gd $199
Straight-pull bolt action. Caliber: .303 British. 5-shot box magazine. 28-inch bbl. Weight: 8.5 lbs. Sights: adj. rear; blade front. Military-type full stock. Note: The Ross was originally issued as a Canadian service rifle in 1907. There were several variations; it was the official weapon at the start of WWI, but has been obsolete for many years. For Ross sporting rifle, see listing under Ross Rifle company.

CENTURY INTERNATIONAL ARMS, INC. — Boca Raton, Florida; (Formerly St. Albans, Vermont)

CENTURION M38/M96 BOLT-ACTION SPORTER
Sporterized Swedish M38/96 Mauser action. Caliber: 6.5x55mm. 5-shot magazine. 24-inch bbl. 44 inches overall. Adj. rear sight. Blade front. Black synthetic or checkered European hardwood Monte Carlo stock. Holden Ironsighter see-through scope mount. Imported 1987 to date.
W/hardwood stock . . . . NiB $178 Ex $127 Gd $82
W/synthetic stock . . . . NiB $194 Ex $153 Gd $102

CENTURION M98 BOLT-ACTION SPORTER
Sporterized VZ24 or 98 Mauser action. Calibers: .270 Win., 7.62x39mm, .308 Win., .30-06. Five shot magazine. 22-inch bbl. 44 inches overall. Weight: 7.5 lbs. W/Millet or Weaver scope base(s), rings and no iron sights. Classic or Monte Carlo laminated hardwood, black synthetic or checkered European hardwood stock. Imported 1992 to date.
M98 Action W/black
synthetic stock (w/o rings). . . . . NiB $229 Ex $178 Gd $121
M98 Action W/hardwood
Stock (w/o rings) . . . . NiB $199 Ex $153 Gd $92
VZ24 Action W/laminated
Hardwood Stock (Elite) . . . . NiB $301 Ex $229 Gd $153
VZ24 Action W/black
synthetic stock . . . . NiB $287 Ex $229 Gd $156
W/Millet base and rings, add $25

CENTURION P-14 SPORTER
Sporterized P-14 action. Caliber: 7mm Rem. Mag., .300 Win. Mag. 5-shot magazine. 24-inch bbl. 43.4 inches overall. Weight: 8.25 lbs. Weaver-type scope base. Walnut stained hardwood or fiberglass stock. Imported 1987 to date.
W/hardwood stock . . . . NiB $219 Ex $178 Gd $117
W/fiberglass stock . . . . NiB $255 Ex $178 Gd $127

ENFIELD SPORTER 4 BOLT-ACTION RIFLE
Sporterized Lee-Enfield action. Caliber: .303 British. 10-shot magazine. 25.25-inch bbl. 44.5 inches overall. Blade front sight, adj. aperture rear. Sporterized beechwood military stock or checkered walnut Monte Carlo stock. Blued finish. Imported 1987 to date.
W/sporterized military stock . . . . NiB $127 Ex $97 Gd $56
W/checkered walnut stock . . . . NiB $178 Ex $153 Gd $97

Chipmunk Bolt-Action
Single-Shot

L1A1 FAL SPORTER . . . . **NiB $841 Ex $663 Gd $505**
Sporterized L1A1 FAL semiautomatic. Caliber: .308 Win. 20.75-inch
bbl. 41 inches overall. Weight: 9.75 lbs. Protected front post sight,
adj. aperture rear. Matte blued finish. Black or camo Bell & Carlson
thumbhole sporter stock w/rubber buttpad. Imported 1988-98.

M-14 SPORTER . . . . **NiB $403 Ex $281 Gd $178**
Sporterized M-14 gas operated semiautomatic action. Caliber: .308
Win. 10-shot magazine. 22-inch bbl. 41 inches overall. Weight:
8.25 lbs. Blade front sight, adj. aperture rear sight. Parkerized finish.
Walnut stock w/rubber recoil pad. Forged receiver. Imported 1991
to date.

TIGER DRAGUNOV . . . . **NiB $3570 Ex 2626 Gd $1249**
Russian SVD semiautomatic sniper rifle. Caliber: 7.62x54R. 5-shot
magazine. 21-inch bbl. 43 inches overall. Weight: 8.5 lbs. Blade
front sight, open rear adj. for elevation. Blued finish. European laminated hardwood thumbhole stock. 4x range-finding scope w/light-
ed reticle and sunshade. Quick detachable scope mount. Imported
1994-95.

CHARTER ARMS CORPORATION — Stratford, Connecticut

AR-7 EXPLORER
SURVIVAL RIFLE . . . . **NiB $127 Ex $92 Gd $61**
Same as Armalite AR-7, except w/black, instead of brown, "wood
grain" plastic stock. See listing of that rifle for specifications. Made
1973-90.

CHIPMUNK RIFLES — Prospect, Oregon MFD. by Rogue Rifle Company (Formerly Oregon Arms Company and Chipmunk Manufacturing, Inc.)

BOLT-ACTION SINGLE-SHOT RIFLE
Calibers: .22 LR. or .22 WMR. 16.13-inch standard or 18.13-inch
bull bbl. Weight: 2.5 lbs. (standard) or 4 lbs. (Bull bbl.) Peep sight
rear; ramp front. Plain or checkered American walnut, laminated or
black hardwood stock. Made 1982 to date.
Standard model
w/plain walnut stock . . . . **NiB $163 Ex $107 Gd $61**
Standard model
w/black hardwood stock . . . . **NiB $143 Ex $97 Gd $61**
Standard model
w/camouflage stock. **NiB $173 Ex $127 Gd $76**
Standard model w/laminated stock . . . . **NiB $159 Ex $127 Gd $87**
Deluxe grade
w/checkered walnut stock. . . . . **NiB $229 Ex $173 Gd $107**
.22 WMR, add **$20**

Charter Arms AR-7 Explorer Survival Rifle
(Disassembled and Stowed in Stock)

CHURCHILL RIFLES — Mfd. in England.
*Imported by Ellett Brothers, Inc., Chapin, SC
(Previously by Kassnar Imports, Inc.)*

HIGHLANDER BOLT-ACTION RIFLE . . . . **NiB $451 Ex $360 Gd $245**
Calibers: .243 Win., .25-06 Rem., .270 Win., .308 Win., .30-06, 7mm Rem. Mag.,
.300 Win. Mag. Four shot magazine (standard); 3-shot (magnum). Bbl. length: 22-
inch (standard); 24-inch (magnum). 42.5 to 44.5 inches overall. Weight: 7.5 lbs.
Adj. rear sight, blade front. Checkered European walnut pistol-grip stock. Imported
1986-91.

"ONE OF ONE THOUSAND" RIFLE . . . . . . **NiB $2575 Ex $2055 Gd $917**
Made for Interarms to commemorate that firm's 20th anniversary.
Mauser-type action. Calibers: .270, 7mm Rem. Mag., .308, .30-06,
.300 Win. Mag., .375 H&H Mag., .458 Win. Mag. Five shot magazine (3-shot in Magnum calibers). 24-inch bbl. Weight: 8 lbs.
Classic-style French walnut stock w/cheekpiece, black forend tip,
checkered pistol grip and forearm, swivel-mounted recoil pad w/car-
tridge trap, pistol-grip cap w/trap for extra front sight, barrel-mounted sling swivel. Limited issue of 1,000 rifles made in 1973. See illustration next page.

REGENT BOLT-ACTION RIFLE . . . . **NiB $566 Ex $510 Gd $386**
Calibers: .243 Win., .25-06 Rem., .270 Win., .308 Win., .30-06, 7mm
Rem. Mag., .300 Win. Mag. Four shot magazine. 22-inch round bbl.
42.5 inches overall. Weight: 7.5 lbs. Ramp front sight w/gold bead;
adj. rear. Hand-checkered Monte Carlo-style stock of select European
walnut; recoil pad. Made 1986-90. See illustration next page.

CIMARRON ARMS — Fredericksburg, Texas

1860 HENRY LEVER-ACTION
Replica of 1860 Henry w/original Henry loading system. Calibers: .44-
40, .44 Special, .45 Colt. 13-shot magazine. 22-inch bbl. (carbine) or
24.25-inch bbl. (rifle). 43 inches overall (rifle). Weight: 9.5 lbs. (rifle).
Bead front sight, open adj. rear. Brass receiver and buttplate. Smooth
European walnut buttstock. Imported 1991 to date.
Carbine model. . . . . **NiB $875 Ex $716 Gd $438**
Rifle model . . . . **NiB $901 Ex $644 Gd $463**
Civil War model
(U.S. issue martially marked). . . . . . **NiB $901 Ex $736 Gd $489**
W/A-engraving, add. **$395**

Churchill "One of One Thousand"

Churchill Regent

1866 YELLOWBOY LEVER-ACTION
Replica of 1866 Winchester. Calibers: .22 LR, 22WMR, .38 Special, .44-40, .45 Colt. 16-inch round bbl. (Trapper), 19-inch round bbl. (Carbine) or 24.25-inch ocatagonal bbl. (rifle). 43 inches overall (rifle). Weight: 9 lbs. (rifle). Bead front sight, open adj. rear. Brass receiver, buttplate and forend cap. Smooth European walnut stock. Imported 1991 to date.

Carbine	NiB $695	Ex $541	Gd $335
Rifle	NiB $818	Ex $566	Gd $360
Indian model (disc.)	NiB $669	Ex $541	Gd $335
Trapper Model (.44-40 WCF only, disc.)	NiB $541	Ex $412	Gd $258
W/A-engraving, add			$425
W/B-engraving, add			$595
W/C-engraving, add			$995

1873 LEVER-ACTION
Replica of 1873 Winchester. Calibers: .22 LR. .22WMR, .357 Magnum, .44-40 or .45 Colt. 16-inch round bbl. (Trapper), 19-inch round bbl. (SRC), 20-inch octagonal bbl. (short rifle), 24.25-inch octagonal bbl. (sporting rifle) and 30-inch octagonal bbl. (express rifle). 43 inches overall (sporting rifle). Weight: 8 lbs. Fixed blade front sight, adj. semi-buckhorn rear or tang peep sight. Walnut stock and forend. Color case-hardened receiver. Imported 1989 to date.

Express Rifle	NiB $875	Ex $644	Gd $463
Short Rifle (disc.)	NiB $850	Ex $592	Gd $402
Sporting Rifle	NiB $721	Ex $566	Gd $381
SRC Carbine	NiB $747	Ex $566	Gd $386
Trapper (disc.)	NiB $613	Ex $489	Gd $299
One of 1000 engraved model	NiB $2214	Ex $1802	Gd $1133

1874 FALLING BLOCK SPORTING RIFLE
Replica of 1874 Sharps Sporting Rifle. Calibers: .45-65, .45-70, .45-90 or .45-120. 32- or 34-inch round or octagonal bbl. Weight: 9.5 to 10 lbs. Blade or globe front sight w/adj. open rear or sporting tang peep sight. Single or double set triggers. Checkered walnut stock and forend w/nose cap. Color case-hardened receiver. Imported 1997 to date.

1874 Sporting Rifle - Billy Dixon Model	NiB $1081	Ex $978	Gd $742
1874 Sporting Rifle - Quigley Model	NiB $1493	Ex $1313	Gd $772
Sharps Sporting No. 1 Rifle	NiB $1025	Ex $798	Gd $541

CLERKE RECREATION PRODUCTS — Santa Monica, California

DELUXE HI-WALL .... **NiB $367 Ex $296 Gd $199**
Same as standard model, except w/adj. trigger, half-octagon bbl., select wood, stock w/cheekpiece and recoil pad. Made 1972-74.

HI-WALL
SINGLE-SHOT RIFLE .... **NiB $357 Ex $301 Gd $178**
Falling-block lever-action similar to Winchester 1885 High Wall S.S. Color casehardened investment-cast receiver. Calibers: .222 Rem., .22-250, .243 Rem., 6mm Rem., .25-06, .270 Win., 7mm Rem. Mag., .30-06, .45-70 Govt. 26-inch medium-weight bbl. Weight: 8 lbs. Furnished w/o sights. Checkered walnut pistol-grip stock and Schnabel forearm. Made 1972-74.

CLIFTON ARMS — Medina, Texas

SCOUT BOLT-ACTION RIFLE
Custom rifle built on the Dakota .76, Ruger .77 or Winchester .70 action. Shilen match-grade barrel cut and chambered to customer's specification. Clifton composite stock fitted and finished to customer's preference. Made 1992-97.

African Scout	NiB $3605	Ex $2935	Gd $2261
Pseudo Scout	NiB $3476	Ex $2055	Gd $1262
Standard Scout	NiB $3450	Ex $2008	Gd $1236
Super Scout	NiB $3579	Ex $2858	Gd $1313

COLT INDUSTRIES, FIREARMS DIVISION — Hartford, Connecticut

NOTE: *On Colt AR-15 Sporter models currently produced (i.e., Competition H-BAR, Sporter Match Target Lightweight, and Sporter Target Rifle), add $200 to pre-ban models made prior to 10-13-94.*

AR-15 A2 DELTA
MATCH H-BAR RIFLE .... **NiB $1648 Ex $1571 Gd $1339**
Similar to AR-15A2 Government Model except w/standard stock and heavy refined bbl. Furnished w/3-9x rubber armored scope and removeable cheekpiece. Made 1986-91.

AR-15 A2 GOVERNMENT
MODEL CARBINE .... **NiB $2189 Ex $1854 Gd $1025**
Caliber: .223 Rem., 5-shot magazine. 16-inch bbl. w/flash suppressor. 35 inches overall. Weight: 5.8 lbs. Telescoping aluminum buttstock; sling swivels. Made 1985-91.

Colt AR-15 A2

Colt AR-15 A2 Delta Match H-BAR

Colt AR-15 A2 Government Model

Colt AR-15 Sporter Competition H-BAR

AR-15 A2 SPORTER II . . . . NiB $1287 Ex $1133 Gd $1025
Same general specifications as standard AR-15 Sporter except heavier bbl., improved pistol-grip. Weight 7.5 lbs.; optional 3x or 4x scope. Made 1985-89.

AR-15 COMPACT 9MM CARBINE . . . . NiB $1699 Ex $1442 Gd $1030
Semiautomatic. Caliber: 9mm NATO. 20-round detachable magazine. Bbl.: 16-inch round. Weight: 6.3 lbs. Adj. rear and front sights. Adj. buttstock. Ribbed round handguard. Made 1985-86.

Colt Stagecoach

Colteer 1-.22

Colteer .22 Autoloader

Coltsman Deluxe

Coltsman 1957 Standard

AR-15 SEMIAUTOMATIC SPORTER
Commercial version of U.S. M16 rifle. Gas-operated. Takedown. Caliber: .223 Rem. (5.56mm). 20-round magazine w/spacer to reduce capacity to 5 rounds. 20-inch bbl. w/flash suppressor. Sights: Rear peep w/windage adjustment in carrying handle; front adj. for windage. 3x scope and mount optional. Black molded buttstock of high-impact synthetic material, rubber buttplate. Barrel surrounded by handguard of black fiberglass w/heat-reflecting inner shield. Swivels, black web sling strap. Weight: w/o accessories, 6.3 lbs. Made 1964-94.
Standard Sporter . . . . NiB $1281 Ex 1025 Gd $697
W/adj. stock, redesigned
forearm (disc. 1988), add $200
W/3x scope and mount, add. $100

AR-15 SPORTER
COMPETITION
H-BAR RIFLE . . . . NiB $1287 Ex 1025 Gd $644
Similar to AR-15 Sporter Target model except w/integral Weaver-type mounting system on a flat-top receiver. 20-inch bbl. w/counter-bored muzzle and 1:9 rifling twist. Made 1991 to date.

AR-15 SPORTER
COMPETITION H-BAR (RS) . . . . NiB $1674 Ex $1339 Gd $819
Similar to AR-15 Sporter Competition H-BAR Model except "Range Selected" for accuracy w/3x9 rubber-clad scope w/mount. Carrying handle w/iron sights. Made 1992-94.

AR-15 SPORTER MATCH TARGET LIGHTWEIGHT
Calibers: .223 Rem., 7.62x39mm, 9mm. 5-shot magazine. 16-inch bbl. (non-threaded after 1994). 34.5-35.5 inches overall. Weight: 7.1 lbs. Redesigned stock and shorter handguard. Made 1991 to date.
Standard LW Sporter (except 9mm) . . . . . NiB $1025 Ex $772 Gd $525
Standard LW Sporter, 9mm . . . . NiB $953 Ex $669 Gd $463
.22 LR conversion (disc. 1994), add $175

AR-15 SPORTER TARGET RIFLE
Caliber: .223 Rem. 5-shot magazine. 20-inch bbl. w/flash suppressor (non-threaded after 1994). 39 inches overall. Weight: 7.5 lbs. Black composition stock, grip and handguard. Sights: post front; adj. aperture rear. Matte black finish. Made 1993 to date.
Sporter Target Rifle . . . . NiB $1133 Ex $953 Gd $618
.22 LR conversion (disc. 1994), add $200

LIGHTNING MAGAZINE RIFLE - LARGE FRAME
Similar to Medium Frame model except w/large frame to accommodate larger calibers: .38-56, .44-60, .45-60, .45-65, .45-85, or .50-95 Express. Standard 22-inch (carbine & baby carbine) or 28-inch round or octagonal bbl. (rifle). Note: Additional bbl. lengths optional. Weight: 8 to 10.5 lbs. Sights: Open rear; bead or blade front. Walnut stock and checkered forearm. Made 1887-94. (6,496 produced)
Rifle . . . . NiB $4120 Ex $3064 Gd $2163
Carbine . . . . NiB $8137 Ex $6180 Gd $4120
Baby Carbine . . . . NiB $10,293 Ex $8234 Gd $5600
.50-95 Express, add 35%

Coltsman 1961 Custom

Coltsman 1961 Standard

Colt-Sauer Grand African

RIFLES

LIGHTNING MAGAZINE RIFLE - MEDIUM FRAME
Slide-action w/12-shot tubular magazine Carbine & Baby Carbine) or 15-shot tubular magazine (rifle). Calibers: .32-20, .38-40, .44-40. Standard 20-inch (Carbine & Baby Carbine) or 26-inch round or octagonal bbl.(rifle). Note: Additional bbl. lengths optional. Weight: 5.5 lbs. (Baby Carbine), 6.25 lbs. (carbine) or 7 to 9 lbs. (rifle). Sights: Open rear; bead or blade front. Walnut stock and checkered forearm. Blue finish w/color casehardened hammer. Made 1884-1902. (89,777 produced)

Rifle . . . . NiB $2266 Ex $1699 Gd $1133
Carbine . . . . NiB $3605 Ex $2755 Gd $1880
Baby Carbine . . . . NiB $5150 Ex $4017 Gd $2781
Military model
w/bayonet
lug & sling swivels . . . . NiB $4957 Ex $3553 Gd $2416

LIGHTNING MAGAZINE RIFLE - SMALL FRAME
Similar to Medium Frame model except w/smaller frame and chambered for .22 caliber only. Standard 24-inch round or octagonal bbl. w/half magazine. Note: Additional bbl. lengths optional. Weight: 6 lbs. Sights: Open rear; bead or blade front. Walnut stock and checkered forearm. Made 1884-1902. (89,912 produced)

Standard Rifle model . . . . NiB $1354 Ex $1025 Gd $695
W/Deluxe or optional features, add **20%**

STAGECOACH .22 AUTOLOADER . . . . NiB $360 Ex $283 Gd $154
Same as Colteer .22 Autoloader except w/engraved receiver, saddle ring, 16.5-inch bbl. Weight: 4 lbs., 10 oz. Made 1965-75.

1-.22 SINGLE-SHOT
BOLT-ACTION RIFLE . . . . NiB $309 Ex $232 Gd $154
Caliber: .22 LR. Long, Short. 20- or 22-inch bbl. Sights: Open rear; ramp front. Pistol-grip stock w/Monte Carlo comb. Weight: 5 lbs. Made 1957-67.

.22 AUTOLOADER . . . . NiB $309 Ex $232 Gd $154
Caliber: .22 LR. 15-round tubular magazine. 19.38-inch bbl. Sights: Open rear; hooded ramp front. Straight-grip stock, Western carbine-style forearm w/bbl. band. Weight: 4.75 lbs. Made 1964-75.

CUSTOM BOLT-ACTION
SPORTING RIFLE . . . . NiB $515 Ex $407 Gd $257
FN Mauser action, side safety, engraved floorplate. Calibers: .30-06, .300 H&H Mag. Five shot box magazine. 24-inch bbl., rampfront sight. Fancy walnut stock. Monte Carlo comb, cheekpiece, pistol-grip, checkered, QD swivels. Weight: 7.25 lbs. Made 1957-61.

DELUXE RIFLE . . . . NiB $875 Ex $669 Gd $463
FN Mauser action. Same as Custom model, except plain floorplate, plainer wood and checkering. Made 1957-61. Value shown is for rifle as furnished by manufacturer w/o rear sight.

MODELS OF 1957 RIFLES
Sako medium action. Calibers: .243, .308. Weight: 6.75 lbs. Other specifications similar to those of models w/FN actions. Made 1957-61.
Custom . . . . NiB $824 Ex $618 Gd $412
Deluxe . . . . NiB $824 Ex $644 Gd $412
Standard . . . . NiB $669 Ex $412 Gd $335

MODEL OF 1961,
CUSTOM RIFLE . . . . NiB $644 Ex $489 Gd $309
Sako action. Calibers: .222, .222 Mag., .223, .243, .264, .270, .308, .30-06, .300 H&H. 23-, 24-inch bbl. Sights: Folding leaf rear; hooded ramp front. Fancy French walnut stock w/Monte Carlo comb, rosewood forend tip and grip cap skip checkering, recoil pad, sling swivels. Weight: 6.5 - 7.5 lbs. Made 1963-65.

MODEL OF 1961, STANDARD RIFLE . . . . . NiB $644 Ex $515 Gd $335
Same as Custom model except plainer, American walnut stock. Made 1963-65.

STANDARD RIFLE . . . . NiB $618 Ex $463 Gd $309
FN Mauser action. Same as Deluxe model except in .243, .30-06, .308, .300 Mag. and stock w/o cheekpiece, bbl. length 22 inches. Made 1957-61. Value shown is for rifle as furnished by manufacturer w/o rear sight.

COLT-SAUER DRILLINGS See Colt shotgun listings.

Colt-Sauer Grand Alaskan

Colt-Sauer Short Action

Cooper Arms — Model 22 Pro Varmint

GRAND AFRICAN . . . . NiB $1854 Ex $1442 Gd $953
Same specifications as standard model except .458 Win. Mag., weight: 9.5 lbs. Sights: Adj. leaf rear; hooded ramp front. Magnum-style stock of Bubinga. Made 1973-85. See illustration previous page.

GRAND ALASKAN . . . . NiB $1854 Ex $1262 Gd $824
Same specifications as standard model except .375 H&H, weight: 8.5 lbs. Sights: Adj. leaf rear; hooded ramp front. Magnum-style stock of walnut.

MAGNUM . . . . NiB $1390 Ex $978 Gd $669
Same specifications as standard model except calibers 7mm Rem. Mag., .300 Win. Mag., .300 Weatherby. Weight: 8.5 lbs. Made 1973-85.

SHORT ACTION . . . . NiB $1236 Ex $953 Gd $644
Same specifications as standard model except shorter action chambered for the following calibers: .22-250, .243 Win., .308 Win. and similar length cartridges. Weight: 7.5 1bs.; 8.25 lbs. (.22-250). Drilled and tapped for scope mount. No front or rear open sights. Made 1973-88.

SPORTING RIFLE,
STANDARD MODEL . . . . NiB $1262 Ex $978 Gd $669
Sauer 80 non-rotating bolt action. Calibers: .25-06, .270 Win., .30-06. Three-round detachable box magazine. 24-inch bbl. Weight: 7.75 lbs., 8.5 lbs. (.25-06). Furnished w/o sights. American walnut stock w/Monte Carlo cheekpiece, checkered pistol grip and forearm, rosewood forend tip and pistol-grip cap, recoil pad. Made 1973-88.

COMMANDO CARBINES — Knoxville, Tennessee, (Formerly Volunteer Enterprises, Inc.)

MARK III SEMIAUTOMATIC CARBINE
Blow-back action, fires from closed bolt. Caliber: .45 ACP. 15- or 30-shot magazine. 16.5-inch bbl. w/cooling sleeve and muzzle brake. Weight: 8 lbs. Sights: peep rear; blade front. "Tommy Gun" style stock and forearm or grip. Made l969-76.
W/horizontal forearm . . . . NiB $438 Ex $335 Gd $232

MARK 9
Same specifications as Mark III and Mark 45 except caliber 9mm Luger. Made 1976-81.
W/horizontal forearm . . . . NiB $463 Ex $371 Gd $252
W/vertical foregrip . . . . NiB $483 Ex $386 Gd $263

MARK 45
Same specifications as Mark III. Has redesigned trigger housing and magazines. Made 1976-88.
W/horizontal forearm . . . . NiB $463 Ex $402 Gd $257
W/vertical f oregrip . . . . NiB $560 Ex $448 Gd $305

CONTINENTAL RIFLES — Manufactured in Belgium for Continental Arms, Corp., New York, N.Y.

DOUBLE RIFLE
Calibers: .270, .303 Sav., .30-40, .348 Win., .30-06, .375 H&H, .400 Jeffrey, .465, .470, .475 No. 2, .500, .600. Side-by-side. Anson-Deeley reinforced boxlock action w/triple bolting lever work. Two triggers. Nonautomatic safety. 24- or 26-inch bbls. Sights: Express rear; bead front. Checkered cheekpiece stock and forend. Weight: From 7 lbs., depending on caliber. Imported 1956-75.
Calibers: .270 to .348 Win. . . . . NiB $5118 Ex $4094 Gd $2784
Calibers: .375 H&H & larger . . . . NiB $6374 Ex $5098 Gd $3467

CZ Model ZKK 600

COOPER FIREARMS of MONTANA, INC. — (Previously COOPER ARMS), Stevensville, Montana

MODEL 21

Similar to Model 36C except in calibers .17 Rem., .17 Mach IV, .221 Fireball, .222, .223, 6x45, 6x47. 24-inch stainless or chrome-moly bbl. 43.5 inches overall. Weight: 8.75 lbs. Made 1994 to date.

21 Benchrest	NiB $1905	Ex $1596	Gd $1025
21 Classic	NiB $978	Ex $818	Gd $463
21 Custom Classic	NiB $1751	Ex $1133	Gd $515
21 Western Classic	NiB $1751	Ex $1133	Gd $515
21 Varminter	NiB $953	Ex $747	Gd $463
21 Varmint Extreme	NiB $1751	Ex $1025	Gd $747

MODEL 22

Bolt-action, single-shot. Calibers: .22 BR. .22-250 Rem., .220 Swift, .243 Win., 6mm PPC, 6.5x55mm, 25-06 Rem., 7.62x39mm 26-inch bbl, 45.63 inches overall. Weight: 8 lbs., 12 oz. Single-stage trigger. AAA Claro walnut stock. Made 1996 to date.

22 Benchrest	NiB $1802	Ex $1468	Gd $978
22 Classic	NiB $1751	Ex $1195	Gd $618
22 Custom Classic	NiB $1236	Ex $1133	Gd $772
22 Western Classic	NiB $1849	Ex $1231	Gd $824
22 Varminter	NiB $1030	Ex $819	Gd $515
22 Pro-Varmint Extreme	NiB $1741	Ex $1025	Gd $721
22 Black Jack	NiB $1741	Ex $1025	Gd $721

MODEL 36 RF/BR 50 . . . . NiB $1777 Ex $1133 Gd $747

Caliber: .22 LR. Bolt-action. Single-shot. 22-inch bbl. 40.5 inches overall. Weight: 6.8 lbs. No sights. Fully-adj. match-grade trigger. Stainless barrel. McMillan benchrest stock. Three mid-bolt locking lugs. Made 1994 to date.

MODEL 36 CF BOLT-ACTION RIFLE

Calibers: .17 CCM, .22 CCM, .22 Hornet. 4-shot mag. 23.75 inch bbl. 42.5 inch overall. Weight: 7 lbs. Walnut or synthetic stock. Made 1992-94.

Marksman	NiB $953	Ex $721	Gd $510
Sportsman	NiB $850	Ex $644	Gd $438
Classic Grade	NiB $1741	Ex $1025	Gd $747
Custom Grade	NiB $1030	Ex $824	Gd $566
Custom Classic Grade	NiB $1751	Ex $1133	Gd $772

MODEL 36 RF BOLT-ACTION RIFLE

Similar to Model 36CF except in caliber .22 LR. Five shot magazine. Weight: 6.5-7 lbs. Made 1992 to date.

BR-50 (22-inch stainless bbl.)	NiB $1339	Ex $1028	Gd $669
Custom Grade	NiB $1030	Ex $804	Gd $541
Custom Classic Grade	NiB $1133	Ex $824	Gd $566
Featherweight	NiB $1095	Ex $876	Gd $595

MODEL 36 TRP-1 SERIES

Similar to Model 36RF except in target configuration w/ ISU or silhouette-style stock. Made 1991-93.

TRP-1 (ISU single-shot)	NiB $927	Ex $747	Gd $438
TRP-1S (Silhouette)	NiB $927	Ex $747	Gd $438

MODEL 38 SINGLE SHOT

Similar to Model 36CF except in calibers .17 or .22 CCM w/3-shot magazine. Weight: 8 lbs. Walnut or synthetic stock. Made 1992-93.

Sporter Standard	NiB $927	Ex $721	Gd $566
Classic Grade	NiB $1025	Ex $819	Gd $566
Custom Grade	NiB $1159	Ex $978	Gd $566
Custom Classic Grade	NiB $1432	Ex $1133	Gd $747

MODEL 40 CLASSIC BOLT-ACTION RIFLE

Calibers: .17 CCM, .17 Ackley Hornet, .22 Hornet, .22K Hornet, .22 CCM, 4- or 5-shot magazine. 23.75-inch bbl. Checkered oil-finished AAA Claro walnut stock. Made 1995-97.

Classic	NiB $1432	Ex $1133	Gd $747
Custom Classic	NiB $1435	Ex $1231	Gd $824
Classic Varminter	NiB $1545	Ex $1231	Gd $824

CUMBERLAND MOUNTAIN ARMS — Winchester, Tennessee

PLATEAU RIFLE

Falling block action w/underlever. Calibers: .40-65, and .45-70. 32-inch round bbl. 48 inches overall. Weight: 10.5 lbs. American walnut stock. Bead front sight, adj. buckhorn rear. Blued finish. Lacquer finish walnut stock w/crescent buttplate. Made 1995 to date.

Standard model	NiB $927	Ex $747	Gd $515
Deluxe model	NiB $1339	Ex $1056	Gd $711

CZ RIFLES — Strankonice, Czechoslovakia (Currently Uhersky Brod and Brno, Czecho.) Mfd. by Ceska Zbrojovka-Nardoni Podnik (Formerly Bohmische Waffenfabrik A.G.)

See also listings under Brno Sporting Rifles and Springfield, Inc.

ZKK 600 BOLT-ACTION RIFLE

Calibers: .270 Win., 7x57, 7x64, .30-06. Five shot magazine. 23.5-inch bbl. Weight: 7.5 lbs. Adj. folding-leaf rear sight, hooded ramp front. Pistol-grip walnut stock. Imported 1990 to date.

Standard model	NiB $542	Ex $434	Gd $295
Deluxe model	NiB $631	Ex $505	Gd $344

ZKK 601 BOLT-ACTION RIFLE

Similar to Model ZKK 600 except w/short action in calibers .223 Rem., .243 Win., .308 Win. 43 inches overall. Weight: 6 lbs., 13 oz. Checkered walnut pistol-grip stock w/Monte Carlo cheekpiece. Imported 1990 to date.

Standard model	NiB $510	Ex $433	Gd $357
Deluxe model	NiB $561	Ex $500	Gd $357

ZKK 602 BOLT-ACTION RIFLE

Similar to Model ZKK 600 except w/Magnum action in calibers .300 Win. Mag., 8x68S, .375 H&H, .458 Win. Mag. 25-inch bbl. 45.5 inches overall. Weight: 9.25 lbs. Imported 1990 to date.

Standard model	NiB $688	Ex $586	Gd $398
Deluxe model	NiB $816	Ex $663	Gd $433

CA Model ZKM 452 LUX Model

CZ 511

CZ Model ZKM 527

CZ 550 LUX Model

ZKM 452 BOLT-ACTION REPEATING RIFLE
Calibers: .22 LR. or .22 WMR. Five, 6- or 10-shot magazine. 25-inch bbl. 43.5 inches overall. Weight: 6 lbs. Adj. rear sight, hooded bead front. Oil-finished beechwood or checkered walnut stock w/Schnabel forend. Imported 1995 to date.

Standard model (22 LR)	NiB $357	Ex $286	Gd $136
Deluxe model (22 LR)	NiB $398	Ex $255	Gd $178
Varmint model (22 LR)	NiB $331	Ex $255	Gd $178
.22 WMR, add			$35

ZKM 527 BOLT-ACTION RIFLE
Calibers: .22 Hornet, .222 Rem., .223 Rem., 7.62x39mm. Five shot magazine. 23.5-inch bbl. 42.5 inches overall. Weight: 6.75 lbs. Adj. rear sight, hooded ramp front. Grooved receiver. Adj. double-set triggers. Oil-finished beechwood or checkered walnut stock . Imported 1995 to date.

Standard model	NiB $505	Ex $398	Gd $280
Classic model	NiB $510	Ex $398	Gd $280
Carbine model (shorter configuration)	NiB $535	Ex $403	Gd $280
Deluxe model	NiB $592	Ex $500	Gd $306

ZKM 537 SPORTER BOLT-ACTION RIFLE
Calibers: .243 Win., .270 Win., 7x57mm, .308 Win., .30-06. Four or 5-shot magazine. 19- or 23.5-inch bbl. 40.25 or 44.75 inches overall. Weight: 7 to 7.5 lbs. Adj. folding leaf rear sight, hooded ramp front. Shrouded bolt. Standard or Mannlicher-style checkered walnut stock. Imported 1992-94.

Standard model	NiB $535	Ex $403	Gd $280
Mannlicher model	NiB $765	Ex $510	Gd $357
Mountain Carbine model	NiB $535	Ex $398	Gd $255

511 SEMI-AUTO RIFLE . . . . NiB $199 Ex $178 Gd $102
Caliber: .22 LR. 8- shot magazine. 22- inch bbl., 38.6 inches

(cont'd.) 511 SEMI-AUTO RIFLE
overall. Weight: 5.39 lbs. Receiver top fitted for telescopic sight mounts. Walnut wood-lacquered checkering stock. Imported 1998 to date.

550 BOLT-ACTION SERIES
Calibers: .243 Win., 6.5x55mm, .270 Win., 7mm Mag., 7x57, 7x64, .30-06, .300 Win Mag., .375 H&H, .416 Rem., .416 Rigby, .458 Win. Mag., 9.3x62. Four or 5-shot detachable magazine. 20.5- or 23.6-inch bbl. Weight: 7.25 to 8 lbs. No sights or Express sights on magnum models. Receiver drilled and tapped for scope mount. Standard or Mannlicher-style checkered walnut stock w/buttpad. Imported 1995 to date.

Standard	NiB $468	Ex $382	Gd $255
Magnum	NiB $586	Ex $464	Gd $306
Delux	NiB $505	Ex $398	Gd $280
Mannlicher	NiB $571	Ex $433	Gd $306
Calibers .416 Rem., .416 Rigby, .458 Win. Mag., add			$70

CZECHOSLOVAKIAN MILITARY RIFLES — Brno, Czechoslovakia, Manufactured by Ceska Zbrojovka

MODEL 1924 (VZ24)
MAUSER MILITARY RIFLE . . . . NiB $257 Ex $196 Gd $129
Basically same as German Kar., 98k and F.N. (Belgian Model 1924.) Caliber: 7.9mm Mauser. Five shot box magazine. 23.25-inch bbl. Weight: 8.5 lbs. Sights: Adj. rear; blade front w/guards. of Belgian-type military stock, full handguard. Mfd. 1924 thru WWII. Many of these rifles were made for export. As produced during the German occupation, this model was known as Gewehr 24t.

Daisy V/L Collector's Kit

Daisy V/L Standard

MODEL 1933 (VZ33) MAUSER
MILITARY CARBINE . . . . **NiB $335 Ex $257 Gd $180**
Modification of German M/98 action w/smaller receiver ring. Caliber: 7.9mm Mauser. 19.25-inch bbl. Weight: 7.5 lbs. Sights: Adj. rear; blade front w/guards. Military-type full stock. Mfd. 1933 thru WWII. A similar model, produced during the German occupation, was designated Gew. 33/40.

DAEWOO PRECISION INDUSTRIES — Manufactured in Korea (Previously Imported by Kimber of America; Daewoo Precision Industries; Nationwide Sports and KBI, Inc.)

DR200 SA SEMIAUTOMATIC SPORTER
Caliber: .223 Rem. (5.56mm). Six or 10-shot magazine. 18.4-inch bbl. 39.25 inches overall. Weight: 9 lbs. Protected post front sight, fully-adj. aperture rear. Forged aluminum receiver w/rotating locking bolt assembly. Synthetic sporterized thumbhole stock. Imported 1994-96.
Sporter model . . . . **NiB $669 Ex $515 Gd $386**
Varmint model. . . . . **NiB $566 Ex $515 Gd $283**

DR300 SA SEMIAUTO-
MATIC SPORTER. . . . . **NiB $592 Ex $505 Gd $335**
Similar to Model Daewoo DR200 except chambered for 7.62x39mm. Imported 1994-96.

DAISY RIFLES — Rogers, Arkansas

Daisy V/L rifles carry the first and only commercial caseless cartridge system. These rifles are expected to appreciate considerably in future years. The cartridge, no longer made, is also a collector's item. Production was discontinued following BATF ruling the V/L model to be a firearm.

COLLECTOR'S KIT. . . . . **NiB $418 Ex $335 Gd $228**
Presentation-grade rifle w/gold plate inscribed w/owner's name and gun serial number mounted on the stock. Also includes a special gun case, pair of brass gun cradles for wall-hanging, 300 rounds of 22 V/L ammunition and a certificate signed by Daisy president Cass S. Hough. Approx. 1,000 manufactured 1968-69.

PRESENTATION
GRADE . . . . **NiB $299 Ex $232 Gd $198**
Same specifications as standard model except w/walnut stock. Approx. 4,000 manufactured 1968-69.

STANDARD RIFLE . . . . **NiB $232 Ex $180 Gd $124**
Single-shot under-lever action. Caliber: .22 V/L (caseless cartridge, propellant ignited by jet of hot air). 18-inch bbl. Weight: 5 lbs. Sights: Adj. open rear, ramp w/blade front. Wood-grained Lustran stock (foam-filled). Approx. 19,000 manufactured 1968-69.

Dakota Model 10 Single-Shot Rifle

Dakota Arms Model 76
African Grade

Dakota Arms Model 76
Classic Grade

Dakota Arms Model 97
Hunter

DAKOTA ARMS, INC. — Sturgis, South Dakota

MODEL 10 SINGLE-SHOT RIFLE

Chambered for most commercially-loaded calibers. 23-inch bbl. 39.5 inches overall. Weight: 5.5 lbs. Top tang safety. No sights. Checkered pistol-grip buttstock and semi-beavertail forearm, QD swivels, rubber recoil pad. Made 1992 to date.

Standard calibers. . . . . **NiB $3275 Ex $2858 Gd $1777**
Magnum calibers. . . . . **NiB $3759 Ex $3013 Gd $2034**

MODEL 22 BOLT-ACTION

SPORTER RIFLE. . . . . **NiB $1339 Ex $1081 Gd $710**
Calibers: .22 LR. .22 Hornet. Five shot magazine. 22-inch bbl. Weight: 6.5 lbs. Adj. trigger. Checkered classic-style Claro or English walnut stock w/black recoil pad. Made 1992 to date.

MODEL 76 AFRICAN

BOLT-ACTION RIFLE. . . . . **NiB $4254 Ex $3811 Gd $2369**
Same general specifications as Model 76 Safari. Calibers: .404 Jeffery, .416 Rigby, .416 Dakota, .450 Dakota. 24-inch bbl. Weight: 8 lbs. Checkered select walnut stock w/two crossbolts. Made 1989 to date.

MODEL 76 ALPINE

BOLT-ACTION RIFLE. . . . . **NiB $2261 Ex $1596 Gd $1066**
Same general specifications as Model 76 Classic except short action w/blind magazine. Calibers: .22-250, .243, 6mm Rem., .250-3000, 7mm-08, .308. 21-inch bbl. Weight: 7.5 lbs. Made 1989-93.

MODEL 76 CLASSIC

BOLT-ACTION RIFLE. . . . . **NiB $2910 Ex $2261 Gd $1545**
Calibers: .257 Roberts, .270 Win., .280 Rem., .30-06, 7mm Rem. Mag., .300 Win. Mag., .338 Win. Mag., .375 H&H Mag., .458 Win. Mag. 21- or 23-inch bbl. Weight: 7.5 lbs. Receiver drilled and

(cont'd.) **MODEL 76 CLASSIC BOLT-ACTION RIFLE**
tapped for sights. Adj. trigger. Classic-style checkered walnut stock w/steel grip cap and solid recoil pad. Right- and left-hand models. Made 1988 to date.

MODEL 76 LONGBOW TACTICAL

BOLT-ACTION RIFLE. . . . . **NiB $4171 Ex $3188 Gd $2158**
Calibers: .300 Dakota Mag., .330 Dakota Mag., .338 Lapua Mag. Blind magazine. Ported 28-inch bbl. 50 to 51 inches overall. Weight: 13.7 lbs. Black or oliver green fiberglass stock w/adj. cheekpiece and buttplate. Receiver drilled and tapped w/one-piece rail mount and no sights. Made 1997 to date.

MODEL 76 SAFARI

BOLT-ACTION RIFLE. . . . . **NiB $4197 Ex $3167 Gd $2086**
Calibers: .300 Win. Mag., .338 Win. Mag., .375 H&H Mag. .458 Win. Mag. 23-inch bbl. w/bbl. band swivel. Weight: 8.5 lbs. Ramp front sight, standing leaf rear. Checkered fancy walnut stock w/ebony forend tip and solid recoil pad. Made 1988 to date.

MODEL 76 TRAVELER SERIES RIFLES

Threadless take-down action w/interchangeable bbl. capability based on the Dakota 76 design. Calibers: .257 through .458 Win (Standard-Classic & Safari) and .416 Dakota, .404 Jeffery, .416 Rigby, .338 Lapua and .450 Dakota Mag. (E/F Family-African Grade). 23- to 24- inch bbl. Weight: 7.5 to 9.5 lbs. Right or left-hand action. X grade (Classic) or XXX grade (Safari or African) oil finish English Bastogne or Claro walnut stock. Made 1999 to date.

Classic Grade. . . . . **NiB $4274 Ex $3219 Gd $2158**
Safari Grade . . . . **NiB $4249 Ex $3244 Gd $2626**
African Grade . . . . **NiB $5401 Ex $4321 Gd $2939**
Interchangeable bbl. assemblies
Classic Grade, add. $1150
Safari Grade, add. $1450
African Grade, add $1595

MODEL 76 VARMINT
BOLT-ACTION RIFLE . . . . NiB $2343 Ex $1828 Gd $1025
Similar to Model 76 Classic except single-shot action w/ heavy bbl. chambered for .17 Rem. to 6mm PPC. Weight: 13.7 lbs. Checkered walnut or synthetic stock. Receiver drilled and tapped for scope mounts and no sights. Made 1994-98.

MODEL 97 HUNTER BOLT-ACTION SERIES
Calibers: .22-250 Rem. to .330 Dakota Mag.(Lightweight), .25-06 to .375 Dakota Mag. (Long Range). 22-, 24- or 26-inch bbl. 43 to 46 inches overall. Weight: 6.16 lbs. to 7.7 lbs. Black composite fiberglass stock w/recoil pad. Fully adj. match trigger. Made 1997 to date.
Lightweight . . . . NiB $1849 Ex $1493 Gd $814
Long Range . . . . NiB $1610 Ex $1287 Gd $875

MODEL 97 VARMINT HUNTER
BOLT-ACTION RIFLE . . . . NiB $1648 Ex $1416 Gd $772
Similar to Model 97 Hunter except single-shot action w/ heavy bbl. chambered .22-250 Rem. to .308 Win. Checkered walnut stock. Receiver drilled and tapped for scope mounts and no sights. Made 1998 to date.

CHARLES DALY RIFLE — Harrisburg, Pennsylvania, *Imported by K.B.I., Inc., Harrisburg, PA, (Previously by Outdoor Sports Headquarters, Inc.)*

EMPIRE GRADE BOLT-ACTION RIFLE (RF)
Similar to Superior Grade except w/checkered California walnut stock w/rosewood grip cap and forearm cap. High polished blued finish and damascened bolt. Made 1998 to date.
Empire Grade (.22 LR) . . . . NiB $312 Ex $250 Gd $170
Empire Grade (.22WMR) . . . . NiB $338 Ex $270 Gd $184
Empire Grade (.22 Hornet) . . . . . . NiB $478 Ex $382 Gd $260

FIELD GRADE BOLT-ACTION RIFLE (RF)
Caliber: .22 LR. 16.25-, 17.5- or 22.63-inch bbl. 32 to 41 inches overall. Single-shot (True Youth) and 6- or 10-shot magazine. Plain walnut-finished hardwood or checkered polymer stock. Blue or stainless finish. Imported 1998 to date.
Field Grade (Standard w/22.63-inch bbl.) . . . . NiB $108 Ex $87 Gd $59
Field Grade (Youth w/17.5-inch bbl.) . . . . NiB $115 Ex $92 Gd $62
Field Grade (True Youth w/16.25-inch bbl.) . . . . NiB $152 Ex $121 Gd $83
Field Grade (Polymer w/stainless action) . . . . NiB $121 Ex $97 Gd $66

FIELD GRADE HUNTER BOLT-ACTION RIFLE
Calibers: .22 Hornet, .223 Rem., .243 Win., .270 Win., 7mm Rem. Mag. .308 Win., .30-06, .300 Win. Mag., .300 Rem. Ultra Mag., .338 Win. Mag. Three, 4-, or 5-shot magazine. 22- or 24-inch bbl. w/o sights. Weight: 7.2 to 7.4 lbs. Checkered walnut or black polymer stock. Receiver drilled and tapped. Blue or stainless finish. Imported 1998 to date.
Field Grade Hunter (walnut stock) . . . . NiB $484 Ex $388 Gd $263
Field Grade Hunter (polymer stock) . . . . . . NiB $504 Ex $403 Gd $274
w/Left-hand model, add $35

HAMMERLESS DRILLING
See listing under Charles Daly shotguns.

HORNET RIFLE . . . . NiB $1212 Ex $969 Gd $659
Same as Herold Rifle. See listing of that rifle for specifications. imported during the 1930s

MAUSER 98
Calibers: .243 Win., .270 Win., 7mm Rem. Mag. .308 Win., .30-06, .300 Win. Mag., .375 H&H, or .458 Win. Mag. Three, 4-, or 5-shot magazine. 23-inch bbl. 44.5 inches overall. Weight: 7.5 lbs. Checkered European walnut (Superior) or fiberglass/graphic (Field) stock w/recoil pad. Ramped front sight, adj. rear. Receiver drilled and tapped w/side saftey. Imported 1998 to date.
Field Grade (standard calibers) . . . . NiB $403 Ex $352 Gd $102
Field Grade (375 H&H and 458 Win. Mag.) . . . . NiB $607 Ex $505 Gd $301
Superior Grade (standard calibers) . . . . NiB $607 Ex $459 Gd $301
Superior Grade (magnum calibers) . . . . NiB $835 Ex $709 Gd $548

MINI-MAUSER 98
Similar to Mauser 98 except w/19.25-inch bbl. chambered for .22 Hornet, .22-250 Rem., .223 Rem., or 7.62x39mm. Five shot magazine. Imported 1998 to date.
Field Grade . . . . NiB $357 Ex $306 Gd$189
Superior Grade . . . . NiB $469 Ex $382 Gd $204

SUPERIOR GRADE BOLT-ACTION RIFLE
Calibers: .22 LR. .22 WMR, .22 Hornet. 20.25- to 22.63-inch bbl. 40.5 to 41.25 inches overall. Five, 6-, or 10-shot magazine. Ramped front sight, adj. rear w/grooved receiver. Checkered walnut stock. Made 1998 to date.
Superior Grade (.22 LR) . . . . NiB $153 Ex $122 Gd $71
Superior Grade (.22WMR) . . . . NiB $178 Ex $138 Gd $92
Superior Grade (.22 Hornet) . . . . . . NiB $342 Ex $291 Gd $178

SEMIAUTOMATIC RIFLE
Caliber: .22 LR. 20.75-inch bbl. 40.5 inches overall. 10-shot magazine. Ramped front sight, adj. rear w/grooved receiver. Plain walnut-finished hardwood stock (Field), checkered walnut (Superior), checkered polymer stock or checkered California walnut stock w/rosewood grip cap and forearm cap (Empire). Blue or stainless finish. Imported 1998 to date.
Field Grade . . . . NiB $112 Ex $92 Gd $56
Field Grade (Polymer w/stainless action) . . . . NiB $124 Ex $102 Gd $61
Superior Grade . . . . NiB $178 Ex $153 Gd $92
Empire Grade . . . . NiB $296 Ex $229 Gd $153

EAGLE ARMS INC. — Geneseo, Illinois (Previously Coal Valley, Illinois)

In 1995, Eagle Arms Inc., became a division of ArmaLite and reintroduced that logo. For current ArmaLite production see models under that listing.

MODEL EA-15 CARBINE
Caliber: .223 Rem. (5.56mm). 30-shot magazine. 16-inch bbl. and collapsible buttstock. Weight: 5.75 lbs. (E1); 6.25 lbs. (E2 w/heavy bbl. & National Match sights). Made 1989 to 94.
E1 Carbine . . . . NiB $804 Ex $644 Gd $438
E2 Carbine . . . . NiB $869 Ex $695 Gd $473

MODEL EA-15 GOLDEN
EAGLE MATCH RIFLE . . . . NiB $1128 Ex $875 Gd $566
Same general specifications as EA-15 Standard, except w/E2-style National Match sights. 20-inch Douglas Heavy Match bbl. NM trigger and bolt-carrier group. Weight: 12.75 lbs. Made 1991 to 94.

MODEL EA-15 SEMIAUTOMATIC RIFLE . . . . . NiB $819 Ex $644 Gd $417
Same as EA-15 Carbine except 20-inch bbl., 39 inches overall and weighs 7 lbs. Made 1989 to date.

EMF AP-74 Semiautomatic

EMF AP74-W Sporter

EMF AP-74 Paratrooper

EMF COMPANY, INC. — Santa Ana, California

MODEL AP-74
SEMI-AUTOMATIC CARBINE . . . . . NiB $304 Ex $257 Gd $160
Calibers: .22 LR or .32 ACP, 15-shot magazine. 20-inch bbl. w/flash reducer. 38 inches overall. Weight: 6.75 lbs. Protected pin front sight; protected rear peep sight. Lightweight plastic buttstock; ventilated snap-out forend. Importation. disc. 1989.

MODEL AP74-W
SPORTER CARBINE . . . . NiB $335 Ex $268 Gd $154
Sporterized version of AP-74 w/wood buttstock and forend. Importation disc. 1988.

MODEL AP74 PARATROOPER . . . . NiB $288 Ex $201 Gd $180
Same general specifications as Model AP74-W except w/folding tubular buttstock. Made in .22 LR. only. Importation disc. 1987.

MODEL 1860 HENRY RIFLE
Calibers: .44-40 and .45 LC. 24.25-inch bbl.; upper-half octagonal w/magazine tube in one-piece steel. 43.75-inches overall. Weight: 9.25 lbs. Varnished American walnut wood stock. Polished brass frame and brass buttplate. Original rifle was patented by B. Tyler Henry and produced by the New Haven Arms Company, when Oliver Winchester was president. Imported 1987 to date.
Deluxe model . . . . NiB $798 Ex $618 Gd $278
Engraved model . . . . NiB $1025 Ex $747 Gd $489

MODEL 1866
YELLOW BOY RIFLE . . . . NiB $592 Ex $510 Gd $299
Calibers: .44-40, .45 LC and .38 Special. Lever-action. Bbl: 24 inches, 43 inches overall. Bead front sight. Exact reproduction. Offered w/blued finish, walnut stock and brass frame.

MODEL 1866 YELLOW BOY CARBINE
Same features as 1866 Yellow Boy Rifle except carbine.
Standard carbine . . . . NiB $613 Ex $402 Gd $257
Engraved carbine . . . . NiB $618 Ex $489 Gd $283

MODEL 1873 SPORTING RIFLE
Calibers: .22 LR. .22 WMR, .357 Mag., .44-40 and .45 LC. 24.25-inch octagonal bbl. 43.25 inches overall. Weight: 8.16 lbs. Color casehardened frame w/blued steel magazine tube. Walnut stock and forend.
Standard Rifle . . . . NiB $772 Ex $618 Gd $386
Engraved Rifle . . . . NiB $901 Ex $592 Gd $402
Boy's Rifle
(Youth Model, .22 LR) . . . . NiB $608 Ex $489 Gd $309

MODEL 1873 SPORTING RIFLE CARBINE
Same features as 1873 sporting rifle except w/19-inch bbl. Overall length: 38.25 inches. Weight: 7.38 lbs. Color casehardened or blued frame.
Standard carbine . . . . NiB $772 Ex $618 Gd $386
Boy's carbine (Youth Model, .22 LR) . . . . . . NiB $608 Ex $489 Gd $309

Erma — EG712

Erma — EGM1

Erma — EM1 22

ERMA-WERKE — Dachau, Germany (Previously imported by Precision Sales International; Nygord Precision Products; Mandall's Shooting Supplies)

MODEL EG72
PUMP-ACTION REPEATER . . . . **NiB $127 Ex $97 Gd $71**
Visible hammer. Caliber: .22 LR. 15-shot magazine. 18.5-inch bbl. Weight: 5.25 lbs. Sights: open rear; hooded ramp front. Receiver grooved for scope mounting. Straight-grip stock, grooved slide handle. Imported 1970-76.

MODEL EG73
. . . . **NiB $270 Ex $235 Gd $127**
Same as Model EG712 except chambered for .22 WMR w/12-shot tubular magazine, 19.3-inch bbl. Imported 1973-97.

MODEL EG712 LEVER-ACTION
REPEATING CARBINE. . . . . **NiB $265 Ex $235 Gd $127**
Styled after Winchester Model 94. Caliber: .22 LR. Long, Short. Tubular magazine holds 15 LR, 17 Long, 21 Short. 18.5-inch bbl. Weight: 5.5 lbs. Sights: Open rear; hooded ramp front. Receiver grooved for scope mounting. Western carbine-style stock and forearm w/bbl. band. Imported 1976-97. Note: A similar carbine of Erma manufacture is marketed in U.S. as Ithaca Model 72 Saddle Gun.

MODEL EGM1
. . . . **NiB $270 Ex $229 Gd $127**
Same as Model EM1 except w/unslotted buttstock, ramp front sight, 5-shot magazine standard. Imported 1970-95.

MODEL EM1 .22
SEMIAUTOMATIC CARBINE . . . . . . **NiB $357 Ex $280 Gd $178**
Styled after U.S. Carbine cal. 30 M1. Caliber: .22 LR. 10- or 15-round magazine. 18-inch bbl. Weight: 5.5 lbs. Carbine-type sights. Receiver grooved for scope mounting. Military stock/handguard. Imported 1966-97.

EUROPEAN AMERICAN ARMORY — Sharpes, Florida

MODEL HW 660 BOLT-ACTION
SINGLE-SHOT RIFLE. . . . . **NiB $819 Ex $669 Gd $412**
Caliber: .22 LR. 26.8-inch bbl., 45.7 inches overall. Weight: 10.8 lbs. Match-type aperture rear sight; Hooded ramp front. Stippled walnut stock. Imported 1992-96.

MODEL HW BOLT-ACTION
SINGLE-SHOT TARGET RIFLE . . . . . **NiB $814 Ex $669 Gd $463**
Same general specification as Model HW 660 except equipped w/target stock. Imported 1995-96.

MODEL SABITTI SP1822
Caliber: .22 LR. 10-round detachable magazine. 18.5 inch bbl. 37.5 inches overall. Weight: 5.25 to 7.15 lbs. No sights. Hammer-forged heavy non-tapered bbl. Scope-mounted rail. Flush-mounted magazine release. Alloy receiver w/non-glare finish. Manual bolt lock. Wide claw extractor. Blowback action. Cross-trigger safety. Imported 1994-96.
Traditional Sporter model . . . . **NiB $200 Ex $160 Gd $108**
**Thumbhole Sporter
model (synthetic stock)**. . . . . **NiB $322 Ex $257 Gd $175**

FABRIQUE NATIONALE HERSTAL — Herstal & Liege, Belgium, (Formerly Fabrique Nationale d'Armes de Guerre)

MODELS 1924, 1934/30 AND
1930 MAUSER MILITARY RIFLES . . . . **NiB $382 Ex $280 Gd $178**
Similar to German Kar. 98k w/straight bolt handle. Calibers: 7mm, 7.65mm and 7.9mm Mauser. Five shot box magazine. 23.5-inch bbl. Weight: 8.5 lbs. Sights: Adj. rear; blade front. Military stock of M/98 pattern w/slight modification. Model differences are minor. Also produced in a short carbine model w/17.25-inch bbl. Note: These rifles were manufactured under contract for Abyssinia, Argentina, Belgium, Bolivia, Brazil, Chile, China, Colombia, Ecuador, Iran, Luxembourg, Mexico, Peru, Turkey, Uruguay and Yugoslavia. Such arms usually bear the coat of arms of the country for which they were made together with the contractor's name and date of manufacture. Also sold commercially and exported to all parts of the world.

F.N. Model 1949

F.N. Model 1950 Mauser

F.N. Deluxe Mauser

F.N. Supreme Mauser

F.N. FAL Semiautomatic

MODEL 1949 SEMIAUTOMATIC
MILITARY RIFLE . . . . **NiB $714 Ex $586 Gd $255**
Gas-operated. Calibers: 7mm, 7.65mm, 7.92mm, .30-06. 10-round box magazine, clip fed or loaded singly. 23.2-inch bbl. Weight: 9.5 lbs. Sights: Tangent rear-shielded post front. Pistol-grip stock, handguard. Note: Adopted by Belgium in 1949; also by Belgian Congo, Brazil, Colombia, Luxembourg, Netherlands, East Indies, and Venezuela. Approx. 160,000 were made.

MODEL 1950 MAUSER
MILITARY RIFLE . . . . **NiB $459 Ex $306 Gd $229**
Same as previous F.N. models of Kar. 98k type except chambered for .30-06.

DELUXE MAUSER BOLT-ACTION
SPORTING RIFLE. . . . . **NiB $709 Ex $612 Gd $357**
American calibers: .220 Swift, .243 Win., .244 Rem., .250/3000, .257 Roberts, .270 Win., 7mm, .300 Sav., .308 Win. European calibers: 7x57, 8x57JS, 8x60S, 9.3x62, 9.5x57, 10.75x68mm. Fiveshot box magazine. 24-inch bbl. Weight: 7.5-8.25 lbs. American model is standard w/hooded ramp front sight and Tri-Range rear; Continental model w/two-leaf rear. Checkered stock w/cheekpiece, pistol-grip, swivels. Made 1947-63.

DELUXE MAUSER —
PRESENTATION GRADE . . . . **NiB $1224 Ex $969 Gd $663**
Same as regular model except w/select grade stock; engraving on receiver, trigger guard, floorplate and bbl. breech. Disc. 1963.

FAL/FNC/LAR SEMIAUTOMATIC
Same as standard FAL military rifle except w/o provision for automatic firing. Gas-operated. Calibers: 7.62mm NATO (.308 Win.) or 5.56mm (.223 Rem.). 10- or 20-round box magazine. 25.5-inch bbl. (including flash hider). Weight: 9 lbs. Sights: Post front; aperture rear. Fixed wood or folding buttstock, pistol-grip, forearm/handguard w/carrying handle and sling swivels. Disc. 1988.
F.N. FAL/LAR model (Light
Automatic Rifle) . . . . **NiB $2422 Ex $2091 Gd $1275**
F.N. FAL/HB model (heavy bbl.) . . . . . . **NiB $2742 Ex $2193 Gd $1491**
F.N. FAL/PARA (Paratrooper) . . . . **NiB $3366 Ex $2703 Gd $1683**
F.N. FNC Carbine
model (.223 cal.). . . . . **NiB $2550 Ex $1826 Gd $1173**
F.N. FNC Carbine model w/flash
suppresser (.223 cal.) . . . . **NiB $2652 Ex $1887 Gd $1224**

SUPREME MAUSER BOLT-ACTION
SPORTING RIFLE. . . . . **NiB $714 Ex $867 Gd $357**
Calibers: .243, .270, 7mm, .308, .30-06. Four shot magazine in .243 and .308; 5-shot in other calibers. 22-inch bbl. in .308; 24-inch in other calibers. Sights: Hooded ramp front, Tri-Range peep rear. Checkered stock w/ Monte Carlo cheekpiece, pistol-grip, swivels. Weight: 7.75 lbs. Made 1957-75.

SUPREME MAGNUM MAUSER
SUPREME MAGNUM MAUSER . . . . **NiB $765 Ex $612 Gd $382**
Calibers: .264 Mag., 7mm Mag., .300 Win. Mag. Specifications same as for standard caliber model except 3-shot magazine capacity.

Finnish Lion Champion

Finnish Lion Match

RIFLES

FEATHER INDUSTRIES, INC. — Boulder, Colorado

See MITCHELL ARMS. For current production.

MODEL AT-9 SEMIAUTOMATIC RIFLE
Caliber: 9mm Parabellum. 10-, 25-, 32-, or 100-shot magazine. 17-inch bbl. 35 inches overall (extended). Hooded post front sight, adj. aperture rear. Weight: 5 lbs. Telescoping wire stock w/composition pistol-grip and barrel-shroud handguard. Matte black finish. Made 1988-95.

Model AT-9	NiB $721	Ex $644	Gd $412
W/32-shot magazine, add			$75
W/100-shot drum magazine, add			$250

MODEL AT-22 .... NiB $231 Ex $180 Gd $124
Caliber: .22 LR. 20-shot magazine. 17-inch bbl. 35 inches overall (extended). Hooded post front sight; adj. aperture rear. Weight: 3.25 lbs. Telescoping wire stock w/composition pistol-grip and barrel shroud handguard. Matte black finish.

MODEL F2 SA CARBINE .... NiB $258 Ex $196 Gd $113
Similar to AT-22, except w/fixed Polymer stock and pistol-grip. Made 1992-95.

MODEL F9 SA CARBINE .... NiB $592 Ex $541 Gd $335
Similar to AT-9, except w/fixed Polymer stock and pistol-grip. Made 1992-95.

FINNISH LION RIFLES — Jyväkylylä, Finland
Manufactured by Valmet Oy, Tourula Works

CHAMPION FREE RIFLE .... NiB $612 Ex $489 Gd $333
Bolt-action single-shot target rifle. Double-set trigger. Caliber: .22 LR. 28.75-inch heavy bbl. Weight: 16 lbs. Sights: Extension rear peep; aperture front. Walnut free-rifle stock w/full pistol-grip, thumbhole, beavertail forend, hook buttplate, palm rest, hand stop, swivel. Made 1965-72.

STANDARD ISU
TARGET RIFLE .... NiB $360 Ex $283 Gd $154
Bolt-action, single-shot. Caliber: .22 LR. 27.5-inch bbl. Weight: 10.5 lbs. Sights: extension rear peep; aperture front. Walnut target stock w/full pistol-grip, checkered beavertail forearm, adj. buttplate, sling swivel. Made 1966-77.

MATCH RIFLE .... NiB $509 Ex $407 Gd $277
Bolt-action, single-shot. Caliber: .22 LR. 28.75-inch heavy bbl. Weight: 14.5 lbs. Sights: Extension rear peep; aperture front. Walnut free-rifle stock w/full pistol-grip, thumbhole, beavertail forearm, hook buttplate, palm rest, hand stop, swivel. Made 1937-72.

STANDARD TARGET RIFLE
Bolt-action, single-shot. Caliber: .22 LR. 27.5-inch bbl. 44.5 inches overall. Weight: 10.5 lbs. No sights; micrometer rear and globe front International-style sights available. Select walnut stock in target configuration. Currently in production.

Standard model	NiB $747	Ex $613	Gd $386
Thumbhole stock model	NiB $804	Ex $644	Gd $438
Standard model	NiB $360	Ex $257	Gd $154
Deluxe model	NiB $386	Ex $309	Gd $206

LUIGI FRANCHI, S.P.A. — Brescia, Italy

CENTENNIAL AUTOMATIC RIFLE
Commemorates Franchi's 100th anniversary (1868-1968). Centennial seal engraved on receiver. Semiautomatic. Take-down. Caliber: .22 LR. 11-shot magazine in buttstock. 21-inch bbl. Weight: 5.13 lbs. Sights: Open rear; gold bead front on ramp. Checkered walnut stock and forend. Deluxe model w/fully engraved receiver, premium grade wood. Made 1968.

Standard model	NiB $357	Ex $265	Gd $178
Engraved model	NiB $423	Ex $331	Gd $224

GRADING: **NiB** = New in Box   **Ex** = Excellent or NRA 95%   **Gd** = Good or NRA 68%

Franchi Deluxe Centennial

Francotte Sidelock Double Rifle

Galil .223 AR Semiautomatic Rifle

Francotte Boxlock Mountain Rifle
w/claw mounts and scope

FRANCOTTE RIFLES — Leige, Belgium
Imported by Armes de Chasse, Hertford, NC (Previously by Abercrombie & Fitch)

BOLT-ACTION RIFLE
Custom rifle built on Mauser style bolt action. Available in three action lengths. Calibers: .17 Bee to .505 Gibbs. Barrel length: 21- to 24.5-inches. Weight: 8 to 12 lbs. Stock dimensions, wood type and style to customer's specifications. Engraving, appointments and finish to customer's preference. Note: Deduct 25% for models w/o engraving.

Short action . . . . NiB $9400 Ex $7350 Gd $4500
Standard action . . . . NiB $7825 Ex $6000 Gd $3600
Magnum Francotte action . . . . . NiB $13,750 Ex $10,800 Gd $7000

BOXLOCK MOUNTAIN RIFLE
Custom single-shot rifle built on Anson & Deeley style boxlock or Holland & Holland style sidelock action. 23- to 26-inch barrels chambered to customer's specification. Stock dimensions, wood type and style to customer's specifications. Engraving, appointments and finish to customer's preference. Note: Deduct 30% for models w/o engraving.

Boxlock . . . . NiB $13,900 Ex $11,700 Gd $7500
Sidelock . . . . NiB $22,438 Ex $17,950 Gd $12,206

DOUBLE RIFLE
Custom side-by-side rifle. Built on Francotte system boxlock or back-action sidelock. 23.5- to 26-inch barrels chambered to customer's specification. Stock dimensions, wood type and style to customer's specifications. Engraving, appointments and finish to customer's preference. Note: Deduct 30% for models w/o engraving.

Boxlock . . . . NiB $18,500 Ex $15,500 Gd $9500
Sidelock . . . . NiB $29,450 Ex $25,000 Gd $15,700

FRENCH MILITARY RIFLE — Saint Etienne, France

MODEL 1936
MAS MILITARY RIFLE . . . . NiB $153 Ex $112 Gd $61
Bolt-action. Caliber: 7.5mm MAS. 5-shot box magazine. 22.5-inch bbl. Weight: 8.25 lbs. Sights: Adj. rear; blade front. Two-piece military-type stock. Bayonet carried in forend tube. Made 1936-1940 by Manufacture Francaise d'Armes et de Cycles de St. Etienne (MAS).

GALIL RIFLES — Manufactured by Israel Military Industries, Israel, Imported by UZI America Inc., North Haven, CT (Previously by Action Arms, Springfield Armory and Magnum Research, Inc.)

AR SEMIAUTOMATIC RIFLE
Calibers: .308 Win. (7.62 NATO), .223 Rem. (5.56mm). 25-shot (.308) or 35-shot (.223) magazine. 16-inch (.223) or 18.5-inch (.308) bbl. w/flash suppressor. Weight: 9.5 lbs. Folding aperture rear sight, post front. Folding metal stock w/carrying handle. Imported 1982-94. Currently select fire models available to law enforcement only.

Model .223 AR . . . . NiB $2266 Ex $1802 Gd $1030
Model .308 AR . . . . NiB $2266 Ex $1802 Gd $1030
Model .223 ARM . . . . NiB $2704 Ex $2060 Gd $1468
Model .308 ARM . . . . NiB $2704 Ex $2060 Gd $1468

SPORTER SEMIAUTOMATIC RIFLE...... NiB $1028 Ex $927 Gd $592
Same general specifications as AR Model except w/hardwood thumb-hole stock and 5-shot magazine. Weight: 8.5 lbs. Imported 1991-94.

GARCIA CORPORATION — Teaneck, New Jersey

BRONCO 22 SINGLE-SHOT RIFLE........ NiB $100 Ex $80 Gd $55
Swing-out action. Takedown. Caliber: .22 LR. Long, Short. 16.5-inch bbl. Weight: 3 lbs. Sights: Open rear-blade front. One-piece stock and receiver, crackle finish. Intro. 1967. Discontinued.

GERMAN MILITARY RIFLES — Mfd. by Ludwig Loewe & Co., Berlin, other contractors and by German arsenals and various plants under German government control

MODEL 24T (GEW. 24T) MAUSER RIFLE .... NiB $515 Ex $360 Gd $232
Same general specifications as Czech Model 24 (VZ24) Mauser Rifle w/minor modification and laminated wood stock. Weight: 9.25 lbs. Made in Czechoslovakia during German occupation; adopted 1940.

MODEL 29/40 (GEW. 29/40)
MAUSER RIFLE .... NiB $360 Ex $257 Gd $154
Same general specifications as Kar. 98K w/minor differences. Made in Poland during German occupation; adopted 1940.

MODEL 33/40 (GEW. 33/40)
MAUSER RIFLE .... NiB $978 Ex $747 Gd $463
Same general specifications as Czech Model 33 (VZ33) Mauser Carbine w/minor modifications and laminated wood stock as found in war-time Model 98K carbines. Made in Czechoslovakia during German occupation; adopted 1940.

MODELS 41 AND 41-W (GEW. 41, GEW. 41-W)
SEMIAUTOMATIC MILITARY RIFLES
Gas-operated, muzzle cone system. Caliber: 7.9mm Mauser. l0-shot box magazine. 22.5-inch bbl. Weight: 10.25 lbs. Sights: Adj. leaf rear; blade front. Military-type stock w/semi-pistol grip, plastic handguard. Note: Model 41 lacks bolt release found on Model 41-W; otherwise, the models are the same. These early models were mfd. in Walther's Zella-Mehlis plant. Made c.1941-43.
Model 41................... NiB $4185 Ex $3347 Gd $2276
Model 41-W .... NiB $3213 Ex $2570 Gd $1748

MODEL 43 (GEW. 43, KAR. 43)
SEMIAUTO MILITARY RIFLES......... NiB $1224 Ex $978 Gd $665
Gas-operated, bbl. vented as in Russian Tokarev. Caliber: 7.9mm Mauser. 10-shot detachable box magazine. 22- or 24-inch bbl. Weight: 9 lbs. Sights: Adj. rear; hooded front. Military-type stock w/semi-pistol-grip, wooden handguard. Note: These rifles are alike except for minor details, have characteristic late WWII mfg. short cuts: cast receiver and bolt cover, stamped steel parts, etc. Gew. 43 may have either 22- or 24-inch bbl. The former length was standardized in late 1944, when weapon designation was changed to "Kar. 43." Made 1943-45.

MODEL 1888 (GEW. 88) MAUSER-
MANNLICHER SERVICE RIFLE.......... NiB $360 Ex $206 Gd $154
Bolt-action w/straight bolt handle. Caliber: 7.9mm Mauser (8x57mm). Five shot Mannlicher box magazine. 29-inch bbl. w/jacket. Weight: 8.5 lbs. Fixed front sight, adj. rear. Military-type full stock. Mfd. by Ludwig Loewe & Co., Haenel, Schilling and other contractors.

MODEL 1888 (KAR. 88) MAUSER-
MANNLICHER CARBINE......... NiB $257 Ex $206 Gd $154
Same general specifications as Gew. 88 except w/18-inch bbl., w/o jacket, flat turned-down bolt handle, weight: 6.75 lbs. Mfd. by Ludwig Loewe & Co., Haenel, Schilling and other contractors.

MODEL 1898 (GEW. 98)
MAUSER MILITARY RIFLE........ NiB $489 Ex $360 Gd $206
Bolt action with straight bolt handle. Caliber: 7.9mm Mauser (8x57mm). Five shot box magazine. 29-inch stepped bbl. Weight: 9 lbs. Sights: Blade front; adj. rear. Military-type full stock w/rounded bottom pistol grip. Adopted 1898.

MODEL 1898A (KAR. 98A)
MAUSER CARBINE .... NiB $407 Ex $360 Gd $154
Same general specifications as Model 1898 (Gew.98) Rifle except has turned-down bolt handle, smaller receiver ring, light 23.5-inch-straight taper bbl., front sight guards, sling is attached to left side of stock, weight: 8 lbs. Note: Some of these carbines are marked "Kar. 98;" the true Kar. 98 is the earlier original M/98 carbine w/17-inch bbl. and is rarely encountered.

MODEL 1898B (KAR. 98B)
MAUSER CARBINE .... NiB $438 Ex $360 Gd $257
Same general specifications as Model 1898 (Gew.98) Rifle except has turned-down bolt handle and sling attached to left side of stock. This is post-WWI model.

MODEL 1898K (KAR. 98K)
MAUSER CARBINE .... NiB $438 Ex $360 Gd $257
Same general specifications as Model 1898 (Gew.98) Rifle except has turned-down bolt handle, 23.5-inch bbl., may have hooded front sight, sling attached to left side of stock, weighs about 8.5 lbs. Adopted in 1935, this was the standard German service rifle of WWII. Note: Late-war models had stamped sheet steel trigger guards and many of the Model 98K carbines made during WWII had laminated wood stocks These weigh .5 to .75 pound more than the previous Model 98K. Value shown is for earlier type.

MODEL VK 98
PEOPLE'S RIFLE ("VOLKSAEWEHR").. NiB $226 Ex $180 Gd $123
Kar. 98K-type action. Caliber: 7.9mm. Single-shot or repeater (latter w/rough hole-in-the-stock 5-shot "magazine" or fitted w/10-shot clip of German Model 43 semiauto rifle). 20.9-inch bbl. Weight: 7 lbs. Fixed V-notch rear sight dovetailed into front receiver ring; front blade welded to bbl. Crude, unfinished, half-length stock w/o buttplate. Last ditch weapon made in 1945 for issue to German civilians. Note: Of value only as a military arms collector's item, this hastily-made rifle should be regarded as unsafe to shoot.

GÉVARM RIFLE — Saint Etienne, France Manufactured by Gevelot

E-1 AUTOLOADING RIFLE .... NiB $178 Ex $153 Gd $102
Caliber: .22 LR. 8-shot clip magazine. 19.5-inch bbl. Sights: Open rear; post front. Pistol-grip stock and forearm of French walnut.

GOLDEN EAGLE RIFLES — Houston, Texas Mfd. by Nikko Firearms Ltd., Tochigi, Japan

MODEL 7000 GRADE I AFRICAN .... NiB $669 Ex $515 Gd $407
Same as Grade I Big Game except: Caliber: .375 H&H Mag. and .458 Win. Mag. two-shot magazine in .458, weight: 8.75 lbs. in .375 and 10.5 lbs. in .458, furnished w/sights. Imported 1976-81.

Golden Eagle Model 7000

Carl Gustaf Model 2000

Carl Gustaf Deluxe

Carl Gustaf Grand Prix

Carl Gustaf Sporter

MODEL 7000 BIG GAME SERIES
Bolt action. Calibers: .22-250, .243 Win., .25-06, .270 Win., Weatherby Mag., 7mm Rem. Mag., .30-06, .300 Weatherby Mag., .300 Win. Mag., .338 Win. Mag. Magazine capacity: 4 rounds in .22-250, 3 rounds in other calibers. 24- or 26-inch bbl. (26-inch only in 338). Weight: 7 lbs., .22-250; 8.75, lbs., other calibers. Furnished w/o sights. Fancy American walnut stock, skip checkered, contrasting wood forend tip and grip cap w/gold eagle head, recoil pad. Imported 1976-81.
Model 7000 Grade I . . . . NiB $701 Ex $561 Gd $382
Model 7000 Grade II. . . . . NiB $766 Ex $613 Gd $417

GREIFELT & CO. — Suhl, Germany

SPORT MODEL 22 HORNET
BOLT-ACTION RIFLE . . . . NiB $2183 Ex $1746 Gd $1188
Caliber: .22 Hornet. Five shot box magazine. 22-inch Krupp steel bbl. Weight: 6 lbs. Sights: Two-leaf rear; ramp front. Walnut stock, checkered pistol-grip and forearm. Made before WWII.

CARL GUSTAF RIFLES — Eskilstuna, Sweden
Mfd. by Carl Gustaf Stads Gevärsfaktori
MODEL 2000 BOLT-ACTION RIFLE
Calibers: .243, 6.5x55, 7x64, .270, .308 Win., .30-06, 7mm Rem. Mag., .300 Win. Mag. Three shot magazine. 24-inch bbl. 44 inches overall. Weight: 7.5 lbs. Receiver drilled and tapped. Hooded ramp front sight, open rear. Adj. trigger. Checkered European walnut stock w/Monte Carlo cheekpiece and Wundhammer palmswell grip. Imported 1991-95
Model 2000
w/o sights . . . . NiB $1410 Ex $1128 Gd $767
Model 2000 w/sights. . . . . NiB $1610 Ex $1287 Gd $875
Model 2000 LUXE . . . . NiB $1746 Ex $1545 Gd $927

DELUXE. . . . . NiB $741 Ex $592 Gd $403
Same specifications as Monte Carlo Standard. Calibers: 6.5x55, 308 Win., .30-06, 9.3x62. Four shot magazine in 9.3x62. Jeweled bolt. Engraved floorplate and trigger guard. Deluxe French walnut stock w/rosewood forend tip. Imported 1970-77.

Hammerli Model 45

Hammerli-Tanner 300M

GRAND PRIX SINGLE-SHOT
TARGET RIFLE .... **NiB $613 Ex $510 Gd $340**
Special bolt action with "world's shortest lock time." Single-stage trigger adjusts down to 18 oz. Caliber: .22 LR. 26.75-inch heavy bbl. w/adj. trim weight. Weight: 9.75 lbs. Furnished w/o sights. Target-type Monte Carlo stock of French walnut, adj. cork buttplate. Imported 1970-77.

MONTE CARLO STANDARD
BOLT-ACTION SPORTING RIFLE .... **NiB $463 Ex $407 Gd $360**
Carl Gustaf 1900 action. Calibers: 6.5x55, 7x64, .270 Win., 7mm Rem. Mag., .308 Win., .30-06, 9.3x62. Five shot magazine, except 4-shot in 9.3x62 and 3-shot in 7mm Rem. Mag. 23.5-inch bbl. Weight: 7 lbs. Sights: Folding leaf rear; hooded ramp front. French walnut Monte Carlo stock w/cheekpiece, checkered forearm and pistol grip, sling swivels. Also available in left-hand model. Imported1970-77.

SPECIAL..................... **NiB $515 Ex $438 Gd $304**
Also designated "Grade II" in U.S. and "Model 9000" in Canada. Same specifications as Monte Carlo Standard. Calibers: .22-250, .243 Win., .25-06, .270 Win., 7mm Rem. Mag., .308 Win., .30-06, .300 Win. Mag. Three shot magazine in magnum calibers. Select wood stock w/rosewood forend tip. Left-hand model avail. Imported 1970-77.

SPORTER.................... **NiB $612 Ex $489 Gd $333**
Also designated "Varmint-Target" in U.S. Fast bolt action w/large Bakelite bolt knob. Trigger pull adjusts down to 18 oz. Calibers: .222 Rem., .22-250, .243 Win., 6.5x55. Five shot magazine except 6-shot in .222 Rem. 26.75-inch heavy bbl. Weight: 9.5 lbs. Furnished w/o sights. Target-type Monte Carlo stock of French walnut. Imported 1970 to date.

STANDARD .... **NiB $566 Ex $463 Gd $309**
Same specifications as Monte Carlo Standard. Calibers: 6.5x55, 7x64, .270 Win., .308 Win., .30-06, 9.3x62. Classic-style stock w/o Monte Carlo. Imported 1970-77.

TROFÉ .... **NiB $818 Ex $618 Gd $422**
Also designated "Grade III" in U.S. and "Model 8000" in Canada. Same specifications as Monte Carlo Standard. Calibers: .22-250, .25-06, 6.5x55, .270 Win., 7mm Rem. Mag., .308 Win., .30-06, .300 Win. Mag. Three shot magazine in magnum calibers. Furnished w/o sights. Fancy wood stock w/rosewood forend tip, high-gloss lacquer finish. Imported 1970-77.

C.G. HAENEL — Suhl, Germany

'88 MAUSER SPORTER .... **NiB $541 Ex $417 Gd $309**
Same general specifications as Haenel Mauser-Mannlicher except w/Mauser 5-shot box magazine.

MAUSER-MANNLICHER
BOLT-ACTION SPORTING RIFLE .. **NiB $489 Ex $386 Gd $231**
Mauser M/88-type action. Calibers: 7x57, 8x57, 9x57mm. Mannlicher clip-loading box magazine, 5-shot. 22- or 24-inch half or full octagon bbl. w/raised matted rib. Double-set trigger. Weight: 7.5 lbs. Sights: Leaf-type open rear; ramp front. Sporting stock w/cheekpiece, checkered pistol-grip, raised side-panels, Schnabel tip, swivels.

HÄMMERLI AG JAGD-UND-SPORTWAFFEN-FABRIK —

Lenzburg, Switzerland, *Imported by Sigarms, Exetre, NH, (Previously by Hammerli USA; Mandall Shooting Supplies, Inc. & Beeman Precision Arms)*

MODEL 45 SMALLBORE BOLT-ACTION
SINGLE-SHOT MATCH RIFLE .... **NiB $680 Ex $566 Gd $360**
Calibers: .22 LR. 22 Extra Long. 27.5-inch heavy bbl. Weight: 15.5 lbs. Sights: Micrometer peep rear; globe front. Free-rifle stock w/cheekpiece, full pistol-grip, thumbhole, beavertail forearm, palm-rest, Swiss-type buttplate, swivels. Made 1945-57.

MODEL 54 SMALLBORE
MATCH RIFLE .... **NiB $690 Ex $566 Gd $335**
Bolt-action, single-shot. Caliber: .22 LR. 27.5-inch heavy bbl. Weight: 15 lbs. Sights: Micrometer peep rear; globe front. Free-rifle stock w/cheekpiece, thumbhole, adj. hook buttplate, palm rest, swivel. Made 1954-57.

MODEL 503 FREE RIFLE .... **NiB $695 Ex $566 Gd $335**
Bolt-action, single-shot. Caliber: .22 LR. 27.5-inch heavy bbl. Weight: 15 lbs. Sights: Micrometer peep rear; globe front. Free-rifle stock w/cheekpiece, thumbhole, adj. hook buttplate, palm rest, swivel. Made 1957-62.

Harrington & Richardson Model 60 Reising

Harrington & Richardson Model 65 Military

Harrington & Richardson Model 150 Leatherneck

MODEL 506 SMALLBORE MATCH RIFLE .... NiB $695 Ex $566 Gd $360
Bolt-action, single-shot. Caliber: .22 LR. 26.75-inch heavy bbl. Weight: 16.5 lbs. Sights: Micrometer peep rear; globe front. Free-rifle stock w/cheekpiece, thumbhole adj. hook buttplate, palmrest, swivel. Made 1963-66.

MODEL OLYMPIA 300 METER BOLT-ACTION
SINGLE-SHOT FREE RIFLE................. NiB $901 Ex $772 Gd $463
Calibers: .30-06, .300 H&H Magnum for U.S.A.; ordinarily produced in 7.5mm, other calibers available on special order. 29.5-inch heavy bbl. Double-pull or double-set trigger. Sights: Micrometer peep rear, globe front. Free-rifle stock w/cheekpiece, full pistol grip, thumbhole, beavertail forend, palmrest, Swiss-type buttplate, swivels. Made 1945-59.

TANNER 300 METER FREE RIFLE .... NiB $927 Ex $850 Gd $463
Bolt-action, single-shot. Caliber: 7.5mm standard, available in most popular centerfire calibers. 29.5-inch heavy bbl. Weight: 16.75 lbs. Sights: Micrometer peep rear; globe front. Free-rifle stock w/cheekpiece, thumbhole, adj. hook buttplate, palmrest, swivel. Intro. 1962. Disc. See Illustration previous page.

HARRINGTON & RICHARDSON, INC. —
Gardner, Massachusetts (Now H&R 1871, INC., Gardner, Mass.)

Formerly Harrington & Richardson Arms Co. of Worcester, Mass. One of the oldest and most distinguished manufacturers of handguns, rifles and shotguns, H&R suspended operations on January 24, 1986. In 1987, New England Firearms was established as an independent company producing selected H&R models under the NEF logo. In 1991, H&R 1871, Inc. was formed from the residual of the parent company and that took over the New England Firearms facility. H&R 1871 produced firearms under both its logo and the NEF brand name until 1999, when the Marlin Firearms Company acquired the assets of H&R 1871.

MODEL 60 REISING SEMI-
AUTOMATIC RIFLE .... NiB $515 Ex $489 Gd $232
Caliber: .45 Automatic. 12- and 20-shot detachable box magazines. 18.25-inch bbl. Weight: 7.5 lbs. Sights: Open rear; blade front. Plain pistol-grip stock. Made 1944-46.

MODEL 65 MILITARY
AUTOLOADING RIFLE .... NiB $309 Ex $247 Gd $129
Also called "General." Caliber: .22 LR. 10-shot detachable box magazine. 23-inch heavy bbl. Weight: 9 lbs. Sights: Redfield 70 rear peep, blade front w/protecting "ears." Plain pistol-grip stock, "Garand" dimensions. Made 1944-46. Note: This model was used as a training rifle by the U.S. Marine Corps.

MODEL 150
LEATHERNECK AUTOLOADER .... NiB $103 Ex $82 Gd $62
Caliber: .22 LR. only. Five shot detachable box magazine. 22-inch bbl. Weight: 7.25 lbs. Sights: Open rear; blade front, on ramp. Plain pistol-grip stock. Made 1949-53.

MODEL 151 .... NiB $154 Ex $88 Gd $72
Same as Model 150 except w/Redfield 70 rear peep sight.

MODEL 155
SINGLE-SHOT RIFLE................... NiB $185 Ex $134 Gd $82
Model 158 action. Calibers: .44 Rem. Mag., .45-70 Govt. 24- or 28-inch bbl. (latter in .44 only). Weight: 7 or 7.5 lbs. Sights: Folding leaf rear; blade front. Straight-grip stock, forearm w/bbl. band, brass cleaning rod. Made 1972-82.

MODEL 157
SINGLE-SHOT RIFLE................... NiB $185 Ex $103 Gd $72
Model 158 action. Calibers: .22 WMR, .22 Hornet, .30-30. 22-inch bbl. Weight: 6.25 lbs. Sights: Folding leaf rear; blade front. Pistol-grip stock, full-length forearm, swivels. Made 1976-86.

Harrington & Richardson
Model 155

Harrington & Richardson
Model 157

Harrington & Richardson
Model 158 Topper Jet

Harrington & Richardson
Model 158C w/extra shotgun barrel

RIFLES

MODEL 158 TOPPER JET SINGLE-SHOT COMBINATION RIFLE
Shotgun-type action w/visible hammer, side lever, auto ejector. Caliber: .22 Rem. Jet. 22-inch bbl. (interchanges with .30-30, .410 ga., 20 ga. bbls.). Weight: 5 lbs. Sights: Lyman folding adj. open rear; ramp front. Plain pistol-grip stock and forearm, recoil pad. Made 1963-67.
Rifle only . . . . **NiB $154 Ex $129 Gd $82**
Interchangeable bbl.
.30-30, shotgun . . . . **NiB $51 Ex $41 Gd $26**

MODEL 158C . . . . **NiB $155 Ex $139 Gd $82**
Same as Model 158 Topper Jet except calibers .22 Hornet, .30-30, .357 Mag., .357 Mag., .44 Mag. Straight-grip stock. Made 1963-86.

MODEL 163 MUSTANG
SINGLE-SHOT RIFLE . . . . **NiB $155 Ex $134 Gd $77**
Same as Model 158 Topper except w/gold-plated hammer and trigger, straight-grip stock and contoured forearm. Made 1964-67.

MODEL 165 LEATHERNECK AUTOLOADER . . . **NiB $129 Ex $113 Gd $77**
Caliber: .22 LR. 10-shot detachable box magazine. 23-inch bbl. Weight: 7.5 lbs. Sights: Redfield 70 rear peep; blade front, on ramp. Plain pistol-grip stock, swivels, web sling. Made 1945-61.

MODEL 171 . . . . **NiB $360 Ex $309 Gd $196**
Model 1873 Springfield Cavalry Carbine replica. Caliber: .45-70. 22-inch bbl. Weight: 7 lbs. Sights: Leaf rear; blade front. Plain walnut stock. Made 1972-81.

MODEL 171 DELUXE . . . . **NiB $412 Ex $360 Gd $257**
Same as Model 171 except engraved action and different sights. Made 1972-86. See illustration next page.

MODEL 172 . . . . **NiB $1281 Ex $1025 Gd $697**
Same as Model 171 Deluxe except silver-plated, w/fancy walnut stock, checkered, w/grip adapter; tang-mounted aperture sight. Made 1972-86.

MODEL 173 . . . . **NiB $4018 Ex $335 Gd $228**
Model 1873 Springfield Officer's Model replica, same as 100th Anniversary Commemorative except w/o plaque on stock. Made 1972-86.

MODEL 174 . . . . **NiB $412 Ex $360 Gd $257**
Little Big Horn Commemorative Carbine. Same as Model 171 Deluxe except w/tang-mounted aperture sight, grip adapter. Made 1972-84.

MODEL 178 . . . . **NiB $412 Ex $360 Gd $257**
Model 1873 Springfield Infantry Rifle replica. Caliber: .45-70. 32-inch bbl. Weight: 8 lbs. 10 oz. Sights: Leaf rear; blade front. Full-length stock w/bbl. bands, swivels, ramrod. Made 1973-86.

MODEL 250 SPORTSTER BOLT-ACTION
REPEATING RIFLE . . . . **NiB $98 Ex $77 Gd $51**
Caliber: .22 LR. 5-shot detachable box magazine. 23-inch bbl. Weight: 6.5 lbs. Sights: Open rear; blade front, on ramp. Plain pistol-grip stock. Made 1948-61.

Harrington & Richardson
Model 171

Harrington & Richardson
Model 171 Deluxe

Harrington & Richardson
Model 172

Harrington & Richardson
Model 173

Harrington & Richardson
Model 174 Little Big Horn Commemorative

Harrington & Richardson
Model 178

MODEL 251 . . . . **NiB $109 Ex $88 Gd $60**
Same as Model 250 except w/Lyman No. 55H rear sight.

**MODEL 265 "REG'LAR" BOLT-
ACTION REPEATING RIFLE** . . . . **NiB $103 Ex $82 Gd $56**
Caliber: .22 LR. 10-shot detachable box magazine. 22-inch bbl.
Weight: 6.5 lbs. Sights: Lyman No. 55 rear peep; blade front, on
ramp. Plain pistol-grip stock. Made 1946-49.

**MODEL 300 ULTRA
BOLT-ACTION RIFLE** . . . . **NiB $515 Ex $438 Gd $232**
Mauser-type action. Calibers: .22-250, .243 Win., .270 Win., .30-06,
.308 Win., 7mm Rem. Mag., .300 Win. Mag. Three round magazine
in 7mm and .300 Mag. calibers, 5-round in others. 22- or 24-inch bbl.
Sights: Open rear; ramp front. Checkered stock w/rollover cheekpiece
and full pistol grip, contrasting wood forearm tip and pistol grip, rubber buttplate, sling swivels. Weight: 7.25 lbs. Made 1965-82.

Harrington & Richardson
Model 300

Harrington & Richardson
Model 301 Carbine

Harrington & Richardson
Model 317P

Harrington & Richardson
Model 330

Harrington & Richardson
Model 360 Ultra

Harrington & Richardson
Model 370 Ultra Medalist

RIFLES

MODEL 301 CARBINE . . . . **NiB $438 Ex $360 Gd $232**
Same as Model 300 except w/18-inch bbl., Mannlicher-style stock,
weighs 7.25 lbs.; not available in caliber .22-250. Made 1967-82.

MODEL 308 AUTOMATIC RIFLE. . . NiB $418 Ex $335 Gd $228
Original designation of the Model 360 Ultra. Made 1965-67.

**MODEL 317 ULTRA WILDCAT
BOLT-ACTION RIFLE** . . . . **NiB $613 Ex $566 Gd $335**
Sako short action. Calibers: .17 Rem. 17/.223 (handload), .222 Rem.,

(cont'd.) **MODEL 317 ULTRA WILDCAT BOLT-ACTION RIFLE**
.223 Rem. Six round magazine. 20-inch bbl. No sights, receiver
dovetailed for scope mounts. Checkered stock w/cheekpiece and
full pistol grip, contrasting wood forearm tip and pistol-grip cap,
rubber buttplate. Weight: 5.25 lbs. Made 1968-76.

**MODEL 317P
PRESENTATION GRADE** . . . . **NiB $721 Ex $592 Gd $412**
Same as Model 317 except w/select grade fancy walnut stock
w/basket weave carving on forearm and pistol-grip. Made 1968-76.

GRADING: **NiB** = New in Box   **Ex** = Excellent or NRA 95%   **Gd** = Good or NRA 68%

Harrington & Richardson
Model 700 Deluxe

Harrington & Richardson
Model 750 Pioneer

Harrington & Richardson
"New" Model 750

Harrington & Richardson
Model 755

MODEL 330 HUNTER'S RIFLE . . . . NiB $309 Ex $257 Gd $180
Similar to Model 300, but w/plainer stock. Calibers: .243 Win., .270 Win., .30-06, .308 Win., 7mm Rem. Mag., .300 Win. Mag. Weight: 7.13 lbs. Made 1967-72.

MODEL 333 . . . . NiB $257 Ex $232 Gd $129
Plainer version of Model 300 w/uncheckered walnut-finished hardwood stock. Calibers: 7mm Rem. Mag. and .30-06. 22-inch bbl. Weight: 7.25 lbs. No sights. Made in 1974.

MODEL 340 . . . . NiB $386 Ex $309 Gd $201
Mauser-type action. Calibers: .243 Win., .308 Win., .270 Win., .30-06, 7x57. 22-inch bbl. Weight: 7.25 lbs. Hand-checkered American walnut stock. Made 1982-84.

MODEL 360
ULTRA AUTOMATIC RIFLE . . . . NiB $417 Ex $335 Gd $232
Gas-operated semiautomatic. Calibers: .243 Win., .308 Win. Three round detachable box magazine. 22-inch bbl. Sights: Open rear; ramp front. Checkered stock w/rollover cheekpiece, full pistol grip, contrasting wood forearm tip and pistol-grip cap, rubber buttplate, sling swivels. Weight: 7.25 lbs. Made 1967-78.

MODEL 361 . . . . NiB $463 Ex $386 Gd $257
Same as Model 360 except w/full rollover cheekpiece for right- or left-hand shooters. Made 1970-73.

MODEL 365 ACE BOLT-ACTION
SINGLE-SHOT RIFLE . . . . NiB $103 Ex $98 Gd $51
Caliber: .22 LR. 22-inch bbl. Weight: 6.5 lbs. Sights: Lyman No. 55 rear peep, blade front, on ramp. Plain pistol-grip stock. Made 1946-47.

MODEL 370 ULTRA MEDALIST . . . NiB $489 Ex $463 Gd $266
Varmint and target rifle based on Model 300. Calibers: .22-250, .243 Win., 6mm Rem. Three round magazine. 24-inch varmint weight bbl. No sights. Target-style stock w/semibeavertail forearm. Weight: 9.5 lbs. Made 1968-73.

MODEL 422 SLIDE-ACTION
REPEATER . . . . NiB $129 Ex $98 Gd $77
Caliber: .22 LR. Long, Short. Tubular magazine holds 21 Short, 17 Long, 15 LR. 24-inch bbl. Weight: 6 lbs. Sights: Open rear; ramp front. Plain pistol-grip stock grooved slide handle. Made 1956-58.

MODEL 450 . . . . NiB $113 Ex $98 Gd $51
Same as Model 451 except w/o front and rear sights.

MODEL 451 MEDALIST
BOLT-ACTION TARGET RIFLE . . . . . . NiB $180 Ex $154 Gd $82
Caliber: .22 LR. Five shot detachable box magazine. 26-inch bbl. Weight: 10.5 lbs. Sights: Lyman No. 524F extension rear; Lyman No. 77 front, scope bases. Target stock w/full pistol-grip and forearm, swivels and sling. Made 1948-61.

Harrington & Richardson
Model 760

Harrington & Richardson
Model 866

Harrington & Richardson
Model 1873 — 100th Anniversary

Harrington & Richardson
Model 5200 Sporter

Harrington & Richardson
Ultra Varmint

MODEL 465 TARGETEER SPECIAL
BOLT-ACTION REPEATER .... **NiB $165 Ex $129 Gd $82**
Caliber: .22 LR. 10-shot detachable box magazine. 25-inch
bbl. Weight: 9 lbs. Sights: Lyman No. 57 rear peep; blade front,
on ramp. Plain pistol-grip stock, swivels, web sling strap. Made
1946-47.

MODEL 700 AUTOLOADER ...... **NiB $283 Ex $257 Gd $129**
Caliber: .22 WMR. 5-shot magazine. 22-inch bbl. Weight: 6.5 lbs.
Sights: Folding leaf rear; blade front, on ramp. Monte Carlo-style
stock of American walnut. Made 1977-86.

MODEL 700 DELUXE .... **NiB $412 Ex $335 Gd $257**
Same as Model 700 Standard except w/select custom polished and
blued finish, select walnut stock, hand checkering, and no iron
sights. Fitted w/H&R Model 432 4x scope. Made 1980-86.

MODEL 750 PIONEER BOLT-ACTION
SINGLE-SHOT RIFLE .... **NiB $93 Ex $72 Gd $51**
Caliber: .22 LR. Long, Short. 22- or 24-inch bbl. Weight: 5 lbs. Sights: Open rear;
bead front. Plain pistol-grip stock. Made 1954-81; redesigned 1982; discont. 1985.

MODEL 751 SINGLE-SHOT RIFLE .... **NiB $77 Ex $57 Gd $36**
Same as Model 750 except w/Mannlicher-style stock. Made 1971.

MODEL 755 SAHARA
SINGLE-SHOT RIFLE .... **NiB $77 Ex $57 Gd $36**
Blow-back action, automatic ejection. Caliber: .22 LR. Long, Short.
18-inch bbl. Weight: 4 lbs. Sights: Open rear; military-type front.
Mannlicher-style stock. Made 1963-71.

MODEL 760 SINGLE-SHOT .... **NiB $93 Ex $72 Gd $51**
Same as Model 755 except w/conventional sporter stock. Made 1965-70.

MODEL 765 PIONEER BOLT-ACTION
SINGLE-SHOT RIFLE . . . . **NiB $72 Ex $57 Gd $36**
Caliber: .22 LR. Long, Short. 24-inch bbl. Weight: 5 lbs. Sights: Open rear; hooded bead front. Plain pistol-grip stock. Made 1948-54.

MODEL 800 LYNX
AUTOLOADING RIFLE . . . . **NiB $129 Ex $103 Gd $67**
Caliber: .22 LR. Five or 10-shot clip magazine. 22-inch bbl. Open sights. Weight: 6 lbs. Plain pistol-grip stock. Made 1958-60.

MODEL 852 FIELDSMAN
BOLT-ACTION REPEATER . . . . **NiB $113 Ex $57 Gd $62**
Caliber: .22 LR. Long, Short. Tubular magazine holds 21 Short, 17 Long, 15 LR. 24-inch bbl. Weight: 5.5 lbs. Sights: Open rear; bead front. Plain pistol-grip stock. Made 1952-53.

MODEL 865 PLAINSMAN
BOLT-ACTION REPEATER . . . . **NiB $103 Ex $82 Gd $51**
Caliber .22 LR. Long, Short. Five shot detachable box magazine. 22- or 24-inch bbl. Weight: 5.25 lbs. Sights: Open rear, bead front. Plain pistol-grip stock. Made 1949-86.

MODEL 866
BOLT-ACTION REPEATER . . . . **NiB $103 Ex $82 Gd $51**
Same as Model 865, except w/Mannlicher-style stock. Made 1971.

MODEL 1873 100TH ANNIVERSARY
(1871-1971) COMMEMORATIVE
OFFICER'S SPRINGFIELD REPLICA . . . **NiB $772 Ex $566 Gd $386**
Model 1873 "trap door" single-shot action. Engraved breech block, receiver, hammer, lock, band and buttplate. Caliber: .45-70. 26-inch bbl. Sights: Peep rear; blade front. Checkered walnut stock w/anniversary plaque. Ramrod. Weight: 8 lbs. 10,000 made 1971.

MODEL 5200 SPORTER
. . . . **NiB $613 Ex $515 Gd $317**
Turn-bolt repeater. Caliber: .22 LR. 24-inch bbl. Classic-style American walnut stock. Adj. trigger. Sights: Peep receiver; hooded ramp front. Weight: 6.5 lbs. Disc. 1983.

MODEL 5200 MATCH RIFLE
. . . . . . **NiB $412 Ex $407 Gd $309**
Same action as 5200 Sporter. Caliber: .22 LR. 28-inch target weight bbl. Target stock of American walnut. Weight: 11 lbs. Made 1982-86.

CUSTER MEMORIAL ISSUE
Limited Edition Model 1873 Springfield Carbine replica, richly engraved and inlaid w/gold, fancy walnut stock, in mahogany display case. Made 1973.
Officers' Model
Limited to 25 pieces. . . . . **NIB $5794 EX $4635 GD $3152**
Enlisted Men's model,
limited to 243 pieces. . . . . **NiB $3219 Ex $2575 Gd $1751**

TARGETEER JR. BOLT-ACTION RIFLE . . . . . **NiB $129 Ex $103 Gd $67**
Caliber: .22 LR. 5-shot detachable box magazine. 20-inch bbl. Weight: 7 lbs. Sights: Redfield 70 rear peep; Lyman No. 17A front. Target stock, junior-size w/pistol grip, swivels and sling. Made 1948-51.

ULTRA SINGLE-SHOT RIFLE
Side-lever single-shot. Calibers: .22-250 Rem., .223 Rem., .25-06 Rem., .308 Win. 22- to 26-inch bbl. Weight: 7-8 lbs. Curly maple or laminated stock. Barrel-mounted scope mount, no sights. Made 1993 to date.
Ultra Hunter (.25-06, .308) . . . . . . **NiB $196 Ex $129 Gd $103**
Ultra Varmint. . . . . **NiB $232 Ex $180 Gd $129**

HARRIS GUNWORKS — Phoenix, Arizona (Formerly McMillan Gun Works)

SIGNATURE ALASKAN
BOLT-ACTION RIFLE . . . . **NiB $3502 Ex $2781 Gd $1854**
Same general specifications as Classic Sporter except w/match-grade bbl. Rings and mounts. Sights: Single-leaf rear, bbl. band front. Checkered Monte Carlo stock w/palmswell and solid recoil pad. Nickel finish. Calibers: LA (long): .270 Win., .280 Rem., .30-06, MA (Magnum): 7mm Rem. Mag., .300 Win. Mag., .300 Wby. Mag., .340 Wby. Mag., .358 Win., .375 H&H Mag. Made 1990 to date.

SIGNATURE CLASSIC SPORTER
The prototype for Harris' Signature Series, this bolt-action rifle is available in three lengths: SA (standard/ short) — from .22-250 to .350 Rem Mag.; LA (long) — .25-06 to .30-06; MA (Magnum) — 7mm STW to .416 Rem. Mag. Four-shot or 3-shot (Magnum) magazine. Bbl. lengths: 22, 24 or 26 inches. Weight: 7 lbs. (short action). No sights; rings and bases provided. Harris fiberglass stock, Fibergrain or wood stock optional. Stainless, matte black or black chrome sulfide finish. Available in right- and left-hand models. Made 1987 to date. Has pre-64 Model 70-style action for dangerous game.
Classic Sporter Standard . . . . . . **NiB $2472 Ex $2163 Gd $1236**
Classic Sporter Stainless . . . . . . **NiB $2668 Ex $2189 Gd $1262**
Talon Sporter . . . . **NiB $2678 Ex $1957 Gd $1339**

SIGNATURE MOUNTAIN RIFLE . . . . . **NiB $3038 Ex $2678 Gd $1365**
Same general specifications as Harris (McMillan) Classic Sporter except w/titanium action and graphite-reinforced fiberglass stock. Weight: 5.5 lbs. Calibers: .270 Win., .280 Rem., .30-06, 7mm Mag., .300 Win. Mag. Other calibers on special order. Made 1995 to date.

SIGNATURE SUPER VARMINTER . . . . . **NiB $2472 Ex $2060 Gd $1236**
Same general specifications as Harris (McMillan) Classic Sporter except w/heavy, contoured bbl., adj. trigger, fiberglass stock and field bipod. Calibers: .223, .22-250, .220 Swift, .244 Win., 6mm Rem., .25-06, 7mm-08, .308 Win., .350 Win. Mag. Made 1995 to date.

TALON SAFARI RIFLE
Same general specifications as Harris (McMillan) Classic Sporter except w/Harris Safari-grade action, match-grade bbl. and "Safari" fiberglass stock. Calibers: Magnum — .300 H&H Mag., .300 Win Mag., .300 Wby. Mag., .338 Win. Mag., .340 Wby. Mag., .375 H&H Mag., .404 Jeffrey, .416 Rem. Mag., .458 Win., Super Mag. — .300 Phoenix, .338 Lapua, .378 Wby. Mag., .416 Rigby, .416 Wby. Mag., .460 Wby. Mag. Matte black finish. Other calibers available on special order, and at a premium, but the "used gun" value remains the same. Imported 1989 to date.
Safari Magnum . . . . **NiB $3759 Ex $2935 Gd $1905**
Safari Super Magnum . . . . **NiB $4165 Ex $3394 Gd $2407**

HECKLER & KOCH, GMBH — Oberndorf/Neckar, Germany Imported by Heckler & Koch, Inc., Sterling, VA

MODEL 911 SEMIAUTO RIFLE . . . . **NiB $1802 Ex $1596 Gd $875**
Caliber: .308 (7.62mm). 5-shot magazine. 19.7-inch bull bbl. 42.4 inches overall. Sights: Hooded post front; adj. aperture rear. Weight: 11 lbs. Kevlar-reinforced fiberglass thumbhole-stock. Imported 1989-93.

MODEL HK91 A-2 SEMIAUTO . . . . **NiB $2266 Ex $1957 Gd $1226**
Delayed roller-locked blow-back action. Caliber: 7.62mm X 51 NATO (308 Win.) 5- or 20-round box magazine. 19-inch bbl. Weight: W/o magazine, 9.37 lbs. Sights L "V" and aperture rear, post front. Plastic buttstock and forearm. Disc. 1991.

Heckler & Koch
Model HK91 A-2

Heckler & Koch
Model HK91 A-3

Heckler & Koch
Model HK93 A-2

Heckler & Koch
Model HK940 Carbine

MODEL HK91 A-3 . . . . **NiB $2575 Ex $2317 Gd $1442**
Same as Model HK91 A-2 except w/retractable metal buttstock,
weighs 10.56 lbs. Disc. 1991.

MODEL HK93 SEMIAUTOMATIC
Delayed roller-locked blow-back action. Caliber: 5.56mm x 45 (.223
Rem.). 5- or 20-round magazine. 16.13-inch bbl. Weight: W/o mag-
azine, 7.6 lbs. Sights: "V" and aperture rear; post front. Plastic butt-
stock and forearm. Disc. 1991.
HK93 A-2 . . . . **NiB $2377 Ex $2214 Gd $1025**
HK93 A-3 w/retractable stock. . . . . . . **NiB $2420 Ex $2163 Gd $1905**

MODEL HK94 SEMIAUTOMATIC CARBINE
Caliber: 9mm Para. 15-shot magazine. 16-inch bbl. Weight: 6.75
lbs. Aperture rear sight, front post. Plastic buttstock and forend or
retractable metal stock. Imported 1983-91.

(cont'd.) MODEL HK94 SEMIAUTOMATIC CARBINE
HK94-A2 w/standard stock. . . . . **NiB $3090 Ex $3038 Gd $2575**
HK94-A3 w/retractable stock . . . . **NiB $4666 Ex $3734 Gd $2539**

MODEL HK300
SEMIAUTOMATIC . . . . **NiB $711 Ex $644 Gd $412**
Caliber: .22 WMR. 5- or 15-round box magazine. 19.7-inch bbl.
w/polygonal rifling. Weight: 5.75 lbs. Sights: V-notch rear; ramp
front. High-luster polishing and bluing. European walnut stock
w/cheekpiece, checkered forearm and pistol-grip. Disc. 1989.

MODEL HK630 SEMIAUTOMATIC. . . . . . **NiB $1210 Ex $978 Gd $592**
Caliber: .223 Rem. Four or 10-round magazine. 24-inch bbl.
Overall length: 42 inches. Weight: 7 lbs. Sights: Open rear; ramp
front. European walnut stock w/Monte Carlo cheekpiece.
Imported 1983-90.

GRADING: **NiB** = New in Box   **Ex** = Excellent or NRA 95%   **Gd** = Good or NRA 68%

Heckler & Koch
Model HK PSG-1

Heckler & Koch
Model SL-8

Heckler & Koch
Model USC Carbine

MODEL HK770 SEMIAUTOMATIC .... NiB $1880 Ex $1545 Gd $824
Caliber: .308 Win. Three or 10-round magazine. Overall length: 44.5 inches. Weight: 8 lbs. Sights: Open rear; ramp front. European walnut stock w/Monte Carlo cheekpiece. Imported 1983-90.

MODEL HK940 SEMIAUTOMATIC .... NiB $2008 Ex $1802 Gd $953
Caliber: .30-06 Springfield. Three or 10-round magazine. Overall length: 47 inches. Weight: 8.8 lbs. Sights: Open rear; ramp front. European walnut stock w/Monte Carlo cheekpiece. Imported 1983-90.

MODEL HK PSG-1
MARKSMAN'S RIFLE .... NiB $10,622 Ex $8497 Gd $5778
Caliber: .308 (7.62mm). Five and 20-shot magazine. 25.6-inch bbl. 47.5 inches overall. Hensoldt 6x42 telescopic sight. Weight: 17.8 lbs. Matte black composite stock w/pistol-grip. Imported 1988 to date.

MODEL SL8-1 RIFLE .... NiB $1648 Ex $1287 Gd $875
Caliber: .223 Win. 10-shot magazine. 20.80- inch bbl. 38.58 inches overall. Weight: 8.6 lbs. Gas-operated, short-stroke piston w/rotary locking bolt. Rear adjustable sight w/ambidextrous safety selector lever. Polymer receiver w/adjustable buttstock. Introduced 1999.

MODEL SR-9
SEMIAUTO RIFLE .... NiB $1802 Ex $1648 Gd $927
Caliber: .308 (7.62mm). Five shot magazine. 19.7-inch bull bbl. 42.4 inches overall. Hooded post front sight; adj. aperture rear. Weight: 11 lbs. Kevlar-reinforced fiberglass thumbhole-stock w/wood grain finish. Imported 1989-93.

MODEL SR-9
TARGET RIFLE. .... NiB $2575 Ex $2008 Gd $1339
Same general specifications as standard SR-9 except w/ PSG-1 trigger group and adj. buttstock. Imported 1992-94.

MODEL USC
CARBINE RIFLE. .... NiB $1133 Ex $1025 Gd $669
Caliber: 45 ACP. 10-shot magazine. 16- inch bbl., 35.43 inches overall. Weight: 6 lbs. Blow-back operating system. Polymer receiver w/integral grips. Rear adjustable sight w/ambidextrous safety selector lever. Introduced 1999.

HERCULES RIFLES

See listings under "W" for Montgomery Ward.

Heym
Model SR-20 Standard

Heym
Model SR-20L Mannlicher

HEROLD RIFLE — Suhl, Germany
Made by Franz Jaeger & Company

BOLT-ACTION REPEATING
SPORTING RIFLE. . . . . **NiB $1287 Ex $1025 Gd $644**
"Herold-Repetierbüchse." Miniature Mauser-type action w/unique 5-shot box magazine on hinged floorplate. Double-set triggers. Caliber: .22 Hornet. 24-inch bbl. Sights: Leaf rear; ramp front. Weight: 7.75 lbs. Fancy checkered stock. Made before WWII. Note: These rifles were imported by Charles Daly and A.F. Stoeger Inc. of New York City and sold under their names.

HEYM RIFLES AMERICA, INC. — Mfd. By Heym, GmbH & Co JAGWAFFEN KD., Gleichamberg, Germany, *(Previously imported by Heym America, Inc.; Heckler & Koch; JagerSport, Ltd.)*

MODEL 55B O/U DOUBLE RIFLE
Kersten boxlock action w/double cross bolt and cocking indicators. Calibers: .308 Win., .30-06, .375 H&H, .458 Win. Mag., .470 N.E. 25-inch bbl. 42 inches overall. Weight: 8.25 lbs. Sights: fixed V-type rear; front ramp w/silver bead. Engraved receiver w/optional sidelocks, interchangeable bbls. and claw mounts. Checkered European walnut stock. Imported from Germany.
Model 55 (boxlock) . . . . **NiB $7500 Ex $6100 Gd $5500**
Model 55 (sidelock . . . . **NiB $11,938 Ex $9550 Gd $6494**
W\Extra rifle bbls., add **$5500**
W/Extra shotgun bbls., add **$2800**

MODEL 88B DOUBLE RIFLE
Modified Anson & Deeley boxlock action w/standing gears, double underlocking lugs and Greener extension w/crossbolt. Calibers: 8x57 JRS, 9.3x74R, .30-06, .375 H&H, .458 Win. Mag., .470 Nitro Express, .500 Nitro Express. Other calibers available on special order. Weight: 8 to 10 lbs. Top tang safety and cocking indicators. Double triggers w/front set. Fixed or 3-leaf express rear sight, front ramp w/silver bead. Engraved receiver w/optional sidelocks. Checkered French walnut stock. Imported from Germany.
Model 88B Boxlock . . . . **NiB $10,969 Ex $8775 Gd $5967**
Model 88B/SS Sidelock . . . . **NiB $13,438 Ex $10,750 Gd $7310**
Model 88B Safari (Magnum) . . . . . . **NiB $14,938 Ex $11,950 Gd $8126**

EXPRESS BOLT-ACTION RIFLE
Same general specifications as Model SR-20 Safari except w/modified magnum Mauser action. Checkered AAA-grade European walnut stock w/cheekpiece, solid rubber recoil pad, rosewood forend tip and grip

(cont'd.) EXPRESS BOLT-ACTION RIFLE
cap. Calibers: .338 Lapua Magnum, .375 H&H, .378 Wby. Mag., .416 Rigby .450 Ackley, .460 Wby. Mag., .500 A-Square, .500 Nitro Express, .600 Nitro Express. Other calibers available on special order, but no change in used gun value. Imported from Germany 1989-95.
Standard Express Magnum . . . . **NiB $5188 Ex $4150 Gd $2822**
600 Nitro Express . . . . **NiB $5500 Ex $4800 Gd $2800**
Left-hand models, add **$600**

SR-20 BOLT-ACTION RIFLE
Calibers: .243 Win., .270 Win., .308 Win., .30-06, 7mm Rem. Mag., .300 Win. Mag., .375 H&H. Five shot (standard) or 3-shot (Magnum) magazine. Bbl. length: 20.5-inch (SR-20L); 24-inch (SR-20N); 26-inch (SR-20G). Weight: 7.75 lbs. Adj. rear sight, blade front. Checkered French walnut stock in Monte Carlo style (N&G Series) or full Mannlicher (L Series). Imported from Germany. Disc. 1992.
SR-20L . . . . **NiB $1880 Ex $1468 Gd $824**
SR-20N . . . . **NiB $2050 Ex $1643 Gd $978**
SR-20G . . . . **NiB $2575 Ex $2008 Gd $1313**

SR-20 CLASSIC BOLT-ACTION RIFLES
Same as SR-20 except w/.22-250 and .338 Win. Mag. plus metric calibers on request. 24-inch (standard) or 25-inch (Magnum) bbl. Checkered French walnut stock. Left-hand models. Imported from Germany since 1985; Sporter version 1989-93.
Classic (Standard) . . . . **NiB $2155 Ex $1724 Gd $1172**
Classic (Magnum) . . . . **NiB $2395 Ex $1916 Gd $1302**
Left-hand models, add **$300**
Classic Sporter (Std.
w/22-inch bbl.) . . . . **NiB $2309 Ex $1848 Gd $1257**
Classic Sporter (Mag.
w/24-inch bbl.) . . . . **NiB $2549 Ex $2039 Gd $1386**

SR-20 ALPINE, SAFARI AND TROPHY SERIES
Same general specifications as Model SR-20 Classic Sporter except Alpine Series w/20-inch bbl., Mannlicher stock, chambered in standard calibers only; Safari Series w/24-inch bbl., 3-leaf express sights and magnum action in calibers .375 H & H, .404 Jeffrey, .425 Express, .458 Win. Mag.; Trophy Series w/Krupp-Special tapered octagon bbl. w/quarter rib and open sights, standard and Magnum calibers. Imported from Germany 1989-93.
Alpine Series . . . . **NiB $2309 Ex $1848 Gd $1257**
Safari Series . . . . **NiB $2356 Ex $1885 Gd $1281**
Trophy Series (Stand. calibers) . . . . **NiB $3013 Ex $2410 Gd $1639**
Trophy Series
(Magnum calibers) . . . . **NiB $3283 Ex $2626 Gd $1786**

J.C. HIGGINS RIFLES

See Sears, Roebuck & Company.

High Standard
Flite-King Pump

High Standard
Hi-Power Deluxe

High Standard
Sport-King Autoloading Carbine

High Standard
Sport-King Deluxe Auto

High Standard
Sport-King Field Auto

High Standard
Sport-King Special Auto

HI-POINT FIREARMS — Dayton, Ohio
MODEL 995 CARBINE
Semiautomatic recoil-operated carbine. Calibers: 9mm Parabellum or 40 S&W. 10-shot magazine. 16.5-inch bbl. 31.5 inches overall. Protected post front sight, aperture rear w/integral scope mount. Matte blue, chrome or Parkerized finish. Checkered polymer grip/frame. Made 1996 to date.
Model 995, 9mm (blue or Parkerized) . . . . . NiB $161 Ex $129 Gd $88
Model 995, .40 S&W (blue or Parkerized) . . . NiB $194 Ex $154 Gd $105
W/laser sights, add $35
W/chrome finish, add $15

HIGH STANDARD SPORTING FIREARMS — East Hartford, Connecticut, (Formerly High Standard Mfg. Co., Hamden, CT)

A long-standing producer of sporting arms, High Standard discontinued its operations in 1984.

FLITE-KING
PUMP RIFLE . . . . NiB $154 Ex $103 Gd $62
Hammerless slide-action. Caliber: .22 LR. .22 Long, .22 Short. Tubular mag. holds 17 LR, 19 Long, or 24 Short. 24-inch bbl. Weight: 5.5 lbs. Sights: Partridge rear; bead front. Monte Carlo stock w/pistol grip, serrated semibeavertail forearm. Made 1962-75.

HI-POWER
DELUXE RIFLE . . . . NiB $541 Ex $360 Gd $206
Mauser-type bolt action, sliding safety. Calibers: .270, .30-06. Four shot magazine. 22-inch bbl. Weight: 7 lbs. Sights: Folding open rear; ramp front. Walnut stock w/checkered pistol-grip and forearm, Monte Carlo comb, QD swivels. Made 1962-66.

Holland & Holland
Best Quality Magazine

Holland & Holland
Royal Deluxe Double

Howa
Model 1500 Hunter

Howa
Model 1500 Lightning

HI-POWER FIELD BOLT-ACTION RIFLE...... NiB $463 Ex $309 Gd $180
Same as Hi-Power Deluxe except w/plain field style stock. Made 1962-66.

**SPORT-KING AUTO-
LOADING CARBINE** .... NiB $154 Ex $93 Gd $72
Same as Sport-King Field Autoloader except w/18.25-inch bbl., Western-style straight-grip stock w/bbl. band, sling and swivels. Made 1964-73.

SPORT-KING DELUXE AUTOLOADER .... NiB $232 Ex $180 Gd $77
Same as Sport-King Special Autoloader except w/checkered stock. Made 1966-75.

SPORT-KING FIELD AUTOLOADER .... NiB $113 Ex $93 Gd $57
Calibers: .22 LR. .22 Long, .22 Short (high speed). Tubular magazine holds 15 LR, 17 Long, or 21 Short. 22.25-inch bbl. Weight: 5.5 lbs. Sights: Open rear; beaded post front. Plain pistol-grip stock. Made 1960-66.

SPORT-KING SPECIAL AUTOLOADER .... NiB $180 Ex $134 Gd $77
Same as Sport-King Field except stock w/Monte Carlo comb and semibeavertail forearm. Made 1960-66.

**HOLLAND & HOLLAND, LTD. — London,
England, *Imported by Holland & Holland, NY, NY***

**NO. 2 MODEL HAMMERLESS
EJECTOR DOUBLE RIFLE** .... NiB $14,938 Ex $11,950 Gd $8126
Same general specifications as Royal Model except plainer finish. Disc. 1960.

BEST QUALITY MAGAZINE RIFLE .... NiB $14,375 Ex $11,500 Gd $7820
Mauser or Enfield action. Calibers: .240 Apex, .300 H&H Mag., .375 H&H Magnum. Four shot box magazine. 24-inch bbl. Weight: 7.25 lbs., 240 Apex; 8.25 lbs., .300 Mag. and .375 Mag. Sights: Folding leaf rear; hooded ramp front. Detachable French walnut stock w/cheekpiece, checkered pistol-grip and forearm, swivels. Currently mfd. Specifications given apply to most models.

DELUXE MAGAZINE RIFLE....... NiB $15,938 Ex $12,750 Gd $8670
Same specifications as Best Quality except w/exhibition-grade stock and special engraving. Currently mfd.

ROYAL DELUXE DOUBLE RIFLE .... NiB $56,875 Ex $45,500 Gd $30,940
Formerly designated "Modele Deluxe." Same specifications as Royal Model except w/exhibition-grade stock and special engraving. Currently mfd.

**ROYAL HAMMERLESS
EJECTOR RIFLE**........ NiB $40,625 Ex $32,500 Gd $22,100
Sidelock. Calibers: .240 Apex, 7mm H&H Mag., .300 H&H Mag., .300 Win. Mag., .30-06, .375 H&H Mag., .458 Win. Mag., .465 H&H Mag. 24- to 28-inch bbls. Weight: From 7.5 lbs. Sights: Folding leaf rear, ramp front. Cheekpiece stock of select French walnut, checkered pistol-grip and forearm. Currently mfd. Same general specifications apply to prewar model.

Husqvarna
Series 1100 Deluxe

Husqvarna
1951 Hi-Power

HOWA RIFLES — Mfg. By Howa Machinery Ltd., Shinkawa-Chonear, Nagoya 452, Japan, Imported by Interarms, Alexandria, VA

See also Mossberg (1500) Smith & Wesson (1500 & 1700) and Weatherby (Vanguard).

MODEL 1500 HUNTER
Similar to Trophy Model except w/standard walnut stock. No Monte Carlo cheekpiece or grip cap. Imported 1988-89.

Standard calibers	NiB $463	Ex $412	Gd $283
Magnum calibers	NiB $444	Ex $360	Gd $253
Stainless steel, add			$85

MODEL 1500 LIGHTNING BOLT-ACTION RIFLE
Similar to Hunter Model except fitted w/black Bell & Carlson Carbelite stock w/checkered grip and forend. Weight: 7.5 lbs. Imported 1988-89.

Standard calibers	NiB $427	Ex $340	Gd $201
Magnum calibers	NiB $444	Ex $360	Gd $253

MODEL 1500 PCS BOLT-ACTION RIFLE
Similar to Hunter Model except in Police Counter Sniper configuration and chambered for .308 Win. only. Walnut or synthetic stock w/checkered grip and forend. Receiver drilled and tapped but w/o sights. Weight: 8.5 to 9.3 lbs. Imported 1999 to date.

PCS Model w/walnut stock	NiB $427	Ex $340	Gd $201
PCS Model w/synthetic stock	NiB $406	Ex $335	Gd $244
Stainless steel, add			$85

MODEL 1500 REALTREE
CAMO RIFLE	NiB $489	Ex $412	Gd $283

Similar to Trophy Model except fitted w/Camo Bell & Carlson Carbelite stock w/checkered grip and forend. Weight: 8 lbs. Stock, action and barrel finished in Realtree camo. Available in standard calibers only. Imported 1993 to date.

MODEL 1500 TROPHY/VARMINT BOLT-ACTION RIFLE
Calibers: .22-250, .223, .243 Win., .270 Win., .308 Win., .30-06, 7mm Mag., .300 Win. Mag., .338 Win. Mag. 22-inch bbl. (standard); 24-inch bbl. (Magnum). 42.5 inches overall (standard). Weight: 7.5 lbs. Adj. rear sight hooded ramp front. Checkered walnut stock w/Monte Carlo cheekpiece. Varmint Model w/24-inch heavy bbl., weight of 9.5 lbs. in calibers .22-250, .223 and .308 only. Imported 1979-93.

Trophy Standard	NiB $544	Ex $422	Gd $247
Trophy Magnum	NiB $504	Ex $407	Gd $283
Varmint (Parkerized finish)	NiB $412	Ex $330	Gd $225
Stainless steel, add			$85

MODEL 1500 WOODGRAIN LIGHTNING RIFLE
Calibers: .243, .270, 7mm Rem. Mag., .30-06. Mag. Five shot magazine 22-inch. 42 inches overall. Weight: 7.5 lbs. Receiver drilled and tapped for scope mount, no sights. Checkered woodgrain synthetic polymer stock. Imported 1993-94.

Standard calibers	NiB $463	Ex $402	Gd $232
Magnum calibers	NiB $529	Ex $427	Gd $298

H-S PRECISION — Rapid City, South Dakota

PRO-SERIES
Custom rifle built on Remington 700 bolt action. Calibers: .22 to .416, 24- or 26-inch bbl. w/fluted option. Aluminum bedding block system w/take-down option. Kevlar/carbon fiber stock to customer's specifications. Appointments and options to customer's preference. Made 1990 to date.

Sporter model	NiB $2034	Ex $1699	Gd $978
Pro-Hunter model (PHR)	NiB $1706	Ex $1365	Gd $928
Long-Range Model	NiB $1931	Ex $1622	Gd $901
Long-Range takedown model	NiB $2254	Ex $1802	Gd $1226
Marksman model	NiB $2034	Ex $1699	Gd $978
Marksman takedown model	NiB $2359	Ex $1880	Gd $1236
Varmint takedown model (VTD)	NiB $2008	Ex $1674	Gd $953
Left-hand models, add			$200

HUNGARIAN MILITARY RIFLES — Budapest, Hungary, Manufactured at Government Arsenal

MODEL 1935M MANN-
LICHER MILITARY RIFLE	NiB $283	Ex $232	Gd $129

Caliber: 8x52mm Hungarian. Bolt action, straight handle. Five shot projecting box magazine. 24-inch bbl. Weight: 9 lbs. Adj. leaf rear sight, hooded front blade. Two-piece military-type stock. Made 1935-40.

MODEL 1943M (GERMAN GEW 98/40) MANNLICHER
MILITARY RIFLE	NiB $335	Ex $257	Gd $154

Modification, during German occupation, of Model 1935M. Caliber: 7.9mm Mauser. Turned-down bolt handle and Mauser M/98-type box magazine; other differences are minor. Made 1940 to end of war in Europe.

Husqvarna 3000
Crown Grade

Husqvarna 4100
Lightweight

Husqvarna 6000
Imperial Custom

RIFLES

HUSQVARNA VAPENFABRIK A.B. — Husqvarna, Sweden

MODEL 456 LIGHTWEIGHT
FULL-STOCK SPORTER . . . . NiB $515 Ex $412 Gd $283
Same as Series 4000/4100 except w/sporting style full stock w/slope-away cheekrest. Weight: 6.5 lbs. Made 1959-70.

SERIES 1000 SUPER GRADE . . . . . . NiB $509 Ex $407 Gd $277
Same as 1951 Hi-Power except w/European walnut sporter stock w/Monte Carlo comb and cheekpiece. Made 1952-56.

SERIES 1100 DELUXE MODEL HI-POWER
BOLT-ACTION SPORTING RIFLE . . . . NiB $515 Ex $412 Gd $280
Same as 1951 Hi-Power, except w/jeweled bolt, European walnut stock. Made 1952-56.

1950 HI-POWER SPORTING RIFLE . . . . . . NiB $451 Ex $360 Gd $245
Mauser-type bolt action. Calibers: .220 Swift, .270 Win. .30-06 (see note below), 5-shot box magazine. 23.75-inch bbl. Weight: 7.75 lbs. Sights: Open rear; hooded ramp front. Sporting stock of Arctic beech, checkered pistol grip and forearm, swivels. Note: Husqvarna sporters were first intro. in U.S. about 1948; earlier models were also available in calibers 6.5x55, 8x57 and 9.3x57. Made 1946-1951.

1951 HI-POWER RIFLE . . . . NiB $483 Ex $386 Gd $263
Same as 1950 Hi-Power except w/high-comb stock, low safety.

SERIES 3000 CROWN GRADE . . . . NiB $489 Ex $360 Gd $232
Same as Series 3100, except w/Monte Carlo comb stock.

SERIES 3100 CROWN GRADE . . . . NiB $489 Ex $360 Gd $232
HVA improved Mauser action. Calibers: .243, .270, 7mm, .30-06, .308 Win. Five shot box magazine. 23.75-inch bbl. Weight: 7.75 lbs. Sights: Open rear; hooded ramp front. European walnut stock, checkered, cheekpiece, pistol-grip cap, black forend tip, swivels. Made 1954-72.

SERIES 4000 LIGHTWEIGHT RIFLE . . . . . . NiB $489 Ex $360 Gd $232
Same as Series 4100 except w/Monte Carlo comb stock and no rear sight.

SERIES 4100 LIGHTWEIGHT RIFLE . . . . . . NiB $484 Ex $360 Gd $206
HVA improved Mauser action. Calibers: .243, .270, 7mm, .30-06, .308 Win. Five shot box magazine. 20.5-inch bbl. Weight: 6.25 lbs. Sights: Open rear; hooded ramp front. Lightweight walnut stock w/cheekpiece, pistol grip, Schnabel forend tip, checkered, swivels. Made 1954-72. See illustration previous page.

SERIES 6000 IMPERIAL CUSTOM GRADE . NiB $644 Ex $515 Gd $335
Same as Series 3100 except fancy-grade stock, 3-leaf folding rear sight, adj. trigger. Calibers: .243, .270, 7mm Rem. Mag. .308, .30-06. Made 1968-70. See illustration previous page.

SERIES 7000 IMPERIAL
MONTE CARLO LIGHTWEIGHT. . . NiB $669 Ex $515 Gd $335
Same as Series 4000 Lightweight except fancy-grade stock, 3-leaf folding rear sight, adj. trigger. Calibers: .243, .270, .308, .30-06. Made 1968-70.

MODEL 8000 IMPERIAL GRADE RIFLE . . . NiB $669 Ex $515 Gd $335
Same as Model 9000 except w/jeweled bolt, engraved floorplate, deluxe French walnut checkered stock, no sights. Made 1971-72.

MODEL 9000 CROWN GRADE RIFLE . . . . NiB $515 Ex $412 Gd $309
New design Husqvarna bolt action. Adj. trigger. Calibers: .270, 7mm Rem. Mag., .30-06, .300 Win. Mag. Five shot box magazine, hinged floorplate. 23.75-inch bbl. Sights: Folding leaf rear; hooded ramp front. Checkered walnut stock w/Monte Carlo cheekpiece, rosewood forend tip and pistol-grip cap. Weight: 7 lbs. 3 oz. Made 1971-72.

SERIES P-3000 PRESENTATION RIFLE . . . . NiB $824 Ex $669 Gd $438
Same as Crown Grade Series 3000 except w/selected stock, engraved action, adj. trigger. Calibers: .243, .270, 7mm Rem. Mag., .30-06. Made 1968-70.

Interarms Mark X
Lightweight Sporter

Interarms Mini-Mark X

Italian Model 38 Military Rifle

INTERARMS RIFLES — Alexandria, Virginia

The following Mark X rifles are manufactured by Zavodi Crvena Zastava, Belgrade, Yugoslavia.

MARK X ALASKAN . . . . NiB $484 Ex $357 Gd $255
Same specifications as Mark X Sporter, except chambered for .375 H&H Mag. and .458 Win. Mag. w/3-round magazine. Stock w/recoil-absorbing cross bolt and heavy duty recoil pad. Weighs 8.25 lbs. Made 1976-84.

MARK X BOLT-ACTION SPORTER SERIES
Mauser-type action. Calibers: .22-250, .243, .25-06, .270, 7x57, 7mm Rem. Mag., .308, .30-06, .300 Win. Mag. Five shot magazine (3-shot in magnum calibers). 24-inch bbl. Weight: 7.5 lbs. Sights: Adj. leaf rear; ramp front, w/hood. Classic-style stock of European walnut w/Monte Carlo comb and cheekpiece, checkered pistol grip and forearm, black forend tip, QD swivels. Made 1972-97.
Mark X Standard . . . . NiB $376 Ex $301 Gd $205
Mark X Camo (Realtree) . . . . NiB $478 Ex $382 Gd $260
American Field, std.
(rubber recoil pad) . . . . NiB $593 Ex $474 Gd $322
American Field, Magnum
(rubber recoil pad) . . . . NiB $631 Ex $505 Gd $344

MARK X CAVALIER . . . . NiB $382 Ex $306 Gd $204
Same specifications as Mark X Sporter except w/contemporary-style stock w/rollover cheekpiece, rosewood forend tip/grip cap, recoil pad. Intro. 1974; Disc.

MARK X CONTINENTAL
MANNLICHER STYLE CARBINE . . . . NiB $408 Ex $357 Gd $229
Same specifications as Mark X Sporter except straight European-style comb stock w/sculptured cheekpiece. Precise double-set triggers and classic "butterknife" bolt handle. French checkering. Weight: 7.25 lbs. Disc.

MARK X LIGHTWEIGHT SPORTER . . . . . . NiB $357 Ex $296 Gd $204
Calibers: .22-250 Rem., .270 Win., 7mm Rem. Mag., .30-06 or 7mm Mag. Four or 5-round magazine. 20-inch bbl. Synthetic Carbolite stock Weight: 7 lbs. Imported 1988-90. (Reintroduced

1994-97.)
MARK X MARQUIS
MANNLICHER STYLE CARBINE . . . . NiB $440 Ex $352 Gd $240
Same specifications as Mark X Sporter except w/20-inch bbl., full-length Mannlicher-type stock w/metal forend/muzzle cap. Calibers: .270, 7x57, .308, .30-06. Imported 1976-84.

MINI-MARK X BOLT-ACTION
RIFLE. . . . . NiB $382 Ex $301 Gd $204
Miniature M98 Mauser action. Caliber: .223 Rem. Five shot magazine. 20-inch bbl. 39.75 inches overall. Weight: 6.25 lbs. Adj. rear sight, hooded ramp front. Checkered hardwood stock. Imported 1987-94.

MARK X VISCOUNT . . . . NiB $382 Ex $306 Gd $204
Same specifications as Mark X Sporter except w/plainer field grade stock. Imported 1974-87.

AFRICAN SERIES . . . . NiB $637 Ex $551 Gd $357
Mauser-type bolt-action. Calibers: .375 H&H Mag., .458 Win. Mag. Three shot magazine. 24-inch bbl. Weight: 8 lbs. Sights: 3-leaf express open rear, ramp front w/hood. English-style stock of European walnut, w/cheekpiece, black forend tip, checkered pistol grip and forearm, recoil pad, QD swivels. Imported 1974-96 by Whitworth Rifle Co., England.

ITALIAN MILITARY RIFLES
Manufactured by government plants at Brescia, Gardone, Terni and Turin, Italy

MODEL 38 MILITARY RIFLE . . . . NiB $102 Ex $92 Gd $51
Modification of Italian Model 1891 Mannlicher-Carcano Military Rifle w/turned-down bolt handle, detachable folding bayonet. Caliber: 7.35mm Italian Service (many arms of this model were later converted to the old 6.5mm caliber). Six shot box magazine. 21.25-inch bbl. Weight: 7.5 lbs. Sights: Adj. rear-blade front. Military straight-grip stock. Adopted 1938.

Ithaca Model 49

Ithaca Model 49
Presentation

Ithaca Model 49R
Sporter

Ithaca Model 72
Saddlegun

Ithaca Model 72
Saddlegun Deluxe

ITHACA GUN COMPANY, INC. — King Ferry, New York, (Formerly Ithaca, NY)

MODEL 49
SADDLEGUN LEVER ACTION
SINGLE-SHOT RIFLE . . . . NiB $148 Ex $133 Gd $61
Martini-type action. Hand-operated rebounding hammer. Caliber: .22 LR. Long, Short. 18-inch bbl. Open sights. Western carbine-style stock. Weight: 5.5 lbs. Made 1961-78.

MODEL 49 SADDLEGUN — DELUXE . . . . . NiB $178 Ex $127 Gd $76
Same as standard Model 49 except w/gold-plated hammer and trigger, figured walnut stock, sling swivels. Made 1962-75.

MODEL 49 SADDLEGUN — MAGNUM . . . NiB $173 Ex $153 Gd $92
Same as standard Model 49 except chambered for .22 WMR cartridge. Made 1962-78.

MODEL 49 SADDLEGUN
—PRESENTATION. . . . . NiB $296 Ex $280 Gd $122
Same as standard Model 49 Saddlegun except w/gold-plated hammer and trigger, engraved receiver, full fancy-figured walnut stock w/gold nameplate. Available in .22 LR or .22 WMR. Made 1962-74.

MODEL 49 SADDLEGUN
— ST. LOUIS BICENTENNIAL . . . . . NiB $296 Ex $280 Gd $122
Same as Model 49 Deluxe except w/commemorative inscription. 200 made in 1964. Top value is for rifle in new, unfired condition.

MODEL 49R SADDLEGUN
REPEATING RIFLE . . . . NiB $270 Ex $250 Gd $102
Similar in appearance to Model 49 Single-Shot. Caliber: .22 LR. Long, Short. Tubular magazine holds 15 LR, 17 Long, 21 Short. 20-inch bbl. Weight: 5.5 lbs. Sights: Open rear-bead front. Western-style stock, checkered grip. Made 1968-71.

Ithaca
Model LSA-65 Standard

Ithaca
Model X5-T

Ithaca
Model X-15

Ithaca
BSA CF-2

MODEL 49 YOUTH SADDLEGUN . . . . NiB $138 Ex $102 Gd $71
Same as standard Model 49 except shorter stock for young shooters.
Made 1961-78.

REPEATING CARBINE . . . . NiB $331 Ex $255 Gd $153
Caliber: .22 LR. Long, Short. Tubular magazine holds 15 LR, 17
Long, 21 Short. 18.5-inch bbl. Weight: 5.5 lbs. Sights: Open rear;
hooded ramp front. Receiver grooved for scope mounting. Western
carbine stock and forearm of American walnut. Made 1973-78.

MODEL 72 SADDLEGUN — DELUXE . . . . NiB $382 Ex $306 Gd $194
Same as standard Model 72 except w/silver-finished and engraved
receiver, octagon bbl., higher grade walnut stock and forearm.
Made 1974-76.

MODEL LSA-65 BOLT
ACTION STANDARD GRADE . . . . . NiB $433 Ex $382 Gd $255
Same as Model LSA-55 Standard Grade except calibers .25-06,
.270, .30-06; 4-shot magazine, 23-inch bbl., weight: 7 lbs. Made
1969-77.

MODEL LSA-65 DELUXE . . . . NiB $510 Ex $459 Gd $280
Same as Model LSA-65 Standard Grade except w/special features of
Model LSA-55 Deluxe. Made 1969-77.

MODEL X5-C LIGHTNING
AUTOLOADER . . . . NiB $178 Ex $127 Gd $76
Takedown. Caliber: .22 LR. Seven shot clip magazine. 22-inch bbl.
Weight: 6 lbs. Sights: Open rear; Ray-bar front. Pistol-grip stock,
grooved forearm. Made 1958-64.

MODEL X5-T LIGHTNING
AUTOLOADER TUBULAR
REPEATING RIFLE . . . . NiB $178 Ex $127 Gd $76
Same as Model X5-C except w/16-shot tubular magazine, stock
w/plain forearm.

MODEL X-15 LIGHTNING
AUTOLOADER . . . . NiB $14 Ex $143 Gd $76
Same general specifications as Model X5-C except forend is not
grooved. Made 1964-67.

BSA CF-2 BOLT-ACTION
REPEATING RIFLE . . . . NiB $306 Ex $280 Gd $173
Mauser-type action. Calibers: 7mm Rem. Mag., .300 Win. Mag.
Three shot magazine. 23.6-inch bbl. Weight: 8 lbs. Sights: Adj. rear;
hooded ramp front. Checkered walnut stock w/Monte Carlo comb,
rollover cheekpiece, rosewood forend tip, recoil pad, sling swivels.
Imported 1976-77. Mfd. by BSA Guns Ltd., Birmingham, England.

Johnson Model 1941

Johnson Sporting Rifle

Iver Johnson Model M-1

JAPANESE MILITARY RIFLES — Tokyo, Japan
Manufactured by Government Plant

MODEL 38 ARISAKA SERVICE RIFLE . . . . . NiB $484 Ex $331 Gd $178
Mauser-type bolt action. Caliber: 6.5mm Japanese. Five shot box magazine. Bbl. lengths: 25.38 and 31.25 inches. Weight: 9.25 lbs. w/long bbl.
Sights: fixed front, adj. rear. Military-type full stock. Adopted in 1905, the
38th year of the Meiji reign hence, the designation "Model 38."

MODEL 38 ARISAKA CARBINE. . . . NiB $484 Ex $331 Gd $178
Same general specifications as Model 38 Rifle except w/19-inch
bbl., heavy folding bayonet, weight 7.25 lbs.

MODEL 44 CAVALRY CARBINE . . . NiB $663 Ex $586 Gd $306
Same general specifications as Model 38 Rifle except w/19-inch
bbl., heavy folding bayonet, weight 8.5 lbs. Adopted in 1911, the
44th year of the Meiji reign, hence the designation, "Model 44."

MODEL 99 SERVICE RIFLE . . . . NiB $388 Ex $204 Gd $153
Modified Model 38. Caliber: 7.7mm Japanese. Five shot box magazine. 25.75-inch bbl. Weight: 8.75 lbs. Sights: Fixed front; adj. aperture
rear; anti-aircraft sighting bars on some early models; fixed rear sight
on some late WWII rifles. Military-type full stock, may have bipod.
Takedown paratroop model was also made during WWII. Adopted in
1939, (Japanese year 2599) from which the designation "Model 99" is
taken. Note: The last Model 99 rifles made were of poor quality; some
with cast steel receivers. Value shown is for earlier type.

JARRETT CUSTOM RIFLES — Jackson, South Carolina

MODEL NO. 2 WALKABOUT
BOLT-ACTION RIFLE. . . . . NiB $2977 Ex $2626 Gd $1596
Custom lightweight rifle built on Remington M700 action. Jarrett
match- grade barrel cut and chambered to customer's specification
in short action calibers only. McMillan fiberglass stock pillar-bed-
ded to action and finished to customer's preference.

MODEL NO. 3 CUSTOM
BOLT-ACTION RIFLE. . . . . NiB $2961 Ex $2472 Gd $1519
Custom rifle built on Remington M700 action. Jarrett match grade barrel cut

(cont'd.) MODEL NO. 3 CUSTOM BOLT-ACTION RIFLE
and chambered to customer's specification. McMillan classic fiberglass stock pil-
lar-bedded to action and finished to customer's preference. made 1989 to date.

MODEL NO. 4 PROFESSIONAL
HUNTER BOLT-ACTION RIFLE . . . . . . NiB $6643 Ex $5562 Gd $4223
Custom magnum rifle built on Winchester M70 "controlled feed"
action. Jarrett match grade barrel cut and chambered to customer's specification in magnum calibers only. Quarter rib w/iron
sights and two Leupold scopes w/Q-D rings and mounts.
McMillan classic fiberglass stock fitted and finished to customer's
preference.

JOHNSON AUTOMATICS, INC. — Providence, Rhode Island

MODEL 1941 SEMIAUTO
MILITARY RIFLE . . . . NiB $2500 Ex $1575 Gd $1200
Short-recoil operated. Removable, air-cooled, 22-inch bbl. Caliber: .30-06,
7mm Mauser. 10-shot rotary magazine. Two-piece wood stock, pistol grip,
perforated metal radiator sleeve over rear half of bbl. Sights: Receiver peep;
protected post front. Weight: 9.5 lbs. Note: The Johnson M/1941 was adopted by the Netherlands government in 1940-41 and the major portion of the
production of this rifle, 1941-43, was on Dutch orders. A quantity was also
bought by the U.S. government for use by Marine Corps parachute troops
(1943) and for Lend Lease. All these rifles were caliber .30-06; the 7mm
Johnson rifles were made for the South American government.

SPORTING RIFLE PROTOTYPE. . . . NiB $13,750 Ex $11,000 Gd $7480
Same general specifications as military rifle except fitted w/sporting
stock, checkered grip and forend. Blade front sight; receiver peep
sight. Less than a dozen made prior to World War II.

IVER JOHNSON ARMS, INC. — Jacksonville, Arkansas, (Formerly of Fitchburg, Massachusetts, and Middlesex, New Jersey)

LI'L CHAMP BOLT-ACTION RIFLE . . . . NiB $93 Ex $67 Gd $51
Caliber: .22 S. L. LR. Single-shot. 16.25-inch bbl. 32.5 inches overall. Weight: 3.25 lbs. Adj. rear sight, blade front. Synthetic compo-

Iver Johnson Model SC30FS

Iver Johnson Survival
Semiautomatic Carbine

Iver Johnson Trailblazer

Iver Johnson Model XX (2X) Bolt-Action Rifle

MODEL M-1 SEMIAUTOMATIC CARBINE
Similar to U.S. M-1 Carbine. Calibers: 9mm Parabellum 30 U.S. Carbine. 15- or 30-shot magazine. 18-inch bbl. 35.5 inches overall. Weight: 6.5 lbs. Sights: blade front, w/guards; adj. peep rear. Walnut, hardwood or collapsible wire stock. Parkerized finish.

Model M-1 (30 cal. w/hardwood). . . . . . . NiB $335 Ex $257 Gd $154
Model M-1 (30 cal. w/walnut) . . . . NiB $360 Ex $268 Gd $165
Model M-1 (30 cal. w/wire) . . . . NiB $412 Ex $335 Gd $170
Model M-1 (9mm w/hardwood) . . . . NiB $242 Ex $227 Gd $191
Model M-1 (9mm w/walnut). . . . . NiB $304 Ex $257 Gd $196
Model M-1 (9mm w/wire) . . . . NiB $360 Ex $299 Gd $185

MODEL PM.30
SEMIAUTOMATIC CARBINE. . . . . . NiB $340 Ex $257 Gd $154
Similar to U.S. Carbine, Cal. 30 M1. 18-inch bbl. Weight: 5.5 lbs. 15- or 30-round detachable magazine. Both hardwood and walnut stock.

MODEL SC30FS
SEMIAUTOMATIC CARBINE. . . . . . NiB $412 Ex $335 Gd $170
Similar to Survival Carbine except w/folding stock. Made 1983 to date.

SURVIVAL SEMIAUTOMATIC CARBINE . . NiB $386 Ex $360 Gd $180
Similar to Model PM.30 except in stainless steel. Made 1983 to date. W/folding high-impact plastic stock add $35.

TRAILBLAZER SEMIAUTO RIFLE. . . . NiB $129 Ex $113 Gd $93
Caliber: .22 LR. 18-inch bbl. Weight: 5.5 lbs. Sights: Open rear, blade front. Hardwood stock. Made 1983-85

MODEL X BOLT-ACTION RIFLE . . . . . NiB $118 Ex $98 Gd $67
Takedown, Single-shot. Caliber: .22 Short, Long and LR. 22-inch bbl. Weight: 4 lbs. Sights: Open rear; blade front. Pistol-grip stock w/knob forend tip. Made 1928-32.

MODEL XX (2X) BOLT-ACTION RIFLE . . . . . . NiB $129 Ex $93 Gd $72
Improved version of Model X w/heavier 24-inch bbl. larger stock (w/o knob tip), weight: 4.5 lbs. Made 1932-55.

MODEL 5100A1
BOLT-ACTION RIFLE. . . . . NiB $5144 Ex $4115 Gd $2799
Single-shot long-range rifle w/removable bolt for breech loading. Caliber: 50BMG. Fluted 29-inch bbl. w/muzzle brake. 51.5 inches overall. Adj. composition stock w/folding bipod. Scope rings; no sights.

K.B.I., INC. — Harrisburg, Pennsylvania
See listing under Armscor; Charles Daly; FEG; Liberty and I.M.I.
SUPER CLASSIC
Calibers: .22 LR, .22 Mag., RF, .22 Hornet. Five or 10-round capacity. Bolt and semiauto action. 22.6- or 20.75-inch bbl. 41.25 or 40.5 inches overall. Weight: 6.4 to 6.7 lbs. Blue finish. Oil-finished American walnut stock w/hardwood grip cap and forend tip. Checkered Monte Carlo comb and cheekpiece. High polish blued barreled action w/damascened bolt. Dovetailed receiver and iron sights. Recoil pad. QD swivel posts.

.22 Long Rifle (M-1500 SC). . . . . NiB $212 Ex $170 Gd $115
.22 Magnum Rimfire (M-1500 SC) . . . . NiB $238 Ex $191 Gd $130
.22 Hornet (M-1800-S) . . . . NiB $380 Ex $304 Gd $207
.22 Long Rifle Semiauto (M-2000 SC). . . . . NiB $238 Ex $191 Gd $130

K.D.F. INC. — Sequin, Texas
MODEL K15 BOLT-ACTION RIFLE
Calibers: (Standard) .22-250, .243 Win., 6mm Rem., .25-06, .270 Win., .280 Rem., 7mm Mag., .30-60; (Magnum) .300 Wby., .300 Win., .338 Win., .340 Wby., .375 H&H, .411 KDF, .416 Rem., .458 Win. Four shot magazine (standard), 3-shot (magnum). 22-inch (standard) or 24-inch (magnum) bbl. 44.5 to 46.5 inches overall. Weight: 8 lbs. Sights optional. Kevlar composite or checkered walnut stock in Classic, European or thumbhole-style. Note: U.S. Manufacture limited to 25 prototypes and pre-production variations.

Standard model . . . . NiB $1777 Ex $1596 Gd $876
Magnum model . . . . NiB $1828 Ex $1442 Gd $927

KDF Model K15
Bolt-Action Rifle

Kel-Tec
Sub-Series Semiautomatic Rifles

KEL-TEC CNC INDUSTRIES, INC. — Cocoa, Florida

SUB-SERIES SEMIAUTOMATIC RIFLES
Semiautomatic blow-back action w/pivoting bbl., takedown. 9mm Parabellum or 40 S&W. Interchangeable grip assembly accepts most double column, high capacity handgun magazines. 16.1-inch bbl. 31.5 inches overall. Weight: 4.6 lbs. Hooded post front sight, flip-up rear. Matte black finish. Tubular buttstock w/grooved polymer buttplate and vented handguard. Made 1997 to date.
Sub-9 Model (9mm)............. NiB $402 Ex $283 Gd $206
Sub-40 Model (40 S&W)......... NiB $489 Ex $402 Gd $257

KIMBER RIFLES — Mfd. By Kimber Manufacturing, Inc., Yonkers, NY (Formerly Kimber of America, Inc.; Kimber of Oregon, Inc.)

Note: From 1980-91, Kimber of Oregon produced Kimber firearms. A redesigned action designated by serialization with a "B" suffix was introduced 1986. Pre-1986 production is recognized as the "A" series but is not so marked. These early models in rare configurations and limited-run calibers command premium prices from collectors. Kimber of America, in Clackamas, Oregon, acquired the Kimber trademark and resumed manufactured of Kimber rifles. During this transition, Nationwide Sports Distributors, Inc. in Pennsylvania and Nevada became exclusive distributors of Kimber products. In 1997, Kimber Manufacturing acquired the trademark with manufacturing rights and expanded production to include a 1911-A1-style semiautomatic pistol, the Kimber Classic 45.
Rifle production resumed in late 1998 with the announcement of an all-new Kimber .22 rifle and a refined Model 84 in both single shot and repeater configurations.

MODEL 82 BOLT-ACTION RIFLE
Small action based on Kimber's "A" Model 82 rimfire receiver w/twin rear locking lugs. Calibers: .22 LR. .22 WRF, .22 Hornet, .218 Bee, .25-20. 5- or 10-shot magazine (.22 LR); 5-shot magazine (22WRF); 3-shot magazine (.22 Hornet). .218 Bee and .25-20 are single-shot. 18- to 25-inch bbl. 37.63 to 42.5 inches overall. Weight: 6 lbs. (Light Sporter), 6.5 lbs. (Sporter), 7.5 lbs. (Varmint); 10.75 lbs. (Target). Right- and left-hand actions are available in distinctive stock styles.
Cascade (disc. 1987)........... NiB $875 Ex $798 Gd $515
Classic (disc. 1988)............ NiB $875 Ex $798 Gd $515
Continental.................. NiB $1352 Ex $1081 Gd $735
Custom Classic
(disc. 1988).................. NiB $933 Ex $747 Gd $508
Mini Classic.................... NiB $586 Ex $469 Gd $318
Super America............... NiB $1596 Ex $1004 Gd $746
Super Continental............ NiB $1535 Ex $1287 Gd $772
1990 Classifications
All-American
Match....................... NiB $901 Ex $772 Gd $541
Deluxe Grade
(disc. 1990).................. NiB $1287 Ex $1004 Gd $798
Hunter
(Laminated stock)............. NiB $824 Ex $669 Gd $438
Super America............... NiB $1287 Ex $1025 Gd $669
Target
(Government Match)........... NiB $875 Ex $818 Gd $644

MODEL 82C CLASSIC BOLT-ACTION RIFLE
Caliber: .22 LR. Four shot or 10-shot magazine. 21-inch air-gauged bbl. 40.5 inches overall. Weight: 6.5 lbs. Receiver drilled and tapped for Warne scope mounts; no sights. Single-set trigger. Checkered Claro walnut stock w/red buttpad and polished steel grip cap. Reintroduced 1993.
Classic model .... NiB $850 Ex $711 Gd $412
Left-hand model, add.................................. $75

Kimber Model 82 Rimfire Classic

Kimber Model 82C Rimfire Classic

Kimber Model 84 Classic

Kimber Model 89 Big Game 375 Caliber

Kimber Model 89 Big Game 375 H&H Caliber

Model 84 Bolt-Action Rifle

Classic (disc. 1988) Compact-medium action based on a scaled-down Mauser-type receiver, designed to accept small base centerfire cartridges. Calibers: .17 Rem., .221 Fireball, .222 Rem., .223 Rem. Five shot magazine. Same general barrel and stock specifications as Model 82.

Classic (discontinued 1988)	NiB $921	Ex $716	Gd $483
Continental	NiB $1224	Ex $978	Gd $665
Custom Classic (disc. 1988)	NiB $1101	Ex $881	Gd $598
Super America (disc. 1988)	NiB $1256	Ex $1004	Gd $683
Super Continental (disc. 1988)	NiB $1319	Ex $1056	Gd $718
1990 Classifications			
Deluxe Grade (disc. 1990)	NiB $1153	Ex $922	Gd $627
Hunter/Sporter (laminated stock)	NiB $1024	Ex $819	Gd $557
Super America (disc. 1991)	NiB $1281	Ex $1025	Gd $697
Super Varmint (disc. 1991)	NiB $1319	Ex $1056	Gd $717
Ultra Varmint (disc. 1991)	NiB $1230	Ex $984	Gd $668

MODEL 89 BIG-GAME RIFLE

Large action combining the best features of the pre-64 Model 70 Winchester and the Mauser 98. Three action lengths are offered in three stock styles. Calibers: .257 Roberts, .25-06, 7x57, .270 Win., .280 Win., .30-06, 7mm Rem. Mag., .300 Win. Mag., .300 H&H, .338 Win., 35

(cont'd.) MODEL 89 BIG-GAME RIFLE

Whelen, .375 H&H, .404 Jeffrey, .416 Rigby, .460 Wby., .505 Gibbs (.308 cartridge family to follow). Five shot magazine (standard calibers); 3-shot magazine (Magnum calibers). 22- to 24-inch bbl. 42 to 44 inches overall. Weight: 7.5 to 10.5 lbs. Model 89 African features express sights on contoured quarter rib, banded front sight. Barrel-mounted recoil lug w/integral receiver lug and twin recoil crosspins in stock.

BGR Long Action

Classic (disc. 1988)	NiB $895	Ex $716	Gd $487
Custom Classic (disc. 1988)	NiB $1153	Ex $922	Gd $627
Super America	NiB $1410	Ex $1128	Gd $767
1990 Classifications			
Deluxe Grade: Featherweight	NiB $1668	Ex $1334	Gd $907
Medium	NiB $1706	Ex $1365	Gd $928
.375 H&H	NiB $1796	Ex $1437	Gd $977
Hunter Grade (laminated stock)			
.270 and .30-06	NiB $1224	Ex $978	Gd $665
.375 H&H	NiB $1539	Ex $1231	Gd $838
Super America: Featherweight	NiB $1925	Ex $1540	Gd $1048
Medium	NiB $2021	Ex $1617	Gd $1100
.375 H&H	NiB $2575	Ex $2060	Gd $1400
African — All calibers	NiB $4629	Ex $3702	Gd $2518

Krico Model 400

KNIGHT'S MANUFACTURING COMPANY — Vero Beach, Florida

SR-15 SEMIAUTOMATIC
MATCH RIFLE . . . . NiB $1648 Ex $1390 Gd $927
AR-15 configuration. Caliber: .223 Rem. (5.56mm). Five or 10-shot magazine. 20-inch w/free-floating, match-grade bbl., 38 inches overall. Weight: 7.9 lbs. Integral Weaver-style rail. Two-stage target trigger. Matte black oxide finish. Black synthetic AR-15A2-style stock and forearm. Made 1997 to date.

SR-15 M-4 SEMIAUTOMATIC CARBINE
Similar to SR-15 rifle except w/16-inch bbl. Sights and mounts optional. Fixed synthetic or collapsible buttstock. Made 1997 to date.
Model SR-15 Carbine (w/collapsible stock) . . . . . NiB $1369 Ex $1236 Gd $875
Model SR-15 Carbine (w/fixed stock) . . . . . . NiB $1369 Ex $1236 Gd $875

SR-15 M-5 SEMIAUTOMATIC RIFLE . . . . NiB $1493 Ex $1313 Gd $978
Caliber: .223 Rem. (5.56mm). Five or 10-shot magazine. 20-inch bbl. 38 inches overall. Weight: 7.6 lbs. Integral Weaver-style rail. Two-stage target trigger. Matte black oxide finish. Black synthetic AR-15A2-style stock and forearm. Made 1997 to date.

SR-25 MATCH RIFLE
Similar to SR-25 Sporter except w/free floating 20- or 24-inch match bbl. 39.5-43.5 inches overall. Weight: 9.25 and 10.75 lbs., respectively. Integral Weaver-style rail. Sights and mounts optional. 1 MOA guaranteed. Made 1993 to date.
Model SR-25 LW Match (w/20-inch bbl.) . . . . . NiB $2729 Ex $2317 Gd $1468
Model SR-25 Match (w/24-inch bbl.) . . . NiB $2729 Ex $2317 Gd $1468
W/RAS (Rail Adapter System), add $300

SR-25 SEMIAUTOMATIC CARBINE
Similar to SR-25 Sporter except w/free floating 16-inch bbl. 35.75 inches overall. Weight: 7.75 lbs. Integral Weaver-style rail. Sights and mounts optional. Made 1995 to date.
Model SR-25 Carbine (w/o sights) . . . . NiB $2678 Ex $2420 Gd $1442
W/RAS (Rail Adapter System), add $300

SR-25 SEMIAUTOMATIC
SPORTER RIFLE . . . . NiB $2781 Ex $2266 Gd $1545
AR-15 configuration. Caliber: .308 Win. (7.62 NATO). Five, 10- or 20-shot magazine. 20-inch bbl. 39.5 inches overall. Weight: 8.75 lbs. Integral Weaver-style rail. Protected post front sight adjustable for elevation, detachable rear adjustable for windage. Two-stage target trigger. Matte black oxide finish. Black synthetic AR-15A2-style stock and forearm. Made 1993-97.

SR-50 SEMIAUTOMATIC LONG
RANGE PRECISION RIFLE . . . . . NiB $6489 Ex $5665 Gd $3296
Gas-operated semiautomatic action. Caliber: .50 BMG. 10-shot magazine. 35.5-inch bbl. 58.5 inches overall. Weight: 31.75 lbs. Integral Weaver-style rail. Two-stage target trigger. Matte black oxide finish. Tubular-style stock. Made 1996 to date.

KONGSBERG RIFLES — Kongsberg, Norway
(Imported by Kongsberg America L.L.C., Fairfield, CT)

MODEL 393 CLASSIC SPORTER
Calibers: .22-250 Rem., .243 Win., 6.5x55, .270 Win., 7mm Rem. Mag., .30-06, .308 Win. .300 Win. Mag., .338 Win. Mag. Three or 4-shot rotary magazine. 23-inch bbl. (Standard) or 26-inch bbl. (magnum). Weight: 7.5 to 8 lbs. 44 to 47 inches overall. No sights w/ dovetailed receiver or optional hooded blade front sight, adjustable rear. Blue finish. Checkered European walnut stock w/rubber buttplate. Imported 1994-98.
Standard calibers . . . . NiB $901 Ex $772 Gd $493
Magnum calibers . . . . NiB $1180 Ex $968 Gd $696
Left-hand model, add $135
W/optional sights, add $50

MODEL 393 DELUXE SPORTER
Similar to Classic Model except w/deluxe European walnut stock. Imported 1994-98.
Standard calibers . . . . NiB $978 Ex $819 Gd $489
Magnum calibers . . . . NiB $1213 Ex $994 Gd $714
Left-hand model, add $135
W/optional sights, add $50

MODEL 393 THUMBHOLE SPORTER
Calibers: 22-250 Rem. or 308 Win. Four shot rotary magazine. 23-inch heavy bbl. Weight: 8.5 lbs. 44 inches overall. No sights, dovetailed receiver. Blue finish. Stippled American walnut thumbhole stock w/adjustable cheekpiece. Imported 1993-98.
Right-hand model . . . . NiB $1390 Ex $1210 Gd $515
Left-hand model . . . . NiB $1678 Ex $1370 Gd $976

KRICO RIFLES — Stuttgart-Hedelfingen, Germany, Mfd. by Sportwaffenfabrik, Kriegeskorte GmbH, *Imported by Mandall Shooting Supplies, Scottsdale, AZ, (Previously by Beeman Precision Arms, Inc.)*

MODEL 260 SEMIAUTOMATIC RIFLE . . . . NiB $628 Ex $566 Gd $360
Caliber: .22 LR. 10-shot magazine. 20-inch bbl. 38.9 inches overall. Weight: 6.6 lbs. Hooded blade front sight; adj. rear. Grooved receiver. Beech stock. Blued finish. Imported 1991 to date.

MODEL 300 BOLT-ACTION RIFLE
Calibers: .22 LR. .22 WMR, .22 Hornet. 19.6-inch bbl. (22 LR), 23.6-inch (22 Hornet). 38.5 inches overall. Weight: 6.3 lbs. Double-set triggers. Sights: Ramped blade front, adj. open rear. Checkered walnut-finished hardwood stock. Blued finish. Imported 1993 to date.
Model 300 Standard . . . . NiB $644 Ex $489 Gd $335
Model 300 Deluxe . . . . NiB $670 Ex $515 Gd $360
Model 300 SA (Monte Carlo walnut stock) . . . . NiB $779 Ex $633 Gd $447
Model 300 Stutzen (full-length walnut stock) . . . . . NiB $901 Ex $772 Gd $515

Krico Model 420

Krico 640 Varmint

MODEL 311 SMALL-BORE RIFLE
Bolt action. Caliber: .22 LR. Five or 10-shot clip magazine. 22-inch bbl. Weight: 6 lbs. Single- or double-set trigger. Sights: Open rear; hooded ramp front; available w/factory-fitted Kaps 2.5x scope. Checkered stock w/cheekpiece, pistol-grip and swivels. Disc.
W/scope sight . . . . NiB $438 Ex $386 Gd $232
W/iron sights only . . . . NiB $360 Ex $257 Gd $206

MODEL 320 BOLT-ACTION SPORTER . . . . NiB $695 Ex $541 Gd $360
Caliber: .22 LR. Five shot detachable box magazine. 19.5-inch bbl. 38.5 inches overall. Weight: 6 lbs. Adj. rear sight, blade ramp front. Checkered European walnut Mannlicher-style stock w/low comb and cheekpiece. Single or double-set triggers. Imported 1986-91.

**MODEL 340 METALLIC
SILHOUETTE
BOLT-ACTION RIFLE . . . . NiB $711 Ex $592 Gd $402**
Caliber: .22 LR. Five shot magazine. 21-inch heavy, bull bbl. 39.5 inches overall. Weight: 7.5 lbs. No sights. Grooved receiver for scope mounts. European walnut stock in off-hand, match-style configuration. Match or double-set triggers. Imported 1983-86.

MODEL 360S BIATHLON RIFLE . . . . . . NiB $1339 Ex $1081 Gd $592
Caliber: .22 LR. Five 5-shot magazines. 21.25-inch bbl. w/snow cap. 40.5 inches overall. Weight: 9.25 lbs. Straight-pull action. Match trigger w/17-oz. pull. Sights: Globe front, adj. match peep rear. Biathlon-style walnut stock w/high comb and adj. butt-plate. Imported 1991 to date.

MODEL 360 S2 BIATHLON RIFLE . . . . . NiB $1313 Ex $1030 Gd $566
Similar to Model 360S except w/pistol-grip activated action. Biathlon-style walnut stock w/black epoxy finish. Imported 1991 to date.

MODEL 400 BOLT-ACTION RIFLE . . . . NiB $869 Ex $695 Gd $473
Caliber: .22 Hornet. Five shot detachable box magazine. 23.5-inch bbl. Weight: 6.75 lbs. Adj. open rear sight, ramp front. European walnut stock. Disc. 1990.

MODEL 420 BOLT-ACTION RIFLE . . . . NiB $901 Ex $721 Gd $489
Same as Model 400 except w/full-length Mannlicher-style stock and double-set triggers. Scope optional, extra. Disc. 1989.

MODEL 440 S BOLT-ACTION RIFLE . . . . . . NiB $844 Ex $675 Gd $458
Caliber: .22 Hornet. Detachable box magazine. 20-inch bbl. 36.5 inches overall. Weight: 7.5 lbs. No sights. French walnut stock w/ventilated forend. Disc. 1988.

MODEL 500 MATCH RIFLE . . . . NiB $3412 Ex $2729 Gd $1856
Caliber: .22 LR. Single-shot. 23.6-inch bbl. 42 inches overall. Weight: 9.4 lbs. Kricotronic electronic ignition system. Sights: Globe front; match micrometer aperture rear. Match-style European walnut stock w/adj. butt.

MODEL 600 BOLT-ACTION RIFLE . . . . . . NiB $1153 Ex $922 Gd $627
Same general specifications as Model 700 except w/short action. Calibers: .17 Rem., .222, .223, .22-250, .243, 5.6x50 Mag. and 308.

MODEL 620 BOLT-ACTION RIFLE . . . . . . NiB $1205 Ex $999 Gd $618
Same as Model 600 except w/short-action-chambered for .308 Win. only and full-length Mannlicher-style stock w/Schnabel forend tip. 20.75-inch bbl. Weight: 6.5 lbs. No longer imported.

**MODEL 640 SUPER SNIPER
BOLT-ACTION REPEATING RIFLE NiB $1410 Ex $1128 Gd $767**
Calibers: .223 Rem., .308 Win. Three shot magazine. 26-inch bbl. 44.25 inches overall. Weight: 9.5 lbs. No sights drilled and tapped for scope mounts. Single or double-set triggers. Select walnut stock w/adj. cheekpiece and recoil pad. Disc. 1989.

MODEL 640 VARMINT RIFLE . . . . NiB $901 Ex $772 Gd $463
Caliber: .222 Rem. Four shot magazine. 23.75-inch bbl. Weight: 9.5 lbs. No sights. European walnut stock. No longer imported.

MODEL 700 BOLT-ACTION RIFLE
Calibers: .17 Rem., .222, .222 Rem. Mag., .223, .22-250, 5.6x50 Mag., .243, 5.6x57 RSW, 6x62, 6.5x55, 6.5x57, 6.5x68 .270 Win., 7x64, 7.5 Swiss, 7mm Mag., .30-06, .300 Win., 8x68S, 9.3x64. 24-inch (standard) or 26-inch (magnum) bbl. 44 inches overall (standard). Weight: 7.5 lbs. Adj. rear sight; hooded ramp front. Checkered European-style walnut stock w/Bavarian cheekpiece and rosewood Schnabel forend tip. Imported 1983 to date.
Model 700 . . . . NiB $1095 Ex $875 Gd $595
Model 700 Deluxe . . . . NiB $1153 Ex $922 Gd $627
Model 700 Deluxe S . . . . NiB $1410 Ex $1127 Gd $767
Model 700 Stutzen . . . . NiB $1224 Ex $978 Gd $665

Krieghoff Teck Boxlock Over/Under

Krieghoff Teck Sidelock Over/Under

Lakefield Model 64B

Lakefield Model 92S Target

Lakefield Mark I

RIFLES

MODEL 720 BOLT-ACTION RIFLE
Same general specifications as Model 700 except in calibers .270 Win. and .30-06 w/full-length Mannlicher-style stock and Schnabel forend tip. 20.75-inch bbl. Weight: 6.75 lbs. Disc. importing 1990.
Sporter Model . . . . NiB $1153 Ex $922 Gd $627
Ltd. Edition . . . . NiB $2369 Ex $2050 Gd $1030

BOLT-ACTION SPORTING RIFLE . . . . NiB $618 Ex $566 Gd $386
Miniature Mauser action. Single- or double-set trigger. Calibers: .22 Hornet, .222 Rem. Four shot clip magazine. 22-24- or 26-inch bbl. Weight: 6.25 lbs. Sights: Open rear; hooded ramp front. Checkered stock w/cheekpiece, pistol-grip, black forend tip, sling swivels. Imported 1956-62.

CARBINE . . . . NiB $669 Ex $541 Gd $360
Same as Krico Sporting Rifle except w/20- or 22-inch bbl., full-length Mannlicher-type stock.

SPECIAL VARMINT RIFLE . . . . NiB $669 Ex $541 Gd $360
Same as Krico Rifle except w/heavy bbl., no sights, weight: 7.25 lbs. Caliber: .222 Rem. only.

KRIEGHOFF RIFLES — Ulm (Donau), Germany, Mfd. by H. Krieghoff Jagd und Sportwaffenfabrik

See also Combination Guns under Krieghoff shotgun listings.

TECK OVER/UNDER RIFLE
Kersten action, double crossbolt, double underlugs. Boxlock. Calibers: 7x57r5, 7x64, 7x65r5, .30-30, .308 Win. .30-06, .300 Win. Mag., 9.3x74r5, .375 H&H Mag. .458 Win. Mag. 25-inch bbls. Weight: 8 to 9.5 lbs. Sights: Express rear; ramp front. Checkered walnut stock and forearm. Made 1967 to date.
Standard calibers . . . . NiB $8961 Ex $6592 Gd $5150
.375 H&H Mag.
(Disc. 1988)
.458 Win. Mag . . . . NiB $9270 Ex $6901 Gd $6180

ULM OVER/
UNDER RIFLE . . . . NiB $14,729 Ex $10,609 Gd $6180
Same general specifications as Teck model except w/sidelocks w/leaf Arabesque engraving. Made 1963 to date.

**Magnum Research Mountain Eagle
Bolt-Action Rifle**

ULM-PRIMUS OVER/UNDER RIFLE...NiB $14,485 Ex $11,587 Gd $7879
Delux version of Ulm model, w/detachable sidelocks, higher grade engraving and stock wood. Made 1963 to date.

LAKEFIELD ARMS LTD. — Ontario, Canada

See also listing under Savage for production since 1994.

MODEL 64B SEMIAUTOMATIC RIFLE......NiB $143 Ex $82 Gd $61
Caliber: .22 LR. 10-shot magazine. 20-inch bbl. Weight: 5.5 lbs. 40 inches overall. Bead front sight, adj. rear. Grooved receiver for scope mounts. Stamped checkering on walnut-finished hardwood stock w/Monte Carlo cheekpiece. Imported 1990-94.

**MODEL 90B
BOLT-ACTION TARGET RIFLE.....NiB $433 Ex $306 Gd $179**
Caliber: .22 LR. Five shot magazine. 21-inch bbl. w/snow cap. 39.63 inches overall. Weight: 8.25 lbs. Adj. receiver peep sight; globe front w/colored inserts. Receiver drilled and tapped for scope mounts. Biathlon-style natural finished hardwood stock w/shooting rails, hand stop and butthook. Made 1991-94.

MODEL 91T/91TR BOLT-ACTION TARGET RIFLE
Calibers: .22 Short, Long, LR. 25-inch bbl. 43.63 inches overall. Weight: 8 lbs. Adj. rear peep sight; globe front w/inserts. Receiver drilled and tapped for scope mounts. Walnut-finished hardwood stock w/shooting rails and hand stop. Model 91TR is a 5-shot clip-fed repeater. Made 1991-94.
Model 91T single-shot.................NiB $347 Ex $260 Gd $102
Model 91TR repeater (.22 LR only)......NiB $357 Ex $204 Gd $112

MODEL 92S TARGET RIFLE.......NiB $287 Ex $229 Gd $156
Same general specifications as Model 90B except w/conventional target-style stock. 8 lbs. No sights, but drilled and tapped for scope mounts. Made 1993-95.

MODEL 93M BOLT ACTION.......NiB $141 Ex $112 Gd $76
Caliber: .22 WMR. Five shot magazine. 20.75-inch bbl. 39.5 inches overall. Weight: 5.75 lbs. Bead front sight, adj. open rear. Receiver grooved for scope mount. Thumb-operated rotary safety. Checkered walnut-finished hardwood stock. Blued finish. Made 1995.

MARK I BOLT-ACTION RIFLE.......NiB $90 Ex $71 Gd $49
Calibers: .22 Short, Long, LR. Single-shot. 20.5-inch bbl. (19-inch Youth Model); available in smoothbore. Weight: 5.5 lbs. 39.5 inches overall. Bead front sight; adj. rear. Grooved receiver for scope mounts. Checkered walnut-finished hardwood stock w/Monte Carlo and pistol-grip. Blued finish. Made 1990-94.

MARK II BOLT-ACTION RIFLE
Same general specifications as Mark I except has repeating action w/10-shot detachable box magazine. .22 LR. only. Made 1992-94.

(cont'd.) MARK II BOLT-ACTION RIFLE
Mark II Standard...................NiB $96 Ex $77 Gd $52
Mark II Youth (19-inch barrel).......NiB $108 Ex $87 Gd $59
Mark II left-hand................NiB $134 Ex $107 Gd $72

LAURONA RIFLES — Mfg. in Eibar, Spain
Imported by Galaxy Imports, Victoria, TX

MODEL 2000X O/U EXPRESS RIFLE
Calibers: .30-06, 8x57 JRS, 8x75 JR, .375 H&H, 9.3x74R Five shot magazine. 24-inch separated bbls. Weight: 8.5 lbs. Quarter rib drilled and tapped for scope mount. Open sights. Matte black chrome finish. Monte Carlo-style checkered walnut buttstock; tulip forearm. Imported 1993 to date.
Standard calibers............NiB $2897 Ex $2317 Gd $1576
Magnum calibers............NiB $3600 Ex $2878 Gd $1958

L.A.R. MANUFACTURING, INC. —
West Jordan, Utah

**BIG BOAR COMPETITOR
BOLT-ACTION RIFLE.........NiB $2383 Ex $1906 Gd $1296**
Single-shot, bull-pup action. Caliber: .50 BMG. 36-inch bbl. 45.5 inches overall. Weight: 28.4 lbs. Made 1994 to date.

LUNA RIFLE — Mehlis, Germany
Mfg. by Ernst Friedr. Büchel

SINGLE-SHOT TARGET RIFLE....NiB $1020 Ex $875 Gd $566
Falling block action. Calibers: .22 LR. .22 Hornet. 29-inch bbl. Weight: 8.25 lbs. Sights: Micrometer peep rear tang; open rear; ramp front. Cheekpiece stock w/full pistol-grip, semibeavertail forearm, checkered, swivels. Made before WWII.

MAGNUM RESEARCH, INC. —
Minneapolis, Minnesota

MOUNTAIN EAGLE BOLT-ACTION RIFLE SERIES
Calibers: .222 Rem., .223 Rem., .270 Win., .280 Rem., 7mm Rem. Mag., 7mm STW, .30-06, .300 Win. Mag., .338 Win. Mag., .340 Wby. Mag., .375 H&H, .416 Rem. Mag. Five shot (std.) or 4-shot (Mag.). 24- or 26-inch bbl. 44 to 46 inches overall. Weight: 7.75 to 9.75 lbs. Receiver drilled and tapped for scope mount; no sights. Blued finish. Fiberglass composite stock. Made 1994 to date.
Standard model..............NiB $1368 Ex $1107 Gd $618
Magnum model..............NiB $1368 Ex $1107 Gd $618
Varmint model (Intro. 1996).........NiB $1368 Ex $1107 Gd $618
Calibers .375 H&H, .416 Rem. Mag., add...............$300

Mannlicher Model L Rifle

Mannlicher
Model M Carbine

RIFLES

Mannlicher Model M Professional

Mannlicher
Model M Rifle

MAGTECH — Las Vegas, Nevada
Mfg. by CBC, Brazil

MODEL MT 122.2/S BOLT-ACTION RIFLE . . . NiB $112 Ex $92 Gd $51
Calibers: .22 Short, Long, Long Rifle. Six or 10-shot clip. Bolt
action. 25-inch free-floating bbl. 43 inches overall. Weight: 6.5 lbs.
Double locking bolt. Red cocking indicator. Safety lever. Brazilian
hardwood finish. Double extractors. Beavertail forearm. Sling
swivels. Imported 1994 to date.

MODEL MT 122.2/R BOLT-ACTION RIFLE . . . NiB $108 Ex $87 Gd $59
Same as Model MT 122.2/S except adj. rear sight and post front sight.

MODEL MT 122.2T BOLT-ACTION RIFLE . . . NiB $115 Ex $92 Gd $62
Same as Model MT 122.2/S except w/adj. micrometer-type rear
sight and ramp front sight.

MANNLICHER SPORTING RIFLES — Steyr,
Austria, Mfg. by Steyr-Daimler-Puch, A.-G.

NOTE: *Certain Mannlicher-Schoenauer models were produced
before WWII. Manufacture of sporting rifles and carbines was
resumed at the Steyr-Daimler-Puch plant in Austria in 1950 during
which time the Model 1950 rifles and carbines were introduced.*

*In 1967, Steyr-Daimler-Puch introduced a series of sporting rifles
with a bolt action that is a departure from the Mannlicher-
Schoenauer system of earlier models. In the latter, the action is
locked by lugs symmetrically arranged behind the bolt head as
well as by placing the bolt handle ahead of the right flank of the
receiver, the rear section of which is open on top for backward
movement of the bolt handle. The current action, made in four
lengths to accommodate different ranges of cartridges, has a
closed-top receiver; the bolt locking lugs are located toward the
rear of the bolt (behind the magazine). The Mannlicher-
Schoenauer rotary magazine has been redesigned as a detachable
box type made of Makrolon. Imported by Gun South, Inc.
Trussville, AL*

MODEL L CARBINE. . . . . NiB $1352 Ex $1081 Gd $735
Same general specifications as Model SL Carbine except w/type "L" action,
weight: 6.2 lbs. Calibers same as for Model L Rifle. Imported 1968-96.

**Mannlicher Model SL
Rifle w/Single-Set Trigger**

MODEL L RIFLE . . . . NiB $1931 Ex $1390 Gd $824
Same general specifications as Model SL Rifle except w/type "L" action, weighs 6.3 lbs. Calibers: .22-250, 5.6x57 (disc. 1991), ..243 Win., 6mm Rem. .308 Win. Imported 1968-96.

MODEL L VARMINT RIFLE . . . . . NiB $1957 Ex $1432 Gd $814
Same general specifications as Model SL Varmint Rifle except w/type "L" action. Calibers: .22-250, .243 Win., .308 Win. Imported 1969-96.

MODEL LUXUS BOLT-ACTION RIFLE
Same general specifications as Models L and M except w/3-shot detachable box magazine and single-set trigger. Full or half-stock w/low-luster oil or high-gloss lacquer finish. Disc. 1996.
Full stock . . . . NiB $2002 Ex $1643 Gd $1183
Half stock . . . . NiB $2570 Ex $1802 Gd $803

MODEL M CARBINE
Same general specifications as Model SL Carbine except w/type "M" action, stock w/recoil pad, weighs 6.8 lbs. Left-hand version w/additional 6.5x55 and 9.3x62 calibers intro. 1977. Imported 1969-96.
Right-hand carbine . . . . NiB $2054 Ex $1442 Gd $772
Left-hand carbine . . . . NiB $2208 Ex $1848 Gd $1389

MODEL M PROFESSIONAL RIFLE . . . . . NiB $1957 Ex $1390 Gd $721
Same as standard Model M Rifle except w/synthetic (Cycolac) stock, weighs 7.5 lbs. Calibers: 6.5x55, 6.5x57, .270 Win., 7x57, 7x64, 7.5 Swiss, .30-06, 8x57JS, 9.3x62. Imported 1977-93.

MODEL M RIFLE
Same general specifications as Model SL Rifle except w/type "M" action, stock w/forend tip and recoil pad; weighs 6.9 lbs. Calibers: 6.5x57, .270 Win., 7x57, 7x64, .30-06, 8x57JS, 9.3x62. Made 1969 to date. Left-hand version also in calibers 6.5x55 and 7.5 Swiss. Imported 1977-96.
Right-hand rifle . . . . NiB $1545 Ex $1081 Gd $721
Left-hand rifle . . . . NiB $2208 Ex $1848 Gd $1389

MODEL S RIFLE . . . . NiB $1545 Ex $1081 Gd $721
Same general specifications as Model SL Rifle except w/type "S" action, 4-round magazine, 25.63-inch bbl., stock w/forend tip and recoil pad, weighs 8.4 lbs. Calibers: 6.5x68, .257 Weatherby Mag., .264 Win. Mag., 7mm Rem. Mag., .300 Win. Mag., .300 H&H Mag., .308 Norma Mag., 8x68S, .338 Win. Mag., 9.3x64, .375 H&H Mag. Imported 1970-96.

MODEL SL CARBINE . . . . NiB $1545 Ex $1081 Gd $721
Same general specifications as Model SL Rifle except w/20-inch bbl. and full-length stock, weight: 6 lbs. Imported 1968-96.

MODEL SL RIFLE . . . . NiB $1545 Ex $1081 Gd $721
Steyr-Mannlicher SL bolt action. Calibers: .222 Rem., .222 Rem., .222 Rem. Mag., .223 Rem. Five shot rotary magazine, detachable. 23.63-inch bbl. Weight: 6 lbs. Single- or double-set trigger (mechanisms interchangeable). Sights: Open rear; hooded ramp front. Half stock of European walnut w/Monte Carlo comb and cheekpiece, skip-checkered forearm and pistol grip, rubber buttpad, QD swivels. Imported 1967-96.

MODEL SL
VARMINT RIFLE . . . . NiB $1133 Ex $1107 Gd $747
Same general specifications as Model SL Rifle except caliber .222 Rem. only, w/25.63-inch heavy bbl., no sights, weighs 7.92 lbs. Imported 1969-96.

MODEL SSG MATCH TARGET RIFLE
Type "L" action. Caliber: .308 Win. (7.62x51 NATO). Five or 10-round magazine, single-shot plug. 25.5-inch heavy bbl. Weight: 10.25 lbs. Single trigger. Sights: Micrometer peep rear; globe front. Target stock, European walnut or synthetic, w/full pistol-grip, wide forearm w/swivel rail, adj. rubber buttplate. Imported 1969 to date.
W/walnut stock . . . . NiB $2266 Ex $1802 Gd $1135
W/synthetic stock . . . . NiB $1359 Ex $1025 Gd $598

MODEL S/T RIFLE . . . . NiB $2055 Ex $1442 Gd $618
Same as Model S Rifle except w/heavy 25.63-inch bbl., weight: 9 lbs. Calibers: 9.3x64, .375 H&H Mag., .458 Win. Mag. Option of 23.63-inch bbl. in latter caliber. Imported 1975-96.

MODEL 1903
BOLT-ACTION
SPORTING CARBINE . . . . NiB $4017 Ex $3914 Gd $515
Caliber: 6.5x53mm (referred to in some European gun catalogs as 6.7x53mm, following the Austrian practice of designating calibers by bullet diameter). Five shot rotary magazine. 450mm (17.7-inch) bbl. Weight: 6.5 lbs. Double-set trigger. Sights: Two-leaf rear; ramp front. Full-length sporting stock w/cheekpiece, pistol-grip, trap buttplate, swivels. Pre-WWII.

MODEL 1905 CARBINE . . . . NiB $1236 Ex $798 Gd $515
Same as Model 1903 except w/19.7-inch bbl.chambered 9x56mm and weight: 6.75 lbs. Pre-WWII.

MODEL 1908 CARBINE . . . . NiB $1339 Ex $1133 Gd $824
Same as Model 1905 except calibers 7x57mm and 8x56mm Pre-WWII.

MODEL 1910 CARBINE . . . . NiB $1545 Ex $1236 Gd $566
Same as Model 1905 except in 9.5x57mm. Pre-WWII.

MODEL 1924 CARBINE . . . . NiB $1648 Ex $1442 Gd $927
Same as Model 1905 except caliber .30-06 (7.62x63mm). Pre-WWII.

MODEL 1950
BOLT-ACTION
SPORTING RIFLE . . . . NiB $1493 Ex $1339 Gd $463
Calibers: .257 Roberts, .270 Win., .30-06. Five shot rotary magazine. 24-inch bbl. Weight: 7.25 lbs. Single trigger or double-set trigger. Redesigned low bolt handle, shotgun-type safety. Sights: Folding leaf open rear; hooded ramp front. Improved half-length stock w/cheekpiece, pistol grip, checkered, ebony forend tip, swivels. Made 1950-52.

Mannlicher-Schoenauer
Model 1950 Carbine

Mannlicher-Schoenauer
Model 1950 Carbine

Mannlicher-Schoenauer
Model 1950 Carbine

Mannlicher-Schoenauer
Model 1950 Carbine

Mannlicher-Schoenauer
Model 1950 Carbine

RIFLES

MODEL 1950 CARBINE . . . . NiB $1751 Ex $1442 Gd $875
Same general specifications as Model 1950 Rifle except w/20-inch bbl., full-length stock, weighs 7 lbs. Made 1950-52.

MODEL 1950
6.5 CARBINE . . . . NiB $1854 Ex $1648 Gd $917
Same as other Model 1950 Carbines except caliber 6.5x53mm, w/18.25-inch bbl., weighs 6.75 lbs. Made 1950-52.

MODEL 1952
IMPROVED CARBINE . . . . NiB $1957 Ex $1334 Gd $803
Same as Model 1950 Carbine except w/swept-back bolt handle, redesigned stock. Calibers: .257, .270, 7mm, .30-06. Made 1952-56.

MODEL 1952 IMPROVED
6.5 CARBINE . . . . NiB $1081 Ex $978 Gd $515
Same as Model 1952 Carbine except caliber 6.5x53mm, w/18.25-inch bbl. Made 1952-56.

MODEL 1952 IMPROVED
SPORTING RIFLE . . . . NiB $1442 Ex $1236 Gd $772
Same as Model 1950 except w/swept-back bolt handle, redesigned stock. Calibers: .257, .270, .30-06, 9.3x62mm. Made 1952-56 and imported exclusively by Stoeger Arms Corp.

MODEL 1956 CUSTOM CARBINE . . . . NiB $901 Ex $721 Gd $489
Same general specifications as Models 1950 and 1952 Carbines except w/redesigned stock w/high comb. Drilled and tapped for scope mounts. Calibers: .243, 6.5mm, .257, .270, 7mm, .30-06, .308. Made 1956-60.

CARBINE, MODEL 1961-MCA . . NiB $2060 Ex $1905 Gd $515
Same as Model 1956 Carbine except w/universal Monte Carlo design stock. Calibers: .243 Win., 6.5mm, .270, .308, .30-06. Made 1961-71.

RIFLE, MODEL 1961-MCA . . . . . NiB $1700 Ex $1236 Gd $566
Same as Model 1956 Rifle except w/universal Monte Carlo design stock. Calibers: .243, .270, .30-06. Made 1961-71.

HIGH VELOCITY
BOLT-ACTION SPORTING RIFLE . . . NiB $2163 Ex $1957 Gd $901
Calibers: 7x64 Brenneke, .30-06 (7.62x63), 8x60 Magnum, 9.3x62, 10.75x68mm. 23.6-inch bbl. Weight: 7.5 lbs. Sights: British-style 3-leaf open rear; ramp front. Half-length sporting stock w/cheek-piece, pistol grip, checkered, trap buttplate, swivels. Also produced in a takedown model. Pre-WWII. See illustration next page.

M72 MODEL L/M CARBINE . . . . . . NiB $927 Ex $669 Gd $412
Same general specifications as M72 Model L/M Rifle except w/20-inch bbl. and full-length stock, weight: 7.2 lbs. Imported 1972 to date.

GRADING: NiB = New in Box   **Ex** = Excellent or NRA 95%   **Gd** = Good or NRA 68%

Mannlicher Schoenauer
High Velocity Bolt-Action Sporting Rifle

Marlin Model 9 9mm Carbine

Marlin Model 9N Nickel-Teflon

M72 MODEL L/M RIFLE . . . . **NiB $824 Ex $747 Gd $515**
M72 bolt-action, type L/M receiver front-locking bolt internal rotary magazine (5-round). Calibers: .22-250, 5.6x57, 6mm Rem., .243 Win., 6.5x57, .270 Win., 7x57, 7x64, .308 Win., .30-06. 23.63-inch bbl. Weight: 7.3 lbs. Single- or double-set trigger (mechanisms interchangeable). Sights: Open rear; hooded ramp front. Half stock of European walnut, checkered forearm and pistol-grip, Monte Carlo cheekpiece, rosewood forend tip, recoil pad QD swivels. Imported 1972-81.

M72 MODEL S RIFLE . . . . **NiB $798 Ex $695 Gd $463**
Same general specifications as M72 Model L/M Rifle except w/magnum action, 4-round magazine, 25.63-inch bbl., weighs 8.6 lbs. Calibers: 6.5x68, 7mm Rem. Mag., 8x68S, 9.3x64, .375 H&H Mag. Imported 1972-81.

M72 MODEL S/T RIFLE . . . . **NiB $1365 Ex $1056 Gd $700**
Same as M72 Model S Rifle except w/heavy 25.63-inch bbl., weighs 9.3 lbs. Calibers: .300 Win. Mag. 9.3x64, .375 H&H Mag., .458 Win. Mag. Option of 23.63-inch bbl. in latter caliber. Imported 1975-81.

MODEL SBS FORESTER RIFLE
Calibers: .243 Win., .25-06 Rem., .270 Win., .6.5x55mm, 6.5x57mm, 7x64mm, 7mm-08 Rem., .30-06, .308 Win. 9.3x64mm. Four shot detachable magazine. 23.6-inch bbl. 44.5 inches overall. Weight: 7.5 lbs. No sights w/drilled and tapped for Browning A-Bolt configuration. Checkered American walnut stock w/Monte Carlo cheekpiece and Pachmayr swivels. Polished or matte blue finish. Imported 1997 to date.
SBS Forester Rifle (standard calibers) . . . . . NiB $814 Ex $644 Gd $407
SBS Forester Mountain Rifle (20-inch bbl.) . . . . NiB $779 Ex $618 Gd $402
For magnum calibers, add. $25
For metric calibers, add $100

MODEL SBS PRO-HUNTER RIFLE
Similar to the Forester Model, except w/ASB black synthetic stock. Matte blue finish. Imported 1997 to date.

(cont'd.) MODEL SBS PRO-HUNTER RIFLE
SBS Pro-Hunter Rifle (standard calibers). . . . . NiB $762 Ex $618 Gd $402
SBS Pro-Hunter Rifle
Mountain Rifle (20-inch bbl.) . . . . NiB $814 Ex $608 Gd $397
SBS Pro-Hunter Rifle (.376 Steyr) . . . . NiB $804 Ex $644 Gd $438
SBS Pro-Hunter Youth/Ladies Rifle . . . . NiB $814 Ex $644 Gd $407
For magnum calibers, add. $25
For metric calibers, add. $100
W/walnut stock . . . . NiB $2208 Ex $1797 Gd $1272
W/synthetic stock . . . . NiB $1771 Ex $1437 Gd $1010

MARLIN FIREARMS CO. — North Haven, Connecticut

MODEL 9 SEMIAUTOMATIC CARBINE
Calibers: 9mm Parabellum. 12-shot magazine. 16.5-inch bbl. 35.5 inches overall. Weight: 6.75 lbs. Manual bolt hold-open. Sights: Hooded post front; adj. open rear. Walnut-finished hardwood stock w/rubber buttpad. Blued or nickel-Teflon finish. Made 1985 to date.
Model 9 . . . . NiB $350 Ex $232 Gd $108
Model 9N, Nickel-Teflon (disc. 1994) . . . . NiB $386 Ex $257 Gd $113

MODEL 15Y/15YN
Bolt-action, single-shot "Little Buckaroo" rifle. Caliber: .22 Short, Long or LR. 16.25-inch bbl. Weight: 4.25 lbs. Thumb safety. Ramp front sight; adj. open rear. One-piece walnut Monte Carlo stock w/full pistol-grip. Made 1984-88. Reintroduced in 1989 as Model 15YN.
Model 15Y . . . . NiB $124 Ex $93 Gd $57
Model 15YN . . . . .NiB $129 Ex $98 Gd $62

MODEL 18 BABY SLIDE-ACTION
REPEATER . . . . NiB $299 Ex $283 Gd $154
Exposed hammer. Solid frame. Caliber: .22 LR, Long Short. Tubular magazine holds 14 Short cartridges. 20-inch bbl., round or octagon. Weight: 3.75 lbs. Sights: Open rear; bead front. Plain straight-grip stock and slide handle. Made 1906-09.

Marlin Model 15Y "Little Buckaroo"

Marlin Model 15YN

Marlin Model 20

Marlin Model 25M Bolt-Action Rifle

Marlin Model 25MB
Midget Magnum

MODEL 20 SLIDE-ACTION
REPEATING RIFLE . . . . **NiB $304   Ex $288   Gd $154**
Exposed hammer. Takedown. Caliber: .22 LR, Long, Short. Tubular magazine: Half-length holds 15 Short, 12 Long, 10 LR; full-length holds 25 Short, 20 Long, 18 LR. 24-inch octagon bbl. Weight: 5 lbs. Sights: Open rear; bead front. Plain straight-grip stock, grooved slide handle. Made 1907-22. Note: After 1920 was designated "Model 20-S."

MODEL 25 BOLT-ACTION RIFLE . . . . **NiB $154   Ex $129   Gd $77**
Caliber: .22 Short, Long or LR 7-shot clip. 22-inch bbl. Weight: 5.5 lbs. Ramp front sight, adj. open rear. One-piece walnut Monte Carlo stock w/full pistol-grip Mar-Shield finish. Made 1984-88.

MODEL 25
SLIDE-ACTION REPEATER . . . . **NiB $427   Ex $283   Gd $154**
Exposed hammer. Takedown. Caliber: .22 Short (also handles 22 CB caps). Tubular magazine holds 15 Short. 23-inch bbl. Weight: 4 lbs. Sights: Open rear; beaded front. Plain straight-grip stock and slide handle. Made 1909-10.

MODEL 25M BOLT ACTION W/SCOPE . . . . **NiB $148   Ex $118   Gd $80**
Caliber: .22 WMR. 7-shot clip. 22-inch bbl. Weight: 6 lbs. Ramp front sight w/brass bead, adj. open rear. Walnut-finished stock w/Monte Carlo styling and full pistol-grip. Sling swivels. Made 1986-88.

MODEL 25MB MIDGET MAGNUM . . . . **NiB $154   Ex $118   Gd $77**
Bolt action. Caliber: .22 WMR. Seven shot capacity.16.25-inch bbl. Weight: 4.75 lbs. Walnut-finished Monte Carlo-style stock w/full pistol grip and abbreviated forend. Sights: Ramp front w/brass bead, adj. open rear. Thumb safety. Made 1986-88.

MODEL 25MG/25MN/25N/25NC BOLT-ACTION RIFLE
Caliber: .22 WMR (Model 25MN) or .22 LR (Model 25N). Seven shot clip magazine. 22-inch bbl. 41 inches overall. Weight: 5.5 to 6 lbs. Adj. open rear sight, ramp front; receiver grooved for scope mounts. One piece walnut-finished hardwood Monte Carlo stock w/pistol grip. Made 1989 to date.
Marlin Model 25MG (Garden Gun) . . . . **NiB $168   Ex $134   Gd $91**
Marlin Model 25MN . . . . **NiB $148   Ex $118   Gd $80**
Marlin Model 25N . . . . **NiB $135   Ex $108   Gd $73**
Marlin Model 25NC (camouflage stock) . . . . **NiB $168   Ex $134   Gd $91**

Marlin Model 39
Carbine

Marlin Model 39
Century Ltd.

Marlin Model 39 Carbine
90th Anniversary

Marlin Model 39 Rifle
Original First Issue

Marlin Model 39A
90th Anniversary Rifle

**MODEL 27 SLIDE-ACTION
REPEATING RIFLE . . . . NiB $402 Ex $232 Gd $154**
Exposed hammer. Takedown. Calibers: .25-20, .32-20. Magazine
(tubular) holds 7 shots. 24-inch octagon bbl. Weight: 5.75 lbs.
Sights: Open rear; bead front. Plain, straight-grip stock, grooved
slide handle. Made 1910-16.

MODEL 27S . . . . NiB $309 Ex $214 Gd $129
Same as Model 27 except w/round bbl., also chambered for .25
Stevens rimfire Made 1920-32.

MODEL 29 SLIDE-ACTION REPEATER . . . . NiB $309 Ex $232 Gd $129
Similar to Model 20 w/23-inch round bbl., half magazine only,
weight 5.75 lbs. Made 1913-16.

MODEL 30/30A AND 30AS LEVER-ACTION
Caliber: .30/30 Win. 6-shot tubular magazine. 20-inch bbl. w/Micro-
Groove rifling. 38.25 inches overall. Weight: 7 lbs. Solid top receiver, offset hammer spur for scope use. Walnut-fin-
ished hardwood stock w/pistol-grip. Mar-Shield finish. Made 1964-2000.
Model 30/30A . . . . NiB $227 Ex $154 Gd $103
Model 30AS . . . . NiB $227 Ex $154 Gd $103
Model 30AS w/4x scope, add $10

MODEL 32 SLIDE-ACTION REPEATER . . . . NiB $566 Ex $412 Gd $232
Hammerless. Takedown. Caliber: .22 LR. Long, Short. Tubular magazine
holds 15 Short, 12 Long, 10 LR; full magazine, 25 Short, 20 Long, 18
LR. 24-inch octagon bbl. Weight: 5.5 lbs. Sights: Open rear; bead front.
Plain pistol-grip stock, grooved slide handle. Made 1914-15.

MODEL 36 LEVER-ACTION REPEATING CARBINE
Calibers: .30-30, .32 Special. 7-shot tubular magazine. 20-inch bbl.
Weight: 6.5 lbs. Sights: Open rear; bead front. Pistol-grip stock,
semibeavertail forearm w/carbine bbl. band. Early production
w/receiver, lever and hammer color casehardened and the remaining metal blued. Late production w/blued receiver. Made 1936-48.
Note: In 1936, this was designated "Model 1936" and was so
marked on the upper tang. In 1937, the model designation was
shortened to "36". An "RC" serial number suffix identifies a
"Regular/Carbine".
Model 1936 (CC receiver,
w/long tang, w/o SN prefix) . . . . NiB $772 Ex $644 Gd $412
Model 1936 (CC receiver,
w/short tang, w/o SN prefix) . . . . NiB $547 Ex $438 Gd $298
Model 1936 (CC receiver, w/SN prefix) . . . NiB $451 Ex $360 Gd $245
Model 36 (CC receiver, w/SN prefix) . . . . . NiB $418 Ex $335 Gd $228
Model 36 (blued receiver, w/SN prefix) . . . NiB $380 Ex $304 Gd $207

Marlin Model 39 — ADL

Marlin Model 39AS

MODEL 36 SPORTING CARBINE

Same as M36 carbine except w/6-shot, (2/3 magazine) and weighs 6.25 lbs.

Model 1936 (CC receiver,
w/long tang, w/o SN prefix) . . . . NiB $772 Ex $618 Gd $412
Model 1936 (CC receiver,
w/short tang, w/o SN prefix) . . . . NiB $566 Ex $489 Gd $309
Model 1936 (CC receiver, w/SN prefix) . . NiB $509 Ex $407 Gd $277
Model 36 (CC receiver, w/SN prefix) . . . . . NiB $463 Ex $371 Gd $252
Model 36 (blued receiver, w/SN prefix) . . . NiB $418 Ex $335 Gd $228

MODEL 36A/36A-DL LEVER-ACTION REPEATING RIFLE

Same as Model 36 Carbine except has 24-inch bbl. w/hooded front sight and 2/3 magazine holding 6 cartridges. Weight: 6.75 lbs. Note: An "A" serial number suffix identifies a Rifle while an "A-DL" suffix designates a Deluxe Model w/checkered stock, semibeavertail forearm, swivels and sling. Made 1936-48.

Model 1936 (CC receiver,
w/long tang, w/o SN prefix) . . . . NiB $1184 Ex $1030 Gd $309
Model 1936 (CC receiver,
w/short tang, w/o SN prefix) . . . . NiB $566 Ex $489 Gd $309
Model 1936 (CC receiver, w/SN prefix) . . . NiB $547 Ex $438 Gd $298
Model 36 (CC receiver, w/SN prefix) . . . . . NiB $483 Ex $386 Gd $263
Model 36 (blued receiver, w/SN prefix) . . . NiB $451 Ex $360 Gd $245
For ADL model, add 25%

MODEL 37 SLIDE-ACTION

REPEATING RIFLE . . . . NiB $412 Ex $360 Gd $154
Similar to Model 29 except w/24-inch bbl. and full magazine. Weight: 5.25 lbs. Made 1913-16.

MODEL 38 SLIDE-ACTION

REPEATING RIFLE . . . . NiB $360 Ex $257 Gd $154
Hammerless. Takedown. Caliber: .22 LR. Long, Short. 2/3 magazine (tubular) holds 15 Short, 12 Long, 10 LR. 24-inch octagon or round bbls. Weight: 5.5 lbs. Sights: Open rear; bead front. Plain shotgun-type pistol-grip buttstock w/hard rubber buttplate, grooved slide handle. Ivory bead front sight; adj. rear. About 20,000 Model 38 rifles were made between 1920-30.

MODEL 39 CARBINE . . . . NiB $257 Ex $180 Gd $129

Same as 39M except w/lightweight bbl., 3/4 magazine (capacity: 18 Short, 14 Long, 12 LR), slimmer forearm. Weight: 5.25 lbs. Made 1963-67.

MODEL 39 90TH

ANNIVERSARY CARBINE . . . . . . NiB $1030 Ex $953 Gd $711
Carbine version of 90th Anniversary Model 39A. 500 made in 1960. Top value is for carbine in new, unfired condition.

MODEL 39 CENTURY LTD. . . . . . . NiB $463 Ex $309 Gd $196

Commemorative version of Model 39A. Receiver inlaid w/brass medallion, "Marlin Centennial 1870-1970." Square lever. 20-inch octagon bbl. Fancy walnut straight-grip stock and forearm; brass forend cap, buttplate, nameplate in buttstock. 35,388 made in 1970.

MODEL 39 LEVER-ACTION

REPEATER . . . . NiB $2060 Ex $1905 Gd $1020
Takedown. Casehardened receiver. Caliber: .22 LR. Long, Short. Tubular magazine holds 25 Short, 20 Long, 18 LR. 24-inch octagon bbl. Weight: 5.75 lbs. Sights: Open rear; bead front. Plain pistol-grip stock and forearm. Made 1922-38.

MODEL 39A

General specifications same as Model 39 except w/blued receiver, round bbl., heavier stock w/semibeavertail forearm, weight 6.5 lbs. Made 1938-60.

Early model (no prefix) . . . . NiB $1191 Ex $953 Gd $648
Late model ("B" prefix) . . . . NiB $966 Ex $772 Gd $525

MODEL 39A 90TH

ANNIVERSARY RIFLE . . . . NiB $1030 Ex $978 Gd $711
Commemorates Marlin's 90th anniversary. Same general specifications as Golden 39A except w/chrome-plated bbl. and action, stock and forearm of select walnut-finely checkered, carved figure of a squirrel on right side of buttstock. 500 made in 1960. Top value is for rifle in new, unfired condition.

MODEL 39A

ARTICLE II RIFLE . . . . NiB $489 Ex $360 Gd $257
Commemorates National Rifle Association Centennial 1871-1971. "The Right to Bear Arms" medallion inlaid in receiver. Similar to Model 39A. Magazine capacity: 26 Short, 21 Long, 19 LR. 24-inch octagon bbl. Fancy walnut pistol-grip stock and forearm; brass forend cap, buttplate. 6,244. Made in 1971.

Marlin Model 56

Marlin Model 57

Marlin Model 60C

Marlin Model 60SS

Marlin Model 62

GOLDEN 39A/39AS RIFLE
Same as Model 39A except w/gold-plated trigger, hooded ramp front sight, sling swivels. Made 1960-87 (39A); Model 39AS 1988 to date.
Golden 39A . . . . NiB $3560 Ex $257 Gd $129
Golden 39AS (W/hammer block safety) . . . . NiB $237 Ex $14 Gd $113

MODEL 39A "MOUNTIE" LEVER-
ACTION REPEATING RIFLE. . . . . . . NiB $360 Ex $309 Gd $180
Same as Model 39A except w/lighter, straight-grip stock, slimmer forearm. Weight: 6.25 lbs. Made 1953-60.

MODEL 39A OCTAGON. . . . . NiB $669 Ex $515 Gd $309
Same as Golden 39A except w/oct. bbl., plain bead front sight, slimmer stock and forearm, no pistol-grip cap or swivels. Made 1973. (2551 produced)

MODEL 39D . . . . NiB $232 Ex $185 Gd $129
Same as Model 39M except w/pistol-grip stock, forearm w/bbl. band. Made 1970-74.

39M ARTICLE II CARBINE. . . . . . . NiB $463 Ex $407 Gd $232
Same as 39A Article II Rifle except w/straight-grip buttstock, square lever, 20-inch octagon bbl., reduced magazine capacity. 3,824m, made in 1971.

GOLDEN 39M
Calibers: .22 Short, Long and LR. Tubular magazine holds 21 Short, 16 Long or 15 LR cartridges. 20-inch bbl. 36 inches overall. Weight: 6 lbs. Gold-plated trigger. Hooded ramp front sight, adj. folding semi-buckhorn rear. Two-piece, straight-grip American black walnut stock. Sling swivels. Mar-Shield finish. Made 1960-87.
Model Golden 39M. . . . . NiB $368 Ex $258 Gd $206
Model 39M Octagon
(octagonal bbl.
made 1973 only). . . . . NiB $438 Ex $407 Gd $309

MODEL 39M "MOUNTIE" CARBINE
Same as Model 39A "Mountie" Rifle except w/20-inch bbl. Weight: 6 lbs. 500 made in 1960. (For values See Marlin 39 90th Anniversary Carbine)

MODEL 39TDS
CARBINE. NiB $309 Ex $206 Gd $129
Same general specifications as Model 39M except takedown style w/16.5-inch bbl. and reduced magazine capacity. 32.63 inches overall. Weight: 5.25 lbs. Made 1988-95.

Marlin Model 70HC w/7-Shot Clip

Marlin Model 70P

MODEL 45 . . . . NiB $288 Ex $232 Gd $129
Semiautomatic action. Caliber: .45 Auto. Seven shot clip.16.5-inch bbl. 35.5 inches overall. Weight: 6.75 lbs. Manual bolt hold-open. Sights: Ramp front sight w/brass bead, adj. folding rear. Receiver drilled and tapped for scope mount. Walnut-finished hardwood stock. Made 1986 to date.

MODEL 49/49DL AUTOLOADING RIFLE
Same as Model 99C except w/two-piece stock, checkered after 1970. Made 1968-71. Model 49DL w/scrollwork on sides of receiver, checkered stock and forearm; made 1971-78.
Model 49. NiB $154 Ex $124 Gd $84
Model 49DL . . . . NiB $161 Ex $129 Gd $88

MODEL 50/50E AUTOLOADING RIFLE
Takedown. Cal: .22 LR. Six shot detachable box mag. 22 inch bbl. Wt: 6 lbs. Sights: Open rear; bead front; Mdl. 50E w/peep rear sight, hooded front. Plain pistol-grip stock, forearm w/finger grooves. Made 1931-34.
Model 50. NiB $170 Ex $129 Gd $77
Model 50E. . . . . NiB $180 Ex $129 Gd $82

MODEL 56 LEVERMATIC RIFLE . . . NiB $257 Ex $196 Gd $103
Same as Model 57 except clip-loading. Magazine holds eight rounds. Weight: 5.75 lbs. Made 1955-64.

MODEL 57 LEVERMATIC RIFLE . . . NiB $257 Ex $196 Gd $103
Lever-action. Cal: .22 LR. 22 Long, 22 Short. Tubular mag. holds 19 LR, 21 Long, 27 Short. 22 inch bbl. Wt: 6.25 lbs. Sights: Open rear, adj. for windage and elevation; hooded ramp front. Monte Carlo-style stock w/pistol-grip. Made 1959-65.

MODEL 57M LEVERMATIC. . . . . . . NiB $257 Ex $196 Gd $113
Same as Model 57 except chambered for 22 WMR cartridge, w/24-inch bbl., 15-shot magazine. Made 1960-69.

MODEL 60 SEMIAUTOMATIC RIFLE . . . . NiB $103 Ex $77 Gd $51
Caliber: .22 LR. 14-shot tubular magazine. 22-inch bbl. 40.5 inches overall. Weight: 5.5 lbs. Grooved receiver. Ramp front sight w/removable hood; adj. open rear. Anodized receiver w/blued bbl. Monte Carlo-style walnut-finished hardwood stock w/Mar-Shield finish. Made 1981 to date. Note: Marketed 1960-1980 under Glenfield promotion logo and w/slightly different stock configuration.

MODEL 60C SELF-LOADING RIFLE . . . . NiB $108 Ex $98 Gd $72
Cal: .22 LR. 14- shot tubular mag. 22 inch Micro-Groove bbl., 40.5 inch overall. Wt: 5.5 lbs. Screw-adjustable open rear and ramp front sights. Aluminum receiver, grooved for scope mount. Hardwood Monte Carlo stock w/Mossy Oak "Break-Up" camouflage pattern. Made 1998 to date.

MODEL 60SS SEMIAUTOMATIC RIFLE
Same general specifications as Model 60 except w/stainless bbl. and magazine tube. Synthetic, uncheckered birch or laminated black/gray birch stock w/nickel-plated swivel studs. Made 1993 to date.
Model 60SB w/uncheckered
birch stock . . . . NiB $206 Ex $154 Gd $93
Model 60SS w/laminated
birch stock . . . . NiB $216 Ex $154 Gd $93
Model 60SSK w/fiberglass stock. . . . . NiB $206 Ex $154 Gd $93

MODEL 62
LEVERMATIC RIFLE. . . . . NiB $489 Ex $360 Gd $232
Lever-action. Calibers: .256 Magnum, .30 Carbine. Four shot clip magazine. 23-inch bbl. Weight: 7 lbs. Sights: Open rear; hooded ramp front. Monte Carlo-style stock w/pistol-grip, swivels and sling. Made in .256 Magnum 1963-66; in .30 Carbine 1966-69.

MODEL 65 BOLT-ACTION
SINGLE-SHOT RIFLE . . . . NiB $93 Ex $62 Gd $41
Takedown. Caliber: .22 LR. Long, Short. 24-inch bbl. Weight: 5 lbs. Sights: Open rear; bead front. Plain pistol-grip stock w/grooved forearm. Made 1932-38. Model 65E is same as Model 65 except w/rear peep sight and hooded front sight.

MODEL 70HC SEMIAUTOMATIC
Caliber: .22 LR. Seven and 15-shot magazine. 18-inch bbl. Weight: 5.5 lbs. 36.75 inches overall. Ramp front sight; adj. open rear. Grooved receiver for scope mounts. Walnut-finished hardwood stock w/Monte Carlo and pistol-grip. Made 1988-96.
Marlin model. . . . . NiB $149 Ex $124 Gd $77
Glenfield model. . . . . NiB $103 Ex $82 Gd $51

MODEL 70P
SEMIAUTOMATIC. . . . . NiB $154 Ex $129 Gd $72
"Papoose" takedown. Caliber: .22 LR. Seven shot clip. 16.25-inch bbl. 35.25 inches overall. Weight: 3.75 lbs. Sights: Ramp front, adj. open rear. Side ejection, manual bolt hold-open. Cross-bolt safety. Walnut-finished hard-wood stock w/abbreviated forend, pistol-grip. Made 1984-94.

MODEL 70PSS
SELF-LOADING CARBINE . . . . NiB $165 Ex $129 Gd $77
"Papoose" takedown carbine. Caliber: .22 LR. Seven shot clip. 16.25- inch bbl., 35.25 inches overall. Weight: 3.25 lbs. Ramp front and adjustable open rear sights. Automatic last-shot hold open (1996). Black fiberglass synthetic stock. Made 1995 to date.

Marlin Model 75C

Marlin Model 80C

Marlin Model 80DL

Marlin Model 81DL

MODEL 75C
SEMIAUTOMATIC . . . . **NiB $154 Ex $103 Gd $77**
Caliber: .22 LR. 13-shot tubular magazine.18-inch bbl. 36.5 inches overall. Weight: 5 lbs. Side ejection. Cross-bolt safety. Sights: Ramp-mounted blade front; adj. open rear. Monte Carlo-style walnut-finished hardwood stock w/pistol-grip. Made 1975-92.

MODEL 80 BOLT-ACTION REPEATING RIFLE
Takedown. Caliber: .22 LR. Long, Short. Eight shot detachable box magazine. 24-inch bbl. Weight: 6 lbs. Sights: Open rear; bead front. Plain pistol-grip stock. Made 1934-39. Model 80E, w/peep rear sight; hooded front, made 1934-40.
Model 80 Standard . . . . **NiB $124 Ex $93 Gd $62**
Model 80E . . . . **NiB $113 Ex $77 Gd $57**

MODEL 80C/80DL BOLT-ACTION REPEATER
Improved version of Model 80. Model 80C w/bead from sight, semi-beavertail forearm; made 1940-70. Model 80DL w/peep rear sight; hooded blade front sight on ramp, swivels; made 1940-65.
Model 80C . . . . **NiB $124 Ex $93 Gd $62**
Model 80DL . . . . **NiB $113 Ex $77 Gd $62**

MODEL 81/81E BOLT-ACTION REPEATER
Takedown. .22 LR. Long, Short. Tubular magazine holds 24 Short, 20 Long, 18 LR. 24-inch bbl. Weight: 6.25 lbs. Sights: Open rear, bead front. Plain pistol-grip stock. Made 1937-40. Model 81E w/peep rear sight; hooded front w/ramp.
Model 81 . . . . **NiB $134 Ex $129 Gd $62**
Model 81E . . . . **NiB $154 Ex $103 Gd $93**

MODEL 81C/81DL BOLT-ACTION REPEATER
Improved version of Model 81 w/same general specifications. Model 81C w/bead front sight, semibeavertail forearm; made 1940-70. Model 81 DL w/peep rear sight, hooded front, swivels; disc. 1965.
Model 81C. . . . . **NiB $154 Ex $129 Gd $62**
Model 81DL . . . . **NiB $170 Ex $134 Gd $77**

MODEL 88-C/88-DL AUTOLOADING
Takedown. Caliber: .22 LR. Tubular magazine in buttstock holds 14 cartridges. 24-inch bbl. Weight: 6.75 lbs. Sights: Open rear; hooded front. Plain pistol-grip stock. Made 1947-56. Model 88-DL w/received peep sight, checkered stock and sling swivels, made 1953-56.
Model 88-C . . . . **NiB $180 Ex $154 Gd $93**
Model 88-DL . . . . **NiB $185 Ex $165 Gd $98**

Marlin Model 93 Musket

Marlin Model 93 Lever Action

Marlin Model 94 Sporting Carbine

MODEL 89-C/89-DL AUTOLOADING RIFLE

Clip magazine version of Model 88-C. Seven shot clip (12-shot in later models); other specifications same. Made 1950-61. Model 89-DL w/receiver peep sight, sling swivels.

Model 89-C . . . . **NiB $170 Ex $134 Gd $93**
Model 89-DL . . . . **NiB $175 Ex $154 Gd $98**

MODEL 92 LEVER-ACTION REPEATING RIFLE

Calibers: .22 Short, Long, LR. .32 Short, Long (rimfire or centerfire by changing firing pin). Tubular magazines holding 25 Short, 20 Long, 18 LR (.22); or 17 Short, 14 Long (.32); 16-inch bbl. model w/shorter magazine holding 15 Short, 12 Long, 10 LR. Bbl. lengths: 16 (.22 cal. only) 24, 26, 28 inches. Weight: 5.5 lbs. w/24-inch bbl. Sights: open rear; blade front. Plain straight-grip stock and forearm. Made 1892-1916. Note: Originally designated "Model 1892."

Model 92 (.22 caliber) . . . . **NiB $1854 Ex $1287 Gd $669**
Model 92 (.32 caliber) . . . . **NiB $1432 Ex $1133 Gd $803**

MODEL 93/93SC CARBINE

Same as Standard Model 93 Rifle except in calibers .30-30 and .32 Special only. Model 93 w/7-shot magazine. 20-inch round bbl., carbine sights, weight: 6.75 lbs. Model 93SC magazine capacity 5 shots, weight 6.5 lbs.

Model 93 Carbine
(w/saddle ring) . . . . **NiB $1545 Ex $1287 Gd $1004**
Model 93 Carbine ("Bullseye")
w/o saddle ring) . . . . **NiB $1030 Ex $917 Gd $566**
Model 93SC Sporting Carbine . . . . **NiB $1648 Ex $1339 Gd $927**

MODEL 93
LEVER-ACTION

REPEATING RIFLE . . . . **NiB $2266 Ex $1854 Gd $1231**
Solid frame or takedown. Calibers: .25-36 Marlin, .30-30, .32 Special, .32-40, .38-55. Tubular magazine holds 10 cartridges. 26-inch round or octagon bbl. standard; also made w/28-, 30- and 32-inch bbls. Weight: 7.25 lbs. Sights: Open rear; bead front. Plain straight-grip stock and forearm. Made 1893-1936. Note: Before 1915 designated "Model 1893."

MODEL 93 MUSKET . . . . **NiB $4017 Ex $2977 Gd $1638**

Same as Standard Model 93 except w/30-inch bbl., angular bayonet, ramrod under bbl., musket stock, full-length military-style forearm. Weight: 8 lbs. Made 1893-1915.

MODEL 94 LEVER-ACTION

REPEATING RIFLE . . . . **NiB $2575 Ex $2060 Gd $1931**
Solid frame or takedown. Calibers: .25-20, .32-20, .38-40, .44-40. 10-shot tubular magazine. 24-inch round or octagon bbl. Weight: 7 lbs. Sights open rear; bead front. Plain straight-grip stock and forearm (also available w/pistol-grip stock). Made 1894-1934. Note: Before 1906 designated "Model 1894."

MODEL 94 LEVER-ACTION COWBOY SERIES

Calibers: .357 Mag., .44-40, .44 Mag., .45 LC. 10-shot magazine. 24-inch tapered octagon bbl. Weight: 7.5 lbs. 41.5 inches overall. Marble carbine front sight, adjustable semi-buckhorn rear. Blue finish. Checkered, straight-grip American black walnut stock w/hard rubber buttplate. Made 1996 to date. Cowboy II introduced in 1997.

Cowboy model (.45 LC) . . . . **NiB $515 Ex $386 Gd $257**
Cowboy II model (.357 Mag.,
.44-40, .44 Mag) . . . . **NiB $515 Ex $386 Gd $257**

MODEL 97 LEVER-ACTION

REPEATING RIFLE . . . . **NiB $2523 Ex $2039 Gd $1957**
Takedown. Caliber: .22 LR. Long, Short. Tubular magazine; full length holds 25 Short, 20 Long, 18 LR; half length holds 16 Short, 12 Long and 10 LR. Bbl. lengths: 16, 24, 26, 28 inches. Weight: 6 lbs. Sights: Open rear; bead front. Plain, straight-grip stock and forearm (also avail. w/pistol-grip stock). Made 1897-1922. Note: Before 1905 designated "Model 1897."

MODEL 98 AUTOLOADING RIFLE . . . . **NiB $154 Ex $98 Gd $77**

Solid frame. Caliber: .22 LR. Tubular magazine holds 15 cartridges. 22-inch bbl. Weight: 6.75 lbs. Sights: Open rear; hooded ramp front. Monte Carlo stock w/cheekpiece. Made 1950-61.

MODEL 99 AUTOLOADING RIFLE . . . . **NiB $154 Ex $98 Gd $77**

Caliber: .22 LR. Tubular magazine holds 18 cartridges. 22-inch bbl. Weight: 5.5 lbs. Sights: Open rear; hooded ramp front. Plain pistol-grip stock. Made 1959-61.

MODEL 99C . . . . **NiB $165 Ex $129 Gd $82**

Same as Model 99 except w/gold-plated trigger, receiver grooved for tip-off scope mounts, Monte Carlo stock (checkered in later production). Made 1962-78.

MODEL 99DL . . . . **NiB $206 Ex $180 Gd $98**

Same as Model 99 except w/gold-plated trigger, jeweled breech bolt, Monte Carlo stock w/pistol-grip, swivels and sling. Made 1960-65.

Marlin Model 336 Cowboy

Marlin Model 336M

Marlin Model 336 Marauder

Marlin Model 336 Sporting Carbine

Marlin Model 336 Zane Grey Century

Marlin Model 336A

Marlin Model 336A-DL

MODEL 99M1 CARBINE . . . . **NiB $216 Ex $154 Gd $103**
Same as Model 99C except styled after U.S. .30 M1 Carbine; 9-shot tubular magazine, 18-inch bbl. Sights: Open rear; military-style ramp front; carbine stock w/handguard and bbl. band, sling swivels. Weight: 4.5 lbs. Made 1966-79.

MODEL 100 BOLT-ACTION
SINGLE-SHOT RIFLE . . . . **NiB $129 Ex $93 Gd $51**
Takedown. Caliber: .22 LR, Long, Short. 24-inch bbl. Weight: 4.5 lbs. Sights: Open rear; bead front. Plain pistol-grip stock. Made 1936-60.

MODEL 100SB . . . . **NiB $124 Ex $98 Gd $62**
Same as Model 100 except smoothbore for use w/22 shot cartridges, shotgun sight. Made 1936-41.

Marlin Model 336DT Deluxe Texan

Marlin Model 336T Texan

MODEL 100 TOM MIX SPECIAL........ **NiB $391 Ex $304 Gd $206**
Same as Model 100 except w/peep rear sight; hooded front; sling.
Made 1936-46.

MODEL 101 .... **NiB $98 Ex $77 Gd $41**
Improved version of Model 100 w/same general specifications,
except w/stock w/beavertail forearm, weighs 5 lbs. Intro. 1951. Disc.

MODEL 101 DL.................. **NiB $103 Ex $72 Gd $41**
Same as Model 101 except has peep rear sight; hooded front,
swivels. Disc.

MODEL 122 SINGLE-SHOT
JUNIOR TARGET RIFLE............. **NiB $77 Ex $51 Gd $36**
Bolt action. Caliber: .22 LR, .22 Long, .22 Short. 22-inch bbl.
Weight: 5 lbs. Sights: Open rear; hooded ramp front. Monte Carlo
stock w/pistol-grip, swivels, sling. Made 1961-65.

MODEL 322 BOLT-ACTION
VARMINT RIFLE .... **NiB $566 Ex $515 Gd $304**
Sako short Mauser action. Caliber: .222 Rem. Three shot clip magazine. 24-inch medium weight bbl. Checkered stock. Sights: Two-
position peep rear; hooded ramp front. Weight: 7.5 lbs. Made 1954-57.

MODEL 336A
LEVER-ACTION RIFLE........... **NiB $309 Ex $180 Gd $163**
Improved version of Model 36A Rifle w/same general specifications
except w/improved action w/round breech bolt. Calibers: .30-30,
.32 Special (disc. 1963), .35 Rem. (intro. 1952). Made 1948-63;
reintroduced 1973, disc. 1980.

MODEL 336A-DL .... **NiB $541 Ex $463 Gd $283**
Same as Model 336A Rifle except w/deluxe checkered stock and
forearm, swivels and sling. Made 1948-63.

MODEL 336AS
LEVER-ACTION RIFLE........... **NiB $232 Ex $165 Gd $113**
Similar to Model 30AS. Caliber: .30-30 Win., Six shot tubular maga-
zine. 20- inch Micro-Groove bbl. 38.25 inches overall. Weight: 7 lbs.
Maine birch pistol grip stock w/swivel studs and hard rubber butt plate.
Tapped for scope mount and receiver sight. Screw-adjustable open
rear and ramp front sight. Checkered walnut finish. Made 1999 to date.

MODEL 336C
LEVER-ACTION CARBINE........ **NiB $283 Ex $227 Gd $154**
Improved version of Model 36 Carbine w/same general specifica-
tions except w/improved action w/round breech bolt. Original cal-
ibers: .30-30 and .32 Win. Spec. Made 1948-83. Note: Caliber .35
Rem. intro. 1953. Caliber .32 Winchester Special disc. 1963.

MODEL 336 COWBOY
LEVER-ACTION RIFLE.......... **NiB $566 Ex $412 Gd $283**
Calibers: .30-30 Win., or .38-55 Win., 6- shot tubular magazine. 24- inch
tapered octagon bbl. 42.5 inches overall. Weight: 7.5 lbs. American black
walnut checkering stock. Marble carbine front sight w/solid top receiver
drilled and tapped for scope mount. Mar-Shield finish. Made 1998 to date.

MODEL 336CS
W/SCOPE .... **NiB $360 Ex $252 Gd $154**
Lever-action w/hammer block safety. Caliber: .30/30 Win. or .35 Rem. Six
shot tubular magazine. 20-inch round bbl. w/Micro-Groove rifling. 38.5
inches overall. Weight: 7 lbs. Ramp front sight w/hood, adj. semi-buckhorn folding rear. Solid top receiver drilled and tapped for scope mount or
receiver sight; offset hammer spur for scope use. American black walnut
stock w/pistol-grip, fluted comb. Mar-Shield finish. Made 1984 to date.

MODEL 336DT
DELUXE TEXAN............... **NiB $412 Ex $407 Gd $309**
Same as Model 336T except w/select walnut stock and forearm, hand-
carved longhorn steer and map of Texas on buttstock. Made 1962-64.

MODEL 336M
LEVER-ACTION RIFLE.......... **NiB $515 Ex $412 Gd $283**
Calibers: .30-30 Win., 6- shot tubular magazine. 20- inch stainless
steel Micro Groove bbl., 38.5 inches overall. Weight: 7 lbs.
American black walnut w/checkered pistol-grip stock. Adjustable
folding semi-buckhorn rear and ramp front sight w/brass bead and
removable Wide-Scan hood. Tapped for receiver sight and scope
mount. Mar-Shield finish. Made 1999 to date.

MODEL 336 MARAUDER .... **NiB $463 Ex $412 Gd $226**
Same as Model 336 Texan Carbine except w/16.25-inch bbl.,
weight: 6.25 lbs. Made 1963-64.

MODEL 336-MICRO GROOVE ZIPPER ... **NiB $541 Ex $463 Gd $304**
General specifications same as Model 336 Sporting Carbine except
caliber .219 Zipper. Made 1955-61.

MODEL 336 OCTAGON .... **NiB $515 Ex $448 Gd $185**
Same as Model 336T except chambered for .30-30 only w/22-inch
octagon bbl. Made 1973.

MODEL 336 SPORTING CARBINE....... **NiB $412 Ex $309 Gd $154**
Same as Model 336A rifle except w/20-inch bbl., weight: 6.25 lbs.
Made 1948-63.

MODEL 336T TEXAN CARBINE .... **NiB $257 Ex $206 Gd $180**
Same as Model 336 Carbine except w/straight-grip stock and is not available
in caliber .32 Special. Made 1953-83. Caliber .44 Magnum made 1963-67.

Marlin Model 336TS Carbine

Marlin Model 444SS

Marlin Model 455 Sporter

MODEL 336TS . . . . **NiB $335 Ex $283 Gd $129**
Lever-action w/hammer-block safety. Caliber: .30-30 Win. Six shot tubular magazine. 18.5-inch Micro-Groove bbl. 37 inches overall. Weight: 6.5 lbs. Ramp front sight, adj. semi-buckhorn folding rear. Straight-grip American black walnut stock. Made 1983-87.

**MODEL 336 ZANE
GREY CENTURY** . . . . **NiB $463 Ex $360 Gd $232**
Similar to Model 336A except w/22-inch octagonal bbl., caliber .30-30, Zane Grey Centennial 1872-1972 medallion inlaid in receiver; select walnut stock w/classic pistol-grip and forearm; brass buttplate, forend cap. Weight: 7 lbs. 10,000 produced (numbered ZG1 through ZG10,000). Made 1972.

**MODEL 444 LEVER-ACTION
REPEATING RIFLE** . . . . **NiB $386 Ex $335 Gd $154**
Action similar to Model 336. Caliber: .444 Marlin. Four shot tubular magazine. 24-inch bbl. Weigh: 7.5 lbs. Sights: Open rear; hooded ramp front. Monte Carlo stock w/straight grip, recoil pad. Carbine-style forearm w/bbl. band. Swivels, sling. Made 1965-71.

MARLIN MODEL 444 SPORTER . . . . **NiB $391 Ex $360 Gd $165**
Same as Model 444 Rifle except w/22-inch bbl., pistol-grip stock and forearm as on Model 336A, recoil pad, QD swivels and sling. Made 1972-83.

**MODEL 444P (OUTFITTER)
LEVER-ACTION RIFLE** . . . . **NiB $475 Ex $360 Gd $180**
Caliber: .444 Marlin. Five shot tubular mag89ine. 18.5-inch ported bbl., 37 inches overall. Weight: 6.75 lbs. Ramp front and adjustable folding rear sights. Black walnut straight grip stock w/cut checkering and Mar-Shield finish. Made 1998 to date.

MODEL 444SS . . . . **NiB $489 Ex $360 Gd $180**
Same general specifications as Model 444 except w/hammer safety. Made 1984 to date.

MODEL 455 BOLT-ACTION SPORTER
FN Mauser action w/Sako trigger. Calibers: .30-06 or .308. Five shot box magazine. 24-inch medium weight stainless-steel bbl. Monte Carlo

(cont'd.) **MODEL 455 BOLT-ACTION SPORTER**
stock w/cheekpiece, checkered pistol grip and forearm. Lyman No. 48 receiver sight; hooded ramp front. Weight: 8.5 lbs. Made 1957-59.
**Model 455 (chambered for .30-06,
1079 produced)** . . . . **NiB $566 Ex $438 Gd $232**
Model 455 (chambered for .308, 59 produced) . . . . **NiB $566 Ex $438 Gd $232**

MODEL 780 BOLT-ACTION REPEATER SERIES
Caliber: .22 LR. Long, Short. Seven shot clip magazine. 22-inch bbl. Weight: 5.5 to 6 lbs. Sights: Open rear; hooded ramp front. Receiver grooved for scope mounting. Monte Carlo stock w/checkered pistol-grip and forearm. Made 1971-88.
Model 780 Standard . . . . **NiB $113 Ex $82 Gd $57**
Model 781 (w/17-shot tubular magazine) . . . **NiB $113 Ex $82 Gd $57**
Model 782 (.22 WMR, w/swivels, sling) . . . . . **NiB $113 Ex $82 Gd $57**
Model 783 (w/12-shot tubular magazine) . . . **NiB $113 Ex $82 Gd $57**

MODEL 795 SELF-LOADING RIFLE . . . . **NiB $129 Ex $103 Gd $82**
Caliber: .22 LR. 10- shot clip. 18- inch Micro-Groove bbl., 37 inches overall. Weight: 5 lbs. Screw-adjustable open rear and ramp front sight. Monte Carlo synthetic stock with checkering swivel studs. Made 1999 to date.

MODEL 880 BOLT-ACTION REPEATER SERIES
Caliber: .22 rimfire. 7-shot magazine. 22-inch bbl. 41 inches overall. Weight: 5.5 to 6 lbs. Hooded ramp front sight; adj. folding rear. Grooved receiver for scope mounts. Checkered Monte Carlo-style walnut stock w/QD studs and rubber recoil pad. Made 1989-97.
Model 880 (.22 LR) . . . . **NiB $185 Ex $134 Gd $77**
Model 880SS (Stainless .22 LR) . . . . **NiB $206 Ex $165 Gd $112**
Model 880SQ (Squirrel .22 LR) . . . . **NiB $219 Ex $175 Gd $119**
Model 881 (w/7-shot tubular magazine . . . . **NiB $190 Ex $139 Gd $77**
Model 882 (.22 WMR) . . . . **NiB $180 Ex $144 Gd $98**
Model 882L (w/laminated hardwood stock) . . . . . . **NiB $190 Ex $139 Gd $77**
Model 882SS (Stainless w/fire sights) . . . . . **NiB $226 Ex $180 Gd $123**
Model 882SSV (Stainless .22 LR) . . . . **NiB $226 Ex $180 Gd $123**
**Model 883 (.22 WMR w/12-
shot tubular magazine)** . . . . **NiB $185 Ex $134 Gd $77**
Model 883N (w/nickel-Teflon finish) . . . . . **NiB $222 Ex $180 Gd $126**
Model 883SS (stainless w/laminated stock) . . . . **NiB $241 Ex $160 Gd $138**

Marlin Model 780

Marlin Model 781

Marlin Model 783

Marlin Model 882L

Marlin Model 883N

MODEL 922 MAGNUM
SELF-LOADING RIFLE . . . . **NiB $360 Ex $283 Gd $103**
Similar to Model 9 except chambered for .22 WMR. Seven shot magazine. 20.5-inch bbl. 39.5 inches overall. Weight: 6.5 lbs. American black walnut stock w/Monte Carlo. Blued finish. Made 1993 to date.

MODEL 980 .22 MAGNUM . . . . . . **NiB $165 Ex $113 Gd $77**
Bolt action. Caliber: .22 WMR. Eight shot clip magazine. 24-inch bbl. Weight: 6 lbs. Sights: Open rear; hooded ramp front. Monte Carlo stock, swivels, sling. Made 1962-70.

MODEL 989 AUTOLOADING RIFLE . . . . **NiB $144 Ex $98 Gd $72**
Caliber: .22 LR. Seven shot clip magazine. 22-inch bbl. Weight: 5.5 lbs. Sights: Open rear; hooded ramp front. Monte Carlo walnut stock w/pistol grip. Made 1962-66.

MODEL 989M2
CARBINE . . . . **NiB $144 Ex $93 Gd $69**
Same as Model 99M1 except clip-loading, 7-shot magazine. Made 1966-79.

MODEL 990 SEMIAUTOMATIC
Caliber: .22 LR. 17-shot tubular magazine. 22-inch bbl. 40.75 inches overall. Weight: 5.5 lbs. Side ejection. Cross-bolt safety. Ramp front sight w/brass bead; adj. semi-buckhorn folding rear. Receiver grooved for scope mount. Monte Carlo-style American black walnut stock w/checkered pistol grip and forend. Made 1979-87.
Model 990 Semiautomatic . . . . **NiB $144 Ex $113 Gd $72**
Model 990L (w/14 rounds,
laminated hardwood stock, QD studs,
black recoil pad; 1992 to date) . . . . **NiB $129 Ex $98 Gd $72**

Marlin Model 980

Marlin Model 989

Marlin Model 989M2

Marlin Model 990

Marlin Model 990L

Marlin Model 995

MODEL 995 SEMIAUTOMATIC . . . . NiB $165 Ex $124 Gd $77
Caliber: .22 LR. Seven shot clip magazine.18-inch bbl. 36.75 inches overall. Weight: 5 lbs. Cross-bolt safety. Sights: Ramp front w/brass bead; adj. folding semi-buckhorn rear. Monte Carlo-style American black walnut stock w/checkered pistol grip and forend. Made 1979-94.

MODEL 1870-1970 CENTENNIAL MATCHED PAIR, MODELS 336 AND 39 . . . . NiB $1931 Ex $1596 Gd $1030
Presentation-grade rifles in luggage-style case. Matching serial numbers. Fancy walnut straight-grip buttstock and forearm brass buttplate and forend cap. Engraved receiver w/inlaid medallion; square lever. 20-inch octagon bbl. Model 336: .30-30, 7-shot, 7 lbs. Model 39: .22 Short, Long, LR, tubular magazine holds 21 Short, 16

***(cont'd.)* MODEL 1870-1970 CENTENNIAL MATCHED PAIR, MODELS 336 AND 39**
Long, 15 LR. 1,000 sets produced. Made 1970. Top value is for rifles in new, unfired condition. See illustration on page 277.

MODEL 1892 LEVER-ACTION RIFLE
See Marlin Model 92.

MODEL 1893 LEVER-ACTION RIFLE
See Marlin Model 93.

MODEL 1894 LEVER-ACTION RIFLE
See Marlin Model 94 Lever-Action Rifle listed previously under this section.

Marlin 1870-1970 Matched Pair

Marlin Model 1894 Carbine

Marlin Model 1894CL

RIFLES

MODEL 1894 CARBINE
Replica of original Model 94. Caliber: .44 Rem. 10-shot magazine. 20-inch round bbl. Weight: 6 lbs. Sight: Open rear; ramp front. Straight-grip stock. Made 1969-84.
Standard Model 1894 Carbine . . . . **NiB $386 Ex $257 Gd $180**
Model 1894 Octagon
(made 1973) . . . . **NiB $412 Ex $335 Gd $185**
Model 1894 Sporter (w/22-inch bbl.,
made 1973) . . . . **NiB $386 Ex $257 Gd $232**

MODEL 1894CL CLASSIC . . . . NiB $463 Ex $335 Gd $180
Calibers: .218 Bee, .25-20 Win., .32-20 Win. Six shot tubular magazine. 22-inch bbl. 38.75 inches overall. Weight: 6.25 lbs. Adj. semibuckhorn folding rear sight, brass bead front. Receiver tapped for scope mounts. Straight-grip American black walnut stock w/Mar-Shield finish. Made 1988-94.

MODEL 1894 COWBOY/COWBOY II
See Marlin Model 94 Cowboy/Cowboy II.

MODEL 1894CS LEVER-ACTION . . . . NiB $412 Ex $360 Gd $154
Caliber: .357 Magnum, .38 Special. Nine shot tubular magazine. 18.5-inch bbl. 36 inches overall. Weight: 6 lbs. Side ejection. Hammer block safety. Square finger lever. Bead front sight, adj. semi-buckhorn folding rear. Offset hammer spur for scope use. Two-piece straight grip American black walnut stock w/white buttplate spacer. Mar-Shield finish. Made 1984 to date.

MODEL 1894M LEVER-ACTION . . . . NiB $309 Ex $257 Gd $154
Caliber: .22 WMR.11-shot tubular magazine. 20-inch bbl. Weight: 6.25 lbs. Sights: Ramp front w/brass bead and Wide-Scan hood; adj. semi-buckhorn folding rear. Offset hammer spur for scope use. Straight-grip American black walnut stock w/white buttplate spacer. Squared finger lever. Made 1986-88.

MODEL 1894S LEVER-ACTION . . . . NiB $360 Ex $283 Gd $180
Calibers: .41 Mag., .44 Rem. Mag., .44 S&W Special, .45 Colt.10-shot tubular magazine. 20-inch bbl.37.5 inches overall. Weight: 6 lbs. Sights and stock same as Model 1894M. Made 1984 to date.

Marlin Model 1894CS

Marlin Model 1894M

Marlin Model 1894S

Marlin Model 1895
.45-70 (New Model)

MODEL 1895 .45-70 REPEATER . . . NiB $618 Ex $309 Gd $154
Model 336-type action. Caliber: .45-70 Government. Four shot magazine. 22-inch bbl. Weight: 7 lbs. Sights: Open rear; bead front. Straight-grip stock, forearm w/metal end cap, QD swivels, leather sling. Made 1972-79.

MODEL 1895
LEVER-ACTION REPEATER . . . . NiB $3090 Ex $2781 Gd $2060
Solid frame or takedown. Calibers: .33 WCF, .38-56, .40-65, .40-70, .40-82, .45-70. Nine shot tubular magazine. 24-inch round or octagongon bbl. standard (other lengths available). Weight: 8 lbs. Sights: Open rear; bead front. Plain stock and forearm (also available w/pistol-grip stock). Made 1895-1915.

MODEL 1895G (GUIDE GUN)
LEVER-ACTION RIFLE . . . . NiB $380 Ex $304 Gd $207
Caliber: .45-70 Govt., 4- shot magazine. 18.5-inch ported bbl., 37 inches overall. Weight: 6.75 lbs. Ramp front and adjustable folding rear sights. Black walnut straight grip stock w/cut checkering and Mar-Shield finish. Made 1998 to date.

MODEL 1895M
LEVER-ACTION RIFLE . . . . NiB $515 Ex $463 Gd $283
Caliber: .450 Marlin. Four shot tubular magazine., 18.5- inch ported bbl. w/Ballard-type rifling. 37 inches overall. Weight: 6.75 lbs. Genuine American black walnut straight-grip stock w/checkering. Ventilated recoil pad. Adjustable folding semi-buckhorn rear and ramp front sights. Mar-Shield finish. Made 1999 to date.

MODEL 1895SS
LEVER-ACTION . . . . NiB $335 Ex $257 Gd $180
Caliber: .45-70 Govt. Four shot tubular magazine. 22-inch bbl. w/Micro-Groove rifling. 40.5 inches overall. Weight: 7.5 lbs. Ramp front sight w/brass bead and Wide-Scan hood; adj. semi-buckhorn folding rear. Solid top receiver tapped for scope mount or receiver sight. Off-set hammer spur for scope use. Two-piece American black walnut stock w/fluted comb, pistol-grip, sling swivels. Made 1984 to date.

MODEL 1897 LEVER-ACTION RIFLE
See Marlin Model 97.

Marlin Model 1895G

Marlin Model 1895M

Marlin Model 1895SS

Marlin Model 1895 Rifle
(Old Model — 1895-1915)

Marlin Model 1897
Cowboy

MODEL 1897 COWBOY
LEVER-ACTION RIFLE . . . . **NiB $618 Ex $515 Gd $283**
Caliber: .22 LR., capacity: 19LR,- 21L,- or 26S,- tubular magazine. 24-inch tapered octagon bbl., 40 inches overall. Weight: 6.5 lbs. Marble front and adjustable rear sight, tapped for scope mount. Black walnut straight grip stock w/cut checkering and Mar-Shield finish. Made 1999 to date.

MODEL 1936 LEVER-ACTION CARBINE
See Marlin Model 36.

MODEL 2000 TARGET RIFLE
Bolt-action single-shot. Caliber: .22 LR. Optional 5-shot adapter kit available. 22-inch bbl. 41 inches overall. Weight: 8 lbs. Globe front sight, adj. peep or aperture rear. two-stage target trigger. Textured composite Kevlar or black/gray laminated stock. Made 1991 to date.
Model 2000 (disc. 1995) . . . . **NiB $489 Ex $417 Gd $257**
Model 2000A w/Adj. comb
(Made 1994 only) . . . . **NiB $541 Ex $438 Gd $257**
Model 2000L w/laminated
stock (intro. 1996) . . . . **NiB $571 Ex $463 Gd $327**

MODEL 7000 . . . . **NiB $212 Ex $170 Gd $115**
Caliber: .22 LR. 10-shot magazine. 18-inch bbl. Weight: 5.5 lbs. Synthetic stocks. No sights; receiver grooved for scope. Semi-auto. Side ejection. Manual bolt hold-open. Cross-bolt safety. Matte finish. Made 1997 to date.
Model 7000 . . . . **NiB $232 Ex $180 Gd $129**
Model 7000T . . . . **NiB $386 Ex $309 Gd $257**

MODEL A-1
AUTOLOADING RIFLE . . . . **NiB $180 Ex $103 Gd $77**
Takedown. Caliber: .22 LR. Six shot detachable box magazine. 24-inch bbl. Weight: 6 lbs. Open rear sight. Plain pistol-grip stock. Made 1935-46.

MODEL A-1C
AUTOLOADING RIFLE . . . . **NiB $154 Ex $93 Gd $62**
Improved version of Model A-1 w/same general specifications, stock w/semibeavertail forend. Made 1940-46.

MODEL A-1DL . . . . **NiB $154 Ex $93 Gd $62**
Same as Model A-1C except w/peep rear sight; hooded front, swivels.

Marlin Model 2000

Marlin Model 2000L

Marlin Model 7000

Marlin Model 7000T

MODEL A-1E . . . . NiB $154 Ex $93 Gd $62
Same as Model A-1 except w/peep rear sight; hooded front.

MODEL MR-7 BOLT-ACTION RIFLE
Calibers: .25-06 Rem., .270 Win., .280 Rem., .308 Win. or .30-06.
Four shot magazine. 22-inch bbl. w/ or w/o sights. 43.31 inches
overall. Weight: 7.5 lbs. Checkered American walnut or birch stock
w/recoil pad and sling-swivel studs. Jeweled bolt w/cocking indica-
tor and 3-position safety. Made from 1996-99.
Model MR-7 . . . . NiB $463 Ex $335 Gd $232
Model MR7B w/birch
stock (Intro. 1998) . . . . NiB $134 Ex $129 Gd $98
Open sights, add $35

MODEL 10 . . . . NiB $103 Ex $82 Gd $56
Same as Marlin Model 101 except w/walnut-finished hardwood
stock. Made 1966-79. Note: Later production w/hot-iron-
stamped wood pistol grip to simulate checkering/carving; plain
forend.

MODEL 20 . . . . NiB $103 Ex $82 Gd $56
Same as Marlin Model 80/780 except w/bead front sight, walnut-
finished hardwood stock. Made 1966-82. Note: Recent production
has stamped pistol-grip to simulate checkering; plain forend.

MODEL 30 . . . . NiB $154 Ex $93 Gd $62
Same as Marlin Model 336C except chambered for .30-30 only,
w/4-shot magazine, plainer stock and forearm of walnut-finished
hardwood. Made 1966-68.

MODEL 30A . . . . NiB $232 Ex $154 Gd $103
Same as Marlin Model 336C except chambered for .30-30 only,
w/checkered stock of walnut-finished hardwood. Made 1969-83.

MODEL 36G . . . . NiB $257 Ex $154 Gd $97
Same as Marlin Model 336C except chambered for .30-30 only,
w/5-shot magazine, plainer stock. Made 1960-65.

MODEL 60 . . . . NiB $77 Ex $51 Gd $36
Same as Marlin Model 99C except w/walnut-finished hardwood
stock. Made 1960-80.

MODEL 70 . . . . NiB $82 Ex $62 Gd $41
Same as Marlin Model 989M2 except w/walnut-finished hardwood
stock; no handguard. Made 1966-69.

MODEL 80G . . . . NiB $82 Ex $62 Gd $41
Same as Marlin Model 80C except w/plain stock, bead front sight.
Made 1960-65.

Marlin Model A-1 Autoloader

Marlin-Glenfield Model 10

Marlin-Glenfield Model 30A

Marlin-Glenfield Model 60

Marlin-Glenfield Model 70

Marlin-Glenfield Model 80G

RIFLES

MODEL 81G . . . . **NiB $77 Ex $51 Gd $41**
Same as Marlin Model 81C except w/plain stock, bead front sight.
Made 1960-65.

MODEL 99G . . . . **NiB $82 Ex $67 Gd $51**
Same as Marlin Model 99C except w/plain stock, bead front sight.
Made 1960-65.

MODEL 101G . . . . **NiB $77 Ex $51 Gd $41**
Same as Marlin Model 101 except w/plain stock. Made 1960-65.

MODEL 989G
AUTOLOADING RIFLE . . . . **NiB $77 Ex $51 Gd $41**
Same as Marlin Model 989 except w/plain stock, bead front sight.
Made 1962-64.

MAUSER SPORTING RIFLES — Oberndorf am Neckar, Germany, Mfg. by Mauser-Werke GmbH, *Imported by Brolin Arms, Pomona, CA, (Previously by Gun South, Inc.; Gibbs Rifle Co.; Precision Imports, Inc. and KDF, Inc.)*

Before the end of WWI the name of the Mauser firm was "Waffenfabrik Mauser A.-G." Shortly after WWI it was changed to "Mauser-Werke A.-G." This information may be used to determine the age of genuine original Mauser sporting rifles made before WWII because all bear either of these firm names as well as the Mauser banner trademark.

The first four rifles listed were manufactured before WWI. Those that follow were produced between World Wars I and II. The early Mauser models can generally be identified by the pistol grip, which is rounded instead of capped, and the M/98 military-type magazine floorplate and catch. The later models have hinged magazine floorplates with lever or button release.

Mauser Model ES340

Mauser Model ES350

NOTE: *The "B" series of Mauser 22 rifles (Model ES340B, MS350B, etc.) were improved versions of their corresponding models and were introduced about 1935.*

PRE-WORLD WAR I MODELS

BOLT-ACTION SPORTING CARBINE
Calibers: 6.5x54, 6.5x58, 7x57, 8x57, 957mm. 19.75-inch bbl. Weight: 7 lbs. Full-stocked to muzzle. Other specifications same as for standard rifle.
Sporting Carbine w/20-inch
bbl. (Type M)..................... NiB $2311 Ex $1849 Gd $1258
Sporting Carbine w/20
or 24-inch bbl. (Type S)............ NiB $2382 Ex $1905 Gd $1296

BOLT-ACTION SPORTING RIFLE
Calibers: 6.5x55, 6.5x58, 7x57, 8x57, 9x57, 9.3x62 10.75x68.5- shot box magazine, 23.5-inch bbl. Weight: 7 to 7.5 lbs. Pear-shaped bolt handle. Double-set or single trigger. Sights: Tangent curve rear; ramp front. Pistol-grip stock, forearm w/Schnabel tip and swivels.
Sporting Rifle (Type A, English export) NiB $24569 Ex $2055 Gd $1398
Sporting Rifle (Type B) .... NiB $1668 Ex $1334 Gd $907

BOLT-ACTION SPORTING RIFLE,
MILITARY MODEL TYPE C .... NiB $708 Ex $566 Gd $385
So called because of stepped M/98-type bbl., military front sight and double-pull trigger. Calibers: 7x57, 8x57, 9x57mm. Other specifications same as for standard rifle.

BOLT-ACTION SPORTING RIFLE
SHORT MODEL TYPE K .... NiB $3670 Ex $2935 Gd $1996
Calibers: 6.5x54, 8x51mm. 19.75-inch bbl. Weight: 6.25 lbs. Other specifications same as for standard rifle.

PRE-WORLD WAR II MODELS

MODEL DSM34 BOLT-ACTION
SINGLE-SHOT SPORTING RIFLE .... NiB $483 Ex $386 Gd $263
Also called "Sport-model." Caliber: .22 LR. 26-inch bbl. Weight: 7.75 lbs. Sights: Tangent curve open rear; Barleycorn front. M/98 military-type stock, swivels. Intro. c. 1935.

MODEL EL320 BOLT-ACTION
SINGLE-SHOT SPORTING RIFLE .... NiB $463 Ex $371 Gd $252
Caliber: .22 LR. 23.5-inch bbl. Weight: 4.25 lbs. Sights: Adj. open rear; bead front. Sporting stock w/checkered pistol grip, swivels.

MODEL EN310 BOLT-ACTION
SINGLE-SHOT SPORTING RIFLE .... NiB $418 Ex $335 Gd $228
Caliber: .22 LR. ("22 Lang fur Buchsen.") 19.75-inch bbl. Weight: 4 lbs. Sights: Fixed open rear, blade front. Plain pistol-grip stock.

MODEL ES340 BOLT-ACTION
SINGLE-SHOT TARGET RIFLE .... NiB $483 Ex $386 Gd $263
Caliber: .22 LR. 25.5-inch bbl. Weight: 6.5 lbs. Sights: Tangent curve rear; ramp front. Sporting stock w/checkered pistol-grip and grooved forearm, swivels.

MODEL ES340B
BOLT-ACTION SINGLE-SHOT
TARGET RIFLE................. NiB $483 Ex $386 Gd $263
Caliber: .22 LR. 26.75-inch bbl. Weight: 8 lbs. Sights: Tangent curve open rear; ramp front. Plain pistol-grip stock, swivels.

MODEL ES350
BOLT-ACTION SINGLE-SHOT
TARGET RIFLE................. NiB $676 Ex $541 Gd $368
"Meistershaftsbuchse" (Championship Rifle). Caliber: .22 LR. 27.5- inch bbl. Weight: 7.75 lbs. Sights: Open micrometer rear; ramp front. Target stock w/checkered pistol-grip and forearm, grip cap, swivels.

MODEL ES350B
BOLT-ACTION SINGLE-SHOT
TARGET RIFLE .... NiB $612 Ex $489 Gd $333
Same general specifications as Model MS350B except single-shot, weight: 8.25 lbs.

MODEL KKW BOLT-ACTION
SINGLE-SHOT TARGET RIFLE........... NiB $483 Ex $386 Gd $263
Caliber: .22 LR. 26-inch bbl. Weight: 8.75 lbs. Sights: Tangent curve open rear; Barleycorn front. M/98 military-type stock, swivels. Note: This rifle has an improved design Mauser 22 action w/separate nonrotating bolt head. In addition to being produced for commercial sale, this model was used as a training rifle by the German armed forces; it was also made by Walther and Gustoff. Intro. just before WWII.

MODEL M410 BOLT-ACTION
REPEATING SPORTING RIFLE .... NiB $869 Ex $695 Gd $473
Caliber: .22 LR. Five shot detachable box magazine. 23.5-inch bbl. Weight: 5 lbs. Sights: Tangent curve open rear; ramp front. Sporting stock w/checkered pistol-grip, swivels.

Mauser Type "A" Pattern No. 1

Mauser Type "B" Pattern No. 60

Mauser Type "M" Pattern No. 270

RIFLES

MODEL MM410B BOLT-ACTION
REPEATING SPORTING RIFLE . . . . **NiB $895 Ex $716 Gd $487**
Caliber: .22 LR. Five shot detachable box magazine. 23.5-inch bbl.
Weight: 6.25 lbs. Sights: Tangent curve open rear; ramp front.
Lightweight sporting stock w/checkered pistol-grip, swivels.

MODEL MS350B BOLT-ACTION
REPEATING TARGET RIFLE . . . . **NiB $895 Ex $7166 Gd $487**
Caliber: .22 LR. Five shot detachable box magazine. Receiver and
bbl. grooved for detachable rear sight or scope. 26.75-inch bbl.
Weight: 8.5 lbs. Sights: Micrometer open rear; ramp front. Target
stock w/checkered pistol grip and forearm, grip cap, sling swivels.

MODEL MS420 BOLT-ACTION
REPEATING SPORTING RIFLE . . . . **NiB $966 Ex $772 Gd $525**
Caliber: .22 LR. Five shot detachable box magazine. 25.5-inch bbl.
Weight: 6.5 lbs. Sights: Tangent curve open rear; ramp front.
Sporting stock w/checkered pistol grip, grooved forearm swivels.

MODEL MS420B BOLT-ACTION
REPEATING TARGET RIFLE . . . . **NiB $804 Ex $644 Gd $438**
Caliber: .22 LR. Five shot detachable box magazine. 26.75-inch bbl.
Weight: 8 lbs. Sights: Tangent curve open rear; ramp front. Target
stock w/checkered pistol grip, grooved forearm, swivels.

STANDARD MODEL RIFLE . . . . NiB $676 Ex $541 Gd $368
Refined version of German Service Kar. 98k. Straight bolt handle.
Calibers: 7mm Mauser (7x57mm), 7.9mm Mauser (8x57mm). Five shot
box magazine. 23.5-inch bbl. Weight: 8.5 lbs. Sights: Blade front; adj.
rear. Walnut stock of M/98 military-type. Note: These rifles were made for
commercial sale and are of the high quality found in the Oberndorf
Mauser sporters. They bear the Mauser trademark on the receiver ring.

TYPE "A" BOLT-ACTION
SPORTING RIFLE. . . . . **NiB $2569 Ex $2055 Gd $1398**
Special British Model. 7x57, 30-06 (7.62x63), 8x60, 9x57, 9.3x62mm. Five shot
box mag. 23.5-inch round bbl. Weight: 7.25 lbs. Mil.-type single trigger. Sights:
Express rear; hooded ramp front. Circassian walnut sporting stock w/checkered
pistol-grip and forearm, w/ or w/o cheekpiece, buffalo horn forend tip and grip
cap, detachable swivels. Variations: Octagon bbl., double-set trigger, shotgun-type
safety, folding peep rear sight, tangent curve rear sight, three-leaf rear sight.

TYPE "A" BOLT-ACTION
SPORTING RIFLE,
MAGNUM MODEL . . . . **NiB $2826 Ex $2261 Gd $1538**
Same general specifications as standard Type "A" except w/Magnum
action, weighs 7.5 to 8.5 lbs. Calibers: .280 Ross, .318 Westley
Richards Express, 10.75x68mm, .404 Nitro Express.

TYPE "A" BOLT-ACTION
SPORTING RIFLE,
SHORT MODEL. . . . . **NiB $2311 Ex $1848 Gd $1258**
Same as standard Type "A" except w/short action, 21.5-inch round
bbl., weight 6 lbs. Calibers: .250-3000, 6.5x54, 8x51mm.

TYPE "B" BOLT-ACTION
SPORTING
RIFLE . . . . **NiB $1739 Ex $1390 Gd $946**
Normal Model. Calibers: 7x57, .30-06 (7.62x63), 8x57, 8x60, 9x57,
9.3x62, 10.7568mm. Five shot box magazine. 23.5-inch round bbl.
Weight: 7.25 lbs. Double-set trigger. Sights: Three-leaf rear, ramp front.
Fine walnut stock w/checkered pistol-grip, Schnabel forend tip, cheekpiece, grip cap, swivels. Variations: Octagon or half-octagon bbl., military-type single trigger, shotgun-type safety, folding peep rear sight, tangent curve rear sight, telescopic sight.

TYPE "K"
BOLT-ACTION
SPORTING RIFLE. . . . . **NiB $3670 Ex $2935 Gd $1996**
Light Short Model. Same specifications as Normal Type "B" model
except w/short action, 21.5-inch round bbl., weight: 6 lbs. Calibers:
.250-3000, 6.5x54, 8x51mm.

TYPE "M"
BOLT-ACTION
SPORTING CARBINE . . . . **NiB $2311 Ex $1849 Gd $1258**
Calibers: 6.5x54, 7x57, .30-06 (7.62x63), 8x51, 8x60, 9x57mm.
Five shot box magazine. 19.75-inch round bbl. Weight: 6 to 6.75
lbs. Double-set trigger, flat bolt handle. Sights: Three-leaf rear; ramp
front. Stocked to muzzle, cheekpiece, checkered pistol-grip and
forearm, grip cap, steel forend cap, swivels. Variations: Military-type
single trigger, shotgun-type trigger, shotgun-type safety, tangent
curve rear sight, telescopic sight.

Mauser Model 66S Standard

Mauser Model 66S Deluxe

Mauser Model 66SP
Super Match Target Rifle

Mauser Model 66ST Carbine

TYPE "S" BOLT-ACTION
SPORTING CARBINE . . . . **NiB $2395 Ex $2008 Gd $1262**
Calibers: 6.5x54 7x57, 8x51, 8x60, 9x57mm. Five-shot box magazine. 19.75-inch round bbl. Weight: 6 to 6.75 lbs. Double-set trigger. Sights: Three-leaf rear; ramp front. Stocked to muzzle, Schnabel forend tip, cheekpiece, checkered pistol-grip w/cap, swivels. Variations: Same as listed for Normal Model Type "B."

POST-WORLD WAR II MODELS

NOTE: *Production of original Mauser sporting rifles (66 series) resumed at the Oberndorf plant in 1965 by Mauser-Jagdwaffen GmbH, now Mauser-Werke Oberndorf GmbH. The Series 2000-3000-4000 rifles, however, were made for Mauser by Friedrich Wilhelm Heym Gewehrfabrik, Muennerstadt, West Germany.*

MODEL 66S BOLT-ACTION STANDARD SPORTING RIFLE
Telescopic short action. Bbls. interchangeable within cal. group. Single- or double-set trigger (interchangeable). Cal: .243 Win., 6.5x57, .270 Win., 7x64, .308 Win., .30-06. Three round mag. 23.6 inch bbl. (25.6inch in 7x64). Wt: 7.3 lbs. (7.5 lbs. in 7x64). Sights: Adj. open rear, hooded ramp front. Select Eur. walnut stock, Monte Carlo w/cheekpiece, rosewood forend tip and pistol-grip cap, skip checkering, recoil pad, sling swivels. Made 1965 to date, export to

(cont'd.) **MODEL 66S BOLT-ACTION STANDARD SPORTING RIFLE**
U.S. disc. 1974. Note: U.S.designation, 1971-73, was "Model 660."
Model 66S . . . . **NiB $2369 Ex $2060 Gd $1030**
W/extra bbl. assembly, add $550

MODEL 66S DELUXE SPORTER
Limited production special order. Model 66S rifles and carbines are available with /elaborate engraving, gold and silver inlays and carved select walnut stocks. Added value is upward of $4500.

MODEL 66S ULTRA
Same general specifications as Model 66S Standard except with 20.9-inch bbl., weight: 6.8 lbs.
Model 66S Ultra . . . . **NiB $1622 Ex $1535 Gd $978**
W/extra bbl. assembly, add $550

MODEL 66SG BIG GAME
Same general specifications as Model 66S Standard except w/25.6-inch bbl., weight 9.3 lbs. Calibers: .375 H&H Mag., .458 Win. Mag. Note: U.S. designation, 1971-73, was "Model 660 Safari."
Model 66SG . . . . **NiB $2987 Ex $1931 Gd $1184**
W/ extra bbl. assembly, add $550

Mauser Model 99

Mauser Model 201

Mauser Model 3000

Mauser Model 4000

MODEL 66SH HIGH PERFORMANCE . . NiB $1575 Ex $1400 Gd $975
Same general specifications as Model 66S Standard except w/25.6-inch bbl., weighs 7.5 lbs. (9.3 lbs. in 9.3x64). Calibers: 6.5x68, 7mm Rem. Mag., 7mm S.E.v. Hoffe, .300 Win. Mag., 8x68S, 9.3x64.

MODEL 66SP SUPER MATCH
BOLT-ACTION TARGET RIFLE. . . . . . . NiB $4120 Ex $3502 Gd $1802
Telescopic short action. Adj. single-stage trigger. Caliber: .308 Win. (chambering for other cartridges available on special order). Three shot magazine. 27.6-inch heavy bbl. w/muzzle brake, dovetail rib for special scope mount. Weight: 12 lbs. Target stock w/wide and deep forearm, full pistol-grip, thumbhole adj. cheekpiece, adj. rubber buttplate.

MODEL 66ST CARBINE
Same general specifications as Model 66S Standard except w/20.9-inch bbl., full-length stock, weight: 7 lbs.
Model 66ST . . . . NiB $6225 Ex $1442 Gd $1004
W/extra bbl. assembly, add $550

MODEL 83 BOLT-ACTION RIFLE . . . . . NiB $2395 Ex $2008 Gd $1236
Centerfire single-shot, bolt-action rifle for 300-meter competition. Caliber: .308 Win. 25.5-inch fluted bbl. Weight: 10.5 lbs. Adj. micrometer rear sight globe front. Fully adj. competition stock. Disc. 1988.

MODEL 96 . . . . NiB $676 Ex $541 Gd $368
Calibers: .25-06, .270 Win., 7x64, .308 Win., .30-06, 7mm Rem. Mag., .300 Win. Mag. 22-inch bbl.; magnums 24-inch. Weight: 6.25 lbs. No sights; drilled and tapped for scope. Walnut stock. 5-shot top-loading magazine. 3-position safety.

MODEL 99 CLASSIC BOLT-ACTION RIFLE
Calibers: .243 Win., .25-06, .270 Win., .30-06, .308 Win., .257 Wby., .270 Wby., 7mm Rem. Mag., .300 Win., .300 Wby. .375 H&H. Four shot magazine (standard), 3-shot (Magnum). Bbl.: 24-inch (standard) or 26-inch (Magnum). 44 inches overall (standard). Weight: 8 lbs. No sights. Checkered European walnut stock w/rosewood grip cap available in Classic and Monte Carlo styles w/High-Luster or oil finish. Disc. importing 1994.
Standard Classic or
Monte Carlo (oil finish). . . . . NiB $1154 Ex $953 Gd $618
Magnum Classic or
Monte Carlo (oil finish). . . . . NiB $1244 Ex $999 Gd $686
Standard Classic or
Monte Carlo (H-L finish). . . . . NiB $1184 Ex $978 Gd $635
Magnum Classic or
Monte Carlo (H-L finish). . . . . NiB $1230 Ex $1045 Gd $718

MODEL 107 BOLT-ACTION RIFLE . . . . NiB $360 Ex $257 Gd $154
Caliber: .22 LR. Mag. Five shot magazine. 21.5-inch bbl. 40 inches overall. Weight: 5 lbs. Receiver drilled and tapped for rail scope mounts. Hooded front sight, adj. rear. Disc. importing 1994.

MODEL 201/201 LUXUS BOLT-ACTION RIFLE
Calibers: .22 LR. .22 Win. Mag. 5-shot magazine. 21-inch bbl. 40 inches overall. Weight: 6.5 lbs. Receiver drilled and tapped for scope mounts. Sights optional. Checkered walnut-stained beech stock w/Monte Carlo. Model 201 Luxus w/checkered European walnut stock QD swivels, rosewood forend and rubber recoil pad. Made 1989 to date. Disc. importing 1994.
Model 201 Standard . . . . NiB $721 Ex $669 Gd $381
Model 201 Magnum . . . . NiB $663 Ex $537 Gd $373
Model 201 Luxus Standard . . . . NiB $747 Ex $669 Gd $386
Model 201 Luxus Magnum . . . . NiB $856 Ex $695 Gd $489

Midland Model 2700 Bolt-Action Rifle

Merkel Model 220

MODEL 2000 BOLT-ACTION
SPORTING RIFLE. . . . . **NiB $587 Ex $489 Gd $309**
Modified Mauser-type action. Calibers: .270 Win., .308 Win., .30-
06. Five-shot magazine. 24-inch bbl. Weight: 7.5 lbs. Sights: Folding
leaf rear; hooded ramp front. Checkered walnut stock w/Monte
Carlo comb and cheekpiece, forend tip, sling swivels. Made 1969-
71. Note: Model 2000 is similar in appearance to Model 3000.

MODEL 2000 CLASSIC BOLT-ACTION SPORTING RIFLE
Calibers: .22-250 Rem., .234 Win., .270 Win., 7mm Mag., .308 Win.,
.30-06, .300 Win. Mag. Three or 5-shot magazine. 24-inch bbl.
Weight: 7.5 lbs. Sights: Folding leaf rear; hooded ramp front.
Checkered walnut stock w/Monte Carlo comb and cheekpiece, forend
tip, sling swivels. Imported 1998. Note: The Model 2000 Classic is
designed to interchange bbl. assemblies within a given caliber group.
Model 2000 Classic. . . . . **NiB $1577 Ex $1262 Gd $858**
Model 2000 Professional
w/Recoil Compensator . . . . **NiB $3213 Ex $2570 Gd $1748**
Model 2000 Sniper. . . . . **NiB $1796 Ex $1437 Gd $977**
Model 2000 Varmint. . . . . **NiB $1639 Ex $1390 Gd $946**
Extra bbl. assembly, add **$895**

MODEL 3000 BOLT-ACTION
SPORTING RIFLE. . . . . **NiB $592 Ex $463 Gd $330**
Modified Mauser-type action. Calibers: .243 Win., .270 Win., .308
Win., .30-06. Five-shot magazine. 22-inch bbl. Weight: 7 lbs. No
sights. Select European walnut stock, Monte Carlo style w/cheek-
piece, rosewood forend tip and pistol-grip cap, skip checkering,
recoil pad, sling swivels. Made 1971-74.

MODEL 3000 MAGNUM . . . . NiB $592 Ex $515 Gd $412
Same general specifications as standard Model 3000, except w/3-
shot magazine, 26-inch bbl., weight: 8 lbs. Calibers: 7mm Rem.
Mag., .300 Win. Mag., .375 H&H Mag.

MODEL 4000 VARMINT RIFLE . . . . NiB $515 Ex $412 Gd $299
Same general specifications as standard Model 3000, except
w/smaller action, folding leaf rear sight; hooded ramp front, rubber
buttplate instead of recoil pad, weight 6.75 lbs. Calibers: .222 Rem.,
.223 Rem. 22-inch bbl. Select European walnut stock w/rosewood
forend tip and pistol-grip cap. French checkering and sling swivels.

McMILLAN GUN WORKS — Phoenix, Arizona
Harris Gunworks

See Harris Gunworks.

GEBRÜDER MERKEL — Suhl, Germany

For Merkel combination guns and drillings, see listings under Merkel shotguns.

OVER/UNDER RIFLES ("BOCK-DOPPELBÜCHSEN")
Calibers: 5.6x35 Vierling, 6.5x58r5, 7x57r5, 8x57JR, 8x60R
Magnum, 9.3x53r5, 9.3x72r5, 9.3x74r5, 10.3x60R as well as
most of the British calibers for African and Indian big game.
Various bbl. lengths, weights. In general, specifications correspond to those of Merkel over/under shotguns. Values of these
over/under rifles (in calibers for which ammunition is obtainable)
are about the same as those of comparable shotgun models cur-
rently manufactured. For more specific data, see Merkel shotgun
models indicated below.
Model 220. . . . . **NiB $9000 Ex $8000 Gd $4000**
Model 220E. . . . . **NiB $9575 Ex $8400 Gd $7400**
Model 221. . . . . **NiB $7438 Ex $5950 Gd $4046**
Model 221E. . . . . **NiB $9813 Ex $7850 Gd $5338**
Model 320. . . . . **NiB $8125 Ex $6500 Gd $4420**
Model 320E. . . . . **NiB $15,000 Ex $12,000 Gd $8160**
Model 321. . . . . **NiB $16,563 Ex $13,250 Gd $9010**
Model 321E. . . . . **NiB $17,500 Ex $14,000 Gd $9520**
Model 322. . . . . **NiB $18,125 Ex $14,500 Gd $9860**
Model 323E. . . . . **NiB $23,125 Ex $18,500 Gd $12,580**
Model 324. . . . . **NiB $26,875 Ex $21,500 Gd $14,620**

MEXICAN MILITARY RIFLE
Mfd. by Government Arsenal, Mexico, D.F.

MODEL 1936 MAUSER MILITARY RIFLE . . . . **NiB $206 Ex $154 Gd $8**
Same as German Kar.98k w/minor variations and U.S. M/1903
Springfield-type knurled cocking piece.

Mossberg Model 25

MIDLAND RIFLES — Mfg. by Gibbs Rifle Company, Inc., Martinsburg, WV

MODEL 2100 BOLT-ACTION
RIFLE......................... NiB $341 Ex $273 Gd $185
Calibers: .22-250, .243 Win., 6mm Rem., .270 Win., 6.5x55, 7x57, 7x64, .308 Win., and .30-06. Springfield 1903 action. Four-shot magazine. 22-inch bbl. 43 inches overall. Weight: 7 lbs. Flip-up rear sight; hooded ramp front. Finely finished and checkered walnut stock w/pistol-grip cap and sling swivels. Steel recoil bar. Action drilled and tapped for scope mounts. Production disc.1997.

MODEL 2600 BOLT-ACTION RIFLE ...... NiB $360 Ex $288 Gd $165
Same general specifications as Model 2100 except no pistol-grip cap, and stock is walnut-finished hardwood. Made 1992-97.

MODEL 2700 BOLT-ACTION RIFLE ...... NiB $360 Ex $283 Gd $180
Same general specifications as Model 2100 except the weight of this rifle as been reduced by utilizing a tapered bbl., anodized aluminum trigger housing and lightened stock. Weight: 6.5 lbs. Disc.

MODEL 2800 LIGHTWEIGHT RIFLE ..... NiB $367 Ex $294 Gd $200
Same general specifications as Model 2100 except w/laminated birch stock. Made 1992-94 and 1996-97.

MITCHELL ARMS. INC. — Fountain Valley, California, (Formerly Santa Ana, CA)

MODEL 15/22 SEMIAUTOMATIC
High Standard-style action. Caliber: .22 LR. 15-shot magazine (10-shot after 10/13/94). 20.5-inch bbl. 37.5 inches overall. Weight: 6.25 lbs. Ramp front sight; adj. open rear. Blued finish. Mahogany stock; Monte Carlo-style American walnut stock on Deluxe model. Made 1994-96.
Model 15/22 SP (Special)
w/plastic buttplate .... NiB $97 Ex $77 Gd $53
Model 15/22 Carbine .... NiB $135 Ex $108 Gd $73
Model 15/22D Deluxe .... NiB $161 Ex $129 Gd $88

MODEL 9300 SERIES BOLT-ACTION RIFLE
Calibers: .22 LR. .22 Mag. Five or 10-shot magazine. 22.5-inch bbl. 40.75 inches overall. Weight: 6.5 lbs. Beaded ramp front sight; adj. open rear. Blued finish. American walnut stock. Made 1994-95.
Model 9302 (.22 LR,
checkered, rosewood caps)............. NiB $238 Ex $191 Gd $130
Model 9302 (.22 Mag.,
checkered, rosewood caps)............. NiB $251 Ex $201 Gd $137
Model 9303 (.22 LR, plain stock) .... NiB $186 Ex $149 Gd $102
Model 9304 (.22 Mag.,
checkered, No rosewood caps).......... NiB $200 Ex $160 Gd $108
Model 9305 (.22 LR, special stock)........ NiB $161 Ex $129 Gd $88

AK-22 SEMIAUTOMATIC RIFLE .... NiB $238 Ex $191 Gd $130
Replica of AK-47 rifle. .22 LR. .22 WMR., 20-shot magazine (.22 LR) 10-shot (.22 WMR). 18-inch bbl. 36 inches overall. Weight: 6.5 lbs. Sights: Post front; open adj. rear. European walnut stock and forend. Matte black finish. Made 1985-94.

CAR-15 22 SEMIAUTOMATIC RIFLE..... NiB $238 Ex $191 Gd $130
Replica of AR-15 CAR rifle. Caliber: .22 LR. 15-shot magazine.16.25-inch bbl. 32 inches overall. Sights: Adj. post front; adj. aperture rear. Telescoping buttstock and ventilated forend. Matte black finish. Made 1990-94.

GALIL 22 SEMIAUTOMATIC RIFLE...... NiB $283 Ex $232 Gd $144
Replica of Israeli Galil rifle. Calibers: .22 LR. .22 WMR., 20-shot magazine (.22 LR), 10-shot (.22 WMR). 18-inch bbl. 36 inches overall. Weight: 6.5 lbs. Sights: Adj. post front; rear adj. for windage. Folding metal stock w/European walnut grip and forend. Matte black finish. Made 1987-93.

M-16A 22 SEMIAUTOMATIC RIFLE ..... NiB $238 Ex $191 Gd $130
Replica of AR-15 rifle. Caliber: .22 LR. 15-shot magazine. 20.5-inch bbl. 38.5 inches overall. Weight: 7 lbs. Sights: Adj. post front, adj. aperture rear. Black composite stock and forend. Matte black finish. Made 1990-94.

MAS 22 SEMIAUTOMATIC RIFLE....... NiB $283 Ex $227 Gd $154
Replica of French MAS bullpup rifle. Caliber: .22 LR. 20-shot magazine. 18-inch bbl. 28 inches overall. Weight: 7.5 lbs. Sights: Adj. post front, folding aperture rear. European walnut buttstock and forend. Matte black finish. Made 1987-93.

PPS SEMIAUTOMATIC RIFLE
Caliber: .22 LR. 20-shot magazine, 50-shot drum. 16.5-inch bbl. 33.5 inches overall. Weight: 5.5 lbs. Sights: Blade front; adj. rear. European walnut stock w/ventilated bbl. shroud. Matte black finish. Made 1989-94.
Model PPS (20-shot) .... NiB $257 Ex $206 Gd $140
Model PPS/50 (50-shot drum)..... NiB $521 Ex $438 Gd $331

O.F. MOSSBERG & SONS, INC. — North Haven, Connecticut, (Formerly New Haven, CT)

MODEL 10 BOLT-ACTION
SINGLE-SHOT RIFLE .... NiB $154 Ex $103 Gd $77
Takedown. Caliber: .22 LR, Long, Short. 22-inch bbl. Weight: 4 lbs. Sights: Open rear; bead front. Plain pistol-grip stock w/swivels, sling. Made 1933-35.

MODEL 14 BOLT-ACTION
SINGLE-SHOT RIFLE .... NiB $165 Ex $103 Gd $77
Takedown. Caliber: .22 LR. Long, Short. 24-inch bbl. Weight: 5.25 lbs. Sights: Peep rear; hooded ramp front. Plain pistol-grip stock w/semi-beavertail forearm, 1.25-inch swivels. Made 1934-35.

MODEL 20 BOLT-ACTION
SINGLE-SHOT RIFLE .... NiB $165 Ex $103 Gd $77
Takedown. Caliber: .22 LR. Long, Short. 24-inch bbl. Weight: 4.5 lbs. Sights: Open rear; bead front. Plain pistol-grip stock and forearm w/finger grooves, sling and swivels. Made 1933-35.

MODEL 25/25A BOLT-ACTION SINGLE-SHOT RIFLE
Takedown. Caliber: .22 LR. Long, Short. 24-inch bbl. Weight: 5 lbs. Sights: Peep rear; hooded ramp front. Plain pistol-grip stock w/semi-beavertail forearm. 1.25-inch swivels. Made 1935-36.
Model 25.......................... NiB $165 Ex $103 Gd $72
Model 25A (Improved Model 25, 1936-38)..... NiB $175 Ex $103 Gd $77

RIFLES

Mossberg Model 35A

Mossberg Model L42A

Mossberg Model 42B

MODEL 26B/26C BOLT-ACTION SINGLE-SHOT
Takedown. Caliber: .22 LR. Long, Short. 26-inch bbl. Weight: 5.5 lbs. Sights; Rear, micrometer click peep or open; hooded ramp front. Plain pistol-grip stock swivels. Made 1938-41.
Model 26B . . . . NiB $175 Ex $134 Gd $77
Model 26C
(No rear sight/swivels) . . . . NiB $154 Ex $103 Gd $62

MODEL 30 BOLT-ACTION
SINGLE-SHOT RIFLE . . . . NiB $134 Ex $103 Gd $72
Takedown. Caliber: .22 LR. Long, Short. 24-inch bbl. Weight: 4.5 lbs. Sights: Peep rear; bead front, on hooded ramp. Plain pistol-grip stock, forearm w/finger grooves. Made 1933-35.

MODEL 34 BOLT-ACTION
SINGLE-SHOT RIFLE . . . . NiB $154 Ex $103 Gd $72
Takedown. Caliber: .22 LR. Long, Short. 24-inch bbl. Weight: 5.5 lbs. Sights: Peep rear; hooded ramp front. Plain pistol-grip stock w/semibeavertail forearm, 1.25-inch swivels. Made 1934-35.

MODEL 35 TARGET GRADE
BOLT-ACTION SINGLE-SHOT RIFLE. . . . . . NiB $335 Ex $227 Gd $84
Caliber: .22 LR. 26-inch heavy bbl. Weight: 8.25 lbs. Sights: Micrometer click rear peep; hooded ramp front. Large target stock w/full pistol grip, cheekpiece, full beavertail forearm, 1.25-inch swivels. Made 1935-37.

MODEL 35A BOLT-ACTION
SINGLE-SHOT RIFLE . . . . NiB $335 Ex $226 Gd $82
Caliber: .22 LR. 26-inch heavy bbl. Weight: 8.25 lbs. Sights: Micrometer click peep rear; hooded front. Target stock w/cheekpiece full pistol grip and forearm, 1.25-inch sling swivels. Made 1937-38.

MODEL 35A-LS . . . . NiB $391 Ex $257 Gd $170
Caliber .22 LR. Same as Model 35A but w/Lyman No. 57 rear sight, 17A front. Target stock w/checkpiece, full pistol-grip and forearm.

MODEL 35B . . . . NiB $381 Ex $247 Gd $165
Same specifications as Model 44B except single-shot. Made 1938-40.

MODEL 40 BOLT-ACTION REPEATER. . . . . . NiB $154 Ex $103 Gd $72
Takedown. Caliber: .22 LR. Long, Short, 16-round tubular magazine. 24-inch bbl. Weight: 5 lbs. Sights: Peep rear; bead front, on hooded ramp. Plain pistol-grip stock, forearm w/finger grooves. Made 1933-35.

MODEL 42 BOLT-ACTION REPEATER. . . . . . NiB $154 Ex $103 Gd $72
Takedown. Caliber: .22 LR. Long, Short. Seven-shot detachable box magazine. 24-inch bbl. Weight: 5 lbs. Sights: Receiver peep, open rear; hooded ramp front. Pistol-grip stock. 1.25-inch swivels. Made 1935-37.

MODEL 42A/L42A BOLT-ACTION REPEATERS
Takedown. Caliber: .22 LR. Long, Short. Seven-shot detachable box magazine. 24-inch bbl. Weight: 5 lbs. Sights: Receiver peep, open rear; ramp front. Plain pistol-grip stock. Made 1937-38. Model L42A (left-hand action) made 1937-1941.
Model 42A. NiB $154 Ex $124 Gd $84
Model L42A. . . . . NiB $238 Ex $191 Gd $130

MODEL 42B/42C BOLT-ACTION REPEATERS
Takedown. Caliber: .22 LR. Long, Short. Five-shot detachable box magazine. 24-inch bbl. Weight: 6 lbs. Sights: Micrometer click receiver peep, open rear hooded ramp front. Plain pistol-grip stock, swivels. Made 1938-41.
Model 42B. NiB $154 Ex $129 Gd $62
Model 42C (No rear peep sight) . . . . . NiB $123 Ex $98 Gd $67

Mossberg Model 42C

Mossberg Model L-43

Mossberg Model 43B

Mossberg Model 44US

Mossberg Model L45A
Left-Hand Model

Mossberg Model 45B

Mossberg Model L46A-LS

Mossberg Model 46B

RIFLES

MODEL 42M BOLT-ACTION REPEATER . . . . NiB $180 Ex $154 Gd $82
Caliber: .22 LR. Long, Short. Seven-shot detachable box magazine. 23-inch bbl. Weight: 6.75 lbs. Sights: Microclick receiver peep, open rear; hooded ramp front. Two-piece Mannlicher-type stock w/cheekpiece and pistol-grip, swivels. Made 1940-50.

MODEL 43/L43 BOLT-ACTION
REPEATERS . . . . NiB $418 Ex $335 Gd $228
Speedlock, adj. trigger pull. Caliber: .22 LR. Seven-shot detachable box

(cont'd.) MODEL 43/L43 BOLT-ACTION REPEATERS
magazine. 26-inch heavy bbl. Weight: 8.25 lbs. Sights: Lyman No. 57 rear; selective aperture front. Target stock w/cheekpiece, full pistol-grip, beavertail forearm, adj. front swivel. Made 1937-38. Model L43 is same as Model 43 except w/left-hand action.

MODEL 43B . . . . NiB $360 Ex $257 Gd $98
Same as Model 44B except w/Lyman No. 57 receiver sight and No. 17A front sight. Made 1938-39.

Mossberg Model 46M

Mossberg Model 50

Mossberg Model 51

Mossberg Model 51M

MODEL 44 BOLT-ACTION REPEATER. . . . . . NiB $257 Ex $206 Gd $93
Takedown. Caliber: .22 LR. Long, Short. Tubular magazine holds 16 LR. 24-inch bbl. Weight: 6 lbs. Sights: Peep rear; hooded ramp front. Plain pistol-grip stock w/semi-beavertail forearm, 1.25-inch swivels. Made 1934-35. Note: Do not confuse this rifle w/later Models 44B and 44US, which are clip repeaters.

**MODEL 44B BOLT-ACTION
TARGET RIFLE . . . . NiB $278 Ex $206 Gd $103**
Caliber: .22 LR. Seven-shot detachable box magazine. Made 1938-41.

MODEL 44US BOLT-ACTION REPEATER
Caliber: .22 LR. Seven shot detachable box magazine. 26-inch heavy bbl. Weight: 8.5 lbs. Sights: Micrometer click receiver peep, hooded front. Target stock, swivels. Made 1943-48. Note: This model was used as a training rifle by the U.S. Armed Forces during WWII.
Model 44US . . . . NiB $257 Ex $232 Gd $93
Model 44US (marked U.S. Property) . . . . . NiB $335 Ex $283 Gd $206

MODEL 45 BOLT-ACTION REPEATER. . . . . . NiB $180 Ex $154 Gd $93
Takedown. Caliber: .22 LR. Long, Short. Tubular magazine holds 15 LR. 18 Long, 22 Short. 24-inch bbl. Weight: 6.75 lbs. Sights: Rear peep; hooded ramp front. Plain pistol-grip stock, 1.25-inch swivels. Made 1935-37.

MODEL 45A, L45A, 45AC BOLT-ACTION REPEATERS
Takedown. Caliber: .22 LR. Long, Short. Tubular magazine holds 15 LR, 18 Long, 22 Short. 24-inch bbl. Weight: 6.75 lbs. Sights: Receiver peep, open rear; hooded blade front sight mounted on ramp. Plain pistol-grip stock, 1.25-inch sling swivels. Made 1937-38. See illustration on previous page.

(cont'd.) MODEL 45A, L45A, 45AC BOLT-ACTION REPEATERS
Model 45A . . . . NiB $180 Ex $144 Gd $98
Model L45A (Left-hand action) . . . . NiB $232 Ex $185 Gd $126
Model 45AC (No receiver peep sight) . . . . . NiB $165 Ex $124 Gd $82

MODEL 45B/45C BOLT-ACTION REPEATERS
Takedown. Caliber: .22 LR. Long, Short. Tubular magazine holds 15 LR, 18 Long, 22 Short. 24-inch bbl. Weight: 6.25 lbs. Open rear sight; hooded blade front sight mounted on ramp. Plain pistol-grip stock w/sling swivels. Made 1938-40.
Model 45B . . . . NiB $161 Ex $129 Gd $88
Model 45C (No sights, made 1935-37) . . . . . NiB $142 Ex $113 Gd $77

MODEL 46 BOLT-ACTION REPEATER. . . . . . NiB $180 Ex $185 Gd $93
Takedown. Caliber: .22 LR. Long, Short. Tubular magazine holds 15 LR, 18 Long, 22 Short. 26-inch bbl. Weight: 7.5 lbs. Sights: Micrometer click rear peep; hooded ramp front. Pistol-grip stock w/cheekpiece, full beavertail forearm, 1.25-inch swivels. Made 1935-37.

MODEL 46A, 46A-LS, L46A-LS BOLT-ACTION REPEATERS
Takedown. Caliber: .22 LR. Long, Short. Tubular magazine holds 15 LR, 18 Long, 22 Short. 26-inch bbl. Weight: 7.25 lbs. Sights: Micrometer click receiver peep, open rear; hooded ramp front. Pistol-grip stock w/cheekpiece and beavertail forearm, quick-detachable swivels. Made 1937-38.
Model 46A . . . . NiB $186 Ex $149 Gd $102
Mdl. 46A-LS (w/Lyman No. 57 receiver sight) . . . . NiB $251 Ex $201 Gd $137
Model L46A-LS (Left-hand action) . . . . NiB $366 Ex $294 Gd $200

Mossberg Model 140B

Mossberg Model 140K

Mossberg Model 144LS

Mossberg Model 146B

**MODEL 46B BOLT-ACTION
REPEATER** . . . . **NiB $148 Ex $118 Gd $80**
Takedown. Caliber: .22 LR. Long, Short. Tubular magazine holds 15
LR, 18 Long, 22 Short. 26-inch bbl. Weight: 7 lbs. Sights: Micrometer
click receiver peep, open rear, hooded front. Plain pistol-grip stock
w/cheekpiece, swivels. Note: Postwar version of this model has full
magazine holding 20 LR, 23 Long, 30 Short. Made 1938-50.

MODEL 46BT . . . . **NiB $212 Ex $170 Gd $115**
Same as Model 46B except w/heavier bbl. and stock. Weight: 7.75
lbs. Made 1938-39.

MODEL 46C . . . . **NiB $206 Ex $154 Gd $93**
Same as Model 46 except w/a heavier bbl. and stock than that
model. Weight: 8.5 lbs. Made 1936-37.

**MODEL 46M
BOLT-ACTION REPEATER** . . . . **NiB $206 Ex $154 Gd $93**
Caliber: .22 LR. Long, Short. Tubular magazine holds 22 Short, 18
Long, 15 LR. 23-inch bbl. Weight: 7 lbs. Sights: Microclick receiver
peep, open rear; hooded ramp front. Two-piece Mannlicher-type
stock w/cheekpiece and pistol-grip, swivels. Made 1940-52.

**MODEL 50
AUTOLOADING RIFLE** . . . . **NiB $180 Ex $144 Gd $98**
Same as Model 51 except w/plain stock w/o beavertail cheekpiece,
swivels or receiver peep sight. Made 1939-42.

MODEL 51 AUTOLOADING RIFLE . . . . **NiB $175 Ex $129 Gd $98**
Takedown. Caliber: .22 LR. Fifteen-shot tubular magazine in buttstock. 24-inch bbl. Weight: 7.25 lbs. Sights: Micrometer click
receiver peep, open rear; hooded ramp front. Cheekpiece stock
w/full pistol grip and beavertail forearm, swivels. Made 1939 only.

MODEL 51M AUTOLOADING RIFLE . . . . . . **NiB $175 Ex $129 Gd $98**
Caliber: .22 LR. Fifteen-shot tubular magazine. 20-inch bbl. Weight:
7 lbs. Sights: Microclick receiver peep, open rear; hooded ramp
front. Two-piece Mannlicher-type stock w/pistol-grip and cheekpiece, hard-rubber buttplate and sling swivels. Made 1939-46.

MODEL 140B SPORTER-TARGET RIFLE . . . . **NiB $175 Ex $129 Gd $98**
Same as Model 140K except w/peep rear sight, hooded ramp front
sight. Made 1957-58.

MODEL 140K BOLT-ACTION REPEATER . . . **NiB $154 Ex $124 Gd $84**
Caliber: .22 LR. .22 Long, .22 Short. Seven-shot clip magazine. 24.5-
inch bbl. Weight: 5.75 lbs. Sights: Open rear; bead front. Monte Carlo
stock w/cheekpiece and pistol-grip, sling swivels. Made 1955-58.

**MODEL 142-A BOLT-ACTION
REPEATING CARBINE** . . . . **NiB $194 Ex $154 Gd $105**
Caliber: .22 Short Long, LR. Seven-shot detachable box magazine. 18-
inch bbl. Weight: 6 lbs. Sights: Peep rear, military-type front. Monte
Carlo stock w/pistol-grip, hinged forearm pulls down to form hand grip;
sling swivels mounted on left side of stock. Made 1949-57.

Mossberg Model 151K

Mossberg Model 151M

Mossberg Model 152

MODEL 142K . . . . **NiB $135 Ex $108 Gd $73**
Same as Model 142 except w/open rear sight. Made 1953-57.

**MODEL 144 BOLT-ACTION
TARGET RIFLE** . . . . **NiB $412 Ex $335 Gd $180**
Caliber: .22 LR. Seven-shot detachable box magazine. 26-inch
heavy bbl. Weight: 8 lbs. Sights: Microclick receiver peep; hooded
front. Pistol-grip target stock w/beavertail forearm, adj. hand stop,
swivels. Made 1949-54. Note: This model designation was resumed
c.1973 to replace Model 144LS, and then disc. again in 1985.

MODEL 144LS. . . . . **NiB $463 Ex $402 Gd $170**
Same as Model 144 except w/Lyman No. 57MS or Mossberg S331
receiver sight and Lyman 17A front sight. Made 1954 to date. Note:
Since 1973, this model has been marketed as Model 144.

MODEL 146B BOLT-ACTION REPEATER . . **NiB $206 Ex $154 Gd $103**
Takedown. Caliber: .22 LR. Long, Short. Tubular magazine holds 30
Short, 23 Long, 20 LR. 26-inch bbl. Weight: 7 lbs. Sights: Micrometer
click rear peep, open rear; hooded front. Plain stock w/pistol-grip, Monte
Carlo comb and cheekpiece, knob forend tip, swivels. Made 1949-54.

MODEL 151K . . . . **NiB $185 Ex $144 Gd $93**
Same as Model 151M except w/24-inch bbl., weight: 6 lbs., w/o
peep sight, plain stock w/Monte Carlo comb and cheekpiece, pistol-
grip knob, forend tip, w/o swivels. Made 1950-51.

MODEL 151M AUTOLOADING RIFLE . . . . **NiB $185 Ex $144 Gd $93**
Improved version of Model 51M w/same general specifications, complete action is instantly removable w/o use of tools. Made 1946-58.

MODEL 152 AUTOLOADING CARBINE . . . **NiB $185 Ex $144 Gd $93**
Caliber: .22 LR. Seven-shot detachable box magazine. 18-inch bbl.
Weight: 5 lbs. Sights: Peep rear; military-type front. Monte Carlo
stock w/pistol-grip, hinged forearm pulls down to form hand grip,
sling mounted on swivels on left side of stock. Made 1948-57.

MODEL 152K . . . . **NiB $165 Ex $129 Gd $82**
Same as Model 152 except w/open instead of peep rear sight. Made
1950-57.

MODEL 320B BOY SCOUT TARGET RIFLE . . . . . **NiB $168 Ex $134 Gd $91**
Same as Model 340K except single-shot w/auto. safety. Made 1960-71.

**MODEL 320K HAMMERLESS
BOLT-ACTION SINGLE-SHOT**. . . . . . **NiB $129 Ex $103 Gd $70**
Same as Model 346K except single-shot, w/drop-in loading plat-
form, automatic safety. Weight: 5.75 lbs. Made 1958-60.

MODEL 321B . . . . **NiB $148 Ex $118 Gd $80**
Same as Model 321K except w/receiver peep sight. Made 1972-75.

**MODEL 321K BOLT-ACTION
SINGLE-SHOT** . . . . **NiB $154 Ex $124 Gd $84**
Same as Model 341 except single-shot. Made 1972-80.

MODEL 333 AUTOLOADING CARBINE . . **NiB $154 Ex $129 Gd $103**
Caliber: .22 LR. 15-shot tubular magazine. 20-inch bbl. Weight:
6.25 lbs. Sights: Open rear; ramp front. Monte Carlo stock w/check-
ered pistol grip and forearm, bbl. band, swivels. Made 1972-73.

MODEL 340B TARGET SPORTER . . . . **NiB $185 Ex $154 Gd $103**
Same as Model 340K except w/peep rear sight, hooded ramp front
sight. Made 1958-81.

**MODEL 340K HAMMERLESS
BOLT-ACTION REPEATER** . . . . **NiB $154 Ex $129 Gd $103**
Same as Model 346K except clip type, 7-shot magazine. Made
1958-71.

MODEL 340M . . . . **NiB $297 Ex $237 Gd $161**
Same as Model 340K except w/18.5-inch bbl., Mannlicher-style
stock w/swivels and sling. Weight: 5.25 lbs. Made 1970-71.

Mossberg Model 320B

Mossberg Model 320K

Mossberg Model 333

Mossberg Model 340B

Mossberg Model 340K

Mossberg Model 341

Mossberg Model 342K

Mossberg Model 346B

Mossberg Model 346K

RIFLES

Mossberg Model 350K
Autoloading — Clip Type

Mossberg Model 351K
Automatic Sporter

Mossberg Model 352K
Carbine

Mossberg Model 353
Carbine

Mossberg Model 377
Plinkster

MODEL 341 BOLT-ACTION REPEATER. . . . . . NiB $129 Ex $98 Gd $72
Caliber: .22 Short. Long, LR. Seven-shot clip magazine. 24-inch bbl. Weight: 6.5 lbs. Sights: Open rear, ramp front. Monte Carlo stock w/checkered pistol-grip and forearm, sling swivels. Made 1972-85.

**MODEL 342K HAMMERLESS
BOLT-ACTION CARBINE.** . . . . NiB $154 Ex $129 Gd $93
Same as Model 340K except w/18-inch bbl., stock w/no cheekpiece, extension forend is hinged, pulls down to form hand grip; sling swivels and web strap on left side of stock. Weight: 5 lbs. Made 1958-74.

MODEL 346B . . . . NiB $154 Ex $129 Gd $93
Same as Model 346K except w/peep rear sight, hooded ramp front sight. Made 1958-67.

**MODEL 346K HAMMERLESS
BOLT-ACTION REPEATER** . . . . NiB $148 Ex $118 Gd $80
Caliber: .22 Short. Long, LR. Tubular magazine holds 25 Short, 20 Long, 18 LR. 24-inch bbl. Weight: 6.5 lbs. Sights: Open rear; bead front. Walnut stock w/Monte Carlo comb, cheekpiece, pistol-grip, sling swivels. Made 1958-71.

**MODEL 350K AUTOLOADING
RIFLE — CLIP TYPE** . . . . NiB $144 Ex $98 Gd $72
Caliber: .22 Short (High Speed), Long, LR. Seven-shot clip magazine.

(cont'd.) **MODEL 350K AUTOLOADING RIFLE — CLIP TYPE**
23.5-inch bbl. Weight: 6 lbs. Sights: Open rear; bead front. Monte Carlo stock w/pistol-grip. Made 1958-71.

MODEL 351C AUTOLOADING CARBINE . . NiB $165 Ex $134 Gd $93
Same as Model 351K except w/18.5-inch bbl., Western carbine-style stock w/barrel band and sling swivels. Weight: 5.5 lbs. Made 1965-71.

**MODEL 351K AUTOLOADING
SPORTER.** . . . . NiB $165 Ex $134 Gd $93
Caliber: .22 LR. Fifteen-shot tubular magazine in buttstock. 24-inch bbl. Weight: 6 lbs. Sights: Open rear; bead front. Monte Carlo stock w/pistol-grip. Made 1960-71.

MODEL 352K AUTOLOADING CARBINE. . . . . . NiB $165 Ex $134 Gd $93
Caliber: .22 Short, Long, LR. Seven-shot clip magazine. 18-inch bbl. Weight: 5 lbs. Sights: Open rear; bead front. Monte Carlo stock w/pistol grip; extension forend of Tenite is hinged, pulls down to form hand grip; sling swivels, web strap. Made 1958-71.

MODEL 353 AUTOLOADING CARBINE . . . NiB $165 Ex $134 Gd $93
Caliber: .22 LR. 7-shot clip magazine. 18-inch bbl. Weight: 5 lbs. Sights: Open rear; ramp front. Monte Carlo stock w/checkered pistol-grip and forearm; black Tenite extension forend pulls down to form hand grip. Made 1972-85.

Mossberg Model 400

Mossberg Model 402

Mossberg Model 472
Brush Gun

Mossberg Model 472
Carbine (Pistol Grip)

Mossberg Model 472
Carbine (Straight Grip)

Mossberg Model 472
"One in Five Thousand"

MODEL 377 PLINKSTER AUTOLOADER ... **NiB $185 Ex $144 Gd $98**
Caliber: .22 LR. Fifteen-shot tubular magazine. 20-inch bbl. Weight: 6.25 lbs. 4x scope sight. Thumbhole stock w/rollover cheekpiece, Monte Carlo comb, checkered forearm; molded of modified polystyrene foam in walnut-finish; sling swivel studs. Made 1977-79.

MODEL 380 SEMIAUTOMATIC RIFLE ..... **NiB $154 Ex $124 Gd $84**
Caliber: .22 LR. Fifteen-shot buttstock magazine. 20-inch bbl. Weight: 5.5 lbs. Sights: Open rear; bead front. Made 1980-85.

MODEL 400 PALOMINO LEVER-ACTION ..... **NiB $257 Ex $196 Gd $103**
Hammerless. Caliber: .22 Short, Long, LR. Tubular magazine holds 20 Short, 17 Long, 15 LR. 24-inch bbl. Weight: 5.5 lbs. Sights: Open rear; bead front. Monte Carlo stock w/checkered pistol-grip; beavertail forearm. Made 1959-64.

MODEL 402 PALOMINO CARBINE ...... **NiB $257 Ex $206 Gd $180**
Same as Model 400 except w/18.5-inch (1961-64) or 20-inch bbl. (1964-71), forearm w/bbl. band, swivels; magazine holds two fewer rounds. Weight: 4.75 lbs. Made 1961-71.

MODEL 430 AUTOLOADING RIFLE ...... **NiB $148 Ex $118 Gd $80**
Caliber: .22 LR. Eighteen-shot tubular magazine. 24-inch bbl. Weight: 6.25 lbs. Sights: Open rear; bead front. Monte Carlo stock w/checkered pistol grip; checkered forearm. Made 1970-71.

MODEL 432 WESTERN-STYLE AUTO ...... **NiB $142 Ex $113 Gd $77**
Same as Model 430 except w/plain straight-grip carbine-type stock and forearm, bbl. band, sling swivels. Magazine capacity: 15 cartridges. Weight: 6 lbs. Made 1970-71.

Mossberg Model 640K
Chuckster

Mossberg Model 640KS

Mossberg Model 640M

Mossberg Model 642K

MODEL 472 BRUSH GUN . . . . NiB $206 Ex $180 Gd $103
Same as Model 472 Carbine w/straight-grip stock except w/18-inch
bbl., weight: 6.5 lbs. Caliber: .30-30. Magazine capacity: 5 rounds.
Made 1974-76.

MODEL 472 LEVER-ACTION CARBINE . . . NiB $185 Ex $154 Gd $103
Calibers: .30-30, .35 Rem. Six shot tubular magazine. 20-inch bbl.
Weight: 6.75 to 7 lbs. Sights: Open rear; ramp front. Pistol-grip or
straight-grip stock, forearm w/bbl. band; sling swivels on pistol-grip
model saddle ring on straight-grip model. Made 1972-79.

MODEL 472 ONE IN FIVE THOUSAND . . . NiB $438 Ex $309 Gd $144
Same as Model 472 Brush Gun except w/Indian scenes etched on
receiver; brass buttplate, saddle ring and bbl. bands, gold-plated
trigger, bright blued finish, select walnut stock and forearm. Limited
edition of 5,000; serial numbered 1 to 5,000. Made in 1974.

MODEL 472 RIFLE . . . . NiB $206 Ex $180 Gd $103
Same as Model 472 Carbine w/pistol-grip stock except w/24-inch
bbl., 5-shot magazine, weight: 7 lbs. Made 1974-76.

MODEL 479
Calibers: .30-30. Six-shot tubular magazine. 20-inch bbl. Weight:
6.75 to 7 lbs. Sights: Open rear; ramp front. Made 1983-85.
Model 479 Rifle . . . . NiB $196 Ex $180 Gd $124
Model 479PCA
(Carbine w/20-inch bbl.) . . . . NiB $196 Ex $180 Gd $124
Model 479RR
(Roy Rogers, 5000 Ltd. Edition) . . . . NiB $335 Ex $283 Gd $124

MODEL 620K HAMMERLESS SINGLE-SHOT
BOLT-ACTION RIFLE . . . . NiB $165 Ex $144 Gd $98
Single shot. Caliber: .22 WMR. 24-inch bbl. Weight: 6 lbs. Sights:
Open rear; bead front. Monte Carlo stock w/cheekpiece, pistol-grip,
sling swivels. Made 1959-60.

MODEL 620K-A . . . . NiB $161 Ex $129 Gd $88
Same as Model 640K except w/sight modification. Made 1960-68.

MODEL 640K CHUCKSTER HAMMERLESS
BOLT-ACTION RIFLE . . . . NiB $165 Ex $144 Gd $98
Caliber: .22 WMR. Five-shot detachable clip magazine. 24-inch bbl.
Weight: 6 lbs. Sights: Open rear; bead front. Monte Carlo stock
w/cheekpiece, pistol grip, sling swivels. Made 1959-84.

MODEL 640KS . . . . NiB $206 Ex $154 Gd $103
Deluxe version of Model 640K w/select walnut stock hand checkering;
gold-plated front sight, rear sight elevator, and trigger. Made 1960-64.

MODEL 640M . . . . NiB $309 Ex $283 Gd $180
Similar to Model 640K except w/heavy receiver and jeweled bolt. 20-inch
bbl., full length Mannlicher-style stock w/Monte Carlo comb and cheekpiece,
swivels and leather sling. 40.75 inches overall. Weight: 6 lbs. Made 1971-73.

MODEL 642K CARBINE . . . . NiB $232 Ex $180 Gd $129
Caliber: .22 WMR. Five-shot detachable clip magazine. 18-inch bbl.
Weight: 5 lbs. 38.25 inches overall. Sights: Open rear; bead front.
Monte Carlo walnut stock w/black Tenite forearm extension that
pulls down to form hand grip. Made 1961-68.

Mossberg Model 800

Mossberg Model 800D

Mossberg Model 800M

Mossberg Model 810

Mossberg Model L

Mossberg Model R

MODEL 800 BOLT-ACTION
CENTERFIRE RIFLE . . . . **NiB $226 Ex $180 Gd $123**
.222 Rem., .22-250, .243 Win., .308 Win. Four-shot mag., 3-shot in .222. 22-inch bbl. Weight: 7.5 lbs. Sights: Folding leaf rear; ramp front. Monte Carlo stock w/cheekpiece, checkered pistol-grip and forearm, sling swivels. Made 1967-79.

MODEL 800D SUPER GRADE. . . . . **NiB $367 Ex $294 Gd $200**
Deluxe version of Model 800 except w/stock w/rollover comb and cheekpiece, rosewood forend tip and pistol-grip cap. Weight: 6.75 lbs. Chambered for all calibers listed for the Model 800 except for .222 Rem. Sling swivels. Made 1970-73.

MODEL 800M . . . . **NiB $283 Ex $257 Gd $154**
Same as Model 800 except w/flat bolt handle, 20-inch bbl., Mannlicher-style stock. Weight: 6.5 lbs. Calibers: .22-250, .243 Win., .308 Win. Made 1969-72.

MODEL 800VT VARMINT/TARGET . . . . . . **NiB $232 Ex $180 Gd $129**
Similar to Model 800 except w/24-inch heavy bbl., no sights. Weight: 9.5 lbs. Calibers: .222 Rem., .22-250, .243 Win. Made 1968-79.

MODEL 810 BOLT-ACTION CENTERFIRE RIFLE
Calibers: .270 Win., .30-06, 7mm Rem. Mag., .338 Win. Mag. Detachable box magazine (1970-75) or internal magazine w/hinged floorplate (1972 to date). Capacity: Four-shot in .270 and .30-06, 3-shot in Magnums. 22-inch bbl. in .270 and .30-06, 24-inch in Magnums. Weight: 7.5 to 8 lbs. Sights: Leaf rear; ramp front. Stock w/Monte Carlo comb and cheekpiece, checkered pistol-grip and forearm, grip cap, sling swivels. Made 1970-79.
Standard calibers . . . . **NiB $335 Ex $268 Gd $182**
Magnum calibers . . . . **NiB $360 Ex $283 Gd $196**

MODEL 1500
MOUNTAINEER
GRADE I CENTERFIRE RIFLE . . . . . . **NiB $386 Ex $309 Gd $232**
Calibers: .223, .243, .270, .30-06, 7mm Mag. 22-inch or 24-inch (7mm Mag.) bbl. Weight: 7 lbs. 10 oz. Hardwood walnut-finished checkered stock. Sights: Hooded ramp front w/gold bead; fully adj. rear. Drilled and tapped for scope mounts. Sling swivel studs. Imported 1986-87.

Musgrave Premier NR5

Musgrave RSA NR1

Musgrave Valiant NR6

Musketeer Mauser Sporter

MODEL 1500 VARMINT BOLT-ACTION RIFLE
Same as Model 1500 Grade I except w/22-inch heavy bbl. Chambered in .222, .22-250, .223 only. High-luster blued finish or Parkerized satin finished stock. Imported from Japan 1986-87.
High-luster blue . . . . NiB $386 Ex $309 Gd $232
Parkerized satin finish . . . . NiB $406 Ex $324 Gd $220

MODEL 1700LS CLASSIC
HUNTER BOLT-ACTION RIFLE . . . . NiB $438 Ex $360 Gd $232
Same as Model 1500 Grade I except w/checkered classic-style stock and Schnabel forend. Chambered in 243, 270, 30-06 only. Imported from Japan 1986-87.

MODEL B BOLT-ACTION RIFLE . . . . NiB $180 Ex $154 Gd $72
Takedown. Caliber: .22 LR. Long, Short. Single-shot. 22-inch bbl. Sights: Open rear; bead front. Plain pistol-grip stock. Made 1930-32.

MODEL K SLIDE-ACTION REPEATER . . . . . NiB $185 Ex $129 Gd $82
Hammerless. Takedown. Caliber: .22 LR. Long, Short. Tubular magazine holds 20 Short, 16 Long, 14 LR. 22-inch bbl. Weight: 5 lbs. Sights: Open rear; bead front. Plain, straight-grip stock. Grooved slide handle. Made 1922-31.

MODELS L42A, L43, L45A, L46A-LS
See Models 42A, 43, 45A and 46A-LS respectively; "L" refers to a left-hand version of those rifles.

MODEL L SINGLE-SHOT RIFLE . . . . NiB $444 Ex $355 Gd $242
Martini-type falling-block lever-action. Takedown. Caliber: .22 LR, Long, Short. 24-inch bbl. Weight: 5 lbs. Sights: Open rear; bead front. Plain pistol-grip stock and forearm. Made 1929-32.

MODEL M SLIDE-ACTION REPEATER . . . . NiB $289 Ex $232 Gd $158
Specifications same as for Model K except w/24-inch octagon bbl., pistol-grip stock, weighs 5.5 lbs. Made 1928-31.

MODEL R BOLT-ACTION REPEATER . . . . . NiB $277 Ex $221 Gd $150
Takedown. Caliber: .22 LR, Long, Short. Tubular magazine. 24-inch bbl. Sights: Open rear; bead front. Plain pistol-grip stock. Made 1930-32.

MUSGRAVE RIFLES, MUSGRAVE MFRS. & DIST. (PTY) LTD. — Bloemfontein, South Africa

PREMIER NR5 BOLT-
ACTION HUNTING RIFLE . . . . NiB $443 Ex $360 Gd $232
Calibers: .243 Win., .270 Win., .30-06, .308 Win., 7mm Rem. Mag. Five-shot magazine. 25.5-inch bbl. Weight: 8.25 lbs. Furnished w/o sights, but drilled and tapped for scope mount. Select walnut Monte Carlo stock w/cheekpiece, checkered pistol-grip and forearm, contrasting pistol-grip cap and forend tip, recoil pad, swivel studs. Made 1971-76.

Navy Arms .45-70 Mauser

Navy Arms 1873 Carbine

Navy Arms Henry
Lever-Action

Navy Arms Model 1873 Carbine

Navy Arms 1874 Sharps Cavalry Carbine

Navy Arms 1874
Sharps Sniper Rifle

RSA NR1 BOLT-ACTION
SINGLE-SHOT TARGET RIFLE . . . . . **NiB $444 Ex $355 Gd $242**
Caliber: .308 Win. (7.62mm NATO). 26.4-inch heavy bbl. Weight:
10 lbs. Sights: Aperture receiver; tunnel front. Walnut target stock
w/beavertail forearm, handguard, bbl. band, rubber buttplate, sling
swivels. Made 1971-76.

VALIANT NR6 HUNTING RIFLE . . . **NiB $407 Ex $309 Gd $201**
Similar to Premier except w/24-inch bbl.; stock w/straight comb,
skip French-style checkering, no grip cap or forend tip. Sights:
Leaf rear; hooded ramp front bead sight. Weight: 7.7lbs. Made
1971-76.

MUSKETEER RIFLES — Washington, D.C.
Mfd. by Firearms International Corp.

MAUSER SPORTER
FN Mauser bolt action. .243, .25-06, .270, .264 Mag., .308, .30-06,
7mm Mag., .300 Win. Mag. Magazine holds 5 standard, 3 Magnum
cartridges. 24-inch bbl. Weight: 7.25 lbs. No sights. Monte Carlo
stock w/checkered pistol-grip and forearm, swivels. Made 1963-72.
Standard Sporter . . . . **NiB $386 Ex $335 Gd $201**
Deluxe Sporter . . . . **NiB $438 Ex $360 Gd $206**
Standard Carbine . . . . **NiB $371 Ex $309 Gd $201**

**Navy Arms
Revolving Carbine**

**Navy Arms
Rolling Block Baby Carbine**

**Navy Arms
Rolling Block Buffalo Rifle**

NAVY ARMS — Ridgefield, New Jersey

.45-70 MAUSER CARBINE........ **NiB $229 Ex $178 Gd $122**
Same as .45-70 Mauser Rifle except w/18-inch bbl., straight-grip stock w/low comb, weight: 7.5 lbs. Disc.

.45-70 MAUSER RIFLE.......... **NiB $204 Ex $163 Gd $111**
Siamese Mauser bolt action. Caliber: .45-70 Govt. Three-round magazine. 24- 0r 26-inch bbl. Weight: 8.5 lbs. w/26-inch bbl. Sights: Open rear; ramp front: Checkered stock w/Monte Carlo comb. Intoduced 1973. Disc.

**MODEL 1873 WINCHESTER
BORDER RIFLE** .... **NiB $790 Ex $663 Gd $301**
Replica of Winchester Model 1873 Short Rifle. Calibers: .357 Mag., .44-40, and .45 Colt. 20- inch bbl., 39.25 inches overall. Weight: 7.6 lbs. Blued full octagonal barrel, color casehardened receiver w/walnut stocks. Made 1999 to date.

MODEL 1873 CARBINE .... **NiB $765 Ex $663 Gd $331**
Similar to Model 1873 Rifle except w/blued receiver, 10-shot magazine, 19-inch round bbl. carbine-style forearm w/bbl. band, weighs 6.75 lbs. Disc. Reissued in 1991 in 44-40 or 45 Colt.

MODEL 1873 LEVER-ACTION RIFLE ..... **NiB $765 Ex $688 Gd $357**
Replica of Winchester Model 1873. Casehardened receiver. Calibers: .22 LR. .357 Magnum, .44-40. 15-shot magazine. 24-inch octagon bbl. Weight: 8 lbs. Sights: Open rear; blade front. Straight-grip stock, forearm w/end cap. Disc. Reissued in 1991 in .44-40 or .45 Colt w/12-shot magazine. Disc. 1994.

MODEL 1873 TRAPPER'S .... **NiB $592 Ex $484 Gd $347**
Same as Model 1873 Carbine, except w/16.5-inch bbl., 8-shot magazine, weighs 6.25 lbs. Disc.

MODEL 1873 SPORTING CARBINE/RIFLE
Replica of Winchester Model 1873 Sporting Rifle. Calibers: .357 Mag. (24.25-inch bbl. only), .44-40 and .45 Colt. 24.25-inch bbl. (Carbine) or 30-inch bbl. (Rifle). 48.75 to 53 inches overall. Weight: 8.14 to 9.3 lbs. Octagonal barrel, casehardened receiver and checkered walnut pistol-grip. Made 1992 to date.
Carbine model................. **NiB $867 Ex $739 Gd $382**
Rifle model .... **NiB $918 Ex $841 Gd $433**

**MODEL 1874 SHARPS
CAVALRY CARBINE**............ **NiB $739 Ex $561 Gd $408**
Replica of Sharps 1874 Cavalry Carbine. Similar to Sniper Model, except w/22-inch bbl. and carbine stock. Caliber: .45-70. Imported 1994 to date.

MODEL 1874 SHARPS SNIPER RIFLE
Replica of Sharps 1874 Sharpshooter's Rifle. Caliber: .45-70. Falling breech, single-shot. 30-inch bbl. 46.75 inches overall. Weight: 8.5 lbs. Double-set triggers. Color casehardened receiver. Blade front sight; rear sight w/elevation leaf. Polished blued bbl. Military three-band stock w/patch box. Imported 1994 to date.
Infantry model (single trigger) .... **NiB $1122 Ex $994 Gd $586**
Sniper model (double set trigger) ...... **NiB $1632 Ex $1428 Gd $688**

ENGRAVED MODELS
Yellowboy and Model 1873 rifles are available in deluxe models w/select walnut stocks and forearms and engraving in three grades. Grade "A" has delicate scrollwork in limited areas. Grade "B" is more elaborate with 40 percent coverage. Grade "C" has highest grade engraving. Add to value:
Grade "A" .... **NiB $223 Ex $178 Gd $121**
Grade "B" .... **NiB $249 Ex $199 Gd $136**
Grade "C" .... **NiB $631 Ex $505 Gd $344**

HENRY LEVER-ACTION RIFLE
Replica of the Winchester Model 1860 Henry Rifle. Caliber: .44-40. Twelve-shot magazine. 16.5-, 22- or 24.25-inch octagon bbl. Weight: 7.5 to 9 lbs. 35.4 to 43.25 inches overall. Sights: Blade front, adjustable ladder rear. European walnut straight grip buttstock w/bbl. and side stock swivels. Imported 1985 to date. Brass or steel receiver. Blued or color casehardened metal.
**Carbine model w/22-inch bbl.,
introduced 1992)** .... **NiB $790 Ex $612 Gd $382**
Military rifle model (w/brass frame) ...... **NiB $790 Ex $612 Gd $382**
Trapper model (w/brass frame) .... **NiB $790 Ex $612 Gd $382**
Trapper model (w/iron frame)............ **NiB $841 Ex $739 Gd $403**
W/"A" engraving, add.................................... **$300**
W/"B" engraving, add.................................... **$500**
W/"C" engraving, add.................................... **$900**

Navy Arms
Yellowboy Carbine

MARTINI TARGET RIFLE . . . . **NiB $484 Ex $408 Gd $265**
Martini single-shot action. Calibers: .444 Marlin, .45-70. 26- or 30-inch half-octagon or full-octagon bbl. Weight: 9 lbs. w/26-inch bbl. Sights: Creedmoor tang peep, open middle, blade front. Stock w/cheekpiece and pistol-grip, forearm w/Schnabel tip, both checkered. Intro. 1972. Disc.

REVOLVING CARBINE . . . . **NiB $586 Ex $484 Gd $331**
Action resembles that of Remington Model 1875 Revolver. Casehardened frame. Calibers: .357 Magnum, .44-40, .45 Colt. Six shot cylinder. 20-inch bbl. Weight: 5 lbs. Sights: Open rear; blade front. Straight-grip stock brass trigger guard and buttplate. Intro. 1968. Disc.

ROLLING BLOCK BABY CARBINE . . . . **NiB $223 Ex $178 Gd $121**
Replica of small Remington Rolling Block single-shot action. Casehardened frame, brass trigger guard. Calibers: .22 LR. .22 Hornet, .357 Magnum, .44-40. 20-inch octagon or 22-inch round bbl. Weight: 5 lbs. Sights: Open rear; blade front. Straight-grip stock, plain forearm, brass buttplate. Imported 1968-81.

ROLLING BLOCK BUFFALO CARBINE. . . . **NiB $392 Ex $357 Gd $306**
Same as Buffalo Rifle except w/18-inch bbl., weigh: 10 lbs.

ROLLING BLOCK BUFFALO RIFLE. . . . . . **NiB $612 Ex $510 Gd $255**
Replica Remington Rolling Block single-shot action. Casehardened frame, brass trigger guard. Calibers: .444 Marlin, .45-70, .50-70. 26- or 30-inch heavy half-octagon or full-octagon bbl. Weight: 11 to 12 lbs. Sights: Open rear; blade front. Straight-grip stock w/brass buttplate, forearm w/brass bbl. band. Made 1971 to date.

ROLLING BLOCK CREEDMOOR RIFLE
Same as Buffalo Rifle except calibers .45-70 and .50-70 only, 28- or 30-inch heavy half-octagon or full-octagon bbl., Creedmoor tang peep sight.
Target model. . . . . **NiB $801 Ex $576 Gd $306**
Deluxe target model (disc. 1998) . . . . . . **NiB $1504 Ex $1224 Gd $994**

YELLOWBOY CARBINE. . . . . **NiB $542 Ex $433 Gd $295**
Similar to Yellowboy Rifle except w/19-inch bbl., 10-shot magazine (14-shot in 22 Long Rifle), carbine-style forearm. Weight: 6.75 lbs. Disc. Reissued 1991 in .44-40 only.

YELLOWBOY LEVER-ACTION REPEATER . . . . . **NiB $637 Ex $510 Gd $306**
Replica of Winchester Model 1866. Calibers: .38 Special, .44-40. 15-shot magazine. 24-inch octagon bbl. Weight: 8 lbs. Sights: Folding leaf rear; blade front. Straight-grip stock, forearm w/end cap. Intro. 1966. Disc. Reissued 1991 in .44-40 only w/12-shot magazine and adj. ladder-style rear sight.

YELLOWBOY TRAPPER'S MODEL. . . . . **NiB $567 Ex $454 Gd $309**
Same as Yellowboy Carbine except w/16.5-inch bbl., 8-round magazine, weighs 6.25 lbs. Disc.

NEW ENGLAND FIREARMS —
Gardner, Massachusetts

In 1987, New England Firearms was established as an independent company producing selected H&R models under the NEF logo. In 1991, H&R 1871, Inc. was formed from the residual of the parent company and that took over the New England Firearms facility. H&R 1871 produced firearms under both its logo and the NEF brand name until 1999, when the Marlin Firearms Company acquired the assets of H&R 1871.

HANDI-RIFLE
Single-shot, break-open action w/side-lever release. Calibers: .22 Hornet, .22-250, .223, .243, .270, .30-30, .30-06, .45-70. 22-inch bbl. Weight: 7 lbs. Sights: Ramp front; folding rear. Drilled and tapped for scope mounts. Walnut-finished hardwood or synthetic stock. Blued finish. Made 1989 to date.
Calibers: .22-250, .243,
.270 and .30-06 . . . . **NiB $204 Ex $143 Gd $97**
Calibers: .22 Hornet, .223,
.30-30 and .45-70 . . . . **NiB $204 Ex $143 Gd $97**

NEWTON SPORTING RIFLES — Buffalo, New York
Mfd. by Newton Arms Co., Charles Newton Rifles Corp. and Buffalo Newton Rifle Co.

BUFFALO SPORTING RIFLE . . . . **NiB $1287 Ex $1081 Gd $772**
Same general specifications as Standard Model — Second Type. Made c. 1922-32 by Buffalo Newton Rifle Co.

MAUSER SPORTING RIFLE . . . . . **NiB $1236 Ex $1123 Gd $721**
Mauser (Oberndorf) action. Caliber: .256 Newton. Five shot box magazine, hinged floorplate. Double-set triggers. 24-inch bbl. Open rear sight, ramp front sight. Sporting stock w/checkered pistol-grip. Weight: 7 lbs. Made c. 1914 by Newton Arms Co.

STANDARD MODEL
SPORTING RIFLE — FIRST TYPE . . . . . . **NiB $1184 Ex $1004 Gd $608**
Newton bolt action, interrupted screw-type breech-locking mechanism, double-set triggers. Calibers: .22, .256, .280, .30, .33, .35 Newton; .30-06. 24-inch bbl. Sights: Open rear or cocking-piece peep; ramp front. Checkered pistol-grip stock. Weight: 7 to 8 lbs., depending on caliber. Made c. 1916-18 by Newton Arms Co.

STANDARD MODEL
SPORTING RIFLE
SECOND TYPE. . . . . **NiB $947 Ex $757 Gd $515**
Newton bolt action, improved design; distinguished by reversed-set trigger and 1917-Enfield-type bolt handle. Calibers: .256, .30, .35 Newton and .30-06. Five-shot box magazine. 24-inch bbl. Sights: Open rear; ramp front. Checkered pistol-grip stock. Weight: 7.75 to 8.25 lbs. Made c. 1921 by Charles Newton Rifle Corp.

RIFLES

Noble Model 10

Noble Model 33

Noble Model 222

Noble Model 236

Noble Model 275

NIKKO FIREARMS, LTD. — Tochiga, Japan
See listings under Golden Eagle Rifles.

NOBLE MFG. CO. — Haydenville, Massachusetts

MODEL 10 BOLT-ACTION
SINGLE-SHOT RIFLE . . . . **NiB $83 Ex $66 Gd $45**
Caliber: .22 LR. Long, Short. 24-inch bbl. Plain pistol-grip stock. Sights: Open rear, bead front. Weight: 4 lbs. Made 1955-58.

MODEL 20 BOLT-ACTION
SINGLE-SHOT RIFLE . . . . **NiB $76 Ex $61 Gd $42**
Manually cocked. Caliber: .22 LR. Long, Short. 22-inch bbl. Weight: 5 lbs. Sights: Open rear; bead front. Walnut stock w/pistol grip. Made 1958-63.

MODEL 33 SLIDE-ACTION REPEATER . . . . **NiB $96 Ex $76 Gd $52**
Hammerless. Caliber: .22 LR. Long, Short. Tubular magazine holds 21 Short, 17 Long, 15 LR. 24-inch bbl. Weight: 6 lbs. Sights: Open rear; bead front. Tenite stock and slide handle. Made 1949-53.

MODEL 33A . . . . **NiB $83 Ex $66 Gd $45**
Same general specifications as Model 33 except w/wood stock and slide handle. Made 1953-55.

MODEL 222 BOLT-ACTION
SINGLE-SHOT RIFLE . . . . **NiB $96 Ex $76 Gd $52**
Manually cocked. Caliber: .22 LR. Long, Short. Barrel integral w/receiver. Overall length: 38 inches. Weight: 5 lbs. Sights: Interchangeable V-notch and peep rear; ramp front. Scope mounting base. Pistol-grip stock. Made 1958-71.

MODEL 236 SLIDE-ACTION
REPEATING RIFLE . . . . **NiB $108 Ex $87 Gd $59**
Hammerless. Caliber: .22 Short, Long, LR. Tubular magazine holds 21 Short, 17 Long, 15 LR. 24-inch bbl. Weight: 5.5 lbs. Sights: Open rear; ramp front. Pistol-grip stock, grooved slide handle. Made 1951 to date.

MODEL 275 LEVER-ACTION RIFLE . . . . **NiB $153 Ex $97 Gd $71**
Hammerless. Caliber: .22 Short, Long, LR. Tubular magazine holds 21 Short, 17 Long, 15 LR. 24-inch bbl. Weight: 5.5 lbs. Sights: Open rear; ramp front. Stock w/semipistol-grip. Made 1958-71.

Parker-Hale
Model 81 Classic

Parker-Hale
Model 87

NORINCO — Mfd. by Northern China Industries Corp., Beijing, China, *Imported by Century International Arms; Interarms; KBI and China Sports, Inc.*

MODEL 81S/AK SEMIAUTOMATIC RIFLE
Semiautomatic Kalashnikov style AK-47 action. Caliber: 7.62x39mm. Five, 30- or 40-shot magazine. 17.5-inch bbl. 36.75 inches overall. Weight: 8.5 lbs. Hooded post front sight, 500 meters leaf rear sight. Oil-finished hardwood (military style) buttstock, pistol grip, forearm and handguard or folding metal stock. Black oxide finish. Imported 1988-89.

Model 81S (w/wood stock) . . . . NiB $1004 Ex $747 Gd $515
Model 81S-1 (w/under-folding metal stock) . . NiB $1153 Ex $922 Gd $627
Model 81S-5/56S-2 (w/side-
folding metal stock) . . . . NiB $1024 Ex $819 Gd $557

MODEL 84S/AK SEMIAUTOMATIC RIFLE
Semiautomatic Kalashnikov style AK-47 action. Caliber: .223 (5.56mm). 30-shot magazine. 16.25-inch bbl. 35.5 inches overall. Weight: 8.75 lbs. Hooded post front sight, 800 meters leaf rear sight. Oil-finished hardwood (military style) buttstock, pistol grip, forearm and handguard; sporterized composite fiberglass stock or folding metal stock. Black oxide finish. Imported 1988-89.

Model 84S (w/wood stock) . . . . NiB $5573 Ex $4458 Gd $312
Model 84S-1 (w/under-folding metal stock) . . . NiB $709 Ex $566 Gd $385
Model 84S-3 (w/fiberglass stock) . . . . NiB $676 Ex $541 Gd $368
Model 84S-5 (w/side-folding metal stock) . . . . NiB $1153 Ex $921 Gd $627

MODEL AK-47 THUMBHOLE SPORTER
Semiautomatic AK-47 sporterized variant. Calibers: .223 (5.56mm) or 7.62x39mm. Five shot magazine. 16.25-inch bbl. or 23.25-inch bbl. 35.5 or 42.5 inches overall. Weight: 8.5 to 10.3 lbs. Adj. post front sight, open adj. rear. Forged receiver w/black oxide finish. Walnut-finished thumbhole stock w/recoil pad. Imported 1991-93.

Model AK-47 Sporter (5.56mm) . . . . NiB $509 Ex $407 Gd $277
Model AK-47 Sporter (7.62x39mm) . . . . . . NiB $483 Ex $386 Gd $263

MODEL MAK 90/91 SPORT
Similar to Model AK-47 Thumbhole Sporter except w/minor modifications implemented to meet importation requirements. Imported 1994-95.

Model Mak 90 (w/16.25-inch bbl.) . . . . . . NiB $489 Ex $412 Gd $283
Model Mak 91 (w/23.25-inch bbl.) . . . . . . NiB $489 Ex $412 Gd $283

OLYMPIC ARMS — Olympia, Washington

PCR SERIES
Gas-operated semi-auto action. Calibers: .17 Rem., .223, 7.62x39, 6x45, 6PPC or 9mm, .40 S&W, 4.5ACP (in carbine version only). Ten-shot magazine. 16-, 20- or 24-inch bbl. Weight: 7 to 10.2 lbs. Black composite stocks. Post front, rear adj. sights; scope ready flat-top. Barrel fluting. William set trigger. Made 1994 to date.

PCR-1/Ultra Match . . . . NiB $989 Ex $875 Gd $515
PCR-2/MultiMatch ML-1 . . . . NiB $1024 Ex $819 Gd $557
PCR-3/MultiMatch ML-2 . . . . NiB $1081 Ex $875 Gd $566
PCR-4/AR-15 Match . . . . NiB $1235 Ex $988 Gd $672
PCR-5/CAR-15 (.223 Rem.) . . . . NiB $989 Ex $721 Gd $438
PCR-5/CAR-15 (9mm,
40S&W, 45ACP) . . . . NiB $824 Ex $716 Gd $463
PCR-5/CAR-15 (.223 Rem.) . . . . NiB $766 Ex $613 Gd $417
PCR-6/A-2 (7.62x39mm) . . . . NiB $804 Ex $644 Gd $438

PARKER-HALE LIMITED — Birmingham, England

MODEL 81 AFRICAN . . . . NiB $901 Ex $721 Gd $463
Same general specifications as Model 81 Classic except in caliber .375 H&H only. Sights: African Express rear; hooded blade front. Barrel-band swivel. All-steel trigger guard. Checkered European walnut stock w/pistol grip and recoil pad. Engraved receiver. Imported 1986-91.

MODEL 81 CLASSIC
BOLT-ACTION RIFLE . . . . NiB $742 Ex $566 Gd $360
Calibers: .22-250, .243 Win., .270 Win., 6mm Rem., 6.5x55, 7x57, 7x64, .308 Win., .30-06, .300 Win. Mag., 7mm Rem. Mag. Four shot magazine. 24-inch bbl. Weight: 7.75 lbs. Sights: Adj. open rear, hooded ramp front. Checkered pistol-grip stock of European walnut. Imported 1984-91.

MODEL 85 SNIPER RIFLE . . . . . . NiB $1802 Ex $1468 Gd $875
Caliber: .308 Win. Ten or 20-shot M-14-type magazine. 24.25-inch bbl. 45 inches overall. Weight: 12.5 lbs. Blade front sight, folding aperture rear. McMillan fiberglass stock w/detachable bipod. Imported 1989-91.

Parker-Hale Model 1100
Lightweight

Parker-Hale Model 1200
Super Clip

MODEL 87 BOLT-ACTION
REPEATING TARGET RIFLE . . . . . **NiB $1416 Ex $1133 Gd $669**
Calibers: .243 Win., 6.5x55, .308 Win., .30-06 Springfield, .300 Win. Mag. Five-shot detachable box magazine. 26-inch bbl. 45 inches overall. Weight: 10 lbs. No sights; grooved for target-style scope mounts. Stippled walnut stock w/adj. buttplate. Sling swivel studs. Parkerized finish. Folding bipod. Imported 1988-91.

MODEL 1000 STANDARD RIFLE . . . . **NiB $412 Ex $335 Gd $201**
Calibers: .22-250, .243 Win., .270 Win., 6mm Rem., .308 Win., .30-06. Four-shot magazine. Bolt action. 22-inch or 24-inch (22-250) bbl. 43 inches overall. 7.25 lbs. Checkered walnut Monte Carlo-style stock w/satin finish. Imported 1984-88.

MODEL 1100 LIGHTWEIGHT
BOLT-ACTION RIFLE . . . . **NiB $489 Ex $412 Gd $278**
Same general specifications as Model 1000 Standard except w/22-inch lightweight profile bbl., hollow bolt handle, alloy trigger guard and floorplate, 6.5 lbs., Schnabel forend. Imported 1984-91.

MODEL 1100M AFRICAN
MAGNUM RIFLE . . . . **NiB $824 Ex $669 Gd $438**
Same as Model 1000 Standard except w/24-inch bbl. in calibers .404 Jeffery, .458 Win. Mag. Weight: 9.5 lbs. Sights: Adj. rear; hooded post front. Imported 1984-91.

MODEL 1200 SUPER CLIP
BOLT-ACTION RIFLE . . . . **NiB $556 Ex $463 Gd $283**
Same as Model 1200 Super except w/detachable box magazine in calibers .243 Win., 6mm Rem., .270 Win. .30-06 and .308 Win., .300 Win. Mag., 7mm Rem. Mag. Imported 1984-91.

MODEL 1200 SUPER BOLT-ACTION
SPORTING RIFLE . . . . **NiB $556 Ex $463 Gd $283**
Mauser-type bolt action. Calibers: .22-250, .243 Win., 6mm Rem., .25-06, .270 Win., .30-06, .308 Win. Four shot magazine. 24-inch bbl. Weight: 7.25 lbs. Sights: Folding open rear, hooded ramp front. European walnut stock w/rollover Monte Carlo cheekpiece, rosewood forend tip and pistol-grip cap, skip checkering, recoil pad, sling swivels. Imported 1968-91.

MODEL 1200 SUPER MAGNUM . . . . **NiB $608 Ex $489 Gd $309**
Same general specifications as 1200 Super except calibers 7mm Rem. Mag. and .300 Win. Mag., 3-shot magazine. Imported 1988-91.

MODEL 1200P PRESENTATION . . . . **NiB $509 Ex $407 Gd $277**
Same general specifications as 1200 Super except w/scroll-engraved action, trigger guard and floorplate, no sights. QD swivels. Calibers: .243 Win. and .30-06. Imported 1969-75.

MODEL 1200V VARMINT . . . . **NiB $541 Ex $438 Gd $381**
Same general specifications as 1200 Super, except w/24-inch heavy bbl., no sights, weight: 9.5 lbs. Calibers: .22-250, 6mm Rem., .25-06, .243 Win. Imported 1969-89.

MODEL 1300C SCOUT . . . . **NiB $721 Ex $618 Gd $489**
Calibers: .243, .308 Win. 10-round magazine. 20-inch bbl. w/muzzle brake. 41 inches overall. Weight: 8.5 lbs. No sights, drilled and tapped for scope. Checkered laminated birch stock w/QD swivels. Imported 1991.

MODEL 2100 MIDLAND
BOLT-ACTION RIFLE . . . . **NiB $335 Ex $278 Gd $180**
Calibers: .22-250, .243 Win., 6mm Rem., .270 Win., 6.5x55, 7x57, 7x64, .308 Win, .30-06. Four-shot box magazine. 22-inch or 24-inch (22-250) bbl. 43-inches overall. Weight: 7 lbs. Sights: Adj. folding rear; hooded ramp front. Checkered European walnut Monte Carlo stock w/pistol-grip. Imported 1984-91.

MODEL 2700 LIGHTWEIGHT . . . . **NiB $360 Ex $283 Gd $180**
Same general specifications as Model 2100 Midland except w/tapered lightweight bbl. and aluminum trigger guard. Weight: 6.5 lbs. Imported 1991.

MODEL 2800 MIDLAND . . . . **NiB $309 Ex $257 Gd $14**
Same general specifications as model 2100 except w/laminated birch stock. Imported 1991.

PEDERSEN CUSTOM GUNS — North Haven, Connecticut, Division of O.F. Mossberg & Sons, Inc.

MODEL 3000 GRADE I
BOLT-ACTION RIFLE . . . . **NiB $1024 Ex $819 Gd $557**
Richly engraved w/silver inlays, full-fancy American black walnut stock. Mossberg Model 810 action. Calibers: .270 Win., .30-06, 7mm Rem. Mag., .338 Win. Mag. Three-shot magazine, hinged floorplate. 22-inch bbl. in .270 and .30-06, 24-inch in Magnums. Weight: 7 to 8 lbs. Sights: Open rear; hooded ramp front. Monte Carlo stock w/roll-over cheekpiece, wraparound hand checkering on pistol grip and forearm, rosewood pistol-grip cap and forend tip, recoil pad or steel buttplate w/trap, detachable swivels. Imported 1973-75.

MODEL 3000 GRADE II . . . . **NiB $766 Ex $613 Gd $417**
Same as Model 3000 Grade I except less elaborate engraving, no inlays, fancy grade walnut stock w/recoil pad. Imported 1973-75.

MODEL 3000 GRADE III . . . . **NiB $637 Ex $510 Gd $347**
Same as Model 3000 Grade I except no engraving or inlays, select grade walnut stock w/recoil pad. Imported 1973-74.

Pedersen Model 3000
Grade I Bolt-Action Rifle

Pedersen Model 3000
Grade III

Plainfield M-1 Carbine

RIFLES

MODEL 4700 CUSTOM
DELUXE LEVER-ACTION RIFLE. . . . . NiB $251 Ex $201 Gd $137
Mossberg Model .472 action. Calibers: .30-30, 35 Rem. Five-shot tubular magazine. 24-inch bbl. Weight: 7.5 lbs. Sights: Open rear, hooded ramp front. Hand-finished black walnut stock and beavertail forearm, barrel band swivels. Imported 1975.

J.C. PENNEY CO., INC. — Dallas, Texas

Firearms sold under the J.C. Penney label were mfd. by Marlin, High Standard, Stevens, Savage and Springfield.

MODEL 2025 BOLT-ACTION REPEATER. . . . . . NiB $71 Ex $41 Gd $36
Takedown. Caliber: .22 RF. 8-shot detachable box magazine. 24-inch bbl. Weight: 6 lbs. Sights: Open rear; bead front. Plain pistol-grip stock. Mfd. by Marlin.

MODEL 2035 BOLT-ACTION REPEATER. . . . . . NiB $71 Ex $41 Gd $36
Takedown. Caliber: .22 RF. Eight-shot detachable box magazine. 24-inch bbl. Weight: 6 lbs. Sights: Open rear; bead front. Plain pistol-grip stock. Mfd. by Marlin.

MODEL 2935 LEVER-ACTION RIFLE . . . . . . NiB $178 Ex $143 Gd $92
Same general specifications as Marlin Model 336.

MODEL 6400 BOLT-ACTION
CENTERFIRE RIFLE . . . . NiB $163 Ex $127 Gd $82
Same general specifications as Savage Model 340.

MODEL 6660
AUTOLOADING RIFLE . . . . NiB $76 Ex $61 Gd $51
Caliber: .22 RF. Tubular magazine. 22-inch bbl. Weight: 5.5 lbs. Sights: Open rear; hooded ramp front. Plain pistol-grip stock. Mfd. by Marlin.

PLAINFIELD MACHINE COMPANY — Dunellen, New Jersey

M-1 CARBINE . . . . NiB $178 Ex $133 Gd $97
Same as U.S. Carbine, Cal. .30, M-1 except also available in caliber 5.7mm (.22 caliber w/necked-down .30 Carbine cartridge case). Current production w/ventilated metal handguard and barrel band w/o bayonet lug; earlier models have standard military-type fittings. Made 1960-77.

M-1 CARBINE,
COMMANDO MODEL . . . . NiB $184 Ex $153 Gd $107
Same as M-1 Carbine except w/paratrooper-type stock w/telescoping wire shoulderpiece. Made 1960-77.

M-1 CARBINE, MILITARY SPORTER . . . . . . NiB $178 Ex $148 Gd $112
Same as M-1 Carbine except w/unslotted buttstock and wood handguard. Made 1960-77.

M-1 DELUXE SPORTER . . . . NiB $184 Ex $153 Gd $107
Same as M-1 Carbine except w/Monte Carlo sporting stock Made 1960-73.

GRADING: **NiB** = New in Box   **Ex** = Excellent or NRA 95%   **Gd** = Good or NRA 68%

Polish Model 1929 Mauser

Purdey Double Rifle

Purdey Bolt-Action Rifle

POLISH MILITARY RIFLES — Manufactured by Government Arsenals at Radom and Warsaw, Poland

MODEL 1898 (KARABIN 98, K98)
MAUSER MILITARY CARBINE. . . . . Nib $275 Ex $178 Gd $127
Same as German Kar. 98A except for minor details. First manufactured during early 1920s.

MODEL 1898 (KARABIN 98, WZ98A)
MAUSER MILITARY RIFLE. . . . . NiB $255 Ex $148 Gd $112
Same as German Kar. 98 used in WWI except for minor details. Manufacture began c. 1921.

MODEL 1929 (KARABIN 29, WZ29)
MAUSER MILITARY RIFLE. . . . . NiB $275 Ex $178 Gd $127
Same as Czech Model 24, mfd. 1929 thru WWII except for minor details. A similar model produced during German occupation was designated Gew. 29/40.

WILLIAM POWELL & SON LTD. — Birmingham, England

DOUBLE-BARREL RIFLE. . . . . NiB $31,250 Ex $25,000 Gd $17,000
Boxlock. Made to order in any caliber during the time that rifle was manufactured. Bbls.: Made to order in any legal length, but 26 inches recommended. Highest grade French walnut buttstock and forearm w/fine checkering. Metal is elaborately engraved. Imported by Stoeger 1938-51.

BOLT-ACTION RIFLE. . . . . NiB $2625 Ex $2100 Gd $1428
Mauser-type bolt action. Calibers: 6x54 through .375 H&H Magnum. Three and 4-shot shot magazine, depending upon chambering. 24-inch bbl. Weight: 7.5 to 8.75 lbs. Sights: Folding leaf rear; hooded ramp front. Cheekpiece stock, checkered forearm and pistol grip, swivels. Imported by Stoeger 1938-51.

JAMES PURDEY & SONS LTD. — London, England

DOUBLE RIFLE
Sidelock action, hammerless, ejectors. Almost any caliber is available but the following are the most popular: .375 Flanged Magnum Nitro Express, .500/465 Nitro Express .470 Nitro Express, .577 Nitro Express. 25.5-inch bbls. (25-inch in .375). Weight: 9.5 to 12.75 lbs. Sights: Folding leaf rear; ramp front. Cheekpiece stock, checkered forearm and pistol-grip, recoil pad, swivels. Currently manufactured to individual measurements and specifications; same general specifications apply to pre-WWII model.
H&H calibers. . . . . NiB $69,375 Ex $55,500 Gd $37,740
NE calibers. . . . . NiB $85,000 Ex $55,500 Gd $37,774

BOLT-ACTION RIFLE. . . . . NiB $22,000 Ex $19,000 Gd $12,000
Mauser-type bolt action. Calibers: 7x57, .300 H&H Magnum, .375 H&H Magnum, 10.75x73. Three shot magazine. 24-inch bbl. Weight: 7.5 to 8.75 lbs. Sights: Folding leaf rear; hooded ramp front. Cheekpiece stock, checkered forearm and pistol-grip, swivels. Currently manufactured; same general specifications apply to pre-WWII model.

RAPTOR ARMS COMPANY, INC. — Newport, New Hampshire

BOLT-ACTION RIFLE
Calibers: .243 Win., .270 Win., .30-06 or .308 Win. Four shot magazine. 22-inch sporter or heavy bbl. Weight: 7.3 to 8 lbs. 42.5 inches overall. No sights w/drilled and tapped receiver or optional blade front, adjustable rear. Blue, stainless or "Taloncote" rust-resistant finish. Checkered black synthetic stock w/Monte Carlo cheepiece and vented recoil pad. Imported 1997 to date.
Raptor Sporter model . . . . NiB $251 Ex $201 Gd $137
Raptor Deluxe Peregrine model (Disc. 1998) . . . . NiB $303 Ex $425 Gd $165
Raptor heavy barrel model . . . . NiB $289 Ex $232 Gd $158
Raptor stainless barrel model . . . . NiB $315 Ex $22 Gd $172

Remington No. 7
Target and Sporting Rifle

REMINGTON ARMS COMPANY — Ilion, New York

To facilitate locating Remington firearms, models are grouped into four categories: Single-shot rifles, bolt-action repeating rifles, slide-action (pump) rifles, and semiautomatic rifles. For a complete listing, please refer to the index.

SINGLE-SHOT RIFLES

NO. 1 SPORTING RIFLE . . . . . . NiB $1905 Ex $1648 Gd 10255
Single-Shot, rolling-block action. Calibers: .40-50, .40-70, .44-77, .50-45, .50-70 Gov't. centerfire and .44 Long, .44 Extra Long, .45-70, .46 Long, .46 Extra Long, .50-70 rimfire. Bbl. lengths: 28- or 30-inch part octagon. Weight: 5 to 7.5 lbs. Sights: Folding leaf rear sight; sporting front, dovetail bases. Plain walnut straight stock; flanged-top, semicarbine buttplate. Plain walnut forend with thin, rounded front end. Made 1868 to 1902.

NO. 1 1/2 SPORTING RIFLE . . . . NiB $3605 Ex $3090 Gd $669
Single-Shot, rolling-block action. Calibers: .22 Short, Long, or Extra Long. 25 Stevens, .32, and .38 rimfire cartridges. .32-20, .38-40 and .44-40 centerfire. Bbl. lengths: 24-, 26-, 28- or 30-inch part octagon. Remaining features similar to Remington No. 1. Made from 1869 to 1902.

NO. 2 SPORTING RIFLE
Single-shot, rolling-block action. Calibers: .22, .25, .32, .38, .44 rimfire or centerfire. Bbl. lengths: 24, 26, 28 or 30 inches. Weight: 5 to 6 lbs. Sights: Open rear; bead front. Straight-grip sporting stock and knobtip forearm of walnut. Made 1873-1910.
Calibers: .22, .25, .32 . . . . NiB $824 Ex $618 Gd $283
Calibers: .38, .44 . . . . NiB $875 Ex $644 Gd $309

NO. 3 CREEDMOOR
AND SCHUETZEN RIFLES
. . . . NiB $7081 to $32,187 Ex $25,7500 to $56,650 Gd $3852 to $17,510
Produced in a variety of styles and calibers, these are collector's items and bring far higher prices than the sporting types. The Schuetzen Special, which has an under-lever action, is especially rare — perhaps fewer than 100 have been made.

NO. 3 HIGH POWER RIFLE
Single-shot, Hepburn falling-block action w/side lever. Calibers: .30-30, .30-40, .32 Special, .32-40, .38-55, .38-72 (high-power cartridges). Bbl. lengths: 26-, 28-, 30-inch. Weight: About 8 lbs. Open sporting sights. Checkered pistol-grip stock and forearm. Made 1893-1907.
Calibers: .30-30, .30-40,
.32 Special, .32-40 . . . . NiB $2060 Ex $1545 Gd $978
Calibers: .38-55, .38-72 . . . . NiB $2254 Ex $1802 Gd $1226

NO. 3 SPORTING RIFLE . . . . NiB $2575 Ex $2060 Gd 1025
Single-shot, Hepburn falling-block action w/side lever. Calibers: .22 WCF, .22 Extra Long, .25-20 Stevens, .25-21 Stevens, .25-25 Stevens, .32 WCF, .32-40 Ballard & Marlin, .32-40 Rem., .38 WCF, .38-40 Rem., 38-

(cont'd.) **NO. 3 SPORTING RIFLE**
.38-50 Rem., .38-55 Ballard & Marlin, .40-60 Ballard & Marlin, .40-60 WCF, .40-65 Rem. Straight, .40-82 WCF, .45-70 Gov., .45-90 WCF, also was supplied on special order in bottle-necked .40-50, .40-70, .40-90, .44-77, .44-90, .44-105, .50-70 Gov., .50-90 Sharps Straight. Bbl. lengths: 26-inch (22, 25, 32 cal. only), 28-inch, 30-inch; half-octagon or full-octagon. Weight: 8 to 10 lbs. Sights: Open rear; blade front. Checkered pistol-grip stock and forearm. Made 1880 to c. 1911.

NO. 4 SINGLE-SHOT RIFLE . . . . NiB $901 Ex $669 Gd $412
Rolling-block action. Solid frame or takedown. Calibers: .22 Short and Long, .22 LR. .25 Stevens R.F., .32 Short and Long R.F. 22.5-inch octagon bbl., 24-inch available in 32 caliber only. Weight: About 4.5 lbs. Sights: Open rear; blade front. Plain walnut stock and forearm. Made 1890-1933.

NO. 4S MILITARY MODEL 22
SINGLE-SHOT RIFLE . . . . NiB $875 Ex $747 Gd $515
Rolling-block action. Calibers: .22 Short only, .22 LR. only. 28-inch bbl. Weight: About 5 lbs. Sights: Military-type rear; blade front. Military-type stock w/handguard, stacking swivel, sling. Has a bayonet stud on the barrel; bayonet and scabbard were regularly supplied. Note: At one time the Military Model was the official rifle of the Boy Scouts of America and was called the Boy Scout Rifle. Made 1913-33.

NO. 5 SPECIAL SINGLE-SHOT RIFLE
Single-shot, rolling-block action. Calibers: 7mm Mauser, .30-30, .30-40 Krag, .303 British, .32-40, .32 Special, .38-55 (high-power cartridges). Bbl. lengths: 24, 26 and 28 inches. Weight: About 7 lbs. Open sporting sights. Plain straight-grip stock and forearm. Made 1902-18. Note: Models 1897 and 1902 Military Rifles, intended for the export market, are almost identical with the No. 5, except for 30-inch bbl. full military stock and weight (about 8.5 lbs.); a carbine was also supplied. The military rifles were produced in caliber 8mm Lebel for France, 7.62mm Russian for Russia and 7mm Mauser for the Central and South American government trade. At one time, Remington also offered these military models to retail buyers.
Sporting model . . . . NiB $837 Ex $669 Gd $455
Military model . . . . NiB $612 Ex $489 Gd $333

NO. 6 TAKEDOWN RIFLE . . . . NiB $541 Ex $381 Gd $206
Single-shot, rolling-block action. Calibers: .22 Short, .22 Long, .22 LR, .32 Short/Long RF. 20-inch bbl. Weight: Avg. 4 lbs. Sights: Open front and rear; tang peep. Plain straight-grip stock, forearm. Made 1901-33.

NO. 7 TARGET AND SPORTING RIFLE . . . . NiB $2511 Ex $2008 Gd $1366
Single-shot. Rolling-block Army Pistol frame. Calibers: .22 Short, .22 LR. 25-10 Stevens R.F. (other calibers as available in No. 2 Rifle were supplied on special order). Half-octagon bbls.: 24-, 26-, 28-inch. Weight: About 6 lbs. Sights: Lyman combination rear; Beach combination front. Fancy walnut stock and forearm, Swiss buttplate available as an extra. Made 1903-11.

Remington
Model 40X Standard Rimfire

Remington
Model 40-XB Centerfire

Remington
Model 40-XB Rimfire

MODEL 33 BOLT-ACTION
SINGLE-SHOT RIFLE . . . . **NiB $206 Ex $144 Gd $98**
Takedown. Caliber: .22 Short, Long, LR. 24-inch bbl. Weight: About 4.5 lbs. Sights: Open rear, bead front. Plain, pistol-grip stock, forearm with grasping grooves. Made 1931-36.

MODEL 33 NRA
JUNIOR TARGET RIFLE . . . . **NiB $309 Ex $257 Gd $103**
Same as Model 33 Standard except has Lyman peep rear sight, Partridge-type front sight, 0.88-inch sling and swivels, weighs about 5 lbs.

MODEL 40X
CENTERFIRE RIFLE . . . . **NiB $1236 Ex $772 Gd $335**
Specifications same as for Model 40X Rimfire (heavy weight). Calibers: .222 Rem., .222 Rem. Mag., 7.62mm NATO, .30-06 (others were available on special order). Made 1961-64. Value shown is for rifle w/o sights.

MODEL 40X HEAVYWEIGHT BOLT-ACTION TARGET RIFLE (RIMFIRE)
Caliber: .22 LR. Single shot. Action similar to Model 722. Click adj. trigger. 28-inch heavy bbl. Redfield Olympic sights. Scope bases. High-comb target stock bedding device, adj. swivel, rubber buttplate. Weight: 12.75 lbs. Made 1955-1964.
With sights . . . . **NiB $1122 Ex $1025 Gd $489**
Without sights . . . . **NiB $1123 Ex $922 Gd $386**

MODEL 40-X SPORTER . . . . **NiB $1610 Ex $1287 Gd $875**
Same general specifications as Model 700 C Custom (see that listing in this section) except in caliber .22 LR. Made 1972-77.

MODEL 40X STANDARD BARREL
Same as Model 40X Heavyweight except has lighter bbl. Weight: 10.75 lbs.
With sights . . . . **NiB $721 Ex $556 Gd $206**
Without sights . . . . **NiB $814 Ex $669 Gd $299**

MODEL 40-XB CENTERFIRE MATCH RIFLE . . **NiB $1236 Ex $772 Gd $381**
Bolt-action, single-shot. Calibers: .222 Rem., .222 Rem. Mag., .223 Rem., .22-250, 6x47mm, 6mm Rem., .243 Win., .25-06, 7mm Rem. Mag., .30-06, .308 Win. (7.62mm NATO), .30-338,

(cont'd.) **MODEL 40-XB CENTERFIRE MATCH RIFLE**
(7.62mm NATO), .30-338, .300 Win. Mag. 27 25-inch standard or heavy bbl. Target stock w/adj. front swivel block on guide rail, rubber buttplate. Weight w/o sights: Standard bbl., 9.25 lbs.; heavy bbl., 11.25 lbs. Value shown is for rifle without sights. Made 1964 to date.

MODEL 40-XB RANGEMASTER CENTERFIRE
Single-shot target rifle with same basic specifications as Model 40-XB Centerfire Match. Additional calibers in .220 Swift, 6mm BR Rem. and 7mm BR Rem., and stainless bbl. only. American walnut or Kevlar (weighs 1 lb. less) target stock with forend stop. Discontinued 1994.
Model 40-XB right-hand model . . . . **NiB $1024 Ex $818 Gd $557**
Model 40-XB left-hand model . . . . **NiB $1095 Ex $875 Gd $595**
For 2-oz. trigger, add **$100**
Model 40-XB KS (Kevlar stock, R.H.) . . . . **NiB $1153 Ex $922 Gd $627**
Model 40-XB KS (Kevlar stock, L.H.) . . . . **NiB $1095 Ex $875 Gd $595**
For 2-oz. trigger, add **$100**
For Repeater model, add **$100**

MODEL 40-XB RANGEMASTER
RIMFIRE MATCH RIFLE . . . . **NiB $824 Ex $711 Gd $335**
Bolt-action, single-shot. Caliber: .22 LR. 28-inch standard or heavy bbl. Target stock with adj. front swivel block on guide rail, rubber buttplate. Weight w/o sights: Standard bbl., 10 lbs.; heavy bbl., 11.25 lbs. Value shown is for rifle without sights. Made 1964-74.

MODEL 40-XB
VARMINT SPECIAL RIFLE . . . . **NiB $1236 Ex $772 Gd $381**
Same general specifications as Model 40-XB Repeater except has synthetic stock (Kevlar). Made 1987-94.

MODEL 40-XBBR BENCH REST RIFLE
Bolt action, single shot. Calibers: .222 Rem., .222 Rem. Mag., .223 Rem., 6x47mm, .308 Win. (7.62mm NATO). 20- or 26-inch unblued stainless-steel bbl. Supplied w/o sights. Weight: With 20-inch bbl., 9.25 lbs., with 26-inch bbl., 12 lbs. (Heavy Varmint class; 7.25 lbs. w/Kevlar stock (Light Varmint class). Made 1969 to date.
Model 40-XBBR (discontinued) . . . . **NiB $895 Ex $716 Gd $487**
Model 40-XBBR KS (Kevlar stock) . . . . . . **NiB $1153 Ex $922 Gd $628**

Remington
Model 40-XB Varmint Special

Remington
Model 40-XBR

Remington
Model 40-XC

Remington
Model 40-XR Custom Sporter Grade II

Remington
Model 40-XR Rimfire Position Rifle

RIFLES

MODEL 40-XC NATIONAL MATCH COURSE RIFLE

Bolt-action repeater. Caliber: .308 Win. (7.62mm NATO). Five shot magazine, clip slot in receiver. 24-inch bbl. Supplied w/o sights. Weight: 11 lbs. Thumb groove stock w/adj. hand stop and sling swivel, adj. buttplate. Made 1974 to date.

Mdl. 40-XC (wood stock) (disc.) . . . . NiB $896 Ex $669 Gd $438
Mdl. 40-XC KS (Kevlar stk. disc. 1994) . . . NiB $1330 Ex $927 Gd $592

MODEL 40-XR CUSTOM SPORTER RIFLE

Caliber: .22 RF. 24-inch contoured bbl. Supplied w/o sights. Made in four grades of checkering, engraving and other custom features. Made 1987 to date.

Grade I . . . . NiB $1133 Ex $953 Gd $721
Grade II . . . . NiB $2055 Ex $1699 Gd $1030
Grade III . . . . NiB $2987 Ex $2214 Gd $1133
Grade IV . . . . NiB $5021 Ex $4841 Gd $2678

MODEL 40-XR RIMFIRE POSITION RIFLE

Bolt action, single shot. Caliber: .22 LR. 24-inch heavy bbl. Supplied w/o sights. Weight: 10 lbs. Position-style stock w/thumb groove, adj. hand stop and sling swivel on guide rail, adj. buttplate. Made 1974 to date.

Model 40-XR . . . . NiB $1133 Ex $953 Gd $541
Model 40-XR KS (Kevlar stock) . . . . NiB $1236 Ex $1025 Gd $618

MODEL 41A TARGETMASTER BOLT-ACTION

SINGLE-SHOT RIFLE . . . . NiB $206 Ex $154 Gd $98
Takedown. Caliber: .22 Short, Long, LR. 27-inch bbl. Weight: About 5.5 lbs. Sights: Open rear; bead front. Plain pistol-grip stock. Made 1936-40.

MODEL 41AS . . . . NiB $206 Ex $154 Gd $98
Same as Model 41A except chambered for .22 Remington Special (.22 W.R.F.).

MODEL 41P . . . . NiB $206 Ex $154 Gd $98
Same as Model 41A except has peep rear sight, hooded front sight.

MODEL 41SB . . . . NiB $185 Ex $129 Gd $103
Same as Model 41A except smoothbore for use with shot cartridges.

MODEL 510A TARGETMASTER

BOLT-ACTION SINGLE-SHOT RIFLE . . . . NiB $161 Ex $129 Gd $88
Takedown. Caliber: 22 Short, Long, LR. 25-inch bbl. Weight: About 5.5 lbs. Sights: Open rear; bead front. Plain pistol-grip stock. Made 1939-62.

MODEL 510P . . . . NiB $173 Ex $139 Gd $96
Same as Model 510A except has peep rear sight, Partridge front on ramp.

Remington
Model 540X

Remington
Model 580

Remington
International Match

Remington
Nylon 10

MODEL 510SB . . . . **NiB $309 Ex $206 Gd $154**
Same as Model 510A except smoothbore for use with shot cartridges, shotgun bead front sight, no rear sight.

MODEL 510X BOLT-ACTION
SINGLE-SHOT RIFLE . . . . **NiB $206 Ex $154 Gd $93**
Same as Model 510A except improved sights. Mfd.1964-66.

MODEL 514 BOLT-ACTION
SINGLE-SHOT . . . . **NiB $154 Ex $129 Gd $93**
Takedown. Caliber: .22 Short, Long, LR. 24-inch bbl. Weight: 4.75
lbs. Sights: Open rear; bead front. Plain pistol-grip stock. Made
1948-71.

MODEL 514BC BOY'S CARBINE . . . . **NiB $165 Ex $134 Gd $98**
Same as Model 514 except has 21-inch bbl., 1-inch shorter stock.
Made 1961-71.

MODEL 514P . . . . **NiB $165 Ex $134 Gd $98**
Same as Model 514 except has receiver peep sight.

MODEL 540-X RIMFIRE TARGET RIFLE . . . **NiB $335 Ex $257 Gd $103**
Bolt-action, single-shot. Caliber: .22 R. 26-inch heavy bbl. Supplied
w/o sights. Weight: About 8 lbs. Target stock w/Monte Carlo cheekpiece and thumb groove, guide rail for hand stop and swivel, adj.
buttplate. Made 1969-74.

MODEL 540-XR POSITION RIFLE . . . . **NiB $360 Ex $283 Gd $153**
Bolt-action, single-shot. Caliber: .22 LR. 26-inch medium-weight bbl.
Supplied w/o sights. Weight: 8 lbs., 13 oz. Position-style stock w/thumb
groove, guide rail for hand stop and swivel, adj. buttplate. Made 1974-84.

MODEL 540-XRJR . . . . **NiB $360 Ex $283 Gd $154**
Same as Model 540-XR except 1.75-inch shorter stock. Made
1974-84.

MODEL 580 BOLT-ACTION
SINGLE-SHOT . . . . **NiB $154 Ex $124 Gd $84**
Caliber: .22 Short, Long, LR. 24-inch bbl. Weight: 4.75 lbs. Sights:
Bead front; U-notch rear. Monte Carlo stock. Made 1967-78.

MODEL 580BR BOY'S RIFLE . . . . . . **NiB $168 Ex $134 Gd $91**
Same as Model 580 except w/1-inch shorter stock. Made 1971-78.

MODEL 580SB SMOOTH BORE . . . **NiB $226 Ex $180 Gd $123**
Same as Model 580 except smooth bore for .22 Long Rifle shot cartridges. Made 1967-78.

INTERNATIONAL FREE RIFLE . . . . . **NiB $978 Ex $721 Gd $412**
Same as Model 40-XB rimfire and centerfire except has free rifle-
type stock with adj. buttplate and hook, adj. palm rest, movable
front sling swivel, 2-oz. trigger. Weight: About 15 lbs. Made
1964-74. Value shown is for rifle with professionally finished
stock, no sights.

INTERNATIONAL MATCH FREE RIFLE . . . **NiB $1030 Ex $901 Gd $489**
Calibers: .22 LR, .222 Rem., .222 Rem. Mag., 7.62mm NATO, .30-
06 (others were available on special order). Model 40X-type bolt-
action, single-shot. 2-oz. adj. trigger. 28-inch heavy bbl. Weight:
About 15.5 lbs. Free rifle-style stock with thumbhole (furnished
semifinished by mfr.); interchangeable and adj. rubber buttplate and
hook buttplate, adj. palm rest, sling swivel. Made 1961-64. Value
shown is for rifle with professionally-finished stock, no sights.

Remington Model 7

Remington Model Seven FS

Remington Model Seven
KS Custom Rifle

NYLON 10 BOLT-ACTION
SINGLE-SHOT RIFLE . . . . **NiB $154 Ex $129 Gd $98**
Caliber: .22 Short, Long, LR. 19.13-inch bbl. Weight: 4.25 lbs. Open rear sight; ramped blade front. Receiver grooved for scope mount. Brown nylon stock. Made 1962-1966.

BOLT-ACTION REPEATING RIFLES

MODEL SEVEN (7) CF BOLT-ACTION RIFLE
Calibers: .17 Rem., .222 Rem., .223 Rem., .243 Win., 6mm Rem., 7mm-08 Rem., .308 Win. Magazine capacity: 5-shot in .17 Rem., .222 Rem., .223 Rem., 4-shot in other calibers. 18.5-inch bbl. Weight: 6.5 lbs. Walnut stock checkering, and recoil pad. Made 1983 to date. .223 Rem. added in 1984.
Standard calibers except
.17 Rem. & .222 Rem. . . . . **NiB $463 Ex $386 Gd $257**
Caliber .17 Rem & .222 Rem. . . . . **NiB $489 Ex $407 Gd $268**

MODEL SEVEN (7)
FS RIFLE. . . . . **NiB $547 Ex $438 Gd $298**
Calibers: .243, 7mm-08 Rem., .308 Win. 18.5-inch bbl. 37.5 inches overall. Weight: 5.25 lbs. Hand layup fiberglass stock, reinforced with DuPont Kevlar at points of bedding and stress. Made 1987-90.

MODEL SEVEN (7) KS RIFLE . . . . . . **NiB $798 Ex $644 Gd $412**
Calibers: .223 Rem., 7mm-08, .308, .35 Rem. and .350 Rem. Mag. 20-inch bbl. Custom-made in Remington's Custom Shop with Kevlar stock. Made 1987 to date.

MODEL SEVEN (7) LS RIFLE . . . . . . **NiB $515 Ex $438 Gd $257**
Calibers: .223 Rem., .243 Win., .260 Rem., 7mm-08 and 308 Win. 20-inch matte bbl. Laminated hardwood stock w/matte brown finish. Weight: 6.5 lbs. Made 2000 to date.

MODEL SEVEN (7) LSS RIFLE . . . . . **NiB $566 Ex $438 Gd $283**
Similar to Model 7 LS except stainless bbl. w/o sights. Calibers: .22-250 Rem., .243 Win. or 7mm-08. Made 2000 to date.

MODEL SEVEN (7) MS CUSTOM RIFLE . . . **NiB $978 Ex $850 Gd $489**
Similar to the standard Model 7 except fitted with a laminated full Mannlicher-style stock. Weight: 6.75 lbs. Calibers: .222 Rem., .22-250, .243, 6mm Rem.,7mm-08, .308, .350 Rem. Additional calibers available on special order. Made 1993 to date.

MODEL SEVEN (7) SS RIFLE . . . . . . **NiB $541 Ex $412 Gd $283**
Same as Model 7 except 20-inch stainless bbl., receiver and bolt; black synthetic stock. Calibers: .243, 7mm-08 or .308. Made 1994 to date.

MODEL SEVEN (7) YOUTH RIFLE. . . . . **NiB $360 Ex $309 Gd $232**
Similar to the standard Model 7 except fitted with hardwood stock with a 12.19-inch pull. Calibers: .243, 6mm, 7mm-08 only. Made 1993 to date.

MODEL 30A BOLT-ACTION
EXPRESS RIFLE. . . . . **NiB $573 Ex $458 Gd $312**
Standard Grade. Modified M/1917 Enfield Action. Calibers: .25, .30, .32 and .35 Rem., 7mm Mauser, .30-06. Five shot box magazine. 22-inch bbl. Weight: About 7.25 lbs. Sights: Open rear; bead front. Walnut stock w/checkered pistol grip and forearm. Made 1921-40. Note: Early Model 30s had a slender forend with Schnabel tip, military-type double-pull trigger.

MODEL 30R CARBINE . . . . **NiB $586 Ex $489 Gd $366**
Same as Model 30A except has 20-inch bbl., plain stock weighs about 7 lbs.

MODEL 30S SPORTING RIFLE . . . . **NiB $701 Ex $561 Gd $382**
Special Grade. Same action as Model 30A. Calibers: .257 Roberts, 7mm Mauser, .30-06. Five shot box magazine. 24-inch bbl. Weight: About 8 lbs. Lyman No. 48 Receiver sight, bead front sight. Special high comb stock with long, full forearm, checkered. Made 1930-40.

MODEL 34 BOLT-ACTION REPEATER. . . . . . **NiB $154 Ex $128 Gd $93**
Takedown. Caliber: .22 Short, Long, LR. Tubular magazine holds 22 Short, 17 Long or 15 LR. 24-inch bbl. Weight: 5.25 lbs. Sights: Open rear; bead front. Plain, pistol-grip stock, forearm w/grasping grooves. Made 1932-36.

Remington Model 30A

Remington Model 30R

Remington Model 30S

Remington Model 34

Remington Model 37 (1937)

Remington Model 37 (1940)

MODEL 34 NRA TARGET RIFLE . . . . **NiB $412 Ex $335 Gd $206**
Same as Model 34 Standard except has Lyman peep rear sight, Partridge-type front sight, .88-inch sling and swivels, weight: About 5.75 lbs.

MODEL 37 RANGEMASTER BOLT-ACTION TARGET RIFLE (I)
Model of 1937. Caliber: .22 LR. Five shot box magazine, single shot adapter also supplied as standard equipment. 28-inch heavy bbl. Weight: About 12 lbs. Remington front and rear sights, scope bases. Target stock, swivels, sling. Note: Original 1937 model had a stock with outside bbl. band similar in appearance to that of the old-style Winchester Model 52, forearm design was modified and bbl. band eliminated in 1938. Made 1937-40.
With factory sights . . . . **NiB $566 Ex $438 Gd $309**
Without sights . . . . **NiB $489 Ex $412 Gd $232**

MODEL 37 RANGEMASTER BOLT-ACTION TARGET RIFLE (II)
Model of 1940. Same as Model of 1937 except has "Miracle" trigger mechanism and Randle-design stock with high comb, full pistol-grip and wide beavertail forend. Made 1940-54.
With factory sights . . . . **NiB $709 Ex $566 Gd $385**
Without sights . . . . **NiB $509 Ex $407 Gd $277**

MODEL 40-XB
CENTERFIRE REPEATER. . . . . **NiB $1075 Ex $860 Gd $585**
Same as Model 40-XB Centerfire except 5-shot repeater. Calibers: .222 Rem., .222 Rem. Mag., .223 Rem., .22-250, 6x47mm, 6mm Rem., .243 Win., .308 Win. (7.62mm NATO). Heavy bbl. only. Discontinued.

MODEL 78 SPORTSMAN
BOLT-ACTION RIFLE . . . . **NiB $289 Ex $232 Gd $158**
Similar to Model 700 ADL except with straight-comb walnut-finished hardwood stock in calibers .223 Rem., .243 Win., .270 Win., .30-06 Springfield and .308 Win. 22-inch bbl. Weight: 7 lbs. Adj. sights. Made 1984-91.

MODEL 341A SPORTSMASTER
BOLT-ACTION REPEATER . . . . **NiB $174 Ex $139 Gd $95**
Takedown. Caliber: .22 Short, Long, LR. Tubular magazine holds 22 Short, 17 Long, 15 LR. 27-inch bbl. Weight: About 6 lbs. Sights: Open rear; bead front. Plain pistol-grip stock. Made 1936-40.

Remington Model 511X

Remington Model 512A

Remington Model 513S

Remington Model 513TR

MODEL 341P . . . . **NiB $200 Ex $160 Gd $108**
Same as Model 341A except has peep rear sight, hooded front sight.

MODEL 341SB . . . . **NiB $206 Ex $232 Gd $154**
Same as Model 341A except smoothbore for use with shot cartridges.

MODEL 511A SCOREMASTER BOLT-ACTION
BOX MAGAZINE REPEATER . . . . **NiB $186 Ex $149 Gd $102**
Takedown. Caliber: 22 Short, Long, LR. Six shot detachable box magazine. 25-inch bbl. Weight: About 5.5 lbs. Sights: Open rear; bead front. Plain pistol-grip stock. Made 1939-62.

MODEL 511P . . . . **NiB $194 Ex $154 Gd $105**
Same as Model 511A except has peep rear sight, Partridge-type blade front on ramp.

MODEL 511X BOLT-ACTION REPEATER . . **NiB $200 Ex $160 Gd $108**
Clip type. Same as Model 511A except improved sights. Made 1964-66.

MODEL 512A SPORTSMASTER
BOLT-ACTION REPEATER . . . . **NiB $174 Ex $139 Gd $95**
Takedown. Caliber: .22 Short, Long, LR. Tubular magazine holds 22 Short, 17 Long, 15 LR. 25-inch bbl. Weight: About 5.75 lbs. Sights: Open rear; bead front. Plain pistol-grip stock w/semibeavertail forend. Made 1940-62.

MODEL 512P . . . . **NiB $226 Ex $180 Gd $123**
Same as Model 512A except has peep rear sight, blade front, on ramp.

MODEL 512X BOLT-ACTION REPEATER . . **NiB $237 Ex $190 Gd $130**
Tubular magazine type. Same as Model 512A except has improved sights. Made 1964-66.

MODEL 513S BOLT-ACTION RIFLE . . . . . . **NiB $515 Ex $463 Gd $283**
Caliber: .22 LR. Six shot detachable box magazine. 27-inch bbl. Weight: About 6.75 lbs. Marble open rear sight, Partridge-type front. Checkered sporter stock. Made 1941-56.

MODEL 513TR MATCHMASTER
BOLT-ACTION TARGET RIFLE . . . . . **NiB $341 Ex $273 Gd $185**
Caliber: .22 LR. Six shot detachable box magazine. 27-inch bbl. Weight: About 9 lbs. Sights: Redfield No. 75 rear; globe front. Target stock. Sling and swivels. Made 1941-69.

MODEL 521TL JUNIOR TARGET
BOLT-ACTION REPEATER . . . . **NiB $303 Ex $242 Gd $165**
Takedown. Caliber: .22 LR. Six shot detachable box magazine. 25-inch bbl. Weight: About 7 lbs. Sights: Lyman No. 57RS rear; dovetailed blade front. Target stock. Sling and swivels. Made 1947-69.

MODEL 522 VIPER . . . . **NiB $154 Ex $103 Gd $77**
Calibers: .22 LR. 10-shot magazine. 20-inch bbl. 40 inches overall. Weight: 4.63 lbs. Checkered black PET resin stock with beavertail forend. Dupont high-tech synthetic lightweight receiver. Matte black finish on all exposed metal. Made 1993 to date.

MODEL 541-S CUSTOM SPORTER . . . . . . **NiB $709 Ex $566 Gd $385**
Bolt-action repeater. Scroll engraving on receiver and trigger guard. Caliber: .22 Short, Long, LR. 5-shot clip magazine. 24-inch bbl. Weight: 5.5 lbs. Supplied w/o sights. Checkered walnut stock w/rosewood-finished forend tip, pistol-grip cap and buttplate. Made 1972-84.

MODEL 541-T BOLT-ACTION RIFLE
Caliber: .22 RF. Clip-fed, Five shot. 24-inch bbl. Weight: 5.88 lbs. Checkered walnut stock. Made 1986 to date; heavy bbl. model intro. 1993.
Model 541-T Standard . . . . **NiB $412 Ex $283 Gd $165**
Model 541-T-HB heavy bbl. . . . . . . **NiB $438 Ex $309 Gd $221**

RIFLES

Remington Model 521TL

Remington Model 541-S

Remington Model 581-S

MODEL 581 CLIP REPEATER
Same general specifications as Model 580 except has 5-shot clip magazine. Made 1967-84.
Model 581 . . . . NiB $161 Ex $129 Gd $88
Model 581 left hand
(made 1969-1984) . . . . NiB $194 Ex $154 Gd $105

MODEL 581-S BOLT-ACTION RIFLE . . . . . NiB $180 Ex $154 Gd $103
Caliber: .22 RF. Clip-fed, 5-shot. 24-inch bbl. Weight: 4.75 lbs. Plain walnut-colored stock. Made 1987-92.

MODEL 582 TUBULAR REPEATER . . . . NiB $168 Ex $134 Gd $91
Same general specifications as Model 580 except has tubular magazine holding 20 Short,15 Long,14 LR. Weight: About 5 lbs. Made 1967-84.

MODEL 591 BOLT-ACTION
CLIP REPEATER . . . . NiB $251 Ex $201 Gd $137
Caliber: 5mm Rimfire Magnum. Four shot clip magazine. 24-inch bbl. Weight: 5 lbs. Sights: Bead front; U-notch rear. Monte Carlo stock. Made 1970-73.

MODEL 592 TUBULAR REPEATER . . . . NiB $186 Ex $149 Gd $102
Same as Model 591 except has tubular magazine holding 10 rounds, weight: 5.5 lbs. Made 1970-73.

MODEL 600 BOLT-ACTION CARBINE
Calibers: .222 Rem., .223 Rem., .243 Win., 6mm Rem., .308 Win., 35 Rem., 5-shot magazine (6-shot in .222 Rem.) 18.5-inch bbl. with ventilated rib. Weight: 6 lbs. Sights: Open rear; blade ramp front. Monte Carlo stock w/pistol-grip. Made 1964-67.
.222 Rem. . . . . NiB $824 Ex $747 Gd $438
.223 Rem. . . . . NiB $1352 Ex $1081 Gd $735
.35 Rem. . . . . NiB $804 Ex $644 Gd $438
Standard calibers . . . . NiB $638 Ex $510 Gd $347

MODEL 600 MAGNUM . . . . NiB $1024 Ex $819 Gd $557
Same as Model 600 except calibers 6.5mm Mag. and .350 Rem. Mag., 4-shot magazine, special Magnum-type bbl. with bracket for scope back-up, laminated walnut and beech stock w/recoil pad. QD swivels and sling; weight: About 6.5 lbs. Made 1965-67.

MODEL 600 MONTANA
TERRITORIAL CENTENNIAL $772
Same as Model 600 except has commemorative medallion embedded in buttstock. Made 1964. Value is for rifle in new, unfired condition.

MODEL 660 STP
Calibers: .222 Rem., 6mm Rem., .243 Win., .308 Win., 5-shot magazine. (6-shot in .222 Rem.) 20-inch bbl. Weight: 6.5 lbs. Sights: Open rear; bead front on ramp. Monte Carlo stock, checkered, black pistol-grip cap and forend tip. Made 1968-71.
.222 Rem. . . . . NiB $624 Ex $500 Gd $340
Other calibers . . . . NiB $580 Ex $463 Gd $315

MODEL 660 MAGNUM . . . . NiB $875 Ex $695 Gd $566
Same as Model 660 except calibers 6.5mm Rem. Mag. and .350 Rem. Mag., 4-shot magazine, laminated walnut-and-beech stock with recoil pad. QD swivels and sling. Made 1968-71.

MODEL 700 ADL CENTERFIRE RIFLE . . . . . NiB $386 Ex $304 Gd $200
Calibers: .22-250, .222 Rem., .25-06, 6mm Rem., .243 Win., .270 Win., .30-06, .308 Win., 7mm Rem. Mag. Magazine capacity: 6-shot in .222 Rem.; 4-shot in 7mm Rem. Mag. Five shot in other calibers. Bbl. lengths: 24-inch in .22-250, .222 Rem., .25-06, 7mm Rem. Mag.; 22-inch in other calibers. Weight: 7 lbs. standard; 7.5 lbs. in 7mm Rem. Mag. Sights: Ramp front; sliding ramp open rear. Monte Carlo stock w/cheekpiece, skip checkering, recoil pad on Magnum. Laminated stock also avail. Made 1962-93.

MODEL 700 APR BOLT-ACTION RIFLE . . NiB $1224 Ex $978 Gd $665
Acronym for African Plains Rifle. Calibers: 7mm Rem. Mag., 7mm STW, 300 Win. Mag., 300 Wby. Mag., 300 Rem. Ultra Mag., 338 Win. Mag., 375 H&H. Three shot magazine. 26-inch bbl. on a magnum action. 46.5 inches overall. Weight: 7.75 lbs. Matte blue finish. Checkered classic-style laminated wood stock w/black magnum recoil pad. Made 1994 to date.

MODEL 700 AS BOLT-ACTION RIFLE
Similar to the Model 700 BDL except with nonreflective matte black metal finish, including the bolt body. Weight: 6.5 lbs. Straight comb synthetic stock made of Arylon, a fiberglass-reinforced thermoplastic resin with nonreflective matte finish. Made 1988-92.
Standard caliber . . . . NiB $470 Ex $376 Gd $255
Magnum caliber . . . . NiB $509 Ex $407 Gd $277

COACH GUN

It's a showdown at the Dry Gulch Saloon.

Your hogleg's run dry and you're the only one between the outlaws and the open prairie. It's Stoeger Coach Gun time.

Cowboy shooting has grown like jimson weed in the last few years, and top competitors count on the Stoeger Coach Gun to pile up points in those crucial shotgun matches. All versions have traditional double triggers for lightning-fast barrel selection in any scenario and conventional barrels with fixed improved cylinder and modified chokes.

Coach Gun
The Coach Gun is available in 12 gauge, 20 gauge, and .410 bore. All models handle 3" shells. Its 20" barrels are proofed for steel shot, and the shooter's hand is well-protected from barrel heat by a husky beavertail fore-end. **MSRP: $320**

Silverado Coach Gun
The Silverado Coach Gun offers the perfect combination of style and performance. This Coach Gun features matte nickel and brown hardwood stocks with a rubbed-oil finish. **MSRP: $375**

Nickel Coach Gun
For those who prefer a distinctive appearance, this Coach Gun is available with nickel-plated frame and barrels and a black Brazilian hardwood stock. This gun makes a big impression at a cowboy shoot, and is suitable for maritime use. **MSRP: $375**

Stoeger
Serving America's Sportsmen Since 1924

Stoeger Industries • 17603 Indian Head Highway, Suite 200, Accokeek, MD 20607 • (301) 283-6300 • www.StoegerIndustries.com
Part of the Benelli USA® family

Uberti . . .
Home on the Range

Reach back across the centuries and fill your hand with a real piece of Americana. Follow the trail of inventors and adventurers through the 19th century as they set the standard for design and craftsmanship across the globe. Uberti historical arms

faithfully replicate the guns that helped forge a new nation. These replicas are the ultimate in fit, finish, attention to authentic detail and accuracy. More than just classic looks, these firearms are the choice of today's collectors and competitive shooters.

A. Uberti

HISTORY REPEATS ITSELF

Remington Model 581

Remington Model 581-S

Remington Model 582

Remington Model 591

Remington Model 592

Remington Model 600

Remington Model 600
Montana Territorial Centennial

Remington Model 660

Remington Model 700 ADL

RIFLES

Remington Model 700
ADL w/Laminated Stock

Remington
Model 700 ADL Left Hand

MODEL 700 AWR
BOLT-ACTION RIFLE . . . . **NiB $1339 Ex $1133 Gd $978**
Acronym for Alaskan Wilderness Rifle, similar to Model 700 APR except w/24-inch stainless bbl. and black chromed action. Matte gray or black Kevlar stock w/straight comb and raised cheekpiece fitted w/black magnum recoil pad. Made 1994 to date.

MODEL 700 BDL CENTERFIRE RIFLE
Same as Model 700 ADL except has hinged floorplate hooded ramp front sight, stock w/black forend tip and pistol-grip cap, cut checkering, QD swivels and sling. Additional calibers: .17 Rem., .223 Rem., .264 Win. Mag., 7mm-08, .280, .300 Sav., .300 Win. Mag., 8mm Rem. Mag., .338 Win. Mag., .35 Whelen. All have 24-inch bbls. Magnums have 4-shot magazine, recoil pad, weighs 7.5 lbs; .17 Rem. has 6-shot magazine, weighs 7 lbs. Made 1962 to date. Made 1973 to date.
Standard calibers except .17 Rem.. . . . . . **NiB $495 Ex $397 Gd $270**
Magnum calibers and .17 Rem. . . . . **NiB $560 Ex $448 Gd $305**
Left-hand, .270 Win. and .30-06. . . . . **NiB $509 Ex $407 Gd $277**
Left-hand, 7mm
Rem. Mag and .222 Rem. . . . . **NiB $566 Ex $489 Gd $412**

MODEL 700 BDL EUROPEAN RIFLE
Same general specifications as Model 700 BDL, except has oil-finished walnut stock. Calibers: .243, .270, 7mm-08, 7mm Mag., .280 Rem., .30-06. Made 1993-95.
Standard calibers. . . . . **NiB $515 Ex $412 Gd $283**
Magnum calibers. . . . . **NiB $515 Ex $473 Gd $360**

MODEL 700 BDL SS BOLT-ACTION RIFLE
Same as Model 700 BDL except w/24-inch stainless bbl., receiver and bolt plus black synthetic stock. Calibers: .223 Rem., .243 Win., 6mm Rem., .25-06 Rem., .270 Win. .280 Rem., 7mm-08, 7mm Rem. Mag., 7mm Wby. Mag., .30-06, .300 Win., .308 Win., .338 Win. Mag., .375 H&H. Made 1992 to date.
Standard calibers. . . . . **NiB $566 Ex $489 Gd $288**
Magnum calibers, add **$80**
DM (detachable magazine), add **$40**
DM-B (muzzle brake), add **$90**

MODEL 700 BDL
VARMINT SPECIAL . . . . **NiB $515 Ex $412 Gd $278**
Same as Model 700 BDL except has 24-inch heavy bbl., no sights, weighs 9 lbs. (8.75 lbs. in 308 Win.). Calibers: .22-250, .222 Rem., .223 Rem., .25-06, 6mm Rem., .243 Win., .308 Win. Made 1967-94.

REMINGTON MODEL 700 CS BOLT-ACTION RIFLE
Similar to Model 700 BDL except with nonreflective matte black metal finish, including the bolt body. Straight comb synthetic stock camouflaged in Mossy Oak Bottomland pattern. Made 1992-94.
Standard calibers. . . . . **NiB $509 Ex $407 Gd $277**
Magnum calibers. . . . . **NiB $547 Ex $438 Gd $298**

MODEL 700 CLASSIC
Same general specifications as Model 700 BDL except has "Classic" stock of high-quality walnut with full-pattern cut-checkering, special satin wood finish; Schnabel forend. Brown rubber buttpad. Hinged floorplate. No sights. Weight: 7 lbs. Also chambered for "Classic" cartridges such as .257 Roberts and .250-3000. Intro. 1981.
Standard calibers. . . . . **NiB $515 Ex $360 Gd $257**
Magnum calibers. . . . . **NiB $566 Ex $412 Gd $278**

MODEL 700 CUSTOM BOLT-ACTION RIFLE
Same general specifications as Model 700 BDL except custom-built; available in choice of grades, each with higher quality wood, different checkering patterns, engraving, high-gloss blued finish. Introduced in 1965.
Model 700 C Grade I . . . . **NiB $1224 Ex $978 Gd $665**
Model 700 C Grade II . . . . **NiB $2125 Ex $1699 Gd $1156**
Model 700 C Grade III . . . . **NiB $2769 Ex $2214 Gd $1506**
Model 700 C Grade IV . . . . **NiB $5086 Ex $4068 Gd $2767**
Model 700 D Peerless . . . . **NiB $196 Ex $1437 Gd $977**
Model 700 F Premier. . . . . **NiB $3419 Ex $2735 Gd $1859**

MODEL 700 FS BOLT-ACTION RIFLE
Similar to Model 700 ADL except with straight comb fiberglass stock reinforced with DuPont Kevlar, finished in gray or gray camo with Old English-style recoil pad. Made 1987-89.
Standard calibers. . . . . **NiB $577 Ex $515 Gd $309**
Magnum calibers. . . . . **NiB $618 Ex $515 Gd $360**

MODEL 700 KS CUSTOM MOUNTAIN RIFLE
Similar to standard Model 700 MTN Rifle, except with custom Kevlar reinforced resin synthetic stock with standard or wood-grain finish. Calibers: .270 Win., .280 Rem., 7mm Rem Mag., .30-06, .300 Win. Mag., .300 Wby. Mag., 8mm Rem. Mag., .338 Win. Mag., .35 Whelen, .375 H&H. Four shot magazine. 24-inch bbl. Weight: 6.75 lbs. Made 1986 to date.
Standard KS stock (disc. 1993) . . . . **NiB $1056 Ex $875 Gd $463**
Wood-grain KS stock. . . . . **NiB $978 Ex $747 Gd $508**
SS Model Stainless Synthetic (1995-97) . . **NiB $1191 Ex $994 Gd $742**
Left-hand model, add **$75**

Remington Model 700 APR

Remington Model 700 BDL

Remington Model 700 BDL Magnum

Remington Model 700 Classic

Remington Model 700 Custom Grade I

Remington Model 700 Custom Grade II

Remington Model 700 Custom Grade III

Remington Model 700 Custom Grade IV

Remington Model 700 FS

RIFLES

Remington Model 700 KS
Custom Mountain Rifle

Remington Model 700
Mountain Rifle Deluxe

Remington Model 700 RS

Remington Model 700 Sendero

Remington Model 700 Safari

MODEL 700 LS BOLT-ACTION RIFLE

Similar to Model 700 ADL except with checkered Monte Carlo-style laminated wood stock with alternating grain and wood color, impregnated with phenolic resin and finished with a low satin luster. Made 1988-93

Standard calibers . . . . NiB $566 Ex $463 Gd $309
Magnum calibers . . . . NiB $592 Ex $473 Gd $335

MODEL 700 LSS BOLT-ACTION RIFLE

Similar to Model 700 BDL except with stainless steel barrel and action. Checkered Monte Carlo-style laminated wood stock with alternating grain and gray tinted color impregnated with phenolic resin and finished with a low satin luster. Made 1996 to date.

Standard calibers . . . . NiB $566 Ex $489 Gd $335
Magnum calibers . . . . NiB $618 Ex $541 Gd $360

MODEL 700 MTN RIFLE

Lightweight version of Model 700. Calibers: .243 Win., .25-06, .257 Roberts, .270 Win., 7x57, 7mm-08 Rem., .280 Rem., .30-06 and .308 Win. Four shot magazine. 22-inch bbl. Weight: 6.75 lbs. Satin blue or stainless finish. Checkered walnut stock and redesigned pistol grip, straight comb, contoured cheekpiece, Old English-style recoil pad and satin oil finish or black synthetic stock with pressed checkering and blind magazine. Made 1986 to date.

(cont'd.) MODEL 700 MOUNTAIN RIFLE

Standard w/blind magazine . . . . NiB $463 Ex $360 Gd $232
Standard w/hinged floorplate (disc. 1994) . NiB $523 Ex $433 Gd $317
DM Model (New 1995) . . . . NiB $577 Ex $463 Gd $309
SS Model stainless synthetic (disc. 1993) . . NiB $474 Ex $360 Gd $257

MODEL 700 RS BOLT-ACTION RIFLE

Similar to the Model 700 BDL except with straight comb DuPont Rynite stock finished in gray or gray camo with Old English style recoil pad. made 1987-90.

Standard calibers . . . . NiB $566 Ex $463 Gd $309
Magnum calibers . . . . NiB $592 Ex $463 Gd $335
.280 Rem. calibers (Limited production) . . . NiB $709 Ex $566 Gd $385

MODEL 700 SAFARI GRADE

Big game heavy magnum version of the Model 700 BDL. 8mm Rem. Mag., .375 H&H Mag., .416 Rem. Mag. and .458 Win. Mag. 24-inch heavy bbl. Weight: 9 lbs. Blued or stainless finish. Checkered walnut stock in synthetic/Kevlar stock with standard matte or wood-grain finish with old English style recoil pad. made 1962 to date.

Safari Classic/Monte Carlo . . . . NiB $1056 Ex $927 Gd $489
Safari KS (Kevlar stock) intro. 1989 . . . . NiB $1230 Ex $1025 Gd $763
Safari KS (Wood-grain) intro. 1992 . . . . . . NiB $1146 Ex $927 Gd $647
Safari KS SS (Stainless) intro. 1993 . . . . . NiB $1430 Ex $1184 Gd $871
Safari left-hand, add $95

Remington Model 721A Deluxe

Remington Model 722A

MODEL 700 SENDERO BOLT-ACTION RIFLE
Same as Model 700 VS except chambered in long action and magnum .25-06 Rem., .270 Win., .280 Rem., 7mm Rem. Mag., .300 Win. Made 1994 to date.
Standard calibers . . . . NiB $669 Ex $566 Gd $335
Magnum calibers, add $30
SF Model (stainless fluted), add $115

MODEL 700 VLS (VARMIT LAMINATED STOCK)
BOLT-ACTION RIFLE. . . . . NiB $592 Ex $463 Gd $309
Same as Model 700 BDL Varmint Special except with 26-inch polished blue barrel. Laminated wood stock with alternating grain and wood color impregnated with phenolic resin and finished with a satin luster. Calibers: .222 Rem., .223 Rem., .22-250 Rem., .243 Win., 7mm-08 Rem., .308 Win. Weight: 9.4 lbs. Made 1995 to date.

MODEL 700 VS BOLT-ACTION RIFLE
Same as Model 700 BDL Varmint Special except w/26-inch matte blue or fluted stainless barrel. Textured black or gray synthetic stock reinforced with Kevlar, fiberglass and graphite with full length aluminum bedding block. Calibers: .22-250 Rem., .220 Swift, .223 Rem., .308 Win. Made 1992 to date.
Model 700 VS . . . . NiB $669 Ex $489 Gd $360
Model 700 VS SF (fluted barrel) . . . . NiB $715 Ex $587 Gd $424
Model 700 VS SF/SF-P
(Fluted & ported barrel) . . . . NiB $882 Ex $747 Gd $574

MODEL 720A BOLT-ACTION
HIGH POWER . . . . NiB $1313 Ex $1133 Gd $978
Modified M/1917 Enfield action. .257 Roberts, .270 Win., .30-06. Five shot box magazine. 22-inch bbl. Weight: About 8 lbs. Sights: Open rear; bead front, on ramp. Pistol-grip stock, checkered. Model 720R has 20-inch bbl.; Model 720S has 24-inch bbl. Made 1941.

MODEL 721A STANDARD GRADE
BOLT-ACTION HIGH-POWER RIFLE . . . . . NiB $412 Ex $360 Gd $299
Calibers: .270 Win., .30-06. Fourshot box magazine. 24-inch bbl. Weight: About 7.25 lbs. Sights: Open rear; bead front, on ramp. Plain sporting stock. Made 1948-62.

MODEL 721A MAGNUM
STANDARD GRADE . . . . NiB $566 Ex $438 Gd $360
Caliber: .264 Win. Mag. or .300 H&H Mag. Same as standard model except has 26-inch bbl. Three shot magazine and recoil pad. Weight: 8.25 lbs.

MODEL 721ADL/BDL DELUXE
Same as Model 721A Standard or Magnum except has deluxe checkered stock and/or select wood.
Model 721ADL Deluxe Grade . . . . NiB $644 Ex $566 Gd $438
Model 721ADL .300 Magnum Deluxe . . . . NiB $766 Ex $644 Gd $487
Model 721BDL Deluxe Special Grade . . . . NiB $651 Ex $541 Gd $400
Model 721BDL .300 Magnum Deluxe . . . . . NiB $724 Ex $608 Gd $459

MODEL 722A STANDARD GRADE SPORTER
Same as Model 721A bolt-action except shorter action. .222 Rem. mag., .243 Win., .257 Roberts, .308 Win., .300 Savage. Four or 5-shot magazine. Weight: 7-8 lbs. .222 Rem. introduced 1950; .244 Rem. introduced 1955. Made 1948-62.
.222 Rem. NiB $418 Ex $335 Gd $228
.244 Rem. NiB $380 Ex $304 Gd $208
.222 Rem. Mag. & .243 Win. . . . . . . NiB $483 Ex $386 Gd $263
Other Calibers . . . . NiB $412 Ex $335 Gd $206

MODEL 722ADL DELUXE GRADE
Same as Model 722A except has deluxe checkered stock.
Standard calibers . . . . NiB $566 Ex $463 Gd $309
.222 Rem. Deluxe Grade . . . . NiB $618 Ex $515 Gd $386
.244 Rem. Deluxe Grade . . . . NiB $721 Ex $644 Gd $386

MODEL 722BDL DELUXE SPECIAL GRADE
Same as Model 722ADL except select wood.
Standard calibers . . . . NiB $566 Ex $515 Gd $412
.222 Rem. Deluxe Special Grade . . . NiB $566 Ex $515 Gd $412
.224 Rem. Deluxe Special Grade . . . NiB $618 Ex $510 Gd $386

MODEL 725 KODIAK
MAGNUM RIFLE . . . . NiB $4120 Ex $3399 Gd $2060
Similar to Model 725ADL. Calibers: .375 H&H Mag., .458 Win. Mag. Three shot magazine. 26-inch bbl. with recoil reducer built into muzzle. Weight: About 9 lbs. Deluxe, reinforced Monte Carlo stock with recoil pad, black forend tip swivels, sling. Fewer than 100 made in 1961.

MODEL 725ADL BOLT-ACTION REPEATING RIFLE
Calibers: .222, .243, .244, .270, .280, .30-06. Four shot box mag. (5-shot in 222). 22-inch bbl. (24-inch in .222). Weight: About 7 lbs. Sights: Open rear, hooded ramp front. Monte Carlo comb stock w/pistol-grip, checkered, swivels. Made 1958-61.
.222 Rem., .243 Win., .244 Rem . . . NiB $741 Ex $592 Gd $403
.270 Win. . . . . NiB $721 Ex $566 Gd $360
.280 Win. . . . . NiB $824 Ex $695 Gd $412
.30-06 . . . . NiB $592 Ex $463 Gd $360

MODEL 788 CENTERFIRE BOLT-ACTION
Calibers: .222 Rem., .22-250, .223 Rem., 6mm Rem., .243 Win., 7mm-08 Rem., .308 Win., .30-30, .44 Rem. Mag. Three shot clip magazine (4-shot in .222 and .223 Rem.). 24-inch bbl. in .22s, 22-inch in other calibers. Weight: 7.5 lbs. with 24-inch bbl.; 7.25 lbs. with 22-inch bbl. Sights: Blade front on ramp; U-notch rear. Plain Monte Carlo stock. Made 1967-84.
.22-250, .223 Rem., 6mm Rem.,
.243 Win., .308 Win. . . . . NiB $386 Ex $283 Gd $196
.30-30 Win. . . . . NiB $449 Ex $366 Gd $259
7mm-08 Rem. NiB $451 Ex $360 Gd $245
.44 Mag. . . . . NiB $495 Ex $397 Gd $270
Left-hand (6mm Rem. and
.308 Win. 1972-79) . . . . NiB $399 Ex $325 Gd $231

Remington Nylon 11

Remington Nylon 12

NYLON 11 BOLT-ACTION
REPEATER . . . . NiB $257 Ex $154 Gd $93
Clip type. Caliber: .22 Short, Long, LR. six or 10-shot clip mag.
19.63-inch bbl. Weight: 4.5 lbs. Sights: Open rear; blade front.
Nylon stock. Made 1962-66.

NYLON 12 BOLT-ACTION
REPEATER . . . . NiB $257 Ex $154 Gd $93
Same as Nylon 11 except has tubular magazine holding 22 Short,
17 Long, 15 LR. Made 1962-66.

SLIDE- AND LEVER-ACTION RIFLES

MODEL SIX (6) SLIDE-ACTION
REPEATER . . . . NiB $418 Ex $335 Gd $228
Hammerless. Calibers: 6mm Rem., .243 Win., .270 Win. 7mm
Express Rem., .30-06, .308 Win. 22-inch bbl. Weight: 7.5 lbs.
Checkered Monte Carlo stock and forearm. Made 1981-88.

MODEL SIX (6) SLIDE-ACTION
REPEATER, PEERLESS GRADE . . . . NiB $1802 Ex $1545 Gd $927
Same as Model Six Standard except has engraved receiver. Made
1981-88.

MODEL SIX (6) SLIDE-ACTION REPEATER, PREMIUM GRADES
Same as Model Six Standard except has engraved receiver with gold
inlay. Made 1981-88.
Peerless D Grade . . . . NiB $1802 Ex $1596 Gd $953
Premier F Grade . . . . NiB $4185 Ex $3347 Gd $2276
Premier Gold F Grade . . . . NiB $5916 Ex $4733 Gd $3219

MODEL 12A, 12B, 12C, 12CS SLIDE-ACTION REPEATERS
Standard Grade. Hammerless. Takedown. Caliber: .22 Short, Long
or LR. Tubular magazine holds 15 Short, 12 Long or 10 LR cartridges. 22- or 24-inch round or octagonal bbl. Open rear sight,
bead front. Plain, half-pistol-grip stock and grooved slide handle of
walnut. Made 1909-36.
Model 12A . . . . NiB $515 Ex $309 Gd $206
Model 12B
(22 Short only w/octagon bbl.) . . . . NiB $644 Ex $489 Gd $309
Model 12C
(w/24-inch octagon bbl.) . . . . NiB $541 Ex $463 Gd $283
Model 12CS
(22 WRF w/24-inch octagon bbl.) . . . . NiB $515 Ex $386 Gd $257

MODEL 14A HIGH POWER
SLIDE-ACTION REPEATING RIFLE . . . . NiB $551 Ex $412 Gd $360
Standard grade. Hammerless. Takedown. Calibers: .25, .30, .32 and
.35 Rem. Five shot tubular magazine. 22-inch bbl. Weight: About
6.75 lbs. Sights: Open rear; bead front. Plain half-pistol-grip stock
and grooved slide handle of walnut. Made 1912-35.

MODEL 14R CARBINE . . . . NiB $875 Ex $695 Gd $412
Same as Model 14R except has 18.5-inch bbl., straight-grip stock,
weight: About 6 lbs.

MODEL 14.5 CARBINE . . . . NiB $875 Ex $669 Gd $386
Same as Model 14A Rifle except has 9-shot magazine, 18.5-inch
bbl.

MODEL 14.5 RIFLE . . . . NiB $978 Ex $695 Gd $463
Similar to Model 14A except calibers: .38-40 and .44-40, 11-shot
full magazine, 22.5-inch bbl. Made 1912 to early 1920's.

MODEL 25A SLIDE-ACTION
REPEATER . . . . NiB $875 Ex $515 Gd $386
Standard Grade. Hammerless. Takedown. Calibers: .25-20, .32-20.
10-shot tubular magazine. 24-inch bbl. Weight: About 5.5 lbs.
Sights: Open rear; bead front. Plain, pistol-grip stock, grooved slide
handle. Made 1923-36.

MODEL 25R CARBINE . . . . NiB $927 Ex $541 Gd $412
Same as Model 25A except has 18-inch bbl. Six shot magazine,
straight-grip stock, weight: About 4.5 lbs.

MODEL 121A
FIELDMASTER
SLIDE-ACTION REPEATER. . . . . NiB $566 Ex $412 Gd $257
Standard Grade. Hammerless. Takedown. Caliber: .22 Short, Long,
LR. Tubular magazine holds 20 Short, 15 Long or 14 LR cartridges.
24-inch round bbl. Weight: 6 lbs. Plain, pistol-grip stock and
grooved semi-beavertail slide handle. Made 1936-54.

MODEL 121S. . . . . NiB $547 Ex $438 Gd $298
Same as Model 121A except chambered for .22 Remington Special
(.22 W.R.F.). Magazine holds 12 rounds. Disc.

MODEL 121SB . . . . NiB $638 Ex $510 Gd $347
Same as Model 121A except smoothbore. Disc.

Remington Model 121A

Remington Model 141A
Gamemaster

Remington Model 572A

Remington Model 572BDL

MODEL 141A GAMEMASTER
SLIDE-ACTION REPEATER . . . . **NiB $412 Ex $283 Gd $196**
Standard Grade. Hammerless. Takedown. Calibers: .30, .32 and .35 Rem. Five shot tubular magazine. 24-inch bbl. Weight: About 7.75 lbs. Sights: Open rear; bead front, on ramp. Plain, pistol-grip stock, semibeavertail forend (slide-handle). Made 1936-50.

MODEL 572A FIELDMASTER
SLIDE-ACTION REPEATER . . . . **NiB $257 Ex $129 Gd $93**
Hammerless. Caliber: .22 Short, Long, LR. Tubular magazine holds 20 Short, 17 Long, 15 LR. 23-inch bbl. Weight: About 5.5 lbs. Sights: Open rear; ramp front. Pistol-grip stock, grooved forearm. Made 1955-88.

MODEL 572BDL DELUXE . . . . **NiB $309 Ex $206 Gd $103**
Same as Model 572A except has blade ramp front sight, sliding ramp rear; checkered stock and forearm. Made 1966 to date.

MODEL 572SB SMOOTH BORE . . . **NiB $322 Ex $257 Gd $175**
Same as Model 572A except smoothbore for .22 LR shot cartridges. Made 1961 to date.

MODEL 760 BICENTENNIAL
COMMEMORATIVE. . . . . **NiB $721 Ex $515 Gd $386**
Same as Model 760 except has commemorative inscription on receiver. Made 1976.

MODEL 760 CARBINE . . . . **NiB $566 Ex $438 Gd $206**
Same as Model 760 Rifle except made in calibers .270 Win., .280 Rem., .30-06 and .308 Win. only, has 18.5-inch bbl., weight: 7.25 lbs. Made 1961-80.

MODEL 760 GAMEMASTER
STANDARD GRADE SLIDE-ACTION REPEATING RIFLE
Hammerless. Calibers: .223 Rem., 6mm Rem., .243 Win., .257 Roberts, .270 Win. .280 Rem., .30-06, .300 Sav., .308 Win., .35 Rem. 22-inch bbl. Weight: About 7.5 lbs. Sights: Open rear; bead front, on ramp. Plain pistol-grip stock, grooved slide handle on early models; current production has checkered stock and slide handle. Made 1952-80.
.222 Rem. . . . . **NiB $1210 Ex $927 Gd $566**
.223 Rem. . . . . **NiB $1390 Ex $1019 Gd $618**
.257 Roberts . . . . **NiB $917 Ex $695 Gd $412**
Other calibers . . . . **NiB $875 Ex $721 Gd $232**

MODEL 760ADL
DELUXE GRADE . . . . **NiB $489 Ex $386 Gd $257**
Same as Model 760 except has deluxe checkered stock, standard or high comb, grip cap, sling swivels. Made 1953-63.

MODEL 760BDL
CUSTOM DELUXE . . . . **NiB $470 Ex $376 Gd $255**
Same as Model 760 Rifle except made in calibers .270, .30-06 and .308 only, has Monte Carlo cheekpiece stock forearm with black tip, basket-weave checkering. Available also in left-hand model. Made 1953-80.

MODEL 760D
PEERLESS GRADE . . . . **NiB $1287 Ex $1030 Gd $772**
Same as Model 760 except scroll engraved, fancy wood. Made 1953-80.

**Remington Model 760
Bicentennial Commemorative**

**Remington Model 760
Gamemaster**

Remington Model 7600 Carbine

Remington Model 7600 Rifle

Remington Nylon 76 Lever-Action

Remington Sportsman 76

MODEL 760F PREMIER GRADE
Same as Model 760 except extensively engraved with game scenes and scroll, finest grade wood. Also available with receiver inlaid with gold; adds 50 percent to value. Made 1953-80.
Premier F Grade . . . . NiB $2511 Ex $2008 Gd $1366
Premier Gold F Grade . . . . NiB $5916 Ex $4733 Gd $3219

**MODEL 7600 SLIDE-ACTION
CARBINE** . . . . NiB $515 Ex $335 Gd $232
Same general specifications as Model 7600 Rifle except has 18.5-inch bbl. and weighs 7.25 lbs. Made 1987 to date.

MODEL 7600 SLIDE-ACTION RIFLE . . . . . . NiB $489 Ex $391 Gd $232
Similar to Model Six except has lower grade finishes. Made 1981 to date.

MODEL 7600 SPECIAL PURPOSE . . . . NiB $463 Ex $360 Gd $206
Same general specification as the Model 7600, except chambered only in .270 or .30-06. Special Purpose matte black finish on all exposed metal. American walnut stock with SP nonglare finish.

NYLON 76 LEVER-ACTION REPEATER . . . . NiB $309 Ex $257 Gd $154
Short-throw lever action. Caliber: .22 LR. 14-shot buttstock tubular magazine. Weight: 4 lbs. Black or brown nylon stock and forend. Made 1962-64. Remington's only lever-action rifle.

SPORTSMAN 76 SLIDE-ACTION RIFLE . . . NiB $299 Ex $232 Gd $154
Caliber: .30-06, 4-shot magazine. 22-inch bbl. Weight: 7.5 lbs. Open rear sight; front blade mounted on ramp. Uncheckered hardwood stock and forend. Made 1985-87.

SEMIAUTOMATIC RIFLES

MODEL FOUR (4) AUTOLOADING RIFLE
Hammerless. Calibers: 6mm Rem., .243 Win., .270 Win. 7mm Express Rem., .30-06, .308 Win. 22-inch bbl. Weight: 7.5 lbs. Sights: Open rear; bead front, on ramp. Monte Carlo checkered stock and forearm. Made 1981-88.
Standard . . . . NiB $721 Ex $592 Gd $257
Peerless Grade (Engr. receiver) . . . . NiB $2060 Ex $1854 Gd $772
Premier Grade (Engr. receiver) . . . . NiB $3799 Ex $3038 Gd $2066
Prem. Gr. (Engr. rec., gold inlay) . . . . . . NiB $6244 Ex $4995 Gd $3397

MODEL FOUR DIAMOND
ANNIVERSARY LTD. EDITION $1030
Same as Model Four Standard except has engraved receiver w/inscription, checkered high-grade walnut stock and forend. Only 1,500 produced. Made 1981 only. (Value for new condition)

MODEL 8A AUTOLOADING RIFLE . . . . . . NiB $772 Ex $618 Gd $865
Standard Grade. Takedown. Calibers: .25, .30, .32 and .35 Rem. Five-shot, clip-loaded magazine. 22-inch bbl. Weight: 7.75 lbs. Sights: Adj. and dovetailed open rear; dovetailed bead front. Half-moon metal buttplate on plain straight-grip walnut stock; plain walnut forearm with thin curved end. Made 1906-1936.

MODEL 16 AUTOLOADING RIFLE . . . . . . NiB $412 Ex $309 Gd $180
Takedown. Closely resembles the Winchester Model 03 semiautomatic rifle. Calibers: .22 Short, .22 LR, 22 Rem. Auto. 15-shot tubular magazine in buttstock. 22-inch bbl. Weight: 5.75 lbs. Sights: Open rear; dovetailed bead front. Plain straight-grip stock and forearm. Made 1914-1928. Note: In 1918 this model was discontinued in all calibers except .22 Rem. Auto; specifications are for that model.

MODEL 24A AUTOLOADING RIFLE . . . . . NiB $412 Ex $283 Gd $180
Standard Grade. Takedown. Calibers: .22 Short only, .22 LR. only. Tubular magazine in buttstock, holds 15 Short or 10 LR. 21-inch bbl. Weight: About 5 lbs. Sights: Dovetailed adj. open rear; dovetailed bead front. Plain walnut straight-grip buttstock; plain walnut forearm. Made 1922-35.

MODEL 81A WOODSMASTER
AUTOLOADER . . . . NiB $541 Ex $412 Gd $232
Standard Grade. Takedown. Calibers: .30, .32 and .35 Rem., .300 Sav. Five shot box magazine (not detachable). 22-inch bbl. Weight: 8.25 lbs. Sights: Open rear; bead front. Plain walnut pistol-grip stock, forearm. Made 1936-50.

MODEL 241A SPEEDMASTER
AUTOLOADER . . . . NiB $309 Ex $257 Gd $154
Standard Grade. Takedown. Calibers: .22 Short only, .22 LR. only. Tubular magazine in buttstock, holds 15 Short or 10 LR. 24-inch bbl. Weight: About 6 lbs. Sights: Open rear, bead front. Plain walnut stock and forearm. Made 1935-51.

MODEL 550A AUTOLOADER . . . . . . NiB $232 Ex $154 Gd $77
Has "Power Piston" or floating chamber, which permits interchangeable use of 22 Short, Long or LR cartridges. Tubular magazine holds 22 Short, 17 Long, 15 LR. 24-inch bbl. Weight: About 6.25 lbs. Sights: Open rear; bead front. Plain, one-piece pistol-grip stock. Made 1941-71.

MODEL 550P . . . . NiB $232 Ex $154 Gd $77
Same as Model 550A except has peep rear sight, blade front, on ramp.

MODEL 550-2G . . . . NiB $309 Ex $232 Gd $129
"Gallery Special." Same as Model 550A except has 22-inch bbl., screweye for counter chain and fired shell deflector.

**Remington Sportsman 742
Canadian Centennial**

MODEL 552A SPEEDMASTER
AUTOLOADER . . . . NiB $232 Ex $154 Gd $77
Caliber: .22 Short, Long, LR. Tubular magazine holds 20 Short, 17 Long, 15 LR. 25-inch bbl. Weight: About 5.5 lbs. Sights: Open rear; bead front. Pistol-grip stock, semi-beavertail forearm. Made 1957-88.

MODEL 552BDL DELUXE . . . . NiB $299 Ex $196 Gd $129
Same as Model 552A except has checkered walnut stock and forearm. Made 1966 to date.

MODEL 552C CARBINE . . . . NiB $257 Ex $154 Gd $103
Same as Model 552A except has 21-inch bbl. Made 1961-77.

MODEL 552GS GALLERY SPECIAL . . . . NiB $299 Ex $196 Gd $129
Same as Model 552A except chambered for .22 Short only. Made 1957-77.

MODEL 740A WOODSMASTER AUTOLOADER
Standard Grade. Gas-operated. Calibers: .30-06 or .308. Four shot detachable box magazine. 22-inch bbl. Weight: About 7.5 lbs. Plain pistol-grip stock, semibeavertail forend with finger grooves. Sights: Open rear; ramp front. Made 1955-60.
Rifle model . . . . NiB $386 Ex $309 Gd $196
Carbine model . . . . NiB $438 Ex $360 Gd $232

MODEL 740ADL/BDL DELUXE
Same as Model 740A except has deluxe checkered stock, standard or high comb, grip cap, sling swivels. Model 740 BDL also has select wood. Made 1955-60.
Model 740 ADL Deluxe Grade . . . . NiB $592 Ex $463 Gd $232
Model 740 BDL Deluxe Special Grade . . . NiB $669 Ex $515 Gd $360

MODEL 742 BICENTENNIAL
COMMEMORATIVE. $721
Same as Model 742 Woodsmaster rifle except has commemorative inscription on receiver. Made 1976. (Value for new condition)

MODEL 742
CANADIAN CENTENNIAL $721
Same as Model 742 rifle except has commemorative inscription on receiver. Made 1967. Value is for rifle in new, unfired condition.

MODEL 742 CARBINE . . . . NiB $669 Ex $463 Gd $196
Same as Model 742 Woodsmaster Rifle except made in calibers .30-06 and .308 only, has 18.5-inch bbl., weight 6.75 lbs. Made 1961-80.

MODEL 742 WOODSMASTER
AUTOMATIC BIG GAME RIFLE . . . . NiB $608 Ex $412 Gd $201
Gas-operated semiautomatic. Calibers: 6mm Rem., .243 Win., .280 Rem., .30-06, .308 Win. Four shot clip magazine. 22-inch bbl. Weight: 7.5 lbs. Sights: Open rear; bead front, on ramp. Checkered pistol-grip stock and forearm. Made 1960-80.

GRADING: NiB = New in Box   Ex = Excellent or NRA 95%   Gd = Good or NRA 68%

Remington Model 7400

Remington Model 7400 Carbine

Remington Nylon 66
Bicentennial Commemorative

Remington Nylon 66 Mohawk

Remington Sportsman 74

MODEL 742BDL CUSTOM DELUXE...... NiB $566 Ex $463 Gd $232
Same as Model 742 Rifle except made in calibers .30-06 and .308 only, has Monte Carlo cheekpiece stock, forearm with black tip, basket-weave checkering. Available in left-hand model. Made 1966-80.

MODEL 742D PEERLESS GRADE......... NiB $1777 Ex $1468 Gd $927
Same as Model 742 except scroll engraved, fancy wood. Made 1961-80.

MODEL 742F PREMIER GRADE
Same as Model 742 except extensively engraved with game scenes and scroll, finest grade wood. Also available with receiver inlaid with gold; adds 50 percent to value. Made 1961-1980.
Premier F Grade .... NiB $3799 Ex $3038 Gd $2066
Premier Gold F Grade .... NiB $5916 Ex $4733 Gd $3219

MODEL 7400 AUTOLOADER
Similar to Model Four w/lower grade finishes. Made 1981 to date.
Model 7400 Standard .... NiB $438 Ex $360 Gd $201
Model 7400 HG
(High gloss finish) .... NiB $444 Ex $355 Gd $242

MODEL 7400 CARBINE .... NiB $438 Ex $309 Gd $232
Caliber: .30-06 only. Similar to the Model 7400 rifle except has 18.5-inch bbl. and weight: 7.25 lbs. Made 1988 to date.

MODEL 7400 SPECIAL PURPOSE........ NiB $438 Ex $335 Gd $206
Same general specification as the Model 7400 except chambered only in .270 or .30-06. Special Purpose matte black finish on metal. American walnut stock with SP nonglare finish. Made 1993-95.

NYLON 66 APACHE BLACK .... NiB $206 Ex $129 Gd $93
Same as Nylon 66 Mohawk Brown except bbl. and receiver cover chrome-plated, black stock. Made 1962-84.

**NYLON 66 BICENTENNIAL
COMMEMORATIVE** .... NiB $232 Ex $154 Gd $103
Same as Nylon 66 except has commemorative inscription on receiver. Made 1976.

NYLON 66MB AUTOLOADING RIFLE..... NiB $206 Ex $129 Gd $93
Similar to the early production Nylon 66 Black Apache except with blued bbl. and receiver cover. Made 1978-87.

**NYLON 66 MOHAWK
BROWN AUTOLOADER** .... NiB $154 Ex $103 Gd $88
Caliber: .22 LR. Tubular magazine in buttstock holds14 rounds. 19.5-inch bbl. Weight: About 4 lbs. Sights: Open rear; blade front. Brown nylon stock and forearm. Made 1959-87.

NYLON 77 CLIP REPEATER........ NiB $180 Ex $129 Gd $93
Same as Nylon 66 except has 5-shot clip magazine. Made 1970-71.

Rossi Model 62 Stainless Rifle

Rossi Model 62 Stainless Carbine

Rossi Model 62 WMR Rifle

Rossi Model 62 SAC Carbine

Rossi Model 62 Gallery Rifle

SPORTSMAN 74 AUTOLOADING RIFLE . . . . . **NiB $335 Ex $237 Gd $154**
Caliber: .30-06, 4-shot magazine. 22-inch bbl. Uncheckered buttstock and forend. Open rear sight; ramped blade front sight. Made 1985-88.

JOHN RIGBY & CO. — London, England

MODEL 275 MAGAZINE SPORTING RIFLE **NiB $6250 Ex $5000+ Gd $3400**
Mauser action. Caliber: .275 High Velocity or 7x57mm 5-shot box magazine. 25-inch bbl. Weight: about 7.5 lbs. Sights: Folding leaf rear; bead front. Sporting stock w/half-pistol-grip, checkered. Specifications given are those of current model; however, in general, they apply also to prewar model.

MODEL 275 LIGHTWEIGHT
MAGAZINE RIFLE . . . . **NiB $5000 Ex $4000+ Gd $2720**
Same as standard .275 rifle except has 21-inch bbl. Weight: 6.75 lbs.

MODEL 350 MAGNUM
MAGAZINE SPORTING RIFLE . . . . . . **NiB $4375 Ex $3500+ Gd $2380**
Mauser action. Caliber: .350 Magnum. Five shot box magazine. 24-inch bbl. Weight: About 7.75 lbs. Sights: Folding leaf rear; bead front. Sporting stock with full pistol-grip, checkered. Currently mfd.

MODEL 416 BIG GAME
MAGAZINE SPORTING RIFLE . . . . . . **NiB $7500 Ex $6000+ Gd $4080**
Mauser action. Caliber: .416 Big Game. Four shot box magazine. 24-inch bbl. Weight: 9 to 9.25 lbs. Sights: Folding leaf rear; bead front. Sporting stock with full pistol-grip, checkered. Currently mfd.

BEST QUALITY HAMMERLESS
EJECTOR DOUBLE RIFLE . . . . . . **NiB $48,750 Ex $39,000+ Gd $26,520**
Sidelocks. Calibers: .275 Magnum, .350 Magnum, .470 Nitro Express. 24- to 28-inch bbls. Weight: 7.5 to 10.5 lbs. Sights: Folding leaf rear; bead front. Checkered pistol-grip stock and forearm.

SECOND QUALITY HAMMERLESS
EJECTOR DOUBLE RIFLE . . . . . . **NiB $21,875 Ex $17,500 Gd $11,900**
Same general specifications as Best Quality double rifle except boxlock.

THIRD QUALITY HAMMERLESS
EJECTOR DOUBLE RIFLE . . . . **NiB $12,375 Ex $9900 Gd $6732**
Same as Second Quality double rifle except plainer finish and not of as high quality.

ROSS RIFLE CO. — Quebec, Canada

MODEL 1910 BOLT-ACTION
SPORTING RIFLE . . . . **NiB $618 Ex $201 Gd $180**
Straight-pull bolt-action with interrupted screw-type lugs. Calibers: .280 Ross, .303 British. Four shot or 5-shot magazine. Bbl. lengths: 22, 24, 26 inches. Sights: Two-leaf open rear; bead front. Checkered sporting stock. Weight: About 7 lbs. Made c. 1910 to end of World War I. Note: Most firearm authorities agree that this and other Ross models with interrupted screw-type lugs are unsafe to fire.

ROSSI RIFLES — Sao Leopoldo, Brazil Manufactured by Amadeo Rossi, S.A.

62 GALLERY MODEL SAC CARBINE
Same as standard Gallery Model except in .22 LR only with 16.25-inch bbl.; weight 5.5 lbs. Imported 1975-98.
Blued finish . . . . **NiB $191 Ex $154 Gd $93**
Nickel finish . . . . **NiB $206 Ex $165 Gd $118**
Stainless. . . . . **NiB $257 Ex $185 Gd $124**

62 GALLERY MODEL MAGNUM . . . . **NiB $196 Ex $165 Gd $103**
Same as standard Gallery Model except chambered for .22 WMR, 10-shot magazine. Imported 1975-98.

Ruger Number One (1)
Light Sporter

Ruger Number One (1)
Medium Sporter

Ruger Number One
"North Americans"

62 GALLERY MODEL SLIDE-ACTION REPEATER
Similar to Winchester Model 62. Calibers: .22 LR. Long, Short or .22 WMR. Tubular magazine holds 13 LR, 16 Long, 20 Short. 23-inch bbl. 39.25 inches overall. Weight: 5.75 lbs. Sights: Open rear; bead front. Straight-grip stock, grooved slide handle. Blued, nickel or stainless finish. Imported 1970-98. Values same as SAC Model.

LEVER-ACTION 65/92 CARBINE
Similar to Winchester Model 92. Caliber: .38 Special/.357 Mag., .44 Mag., .44-40, .45 LC. 8- or 10-shot magazine. 16-, 20- or 24-inch round or half-octagonal bbl. Weight: 5.5 to 6 lbs. 33.5- to 41.5-inches overall. Satin blue, chrome or stainless finish. Brazilian hardwood buttstock and forearm. Made 1978-98.

Model M92 SRC .45LC	NiB $360	Ex $283	Gd $196
Model M92 SRC .38/357, .44 Mag	NiB $360	Ex $283	Gd $196
Model M92 w/octagon bbl	NiB $386	Ex $206	Gd $201
Model M92 LL Lever	NiB $360	Ex $232	Gd $180
Engraved, add			$75
Chrome, add			$25
Stainless, add			$75

RUGER RIFLES — Southport, Connecticut Manufactured by Sturm, Ruger & Co.

NUMBER ONE (1) LIGHT SPORTER . . . . . . NiB $669 Ex $541 Gd $257
Same as No.1 Standard except has 22-inch bbl., folding leaf rear sight on quarter-rib and ramp front sight, Henry pattern forearm. Made 1966 to date.

NUMBER ONE (1) MEDIUM SPORTER . . . NiB $618 Ex $489 Gd $283
Same as No. 1 Light Sporter except has 26-inch bbl. 22-inch in 45-70); weight: 8 lbs (7.25 lbs. in .45-70). Calibers: 7mm Rem. Mag., .300 Win. Mag., .45-70. Made 1966 to date.

**NUMBER ONE (1) "NORTH AMERICANS"
PRESENTATION RIFLE** $52,560
Same general specifications as the Ruger No. 1 Standard except highly

(cont'd.) **NUMBER ONE (1) "NORTH AMERICANS" PRESENTATION RIFLE**
customized with elaborate engravings, carvings, fine-line checkering and gold inlays. A series of 21 is planned, each rifle depicting a North American big-game animal, chambered in the caliber appropriate to the game. Stock is of Northern California English walnut. Comes in trunk-style Huey case with Leupold scope and other accessories.

**NUMBER ONE (1) RSI INTERNATIONAL
SINGLE-SHOT RIFLE** . . . . NiB $618 Ex $463 Gd $299
Similar to the No. 1 Light Sporter except with lightweight 20-inch bbl. and full Mannlicher-style forend, in calibers .243 Win., .270 Win., 7x57mm, .30-06. Weight: 7.25 lbs.

**NUMBER ONE (1)
SPECIAL VARMINTER** . . . . NiB $618 Ex $463 Gd $299
Same as No. 1 Standard except has heavy 24-inch bbl. with target scope bases, no quarter-rib. Weight: 9 lbs. Calibers: .22-250, .25-06, 7mm Rem. Mag., .300 Win. Mag. Made 1966 to date.

**NUMBER ONE (1)
STANDARD RIFLE** . . . . NiB $608 Ex $438 Gd $283
Falling-block single-shot action with Farquharson-type lever. Calibers: .22-250, .243 Win., 6mm Rem., .25-06, .270 Win., .30-06, 7mm Rem. Mag., .300 Win. Mag. 26-inch bbl. Weight: 8 lbs. No sights, has quarter-rib for scope mounting. Checkered pistol-grip buttstock and semi-beavertail forearm, QD swivels, rubber buttplate. Made 1966 to date.

NUMBER ONE (1) TROPICAL RIFLE. . . . . . NiB $669 Ex $536 Gd $309
Same as No. 1 Light Sporter except has heavy 24-inch bbl.; calibers are .375 H&H .404 Jeffery, .416 Rigby, and .458 Win. Mag. Weight: 8.25 to 9 lbs. Made 1966 to date.

**NUMBER THREE (3) SINGLE-SHOT
CARBINE** . . . . NiB $463 Ex $412 Gd $232
Falling-block action with American-style lever. Calibers: .22 Hornet .223 Rem., .30-40 Krag, .357 Win., .44 Mag., .45-70. 22-inch bbl. Weight: 6 lbs. Sights: Folding leaf rear; gold bead front. Carbine-style stock w/curved buttplate, forearm with bbl. band. Made 1972-87.

Ruger Number One "North Americans" Presentation Set

Ruger No. 1
International

Ruger No. 1
Special Varminter

Ruger No. 1
Standard Rifle

Ruger No. 1 Tropical Rifle

RIFLES

Ruger No. 3 Single-Shot Carbine

Ruger Model 10/22
Standard Rifle

Ruger Model 10/22
Deluxe Rifle

Ruger Model 44
Autoloading Carbine

MODEL 10/22 AUTOLOADING CARBINE

Caliber: .22 LR. Detachable 10-shot rotary magazine. 18.5-inch bbl. Weight: 5 lbs. Sights: Folding leaf rear; bead front. Carbine-style stock with bbl. band and curved buttplate (walnut stock discontinued 1980). Made 1964 to date. International and Sporter versions discontinued 1971.

10/22 Standard Carbine (Walnut stock) . . . . NiB $257 Ex $196 Gd $103
10/22 Int'l. (w/Mannlicher
style stock, swivels) Disc.1971. . . . . NiB $566 Ex $412 Gd $309
10/22 RB (Birch stock, blued) . . . . NiB $180 Ex $129 Gd $93
K10/22 RB (Birch stock, stainless) . . . . NiB $185 Ex $154 Gd $103
10/22 Sporter (MC stock,
flat buttplate, swivels) Disc.1971. . . . . NiB $185 Ex $154 Gd $103
10/22 SP Deluxe Sporter (made since 1966). . . . NiB $238 Ex $190 Gd $130
10/22 RBI Int'l. (blued); made since 1994 . . NiB $226 Ex $1780 Gd $123
10/22 RBI Int'l. (stainless); made since 1995 . . . . NiB $251 Ex $201 Gd $137

MODEL 44 AUTOLOADING CARBINE

Gas-operated. Caliber: .44 Magnum. Four shot tubular magazine (with magazine release button since 1967). 18.5-inch bbl. Weight: 5.75 lbs. Sights: Folding leaf rear; gold bead front. Carbine-style stock w/bbl. band and curved buttplate. Made 1961-86. International and Sporter versions discontinued 1971.

Model 44 Standard autoloading carbine. . . NiB $463 Ex $360 Gd $247
Model 44 Int'l (w/Mannlicher-
style stock, swivels). . . . . NiB $611 Ex $515 Gd $412
Mdl. 44 Sporter (MC stk. w/fingergroove). . . NiB $618 Ex $669 Gd $463
Model 44RS Carbine
(w/rear peep sight, disc. 1978) . . . . NiB $566 Ex $412 Gd $304

MODEL 77 BOLT-ACTION RIFLE

Receiver with integral scope mount base or with round top. Short stroke or magnum length action (depending on caliber) in the former type receiver, magnum only in the latter. .22-250, .220 Swift, 6mm Rem., .243 Win., .250-3000, .25-06, .257 Roberts, 6.5 Rem. Mag., .270 Win., 7x57mm,

(cont'd.) MODEL 77 BOLT-ACTION RIFLE

7mm-08 7mm Rem. Mag., .280 Rem., .284 Win., .308 Win., .30-06, .300 Win. Mag. .338 Win. Mag., .350 Rem. Mag., .458 Win. Mag. Five shot magazine standard, 4-shot in .220 Swift, 3-shot in magnum calibers. 22 24- or 26-inch bbl. (depending on caliber). Weight: About 7 lbs.; .458 Mag. model, 8.75 lbs. Round-top model furnished w/folding leaf rear sight and ramp front; integral base model furnished w/scope rings,with or w/o open sights. Stock w/checkered pistol grip and forearm, pistol-grip cap, rubber recoil pad, QD swivel studs. Made 1968-92.

Model 77, integral base, no sights . . . . NiB $463 Ex $391 Gd $206
6.5 Rem. Mag., add. $75
.284 Win., add $30
.338 Win. Mag., add $50
.350 Rem. Mag., 6.5 Rem. Mag., add $75
Model 77RL Ultra Light, no sights, ... NiB $463 Ex $360 Gd $232
Model 77RL Ultra Light, open sights . . . . . . NiB $474 Ex $381 Gd $257
Model 77RS, integral base, open sights . . . NiB $470 Ex $375 Gd $255
.338 Win. Mag., .458 Win. Mag.,
with standard stock, add. $75
Model 77RSC, .458 Win. Mag. with
fancy Circassian walnut stock, add $525
Model 77RSI International, Mannlicher
stock, short action, 18.5-inch bbl., 7 lbs. . . . . NiB $463 Ex $360 Gd $232
Model 77ST, round top, open sights . . . . . . NiB $474 Ex $371 Gd $288
.338 Win. Mag., add. $50
Model 77V, Varmint,
integral base, no sights . . . . NiB $463 Ex $391 Gd $206
Model 77NV, Varmint, integral base, no sights, stainless
steel barrel, laminated wood stock . . . . NiB $489 Ex $402 Gd $257

MODEL 77 MARK II ALL-WEATHER RIFLE . . . NiB $463 Ex $360 Gd $232

Revised Model 77 action. Same general specifications as Model M-77 Mark II except with stainless bbl. and action. Zytel injection-molded stock. Calibers: .223, .243, .270, .308, .30-06, 7mm Mag., .300 Win. Mag., .338 Win. Mag. Made 1990 to date.

Ruger Model 77 Round Top Receiver

Ruger Model 77
Ultra-Light Carbine

Ruger Model 77
International Carbine

Ruger Model 77
Varmint Rifle

Ruger Model 77 Mark II
All-Weather Rifle

MODEL 77 MARK II BOLT-ACTION RIFLE

Revised Model 77 action. Same general specifications as Model M-77 except with new 3-position safety and fixed blade ejector system. Calibers .22 PPC, .223 Rem., 6mm PPC, 6.5x55 Swedish, .375 H&H, .404 Jeffery and .416 Rigby also available. Weight: 6 to 10.25 lbs. Made 1989 to date.

Model 77 MKIIR, integral base, no sights . . NiB $463 Ex $360 Gd $232
Left-hand Model 77LR MKII, add $25
Model 77RL MKII, Ultra Light, no sights. . . NiB $463 Ex $391 Gd $206
Model 77RLS MKII, Ultra
Light, open sights . . . . NiB $463 Ex $402 Gd $257
Model 77RS MKII, integral base, open sights . . . NiB $470 Ex $376 Gd $255
Model 77RS MKII, Express, with fancy French
walnut stock, integral base, open sights . NiB $1236 Ex $1004 Gd $669
Model 77RSI MKII,
International, Mannlicher . . . . NiB $509 Ex $407 Gd $277
Model 77RSM MKII magnum, with fancy Circassian
walnut stock, integral base, open sights. . . . . NiB $1329 Ex $1020 Gd $711
Model 77VT (VBZ or VTM)
MKII Varmint/Target stainless steel action,
laminated wood stock. . . . . NiB $489 Ex $402 Gd $257

MODEL 77/.22 HORNET BOLT-ACTION RIFLE

Mini-Sporter built on the 77/.22 action in caliber .22 Hornet. Six shot rotary magazine. 20- inch bbl. 40 inches overall. Weight: 6 lbs. Receiver machined for Ruger rings (included). Beaded front sight and open adj. rear, or no sights. Blued or stainless finish. Checkered American walnut stock. Made 1994 to date.

(cont'd.) MODEL 77/.22 HORNET BOLT-ACTION RIFLE

Model 77/.22RH (rings, no sights) . . . . NiB $335 Ex $309 Gd $206
Model 77/.22RSH (rings & sights). . . . . NiB $360 Ex $309 Gd $206
Model 77/.22VHZ (S/S w/
laminated wood stock) . . . . NiB $386 Ex $360 Gd $232

MODEL 77/.22 RIMFIRE BOLT-ACTION RIFLE

Calibers: .22 LR. or .22 WMR. 10-shot (.22 LR) or 9-shot (.22 WMR) rotary magazine. 20-inch bbl. 39.75 inches overall. Weight: 5.75 lbs. Integral scope bases; with or w/o sights. Checkered American walnut or Zytel injection-molded stock. Stainless or blued finish. Made 1983 to date. (Blued); stainless. Introduced 1989.

77/.22 R, rings, no sights, walnut stock . . . . . . NiB $354 Ex $283 Gd $193
77/.22 RS, rings, sights, walnut. . . . . NiB $360 Ex $283 Gd $206
77/.22 RP, rings, no sights, synthetic stock . . . . NiB $289 Ex $232 Gd $158
77/.22 RSP, rings, sights, synthetic stock . . . . . NiB $315 Ex $252 Gd $172
K77/.22 RP, S/S rings, no sights, synthetic . . . . NiB $367 Ex $294 Gd $200
K77/.22 RSP, S/S, rings, sights, synthetic . . . . . NiB $380 Ex $304 Gd $207
77/.22 RM, .22 WMR,
rings, no sights, walnut . . . . NiB $360 Ex $283 Gd $196
77/.22 RSM, .22 WMR, rings, sights, walnut . . . NiB $386 Ex $299 Gd $206
K77/.22 RSMP, .22 WMR, S/S, rings,
sights, synthetic. . . . . NiB $380 Ex $304 Gd $207
K77/.22 RMP, .22 WMR,
S/S, no sights, synthetic . . . . NiB $354 Ex $283 Gd $193
K77/.22 VBZ, .22 WMR,
no sights, laminated. (1993) . . . . NiB $380 Ex $304 Gd $207

Ruger Model 77 Mark II

Ruger Model 77/.22 Rimfire

Ruger Model 77/.22 All Weather

Ruger Model 77/.44 All Weather

MODEL 77/.44 BOLT-ACTION
Short-action, carbine-style M77 similar to the 77/.22RH. Chambered .44 Rem. Mag. Four shot rotary magazine. 18.5-inch bbl. 38.25 inches overall. Weight: 6 lbs. Gold bead front sight, folding adjustable rear w/integral scope base and Ruger rings. Blue or stainless finish. Synthetic or checkered American walnut stock w/rubber buttpad and swivels. Made 1997 to date.
Model 77/.44 blued............ NiB $489 Ex $360 Gd $232
Model 77/.44 stainless........... NiB $505 Ex $371 Gd $237

MODEL 96 LEVER ACTION CARBINE
Caliber: .22 LR. .22 Mag., .44 Mag. Detachable 10-, 9- or 4-shot magazine. 18.5-inch bbl. Weight: 5.25 lbs. Front gold bead sights. Drilled and tapped for scope. American hardwood stock. Made 1996 to date.
.22 Long Rifle .... NiB $257 Ex $206 Gd $134
.22 Magnum .... NiB $268 Ex $232 Gd $144
.44 Magnum .... NiB $444 Ex $355 Gd $242

MINI-14 SEMIAUTOMATIC RIFLE
Gas-operated. Caliber: .223 Rem. (5.56mm). 5-, 10- or 20-shot box magazine. 18.5-inch bbl. Weight: About 6.5 lbs. Sights: Peep rear; blade front mounted on removable barrel band. Pistol-grip stock w/curved buttplate, handguard. Made 1976 to date.
Mini-14/5 blued .... NiB $541 Ex $505 Gd $309
K-Mini-14/5 stainless steel .... NiB $566 Ex $515 Gd $360

(cont'd.) MINI-14 SEMIAUTOMATIC RIFLE
Mini-14/5F blued, folding stock .... NiB $721 Ex $608 Gd $412
K-Mini-14/5F stainless, folding stock ..... NiB $747 Ex $618 Gd $438
Mini-14 Ranch Rifle,
scope model, 6.25 lbs. .... NiB $566 Ex $515 Gd $309
K-Mini-1H Ranch Rifle,
scope model, stainless.................. NiB $592 Ex $541 Gd $334

MINI-THIRTY (30) AUTOLOADER
Caliber: 7.62 x 39mm. 5-shot detachable magazine. 18.5-inch bbl. 37.25 inches overall. Weight: 7 lbs. 3 oz. Designed for use with telescopic sights. Walnut stained stock. Sights: Peep rear; blade front mounted on bbl. band. Blued or stainless finish. Made 1986 to date.
Blued........................ NiB $566 Ex $515 Gd $299
Stainless..................... NiB $592 Ex $566 Gd $309

PC SERIES SEMIAUTOMATIC CARBINES
Calibers: 9mm Parabellum or .40 S&W. 10-shot magazine. 15.25-inch bbl. Weight: 6.25 lbs. Integral Ruger scope mounts with or without sights. Optional blade front sight, adjustable open rear. Matte black oxide finish. Matte black Zytel stock w/checkered pistol-grip and forearm. Made 1997 to date.
Model PC9 (w/o sights).......... NiB $437 Ex $386 Gd $232
Model PC40 (w/o sights)......... NiB $463 Ex $412 Gd $257
W/adjustable sights, add $40

RIFLES

Ruger Model 96 Lever-Action

Ruger Model 96/44M Lever-Action

Ruger Mini-14 Semiautomatic

Ruger Mini-14 with Folding Stock

Ruger Mini-Thirty Autoloader

Ruger Model PC9 Carbine

Ruger Model PC9 w/Ghost Ring Sights

RUSSIAN MILITARY RIFLES — Principal U.S.S.R. Arms Plant, Tula

MODEL 1891
MOSIN MILITARY RIFLE . . . . **NiB $412 Ex $103 Gd $57**
Nagant system bolt action. Caliber: 7.62mm Russian. Five shot box magazine. 31.5-inch bbl. Weight: About 9 lbs. Sights: Open rear; blade front. Full stock w/straight grip. Specifications given are for WWII version; earlier types differ slightly. Note: In 1916, Remington Arms Co. and New England Westinghouse Co. produced 250,000 of these rifles on a contract from the Imperial Russian Government. Few were delivered to Russia and the balance bought by the U.S. Government for training in 1918. Eventually, many of these rifles were sold to N.R.A. members for about $3 each by the Director of Civilian Marksmanship.

TOKAREV MODEL 40 SEMIAUTOMATIC
MILITARY RIFLE . . . . **NiB $772 Ex $360 Gd $206**
Gas-operated. Caliber: 7.62mm Russian. 10-shot detachable box magazine. 24.5-inch bbl. Muzzle brake. Weight: About 9 lbs. Sights: Leaf rear, hooded post front. Full stock w/pistol grip. Differences among Models 1938, 1940 and 1941 are minor.

SAKO RIFLES — Riihimaki, Finland Manufactured by Sako L.T.D.

Formerly imported by Stoeger Industries, Wayne NJ (formerly by Garcia Corp.) until 2000. Imported by Beretta USA 2001 to date.

MODEL 72 . . . . **NiB $978 Ex $772 Gd $566**
Single model designation replacing Vixen Sporter, Vixen Carbine, Vixen Heavy Barrel, Forester Sporter, Forester Carbine, Forester Heavy Barrel, Finnbear Sporter, and Finnbear Carbine, with same specifications, except all but heavy barrel models fitted with open rear sight. Values same as for corresponding earlier models. Imported 1972-74.

MODEL 73 LEVER-ACTION RIFLE . . . . . . **NiB $1030 Ex $875 Gd $566**
Same as Finnwolf except has 3-shot clip magazine, flush floorplate; stock has no cheekpiece. Imported 1973-75.

MODEL 74 CARBINE . . . . **NiB $978 Ex $644 Gd $505**
Long Mauser-type bolt action. Caliber: .30-06. Five shot magazine. 20-inch bbl. Weight: 7.5 lbs. No sights. Checkered Mannlicher-type full stock of European walnut, Monte Carlo cheekpiece. Imported 1974-78.

MODEL 74 HEAVY BARREL RIFLE,
LONG ACTION . . . . **NiB $978 Ex $644 Gd $412**
Same specifications as short action except w/24-inch heavy bbl., weighs 8.75 lbs.; magnum w/4-shot magazine. Calibers: .25-06, 7mm Rem. Mag. Imported 1974-78.

MODEL 74 HEAVY BARREL RIFLE,
MEDIUM ACTION . . . . **NiB $978 Ex $644 Gd $412**
Same specifications as short action except w/23-inch heavy bbl., weighs 8.5 lbs. Calibers: .220 Swift, .22-250, .243 Win., .308 Win. Imported 1974-78.

MODEL 74 HEAVY BARREL RIFLE,
SHORT ACTION . . . . **NiB $1030 Ex $824 Gd $463**
Mauser-type bolt action. Calibers: .222 Rem., .223 Rem. Five shot magazine. 23.5-inch heavy bbl. Weight: 8.25 lbs. No sights. Target-style checkered European walnut stock w/beavertail forearm. Imported 1974-78.

MODEL 74 SUPER SPORTER,
LONG ACTION . . . . **NiB $978 Ex $678 Gd $412**
Same specifications as short action except w/24-inch bbl., weight: 8 lbs.; magnums have 4-shot magazine, recoil pad. Calibers: .25-06, .270 Win. 7mm Rem. Mag., .30-06, .300 Win. Mag., .338 Win. Mag., .375 H&H Mag. Imported 1974-78.

MODEL 74 SUPER SPORTER,
MEDIUM ACTION . . . . **NiB $1004 Ex $695 Gd $438**
Same specifications as short action except weight: 7.25 lbs. Calibers: .220 Swift, .22-250, .243 Win. Imported 1974-78.

MODEL 74 SUPER SPORTER,
SHORT ACTION . . . . **NiB $1004 Ex $669 Gd $412**
Mauser-type bolt action. Calibers: .222 Rem., .223 Rem. Five shot magazine. 23.5-inch bbl. Weight: 6.5 lbs. No sights. Checkered European walnut stock w/Monte Carlo cheekpiece, QD swivel studs. Imported 1974, now disc.

MODEL 75 DELUXE . . . . **NiB $1281 Ex 1025 Gd $697**
Same specifications as Sako 75 Hunter Model except w/hinged floor plate, deluxe high gloss checkered walnut stock w/rosewood forend cap and grip cap w/silver inlay. Imported 1998 to date.

MODEL 75 HUNTER . . . . **NiB $1004 Ex $747 Gd $515**
New bolt action design available in four action lengths fitted with a new bolt featuring three front locking lugs with an external extractor positioned under the bolt. Calibers: .17 Rem., .222 Rem., .223 Rem., (I); .22-250 Rem., .243 Win., 7mm-08 Rem., .308 Win., (III); .25-06 Rem., .270 Win., .280 Rem., .30-06, (IV); 7mm Rem Mag., .300 Win. Mag., .300 Wby. Mag., .338 Win. Mag. 7mm STW, .300 Wby. Mag., .340 Wby. Mag., .375 H&H Mag. and .416 Rem. Mag.,(V). 4-, 5- or 6-shot magazine w/detachable magazine. 22-, 24-, and 26-inch bbls. 41.75 to 45.6 inches over all. Weight: 6.3 to 9 lbs. Sako dovetail scope base integral with receiver with no sights. Checkered high-grade walnut stock w/recoil pad and sling swivels. Made 1997 to date.

MODEL 75 STAINLESS SYNTHETIC . . . . . **NiB $1062 Ex $850 Gd $578**
Similar to Model 75 Hunter except chambered for .22-250 Rem., .243 Win., .25-06 Rem., .270 Win., 7mm-08 Rem., 7mm STW, .30-06, .308 Win., 7mm Rem Mag., .300 Win. Mag., .338 Win. Mag. or .375 H&H Mag. 22-, 24-, and 26-inch bbls. Black composite stock w/soft rubber grips inserts. Matte stainless steel finish. Made 1997 to date.

MODEL 75 VARMINT RIFLE . . . . . . **NiB $772 Ex $566 Gd $386**
Similar to Model 75 Hunter except chambered .17 Rem., .222 Rem., .223 Rem. and .22-250 Rem. 24-inch bbl. Matte lacquered walnut stock w/beavertail forearm. Made 1998 to date.

MODEL 78 SUPER HORNET SPORTER. . . . **NiB $566 Ex $438 Gd $283**
Same specifications as Model 78 Rimfire except chambered for .22 Hornet, 4-shot magazine. Imported 1977-87.

MODEL 78 SUPER RIMFIRE SPORTER . . . . **NiB $515 Ex $412 Gd $232**
Bolt action. Caliber: .22 LR. Five shot magazine. 22.5-inch bbl. Weight, 6.75 lbs. No sights. Checkered European walnut stock, Monte Carlo cheekpiece. Imported 1977-86.

CLASSIC BOLT-ACTION RIFLE
Medium Action (.243. Win.) or Long Action (.270 Win. .30-06, 7mm Rem. Mag.). American walnut stock. Made 1980-86. Reintroduced in 1993 w/matte lacquer finish stock, 22- or 24-inch bbl., overall length of 42 to 44 inches, weight 6.88 to 7.25lbs. Imported 1992-97.
Standard calibers . . . . **NiB $869 Ex $695 Gd $473**
Magnum caliber . . . . **NiB $933 Ex $747 Gd $508**
Left-hand models . . . . **NiB $946 Ex $757 Gd $515**

Sako Model 73

Sako Model 74 Carbine

Sako Model 74 Super Sporter

Sako Model 74 Super Rimfire

Sako Model 75 Hunter

Sako 75 Stainless Synthetic

Sako Model 75 Varmint Rifle

Sako Classic

RIFLES

Sako Deluxe Lightweight

Sako Fiberglass

Sako Finnfire

Sako Finnfire Heavy Barrel

Sako Finnwolf

DELUXE GRADE AI . . . . **NiB $978 Ex $669 Gd $438**
Same specifications as Standard Grade except w/22 lines to the inch
French checkering, rosewood grip cap and forend tip, semibeaver-
tail forend. Disc.

DELUXE GRADE AII . . . . **NiB $1004 Ex $695 Gd $463**
Same specifications as Standard Grade except w/22 lines per inch
French checkering, rosewood grip cap and forend tip, semi beaver-
tail forend. Disc.

DELUXE GRADE AIII . . . . **NiB $1313 Ex $1009 Gd $618**
Same specifications as w/standard except w/French checkering,
rosewood grip cap and forend tip, semibeavertail forend. Disc.

DELUXE LIGHTWEIGHT
BOLT-ACTION RIFLE . . . . **NiB $1088 Ex $870 Gd $592**
Same general specifications as Hunter Lightweight except w/beauti-
fully grained French walnut stock; superb high-gloss finish, fine
hand-cut checkering, rosewood forend tip and grip cap. Imported
1985-97.

FIBERCLASS BOLT-ACTION
RIFLE . . . . **NiB $1030 Ex $927 Gd $541**
All-weather fiberglass stock version of Sako barreled long action.
Calibers: .25-06, .270, .30-06, 7mm Rem. Mag., .300 Win. Mag.,
.338 Win. Mag., .375 H&H Mag. Bbl. length: 22.5 inches. Overall
length: 44.25 inches. Weight: 7.25 lbs. Imported 1984-96.

FINNBEAR CARBINE . . . . **NiB $1133 Ex $824 Gd $489**
Same as Finnbear Sporter except w/20-inch bbl., Mannlicher-type
full stock. Imported 1971. Disc.

FINNBEAR SPORTER . . . . **NiB $1081 Ex $824 Gd $489**
Long Mauser-type bolt action. Calibers: .25-06, .264 Mag. .270,
.30-06, .300 Win. Mag., .338 Mag., 7mm Mag., .375 H&H Mag.
Magazine holds 5 standard or 4 magnum cartridges. 24-inch bbl.
Weight: 7 lbs. Hooded ramp front sight. Sporter stock w/Monte
Carlo cheekpiece, checkered pistol-grip and forearm, recoil pad,
swivels. Imported 1961-71.

FINNFIRE BOLT-ACTION RIFLE
Mini-Sporter built for rimfires on a scaled-down Sako design.
Caliber: .22 LR. 5- or 10-shot magazine. 22-inch bbl. 39.5 inches
overall. Weight: 5.25 lbs. Receiver machined for 11mm dovetail
scope rings. Beaded blade front sight, open adj. rear. Blued finish.
Checkered European walnut stock. Imported 1994 to date.
Hunter model . . . . **NiB $721 Ex $608 Gd $438**
Varmint model. . . . . **NiB $819 Ex $618 Gd $463**
Sporter model . . . . **NiB $933 Ex $747 Gd $508**

FINNWOLF LEVER-ACTION RIFLE . . . . **NiB $998 Ex $798 Gd $543**
Hammerless. Calibers: .243 Win., .308 Win. Four shot clip magazine. 23-inch bbl. Weight: 6.75 lbs. Hooded ramp front sight. Sporter
stock w/Monte Carlo cheekpiece, checkered pistol-grip and forearm,
swivels (available w/right- or left-hand stock). Imported 1963-72.

Sako Forester Sporter

Sako Golden Anniversary

Sako Hunter Lightweight

FINSPORT 2700 . . . . **NiB $875 Ex $721 Gd $463**
Bolt-action centerfire rifle. Calibers: .270, .30-06, 7mm Rem. Mag., .300 Win. Mag. Bbl. length: 24 inches. Weight: 8 lbs. Imported 1984-86.

FORESTER CARBINE . . . . **NiB $1081 Ex $953 Gd $489**
Same as Forester Sporter except w/20-inch bbl., Mannlicher-type full stock. Imported 1958-71.

FORESTER HEAVY BARREL . . . . . . **NiB $1030 Ex $927 Gd $438**
Same as Forester Sporter except w/24-inch heavy bbl. Weight 7.5 lbs. Imported 1958-71.

FORESTER SPORTER . . . . **NiB $1133 Ex $953 Gd $463**
Medium-length Mauser-type bolt action. Calibers: .22-250, .243 Win., .308 Win. Five shot magazine. 23-inch bbl. Weight: 6.5 lbs. Hooded ramp front sight. Sporter stock w/Monte Carlo cheekpiece, checkered pistol grip and forearm, swivels. Imported 1957-71.

GOLDEN ANNIVERSARY MODEL . . . . **NiB $2668 Ex $2024 Gd $1339**
Special presentation-grade rifle issued in 1973 to commemorate Sako's 50th anniversary. 1,000 (numbered 1 to 1,000) made. Same specifications as Deluxe Sporter: Long action, 7mm Rem. Mag. receiver, trigger guard and floorplate decorated w/gold oak leaf and acorn motif. Stock of select European walnut, checkering bordered w/hand-carved oak leaf pattern.

HIGH-POWER MAUSER SPORTING RIFLE . . . . . . **NiB $1030 Ex $927 Gd $721**
FN Mauser action. Calibers: .270, .30-06. Five shot magazine. 24-inch bbl. Sights: Open rear leaf; Partridge front; hooded ramp. Checkered stock w/Monte Carlo comb and cheekpiece. Weight: 7.5 lbs. Imported 1950-57.

HUNTER LIGHTWEIGHT BOLT-ACTION RIFLE
5- or 6-shot magazine. Bbl. length: 21.5 inches, AI; 22 inches, AII; 22.5 inches, AIII. Overall length: 42.25-44.5 inches. Weight: 5.75 lbs., AI; 6.75 lbs. AII; 7.25 lbs., AIII. Monte Carlo-style European walnut stock, oil finished. Hand-checkered pistol-grip and forend. Imported 1985-97. Left-hand version intro. 1987.
AI (Short Action) .17 Rem. . . . . **NiB $1004 Ex $721 Gd $515**
.222 Rem., .223 Rem. . . . . **NiB $978 Ex $747 Gd $515**
AII (medium action)
.22-250 Rem., .243 Win., .308 Win. . . . . . . **NiB $875 Ex $721 Gd $463**

(cont'd.) **HUNTER LIGHTWEIGHT BOLT-ACTION RIFLE**
AII1 (long action) .25-06 Rem.,
.270 Win., .30-06 . . . . **NiB $933 Ex $747 Gd $508**
.338 Win. Mag. . . . . **NiB $1070 Ex $870 Gd $615**
.375 H&H Mag. . . . . **NiB $1167 Ex $948 Gd $667**
Left-hand model (standard cal.) . . . . **NiB $1197 Ex $958 Gd $651**
Magnum calibers. . . . . **NiB $1455 Ex $1179 Gd $827**

LAMINATED STOCK BOLT-ACTION RIFLES
Similar in style and specifications to Hunter Grade except w/stock of resin-bonded hardwood veneers. Available 18 calibers in AI (Short), AII (Medium) or AV action, left-hand version in 10 calibers, AV only. Imported 1987-95.
Short or medium action . . . . **NiB $978 Ex $798 Gd $515**
Long action/Magnum . . . . **NiB $1004 Ex $824 Gd $541**

MAGNUM MAUSER . . . . **NiB $1442 Ex $1133 Gd $798**
Similar specifications as Standard Model except w/recoil pad and redesigned longer AIII action to handle longer magnum cartridges. Calibers: .300 H&H Magnum, .375 H&H Magnum, standard at time of introduction. Disc.

MANNLICHER-STYLE CARBINE
Similar to Hunter Model except w/full Mannlicher-style stock and 18.5-inch bbl. Weighs 7.5 lbs. Chambered in .243, .25-06, .270, .308, .30-06, 7mm Rem. Mag., .300 Win. Mag., .338 Win. Mag., .375 H&H. Intro. in 1977. Disc.
Standard calibers . . . . **NiB $1184 Ex $901 Gd $566**
Magnum calibers (except .375) . . . . **NiB $1210 Ex $927 Gd $618**
.375 H&H . . . . **NiB $1226 Ex $953 Gd $644**

SAFARI GRADE . . . . **NiB $2395 Ex $1833 Gd $1004**
Classic bolt-action. Calibers: .300 Win. Mag., .338 Win. Mag., .375 H&H. Oil-finished European walnut stock w/hand-checkering. Barrel band swivel, express-type sight rib; satin or matte blue finish. Imported 1980-96.

SPORTER DELUXE . . . . **NiB $1184 Ex $901 Gd $566**
Same as Vixen, Forester, Finnbear and Model 74 except w/fancy French walnut stock w/skip checkering, rosewood forend tip and pistol-grip cap, recoil pad, inlaid trigger guard and floorplate. Disc.

Sako Mannlicher-Style Carbine

Sako Sporter Deluxe

Sako TRG-21
Target Rifle

STANDARD GRADE AI . . . . **NiB $978 Ex $695 Gd $360**
Short bolt-action. Calibers: .17 Rem., .222 Rem., .223 Rem. Five shot maga-zine. 23.5-inch bbl. Weight: 6.5 lbs. No sights. Checkered European walnut stock w/Monte Carlo cheekpiece, QD swivel studs. Imported 1978-85.

STANDARD GRADE AII. . . . . **NiB $989 Ex $711 Gd $386**
Medium bolt-action. Calibers: .22-250 Rem., .243 Win., .308 Win. 23.5-inch bbl. in .22-250; 23-inch bbl. in other calibers. Five shot magazine. Weight: 7.25 lbs. Checkered European walnut stock w/Monte Carlo cheekpiece, QD swivel studs. Imported 1978-85.

STANDARD GRADE AIII . . . . **NiB $1025 Ex $747 Gd $438**
Long bolt action. Calibers: .25-06 Rem., .270 Win., .30-06, 7mm Rem. Mag., .300 Win. Mag., .338 Win. Mag., .375 H&H. 24-inch bbl. 4-shot magazine. Weight: 8 lbs. Imported 1978-84.

SUPER DELUXE RIFLE . . . . **NiB $2317 Ex $2034 Gd $1184**
Available in AI, AII, AIII calibers. Select European walnut stock, hand-checkered, deep oak leaf hand-engraved design. Disc.

TRG-BOLT-ACTION TARGET RIFLE
Caliber: .308 Win., .330 Win. or .338 Lapua Mag. Detachable 10-shot magazine. 25.75- or 27.2-inch bbl. Weight: 10.5 to 11 lbs. Blued action w/stainless barrel. Adjustable two-stage trigger. modular reinforced polyurethane target stock w/adj. cheekpiece and buttplate. Options: Muzzle break; detachable bipod; QD sling swivels and scope mounts w/1-inch or 30mm rings. Imported 1993 to date.
(cont'd.) **TRG-BOLT-ACTION TARGET RIFLE**

TRG-21 .308 Win . . . . **NiB $2575 Ex $2050 Gd $1390**
TRG-22 .308 Win. . . . . **NiB $2640 Ex $2111 Gd $1436**
TRG-41 .338 Lapua. . . . . **NiB $3084 Ex $2467 Gd $1678**
TRG-42 .300 Win. or .338 Lapua . . . . . **NiB $3155 Ex $2532 Gd $1716**

TRG-S BOLT-ACTION RIFLE
Calibers: .243, 7mm-08, .270, .30-06, 7mm Rem. Mag., .300 Win. Mag., .338 Win. Mag. Five shot magazine (standard calibers), 4-shot (magnum), 22- or 24-inch bbl. 45.5 inches overall. Weight: 7.75 lbs. No sights. Reinforced polyurethane stock w/Monte Carlo. Intro. in 1993.
Standard calibers. . . . . **NiB $721 Ex $644 Gd $386**
Magnum calibers. . . . . **NiB $766 Ex $613 Gd $417**

VIXEN CARBINE . . . . **NiB $1081 Ex $953 Gd $824**
Same as Vixen Sporter except w/20-inch bbl., Mannlicher-type full stock. Imported 1947-71.

VIXEN HEAVY BARREL . . . . **NiB $1030 Ex $824 Gd $448**
Same as Vixen Sporter except calibers .222 Rem., .222 Rem. Mag., .223 Rem., heavy bbl., target-style stock w/beavertail forearm. Weight: 7.5 lbs. Imported 1947-71.

VIXEN SPORTER . . . . **NiB $1081 Ex $978 Gd $463**
Short Mauser-type bolt-action. Cals.: .218 Bee, .22 Hornet, .222 Rem., .222 Rem. Mag., .223 Rem. Five shot magazine. 23.5-inch bbl. Weight: 6.5 lbs. Hooded ramp front sight. Sporter stock w/Monte Carlo cheek-piece, checkered pistol-grip and forearm, swivels. Imported 1946-71.

Sako TRG-S Bolt-Action Rifle

Sako Vixen Heavy Barrel

Sako Vixen Sporter

J. P. SAUER & SOHN — Eckernforde, Germany, (Formerly Suhl, Germany), Imported by Sigarms Exeter, NH , (Previously by Paul Company Inc. and G.U. Inc.)

MAUSER BOLT-ACTION
SPORTING RIFLE . . . . NiB $1287 Ex $1020 Gd $695
Calibers: 7x57 and 8x57mm most common, but these rifles were produced in a variety of calibers including most of the popular Continental calibers as well as our .30-06. Five shot box magazine. 22- or 24-inch Krupp steel bbl., half-octagon w/raised matted rib. Double-set trigger. Weight: 7.5 lbs. Sights: Three-leaf open rear; ramp front. Sporting stock w/cheekpiece, checkered pistol grip, raised side-panels, Schnabel tip, swivels. Also made w/20-inch bbl. and full-length stock. Mfd. before WWII.

MODEL S-90 BOLT-ACTION RIFLES
Calibers: .243 Win., .308 Win. (Short action); .25-06, .270 Win., .30-06 (Medium action); 7mm Rem. Mag., .300 Win. Mag., .300 Wby., .338 Win., .375 H&H (Magnum action). Four shot (standard) or 3-shot magazine (magnum). Bbl. length: 20-inch (Stutzen), 24-inch. Weight: 7.6 to 10.75 lbs. Adjustable (Supreme) checkered Monte Carlo style stock. contrasting forend and pistol grip cap w/high-gloss finish or European (Lux) checkered Classic-style European walnut stock w/satin oil finish. Imported 1983-89.
S-90 Standard . . . . NiB $1030 Ex $901 Gd $489
S-90 Lux . . . . NiB $1236 Ex $978 Gd $515
S-90 Safari. . . . . NiB $1210 Ex $953 Gd $515
S-90 Stutzen . . . . NiB $1030 Ex $901 Gd $489
S-90 Supreme . . . . NiB $1339 Ex $1081 Gd $721
Grade I engraving, add $600
Grade II engraving, add $800
Grade III engraving add $1000
Grade IV engraving, add $1500

MODEL 200 BOLT-ACTION RIFLES
Calibers: .243 Win., .25-06, .270 Win., 7mm Rem Mag., .30-06, .308 Win., .300 Win. Mag., Detachable box magazine. 24-inch (American) or 26-inch (European) interchangeable bbl. Standard (steel) or lightweight (alloy) action. Weight: 6.6 to 7.75 lbs. 44 inches overall. Stock options: American Model w/checkered Monte Carlo style 2-piece stock contrasting forend and pistol grip cap w/high gloss finish and no sights. European walnut stock w/Schnabel forend, satin oil finish and iron sights. Contemporary Model w/synthetic carbon fiber stock. Imported 1986-93.
Standard model. NiB $1262 Ex $952 Gd $592

(cont'd.) MODEL 200 BOLT-ACTION RIFLES
Lightweight model . . . . NiB $1030 Ex $901 Gd $489
Contemporary model . . . . NiB $1133 Ex $953 Gd $541
American model . . . . NiB $1236 Ex $978 Gd $541
European model . . . . NiB $1262 Ex $1004 Gd $566
Left-hand model, add $125
Magnum calibers, add. $115
Interchangeable barrel assembly, add $295

MODEL 202 BOLT-ACTION RIFLES
Calibers: .243 Win., 6.5x55, 6.5x57, 6.6x68, .25-06, .270 Win., .280 7x64, .308, .30-06, Springfield, 7mm Rem. Mag., .300 Win. Mag., .300 Wby. Mag., 8x68S, .338 Win. Mag., .375 H&H Mag. Removable 3-shot box magazine. 23.6- and 26-inch interchangable bbl. 44.3 and 46 inches overall. Modular receiver drilled and tapped for scope bases. Adjustable two-stage trigger w/dual release safety. Weight: 7.7 to 8.4 lbs. Stock options: Checkered Monte Carlo-style select American walnut two-piece stock; Euro-classic French walnut two-piece stock w/semi Schnabel forend and satin oil finish; Super Grade Claro walnut two-piece stock fitted w/rosewood forend and grip cap w/high-gloss epoxy finish. Imported 1994 to date.
Standard model. NiB $1184 Ex $747 Gd $489
Euro-Classic model . . . . NiB $1226 Ex $772 Gd $489
Super Grade model . . . . NiB $1236 Ex $798 Gd $515
Left-hand model, add $150
Magnum calibers, add. $125
Interchangeable barrel assembly, add $295

SAVAGE INDUSTRIES — Westfield, Massachusetts, (Formerly Chicopee Falls, MA and Utica, NY)

MODEL 3 BOLT-ACTION
SINGLE-SHOT RIFLE . . . . NiB $154 Ex $129 Gd $77
Takedown. Caliber: .22 Short, Long, LR. 26-inch bbl. on prewar rifles, postwar production w/24-inch bbl. Weight: 5 lbs. Sights: Open rear; bead front. Plain pistol-grip stock. Made 1933-52.

MODEL 3S. . . . . NiB $190 Ex $154 Gd $93
Same as Model 3 except w/peep rear sight, hooded front. Made 1933-42.

MODEL 3ST. . . . . NiB $196 Ex $180 Gd $98
Same as Model 3S except fitted w/swivels and sling. Made 1933-42.

Savage Model 3

Savage Model 4

Savage Model 5

Savage Model 6

Savage Model 19 NRA (1933)

Savage Model 20

MODEL 4 BOLT-ACTION REPEATER. . . . . . . NiB $180 Ex $139 Gd $98
Takedown. Caliber: .22 Short, Long, LR. Five shot detachable box magazine. 24-inch bbl. Weight: 5.5 lbs. Sights: Open rear; bead front. Checkered pistol-grip stock on prewar models, early production had grooved forearm; postwar rifles have plain stocks. Made 1933-65.

MODEL 4M . . . . NiB $154 Ex $88 Gd $72
Same as Model 4 except chambered for .22 Rimfire Magnum. Made 1961-65.

MODEL 4S. . . . . NiB $196 Ex $98 Gd $77
Same as Model 4 except w/peep rear sight, hooded front. Made 1933-42.

MODEL 5 BOLT-ACTION
REPEATER . . . . NiB $180 Ex $98 Gd $77
Same as Model 4 except w/tubular magazine (holds 21 Short, 17 Long, 15 LR), weight: 6 lbs. Made 1936-61.

MODEL 5S. . . . . NiB $180 Ex $144 Gd $98
Same as Model 5 except w/peep rear sight, hooded front. Made 1936-42.

MODEL 6 AUTOLOADING RIFLE. . . . . NiB $180 Ex $154 Gd $103
Takedown. Caliber: .22 Short, Long, LR. Tubular magazine holds 21 Short, 17 Long, 15 LR. 24-inch bbl. Weight: 6 lbs. Sights: Open rear; bead front. Checkered pistol-grip stock on prewar models, postwar rifles have plain stocks. Made 1938-68.

MODEL 6S. . . . . NiB $196 Ex $165 Gd $108
Same as Model 6 except w/peep rear sight, bead front. Made 1938-42.

MODEL 7 AUTOLOADING RIFLE. . . . . NiB $206 Ex $180 Gd $113
Same general specifications as Model 6 except w/5-shot detachable box magazine. Made 1939-51.

MODEL 7S. . . . . NiB $185 Ex $124 Gd $103
Same as Model 7 except w/peep rear sight, hooded front. Made 1938-42.

MODEL 19 BOLT-ACTION TARGET RIFLE. . . . . . NiB $360 Ex $257 Gd $154
Model of 1933. Speed lock. Caliber: .22-LR. Five shot detachable box magazine. 25-inch bbl. Weight: 8 lbs. Adj. rear peep sight, blade front on early models, later production equipped w/extension rear sight, hooded front. Target stock w/full pistol-grip and beavertail forearm. Made 1933-46.

Savage Model 23AA

Savage Model 29

Savage Model 40

Savage Model 45

MODEL 19 NRA BOLT-ACTION
MATCH RIFLE . . . . NiB $515 Ex $463 Gd $232
Model of 1919. Caliber: .22 LR. Five shot detachable box magazine.
25-inch bbl. Weight: 7lbs. Sights: Adj. rear peep; blade front. Full
military stock w/pistol-grip. Made 1919-33.

MODEL 19H . . . . NiB $592 Ex $489 Gd $309
Same as standard Model 19 (1933) except chambered for .22
Hornet, w/Model 23D-type bolt mechanism, loading port and mag-
azine. Made 1933-42.

MODEL 19L . . . . NiB $360 Ex $257 Gd $154
Same as standard Model 19 (1933) except equipped w/Lyman No.
48Y receiver sight, 17A front sight. Made 1933-42.

MODEL 19M . . . . NiB $463 Ex $412 Gd $180
Same as standard Model 19 (1933) except w/heavy 28-inch bbl.
w/scope bases, weight: 9.25 lbs. Made 1933-42.

MODEL 20-1926
HI-POWER . . . . NiB $463 Ex $360 Gd $257
Same as Model 1920 except w/24-inch medium weight bbl.,
improved stock, Lyman 54 rear peep sight, weight: 7 lbs. Made
1926-29.

MODEL 23A BOLT-ACTION
SPORTING RIFLE. . . . . NiB $247 Ex $170 Gd $134
Caliber: 22 LR. Five shot detachable box magazine. 23-inch bbl.
Weight: 6 lbs. Sights: Open rear, blade or bead front. Plain pistol-
grip stock w/slender forearm and Schnabel tip. Made 1923-33.

MODEL 23AA . . . . NiB $304 Ex $257 Gd $165
Model of 1933. Improved version of Model 23A w/same general
specifications except w/speed lock, improved stock, weighs 6.5 lbs.
Made 1933-42.

MODEL 23B . . . . NiB $283 Ex $180 Gd $129
Same as Model 23A except caliber .25-20, 25-inch bbl. Model of 1933
w/improved stock w/full forearm instead of slender forearm w/Schnabel
found on earlier production. Weight: 6.5 lbs. Made 1923-42.

MODEL 23C . . . . NiB $309 Ex $227 Gd $134
Same as Model 23B except caliber .32-20. Made 1923-42.

MODEL 23D . . . . NiB $386 Ex $257 Gd $180
Same as Model 23B except caliber .22 Hornet. Made 1933-47.

MODEL 25 SLIDE-ACTION REPEATER . . . . NiB $515 Ex $360 Gd $206
Takedown. Hammerless. Caliber: .22 Short, Long, LR. Tubular magazine holds 20 Short, 17 Long, 15 LR. 24-inch octagon bbl. Weight:
5.75 lbs. Sights: Open rear; blade front. Plain pistol-grip stock,
grooved slide handle. Made 1925-29.

MODEL 29 SLIDE-ACTION
REPEATER . . . . NiB $438 Ex $309 Gd $206
Takedown. Hammerless. Caliber: .22 Short, Long, LR. Tubular magazine holds 20 Short, 17 Long, 15 LR. 24-inch bbl., octagon on prewar,
round on postwar production. Weight: 5.5 lbs. Sights: Open rear; bead
front. Stock w/checkered pistol grip and slide handle on prewar, plain
stock and grooved forearm on postwar production. Made 1929-67.

MODEL 40 BOLT-ACTION
SPORTING RIFLE. . . . . NiB $386 Ex $232 Gd $185
Standard Grade. Calibers: .250-3000, .300 Sav., .30-30, .30-06. Four shot
detachable box magazine. 22-inch bbl. in calibers .250-3000 and .30-30; 24-
inch in .300 Sav. and .30-06. Weight: 7.5 lbs. Sights: Open rear; bead front, on
ramp. Plain pistol-grip stock w/tapered forearm and Schnabel tip. Made 1928-
40.

MODEL 45 SUPER SPORTER. . . . . . . NiB $541 Ex $407 Gd $257
Special Grade. Same as Model 40 except w/checkered pistol-grip

Savage Model 60

Savage Model 63K

Savage Model 71 "Stevens Favorite"

MODEL 60 AUTOLOADING RIFLE.......NiB $154 Ex $103 Gd $80
Caliber: .22 LR. 15-shot tubular magazine. 20-inch bbl. Weight: 6 lbs. Sights: Open rear, ramp front. Monte Carlo stock of walnut w/checkered pistol-grip and forearm. Made 1969-72.

**MODEL 63K KEY LOCK BOLT-ACTION
SINGLE-SHOT RIFLE.............NiB $103 Ex $72 Gd $51**
Trigger locked w/key. Caliber: .22 Short, Long, LR. 18-inch bbl. Weight: 4 lbs. Sights: Open rear; hooded ramp front. Full-length stock w/pistol grip, swivels. Made 1970-72.

MODEL 63KM...................NiB $118 Ex $77 Gd $62
Same as Model 63K except chambered for .22 WMR. Made 1970-72.

MODEL 64F AUTOLOADING RIFLE.......NiB $103 Ex $77 Gd $62
Same general specifications as Model 64G except w/black graphite/polymer stock. Weight: 5 lbs. Made 1997 to date.

MODEL 64G AUTOLOADING RIFLE.......NiB $113 Ex $93 Gd $72
Caliber: 22 LR. 10-shot magazine. 20-inch bbl. Weight: 5.5 lbs. 40 inches overall. Sights: Adj. open rear; bead front. Grooved receiver for scope mounts. Stamped checkering on walnut-finished hardwood stock w/Monte Carlo cheekpiece. Made 1996 to date.

**MODEL 71 "STEVENS FAVORITE"
SINGLE-SHOT LEVER-ACTION RIFLE.....NiB $257 Ex $180 Gd $129**
Replica of original Stevens Favorite issued as a tribute to Joshua Stevens, "Father of .22 Hunting." Caliber: .22 LR. 22-inch full-octagon bbl. Brass-plated hammer and lever. Sights: Open rear; brass blade front. Weight: 4.5 lbs. Plain straight-grip buttstock and Schnabel forend; brass commemorative medallion inlaid in buttstock, brass crescent-shaped buttplate. 10,000 produced. Made in 1971 only. Top value is for new, unfired gun.

**MODEL 90 AUTO-LOADING
CARBINE......................NiB $154 Ex $124 Gd $84**
Similar to Model 60 except w/16.5-inch bbl. w/folding leaf rear sight, bead front. 10-shot tubular magazine. Uncheckered, carbine-

(cont'd.) MODEL 90 AUTOLOADING CARBINE
style walnut stock w/bbl. Band and sling swivels. Weight: 5.75 lbs. Made 1969-72.

MODEL 93G BOLT-ACTION RIFLE.......NiB $154 Ex $129 Gd $93
Caliber: .22 Win Mag. 5-shot magazine. 20.75-inch bbl. 39.5 inches overall. Weight: 5.75 lbs. Sights: Adj. open rear; bead front. Grooved receiver for scope mounts. Stamped checkering on walnut-finished hardwood stock w/Monte Carlo cheekpiece. Made 1996 to date.

MODEL 93F BOLT-ACTION RIFLE........NiB $129 Ex $82 Gd $77
Same general specifications as Model 93G except w/black graphite/polymer stock. Weight: 5.2 lbs. Made 1997 to date.

NOTE: MODEL 99 LEVER-ACTION REPEATER
Introduced in 1899, this model has been produced in a variety of styles and calibers. Original designation "Model 1899" was changed to "Model 99" c.1920. Earlier rifles and carbines — similar to Models 99A, 99B and 99H — were supplied in calibers .25-35, .30-30, .303 Sav., .32-40 and .38-55. Post-WWII Models 99A, 99C, 99CD, 99DE, 99DL, 99F and 99PE have top tang safety other 99s have slide safety on right side of trigger guard. Models 99C and 99CD have detachable box magazine instead of traditional Model 99 rotary magazine.

MODEL 99A (I)................NiB $875 Ex $669 Gd $283
Hammerless. Solid frame. Calibers: .30-30, .300 Sav., .303 Sav. Five-shot rotary magazine. 24-inch bbl. Weight: 7.25 lbs. Sights: Open rear; bead front, on ramp. Plain straight-grip stock, tapered forearm. Made 1920-36.

MODEL 99A (II)...............NiB $824 Ex $772 Gd $463
Current model. Similar to original Model 99A except w/top tang safety, 22-inch bbl., folding leaf rear sight, no crescent buttplate. Calibers: .243 Win., .250 Sav., .300 Sav., .308 Win. Made 1971-82.

MODEL 99B.................NiB $1025 Ex $819 Gd $489
Takedown. Otherwise same as Model 99A except weight: 7.5 lbs. Made 1920-36.

Savage Model 90

Savage Model 99A 1971 Issue

Savage Model 99C

Savage Model 99CD

Savage Model 99DE

MODEL 99C . . . . **NiB $1025 Ex $927 Gd $309**
Current model. Same as Model 99F except w/clip magazine instead of rotary. Calibers: .243 Win., .284 Win., .308 Win. Four shot detachable magazine holds one round less in .284. Weight: 6.75 lbs. Made 1965 to date.

MODEL 99CD . . . . **NiB $618 Ex $541 Gd $309**
Deluxe version of Model 99C. Calibers: .243 Win., .250 Sav., .308 Win. Hooded ramp front sight. Weight: 8.25 lbs. Stock w/Monte Carlo comb and cheekpiece, checkered pistol-grip, grooved forearm, swivels and sling. Made 1975 to 81.

MODEL 99DE CITATION GRADE. . . . . **NiB $875 Ex $592 Gd $412**
Same as Model 99PE except w/less elaborate engraving. Made 1968-70.

MODEL 99DL DELUXE . . . . **NiB $412 Ex $309 Gd $206**
Postwar model. Calibers: .243 Win., .308 Win. Same as Model 99F, except w/high comb Monte Carlo stock, sling swivels. Weight: 6.75 lbs. Made 1960-73.

MODEL 99E CARBINE (I) . . . . **NiB $772 Ex $618 Gd $335**
Pre-WWII type. Solid frame. Calibers: .22 Hi-Power, .250/3000, .30/30, .300 Sav., .303 Sav. w/22-inch bbl.; .300 Sav. 24-inch. Weight: 7 lbs. Other specifications same as Model 99A. Made 1920-36.

MODEL 99E CARBINE (II) . . . . **NiB $402 Ex $268 Gd $154**
Current model. Solid frame. Calibers: .250 Sav., .243 Win., .300 Sav., .308 Win. 20- or 22-inch bbl. Checkered pistol-grip stock and forearm. Made 1960-89.

Savage Model 99E 1969 Issue

Savage Model 99EG (Post WWII)

Savage Model 99F

Savage Model 99G

Savage Model 99PE Early Issue

Savage Model 99PE Late Issue

MODEL 99EG (I) . . . . **NiB $803 Ex $669 Gd $386**
Pre-WWII type. Solid frame. Plain pistol-grip stock and forearm. Otherwise same as Model G. Made 1936-41.

MODEL 99EG (II) . . . . **NiB $618 Ex $412 Gd $309**
Post-WWII type. Same as prewar model except w/checkered stock and forearm. Calibers: .250 Sav., .300 Sav., .308 Win. (intro. 1955), .243 Win., and .358 Win. Made 1946-60.

MODEL 99F
FEATHERWEIGHT (I) . . . . **NiB $875 Ex $618 Gd $427**
Pre-WWII type. Takedown. Specifications same as Model 99E, except weight: 6.5 lbs. Made 1920-42.

MODEL 99F
FEATHERWEIGHT (II) . . . . **NiB $566 Ex $360 Gd $206**
Postwar model. Solid frame. Calibers: .243 Win., .300 Sav., .308 Win. 22-inch bbl. Checkered pistol-grip stock and forearm. Weight: 6.5 lbs. Made 1955-73.

MODEL 99G . . . . **NiB $875 Ex $618 Gd $427**
Takedown. Checkered pistol-grip stock and forearm. Weight: 7.25 lbs. Other specifications same as Model 99E. Made 1920-42.

MODEL 99H CARBINE . . . . **NiB $824 Ex $515 Gd $360**
Solid frame. Calibers: .250/3000, .30/30, .303 Sav. 20-inch special weight bbl. Walnut carbine stock w/metal buttplate; walnut forearm w/bbl. band. Weight: 6.5 lbs. Open rear sights; ramped blade front sight. Other specifications same as Model 99A. Made 1931-42.

MODEL 99K . . . . **NiB $2266 Ex $1931 Gd $1020**
Deluxe version of Model G w/similar specifications except w/fancy stock and engraving on receiver and bbl. Lyman peep rear sight and folding middle. Made 1931-42.

MODEL 99PE PRESENTATION GRADE . . . **NiB $1854 Ex $1596 Gd $721**
Same as Model 99DL except w/engraved receiver (game scenes on sides), tang and lever, fancy walnut Monte Carlo stock and forearm w/hand checkering, QD swivels. Calibers: .243, .284, .308. Made 1968-70.

Savage Model 99R (Pre-WWII)

Savage Model 99R (Post-WWII)

Savage Model 99RS (Pre-WWII)

Savage Model 99T

RIFLES

MODEL 99R (I) . . . . **NiB $875 Ex $618 Gd $438**
Pre-WWII type. Solid frame. Calibers: .250-3000 (22-inch bbl.),
.300 Sav. (24-inch bbl.). Weight: 7.5 lbs. Special large pistol-grip
stock and forearm, checkered. General specifications same as other
Model 99 rifles. Made 1936-42.

MODEL 99R (II) . . . . **NiB $803 Ex $412 Gd $283**
Post-WWII type. Same as prewar mod except w/24-inch bbl. only,
w/screw eyes for sling swivels. Calibers: .250 Sav., .300 Sav., .308
Win., .243 Win. and .358 Win. Made 1946-60.

MODEL 99RS (I) . . . . **NiB $798 Ex $541 Gd $412**
Pre-WWII type. Same as prewar Model 99R except equipped
w/Lyman rear peep sight and folding middle sight, quick detachable
swivels and sling. Made 1936-42.

MODEL 99RS (II). . . . . **NiB $798 Ex $515 Gd $386**
Post-WWII type. Same as postwar Model 99RS except equipped
w/Redfield 70LH receiver sight, blank in middle sight slot. Made 1946-58.

MODEL 99T . . . . **NiB $803 Ex $438 Gd $324**
Featherweight. Solid frame. Calibers: .22 Hi-Power, .30/30, .303
Sav. w/20-inch bbl.; .300 Sav. w/22-inch bbl. Checkered pistol-grip
stock and beavertail forearm. Weight: 7 lbs. General specifications
same as other Model 99 rifles. Made 1936-42.

MODEL 99-358. . . . . **NiB $566 Ex $412 Gd $309**
Similar to current Model 99A except caliber .358 Win. has grooved
forearm, recoil pad, swivel studs. Made 1977-80.

MODEL 110 SPORTER
BOLT-ACTION RIFLE. . . . . **NiB $216 Ex $154 Gd $103**
Calibers: .243, .270, .308, .30-06. Four shot box magazine. 22-inch
bbl. Weight: About 6.75 lbs. Sights: Open rear; ramp front. Standard
sporter stock with checkered pistol-grip. Made 1958-63.

MODEL 110B BOLT-ACTION RIFLE
Same as Model 110E except with checkered select walnut Monte
Carlo-style stock (early models) or brown laminated stock (late mod-
els). Calibers: .243 Win., .270 Win. .30-06, 7mm Rem. Mag., .338
Win. Mag. Made 1976 to date.
Early model . . . . **NiB $322 Ex $257 Gd $175**
Laminated
stock model. . . . . **NiB $341 Ex $273 Gd $185**

MODEL 110BL . . . . **NiB $380 Ex $304 Gd $207**
Same as Model 110B except has left-hand action.

MODEL 110C
Calibers: .22-250, .243, .25-06, .270, .308, .30-06, 7mm Rem.
Mag., .300 Win. Mag. Four shot detachable clip magazine (3-shot
in Magnum calibers). 22-inch bbl. (24-inch in .22-250 Magnum calibers). Weight: 6.75 lbs., Magnum, 7.75 to 8 lbs. Sights: Open rear;
ramp front. Checkered Monte Carlo-style walnut stock (Magnum
has recoil pad). Made 1966-88.
Standard
calibers . . . . **NiB $597 Ex $360 Gd $180**
Magnum
calibers . . . . **NiB $644 Ex $386 Gd $206**

Savage Model 110

Savage Model 110B

Savage Model 110BL

Savage Model 110C

Savage Model 110E

Savage Model 110 MCL

MODEL 110CL
Same as Model 110C except has left-hand action. (Available only in .243 Win., .30-06, .270 Win. and 7mm Mag.) Made 1963-66.
Standard calibers . . . . NiB $360 Ex $283 Gd $196
Magnum calibers . . . . NiB $386 Ex $288 Gd $206

MODEL 110CY
YOUTH/LADIES RIFLE . . . . NiB $360 Ex $309 Gd $180
Same as Model 110G except with walnut-finished hardwood stock with 12.5-inch pull. Calibers: .243 Win. and .300 Savage. Made 1991 to date.

MODEL 110D
Similar to Model 110C except has internal magazine with hinged floorplate. Calibers: .243 Win., .270 Win., .30-06, 7mm Rem. Mag., .300 Win. Mag. Made 1972-88.
Standard calibers . . . . NiB $354 Ex $283 Gd $193
Magnum calibers . . . . NiB $380 Ex $304 Gd $207

MODEL 110DL
Same as Model 110D except has left-hand action. Discontinued.
Standard calibers . . . . NiB $418 Ex $335 Gd $228
Magnum calibers . . . . NiB $451 Ex $360 Gd $245

Savage Model 110P

Savage Model 110PE

MODEL 110E. . . . . **NiB $299 Ex $206 Gd $154**
Calibers: .22-250, .223 Rem., .243 Win., .270 Win., .308, 7mm Rem. Mag., .30-06. Four shot box magazine (3-shot in Magnum). 20- or 22-inch bbl. (24-inch stainless steel in Magnum). Weight: 6.75 lbs.; Magnum, 7.75 lbs. Sights: Open rear; ramp front. Plain Monte Carlo stock on early production; current models have checkered stocks of walnut-finished hardwood (Magnum has recoil pad). Made 1963-89.

MODEL 110EL. . . . . **NiB $315 Ex $252 Gd $172**
Same as Model 110E except has left-hand action made in .30-06 and 7mm Rem. Mag. only. Made 1969-73.

MODEL 110F/110K BOLT-ACTION RIFLE
Same as Model 110E except Model 110F has black Rynite synthetic stock, swivel studs; made 1988-93. Model 110K has laminated camouflage stock; made 1986-88.
Model 110F, adj. sights . . . . **NiB $354 Ex $283 Gd $193**
Model 110FNS, no sights . . . . **NiB $367 Ex $294 Gd $200**
Model 110K, standard calibers . . . . **NiB $380 Ex $304 Gd $207**
Model 110K, magnum calibers . . . . **NiB $432 Ex $345 Gd $235**

MODEL 110FM SIERRA ULTRA LIGHT. . . . . **NiB $360 Ex $283 Gd $185**
Calibers: .243 Win., .270 Win., .30-06, .308 Win. Five shot magazine. 20-inch bbl. 41.5 inches overall. Weight: 6.25 lbs. No sights w/drilled and tapped receiver. Black graphite/fiberglass composition stock. Non-glare matte blue finish. Made 1996 to date.

MODEL 110FP POLICE RIFLE . . . . . **NiB $397 Ex $299 Gd $196**
Calibers: .223, .308 Win. Four shot magazine. 24-inch bbl. 45.5 inches overall. Weight: 9 lbs. Black Rynite composite stock. Matte blue finish. Made 1990 to date.

MODEL 110G BOLT-ACTION RIFLE
Calibers: .223, .22-250, .243 Win., .270, 7mm Rem. Mag., .308 Win., .30-06, .300 Win. Mag. Five shot (standard) or 4-shot magazine (magnum). 22- or 24-inch bbl. 42.38 overall (standard). Weight: 6.75 to 7.5 lbs. Ramp front sight, adj. rear. Checkered walnut-finished hardwood stock with rubber recoil pad. Made 1989-93.
Model 110G, standard calibers . . . . **NiB $360 Ex $257 Gd $154**
Model 110G, magnum calibers . . . . **NiB $386 Ex $283 Gd $196**
Model 110GLNS, left-hand, no sights . . . . . **NiB $392 Ex $314 Gd $213**

MODEL 110GV VARMINT RIFLE . . . . **NiB $360 Ex $283 Gd $180**
Similar to the Model 110G except fitted with medium-weight varmint bbl. with no sights. Receiver drilled and tapped for scope mounts. Calibers .22-250 and .223 only. Made 1989-93.

MODEL 110M MAGNUM
Same as Model 110MC except calibers: 7mm Rem. Mag. .264, .300 and .338 Win. 24-inch bbl. Stock with recoil pad. Weight: 7.75 to 8 lbs. Made 1963-69.
Model 110M Magnum . . . . **NiB $402 Ex $386 Gd $206**
Model 110ML Magnum. . . . . **NiB $427 Ex $412 Gd $386**

MODEL 110MC
Same as Model 110 except has Monte Carlo-style stock. Calibers: .22-250, .243 Win., .270, .308, .30-06. 24-inch bbl. in .22-250. Made 1959-69.
Model 110MC. . . . . **NiB $232 Ex $180 Gd $113**
Model 110MCL. . . . . **NiB $238 Ex $191 Gd $130**

MODEL 110P PREMIER GRADE
Calibers: .243 Win., 7mm Rem. Mag., .30-06. Four shot magazine (3-shot in Magnum). 22-inch bbl. (24-inch stainless steel in Magnum). Weight: 7 lbs.; Magnum, 7.75 lbs. Sights: Open rear folding leaf; ramp front. French walnut stock w/Monte Carlo comb and cheekpiece, rosewood forend tip and pistol-grip cap, skip checkering, sling swivels (Magnum has recoil pad). Made 1964-70.
Calibers .243 Win. and .30-06. . . . . **NiB $463 Ex $335 Gd $232**
Caliber 7mm Rem. Mag. . . . . **NiB $479 Ex $360 Gd $257**

MODEL 110PE PRESENTATION GRADE
Same as Model 110P except has engraved receiver, floorplate and trigger guard, stock of choice grade French walnut. Made 1968-70.
Calibers .243 Win. and .30-06. . . . . **NiB $709 Ex $566 Gd $385**
Caliber 7mm Rem. Mag. . . . . **NiB $766 Ex $613 Gd $417**

MODEL 110PEL PRESENTATION GRADE
Same as Model 110PE except has left-hand action.
Calibers .243 Win. and .30-06. . . . . **NiB $766 Ex $613 Gd $417**
Caliber 7mm Rem. Mag. . . . . **NiB $838 Ex $669 Gd $455**

MODEL 110PL PREMIER GRADE
Same as Model 110P except has left-hand action.
Calibers .243 Win. and .30-06. . . . . **NiB $489 Ex $360 Gd $232**
Caliber 7mm Rem. Mag. . . . . **NiB $510 Ex $360 Gd $257**

MODEL 110S/110V
Same as Model 110E except Model 110S in .308 Win. only; discontinued 1985. Model 110V in .22-250 and .223 Rem. w/heavy 2-inch barrel, 47 inches overall, weight: 9 lbs. Discontinued. 1989.
Model 110S. . . . . **NiB $354 Ex $283 Gd $193**
Model 110V. . . . . **NiB $380 Ex $303 Gd $207**

Savage Model 111 Chieftain

Savage Model 111F

Savage Model 112V

Savage Model 116FCSAK

MODEL 111 CHIEFTAIN BOLT-ACTION RIFLE
Calibers: .243 Win., .270 Win., 7x57mm, 7mm Rem. Mag. .30-06. 4-shot clip magazine (3-shot in Magnum). 22-inch bbl. (24-inch in Magnum). Weight: 7.5 lbs., 8.25 lbs. Magnum. Sights: Leaf rear; hooded ramp front. Select walnut stock w/Monte Carlo comb and cheekpiece, checkered, pistol-grip cap, QD swivels and sling. Made 1974-79.
Standard calibers . . . . NiB $412 Ex $335 Gd $206
Magnum calibers . . . . NiB $465 Ex $376 Gd $263

MODELS 111F, 111FC, 111FNS CLASSIC HUNTERS
Similar to the Model 111G except with graphite/fiberglass composite stock. Weight: 6.25 lbs. Made 1994 to date.
Model 111F (Box mag., right/left hand) . . . NiB $360 Ex $232 Gd $180
Model 111FC (Detachable magazine) . . . . . NiB $438 Ex $309 Gd $206
Model 111FNS (Box mag.,
no sights, R/L hand) . . . . NiB $335 Ex $268 Gd $183

MODELS 111G, 111GC, 111GNS CLASSIC HUNTERS
Calibers: .22-250 Rem., .223 Rem., .243 Win., .25-06 Rem. .250 Sav., .270 Win., 7mm-08 Rem., 7mm Rem. Mag., .30-06, .300 Sav., .300 Win. Mag., .308 Win., .338 Win. 22- or 24-inch bbl. Weight: 7 lbs. Ramp front sight, adj. open rear. Walnut-finished hardwood stock. Blued finish. Made 1994 to date.
Model 111G (Box mag., right/left hand) . . . NiB $360 Ex $283 Gd $154
Model 111GC (Detachable
mag., R/L hand) . . . . NiB $381 Ex $288 Gd $165
Model 111GNS (Box mag., no sights) . . . . . NiB $340 Ex $257 Gd $129

MODEL 112BV,112BVSS HEAVY VARMINT RIFLES
Similar to the Model 110G except fitted with 26-inch heavy bbl. Laminated wood stock with high comb. .22-250 and .223 only.

(cont'd.) MODEL 112BV,112BVSS HEAVY VARMINT RIFLES
Model 112BV (Made 1993-94) . . . . NiB $566 Ex $412 Gd $299
Model 112BVSS (Fluted stainless
bbl.; made since 1994) . . . . NiB $592 Ex $438 Gd $335

MODEL 112FV,112FVS,112FVSS VARMINT RIFLES
Similar to the Model 110G except fitted with 26-inch heavy bbl. and Dupont Rynite stock. Calibers: .22-250, .223 and .220 Swift (112FVS only). Blued or stainless finish. Made 1991 to date.
Model 112FV (blued) . . . . NiB $354 Ex $283 Gd $193
Model 112FV-S (blued, single
shot), disc. 1993 . . . . NiB $386 Ex $360 Gd $216
Model 112FVSS (stainless) . . . . NiB $515 Ex $438 Gd $257
Model 112 FVSS-S (stainless, single shot) . . NiB $541 Ex $463 Gd $283

MODEL 112V VARMINT RIFLE . . . . NiB $406 Ex $324 Gd $220
Bolt action, single shot. Caliber: .220 Swift, .222 Rem., .223 Rem., .22-250, .243 Win., .25-06. 26-inch heavy bbl. with scope bases. Supplied w/o sights. Weight: 9.25 lbs. Select walnut stock in varmint style w/checkered pistol-grip, high comb, QD sling swivels. Made 1975-79.

MODEL 114C, 114CE, 114CU RIFLES
Calibers: .270 Win., 7mm Rem. Mag., .30-06, .300 Win. Mag. 22- or 24-inch bbl. Weight: 7 lbs. Detachable 3- or 4-shot magazine. Ramp front sight; adjustable, open rear; (114CU has no sights). Checkered select walnut stock w/oil finish, red butt pad. Schnabel forend and skip-line checkering (114CE). High-luster blued finish. Made 1991 to date.
Model 114C (Classic) . . . . NiB $489 Ex $412 Gd $237
Model 114CE (Classic European) . . . . NiB $494 Ex $412 Gd $242
Model 114CU (Classic Ultra) . . . . NiB $510 Ex $386 Gd $257

Savage Model 170C Carbine

Savage Model 219

Savage Model 219L

MODELS 116FSAK, 116FCSAK BOLT-ACTION RIFLES
Similar to the Model 116FSK except in calibers .270 Win., .30-06, 7mm Mag., .300 Win. Mag., .338 Win. Mag. Fluted 22-inch stainless bbl. w/adj. muzzle brake. Weight: 6.5 lbs. Made 1994 to date.
Model 116FSAK . . . . NiB $515 Ex $463 Gd $283
Model 116FCSAK (detachable mag.) . . . . . . NiB $566 Ex $469 Gd $309

MODELS 116FSC, 116FSS BOLT-ACTION RIFLES
Improved Model 110 with satin stainless action and bbl. Calibers: .223, .243, .270, .30-06, 7mm Rem. Mag., .300 Win. Mag., .338 Win. Mag. 22- or 24-inch bbl. Four or 5-shot capacity. Weight: About 7.5 lbs. Black Rynite stock w/recoil pad and swivel studs. Receiver drilled and tapped for scope mounts, no sights. Made 1991 to date.
Model 116FSS . . . . NiB $541 Ex $463 Gd $283
Model 116FSC, detachable magazine . . . . . NiB $566 Ex $489 Gd $309

MODEL 116FSK KODIAK RIFLE . . . . NiB $592 Ex $412 Gd $309
Similar to the Model 116FSS except with 22-inch bbl. chambered for 338 Win. Mag. only. "Shock Suppressor" recoil reducer. Made 1993 to date.

MODEL 116SE, 116US RIFLES
Calibers: .270 Win., 7mm Rem Mag., .30-06, .300 Win. Mag. (116US); .300 Win. Mag., .338 Win. mag., .425 Express, .458 Win. Mag. (116SE). 24-inch stainless barrel (with muzzle brake 116SE only). 45.5 inches overall. Weight: 7.2 to 8.5 lbs. Three shot magazine. 3-leaf Express sights 116SE only. Checkered Classic style select walnut stock with ebony forend tip. Stainless finish. Made 1994 to date.
Model 116SE (Safari Express) . . . . . NiB $901 Ex $695 Gd $463
Model 116US (Ultra Stainless) . . . . NiB $669 Ex $515 Gd $335

MODEL 170 PUMP-ACTION
CENTERFIRE RIFLE . . . . NiB $247 Ex $196 Gd $129
Calibers: .30-30, .35 Rem. Three shot tubular magazine. 22-inch bbl. Weight: 6.75 lbs. Sights: Folding leaf rear; ramp front. Select walnut stock w/checkered pistol-grip Monte Carlo comb, grooved slide handle. Made 1970-81.

MODEL 170C CARBINE . . . . NiB $283 Ex $201 Gd $129
Same as Model 170 Rifle except has 18.5-inch bbl., straight comb stock, weight: 6 lbs.; caliber .30-30 only. Made 1974-81.

MODEL 219 SINGLE-SHOT RIFLE
Hammerless. Takedown. Shotgun-type action with top lever. Calibers: .22 Hornet, .25-20, .32-20, .30-30. 26-inch bbl. Weight: about 6 lbs. Sights: Open rear; bead front. Plain pistol-grip stock and forearm. Made 1938-65.
Model 219 . . . . NiB $257 Ex $180 Gd $124
Model 219L (w/side lever, made 1965-67) . . NiB $180 Ex $129 Gd $93

MODEL 221-229 UTILITY GUNS
Same as Model 219 except in various calibers, supplied in combination with an interchangeable shotgun bbl. All versions discontinued.
Model 221 (.30-30,12-ga. 30-inch bbl.) . . . . NiB $180 Ex $144 Gd $98
Model 222 (.30-30,16-ga. 28-inch bbl.) . . . . NiB $161 Ex $129 Gd $88
Model 223 (.30-30, 20-ga. 28-inch bbl.) . . . . NiB $142 Ex $113 Gd $77
Model 227 (.22 Hornet, 12-ga. 30-inch bbl.) . . NiB $194 Ex $154 Gd $105
Model 228 (.22 Hornet, 16-ga. 28-inch bbl.) . NiB $186 Ex $149 Gd $102
Model 229 (.22 Hornet, 20-ga. 28-inch bbl.) . . NiB $180 Ex $144 Gd $98

MODEL 340 BOLT-ACTION REPEATER
Calibers: .22 Hornet, .222 Rem., .223 Rem., .225 Win., .30-30. Clip magazine; 4-shot capacity (3-shot in 30-30). Bbl. lengths: Originally 20-inch in .30-30, 22-inch in .22 Hornet; later 22-inch in .30-30, 24-inch in other calibers. Weight: 6.5 to 7.5 lbs. depending on caliber and vintage. Sights: Open rear (folding leaf on recent production); ramp front. Early models had plain pistol-grip stock, checkered since 1965. Made 1950-85. (Note: Those rifles produced between 1947-1950 were .22 Hornet Stevens Model .322 and .30-30 Model .325. The Savage model, however, was designated Model .340 for all calibers.)
Pre-1965 with plain stock . . . . NiB $309 Ex $196 Gd $129
Current model . . . . NiB $206 Ex $165 Gd $112
Savage Model 340C Carbine . . . . . . NiB $309 Ex $196 Gd $129

Savage Model 340

Savage Model 340C Carbine

Savage Model 1895 Replica

MODEL 340S DELUXE . . . . **NiB $360 Ex $257 Gd $144**
Same as Model 340 except has checkered stock, screw eyes for
sling, peep rear sight, hooded front. Made 1955-60.

MODEL 342 . . . . **NiB $350 Ex $257 Gd $154**
Designation, 1950 to 1955, of Model 340 .22 Hornet.

MODEL 342S DELUXE . . . . **NiB $386 Ex $283 Gd $154**
Designation, 1950 to 1955, of Model 340S .22 Hornet.

**ANNIVERSARY MODEL
1895 LEVER-ACTION** . . . . **NiB $1545 Ex $1339 Gd $1030**
Replica of Savage Model 1895 Hammerless Lever-Action Rifle issued
to commemorate the 75th anniversary (1895-1970) of Savage Arms.
Caliber: .308 Win. Five shot rotary magazine. 24-inch full-octagon
bbl. Engraved receiver. Brass-plated lever. Sights: Open rear; brass
blade front. Plain straight-grip buttstock, Schnabel-type forend; brass
medallion inlaid in buttstock, brass crescent-shaped buttplate. 9,999
produced. Made in 1970 only. Top value is for new, unfired specimen.

**MODEL 1903 SLIDE-ACTION
REPEATER** . . . . **NiB $386 Ex $257 Gd $196**
Hammerless. Takedown. Caliber: .22 Short, Long, LR. Detachable box
magazine. 24-inch octagon bbl. Weight: About 5 lbs. Sights: Open rear;
bead front. Pistol-grip stock, grooved slide handle. Made 1903-21.

**MODEL 1904 BOLT-ACTION
SINGLE-SHOT RIFLE** . . . . **NiB $154 Ex $103 Gd $51**
Takedown. .22 Short, Long, LR. 18-inch bbl. Weight: About 3 lbs. Sights:
Open rear; bead front. Plain, straight-grip, one-piece stock. Made 1904-17.

**MODEL 1905 BOLT-ACTION
SINGLE-SHOT RIFLE** . . . . **NiB $154 Ex $103 Gd $51**
Takedown. .22 Short, Long, LR. 22-inch bbl. Weight: About 5 lbs.
Sights: Open rear; bead front. Plain, straight-grip one-piece stock.
Made 1905-19.

**MODEL 1909 SLIDE-ACTION
REPEATER** . . . . **NiB $378 Ex $257 Gd $180**
Hammerless. Takedown. Similar to Model 1903 except has 20-inch
round bbl., plain stock and forearm, weight: about 4.75 lbs. Made
1909-15.

**MODEL 1912
AUTOLOADING RIFLE** . . . . **NiB $489 Ex $299 Gd $154**
Takedown. Caliber: 22 LR. only. Seven shot detachable box maga-
zine. 20-inch bbl., plain stock and forearm. Made 1912-16.

**MODEL 1914 SLIDE-ACTION
REPEATER** . . . . **NiB $381 Ex $257 Gd $180**
Hammerless. Takedown. Caliber: .22 Short, Long, LR, Tubular mag-
azine holds 20 Short, 17 Long, 15 LR. 24-inch octagon bbl. Weight:
About 5.75 lbs. Sights: Open rear; bead front. Plain pistol-grip stock,
grooved slide handle. Made 1914-24.

MODEL 1920 HI-POWER BOLT-ACTION RIFLE
Short Mauser-type action. Calibers: .250/3000, .300 Sav. Five shot
box magazine. 22-inch bbl. in .250 cal.; 24-inch in .300 cal.
Weight: About 6 lbs. Sights: Open rear; bead front. Checkered pis-
tol-grip stock w/slender forearm and Schnabel tip. Made 1920-26.
**Model 1920
Hi-Power
(.250-3000 Sav.)** . . . . **NiB $566 Ex $386 Gd $232**
**Model 1920
Hi-Power
(.300 Sav.)** . . . . **NiB $515 Ex $335 Gd $206**

NOTE: *In 1965, Savage began the importation of rifles manufactured
by J. G. Anschutz GmbH, Ulm, West Germany. Models designated
"Savage/Anschutz" are listed in this section, those marketed in the
U.S. under the "Anschutz" name are included in that firm's listings.
Anschutz rifles are now distributed in the U.S. by Precision Sales
Int'l., Westfield, Mass. See "Anschutz" for detailed specifications.*

Savage/Anschutz Mark 10D

Savage-Stevens Model 34

Savage-Stevens Model 35

MARK 10 BOLT-ACTION
TARGET RIFLE . . . . **NiB $463 Ex $304 Gd $206**
Single shot. Caliber: .22 LR. 26-inch bbl. Weight: 8.5 lbs. Sights:
Anschutz micrometer rear; globe front. Target stock w/full pistol-grip
and cheekpiece, adj. hand stop and swivel. Made 1967-72.

MARK 10D . . . . **NiB $489 Ex $309 Gd $206**
Same as Mark 10 except has redesigned stock with Monte Carlo
comb, different rear sight. Weight: 7.75 lbs. Made 1972.

MODEL 54
CUSTOM SPORTER . . . . **NiB $695 Ex $566 Gd $309**
Same as Anschutz Model 1422D.

MODEL 54M . . . . **NiB $850 Ex $592 Gd $360**
Same as Anschutz Model 1522D.

MODEL 64 BOLT-ACTION
TARGET RIFLE . . . . **NiB $566 Ex $412 Gd $257**
Same as Anschutz Model 1403.

MODEL 153 BOLT-ACTION
SPORTER . . . . **NiB $618 Ex $412 Gd $283**
Caliber: .222 Rem. Three shot clip magazine. 24-inch bbl. Sights:
Folding leaf open rear; hooded ramp front. Weight: 6.75 lbs. French
walnut stock w/cheekpiece, skip checkering, rosewood forend tip
and grip cap, swivels. Made 1964-67.

MODEL 153S . . . . **NiB $695 Ex $489 Gd $309**
Same as Model 153 except has double-set trigger. Made 1965-67.

MODEL 164 CUSTOM SPORTER . . . . **NiB $515 Ex $360 Gd $206**
Same as Anschutz Model 1416.

MODEL 164M . . . . **NiB $592 Ex $386 Gd $232**
Same as Anschutz Model 1516.

MODEL 184 SPORTER . . . . **NiB $566 Ex $412 Gd $206**
Same as Anschutz Model 1441.

NOTE: *Since J. Stevens Arms (see also separate listing) is a division
of Savage Industries, certain Savage models carry the "Stevens"
name.*

MODEL 34 BOLT-ACTION
REPEATER . . . . **NiB $144 Ex $88 Gd $51**
Caliber: .22 Short, Long, LR. 20-inch bbl. Weight: 4.75 lbs. Sights:
Open rear; bead front. Plain pistol-grip stock. Made 1965-80.

MODEL 34M . . . . **NiB $129 Ex $93 Gd $62**
Same as Model 34 except chambered for 22 WMR. Made 1969-73.

MODEL 35 . . . . **NiB $129 Ex $93 Gd $62**
Bolt-action repeater. Caliber: 22 LR. Six shot clip magazine. 22-inch
bbl. Weight: About 5 lbs. Sights: Open rear; ramp front. Monte Carlo
stock w/checkered pistol grip and forearm. Made 1982 to date.

MODEL 35M . . . . **NiB $154 Ex $103 Gd $67**
Same as Model 35 except chambered for 22 WMR. Made 1982 to
date.

MODEL 46 BOLT-ACTION
RIFLE . . . . **NiB $139 Ex $93 Gd $62**
Caliber: .22 Short, Long, LR. Tubular magazine holds 22 Short, 17
Long, 15 LR. 20-inch bbl. Weight: 5 lbs. Plain pistol-grip stock on
early production; later models have Monte Carlo stock w/checker-
ing. Made 1969-73.

MODEL 65
BOLT-ACTION RIFLE . . . . **NiB $154 Ex $103 Gd $62**
Caliber: .22 Short, Long, LR. Five shot clip magazine. 20-inch bbl.
Weight: 5 lbs. Sights: Open rear; ramp front. Monte Carlo stock
w/checkered pistol grip and forearm. Made 1969-73.

Savage-Stevens Model 46

Savage-Stevens Model 65

Savage-Stevens Model 72 — Crackshot

Savage-Stevens Model 73

Savage-Stevens Model 80

MODEL 65M . . . . **NiB $154 Ex $113 Gd $72**
Same as Model 65 except chambered for .22 WMR, has 22-inch
bbl., weighs 5.25 lbs. Made 1969-81.

NOTE: *The Model 72 is a "Favorite"-type single-shot unlike the
smaller, original "Crackshot" made by Stevens from 1913-39.*

**MODEL 72 CRACKSHOT SINGLE-SHOT
LEVER-ACTION RIFLE** . . . . **NiB $257 Ex $206 Gd $129**
Falling-block action. Casehardened frame. Caliber: .22 Short, Long,
LR. 22-inch octagon bbl. Weight: 4.5lbs. Sights: Open rear; bead front.
Plain straight-grip stock and forend of walnut. Made 1972 to date.

MODEL 73 BOLT-ACTION SINGLE-SHOT . . . **NiB $103 Ex $82 Gd $62**
Caliber: .22 Short, Long, LR. 20-inch bbl. Weight: 4.75 lbs. Sights:
Open rear; bead front. Plain pistol-grip stock. Made 1965-80.

MODEL 73Y YOUTH MODEL . . . . **NiB $108 Ex $88 Gd $62**
Same as Model 73 except has 18-inch bbl., 1.5-inch shorter buttstock, weight: 4.5 lbs. Made 1965-80.

**MODEL 74
LITTLE FAVORITE** . . . . **NiB $175 Ex $163 Gd $93**
Same as Model 72 Crackshot except has black-finished frame, 22-
inch round bbl., walnut-finished hardwood stock. Weight: 4.75 lbs.
Made 1972-74.

**MODEL 80
AUTOLOADING RIFLE** . . . . **NiB $154 Ex $124 Gd $84**
Caliber: 22 LR. 15-shot tubular magazine. 20-inch bbl.
Weight: 6 lbs. Sights: Open rear, bead front. Monte Carlo
stock of walnut w/checkered pistol-grip and forearm. Made
1976 to date. (Note: This rifle is essentially the same as the
Model 60 of 1969-72 except for a different style of checkering, side instead of top safety and plain bead instead of ramp
front sight.)

**MODEL 88
AUTOLOADING RIFLE** . . . . **NiB $165 Ex $154 Gd $93**
Similar to Model 60 except has walnut-finished hardwood stock,
plain bead front sight. Weight: 5.75 lbs. Made 1969-72.

Savage-Stevens Model 89

Savage-Stevens Model 987-T

MODEL 89 SINGLE-SHOT
LEVER-ACTION CARBINE . . . . **NiB $92 Ex $77 Gd $51**
Martini-type action. Caliber: .22 Short, Long, LR. 18.5-inch bbl. Weight: 5 lbs. Sights: Open rear; bead front. Western-style carbine stock w/straight grip, forearm with bbl. band. Made 1976-89.

MODEL 987-T
AUTOLOADING RIFLE . . . . **NiB $154 Ex $124 Gd $84**
Caliber: .22 LR. 15-shot tubular magazine. 20-inch bbl. Weight: 6 lbs. Sights: Open rear; ramp front. Monte Carlo stock w/checkered pistol grip and forearm. Made 1981-89.

"STEVENS FAVORITE"
See Savage Model 71.

V.C. SCHILLING — Suhl, Germany

MAUSER-MANNLICHER
BOLT ACTION SPORTING RIFLE . . **NiB $837 Ex $669 Gd $455**
Same general specifications as given for the Haenel Mauser-Mannlicher Sporter. See separate listing.

'88 MAUSER SPORTER . . . . **NiB $804 Ex $644 Gd $438**
Same general specifications as Haenel '88 Mauser Sporter. See separate listing.

SCHULTZ & LARSEN GEVAERFABRIK — Otterup, Denmark

MATCH RIFLE NO. 47 . . . . **NiB $721 Ex $669 Gd $489**
Caliber: .22 LR. Bolt-action, single-shot, set trigger. 28.5-inch heavy bbl. Weight: 14 lbs. Sights: Micrometer receiver, globe front. Free-rifle stock w/cheekpiece, thumbhole, adj. Schuetzen-type buttplate, swivels, palmrest.

FREE RIFLE MODEL 54 . . . . **NiB $978 Ex $798 Gd $515**
Calibers: 6.5x55mm or any standard American centerfire caliber. Schultz & Larsen M54 bolt-action, single-shot, set trigger. 27.5-inch heavy bbl. Weight: 15.5 lbs. Sights: Micrometer receiver; globe front. Free-rifle stock w/cheekpiece, thumbhole, adj. Schuetzen-type buttplate, swivels, palm rest.

MODEL 54J
SPORTING RIFLE . . . . **NiB $695 Ex $566 Gd $360**
Calibers: .270 Win., .30-06, 7x61 Sharpe & Hart. Schultz & Larsen bolt action. Three-shot magazine. 24-inch bbl. in .270 and .30-06, 26-inch in 7x61 S&H. Checkered stock w/Monte Carlo comb and cheekpiece. Value shown is for rifle less sights.

SEARS, ROEBUCK & COMPANY — Chicago, Illinois

The most encountered brands or model designations used by Sears are J. C. Higgins and Ted Williams. Firearms sold under these designations have been mfd. by various firms including Winchester, Marlin, Savage, Mossberg, etc.

MODEL 2C
BOLT-ACTION RIFLE . . . . **NiB $102 Ex $82 Gd $61**
Caliber: .22RF. Seven shot clip mag. 21-inch bbl. Weight: 5 lbs. Sights: Open rear; ramp front. Plain Monte Carlo stock. Mfd. by Win.

MODEL 42
BOLT-ACTION REPEATER . . . . **NiB $102 Ex $82 Gd $55**
Takedown. Caliber: .22RF. Eight shot detachable box magazine. 24-inch bbl. Weight: 6 lbs. Sights: Open rear; bead front. Plain pistol-grip stock. Mfd. by Marlin.

MODEL 42DL
BOLT-ACTION REPEATER . . . . **NiB $102 Ex $82 Gd $61**
Same general specifications as Model 42 except fancier grade w/peep sight, hooded front sight and swivels.

MODEL 44DL
LEVER-ACTION RIFLE . . . . **NiB $178 Ex $138 Gd $92**
Caliber: .22RF. Tubular magazine holds 19 LR cartridges. 22-inch bbl. Weight: 6.25 lbs. Sights: Open rear; hooded ramp front. Monte Carlo-style stock w/pistol grip. Mfd. by Marlin.

MODEL 53
BOLT-ACTION RIFLE . . . . **NiB $229 Ex $153 Gd $112**
Calibers: .243, .270, .308, .30-06. Four-shot magazine. 22-inch bbl. Weight: 6.75 lbs. Sights: Open rear; ramp front. Standard sporter stock w/pistol-grip, checkered. Mfd. by Savage.

Sedgley Springfield Sporter

Sedgley Springfield — Left Hand

Sedgley Springfield Mannlicher

MODEL 54 LEVER-ACTION
RIFLE . . . . **NiB $178 Ex $153 Gd $102**
Similar general specifications as Winchester Model 94 carbine. Made in .30-30 caliber only. Mfd. by Winchester.

MODEL 103 SERIES
BOLT-ACTION REPEATER . . . . **NiB $184 Ex $76 Gd $56**
Same general specifications as Model 103.2 w/minor changes. Mfd. by Marlin.

MODEL 103.2 BOLT-ACTION
REPEATER . . . . **NiB $102 Ex $76 Gd $56**
Takedown. Caliber: .22RF. Eight-shot detachable box magazine. 24-inch bbl. Weight: 6 lbs. Sights: Open rear; bead front. Plain pistol-grip stock. Mfd. by Marlin.

R. F. SEDGLEY, INC. — Philadelphia, Pennsylvania

SPRINGFIELD SPORTER . . . . **NiB $1313 Ex $1030 Gd $515**
Springfield '03 bolt action. Calibers: .220 Swift, .218 Bee, .22-3000, R, .22-4000, .22 Hornet, .25-35, .250-3000, .257 Roberts, .270 Win., 7mm, .30-06. 24-inch bbl. Weight: 7.5 lbs. Sights: Lyman No. 48 receiver; bead front on matted ramp. Checkered walnut stock, grip cap, sling swivels. Disc. 1941.

SPRINGFIELD LEFT-HAND SPORTER . . . **NiB $1493 Ex $1226 Gd $798**
Bolt-action reversed for left-handed shooter; otherwise the same as standard Sedgley Springfield Sporter. Disc. 1941.

SEDGLEY SPRINGFIELD
MANNLICHER-TYPE SPORTER . . . . **NiB $1596 Ex $1313 Gd $927**
Same as standard Sedgley Springfield Sporter except w/20-inch bbl., Mannlicher-type full stock w/cheekpiece, weight: 7.75 lbs. Disc. 1941.

SHILEN RIFLES, INC. — Ennis, Texas

DGA BENCHREST RIFLE . . . . . . **NiB $1493 Ex $1107 Gd $824**
DGA single-shot bolt-action. Calibers as listed for Sporter. 26-inch medium-heavy or heavy bbl. Weight: From 10.5 lbs. No sights. Fiberglass or walnut stock, classic or thumbhole pattern. Currently manufactured.

DGA SPORTER . . . . **NiB $1545 Ex $1025 Gd $711**
DGA bolt action. Calibers: .17 Rem., .222 Rem., .223 Rem. .22-250, .220 Swift, 6mm Rem., .243 Win., .250 Sav., .257 Roberts, .284 Win., .308 Win., .358 Win. Three shot blind magazine. 24-inch bbl. Average weight: 7.5 lbs. No sights. Select Claro walnut stock w/cheekpiece, pistol grip, sling swivel studs. Currently manufactured.

DGA VARMINTER . . . . **NiB $1437 Ex $1081 Gd $736**
Same as Sporter except w/25-inch medium-heavy bbl. Weight: 9 lbs.

SHILOH RIFLE MFG. Co. — Big Timber, Montana (Formerly Shiloh Products)

SHARPS MODEL 1874 BUSINESS RIFLE . . . . **NiB $1081 Ex $1004 Gd $618**
Replica of 1874 Sharps similar to No. 3 Sporting Rifle. .32-40, .38-55, .40-50 BN, .40-70 BN, .40-90 BN, .45-70 ST, .45-90 ST, .50-70 ST, .50-100 ST. 28-inch round heavy bbl. Blade front sight, buckhorn rear. Double-set triggers. Straight-grip walnut stock w/steel crescent buttplate. Made 1986 to date.

SHARPS MODEL 1874 LONG
RANGE EXPRESS RIFLE . . . . **NiB $1648 Ex $1596 Gd $1025**
Replica of 1874 Sharps w/single-shot falling breech action. .32-40, .38-55, .40-50 BN, .40-70 BN, .40-90 BN, .45-70 ST, .45-90 ST, .45-110 ST, .50-70 ST, .50-90 ST, .50-110 ST. 34-inch tapered octagon bbl. 51 inches overall. Weight: 10.75 lbs. Globe front sight, sporting tang peep rear. Walnut buttstock w/pistol-grip and Schnabel-style forend. Color casehardened action w/double-set triggers Made 1986 to date.

Shilen DGA Benchrest Rifle

Shilen DGA Sporter

Shilen DGA Varminter

RIFLES

SHARPS MODEL 1874 SADDLE RIFLE . . NiB $1133 Ex $1025 Gd $618
Similar to 1874 Express Rifle except w/30-inch bbl., blade front sight and buckhorn rear. Made 1986 to date.

**SHARPS MODEL 1874
SPORTING RIFLE NO. 1 . . . . NiB $1226 Ex 1025 Gd $644**
Similar to 1874 Express Rifle except w/30-inch bbl., blade front sight and buckhorn rear. Made 1986 to date.

**SHARPS MODEL 1874
SPORTING RIFLE NO. 3 . . . . NiB $1030 Ex $901 Gd $592**
Similar to 1874 Sporting Rifle No. 1 except w/straight-grip stock w/steel crescent buttplate. Made 1986 to date.

SHARPS MODEL 1874 MONTANA ROUGHRIDER
Similar to 1874 Sporting Rifle No. 1 except w/24- to 34-inch half-octagon or full-octagon bbl. Standard or deluxe walnut stock w/pistol-grip or military-style buttstock. Made 1989 to date.
Standard model . . . . NiB $1025 Ex $618 Gd $541
Deluxe model . . . . NiB $1159 Ex $875 Gd $515

SIG SWISS INDUSTRIAL COMPANY —
Neuhausen-Rhine Falls, Switzerland

AMT SEMIAUTOMATIC RIFLE . . . . NiB $4146 Ex $4094 Gd $2781
.308 Win.(7.62 NATO). 5, 10, or 20-shot magazine. 18.5-inch bbl. w/flash suppressor. Weight: 9.5 lbs. Sights: Adj. aperture rear, post front. Walnut buttstock and forend w/synthetic pistol grip. Imported 1980-88.

AMT SPORTING RIFLE . . . . NiB $3862 Ex $2832 Gd $2055
Semiautomatic version of SG510-4 automatic assault rifle based on Swiss Army SIGW57. Roller-delayed blowback action. Caliber: 7.62x51mm NATO (.308 Win.). Five, 10- and 20-round magazines. 19-inch bbl. Weight: 10 lbs. Sights, aperture rear, post front. Wood buttstock and forearm, folding bipod. Imported 1960-88.

PE57 SEMIAUTOMATIC RIFLE . . . . NiB $5144 Ex $4115 Gd $2799
Caliber: 7.5 Swiss. 24-shot magazine. 23.75-inch bbl. Weight: 12.5 lbs. Sights: Adj. aperture rear; post front. High-impact synthetic stock. Imported from Switzerland during the 1980s.

GRADING: **NiB** = New in Box   **Ex** = Excellent or NRA 95%   **Gd** = Good or NRA 68%

Smith & Wesson
Model 1500DL

Smith & Wesson
Model 1700 LS Classic Hunter

Springfield Armory
BM-59

SMITH & WESSON — Springfield, Massachusetts, Mfd. by Husqvarna, Vapenfabrik A.B., Huskvarna, Sweden & Howa Machonery LTD., Shinkawa-Chonear, Nagota 452, Japan

MODEL 1500 . . . . NiB $360 Ex $283 Gd $180
Bolt-action. .243 Win., .270 Win., .30-06, 7mm Rem. Mag. 22-inch bbl. (24-inch in 7mm Rem. Mag.). Weight: 7.5 lbs. American walnut stock w/Monte Carlo comb and cheekpiece, cut checkering. Sights: Open rear, hooded ramp, gold beadfront. This model was also imported by Mossberg (see separate listings); Imported 1979-84.

MODEL 1500DL DELUXE . . . . NiB $360 Ex $283 Gd $185
Same as standard model, except w/o sights; w/engine-turned bolt, decorative scroll on floorplate, French checkering. Imported 1983-84.

MODEL 1700 LS "CLASSIC HUNTER" . . . . NiB $412 Ex $360 Gd $206
Bolt action. Calibers: .243 Win., .270 Win., .30-06, 5-shot magazine. 22-inch bbl. Weight: 7.5 lbs. Solid recoil pad, no sights, Schnabel forend, checkered walnut stock. Imported 1983-84.

MODEL A BOLT-ACTION RIFLE . . . . NiB $489 Ex $360 Gd $247
Similar to Husqvarna Model 9000 Crown Grade. Mauser-type bolt action. Calibers: .22-250, .243 Win., .270 Win., .308 Win., .30-06, 7mm Rem. Mag., .300 Win. Mag. Five shot magazine except 3-round capacity in latter two calibers. 23.75-inch bbl. Weight: 7 lbs. Sights: Folding leaf rear; hooded ramp front. Checkered walnut stock w/Monte Carlo cheekpiece, rosewood forend tip and pistol-grip cap, swivels. Made 1969-72.

MODEL B . . . . NiB $438 Ex $314 Gd $180
Same as Model A except w/20.25-inch extra-light bbl., Monte Carlo cheekpiece w/Schnabel-style forearm, weight: 6 lbs., 10 oz. Calibers: .243 Win., .30-06.

MODEL C . . . . NiB $438 Ex $319 Gd $180
Same as Model B except w/cheekpiece stock w/straight comb.

MODEL D . . . . NiB $566 Ex $412 Gd $283
Same as Model C except w/full-length Mannlicher-style forearm.

MODEL E. . . . . NiB $566 Ex $412 Gd $283
Same as Model B except w/full-length Mannlicher-style forearm.

SPRINGFIELD, INC. — Colona, Illinois (Formerly Springfield Armory of Geneseo, Ill.)

This is a private firm not to be confused with the former U.S. Government facility in Springfield, Mass.

BM-59 SEMIAUTOMATIC RIFLE
Gas-operated. Caliber: .308 Win. (7.62mm NATO). 20-shot detachable box magazine. 19.3-inch bbl. w/flash suppressor. About 43 inches overall. Weight: 9.25 lbs. Adj. military aperture rear sight, square post front; direct and indirect grenade launcher sights. European walnut stock w/handguard or folding buttstock (Alpine Paratrooper). Made 1981-90.

Standard model . . . . NiB $2054 Ex $1643 Gd $1118
Paratrooper model . . . . NiB $2060 Ex $1674 Gd $1313

**Springfield Armory
SAR-8 Sporter Rifle**

M-1 GARAND SEMIAUTOMATIC RIFLE
Gas-operated. Calibers: .308 Win. (7.62 NATO), .30-06. Eight shot stripper clip. 24-inch bbl. 43.5 inches overall. Weight: 9.5 lbs. Adj. aperture rear sight, military square blade front. Standard "Issue-grade" walnut stock or folding buttstock. Made 1979-90.

Standard model	NiB $921	Ex $695	Gd $463
National match	NiB $927	Ex $721	Gd $515
Ultra match	NiB $978	Ex $875	Gd $566
Sniper model	NiB $978	Ex $875	Gd $566
Tanker model	NiB $772	Ex $669	Gd $386
Paratrooper w/folding stock	NiB $1004	Ex $772	Gd $541

MATCH M1A
Same as Standard M1A except w/National Match-grade bbl. w/modified flash suppressor, National Match sights, turned trigger pull, gas system assembly in one unit, modified mainspring guide glass-bedded walnut stock. Super Match M1A w/premium-grade heavy bbl. (weighs 10 lbs).

Match M1A	NiB $1545	Ex $1329	Gd $824
Super Match M1A	NiB $1751	Ex $1339	Gd $953

STANDARD M1A SEMIAUTOMATIC
Gas-operated. Similar to U.S. M14 service rifle except w/o provision for automatic firing. Caliber: 7.65mm NATO (.308 Win.). Five, 10- or 20-round detachable box magazine. 25.13-inch bbl w/flash suppressor. Weight: 9 lbs. Sights: Adj. aperture rear; blade front. Fiberglass, birch or walnut stock, fiberglass handguard, sling swivels. Made 1974 to date.

W/fiberglass or birch stock	NiB $1051	Ex $798	Gd $515
W/walnut stock	NiB $1196	Ex $983	Gd $712

M-6 SCOUT RIFLE/SHOTGUN COMBO
Similar to (14-inch) short-barrel Survival Gun provided as backup weapon to U.S. combat pilots. Calibers: .22 LR/.410 and .22 Hornet/.410. 18.5-inch bbl. 32 inches overall. Weight: 4 lbs. Parkerized or stainless steel finish. Folding detachable stock w/storage for fifteen .22 LR cartridges and four .410 shells. Drilled and tapped for scope mounts. Intro. 1982 and imported from Czech Republic 1995 to date.

First Issue (no trigger guard)	NiB $196	Ex $1504	Gd $103
Second Issue (w/trigger guard)	NiB $165	Ex $129	Gd $93

SAR-8 SPORTER RIFLE
Similar to H&K 911 semiautomatic rifle. Calibers: .308 Win., (7.62x51) NATO. Detachable 5- 10- or 20-shot magazine. 18- or 20-inch bbl. 38.25 or 45.3 inches overall. Weight: 8.7 to 9.5 lbs. Protected front post and rotary adj. rear sight. Delayed roller-locked blow-back action w/fluted chamber. Kevlar-reinforced fiberglass thumb-hole style wood stock. Imported 1990 to date.

SAR-8 w/wood stock (disc. 1994)	NiB $1327	Ex $1081	Gd $768
SAR-8 w/thumb-hole stock	NiB $1056	Ex $875	Gd $592

SAR-48, SAR-4800
Similar to Browning FN FAL/LAR semiautomatic rifle. Calibers: .233 Rem. (5.56x45) and 3.08 Win. (7.62x51) NATO. Detachable 5- 10- or 20-shot magazine. 18- or 21-inch chrome-lined bbl. 38.25 or 45.3 inches overall. Weight: 9.5 to 13.25 lbs. Protected post front and adj. rear sight. Forged receiver and bolt w/adj. gas system. Pistol-grip or thumb-hole style; synthetic or wood stock. Imported 1985; reintroduced 1995.

SAR-48 w/pistol-grip stock (disc. 1989)	NiB $1184	Ex $1004	Gd $592
SAR-48 w/wood stock (disc. 1989)	NiB $2357	Ex $1905	Gd $1329
SAR-48 w/folding stock (disc. 1989)	NiB $2651	Ex $2137	Gd $1480
SAR-48 w/thumb-hole stock	NiB $1211	Ex $973	Gd $668

SQUIRES BINGHAM CO., INC. —
Makati, Rizal, Philippines

**MODEL 14D DELUXE BOLT-ACTION
REPEATING RIFLE** . . . . NiB $102 Ex $76 Gd $51
Caliber: .22 LR. Five shot box magazine. 24-inch bbl. Sights: V-notch rear; hooded ramp front. Receiver grooved for scope mounting. Pulong Dalaga stock w/contrasting forend tip and grip cap, checkered forearm and pistol-grip. Weight: 6 lbs. Disc.

MODEL 15 . . . . NiB $127 Ex $82 Gd $76
Same as Model 14D except chambered for .22 WMR. Importation. Disc.

MODEL M16 SEMIAUTOMATIC RIFLE . . . . NiB $122 Ex $127 Gd $92
Styled after U.S. M16 military rifle. Caliber: .22 LR. 15-shot box magazine. 19.5-inch bbl. w/muzzle brake/flash hider. Rear sight in carrying handle, post front on high ramp. Black-painted mahogany buttstock and forearm. Weight: 6.5 lbs. Importation. Disc.

MODEL M20D DELUXE . . . . NiB $204 Ex $178 Gd $97
Caliber: .22 LR. 15-shot box magazine. 19.5-inch bbl. w/muzzle brake/flash hider. Sights: V-notch rear; blade front. Receiver grooved for scope mounting. Pulong Dalaga stock w/contrasting forend tip and grip cap, checkered forearm/pistol-grip. Weight: 6 lbs. Importation. Disc.

STANDARD ARMS COMPANY —
Wilmington, Delaware

MODEL G AUTOMATIC RIFLE . . . . NiB $618 Ex $309 Gd $201
Gas-operated. Autoloading. Hammerless. Takedown. .25-35, .30-30, .25 Rem., .30 Rem., .35 Rem. Magazine capacity: 4 rounds in .35 Rem., 5 rounds in other calibers. 22.38-inch bbl. Weight: 7.75 lbs. Sights: Open sporting rear; ivory bead front. Shotgun-type stock. Made c. 1910. Note: This was the first gas-operated rifle manufactured in the U.S. While essentially an autoloader, the gas port can be closed and the rifle may be operated as a slide-action repeater.

RIFLES

Star
Rolling Block Carbine

MODEL M HAND-OPERATED RIFLE . . . . . NiB $309 Ex $283 Gd $154
Slide-action repeater w/same general specifications as Model G except lacks autoloading feature. Weight: 7 lbs.

STAR — Eibar, Spain
Mfd. by Bonifacio Echeverria, S.A.

ROLLING BLOCK CARBINE . . . . . NiB $206 Ex $165 Gd $112
Single-shot action similar to Remington Rolling Block. .30-30, .357 Mag., .44 Mag. 20-inch bbl. Weight: 6 lbs. Sights: Folding leaf rear; ramp front. Walnut straight-grip stock w/crescent buttplate, forearm w/bbl. band. Imported 1973-75.

STERLING — Imported by Lanchester U.S.A., Inc., Dallas, Texas

MARK 6 SEMIAUTOMATIC CARBINE . . . . . NiB $772 Ex $592 Gd $407
Caliber: 9mm Para. 34-shot magazine. Bbl.: 16.1 inches. Weight: 7.5 lbs. Flip-type rear peep sight, ramp front. Folding metal skeleton stock. Made 1983-94.

J. STEVENS ARMS CO. — Chicopee Falls, Massachusetts, Div. of Savage Industries, Westfield, Mass.

J. Stevens Arms eventually became a division of Savage Industries. Consequently, the "Stevens" brand name is used for some rifles by Savage; see separate Savage-Stevens listings under Savage.

NO. 12 MARKSMAN SINGLE-SHOT RIFLE. . NiB $204 Ex $153 Gd $76
Lever-action, tip-up. Takedown. Calibers: .22 LR, .25 R.F., .32 R.F. 22-inch bbl. Plain straight-grip stock, small tapered forearm.

NO. 14 LITTLE SCOUT
SINGLE-SHOT RIFLE. . . . . NiB $204 Ex $97 Gd $51
Caliber: .22 RF. 18-inch bbl. One-piece slab stock readily distinguishes it from the No. 14X that follows. Made 1906-1910.

NO. 14.5 LITTLE SCOUT
SINGLE-SHOT RIFLE . . . . NiB $204 Ex $102 Gd $76
Rolling block. Takedown. Caliber: .22 LR. 18- or 20-inch bbl. Weight: 2.75 lbs. Sights: open rear; blade front. Plain straight-grip stock, small tapered forearm.

MODEL 15 . . . . NiB $178 Ex $102 Gd $92
Same as Stevens-Springfield Model 15 except w/24-inch bbl., weight: 5 lbs., w/redesigned stock. Made 1948-65.

MODEL 15Y YOUTH'S RIFLE . . . . NiB $153 Ex $97 Gd $82
Same as Model 15 except w/21-inch bbl., short buttstock, weight: 4.75 lbs. Made 1958-65.

NO. 44 IDEAL
SINGLE-SHOT RIFLE. . . . . NiB $759 Ex $607 Gd $413
Rolling block. Lever-action. Takedown. Calibers: .22 LR. .25 R.F., .32 R.F., .25-20 S.S., .32-20, .32-40, .38-40, .38-55, .44-40. Bbl. lengths: 24-inch, 26-inch (round, half-octagon, full-octagon). Weight: 7 lbs w/26-inch round bbl. Sights: Open rear; Rocky Mountain front. Plain straight-grip stock and forearm. Made 1894-32.

NO. 44.5 IDEAL SINGLE-SHOT RIFLE . . . . NiB $957 Ex $765 Gd $520
Falling-block. Lever-action rifle. Aside from the new design action intro. 1903, specifications of this model are the same as those of Model 44. Model 44X disc. 1916.

NOS. 45 TO 54 IDEAL SINGLE-SHOT RIFLES
These are higher-grade models, differing from the standard No. 44 and 44.5 chiefly in finish, engraving, set triggers, levers, bbls., stock, etc. The Schuetzen types (including the Stevens-Pope models) are in this series. Model Nos. 45 to 54 were intro. 1896 and originally had the No. 44-type rolling-block action, which was superseded in 1903 by the No. 44.5-type falling-block action. These models were all disc. about 1916. Generally speaking, the 45-54 series rifles, particularly the Stevens Pope and higher grade Schuetzen models are collector's items, bringing much higher prices than the ordinary No. 44 and 44.5.

MODEL 66 BOLT-ACTION
REPEATING RIFLE . . . . NiB $178 Ex $102 Gd $87
Takedown. Caliber: .22 Short, Long, LR. Tubular magazine holds 13 LR, 15 Long, 19 Short. 24-inch bbl. Weight: 5 lbs. Sights: Open rear, bead front. Plain pistol-grip stock w/grooved forearm. Made 1931-35.

NO. 70 VISIBLE LOADING
SLIDE-ACTION . . . . NiB $306 Ex $255 Gd $102
Exposed hammer. Caliber: .22 LR., Long, Short. Tubular magazine holds 11 LR., 13 Long, 15 Short. 22-inch bbl. Weight: 4.5 lbs. Sights: Open rear; bead front. Plain straight-grip stock, grooved slide handle. Made 1907-34. Note: Nos. 702, 71, 712, 72, 722 essentially the same as No. 70, differing chiefly in bbl. length or sight tooling.

MODEL 87 AUTOLOADING RIFLE. . . . . NiB $178 Ex $127 Gd $92
Takedown. Caliber: .22 LR. 15-shot tubular magazine. 24-inch bbl. (20-inch on current model). Weight: 6 lbs. Sights: Open rear, bead front. Pistol-grip stock. Made 1938 to date. Note: This model originally bore the "Springfield" brand name, disc. in 1948.

MODEL 322 HI-POWER
BOLT-ACTION CARBINE. . . . . NiB $306 Ex $255 Gd $127
Caliber: .22 Hornet. 4-shot detachable magazine. 21-inch bbl. Weight: 6.75 lbs. Sights: Open rear; ramp front. Pistol-grip stock. Made 1947-50 (See Savage models 340, 342.)

Stevens No. 14 Little Scout

Stevens No. 14.5 Little Scout

Stevens No. 44 Ideal

Stevens Ideal Schuetzen Rifle

Stevens Model 87

MODEL 322-S . . . . **NiB $357 Ex $280 Gd $153**
Same as Model 325 except w/peep rear sight. (See Savage models 340S, 342S.)

**MODEL 325 HI-POWER
BOLT-ACTION CARBINE** . . . . **NiB $306 Ex $255 Gd $127**
Caliber: .30-30. Three shot detachable box magazine. 21-inch bbl. Weight: 6.75 lbs. Sights: Open rear; bead front. Plain pistol-grip stock. Made 1947-50. (See Savage Model 340.)

MODEL 325-S . . . . **NiB $357 Ex $280 Gd $153**
Same as Model 325 except w/peep rear sight. (See Savage Model 340S.)

**NO. 414 ARMORY MODEL
SINGLE-SHOT RIFLE** . . . . **NiB $510 Ex $433 Gd $280**
No. 44-type lever-action. Calibers: .22 LR only, .22 Short only. 26-inch bbl. Weight: 8 lbs. Sights: Lyman receiver peep; blade front. Plain straight-grip stock, military-type forearm, swivels. Made 1912-32.

**MODEL 416 BOLT-ACTION
TARGET RIFLE** . . . . **NiB $332 Ex $229 Gd $184**
Caliber: .22 LR. Five shot detachable box magazine. 26-inch heavy bbl. Weight: 9.5 lbs. Sights: Receiver peep; hooded front. Target stock, swivels, sling. Made 1937-49.

**NO. 419 JUNIOR TARGET MODEL
BOLT-ACTION SINGLE-SHOT RIFLE** . . . . . . **NiB $357 Ex $255 Gd $178**
Takedown. Caliber: .22 LR. 26-inch bbl. Weight: 5.5 lbs. Sights: Lyman No. 55 rear peep; blade front. Plain junior target stock w/pistol grip and grooved forearm, swivels, sling. Made 1932-36.

**BUCKHORN MODEL 053 BOLT-ACTION
SINGLE-SHOT RIFLE** . . . . **NiB $141 Ex $112 Gd $76**
Takedown. Calibers: .22 Short, Long, LR., .22 WRF. .25 Stevens R.F. 24-inch bbl. Weight: 5.5 lbs. Sights: Receiver peep; open middle; hooded front. Sporting stock w/pistol-grip and black forend tip. Made 1935-48.

BUCKHORN MODEL 53 . . . . **NiB $184 Ex $153 Gd $92**
Same as Buckhorn Model 053 except w/open rear sight and plain bead front sight.

Stevens No. 414 Armory

Stevens Model 416

Stevens Buckhorn Model 53

Stevens Buckhorn Model 055

Stevens Buckhorn Model 56

BUCKHORN 055 . . . . **NiB $184 Ex $153 Gd $92**
Takedown. Same as Model 056 except in single-shot configuration. Weight: 5.5 lbs. Caliber: .22 LR., Long, Short. 24-inch bbl. Weight: 6 lbs. Sights: Receiver peep, open middle, hooded front. Made 1935-48.

BUCKHORN MODEL 056
BOLT-ACTION . . . . **NiB $189 Ex $153 Gd $97**
Takedown. Caliber: .22 LR., Long, Short. Five shot detachable box magazine. 24-inch bbl. Weight: 6 lbs. Sights: Receiver peep, open middle, hooded front. Sporting stock w/pistol grip and black forend tip. Made 1935-48.

BUCKHORN
MODEL 56 . . . . **NiB $178 Ex $127 Gd $92**
Same as Buckhorn Model 056 except w/open rear sight and plain bead front sight.

BUCKHORN NO. 057 . . . . **NiB $163 Ex $102 Gd $76**
Same as Buckhorn Model 076 except w/5-shot detachable box magazine. Made 1939-48.

BUCKHORN NO. 57 . . . . **NiB $163 Ex $102 Gd $76**
Same as Buckhorn Model 76 except w/5-shot detachable box magazine. Made 1939-48.

BUCKHORN MODEL 066
BOLT-ACTION REPEATING RIFLE . . . . **NiB $229 Ex $178 Gd $102**
Takedown. Caliber: .22 LR, Long, Short. Tubular magazine holds 21 Short, 17 Long, 15 LR. 24-inch bbl. Weight: 6 lbs. Sights: Receiver peep; open middle; hooded front. Sporting stock w/pistol grip and black forend tip. Made 1935-48.

BUCKHORN MODEL 66 . . . . **NiB $163 Ex $102 Gd $76**
Same as Buckhorn Model 066 except w/open rear sight, plain bead front sight.

BUCKHORN NO. 076
AUTOLOADING RIFLE . . . . **NiB $178 Ex $153 Gd $97**
Takedown. Caliber: .22 LR. 15-shot tubular magazine. 24-inch bbl. Weight: 6 lbs. Sights: Receiver peep; open middle; hooded front. Sporting stock w/pistol grip, black forend tip. Made 1938-48.

BUCKHORN NO. 76 . . . . **NiB $178 Ex $153 Gd $92**
Same as Buckhorn No. 076 except w/open rear sight, plain bead front sight.

CRACKSHOT NO. 26
SINGLE-SHOT RIFLE . . . . **NiB $255 Ex $199 Gd $127**
Lever-action. Takedown. Calibers: .22 LR, .32 R.F. 18-inch or 22-inch bbl. Weight: 3.25 lbs. Sights: Open rear; blade front. Plain straight-grip stock, small tapered forearm. Made 1913-39.

Stevens Buckhorn Model 066

Stevens Buckhorn Model 66

Stevens Buckhorn Model 76

Stevens Crackshot No. 26

RIFLES

CRACKSHOT NO. 26.5 . . . . **NiB $296 Ex $178 Gd $153**
Same as Crackshot No. 26 except w/smoothbore bbl. for shot cartridges.

FAVORITE NO. 17
SINGLE-SHOT RIFLE . . . . **NiB $280 Ex $178 Gd $127**
Lever-action. Takedown. Calibers: .22 LR, .25 R.F., .32 R.F. 24-inch round bbl; other lengths were available. Weight: 4.5 lbs. Sights: Open rear; Rocky Mountain front. Plain straight-grip stock, small tapered forearm. Made 1894-1935.

FAVORITE NO. 18 . . . . **NiB $357 Ex $255 Gd $127**
Same as Favorite No. 17 except w/Vernier peep rear sight, leaf middle sight, Beach combination front sight.

FAVORITE NO. 19 . . . . **NiB $382 Ex $280 Gd $153**
Same as Favorite No. 17 except w/Lyman combination rear sight, leaf middle sight, Lyman front sight.

FAVORITE NO. 20 . . . . **NiB $357 Ex $280 Gd $178**
Same as Favorite No. 17 except w/smoothbore barrel.

FAVORITE NO. 27 . . . . **NiB $382 Ex $280 Gd $194**
Same as Favorite No. 17 except w/octagon bbl.

FAVORITE NO. 28 . . . . **NiB $357 Ex $255 Gd $178**
Same as Favorite No. 18 except w/octagon bbl.

FAVORITE NO. 29 . . . . **NiB $382 Ex $255 Gd $178**
Same as Favorite No. 19 except w/octagon bbl.

WALNUT HILL NO. 417-0
SINGLE-SHOT TARGET RIFLE . . . . **NiB $892 Ex $688 Gd $433**
Lever-action. Calibers: .22 LR only, .22 Short only, .22 Hornet. 28-inch heavy bbl. (extra heavy 29-inch bbl. also available). Weight: 10.5 lbs. Sights: Lyman No. 52L extension rear; 17A front, scope bases mounted on bbl. Target stock w/full pistol-grip, beavertail forearm, bbl. band, swivels, sling. Made 1932-47.

WALNUT HILL NO. 417-1 . . . . . . **NiB $918 Ex $892 Gd $510**
Same as No. 417-0 except w/Lyman No. 48L receiver sight.

WALNUT HILL NO. 417-2 . . . . . . **NiB $969 Ex $892 Gd $535**
Same as No. 417-0 except w/Lyman No. 144 tang sight.

WALNUT HILL NO. 417-3 . . . . . . **NiB $908 Ex $765 Gd $408**
Same as No. 417-0 except w/o sights.

WALNUT HILL NO. 417.5
SINGLE-SHOT RIFLE . . . . **NiB $918 Ex $841 Gd $459**
Lever-action. Calibers: .22 LR, .22 WMR, .25 R.F., .22 Hornet. 28-inch bbl. Weight: 8.5 lbs. Sights: Lyman No. 144 tang peep, folding middle; bead front. Sporting stock w/pistol-grip, semi-beavertail forearm, swivels, sling. Made 1932-40.

WALNUT HILL NO. 418
SINGLE-SHOT RIFLE . . . . **NiB $561 Ex $408 Gd $331**
Lever-action. Takedown. Calibers: .22 LR only, .22 Short only. 26-inch bbl. Weight: 6.5 lbs. Sights: Lyman No. 144 tang peep; blade front. Pistol-grip stock, semi-beavertail forearm, swivels, sling. Made 1932-40.

Stevens Walnut Hill
No. 417-1

Stevens Walnut Hill
No. 417.5

Stevens Walnut Hill
No. 418

WALNUT HILL NO. 418.5 . . . . NiB $637 Ex $561 Gd $398
Same as No. 418 except also available in calibers .22 WRF and .25
Stevens R.F., w/Lyman No. 2A tang peep sight, bead front sight.

MODEL 15 SINGLE-SHOT
BOLT-ACTION RIFLE . . . . NiB $153 Ex $102 Gd $76
Takedown. Caliber: .22 LR, Long, Short. 22-inch bbl. Weight: 4 lbs.
Sights: Open rear, bead front. Plain pistol-grip stock. Made 1937-48.

MODEL 82 BOLT-ACTION
SINGLE-SHOT RIFLE . . . . NiB $127 Ex $107 Gd $76
Takedown. Caliber: .22 LR, Long, Short. 22-inch bbl. Weight: 4 lbs.
Sights: Open rear; gold bead front. Plain pistol-grip stock w/grooved
forearm. Made 1935-39.

MODEL 83 BOLT-ACTION
SINGLE-SHOT RIFLE . . . . NiB $153 Ex $92 Gd $71
Takedown. Calibers: .22 LR, Long, Short; .22 WRF, .25 Stevens R.F.
24-inch bbl. Weight: 4.5 lbs. Sights: Peep rear; open middle; hooded front. Plain pistol-grip stock w/grooved forearm. Made 1935-39.

MODEL 84 . . . . NiB $178 Ex $153 Gd $97
Same as Model 86 except w/5-shot detachable box magazine. Pre-
1948 rifles of this model were designated Springfield Model 84,
later known as Stevens Model 84. Made 1940-65.

MODEL 84-S (084) . . . . NiB $178 Ex $153 Gd $97
Same as Model 84 except w/peep rear sight and hooded front sight.
Pre-1948 rifles of this model were designated Springfield Model
084, later known as Stevens Model 84-S. Disc.

MODEL 85 . . . . NiB $194 Ex $112 Gd $82
Same as Stevens Model 87 except w/5-shot detachable box magazine. Made
1939 to date. Pre-1948 rifles of this model were designated Springfield Model 85,
currently known as Stevens Model 85. Earlier models command slight premiums.

MODEL 85-S (085) . . . . NiB $178 Ex $127 Gd $92
Same as Model 85 except w/peep rear sight and hooded front sight.
Pre-1948 models were designated Springfield Model 085; also
known as Stevens Model 85-S.

MODEL 86
BOLT-ACTION . . . . NiB $178 Ex $127 Gd $92
Takedown. Caliber: .22 LR, Long, Short. Tubular magazine holds 15
LR, 17 Long, 21 Short. 24-inch bbl. Weight: 6 lbs. Sights: Open
rear, gold bead front. Pistol-grip stock, black forend tip on later production. Made 1935-65. Note: The Springfield brand name was
disc. in 1948.

MODEL 86-S (086) . . . . NiB $184 Ex $153 Gd $102
Same as Model 86 except w/peep rear sight and hooded front sight.
Pre-1948 rifles of this model were designated as Springfield Model
086, later known as Stevens Model 86-S. Disc.

MODEL 87-S (087) . . . . NiB $194 Ex $178 Gd $107
Same as Stevens Model 87 except w/peep rear sight and
hooded front sight. Pre-1948 rifles of this model were designated as Springfield Model 087, later known as Stevens Model
87-S. Disc.

STEYR-DAIMLER-PUCH A.-G. — Steyr, Austria

See also listings under Mannlicher.

AUG-SA
SEMIAUTOMATIC RIFLE . . . . NiB $3856 Ex $3085 Gd $2098
Gas-operated. Caliber: .223 Rem. (5.56mm). 30- or 40-shot magazine. 20-inch bbl. standard; optional 16-inch or 24-inch heavy bbl.
w/folding bipod. 31 inches overall. Weight: 8.5 lbs. Sights: Integral
1.5x scope and mount. Green high-impact synthetic stock w/folding
vertical grip.

Stevens-Springfield
Model 15

Stevens-Springfield
Model 82

Stevens-Springfield
Model 83

Stevens-Springfield
Model 84

Stevens-Springfield
Model 85

Stevens-Springfield
Model 86-S

RIFLES

SMALL BORE CARBINE. . . . . **NiB $547 Ex $438 Gd $298**
Bolt-action repeater. Caliber: .22 LR. Five shot detachable box magazine. 19.5-inch bbl. Sights: Leaf rear; hooded bead front. Mannlicher-type stock, checkered, swivels. Made 1953-67.

STOEGER RIFLE — Mfd. by Franz Jaeger & Co., Suhl, Germany; dist. in the U.S. by A. F. Stoeger, Inc., New York, N.Y.

HORNET RIFLE . . . . **NiB $1287 Ex $901 Gd $566**
Same specifications as Herold Rifle, designed and built on a Miniature Mauser-type action. See listing under Herold Bolt-Action Repeating Sporting Rifle for additional specifications. Imported during the 1930s.

SURVIVAL ARMS — Orange, CT

AR-7 EXPLORER . . . . **NiB $143 Ex $102 Gd $61**
Caliber: .22 LR. Eight shot magazine. Weight: 3 lbs. Polymer stocks. Drift adj. sights. Disassembles into five separate elements, allowing

(cont'd.) **AR-7 EXPLORER**
barrel, action and magazine to fit into buttstock; assembles quickly w/o tools. Choice of camo, silvertone or black matte finishes. Made 1992-95.

THOMPSON/CENTER ARMS — Rochester, New Hampshire

CONTENDER CARBINE
Calibers: .22 LR, .22 Hornet, .222 Rem., .223 Rem., 7mm T.C.U., 7x30 Waters, .30-30 Win., .35 Rem., .44 Mag., .357 Rem. Max. and .410 bore. 21-inch interchangeable bbls. 35 inches overall. Adj. iron sights. Checkered American walnut or Rynite stock and forend. Made 1985 to date.

Standard model (rifle calibers)	NiB $412	Ex $309	Gd $232
Standard model (.410 bore)	NiB $472	Ex $381	Gd $266
Rynite stock model (rifle calibers)	NiB $535	Ex $463	Gd $373
Rynite stock model (.410 bore).	NiB $560	Ex $484	Gd $387
Extra bbls. (rifle calibers)	NiB $256	Ex $211	Gd $153
Extra bbls. (.410 bore).	NiB $272	Ex $221	Gd $158
Youth model (all calibers and .410 bore)	NiB $360	Ex $283	Gd $180

Thompson/Center
Contender Carbine

Thompson/Center
TCR '83 Aristocrat

Thompson/Center
TCR '87 Hunter

CONTENDER CARBINE
SURVIVAL SYSTEM . . . . **NiB $592 Ex $412 Gd $309**
Similar to standard Contender Carbine w/Rynite stock and forend. Comes w/two 16.25-inch bbls. chambered in .223 and .45/.410 bore. Camo Cordura case.

STAINLESS CONTENDER CARBINE
Same as standard Contender Carbine Model, except stainless steel w/blued sights. Calibers: .22 LR, .22 Hornet, .223 Rem., 7-30 Waters, .30-30 Win., .410. Walnut or Rynite stock and forend. Made 1993 to date.
Walnut stock model. . . . . **NiB $463 Ex $386 Gd $257**
Rynite stock model . . . . **NiB $438 Ex $360 Gd $247**
Youth stock model. . . . . **NiB $412 Ex $335 Gd $232**
Extra bbls. (rifle calibers). . . . . **NiB $226 Ex $180 Gd $123**

TCR '83 ARISTOCRAT MODEL
Break frame, overlever action. Calibers: .223 Rem., .22/250 Rem., .243 Win., 7mm Rem. Mag., .30-06 Springfield. Interchangeable bbls.: 23 inches in length. Weight: 6 lbs., 14 oz. American walnut stock and forearm, checkered, black rubber recoil pad, cheekpiece. Made 1983-87.
TCR '83 Standard model . . . . **NiB $438 Ex $386 Gd $206**
TCR '83 Aristocrat. . . . . **NiB $510 Ex $360 Gd $232**
Extra bbls. (rifle calibers). . . . . **NiB $226 Ex $180 Gd $123**

TCR '87 HUNTER RIFLE
Similar to TCR '83 except in calibers .22 Hornet, ..222 Rem., 223 Rem., .22-250 Rem., .243 Win., .270 Win., 7mm-08, .308 Win., .30-06, .32-40 Win. Also 12-ga. slug and 10- and 12-ga. field bbls. 23-inch standard or 25.88-inch heavy bbl. interchangeable. 39.5 to 43.38 inches overall. Weight: 6 lbs., 14 oz. to 7.5 lbs. Iron sights optional. Checkered American black walnut buttstock w/fluted end. Disc. 1993.

(cont'd.) TCR '87 HUNTER RIFLE
Standard model. . . . . **NiB $515 Ex $412 Gd $232**
Extra bbl. (rifle calibers and
10- or 12-ga. Field) . . . . **NiB $245 Ex $196 Gd $133**
Extra bbl. (12-ga. slug) . . . . **NiB $289 Ex $232 Gd $158**

TIKKA RIFLES — Mfg. by Sako, Ltd. of Riihimaki, Finland & Armi Marocchi in Italy

Imported by Beretta USA

Note: *Tikka New Generation, Battue and Continental series bolt action rifles are being manufactured by Sako, Ltd., in Finland. Tikka O/U rifles (previously Valmet) are being manufactured in Italy by Armi Marocchi. For earlier importation see additional listings under Ithaca LSA and Valmet 412S models.*

MODEL 412S DOUBLE RIFLE
Calibers: .308 Win., .30-06, 9.3x74R. 24-inch bbl. w/quarter rib machined for scope mounts; automatic ejectors (9.3x74R only). 40 inches overall. Weight: 8.5 lbs. Ramp front and folding adj. rear sight. Barrel selector on trigger and cocking indicators in tang. European walnut buttstock and forearm. Model 412S was replaced by the 512S version in 1994. Imported 1989-93.
Model 412S
(disc. 1993) . . . . **NiB $1432 Ex $1030 Gd $772**
Extra barrel assembly
(O/U shotgun), add. **$650**
Extra barrel assembly
(O/U Combo), add **$775**
Extra barrel assembly
(O/U rifle), add. **$995**

Tikka Model 412S
Double Rifle

Tikka Model LSA55
Deluxe

Tikka Model LSA65
Deluxe

Tikka Model M55
Deluxe

Tikka Model M55
Standard

MODEL 512S DOUBLE RIFLE
Formerly Valmet 412S. In 1994, following the joint venture of 1989, the model designation was changed to 512S. Imported 1994 to date.
Model 512S......................NiB $1442 Ex $1313 Gd $953
Extra barrel assembly
(O/U rifle), add..$755

LSA55 DELUXE...............NiB $515 Ex $463 Gd $386
Same as LSA55 Standard except w/rollover cheekpiece, rosewood grip cap and forend tip, skip checkering, high-luster blue. Imported 1965-88.

LSA55 SPORTER...............NiB $508 Ex $407 Gd $277
Same as LSA55 except has 22.8-inch heavy bbl. w/o sights, special stock w/beavertail forearm, not available in 6mm Rem. Weighs 9 lbs. Imported 1965-88.

LSA55 STANDARD
BOLT-ACTION REPEATER.......NiB $463 Ex $335 Gd $206
Mauser-type action. Calibers: .222 Rem., .22-250, 6mm Rem. Mag., .243 Win., .308 Win. Thrree shot clip magazine. 22.8-inch bbl. Weight: 6.8 lbs. Sights: Folding leaf rear; hooded ramp front. Checkered walnut stock w/Monte Carlo cheekpiece, swivels. Made 1965-88.

LSA65 DELUXE................NiB $541 Ex $463 Gd $309
Same as LSA65 Standard except w/special features of LSA55 Deluxe. Imported 1970-88.

LSA65 STANDARD.............NiB $438 Ex $335 Gd $206
Same as LSA55 Standard except calibers: .25-06, 6.5x55 .270 Win., .30-06. Five shot magazine, 22-inch bbl., weight: 7.5 lbs. Imported 1970-88.

MODEL M 55
Bolt action. Calibers: .222 Rem., .22-250 Rem., .223 Rem. .243 Win., .308 Win. (6mm Rem. and 17 Rem. available in Standard and Deluxe models only). 23.2-inch bbl. (24.8-inch in Sporter and Heavy Barrel models). 42.8 inches overall (44 inches in Sporter and Heavy Barrel models). Weight: 7.25 to 9 lbs. Monte Carlo-style stock w/pistol-grip. Sling swivels. Imported 1965-88.
Continental ....NiB $669 Ex $489 Gd $340
Deluxe model ....NiB $711 Ex $494 Gd $360
Sporter........................NiB $644 Ex $515 Gd $335
Sporter w/sights ....NiB $669 Ex $489 Gd $339
Standard ....NiB $592 Ex $463 Gd $309
Super Sporter ....NiB $747 Ex $608 Gd $360
Super Sporter w/sights ....NiB $814 Ex $386 Gd $412
Trapper ....NiB $680 Ex $463 Gd $335

Tikka Model M65 Sporter

Tikka Model M65 Wild Boar

MODEL M65
Bolt action. Calibers: .25-06, .270 Win., .308 Win., .30-06, 7mm Rem. Mag., .300 Win. Mag. (Sporter and Heavy Bbl. models in .270 Win., .308 Win. and .30-06 only). 22.4-inch bbl. (24.8-inch in Sporter and Heavy Bbl. models). 43.2 inches overall (44 inches in Sporter, 44.8 inches in Heavy Bbl.). Weight: 7.5 to 9.9 lbs. Monte Carlo-style stock w/pistol-grip. Disc. 1989.

Continental	NiB $669	Ex $489	Gd $340
Deluxe Magnum	NiB $747	Ex $608	Gd $3407
Deluxe model	NiB $695	Ex $489	Gd $335
Magnum	NiB $644	Ex $438	Gd $360
Sporter	NiB $515	Ex $463	Gd $309
Sporter w/sights	NiB $700	Ex $566	Gd $360
Standard	NiB $592	Ex $463	Gd $309
Super Sporter	NiB $819	Ex $618	Gd $412
Super Sporter w/sights	NiB $824	Ex $644	Gd $463
Super Sporter Master	NiB $1030	Ex $850	Gd $515

MODEL M65 WILDBOAR .... NiB $695 Ex $566 Gd $402
Same general specifications as Model M 65 except 20.8-inch bbl., overall length of 41.6 inches, weight: of 7.5 lbs. Disc. 1989.

NEW GENERATION RIFLES
Short-throw bolt available in three action lengths. Calibers: .22-250 Rem., .223 Rem., .243 Win., .308 Win., (medium action) .25-06 Rem., .270 Win., .30.06, (Long Action) 7mm Rem. Mag., .300 Win. Mag., .338 Win. Mag., (Magnum Action). 22- to 26-inch bbl. 42.25 to 46 inches overall. Weight: 7.2 to 8.5 lbs. Available w/o sights or w/hooded front and open rear sight on quarter rib. Quick-release 3- or 5-shot detachable magazine w/recessed side release. Barrel selector on trigger and cocking indicators in tang. European walnut buttstock and forearm matte lacquer finish. Imported 1989-94.

Standard calibers	NiB $772	Ex $608	Gd $386
Magnum calibers	NiB $798	Ex $618	Gd $412

PREMIUM GRADE RIFLE
Similar to New Generation rifles except w/hand-checkered deluxe wood stock w/roll-over check-piece and rosewood grip cap and forend tip. High polished blued finish. Imported 1989-94.

Standard calibers	NiB $819	Ex $669	Gd $412
Magnum calibers	NiB $901	Ex $669	Gd $489

WHITETAIL BOLT-ACTION RIFLE SERIES
New Generation design in multiple model configurations and three action lengths chambered .22-250 to .338 Win. Mag.

BATTUE MODEL
Similar to Hunter Model except designed for snapshooting w/hooded front and open rear sights on quarter rib. Blued finish. Checkered select walnut stock w/matt lacquered finish. Imported 1991-97.

Battue model (standard w/sights)	NiB $587	Ex $463	Gd $309
Magnum calibers, add			$40

CONTINENTAL MODEL
Similar to Hunter Model except w/prone-style stock w/wider forearm and 26-inch heavy bbl. chambered for 17 Rem., .22-250 Rem., .223 Rem., .308 Win. (Varmint); .25-06 Rem., .270 Win., 7mm Rem. Mag., .300 Win. Mag. (Long Range). Weight: 8.6 lbs. Imported 1991 to date.

Continental Long-Range model	NiB $695	Ex $489	Gd $340
Continental Varmint model	NiB $644	Ex $489	Gd $335
Magnum calibers, add			$40

SPORTER MODEL .... NiB $875 Ex $695 Gd $541
Similar to Hunter Model except 23.5-inch bbl. Five shot detachable mazigine. Chambered .22-250 Rem., .223 Rem., .308 Win. Weight: 8.6 lbs. Adjustable buttplate and cheekpiece w/stippled pistol grip and forend. Imported 1998 to date.

WHITETAIL HUNTER MODEL
Calibers: .22-250 Rem., .223 Rem., .243 Win., .25-06 Rem., .270 Win., 7mm Rem. Mag., .308 Win .30.06, .300 Win. Mag., .338 Win. Mag. Three or 5-shot detachable box magazine. 20.5- to 24.5-inch bbl. with no sights. 42 to 44.5 inches overall. Weight: 7 to 7.5 lbs. Adj. single-stage or single-set trigger. Blued or stainless finish. All-Weather synthetic or checkered select walnut stock w/matt lacquered finish. Imported 1991 to date.

Standard model	NiB $592	Ex $463	Gd $309
Deluxe model	NiB $721	Ex $566	Gd $386
Synthetic model	NiB $695	Ex $463	Gd $335
Stainless model	NiB $700	Ex $510	Gd $335
Magnum calibers, add			$40
Left-hand model, add			$70

Tikka
Continental/Varmint

Tikka
New Generation

Tikka
Premium Grade

Tikka
Whitetail/Battue

Tikka
Whitetail Hunter Deluxe

Tikka
Whitetail Hunter Synthetic

Tikka
Whitetail Hunter Stainless Synthetic

UBERTI RIFLES — Lakeville, Connecticut
Mfd. By Aldo Uberti, Ponte Zanano, Italy
Imported by Stoeger Industries, Accokeek, MD

MODEL 1866 SPORTING RIFLE
Replica of Winchester Model 1866 lever-action repeater. Calibers: .22 LR, .22 WMR, .38 Spec., .44-40, .45 LC. 24.25-inch octagonal bbl. 43.25 inches overall. Weight: 8.25 lbs. Blade front sight, rear elevation leaf. Brass frame and buttplate. Bbl., magazine tube, other metal parts blued. Walnut buttstock and forearm.

Model 1866 Rifle	NiB $772	Ex $592	Gd $309
Model 1866 Carbine (19-inch round bbl.)	NiB $664	Ex $541	Gd $335
Model 1866 Trapper (16-inch bbl.) Disc. 1989	NiB $592	Ex $463	Gd $330
Model 1866 Rimfire (Indian Rifle)	NiB $541	Ex $438	Gd $309
Model 1866 Rimfire (Indian Carbine)	NiB $515	Ex $417	Gd $304

Uberti Model
1873 Carbine

Ultra Model 2200

Ultra Light Model 28

MODEL 1873 SPORTING RIFLE

Replica of Winchester Model 1873 lever-action repeater. Calibers: .22 LR, .22 WMR, .38 Spec., .357 Mag., .44-40, .45 LC. 24.25- or 30-inch octagonal bbl. 43.25 inches overall. Weight: 8 lbs. Blade front sight; adj. open rear. Color case-hardened frame. Bbl., magazine tube, hammer, lever and buttplate blued. Walnut buttstock and forearm.

Model 1873 Rifle . . . . NiB $850 Ex $608 Gd $360
Model 1873 Carbine
(19-inch round bbl.) . . . . NiB $747 Ex $577 Gd $350
Model 1873 Trapper
(16-inch bbl.)
Disc. 1990 . . . . NiB $695 Ex $515 Gd $335

HENRY RIFLE

Replica of Henry lever-action repeating rifle. Calibers: .44-40, .45 LC. 24.5-inch half-octagon bbl. 43.75 inches overall. Weight: 9.25 lbs. Blade front sight; rear sight adj. for elevation. Brass frame, buttplate and magazine follower. Bbl., magazine tube and remaining parts blued. Walnut buttstock.

Henry Rifle . . . . NiB $798 Ex $566 Gd $386
Henry Carbine (22.5-inch bbl.) . . . . NiB $772 Ex $541 Gd $360
Henry Trapper
(16- or 18-inch bbl.) . . . . NiB $721 Ex $577 Gd $392
Steel frame, add. $85

ULTRA-HI PRODUCTS COMPANY — Hawthorne, New Jersey

MODEL 2200 SINGLE-SHOT

BOLT-ACTION RIFLE . . . . NiB $154 Ex $113 Gd $77
Caliber: .22 LR, Long, Short. .23-inch bbl. Weight: 5 lbs. Sights: Open rear; blade front. Monte Carlo stock w/pistol grip. Made in Japan. Intro. 1977; Disc.

ULTRA LIGHT ARMS COMPANY — Granville, West Virginia

MODEL 20 BOLT-ACTION RIFLE

Calibers: .22-250 Rem., .243 Win., 6mm Rem., .250-3000 Savage, .257 Roberts, .257 Ack., 7mm Mauser, 7mm Ack., 7mm-08 Rem., .284 Win., .300 Savage, .308 Win., .358 Win. Box magazine. 22-inch ultra light bbl. Weight: 4.75 lbs. No sights. Synthetic stock of Kevlar or graphite finished, seven different colors. Nonglare matte or bright metal finish. Medium-length action available L.H. models. Made 1985 to date.
Standard model . . . . NiB $2292 Ex $1905 Gd $1025
Left-hand model . . . . NiB $2066 Ex $1674 Gd $1171

MODEL 20S BOLT-ACTION RIFLE

Same general specifications as Model 20 except w/short action in calibers 17 Rem., .222 Rem., .223 Rem., .22 Hornet only.
Standard model . . . . NiB $2317 Ex $1931 Gd $1030
Left-hand model . . . . NiB $2157 Ex $1746 Gd $1221

MODEL 24 BOLT-ACTION RIFLE

Same general specifications as Model 20 except w/long action in calibers .25-06, .270 Win., .30-06 and 7mm Express only.
Standard model . . . . NiB $2395 Ex $1947 Gd $1025
Left-hand model . . . . NiB $2099 Ex $1699 Gd $1189

MODEL 28 BOLT-ACTION RIFLE . . . . . NiB $2575 Ex $1844 Gd $1133
Same general specifications as Model 20 except w/long magnum action in calibers .264 Win. Mag., 7mm Rem. Mag., .300 Win. Mag., .338 Win. Mag. only. Offered w/recoil arrester. Left-hand model available.

MODEL 40 BOLT-ACTION RIFLE

Similar to Model 28 except in calibers .300 Wby. and .416 Rigby. Weight: 5.5 lbs. Made 1994 to date.
Standard model . . . . NiB $2575 Ex $1844 Gd $1133
Left-hand, model . . . . NiB $2543 Ex $2055 Gd $1431

U.S. Model 1903-A1
Springfield

U.S. Model 1903-A3
Springfield

U.S. Model 1917
Enfield

UNIQUE RIFLE — Hendaye, France
Mfd. by Manufacture d'Armes des Pyrénées Francaises

T66 MATCH RIFLE. . . . . **NiB $489 Ex $412 Gd $283**
Single-shot bolt-action rifle. Caliber: .22 LR. 25.5-inch bbl. Weight: 10.5 lbs. Sights: Micrometer aperture rear; globe front. French walnut target stock w/Monte Carlo comb, bull pistol-grip, wide and deep forearm, stippled grip surfaces, adj. swivel on accessory track, adj. rubber buttplate. Made 1966. Disc.

U.S. MILITARY RIFLES — Mfd. by Springfield Armory, Remington Arms Co., Winchester Repeating Arms Co., Inland Mfg. Div. of G.M.C., and other contractors. See notes.

Unless otherwise indicated, the following U.S. military rifles were mfg. at Springfield Armory, Springfield, Mass.

MODEL 1898
KRAG-JORGENSEN CARBINE . . . **NiB $1931 Ex $1725 Gd $978**
Same general specifications as Model 1898 Rifle except w/22-inch bbl., weight: 8 lbs., carbine-type stock. Note: The foregoing specifications apply, in general, to Carbine models 1896 and 1899, which differed from Model 1898 only in minor details.

MODEL 1898
KRAG-JORGENSEN MILITARY RIFLE . . . **NiB $1931 Ex $1625 Gd $978**
Bolt action. Caliber: .30-40 Krag. 5-shot hinged box magazine. 30-inch bbl. Weight: 9 lbs. Sights: Adj. rear; blade front. Military-type stock, straight grip. Note: The foregoing specifications apply, in general, to Rifle models 1892 and 1896, which differed from Model 1898.

MODEL 1903 MARK I SPRINGFIELD . . . **NiB $1905 Ex $1699 Gd $798**
Same as Standard Model 1903 except altered to permit use of the Pedersen Device. This device, officially designated "U.S. Automatic Pistol Model 1918," converted the M/1903 to a semiautomatic weapon firing a .30 caliber cartridge similar to .32 automatic pistol ammunition. Mark I rifles have a slot milled in the left side of the receiver to serve as an ejection port when the Pedersen Device was in

(cont'd.) MODEL 1903 MARK I SPRINGFIELD
use; these rifles were also fitted w/a special sear and cut-off. Some 65,000 of these devices were manufactured and, presumably, a like number of M/1903 rifles were converted to handle them. During the early 1930s, all Pedersen Devices were ordered destroyed and the Mark I rifles were reconverted by replacement of the special sear and cut-off w/standard components. Some 20-odd specimens are known to have escaped destruction and are in government museums and private collections. Probably more are extant. Rarely is a Pedersen Device offered for sale, so a current value cannot be assigned. However, many of the altered rifles were bought by members of the National Rifle Association through the Director of Civilian Marksmanship. Value shown is for the Mark I rifle w/o the Pedersen Device.

MODEL 1903 NATIONAL
MATCH SPRINGFIELD . . . . **NiB $1596 Ex $1416 Gd $818**
Same general specifications as Standard Model 1903 except specially selected w/star-gauged bbl., Type C pistol-grip U.S. Model 1903 National Match Springfield (Con't) stock, polished bolt assembly; early types have headless firing pin assembly and reversed safety lock. Produced especially for target shooting.

MODEL 1903 SPRINGFIELD MILITARY RIFLE
Modified Mauser-type bolt action. Caliber: .30-06. 5-shot box magazine. 23.79-inch bbl. Weight: 8.75 lbs. Sights: Adj. rear; blade front. Military-type stock straight grip. Note: M/1903 rifles of Springfield manufacture w/serial numbers under 800,000 (1903-1918) have case-hardened receivers; those between 800,000 and 1,275,767 (1918-1927) were double heat-treated; rifles numbered over 1,275,767 have nickle steel bolts and receivers. Rock Island production from No. 1 to 285,507 have case-hardened receivers. Improved heat treatment was adopted in May 1918 with No. 285,207; about three months later, with No. 319,921, the use of nickel steel was begun, but the production of some double-heat-treated carbon-steel receivers and bolts continued. Made 1903-30 at Springfield Armory during WWI, M/1903 rifles were also made at Rock Island Arsenal, Rock Island, Ill.
W/case-hardened receiver. . . . . . **NiB $5150 Ex $4377 Gd $1905**
W/double heat-treated receiver . . . **NiB $4068 Ex $3347 Gd $1339**
W/nickel steel receiver . . . . **NiB $1493 Ex $1287 Gd $772**

MODEL 1903 SPRINGFIELD SPORTER. . **NiB $1281 Ex $1025 Gd $697**
Same general specifications as National Match except w/sporting design stock, Lyman No. 48 receiver sight.

U.S. Carbine Caliber .30, M1 (Grand)

U.S. Carbine Caliber .30, M1

MODEL 1903 STYLE T
SPRINGFIELD MATCH RIFLE . . . . NiB $1481 Ex $1184 Gd $805
Same specifications as Springfield Sporter except w/heavy bbl. (26-, 28- or 30-inch), scope bases, globe front sight, weight: 12.5 lbs. w/26-inch bbl.

MODEL 1903 TYPE A
SPRINGFIELD FREE RIFLE . . . . . . NiB $1771 Ex $1416 Gd $963
Same as Style T except made w/28-inch bbl. only, w/Swiss buttplate, weight: 13.25 lbs.

MODEL 1903 TYPE B
SPRINGFIELD FREE RIFLE . . . . . NiB $2349 Ex $1880 Gd $1278
Same as Type A, except w/cheekpiece stock, palm rest, Woodie double-set triggers, Garand fast firing pin, weight: 14.75 lbs.

MODEL 1903-A1 SPRINGFIELD
Same general specifications as Model 1903 except may have Type C pistol-grip stock adopted in 1930. The last Springfields produced at the Springfield Armory were of this type; final serial number was 1,532,878, made in 1939. Note: Late in 1941, Remington Arms Co., Ilion, N.Y., began production, under government contract, of Springfield rifles of this type w/a few minor modifications. These rifles are numbered 3,000,001-3,348,085 and were manufactured before the adoption of Model 1903-A3.
Springfield manufacture . . . . NiB $1287 Ex $1133 Gd $618
Remington manufacture . . . . NiB $837 Ex $669 Gd $455

MODEL 1903-A3 SPRINGFIELD . . . . NiB $1545 Ex $1339 Gd $335
Same general specifications as Model 1903-A1, except modified to permit increased production and lower cost; may have either straight-grip or pistol-grip stock, bolt is not interchangeable w/earlier types, w/receiver peep sight, many parts are stamped sheet steel, including the trigger guard and magazine assembly. Quality of these rifles, lower than that of other 1903 Springfields, reflects the emergency conditions under which they were produced. Mfd. during WWII by Remington Arms Co. and L. C. Smith Corona Typewriters, Inc.

MODEL 1922-M1 22
SPRINGFIELD TARGET RIFLE . . . . NiB $1127 Ex $901 Gd $613
Modified Model 1903. Caliber: .22 LR. Five shot detachable box magazine. 24.5-inch bbl. Weight: 9 lbs. Sights: Lyman No. 48C receiver, blade front. Sporting-type stock similar to that of Model 1903 Springfield Sporter. Issued 1927. Note: The earlier Model 1922, which is seldom encountered, differs from the foregoing chiefly in the bolt mechanism and magazine.

M2 22 SPRINGFIELD TARGET RIFLE . . . . NiB $1231 Ex $953 Gd $515
Same general specifications as Model 1922-M1 except w/speedlock, improved bolt assembly adj. for headspace. Note: These improvements were later incorporated in many rifles of the preceding models (M1922, M1922MI) and arms so converted were marked "M1922M2" or "M1922MII."

NOTE: *The WWII-vintage .30-caliber U.S. Carbine was mfd. by Inland Mfg. Div. of G.M.C., Dayton, OH; Winchester Repeating Arms Co., New Haven, CT, and other contractors: International Business Machines Corp., Poughkeepsie, NY; National Postal Meter Co., Rochester, NY; Quality Hardware & Machine Co., and Rock-Ola Co., Chicago, IL; Saginaw Steering Gear Div. of G.M.C., Saginaw, MI; Standard Products Co., Port Clinton, OH; Underwood-Elliott-Fisher Co., Hartford, CT.*

CALIBER .30, M1
(GARAND) MIL. RIFLE . . . . NiB $1287 Ex $1081 Gd $1004
Clip-fed, gas-operated, air-cooled semiautomatic. Uses a clip containing 8 rounds. 24-inch bbl. Weight: W/o bayonet, 9.5 lbs. Sights: Adj. peep rear; blade front w/guards. Pistol-grip stock, handguards. Made 1937-57. Note: Garand rifles have also been produced by Winchester Repeating Arms Co., Harrington & Richardson Arms Co., and International Harvester Co. Deduct 25% for arsenal-assembled mismatches.

CALIBER .30, M1,
NATIONAL MATCH . . . . NiB $2163 Ex $1596 Gd $618
Accurized target version of the Garand. Glass-bedded stock; match grade bbl., sights, gas cylinder. "NM" stamped on bbl. forward of handguard.

NOTE: *The U.S. Model 1917 Enfield was mfd. 1917-18 by Remington Arms Co. of Delaware (later Midvale Steel & Ordnance Co., Eddystone, PA); Remington Arms Co., Ilion, NY; Winchester Repeating Arms Co., New Haven, CT.*

MODEL 1917 ENFIELD MILITARY RIFLE . . NiB $819 Ex $695 Gd $257
Modified Mauser-type bolt action. Caliber: .30-06. Five shot box magazine. 26-inch bbl. Weight: 9.25 lbs. Sights: Adj. rear; blade front w/guards. Military-type stock w/semi-pistol-grip. This design originated in Great Britain as the, "Pattern 14" and was mfd. in caliber .303 for the British Government in three U.S. plants. In 1917, the U.S. Government contracted w/these firms to produce the same rifle in caliber .30-06; over two million of these Model 1917 Enfields were mfd. While no more were produced after WWI, the U.S. supplied over a million of them to Great Britain during WWII.

Uzi Semiautomatic
Model B Carbine

RIFLES

Valmet M-62S

Valmet Hunter

**CARBINE,
CALIBER 30, M1** . . . . **NiB $741 Ex $592 Gd $403**
Gas-operated (short-stroke piston), semiautomatic. 15- or 30-round detachable box magazine. 18-inch bbl. Weight: 5.5 lbs. Sights: adj. rear; blade front sight w/guards. Pistol-grip stock w/handguard, side-mounted web sling. Made 1942-45. In 1963, 150,000 surplus M1 Carbines were sold at $20 each to members of the National Rifle Assn. by the Dept. of the Army. Note: For Winchester and Rock-Ola, add 30%; for Irwin Pedersen, add 80%. Quality Hardware did not complete its production run. Guns produced by other manufacturers were marked "Unquality" & command premium prices.

U.S. REPEATING ARMS CO.

See Winchester Rifle listings.

UNIVERSAL SPORTING GOODS, INC. — Miami, Florida

DELUXE CARBINE. . . . . **NiB $331 Ex $280 Gd $153**
Same as standard model except also available in caliber .256, w/deluxe walnut Monte Carlo stock and handguard. Made 1965 to date.

STANDARD M-1 CARBINE . . . . **NiB $229 Ex $178 Gd $127**
Same as U.S. Carbine, Cal. .30, M1 except may have either wood or metal handguard, bbl. band w/ or w/o bayonet lug; 5-shot magazine standard. Made 1964 to date.

UZI CARBINE — Mfd. by Israel Military Industries, Israel

SEMIAUTOMATIC MODEL B CARBINE
Calibers: 9mm Parabellum, .41 Action Express, .45 ACP. 20- to 50-round magazine. 16.1-inch bbl. Weight: 8.4 lbs. Metal folding stock. Front post-type sight, open rear, both adj. Imported by Action Arms 1983-89. NFA (Selective Fire) models imported by UZI America, INC., 1994 to date.
Model B Carbine (9mm or .45 ACP). . . . NiB $1313 Ex $1081 Gd $695
Model B Carbine (.41 AE). . . . . NiB $1539 Ex $1231 Gd $837
Centerfire conversion unit, add $250
Rimfire conversion unit, add. $175

SEMIAUTOMATIC
MINI CARBINE . . . . **NiB $2523 Ex $2060 Gd $1442**
Similar to Uzi Model B except with 19.75-inch bbl.and chambered 9mm Parabellum only. 20-round magazine. Weight: 7.2 lbs. Imported 1989.

**Vickers Jubilee
Single-Shot Target Rifle**

VALMET OY — Jyväskylä, Finland

M-62S SEMIAUTOMATIC RIFLE . . . . NiB $1834 Ex $1468 Gd $998
Semiautomatic version of Finnish M-62 automatic assault rifle based on Russian AK-47. Gas-operated rotating bolt action. Caliber: 7.62mmX39 Russian. 15- and 30-round magazines. 16.63-inch bbl. Weight: 8 lbs. w/metal stock. Sights: Tangent aperture rear; hooded blade front w/luminous flip-up post for low-light use. Tubular steel or wood stock. Intro. 1962. Disc.

M-71S . . . . NiB $1854 Ex $1622 Gd $901
Same specifications as M-62S except caliber 5.56mmx45 (.223 Rem.), w/open rear sight, reinforced resin or wood stock, weight: 7.75 lbs. w/former. Made 1971-89.

M-76 SEMIAUTOMATIC RIFLE
Semiautomatic assault rifle. Gas-operated, rotating bolt action. Caliber: 223 Rem. 15- and 30-shot magazines. Made 1984-89.
Wood stock . . . . NiB $1539 Ex $1231 Gd $883
Folding stock . . . . NiB $1925 Ex $1540 Gd $1048

M-78 SEMIAUTOMATIC RIFLE . . . . NiB $1739 Ex $1390 Gd $946
Caliber: 7.62x51 (NATO). 24.13-inch bbl. Overall length: 43.25 inches. Weight: 10.5 lbs.

M-82 SEMIAUTOMATIC CARBINE . . . . NiB $2575 Ex $2008 Gd $1004
Caliber: .223 Rem. 15- or 30-shot magazine. 17-inch bbl. 27 inches overall. Weight: 7.75 lbs.

MODEL 412 S DOUBLE RIFLE . . . . NiB $1352 Ex $1081 Gd $735
Boxlock. Manual or automatic extraction. Calibers: .243, .308, .30-06, .375 Win., 9.3x74R. Bbls.: 24-inch over/under. Weight: 8.63 lbs. American walnut checkered stock and forend.

HUNTER SEMIAUTOMATIC RIFLE . . . . NiB $978 Ex $772 Gd $515
Similar to M-78 except in calibers .223 Rem. (5.56mm), .243 Win., .308 Win. (7.62 NATO) and .30-06. Five , 9- or 15-shot magazine. 20.5-inch plain bbl. 42 inches overall. Weight: 8 lbs. Sights: Adj. combination scope mount/rear; blade front, mounted on gas tube. Checkered European walnut buttstock and extended checkered forend and handguard. Imported 1986-89.

VICKERS LTD. — Crayford, Kent, England

**JUBILEE MODEL SINGLE-SHOT-
TARGET RIFLE . . . . NiB $438 Ex $335 Gd $206**
Round-receiver Martini-type action. Caliber: .22 LR. 28-inch heavy bbl. Weight: 9.5 lbs. Sights: Parker-Hale No. 2 front; Perfection rear peep. One-piece target stock w/full forearm and pistol-grip. Made before WWII.

EMPIRE MODEL . . . . NiB $489 Ex $360 Gd $232
Similar to Jubilee Model except w/27- or 30-inch bbl., straight-grip stock, weight: 9.25 lbs. w/30-inch bbl. Made before WWII.

VOERE — Manufactured in Kufstein, Austria Imported by JagerSport, Cranston, Rhode Island

**VEC-91 LIGHTNING
BOLT-ACTION RIFLE . . . . NiB $2511 Ex $2008 Gd $1366**
Features unique electronic ignition system to activate or fire caseless ammunition. Calibers: .5.56 UCC (.222 Cal.), 6mm UCC caseless. Five shot magazine. 20-inch bbl. 39 inches overall. Weight: 6 lbs. Open adj. rear sight. Drilled and tapped for scope mounts. European walnut stock w/cheekpiece. Twin forward locking lugs. Imported 1992 to date.

VOERE, VOELTER & COMPANY — Vaehrenbach, Germany

Mauser-Werke acquired Voere in 1987 and all models are now marketed under new designations.

MODEL 1007 BIATHLON REPEATER . . . . . NiB $360 Ex $283 Gd $180
Caliber: 22 LR. Five shot magazine. 19.5-inch bbl. 39 inches overall. Weight: 5.5 lb. Sights: Adj. rear, blade front. Plain beechwood stock. Imported 1984-86.

MODEL 1013 BOLT-ACTION REPEATER . . . . . NiB $669 Ex $463 Gd $309
Same as Model 1007 except w/military-style stock in 22 WMR caliber. Double-set triggers optional. Imported 1984-86 by KDF, Inc.

MODEL 2107 BOLT-ACTION REPEATER
Caliber: 22 LR. Five or 8-shot magazine. 19.5-inch bbl. 41 inches overall. Weight: 6 lbs. Sights: Adj. rear sight, hooded front. European hardwood Monte Carlo-style stock. Imported 1986 by KDF, Inc.
Standard model . . . . NiB $360 Ex $232 Gd $154
Deluxe model . . . . NiB $412 Ex $283 Gd $206

WALTHER RIFLES — Mfd. by the German firms of Waffenfabrik Walther and Carl Walther Sportwaffenfabrik

The following Walther rifles were mfd. before WWII by Waffenfabrik Walther, Zella-Mehlis (Thür.), Germany.

**MODEL 1 AUTOLOADING
RIFLE (LIGHT) . . . . NiB $716 Ex $618 Gd $360**
Similar to Standard Model 2 but w/20-inch bbl., lighter stock, weight: 4.5 lbs.

MODEL 2 AUTOLOADING RIFLE . . . . NiB $695 Ex $566 Gd $335
Bolt-action, may be used as autoloader, manually operated repeater or single-shot. Caliber: .22 LR. Five or 9-shot detachable box magazine. 24.5-inch bbl. Weight: 7 lbs. Sights: Tangent-curve rear; ramp front. Sporting stock w/checkered pistol grip, grooved forearm, swivels. Disc.

RIFLES

Walther Model 1

Walther Model 2

Walther Model GX-1

Walther Model KKM-S

Walther Model U.I.T.
Super Match

OLYMPIC BOLT-ACTION
MATCH RIFLE . . . . **NiB $1191 Ex $952 Gd $648**
Single-shot. Caliber: .22 LR. 26-inch heavy bbl. Weight: 13 lbs.
Sights: Micrometer extension rear; interchangeable front. Target
stock w/checkered pistol-grip, thumbhole, full beavertail forearm
covered w/corrugated rubber, palm rest, adj. Swiss-type buttplate,
swivels. Disc.

MODEL V BOLT-ACTION
SINGLE-SHOT RIFLE . . . . **NiB $566 Ex $402 Gd $283**
Caliber: .22 LR. 26-inch bbl. Weight: 7 lbs. Sights: Open rear; ramp
front. Plain pistol-grip stock w/grooved forearm. Disc.

MODEL V MEISTERBÜCHSE
(CHAMPION) . . . . **NiB $644 Ex $463 Gd $304**
Same as standard Model V except w/micrometer open rear sight and
checkered pistol-grip. Disc.

POST WWII MODELS
*The Walther rifles listed below have been manufactured since WWII
by Carl Walther Sportwaffenfabrik, Ulm (Donau), Germany.*

MODEL GX-1 FREE RIFLE . . . . . . **NiB $1931 Ex $1416 Gd $798**
Bolt-action, single-shot. Caliber: .22 LR. 25.5-inch heavy bbl.
Weight: 15.9 lbs. Sights: Micrometer aperture rear; globe front.
Thumbhole stock w/adj. cheekpiece and buttplate w/removable
hook, accessory rail. Left-hand stock available. Accessories furnished include hand stop and sling swivel, palm rest, counterweight assembly.

MODEL KKJ SPORTER . . . . **NiB $1236 Ex $1004 Gd $510**
Bolt action. Caliber: .22 LR. Five shot box magazine. 22.5-inch
bbl. Weight: 5.5 lbs. Sights: Open rear; hooded ramp front.
Stock w/cheekpiece, checkered pistol-grip and forearm, sling
swivels. Disc.

MODEL KKJ-HO . . . . NiB $1493 Ex $1287 Gd $953
Same as Model KKJ except chambered for .22 Hornet. Disc.

MODEL KKJ-MA . . . . NiB $1287 Ex $1133 Gd $505
Same as Model KKJ except chambered for .22 WMR. Disc.

**MODEL KKM INTERNATIONAL
MATCH RIFLE** . . . . NiB $953 Ex $772 Gd $515
Bolt-action, single-shot. Caliber: .22 LR. 28-inch heavy bbl. Weight: 15.5 lbs. Sights: Micrometer aperture rear; globe front. Thumbhole stock w/high comb, adj. hook buttplate, accessory rail. Left-hand stock available. Disc.

MODEL KKM-S . . . . NiB $1004 Ex $824 Gd $541
Same specifications as Model KKM, except w/adj. cheekpiece. Disc.

MOVING TARGET MATCH RIFLE . . . . NiB $953 Ex $695 Gd $443
Bolt-action, single-shot. Caliber: .22 LR. 23.6-inch bbl. w/weight. Weight: 8.6 lbs. Supplied w/o sights. Thumbhole stock w/adj. cheekpiece and buttplate. Left-hand stock available.

PRONE 400 TARGET RIFLE . . . . NiB $798 Ex $644 Gd $412
Bolt-action, single-shot. Caliber: .22 LR. 25.5-inch heavy bbl. Weight: 10.25 lbs. Supplied w/o sights. Prone stock w/adj. cheekpiece and buttplate, accessory rail. Left-hand stock available. Disc.

MODEL SSV VARMINT RIFLE . . . . . NiB $742 Ex $618 Gd $412
Bolt-action, single-shot. Calibers: .22 LR, .22 Hornet. 25.5-inch bbl. Weight: 6.75 lbs. Supplied w/o sights. Monte Carlo stock w/high cheekpiece, full pistol grip and forearm. Disc.

MODEL U.L.T. SPECIAL MATCH RIFLE . . . . . NiB $1287 Ex $953 Gd $669
Bolt-action, single-shot. Caliber: .22 LR. 25.5-inch bbl. Weight: 10.2 lbs. Sights: Micrometer aperture rear; globe front. Target stock w/high comb, adj. buttplate, accessory rail. Left-hand stock avail. Disc. 1993.

MODEL U.L.T. SUPER MATCH RIFLE . . . . . . NiB $1313 Ex $978 Gd $695
Bolt-action, single-shot. Caliber: .22 LR. 25.5-inch heavy bbl. Weight: 10.2 lbs. Micrometer aperture rear; globe front. Target stock w/support for off-hand shooting, high comb, adj. buttplate and swivel. Left-hand stock available. Disc. 1993.

MONTGOMERY WARD — Chicago, Illinois
Western Field and Hercules Models

Firearms under the "private label" names of Western Field and Hercules are manufactured by such firms as Mossberg, Stevens, Marlin, and Savage for distribution and sale by Montgomery Ward.

**MODEL 14M-497B WESTERN FIELD
BOLT-ACTION RIFLE** . . . . NiB $102 Ex $82 Gd $55
Caliber: .22 RF. Seven shot detachable box magazine. 24-inch bbl. Weight: 5 lbs. Sights: Receiver peep; open rear; hooded ramp front. Pistol-grip stock. Mfg. by Mossberg.

**MODEL M771 WESTERN FIELD
LEVER-ACTION RIFLE** . . . . NiB $153 Ex $127 Gd $97
Calibers: .30-30, .35 Rem. Six shot tubular magazine. 20-inch bbl. Weight: 6.75 lbs. Sights: Open rear; ramp front. Pistol-grip or straight stock, forearm w/barrel band. Mfg. by Mossberg.

**MODEL M772 WESTERN FIELD
LEVER-ACTION RIFLE** . . . . NiB $178 Ex $153 Gd $102
Calibers: .30-30, .35 Rem. Six shot tubular magazine. 20-inch bbl. Weight: 6.75 lbs. Sights: Open rear; ramp front. Pistol-grip or straight stock, forearm w/bbl. band. Mfg. by Mossberg.

**MODEL M775
BOLT-ACTION RIFLE.** . . . . NiB $112 Ex $97 Gd $71
Calibers: .222 Rem., .22-250, .243 Win., .308 Win. Four shot magazine. Weight: 7.5 lbs. Sights: Folding leaf rear; ramp front. Monte Carlo stock w/cheekpiece, pistol-grip. Mfg by Mossberg.

**MODEL M776
BOLT-ACTION RIFLE.** . . . . NiB $204 Ex $178 Gd $127
Calibers: .222 Rem., .22-250, .243 Win., .308 Win. Four shot magazine. Weight: 7.5 lbs. Sights: Folding leaf rear; ramp front. Monte Carlo stock w/cheekpiece, pistol-grip. Mfg. by Mossberg.

**MODEL M778
LEVER-ACTION** . . . . NiB $199 Ex $153 Gd $102
Calibers: .30-30, .35 Rem. 6-shot tubular magazine. 20-inch bbl. Weight: 6.75 lbs. Sights: Open rear; ramp front. Pistol-grip or straight stock, forearm w/bbl. band. Mfg. by Mossberg.

**MODEL M780
BOLT-ACTION RIFLE.** . . . . NiB $204 Ex $178 Gd $127
Calibers: .222 Rem., .22-250, .243 Win., .308 Win. Four shot magazine. Weight: 7.5 lbs. Sights: Folding leaf rear; ramp front. Monte Carlo stock w/cheekpiece, pistol grip. Mfg. by Mossberg.

**MODEL M782
BOLT-ACTION RIFLE.** . . . . NiB $204 Ex $178 Gd $127
Same general specifications as Model M780.

MODEL M808 . . . . NiB $107 Ex $87 Gd $60
Takedown. Caliber: .22RF. 15-shot tubular magazine. Bbls.: 20- and 24-inch. Weight: 6 lbs. Sights: Open rear; bead front. Pistol-grip stock. Mfg. by Stevens.

MODEL M832 BOLT-ACTION RIFLE. . . . . NiB $112 Ex $92 Gd $61
Caliber: .22 RF. Seven shot clip magazine. 24-inch bbl. Weight: 6.5 lbs. Sights: Open rear; ramp front. Mfg. by Mossberg.

MODEL M836 . . . . NiB $117 Ex $92 Gd $71
Takedown. Caliber: .22RF. 15-shot tubular magazine. Bbls.: 20- and 24-inch. Weight: 6 lbs. Sights: Open rear; bead front. Pistol-grip stock. Mfg. by Stevens.

MODEL M865 LEVER-ACTION CARBINE. . . NiB $143 Ex $102 Gd $87
Hammerless. Caliber: .22RF. Tubular magazine. Made w/both 18.5-inch and 20-inch bbls., forearm w/bbl. band, swivels. Weight: 5 lbs. Mfg. by Mossberg.

**MODEL M894
AUTO-LOADING CARBINE** . . . . NiB $127 Ex $102 Gd $76
Caliber: .22 RF. 15-shot tubular magazine. 20-inch bbl. Weight: 6 lbs. Sights: Open rear; ramp front. Monte Carlo stock w/pistol-grip. Mfg. by Mossberg.

MODEL M-SD57 . . . . NiB $112 Ex $92 Gd $61
Takedown. Caliber: .22RF. 15-shot tubular magazine. Bbls.: 20- and 24-inch. Weight: 6 lbs. Sights: Open rear; bead front. Pistol-grip stock. Mfg. by Stevens.

WEATHERBY, INC. — Atascadero, CA
(Formerly South Gate, CA)

CROWN CUSTOM RIFLE . . . . . NiB $5871 Ex $3991 Gd $2034
Calibers: .240, .30-06, .257, .270, 7mm, .300, and .340. Bbl.: Made to order. Super fancy walnut stock. Also available w/engraved barreled action including gold animal overlay.

Weatherby Mark V Classicmark I

Weatherby Crown Custom

Weatherby Fiberguard

Weatherby Fibermark

DELUXE .378 MAGNUM RIFLE . . . . . . **NiB $2678 Ex $1931 Gd $1287**
Same general specifications as Deluxe Magnum in other calibers except caliber .378 W. M. Schultz & Larsen action; 26-inch bbl. Disc. 1958.

DELUXE MAGNUM RIFLE . . . . . **NiB $1952 Ex $1442 Gd $1030**
Calibers: .220 Rocket, .257 Weatherby Mag., .270 W.M. 7mm W.M., .300 W.M., .375 W.M. Specially processed FN Mauser action. 24-inch bbl. (26-inch in .375 cal.). Monte Carlo-style stock w/cheekpiece, black forend tip, grip cap, checkered pistol-grip and forearm, quick-detachable sling swivels. Value shown is for rifle w/o sights. Disc. 1958.

DELUXE RIFLE . . . . **NiB $1390 Ex $1056 Gd $747**
Same general specifications as Deluxe Magnum except chambered for standard calibers such as .270, .30-06, etc. Disc. 1958.

FIBERGUARD RIFLE . . . . **NiB $695 Ex $566 Gd $386**
Same general specifications as Vanguard except for fiberglass stock and matte metal finish. Disc, 1988.

FIBERMARK RIFLE . . . . **NiB $1231 Ex $901 Gd $592**
Same general specifications as Mark V except w/molded fiberglass stock, finished in a nonglare black wrinkle finish. The metal is finished in a non-glare matte finish. Disc. 1993.

MARK V ACCUMARK BOLT-ACTION REPEATING
Weatherby Mark V magnum action. Calibers: .257 Wby., .270 Wby., 7mm Rem. Mag., 7mm Wby., 7mm STW, .300 Win. Mag., .300 Wby.

(cont'd.) MARK V ACCUMARK BOLT ACTION REPEATING
Mag., .30-338 Wby., .30-378 Wby. and .340 Wby. 26- or 28-inch stainless bbl. w/black oxide flutes. 46.5 or 48.5 inches overall. Weight: 8 to 8.5 lbs. No sights, drilled and tapped for scope. Stainless finish w/blued receiver. H-S Precision black synthetic stock w/aluminum bedding plate, recoil pad and sling swivels. Imported 1996 to date.
**Mark V Accumark (.30-338
& .30-378 Wby. Mag.)** . . . . **NiB $1352 Ex $1081 Gd $735**
Mark V Accumark (All other calibers) . . . . **NiB $1153 Ex $922 Gd $627**
Mark V Left-Action, add **$75**

**MARK V ACCUMARK
LIGHT WEIGHT RIFLE** . . . . **NiB $1251 Ex $1056 Gd $618**
Similar to the Mark V Accumark except w/LightWeight Mark V action designed for standard calibers w/sixlocking lugs rather than nine. 24-inch stainless bbl. Weight: 5.75 lbs. Gray or black Monte Carlo-style composite Kevlar/fiberglass stock w/Pachmayr "Decelerator" pad. No sights. Imported 1997 to date.

MARK V CLASSICMARK I RIFLE
Same general specifications as Mark V except w/checkered select American Claro walnut stock w/oil finish and presentation recoil pad. Satin metal finish. Imported 1992-93.
Calibers .240 to .300 Wby. . . . . . . **NiB $1107 Ex $772 Gd $463**
Caliber .340 Wby. . . . . **NiB $1128 Ex $798 Gd $463**
Caliber .378 Wby. . . . . **NiB $1313 Ex $798 Gd $463**
Caliber .416 Wby. . . . . **NiB $1184 Ex $850 Gd $463**
Caliber .460 Wby. . . . . **NiB $1287 Ex $927 Gd $489**

Weatherby Mark V Deluxe

Weatherby Mark V Euromark

Weatherby Mark V Lazermark

Weatherby Mark V Safari Grade

MARK V CLASSICMARK LL RIFLE
Same general specifications as Classicmark I except w/checkered select American walnut stock w/oil finish steel grip cap and Old English recoil pad. Satin metal finish. Right-hand only. Imported 1992-93.
Calibers .240 to .340 Wby.
(26-inch bbl.)............... NiB $1390 Ex $1081 Gd $721
Caliber .378 Wby. .... NiB $1442 Ex $1107 Gd $772
Caliber .416 Wby. .... NiB $1571 Ex $1334 Gd $922
Caliber .460 Wby. .... NiB $1622 Ex $1365 Gd $953

MARK V DELUXE RIFLE........ NiB $1025 Ex $747 Gd $494
Similar to Mark V Sporter except w/Lightweight Mark V action designed for standard calibers w/sixlocking lugs rather than nine, 4- or 5-shot magazine. 24-inch bbl. 44 inches overall. Weight: 6.75 lbs. Checkered Monte Carlo American walnut stock w/rosewood forend and pistol grip and diamond inlay. Imported 1997 to date.

WEATHERBY MARK V DELUXE BOLT-ACTION SPORTING RIFLE
Mark V action, right or left hand. Calibers: .22-250, .30-06- .224 Weatherby Varmintmaster; .240, .257, .270, 7mm, .300, .340, .375, .378, .416, .460 Weatherby Magnums. Box magazine holds 2 to 5 cartridges depending on caliber. 24- or 26-inch bbl. Weight: 6.5 to 10.5 lbs. Monte Carlo-style stock w/cheekpiece, skip checkering, forend tip, pistol-grip cap, recoil pad, QD swivels. Values shown are for rifles w/o sights. Made in Germany 1958-69; in Japan 1970-94. Values shown for Japanese production.
Calibers .22-250, .224 .... NiB $1056 Ex $808 Gd $556
Caliber .375 H&H Magnum .... NiB $1133 Ex $953 Gd $644
Caliber .378 Weatherby Magnum ...... NiB $1313 Ex $1030 Gd $798
Caliber .416 Weatherby Magnum ...... NiB $1390 Ex $1081 Gd $721
Caliber .460 Weatherby Magnum ..... NiB $1802 Ex $13265 Gd $978

MARK V EUROMARK BOLT-ACTION RIFLE
Same general specifications as other Mark V rifles except w/hand-rubbed, satin oil finish Claro walnut stock and nonglare special process blue matte barreled action. Left-hand models available. Imported 1986-93. Reintroduced 1995.
Caliber .378 Wby. Mag......... NiB $1390 Ex $1081 Gd $721
Caliber .416 Wby. Mag......... NiB $1493 Ex $1159 Gd $824
Caliber .460 Wby Mag......... NiB $1777 Ex $1365 Gd $978
Other calibers .... NiB $953 Ex $716 Gd $463

MARK V LAZERMARK RIFLE
Same general specifications as Mark V except w/laser-carved stock.
Caliber .378 Wby. Mag......... NiB $1880 Ex $1469 Gd $819
Caliber .416 Wby. Mag......... NiB $1880 Ex $1468 Gd $819
Caliber .460 Wby. Mag......... NiB $2214 Ex $1545 Gd $1004
Other calibers .... NiB $1334 Ex $1025 Gd $644

MARK V SAFARI GRADE RIFLE....... NiB $2183 Ex $1746 Gd $1188
Same general specifications as Mark V except extra capacity magazine, bbl. sling swivel, and express rear sight typical "Safari" style.

MARK V SPORTER RIFLE
Sporter version of Mark V Magnum w/low-luster metal finish. Checkered Carlo walnut stock w/o grip cap or forend tip. No sights. Imported 1993 to date.
Calibers .257 to .300 Wby......... NiB $963 Ex $798 Gd $412
.340 Weatherby .... NiB $1025 Ex $644 Gd $438
.375 H&H .... NiB $1056 Ex $747 Gd $541

MARK V LIGHTWEIGHT SPORTER RIFLE.. NiB $927 Ex $747 Gd $412
Similar to Mark V Sporter except w/Lightweight Mark V action designed for standard calibers w/six locking lugs rather than nine. Imported 1997 to date.

Weatherby Mark XXII Deluxe
.22 Automatic Sporter

Weatherby Vanguard (I) VGL
Bolt-Action Sporting Rifle

Weatherby Varmintmaster

MARK V STAINLESS RIFLE

Similar to the Mark V Magnum except in 400-series stainless steel w/bead-blasted matte finish. Weight: 8 lbs. Monte Carlo synthetic stock w/aluminum bedding block. Imported 1995 to date.

Mark V Stainless (.30-.378 Wby.). . NiB $1159 Ex $942 Gd $489
Mark V Stainless (.375 H&H.) . . . . NiB $1159 Ex $942 Gd $489
All other calibers. . . . . NiB $1004 Ex $716 Gd $489
W/fluted bbl., add. $100

MARK V (LW) STAINLESS RIFLE . . . . NiB $798 Ex $613 Gd $407

Similar to the Mark V (standard calibers) except in 400-series stainless steel w/bead-blasted matte finish. Five shot magazine. 24-inch bbl. 44 inches overall. Weight: 6.5 lbs. Monte Carlo synthetic stock w/aluminum bedding block. Imported 1995 to date.

MARK V SLS RIFLE

Acronym for Stainless Laminated Sporter. Similar to the Mark V Magnum Sporter, except w/stainless 400-series action and 24- or 26-inch stainless bbl. Laminated wood stock. Weight: 8.5 lbs. Black oxide bead-blasted matte blue finish. Imported 1997 to date.

Mark V SLS (.340 Wby.) . . . . NiB $1159 Ex $942 Gd $489
All other calibers. . . . . NiB $1004 Ex $716 Gd $489

MARK V SYNTHETIC RIFLE

Similar to the Mark V Magnum except w/Monte Carlo synthetic stock w/aluminum bedding block. 24- or 26-inch standard tapper or fluted bbl. Weight: 7.75 to 8 lbs. Matte blue finish. Imported 1995 to date.

Mark V Synthetic (.340 Wby.) . . . . NiB $1004 Ex $716 Gd $463
Mark V Synthetic (.30-378 Wby.) . . . . NiB $1025 Ex $695 Gd $463
All other calibers . . . . NiB $747 Ex $566 Gd $386
W/fluted bbl., add. $100

MARK V ULTRA LIGHT WEIGHT RIFLE

Similar to the Mark V Magnum except w/skeletonized bolt handle. 24- or 26-inch fluted stainless bbl. chambered .257 Wby., .270 Wby., 7mm Rem. Mag., 7mm Wby., .300 Win. Mag., .300 Wby. Monte Carlo synthetic stock w/aluminum bedding block. Weight: 6.75 lbs. Imported 1998 to date.

(cont'd.) MARK V ULTRA LIGHT WEIGHT RIFLE

Mark V Ultra Lightweight
(standard calibers). . . . . NiB $1880 Ex $1442 Gd $747
Mark V Ultra Lightweight
(Weatherby calibers) . . . . NiB $1905 Ex $1493 Gd $772
Mark V Ultra Lightweight
(Left-hand action), add $100

MARK XXII DELUXE .22 AUTOMATIC

SPORTER, CLIP-FED MODEL . . . . NiB $510 Ex $463 Gd $335
Semiautomatic w/single-shot selector. Caliber: .22 LR. Five and 10-shot clip magazines. 24-inch bbl. Weight: 6 lbs. Sights: Folding leaf open rear; ramp front. Monte Carlo-type stock w/cheekpiece, pistol-grip, forend tip, grip cap, skip checkering, QD swivels. Intro. 1964. Made in Italy 1964-69; in Japan, 1970-1981; in the U.S., 1982-90.

MARK XXII, TUBULAR

MAGAZINE MODEL . . . . NiB $407 Ex $330 Gd $200
Same as Mark XXII, clip-fed model except w/15-shot tubular magazine. Made in Japan 1973-81; in the U.S.,1982-90.

VANGUARD (I) BOLT-ACTION SPORTING RIFLE

Mauser-type action. Calibers: .243 Win., .25-06, .270 Win., 7mm Rem. Mag., .30-06, .300 Win. Mag. Five shot magazine; (3-shot in Magnum calibers). 24-inch bbl. Weight: 7 lbs. 14 oz. No sights. Monte Carlo-type stock w/cheekpiece, rosewood forend tip and pistol-grip cap, checkering, rubber buttpad, QD swivels. Imported 1970-84.

Vanguard Standard . . . . NiB $463 Ex $386 Gd $232
Vanguard VGL (w/shorter
20-inch bbl., plain checkered
stock matte finish, 6.5 lbs . . . . NiB $438 Ex $360 Gd $237
Vanguard VGS (w/24-inch
bbl., plain checkered stock,
matte finish. . . . . NiB $489 Ex $371 Gd $257
Vanguard VGX
(w/higher grade finish) . . . . NiB $541 Ex $438 Gd $283

Westley Richards
Best Quality Double

Westley Richards
Best Quality Magazine Rifle

VANGUARD CLASSIC I RIFLE..... NiB $494 Ex $381 Gd $263
Same general specifications as Vanguard VGX Deluxe except w/hand-checkered classic-style stock, black buttpad and satin finish. Calibers .223 Rem., .243 Win. .270 Win., 7mm-08, 7mm Rem. Mag., .30-06 and .308 Win. Imported 1989-94.

VANGUARD CLASSIC II RIFLE .... NiB $716 Ex $592 Gd $386
Same general specifications as Vanguard VGX Deluxe except custom checkered classic-style American walnut stock w/black forend tip, grip cap and solid black recoil pad, satin finish. Imported 1989-94.

VANGUARD VGX DELUXE .... NiB $644 Ex $510 Gd $360
Calibers: .22-250 Rem., .243 Rem., .270 Wby. Mag., .270 Win., 7mm Rem. Mag., .30-06, .300 Win. Mag., .300 Wby. Mag., .338 Win. Mag. Three or 5-round capacity. 24-inch bbl. About 44 inches overall. Weight: 7 to 8.5 lbs. Custom checkered American walnut stock w/Monte Carlo and recoil pad. Rosewood forend tip and pistol-grip cap. High-luster finish. Disc. 1994.

VARMINTMASTER BOLT-ACTION RIFLE. . NiB $1854 Ex $1437 Gd $772
Calibers: .224 Wby., .22-250, 4-shot magazine. 26-inch bbl. 45 inches overall. Weight: 7.75 lbs. Checkered walnut stock. No sights. Disc.

WEATHERMARK RIFLE
Same gen. specs. as Classicmark except w/checkered blk. Weathermark composite stock. Mark V bolt act. Cal: .240, .257, .270, .300, .340, .378, .416 and .460 Weatherby Mag.; plus .270 Win., 7mm Rem. Mag., .30-06 and .375 H&H Mag. Wt: 8 to 10 lbs. Right-hand only. Imp. 1992-94.
Calibers .257 to .300 Wby........	NiB $716	Ex $541	Gd $360
Caliber .340 Weatherby..........	NiB $747	Ex $566	Gd $371
Caliber .375 H&H..............	NiB $978	Ex $669	Gd $463
Other non-Wby. calibers........	NiB $715	Ex $510	Gd $360

WEATHERMARK ALASKAN RIFLE....... NiB $798 Ex $644 Gd $438
Same general specifications as Weathermark except w/nonglare electroless nickel finish. Right-hand only. Imported 1992-94.

WEIHRAUCH — Melrichstadt, West Germany
Imported by European American Armory, Sharpes, FL.

MODEL HW 60 TARGET RIFLE.... NiB $644 Ex $566 Gd $360
Single-shot. Caliber: .22 LR. 26.75-inch bbl. Walnut stock. Adj. buttplate and trigger. Hooded ramp front sight. Push button safety. Imported 1995-97.

MODEL HW 66 BOLT-ACTION RIFLE .... NiB $592 Ex $505 Gd $309
Caliber: .22 Hornet. 22.75-inch bbl. 41.75 inches overall. Weight: 6.5 lbs. Walnut stock w/cheekpiece. Hooded blade ramp front sight. Checkered pistol grip and forend. Imported 1989-90.

**MODEL HW 660 MATCH
BOLT-ACTION RIFLE........... NiB $875 Ex $747 Gd $412**
Caliber: .22 LR. 26-inch bbl. 45.33 inches overall. Weight: 10.75 lbs. Walnut or laminated stock w/adj. cheekpiece and buttplate. Checkered pistol grip and forend. Adj. trigger. Imported 1991 to date.

WESTERN FIELD RIFLES

See listings under "W" for Montgomery Ward.

WESTLEY RICHARDS & CO., LTD. — London, England

**BEST QUALITY
DOUBLE RIFLE......... NiB $34,375 Ex $27,500 Gd $18,700**
Boxlock, hammerless, ejector. Hand-detachable locks. Calibers: .30-06, .318 Accelerated Express, .375 Mag., .425 Mag. Express, .465 Nitro Express, .470 Nitro Express. 25-inch bbls. Weight: 8.5 to 11 lbs. Sights: leaf rear; hooded front. French walnut stock w/cheekpiece, checkered pistol grip and forend.

BEST QUALITY MAGAZINE RIFLE
Mauser or Magnum Mauser action. Calibers: 7mm High Velocity, .30-06, .318 Accelerated Express, .375 Mag., .404 Nitro Express, .425 Mag. Bbl. lengths: 24-inch; 7mm, 22-inch; .425 caliber, 25-inch. Weight 7.25 to 9.25 lbs. Sights: Leaf rear; hooded front.
Standard action.............	NiB $8688	Ex $6950	Gd $4726
Magnum action..........	NiB $12,813	Ex $10,250	Gd $6970

WICHITA ARMS — Wichita, Kansas

MODEL WCR CLASSIC BOLT-ACTION RIFLE
Single-shot. Calibers: .17 Rem through .308 Win. 21-inch octagon bbl. Hand-checkered walnut stock. Drilled and tapped for scope w/no sights. Right or left-hand action w/Canjar trigger. Non-glare blued finish. Made 1978 to date.
Right-hand model..........	NiB $3347	Ex $2575	Gd $1648
Left-hand model............	NiB $3264	Ex $2647	Gd $1858

MODEL WSR SILHOUETTE BOLT-ACTION RIFLE
Single-shot, bolt action, chambered in most standard calibers. Right or left-hand action w/fluted bolt. Drilled and tapped for scope mount with no sights. 24-inch bbl. Canjar trigger. Metallic gray Fiberthane stock w/vented rubber recoil pad. Made 1983-95.
Right-hand model..........	NiB $2523	Ex $1828	Gd $1236
Left-hand model............	NiB $2466	Ex $2008	Gd $1423

Wickliffe '76 Standard
Single-Shot Rifle

Winchester Model 1873
Lever-Action Rifle

MODEL WMR STAINLESS
MAGNUM BOLT-ACTION RIFLE . . . . **NiB $2060 Ex $1746 Gd $1025**
Single-shot or w/blind magazine action chambered .270 Win. through .458 Win. Mag. Drilled and tapped for scope with no sights. Fully adj. trigger. 22- or 24-inch bbl. Hand-checkered select walnut stock. Made 1980-84.

MODEL WVR VARMINT RIFLE
Calibers: .17 Rem through .308 Win. Three shot magazine. Right or left-hand action w/jeweled bolt. 21-inch bbl. w/o sights. Drilled and tapped for scope. Hand-checkered American walnut pistol-grip stock. Made 1978 to date.
Right-hand model . . . . **NiB $2575 Ex $1844 Gd $1133**
Left-hand model . . . . **NiB $2530 Ex $2060 Gd $1458**

WICKLIFFE RIFLES — Wickliffe, Ohio
Mfd. by Triple S Development Co., Inc.

'76 COMMEMORATIVE
MODEL. . . . . **NiB $1236 Ex $978 Gd $798**
Limited edition of 100. Same as Deluxe Model except w/filled etching on receiver sidewalls, U.S. silver dollar inlaid in stock, 26-inch bbl. only, comes in presentation case. Made in 1976 only.

'76 DELUXE MODEL . . . . **NiB $509 Ex $407 Gd $277**
Same as Standard Model except w/22-inch bbl. in .30-06 only; high-luster blued finish, fancy-grade figured American walnut stock w/nickel silver grip cap.

'76 STANDARD MODEL
SINGLE-SHOT RIFLE . . . . **NiB $432 Ex $345 Gd $235**
Falling-block action. Calibers: .22 Hornet, .223 Rem., .22-250, .243 Win., .25-06, .308 Win., .30-06, .45-70. 22-inch lightweight bbl. (.243 and .308 only) or 26-inch heavy sporter bbl. Weight: 6.75 or 8.5 lbs., depending on bbl. No sights. Select American walnut Monte Carlo stock w/right or left cheekpiece and pistol-grip, semi-beavertail forearm. Intro. 1976. Disc.

STINGER MODEL . . . . **NiB $451 Ex $360 Gd $245**
Falling block, single-shot. Calibers: .22 Hornet and .223 Rem. .22-inch bbl. w/no sights. American walnut Monte Carlo stock w/continental-type forend. Made 1979-80.

TRADITIONALIST MODEL . . . . **NiB $453 Ex $350 Gd $242**
Falling block single-shot. Calibers: .30-06, .45-70. 24-inch bbl. w/open sights. Hand-checkered. American walnut classic-style buttstock and forearm. Made 1979-80.

WILKINSON ARMS CO. — Covina, California

TERRY CARBINE . . . . **NiB $489 Ex $376 Gd $257**
Caliber: 9mm Para. Semiautomatic. 30-shot magazine. 16-inch bbl. 30 inches overall. Weight: 6 lbs. Dovetailed receiver for scope mounting. Bolt-type safety. Ejection port w/automatic trap door. Blowback action. Fires from closed bolt. Made 1975 to date.

TED WILLIAMS RIFLES

See Sears, Roebuck and Company.

WINCHESTER RIFLES — Winchester
Repeating Arms Company, New Haven,
Connecticut

EARLY MODELS 1873 – 1918

NOTE: *Most Winchester rifles manufactured prior to 1918 used the date of approximate manufacture as the model number. For example, the Model 1894 repeating rifle was manufactured from 1894 to 1937. When Winchester started using two-digit model numbers after 1918, the "18" was dropped and the rifle was then called the Model 94. The Model 1892 was called the Model 92, etc.*

Winchester Model 1886
w/Case-colored Receiver

Winchester Model 1886
w/Blued Receiver

Winchester Model 1886 Saddle-Ring Carbine

**At Right: Close-up barrel engraving on Winchester
Model 1873 One of One Thousand.**

MODEL 1873 LEVER-ACTION
CARBINE . . . . NiB $9592 Ex $7673 Gd $5218
Same as Standard Model 1873 Rifle except w/20-inch bbl., 12-shot
magazine, weight: 7.25 lbs.

MODEL 1873 LEVER-ACTION
RIFLE . . . . NiB $8949 Ex $7158 Gd $4868
Calibers: .32-20, .38-40, .44-40; a few were chambered for .22 rimfire. 15-shot magazine, also made w/6-shot half magazine. 24-inch
bbl. (round, half-octagon, octagon). Weight: 8.5 lbs. Sights: Open
rear; bead or blade front. Plain straight-grip stock and forearm.
Made 1873-1924. 720,610 rifles of this model were mfd.

MODEL 1873 —
ONE OF ONE THOUSAND . . . . NiB $195,700+ Ex $82,400+ Gd $51,500+
During the late 1870s, Winchester offered Model 1873 rifles of
superior accuracy and extra finish, designated "One of One
Thousand" grade, at $100. These rifles are marked "1 of 1000" or
"One of One Thousand." Only 136 of this model are known to have
been manufactured. This is one of the rarest of shoulder arms and,
because so few have been sold in recent years, it is extremely difficult to assign a value; however, an "excellent" specimen would
probably bring a price upward of $200,000.

MODEL 1873 SPECIAL
SPORTING RIFLE . . . . NiB $10,300 Ex $8755 Gd $5150
Same as Standard Model 1873 Rifle except this type has receiver case-
hardened in colors, pistol-grip stock of select walnut, octagon bbl. only.

MODEL 1885 SINGLE-SHOT RIFLE
Designed by John M. Browning, this falling-block, lever-action rifle was
manufactured from 1885 to 1920 in a variety of models and chambered
for most of the popular cartridges of the period — both rimfire and centerfire — from .22 to .50 caliber. There are two basic styles of frames,

(cont'd.) MODEL 1885 SINGLE-SHOT RIFLE
low-wall and high-wall. The low-wall was chambered only for the
lower-powered cartridges, while the high-wall was supplied in all calibers and made in three basic types. The standard model for No. 3 and
heavier barrels is the type commonly encountered; the thin-walled version was supplied with No. 1 and No. 2 light barrels and the thick-
walled action in the heavier calibers. Made in both solid frame and
takedown versions. Barrels were available in five weights ranging from
the lightweight No. 1 to the extra-heavy No. 5 in round, half-octagon
and full-octagon styles. Many other variations were also offered.

MODEL 1885 HIGH-WALL
SPORTING RIFLE . . . . NiB $3605+ Ex $1957+ Gd $1545
Solid frame or takedown. No. 3, 30-inch bbl., standard. Weight: 9.5
lbs. Standard trigger and lever. Open rear sights; blade front sight.
Plain stock and forend.

MODEL 1885 LOW-WALL
SPORTING RIFLE. . . . . NiB $1668 Ex $1334 Gd $907
Solid frame. No. 1, 28-inch round or octagon bbl. Weight: 7 lbs.
Open rear sight; blade front sight. Plain stock and forend.

MODEL 1885
SCHUETZEN RIFLE . . . . NiB $5659 Ex $4563 Gd $3079
Solid frame or takedown. High-wall action. Schuetzen double-set
trigger. Spur finger lever. No. 3, 30-inch octagon bbl. Weight: 12
lbs. Vernier rear peep sight; wind-gauge front sight. Fancy walnut
Schuetzen stock with checkered pistol-grip and forend. Schuetzen
buttplate; adj. palm rest.

MODEL 1885
SPECIAL SPORTING RIFLE . . . . . NiB $2575+ Ex $2060+ Gd $1442
Same general specifications as the standard high-wall model except
with checkered fancy walnut stock and forend.

Winchester Model 1890

Winchester Model 1892

MODEL 1885 SINGLE-SHOT
MUSKET . . . . **NiB $1281 Ex $1025 Gd $697**
Solid frame. Low-wall. .22 Short and Long Rifle. 28-inch round bbl. Weight: 8.6 lbs. Lyman rear peep sight; blade front sight. Military-type stock and forend. Note: The U.S. Government purchased a large quantity of these muskets during World War I for training purposes.

MODEL 1885 SINGLE-SHOT
"WINDER" MUSKET . . . . **NiB $978 Ex $814 Gd $515**
Solid frame or takedown. High-wall. Plain trigger. 28-inch round bbl. Weight: 8.5 lbs. Musket rear sight; blade front sight. Military-type stock and forend w/bbl. band and sling stud/rings.

MODEL 1886 LEVER-ACTION RIFLE
Solid frame or takedown. .33 Win., .38-56, .38-70, .40-65, .40-70, .40-82, .45-70, .45-90, .50-100, .50-110. The .33 Win. and .45-70 were the last calibers in which this model was supplied. Eight shot tubular magaine; also 4-shot half-magazine. 26-inch bbl. (round, half-octagon, octagon). Weight: 7.5 lbs. Sights: Open rear; bead or blade front. Plain straight-grip stock and forend or standard models. Made 1886-1935.
Standard model . . . . **NiB $5086 Ex $4068 Gd $2767**
Takedown model . . . . **NiB $6303 Ex $5042 Gd $3429**
Deluxe model (pistol-grip and
high-quality walnut) . . . . **NiB $10,300 Ex $9785 Gd $6180**

MODEL 1886 SADDLE-RING
CARBINE . . . . **NiB $12,425 Ex $9939 Gd $6759**
Same as standard rifle except with 22-inch bbl., carbine buttstock and forend. Carbine rear sight. Saddle ring on left side of receiver.

MODEL 1890 SLIDE-ACTION RIFLE
Visible hammer. Calibers: .22 Short, Long, LR; .22 WRF (not interchangeable). Tubular magazine holds 15 Short, 12 Long, 11 LR; 12 WRF. 24-inch octagon bbl. Weight: 5.75 lbs. Sights: Open rear; bead front. Plain straight-grip stock, grooved slide handle. Originally solid frame; after No. 15,499, all rifles of this model were takedown-type. Fancy checkered pistol-grip stock, nickel-steel bbl. supplied at extra cost, which can also increase the value by 100% or more. Made 1890-1932.
Blue WRF . . . . **NiB $1905 Ex $1545 Gd $978**
Blue (.22 LR) . . . . **NiB $1957 Ex $1905 Gd $1004**
Color casehardened receiver . . . . **NiB $6303 Ex $5042 Gd $3429**

MODEL 1892 LEVER-ACTION
RIFLE . . . . **NiB $2440 Ex $1952 Gd $1328**
Solid frame or takedown. Calibers: .25-20, .32-20, .38-40, .44-40. 13-shot tubular magazine; also 7-shot half-magazine. 24-inch bbl. (round, octagon, half-octagon). Weight: from 6.75 lbs. up. Sights: Open rear; bead front. Plain straight-grip stock and forend. Pistol-grip fancy walnut stocks were available at extra cost and also doubles the value of the current value for standard models.

MODEL 1892 SADDLE-RING
CARBINE . . . . **NiB $2575 Ex $2266 Gd $1648**
Same general specifications as the Model 1892 rifle except carbine buttstock, forend and sights. 20-inch bbl. Saddle ring on left side of receiver.

MODEL 1894 LEVER-ACTION
RIFLE . . . . **NiB $1925 Ex $1540 Gd $1048**
Solid frame or takedown. .25-35, .30-30, .32-40, .32 Special, .38-55. Seven shot tubular magazine or 4-shot half-magazine. 26-inch bbl. (round, octagon, half-octagon). Weight: about 7.35 lbs. Sights: Open rear; bead front. Plain straight-grip stock and forearm on standard model; crescent-shaped or shotgun-style buttplate. Made 1894-1937. See also Winchester Model 94 for later variations of this model.

MODEL 1894 LEVER-ACTION DELUXE. NiB $2382 Ex $1905 Gd $1296
Same general specifications as the standard rifle except checkered pistol-grip buttstock and forend using high-grade walnut. Engraved versions are considerably higher in value.

MODEL 1894 SADDLE-RING
CARBINE . . . . **NiB $1545 Ex $1437 Gd $978**
Same general specifications as the Model 1894 standard rifle except 20-inch bbl., carbine buttstock, forend, and sights. Saddle ring on left side of receiver. Weight: about 6.5 lbs.

MODEL 1894 STANDARD CARBINE . . . **NiB $1281 Ex $1025 Gd $697**
Same general specifications as Saddle-Ringle Carbine except shotgun type buttstock and plate, no saddle ring, standard open rear sight. Sometimes called "Eastern Carbine." See also Winchester Model 94 carbine.

1895 LEVER-ACTION
CARBINE . . . . **NiB $2769 Ex $2214 Gd $1506**
Same as Model 95 Standard Rifle except has 22-inch bbl., carbine-style buttstock and forend, weight: About 8 lbs., calibers .30-40 Krag, .30-03, .30-06 and .303, solid frame only.

1895 LEVER-ACTION RIFLE . . . . **NiB $3090 Ex $1905 Gd $1030**
Calibers: .30-40 Krag, .30-03, .30-60, .303 British, 7.62mm Russian, .35 Win., .38-72, .40-72, .405 Win. Four shot box magazine except .30-40 and .303, which have 5-shot magazines. Bbl. lengths: 24-, 26-, 28-inches (round, half-octagon, octagon). Weight: About 8.5 lbs. Sights: Open rear; bead or blade front. Plain straight-grip stock and forend (standard). Both solid frame and takedown models were made from1897-1931.

MODEL (1897) LEE BOLT-ACTION RIFLE
Straight-pull bolt-action. .236 U.S. Navy, 5-shot box magazine, clip loaded. 24- and 28-inch bbl. Weight: 7.5 to 8.5 lbs. Sights: Folding leaf rear sight on musket; open sporting sight on sporting rifle.
Musket model . . . . **NiB $1802 Ex $1648 Gd $1004**
Sporting rifle . . . . **NiB $1905 Ex $1699 Gd $1004**

Winchester Model 1894

Winchester Model 1894
Fancy-Grade Takedown

Winchester Model 1894
Saddle-Ring Carbine

Winchester Model 1895
Carbine

Winchester Model 1895
Rifle

Winchester Model 1897
Lee Sporting Rifle

MODEL 1900 BOLT-ACTION
SINGLE-SHOT RIFLE . . . . **NiB $547 Ex $438 Gd $298**
Takedown. Caliber: .22 Short and Long. 18-inch bbl. Weight:
2.75 lbs. Open rear sight; blade front sight. One-piece, straight-
grip stock. Made from 1899 to 1902.

MODEL 1902
BOLT-ACTION
SINGLE-SHOT RIFLE . . . . **NiB $412 Ex $309 Gd $206**
Takedown. Basically the same as Model 1900 with minor
improvements. Calibers: .22 Short and Long, .22 Extra Long, .22
LR. Weight: 3 lbs. Made 1902-1931.

MODEL 1903
SELF-LOADING RIFLE . . . . **NiB $1004 Ex $772 Gd $489**
Takedown. Caliber: .22 WRA. 10-shot tubular magazine in buttstock. 20-inch bbl. Weight: 5.75 lbs. Sights: Open rear; bead
front. Plain straight-grip stock and forearm (fancy grade illustrated). Made 1903-36.

MODEL (1904) 99 THUMB-TRIGGER BOLT-ACTION
SINGLE-SHOT RIFLE . . . . **NiB $766 Ex $613 Gd $417**

(cond't) **MODEL (1904) 99**
Takedown. Same as Model 1902 except fired by pressing a button behind the cocking piece. Made 1904-23.

MODEL 1904 BOLT-ACTION
SINGLE-SHOT RIFLE . . . . **NiB $412 Ex $309 Gd $206**
Similar to Model 1902. Takedown. Caliber: 22 Short, Long Extra
Long, LR. 21-inch bbl. Weight: 4 lbs. Made 1904-31.

MODEL 1905
SELF-LOADING RIFLE . . . . **NiB $747 Ex $515 Gd $438**
Takedown. Calibers: .32 Win. S. and L., .35 Win. S. and L. Five
or 10-shot detachable box magazine. 22-inch bbl. Weight: 7.5
lbs. Sights: Open rear; bead front. Plain pistol-grip stock and
forearm. Made 1905-20.

MODEL 1906
SLIDE-ACTION REPEATER . . . . . **NiB $824 Ex $772 Gd $515**
Takedown. Visible hammer. Caliber: .22 Short, Long, LR. Tubular
magazine holds 20 Short, 16 Long or 14 LR. 20-inch bbl.
Weight: 5 lbs. Sights: Open rear; bead front. Straight-grip stock
and grooved forearm. Made 1906-32.

Winchester Model 1902

Winchester Model 1903

Winchester Model 1904

Winchester Model 1905

Winchester Model 1906

Winchester Model 1907

Winchester Model 1910

MODEL 1907 SELF-LOADING RIFLE . . . . . **NiB $638 Ex $510 Gd $347**
Takedown. Caliber: .351 Win. S. and L. Five or 10-shot detachable box magazine. 20-inch bbl. Weight: 7.75 lbs. Sights: Open rear; bead front. Plain pistol-grip stock and forearm. Made 1907-57.

MODEL 1910 SELF-LOADING RIFLE . . . . . **NiB $766 Ex $613 Gd $417**
Takedown. Caliber: .401 Win. S. and L. Four shot detachable box magazine. 20-inch bbl. Weight: 8.5 lbs. Sights: Open rear; bead front. Plain pistol-grip stock and forearm. Made 1910-36.

**Winchester Model 43
Special Grade**

MODEL 43 BOLT-ACTION

SPORTING RIFLE. . . . . NiB $778 Ex $618 Gd $412
Standard Grade. Calibers: .218 Bee, .22 Hornet, .25-20, .32-20 (latter two discontinued 1950). Three shot detachable box magazine. 24-inch bbl. Weight: 6 lbs. Sights: Open rear, bead front on hooded ramp. Plain pistol-grip stock with swivels. Made 1949-57.

MODEL 43 SPECIAL GRADE. . . . . NiB $1009 Ex $772 Gd $510
Same as Standard Model 43 except has checkered pistol-grip and forearm, grip cap.

MODEL 47 BOLT-ACTION

SINGLE-SHOT RIFLE . . . . NiB $360 Ex $283 Gd $180
Caliber: .22 Short, Long, LR. 25-inch bbl. Weight: 5.5 lbs. Sights: Peep or open rear; bead front. Plain pistol-grip stock. Made 1949-54.

MODEL 52 BOLT-ACTION TARGET RIFLE
Standard bbl. First type. .22 LR. Five shot box magazine. 28-inch bbl. Weight: 8.75 lbs. Sights: Folding leaf peep rear; blade front sight; standard sights various other combinations available. Scope bases. Semi-military-type target stock w/pistol grip; original model has grasping grooves in forearm; higher comb and semi-beavertail forearm on later models. Numerous changes were made in this model; the most important was the adoption of the speed lock in 1929. Model 52 rifles produced before this change are generally referred to as "slow lock" models. Last arms of this type bore serial numbers followed by the letter "A." Made 1919-37.
Slow Lock model . . . . NiB $547 Ex $438 Gd $298
Speed Lock model . . . . NiB $741 Ex $592 Gd $403

MODEL 52 HEAVY BARREL . . . . . . NiB $804 Ex $644 Gd $438
First type speed lock. Same general specifications as Standard Model 52 of this type except has heavier bbl., Lyman No. 17G front sight, weight: 10 lbs.

MODEL 52 INTERNATIONAL MATCH RIFLE
Similar to Model 52-D Heavy Barrel except has special lead-lapped bbl., laminated "free rifle"-style stock with high comb, thumbhole, hook buttplate, accessory rail, handstop/swivel assembly, palm rest. Weight: 13.5 lbs. Made 1969-78.
With standard trigger . . . . NiB $1030 Ex $978 Gd $798
With Kenyon or I.S.U. trigger . . . . . NiB $709 Ex $566 Gd $385

MODEL 52 INTERNATIONAL PRONE . . NiB $1056 Ex $1025 Gd $803
Similar to Model 52-D Heavy Barrel except has special lead-lapped bbl., prone stock with full pistol-grip, rollover cheekpiece removable for bore-cleaning. Weight 11.5 lbs. Made 1975-80.

MODEL 52 SPORTING RIFLE
First type. Same as Standard Model 52 of this type except has lightweight 24-inch bbl., Lyman No. 48 receiver sight and gold bead front sight on hooded ramp, deluxe checkered sporting stock with cheekpiece, black forend tip, etc. Weight: 7.75 lbs. Made 1934-58. Reintroduced 1993.

(cont'd.) MODEL 52 SPORTING RIFLE
Model 52 Sporter	NiB $2511	Ex $2008	Gd $1366
Model 52A Sporter	NiB $3599	Ex $2879	Gd $1958
Model 52B Sporter	NiB $2826	Ex $2261	Gd $1537
Model 52C Sporter	NiB $3541	Ex $2832	Gd $1926

**Model 52 C Sporter
(1993 BAC re-issue) . . . . NiB $669 Ex $510 Gd $340**

MODEL 52-B BOLT-ACTION RIFLE
Standard bbl. Extensively redesigned action. Supplied with choice of "Target" stock, an improved version of the previous Model 52 stock, or "Marksman" stock with high comb, full pistol grip and beavertail forearm. Weight: 9 lbs. Offered with a wide choice of target sight combinations (Lyman, Marble-Goss, Redfield, Vaver, Winchester), value shown is for rifle less sight equipment. Other specifications as shown for first type. Made 1935-47. Reintroduced 1997.
Target model . . . . NiB $824 Ex $669 Gd $9253
**BAC model
(1997 BAC re-issue). . . . . NiB $638 Ex $510 Gd $347**
USRAC Sporting model . . . . NiB $669 Ex $511 Gd $360

MODEL 52-B BULL GUN
HEAVY BARREL. . . . . NiB $869 Ex $695 Gd $473
Same specifications as Standard Model 52-B except Bull Gun has extra heavy bbl., Marksman stock only, weight: 12 lbs. Heavy Bbl. model weight: 11 lbs. Made 1940-47.

MODEL 52-C BOLT-ACTION RIFLE
Improved action with "Micro-Motion" trigger mechanism and new-type "Marksman" stock. General specifications same as shown for previous models. Made 1947-61, Bull Gun from 1952. Value shown is for rifle less sights.
**Bull Gun (extra heavy barrel,
Wt. 12 lbs.) . . . . NiB $1030 Ex $824 Gd $566**
**Standard barrel
(Wt. 9.75 lbs.) . . . . NiB $824 Ex $669 Gd $556**
**Target model
(heavy barrel) . . . . NiB $875 Ex $975 Gd $566**

NOTE: *Following WWI, Winchester had financial difficulties and, like many other firearm firms of the day, failed. However, Winchester continued to operate in the hands of receivers. Then, in 1931, The Western Cartridge Co. — under the leadership of John Olin — purchased all assets of the firm. After that, Winchester leaped ahead of all other firms of the day in firearm and ammunition development.*
The first sporting firearm to come out of the Winchester plant after WWI was the Model 20 shotgun, but this was quickly followed by the famous Model 52 bolt-action rifle. This was also a time when Winchester dropped the four-digit model numbers and began using two-digit numbers instead. This model-numbering procedure, with one exception (Model 677), continued for the next several years.

Winchester Model 47

Winchester Model 52
Standard Barrel

Winchester Model 52
International Match

Winchester Model 52
International Prone Target

RIFLES

MODEL 52-D BOLT-ACTION
TARGET RIFLE . . . . **NiB $824 Ex $772 Gd $407**
Redesigned Model 52 action, Single-Shot. Caliber: .22 LR. 28-inch standard or heavy bbl., free-floating, with blocks for standard target scopes. Weight: With standard bbl., 9.75 lbs., with heavy barrel, 11 lbs. Restyled Marksman stock with accessory channel and forend stop, rubber buttplate. Made 1961-78. Value shown is for rifle without sights.

MODEL 53 LEVER-ACTION
REPEATER . . . . **NiB $2183 Ex $1746 Gd $1188**
Modification of Model 92. Solid frame or takedown. Calibers: .25-20, .32-20, .44-40. Six shot tubular half-magazine in solid frame model. 7-shot in takedown. 22-inch nickel steel bbl. Weight: 5.5 to 6.5 lbs. Sights: Open rear; bead front. Redesigned straight-grip stock and forearm. Made 1924-32.

MODEL 54 BOLT-ACTION
HIGH POWER SPORTING RIFLE (I) . . . . . **NiB $927 Ex $824 Gd $566**
First type. Calibers: .270 Win., 7x57mm, .30-30, .30-06, 7.65x53mm, 9x57mm. Five shot box magazine. 24-inch bbl. Weight: 7.75 lbs. Sights: Open rear; bead front. Checkered stock w/pistol grip, tapered forearm w/Schnabel tip. This type has two-piece firing pin. Made 1925-30.

MODEL 54 BOLT-ACTION
HIGH POWER SPORTING RIFLE (II) . . . . . **NiB $978 Ex $850 Gd $515**
Standard Grade. Improved type with speed lock and one-piece firing pin. Calibers: .22 Hornet, .220 Swift, .250/3000, .257 Roberts, .270 Win., 7x57mm, .30-06. Five shot box magazine. 24-inch bbl., 26-inch in cal. .220 Swift. Weight: About 8 lbs. Sights: Open rear, bead front on ramp. NRA-type stock w/checkered pistol-grip and forearm. Made 1930-36. Add $200 for .22 Hornet caliber.

MODEL 54 CARBINE (I) . . . . **NiB $1030 Ex $824 Gd $541**
First type. Same as Model 54 rifle except has 20-inch bbl., plain lightweight stock with grasping grooves in forearm. Weight: 7.25 lbs.

MODEL 54 CARBINE (II) . . . . **NiB $1030 Ex $875 Gd $566**
Improved type. Same as Model 54 Standard Grade Sporting Rifle of this type except has 20-inch bbl. Weight: About 7.5 lbs. This model may have either NRA-type stock or the lightweight stock found on the first-type Model 54 Carbine.

MODEL 54 NATIONAL
MATCH RIFLE . . . . **NiB $1062 Ex $850 Gd $578**
Same as Standard Model 54 except has Lyman sights, scope bases, Marksman-type target stock, weighs 9.5 lbs. Same calibers as Standard Model.

MODEL 54 SNIPER'S
MATCH RIFLE . . . . **NiB $1545 Ex $1287 Gd $515**
Similar to the earlier Model 54 Sniper's Rifle except has Marksman-type target stock, scope bases, weight: 12.5 lbs. Available in same calibers as Model 54 Standard Grade.

MODEL 54 SNIPER'S RIFLE . . . . . . **NiB $1159 Ex $927 Gd $618**
Same as Standard Model 54 except has heavy 26-inch bbl., Lyman No. 48 rear peep sight and blade front sight semi-military stock, weight: 11.75 pounds, cal. .30-06 only.

MODEL 54 SUPER GRADE . . . . . **NiB $1545 Ex $1287 Gd $824**
Same as Standard Model 54 Sporter except has deluxe stock with cheekpiece, black forend tip, pistol-grip cap, quick detachable swivels, 1-inch sling strap. See illustration previous page.

Winchester Model 52-B
Standard Barrel

Winchester Model 52-B
Sporter

Winchester Model 52-C
Heavy Barrel

Winchester Model 53

Winchester Model 54
Super Grade

MODEL 54 TARGET RIFLE.......NiB $1062 Ex $850 Gd $578
Same as Standard Model 54 except has 24-inch medium-weight bbl. (26-inch in cal. .220 Swift), Lyman sights, scope bases, Marksman-type target stock, weight: 10.5 lbs., same calibers as Standard Model.

MODEL 55 "AUTOMATIC"
SINGLE-SHOT.................NiB $309 Ex $232 Gd $154
Caliber: .22 Short, Long, LR. 22-inch bbl. Sights: Open rear, bead front. One-piece walnut stock. Weight: About 5.5 lbs. Made 1958-60.

MODEL 55 LEVER-ACTION REPEATER
Modification of Model 94. Solid frame or takedown. Calibers: .25-35, .30-30, .32 Win. Special. Three shot tubular half magazine. 24-inch nickel steel bbl. Weight: About 7 lbs. Sights: Open rear; bead front. Made 1924-32.
Standard model (straight grip) ....NiB $1224 Ex $978 Gd $665
Deluxe model (pistol grip) ....NiB $3213 Ex $2570 Gd $1748

MODEL 56 BOLT-ACTION
SPORTING RIFLE.............NiB $1236 Ex $1025 Gd $592
Solid frame. Caliber: .22 LR., .22 Short. Five or 10-shot detachable box magazine. 22-inch bbl. Weight: 4.75 lbs. Sights: Open rear; bead front. Plain pistol-grip with Schnabel forend. Made 1926-29.

MODEL 57 BOLT-ACTION RIFLE
Solid frame. Same as Model 56 except available (until 1929) in .22 Short as well as LR with 5- or 10-shot magazine. Has semi-military style target stock, bbl. band on forend, swivels and web sling, Lyman peep rear sight, weight: 5 lbs. Mfd. 1926-36.
Sporter model ....NiB $695 Ex $566 Gd $412
Target model ....NiB $644 Ex $592 Gd $438

MODEL 58 BOLT-ACTION
SINGLE-SHOT.................NiB $418 Ex $335 Gd $228
Similar to Model 52. Takedown. Caliber: .22 Short, Long LR. 18-inch bbl. Weight: 3 lbs. Sights, Open rear; blade front. Plain, flat, straight-grip hardwood stock. Not serial numbered. Made 1928-31.

MODEL 59 BOLT-ACTION
SINGLE-SHOT.................NiB $541 Ex $412 Gd $283
Improved version of Model 58, has 23-inch bbl., redesigned stock w/pistol grip, weight: 4.5 lbs. Made 1930.

MODEL 60, 60A BOLT-ACTION SINGLE-SHOT
Redesign of Model 59. Caliber: .22 Short, Long, LR. 23-inch bbl. (27-inch after 1933). Weight: 4.25 lbs. Sights: Open rear, blade front. Plain pistol-grip stock. Made 1930-34 (60), 1932-39 (60A).
Model 60.....................NiB $309 Ex $206 Gd $144
Model 60A....................NiB $386 Ex $216 Gd $154

Winchester Model 55
"Automatic" Single-Shot

Winchester Model 55
Lever-Action

Winchester Model 56

Winchester Model 57
Target

MODEL 60A TARGET RIFLE . . . . . . NiB $463 Ex $386 Gd $257
Essentially the same as Model 60 except has Lyman peep rear sight
and square top front sight, semi-military target stock and web sling,
weight: 5.5 lbs. Made 1932-39.

MODEL 61 HAMMERLESS SLIDE-ACTION REPEATER
Takedown. Caliber: .22 Short, Long, LR. Tubular magazine holds 20
Short, 16 Long, 14 LR. 24-inch round bbl. Weight: 5.5 lbs. Sights:
Open rear; bead front. Plain pistol-grip stock, grooved semi-beaver-
tail slide handle. Also available with 24-inch full-octagon bbl. and
only calibers .22 Short, .22 LR or .22 WRF. Note: Octagon barrel
model discontinued 1943-44; assembled 1948.
Model 61 (round barrel) . . . . NiB $766 Ex $613 Gd $417
Model 61 (grooved receiver) . . . . . . NiB $966 Ex $772 Gd $525
Model 61 (octagon barrel) . . . . . NiB $1668 Ex $1334 Gd $907

MODEL 61 MAGNUM . . . . NiB $953 Ex $772 Gd $489
Same as Standard Model 61 except chambered for .22 WMR; magazine holds 12 rounds. Made 1960-63.

MODEL 62 VISIBLE HAMMER. . . . . NiB $644 Ex $515 Gd $360
Modernized version of Model 1890. Caliber: .22 Short, Long, LR.
23-inch bbl. Weight: 5.5 lbs. Plain straight-grip stock, grooved semi-
beavertail slide handle. Also available in Gallery Model chambered
for .22 Short only. Made 1932-1959. Note: Pre-WWII model (small
forearm) commands 25% higher price.

MODEL 63 SELF-LOADING RIFLE
Takedown. Caliber: .22 LR High Speed only. 10-shot tubular magazine
in buttstock. 23-inch bbl. Weight: 5.5 lbs. Sights: Open rear, bead
front. Plain pistol-grip stock and forearm. Originally available with 20-
inch bbl. as well as 23-inch. Made 1933-59. Reintroduced 1997.
Model 63 w/23-inch bbl. . . . . NiB $895 Ex $716 Gd $487
Model 63 w/20-inch bbl. . . . . NiB $1352 Ex $1081 Gd $735

(cont'd.) **MODEL 63 SELF-LOADING RIFLE**
Model 63 grooved receiver) . . . . NiB $1242 Ex $994 Gd $676
Model 63 Grade I (1997 BAC reissue) . . . . NiB $727 Ex $583 Gd $396
Model 63 High Grade (1997 BAC reissue). . . NiB $1313 Ex $1025 Gd $669

MODEL 64 DELUXE DEER RIFLE . . . . . . NiB $1281 Ex $1025 Gd $697
Same as Standard Model 64 calibers .30-30 and .32 Win. Special,
except has checkered pistol-grip and semi-beavertail forearm,
swivels and sling, weighs 7.75 lbs. Made 1933-56.

MODEL 64 LEVER-ACTION REPEATER
Standard Grade. Improved version of Models 94 and 55. Solid
frame. Calibers: .25-35, .30-30, .32 Win. Special. Five shot tubular
two-thirds magazine. 20- or 24-inch bbl. Weight: About 7 lbs.
Sights: Open rear; bead front on ramp w/sight cover. Plain pistol-
grip stock and forearm. Made 1933-56. Production resumed in
1972 (caliber .30-30, 24-inch bbl.). Discontinued 1974.
Original model . . . . NiB $850 Ex $721 Gd $541
1972-74 model . . . . NiB $669 Ex $489 Gd $360

MODEL 64 .219 ZIPPER . . . . . . NiB $2440 Ex $1952 Gd $1328
Same as Standard Grade Model 64 except has 26-inch bbl., peep
rear sight. Made 1937-47.

MODEL 65 LEVER-ACTION
REPEATER . . . . NiB $2569 Ex $2055 Gd $1398
Improved version of Model 53. Solid frame. Calibers: .25-20 and
.32-20. Six-shot tubular half-magazine. 22-inch bbl. Weight: 6.5
lbs. Sights: Open rear, bead front on ramp base. Plain pistol-grip
stock and forearm. made 1933-47.

MODEL 65 .218 BEE . . . . NiB $2769 Ex $2214 Gd $1506
Same as Standard Model 65 except has 24-inch bbl., peep rear
sight. Made 1938-47.

Winchester Model 58

Winchester Model 59

Winchester Model 60A

Winchester Model 61

Winchester Model 62

Winchester Model 63

MODEL 67 BOLT-ACTION
SINGLE-SHOT RIFLE . . . . NiB $206 Ex $180 Gd $103
Takedown. Calibers: .22 Short, Long, LR, .22 LR shot (smoothbore), .22 WRF. 27-inch bbl. Weight: 5 lbs. Sights: Open rear, bead front. Plain pistol-grip stock (original model had grasping grooves in forearm). Made 1934-63.

MODEL 67 BOY'S RIFLE . . . . NiB $232 Ex $180 Gd $113
Same as Standard Model 6 except has shorter stock, 20-inch bbl., weighs 4.25 lbs.

MODEL 68 BOLT-ACTION
SINGLE-SHOT . . . . NiB $257 Ex $180 Gd $139
Same as Model 67 except has rear peep sight. Made 1934-1946.

MODEL 69 BOLT-ACTION RIFLE . . NiB $370 Ex $283 Gd $154
Takedown. Caliber: .22 S, L, LR. Five or 10-shot box magazine. 25-inch bbl. Weight: 5.5 lbs. Peep or open rear sight. Plain pistol-grip stock. Rifle cocks on closing motion of the bolt. Made 1935-37.

MODEL 69A BOLT-ACTION RIFLE
Same as the Model 69 except cocking mechanism was changed to cock the rifle by the opening motion of the bolt. Made 1937-63. Note: Models with grooved receivers command 20% higher prices.
Model 69A standard . . . . NiB $418 Ex $335 Gd $228

Cont'd) **MODEL 69A BOLT-ACTION RIFLE**
Match Mdl. w/Lyman No. 57E
W receiver sight . . . . NiB $509 Ex $407 Gd $277
*(*Target Model w/Winchester
peep rear sight, swivels, sling . . . . . NiB $612 Ex $489 Gd $333

MODEL 70
Introduced in 1937, the Model 70 Bolt-Action Repeating Rifle was offered in several styles and calibers. Only minor design changes were made over a period of 27 years and more than 500,000 of these rifles were sold. The original model was dubbed "The Rifleman's Rifle." In 1964, the original Model 70 was superseded by a revised version with redesigned action, improved bolt, swaged (free-floating) barrel, restyled stock. This model again underwent major changes in 1972. Most visible: New stock with contrasting forend tip and grip cap, cut checkering (instead of impressed as in predecessor) knurled bolt handle. The action was machined from a solid block of steel with barrels made from chrome molybdenum steel. Other changes in the design and style of the Model 70 continued. The XTR models were added in 1978 along with the Model 70A, the latter omitting the white liners, forend caps and floor plates. In 1981, an XTR Featherweight Model was added to the line, beginning with serial number G1,440,000. This version featured lighter barrels, fancy-checkered stocks with Schnabel forend. After U.S. Repeating Arms took over the Winchester plant, the Model 70 went through even more changes as described under that section of Winchester rifles.

Winchester Model 64
Deer Rifle

Winchester Model 64
Standard

Winchester Model 64
1972-74 Type

Winchester Model 65

Winchester Model 67

Winchester Model 68

Winchester Model 69

Winchester Model 69 Match

GRADING: **NiB** = New in Box **Ex** = Excellent or NRA 95% **Gd** = Good or NRA 68%

Winchester Model 70
Basic Post-WWII Model

Winchester Model 70
Standard Model

Winchester Model 70
Super Grade

Winchester Model 70
African (1964)

Winchester Model 70
Deluxe (1964)

PRE-1964 MODEL 70

MODEL 70
AFRICAN RIFLE . . . . **NiB $5150 Ex $4583 Gd $2575**
Same general specifications as Super Grade Model 70 except w/25-inch bbl., 3-shot magazine, Monte Carlo stock w/recoil pad. Weight: 9.5 lbs. Caliber: .458 Winchester Magnum. Made 1956–63.

MODEL 70 ALASKAN
Same as Standard Model 70 except calibers .338 Win. Mag., .375 H&H Mag.; 3-shot magazine in .338, 4-shot in .375 caliber; 25-inch bbl.; stock w/recoil pad. Weight: 8 lbs. in .338; 8.75 lbs. in .375 caliber. Made 1960–63.
.338 Win.
Mag. . . . . **NiB $1796 Ex $1437 Gd $977**
.375 H&H . . . . **NiB $2311 Ex $1849 Gd $1258**

MODEL 70 BULL GUN . . . . **NiB $4120 Ex $3605 Gd $2060**
Same as Standard Model 70 except w/heavy 28-inch bbl., scope bases, Marksman stock, weighs 13.25 lbs., caliber .300 H&H Magnum and .30-06 only. Disc. 1963.

MODEL 70 FEATHERWEIGHT SPORTER
Same as Standard Model 70 except w/redesigned stock and 22-inch bbl., aluminum trigger guard, floorplate and buttplate. Calibers: .243 Win., .264 Win. Mag., .270 Win., .308 Win., .30-06, .358 Win. Weight: 6.5 lbs. Made 1952–63.
.243 Win. . . . . **NiB $1024 Ex $818 Gd $557**
.264 Win. . . . . **NiB $1539 Ex $1231 Gd $837**
.270 Win. . . . . **NiB $1281 Ex $1025 Gd $697**
.30-06 Springfield . . . . **NiB $966 Ex $772 Gd $525**
.308 Win. . . . . **NiB $895 Ex $716 Gd $487**
.358 Win. . . . . **NiB $2183 Ex $1746 Gd $1188**

Winchester Model 70
Standard Weight Target Rifle

Winchester Model 70
Heavy Weight Target Rifle

Winchester Model 70
Bull Gun

Winchester Model 70
(Pre-1964) Standard Model

RIFLES

MODEL 70 NATIONAL
MATCH RIFLE . . . . **NiB $2060 Ex $1983 Gd $1442**
Same as Standard Model 70 except w/scope bases, Marksman-type
target stock, weight: 9.5 lbs. caliber .30-06 only. Disc. 1960.

MODEL 70 STANDARD GRADE
Calibers: .22 Hornet, .220 Swift, .243 Win., .250-3000, .257 Roberts, .270
Win., 7x57mm, .30-06, .308 Win., .300 H&H Mag., .375 H&H Mag. Five
shot box magazine (4-shot in Magnum calibers). 24-inch bbl. standard; 26-
inch in .220 Swift and .300 Mag.; 25-inch in .375 Mag.; at one time a 20-
inch bbl. was available. Sights: Open rear; hooded ramp front. Checkered
walnut stock; Monte Carlo comb standard on later production. Weight:
From 7.75 lbs. depending on caliber and bbl. length. Made 1937–63.

.22 Hornet (1937-58)	NiB $1996	Ex $1596	Gd $1086
.220 Swift (1937-63)	NiB $1410	Ex $1128	Gd $767
.243 Win. (1955-63)	NiB $1153	Ex $922	Gd $627
.250-3000 Sav. (1937-49)	NiB $2569	Ex $2055	Gd $1398
.257 Roberts (1937-59)	NiB $1796	Ex $1437	Gd $977
.264 Win. Mag. (1959-63) limited	NiB $1281	Ex $1025	Gd $697
.270 Win. (1937-63)	NiB $1024	Ex $818	Gd $557
7x57mm Mauser (1937-49)	NiB $2826	Ex $2261	Gd $1538
7.65 Argentine (1937 only) limited			Very Rare
.30-06 Springfield (1937-63)	NiB $837	Ex $669	Gd $455
.308 Win. (1952-63) special order			Very Rare
.300 H&H (1937-63)	NiB $1481	Ex $1184	Gd $805
.300 Sav. (1944-50) limited			Rare
.300 Win. Mag. (1962-63)	NiB $1925	Ex $1540	Gd $1048
.338 Win. Mag. (1959-63)			
special order only	NiB $1834	Ex $1468	Gd $998
.35 Rem. (1941-47) limited			Very Rare
.358 Win. (1955-58)			Very Rare
.375 H&H (1937-63)	NiB $2311	Ex $1849	Gd $1258
.458 Win. Mag. (1956-63)			
Super Grade only	NiB $4629	Ex $3703	Gd $2518
9x57 Mauser (1937 only) limited.			Very Rare

MODEL 70 SUPER GRADE
Same as Standard Grade Model 70 except w/deluxe stock w/cheek-
piece, black forend tip, pistol-grip cap, quick detachable swivels,
sling. Disc. 1960. Prices for Super Grade models also reflect rarity
in both production and caliber. Values are generally twice that of
standard models of similar configuration.

MODEL 70 SUPER GRADE FEATHERWEIGHT
Same as Standard Grade Featherweight except w/deluxe stock
w/cheekpiece, black forend tip, pistol-grip cap, quick detachable
swivels, sling. Disc. 1960. Note: SG-FWs are very rare, but unless
properly documented will not command premium prices. Prices for
authenticated Super Grades Featherweight models are generally 4 to
5 times that of a standard production Featherweight model w/simi-
lar chambering.

MODEL 70 TARGET RIFLE
Same as Standard Model 70 except w/24-inch medium-weight bbl.,
scope bases, Marksman stock, weight 10.5 lbs. Originally offered in
all of the Model 70 calibers, this rifle was available later in calibers
.243 Win. and .30-06. Disc. 1963. Values are generally twice that
of standard models of similar configuration.

MODEL 70 TARGET
HEAVY WEIGHT . . . . **NiB $3708 Ex $1849 Gd $1210**
Same general specifications as Standard Model 70 except w/either
24- or 26-inch heavy weight bbl. weight: 10.5 lbs. No checkering.
.243 and .30-06 calibers.

MODEL 70 TARGET
BULL BARREL . . . . **NiB $4120 Ex $2266 Gd $1643**
Same general specifications as Standard Model 70 except 28-inch
heavy weight bbl. and chambered for either .30-06 or .300 H&H
Mag. Drilled and tapped for front sight base. Receiver slotted for
clip loading. Weight: 13.25 lbs.

Winchester Model 70
International Army Match (1964)

Winchester Model 70
Mannlicher (1964)

Winchester Model 70
Standard (1964)

Winchester Model 70
Target (1964)

MODEL 70
VARMINT RIFLE . . . . NiB $1236 Ex $1159 Gd $1004
Same general specifications as Standard Model 70 except w/26-inch heavy bbl., scope bases, special varminter stock. Calibers: .220 Swift, .243 Win. Made 1956–63.

MODEL 70
WESTERNER . . . . NiB $1184 Ex $1025 Gd $901
Same as Standard Model 70 except calibers .264 Win. Mag., .300 Win. Mag.; 3-shot magazine; 26-inch bbl. in former caliber, 24-inch in latter. Weight: 8.25 lbs. Made 1960–63.

1964-TYPE MODEL 70

MODEL 70 AFRICAN . . . . NiB $1133 Ex $695 Gd $510
Caliber: .458 Win. Mag. Three shot magazine. 22-inch bbl. Weight: 8.5 lbs. Special "African" sights. Monte Carlo stock w/ebony forend tip, hand-checkering, twin stock-reinforcing bolts, recoil pad, QD swivels. Made 1964–71.

MODEL 70 DELUXE . . . . NiB $1025 Ex $747 Gd $438
Calibers: .243, .270 Win., .30-06, .300 Win. Mag. Five shot box magazine (3-shot in Magnum). 22-inch bbl. (24-inch in Magnum). Weight: 7.5 lbs. Sights: Open rear; hooded ramp front. Monte Carlo stock w/ebony forend tip, hand-checkering, QD swivels, recoil pad on Magnum. Made 1964–71.

MODEL 70 INTERNATIONAL
ARMY MATCH RIFLE. . . . . NiB $978 Ex $814 Gd $592
Caliber: .308 Win. (7.62 NATO). Five shot box magazine. 24-inch heavy barrel. Externally adj. trigger. Weight: 11 lbs. ISU stock w/military oil finish, forearm rail for standard accessories, vertically adj. buttplate. Made in 1971. Value shown is for rifle w/o sights.

MODEL 70 MAGNUM
Calibers: 7mm Rem. Mag.; .264, .300, .338 Win. Mag.; .375 H&H Mag. Three shot magazine. 24-inch bbl. Weight: 7.75 to 8.5 lbs. Sights: Open rear; hooded ramp front. Monte Carlo stock w/cheekpiece, checkering, twin stock-reinforcing bolts, recoil pad, swivels. Made 1964–71.
Caliber .375 H&H Mag. . . . . NiB $708 Ex $566 Gd $385
Other calibers . . . . NiB $483 Ex $386 Gd $263

MODEL 70 MANNLICHER . . . . NiB $721 Ex $618 Gd $515
Calibers: .243, .270, .308 Win., .30-06. Five shot box magazine. 19-inch bbl. Sights: open rear; hooded ramp front. Weight: 7.5 lbs. Mannlicher-style stock w/Monte Carlo comb and cheekpiece, checkering, steel forend cap, QD sling swivels. Made 1969–71.

MODEL 70 STANDARD. . . . . NiB $438 Ex $360 Gd $237
Calibers: .22-250, .222 Rem., .225, .243, .270, .308 Win., .30-06. Five shot box magazine. 22-inch bbl. Weight: 7.5 lbs. Sights: Open rear; hooded ramp front. Monte Carlo stock w/cheekpiece, checkering, swivels. Made 1964–71.

Winchester Model 70
African (1972)

MODEL 70 TARGET . . . . **NiB $676 Ex $541 Gd $368**
Calibers: .308 Win. (7.62 NATO) and .30-06. Five shot box magazine. 24-inch heavy bbl. Blocks for target scope. No factory sights installed, but drilled and tapped for front and rear sights. Weight: 10.25 lbs. High-comb Marksman-style stock, aluminum hand stop, swivels. Straight-grain, one-piece stock w/sling swivels, but no checkering. Made 1964–71.

MODEL 70 VARMINT . . . . **NiB $484 Ex $386 Gd $288**
Same as Model 70 Standard except w/24-inch target weight bbl., blocks for target scope. No factory sights installed, but drilled and tapped for front and rear sights. Available in calibers .22-250, .222 Rem., and .243 Win. only. Weight: 9.75 lbs. Made 1964–71.

1972-TYPE MODEL 70

MODEL 70 AFRICAN . . . . **NiB $766 Ex $613 Gd $417**
Similar to Model 70 Magnum except w/22-inch bbl. caliber .458 Win. Mag. w/special African open rear sight, reinforced stock w/ebony forend tip, detachable swivels and sling; front sling swivel stud attached to bbl. Weight: 8.5 lbs. Made 1972-92.

MODEL 70 CLASSIC SM
Similar to Model 70 Classic Sporter except w/checkered black composite stock and matte metal finish. Made 1994-96.
Model 70 Classic SM . . . . **NiB $484 Ex $407 Gd $257**
Caliber .375 H&H . . . . **NiB $592 Ex $463 Gd $309**
W/BOSS, add. **$100**
W/open sights, add **$40**

MODEL 70 CLASSIC SPORTER
Similar to Model 70 Sporter except w/pre-64-style action w/controlled round feeding, classic-style stock. Optional open sights. Made 1994 to date.
Standard model . . . . **NiB $443 Ex $371 Gd $103**
W/BOSS, add. **$100**
W/open sights, add **$40**

MODEL 70 CLASSIC SPORTER STAINLESS
Similar to Model 70 Classic Sporter except w/matte stainless steel finish. Weight: 7.5 lbs. No sights. Made 1994 to date.
Standard model . . . . **NiB $633 Ex $541 Gd $283**
Magnum model . . . . **NiB $695 Ex $566 Gd $335**
W/BOSS, add. **$100**

MODEL 70 CUSTOM SHARPSHOOTER
Calibers: .22-250, .223, .308 Win., .300 Win. Mag. 24- or 26-inch bbl. 44.5 inches overall (24-inch bbl.). Weight: 11 lbs. Custom-fitted, hand-honed action. McMillan A-2 target-style stock. Matte blue or stainless finish. Made 1992-96.
Model 70 Custom
Sharpshooter (blued). . . . . **NiB $1828 Ex $1390 Gd $901**
Model 70 Custom
Sharpshooter (stainless) . . . . **NiB $1914 Ex $1442 Gd $953**

MODEL 70 CUSTOM SPORTING SHARPSHOOTER
Similar to Custom Sharpshooter Model except w/sporter-style gray composite stock. Stainless 24- or 26-inch bbl. w/blued receiver. Calibers: .270, 7mm STW, .300 Win. Mag. Made 1993 to date.
Model 70 Custom Sharpshooter
blued (disc. 1995). . . . . **NiB $1828 Ex $1390 Gd $901**
Model 70 Custom Sharpshooter, stainless . **NiB $1905 Ex $1442 Gd $953**

**MODEL 70 GOLDEN 50TH ANNIVERSARY EDITION
BOLT-ACTION RIFLE** **$1030**
Caliber: .300 Win. Three shot magazine. 24-inch bbl. 44.5 inches overall. Weight: 7.75 lbs. Checkered American walnut stock. Hand-engraved American scroll pattern on bbl., receiver, magazine cover, trigger guard and pistol-grip cap. Sights: Adj. rear; hooded front ramp. Inscription on bbl. reads "The Rifleman's Rifle 1937–1987." Only 500 made 1986–87. (Value for guns in new condition)

MODEL 70 FEATHERWEIGHT CLASSIC . . . . . . **NiB $547 Ex $438 Gd $298**
Similar to Model 70 XTR Featherweight except w/controlled-round feeding system. Calibers: .270, .280 and .30-06. Made 1992 to date.

**MODEL 70 INTERNATIONAL
ARMY MATCH** . . . . **NiB $927 Ex $798 Gd $515**
Caliber: .308 Win. (7.62mm NATO). Five shot magazine, clip slot in receiver bridge. 24-inch heavy barrel. Weight: 11 lbs. No sights, but drilled and tapped for front and rear iron sights, and/or scope mounts. ISU target stock. Intro. 1973; disc.

MODEL 70 LIGHTWEIGHT . . . . **NiB $592 Ex $360 Gd $144**
Calibers: .22-250 and .223 Rem.; .243, .270 and .308 Win.; .30-06 Springfield. Five shot mag. capacity (6-shot .223 Rem.). 22-inch barrel. 42 to 42.5 inches overall. Weight: 6 to 6.25 lbs. Checkered classic straight stock. Sling swivel studs. Made 1986-95.

MODEL 70 MAGNUM
Same as Model 70 except w/3-shot magazine, 24-inch bbl., reinforced stock w/recoil pad. Weight: 7.75 lbs. (except 8.5 lbs. in .375 H&H Mag.). Calibers: .264 Win. Mag., 7mm Rem. Mag., .300 Win. Mag., .338 Win. Mag., .375 H&H Mag. Made 1972-80.
.375 H&H Magnum . . . . **NiB $669 Ex $500 Gd $300**
Other magnum calibers . . . . **NiB $566 Ex $375 Gd $295**

MODEL 70 STANDARD. . . . . **NiB $418 Ex $335 Gd $228**
Same as Model 70A except w/5-shot magazine, Monte Carlo stock w/cheekpiece, black forend tip and pistol-grip cap w/white spacers, checkered pistol grip and forearm, detachable sling swivels. Same calibers plus .225 Win. Made 1972-80.

MODEL 70 STANDARD CARBINE . . . . **NiB $425 Ex $340 Gd $230**
Same general specifications as Standard Model 70 except 19-inch bbl. and weight: 7.25 lbs. Shallow recoil pad. Walnut stock and forend w/traditional Model 70 checkering. Swivel studs. No sights, but drilled and tapped for scope mount.

Winchester Model 70
Featherweight

Winchester Model 70
Golden 50th Anniversary

Winchester Model 70
Featherweight Classic

Winchester Model 70
Lightweight

Winchester Model 70
Magnum

Winchester Model 70
Carbine

MODEL 70 SPORTER DBM

Same general specifications as Model 70 Sporter SSM except w/detachable box magazine. Calibers: .22-250 (disc. 1994), .223 (disc. 1994), .243 (disc. 1994), .270, 7mm Rem. Mag., .308 (disc. 1994), .30-06, .300 Win. Mag. Made 1992-94.

Model 70 DBM.....................NiB $489 Ex $407 Gd $257
Model 70 DBM-S (w/iron sights) .... NiB $509 Ex $407 Gd $277

MODEL 70 STAINLESS SPORTER SSM .... NiB $509 Ex $407 Gd $277

Same general specifications as Model 70 XTR Sporter except w/checkered black composite stock and matte finished receiver, bbl. and other metal parts. Calibers: .270, 7mm Rem. Mag., .30-06, .300 Win. Mag., .338 Win. Mag. Weight: 7.75 lbs. Made 1992-94.

MODEL 70 CLASSIC SUPER GRADE ..... NiB $824 Ex $747 Gd $407

Calibers: .270, 7mm Rem. Mag., .30-06, .300 Win. Mag., .338 Win. Mag. Five shot magazine (standard), 3-shot (magnum). 24-inch bbl.

(cont'd.) MODEL 70 CLASSIC SUPER GRADE

44.5 inches overall. Weight: 7.75 lbs. Checkered walnut stock w/sculptured cheekpiece and tapered forend. Scope bases and rings, no sights. Controlled-round feeding system. Made 1990 to date.

MODEL 70 TARGET.............NiB $850 Ex $773 Gd $412

Calibers: .30-06 and .308 Win. (7.62mm NATO). 5-shot magazine. 26-inch heavy bbl. Weight: 10.5 lbs. No sights, but drilled and tapped for scope mount and open sights. High-comb Marksman-style target stock, aluminum hand stop and swivels. Intro. 1972. Disc.

MODEL 70 ULTRA MATCH.......NiB $875 Ex $798 Gd $438

Similar to Model 70 Target but custom grade w/26-inch heavy bbl. w/deep counterbore, glass bedding, externally adj. trigger. Intro. 1972. Disc.

Winchester Model 70
XTR Sporter

Winchester Model 70A

MODEL 70 VARMINT (HEAVY BARREL)

Same as Model 70 Standard except w/medium-heavy, counter-bored 26-inch bbl., no sights, stock w/less drop. Weight: 9 lbs. Calibers: .22-250 Rem., .223 Rem., .243 Win., .308 Win. Made 1972-93. Model 70 SHB, in .308 Win. only w/black synthetic stock and matte blue receiver/bbl. Made 1992-93.

Model 70 Varmint . . . . NiB $669 Ex $541 Gd $288
Model 70 SHB (synthetic heavy barrel) . . . NiB $474 Ex $386 Gd $257

MODEL 70 WIN-CAM RIFLE . . . . . . NiB $463 Ex $360 Gd $206

Caliber: .270 Win. and .30-06 Springfield. 24-inch barrel. Camouflage one-piece laminated stock. Recoil pad. Drilled and tapped for scope. Made 1986 to date.

MODEL 70 WINLITE BOLT-ACTION RIFLE . . . . NiB $644 Ex $463 Gd $340

Calibers: .270 Win., .280 Rem., .30-06 Springfield, 7mm Rem., .300 Win. Mag., and .338 Win. Mag. Five shot magazine; 3-shot for Magnum calibers. 22-inch bbl.; 24-inch for Magnum calibers. 42.5 inches overall; 44.5, Magnum calibers. Weight: 6.25 to 7 lbs. Fiberglass stock w/rubber recoil pad, sling swivel studs. Made 1986-90.

MODEL 70 WIN-TUFF BOLT-ACTION RIFLE

Calibers: .22-250, .223, .243, .270, .308 and .30-06 Springfield. 22-inch bbl. Weight: 6.25–7 lbs. Laminated dye-shaded brown wood stock w/recoil pad. Barrel drilled and tapped for scope. Swivel studs. FWT Model made 1986–94. LW Model intro. 1992.

Featherweight model. . . . . NiB $515 Ex $386 Gd $268
Lightweight model (Made 1992–93) . . . . . . NiB $463 Ex $350 Gd $237

MODEL 70 XTR FEATHERWEIGHT . . . . NiB $483 Ex $386 Gd $263

Similar to Standard Win. Model 70 except lightweight American walnut stock w/classic Schnabel forend, checkered. 22-inch bbl., hooded blade front sight, folding leaf rear sight. Stainless-steel magazine follower. Weight: 6.75 lbs. Made 1984-94.

MODEL 70 XTR SPORTER RIFLE . . . . NiB $515 Ex $386 Gd $257

Calibers: .264 Win. Mag., 7mm Rem. Mag., .300 Win. Mag., .200 Weatherby Mag., and .338 Win. Mag. Three shot magazine. 24-inch barrel. 44.5 inches overall. Weight: 7.75 lbs. Walnut Monte Carlo stock. Rubber buttpad. Receiver tapped and drilled for scope mounting. Made 1986-94.

MODEL 70 XTR SPORTER MAGNUM . . . . NiB $515 Ex $386 Gd $267

Calibers: .264 Win. Mag., 7mm Rem. Mag., .300 Win. Mag., .338 Win. Mag. Three shot magazine. 24-inch bbl. 44.5 inches overall. Weight: 7.75 lbs. No sights furnished, optional adj. folding leaf rear; hooded ramp. Receiver drilled and tapped for scope. Checkered

American walnut Monte Carlo-style stock w/satin finish. Made 1986-94.

MODEL 70 XTR

SPORTER VARMINT . . . . NiB $474 Ex $386 Gd $257
Same general specifications as Model 70 XTR Sporter, except in calibers .223, .22-250, .243 only. Checkered American walnut Monte Carlo-style stock w/cheekpiece. Made 1986-94.

MODEL 70A . . . . NiB $371 Ex $283 Gd $201

Calibers: .222 Rem., .22-250, .243 Win., .25-06, .270 Win., .30-06, .308 Win. Four shot magazine. 22-inch bbl. (except 24- or 26-inch in 25-06). Weight: 7.5 lbs. Sights: Open rear; hooded ramp front. Monte Carlo stock w/checkered pistol grip and forearm, sling swivels. Made 1972-78.

MODEL 70A MAGNUM . . . . NiB $386 Ex $283 Gd $206

Same as Model 70A except w/3-shot magazine, 24-inch bbl., recoil pad. Weight: 7.75 lbs. Calibers: .264 Win. Mag., 7mm Rem. Mag., .300 Win. Mag. Made 1972-78

MODEL 70 ULTIMATE CLASSIC BOLT-ACTION RIFLE

Calibers: .25-06 Rem., .264 Win., .270 Win., .270 Wby. Mag., .280 Rem., 7mm Rem. Mag., 7mm STW, .30-06, Mag., .300 Win. Mag., .300 Wby. Mag., .300 H&H Mag., .338 Win. Mag., .340 Wby. Mag., .35 Whelen, .375 H&H Mag., .416 Rem. Mag. and .458 Win. Mag. Three, 4- or 5-shot magazine. 22- 24- 26-inch stainless bbl. in various configurations including: full-fluted tapered round, half round and half octagonal or tapered full octagonal. Weight: 7.75 to 9.25 lbs. Checkered fancy walnut stock. Made 1995 to date.

Model 70
Ultimate Classic . . . . NiB $2369 Ex $1905 Gd $1004
For Mag. calibers (.375 H&H,
.416 and .458), add. $250

MODEL 70 LAMINATED STAINLESS

BOLT-ACTION RIFLE . . . . NiB $875 Ex $747 Gd $407
Calibers: .270 Win., .30-06 Spfld., 7mm Rem. Mag., .300 Win. Mag., and .338 Win. Mag. Five shot magazine. 24-inch bbl. 44.75 inches overall. Weight: 8 to 8.525 lbs. Gray/Black laminated stock. Made 1998 to date.

MODEL 70 CHARACTERISTICS

MODEL 70 FIRST MODEL (SERIAL NUMBERS 1 – 80,000)

First manufactured in 1936; first sold in 1937. Receiver drilled for Lyman No. 57W or No. 48WJS receiver peep sights. Also drilled and tapped for Lyman or Fecker scope sight block. Weight w/24-inch bbl. in all calibers except .375 H&H Mag.: 8.25 lbs. 9 lbs. in H&H

Cross-sectional view of the pre-1964 Winchester Model 70's speed lock action. This action cocks on the opening movement of the bolt with polished, smooth-functioning cams and guide lug, insuring fast and smooth operation.

MODEL 70 SECOND MODEL (SERIAL NUMBERS 80,000 – 350,000)

All civilian production of Winchester Model 70 rifles halted during World War II. Production resumed in 1947 w/improved safety and integral front-sight ramp. Serial numbers started at around 80,000. This model type was produced until 1954, ending around serial number 350,000.

MODEL 70 THIRD MODEL (SERIAL NUMBERS 350,000 – 400,000)

This variety was manufactured from 1954 to 1960 and retained many features of the Second Model except that a folding rear sight replaced the earlier type and front-sight ramps were brazed onto the bbl. rather than being an integral part of the bbl. The Model 70 Featherweight Rifle was intro. in 1954 in .308 WCF caliber. It was fitted w/light 22-inch bbl. and was also available w/either a Monte Carlo or Standard stock. The .243 Win. cartridge was added in 1955 in all grades of the Winchester Model 70 except the National Match and Bull Gun models. The .358 Win. cartridge was also intro. in 1955, along w/new Varmint Model chambered in .243 caliber only.

MODEL 70 FOURTH MODEL (SERIAL NUMBERS 400,000 – 500,000)

Different markings were inscribed on the barrels of these models and new magnum calibers were added; that is, .264 Win Mag., .338 Win. Mag, and .458 Win. Mag. All bbls. of this variation were about 0.13 inch shorter than previous ones. The .22 Hornet and .257 Roberts were disc. in 1962; the .358 Win. caliber in 1963.

MODEL 70 FIFTH MODEL (SERIAL NUMBERS 500,000 TO ABOUT 570,000)

These rifles may be recognized by slightly smaller checkering patterns and slightly smaller lightweight stocks. Featherweight bbls. were marked "Featherweight." Webbed recoil pads were furnished on magnum calibers.

POST-1964 MODEL 70 RIFLES

In 1964, the Winchester-Western Division of Olin Industries claimed that they were losing money on every Model 70 they produced. Both labor and material costs had increased to a level that could no longer be ignored. Other models followed suit. Consequently, sweeping changes were made to the entire Winchester line. Many of the older, less popular models were discontinued. Models that were to remain in production were modified for lower production costs.

1964 WINCHESTER MODEL 70 RIFLES
SERIAL NUMBERS 570,000 TO ABOUT 700,000)

The first version of the "New Model 70s" utilized a free-floating barrel, swaged rifle bore, new stock and sights, new type of bolt and receiver, and a different finish throughout on both the wood and metal parts. The featherweight grade was dropped, but six other grades were available in this new line:

Standard
Deluxe (Replaced Previous Super Grade)
Magnum
Varmint
Target
African

1966 MODEL 70 RIFLES
(SERIAL NUMBERS 700,000-G TO ABOUT 1,005,000)

In general, this group of Model 70s had fancier wood checkering, cross-bolt stock reinforcement, improved wood finish and improved action. One cross-bolt reinforcement was used on standard guns. Magnum calibers, however, used an additional forward cross-bolt and red recoil pad. The free-floating barrel clearance forward of the breech taper was reduced in thickness. Impressed checkering was used on the Deluxe models until 1968. Hand checkering was once again used on Deluxe and Carbine models in 1969; the big, red "W" was removed from all grip caps. A new, red safety-indicator and undercut cheekpiece was introduced in 1971.

1972 MODEL 70 RIFLES
(SERIAL NUMBERS G1,005,000 TO ABOUT G1,360,000)

Both the barrels and receivers for this variety of Model 70s were made from chrome molybdenum (C-M) steel. The barrels were tapered w/spiral rifling, ranging in length from 22 to 24 inches. Calibers .222 Rem., .225 Win. .22-250, .243 Win., .25-06, .270, .308 Win., .30-06 and .458 WM used the 22-inch length, while the following calibers used the 24-inch length: .222 Rem., .22-250, .243 Win., .264 Win. Mag., 7mm Mag., .300 and .375 H&H Mag. The .225 Win caliber was dropped in 1973; Mannlicher stocks were also disc. in 1973. The receiver for this variety of Model 70s was machined from a block of C-M steel. A new improved anti-bind bolt was introduced along with a new type of ejector. Other improvements included hand-cut checkering, pistol-grip stocks with pistol-grip and dark forend caps. An improved satin wood finish was also utilized.

1978 MODEL 70 RIFLES
(SERIAL NUMBERS BEGAN AROUND G1,360,000)

This variety of Model 70 was similar to the 1972 version except that a new XTR style was added which featured high-luster wood and metal finishes, fine-cut checkering, and similar embellishments. All Model 70 rifles made during this period used the XTR style; no standard models were available. In 1981, beginning with serial number G1,440,000 (approximately), a Featherweight version of the Model 70 XTR was introduced. The receiver was identical to the 1978 XTR, but lighter barrels were fitted. Stocks were changed to a lighter design with larger scroll checkering patterns and a Schnabel forend with no Monte Carlo comb. A satin sheen stock finish on the featherweight version replaced the high-luster finish used on the other XTR models. A new-style red buttplate with thick, black rubber liner was used on the Featherweight models. The grip cap was also redesigned for this model.

**Winchester Model 70
Black Shadow**

**Winchester Model 70
Classic Camo**

U.S. REPEATING ARMS MODEL 70 — 1982 TO DATE

In the early 1980s, negotiations began between Olin Industries and an employee-based corporation. The result of these negotiations ended with Olin selling all tools, machinery, supplies, etc. at the New Haven plant to the newly-formed corporation which was eventually named U.S. Repeating Arms Company. Furthermore, U.S. Repeating Arms Company purchased the right to use the Winchester name and logo. Winchester Model 70s went through very few changes the first two years after the transistion. However, in 1984, the Featherweight Model 70 XTR rifles were offered in a new short action for .22-250 Rem., .223 Rem., .243 Win. and .308 Win. calibers, in addition to their standard action which was used for the longer cartridges. A new Model 70 lightweight carbine was also introduced this same year. Two additional models were introduced in 1985 — the Model 70 Lightweight Mini-Carbine Short Action and the Model 70 XTR Sporter Varmint. The Model 70 Winlite appeared in the 1986 "Winchester" catalog, along with two economy versions of the Model 70 — the Winchester Ranger and the Ranger Youth Carbine. Five or six different versions of the Winchester Model 70 had been sufficient for 28 years (1937 - 1964). Now, changes in design and the addition of new models each year seemed to be necessary to keep the rifle alive. New models were added, old models dropped, changed in design, etc., on a regular basis. The trend continues. Still, the Winchester Model 70 Bolt-Action Repeating Rifle — in any of its variations — is the most popular bolt-action rifle ever built.

MODEL 70 BLACK SHADOW . . . . . NiB $397 Ex $309 Gd $232
Calibers: .243 Win., .270 Win., .300 Win. Mag., .308 Win., .338 Win. Mag., .30-06 Spfld., 7mm STW, 7mm Rem. Mag. and 7mm-08 Rem. Three 4- or 5-shot magazine. 20- 24- 25- or 26-inch bbls. 39.5 to 46.75 inches overall.Weight: 6.5 to 8.25 lbs. Composite, Walnut or Gray/Black laminated stocks. Made 1998 to date.

**MODEL 70 CLASSIC
CAMO BOLT-ACTION RIFLE . . . . . . NiB $850 Ex $772 Gd $412**
Calibers: .270 Win., 30-06 Spfld., 7mm Rem. Mag., .300 Win. Mag. Three or 5-shot magazine. 24- or 26-inch bbl. 44.75 to 46.75 inches overall. Weight; 7.25 to 7.5 lbs. Mossy Oak finish and composite stock. Made 1998 to date.

**MODEL 70 CLASSIC
COMPACT BOLT-ACTION RIFLE . . . NiB $509 Ex $407 Gd $277**
Calibers: .243 Win., .308 Win., and 7mm-08 Rem. Three shot magazine. 20-inch bbl., 39.5 inches overall. Weight: 6.5 lbs. Walnut stock. Made 1998 to date.

**MODEL 70 CLASSIC LAREDO RANGE HUNTER
BOLT-ACTION RIFLE**
Calibers: 7mm STW, 7mm Rem. mag., .300 Win. Mag. Three shot magazine. 26-inch bbl. 46.75 inches overall. Weight: 9.5 lbs. Composite stock. Made 1996 to date.
Classic Laredo . . . . NiB $669 Ex $541 Gd $407
**Classic Laredo Fluted
(Made 1998 to date) . . . . NiB $695 Ex $566 Gd $386**
Bossâ Classic Laredo . . . . NiB $676 Ex $541 Gd $368

MODEL 70 COYOTE . . . . NiB $561 Ex $463 Gd $283
Calibers: .22-250 Rem., .223 Rem., and .243 Win. Five or 6-shot magazine. 24- inch bbl., 44 inches overall. Weight: 9 lbs. Medium-heavy stainless steel barrel w/laminated stock. Reverse taper forend. Made 1999 to date.

**MODEL 70 RANGER
COMPACT RIFLE . . . . NiB $386 Ex $294 Gd $180**
Calibers: .22-250 Rem., .223 Rem., .243 Win., 7mm-08 Rem., Mag., and .308 Win. Five or 6-shot magazine. 20- or 22-inch bbl. 41 inches overall. Weight: 6.5 lbs. Adjustable TRUGLO front and rear fiber optic sights. Push-feed action. Made 1999 to date.

**MODEL 70
STEALTH RIFLE . . . . NiB $695 Ex $603 Gd $333**
Varminter style bolt-action rifle. Calibers: .22-250 Rem., .223 Rem., and .308 Win. Five or 6-shot magazine. 26- inch bbl. 46 inches overall. Weight: 10.75 lbs. Black synthetic stock w/Pillar Plus Accu Block and full-length aluminum bedding block. Matte blue finish. Made 1999 to date.

MODEL 71 LEVER-ACTION REPEATER
Solid frame. Caliber: .348 Win. Four shot tubular magazine. 20- or 24-inch bbl. Weight: 8 lbs. Sights: Open or peep rear; bead front on ramp w/hood. Walnut stock. Made 1935–57.
**Special Grade (checkered pistol-grip
and forearm, grip cap, quick-detachable
swivels and sling . . . . NiB $1931 Ex $1545 Gd $1004**
**Special Grade Carbine
(20-inch bbl.; disc. 1940) . . . . NiB $2440 Ex $1952 Gd $1328**
**Standard Grade
(lacks checkering,
grip cap, sling and swivels) . . . . NiB $1133 Ex $978 Gd $541**
**Standard Grade
Carbine (20-inch
bbl.; disc. 1940) . . . . NiB $2060 Ex $1648 Gd $1025**

Winchester Model 72

Winchester Model 74

Winchester Model 75
Sporting

Winchester Model 88
Pre-1965

MODEL 72 BOLT-ACTION REPEATER. . . . . NiB $463 Ex $335 Gd $206
Tubular magazine. Takedown. Caliber: .22 Short, Long, LR. Magazine holds 20 Short, 16 Long or 15 LR. 25-inch bbl. Weight: 5.75 lbs. Sights: Peep or open rear; bead front. Plain pistol-grip stock. Made 1938–59.

MODEL 73 LEVER-ACTION REPEATER
See Model 1873 rifles, carbines, "One of One Thousand" and other variations of this model at the beginning of Winchester Rifle Section. Note: The Winchester Model 1873 was the first lever-action repeating rifle bearing the Winchester name.

MODEL 74 SELF-LOADING RIFLE . . . . NiB $283 Ex $232 Gd $154
Takedown. Calibers: .22 Short only, .22 LR only. Tubular magazine in buttstock holds 20 Short, 14 LR. 24-inch bbl. Weight: 6.25 lbs. Sights: Open rear; bead front. Plain pistol-grip stock, one-piece. Made 1939–55.

MODEL 75 SPORTING RIFLE . . . . . NiB $818 Ex $721 Gd $412
Same as Model 75 Target except has 24-inch bbl., checkered sporter stock, open rear sight; bead front on hooded ramp, weight: 5.5 lbs.

MODEL 75 TARGET RIFLE. . . . . . . NiB $566 Ex $412 Gd $257
Caliber: .22 LR. 5- or 10-shot box magazine. 28-inch bbl. Weight: 8.75 lbs. Target sights (Lyman, Redfield or Winchester). Target stock w/pistol grip and semi-beavertail forearm, swivels and sling. Made 1938–59.

MODEL 77 SEMIAUTOMATIC RIFLE,
CLIP TYPE . . . . NiB $283 Ex $232 Gd $144
Solid frame. Caliber: .22 LR. Eight shot clip magazine. 22-inch bbl. Weight: About 5.5 lbs. Sights: Open rear; bead front. Plain, one-piece pistol-grip stock. Made 1955–63.

MODEL 77,
TUBULAR MAGAZINE . . . . NiB $283 Ex $232 Gd $154
Same as Model 77. Clip type except has tubular magazine holding 15 rounds. Made 1955–63.

MODEL 86 CARBINE AND RIFLE
See Model 1886 at beginning of Winchester Rifle section.

MODEL 88 CARBINE
Same as Model 88 Rifle except has 19-inch bbl., plain carbine-style stock and forearm with bbl. band. Weight: 7 lbs. Made 1968-73.
88 Carbine. . . . . NiB $644 Ex $510 Gd $335
.284 Win. . . . . NiB $1339 Ex $1236 Gd $927

MODEL 88 LEVER-ACTION RIFLE
Hammerless. Calibers: .243 Win., .284 Win., .308 Win., .358 Win. Four shot box magazine. 3-shot in pre-1963 models and in .284. 22-inch bbl. Weight: About 7.25 lbs. One-piece walnut stock with pistol-grip, swivels (1965 and later models have basket-weave ornamentation instead of checkering). Made 1955–1973. Note: .243 and .358 introduced 1956, later discontinued 1964; .284 introduced 1963.
Model 88 (checkered stock) . . . . NiB $669 Ex $515 Gd $345
Model 88 (basketweave stock) . . . . NiB $566 Ex $463 Gd $315
.284 Win. . . . . NiB $1095 Ex $875 Gd $595
.358 Win. . . . . NiB $1281 Ex $1025 Gd $697

MODEL 92 LEVER-ACTION RIFLE
Similar to the original Model 1892. Calibers: .357 Mag., .44-40, .44 Mag., .45 LC. 10-shot magazine. 24-inch round bbl. Weight: 6.25 lbs. 41.25 inches overall. Bead front sight, adjustable buckhorn rear. Etched receiver and gold trigger. Blue finish. Smooth straight-grip walnut stock and forewarn w/ metal grip cap. Made 1997 to date.
Standard Rifle . . . . NiB $580 Ex $463 Gd $315
Short Rifle w/20-inch bbl. (.44 Mag. only) . . . . NiB $560 Ex $448 Gd $305

Winchester Model 70
Coyote

Winchester Model 70
Ranger Compact

Winchester Model 70
Stealth

Winchester Model 94
Traditional

RIFLES

MODEL 94
ANTIQUE CARBINE . . . . NiB $283 Ex $257 Gd $180
Same as standard Post-64 Model 94 Carbine except has decorative scrollwork and casehardened receiver, brass-plated loading gate, saddle ring; caliber .30-30 only. Made 1964–84.

MODEL 94 CARBINE
Same as Model 1894 Rifle except 20-inch round bbl., 6-shot full-length magazine. Weight: About 6.5 lbs. Originally made in calibers .25-35, .30-30, .32 Special and .38-55. Original version discontinued 1964. See 1894 Models at beginning of Winchester Rifle Section.
Pre-World War II
(under No. 1,300,000) . . . . NiB $1281 Ex $1025 Gd $697
Postwar, pre-1964
(under No. 2,700,000) . . . . NiB $708 Ex $566 Gd $385

MODEL 94
CLASSIC CARBINE . . . . NiB $391 Ex $283 Gd $232
Same as Canadian Centennial '67 Commemorative Carbine except without commemorative details; has scroll-engraved receiver, gold-plated loading gate. Made 1968–70.

MODEL 94
CLASSIC RIFLE . . . . NiB $371 Ex $257 Gd $232
Same as Model 67 Rifle except without commemorative details; has scroll-engraved receiver, gold-plated loading gate. Made 1968–70.

MODEL 94
DELUXE CARBINE. . . . . NiB $367 Ex $294 Gd $200
Caliber: .30-30 Win. Six shot magazine. 20-inch bbl. 37.75 inches overall. Weight: 6.5 lbs. Semi-fancy American walnut stock with rubber buttpad, long forearm and specially cut checkering. Engraved with "Deluxe" script. Made 1987 to date.

MODEL 94 LONG BARREL RIFLE. . . . . . . NiB $335 Ex $283 Gd $154
Caliber: .30-30 Win. Seven round magazine. 24-inch bbl. 41.75 inches overall. Weight: 7 lbs. American walnut stock. Blade front sight. Made 1987 to date.

MODEL 94 TRAPPER. . . . . NiB $335 Ex $257 Gd $165
Same as Winchester Model 94 Carbine except 16-inch bbl. and weight: 6 lbs., 2 oz. Made 1980 to date.

MODEL 94 WIN-TUFF RIFLE . . . . . NiB $309 Ex $232 Gd $165
Caliber: .30-30 Win. Six round magazine. 20-inch bbl. 37.75 inches overall. Weight: 6.5 lbs. Brown laminated wood stock. Made 1987 to date.

MODEL 94 WRANGLER CARBINE
Same as standard Model 94 Carbine except has 16-inch bbl., engraved receiver and chambered for .32 Special & .38-55 Win.
Wrangler, Top
Eject (disc.1984) . . . . NiB $335 Ex $257 Gd $180
Wrangler II,
Angle Eject (disc. 1985) . . . . NiB $283 Ex $196 Gd $154

Winchester Model 94
Long Barrel

Winchester Model 94
Win-Tuff

Winchester Model 94
Wrangler II Angle Eject

Winchester Model 94
XTR Big Bore

Winchester Model 94
XTR 7-30 Waters

MODEL 94 XTR BIG BORE . . . . **NiB $366 Ex $263 Gd $165**
Modified Model 94 action for added strength. Caliber: .375 Win.
20-inch bbl. Rubber buttpad. Checkered stock and forearm. Weight:
6.5 lbs. Made 1978 to date.

**MODEL 94 XTR
LEVER-ACTION RIFLE** . . . . **NiB $309 Ex $206 Gd $144**
Same general specifications as standard Angle Eject M94 except
chambered .30-30 and 7-30 Waters and has 20- or 24-inch bbl.
Weight: 7 lbs. Made 1985 to date by U.S. Repeating Arms.

MODEL 94 COMMEMORATIVES

MODEL 94 ANTLERED GAME. . . . . **NiB $676 Ex $541 Gd $368**
Standard Model 94 action. Gold-colored medallion inlaid in
stock. Antique gold-plated receiver, lever tang and bbl. bands.
Medallion and receiver engraved with elk, moose, deer and cari-
bou. 20.5-inch bbl. Curved steel buttplate. In .30-30 caliber.
19,999 made in 1978.

**MODEL 94 BICENTENNIAL
'76 CARBINE** . . . . **NiB $824 Ex $695 Gd $505**
Same as Standard Model 94 Carbine except caliber .30-30 Win.
only; antique silver-finished, engraved receiver; stock and forearm
of fancy walnut, checkered, Bicentennial medallion embedded in
buttstock, curved buttplate. 20,000 made in 1976.

MODEL 94 BUFFALO BILL COMMEMORATIVE
Same as Centennial '66 Rifle except receiver is black-chromed,
scroll-engraved and bears name "Buffalo Bill"; hammer, trigger,
loading gate, saddle ring, forearm cap, and buttplate are nickel-
plated; Buffalo Bill Memorial Assn. commemorative medallion
embedded in buttstock; "Buffalo Bill Commemorative" inscribed
on bbl., facsimile signature "W.F. Cody, Chief of Scouts" on tang.
Carbine has 20-inch bbl., 6-shot magazine, 7-lb. weight. 112,923
made in 1968.
Carbine . . . . **NiB $580 Ex $463 Gd $315**
Rifle. . . . . **NiB $612 Ex $489 Gd $333**
Matched carbine rifle set. . . . . . . **NiB $1410 Ex $1128 Gd $767**

Winchester Model 66
Commemorative

Winchester Model 94
Chief Crazy Horse Commemorative

CANADIAN CENTENNIAL '67 COMMEMORATIVE
Same as Centennial '66 Rifle except receiver engraved with maple leaves and forearm cap is black-chromed, buttplate is blued, commemorative inscription in gold on barrel and top tang: "Canadian Centennial 1867–1967." Carbine has 20-inch bbl., 6-shot magazine, weight: 7 lb., 90,398 made in 1967.

Carbine . . . . NiB $580 Ex $463 Gd $315
Rifle . . . . NiB $612 Ex $489 Gd $333
Matched carbine/rifle set . . . . . . NiB $1352 Ex $1081 Gd $735

CENTENNIAL '66 COMMEMORATIVE
Commemorates Winchester's 100th anniversary. Standard Model 94 action. Caliber: .30-30. Full-length magazine holds 8 rounds. 26-inch octagon bbl. Weight: 8 lbs. Gold-plated receiver and forearm cap. Sights: Open rear; post front. Saddle ring. Walnut buttstock and forearm with high-gloss finish, solid brass buttplate. Commemorative inscription on bbl. and top tang of receiver. 100,478 made in 1966.

Carbine . . . . NiB $580 Ex $463 Gd $315
Rifle . . . . NiB $612 Ex $489 Gd $333
Matched carbine/
rifle set . . . . NiB $1410 Ex $1128 Gd $767

MODEL 94 CHEYENNE
COMMEMORATIVE . . . . NiB $1018 Ex $850 Gd $694
Available in Canada only. Same as Standard Model 94 Carbine except chambered for .44-40. 11,225 made in 1977.

MODEL 94
CHIEF CRAZY HORSE
COMMEMORATIVE . . . . NiB $709 Ex $566 Gd $385
Cailber: .38-55, 7-shot tubular magazine. 24-inch bbl., 41.75 inches overall. Walnut stock with medallion of the United Sioux Tribes; buttstock and forend also decorated with brass tacks. Engraved receiver. Open rear sights; bead front sight. 19,999 made in 1983.

MODEL 94 COLT COMMEMORATIVE
CARBINE SET . . . . NiB $3856 Ex $3085 Gd $2098
Standard Model 94 action. Caliber: .44-40 Win. 20-inch bbl. Weight: 6.25 lbs. Features the horse-and-rider trademark and distinctive WC monogram in gold etching on left side of receiver. Sold in set with Colt Single Action Revolver chambered for same caliber. See illustration next page.

MODEL 94 COWBOY COMMEMORATIVE CARBINE
Same as Standard Model 94 Carbine except caliber .30-30 only; nickel-plated receiver, tangs, lever, bbl. bands; engraved receiver, "Cowboy Commemorative" on bbl., commemorative medallion embedded in buttstock; curved buttplate. 20,915 made in 1970. Nickel-silver medallion inlaid in stock. Antique silver-plated receiver engraved with scenes of the old frontier. Checkered walnut stock and forearm. 19,999 made in 1970.

Cowboy
Carbine . . . . NiB $580 Ex $463 Gd $315
Cowboy
Carbine
(1 of 300) . . . . NiB $3728 Ex $2982 Gd $2028

MODEL 94 GOLDEN SPIKE COMMEMORATIVE
CARBINE . . . . NiB $509 Ex $407 Gd $277
Same as Standard Model 94 Carbine except caliber .30-30 only; gold-plated receiver, tangs and bbl. bands; engraved receiver, commemorative medallion embedded in stock. 64,758 made in 1969.

MODEL 94 ILLINOIS
SESQUICENTENNIAL
COMMEMORATIVE CARBINE . . . . . NiB $509 Ex $407 Gd $277
Same as Standard Model 94 Carbine except caliber .30-30 only; gold-plated buttplate, trigger, loading gate, and saddle ring; receiver engraved with profile of Lincoln, commemorative inscription on receiver, bbl.; souvenir medallion embedded in stock. 31,124 made in 1968.

MODEL 94 LEGENDARY
FRONTIERSMEN
COMMEMORATIVE . . . . NiB $676 Ex $541 Gd $368
Standard Model 94 action. Caliber: .39-55. 24-inch round bbl. Nickel-silver medallion inlaid in stock. Antique silver-plated receiver engraved with scenes of the old frontier. Checkered walnut stock and forearm. 19,999 made in 1979.

MODEL 94
LEGENDARY LAWMEN
COMMEMORATIVE . . . . NiB $676 Ex $541 Gd $368
Same as Standard Model 94 Carbine except .30-30 Win. only; antique silver-plated receiver engraved with action law-enforcement scenes. 16-inch Trapper bbl., antique silver-plated bbl. bands. 19,999 made in 1978.

**Winchester Colt
Commemorative Set**

**Winchester Model 94
NRA Centennial**

MODEL 94 LONE STAR COMMEMORATIVE
Same as Theodore Roosevelt Rifle except yellow-gold plating; "Lone Star" engraving on receiver and bbl., commemorative medallion embedded in buttstock. 30,669 made in 1970.
Rifle or carbine . . . . NiB $580 Ex $463 Gd $315
Matched carbine/rifle set . . . . . . NiB $1410 Ex $1128 Gd $768

MODEL 94 NRA
CENTENNIAL MUSKET . . . . NiB $547 Ex $438 Gd $298
Commemorates 100th anniversary of National Rifle Association of America. Standard Model 94 action. Caliber: .30-30. Seven shot magazine. 26-inch bbl. Sights: Military folding rear; blade front. Black chrome-finished receiver engraved "NRA 1871–1971" plus scrollwork. Barrel inscribed "NRA Centennial Musket." Musket-style buttstock and full-length forearm; commemorative medallion embedded in buttstock. Weight: 7.13 lbs. Made in 1971.

MODEL 94 NRA
CENTENNIAL RIFLE . . . . NiB $580 Ex $463 Gd $315
Same as Model 94 Rifle except has commemorative details as in NRA Centennial Musket (barrel inscribed "NRA Centennial Rifle"); caliber .30-30, 24-inch bbl., QD sling swivels. Made in 1971.

MODEL 94 NRA
CENTENNIAL MATCHED SET . . . . NiB $1224 Ex $978 Gd $665
Rifle and musket were offered in sets with consecutive serial numbers. Note: Production figures not available. These rifles offered in Winchester's 1972 catalog.

MODEL 94
NEBRASKA CENTENNIAL
COMMEMORATIVE CARBINE . . . . NiB $1739 Ex $1365 Gd $946
Same as Standard Model 94 Carbine except caliber .30-30 only; gold-plated hammer, loading gate, bbl. band, and buttplate; souvenir medallion embedded in stock, commemorative inscription on bbl. 2,500 made in 1966.

MODEL 94 THEODORE ROOSEVELT
COMMEMORATIVE RIFLE/CARBINE
Standard Model 94 action. Caliber: .30-30. Rifle has 6-shot half-magazine, 26-inch octagon bbl., weight: 7.5-lb. Carbine has 6-shot full magazine, 20-inch bbl., weight: 7-lb. White gold-plated receiver, upper tang, and forend cap; receiver engraved with American Eagle, "26th President 1901–1909," and Roosevelt's signature. Commemorative medallion embedded in buttstock. Saddle ring. Half pistol-grip, contoured lever. 49,505 made in 1969.
Carbine . . . . NiB $547 Ex $438 Gd $298
Rifle. . . . . NiB $580 Ex $463 Gd $315
Matched set. . . . . NiB $1352 Ex $1081 Gd $735

MODEL 94
TEXAS RANGER
ASSOCIATION CARBINE . . . . . NiB $3341 Ex $2673 Gd $1818
Same as Texas Ranger Commemorative Model 94 except special edition of 150 carbines, numbered 1 through 150, with hand-checkered full-fancy walnut stock and forearm. Sold only through Texas Ranger Association. Made in 1973.

Winchester Model 100

MODEL 94 TEXAS RANGER
COMMEMORATIVE CARBINE. . . . . NiB $959 Ex $767 Gd $522
Same as Standard Model 94 Carbine except caliber .30-30 Win. only, stock and forearm of semi-fancy walnut, replica of Texas Ranger star embedded in buttstock, curved buttplate. 5,000 made in 1973.

MODEL 94 TRAPPER
Same as Winchester Model 94 Carbine except w/16-inch bbl. and weighs 6 lbs. 2 oz. Angle Eject introduced in 1985 also chambered for .357 Mag., .44 Mag. and .45 LC. Made 1980 to date.
94 Trapper, Top Eject (disc. 1984) . . . . NiB $335 Ex $257 Gd $180
94 Trapper, Angle Eject (.30-30) . . . . NiB $309 Ex $201 Gd $129
.357 Mag., .44 Mag. or .45 LC., add. $25

MODEL 94 JOHN WAYNE
COMMEMORATIVE CARBINE. . . . NiB $1224 Ex $978 Gd $665
Standard Model 94 action. Caliber: .32-40. 18.5-inch bbl. Receiver is pewter-plated with engraving of Indian attack and cattle drive scenes. Oversized bow on lever. Nickel-silver medallion in buttstock bears a bas-relief portrait of Wayne. Selected American walnut stock with deep-cut checkering. Introduced by U.S. Repeating Arms in 1981.

MODEL 94 WELLS FARGO & CO.
COMMEMORATIVE CARBINE. . . . . NiB $676 Ex $541 Gd $368
Same as Standard Model 94 Carbine except .30-30 Win. only; antique silver-finished, engraved receiver; stock and forearm of fancy walnut, checkered, curved buttplate. Nickel-silver stagecoach medallion (inscribed "Wells Fargo & Co. —1852–1977—125 Years") embedded in buttstock. 20,000 made in 1977.

MODEL 94 O. F. WINCHESTER
COMMEMORATIVE RIFLE. . . . . NiB $933 Ex $747 Gd $507
Standard Model 94 action. Caliber: .38-55. 24-inch octagonal bbl. Receiver is satin gold-plated with distinctive engravings. Stock and forearm semi-fancy American walnut with high grade checkering.

MODEL 94 WRANGLER CARBINE
Same as standard Model 94 Carbine except w/16-inch bbl., engraved receiver and chambered for .32 Special and .38-55 Win. Angle Eject introduced in 1985 as Wrangler II, also chambered for .30-30 Win., .44 Mag. and .45 LC. Made 1980-86. Re-introduced in 1992.
94 Wrangler, Top Eject (disc. 1984) . . . . . . NiB $288 Ex $232 Gd $154
94 Wrangler II, Angle Eject (.30-30) . . . . . . NiB $283 Ex $206 Gd $144
.44 Mag. or .45 LC., add. $25

MODEL 94 WYOMING DIAMOND JUBILEE
COMMEMORATIVE CARBINE . . . . NiB $1925 Ex $1540 Gd $1048
Same as Standard Model 94 Carbine except caliber .30-30 Win. only, receiver engraved and casehardened in colors, brass saddle ring and loading gate, souvenir medallion embedded in buttstock, commemorative inscription on bbl. 1,500 made in 1964.

MODEL 94 ALASKAN PURCHASE CENTENNIAL
COMMEMORATIVE CARBINE . . . . NiB $2054 Ex $1643 Gd $1118
Same as Wyoming issue except different medallion and inscription. 1,501 made in 1967.

MODEL 94 XTR BIG BORE
Modified Model 94 action for added strength. Calibers: .307 Win., .356 Win., .375 Win. or .444 Marlin. 20-inch bbl. Six shot magazine. Rubber buttpad. Checkered stock and forearm. Weight: 6.5 lbs. Made 1978 to date.
94 XTR BB, Top Eject (disc. 1984). . . . . NiB $366 Ex $257 Gd $154
94 XTR BB, Angle Eject (intro. 1985) . . . . . NiB $283 Ex $201 Gd $134
.356 Win. or .375 Win., add. $150

MODEL 94 XTR LEVER-ACTION RIFLE
Same general specifications as standard M94 and Angle Eject M94 except chambered for .30-30 Win. and 7-30 Waters and has 20- or 24-inch bbl. Weight: 6.5 to 7 lbs. Made 1978-88 by U.S. Repeating Arms.
94 XTR Top Eject (disc. 1984) . . . . NiB $335 Ex $242 Gd $154
94 XTR Angle Eject (.30-30) . . . . NiB $304 Ex $232 Gd $139
94 XTR Deluxe Angle Eject (.30-30) . . . . . . NiB $386 Ex $304 Gd $196
7-30 Waters, add. $80

MODEL 100 AUTOLOADING RIFLE. . . . . . NiB $566 Ex $438 Gd $283
Gas-operated semiautomatic. Calibers: .243, .284, .308 Win. Four shot clip magazine (3-shot in .284). 22-inch bbl. Weight: 7.25 lbs. Sights: Open rear; hooded ramp front. One-piece stock w/pistol grip, basket-weave checkering, grip cap, sling swivels. Made 1961–73.

MODEL 100 CARBINE . . . . NiB $618 Ex $489 Gd $309
Same as Model 100 Rifle except has 19-inch bbl., plain carbine-style stock and forearm with bbl. band. Weight: 7 lbs. Made 1967–73.

MODEL 121 DELUXE . . . . NiB $161 Ex $129 Gd $88
Same as Model 121 Standard except has ramp front sight, stock with fluted comb and sling swivels. Made 1967–73.

MODEL 121 STANDARD
BOLT-ACTION SINGLE SHOT. . . . . . NiB $154 Ex $124 Gd $84
Caliber: .22 Short, Long, LR. 20.75-inch bbl. Weight: 5 lbs. Sights: Open rear; bead front. Monte Carlo-style stock. Made 1967–73.

MODEL 121 YOUTH. . . . . NiB $154 Ex $124 Gd $93
Same as Model 121 Standard except has 1.25-inch shorter stock. Made 1967–73.

MODEL 131 BOLT-ACTION REPEATER. . . . . NiB $174 Ex $139 Gd $95
Caliber: .22 Short, Long or LR. Seven shot clip magazine. 20.75-inch bbl. Weight: 5 lbs. Sights: Open rear; ramp front. Plain Monte Carlo stock. Made 1967–73.

MODEL 135 . . . . NiB $161 Ex $129 Gd $88
Same as Model 131 except chambered for .22 WMR cartridge. Magazine holds 5 rounds. Made in 1967.

MODEL 141
BOLT-ACTION
TUBULAR REPEATER. . . . . NiB $196 Ex $154 Gd $98
Same as Model 131 except has tubular magazine in buttstock; holds 19 Short, 15 Long, 13 LR. Made 1967–73.

Winchester Model 250
Standard

Winchester Model 270
Standard

MODEL 145 . . . . NiB $185 Ex $154 Gd $98
Same as Model 141 except chambered for .22 WMR; magazine holds 9 rounds. Made in 1967.

MODEL 150 LEVER-ACTION CARBINE . . . . . . NiB $154 Ex $129 Gd $77
Same as Model 250 except has straight loop lever, plain carbine-style straight-grip stock and forearm with bbl. band. Made 1967–73.

MODEL 190 CARBINE . . . . NiB $154 Ex $129 Gd $77
Same as Model 190 rifle except has carbine-style forearm with bbl. band. Made 1967–73.

MODEL 190 SEMIAUTOMATIC RIFLE . . . . NiB $134 Ex $103 Gd $67
Same as current Model 290 except has plain stock and forearm. Made 1966–78.

MODEL 250 DELUXE RIFLE . . . . . . NiB $232 Ex $180 Gd $103
Same as Model 250 Standard Rifle except has fancy walnut Monte Carlo stock and forearm, sling swivels. Made 1965–71.

MODEL 250 STANDARD
LEVER-ACTION RIFLE . . . . NiB $154 Ex $124 Gd $84
Hammerless. Caliber: .22 Short, Long or LR. Tubular magazine holds 21 Short, 17 Long, 15 LR. 20.5-inch bbl. Sights: Open rear; ramp front. Weight: About 5 lbs. Plain stock and forearm on early production; later model has checkering. Made 1963–73.

MODEL 255 DELUXE RIFLE . . . . . . NiB $232 Ex $196 Gd $82
Same as Model 250 Deluxe Rifle except chambered for .22 WMR cartridge. Magazine holds 11 rounds. Made 1965–73.

MODEL 255 STANDARD RIFLE. . . NiB $194 Ex $1545 Gd $105
Same as Model 250 Standard Rifle except chambered for .22 WMR cartridge. Magazine holds 11 rounds. Made 1964–70.

MODEL 270 DELUXE RIFLE . . . . NiB $200 Ex $154 Gd $93
Same as Model 270 Standard Rifle except has fancy walnut Monte Carlo stock and forearm. Made 1965–73.

MODEL 270 STANDARD
SLIDE-ACTION RIFLE . . . . NiB $133 Ex $103 Gd $72
Hammerless. Caliber: .22 Short, Long or LR. Tubular magazine holds 21 Short, 17 Long, 15 LR. 20.5-inch bbl. Sights: Open rear; ramp front. Weight: About 5 lbs. Early production had plain walnut stock and forearm (slide handle); latter also furnished in plastic (Cycolac); last model has checkering. Made 1963–73.

MODEL 275 DELUXE RIFLE . . . . . . NiB $232 Ex $180 Gd $103
Same as Model 270 Deluxe Rifle except chambered for .22 WMR cartridge. Tubular magazine holds 11 rounds. Made 1965–70.

MODEL 275
STANDARD RIFLE . . . . NiB $165 Ex $129 Gd $93
Same as Model 270 Standard Rifle except chambered for .22 WMR cartridge. Magazine holds 11 rounds. Made 1964–70.

MODEL 290 DELUXE RIFLE . . . . . . NiB $232 Ex $196 Gd $82
Same as Model 290 Standard Rifle except has fancy walnut Monte Carlo stock and forearm. Made 1965–73.

MODEL 290 STANDARD SEMIAUTOMATIC RIFLE
Caliber: .22 Long or LR. Tubular magazine holds 17 Long, 15 LR. 20.5-inch bbl. Sights: Open rear; ramp front. Weight: About 5 lbs. Plain stock and forearm on early production; current model has checkering. Made 1963–77.
W/plain stock/forearm . . . . NiB $232 Ex $196 Gd $82
W/checkered
stock/forearm . . . . NiB $257 Ex $206 Gd $98

MODEL 310 BOLT-ACTION
SINGLE SHOT . . . . NiB $257 Ex $201 Gd $139
Caliber: .22 Short, Long, LR. 22-inch bbl. Weight: 5.63 lbs. Sights: Open rear; ramp front. Monte Carlo stock w/checkered pistol-grip and forearm, sling swivels. Made 1972–75.

MODEL 320 BOLT-ACTION
REPEATER . . . . NiB $299 Ex $257 Gd $154
Same as Model 310 except has 5-shot clip magazine. Made 1972–74.

MODEL 490
SEMIAUTOMATIC RIFLE . . . . NiB $299 Ex $232 Gd $154
Caliber: .22 LR. 5-shot clip magazine. 22-inch bbl. Weight: 6 lbs. Sights: Folding leaf rear; hooded ramp front. One-piece walnut stock w/checkered pistol grip and forearm. Made 1975–77.

MODEL 670 BOLT-ACTION
SPORTING RIFLE. . . . . NiB $360 Ex $257 Gd $185
Calibers: .225 Win., .243 Win., .270 Win., .30-06, .308 Win. Four shot magazine. 22-inch bbl. Weight: 7 lbs. Sights: Open rear; ramp front. Monte Carlo stock w/checkered pistol-grip and forearm. Made 1967–73.

Winchester Model 310

Winchester Model 320

Winchester Model 490
Rifle

Winchester Model 670
Bolt-Action Rifle

Winchester Model 670
Magnum

Winchester Model 770

MODEL 670 CARBINE . . . . **NiB $360 Ex $288 Gd $191**
Same as Model 670 Rifle except has 19-inch bbl. Weight: 6.75 lbs.
Calibers: .243 Win., .270 Win., .30-06. Made 1967–70.

MODEL 670 MAGNUM . . . . **NiB $407 Ex $283 Gd $221**
Same as Model 670 Rifle except has 24-inch bbl., reinforced
stock with recoil pad with slightly different checkering pattern.
Weight: 7.25 lbs. Calibers: .264 Win. Mag., 7mm Rem. Mag.,
.300 Win. Mag. Open rear sight; ramp front sight with hood.
Made 1967–70.

MODEL 770 BOLT-ACTION
SPORTING RIFLE. . . . . **NiB $386 Ex $283 Gd $206**
Model 70-type action. Calibers: .22-250, .222 Rem., .243, .270
Win., .30-06. Four shot box magazine. 22-inch bbl. Sights: Open
rear; hooded ramp front. Weight: 7.13 lbs. Monte Carlo stock,
checkered pistol-grip and forend; sling swivels. Made 1969–71.

MODEL 770 MAGNUM . . . . **NiB $412 Ex $335 Gd $257**
Same as Standard Model 770 except 24-inch bbl., weight: 7.25 lbs., recoil
pad. Calibers: 7mm Rem. Mag., .264 and .300 Win. Mag. Made 1969–71.

**Winchester Model 9422
Boy Scouts of America Commemorative**

**Winchester Model 9422
Eagle Scout Limited Edtion**

**Winchester Model 9422
WinCam**

**Winchester Model 9422
XTR Classic**

MODEL 9422 LEVER-ACTION RIMFIRE RIFLES

Similar to the standard Model 94 except chambered for .22 Rimfire. Calibers: .22 Short, Long, LR. (9422) or .22 WMR (9422M). Tubular magazine holds 21 or 15 Short.17 or 12 Long, 15 or 11 LR (9422 or Trapper) or 11 or 8 WRM (9422M or Trapper M). 16.5- or 20.5 inch bbl. 33.125- to 37.125 inches overall. Weight: 5.75 to 6.25 lbs. Open rear sight; hooded ramp front. Carbine-style stock and barrel-band forearm. Stock options: Walnut (Standard), laminated brown (WinTuff), laminated green (WinCam). Made 1972 to date.

Walnut (Standard)	NiB $355	Ex $283	Gd $180
WinCam	NiB $360	Ex $288	Gd $185
WinTuff	NiB $303	Ex $242	Gd $165
Legacy	NiB $391	Ex $335	Gd $180
Trapper (16.5-inch bbl.)	NiB $345	Ex $268	Gd $180
XTR Classic	NiB $489	Ex $463	Gd $309
High Grade Series I	NiB $427	Ex $360	Gd $227
High Grade Series II	NiB $386	Ex $283	Gd $206
25th Anniversary Edition			
Grade I(1of 2500)	NiB $566	Ex $463	Gd $360
25th Anniversary Edition			
High Grade (1of 250)	NiB $1231	Ex $1004	Gd $695
Boy Scout			
Commemorative (1of 15,000)	NiB $669	Ex $556	Gd $360
Eagle Scout			
Commemorative (1of 1000)	NiB $3470	Ex $2775	Gd $1888
22 WRM, add			10%

DOUBLE XPRESS RIFLE

NiB $2826   Ex $2261   Gd $1538

Over/under double rifle. Caliber: .30-06. 23.5-inch bbl. Weight: 8.5 lbs. Made for Olin Corp. by Olin-Kodensha in Japan. Introduced 1982.

RANGER YOUTH
BOLT-ACTION CARBINE

NiB $360   Ex $257   Gd $154

Calibers: .223 (discontinued 1989), .243 Win., and .308 Win. Four and 5-shot magazine. Bbl.: 20-inch. Weight: 5.75 lbs. American hardwood stock. Open rear sight. Made 1985 to date by U.S. Repeating Arms.

RANGER LEVER-ACTION CARBINE

NiB $251   Ex $200   Gd $137

Caliber: .30-30. Five shot tubular magazine. Bbl.: 20-inch round. Weight: 6.5 lbs. American hardwood stock. Economy version of Model 94. Made 1985 to date by U.S. Repeating Arms.

RANGER BOLT-ACTION CARBINE

NiB $335   Ex $268   Gd $182

Calibers: .223 Rem., .243 Win., .270, .30-06, 7mm Rem. (discontinued 1985), Mag. Three and 4-shot magazine. Bbl.: 24-inch in 7mm; 22-inch in .270 and .30-06. Open sights. American hardwood stock. Made 1985 to date by U.S. Repeating Arms.

MODEL 1892 GRADE I LEVER-ACTION RIFLE

Similar to the original Model 1892. Calibers: .357 Mag., .44-40, .44 Mag., .45 LC. 10-shot magazine. 24-inch round bbl. Weight: 6.25 lbs. 41.25 inches overall. Bead front sight, adjustable buckhorn rear. Etched receiver and gold trigger. Blue finish. Smooth straight-grip walnut stock and forearm w/ metal grip cap. Made 1997 to date.

Standard Rifle	NiB $685	Ex $597	Gd $335
Short Rifle w/20-inch bbl.			
(.44 Mag. only)	NiB $560	Ex $448	Gd $305

MODEL 1892 GRADE
II LEVER-ACTION RIFLE

NiB $1159   Ex $1004   Gd $613

Similar to the Grade I Model 1892 except w/gold appointments and receiver game scene. Chambered .45 LC only. Limited production of 1,000 in 1997.

Winslow Commander Grade

Winslow Crown Grade

Winslow Regent Grade
Bushmaster Stock

RIFLES

WINSLOW ARMS COMPANY — Camden, South Carolina

BOLT-ACTION SPORTING RIFLE

Action: FN Supreme Mauser, Mark X Mauser, Remington 700 and 788, Sako, Winchester 70. Standard calibers: .17-222, .17-223, .222 Rem., .22-250, .243 Win., 6mm Rem., .25-06, .257 Roberts, .270 Win., 7x57, .280 Rem., .284 Win., .308 Win., .30-06, .358 Win. Magnum calibers: .17-222 Mag., .257 Wby., .264 Win., .270 Wby., 7mm Rem., 7mm Wby., .300 H&H, .300 Wby., .300 Win., .308 Norma, 8mm Rem., .338 Win., .358 Norma, .375 H&H, .375 Wby., .458 Win. Three-shot magazine in standard calibers, 2-shot in magnum. 24-inch barrel in standard calibers, 26-inch in magnum. Weight: With 24-inch bbl., 7 to 7.5 lbs.; with 26-inch bbl., 8 to 9 lbs. No sights. Stocks: "Bushmaster" with slender pistol-grip and beavertail forearm, "Plainsmaster" with full curl pistol-grip and flat forearm; both styles have Monte Carlo cheekpiece. Values shown are for basic rifle in each grade; extras such as special fancy wood, more elaborate carving, inlays and engraving can increase these figures considerably. Made 1962–89.

Commander
Grade . . . . NiB $515 Ex $489 Gd $345
Regal Grade. . . . . NiB $633 Ex $608 Gd $412

(cont'd.) **BOLT-ACTION SPORTING RIFLE**
Regent Grade . . . . .NiB $772 Ex $669 Gd $484
Regimental Grade . . . . NiB $9102 Ex $922 Gd $618
Crown
Grade . . . . NiB $1442 Ex $1236 Gd $978
Royal
Grade . . . . NiB $1648 Ex $1442 Gd $1081
Imperial
Grade . . . . NiB $3605 Ex $3090 Gd $2266
Emperor
Grade . . . . NiB $6595 Ex $5871 Gd $4115

ZEPHYR DOUBLE RIFLES
Manufactured by Victor Sarasqueta Company — Eibar, Spain

DOUBLE RIFLE. . . . . NiB $20,625 Ex $16,500 Gd $11,225
Boxlock. Calibers: Available in practically every caliber from .22 Hornet to .505 Gibbs. Bbls.: 22 to 28 inches standard, but any lengths were available on special order. Weight: 7 lbs. for the smaller calibers up to 12 or more lbs. for the larger calibers. Imported by Stoeger from about 1938 to 1951.

Twenty-Seventh Edition
GUN TRADER'S GUIDE

Shotguns

American Arms
Bristol (Sterling) Over/Under

American Arms
Derby Hammerless Double

American Arms
Gentry/York Hammerless Double

American Arms
Silver Over/Under

American Arms
Camper Special

ALDENS SHOTGUN — Chicago, Illinois

MODEL 670 CHIEFTAIN SLIDE ACTION . . NiB $217 Ex $183 Gd $118
Hammerless. Gauges: 12, 20 and others. 3-shot tubular magazine.
Bbl.: 26- to 30-inch; various chokes. Weight: 6.25 to 7.5 lbs.
depending on bbl. length and ga. Walnut-finished hardwood stock.

AMERICAN ARMS — N. Kansas City, Missouri

See also Franchi Shotguns.

BRISTOL (STERLING) O/U . . . . NiB $709 Ex $561 Gd $383
Boxlock w/Greener crossbolt and engraved sideplates. Single selective trigger. Selective automatic ejectors. Gauges: 12, 20; 3-inch
chambers. 26-, 28-, 30-, or 32-inch vent-rib bbls. w/screw-in choke
tubes (Improved Cylinder/Modified/Full). Weight: 7 lbs. Antique-silver
receiver w/game scene or scroll engraving. Checkered full pistol-grip-
style buttstock and forearm w/high-gloss finish. Imported 1986-88
with the model designation Bristol; redesignated Sterling 1989-90.

BRITTANY HAMMERLESS DOUBLE . . . . . . NiB $704 Ex $571 Gd $383
Boxlock w/engraved case-colored receiver. Single selective trigger.
Selective automatic ejectors. Gauges: 12, 20. 3-inch chambers. Bbls.:

(cont'd.) **BRITTANY HAMMERLESS DOUBLE**
25- or 27-inch w/screw-in choke tubes (IC/M/F). Weight: 6.5 lbs. (20
ga.). Checkered English-style walnut stock w/semi-beavertail forearm or pistol-grip stock w/high-gloss finish. Imported 1989 to date.

CAMPER SPECIAL . . . . NiB $108 Ex $87 Gd $59
Similar to the Single Barrel except takedown model w/21-inch
bbl., M choke and pistol-grip stock. Made in 1989 only.

COMBO . . . . NiB $198 Ex $158 Gd $107
Similar to the Single-Barrel model except available w/interchange-
able rifle and shotgun bbls. .22 LR/20-ga. shotgun or .22 Hornet/12-
ga. shotgun. Rifle bbl. has adj. rear sights; blade-type front sight.
Made in 1989.

DERBY HAMMERLESS DOUBLE
Sidelock w/engraved sideplates. Single non-selective or double triggers. Selective automatic ejectors. Gauges: 12, 20, 28 and .410. 3
inch chambers. Bbls.: 26-inch (IC/M) or 28-inch (M/F). Weight: 6
lbs. (20 ga.). Checkered English-style walnut stock and splinter forearm w/hand-rubbed oil finish. Engraved frame/sideplates w/antique
silver finish. Imported 1986-94.
12 or 20 ga. . . . . NiB $893 Ex $765 Gd $459
28 or .410 ga. (disc. 1991) . . . . NiB $957 Ex $765 Gd $520

**American Arms
WS/SS Hammerless Double**

F.S. SERIES O/U
Greener crossbolt in Trap and Skeet configuration. Single selective trigger. Selective automatic ejectors. 12 gauge only. 26-, 28-, 30-, or 32-inch separated bbls. Weight: 6.5 to 7.25 lbs. Black or chrome receiver. Checkered walnut buttstock and forearm. Imported 1986-87.

Model F.S. 200 Boxlock	NiB $704	Ex $561	Gd $383
Model F.S. 300 Boxlock	NiB $842	Ex $689	Gd $485
Model F.S. 400 Sidelock	NiB $1173	Ex $964	Gd $663
Model F.S. 500 Sidelock	NiB $1173	Ex $969	Gd $663

GENTRY/YORK HAMMERLESS DOUBLE
Chrome, coin-silver or color casehardened boxlock receiver w/scroll engraving. Double triggers. Extractors. Gauges: 12, 16, 20, 28, .410. 3-inch chambers (16 and 28 have 2.75-inch). Bbls.: 26-inch (IC/M) or 28-inch (M/F, 12, 16 and 20). Weight: 6.75 lbs. (12 ga.). Checkered walnut buttstock w/pistol-grip and beavertail forearm; both w/semi-gloss oil finish. Imported as York from 1986-88, redesignated Gentry 1989 to date.

Gentry 12, or 16 or 20 ga.	NiB $638	Ex $459	Gd $306
Gentry 28 or .410 ga.	NiB $689	Ex $561	Gd $398
York 12, 16 or 20 ga. (disc. 1988)	NiB $504	Ex $403	Gd $274
York 28 or .410 ga. (disc. 1988)	NiB $606	Ex $485	Gd $329

GRULLA #2 HAMMERLESS DOUBLE
True sidelock w/engraved detachable sideplates. Double triggers. Extractors and cocking indicators. Gauges: 12, 20, .410 w/3-inch chambers; 28 w/2.75-inch. 26-inch bbl. Imported 1989 to date.

Standard model	NiB $3181	Ex $2545	Gd $1731
Two-bbl. set (disc. 1995)	NiB $4144	Ex $3315	Gd $2254

SILVER I O/U
Boxlock. Single selective trigger. Extractors. Gauges: 12, 20 and .410 w/3-inch chambers; 28 w/2.75 inch. Bbls.: 26-inch (IC/M), 28-inch (M/F, 12 and 20 ga. only). Weight: 6.75 lbs. (12 ga.). Checkered walnut stock and forearm. Antique-silver receiver w/scroll engraving. Imported 1987 to date.

12 or 20 ga.	NIB $536	EX. $433	GD $281
28 or .410 ga.	NIB $574	EX $459	GD $312

SILVER II O/U
Similar to Model Silver I except w/selective automatic ejectors and 26-inch bbls. w/screw-in tubes (12 and 20 ga.). Fixed chokes (28 and .410). Made 1987 to date.

12 or 20 ga	NiB $669	Ex $536	Gd $364
28 or .410 ga.	NiB $733	Ex $587	Gd $399
Upland Lite II	NiB $810	Ex $648	Gd $441
Two-bbl. set	NiB $1052	Ex $842	Gd $572

SILVER LITE O/U
Similar to Model Silver II except w/blued, engraved alloy receiver. Available in 12 and 20 ga. only. Imported from 1990-92.

Standard Model	NiB $689	Ex $561	Gd $408
Two-bbl. Set	NiB $1085	Ex $867	Gd $590

SILVER SKEET/TRAP
NiB $829 Ex $663 Gd $452
Similar to the Silver II Model except has 28-inch (Skeet) or 30-inch (Trap) ported bbls. w/target-style rib and mid-bead sight. Imported 1992-94.

SILVER SPORTING O/U
NiB $842 Ex $704 Gd $459
Boxlock. Single selective trigger. Selective automatic ejectors. Gauges: 12, 2.75-inch chambers. 28-inch bbls.w/Franchoke tubes (SK, IC, M and F). Weight: 7.5 lbs. Checkered walnut stock and forearm. Special broadway rib and vented side ribs. Engraved receiver w/chrome-nickel finish. Imported from 1990 to date.

SINGLE-SHOT SHOTGUN
Break-open action. Gauges: 10 (3.5), 12, 20, .410, 3-inch chamber. Weight: about 6.5 lbs. Bead front sight. Walnut-finished hardwood stock w/checkered grip and forend. Made from 1988 to 1990.

10 ga. (3.5-inch)	NiB $128	Ex $102	Gd $69
12, 20 or .410 ga.	NiB $108	Ex $87	Gd $59
Multi-choke bbl., add			$30

SLUGGER SINGLE-SHOT SHOTGUN
NiB $121 Ex $97 Gd $66
Similar to the Single-Shot model except in 12 and 20 ga. only w/24-inch slug bbl. Rifle-type sights and recoil pad. Made from 1989 to 1990.

TS/OU 12 SHOTGUN
NiB $714 Ex $587 Gd $398
Turkey Special. Boxlock. Single selective trigger. Selective automatic ejectors. Gauge: 12, 3.5-inch chambers. Bbls.: 24-inch O/U w/screw-in choke tubes (IC, M, F). Weight: 6 lbs. 15 oz. Checkered European walnut stock and beavertail forearm. Matte blue metal finish. Imported 1987 to date.

TS/SS 10 HAMMERLESS DOUBLE
NiB $669 Ex $536 Gd $364
Turkey Special. Same general specifications as Model WS/ SS 10, except w/26-inch side-by-side bbls., screw-in choke tubes (F/F) and chambered for 10-ga. 3.5-inch shells. Weight: 10 lbs., 13 oz. Imported 1987 to 1993.

TS/SS 12 HAMMERLESS DOUBLE
NiB $612 Ex $510 Gd $332
Same general specifications as Model WS/SS 10 except in 12 ga. w/26-inch side-by-side bbls. and 3 screw-in choke tubes (IC/M/F). Weight: 7 lbs., 6 oz. Imported 1987 to date.

WS/OU 12 SHOTGUN
NiB $648 Ex $510 Gd $342
Waterfowl Special. Boxlock. Single selective trigger. Selective automatic ejectors. Gauge: 12; 3.5-inch chambers. Bbls.: 28-inch O/U w/screw-in tubes (IC/M/F). Weight: 7 lbs. Checkered European walnut stock and beavertail forearm. Matte blue metal finish. Imported 1987 to date.

WS/SS 10 HAMMERLESS DOUBLE
NiB $714 Ex $587 Gd $398
Waterfowl Special. Boxlock. Double triggers. Extractors. Gauge: 10; 3.5-inch chambers. Bbls.: 32-inch side/side choked F/F. Weight: About 11 lbs. Checkered walnut stock and beavertail forearm w/satin finish. Parkerized metal finish. Imported from 1987 to 1995.

SHOTGUNS

Armalite AR-17
Golden Gun

Armsport 1050

Armsport 1125

WT/OU 10 Shotgun . . . . NiB $918 Ex $740 Gd $500
Same general specifications as Model WS/OU 12 except chambered
for 10-ga. 3.5-inch shells. Extractors. Satin wood finish and matte
blue metal. Imported 1987 to date.

ARMALITE, INC. — Costa Mesa, California

AR-17 GOLDEN GUN. . . . . NiB $638 Ex $510 Gd $398
Recoil-operated semiautomatic. High-test aluminum bbl. and
receiver housing. 12 ga. only. 2-shot. 24-inch bbl. w/inter-
changeable choke tubes: IC/M/F. Weight: 5.6 lbs.
Polycarbonate stock and forearm recoil pad. Gold-anodized
finish standard, also made w/black finish. Made 1964-65.
Fewer than 2,000 produced.

ARMSCOR (Arms Corp.) — Manila, Philippines, *Imported until 1991 by Armscor Precision, San Mateo, CA; 1991-95 by Ruko Products, Inc., Buffalo NY: Currently imported by K.B.I., Harrisburg, PA*

MODEL M-30 FIELD PUMP SHOTGUN
Double slide-action bars w/damascened bolt. Gauge: 12 only w/3-
inch chamber. Bbl.: 28-inch w/fixed chokes or choke tubes. Weight:
7.6 lbs. Walnut or walnut finished hardwood stock.
**Model M30-F (w/hard-
wood stock and fixed chokes)** . . . . . NiB $230 Ex $179 Gd $92
**Model M-30F (w/hard-
wood stock and choke tubes)** . . . . . . NiB $255 Ex $184 Gd $97
**Model M-30F/IC (w/walnut
stock and choke tubes)** . . . . NiB $265 Ex $189 Gd $102

MODEL M-30 RIOT PUMP
Double-action slide bar w/damascened bolt. Gauge: 12 only w/3-
inch chamber. Bbls: 18.5 and 20-inch w/IC bore. 5- or 7-shot magazine. Weight: 7 lbs, 2 ozs. Walnut finished hardwood stock.

(cont'd.) MODEL M-30 RIOT PUMP
Model M-30R6 (5-shot magazine). . . . . . . NiB $179 Ex $153 Gd $100
Model M-30R8 (7-shot magazine). . . . . . . NiB $189 Ex $163 Gd $102

MODEL M-30 SPECIAL COMBO
Simlar to Special Purpose Model except has detachable synthetic
stock that removes to convert to pistol-grip configuration.
Model M-30C (disc. 1995) . . . . NiB $214 Ex $179 Gd $122
Model M-30RP (disc. 1995) . . . . . NiB $223 Ex $179 Gd $121

MODEL M-30 SPECIAL PURPOSE
Double-action slide bar w/damascened bolt. 7-shot magazine.
Gauge: 12 only w/3-inch chamber. 20-inch bbl. w/cylinder choke.
Iron sights (DG Model) or venter handguard (SAS Model). Weight:
7.5 lbs. Walnut finished hardwood stock.
Model M-30DG (Deer Gun) . . . . NiB $210 Ex $168 Gd $114
Model M-30SAS (Special Air Services) . . . . . . NiB $236 Ex $189 Gd $129

ARMSPORT, INC. — Miami, Florida

1000 SERIES HAMMERLESS DOUBLES
Side-by-side w/engraved receiver, double triggers and extractors.
Gauges: 10 (3.5), 12, 20, .410- 3-inch chambers. Model 1033: 10 ga.,
32-inch bbl. Model 1050/51: 12 ga., 28-inch bbl., M/F choke. Model
1052/53: 20 ga., 26-inch bbl., I/M choke. Model 1054/57: .410 ga.,
26-inch bbl., I/M. Model 1055: 28 ga., Weight: 5.75 to 7.25 lbs. European
walnut buttstock and forend. Made in Italy. Importation disc. 1993.
Model 1033 (10 ga. disc. 1989) . . . . . . NiB $735 Ex $589 Gd $400
Model 1050 (12 ga. disc. 1993) . . . . . . NiB $651 Ex $602 Gd $381
Model 1051 (12 ga. disc. 1985) . . . . . . NiB $413 Ex $330 Gd $225
Model 1052 (20 ga. disc. 1985) . . . . . . NiB $385 Ex $308 Gd $209
Model 1053 (20 ga. disc. 1993) . . . . . . NiB $694 Ex $555 Gd $377
Model 1054 (.410 disc. 1992). . . . . NiB $771 Ex $617 Gd $419
Model 1055 (28 ga. disc. 1992) . . . . . . NiB $455 Ex $364 Gd $248
Model 1057 (.410 disc. 1985). . . . . NiB $491 Ex $393 Gd $266

MODEL 1125 SINGLE-SHOT SHOTGUN . . . . NiB $92 Ex $77 Gd $51
Bottom-opening lever. Gauges: 12, 20. 3-inch chambers. Bead front
sight. Plain stock and forend. Imported 1987-89.

Armsport 2700

Armsport 2741

MODEL 2700 GOOSE GUN
Similar to the 2700 Standard Model except 10 ga. w/3.5-inch chambers. Double triggers w/28-inch bbl. choked IC/M or 32-inch bbl., F/F. 12mm wide vent rib. Weight: 9.5 lbs. Canada geese engraved on receiver. Antiqued silver-finished action. Checkered European walnut stock w/rubber recoil pad. Imported from Italy 1986 to 1993.

W/fixed chokes . . . . NiB $995 Ex $791 Gd $536
W/choke tubes . . . . NiB $1097 Ex $867 Gd $587

MODEL 2700 OVER/UNDER SERIES
Hammerless, takedown shotgun w/engraved receiver. Selective single or double triggers. Gauges: 10, 12, 20, 28 and .410. Bbl.: 26-or 28-inch w/fixed chokes or choke tubes. Weight: 8 lbs. Checkered European walnut buttstock and forend. Made in Italy. Importation disc. 1993.

Model 2701 12 ga. (disc. 1985) . . . . NiB $504 Ex $403 Gd $274
Model 2702 12 ga. . . . . NiB $542 Ex $434 Gd $295
Model 2703 20 ga. (disc. 1985) . . . . NiB $529 Ex $423 Gd $288
Model 2704 20 ga. . . . . NiB $574 Ex $459 Gd $312
Model 2705 (.410, DT, fixed chokes) . . . . . NiB $669 Ex $536 Gd $364
Model 2730/31 (Boss-style action,
SST Choke tubes) . . . . NiB $759 Ex $610 Gd $413
Model 2733/35 (Boss-style
action, extractors) . . . . NiB $702 Ex $561 Gd $381
Model 2741 (Boss-style
action, ejectors) . . . . NiB $606 Ex $485 Gd $329
Model 2742 Sporting Clays
(12 ga./choke tubes) . . . . NiB $733 Ex $587 Gd $399
Model 2744 Sporting Clays
(20 ga./choke tubes) . . . . NiB $746 Ex $597 Gd $406
Model 2750 Sporting Clays
(12 ga./sideplates) . . . . NiB $797 Ex $638 Gd $434
Model 2751 Sporting Clays
(20 ga./sideplates) . . . . NiB $829 Ex $663 Gd $451

MODEL 2755 SLIDE-ACTION SHOTGUN
Gauge: 12 w/3-inch chamber. Tubular magazine. Bbls.: 28- or 30-inch w/fixed choke or choke tubes. Weight: 7 lbs. European walnut stock. Made in Italy 1986-87.

Standard model, fixed choke . . . . . NiB $332 Ex $281 Gd $173
Standard model, choke tubes . . . . . NiB $510 Ex $398 Gd $275
Police model, 20-inch bbl. . . . . NiB $301 Ex $255 Gd $163

MODEL 2900 TRI-BARREL (TRILLING) SHOTGUN
Boxlock. Double triggers w/top-tang bbl. selector. Extractors. Gauge: 12; 3-inch chambers. Bbls.: 28-inch (IC, M and F). Weight: 7.75 lbs. Checkered European walnut stock and forearm. Engraved silver receiver. Imported 1986-87 and 1990-93.

Model 2900 (fixed chokes) . . . . NiB $2071 Ex $1658 Gd $1127
Model 2900 (choke tubes) . . . . . NiB $2799 Ex $2239 Gd $1523
Deluxe grades, add $500

ARRIETA, S.L. — Elgoibar, Spain
Imported by New Engkand Arms Corp., Wingshooting Adventures Quality Arms, Griffin & Howe and Orvis.

Custom double-barreled shotguns with frames scaled to individual gauges. Standard gauges are 12 and 16 gauge. Add: 5% for small gauges (20, 24, 28, 32 and .410 bore) on currently manufactured models; $900 for single trigger (most actions); 5% for matched pairs; 10% for rounded action on standard models; extra bbls., add $1375 to $2000 per set.

MODEL 557 STANDARD
Gauges: 12, 16 or 20. Demi-Bloc steel barrels, detachable engraved sidelocks, double triggers, ejectors NiB $3000 Ex $1500 Gd $850

MODEL 570 LIEJA
Gauges: 12, 16 or 20. Non-detachable sidelocks.
. . . . NiB $3750 Ex $1875 Gd $1025

MODEL 578 VICTORIA
Gauges: 12, 16 or 20. Similar to Model 570 but with fine English scrollwork. . . . . NiB $4050 Ex $2075 Gd $1190

LIGERA MODEL
Available in all gauges. Lightweight 12 ga. has 2-inch chambers, lightweight or standard action. Includes unique frame engraving and Turkish wood upgrade. Wt. approx. 6 pounds
. . . . NiB $5300 Ex $3875 Gd $2775

MODEL 590 REGINA
Gauges: 12, 16 or 20. Similar to Model 570 but has more elaborate engraving. . . . . NiB $3250 Ex $2875 Gd $1950

MODEL 595 PRINCIPE
Available in all gauges, sidelock, engraved hunting scenes, ejectors, double triggers. . . . . NiB $5250 Ex $4010 Gd $3100

MODEL 600 IMPERIAL
Gauges: 12, 16 or 20. Self-opening action, very ornate engraving throughout. . . . . NiB $4450 Ex $3575 Gd $2250

MODEL 601 IMPERIAL TYRO
Available in all gauges, sidelock, nickel plating, ejectors, single selective trigger, border engraving. NiB $6450 Ex $3525 Gd $2850

MODEL 801
Available in all gauges, detachable sidelocks, ejectors, coin-wash finish, Churchill-style engraving. NiB $8000 Ex $6550 Gd $5275
With self-opening action (models 801 through 875) . . . add $900

SHOTGUNS

AyA Model 53E

AyA Model 76

AyA Model 117

MODEL 802
Gauges: 12, 16 or 20. Similar to Model 801 except with non-detachable sidelocks, finest Holland-style engraving.
. . . . **NiB $8250 Ex $6775 Gd $5225**

BOSS ROUND BODY
Available in all gauges, Boss pattern best quality engraving, wood upgrade.. . . . . **NiB $9525 Ex $7250 Gd $5995**

MODEL 803
Available in all gauges. Similar to Model 801 except finest Purdey-style engraving. . . . . **NiB $6275 Ex $4895 Gd $3595**

MODEL 871
Available in all gauges. Rounded frame sidelock action with Demi-Bloc barrels, scroll engraving, ejectors,double triggers. . . . .
. . . . **NiB $4575 Ex $3825 Gd $2275**

MODEL 871 EXTRA FINISH
Similar to Model 871 except with standard game scene engraving with woodcock and ruffed grouse.**NiB $5800 Ex $4375 Gd $3575**

RENAISSANCE MODEL
Available in all gauges. Best quality sidelock, custom engraving, wood upgrade, manufactured in Spain in made in Italy. Prices range from $8,000 to $17,000 depending on engraving and wood options.

MODEL 872
Available in all gauges, rounded frame sidelock action, Demi-Bloc barrels, elaborate scroll engraving with third lever fastener.
. . . . **NiB $11,275 Ex $9225 Gd $6100**

MODEL 873
Available in all gauges. Sidelock, gold line engraved action, ejectors, single selective trigger. . . . . **NiB $7675 Ex $4795 Gd $3475**

MODEL 874
Available in all gauges. Sidelock, gold line engraved action, Demi-Bloc barrels.. . . . . **NiB $8250 Ex $5990 Gd $4775**

MODEL 875
Available in all gauges. Custom model built to individual specifications only, elaborate engraving, gold inlays.
. . . . **NiB $14,000 Ex $11,975 Gd $9600**

MODEL 931
Available in all gauges. Self-opening action, elaborate engraving, H&H selective ejectors. . . . . **NiB $14,995 Ex $12,595 Gd $9650**

ASTRA SHOTGUNS — Guernica, Spain
Manufactured by Unceta y Compania

MODEL 650 O/U SHOTGUN
Hammerless, takedown w/double triggers. 12 ga. w/.75-inch chambers. Bbls.: 28-inch (M/F or SK/SK); 30-inch (M/F). Weight: 6.75 lbs. Checkered European walnut buttstock and forend.
W/extractors . . . . NiB $561 Ex $434 Gd $306
W/ejectors . . . . NiB $689 Ex $551 Gd $357

MODEL 750 O/U SHOTGUN
Similar to the Model 650 except w/selective single trigger and ejectors. Made in field, skeet and trap configurations since 1980.
Field model w/extractors. . . . . NiB $638 Ex $510 Gd $347
Field model w/ejectors . . . . NiB $759 Ex $607 Gd $413
Trap or Skeet . . . . NiB $886 Ex $709 Gd $482

AYA (Aguirre Y Aranzabal) — Eibar, Spain
(Previously Mfd. by Diarm, *Imported by Armes De Chasse, Hertford, NC*

MODEL 1 HAMMERLESS DOUBLE
A Holland & Holland sidelock similar to the Model 2 except in 12 and 20 ga. only, w/special engraving and exhibition-grade wood. Weight: 5-8 lbs., depending on ga. Imported by Diarm until 1987, since 1992 by Armes de Chasse.
Model 1 Standard . . . . NiB $6526 Ex $3115 Gd $1872
Model 1 Deluxe. . . . . NiB $8008 Ex $3640 Gd $2080

AyA Matador II

AyA Model XXV Boxlock

MODEL 2
HAMMERLESS DOUBLE
Sidelock action w/selective single or double triggers automatic ejectors and safety. Gauges: 12, 20, 28, (2.75-inch chambers); .410 (3-inch chambers). Bbls.: 26- or 28-inch w/various fixed choke combinations. Weight: 7 lbs. (12 ga.). English-style straight walnut buttstock and splinter forend. Imported by Diarm until 1987, since 1992 by Armes de Chasse.

12 or 20 ga. w/double triggers	NiB $3011	Ex $1508	Gd $1144
12 or 20 ga. w/single trigger	NiB $3068	Ex $2340	Gd $1243
28 or .410 ga. w/double triggers	NiB $3094	Ex $2345	Gd $1274
28 or .410 ga. w/single trigger	NiB $3120	Ex $2479	Gd $1274
Extra set of bbls., add			$1325

MODEL 4
HAMMERLESS DOUBLE
Lightweight Anson & Deely boxlock, scalloped frame. Gauges: 12, 16, 20, 28, and .410. Bbls.: 25- to 28-inch w/concave rib. Importation disc. 1987 and resumed in 1992 by Armes de Chasse.

12 ga.	NiB $1196	Ex $1144	Gd $520
16 ga. (early importation)	NiB $618	Ex $494	Gd $336
20 ga.	NiB $884	Ex $702	Gd $468
28 ga.	NiB $1014	Ex $780	Gd $442
.410 ga.	NiB $1019	Ex $780	Gd $468
Deluxe grades, add			$500

MODEL 37 SUPER
O/U SHOTGUN . . . . NiB $3374 Ex $2699 Gd $1836
Sidelock. automatic ejectors. Selective single trigger. Made in all gauges, bbl. lengths and chokes. Vent rib bbls. Elaborately engraved. Checkered stock (w/straight or pistol grip) and forend. Disc. 1995.

MODEL 37 SUPER A
O/U SHOTGUN . . . . NiB $5974 Ex $4779 Gd $3250
Similar to the Standard Model 37 Super except has nickel steel frame and is fitted w/detachable sidelocks engraved w/game scenes. Importation disc. 1987 and resumed 1992 by Armes de Chasse.

MODEL 53E . . . . NiB $2334 Ex $1867 Gd $1270
Same general specifications as Model 117 except more elaborate engraving and select figured wood. Importation disc. 1987 and resumed in 1992 by Armes de Chasse.

MODEL 56 HAMMERLESS DOUBLE
Pigeon weight Holland & Holland sidelock w/Purdey-style third lug and sideclips. Gauges: 12, 16, 20. Receiver has fine-line scroll and rosette engraving; gold-plated locks. Importation disc. 1987 and resumed 1992 by Armes de Chasse.

12 ga. . . . . NiB $7384 Ex $3484 Gd $2912

16 ga. (early importation)	NiB $6760	Ex $2340	Gd $1591
20 ga. (early importation)	NiB $7540	Ex $3614	Gd $2184

MODEL 76 HAMMERLESS DOUBLE NiB $716 Ex $572 Gd $389
Anson & Deeley boxlock. Auto ejectors. Selective single trigger. Gauges: 12, 20 (3-inch). Bbls.: 26-, 28-, 30-inch (latter in 12 ga. only), any standard choke combination. Checkered pistol-grip stock/beavertail forend. Disc.

MODEL 76—.410 GA. . . . . NiB $846 Ex $676 Gd $460
Same general specifications as 12 and 20 ga. Model 76 except chambered for 3-inch shells in .410, has extractors, double triggers, 26-inch bbls. only, English-style stock w/straight grip and small forend. Disc.

MODEL 117 HAMMERLESS DOUBLE . . NiB $942 Ex $754 Gd $513
Holland & Holland-type sidelocks, hand-detachable. Engraved action. Automatic ejectors. Selective single trigger. Gauges: 12, 20 (3-inch). Bbls.: 26-, 27-, 28-, 30-inch; 27- and 30-inch in 12 ga. only; any standard choke combination. Checkered pistol-grip stock and beavertail forend of select walnut. Manufactured in 1985.

BOLERO . . . . NiB $494 Ex $406 Gd $286
Same general specifications as Matador except non-selective single trigger and extractors. Gauges: 12 16, 20, 20 Magnum (3-inch), .410 (3-inch). Note: This model, prior to 1956, was designated F. I. Model 400 by the importer. Made 1955-63.

CONTENTO OVER/UNDER SHOTGUN
Boxlock w/Woodward side lugs and double internal bolts. Gauge: 12 (2.75-inch chambers). Bbls.: 26-, 28-inch field; 30-, 32-inch trap; fixed chokes as required or screw-in choke tubes. Hand-checkered European walnut stock and forend. Single selective trigger and automatic ejectors.

M.K.2	NiB $942	Ex $754	Gd $513
M.K.3	NiB $1638	Ex $1310	Gd $891
W/Interchangeable single bbl., add			$400

MATADOR HAMMERLESS DOUBLE NiB $488 Ex $390 Gd $265
Anson & Deeley boxlock. Selective automatic ejectors. Selective single trigger. Gauges: 12, 16, 20, 20 Magnum (3-inch). Bbls.: 26-, 28-, 30-inch; any standard choke combination. Weight: 6.5 to 7.5 lbs., depending on ga. and bbl. length. Checkered pistol-grip stock and beavertail forend. Note: This model, prior to 1956, was designated F. I. Model 400E by the U.S. importer, Firearms Int'l. Corp. of Washington, D.C. Made 1955-63.

SHOTGUNS

MATADOR II . . . . **NiB $552 Ex $442 Gd $301**
Improved version of Matador w/same general specifications except has vent-rib bbls. Made 1964-69.

MATADOR III . . . . **NiB $812 Ex $650 Gd $442**
Same general specifications as AyA Matador II. Made 1970-85.

MODEL XXV BOXLOCK
Anson & Deeley boxlock w/double locking lugs. Gauges: 12 and 20. 25-inch chopper lump, satin blued bbls. w/Churchill rib. Weight: 5 to 7 lbs. Double triggers. Automatic safety and ejectors. Color-case-hardened receiver w/Continental-style scroll and floral engraving. European walnut stock. Imported 1979-86 and 1991 to date.
12 or 20 ga. . . . . **NiB $2600 Ex $1451 Gd $832**
Extra set of bbls., add $1050

MODEL XXV SIDELOCK
Holland & Holland-type sidelock. Gauges: 12, 20, 28 and .410; 25-, 26-, 27- 28-, 29-, and 32-inch bbls. Chopper lump, satin blued bbls. w/Churchill rib. Weight: 5 to 7 lbs. Double triggers standard or selective or non-selective single trigger optional. Automatic safety and ejectors. Cocking indicators. Color-casehardened or coin-silver-finished receiver w/Continental-style scroll and floral engraving. Select European walnut stock w/hand-cut checkering and oil finish. Imported 1979-86 and 1991 to date.
12 or 20 ga. . . . . **NiB $3744 Ex $1820 Gd $1035**
28 ga. (disc. 1997) . . . . **NiB $2281 Ex $1804 Gd $1241**
.410 ga. (disc. 1997) . . . . **NiB $2617 Ex $2092 Gd $1423**
Single trigger, add $75
Single selective trigger, add $120
Extra set of bbls., add $1700

BAIKAL SHOTGUNS — Izhevsk and Tula, Russia

MODEL IJ-18M SINGLE SHOT . . . . **NiB $64 Ex $51 Gd $35**
Hammerless w/cocking indicator. Automatic ejector. Manual safety. Gauges: 12 , 20, 16 w/2.75-inch chamber or .410 w/3-inch chamber. Bbls.: 26-, 28-inch w/fixed chokes (IC, M, F). Weight: 5.5 to 6 lbs. Made in Russia.

MODEL IJ-27 FIELD O/U . . . . **NiB $357 Ex $281 Gd $194**
Boxlock. Double triggers w/extractors. 12 ga.; 2.75-inch chambers. Bbls.: 26-inch, IC/M; 28-inch, M/F w/fixed chokes. Weight: 6.75 lbs. Made in Russia.

MODEL IJ-43 FIELD SIDE-BY-SIDE
Side-by-side; boxlock. Double triggers; extractors. 12 or 20 ga. w/2.75-inch chambers. Bbls: 20-inch cylinder bbl and 26-or 28-inch modified full bbl. Weight: 6.75 to 7 lbs. Checkered walnut stock, forend. Blued, engraved receiver. Imported 1994-96.
Model IJ-43 Field w/20-inch bbls . . . . **NiB $236 Ex $189 Gd $129**
Model IJ-43 Field
w/26- or 28-inch bbls . . . . **NiB $210 Ex $168 Gd $114**

IZH-43 SERIES SIDE-BY-SIDE
Boxlock. Gauges: 12, 16, 20 or .410 w/2.75- or 3-inch chambers. Bbls.: 20-, 24-, 26- or 28-inch w/fixed chokes or choke tubes. Single selective or double triggers. Weight: 6.75 lbs. Checkered hardwood (standard on Hunter II Model) or walnut stock and forend (standard on Hunter Model). Blued, engraved receiver. Imported 1994 to date.
Model IZH-43Hunter
(12 ga. w/walnut stock) . . . . **NiB $337 Ex $291 Gd $133**
Model IZH-43 Hunter
(20, 16 or .410 ga.) . . . . **NiB $338 Ex $270 Gd $184**

(cont'd.) IZH-43 SERIES SIDE-BY-SIDE
Model IZH-43 Hunter II
(12 ga. w/external hammers) . . . . . **NiB $351 Ex $281 Gd $191**
Model IZH-43 Hunter II
(12 ga. hammerless) . . . . **NiB $223 Ex $179 Gd $121**
Model IZH-43 Hunter II
(20, 16 or .410 ga.) . . . . **NiB $235 Ex $189 Gd $129**
Hunter II w/walnut stock, add $35
Hunter II w/single selective trigger, add $45

MODEL IJ-27 O/U
Boxlock. Single selective trigger w/automatic ejectors or double triggers w/extractors. Gauges: 12 or 20 w/2.75-inch chambers. Bbls.: 26-inch or 28-inch w/fixed chokes. Weight: 7 lbs. Checkered European hardwood stock and forearm. Made in Russia.
Model IJ-27 (w/double
triggers and extractors.) . . . . **NiB $337 Ex $281 Gd $133**
Model IJ-27
(single selective
trigger and ejectors) . . . . **NiB $357 Ex $296 Gd $153**

BAKER SHOTGUNS — Batavia, New York Made 1903-1933 by Baker Gun Company

BATAVIA LEADER HAMMERLESS DOUBLE
Sidelock. Plain extractors or automatic ejectors. Double triggers. Gauges: 12, 16, 20. Bbls.: 26- to 32-inch; any standard boring. Weight: About 7.75 lbs. (12 ga. w/30-inch bbls.). Checkered pistol-grip stock and forearm.
W/plain extractors . . . . **NiB $819 Ex $361 Gd $258**
W/automatic ejectors . . . . **NiB $850 Ex $438 Gd $258**

BATAVIA EJECTOR . . . . **NiB $1082 Ex $819 Gd $556**
Same general specifications as the Batavia Leader except higher quality and finer finish throughout; has Damascus or homotensile steel bbls., checkered pistol-grip stock and forearm of select walnut; automatic ejectors standard; 12 and 16 ga. only. Deduct 60% for Damascus bbls.

BATAVIA SPECIAL . . . . **NiB $515 Ex $309 Gd $206**
Same general specifications as the Batavia Leader except 12 and 16 ga. only; extractors, homotensile steel bbls.

BLACK BEAUTY
Same general specifications as the Batavia Leader except higher and finer finish throughout; has line engraving, special steel bbls., select walnut stock w/straight, full or half-pistol-grip.
Black Beauty w/plain extractors . . . **NiB $567 Ex $335 Gd $258**
Black Beauty Special
w/plain extractors . . . . **NiB $1025 Ex $644 Gd $412**
Black Beauty Special
w/automatic ejectors . . . . **NiB $1082 Ex $773 Gd $515**

GRADE R
High-grade gun w/same general specifications as the Batavia Leader except has fine Damascus or Krupp fluid steel bbls., engraving in line, scroll and game scene designs, checkered stock and forearm of fancy European walnut; 12 and 16 ga. only. Deduct 60% for Damascus bbls.
Non-ejector . . . . **NiB $1391 Ex $1009 Gd $670**
W/automatic ejectors . . . . **NiB $1391 Ex $1009 Gd $670**

GRADE S
Same general specifications as the Batavia Leader except higher quality and finer finish throughout; has Flui-tempered steel bbls., line and scroll engraving, checkered stock w/half-pistol-grip and

Benelli Executive Grade I

Benelli Executive Grade II

Benelli Executive Grade III

SHOTGUNS

(cont'd.) **GRADE S**
forearm of semi-fancy imported walnut; 10, 12 and 16 ga.
Non-ejector . . . . NiB $1082 Ex $773 Gd $515
W/automatic ejectors . . . . NiB $1391 Ex $1009 Gd $670

PARAGON, EXPERT AND DELUXE GRADES
Made to order only, these are the higher grades of Baker hammer-less sidelock double-bbl. shotguns. After 1909, the Paragon Grade, as well as the Expert and Deluxe intro. that year, had a crossbolt in addition to the regular Baker system taper wedge fastening. There are early Paragon guns w/Damascus bbls. and some are non-ejector, but this grade was also produced w/automatic ejectors and w/the finest fluid steel bbls., in lengths to 34 inches, standard on Expert and Deluxe guns.
Differences among the three models are in overall quality, finish, engraving and grade of fancy figured walnut in the stock and fore-arm; Expert and Deluxe wood may be carved as well as checkered. Choice of straight, full or half-pistol grip was offered. A single trig-ger was available in the two higher grades. The Paragon was avail-able in 10 ga (Damascus bbls. only), and the other two models were regularly produced in 12, 16 and 20 ga.
Paragon grade, non-ejector . . . . . NiB $1796 Ex $1437 Gd $977
Paragon grade,
Automatic ejectors . . . . NiB $2054 Ex $1643 Gd $1085
Expert grade . . . . NiB $2955 Ex $2364 Gd $1607
Deluxe grade . . . . NiB $4185 Ex $3348 Gd $2276
For single trigger, add $250

BELKNAP SHOTGUNS — Louisville, Kentucky

MODEL B-68 SINGLE-SHOT SHOTGUN . . NiB $123 Ex $98 Gd $67
Takedown. Visible hammer. Automatic ejector. Gauges: 12, 16, 20 and .410. Bbls.: 26-inch to 36-inch; F choke. Weight: 6 lbs. Plain pistol-grip stock and forearm.

MODEL B-63 SINGLE-SHOT SHOTGUN . . . . NiB $109 Ex $88 Gd $60
Takedown. Visible hammer. Automatic ejector. Gauges: 12, 20 and .410. Bbls.: 26- to 36-inch, F choke. Weight: Average 6 lbs. Plain pistol-grip stock and forearm.

MODEL B-63E SINGLE-SHOT SHOTGUN . . . . NiB $109 Ex $88 Gd $60
Same general specifications as Model B-68 except has side lever opening instead of top lever.

**MODEL B-64 SLIDE-ACTION
SHOTGUN** . . . . NiB $236 Ex $180 Gd $123
Hammerless. Gauges: 12, 16, 20 and .410. Three shot tubular mag-azine. Various bbl. lengths and chokes from 26-inch to 30-inch. Weight: 6.25 to 7.5 lbs. Walnut-finished hardwood stock.

**MODEL B-65C AUTOLOADING
SHOTGUN** . . . . NiB $367 Ex $294 Gd $200
Browning-type lightweight alloy receiver. 12 ga. only. Four shot tubular magazine. Bbl.: plain, 28-inch. Weight: About 8.25 lbs. Disc. 1949.

BENELLI SHOTGUNS — Urbino, Italy
Imported by Benelli USA, Accokeek, MD

**MODEL 121 M1 MILITARY/POLICE
AUTOLOADING SHOTGUN** . . . . NiB $468 Ex $400 Gd $260
Gauge: 12. Seven shot magazine. 19.75-inch bbl. 39.75 inches overall. Cylinder choke, 2.75-inch chamber. Weight: 7.4 lbs. Matte black finish and European hardwood stock. Post front sight, fixed buckhorn rear sight. Imported in 1985.

BLACK EAGLE AUTOLOADING SHOTGUN
Two-piece aluminum and steel receiver. Ga: 12; 3-inch chamber. Four shot magazine. Screw-in choke tubes (SK, IC, M, IM, F). Bbls.: Ventilated rib; 21, 24, 26 or 28 inches w/bead front sight; 24-inch rifled slug. 42.5 to 49.5 inches overall. Weight: 7.25 lbs. (28-inch bbl.). Matte black lower receiver w/blued upper receiver and bbl. Checkered walnut stock w/high-gloss finish and drop adjustment. Imported from 1989-90 and 1997-98.
Limited edition . . . . NiB $1820 Ex $1560 Gd $1040
Competition model . . . . NiB $1066 Ex $822 Gd $468
Slug model (disc. 1992) . . . . NiB $754 Ex $520 Gd $364
Standard model (disc. 1992) . . . . NiB $858 Ex $676 Gd $406

Benelli Legacy
Limited Edition (Only 250 Made)

Benelli M1 – Super 90 w/Pistol Grip

BLACK EAGLE EXECUTIVE
Custom Black Eagle Series. Montefeltro-style rotating bolt w/three locking lugs. All-steel lower receiver engraved, gold inlay by Bottega Incisione di Cesare Giovanelli. 12 ga. only. 21-, 24-, 26-, or 28-inch vent-rib bbl. w/5 screw-in choke tubes (Type I) or fixed chokes. Custom deluxe walnut stock and forend. Built to customer specifications on special order.

(cont'd.) BLACK EAGLE EXECUTIVE
Executive Grade I . . . . NiB $3894 Ex $3115 Gd $2118
Executive Grade II . . . . NiB $4226 Ex $3380 Gd $2298
Executive Grade III . . . . NiB $4973 Ex $3978 Gd $2705

LEGACY AUTOLOADING SHOTGUN
Gauges: 12 and 20 ga. w/3-inch chambers. 24- 26- or 28-inch bbl. 47.63 to 49.62 inches overall. Weight: 5.8 to 7.5 lbs. Four shot magazine. Five screw-in choke tubes. Lower alloy receiver and upper steel reciever cover. Features Benelli's inertia recoil operating system. Imported 1998 to date. See illustration next page.
Legacy model . . . . NiB $1170 Ex $936 Gd $780
Legacy model Limited edition . . . NiB $1768 Ex $1482 Gd $884

M1 SUPER 90
AUTO-LOADING SHOTGUN . . . . . NiB $832 Ex $702 Gd $416
Gauge: 12. 7-shot magazine. Cylinder choke. 19.75-inch bbl. 39.75 inches overall. Weight: 7 lbs., 4 oz. to 7 lbs., 10 oz. Matte black finish. Stock and forend made of fiberglass-reinforced polymer. Sights: Post front, fixed buckhorn rear, drift adj. Introduced 1985; when the model line expanded in 1989, this configuration was discontinued.

M1 SUPER 90 DEFENSE AUTOLOADER . . . . . NiB $962 Ex $754 Gd $390
Same general specifications as Model Super 90 except w/pistol-grip stock. Available w/Ghost-Ring sight option. Imported 1986-98.

M1 SUPER 90
ENTRY AUTOLOADER . . . . NiB $832 Ex $702 Gd $378
Same gen. specifications as Model Super 90 except w/5-shot magazine. 14-inch bbl. 35.5 inches overall. Weight: 6.5 lbs. Standard or pistol-grip stock. Imported 1992 to date. Special permit required for under 18 inch bbl. firearms.

M1 SUPER 90 FIELD
Inertia-recoil semiautomatic shotgun. Gauge: 12; 3-inch chamber. Three shot magazine. Bbl.: 21, 24, 26 or 28 inches. 42.5 to 49.5 inches overall. Choke: SK, IC, M, IM, F. Matte receiver. Standard polymer stock or satin walnut (26- or 28-inch bbl. only). Bead front sight. Imported from 1990 to date.
W/Realtree camo . . . . NiB $728 Ex $598 Gd $364
W/polymer stock . . . . NiB $614 Ex $442 Gd $312
W/walnut stock . . . . NiB $650 Ex $468 Gd $338

M1 SUPER 90 SLUG AUTOLOADER
Same general specifications as M1 Super 90 Field except w/5-shot magazine. 18.5-inch bbl. Cylinder bore. 39.75 inches overall. Weight: 6.5 lbs. Polymer standard stock. Rifle or Ghost-Ring sights. Imported 1986-98.
W/rifle sights . . . . NiB $676 Ex $520 Gd $416
W/ghost-ring sights . . . . NiB $728 Ex $546 Gd $416
W/Realtree camo finish, add $100

M1 SUPER 90 SPORTING
SPECIAL AUTOLOADER . . . . NiB $780 Ex $676 Gd $390
Same general specifications as M1 Super 90 Field except w/18.5-inch bbl. 39.75 inches overall. Weight: 6.5 lbs. Ghost-ring sights. Polymer stock. Imported 1994-98.

M1 SUPER 90 TACTICAL AUTOLOADER
Same general specifications as M1 Super 90 Field except w/18.5-inch bbl. Five shot magazine. IC, M, or F choke. 39.75 inches overall. Weight: 6.5 lbs. Rifle or Ghost-Ring sights. Polymer pistol-grip or standard stock. Imported 1994 to date.
W/rifle sights . . . . NiB $780 Ex $676 Gd $390
W/ghost-ring sights . . . . NiB $826 Ex $671 Gd $473
W/pistol-grip stock, add $25

M3 SUPER 90 PUMP/AUTOLOADER
Inertia-recoil semiautomatic and/or pump action. Gauge: 12. Seven shot magazine. Cylinder choke. 19.75-inch bbl. 41 inches overall (31 inches folded). Weight: 7 to 7.5 lbs. Matte black finish. Stock: standard synthetic, pistol-grip or folding tubular steel. Standard rifle or Ghost-Ring sights. Imported 1989 to date. Caution:

Benelli Montefeltro Super 90 Left-Handed Model

Benelli Montefeltro Realtree Camo

(cont'd.) M3 SUPER 90 PUMP/AUTOLOADER
Increasing the magazine capacity to more than 5 rounds in M3 shotguns w/pistol-grip stocks violates provisions of the 1994 Crime Bill. This model may be used legally only by the military and law-enforcement agencies.

Standard model . . . . NiB $853 Ex $707 Gd $411
Pistol-grip model . . . . NiB $976 Ex $780 Gd $530
W/folding stock . . . . NiB $1034 Ex $827 Gd $563
W/laser sight . . . . NiB $1294 Ex $1035 Gd $704
For ghost ring sights, add $50

MONTEFELTRO/SUPER 90 SEMIAUTOMATIC
Gauges: 12 or 20 gauge w/3-inch chamber. 21- 24- 26- or 28-inch bbl. 43.7 to 49.5 inches overall. Weight: 5.3 to 7.5 lbs. 4-shot magazine. Five screw-in choke tubes (C, IC, M, IM, F). High gloss or satin walnut or Realtree Camo stock. Blued metal finish. Imported 1987 to date.

Standard Hunter model . . . . NiB $853 Ex $709 Gd $411
Slug model (disc. 1992) . . . . NiB $676 Ex $520 Gd $312
Turkey model . . . . NiB $676 Ex $598 Gd $312
Uplander model . . . . NiB $676 Ex $520 Gd $312
Limited Edition (1995-96) . . . . . . NiB $1852 Ex $1482 Gd $100
20 ga. w/Realtree camo . . . . NiB $716 Ex $572 Gd $389
20 ga. Youth Model w/short stock, add $40
Left-hand model, add $25

SL 121V SEMIAUTO (SL-80 SERIES) . . . NiB $546 Ex $312 Gd $260
Recoil-operated semiautomaticw/split receiver design. Gauge: 12. Five shot capacity. 26-, 28- or 30-inch ventilated rib bbl. (26-inch choked M, IM, IC, 28-inch, F, M, IM; 30-inch, F choke - Mag.). Straight walnut stock w/hand-checkered pistol grip and forend. Importation disc. in 1985.

SL 121V SLUG SHOTGUN
(SL-80 SERIES) . . . . NiB $556 Ex $338 Gd $270
Same general specifications as Benelli SL 121V except designed for rifled slugs and equipped w/rifle sights. Disc. in 1985.

SL 123V SEMIAUTO (SL-80 SERIES) . . . NiB $468 Ex $374 Gd $255
Gauge: 12. 26- and 28-inch bbls. 26-inch choked IM, M, IC; 28-inch choked F, IM, M. Disc. in 1985.

SL 201 SEMIAUTOMATIC
(SL-80 SERIES) . . . . NiB $416 Ex $333 Gd $227
Gauge: 20. 26-inch bbl. Mod. choke. Weight: 5 lbs., 10 oz. Ventilated rib. Disc. in 1985.

SPORT AUTOLOADING SHOTGUN . . NiB $976 Ex $780 Gd $530
Similar to the Black Eagle Competition model except has one-piece matte-finished alloy receiver w/inscribed red Benelli logo. 26 or 28 inches bbl. w/2 inchangable carbon fiber vent ribs. Oil-finished checkered walnut stock w/adjustable buttpad and buttstock. Imported 1997 to date.

SUPER BLACK EAGLE AUTOLOADING SHOTGUN
Same general specifications as Black Eagle except w/3.5-inch chamber that accepts 2.75-, 3- and 3.5-inch shells. Two shot magazine (3.5-inch), 3-shot magazine (2.75- or 3-inch). High-gloss, satin finish or camo stock. Realtree camo, matte black or blued metal finish. Imported 1991 to date.

Standard model . . . . NiB $1034 Ex $827 Gd $563
Realtree camo . . . . NiB $1164 Ex $931 Gd $633
Custom slug model . . . . NiB $976 Ex $780 Gd $530
Limited edition . . . . NiB $1852 Ex $1482 Gd $1008
W/wood stock, add $25
Left-hand model, add $30

BERETTA USA CORP. — Accokeek, Maryland Mfd. by Fabbrica D'Armi Pietro Beretta S.p.A. in Gardone Val Trompia (Brescia), Italy
Imported by Beretta USA (Previously by Garcia Corp.)

MODEL 57E O/U
Same general specifications as Golden Snipe, but higher quality throughout. Imported 1955-67.
W/non-selective single trigger . . . NiB $1035 Ex $910 Gd $494
W/selective single trigger . . . . NiB $1072 Ex $858 Gd $583

MODEL 409PB
HAMMERLESS DOUBLE . . . . NiB $988 Ex $676 Gd $411
Boxlock. Double triggers. Plain extractors. Gauges: 12, 16, 20, 28. Bbls.: 27.5-, 28.5- and 30-inch, IC/M choke or M/F choke. Weight: from 5.5 to 7.75 lbs., depending on ga. and bbl. length. Straight or pistol-grip stock and beavertail forearm, checkered. Imported 1934-64.

MODEL 410E
Same general specifications as Model 409PB except has automatic ejectors and is of higher quality throughout. Imported 1934-64.
Model 410E (12 ga.) . . . . NiB $1300 Ex $1144 Gd $728
Model 410E (20 ga.) . . . . NiB $1788 Ex $1430 Gd $972
Model 410E (28 ga.) . . . . NiB $4550 Ex $3640 Gd $2475

SHOTGUNS

Beretta Model 682 Over/Under Sporting

Beretta Model 682 Over/Under Trap

MODEL 410 10-GA. MAGNUM . . NiB $1236 Ex $988 Gd $672
Same as Model 410E except heavier construction. Plain extractors. Double triggers. 10-ga. Magnum, 3.5-inch chambers. 32-inch bbls., both F choke. Weight: about 10 lbs. Checkered pistol-grip stock and forearm, recoil pad. Imported 1934-84.

MODEL 411E
Same general specifications as Model 409PB except has sideplates, automatic ejectors and is of higher quality throughout. Imported 1934-64.
Model 411E (12 ga.) . . . . NiB $1944 Ex $1555 Gd $1058
Model 411E (20 ga.) . . . . NiB $2536 Ex $2028 Gd $1379
Model 411E (28 ga.) . . . . NiB $4674 Ex $3739 Gd $2543

MODEL 424 HAMMERLESS
DOUBLE . . . . NiB $1424 Ex $1139 Gd $775
Boxlock. Light border engraving. Plain extractors. Gauges: 12, 20; chambers 2.75-inch in former, 3-inch in latter. Bbls.: 28-inch M/F choke, 26-inch IC/M choke. Weight: 5 lbs. 14 oz. to 6 lbs. 10 oz., depending on ga. and bbl. length. English-style straight-grip stock and forearm, checkered. Imported 1977-84.

MODEL 426E . . . . NiB $1924 Ex $1456 Gd $1014
Same as Model 424 except action body is finely engraved, silver pigeon inlaid in top lever; has selective automatic ejectors and selective single trigger, stock and forearm of select European walnut. Imported 1977-84.

MODEL 450 SERIES HAMMERLESS DOUBLES
Custom English-style sidelock. Single, non-selective trigger or double triggers. Manual safety. Selective automatic ejectors. Gauge: 12; 2.75- or 3-inch chambers. Bbls.: 26, 28 or 30 inches choked to customers' specifications. Weight: 6.75 lbs. Checkered high-grade walnut stock. Receiver w/coin-silver finish. Imported 1948 to date.
Model 450 EL (disc. 1982) . . . . . NiB $7664 Ex $6131 Gd $4169
Model 450 EELL (disc. 1982) . . . NiB $8126 Ex $6500 Gd $4420
Model 451 (disc. 1987) . . . . NiB $6624 Ex $5299 Gd $3604
Model 451 E (disc. 1989) . . . . . NiB $7273 Ex $5819 Gd $3957
Model 451 EL (disc. 1985) . . . . . NiB $12,936 Ex $10,348 Gd $7037
Model 451 EELL (disc. 1990) . . . NiB $14,202 Ex $11,362 Gd $7726
Model 452 (intro. 1990) . . . . . NiB $20,750 Ex $18,200 Gd $12,376
Model 452 EELL (intro. 1992) . . NiB $30,226 Ex $24,180 Gd $16,442
Extra set of bbls., add 30%

MODEL 470 SERIES HAMMERLESS DOUBLE
Gauge: 12 and 20 ga. w/3-inch chambers. 26- or 28-inch bbl. Weight: 5.9 to 6.5 lbs. Low profile, improved box lock action w/single selective trigger. Selected walnut, checkered stock and forend. Metal front bead sight. Scroll-engraved receiver w/gold inlay and silver chrome finish. Imported 1999 to date.

(cont'd.) MODEL 470 SERIES HAMMERLESS DOUBLE
Model 470 Silver Hawk 12 ga. . . . . . NiB $2406 Ex $1924 Gd $1309
Model 470 Silver Hawk 20 ga. . . . . . NiB $2594 Ex $2075 Gd $1411
Model 470 EL Silver Hawk 12 ga. . . . NiB $4024 Ex $4024 Gd $2189
Model 470 EL Silver Hawk 20 ga. . . . NiB $4192 Ex $4192 Gd $2281
Model 470 EELL (Jubilee II) 12 ga. . . . NiB $7924 Ex $7924 Gd $4311
Model 470 EELL (Jubilee II) 20 ga. . . . NiB $8386 Ex $6708 Gd $4561
Extra set of bbls., add 30%

MODEL 625 S/S HAMMERLESS DOUBLE
Boxlock. Gauges: 12 or 20. Bbls.: 26-, 28- or 30-inch w/fixed choke combinations. Single selective or double triggers w/extractors. Checkered English-style buttstock and forend. Imported 1984-87.
W/double triggers . . . . NiB $942 Ex $754 Gd $513
W/single selective trigger . . . . NiB $1106 Ex $884 Gd $601
20 ga., add. $150

MODEL 626 S/S HAMMERLESS DOUBLE
Field Grade side-by-side. Boxlock action w/single selective trigger, extractors and automatic safety. Gauges: 12 (2.75-inch chambers); 20 (3-inch chambers). Bbls.: 26- or 28-inch w/Mobilchoke or various fixed-choke combinations. Weight: 6.75 lbs. (12 ga.). Bright chrome finish. Checkered European walnut buttstock and forend in straight English style. Imported 1985-94.
Model 626 Field (disc. 1988) . . . . . NiB $1196 Ex $988 Gd $494
Model 626 Onyx . . . . NiB $1326 Ex $1066 Gd $774
Model 626 Onyx (3.5-inch
Magnum, disc. 1993) . . . . NiB $1424 Ex $1139 Gd $775
20 ga., add. $200

MODEL 627 S/S HAMMERLESS DOUBLE
Same as Model 626 S/S except w/engraved sideplates and pistol-grip or straight English-style stock. Imported 1985-94.
Model 627 EL Field . . . . NiB $2485 Ex $1971 Gd $1341
Model 627 EL Sport . . . . NiB $2506 Ex $2028 Gd $1379
Model 627 EELL . . . . NiB $4486 Ex $3588 Gd $2440

MODEL 682 O/U SHOTGUN
Hammerless takedown w/single selective trigger. Gauges: 12, 20, 28, .410. Bbls.: 26- to 34-inch w/fixed chokes or Mobilchoke tubes. Checkered European walnut buttstock/forend in various grades and configurations. Imported 1984 to date.
Model 682 Comp Skeet . . . . . . NiB $1944 Ex $1555 Gd $1058
Model 682 Comp Skeet Deluxe . . . . . NiB $2854 Ex $2283 Gd $1553
Mdl. 682 Comp Super Skeet . . . . NiB $2334 Ex $1867 Gd $1270
Mdl. 682 Comp Skeet 2-bbl.
set (disc. 1989) . . . . NiB $4804 Ex $3843 Gd $2614
Mdl. 682 Comp Skeet
4 bbl. Set (disc. 1996) . . . . NiB $5526 Ex $4420 Gd $3006

Beretta Model 687EL

Beretta Model 687EEL

(cont'd.) MODEL 682 O/U SHOTGUN

Mdl. 682 Sporting Continental . . . . NiB $1944 Ex $1555 Gd $1058
Mdl. 682 Sporting Combo . . . . NiB $3056 Ex $2444 Gd $1662
Mdl. 682 Sporting Gold . . . . NiB $1814 Ex $1451 Gd $987
Mdl. 682 Sporting Super Sport . . . . NiB $1982 Ex $1586 Gd $1078
Mdl. 682 Comp Trap Gold X . . . . NiB $1944 Ex $1555 Gd $1058
Mdl. 682 Comp Trap Top Sgle. (1986-95) . . . NiB $1886 Ex $1508 Gd $994
Mdl. 682 Comp Trap Live Pig. (1990-98) . . . NiB $2502 Ex $2002 Gd $1361
Mdl. 682 Comp Mono/ComboTrp. Gld. X . . NiB $2706 Ex $2236 Gd $1520
Mdl. 682 Comp Mono Trap (1985-88) . . . . . . NiB $1684 Ex $1347 Gd $916
Mdl. 682 Super Trap Gold X (1991-95) . . . . NiB $2016 Ex $1612 Gd $1096
Mdl. 682 Sup. Trap
Combo Gld. X (1991-97) . . . . NiB $2854 Ex $2283 Gd $1553
Mdl. 682 Super Trap
Top Sgle. Gld. X (1991-95) . . . . NiB $2074 Ex $1659 Gd $1128
Mdl. 682 Sup. Trap Unsingle (1992-94) . . . . NiB $1944 Ex $1555 Gd $1058

MODEL 686 O/U SHOTGUN
Low-profile improved boxlock action. Single selective trigger. Selective
automatic ejectors. Gauges: 12, 20, 28 w/3.5- 3- or 2.75-inch chambers, depending upon ga. Bbls.: 26-, 28-, 30-inch w/fixed chokes or
Mobilchoke tubes. Weight: 5.75 to 7.5 lbs. Checkered American wal-
nut stock and forearm of various qualities, depending upon model.
Receiver finishes also vary, but all have blued bbls. Sideplates to sim-
ulate sidelock action on EL models. Imported 1988 to date.
Model 686 Field Onyx . . . . NiB $1336 Ex $993 Gd $572
Mdl. 686 (3.5-inch Mag., disc.
1993 & reintro.1996) . . . . NiB $1404 Ex $1014 Gd $676
Model 686 EL Gold Perdiz (1992-97) . . . . NiB $1684 Ex $1347 Gd $916
Model 686 Essential (1994-96) . . . . NiB $930 Ex $744 Gd $505
Model 686 Silver Essential (1997-98) . . . . NiB $1036 Ex $829 Gd $564
Model 686 Sil. Pig. Onyx (intro. 1996) . . . . NiB $1359 Ex $1087 Gd $738
Mdl. 686 Sil. Perdiz Onyx (disc. 1996) . . . . NiB $1322 Ex $1058 Gd $719
Model 686 Sil. Pig./Perdiz Onyx Combo . . . . . NiB $1894 Ex $1515 Gd $823
Model 686 L Silver Perdiz (disc. 1994) . . . . NiB $1072 Ex $858 Gd $583
Model 686 Skeet Silver Pigeon (1996-98) . . . . . NiB $1137 Ex $909 Gd $619
Model 686 Skeet Silver Perdiz (1994-96) . . . . . NiB $1358 Ex $1087 Gd $738
Model 686 Skeet Sil. Pig./Perdiz Combo . . . . . NiB $1358 Ex $1087 Gd $738
Model 686 Sporting Special (1987-93) . . . . NiB $1565 Ex $1252 Gd $852
Model 686 Sporting English (1991-92) . . . . NiB $1644 Ex $1316 Gd $894
Model 686 Sporting Onyx
w/fixed chokes (1991-92) . . . . NiB $1565 Ex $1252 Gd $852
Model 686 Sporting Onyx
w/tubes (intro. 1992) . . . . NiB $1179 Ex $943 Gd $644
Mdl. 686 Sporting Onyx Gld. (disc. 1993) . . . NiB $1709 Ex $1367 Gd $930
Mdl. 686 Sporting Sil. Pig. (intro. 1996) . . . . . NiB $1393 Ex $1115 Gd $758
Model 686 Sporting Sil. Perdiz (1993-96) . . . . NiB $1358 Ex $1087 Gd $738
Mdl. 686 Sporting Coll. Sport (1996-97) . . . NiB $1036 Ex $829 Gd $564
Model 686 Sporting Combo . . . . NiB $2423 Ex $1939 Gd $1319

Model 686 Trap International (1994-95) . . . . . NiB $993 Ex $795 Gd $541
Model 686 Trap Silver Pigeon (intro. 1997) . . . NiB $1072 Ex $858 Gd $583
Model 686 Trap Top Mono (intro. 1998) . . . NiB $1108 Ex $886 Gd $602
Model 686 Ultralight Onyx (intro. 1992) . . . NiB $1423 Ex $1138 Gd $774
Mdl. 686 Ultralight Del. Onyx (intro. 1998) . . . . NiB $1788 Ex $1430 Gd $972

MODEL 687 O/U SHOTGUN
Same as Model 686 except w/decorative sideplates and varying
grades of engraving and game-scene motifs.
Model 687 L Onyx (disc. 1991) . . . . NiB $1322 Ex $1058 Gd $719
Model 687 L Onyx Gold Field (1988-89) . . NiB $1502 Ex $1201 Gd $816
Model 687 L Onyx Silver Pigeon . . . . NiB $1930 Ex $1544 Gd $1049
Model 687 EL Onyx (disc. 1990) . . . . NiB $2609 Ex $2087 Gd $1420
Model 687 EL Gold Pigeon . . . . NiB $2995 Ex $2396 Gd $1630
Model 687 EL Gold Pigeon Sm. Fr. . . . . . NiB $2788 Ex $2230 Gd $1516
Mdl. 687 EL Gld. Pig. Sporting (Int. 1993) . . . NiB $4139 Ex $3311 Gd $2252
Model 687 EELL Diamond Pigeon . . . . . NiB $34139 Ex $3311 Gd $2252
Mdl. 687 EELL Diamond Pig. Skeet . . . . . . NiB $3997 Ex $3197 Gd $2175
Mdl. 687 EELL Diam. Pig. Sporting . . . . . NiB $4218 Ex $3375 Gd $2294
Mdl. 687 EELL Diam. Pig. X Trap . . . . . . NiB $3682 Ex $2945 Gd $2003
Mdl. 687 EELL Diam. Pig. Mono Trap . . . . NiB $3790 Ex $3032 Gd $2061
Mdl. 687 EELL Diam. Pig. Trap Combo . . . NiB $5141 Ex $4112 Gd $2797
Model 687 EELL Field Combo . . . . NiB $4283 Ex $3426 Gd $2330
Model 687 EELL Skeet 4-bbl. set . . . . NiB $7078 Ex $5662 Gd $3850
Model 687 EELL Gallery Special . . . . NiB $6571 Ex $5256 Gd $3574
Model 687 EELL Gallery Special Combo . . . NiB $7936 Ex $6349 Gd $4317
Model 687 EELL Gallery Special pairs . NiB $15,730 Ex $12,584 Gd $8557
Model 687 Sporting English (1991-92) . . . NiB $2074 Ex $1659 Gd $1127
Mdl. 687 Sporting Sil. Pig. (intro. 1996) . NiB $1851 Ex $1481 Gd $1008
Mdl. 687 Sporting Sil. Perdiz (1993-96) . . NiB $1930 Ex $1544 Gd $1143

MODEL 1200 SERIES SEMIAUTOLOADING SHOTGUN
Short recoil action. Gauge: 12; 2.75- or 3-inch chamber. Six shot magazine. 24-,
26- or 28-inch vent-rib bbl. w/fixed chokes or Mobilchoke tubes. Weight: 7.25 lbs.
Matte black finish. Adj. technopolymer stock and forend. Imported 1988 to date.
Model 1200 w/fixed choke (disc. 1989) . . . . . . NiB $546 Ex $437 Gd $296
Model 1200 Riot (disc. 1989) . . . . NiB $560 Ex $448 Gd $305
Model 1201 w/Mobilchoke (disc. 1994) . . . . . . NiB $575 Ex $460 Gd $313
Model 1201 Riot . . . . NiB $618 Ex $495 Gd $336
W/Pistol-grip stock, add $72
W/Tritium sights, add $56

MODEL A-301 AUTOLOADING SHOTGUN . . . .
. . . . NiB $448 Ex $359 Gd $244
Field Gun. Gas-operated. Scroll-decorated receiver. Gauge: 12 or 20; 2.75-inch
chamber in former, 3-inch in latter. Three shot magazine. Bbl.: Ventilated rib; 28-
inch F or M choke, 26-inch IC. Weight: 6 lbs., 5 oz. – 6 lbs., 14 oz., depending
on gauge and bbl. length. Checkered pistol-grip stock/forearm. Imported 1977-
82.

SHOTGUNS

Beretta Model A-303

Beretta Model A-390 Field

Beretta Model AL-2

MODEL A-301 MAGNUM. . . . . . . NiB $462 Ex $369 Gd $251
Same as Model A-301 Field Gun except chambered for 12 ga. Three inch Magnum shells, 30-inch F choke bbl. only, stock w/recoil pad. Weight: 7.25 lbs.

MODEL A-301 SKEET GUN. . . . . . NiB $488 Ex $390 Gd $265
Same as Model A-301 Field Gun except 26-inch bbl. SK choke only, skeet-style stock, gold-plated trigger.

MODEL A-301 SLUG GUN. . . . . . NiB $456 Ex $364 Gd $248
Same as Model A-301 Field Gun except has plain 22-inch bbl., slug choke, w/rifle sights. Weight: 6 lbs., 14 oz.

MODEL A-301 TRAP GUN . . . . . . NiB $488 Ex $390 Gd $265
Same as Model A-301 Field Gun except has 30-inch bbl. in F choke only, checkered Monte Carlo stock w/recoil pad, gold-plated trigger. Blued bbl. and receiver. Weight: 7 lbs., 10 oz. Imported 1978-82.

MODEL A-302 SEMIAUTOLOADING SHOTGUN
Similar to gas-operated Model 301. Hammerless, takedown shotgun w/tubular magazine and Mag-Action that handles both 2.75- and 3-inch Magnum shells. Gauge: 12 or 20; 2.75- or 3-inch Mag. chambers. Bbl.: Vent or plain; 22-inch/Slug (12 ga.); 26-inch/IC (12 or 20) 28-inch/M (20 ga.), 28-inch/Multi-choke (12 or 20 ga.) 30-inch/F (12 ga.). Weight: 6.5 lbs., 20 ga.; 7.25.lbs., 12 ga. Blued/ black finish. Checkered European walnut, pistol-grip stock and forend. Imported 1983 to c. 1987.
Standard model w/fixed choke . . . . NiB $462 Ex $369 Gd $251
Standard model w/multi-choke. . . . NiB $514 Ex $411 Gd $280

MODEL A-302 SUPER LUSSO. . NiB $2288 Ex $2054 Gd $1352
A custom A-302 in presentation grade w/hand-engraved receiver and custom select walnut stock.

MODEL A-303 SEMIAUTOLOADER
Similar to Model 302, except w/target specifications in Trap, Skeet and Youth configurations, and weighs 6.5 to 8 lbs. Imported 1983-96.
Field and Upland models. . . . . NiB $544 Ex $513 Gd $474
Skeet and Trap (disc. 1994) . . . . . . NiB $674 Ex $539 Gd $366
Slug model (disc. 1992). . . . . NiB $739 Ex $591 Gd $401

(cont'd.) MODEL A-303 SEMIAUTOLOADER
Sporting Clays . . . . NiB $759 Ex $617 Gd $419
Super Skeet . . . . NiB $1129 Ex $903 Gd $615
Super Trap . . . . NiB $1072 Ex $858 Gd $583
Waterfowl/Turkey (disc. 1992) . . . . NiB $707 Ex $565 Gd $385
Mobil choke, add. $50

MODEL A-303 YOUTH GUN . . . . . NiB $676 Ex $468 Gd $260
Locked-breech, gas-operated action. Ga: 12 and 20; 2-shot magazine. Bbls.: 24, 26, 28, 30 or 32-inches, vent rib. Weight: 7 lbs. (12 ga.), 6 lbs. (20 ga.). Crossbolt safety. Length of pull shortened to 12.5 inches. Imported 1988-96.

MODEL A-390 SEMIAUTOMATIC SHOTGUN
Gas-operated, self-regulating action designed to handle any size load. Gauges: 12 or 20 w/ 3-inch chamber. 3-shot magazine. Bbl.: 24, 26, 28 or 30 inches w/vent rib and Mobilchoke tubes. Weight: 7.5 lbs. Select walnut stock w/adj. comb. Blued or matte black finish. Imported 1992-96. Superseded by AL-390 series.
Standard model/Slug model . . . . . . NiB $566 Ex $452 Gd $308
Field model/Silver Mallard . . . . NiB $578 Ex $461 Gd $315
Deluxe model/Gold Mallard . . . . . . NiB $630 Ex $504 Gd $343
Turkey/Waterfowl model (matte finish) . . . NiB $592 Ex $473 Gd $315
For 20 ga., add $35

MODEL A-390 TARGET
Similar to the Model 390 Field except w/2.75-inch chamber. Skeet: 28-inch ported bbl. w/wide vent rib and fixed choke (SK). Trap: 30- or 32-inch w/Mobilchoke tubes. Weight: 7.5 lbs. Fully adj. buttstock. Imported from 1993-96.
Sport Trap model . . . . NiB $578 Ex $463 Gd $315
Sport Skeet model . . . . NiB $566 Ex $452 Gd $308
Sporting Clays model (unported). . . NiB $586 Ex $468 Gd $318
Super Trap model (ported). . . . . NiB $774 Ex $619 Gd $421
Super Skeet model (ported). . . . . . . NiB $760 Ex $608 Gd $414
W/ported bbl., add $85
20 ga., add. $35

MODEL AL-1 FIELD GUN. . . . . . . NiB $448 Ex $359 Gd $244
Same as Model AL-2 gas-operated Field Gun except has bbl. w/o rib, no engraving on receiver. Imported 1971-73.

Beretta Model AL-391
Urika Gold Sporting

Beretta Model AL-391
Urika Gold Trap

MODEL AL-2 AUTOLOADING SHOTGUN

Field Gun. Gas-operated. Engraved receiver (1968 version, 12 ga. only, had no engraving). Gauge: 12 or 20. 2.75-inch chamber. Three shot magazine. Bbls.: Vent rib; 30-inch F choke, 28-inch F or M choke, 26-inch IC. Weight: 6.5 to 7.25 lbs, depending on ga. and bbl. length. Checkered pistol-grip stock and forearm. Imported 1968-75.

W/Plain receiver . . . . NiB $370 Ex $296 Gd $202
W/Engraved receiver . . . . NiB $514 Ex $411 Gd $280

MODEL AL-2 MAGNUM . . . . NiB $462 Ex $369 Gd $251

Same as Model AL-2 Field Gun except chambered for 12 ga. 3-inch Magnum shells; 30-inch F or 28-inch M choke bbl. only. Weight: About 8 lbs. Imported 1973-75.

MODEL AL-2 SKEET GUN . . . . NiB $436 Ex $348 Gd $237

Same as Model AL-2 Field Gun except has wide rib, 26-inch bbl. in SK choke only, checkered pistol-grip stock and beavertail forearm. Imported 1973-75.

MODEL AL-2 TRAP GUN . . . . NiB $422 Ex $338 Gd $230

Same as Model AL-2 Field Gun except has wide rib, 30 inch bbl. in F choke only, beavertail forearm. Monte Carlo stock w/recoil pad. Weight: About 7.75 lbs. Imported 1973-75.

MODEL AL-3

Similar to corresponding AL-2 models in design and general specifications. Imported 1975-76.

Field model . . . . NiB $436 Ex $348 Gd $237
Magnum model . . . . NiB $448 Ex $359 Gd $244
Skeet model . . . . NiB $456 Ex $364 Gd $248
Trap model . . . . NiB $410 Ex $328 Gd $223

MODEL AL-3 DELUXE TRAP GUN . . . . NiB $890 Ex $712 Gd $485

Same as standard Model AL-3 Trap Gun except has fully-engraved receiver, gold-plated trigger and safety, stock and forearm of premium-grade European walnut, gold monogram escutcheon inlaid in buttstock. Imported 1975-76.

AL390 FIELD SHOTGUN

Lightweight version of A-390 series. Gauges: 12 or 20 ga. 22- 24-, 26-, 28-, or 30-inch bbl., 41.7 to 47.6 inches overall. Weight: 6.4 to 7.5 lbs. Imported 1997 to date.
Mdl. AL390 Field/Sil. Mallard (12 or 20 ga.) . . . NiB $678 Ex $543 Gd $369
Mdl. AL390 Field/Sil. Mallard Yth. (20 ga.) . . . . NiB $686 Ex $549 Gd $372
Model AL390 Field/Slug (12 ga. only) . . . . NiB $662 Ex $530 Gd $360
Model AL390 Silver Mallard camouflage . . . NiB $740 Ex $593 Gd $401
Model AL390 Silver Mallard synthetic . . . . NiB $694 Ex $555 Gd $378
Model AL390 Gold Mallard (12 or 20 ga.) . NiB $772 Ex $618 Gd $420
Model AL390 NWTF Spec. camouflage . . . NiB $928 Ex $743 Gd $505
Model AL390 NWTF Spec. synthetic . . . . . NiB $741 Ex $593 Gd $402

(cont'd.) MODEL AL390 FIELD SHOTGUN

Mdl. AL390 NWTF Spec. Yth. . . . . NiB $790 Ex $442 Gd $281

AL390 SPORT SPORTING SHOTGUN

Similar to Model AL-390 Sport Skeet. Gauges: 12 or 20 ga., 28- or 30-inch bbls. Weight: 6.8 to 8 lbs. Imported 1997 to date.
Model AL390 Sport Sporting . . . . NiB $694 Ex $555 Gd $378
Model AL390 Sport Sporting Collection . . . . . . NiB $639 Ex $593 Gd $402
Mdl. AL390 Sport Sporting
Yth. (20 ga. only) . . . . NiB $662 Ex $530 Gd $360
Model AL390 Sport Gold Sporting . . . . NiB $928 Ex $743 Gd $505
Mdl. AL390 EELL Sport
Diamond Sporting. . . . . NiB $3424 Ex $2739 Gd $1863
W/Ported bbl., add $75

AL390 SPORT SKEET SHOTGUN

Gauges: 12 ga. only. 26- or 28-inch bbl. w/3-shot chamber. Weight: 7.6 to 8 lbs. Matte finish wood and metal. Imported 1997 to date.
Model AL390 Sport Skeet . . . . NiB $707 Ex $565 Gd $385
Mdl. AL390 Sport Super Skeet (Semi-Auto) . . . . NiB $967 Ex $773 Gd $526
W/ported bbl., add $95

BERETTA AL390 SPORT TRAP SHOTGUN

Gauges: 12 ga. only. 30- or 32-inch bbl. w/3-shot chamber. Weight: 7.8 to 8.25 lbs. Matte finish wood and metal. Black recoil rubber pad. Imported 1997 to date.
Model AL390 Sport Trap . . . . NiB $707 Ex $565 Gd $385
Model AL390 Sport Super Trap . . . NiB $1015 Ex $812 Gd $552
Multi-choke bbl. (30" only), add $40
Ported bbl., add $95

AL391 URIKA AUTOLOADING SHOTGUN

Gauge: 12 and 20 ga. w/3-inch chambers. 28- 30- or 32-inch bbl. Weight: 6.6 to 7.7 lbs. Self-compensating gas valve. Adjustable synthetic and walnut stocks w/ five interchangeable chokes. Imported 2000 to date.
Model AL391 Urika. . . . . NiB $815 Ex $662 Gd $443
Model AL391 Urika synthetic . . . . NiB $833 Ex $667 Gd $453
Model AL391 Urika camo
w/Realtree Hardwoods . . . . NiB $920 Ex $736 Gd $500
Model AL391 Urika
Gold w/black receiver . . . . NiB $965 Ex $772 Gd $524
Model AL391 Urika Gold
w/silver receiver, lightweight . . . . NiB $1044 Ex $835 Gd $568
Model AL391 Urika Youth. . . . . NiB $823 Ex $659 Gd $449
Model AL391 Urika Sporting . . . . NiB $939 Ex $751 Gd $511
Model AL391 Urika Gold
Sporting w/black receiver. . . . . NiB $1009 Ex $807 Gd $548
Model AL391 Urika
Gold Sporting w/silver receiver . . . . NiB $1080 Ex $863 Gd $587
Model AL391 Urika Trap. . . . . NiB $947 Ex $758 Gd $515
Model AL391 Gold Trap . . . . NiB $1044 Ex $835 Gd $568

SHOTGUNS

Beretta Model BL-1

Beretta Model BL3

Beretta Model BL-6

Beretta Model ASEL

MODEL ASE 90 O/U SHOTGUN

Competition-style receiver w/coin-silver finish and gold inlay featuring drop-out trigger group. Gauge: 12; 2.75-inch chamber. Bbls.: 28- or 30-inch w/fixed or Mobilchoke tubes; vent rib. Weight: 8.5 lbs. (30-inch bbl.). Checkered high-grade walnut stock. Imported 1992 to date.

Pigeon, Skeet, Trap models .... NiB $7606 Ex $6084 Gd $4137
Sporting Clays model. .... NiB $7794 Ex $6235 Gd $4240
Trap Combo model. .... NiB $12,026 Ex $9620 Gd $6542
Deluxe (introduced 1996) .... NiB $13,976 Ex $11,180 Gd $7602

MODEL ASE SERIES O/U SHOTGUN

Boxlock. Single non-selective trigger. Selective automatic ejectors. gauges: 12 and 20. Bbls. 26-, 28-, 30-inch; IC and M choke or M and F choke. Weight: about 5.75-7 lbs. Checkered pistol-grip stock and forearm. Receiver w/various grades of engraving. Imported 1947-64.

Model ASE (light scroll engraving) .... NiB $2137 Ex $1710 Gd $1163
Model ASEL (half coverage engraving) .... NiB $3074 Ex $2460 Gd $1672
Model ASEELL (full coverage engraving) ... NiB $4711 Ex $3769 Gd $2564
For 20 ga. models, add 95%

MODEL BL-1/BL-2 O/U

Boxlock. Plain extractors. Double triggers.12 gauge, 2.75-inch chambers only. Bbls.: 30-and 28-inch M/F choke, 26-inch IC/M choke. Weight: 6.75-7 lbs., depending on bbl. length. Checkered pistol-grip stock and forearm. Imported 1968-73.

Model BL-1. .... NiB $390 Ex $312 Gd $212
Model BL-2 (single selective trigger) .... NiB $488 Ex $390 Gd $265

MODEL BL-2/S .... NiB $500 Ex $400 Gd $272

Similar to Model BL-1, except has selective "Speed-Trigger," vent-rib bbls., 2.75- or 3-inch chambers. Weight: 7-7.5 lbs. Imported 1974-76.

MODEL BL-3 .... NiB $722 Ex $577 Gd $392

Same as Model BL-1, except has deluxe engraved receiver, selective single trigger, vent-rib bbls., 12 or 20 ga., 2.75-inch or 3-inch chambers in former, 3-inch in latter. Weight: 6-7.5 lbs. depending on ga. and bbl. length. Imported 1968-76.

MODELS BL-4, BL-5 AND BL-6

Higher grade versions of Model BL-3 w/more elaborate engraving and fancier wood; Model BL-6 has sideplates. Selective automatic ejectors standard. Imported 1968-76.

Model BL-4 .... NiB $878 Ex $702 Gd $477
Model BL-5 .... NiB $1164 Ex $931 Gd $633
Model BL-6 (1973-76) .... NiB $1462 Ex $1170 Gd $796

SERIES BL SKEET GUNS

Models BL-3, BL-4, BL-5 and BL-6 w/standard features of their respective grades plus wider rib and skeet-style stock, 26-inch bbls. SK choked. Weight: 6-7.25 lbs. depending on ga.

Model BL-3 skeet gun .... NiB $780 Ex $624 Gd $424
Model BL-4 skeet gun .... NiB $904 Ex $723 Gd $492
Model BL-5 skeet gun .... NiB $1202 Ex $962 Gd $654
Model BL-6 skeet gun .... NiB $1632 Ex $1305 Gd $887

SERIES BL TRAP GUNS

Models BL-3, BL-4, BL-5 and BL-6 w/standard features of their respective grades plus wider rib and Monte Carlo stock w/recoil pad; 30-inch bbls., improved M/F or both F choke. Weight: About 7.5 lbs.

Model BL-3 trap gun .... NiB $696 Ex $556 Gd $379
Model BL-4 trap gun .... NiB $774 Ex $619 Gd $421
Model BL-5 trap gun .... NiB $1202 Ex $962 Gd $654
Model BL-6 trap gun .... NiB $1554 Ex $1243 Gd $846

MODEL FS-1 FOLDING SINGLE .... NiB $234 Ex $156 Gd $104

Formerly "Companion." Folds to length of bbl. Hammerless. Underlever. Gauge: 12, 16, 20, 28 or .410. Bbl.: 30-inch in 12 ga., 28-inch in 16 and 20 ga.; 26-inch in 28 and .410 ga.; all F choke. Checkered semipistol-grip stock/forearm. Weight: 4.5-5.5 lbs. depending on ga. Disc. 1971.

GOLDEN SNIPE O/U

Same as Silver Snipe (see page 430) except has automatic ejectors, vent rib is standard feature. Imported 1959-67.

W/non-selective single trigger .... NiB $1035 Ex $884 Gd $468
W/selective single trigger, add $100

Beretta Model GR-2

Beretta FS-1 Folding

Beretta Mark II Trap

Beretta S58 Trap

MODEL GR-2 HAMMERLESS DOUBLE . . . NiB $967 Ex $773 Gd $526
Boxlock. Plain extractors. Double triggers. Gauges: 12, 20; 2.75-inch chambers in former, 3-inch in latter. Bbls.: Vent rib; 30-inch M/F choke (12 ga. only); 28-inch M/F choke, 26-inch IC/M choke. Weight: 6.5 to 7.5 lbs. depending on ga. and bbl. length. Checkered pistol-grip stock and forearm. Imported 1968-76.

MODEL GR-3 . . . . NiB $1097 Ex $877 Gd $596
Same as Model GR-2 except has selective single trigger chambered for 12-ga. Three inch or 2.75-inch shells. Magnum model has 30-inch M/F choke bbl., recoil pad. Weight: about 8 lbs. Imported 1968-76.

MODEL GR-4 . . . . NiB $1503 Ex $1202 Gd $817
Same as Model GR-2 except has automatic ejectors and selective single trigger, higher grade engraving and wood. 12 ga., 2.75-inch chambers only. Imported 1968-76.

GRADE 100 O/U
SHOTGUN . . . . NiB $1944 Ex $1555 Gd $1058
Sidelock. Double triggers. Automatic ejectors. 12 ga. only. Bbls.: 26-, 28-, 30-inch, any standard boring. Weight: About 7.5 lbs. Checkered stock and forend, straight or pistol grip. Disc.

GRADE 200 . . . . NiB $2535 Ex $2028 Gd $1379
Same general specifications as Grade 100 except higher quality; bores and action parts hard chrome plated. Disc.

MARK II SINGLE-BARREL TRAP GUN . . . . NiB $586 Ex $468 Gd $318
Boxlock action similar to that of Series "BL" over-and-unders. Engraved receiver. Automatic ejector. 12 ga. only. 32- or 34-inch bbl. w/wide vent rib. Weight: About 8.5 lbs. Monte Carlo stock w/pistol grip and recoil pad, beavertail forearm. Imported 1972-76.

MODEL S55B O/U
SHOTGUN . . . . NiB $624 Ex $572 Gd $442
Boxlock. Plain extractors. Selective single trigger. Gauges: 12, 20; 2.75- or 3-inch chambers in former, 3-inch in latter. Bbls. vent rib; 30-inch M/F choke or both F choke in 12-ga. Three inch Magnum only; 28-inch M/F choke; 26 inch IC/M choke. Weight: 6.5 to 7.5 lbs. depending on ga. and bbl. length. Checkered pistol-grip stock and forearm. Introduced in 1977. Disc.

MODEL S56E . . . . NiB $884 Ex $624 Gd $416
Same as Model S55B except has scroll-engraved receiver selective automatic ejectors. Introduced in 1977. Disc.

MODEL S58 SKEET GUN . . . . NiB $832 Ex $572 Gd $416
Same as Model S56E except has 26-inch bbls. of Boehler Antinit Anticorro steel, SK choked, w/wide vent rib; skeet-style stock and forearm. Weight: 7.5 lbs. Introduced in 1977.

MODEL S58 TRAP GUN . . . . NiB $827 Ex $442 Gd $416
Same as Model S58 Skeet Gun except has 30-inch bbls. bored IM/F Trap, Monte Carlo stock w/recoil pad. Weight: 7 lbs. 10 oz. Introduced in 1977. Disc.

SILVER HAWK FEATHERWEIGHT
HAMMERLESS DOUBLE-BARREL SHOTGUN
Boxlock. Double triggers or non-selective single trigger. Plain extractor. Gauges: 12, 16, 20, 28, 12 Mag. Bbls.: 26- to 32-inch w/high matted rib, all standard choke combinations. Weight: 7 lbs. (12 ga. w/26-inch bbls.). Checkered walnut stock w/beavertail forearm. Disc. 1967.
W/double triggers . . . . NiB $676 Ex $494 Gd $312
For non-selective single trigger, add $65

SHOTGUNS

Beretta S682 Gold E Trap

Beretta S682 Gold E Double Trap

Beretta S682 Gold E X Trap

SILVER SNIPE O/U SHOTGUN

Boxlock. Non-selective or selective single trigger. Plain extractor. Gauges: 12, 20, 12 Mag., 20 Mag. Bbls.: 26-, 28-, 30-inch; plain or vent rib; chokes IC/M, M/F, SK number 1 and number 2, F/F. Weight: From about 6 lbs. in 20 ga. to 8.5 lbs. in 12 ga. (Trap gun). Checkered walnut pistol-grip stock and forearm. Imported 1955-67.

W/plain bbl., non-selective trigger	NiB $754	Ex $676	Gd $38
W/vent rib bbl., non-selective single trigger	NiB $780	Ex $702	Gd $364
For selective single trigger, add			$65

MODEL SL-2 PIGEON SERIES PUMP GUN

Hammerless. Takedown.12 ga. only. Three shot magazine. Bbls.: Vent rib; 30-inch F choke, 28-inch M, 26-inch IC. Weight: 7-7.25 lbs., depending on bbl. length. Receiver w/various grades of engraving. Checkered pistol-grip stock and forearm. Imported 1968-71.

Model SL-2	NiB $411	Ex $329	Gd $224
Silver Pigeon	NiB $336	Ex $268	Gd $182
Gold Pigeon	NiB $523	Ex $418	Gd $284
Ruby Pigeon	NiB $673	Ex $538	Gd $365

SERIES "SO" SERIES SHOTGUNS

Jubilee Series introduced in 1998. The Beretta Boxlock is made with mechanical works from a single block of hot forged, high-resistance steel. The gun is richly engraved in scroll and game scenes. All engraving is signed by master engravers. High-quality finishing on the inside with high polishing of all internal points. Sidelock. Selective automatic ejectors. Selective single trigger or double triggers. 12 ga. only, 2.75- or 3-inch chambers. Bbls.: Vent rib (wide type on skeet and trap guns); 26-, 27-, 29-, 30-inch; any combination of standard chokes. Weight: 7 to 7.75 lbs., depending on bbl. length, style of stock and density of wood. Stock and forearm of select walnut, finely checkered; straight or pistol-grip, field, skeet and trap guns have appropriate styles of stock and forearm. Models differ chiefly in quality of wood and grade of engraving. Models SO-3EL, SO-3EELL, SO4 and SO-5 have hand-detachable locks. "SO-4" is used to designate skeet and trap models derived from Model SO-3EL, but with less elaborate engraving. Models SO3EL and SO-3EELL are similar to the earlier SO-4 and SO-5, respectively. Imported 1933 to date.

(cont'd.) SERIES "SO" SERIES SHOTGUNS

Jubilee O/U 410-28-20-12			
	NiB $8124 to 17,933	Ex $6500 to 14,347	Gd $4420 to 9756
Jubilee II Side-by-side			
	NiB $8472 to 19,441	Ex $6778 to 14,637	Gd $4608 to 9953
Mdl. SO-2	NiB $4039 to 8573	Ex $3231 to 4570	Gd $2198 to 3107
Mdl. SO-3	NiB $5648 to 7143	Ex $4519 to 6629	Gd $3072 to 4508
Mdl. SO-3EL	NiB $6757 to 9145	Ex $5405 to 7773	Gd $3675 to 5286
Mdl. SO-3EELL	NiB $9652 to 10,861	Ex $7722 to 11,434	Gd $5251 to 7775
Mdl. SO-4 Field, Skeet or Trp gun			
	NiB $6143 to 8313	Ex $4914 to 9147	Gd $3342 to 6220
Model SO-5 Sporting, Skt. or Trp.			
	NiB $10,792 to 11,830	Ex $6331 to 9880	Gd $5871 to 7768
W/extra bbl. set, add			25%

MODELS SO-6 AND SO-9 PREMIUM GRADE SHOTGUNS

High-grade over/unders in the SO series. Gauges: 12 ga. only (SO-6); 12, 20, 28 and .410 (SO-9). Fixed or Mobilchoke (12 ga. only). Sidelock action. Silver or casehardened receiver (SO-6); English custom hand-engraved scroll or game scenes (SO-9). Supplied w/leather case and accessories. Imported from about 1990 to date.

SO-6 O/U	NiB $6923 to 7996	Ex $5538 to 6812	Gd $3766 to 4632
SO-6 EELL O/U	NiB $8516 to 5714	Ex $6812 to 8730	Gd $4632 to 5937
SO-9 O/U			$22,828 to 48,667
SO-9 EELL special engraver			$52,000 to 93,600
W/extra bbl. set, add			25%

MODEL SO6/SO-7 S/S DOUBLES

Side-by-side shotgun w/same general specifications as SO Series over/unders except higher grade w/more elaborate engraving, fancier wood.

SO-6 SxS (imported 1948-82)	$5,538 to 6,812
SO-7 SxS (imported 1948-90)	6,812 to 8,731

MODEL TR-1 SINGLE-SHOT TRAP GUN ...... NiB $349 Ex $280 Gd $190
Hammerless. Underlever action. Engraved frame.12 ga. only. 32-inch bbl. w/vent rib. Weight: About 8.25 lbs. Monte Carlo stock w/pistol grip and recoil pad, beavertail forearm. Imported 1968-71.

MODEL TR-2 .... NiB $393 Ex $314 Gd $213
Same as Model TR-1 except has extended ventilated rib. Imported 1969-73.

Beretta Model SO-2

Beretta Model SO-3

Beretta Model SO-4

Beretta Model SO-5

Beretta Model SO-7

VICTORIA PINTAIL (ES100) SEMIAUTOLOADER
Short Montefeltro-type recoil action. Gauge: 12 w/3-inch chamber. Bbl.: 24-inch slug, 24-, 26- or 28-inch vent rib w/Mobilchoke tubes. Weight: 7 lbs. to 7 lbs., 5 oz. Checkered synthetic or walnut buttstock and forend. Matte finish on both metal and stock. Imported 1993 to date.

Field model w/synthetic
stock (intro. 1998) . . . . NiB $607 Ex $486 Gd $330
Field model w/walnut stock (disc. 1998) . . . . . . NiB $565 Ex $451 Gd $307
Rifled slug model w/synthetic
stock (intro. 1998) . . . . NiB $750 Ex $600 Gd $408
Standard slug model
w/walnut stock (disc. 1998) . . . . NiB $536 Ex $429 Gd $291
Wetland Camo model (intro. 2000) . . . . . . NiB $707 Ex $566 Gd $385

VINCENZO BERNARDELLI —
Gardone V.T. (Brescia), Italy

Previously imported by Armsport, Miami, FL (formerly by Magnum Research, Inc., Quality Arms, Stoeger Industries, Inc. & Action Arms, LTD).

115 SERIES O/U SHOTGUNS
Boxlock w/single trigger and ejectors. 12 ga. only. 25.5-, 26.75-, and 29.5-inch bbls. Concave top and vented middle rib. Anatomical grip stock. Blued or coin-silver finish w/various grades of engraving. Imported 1985-97.

(cont'd.) 115 SERIES O/U SHOTGUNS
Hunting Model 115 (disc. 1990) . . . . . NiB $1851 Ex $1481 Gd $1008
Hunting Model 115E (disc. 1990) . . . . . NiB $5569 Ex $4455 Gd $3029
Hunting Model 115L (disc. 1990) . . . . . NiB $3074 Ex $2460 Gd $1672
Hunting Model 115S (disc. 1990) . . . . NiB $2609 Ex $2087 Gd $1419
Target Model 115 (disc. 1992) . . . . NiB $2074 Ex $1659 Gd $1127
Target Model 115E (disc. 1992) . . . . . . NiB $6285 Ex $5025 Gd $3418
Target Model 115L (disc. 1992) . . . . . NiB $3895 Ex $3117 Gd $2119
Target Model 115S (disc. 1992) . . . . . . NiB $2788 Ex $2231 Gd $1516
Trap/Skeet Model 115S
(imported 1996-97) . . . . NiB $2853 Ex $2282 Gd $1552
Sporting Clays Model 115S
(imported 1995-97) . . . . NiB $4218 Ex $3375 Gd $2294

BRESCIA
HAMMER DOUBLE . . . . NiB $976 Ex $780 Gd $530
Back-action sidelock. Plain extractors. Double triggers. Gauges: 12, 20. Bbls.: 27.5 or 29.5-inch M/F choke in 12 ga. 25.5-inch IC/M choke in 20 ga.. Weight: From 5.75 to 7 lbs., depending on ga. and bbl. length. English-style stock and forearm, checkered. No longer imported.

ELIO . . . . NiB $1164 Ex $931 Gd $633
Lightweight game gun, 12 ga. only, w/same general specifications as Standard Gamecock (S. Uberto 1) except weight: About 6 to 6.25 lbs.; has automatic ejectors, fine English-pattern scroll engraving. No longer imported. See illustration next page.

Bernardelli Gamecock

Bernardelli Standard Gamecock

Bernardelli Gardone

Bernardelli Italia

Bernardelli Roma 6

Bernardelli Elio

GAMECOCK, PREMIER
(ROME 3)
Same general specifications as Standard Gamecock (S. Uberto 1) except has sideplates, auto ejectors, single trigger. No longer imported.
Roma 3 (disc. 1989,
Reintroduced 1993-97) . . . . NiB $1626 Ex $1300 Gd $884
Roma 3E (disc. 1950) Roma 3M
w/single trigger (disc. 1997) . . . . NiB $1814 Ex $1451 Gd $987

GAMECOCK, STANDARD
(S. UBERTO 1) HAMMERLESS
DOUBLE-BARREL SHOTGUN . . . . NiB $1125 Ex $901 Gd $613
Boxlock. Plain extractors. Double triggers. Gauges: 12, 16, 20; 2.75-inch chambers in 12 and 16, 3-inch in 20 ga. Bbls. 25.5-inch IC/M choke; 27.5-inch M/F choke. Weight: 5.75-6.5 lbs., depending on ga. and bbl. length. English-style straight-grip stock and forearm, checkered. No longer imported.

GARDONE HAMMER DOUBLE . . . NiB $2525 Ex $2020 Gd $1373
Same general specifications as Brescia except for higher grade engraving and wood, but not as high as the Italia. Half-cock safety. Disc. 1956.

HEMINGWAY HAMMERLESS DOUBLE
Boxlock. Single or double triggers w/hinged front. Selective automatic ejectors. Gauges: 12 and 20 w/2.75- or 3-inch chambers, 16 and 28 w/2.75-inch. Bbls.: 23.5- to 28-inch w/fixed chokes. Weight: 6.25 lbs. Checkered English-style European walnut stock. Silvered and engraved receiver.
Standard model . . . . NiB $2020 Ex $1615 Gd $1098
Deluxe model
w/sideplates (disc. 1993) . . . . . . NiB $2358 Ex $1886 Gd $1282
For single trigger, add $100

ITALIA . . . . NiB $3424 Ex $2739 Gd $1862
Same general specifications as Brescia except higher grade engraving and wood. Disc. 1986.

ROMA 4 AND ROMA 6
Same as Premier Gamecock (Rome 3) except higher grade engraving and wood, double triggers. Disc. 1997.
Roma 4 (disc. 1989) . . . . NiB $1294 Ex $1035 Gd $704
Roma 4E (disc. 1997) . . . . NiB $1626 Ex $1300 Gd $884
Roma 6 (disc. 1989) . . . . NiB $1332 Ex $1066 Gd $725
Roma 6E (disc. 1997) . . . . NiB $2016 Ex $1612 Gd $1096

ROMA 7, 8, AND 9
Side-by-side. Anson & Deeley boxlock; hammerless. Ejectors; double triggers. 12 ga. Barrels: 27.5-or 29.5-inch. M/F chokes. Fancy hand-checkered European walnut straight or pistol-grip stock, forearm. Elaborately engraved, silver-finished sideplates. Imported 1994-97.
Roma 7 . . . . NiB $2405 Ex $1924 Gd $1308
Roma 8 . . . . NiB $2925 Ex $2340 Gd $1591
Roma 9 . . . . NiB $3634 Ex $2907 Gd $1977

S. UBERTO 2 . . . . **NiB $1423 Ex $1138 Gd $774**
Same as Standard Gamecock (S. Uberto 1) except higher grade engraving and wood. Currently imported.

S. UBERTO F.S.
Same as Standard Gamecock except w/higher grade engraving, wood and has auto-ejectors. Disc. 1989, reintroduced 1993-97.
Model FS . . . . **NiB $1788 Ex $1430 Gd $972**
Model V.B. Incisio . . . . **NiB $2037 Ex $1630 Gd $1108**
W/single trigger, add $75

HOLLAND V.B. SERIES SHOTGUNS
Holland & Holland-type sidelock action. Auto-ejectors. Double triggers. 12 ga. only. Bbl. length or choke to custom specification. Silver-finish receiver (Liscio) or engraved coin finish receiver (Incisio). Extra-select wood and game scene engraving (Lusso). Checkered stock (straight or pistol-grip). Imported 1992-97.
Model V.B. Liscio. . . . . **NiB $6234 Ex $4987 Gd $3391**
Model V.B. Incisio . . . . **NiB $7736 Ex $6188 Gd $4208**
Model V.B. Lusso. . . . . **NiB $9223 Ex $7379 Gd $5018**
Model V.B. Extra. . . . . **NiB $10,726 Ex $8580 Gd $5834**
Model V.B. Gold. . . . . **NiB $37,636 Ex $30,108 Gd $20,473**
Engraving Pattern
No. 4, add $950
Engraving Pattern
No. 12, add $4450
Engraving Pattern No. 20, add $8750
Single trigger, add $595

Bernardelli Uberto 2

Bernardelli Uberto F.S.

BOSS & COMPANY — London, England

HAMMERLESS DOUBLE-BARREL
SHOTGUN . . . . **NiB $62,676 Ex $50,000 Gd $32,800**
Sidelock. Automatic ejectors. Double triggers, non-selective or selective single trigger. Made in all gauges, bbl. lengths and chokes. Checkered stock and forend, straight or pistol-grip.

HAMMERLESS O/U
SHOTGUN . . . . **NiB $109,683 Ex $80,500 Gd $40,000**
Sidelock. Automatic ejectors. Selective single trigger. Made in all gauges, bbl. lengths and chokes. Checkered stock and forend, straight or pistol-grip. Disc.

Bernardelli V.B. Holland Liscio

BREDA MECCANICA BRESCIANA — Brescia, Italy, *formerly ERNESTO BREDA, Milan, Italy*

AUTOLOADING SHOTGUN
Recoil-operated. 12 ga, 2.75-inch chamber. Four shell tubular magazine. Bbls.: 25.5- and 27.5-inch, plain, matted or vent rib, IC, M or F choke; current model has 26-inch vent-rib bbl. w/interchangeable choke tubes. Weight: About 7.25 lbs. Checkered straight or pistol-grip stock and forearm. Disc. 1988.
W/plain bbl. **NiB $457 Ex $366 Gd $248**
W/raised matted rib bbl. . . . . **NiB $509 Ex $407 Gd $277**
W/vent rib bbl. . . . . **NiB $535 Ex $427 Gd $290**
W/vent rib,
interchangeable choke tubes. . . . . **NiB $554 Ex $443 Gd $301**

MAGNUM
Same general specifications as standard model except chambered for 12-ga. 3-inch Magnum, 3-shot magazine; latest model has 29-inch vent-rib bbl. Disc. 1988.
W/plain bbl. **NiB $581 Ex $479 Gd $325**
W/vent rib bbl. . . . . **NiB $594 Ex $489 Gd $333**

Boss Hammerless
Double-Barrel

SHOTGUNS

American Browning Grade I
(see page 435)

American Browning Special
(see page 435)

BRETTON SHOTGUNS — St. Etienne (Cedex1), France

BABY STANDARD SPRINT O/U .... **NiB $1025 Ex $917 Gd $567**
Inline sliding breech action. 12 or 20 gauge w/2.75-inch chambers. 27.5-inch separated bbls. w/vent rib and choke tubes. Weight: 4.8 to 5 lbs. Engraved alloy receiver. Checkered walnut buttstock and forearm w/satin oil finish. Imported 1992 to date.

SPRINT DELUXE O/U .... **NiB $922 Ex $798 Gd $510**
Similar to the Standard Model except w/engraved coin-finished receiver and chambered 12, 16 and 20 ga. Discontinued 1994.

FAIR PLAY O/U .... **NiB $978 Ex $819 Gd $489**
Lightweight action similar to the Sprint Model except w/hinged action that pivots open and is chambered 12 or 20 gauge only.

BRNO SHOTGUNS — Brno and Uherski Brod, Czech Republic, (formerly Czechoslovakia)

500 O/U SHOTGUN .... **NiB $875 Ex $747 Gd $438**
Hammerless boxlock w/double triggers and ejectors.12 ga. w/2.75-inch chambers. 27.5-inch bbls.. choked M/F. 44 inches overall. Weight: 7 lbs. Etched receiver. Checkered walnut stock w/classic style cheekpiece. Imported 1987-91.

500 SERIES O/U COMBINATION GUNS
Similar to the 500 Series over/under shotgun, except w/lower . bbl. chambered in rifle calibers and set trigger option. Imported 1987-95.
Model 502 12/222, 12/243 (disc. 1991)..... NiB $1073 Ex $859 Gd $584
Model 502 12/308, 12/30.06 (disc. 1991) ... NiB $1120 Ex $896 Gd $609
Model 571 12/6x65R (disc. 1993) .... NiB $965 Ex $773 Gd $525
Model 572 12/7x65R (imported since 1992)..... NiB $1042 Ex $834 Gd $566
Model 584 12/7x57R (imported since 1992) ..... NiB $1073 Ex $859 Gd $584
Sport Series 4-bbl. set (disc. 1991) .... NiB $2858 Ex $2286 Gd $1554

CZ 581 SOLO O/U SHOTGUN .... **NiB $814 Ex $651 Gd $443**
Hammerless boxlock w/double triggers, ejectors and automatic safety. 12 ga. w/2.75- or 3-inch chambers. 28-inch bbls. choked M/F. Weight: 7.5 lbs. Checkered walnut stock. Disc. 1996.

SUPER SERIES O/U SHOTGUN
Hammerless sidelock w/selective single or double triggers and ejectors. 12 ga. w/2.75- or 3-inch chambers. 27.5-inch bbls. choked M/F. 44.5 inches overall. Weight: 7.25 lbs. Etched or engraved side

(cont'd.) **SUPER SERIES O/U SHOTGUN**
plates. Checkered European walnut stock w/classic-style cheekpiece. Imported 1987-91.
Super Series Shotgun (disc. 1992).......... NiB $1026 Ex $821 Gd $558
Super Series Combo (disc. 1992) .... NiB $1204 Ex $963 Gd $654
Super Ser. 3-bbl. set (disc. 1990)......... NiB $2400 Ex $1920 Gd $1306
Super Series engraving, add $1250

ZH 300 SERIES O/U SHOTGUNS
Hammerless boxlock w/double triggers. Gauge: 12 or 16 w/2.75- or 3-inch chambers. Bbls.: 26, 27.5 or 30 inches; choked M/F. Weight: 7 lbs. Skip-line checkered walnut stock w/classic-style cheekpiece. Imported 1986-93.
Model 300 (disc. 1993) .... NiB $587 Ex $470 Gd $319
Model 301 Field (disc. 1991) .... NiB $602 Ex $481 Gd $327
Model 302 Skeet (disc. 1992) .... NiB $673 Ex $538 Gd $366
Model 303 Trap (disc. 1992) .... NiB $700 Ex $560 Gd $381

ZH 300 SERIES O/U COMBINATION GUNS
Similar to the 300 Series over/under shotgun except lower bbl. chambered in rifle calibers.
Model 300 Combo
8-bbl. Set (disc. 1991) .... NiB $3341 Ex $2673 Gd $1818
Model 304 12 ga./7x57R (disc. 1995) .... NiB $676 Ex $541 Gd $368
Model 305 12 ga./5.6x52R (disc. 1993) ...... NiB $766 Ex $613 Gd $417
Model 306 12 ga./5.6x50R (disc. 1993) ...... NiB $804 Ex $644 Gd $438
Model 307 12 ga./.22 Hornet
(Imported since 1995) .... NiB $709 Ex $567 Gd $385
Model 324 16 ga./7x57R (disc. 1987 .... NiB $741 Ex $592 Gd $403

ZP 149 HAMMERLESS DOUBLE
Sidelock action w/double triggers, automatic ejectors and automatic safety.12 ga. w/2.75- or 3-inch chambers. 28.5-inch bbls. choked M/F. Weight: 7.25 lbs. Checkered walnut buttstock w/cheekpiece.
Standard model .... NiB $612 Ex $489 Gd $333
Engraved model .... NiB $670 Ex $536 Gd $365

BROLIN ARMS, INC. — Pomona, California

ARMS HAWK PUMP SHOTGUN, FIELD SERIES
Slide-action. Gauge: 12 ga. w/3-inch chamber. 24-, 26-, 28- or 30-inch bbl. 44 and 50 inches overall. Weight: 7.3 to 7.6 lbs. Cross-bolt safety. Vent rib bbl. w/screw-in choke tube and bead sights. Non-reflective metal finish. Synthetic or oil-finished wood stock w/swivel studs. Made 1997-98.
Synthetic stock model .... NiB $223 Ex $179 Gd $121
Wood stock model.............. NiB $210 Ex $168 Gd $114

ARMS HAWK PUMP SHOTGUN COMBO MODEL
Similar to the Field Model except w/extra 18.5- or 22-inch bbl. w/bead or rifle sight. Made 1997-98.
Synthetic stock model . . . . NiB $249 Ex $199 Gd $136
Wood stock model. . . . . NiB $236 Ex $188 Gd $129

ARMS HAWK PUMP SHOTGUN LAWMAN MODEL
Similar to the Field Model except has 18.5-inch bbl. w/cylinder bore fixed choke. Weight: 7 lbs. Dual operating bars. Bead, rifle or ghost ring sights. Black synthetic or wood stock. Matte chrome or satin nickel finish. Made 1997-99.
Synthetic stock model . . . . NiB $210 Ex $168 Gd $114
Wood stock model . . . . NiB $198 Ex $158 Gd $107
Rifle sights, add $20
Ghost ring sights, add $35
Satin nickel finish (disc. 1997), add $25

ARMS HAWK SLUG MODEL
Similar to the Field Model except has 18.5- or 22-inch bbl. w/IC fixed choke or 4-inch extended rifled choke. Rifle or ghost ring sights or optional cantilevered scope mount. Black synthetic or wood stock. Matte blued finish. Made 1998-99.
Synthetic stock model . . . . NiB $210 Ex $168 Gd $114
Wood stock model . . . . NiB $198 Ex $158 Gd $107
W/rifled bbl., add $20
W/cantilevered scope mount, add $35

ARMS HAWK TURKEY SPECIAL
Similar to the Field Model except has 22-inch vent-rib bbl. w/extended extra-full choke. Rifle or ghost ring sights or optional cantilevered scope mount. Black synthetic or wood stock. Matte blued finish. Made 1998-99.
Synthetic stock model . . . . NiB $204 Ex $163 Gd $111
Wood stock model . . . . NiB $192 Ex $153 Gd $104
W/cantilevered
scope mount, add $25

BROWNING SHOTGUNS —
Morgan (formerly Ogden), Utah
AMERICAN BROWNING SHOTGUNS

Designated "American" Browning because they were produced in Ilion, New York, the following Remington-made Brownings are almost identical to the Remington Model 11A and Sportsman and the Browning Auto-5. They are the only Browning shotguns manufactured in the U.S. during the 20th century and were made for Browning Arms when production was suspended in Belgium because of WW II.

NOTE: *Fabrique Nationale Herstal (formerly Fabrique Nationale d'Armes de Guerre) of Herstal, Belgium, is the longtime manufacturer of Browning shotguns dating back to 1900. Miroku Firearms Mfg. Co. of Tokyo, Japan, bought into the Browning company and has, since the early 1970s, undertaken some of the production. The following shotguns were manufactured for Browning by these two firms.*

GRADE I AUTOLOADER (AUTO-5)
Recoil-operated autoloader. Similar to the Remington Model 11A except w/different style engraving and identified w/the Browning logo. Gauges: 12, 16 or 20. Plain 26- to 32-inch bbl. w/any standard boring. Two or four shell tubular magazine w/magazine cut-off. Weight: About 6.88 lbs. (20 ga.) to 8 lbs. (12 ga.). Checkered pistol-grip stock and forearm. Made 1940-49.

(cont'd.) GRADE I AUTOLOADER (AUTO-5)
American Browning Grade I
Auto-5, 12 or 16 ga. . . . . NiB $695 Ex $592 Gd $258
20 ga., add. 20%

SPECIAL 441
Same general specifications as Grade I except supplied w/raised matted rib or vent rib. Disc. 1949.
W/raised matted rib . . . . NiB $773 Ex $670 Gd $335
W/vent rib . . . . NiB $798 Ex $695 Gd $335
20 ga., add. 20%

SPECIAL SKEET MODEL . . . . NiB $676 Ex $541 Gd $368
Same general specifications as Grade I except has 26-inch bbl. w/vent rib and Cutts Compensator. Disc. 1949.

UTILITY FIELD GUN. . . . . NiB $515 Ex $309 Gd $206
Same general specifications as Grade I except has 28-inch plain bbl. w/Poly Choke. Disc. 1949.

MODEL 12 PUMP SHOTGUN
Special limited edition Winchester Model 12. Gauge: 20 or 28. Five-shot tubular magazine. 26-inch bbl., M choke. 45 inches overall. Weight: about 7 lbs. Grade I has blued receiver, checkered walnut stock w/matte finish. Grade V has engraved receiver, checkered deluxe walnut stock w/high-gloss finish. Made 1988-92. See illustration next page.
Grade I,
20 ga. (8600) . . . . NiB $580 Ex $464 Gd $315
Grade I, 28 ga. . . . . NiB $612 Ex $489 Gd $333
Grade V,
20 ga (4000) . . . . NiB $1024 Ex $819 Gd $556
Grade V, 28 ga . . . . NiB $998 Ex $798 Gd $543

MODEL 42 LIMITED EDITION SHOTGUN
Special limited edition Winchester Model 42 pump shotgun. Same general specifications as Model 12 except w/smaller frame in .410 ga. and 3-inch chamber. Made 1991-93.
Grade I
(6000 produced) . . . . NiB $638 Ex $510 Gd $347
Grade
(6000 produced) . . . . NiB $1024 Ex $819 Gd $557
2000 BUCK SPECIAL. . . . . NiB $406 Ex $324 Gd $220
Same as Field Model except has 24-inch plain bbl. Bored for rifled slug and buck shot, fitted w/rifle sights (open rear, ramp front). 12 ga., 2.75-inch or 3-inch chamber; 20 ga., 2.75-inch chamber. Weight: 12 ga., 7 lbs., 8 oz.; 20 ga., 6 lbs., 10 oz. Made 1974-81 by FN.

2000 GAS AUTOMATIC SHOTGUN, FIELD MODEL
Gas-operated. Gauge: 12 or 20. 2.75-inch chamber. Four-shot magazine. Bbl.: 26-, 28-, 30-inch, any standard choke plain matted bbl. (12 ga. only) or vent rib. Weight: 6 lbs. 11 oz.-7 lbs. 12 oz. depending on ga. and bbl. length. Checkered pistol-grip stock/forearm. Made 1974-81 by FN; Assembled in Port gal.
W/plain
matted bbl. . . . . NiB $567 Ex $335 Gd $232
W/vent rib bbl. . . . . NiB $577 Ex $361 Gd $237

2000 MAGNUM MODEL . . . . NiB $577 Ex $361 Gd $237
Same as Field Model except chambered for 3-inch shells, three-shot magazine. Bbl.: 26- (20 ga. only), 28-, 30- or 32-inch (latter two 12 ga. only); any standard choke; vent rib. Weight: 6 lbs., 11 oz.-7 lbs., 13 oz. depending on ga. and bbl. Made 1974-81 by FN.

SHOTGUNS

Browning Model 12 Limited Editon Grade I

Browning Model 12 Limited Editon Grade V

Browning Model 42 Limited Editon Grade V

Browning M2000 Vent Rib

Browning Model A-500

2000 SKEET MODEL . . . . **NiB $444 Ex $355 Gd $242**
Same as Field Model except has skeet-style stock w/recoil pad, 26-inch vent-rib bbl., SK choke. 12 or 20 ga., 2.75-inch chamber. Weight: 8 lbs., 1 oz. (12 ga.); 6 lbs., 12 oz. (20 ga.) Made 1974-81 by FN.

2000 TRAP MODEL . . . . **NiB $444 Ex $355 Gd $242**
Same as Field Model except has Monte Carlo stock w/recoil pad, 30- or 32-inch bbl. w/high-post vent rib and receiver extension, M/I/F chokes. 12 ga., 2.75-inch chamber. Weight: About 8 lbs., 5 oz. Made 1974-81 by FN.

A-500G GAS-OPERATED SEMIAUTOMATIC
Same general specifications as Browning Model A-500R except gas-operated. Made 1990-93.
Buck Special . . . . **NiB $568 Ex $458 Gd $318**
Hunting model . . . . **NiB $581 Ex $469 Gd $325**

A-500G SPORTING CLAYS . . . . **NiB $581 Ex $469 Gd $325**
Same general specifications as Model A-500G except has matte blued receiver w/"Sporting Clays" logo. 28- or 30-inch bbl. w/Invector choke tubes. Made 1992-93.

A-500R SEMIAUTOMATIC
Recoil-operated. Gauge: 12. 26- to 30-inch vent-rib bbls. 24-inch Buck Special. Invector choke tube system. 2.75- or 3-inch Magnum cartridges. Weight: 7 lbs., 3 oz.-8 lbs., 2 oz. Cross-bolt safety. Gold-plated trigger. Scroll-engraved receiver. Gloss-finished walnut stock

(cont'd.) **A-500R SEMIAUTOMATIC**
and forend. Made by FN from 1987-93.
Hunting model . . . . **NiB $573 Ex $458 Gd $312**
Buck Special . . . . **NiB $612 Ex $489 Gd $333**

A-BOLT SERIES SHOTGUN
Bolt-action repeating single-barrel shotgun. 12 ga. only w/3-inch chambers, 2-shot magazine. 22- or 23-inch rifled bbl., w/or w/o a rifled invector tube. Receiver drilled and tapped for scope mounts. Bbl. w/ or w/o open sights. Checkered walnut or graphite/fiberglass composite stock. Matte black metal finish. Imported 1995-98.
Stalker model w/
composite stock . . . . **NiB $406 Ex $324 Gd $220**
Hunter model w/walnut stock . . . . **NiB $386 Ex $309 Gd $210**
W/rifled bbl., add $95
W/open sights, add $25

AUTOLOADING SHOTGUNS, GRADES II, III AND IV
These higher grade models differ from the Standard or Grade I in general quality, grade of wood, checkering, engraving, etc., otherwise specifications are the same. Grade IV guns, sometimes called Midas Grade, are inlaid w/yellow and green gold. Disc. in 1940.
Grade II, plan bbl. . . . . **NiB $1390 Ex $1184 Gd $805**
Grade III, plain bbl. . . . . **NiB $2729 Ex $2369 Gd $1611**
Grade IV, plain bbl. . . . . **NiB $4094 Ex $3811 Gd $3621**
For raised matte rib bbl., add 15%
For vent rib bbl., add 30%

Browning Model A-Bolt Hunter

Browning Model A-Bolt Stalker

Browning Automatic-5 Gold Classic

Browning Automatic-5 Buck Special

Browning Automatic-5 Classic

AUTOMATIC-5, LIGHT 20

Same general specifications as Standard Model except lightweight and 20 ga. Bbl.: 26- or 28-inch; plain or vent rib. Weight: About 6.25-6.5 lbs. depending on bbl. Made 1958-76 by FN, since then by Miroku.

FN manuf., plain bbl..	NiB $663	Ex $530	Gd $360
FN manuf., vent-rib bbl.	NiB $876	Ex $798	Gd $463
Miroku manuf., vent rib,fixed choke	NiB $798	Ex $613	Gd $309
Miroku manuf., vent rib, invectors	NiB $850	Ex $670	Gd $360

AUTOMATIC-5, BUCK SPECIAL MODELS

Same as Light 12, Magnum 12, Light 20, Magnum 20, in respective gauges, except 24-inch plain bbl. bored for rifled slug and buckshot, fitted w/rifle sights (open rear, ramp front). Weight: 6.13-8.25 lbs. depending on ga. Made 1964-76 by FN, since then by Miroku.

FN manuf., w/plain bbl.	NiB $876	Ex $613	Gd $350
Miroku manuf.,	NiB $747	Ex $566	Gd $335
W/3-inch mag. rec., add			10%

AUTOMATIC-5 CLASSIC ...... NiB $1128 Ex $876 Gd $773
Gauge: 12. 5-shot capacity. 28-inch vent rib bbl./M choke. 2.75-

(cont'd.) AUTOMATIC-5 CLASSIC

inch chamber. Engraved silver-gray receiver. Gold-plated trigger. Crossbolt safety. High-grade, hand-checkered select American walnut stock w/rounded pistol grip. 5,000 issued; made in Japan in 1984, engraved in Belgium.

AUTOMATIC-5 GOLD CLASSIC..... NiB $3914 Ex $3244 Gd $2369

Same general specifications as Automatic-5 Classic except engraved receiver inlaid w/gold. Pearl border on stock and forend plus fine-line hand-checkering. Each gun numbered "1 of Five Hundred," etc. 500 issued in 1984; made in Belgium.

AUTOMATIC-5, LIGHT 12

12 ga. only. Same general specifications as Standard Model except lightweight (about 7.25 lbs.), has gold-plated trigger. Guns w/rib have striped matting on top of bbl. Fixed chokes or Invector tubes. Made 1948-76 by FN, since then by Miroku.

FN manuf., plain bbl.	NiB $580	Ex $463	Gd $315
FN manuf., raised matte rib	NiB $670	Ex $566	Gd $438
FN manuf., ventilated rib	NiB $876	Ex $747	Gd $463
Miroku manuf., vent rib, fixed choke	NiB $580	Ex $463	Gd $315
Miroku manuf., vent rib, invectors	NiB $798	Ex $613	Gd $360

Browning Auto-5 Sweet Sixteen (New Model)

Browning Model B-80 Upland Special

Browning BPS Hunter

Browning BPS Youth & Ladies Model

AUTOMATIC-5, MAGNUM 12 GAUGE
Same general specifications as Standard Model. Chambered for 3-inch Magnum 12-ga. shells. Bbl.: 28-inch M/F, 30- or 32-inch F/F, plain or vent rib. Weight: 8.5-9 lbs. depending on bbl. Buttstock has recoil pad. Made 1958-76 by FN, since then by Miroku. Fixed chokes or Invector tubes.

FN manuf., plain bbl. . . . . NiB $792 Ex $633 Gd $431
FN manuf., vent rib bbl. . . . . NiB $858 Ex $687 Gd $467
Miroku manuf., vent rib, fixed chokes . . NiB $644 Ex $515 Gd $350
Miroku manuf., vent rib, invectors . . . . NiB $732 Ex $586 Gd $399

AUTOMATIC-5, MAGNUM 20 GAUGE
Same general specifications as Standard Model except chambered for 3-inch Magnum 20-ga. shell. Bbl.: 26- or 28-inch, plain or vent rib. Weight: 7 lbs., 5 oz.-7 lbs., 7 oz. depending on bbl. Made 1967-76 by FN, since then by Miroku.

FN manuf., plain bbl. . . . . NiB $785 Ex $628 Gd $427
FN manuf., vent rib bbl. . . . . NiB $829 Ex $649 Gd $450
Miroku manuf., vent rib, invectors . NiB $649 Ex $519 Gd $352

AUTOMATIC-5, SKEET MODEL
12 ga. only. Same general specifications as Light 12. Bbl.: 26-or 28-inch, plain or vent rib, SK choke. Weight: 7 lbs., 5 oz.-7 lbs., 10 oz. depending on bbl. Made by FN prior to 1976, since then by Miroku.

FN manuf., plain bbl. . . . . NiB $732 Ex $586 Gd $399
FN manuf., vent rib bbl. . . . . NiB $777 Ex $621 Gd $422
Miroku manuf., vent rib bbl. . . . . . NiB $585 Ex $468 Gd $318

AUTOMATIC-5 STALKER
Same general specifications as Automatic-5 Light and Magnum models except w/matte blue finish and black graphite fiberglass

(cont'd.) AUTOMATIC-5 STALKER
stock and forearm. Made 1992 to date.
Light model . . . . NiB $796 Ex $6377 Gd $434
Magnum model . . . . NiB $845 Ex $676 Gd $459

AUTOMATIC-5, STANDARD (GRADE I)
Recoil-operated. Gauge: 12 or 16 (16-gauge guns made prior to WW II were chambered for 2-inch shells; standard 16 disc. 1964). Four shell magazine in 5-shot model, prewar guns were also available in 3-shot model. Bbls.: 26- to 32-inch; plain, raised matted or vent rib; choice of standard chokes. Weight: About 8 lbs., in 12 ga., 7.5 lbs., in 16 ga. Checkered pistol-grip stock and forearm. (Note: Browning Special, disc. about 1940.) Made 1900-73 by FN.

Grade I, plain bbl. . . . . NiB $636 Ex $508 Gd $346
Grade I or Browning Special,
Raised matted rib . . . . NiB $812 Ex $650 Gd $441
Grade I or Browning Special, vent rib . . . . NiB $836 Ex $670 Gd $455

AUTOMATIC-5, SWEET 16
16 ga. Same general specifications as Standard Model except light-weight (about 6.75 lbs.), has gold plated trigger. Guns w/rib have striped matting on top of bbl. Made 1937-76 by FN.

W/plain bbl. . . . . $NiB $724 Ex $579 Gd $393
W/raised matted or ventilated rib . . . . NiB $796 Ex $637 Gd $434

AUTO-5,
SWEET SIXTEEN NEW MODEL . . . . NiB $892 Ex $714 Gd $485
Reissue of popular 16-gauge Hunting Model w/5-shot capacity, 2.75-inch chamber, scroll-engraved blued receiver, high-gloss French walnut stock w/rounded pistol grip. 26- or 28-inch vent-rib bbl. F choke tube. Weight: 7 lbs., 5 oz. Reintro. 1987-93.

Browning BPS
Waterfowl – Mossy Oak Shadow Grass

Browning BPS Stalker

AUTOMATIC-5, TRAP MODEL .... NiB $876 Ex $669 Gd $412
12 ga. only. Same general specifications as Standard Model except
has trap-style stock, 30-inch vent-rib bbl. F choke. Weight: 8.5 lbs.
Disc. 1971.

MODEL B-80 GAS-OPERATED
AUTOMATIC .... NiB $509 Ex $407 Gd $277
Gauge: 12 or 20; 2.75-inch chamber. Four shot magazine. Bbl.: 26-, 28-
or 30-inch, any standard choke, vent-rib bbl. w/fixed chokes or Invector
tubes. Weight: 6 lbs., 12 oz.-8 lbs., 1 oz. depending on ga. and bbl.
Checkered pistol-grip stock and forearm. Made 1981-87.

MODEL B-80 PLUS .... NiB $560 Ex $448 Gd $305
Same general specifications as Browning Model B-80 except chambered for 3-inch shotshells. Made 1988 only.

MODEL B-80 SUPERLIGHT .... NiB $509 Ex $407 Gd $277
Same as Standard Model except weighs 1 lb. less.

MODEL B-80 UPLAND SPECIAL .. NiB $521 Ex $417 Gd $283
Gauge: 12 or 20. 22-inch vent-rib bbl. Invector choke tube system.
2.75-inch chambers. 42 inches overall. Weight: 5 lbs., 7 oz. (20 ga.);
6 lbs., 10 oz. (12 ga.). German nickel silver sight bead. Crossbolt
safety. Checkered walnut straight-grip stock and forend. Disc. 1988.

BPS GAME GUN DEER SPECIAL ... NiB $451 Ex $360 Gd $245
Same general specifications as Standard BPS model except has
20.5-inch bbl. w/adj. rifle-style sights. Solid scope mounting system. Checkered walnut stock w/sling swivel studs. Made from
1992 to date.

BPS GAME GUN TURKEY SPECIAL ...... NiB $464 Ex $371 Gd $252
Same general specifications as Standard BPS model except w/matte
blue metal finish and satin-finished stock. Chambered for 12 ga. 3-
inch only. 20.5-inch bbl. w/extra full invector choke system.
Receiver drilled and tapped for scope. Made 1992 to date.

BPS PIGEON GRADE .... NiB $612 Ex $489 Gd $333
Same general specifications as Standard BPS model except w/select
grade walnut stock and gold-trimmed receiver. Available in 12 ga.
only w/26- or 28-inch vent-rib bbl. Made 1992 to date.

BPS PUMP INVECTOR STALKER
Same general specifications as BPS Pump Shotgun except in 10
and 12 ga. w/Invector choke system, 22-, 26-, 28- or 30-inch
bbls.; matte blue metal finish w/matte black stock. Made 1987
to date.
12 ga. model (3-inch) .... NiB $432 Ex $345 Gd $235
10- & 12 ga. model (3.5-inch) .... NiB $598 Ex $479 Gd $325

BPS PUMP SHOTGUN
Takedown. Gauges: 10, 12 (3.5-inch chamber); 12, 20 and .410 (3-
inch) and 28 ga. chambered 2.75-inch. Bbls.: 22-, 24-, 26-, 28-, 30-,
or 32-inch; fixed choke or Invector tubes. Weight: 7.5 lbs. (w/28-inch
bbl.). Checkered select walnut pistol-grip stock and semi-beavertail
forearm, recoil pad. Introduced in 1977. Made by Miroku.
Model BPS Magnum Hunter .... NiB $612 Ex $489 Gd $333
Model BPS Magnum Stalker .... NiB $592 Ex $474 Gd $322
Model BPS Magnum Camo .... NiB $669 Ex $536 Gd $365
Model BPS Hunter .... NiB $509 Ex $407 Gd $277
Model BPS Upland .... NiB $509 Ex $407 Gd $277
Model BPS Stalker (26- 28- or 30-inch bbl.) ... NiB $489 Ex $391 Gd $266
Model BPS Stalker 24-inch bbl .... NiB $515 Ex $412 Gd $280
Model BPS Game Gun—Turkey Special ...... NiB $547 Ex $438 Gd $298
Model BPS Game Gun—fully rifled bbl....... NiB $618 Ex $494 Gd $336
Model BPS Hunter 20 ga. .... NiB $509 Ex $407 Gd $277
Model BPS Upland 20 ga. .... NiB $509 Ex $407 Gd $277
Model BPS Micro .... NiB $509 Ex $407 Gd $277
Model BPS Hunter 28 ga. .... NiB $541 Ex $433 Gd $295
Model BPS Bore Hunter .410 .... NiB $541 Ex $433 Gd $295
Model BPS Buck Spec. (10 or 12 ga., 3.5-inch) .... NiB $580 Ex $464 Gd $315
Model BPS Buck Spec. (12 or 20 ga.) .... NiB $406 Ex $324 Gd $220
Model BPS Waterfowl
(10 or 12 ga., 3.5-inch) .... NiB $638 Ex $510 Gd $347
W/fixed choke, deduct $50

BPS YOUTH AND LADIES' MODEL
Lightweight (6 lbs., 11 oz.) version of BPS Pump Shotgun in 20 ga. w/22-
inch bbl. and floating vent rib, F choke (invector) tube. Made 1986 to date.
Standard Invector model (disc. 1994) .... NiB $380 Ex $304 Gd $207
Invector Plus model .... NiB $418 Ex $335 Gd $228

BSA 10 SEMIAUTOMATIC SHOTGUN
Gas-operated short-stroke action. 10 ga.; 3.5-inch chamber. Five shot magazine. Bbls.: 26-, 28-or 30-inch w/Invector tubes and vent rib. Weight: 10.5
lbs. Checkered select walnut buttstock and forend. Blued finish. Made 1993
to date. Note: Although intro. as the BSA 10, this model is now marketed
as the Gold Series. See separate listing for pricing.

B-SS SIDE-BY-SIDE
Boxlock. Automatic ejectors. Non-selective single trigger (early production) or selective-single trigger (late production). Gauges: 12 or
20 w/3-inch chambers. Bbls.: 26-, 28-, or 30-inch; IC/M, M/F, or F/F
chokes; matte solid rib. Weight: 7 to 7.5 lbs. Checkered straight-grip
stock and beavertail forearm. Made 1972-88 by Miroku.
Standard model (early/NSST) .... NiB $547 Ex $438 Gd $298
Standard model (late/SST) .... NiB $638 Ex $510 Gd $347
Grade II (antique silver receiver) .... NiB $1095 Ex $876 Gd $595
20 ga. models, add $100

Browning B-SS 20 Gauge Sporter

Browning BT-99 Competition Trap

B-SS SIDE-BY-SIDE SIDELOCK
Same general specifications as B-SS boxlock models except sidelock version available in 26- or 28-inch bbl. lengths. 26-inch choked IC/M; 28-inch, M/F. Double triggers. Satin-grayed receiver engraved w/rosettes and scrolls. German nickel-silver sight bead. Weight: 6.25 lbs. to 6 lbs., 11 oz. 12 ga. made in 1983; 20 ga. Made in 1984. Disc. 1988.
12 ga. model . . . . NiB $922 Ex $695 Gd $979
20 ga. model . . . . NiB $2464 Ex $1971 Gd $1341

B-SS S/S 20 GAUGE SPORTER . . . . NiB $743 Ex $594 Gd $404
Same as standard B-SS 20 ga. except has selective single trigger, straight-grip stock. Introduced 1977. Disc. 1987.

BT-99 GRADE I SINGLE BBL. TRAP . . . . . . NiB $799 Ex $640 Gd $435
Boxlock. Automatic ejector. 12 ga. only. 32- or 34-inch vent rib bbl., M, IM or F choke. Weight: About 8 lbs. Checkered pistol-grip stock and beavertail forearm, recoil pad. Made 1971-76 by Miroku.

BT-99 MAX
Boxlock. 12 ga. only w/ejector selector and no safety. 32- or 34-inch ported bbl. w/high post vent rib. Checkered select walnut buttstock and finger-grooved forend w/high luster finish. Engraved receiver w/blued or stainless metal finish. Made 1995-96.
Blued . . . . NiB $1177 Ex $941 Gd $641
Stainless . . . . NiB $1769 Ex $1415 Gd $962

BT-99 PLUS
Similar to the BT-99 Competition except w/Browning Recoil Reduction System. Made 1989-95.
Grade I . . . . NiB $1153 Ex $922 Gd $627
Pigeon grade . . . . NiB $1319 Ex $1056 Gd $718
Signature grade . . . . NiB $1281 Ex $1025 Gd $697
Stainless model . . . . NiB $1410 Ex $1128 Gd $767
Golden Clays . . . . NiB $2440 Ex $2261 Gd $2003

BT-99 PLUS MICRO . . . . NiB $1191 Ex $953 Gd $648
Same general specifications as BT-99 Plus except scaled down for smaller shooters. 30-inch bbl. w/adj. rib and Browning's recoil reducer system. Made 1991 to date.

BT-100 COMPETITION TRAP SPECIAL
Same as BT-99 except has super-high wide rib and standard Monte Carlo or fully adj. stock. Available w/adj. choke or Invector Plus tubes w/optional porting. Made 1976-94.
Grade I w/fixed
choke (disc. 1992). . . . . NiB $882 Ex $726 Gd $480
Grade I w/Invectors . . . . NiB $1095 Ex $876 Gd $595
Grade I stainless (disc. 1994) . . . . NiB $1153 Ex $922 Gd $627
Grade I Pigeon Grade (disc. 1994) . . . . . NiB $1062 Ex $850 Gd $578

BT-100 SINGLE-SHOT TRAP
Similar to the BT-99 Max, except w/additional stock options and removable trigger group. Made 1995 to date.
Model BT-100 Grade I blued. . . . . NiB $1416 Ex $1133 Gd $770
Model BT-100 stainless . . . . NiB $1642 Ex $1313 Gd $893
Model BT-100 satin . . . . NiB $1319 Ex $1056 Gd $718
Model BT-100 w/adj. comb, add $250
Thumbhole stock, add $295
Replacement trigger assembly, add $495
Fixed choke, deduct $65

CITORI HUNTING O/U MODELS
Boxlock. Gauges: 12, 16 (disc. 1989), 20, 28 (disc. 1992) and .410 bore (disc. 1989). Bbl. lengths: 24-, 26-, 28-, or 30-inch w/vent rib. Chambered 2.75-, 3- or 3.5-inch mag. Chokes: IC/M, M/F (Fixed Chokes); Standard Invector, or Invector plus choke systems. Overall length ranges from 41-47 inches. 2.75-, 3- or 3-inch Mag. loads, depending on ga. Weight: 5.75 lbs. to 7 lbs. 13 oz. Single selective, gold-plated trigger. Medium raised German nickel-silver sight bead. Checkered, rounded pistol-grip walnut stock w/beavertail forend. Invector Chokes and Invector Plus became standard in 1988 and 1995, respectively. Made from 1973 to date by Miroku.
Grade I (disc. 1994) . . . . NiB $804 Ex $644 Gd $438
Grade I - 3.5-inch Mag.(1989 to date) . . . NiB $1088 Ex $870 Gd $592
Grade II (disc. 1983). . . . . NiB $998 Ex $798 Gd $543
Grade III (1985-95) . . . . NiB $1153 Ex $922 Gd $627
Grade V (disc. 1984) . . . . NiB $1610 Ex $1288 Gd $876
Grade VI (1985-95) . . . . NiB $1796 Ex $1437 Gd $977
Model Sporting Hunter
(12 and 20 ga.; 1998 to date) . . . . NiB $966 Ex $773 Gd $525
Model Satin Hunter
(12 ga. only; 1998 to date). . . . . NiB $869 Ex $695 Gd $473
Mdls. w/o Inv. choke syst., deduct $120
For 3.5-inch Mag., add $90
For disc. ga 16, 28 and .410, add 15%

CITORI LIGHTNING O/U MODELS
Same general specifications as the Citori Hunting models except w/classic Browning rounded pistol-grip stock. Made from 1988 to date by Miroku.
Grade I . . . . NiB $824 Ex $659 Gd $448
Grade III . . . . NiB $1242 Ex $994 Gd $676
Grade VI . . . . NiB $1796 Ex $1437 Gd $977
Gran Lightning model . . . . NiB $1319 Ex $1056 Gd $718
Feather Model (alloy receiver) . . . . NiB $998 Ex $798 Gd $543
Feather Combo model (2-bbl. set) . . . . NiB $2382 Ex $1906 Gd $1296
Privilege Mdl. (engraved w/sideplates) . . . . NiB $4629 Ex $3703 Gd $2518
Micro model, add 10%
Models w/o Invector
choke system, deduct $120
28 and .410 ga., add 15%

Browning BT-100 Monte Carlo Stock

Browning BT-100 Competition Trap

Browning Citori Lightning

Browning Citori Gran Lightning

Browning Citori Skeet Gun

CITORI SKEET GUN

Same as Hunting model except has skeet-style stock and forearm, 26- or 28-inch bbls., both bored SK choke. Available w/either standard vent rib or special target-type, high-post, wide vent rib. Weight (w/26-inch bbls.): 12 ga., 8 lbs., 20 ga., 7 lbs. Made 1974 to date by Miroku.

Grade I . . . . NiB $1437 Ex $978 Gd $566
Grade II . . . . NiB $1095 Ex $876 Gd $595
Grade III . . . . NiB $1281 Ex $1025 Gd $697
Grade VI (disc. 1995) . . . . NiB $1925 Ex $1540 Gd $1048
Golden Clays. . . . . NiB $2125 Ex $1700 Gd $1156
28 and .410 ga., add 15%
3-bbl. Set, Grade I (disc. 1996). . . . . . . NiB $2254 Ex $1803 Gd $1226
3-bbl. Set, Grade III (disc. 1996) . . . . . NiB $2440 Ex $1952 Gd $1318
3-bbl. Set, Grade VI (disc. 1994). . . . . . NiB $2769 Ex $2214 Gd $1506
3-bbl. Set, Golden Clays (disc. 1995) . . . . NiB $3599 Ex $27879 Gd $1958
4-bbl. Set, Grade I . . . . NiB $3295 Ex $2636 Gd $1792
4-bbl. Set, Grade III . . . . NiB $3670 Ex $2935 Gd $1996
4-bbl. Set, Grade VI (disc. 1994). . . . . . NiB $3599 Ex $3085 Gd $2139
4-bbl. Set, Golden Clays (disc. 1995) . . NiB $4571 Ex $3657 Gd $2486

CITORI SPORTING CLAYS

Similar to the standard Citori Lightning model except Classic-style stock with rounded pistol-grip. 30-inch back-bored bbls. with Invector Plus tubes. Receiver with "Lightning Sporting Clays Edition" logo. Made 1989 to date.

(cont'd.) CITORI SPORTING CLAYS

GTI model (disc. 1995). . . . . NiB $1262 Ex $876 Gd $541
GTI Golden Clays model (1993-94) . . . NiB $1925 Ex $1540 Gd $1048
Lightning model (intro. 1989). . . . . NiB $1113 Ex $891 Gd $606
Lightning Golden Clays (1993-98) . . . . NiB $1996 Ex $1596 Gd $1086
Lightning Pigeon Grade (1993-94) . . . . . . NiB $1191 Ex $953 Gd $648
Micro Citori Lightning model
(w/low rib) . . . . NiB $1327 Ex $876 Gd $556
Special Sporting model (intro. 1989) . . . . NiB $1359 Ex $901 Gd $580
Special Sporting
Golden Clays (1993-98) . . . . NiB $2286 Ex $1828 Gd $1243
Special Sporting Pigeon Gr. (1993-94) . . . NiB $1224 Ex $979 Gd $665
Ultra mdl. (intro. 1995-previously GTI) . NiB $1256 Ex $1004 Gd $683
Ultra Golden Clays (intro. 1995) . . . . . NiB $2311 Ex $1849 Gd $1258
Model 325 (1993-94) . . . . NiB $1191 Ex $953 Gd $648
Model 325 Golden Clays (1993-94) . . . NiB $1963 Ex $1571 Gd $1068
Model 425 Grade I (intro. 1995) . . . . . . NiB $1281 Ex $1025 Gd $697
Model 425 Golden Clays (intro. 1995) . . . . NiB $2311 Ex $1849 Gd $1258
Model 425 WSSF (intro. 1995) . . . . NiB $1224 Ex $979 Gd $665
Model 802 Sporter (ES)
Extended Swing (intro. 1996 . . . . NiB $1352 Ex $1082 Gd $735
For 2 bbl. set add $850
For adjustable stock, add $200
For high rib, add $85
For ported barrels, add $65

Browning Citori Superlight Field Shotgun

Browning Citori Trap

Browning Citori White Lightning Over/Under

Browning Citori Sporting Hunter Over/Under

Browning Gold Hunter

Browning Liége Over/Under Shotgun

CITORI SUPERLIGHT O/U FIELD SHOTGUNS
Similar to the Citori Hunting model except w/straight-grip stock and Schnabel forend tip. Made by Miroku 1982 to date.

Grade I . . . . NiB $1256 Ex $1004 Gd $683
Grade III . . . . NiB $1666 Ex $1332 Gd $906
Grade V (disc. 1985) . . . . NiB $2167 Ex $1733 Gd $1179
Grade VI . . . . NiB $2502 Ex $2001 Gd $1364
Models w/o Invector choke system, deduct $120
28 and .410 ga., add 15%

CITORI TRAP GUN
Same as Hunting model except 12 ga. only, has Monte Carlo or fully adjustable stock and beavertail forend, trap-style recoil pad; 20- or 32-inch bbls.; M/F, IM/F, or F/F. Available with either standard vent rib or special target-type, high-post, wide vent rib. Weight: 8 lbs. Made from 1974 to date by Miroku.

(cont'd.) CITORI TRAP GUN
Grade I Trap. . . . . NiB $1380 Ex $1104 Gd $751
Grade I Trap Pigeon grade (disc. 1994) . NiB $1666 Ex $1332 Gd $9065
Grade I Trap Signature grade (disc. 1994) . . . NiB $1632 Ex $1305 Gd $887
Grade I Plus Trap (disc. 1994) . . . NiB $1715 Ex $1372 Gd $933
Grade I Plus Trap
w/ported bbls. (disc. 1994) . . . . . NiB $1832 Ex $1465 Gd $997
Grade I Plus Trap
Combo (disc. 1994) . . . . NiB $3975 Ex $3180 Gd $2162
Grade I Plus Trap
Golden Clays (disc. 1994) . . . . . NiB $1715 Ex $1372 Gd $933
Grade II w/HP rib (disc. 1984) . . NiB $1498 Ex $1198 Gd $815
Grade III Trap . . . . NiB $1832 Ex $1466 Gd $997
Grade V Trap (disc. 1984) . . . . . NiB $2000 Ex $1600 Gd $1088
Grade VI Trap (disc. 1994). . . . . NiB $2335 Ex $1867 Gd $1270
Grade VI Trap
Golden Clays (disc. 1994) . . . . NiB $2837 Ex $2269 Gd $1543

CITORI UPLAND SPECIAL O/U SHOTGUN
A shortened version of the Hunting model fitted with 24-inch bbls. and straight-grip stock.

Upland Special 12, 20 ga. models. . . . . . NiB $1130 Ex $903 Gd $614
Upland Spec. 16 ga. mdl. (disc. 1989) . . NiB $1331 Ex $1064 Gd $724
Models w/o Inv. choke sys., deduct $120

CITORI WHITE LIGHTNING O/U SHOTGUN
Similar to the standard Citori Lightning model except w/silver nitride receiver w/scroll and rosette engraving. Satin wood finish w/round pistol grip. Made 1998 to date.

12, 20 ga. models. . . . . NiB $1331   Ex $1064   Gd $724
28, .410 ga. models (Intro. 2000) . . . . . NiB $1447   Ex $1158   Gd $787

CITORI WHITE UPLAND SPECIAL . . . . . . NiB $1163   Ex $930   Gd $632
Similar to the standard Citori Upland model except w/silver nitride receiver w/scroll and rosette engraving. Satin wood finish w/round pistol grip. Made 2000 to date.

DOUBLE AUTOMATIC (STEEL RECEIVER)
Short recoil system. Takedown. 12 ga. only. Two shots. Bbls.: 26-, 28-, 30-inch; any standard choke. Checkered pistol-grip stock and forend. Weight: About 7.75 lbs. Made 1955-1961.

With plain bbl. . . . . NiB $598 Ex $479 Gd $325
With recessed-rib bbl. . . . . NiB $760 Ex $608 Gd $413

GOLD DEER HUNTER AUTOLOADING SHOTGUN
Similar to the Standard Gold Hunter model except chambered 12 ga. only. 22-inch bbl. W/rifled bore or smooth bore w/5-inch rifled invector tube. Cantilevered scope mount. Made 1997 to date.

Gold Deer Hunter (w/standard finish) . . . . NiB $760 Ex $608 Gd $413
Field model (w/Mossy Oak finish) . . . . . . NiB $638 Ex $510 Gd $347

GOLD HUNTER SERIES
Self-cleaning, gas-operated, short-stroke action. Gauges: 10 or 12 (3.5-inch chamber); 12 or 20 (3-inch chamber). 26-, 28-, or 30-inch bbl. w/Invector or Invector Plus choke tubes. Checkered walnut stock. Polished or matte black metal finish. Made 1994 to date.

Gold Hunter (Light 10 ga. 3.5-inch w/wal. St.) . . . . NiB $856 Ex $685 Gd $466
Gold Hunter (12 ga. 3.5-inch) . . . . NiB $804 Ex $644 Gd $438
Gold Hunter (12 or 20 ga. 3-inch) . . . . NiB $515 Ex $412 Gd $280
Gld. Hunter Clas. Mdl. (12 or 20 Ga. 3-inch) . . . . . NiB $547 Ex $438 Gd $298
Gld. Hunter High Gr.
Classic (12 or 20 ga. 3-inch) . . . . NiB $1127 Ex $901 Gd $613
Gold Deer Hunter
(12 ga. w/22-inch bbl.) . . . . NiB $580 Ex $464 Gd $315
Gold Turkey Hunter Camo
(12 ga. w/24-inch bbl.) . . . . NiB $534 Ex $427 Gd $290
Gold Waterfowl Hunter
Camo (12 ga. w/24-inch bbl.) . . . . NiB $515 Ex $412 Gd $280

GOLD STALKER SERIES
Self-cleaning, gas-operated, short-stroke action. Gauges: 10 or 12 (3.5-inch chamber); 12 or 20 (3-inch chamber). 26-, 28-, or 30-inch bbl. w/Invector or Invector Plus choke tubes. Graphite/fiberglass composite stock. Polished or matte black metal finish. Made 1998 to date.

Gold Stalker (Light 10 ga.
3.5-inch w/composite stock). . . . . NiB $837 Ex $669 Gd $455
Gold Stalker (12 ga. 3.5-inch) . . . . NiB $766 Ex $613 Gd $417
Gold Stalker (12 or 20 ga. 3-inch) . . . . NiB $509 Ex $407 Gd $277
Gold Stalker Classic
Model (12 or 20 ga. 3-inch) . . . . NiB $515 Ex $412 Gd $280
Gold Deer Stalker
(12 ga. w/22-inch bbl.) . . . . NiB $580 Ex $464 Gd $315
Gold Turkey Stalker Camo
(12 ga. w/24-inch bbl.) . . . . NiB $534 Ex $427 Gd $290

Browning Over/Under Gold Classic

(cont'd.) GOLD STALKER SERIES
Gold Waterfowl Stalker
Camo (12 Ga. w/24-inch bbl.) . . . . NiB $901 Ex $474 Gd $412

GOLD SPORTING SERIES
Similar to Gold Hunter Series except w/2.75-inch chamber and 28- or 30-inch ported bbl. w/Invector Plus chokes. Made 1999 to date.

Gold Sporting Clays (standard) . . . . NiB $786 Ex $670 Gd $521
Gold Sporting Clays (youth or ladies) . . . . . NiB $804 Ex $685 Gd $531
Gold Sporting Clays w/Eng. nick. rec. . . . NiB $1230 Ex $1025 Gd $763

LIEGE O/U SHOTGUN (B26/27)
Boxlock. Automatic ejectors. Non-selective single trigger. 12 ga. only. Bbls.: 26.5-, 28-, or 30-inch; 2.75-inch chambers in 26.5- and 28-inch, 3-inch in 30-inch, IC/M, M/F, or F/F chokes; vent rib. Weight: 7 lbs., 4 oz. to 7 lbs., 14 oz., depending on bbls. Checkered pistol-grip stock and forearm. Made 1973-75 by FN.

Liège (B-26 BAC production) . . . . NiB $881 Ex $705 Gd $479
Liège (B-27 FN prod.) Stand. Game Mdl. . . NiB $851 Ex $681 Gd $462
Deluxe Game model . . . . NiB $962 Ex $769 Gd $523
Grand Delux Game model . . . . NiB $1177 Ex $941 Gd $641
Deluxe Skeet model . . . . NiB $999 Ex $799 Gd $543
Deluxe Trap model . . . . NiB $984 Ex $787 Gd $535
COL Commemorative model . . . . NiB $1407 Ex $1125 Gd $764

LIGHT SPORTING 802ES . . . . . . NiB $1281 Ex $1025 Gd $697
Over/under. Invector-plus choke tubes. 12 ga. only with 28-inch bbl. Weight: 7 lbs., 5 oz.

LIGHTNING SPORTING CLAYS
Similar to the standard Citori Lightning model except Classic-style stock with rounded pistol grip. 30-inch back-bored bbls. with Invector Plus tubes. Receiver with "Lightning Sporting Clays Edition" logo. Made 1989 to date.

Standard model . . . . NiB $1129 Ex $876 Gd $590
Pigeon grade . . . . NiB $1191 Ex $953 Gd $648

O/U CLASSIC . . . . NiB $2125 Ex $1700 Gd $1156
Gauge: 20, 2.75-inch chambers. 26-inch blued bbls. choked IC/M. Gold-plated, single selective trigger. Manual, top-tang-mounted safety. Engraved receiver. High grade, select American walnut straight-grip stock with Schnabel forend. Fine-line checkering with pearl borders. High-gloss finish. 5,000 issued in 1986; made in Japan, engraved in Belgium.

O/U GOLD CLASSIC . . . . NiB $5144 Ex $4115 Gd $2799
Same general specifications as Over/Under Classic except more elaborate engravings, enhanced in gold, including profile of John M. Browning. Fine oil finish. 500 issued; made in 1986 in Belgium.

RECOILLESS TRAP SHOTGUN
The action and bbl. are driven forward when firing to achieve 72 percent less recoil. 12 ga, 2.75-inch chamber. 30-inch bbl. with Invector Plus tubes; adjustable vent rib. 51.63 inches overall. Weight: 9 lbs. Adj. checkered walnut buttstock and forend. Blued finish. Made from 1993-96.

Browning Superposed Broadway 12 Trap

Browning Superposed Grade I Lightning

Left Side

Right Side

Browning Superposed Bicentennial

Browning Superposed Grade IV Diana (Postwar)

Browning Superposed Grade V Midas (Postwar)

(cont'd.) RECOILLESS TRAP SHOTGUN
Standard model . . . . NiB $869 Ex $695 Gd $473
Micro model (27-inch bbl.) . . . . NiB $895 Ex $716 Gd $487
Signature model (27-inch bbl.) . . . . NiB $1309 Ex $1048 Gd $745

SUPERPOSED BICENTENNIAL
COMMEMORATIVE . . . . NiB $13,197 Ex $10,558 Gd $7180
Special limited edition issued to commemorate U.S. Bicentennial.
51 guns, one for each state in the Union plus one for Washington,
D.C. Receiver with sideplates has engraved and gold-inlaid hunter
and wild turkey on right side, U.S. flag and bald eagle on left side,
together with state markings inlaid in gold, on blued background.
Checkered straight-grip stock and Schnabel-style forearm of highly-
figured American walnut. Velvet-lined wood presentation case.
Made in 1976 by FN. Value shown is for gun in new, unfired condition. See illustration next page.

SUPERPOSED
BROADWAY 12 TRAP . . . . NiB $1963 Ex $1571 Gd $1067
Same as Standard Trap Gun except has 30- or 32-inch bbls. with
wider Broadway rib. Disc. 1976.

SUPERPOSED SHOTGUNS, HUNTING MODELS
Over/under boxlock. Selective automatic ejectors. Selective single
trigger; earlier models (worth 25% less) supplied w/double triggers,
twin selective triggers or non-selective single trigger. Gauges: 12, 20
(intro. 1949, 3-inch chambers in later production), 28, .410 (latter
two ga. intro. 1960). Bbls.: 26.5-, 28-, 30-, 32-inch, raised matted
or vent rib, prewar Lightning Model made w/ribbed bbl., postwar
version supplied only w/vent rib; any combination of standard
chokes. Weight (w/26.5-inch vent-rib bbls.): Standard 12, 7 lbs., 11
oz., Lightning 12, 7 lbs., 6 oz.; Standard 20, 6 lbs., 8 oz.; Lightning
20, 6 lbs., 4 oz.; Lightning 28, 6 lbs., 7 oz.; Lightning .410, 6 lbs.,
10 oz. Checkered pistol-grip stock/forearm.
Higher grades (Pigeon, Pointer, Diana, Midas, Grade VI) differ from
standard Grade I models in overall quality, engraving, wood and
checkering; otherwise, specifications are the same. Midas Grade
and Grade VI guns are richly gold inlaid. Made by FN 1928-1976.
Prewar models may be considered as disc. in 1940 when Belgium
was occupied by Germany. Grade VI offered 1955-1960. Pointer
Grade disc. in 1966, Grade I Standard in 1973, Pigeon Grade in
1974. Lightning Grade I, Diana and Midas Grades were not offered
after 1976.
Grade I standard weight . . . . NiB $1692 Ex $1353 Gd $921
Grade I Lightning . . . . NiB $2054 Ex $1643 Gd $1117
Grade I Lightning, prewar,
matted bbl., no rib . . . . NiB $2996 Ex $2373 Gd $1614
Grade II—Pigeon . . . . NiB $3109 Ex $2486 Gd $1691

Browning Superposed Ltd.
Pintail Duck Issue

(cont'd.) **SUPERPOSED SHOTGUNS**

Grade III—Pointer . . . . NiB $3026 Ex $2420 Gd $1646
Grade IV—Diana . . . . NiB $3727 Ex $2982 Gd $2028
Grade V—Midas . . . . NiB $9335 Ex $7468 Gd $5078
Grade VI . . . . NiB $6303 Ex $5042 Gd $3429
Add for 20 ga. 20%
Add for 28 ga. 75%
Add for .410. . . . . 45%
Values shown are for models w/ventilated rib.
If gun has raised matted rib, deduct 10%

**SUPERPOSED LIGHTNING AND SUPERLIGHT MODELS
(REISSUE B-25)**
Reissue of popular 12-and 20-ga. Superposed shotguns. Lightning models available in 26.5- and 28-inch bbl. lengths w/2.75- or 3-inch chambering, full pistol grip. Superlight models available in 26.5-inch bbl. lengths w/2.75-inch chambering only, and straight-grip stock w/Schnabel forend. Both have hand-engraved receivers, fine-line checkering, gold-plated single selective trigger, automatic selective ejectors, manual safety. Weight: 6 to 7.5 lbs. Reintroduced 1985.

Grade I, Standard . . . . NiB $1668 Ex $1334 Gd $907
Grade II, Pigeon . . . . NiB $3084 Ex $2467 Gd $1678
Grade III, Pointer . . . . NiB $3856 Ex $3085 Gd $2098
Grade IV, Diana . . . . NiB $4243 Ex $3394 Gd $2308
Grade V, Midas . . . . NiB $5530 Ex $4424 Gd $3008
W/extra bbls., add 45%

SUPERPOSED MAGNUM . . . . . . NiB $1610 Ex $1288 Gd $876
Same as Grade I except chambered for 12-ga. 3-inch shells, 30-inch vent-rib bbls., stock w/recoil pad. Weight: About 8.25 lbs. Disc. 1976.

**SUPERPOSED LTD.
BLACK DUCK ISSUE** . . . . NiB $7210 Ex $5768 Gd $3922
Gauge: 12. Superposed Lightning action. 28-inch vent-rib bbls. Choked M/F. 2.75-inch chambers. Weight: 7 lbs., 6 oz. Gold-inlaid receiver and trigger guard engraved w/black duck scenes. Gold-plated, single selective trigger. Top-tang mounted manual safety. Automatic, selective ejectors. Front and center ivory sights. High-grade, hand-checkered, hand-oiled select walnut stock and forend. 500 issued in 1983.

**SUPERPOSED LTD.
MALLARD DUCK ISSUE** . . . . . NiB $7404 Ex $5923 Gd $4027
Same general specifications as Ltd. Black Duck issue except mallard duck scenes engraved on receiver and trigger guard, dark French walnut stock w/rounded pistol-grip. 500 issued in 1981.

**SUPERPOSED LTD.
PINTAIL DUCK ISSUE** . . . . NiB $7590 Ex $6072 Gd $4129
Same general specifications as Ltd. Black Duck issue except pintail duck scenes engraved on receiver and trigger guard. Stock is of dark French walnut w/rounded pistol-grip. 500 issued in 1982.

SUPERPOSED, PRESENTATION GRADES
Custom versions of Super-Light, Lightning Hunting, Trap and Skeet

(cont'd.) **SUPERPOSED, PRESENTATION GRADES**
Models, w/same general specifications as those of standard guns, but of higher overall quality. The four Presentation grades differ in receiver finish (grayed or blued), engraving gold inlays, wood and checkering. Presentation 4 has sideplates. Made by FN, these models were Intro. in 1977.

Presentation 1 . . . . NiB $3084 Ex $2467 Gd $1678
Presentation 1, gold-inlaid. . . . . NiB $3541 Ex $2832 Gd $1926
Presentation 2 . . . . NiB $3985 Ex $3188 Gd $2168
Presentation 2, gold-inlaid. . . . . NiB $4700 Ex $3759 Gd $2556
Presentation 3, gold-inlaid. . . . . NiB $6083 Ex $4867 Gd $3309
Presentation 4 . . . . NiB $6818 Ex $5454 Gd $3709
Presentation 4, gold-inlaid. . . . . NiB $8820 Ex $7056 Gd $4798

SUPERPOSED SKEET GUNS, GRADE I
Same as standard Lightning 12, 20, 28 and .410 Hunting models, except has skeet-style stock and forearm, 26.5- or 28-inch vent-rib bbls. w/SK choke. Available also in All Gauge Skeet Set: Lightning 12 w/one removable forearm and three extra sets of bbls. in 20, 28 and .410 ga. in fitted luggage case. Disc. 1976. (For higher grades see listings for comparable Hunting models)

12 or 20 ga. . . . . NiB $1867 Ex $1494 Gd $1016
28 or .410 ga. . . . . NiB $2311 Ex $1849 Gd $1258
All ga. skeet set . . . . NiB $5916 Ex $4732 Gd $3219

**SUPERPOSED SUPER
LIGHT MODEL** . . . . NiB $1834 Ex $1468 Gd $998
Ultralight field gun version of Standard Lightning Model has classic straight-grip stock and slimmer forearm. Available only in 12 and 20 gauges (2.75-inch chambers), w/26.5-inch vent-rib bbls. Weight: 6.5 lbs., (12 ga.); 6 lbs., (20 ga.). Made 1967-76.

SUPERPOSED TRAP GUN . . . . . NiB $1899 Ex $1519 Gd $1033
Same as Grade I except has trap-style stock, beavertail forearm, 30-inch vent-rib bbls., 12 ga. only. Disc. 1976. (For higher grades see listings for comparable hunting models)

TWELVETTE DOUBLE AUTOMATIC
Lightweight version of Double Automatic w/same general specifications except aluminum receiver. Bbl. w/plain matted top or vent rib. Weight: 6.75 to 7 lbs., depending on bbl. Receiver is finished in black w/gold engraving; 1956-1961 receivers were also anodized in gray, brown and green w/silver engraving. Made 1955-71

W/plain bbl. . . . . NiB $547 Ex $438 Gd $298
W/vent rib bbl. . . . . NiB $676 Ex $541 Gd $369

CENTURY INTERNATIONAL ARMS INC. — St. Albans, VT

CENTURION . . . . NiB $338 Ex $270 Gd $184
O/U boxlock action with double triggers and extractors. 12 ga. w/2.75-inch chamber. Bbls: 28-inch choked modified/full with ventilated rib. Weight: 7-1/4 lbs. Checkered European walnut buttstock and forend. Polished blue finish. Imported 1993 to date.

SHOTGUNS

Churchill Automatic Shotgun

Churchill Windsor Grade Side-by-Side Shotgun

Churchill Windsor Grade Flyweight Shotgun

CHURCHILL SHOTGUNS — Italy and Spain Imported by Ellett Brothers, Inc., Chapin, SC; previously by Kassnar Imports, Inc., Harrisburg, PA

AUTOMATIC SHOTGUN

Gas-operated. Gauge: 12, 2.75- or 3-inch chambers. Five shot magazine w/cutoff. Bbl.: 24-, 25-, 26-, 28-inch w/ICT choke tubes. Checkered walnut stock w/satin finish. Imported from Italy 1990-94.

Standard model	NiB $514	Ex $411	Gd $280
Turkey model	NiB $540	Ex $432	Gd $293

MONARCH O/U SHOTGUN

Hammerless, takedown w/engraved receiver. Selective single or double triggers. Gauges: 12, 20, 28, .410; 3-inch chambers. Bbls.: 25- or 26-inch (IC/M); 28-inch (M/F). Weight: 6.5-7.5 lbs. Checkered European walnut buttstock and forend. Made in Italy 1986-93.

W/double triggers	NiB $469	Ex $382	Gd $260
W/single trigger	NiB $536	Ex $428	Gd $291

REGENT O/U SHOTGUNS

Gauges: 12 or 20; 2.75-inch chambers. 27-inch bbls. w/interchangeable choke tubes and wide vent rib. Single selective trigger, selective automatic ejectors. Checkered pistol-grip stock in fancy walnut. Imported from Italy 1984-88 and 1990-94.

Regent V(disc. 1988)	NiB $976	Ex $780	Gd $530
Regent VII w/ sideplates (disc. 1994)	NiB $1106	Ex $884	Gd $601

REGENT SKEET

NiB $812 Ex $650 Gd $442

12 or 20 ga. w/2.75-inch chambers. Selective automatic ejectors, single-selective trigger. 26-inch over/under bbls. w/vent rib. Weight: 7 lbs. Made in Italy 1984-88.

REGENT TRAP

NiB $826 Ex $660 Gd $440

12-ga. competition shotgun w/2.75-inch chambers. 30-inch over/under bbls. choked IM/F, vent side ribs. Weight: 8 lbs. Selective automatic ejectors, single selective trigger. Checkered Monte Carlo stock w/Supercushion recoil pad. Made in Italy 1984-88.

SPORTING CLAYS O/U

NiB $864 Ex $692 Gd $470

Same general specifications as Windsor IV except in 12 ga. only w/28-inch ported bbls. and choke tubes. Selective automatic ejectors. Weight: 7.5 lbs. Made from 1992-94.

WINDSOR O/U SHOTGUNS

Hammerless, boxlock w/engraved receiver, selective single trigger. Extractors or ejectors. Gauges: 12, 20, 28 or .410; 3-inch chambers. Bbls.: 24 to 30 inches w/fixed chokes or choke tubes. Weight: 6 lbs., 3 oz. (Flyweight) to 7 lbs., 10 oz. (12 ga.). Checkered straight (Flyweight) or pistol-grip stock and forend of European walnut. Imported from Italy 1984-93.

Windsor III w/fixed chokes	NiB $648	Ex $518	Gd $352
Windsor III w/choke tubes	NiB $812	Ex $649	Gd $442
Windsor IV w/fixed chokes (disc. 1993)	NiB $757	Ex $605	Gd $411
Windsor IV w/choke tubes	NiB $757	Ex $540	Gd $263

WINDSOR SIDE-BY-SIDE SHOTGUNS

Boxlock action w/double triggers, ejectors or extractors and automatic safety. Gauges: 10, (3.5-inch chambers); 12, 20, 28, .410 (3-inch chambers), 16 (2.75-inch chambers). Bbls.: 23 to 32 inches w/various fixed choke or choke tube combinations. Weight: 5 lbs., 12 oz. (Flyweight) to 11.5 lbs. (10 ga.). European walnut buttstock and forend. Imported from Spain 1984-90.

Windsor I 10 ga.	NiB $730	Ex $584	Gd $397
Windsor I 12 thru .410 ga.	NiB $555	Ex $444	Gd $302
Windsor II 12 or 20 ga.	NiB $520	Ex $416	Gd $283
Windsor VI 12 or 20 ga.	NiB $760	Ex $608	Gd $413

E.J. CHURCHILL, LTD. —
Surrey (previously London), England

The E.J. Churchill shotguns listed below are no longer imported.

E.J. Churchill Premiere

PREMIERE QUALITY HAMMERLESS DOUBLE
Sidelock. Automatic ejectors. Double triggers or selective single trigger. Gauges: 12, 16, 20, 28. Bbls.: 25-, 28- 30-, 32-inch; any degree of boring. Weight: 5-8 lbs. depending on ga. and bbl. length. Checkered stock and forend, straight or pistol-grip.
W/double triggers.............. NiB $17,898 Ex $14,508 Gd $10,400
W/selective single trigger, add...................................10%

FIELD MODEL HAMMERLESS DOUBLE
Sidelock Hammerless ejector gun w/same general specifications as Premiere Model but of lower quality.
W/double triggers .... NiB $9880 Ex $7800 Gd $6760
W/selective single trigger, add 10%

PREMIERE QUALITY O/U SHOTGUN
Sidelock. Automatic ejectors. Double triggers or selective single trigger. Gauges: 12, 16, 20, 28. Bbls.: 25-, 28-, 30-, 32-inch, any degree of boring. Weight: 5-8 lbs. depending on ga. and bbl. length. Checkered stock and forend, straight or pistol-grip.
W/double triggers.............. NiB $20,150 Ex $16,120 Gd $10,961
W/selective single trigger, add..................................10%
Raised vent rib, add...15%

UTILITY MODEL HAMMERLESS DOUBLE-BARREL
Anson & Deeley boxlock action. Double triggers or single trigger. Gauges: 12, 16, 20, 28, .410. Bbls.: 25-, 28-, 30-, 32-inch, any degree of boring. Weight: 4.5-8 lbs. depending on ga. and bbl. length. Checkered stock and forend, straight or pistol-grip.
W/double triggers .... NiB $6500 Ex $4680 Gd $3380
W/selective single trigger, add 10%

XXV PREMIERE
HAMMERLESS DOUBLE ... NiB $17,226 Ex $13,780 Gd $9370
Sidelock. Assisted opening. Automatic ejectors. Double triggers. Gauges: 12, 20. 25-inch bbls. w/narrow, quick-sighting rib; any standard choke combination. English-style straight-grip stock and forearm, checkered.

XXV IMPERIAL .... NiB $14,332 Ex $11,466 Gd $7797
Similar to XXV Premiere but no assisted opening feature.

XXV HERCULES .... NiB $10,004 Ex $8002 Gd $5442
Boxlock, otherwise specifications same as for XXV Premiere.

XXV REGAL................ NiB $5526 Ex $4420 Gd $3006
Similar to XXV Hercules but w/o assisted opening feature. Gauges: 12, 20, 28, .410.

CLASSIC DOUBLES — Tochigi, Japan

Imported by Classic Doubles International, St. Louis, MO, and previously by Olin as Winchester Models 101 and 23.

MODEL 101 O/U SHOTGUN
Boxlock. Engraved receiver w/single selective trigger, auto ejectors and combination bbl. selector and safety. Gauges: 12, 20, 28 or .410, 2.75-, 3-inch chambers, 25.5- 28- or 30-inch vent-rib bbls. Weight: 6.25 – 7.75 lbs. Checkered French walnut stock. Imported 1987-90.

(cont'd.) MODEL 101 O/U SHOTGUN
Classic I Field .... NiB $1554 Ex $1242 Gd $846
Classic II Field..................... NiB $1756 Ex $1404 Gd $955
Classic Sporter .... NiB $1886 Ex $1508 Gd $1025
Classic Sporter combo .... NiB $3056 Ex $2444 Gd $1662
Classic Trap...................... NiB $1528 Ex $1222 Gd $831
Classic Trap Single................. NiB $1554 Ex $1243 Gd $846
Classic Trap combo .... NiB $2276 Ex $1820 Gd $1238
Classic Skeet .... NiB $1626 Ex $1300 Gd $884
Classic Skeet
2-bbl. set........................ NiB $2464 Ex $1971 Gd $1341
Classic Skeet
4-bbl. set........................ NiB $4226 Ex $3380 Gd $2298
ClassicWaterfowler .... NiB $1294 Ex $1035 Gd $704
For Grade II (28 ga.), add $750
For Grade II (.410 ga.), add $250

MODEL 201 SIDE-BY-SIDE SHOTGUN
Boxlock. Single selective trigger, automatic safety and selective ejectors. Gauges: 12 or 20; 3-inch chambers. 26- or 28-inch vent-rib bbl., fixed chokes or internal tubes. Weight: 6 to 7 lbs. Checkered French walnut stock and forearm. Imported 1987-90.
Field model....................... NiB $1565 Ex $1252 Gd $852
Skeet model .... NiB $1851 Ex $1481 Gd $1008
With internal choke tubes, add............................$100

MODEL 201
SMALL BORE SET .... NiB $4674 Ex $3739 Gd $2543
Same general specifications as the Classic Model 201 except w/smaller frame, in 28 ga. (IC/M) and .410 (F/M). Weight: 6-6.5 lbs. Imported 1987-90.

COGSWELL & HARRISON, LTD. —
London, England

AMBASSADOR HAMMERLESS
DOUBLE-BARREL SHOTGUN .... NiB $5720 Ex $5122 Gd $3224
Boxlock. Sideplates w/game scene or rose scroll engraving. Automatic ejectors. Double triggers. Gauges: 12, 16, 20. Bbls.: 26- 28-, 30-inch; any choke combination. Checkered straight-grip stock and forearm. Disc.

Colt Auto Shotgun
Ultra Light Standard

Colt Custom
Hammerless Double

Colt Standard Pump

Cogswell & Harrison
Best Quality
Hammerless Sidelock

Colt-Sauer
Drilling

AVANT TOUT SERIES HAMMERLESS DOUBLE-BARREL SHOTGUNS

Boxlock. Sideplates (except Avant Tout III Grade). Automatic ejectors. Double triggers or single trigger (selective or non-selective). Gauges: 12, 16, 20. Bbls.: 25-, 27:5-, 30-inch, any choke combination. Checkered stock and forend, straight grip standard. Made in three models (Avant Tout I or Konor, Avant Tout II or Sandhurst, Avant Tout III or Rex) which differ chiefly in overall quality of engraving, grade of wood, checkering, etc. General specifications are the same. Disc.

Avant Tout I	NiB $3504	Ex $2803	Gd $1906
Avant Tout II	NiB $3056	Ex $2444	Gd $1662
Avant Tout III	NiB $2334	Ex $1867	Gd $1270
Single trigger, non-selective, add.			$225
Single trigger, selective, add			$395

BEST QUALITY HAMMERLESS SIDELOCK DOUBLE-BARREL SHOTGUN

Hand-detachable locks. Automatic ejectors. Double triggers or single trigger (selective or non-selective). Gauges: 12, 16, 20. Bbls.: 25-, 26-, 28-, 30-inch, any choke combination. Checkered stock and forend, straight grip standard.

Victor model	NiB $9913	Ex $7931	Gd $5392
Primic model (disc.).	NiB $6856	Ex $5485	Gd $3729
Single trigger, non-selective, add			$225
Single trigger, selective, add			$395

HUNTIC MODEL HAMMERLESS DOUBLE

Sidelock. Automatic ejectors. Double triggers or single trigger (selective or non-selective). Gauges: 12, 16, 20. Bbls.: 25-, 27.5-, 30-inch; any choke combination. Checkered stock and forend, straight grip standard. Disc.

(cont'd.) HUNTIC MODEL HAMMERLESS DOUBLE

W/double triggers	NiB $4222	Ex $3380	Gd $2298
Single trigger, non-selective, add.			$225
Single trigger, selective, add			$350

MARKOR HAMMERLESS DOUBLE

Boxlock. Non-ejector or ejector. Double triggers. Gauges: 12, 16, 20. Bbls.: 27.5 or 30-inch; any choke combination. Checkered stock and forend, straight grip standard. Disc.

Non-ejector	NiB $1756	Ex $1404	Gd $955
Ejector model	NiB $2146	Ex $1716	Gd $1167

REGENCY HAMMERLESS DOUBLE . . . . . . NiB $2984 Ex $2387 Gd $1622
Anson & Deeley boxlock action. Automatic ejectors. Double triggers. Gauges: 12, 16, 20. Bbls.: 26-, 28-, 30-inch, any choke combination. Checkered straight-grip stock and forearm. Introduced in 1970 to commemorate the firm's bicentennial, this model has deep scroll engraving and the name "Regency" inlaid in gold on the rib. Disc.

COLT INDUSTRIES — Hartford, Connecticut
Auto Shotguns were made by Franchi and are similar to corresponding models of that manufacturer.

AUTO SHOTGUN — ULTRA LIGHT STANDARD
Recoil-operated. Takedown. Alloy receiver. Gauges: 12, 20. Mag. holds 4 shells. Bbls.: plain, solid or vent rib, chrome-lined; 26-inch IC or M choke, 28-inch M or F choke, 30-inch F choke, 32-inch F choke. Weight: 12 ga., about 6.25 lbs. Checkered pistol-grip stock and forearm. Made 1964-66.

W/plain bbl.	NiB $488	Ex $390	Gd $265
W/solid rib bbl.	NiB $358	Ex $286	Gd $194
W/vent rib bbl.	NiB $384	Ex $307	Gd $209

**Charles Daly Over/Under
Field Grade (Postwar)**

AUTO SHOTGUN — MAGNUM CUSTOM
Same as Magnum except has engraved receiver, select walnut stock and forearm. Made 1964-66.
W/Solid-rib bbl.	NiB $552	Ex $442	Gd $301
W/ventilated rib bbl.	NiB $618	Ex $494	Gd $336

AUTO SHOTGUN — ULTRA LIGHT CUSTOM
Same as Standard Auto except has engraved receiver, select walnut stock and forearm. Made 1964-66.
W/solid-rib bbl.	NiB $456	Ex $364	Gd $248
W/ventilated-rib bbl.	NiB $488	Ex $390	Gd $265

AUTO SHOTGUN — MAGNUM
Same as Standard Auto except steel receiver, 3-inch Magnum shells, 30- and 32-inch bbls. in 12 ga., 28-inch in 20 ga. Weight: 12 ga., about 8.25 lbs. Made 1964-66.
W/plain bbl.	NiB $436	Ex $348	Gd $237
W/solid-rib bbl.	NiB $488	Ex $390	Gd $265
W/ventilated rib bbl.	NiB $514	Ex 3411	Gd $280

CUSTOM HAMMERLESS DOUBLE — NiB $774   Ex $619   Gd $421
Boxlock. Double triggers. Auto ejectors. Gauges: 12 Mag., 16. Bbls.: 26-inch IC/M; 28-inch M/F; 30-inch F/F. Weight: 12 ga., about 7.5 lbs. Checkered pistol-grip stock and beavertail forearm. Made in 1961.

STANDARD PUMP SHOTGUN — NiB $345   Ex $276   Gd $187
Takedown. Gauges: 12, 16, 20. Magazine holds 4 shells. Bbls.: 26-inch IC; 28-inch M or F choke; 30-inch F choke. Weight: About 6 lbs. Plain pistol-grip stock and forearm. Made 1961-65 by Manufrance.

CUSTOM PUMP — NiB $380   Ex $304   Gd $206
Same as Standard Pump shotgun except has checkered stock, vent-rib bbl. Weight: About 6.5 lbs. Made 1961-63 by Manufrance.

SAUER DRILLING — NiB $3036   Ex $2428   Gd $1652
Three-bbl. combination gun. Boxlock. Set rifle trigger. Tang bbl. selector, automatic rear sight positioner. 12 ga. over .30-06 or .243 rifle bbl. 25-inch bbls., F and M choke. Weight: About 8 lbs. Folding leaf rear sight, blade front w/brass bead. Checkered pistol-grip stock and beavertail forearm, recoil pad. Made 1974 to date by J. P. Sauer & Sohn, Eckernförde, Germany.

CONNECTICUT VALLEY CLASSICS — Westport, Connecticut

SPORTER O/U
Gauge: 12; 3-inch chamber. Bbls.: 28-, 30- or 32-inch w/ screw-in tubes. Weight: 7.75 lbs. Engraved stainless or nitrided receiver; blued bbls. Checkered American black walnut buttstock and forend w/low-luster satin finish. Made from 1993 to date.
Classic Sporter	NiB $2074	Ex $1659	Gd $1128
Stainless Classic Sporter	NiB $2464	Ex $1971	Gd $1341

FIELD O/U
Similar to the standard Classic Sporter over/under model except w/30-inch bbls. only and non-reflective matte blued finish on both bbls. and receiver for Waterfowler; other grades w/different degrees of embellishment; Grade I the lowest and Grade III the highest. Made 1993 to date.
Grade I	NiB $2329	Ex $2030	Gd $1380
Grade II	NiB $2709	Ex $2167	Gd $1474
Grade III	NiB $3074	Ex $2460	Gd $1672
Waterfowler	NiB $2423	Ex $1939	Gd $1319

CHARLES DALY, INC. — New York, New York

The pre-WWII Charles Daly shotguns, w/the exception of the Commander, were manufactured by various firms in Suhl, Germany. The postwar guns, except for the Novamatic series, were produced by Miroku Firearms Mfg. Co., Tokyo. Miroku ceased production in 1976 and the Daly trademark was acquired by Outdoor Sports Headquarters, in Dayton, Ohio. OSHI continued to market O/U shotguns from both Italy and Spain under the Daly logo. Automatic models were produced in Japan for distribution in the USA. In 1996, KBI, Inc. in Harrisburg, PA acquired the Daly trademark and currently imports firearms under that logo.

COMMANDER O/U SHOTGUN
Daly-pattern Anson & Deeley system boxlock action. Automatic ejectors. Double triggers or Miller selective single trigger. Gauges: 12, 16, 20, 28, .410. Bbls.: 26- to 30-inch, IC/M or M/F choke. Weight: 5.25 to 7.25 lbs. depending on ga. and bbl. length. Checkered stock and forend, straight or pistol grip. The two models, 100 and 200, differ in general quality, grade of wood, checkering, engraving, etc.; otherwise specs are the same. Made in Belgium c. 1939.
Model 100	NiB $515	Ex $411	Gd $286
Model 200	NiB $682	Ex $546	Gd $371
Miller single trigger, add			$100

HAMMERLESS DOUBLE-BARREL SHOTGUN
Daly-pattern Anson & Deeley system boxlock action. Automatic ejectors except "Superior Quality" is non-ejector. Double triggers. Gauges: 10, 12, 16, 20, 28, .410. Bbls.: 26- to 32-inch, any combination of chokes. Weight: from 4 to 8.5 lbs. depending on ga. and bbl. length. Checkered pistol-grip stock and forend. The four grades—Regent Diamond, Diamond, Empire, Superior—differ in general quality, grade of wood, checkering, engraving, etc.; otherwise specifications are the same. Disc. about 1933.
Diamond quality	NiB $11,376	Ex $9100	Gd $6188
Empire quality	NiB $5526	Ex $4420	Gd $3006
Regent Diamond quality	NiB $13,650	Ex $10,920	Gd $7426
Superior quality	NiB $1236	Ex $988	Gd $672

SHOTGUNS

Charles Daly Diamond
GTX DL Hunter

Charles Daly Empire
EDL Hunter

HAMMERLESS DRILLING

Daly pattern Anson & Deeley system boxlock action. Plain extractors. Double triggers, front single set for rifle bbl. Gauges: 12, 16, 20, .25-20, .25-35, .30-30 rifle bbl. Supplied in various bbl. lengths and weights. Checkered pistol-grip stock and forend. Auto rear sight operated by rifle bbl. selector. The three grades — Regent Diamond, Diamond, Superior—differ in general quality, grade of wood, checkering, engraving, etc.; otherwise, specifications are the same. Disc. about 1933.

Diamond quality . . . . NiB $6176 Ex $4940 Gd $3359
Regent Diamond quality . . . NiB $13,326 Ex $10,661 Gd $7249
Superior quality . . . . NiB $3374 Ex $2699 Gd $1836

HAMMERLESS DOUBLE

EMPIRE GRADE . . . . NiB $917 Ex $772 Gd $583
Boxlock. Plain extractors. Non-selective single trigger. Gauges: 12, 16, 20; 3-inch chambers in 12 and 20, 2.75-inch in 16 ga. Bbls.: vent rib; 26-, 28-, 30-inch (latter in 12 ga. only); IC/M, M/F, F/F. Weight: 6 to 7.75 lbs., depending on ga. and bbls. Checkered pistol-grip stock and beavertail forearm. Made 1968-71.

1974 WILDLIFE COMMEMORATIVE . . . . NiB $2204 Ex $1763 Gd $1199
Limited issue of 500 guns. Similar to Diamond Grade over/under. 12-ga. trap and skeet models only. Duck scene engraved on right side of receiver, fine scroll on left side. Made in 1974.

NOVAMATIC LIGHTWEIGHT AUTOLOADER

Same as Breda. Recoil-operated. Takedown.12 ga., 2.75-inch chamber. Four shell tubular magazine. Bbls.: Plain vent rib; 26-inch IC or Quick-Choke w/three interchangeable tubes, 28-inch M or F choke. Weight (w/26-inch vent-rib bbl.): 7 lbs., 6 oz. Checkered pistol-grip stock and forearm. Made 1968 by Ernesto Breda, Milan, Italy.

W/plain bbl. . . . . NiB $422 Ex $338 Gd $230
W/vent rib bbl. . . . . NiB $456 Ex $364 Gd $248
W/Quick-Choke, add $20

NOVAMATIC SUPER LIGHTWEIGHT

Lighter version of Novamatic Lightweight. Gauges: 12, 20. Weight (w/26-inch vent-rib bbl.): 12 ga., 6 lbs., 10 oz., 20 ga., 6 lbs. SK choke available in 26-inch vent-rib bbl. 28-inch bbls. in 12 ga. only. Quick-Choke in 20 ga. w/plain bbl. Made 1968 by Ernesto Breda, Milan, Italy.

12 ga., plain bbl. . . . . NiB $384 Ex $307 Gd $209
12 ga., vent rib bbl. NiB $422 Ex $338 Gd $230
20 ga., plain bbl. . . . . NiB $390 Ex $312 Gd $212
20 ga., plain bbl. w/Quick-Choke . . . . NiB $422 Ex $338 Gd $230
20 ga., vent rib bbl. NiB $448 Ex $359 Gd $245

NOVAMATIC SUPER LIGHTWEIGHT

20 GA. MAGNUM . . . . NiB $448 Ex $359 Gd $244
Same as Novamatic Super Lightweight 2, except 3-inch chamber, has 3-shell magazine, 28-inch vent-rib bbl., F choke.

NOVAMATIC

12 GA. MAGNUM . . . . NiB $456 Ex $364 Gd $248
Same as Novamatic Lightweight, except chambered for 12-ga. Magnum 3-inch shell. Has 3-shell magazine, 30-inch vent rib bbl., F choke, and stock w/recoil pad. Weight: 7.75 lbs.

Post-War Charles Daly shotguns were imported by Sloan's Sporting Goods trading as Charles Daly in New York. In 1976, Outdoor Sports Headquarters acquired the Daly trademark and continued to import European-made shotguns under that logo. In 1996, KBI, Inc., in Harrisburg, PA, acquired the Daly trademark and currently imports firearms under that logo.

NOVAMATIC TRAP GUN . . . . NiB $488 Ex $390 Gd $265
Same as Novamatic Lightweight except has 30-inch vent rib bbl., F choke and Monte Carlo stock w/recoil pad. Weight: 7.75 lbs.

O/U SHOTGUNS (PREWAR)

Daly-pattern Anson & Deeley-system boxlock action. Sideplates. Auto ejectors. Double triggers. Gauges: 12, 16, 20. Supplied in various bbl. lengths and weights. Checkered pistol-grip stock and forend. The two grades — Diamond and Empire — differ in general quality, grade of wood, checkering, engraving, etc.; otherwise specifications are the same. Disc. about 1933.

Diamond
Quality . . . . NiB $5714 Ex $4571 Gd $3109
Empire
Quality . . . . NiB $4356 Ex $3484 Gd $2369

O/U SHOTGUNS (POSTWAR)

Boxlock. Auto ejectors or selective auto/manual ejection. Selective single trigger. Gauges: 12, 12 Magnum (3-inch chambers), 20 (3-inch chambers), 28, .410. Bbls.: Vent rib; 26-, 28-, 30-inch; standard choke combinations. Weight: 6 to 8 lbs. depending on ga. and bbls. Select walnut stock w/pistol grip, fluted forearm checkered; Monte Carlo comb on trap guns; recoil pad on 12-ga. mag. and trap models. The various grades differ in quality of engraving and wood. Made 1963-76.

Diamond grade . . . . NiB $1294 Ex $1035 Gd $704
Field grade . . . . NiB $716 Ex $572 Gd $389
Superior grade . . . . NiB $942 Ex $754 Gd $513
Venture grade . . . . NiB $682 Ex $546 Gd $371

Charles Daly
Field Semiauto

Charles Daly Field III
Over/Under

SEXTUPLE MODEL SINGLE-BARREL TRAP GUN
Daly-pattern Anson & Deeley system boxlock action. Six locking bolts. Auto ejector. 12 ga. only. Bbls.: 30-, 32-, 34-inch, vent rib. Weight: 7.5 to 8.25 lbs. Checkered pistol-grip stock and forend. The two models made Empire and Regent Diamond differ in general quality, grade of wood, checkering, engraving, etc., otherwise specifications are the same. Disc. about 1933.

Regent Diamond quality (Linder) . . . . NiB $552 Ex $442 Gd $301
Empire quality (Linder) . . . . NiB $4934 Ex $3947 Gd $2684
Regent Diamond quality (Sauer) . . . . . . NiB $3504 Ex $2803 Gd $1906
Empire quality (Sauer) . . . . NiB $2594 Ex $2075 Gd $1411

SINGLE-SHOT TRAP GUN
Daly-pattern Anson & Deeley system boxlock action. Auto ejector. 12 ga. only. Bbls.: 30-, 32-, 34-inch, vent rib. Weight: 7.5 to 8.25 lbs. Checkered pistol-grip stock and forend. This model was made in Empire Quality only. Disc. about 1933.

Empire grade (Linder) . . . . NiB $4356 Ex $3484 Gd $2369
Empire grade (Sauer) . . . . NiB $2146 Ex $1716 Gd $1167

SUPERIOR GRADE SINGLE-SHOT TRAP . . NiB $774 Ex $619 Gd $421
Boxlock. Automatic ejector. 12 ga. only. 32- or 34-inch vent-rib bbl., F choke. Weight: About 8 lbs. Monte Carlo stock w/pistol grip and recoil pad, beavertail forearm, checkered. Made 1968-76.

DIAMOND GRADE O/U
Boxlock. Single selective trigger. Selective automatic ejectors. Gauges: 12 and 20, 3-inch chambers (2.75 target grade). Bbls.: 26, 27- or 30-inch w/fixed chokes or screw-in tubes. Weight: 7 lbs. Checkered European walnut stock and forearm w/oil finish. Engraved antique silver receiver and blued bbls. Made 1984-90.

Standard model . . . . NiB $812 Ex $649 Gd $442
Skeet model . . . . NiB $887 Ex $709 Gd $483
Trap model . . . . NiB $948 Ex $758 Gd $516

DIAMOND GTX DL HUNTER O/U SERIES
Sidelock. Single selective trigger and selective auto ejectors. Gauges: 12, 20, 28 ga. or .410 bore. 26-, 28- and 30-inch bbls w/3-inch chambers (2.75-inch 28 ga.). Choke tubes (12 and 20 ga.), Fixed chokes (28 and 410). Weight: 5-8 lbs. Checkered European walnut stock w/hand-rubbed oil finish and recoil pad. Made 1997 to date.

Diamond GTX DL Hunter . . . . NiB $9816 Ex $7852 Gd $5339
Diamond GTX EDL Hunter . . . . NiB $12,122 Ex $9698 Gd $6595
Diamond GTX Sporting (12 or 20 ga.) . . . . NiB $5454 Ex $4363 Gd $2967
Diamond GTX Skeet (12 or 20 ga.) . . . . NiB $5064 Ex $4051 Gd $2755
Diamond GTX Trap (12 ga. only) . . . . . NiB $5266 Ex $4212 Gd $2864

EMPIRE DL HUNTER O/U . . . . . NiB $1196 Ex $1014 Gd $624
Boxlock. Ejectors. Single selective trigger. Gauges:12, 20, 28 ga. and .410 bore. 26- or 28- inch bbls. w/3-inch chambers (2.75-inch 28 ga.). Choke tubes (12 and 20 ga.), Fixed chokes (28 and .410). Engraved coin-silver receiver w/game scene. Imported 1997 to date.

EMPIRE EDL HUNTER SERIES
Similar to Empire DL Hunter except engraved sideplates. Made 1998 to date.

Empire EDL Hunter . . . . NiB $1202 Ex $962 Gd $654
Empire Sporting . . . . NiB $1170 Ex $936 Gd $636
Empire Skeet . . . . NiB $1138 Ex $910 Gd $619
Empire Trap . . . . NiB $1202 Ex $962 Gd $654
28 ga., add $95
.410 ga, add $120
Multi-chokes w/Monte
Carlo stock, add $125

DSS HAMMERLESS DOUBLE . . . . . NiB $682 Ex $546 Gd $371
Boxlock. Single selective trigger. Selective automatic ejectors. Gauges: 12 and 20; 3-inch chambers. 26-inch bbls. w/screw-in choke tubes. Weight: 6.75 lbs. Checkered walnut pistol-grip stock and semi-beavertail forearm w/recoil pad. Engraved antique silver receiver and blued bbls. Made from 1990 to date.

FIELD GRADE O/U . . . . NiB $500 Ex $400 Gd $272
Boxlock. Single selective trigger. Extractors. Gauges: 12 and 20; 3-inch chambers. Bbls.: 26-inch, IC/M; 28-inch, M/F. Weight: 6.75 lbs. (12 ga.). Checkered walnut stock and forearm w/semi-gloss finish and recoil pad. Engraved color-casehardened receiver and blued bbls. Made from 1989 to date.

FIELD SEMIAUTO SHOTGUN . . . . . NiB $384 Ex $307 Gd $209
Recoil-operated. Takedown. 12-ga. and 12-ga. Magnum. Bbls.: 27- and 30-inch; vent rib. Made 1982-88.

FIELD III O/U SHOTGUN . . . . NiB $514 Ex $411 Gd $280
Boxlock. Plain extractors. Non-selective single trigger. Gauges: 12 or 20. Bbls.: vent rib; 26- and 28-inch; IC/M, M/F. Weight: 6 to 7.75 lbs. depending on ga. and bbls. Chrome-molybdenum steel bbls. Checkered pistol-grip stock and forearm. Made from 1982 to date.

LUX O/U . . . . NiB $748 Ex $598 Gd $407
Similar to the Field Grade except w/selective automatic ejectors and choke tubes. Gauges: 12, 20, 28 and .410. Receiver w/antique silver finish and blued bbls. Made from 1989 to date.

SHOTGUNS

Charles Daly Over/Under
Presentation Grade

Charles Daly Over/Under
Superior II

Davidson Model 63B
Double-Barrel Shotgun

MULTI-XII SELF-LOADING SHOTGUN . . . . . . NiB $514 Ex $411 Gd $280
Similar to the gas-operated field semiauto except w/new Multi-Action gas system designed to shoot all loads w/o adjustment. 12 ga. w/3-inch chamber. 27-inch bbl. w/Invector choke tubes, vent rib. Made in Japan from 1987 to date.

O/U
PRESENTATION GRADE . . . . . . .NiB $1098 Ex $879 Gd $598
Purdey boxlock w/double cross-bolt. Gauges: 12 or 20. Engraved receiver w/single selective trigger and auto-ejectors. 27-inch chrome-molybdenum steel, rectified, honed and internally chromed, vent-rib bbls. Hand-checkered deluxe European walnut stock. Made 1982-86.

O/U
Superior II Shotgun . . . . NiB $934 Ex $747 Gd $508
Boxlock. Plain extractors. Non-selective single trigger. Gauges: 12 or 20. Bbls.: chrome-molybdenum vent rib 26-, 28-, 30-inch, latter in magnum only, assorted chokes. Silver engraved receiver. Checkered pistol-grip stock and forearm. Made from 1982 to date.

SPORTING CLAYS O/U . . . . NiB $813 Ex $650 Gd $442
Similar to the Field Grade except in 12 ga. only w/ported bbls. and internal choke tubes. Made from 1990 to date.

DAKOTA ARMS, INC. — Sturgis, South Dakota

CLASSIC FIELD GRADE
S/S SHOTGUN . . . . NiB $7768 Ex $6131 Gd $4036
Boxlock. Gauge: 20 ga. 27-inch bbl. w/fixed chokes. Double triggers. Selective ejectors. Color-casehardened receiver. Weight: 6 lbs. Checkered English walnut stock and splinter forearm w/hand-rubbed oil finish. Made 1996 to date.

PREMIUM GRADE
S/S SHOTGUN . . . . NiB $14,456 Ex $10,608 Gd $6760
Similar to Classic Field Grade model except w/50% engraving coverage. Exhibition grade English walnut stock. Made 1996 to date.

AMERICAN LEGEND
S/S SHOTGUN . . . . NiB $17,290 Ex $14,040 Gd $9880
Limited edition built to customer's specifications. Gauge: 20 ga. 27-inch bbl. Double triggers. Selective ejectors. Fully engraved, coin-silver finished receiver w/gold inlays. Weight: 6 lbs. Hand checkered special-selection English walnut stock and forearm. Made 1996 to date.

DARNE S.A. — Saint-Etienne, France

HAMMERLESS DOUBLE-BARREL SHOTGUNS
Sliding-breech action w/fixed bbls. Auto ejectors. Double triggers. Gauges: 12, 16, 20, 28; also 12 and 20 Magnum w/3-inch chambers. Bbls.: 27.5-inch standard, 25.5- to 31.5-inch lengths available; any standard choke combination. Weight: 5.5 to 7 lbs. depending on ga. and bbl. length. Checkered straight-grip or pistol-grip stock and forearm. The various models differ in grade of engraving and wood. Manufactured 1881-1979.
Model R11
(Bird Hunter) . . . . NiB $1560 Ex $1404 Gd $728
Model R15
(Pheasant Hunter) . . . . NiB $2328 Ex $1829 Gd $1171
Model R16
(Magnum) . . . . NiB $3640 Ex $3016 Gd $1872
Model V19
(Quail Hunter) . . . . NiB $4680 Ex $4160 Gd $3640
Model V22 . . . . NiB $5266 Ex $4420 Gd $2402
Model V Hors Série No. 1 . . . . NiB $6630 Ex $5720 Gd $4555

Exel Model 101

Exel Model 200
Side-by-Side Shotgun

DAVIDSON GUNS — Mfd. by Fabrica de Armas ILJA, Eibar, Spain; distributed by Davidson Firearms Co., Greensboro, North Carolina

MODEL 63B DOUBLE-BARREL

SHOTGUN . . . . NiB $366 Ex $293 Gd $199
Anson & Deeley boxlock action. Frame engraved and nickel plated. Plain extractors. Auto safety. Double triggers. Gauges: 12, 16, 20, 28, .410. Bbl. lengths: 25 (.410 only), 26, 28, 30 inches (latter 12 ga. only). Chokes: IC/ M, M/F, F/F. Weight: 5 lbs., 11 oz. (.410) to 7 lbs. (12 ga.). Checkered pistol-grip stock and forearm of European walnut. Made 1963. Disc.

MODEL 63B MAGNUM
Similar to standard Model 63B except chambered for 10 ga. 3.5-inch, 12 and 20 ga. 3-inch Magnum shells; 10 ga. has 32-inch bbls., choked F/F. Weight: 10 lb., 10 oz. Made from 1963. Disc.
12- and 20 ga. magnum . . . . NiB $427 Ex $342 Gd $233
10 ga. magnum. . . . . NiB $504 Ex $403 Gd $274

MODEL 69SL DOUBLE-BARREL

SHOTGUN. . . . . NiB $632 Ex $525 Gd $390
Sidelock action w/detachable sideplates, engraved and nickel plated. Plain extractors. Auto safety. Double triggers. 12 and 20 ga. Bbls.: 26-inch IC/M, 28-inch M/F. Weight: 12 ga., 7 lbs., 20 ga., 6.5 lbs. Pistol-grip stock and forearm of European walnut, checkered. Made 1963-76.

MODEL 73 STAGECOACH

HAMMER DOUBLE . . . . NiB $338 Ex $270 Gd $184
Sidelock action w/detachable sideplates and exposed hammers. Plain extractors. Double triggers. Gauges: 12, 20, 3-inch chambers. 20-inch bbls, M/F chokes. Weight: 7 lbs., 12 ga.; 6.5 lbs., 20 ga. Checkered pistol-grip stock and forearm. Made from 1976. Disc.

EXEL ARMS OF AMERICA — Gardner, Massachusetts

SERIES 100 O/U SHOTGUN
Gauge: 12. Single selective trigger. Selective auto ejectors. Hand-checkered European walnut stock w/full pistol grip, tulip forend. Black metal finish. Chambered for 2.75-inch shells (Model 103 for 3-inch). Weight: 6. 88 to 7.88 lbs. Disc 1988.
Model 101, 26-inch bbl., IC/M . . . . NiB $478 Ex $383 Gd $260
Model 102, 28-inch bbl., IC/IM . . . . NiB $484 Ex $388 Gd $263
Model 103, 30-inch bbl., M/F . . . . NiB $504 Ex $403 Gd $274
Model 104, 28-inch bbl., IC/IM . . . . NiB $555 Ex $444 Gd $302
Model 105, 28-inch bbl., 5 choke tubes . . . . . . NiB $702 Ex $561 Gd $381
Model 106, 28-inch bbl., 5 choke tubes . . . . . . NiB $848 Ex $673 Gd $459
Model 107 Trap, 30-inch bbl., Full or 5 tubes . . . . . NiB $912 Ex $709 Gd $580

SERIES 200 SIDE-BY-SIDE

SHOTGUN . . . . NiB $504 Ex $403 Gd $274
Gauges: 12, 20, 28 and .410. Bbls.: 26-, 27- and 28-inch; various choke combinations. Weight: 7 lbs. average. American or European-style stock and forend. Made 1985 to 87.

SERIES 300 O/U

SHOTGUN . . . . NiB $574 Ex $459 Gd $312
Gauge: 12. Bbls.: 26-, 28- and 29-inch. Non-glare black-chrome matte finish. Weight: 7 lbs. average. Selective auto ejectors, engraved receiver. Hand-checkered European walnut stock and forend. Made 1985-86.

FABARM SHOTGUNS — Brescia, Italy

Currently imported by Heckler & Koch, Inc., of Sterling, VA (previously by Ithaca Acquisition Corp., St. Lawrence Sales, Inc. and Beeman Precision Arms, Inc.)

See Current listings under "Heckler & Koch."

FIAS — Fabrica Italiana Armi Sabatti Gardone Val Trompia, Italy

GRADE I O/U
Boxlock. Single selective trigger. Gauges: 12, 20, 28, .410; 3-inch chambers. Bbls.: 26-inch IC/M; 28-inch M/F; screw-in choke tubes. Weight: 6.5 to 7.5 lbs. Checkered European walnut stock and forearm. Engraved receiver and blued finish.
12 ga. model . . . . NiB $478 Ex $382 Gd $260
20 ga. model . . . . NiB $542 Ex $433 Gd $295
28 and .410 ga. models. . . . . NiB $702 Ex $561 Gd $382

FOX SHOTGUNS — Made by A. H. Fox Gun Co., Philadelphia, PA, 1903 to 1930, and since then by Savage Arms, originally of Utica, NY, now of Westfield, MA. In 1993, Connecticut Manufacturing Co. of New Britain, CT, reintroduced selected models.

Values shown are for 12 and 16 ga. doubles made by A. H. Fox. Twenty gauge guns often are valued up to 75% higher. Savage-made Fox models generally bring prices 25% lower. With the exception of Model B, production of Fox shotguns was discontinued about 1942.

Fox Model B

Fox Sterlingworth

Fox Grade AE

Fox Grade CE

MODEL B-SE................... NiB $717 Ex $573 Gd $390
Same as Model B except has selective ejectors and single trigger. Made 1966-89.

HAMMERLESS DOUBLE-BARREL SHOTGUNS
The higher grades have the same general specifications as the standard Sterlingworth model, w/differences chiefly in workmanship and materials. Higher grade models are stocked in fine select walnut; quantity and quality of engraving increases w/grade and price. Except for Grade A, all other grades have auto ejectors.

Grade A .... NiB $2889 Ex $2287 Gd $1555
Grade AE .... NiB $3303 Ex $2642 Gd $1796
Grade BE .... NiB $4584 Ex $3667 Gd $2494
Grade CE .... NiB $5820 Ex $4656 Gd $3166
Grade DE .... NiB $11,394 Ex $10,428 Gd $10,803
Grade FE .... NiB $21,357 Ex $17,085 Gd $11,618
Grade XE .... NiB $7427 Ex $5941 Gd $3765
Kautzky selective single trigger, add........................$350
Ventilated rib, add $450
Beavertail forearm, add $275
20 ga., add 60%

SINGLE-BARREL TRAP GUNS
Boxlock. Auto ejector.12 ga. only. 30- or 32-inch vent-rib bbl. Weight: 7.5 to 8 lbs. Trap-style stock and forearm of select walnut, checkered, recoil pad optional. The four grades differ chiefly in quality of wood and engraving; Grade M guns, built to order, have finest Circassian walnut. Stock and receiver are elaborately engraved and inlaid w/gold. Disc. 1942. Note: In 1932, the Fox Trap Gun was redesigned and those manufactured after that date have a stock w/full pistol grip and Monte Carlo comb; at the same time frame was changed to permit the rib line to extend across it to the rear.

Grade JE .... NiB $5042 Ex $4033 Gd $2743
Grade KE .... NiB $5737 Ex $4590 Gd $3121
Grade LE .... NiB $7948 Ex $6359 Gd $4324
Grade ME .... NiB $14,611 Ex $11,689 Gd $7948

"SKEETER" DOUBLE-BARREL SHOTGUN
.... NiB $4584 Ex $3667 Gd $2494
Boxlock. Gauge: 12 or 20. Bbls.: 28 inches w/full-length vent rib. Weight: Approx. 7 lbs. Buttstock and beavertail forend of select American walnut, finely checkered. Soft rubber recoil pad and ivory bead sights. Made in early 1930s.

STERLINGWORTH DELUXE
Same general specifications as Sterlingworth except 32-inch bbl. also available, recoil pad, ivory bead sights.
W/plain extractors............. NiB $1651 Ex $1321 Gd $899
W/automatic ejectors .... NiB $2034 Ex $1627 Gd $1107
20 ga., add..45%

STERLINGWORTH HAMMERLESS DOUBLE
Boxlock. Double triggers (Fox-Kautzky selective single trigger extra). Plain extractors (auto ejectors extra). Gauges: 12,16, 20. Bbl. lengths: 26-, 28-, 30-inch; chokes F/F, M/F, C/M (any combination of C to F choke borings was available at no extra cost). Weight: 12 ga., 6.88 to 8.25 lbs.; 16 ga., 6 to 7 lbs.; 20 ga., 5.75 to 6.75 lbs. Checkered pistol-grip stock and forearm.
W/plain extractors .... NiB $1524 Ex $1219 Gd $829
W/automatic ejectors .... NiB $1944 Ex $1555 Gd $1056
Selective single trigger, add 25%

MODEL B HAMMERLESS DOUBLE ...... NiB $300 Ex $240 Gd $163
Boxlock. Double triggers. Plain extractor. Gauges: 12, 16, 20, .410. 24- to 30-inch bbls., vent rib on current production; chokes: M/F, C/M, F/F (.410 only). Weight: About 7.5 lbs., 12 ga. Checkered pistol-grip stock and forend. Made about 1940-85.

MODEL B-ST.................. NiB $478 Ex $382 Gd $260
Same as Model B except has non-selective single trigger. Made 1955-66.

MODEL B-DE .... NiB $506 Ex $405 Gd $275
Same as Model B-ST except frame finished in satin chrome, select walnut buttstock w/checkered pistol grip and beavertail forearm. Made 1965-66.

MODEL B-DL .... NiB $564 Ex $451 Gd $307
Same as Model B-ST except frame finished in satin chrome, select walnut buttstock w/checkered pistol grip side panels, beavertail forearm. Made 1962-66.

Franchi Model 500
Standard Autoloader

Franchi Model 520 Deluxe

Franchi Model 520
Eldorado Gold

STERLINGWORTH SKEET AND UPLAND GAME GUN
Same general specifications as the standard Sterlingworth except has 26- or 28-inch bbls. w/skeet boring only, straight-grip stock. Weight: 7 lbs. (12 ga.).

W/plain extractors.	NiB $2279	Ex $1823	Gd $1239
W/automatic ejectors	NiB $2735	Ex $2188	Gd $1487
20 ga., add. 45%

SUPER HE GRADE. . . . . NiB $5322 Ex $4257 Gd $2896
Long-range gun made in 12 ga. only (chambered for 3-inch shells on order), 30- or 32-inch full choke bbls., auto ejectors standard. Weight: 8.75 to 9.75 lbs. General specifications same as standard Sterlingworth.

CMC HAMMERLESS DOUBLE-BARREL SHOTGUNS
High-grade doubles similar to the original Fox models. 20 ga. only. 26-28- or 30-inch bbls. Double triggers automatic safety and ejectors. Weight: 5.5 to 7 lbs. Custom Circassian walnut stock w/hand-rubbed oil finish. Custom stock configuration: straight, semi- or full pistol-grip stock w/traditional pad, hard rubber plate checkered or skeleton butt; Schnabel, splinter or beavertail forend. Made 1993 to date.

CE grade	NiB $7994	Ex $6395	Gd $4349
XE grade	NiB $8438	Ex $6750	Gd $4590
DE grade	NiB $12,344	Ex $9875	Gd $6715
FE grade	NiB $16,563	Ex $13,250	Gd $9010
Exhibition grade	NiB $23,744	Ex $18,995	Gd $12,917

LUIGI FRANCHI S.P.A. — Brescia, Italy

MODEL 48/AL ULTRA LIGHT SHOTGUN
Recoil-operated, takedown, hammerless shotgun w/tubular magazine. Gauges: 12 or 20 (2.75-inch); 12-ga. Magnum (3-inch chamber). Bbls.: 24- to 32-inch w/various choke combinations. Weight: 5 lbs., 2 oz. (20 ga.) to 6.25 lbs. (12 ga.). Checkered pistol-grip walnut stock and forend w/high-gloss finish.

Standard model	NiB $496	Ex $403	Gd $284
Hunter or magnum models	NiB $534	Ex $433	Gd $305

MODEL 500 STANDARD AUTOLOADER . . . . NiB $402 Ex $321 Gd $218
Gas-operated. 12 gauge. Four shot magazine. Bbls.: 26-, 28-inch; vent rib; IC, M, IM, F chokes. Weight: About 7 lbs. Checkered pistol-grip stock and forearm. Made 1976-80.

MODEL 520 DELUXE . . . . NiB $447 Ex $357 Gd $243
Same as Model 500 except higher grade w/engraved receiver. Made 1975-79.

MODEL 520 ELDORADO GOLD . . . . NiB $953 Ex $760 Gd $515
Same as Model 520 except custom grade w/engraved and gold-inlaid receiver, finer quality wood. Intro. 1977.

MODEL 610VS SEMIAUTOMATIC SHOTGUN
Gas-operated Variopress system adjustable to function w/2.75- or 3-inch shells. 12 gauge. Four shot magazine. 26- or 28-inch vent rib bbls. w/Franchoke tubes. Weight: 7 lbs., 2 oz. 47.5 inches overall. Alloy receiver w/four-lug rotating bolt and loaded chamber indicator. Checkered European walnut buttstock and forearm w/satin finish. Imported 1997-98.

Standard SV model	NiB $574	Ex $459	Gd $312
Engraved SVL model	NiB $631	Ex $505	Gd $344

MODEL 612 VARIOPRESS AUTOLOADING SHOTGUN
Gauge: 12 ga. Only. 24- to 28-inch bbl. 45 to 49-inches overall. Weight: 6.8 to 7 lbs. Five shot magazine. Bead type sights with C, IC, M chokes. Blued, matte or Advantage camo finish. Imported 1999 to date.

Model 612 satin walnut stock w/blued finish.	NiB $447	Ex $357	Gd $243
Model 612 synthetic stock w/matte finish.	NiB $478	Ex $382	Gd $260
Model 612 Advantage stock and finish	NiB $542	Ex $433	Gd $295
Model 612 Defense	NiB $414	Ex $331	Gd $225
Model 612 Sporting.	NiB $759	Ex $607	Gd $413

MODEL 620 VARIOPRESS AUTOLOADING SHOTGUN
Gauge: 20 ga. Only. 24- 26- or 28-inch bbl. 45 to 49-inches overall. Weight: 5.9 to 6.1 lbs. Five shot magazine. Bead type sights with C, IC, M chokes. Satin walnut or Advantage camo stock. Imported 1999 to date.

Model 620 satin walnut stock w/matte finish	NiB $447	Ex $357	Gd $243
Model 620 Advantage camo stock and finish	NiB $542	Ex $433	Gd $295
Model 620 Youth (short stock).	NiB $453	Ex $362	Gd $246

Franchi 612 Variopress Advantage

Franchi 612 Variopress Sporting

Franchi 612 Variopress

Franchi 620 Variopress Advantage

Franchi 620 Variopress

Franchi Model 2004
Trap Single Barrel

MODEL 2003 TRAP O/U . . . . **NiB $1224 Ex $1117 Gd $816**
Boxlock. Auto ejectors. Selective single trigger. 12 ga. Bbls.: 30-, 32-inch IM/F, F/F, high-vent rib. Weight (w/30-inch bbl.): 8.25 lbs. Checkered walnut beavertail forearm and stock w/straight or Monte Carlo comb, recoil pad. Luggage-type carrying case. Introduced 1976. Disc.

MODEL 2004 TRAP SINGLE BARREL . . . **NiB $1257 Ex $1005 Gd $683**
Same as Model 2003 except single bbl., 32- or 34-inch. Full choke. Weight (w/32-inch bbl.): 8.25 lbs. Introduced 1976. Disc.

MODEL 2005 COMBINATION TRAP . . . **NiB $1830 Ex $1464 Gd $995**
Model 2004/2005 type gun w/two sets of bbls., single and over/under. Introduced 1976. Disc.

MODEL 2005/3 COMBINATION TRAP . . . . . **NiB $2544 Ex $2035 Gd $1384**
Model 2004/2005 type gun w/three sets of bbls., any combination of single and over/under. Introduced 1976. Disc.

MODEL 3000/2 COMBINATION TRAP . . . . . **NiB $2863 Ex $2290 Gd $1558**
Boxlock. Automatic ejectors. Selective single trigger. 12 ga. only. Bbls.: 32-inch over/under choked F/IM, 34-inch underbarrel M choke; high vent rib. Weight (w/32-inch bbls.): 8 lbs., 6 oz. Choice of six different castoff buttstocks. Introduced 1979. Disc.

AIRONE HAMMERLESS DOUBLE . . . . . . **NiB $1175 Ex $940 Gd $640**
Boxlock. Anson & Deeley system action. Auto ejectors. Double triggers. 12 ga. Various bbl. lengths, chokes, weights. Checkered straight-grip stock and forearm. Made 1940-50.

ALCIONE O/U SHOTGUN
Hammerless, takedown shotgun w/engraved receiver. Selective single trigger and ejectors. 12 ga. w/3-inch chambers. Bbls.: 26-inch (IC/M, 28-inch (M/F). Weight: 6.75 lbs. Checkered French walnut buttstock and forend. Imported from Italy 1982-89.
Standard model . . . . **NiB $670 Ex $536 Gd $364**
SL model
(disc. 1986) . . . . **NiB $1141 Ex $913 Gd $621**

ALCIONE FIELD (97-12 IBS) O/U
Similar to the Standard Alcione model except w/nickel-finished receiver. 26- or 28-inch bbls. w/Franchoke tubes. Imported 1998 to date.
Standard Field model . . . . **NiB $861 Ex $688 Gd $468**
SL Field model
(w/sideplates, disc.) . . . . **NiB $1052 Ex $841 Gd $572**

ALCIONE SPORT (SL IBS) O/U........ NiB $1014 Ex $811 Gd $552
Similar to the Alcione Field model except chambered for 2.75 or 3-inch shells. Ported 29-inch bbls. w/target vent rib and Franchoke tubes.

ALCIONE 2000 SX O/U SHOTGUN.... NiB $1486 Ex $1188 Gd $808
Similar to the Standard Alcione model except w/silver finished receiver and gold inlays. 28-inch bbls. w/Franchoke tubes. Weight: 7.25 lbs. Imported 1996-97.

ARISTOCRAT FIELD
MODEL O/U .... NiB $593 Ex $474 Gd $322
Boxlock. Selective auto ejectors. Selective single trigger. 12 ga. Bbls.: 26-inch IC/M; 28- and 30-inch M/F choke, vent rib. Weight (w/26-inch bbls.): 7 lbs. Checkered pistol-grip stock and forearm. Made 1960-69.

ARISTOCRAT DELUXE AND SUPREME GRADES
Available in Field, Skeet and Trap models w/the same general specifications as standard guns of these types. Deluxe and Supreme Grades are of higher quality, w/stock and forearm of select walnut, elaborate relief engraving on receiver, trigger guard, tang and top lever. Supreme game birds inlaid in gold. Made 1960-66.
Deluxe grade .... NiB $1060 Ex $848 Gd $576
Supreme grade .... NiB $1524 Ex $1219 Gd $829

ARISTOCRAT IMPERIAL AND MONTE CARLO GRADES
Custom guns made in Field, Skeet and Trap models w/the same general specifications as standard for these types. Imperial and Monte Carlo grades are of highest quality w/stock and forearm of select walnut, fine engraving — elaborate on the latter grade. Made 1967-69.
Imperial grade .... NiB $2799 Ex $2239 Gd $1523
Monte Carlo grade .... NiB $3946 Ex $3157 Gd $2147

ARISTOCRAT MAGNUM MODEL....... NiB $666 Ex $532 Gd $362
Same as Field Model except chambered for 3-inch shells, has 32-inch bbls. choked F/F; stock has recoil pad. Weight: About 8 lbs. Made 1962-65.

ARISTOCRAT SILVER KING....... NiB $769 Ex $615 Gd $418
Available in Field, Magnum, Meet and Trap models w/the same general specifications as standard guns of these types. Silver King has stock and forearm of select walnut more elaborately engraved silver-finished receiver. Made 1962-69.

ARISTOCRAT SKEET MODEL ..... NiB $729 Ex $583 Gd $397
Same general specifications as Field Model except made only w/26-inch vent-rib bbls. w/SK chokes No. 1 and No. 2, skeet-style stock and forearm. Weight: About 7.5 lbs. Later production had wider (10mm) rib. Made 1960-69.

ARISTOCRAT TRAP MODEL ...... NiB $736 Ex $588 Gd $400
Same general specifications as Field Model except made only w/30-inch vent-rib bbls., M/F choke, trap-style stock w/recoil pad, beavertail forearm. Later production had Monte Carlo comb, 10mm rib. Made 1960-69.

ASTORE HAMMERLESS DOUBLE....... NiB $1014 Ex $811 Gd $552
Boxlock. Anson & Deeley system action. Plain extractors. Double triggers. 12 ga. Various bbl. lengths, chokes, weights. Checkered straight-grip stock and forearm. Made 1937-60.

ASTORE II .... NiB $1269 Ex $1015 Gd $691
Similar to Astore S but not as high grade. Furnished w/either plain extractors or auto ejectors, double triggers, pistol-grip stock. Bbls.: 27-inch IC/IM; 28-inch M/F chokes. Currently manufactured for Franchi in Spain.

Franchi Astore 5

ASTORE 5 .... NiB $2059 Ex $1647 Gd $1120
Same as Astore except has higher grade wood, fine engraving. automatic ejectors, single trigger, 28-inch bbl. M/F or IM/F chokes are standard on current production. Disc.

STANDARD MODEL AUTOLOADER
Recoil operated. Light alloy receiver. Gauges: 12, 20. Four shot magazine. Bbls.: 26-, 28-, 30-inch; plain, solid or vent rib, IC/ M, F chokes. Weight: 12 ga., about 6.25 lbs. 20 ga., 5.13 lbs. Checkered pistol-grip stock and forearm. Made 1950 to date.
W/plain bbl. .... NiB $478 Ex $321 Gd $251
W/solid rib .... NiB $427 Ex $342 Gd $233
W/vent rib..................... NiB $459 Ex $367 Gd $250

CROWN, DIAMOND AND IMPERIAL GRADE
Same general specifications as Standard Model except these are custom guns of the highest quality. Crown Grade has hunting scene engraving, Diamond Grade has silver-inlaid scroll engraving; Imperial Grade has elaborately engraved hunting scenes w/figures inlaid in gold. Stock and forearm of fancy walnut. Made 1954-75.
Crown grade .... NiB $1651 Ex $1321 Gd $899
Diamond grade .... NiB $2161 Ex $1729 Gd $1176
Imperial grade .... NiB $2742 Ex $2193 Gd $1491

STANDARD MODEL MAGNUM
Same general specifications as Standard model except has 3-inch chamber, 32-inch (12 ga.) or 28-inch (20 ga.) F choke bbl., recoil pad. Weight: 12 ga., 8.25 lbs.; 20 ga., 6 lbs. Formerly designated "Superange Model." Made 1954-88.
W/plain bbl. .... NiB $475 Ex $379 Gd $258
W/vent rib .... NiB $501 Ex $401 Gd $272

DYNAMIC-12
Same general specifications and appearance as Standard Model, except 12 ga. only, has heavier steel receiver. Weight: About 7.25 lbs. Made 1965-72.
W/plain bbl. .... NiB $376 Ex $301 Gd $205
W/vent rib..................... NiB $414 Ex $331 Gd $225

DYNAMIC-12 SLUG GUN .... NiB $427 Ex $342 Gd $232
Same as standard gun except 12 ga. only, has heavier steel receiver. Made 1965-72.

DYNAMIC-12 SKEET GUN .... NiB $528 Ex $422 Gd $288
Same general specifications and appearance as Standard model except has heavier steel receiver, made only in 12 ga. w/26-inch vent-rib bbl., SK choke, stock and forearm of extra fancy walnut. Made 1965-72.

ELDORADO MODEL .... NiB $555 Ex $444 Gd $302
Same general specifications as Standard model except highest grade w/gold-filled engraving, stock and forearm of select walnut, furnished w/vent-rib bbl. only. Made 1954-75.

Franchi Falconet Over/Under Buckskin

Franchi Crown Grade

Franchi Diamond Grade

Franchi Eldorado

FALCONET INTERNATIONAL SKEET MODEL... NiB $1120 Ex $896 Gd $609
Similar to Standard Skeet model but higher grade. Made 1970-74.

**FALCONET INTERNATIONAL
TRAP MODEL** . . . . **NiB $1143 Ex $915 Gd $622**
Similar to Standard model but higher grade; w/straight or Monte Carlo comb stock. Made 1970-74.

FALCONET O/U FIELD MODELS
Boxlock. Auto ejectors. Selective single trigger. Gauges: 12, 16, 20, 28, .410. Bbls.: 24-, 26-, 28-, 30-inch; vent rib. Chokes: C/IC, IC/M, M/F. Weight: from about 6 lbs. Engraved lightweight alloy receiver, light-colored in Buckskin model, blued in Ebony model, pickled silver in Silver model. Checkered walnut stock and forearm. Made 1968-75.
Buckskin or Ebony model . . . . **NiB $694 Ex $555 Gd $377**
Silver model . . . . **NiB $771 Ex $617 Gd $419**

FALCONET STANDARD SKEET MODEL . . . . . **NiB $969 Ex $775 Gd $527**
Same general specifications as Field models except made only w/26-inch bbls. w/SK chokes No. 1 and No. 2, wide vent rib, color-casehardened receiver skeet-style stock and forearm. Weight: 12 ga., about 7.75 lbs. Made 1970-74.

FALCONET STANDARD TRAP MODEL . . . . . . **NiB $958 Ex $766 Gd $521**
Same general specifications as Field models except made only in 12 ga. w/30-inch bbls., choked M/F, wide vent rib, color-casehardened receiver, Monte Carlo trap style stock and forearm, recoil pad. Weight: About 8 lbs. Made 1970-74.

HAMMERLESS SIDELOCK DOUBLES
Hand-detachable locks. Self-opening action. Auto ejectors. Double triggers or single trigger. Gauges: 12,16, 20. Bbl. lengths, chokes, weights according to customer's specifications. Checkered stock and forend, straight or pistol grip. Made in six grades — Condor, Imperiale, Imperiale S, Imperiale Montecarlo No. 5, Imperiale Montecarlo No.11, Imperiale Montecarlo Extra — which differ chiefly in overall quality, engraving, grade of wood, checkering, etc.; general specifications are the same. Only the Imperiale Montecarlo Extra Grade is currently manufactured.
Condor grade . . . . **NiB $8427 Ex $6741 Gd $4585**
Imperiale, Imperiale S grades . . . . **NiB $11,982 Ex $9585 Gd $6518**
**Imperiale Monte Carlo
grades No. 5, 11** . . . . **NiB $16,862 Ex $13,489 Gd $9173**
Imperiale Monte Carlo Extra grade . . . . . **NiB $19,613 Ex $15,690 Gd $10,669**

HUNTER MODEL
Same general specifications as Standard Model except higher grade w/engraved receiver; furnished w/ribbed bbl. only. Made 1950 to 90.
W/solid rib . . . . **NiB $435 Ex $348 Gd $237**
W/vent rib . . . . **NiB $468 Ex $374 Gd $254**

HUNTER MODEL MAGNUM . . . . **NiB $528 Ex $422 Gd $288**
Same as Standard Model Magnum except higher grade w/engraved receiver, vent rib bbl. only. Formerly designated "Wildfowler Model." Made 1954-73.

PEREGRINE MODEL 400 . . . . **NiB $720 Ex $576 Gd $392**
Same general specifications as Model 451 except has steel receiver. Weight (w/26.5-inch bbl.): 6 lbs., 15 oz. Made 1975-78.

PEREGRINE MODEL 451 O/U . . . . **NiB $720 Ex $518 Gd $352**
Boxlock. Lightweight alloy receiver. Automatic ejectors. Selective single trigger. 12 ga. Bbls.: 26.5-, 28-inch; choked C/IC, IC/M, M/F; vent rib. Weight (w/26.5-inch bbls.): 6 lbs., 1 oz. Checkered pistol-grip stock and forearm. Made 1975-78.

PG-80 GAS-OPERATED SEMIAUTOMATIC SHOTGUN
Gas-operated, takedown, hammerless shotgun w/tubular magazine. 12 ga. w/2.75-inch chamber. Five shot magazine. Bbls.: 24 to 30 inches w/vent rib. Weight: 7.5 lbs. Gold-plated trigger. Checkered pistol-grip stock and forend of European walnut. Imported from Italy 1985-90.
Prestige model . . . . **NiB $568 Ex $455 Gd $309**
Elite model . . . . **NiB $635 Ex $508 Gd $346**

SKEET GUN . . . . **NiB $511 Ex $409 Gd $277**
Same general specifications and appearance as Standard Model except made only w/26-inch vent-rib bbl., SK choke. Stock and forearm of extra fancy walnut. Made 1972-74.

SLUG GUN . . . . **NiB $393 Ex $314 Gd $213**
Same as Standard Model except has 22-inch plain bbl., Cyl. bore, folding leaf open rear sight, gold bead front sight. Made 1960 to date.

Franchi Hunter Model
w/Ventilated Rib

Franchi Black Magic
48/AL Semiautomatic

Francotte Model 8446

Francotte Model 6886

TURKEY GUN . . . . **NiB $478 Ex $382 Gd $260**
Same as Standard Model Magnum except higher grade w/turkey scene engraved receiver, 12 ga. only, 36-inch matted-rib bbl., Extra Full choke. Made 1963-65.

BLACK MAGIC 48/AL SEMIAUTOMATIC
Similar to the Franchi Model 48/AL except w/Franchoke screw-in tubes and matte black receiver w/Black Magic logo. Gauge: 12 or 20, 2.75-inch chamber. Bbls.: 24-, 26-, 28-inch w/vent rib; 24-inch rifled slug w/sights. Weight: 5.2 lbs. (20 ga.). Checkered walnut buttstock and forend. Blued finish.
Standard model . . . . **NiB $554 Ex $443 Gd $301**
Slug bbl. model . . . . **NiB $596 Ex $476 Gd $323**

FALCONET 2000 O/U . . . . **NiB $1296 Ex $1037 Gd $705**
Boxlock. Single selective trigger. Selective automatic ejectors. Gauge: 12, 2.75-inch chambers. Bbls.: 26-inch w/Franchoke tubes; IC/M/F. Weight: 6 lbs. Checkered walnut stock and forearm. Engraved silver receiver w/gold-plated game scene. Imported from 1992-93.

LAW-12 SHOTGUN. . . . . **NiB $575 Ex $460 Gd $312**
Similar to the SPAS-12 Model except gas-operated semiautomatic action only, ambidextrous safety, decocking lever and adj. sights. Made 1983-94.

SPAS-12 SHOTGUN
Selective operating system functions as a gas-operated semi-automatic or pump action. Gauge: 12, 2.75-inch chamber. Seven shot magazine. Bbl.: 21.5 inches w/cylinder bore and muzzle protector or optional screw-in choke tubes, matte finish. 41 inches overall w/fixed stock. Weight: 8.75 lbs. Blade front sight, aperture rear sight. Folding or black nylon buttstock w/pistol grip and forend, non-reflective anodized finish. Made 1983-94.
Fixed stock model . . . . **NiB $886 Ex $709 Gd $482**
Folding stock model . . . . **NiB $1014 Ex $811 Gd $552**
Optional choke tubes, add **$125**

SPORTING 2000
O/U . . . . **NiB $1332 Ex $1066 Gd $724**
Similar to the Franchi Falconet 2000. Boxlock. Single selective trigger. Selective automatic ejectors. Gauge: 12; 2.75-inch chambers. Ported (1992-93) or unported 28-inch bbls., w/vent rib. Weight: 7.75 lbs. Blued receiver. Bead front sight. Checkered walnut stock and forearm; plastic composition buttplate. Imported from 1992-93 and 1997 to date.

AUGUSTE FRANCOTTE & CIE., S.A. — Liège, Belgium

Francotte shotguns for many years were distributed in the U.S. by Abercrombie & Fitch of New York City. This firm has used a series of model designations for Francotte guns which do not correspond to those of the manufacturer. Because so many Francotte owners refer to their guns by the A & F model names and numbers, the A & F series is included in a listing separate from that of the standard Francotte numbers.

BOXLOCK HAMMERLESS DOUBLES
Anson & Deeley system. Side clips. Greener crossbolt on models 6886, 8446, 4996 and 9261; square crossbolt on Model 6930, Greener-Scott crossbolt on Model 8457, Purdey bolt on Models 11/18E and 10/18E/628. Auto ejectors. Double triggers. Made in all standard gauges, barrel lengths, chokes, weights. Checkered stock and forend, straight or pistol-grip. The eight models listed vary chiefly in fastenings as described above, finish and engraving, etc.; general specifications are the same. Disc.
Model 6886 . . . . **NiB $3379 Ex $2703 Gd $1838**
Model 8446 (Francotte Special),
6930, 4996 . . . . **NiB $3819 Ex $3055 Gd $2078**
Model 8457,
9261 (Francotte Original), 11/18E . . . . **NiB $4909 Ex $3950 Gd $2670**
Model 10/18E/628 . . . . **NiB $6241 Ex $4993 Gd $3396**

Franchi LAW-12

Franchi SPAS-12

Franchi Sporting 2000

Francotte Model
10/18E628

Francotte Model 9261

BOXLOCK HAMMERLESS DOUBLES — A & F SERIES

Boxlock, Anson & Deeley type. Crossbolt. Sideplate on all except Knockabout Model. Side clips. Auto ejectors. Double triggers. Gauges: 12, 16, 20, 28, .410. Bbls.: 26- to 32-inch in 12 ga., 26- and 28-inch in other ga.; any boring. Weight: 4.75 to 8 lbs. depending on ga. and bbl. length. Checkered stock and forend; straight, half or full pistol grip. The seven grades (No. 45 Eagle Grade, No. 30, No. 25, No. 20, No. 14, Jubilee Model, Knockabout Model) differ chiefly in overall quality, engraving, grade of wood, checkering, etc.; general specifications are the same. Disc.

Jubilee model
No. 14 .... NiB $2091 Ex $1673 Gd $1137
Jubilee model
No. 18..................... NiB $2748 Ex $2198 Gd $1495
Jubilee model
No. 20 .... NiB $3507 Ex $2805 Gd $1907
Jubilee model
No. 25 .... NiB $3781 Ex $3024 Gd $2056

(cont'd.) BOXLOCK HAMMERLESS DOUBLES — A & F SERIES
Jubilee model
No. 30 .... NiB $5754 Ex $4602 Gd $3129
Eagle grade
No. 45 .... NiB $8025 Ex $6420 Gd $4366
Knockabout model .... NiB $2454 Ex $1963 Gd $1335

BOXLOCK HAMMERLESS DOUBLES (SIDEPLATES)
Anson & Deeley system. Reinforced frame w/side clips. Purdey-type bolt except on Model 8455, which has Greener crossbolt. Auto ejectors. Double triggers. Made in all standard gauges, bbl. lengths, chokes, weights. Checkered stock and forend, straight or pistol grip. Models 10594, 8455 and 6982 are of equal quality, differing chiefly in style of engraving; Model 9/40E/38321 is a higher grade gun in all details and has fine English-style engraving. Present models quoted and built to customer specifications.

Models 10594, 8455, 6982 .... NiB $4966 Ex $3973 Gd $2702
Model 9/40E/38321 .... NiB $6057 Ex $4845 Gd $3295

Galef Silver Snipe Over/Under Shotgun

Galef Companion Folding Single-Barrel Shotgun

Galef Zabala Hammerless Double-Barrel Shotgun

FINE O/U SHOTGUN **$9180**
Model 9/40.SE. Boxlock, Anson & Deeley system. Auto ejectors. Double triggers. Made in all standard gauges; bbl. length, boring to order. Weight: About 6.75 lbs. 12 ga. Checkered stock and forend, straight or pistol grip. Currently manufactured to customer specifications.

FINE SIDELOCK
HAMMERLESS DOUBLE . . . . NiB **$24,544** Ex **$19,635** Gd **$13,352**
Model 120.HE/328. Automatic ejectors. Double triggers. Made in all standard ga.; bbl. length, boring, weight to order. Checkered stock and forend, straight or pistol-grip. Currently manufactured to customer specifications.

HALF-FINE O/U SHOTGUN . . . . NiB **$10,104** Ex **$8083** Gd **$5447**
Model SOB.E/11082. Boxlock, Anson & Deeley system. Auto ejectors. Double triggers. Made in all standard gauges; barrel length, boring to order. Checkered stock and forend, straight or pistol grip. Note: This model is similar to No. 9/40.SE except general quality lower. Disc.

GALEF SHOTGUNS — Manufactured for J. L. Galef & Son, Inc., New York, New York, by M. A. V. I., Gardone F. T., Italy, by Zabala Hermanos, Eiquetta, Spain, and by Antonio Zoli, Gardone V. T., Italy

SILVER SNIPE OVER/UNDER SHOTGUN . . . . NiB **$516** Ex **$413** Gd **$280**
Boxlock. Plain extractors. Single trigger. Gauges: 12, 20; 3-inch chambers. Bbls: 26-, 28-, 30-inch (latter in 12 ga. only); IC/M, M/F chokes; vent rib. Weight: 12 ga. w/28-inch bbls., 6.5 lbs. Checkered walnut pistol-grip stock and forearm. Introduced by Antonio Zoli in 1968. Disc. See illustration previous page.

GOLDEN SNIPE . . . . NiB **$595** Ex **$476** Gd **$324**
Same as Silver Snipe, except has selective automatic ejectors. Made by Antonio Zoli 1968 to date.

MONTE CARLO TRAP
SINGLE-BARREL SHOTGUN . . . . NiB **$249** Ex **$199** Gd **$136**
Hammerless. Underlever. Plain extractor. 12 ga. 32-inch bbl., F choke, vent rib.

(cont'd.) MONTE CARLO TRAP SINGLE-BARREL SHOTGUN
Weight: About 8.25 lbs. Checkered pistol-grip stock w/Monte Carlo comb and recoil pad, beavertail forearm. Introduced by M. A. V. I. in 1968. Disc.

SILVER HAWK HAMMERLESS DOUBLE . . . . . . NiB **$502** Ex **$401** Gd **$272**
Boxlock. Plain extractors. Double triggers. Gauges: 12, 20; 3-inch chambers. Bbls.: 26-, 28-, 30-inch (latter in 12 ga. only); IC/M, M/F chokes. Weight: 12 ga. w/26-inch bbls., 6 lbs. 6 oz. Checkered walnut pistol-grip stock and beavertail forearm. Made by Antonio Zoli 1968-72.

COMPANION FOLDING SINGLE-BARREL SHOTGUN
Hammerless. Underlever. Gauges: 12 Mag., 16, 20 Mag., 28, .410. Bbls.: 26-inch (.410 only), 28-inch (12, 16, 20, 28), 30-inch (12-ga. only); F choke; plain or vent rib. Weight: 4.5 lbs. for .410 to 5 lbs., 9 oz. for 12 ga. Checkered pistol-grip stock and forearm. Made by M. A. V. I. from 1968 to date.
W/plain bbl. . . . . NiB **$126** Ex **$101** Gd **$69**
W/ventilated rib . . . . NiB **$166** Ex **$134** Gd **$91**

ZABALA HAMMERLESS DOUBLE-BARREL SHOTGUN
Boxlock. Plain extractors. Double triggers. Gauges: 10 Mag., 12 Mag., 16, 20 Mag., 28, .410. Bbls.: 22-, 26-, 28-, 30-, 32-inch; IC/IC, IC/M, M/F chokes. Weight: 12 ga. w/28-inch bbls., 7.75 lbs. Checkered walnut pistol-grip stock and beavertail forearm, recoil pad. Made by Zabala from 1972 to date. See illustration previous page.
10 ga. . . . . NiB **$287** Ex **$229** Gd **$156**
Other ga. . . . . NiB **$210** Ex **$168** Gd **$114**

GAMBA — Gardone V. T. (Brescia), Italy

DAYTONA COMPETITION O/U
Boxlock w/Boss-style locking system. Anatomical single trigger; optional adj., single-selective release trigger. Selective automatic ejectors. Gauge: 12 or 20; 2.75- or 3-inch chambers. Bbls.: 26.75-, 28-, 30- or 32-inch choked SK/SK, IM/F or M/F. Weight: 7.5 to 8.5 lbs. Black or chrome receiver w/blued bbls. Checkered select walnut stock and forearm w/oil finish. Imported by Heckler & Koch until 1992.
American Trap model. . . . . NiB **$5419** Ex **$4335** Gd **$2948**
Pigeon, Skeet, Trap models . . . . NiB **$6241** Ex **$4993** Gd **$3396**

SHOTGUNS

Garbi Model 200

Golden Eagle
Model 5000 Grade II Field

(cont'd.) DAYTONA COMPETITION O/U
Sporting model . . . . NiB $5164 Ex $4131 Gd $2809
Sideplate model . . . . NiB $10,614 Ex $8491 Gd $5774
Engraved models
NiB $9562 to $12,750 Ex $7650 to $10,200 Gd $5202 to $6936
Sidelock model . . . . NiB $27,412 Ex $21,930 Gd $14,912

GARBI SHOTGUNS — Eibar, Spain

MODEL 100
SIDELOCK SHOTGUN . . . . NiB $3805 Ex $3044 Gd $2070
Gauges: 12, 16, 20 and 28. Bbls.: 25-, 28-, 30-inch. Action: Holland
& Holland pattern sidelock; automatic ejectors and double trigger.
Weight: 5 lbs., 6 oz. to 7 lbs. 7 oz. English-style straight grip stock
w/fine-line hand-checkered butt; classic forend. Made 1985 to date.

MODEL 101
SIDELOCK SHOTGUN . . . . NiB $4839 Ex $3871 Gd $2632
Same general specifications as Model 100 except the sidelocks
are handcrafted w/hand-engraved receiver; select walnut straight-
grip stock.

MODEL 102
SIDELOCK SHOTGUN . . . . NiB $5182 Ex $4145 Gd $2819
Similar to the Model 101 except w/large scroll engraving. Made
1985-93.

MODEL 103 HAMMERLESS DOUBLE
Similar to Model 100 except w/Purdey-type, higher grade engraving.
Model 103A Standard . . . . NiB $5259 Ex $4207 Gd $2861
Model 103A Royal Deluxe. . . . . NiB $9810 Ex $7848 Gd $5337
Model 103B . . . . NiB $7924 Ex $6339 Gd $4310
Model 103B Royal Deluxe . . . . NiB $14,018 Ex $11,214 Gd $7625

MODEL 200
HAMMERLESS DOUBLE . . . . . . NiB $7847 Ex $6277 Gd $4269
Similar to Model 100 except w/double heavy-duty locks. Continental-style
floral and scroll engraving. Checkered deluxe walnut stock and forearm.

GARCIA CORPORATION — Teaneck, New Jersey

BRONCO 22/.410 O/U COMBO . . . . NiB $121 Ex $97 Gd $66
Swing-out action. Takedown. 18.5-inch bbls.; .22 LR over, .410 ga.
under. Weight: 4.5 lbs. One-piece stock and receiver, crackle finish.
Intro. In 1976. Disc.

BRONCO .410 SINGLE SHOT. . . . . NiB $96 Ex $76 Gd $52
Swing-out action. Takedown. .410 ga. 18.5-inch bbl. Weight: 3.5 lbs.
One-piece stock and receiver, crackle finish. Intro. In 1967. Disc.

GOLDEN EAGLE FIREARMS INC. — Houston, Texas, Mfd. By Nikko Firearms Ltd., Tochigi, Japan

EAGLE MODEL 5000
GRADE I FIELD O/U . . . . NiB $867 Ex $781 Gd $520
Receiver engraved and inlaid w/gold eagle head. Boxlock. Auto
ejectors. Selective single trigger. 12, 20 ga.; 2.75- or 3-inch chambers, 12 ga., 3-inch, 20 ga. Bbls.: 26-, 28-, 30-inch (latter only in 12-
ga. 3-inch Mag.); IC/M, M/F chokes; vent rib. Weight: 6.25 lbs., 20
ga.; 7.25 lbs., 12 ga.; 8 lbs., 12-ga. Mag. Checkered pistol-grip stock
and semi-beavertail forearm. Imported 1975-82. Note: Guns marketed 1975-76 under the Nikko brand name have white receivers;
since 1976 are blued.

EAGLE MODEL 5000
GRADE I SKEET . . . . NiB $957 Ex $765 Gd $520
Same as Field model except has 26- or 28-inch bbls. w/wide (11
mm) vent rib, SK choked. Imported 1975-82.

EAGLE MODEL 5000
GRADE I TRAP . . . . NiB $914 Ex $731 Gd $497
Same as Field model except has 30-, or 32-inch bbls. w/wide (11
mm) vent rib (M/F, IM/F, F/F chokes), trap-style stock w/recoil pad.
Imported 1975-82.

EAGLE MODEL 5000
GRADE II FIELD . . . . NiB $999 Ex $799 Gd $543
Same as Grade I Field model except higher grade w/fancier wood,
more elaborate engraving and "screaming eagle" inlaid in gold.
Imported 1975-82.

EAGLE MODEL 5000
GRADE II SKEET . . . . NiB $1029 Ex $823 Gd $560
Same as Grade I Skeet model except higher grade w/fancier wood,
more elaborate engraving and "screaming eagle" inlaid in gold;
inertia trigger, vent side ribs. Imported 1975-82.

EAGLE MODEL 5000
GRADE II TRAP . . . . NiB $1046 Ex $837 Gd $569
Same as Grade I Trap model except higher grade w/fancier wood,
more elaborate engraving and "screaming eagle" inlaid in gold;
inertia trigger, vent side ribs. Imported 1975-82.

EAGLE MODEL 5000
GRADE III GRANDEE . . . . NiB $2742 Ex $2193 Gd $1491
Best grade, available in Field, Skeet and Trap models w/same
general specifications as lower grades. Has sideplates w/game
scene engraving, scroll on frame and bbls., fancy wood (Monte
Carlo comb, full pistol-grip and recoil pad on Trap model). Made
1976-82.

Gorosabel
Model 504 Shotgun

Greener Empire Model
Hammerless

GOROSABEL SHOTGUNS — Spain

MODEL 503 SHOTGUN . . . . **NiB $886 Ex $709 Gd $482**
Gauges: 12, 16, 20 and .410. Action: Anson & Deely-style boxlock. Bbls.: 26-, 27-, and 28-inch. Select European walnut, English or pistol grip, sliver or beavertail forend, hand-checkering. Scalloped frame and scroll engraving. Intro. 1985; disc..

MODEL 504 SHOTGUN . . . . **NiB $957 Ex $765 Gd $520**
Gauge: 12 or 20. Action: Holland & Holland-style sidelock. Bbl.: 26-, 27-, or 28-inch. Select European walnut, English or pistol grip, sliver or beavertail forend, hand-checkering. Holland-style large scroll engraving. Inro. 1985; disc..

MODEL 505 SHOTGUN . . . . . . **NiB $1332 Ex $1065 Gd $724**
Gauge: 12 or 20. Action: Holland & Holland-style sidelock. Bbls.: 26-, 27-, or 28-inch. Select European walnut, English or pistol grip, silver or beavertail forend, hand-checkering. Purdey-style fine scroll and rose engraving. Intro. 1985; disc..

STEPHEN GRANT — London, England

**BEST QUALITY SELF-OPENER DOUBLE-BARREL
SHOTGUN** . . . . **NiB $15,313 Ex $12,250 Gd $8330**
Sidelock, self-opener. Gauges: 12, 16 and 20. Bbls.: 25 to 30 inches standard. Highest-grade English or European walnut straight-grip buttstock and forearm w/Greener type lever. Imported by Stoeger in the 1950s.

**BEST QUALITY SIDE-LEVER DOUBLE-BARREL
SHOTGUN** . . . . **NiB $13,125 Ex $10,500 Gd $7140**
Sidelock, self-lever. Gauges: 12, 16 and 20. Bbls.: 25 to 30 inches standard. Highest-grade English or European walnut straight-grip buttstock and forearm w/Greener type lever. Imported by Stoeger in the 1950s.

W. W. GREENER, LTD. — Birmingham, England

EMPIRE MODEL HAMMERLESS DOUBLES
Boxlock. Non-ejector or w/automatic ejectors. Double triggers. 12 ga. only (2.75-inch or 3-inch chamber). Bbls.: 28- to 32-inch; any choke combination. Weight: from 7.25 to 7.75 lbs. depending on bbl. length. Checkered stock and forend, straight- or half-pistol grip. Also furnished in "Empire Deluxe Grade," this model has same general specs, but deluxe finish.

Empire model, non-ejector	NiB $1996	Ex $1596	Gd $1086
Empire model, ejector	NiB $2183	Ex $1746	Gd $1188
Empire Deluxe model, non-ejector . . .	NiB $2028	Ex $1623	Gd $1103
Empire Deluxe model, ejector	NiB $2311	Ex $1849	Gd $1258

FAR-KILLER MODEL GRADE FH35
HAMMERLESS DOUBLE-BARREL SHOTGUN
Boxlock. Non-ejector or w/automatic ejectors. Double triggers. Gauges: 12 (2.75-inch or 3-inch), 10, 8. Bbls.: 28-, 30- or 32-inch. Weight: 7.5 to 9 lbs. in 12 ga. Checkered stock, forend; straight or half-pistol grip. See illustration next page.

Non-ejector, 12 ga.	NiB $2826	Ex $2261	Gd $1538
Ejector, 12 ga.	NiB $3419	Ex $2735	Gd $1859
Non-ejector, 10 or 8 ga.	NiB $2891	Ex $2312	Gd $1573
Ejector, 10 or 8 ga.	NiB $3818	Ex $3054	Gd $2076

G. P. (GENERAL PURPOSE)
SINGLE BARREL . . . . **NiB $451 Ex $360 Gd $245**
Greener Improved Martini Lever Action. Takedown. Ejector. 12 ga. only. Bbl. lengths: 26-, 30-, 32-inch. M or F choke. Weight: 6.25 to 6.75 lbs. depending on bbl. length. Checkered straight-grip stock and forearm.

HAMMERLESS EJECTOR
DOUBLE-BARREL SHOTGUNS
Boxlock. Auto ejectors. Double triggers, non-selective or selective single trigger. Gauges: 12, 16, 20, 28, .410 (two latter gauges not supplied in Grades DH40 and DH35). Bbls.: 26-, 28-, 30-inch; any choke combination. Weight: From 4.75 to 8 lbs. Depending on ga. and bbl. length. Checkered stock and forend, straight- or half-pistol grip. The Royal, Crown, Sovereign and Jubilee Models differ in quality, engraving, grade of wood, checkering, etc. General specifications are the same.

Royal Model Grade DH75	NiB $4629	Ex $3703	Gd $2518
Crown Model Grade DH55	NiB $3419	Ex $2735	Gd $1859
Sovereign Model Grade DH40	NiB $3007	Ex $2405	Gd $1636
Jubilee Model Grade DH35	NiB $2492	Ex $1993	Gd $1354
W/selective single trigger, add.			$330
W/non-selective single trigger, add			$250

GREIFELT & COMPANY — Suhl, Germany

GRADE NO. 1 O/U SHOTGUN
Anson & Deeley boxlock, Kersten fastening. Auto ejectors. Double triggers or single trigger. Elaborately engraved. Gauges: 12, 16, 20, 28, .410. Bbls.: 26- to 32-inch, any combination of chokes, vent or solid matted rib. Weight: 4.25 to 8.25 lbs. depending on ga. and bbl. length. Straight- or pistol-grip stock, Purdey-type forend, both checkered. Manufactured prior to World War II.

W/solid matted-rib bbl.,
except .410 & 28 ga. . . . . **NiB $3470 Ex $2776 Gd $1888**
W/solid matted-rib bbl., .410 & 28 ga
. . . . **NiB $4346 Ex $3476 Gd $2364**
W/ventilated rib, add $395
W/single trigger, add. $425

SHOTGUNS

Francotte Model
10/18E628

Greener Hammerless
Ejector Double-Barrel
Shotguns: Jubilee, Royal
and Sovereign

Greifelt Grade No. 1
Over-and-Under Shotgun

MODEL 22 HAMMERLESS DOUBLE. . . NiB $1912 Ex $1530 Gd $1039
Anson & Deeley boxlock. Plain extractors. Double triggers. Gauges:
12 and 16. Bbls.: 28- or 30-inch, M/F choke. Checkered stock and
forend, pistol grip and cheekpiece standard, English-style stock also
supplied. Manufactured since World War II.

MODEL 22E
HAMMERLESS DOUBLE . . . . . . NiB $2543 Ex $2034 Gd $1383
Same as Model 22 except has automatic ejectors.

MODEL 103
HAMMLERLESS DOUBLE . . . . . NiB $1848 Ex $1478 Gd $1005
Anson & Deeley boxlock. Plain extractors. Double triggers. Gauges:
12 and 16. Bbls.: 28- or 30-inch, M and F choke. Checkered stock
and forend, pistol grip and cheekpiece standard, English-style stock
also supplied. Manufactured since World War II.

MODEL 103E
HAMMERLESS DOUBLE . . . . . . NiB $1964 Ex $1571 Gd $1068
Same as Model 103 except has automatic ejectors.

MODEL 143E O/U SHOTGUN
General specifications same as pre-war Grade No. 1 Over-and-Under, except
this model is not supplied in 28 and .410 ga. or w/32-inch bbls. Model 143E
is not as high quality as the Grade No. 1 gun. Mfd. Since World War II.
W/raised matted rib,
double triggers . . . . NiB $2259 Ex $1808 Gd $1229
W/ventilated rib,
selective single trigger . . . . NiB $2775 Ex $2220 Gd $1510

HAMMERLESS DRILLING (THREE-BARREL
COMBINATION GUN) . . . . NiB $3608 Ex $2886 Gd $1962
Boxlock. Plain extractors. Double triggers, front single set for rifle
bbl. Gauges: 12, 16, 20; rifle bbl. in any caliber adapted to this type
of gun. 26-inch bbls. Weight: About 7.5 lbs. Auto rear sight operated by rifle bbl. selector. Checkered stock and forearm, pistol-grip
and cheekpiece standard. Manufactured prior to WW II. Note: Value
shown is for guns chambered for cartridges readily obtainable. If
rifle bbl. is an odd foreign caliber, value will be considerably less.

GRADE NO. 3 O/U SHOTGUN
Same general specifications as Grade No. 1 except less fancy
engraving. Manufactured prior to World War II.
W/solid matted-rib bbl.,
except .410 & 28 ga. . . . . NiB $2775 Ex $2220 Gd $1510
W/solid matted-rib bbl.,
.410 & 28 ga. . . . . NiB $3302 Ex $2642 Gd $1796
W/ventilated rib, add $395
W/single trigger, add. $425

O/U COMBINATION GUN
Similar in design to this maker's over-and-under shotguns. Gauges: 12, 16, 20, 28, .410; rifle bbl. in any caliber adapted to this type of gun. Bbls.: 24- or 26-inch, solid matted rib. Weight: From 4.75 to 7.25 lbs. Folding rear sight. Manufactured prior to WWII. Note: Values shown are for gauges other than .410 w/rifle bbl. Chambered for a cartridge readily obtainable; if in an odd foreign caliber, value will be considerably less. .410 ga. increases in value by about 50%.
W/non-automatic ejector . . . . . **NiB $5916 Ex $4733 Gd $3219**
W/automatic ejector . . . . **NiB $6760 Ex $5407 Gd $3677**

HARRINGTON & RICHARDSON ARMS COMPANY — Gardner, Massachusetts, Now H&R 1871, Inc.

Formerly Harrington & Richardson Arms Co. of Worcester, Mass. One of the oldest and most distinguished manufacturers of handguns, rifles and shotguns, H&R suspended operations on January 24, 1986. In 1987, New England Firearms was established as an independent company producing selected H&R models under the NEF logo. In 1991, H&R 1871, Inc. was formed from the residual of the parent company and then took over the New England Firearms facility. H&R 1871 produced firearms under both their logo and the NEF brand name until 1999, when the Marlin Firearms Company acquired the assets of H&R 1871.

**Harrington & Richardson
No. 3, 5, 6, 7 and 8 Shotguns**

NO. 3 HAMMERLESS
SINGLE-SHOT SHOTGUN . . . . **NiB $112 Ex $76 Gd $51**
Takedown. Automatic ejector. Gauges: 12, 16, 20, .410. Bbls.: plain, 26- to 32-inch, F choke. Weight: 6.5 to 7.25 lbs. depending on ga. and bbl. length. Plain pistol-grip stock and forend. Disc. 1942.

NO. 5 STANDARD LIGHTWEIGHT
HAMMER SINGLE . . . . **NiB $133 Ex $82 Gd $56**
Takedown. Auto ejector. Gauges: 24, 28, .410. Bbls.: 26- or 28-inch, F choke. Weight: About 4 to 4.75 lbs. Plain pistol-grip stock/forend. Disc. 1942.

NO. 6 HEAVY BREECH SINGLE-SHOT
HAMMER SHOTGUN . . . . **NiB $133 Ex $82 Gd $56**
Takedown. Automatic ejector. Gauges: 10, 12, 16, 20. Bbls.: Plain, 28- to 36-inch, F choke. Weight: About 7 to 7.25 lbs. Plain stock and forend. Disc. 1942.

NO. 7 OR 9 BAY STATE SINGLE-SHOT
HAMMER SHOTGUN . . . . **NiB $133 Ex $82 Gd $56**
Takedown. Automatic ejector. Gauges: 12, 16, 20, .410. Bbls.: Plain 26- to 32-inch, F choke. Weight: 5.5 to 6.5 lbs. depending on ga. and bbl. length. Plain pistol-grip stock and forend. Disc. 1942.

NO. 8 STANDARD SINGLE-SHOT
HAMMER SHOTGUN . . . . **NiB $153 Ex $92 Gd $61**
Takedown. Automatic ejector. Gauges: 12, 16, 20, 24, 28, .410. Bbl.: plain, 26- to 32-inch, F choke. Weight: 5.5 to 6.5 lbs. depending on ga. and bbl. length. Plain pistol-grip stock and forend. Made 1908-42.

MODEL 348 GAMESTER
BOLT-ACTION SHOTGUN . . . . **NiB $112 Ex $76 Gd $51**
Takedown. 12 and 16 ga. Two shot tubular magazine, 28-inch bbl, F choke. Plain pistol-grip stock. Weight: About 7.5 lbs. Made 1949-54.

MODEL 349 GAMESTER DELUXE . . . . **NiB $153 Ex $82 Gd $56**
Same as Model 348 except has 26-inch bbl. W/adj. choke device, recoil pad. Made 1953-55.

MODEL 351 HUNTSMAN
BOLT-ACTION SHOTGUN . . . . **NiB $159 Ex $127 Gd $87**
Takedown. 12 and 16 ga. Two shot tubular magazine. Pushbutton safety. 26-inch bbl. w/H&R variable choke. Weight: About 6.75 lbs. Monte Carlo stock w/recoil pad. Made 1956-58.

MODEL 400 PUMP . . . . **NiB $223 Ex $178 Gd $121**
Hammerless. Gauges: 12, 16, 20. Tubular magazine holds 4 shells. 28-inch bbl., F choke. Weight: About 7.25 lbs. Plain pistol-grip stock (recoil pad in 12 and 16 ga.), grooved slide handle. Made 1955-67.

Harrington & Richardson
Model 400 Pump

Harrington & Richardson
Model 403 Autoloading

Harrington & Richardson
Model 404C

Harrington & Richardson
Model 440

Harrington & Richardson
Model 442

MODEL 401 . . . . **NiB $223 Ex $178 Gd $121**
Same as Model 400 except has H&R variable choke. Made
1956-63.

MODEL 402 . . . . **NiB $236 Ex $189 Gd $129**
Similar to Model 400 except .410 ga., weight: About 5.5 lbs. Made
1959-67.

MODEL 403 AUTOLOADING
SHOTGUN . . . . **NiB $242 Ex $194 Gd $132**
Takedown. .410 ga. Tubular magazine holds four shells. 26-inch
bbl., F choke. Weight: About 5.75 lbs. Plain pistol-grip stock and
forearm. Made in 1964.

MODEL 404/404C . . . . **NiB $287 Ex $230 Gd $156**
Boxlock. Plain extractors. Double triggers. Gauges: 12, 20, .410.
Bbls.: 28-inch in 12 ga. (M/F choke), 26-inch in 20 ga. (IC/M and
.410 (F/F). Weight: 5.5 to 7.25 lbs. Plain walnut-finished hardwood
stock and forend on Model 404; 404C checkered. Made in Brazil by
Amadeo Rossi 1969-1972.

MODEL 440 PUMP . . . . **NiB $185 Ex $148 Gd $101**
Hammerless. Gauges: 12, 16, 20. 2.75-inch chamber in 16 ga., 3-
inch in 12 and 20 ga. Three shot magazine. Bbls.: 26-, 28-, 30-inch;
IC, M, F choke. Weight: 6.25 lbs. Plain pistol-grip stock and slide
handle, recoil pad. Made 1968-73.

MODEL 442 . . . . **NiB $236 Ex $189 Gd $129**
Same as Model 440 except has vent rib bbl., checkered stock and
forearm, weight: 6.75 lbs. Made 1969-73.

ULTRA SLUG SERIES . . . . **NiB $198 Ex $158 Gd $107**
Singel shot 12 or 20 ga w/3-inch chamber w/heavy-wall 24-inch
fully rifled bbl. w/scope . Weight: 9 lbs. Walnut-stained Monte Carlo
stock, sling swivels, black nylon sling. Made 1995 to date.

MODEL 1212 FIELD . . . . **NiB $339 Ex $270 Gd $184**
Boxlock. Plain extractors. Selective single trigger. 12 ga., 2.75-inch
chambers. 28-inch bbls., IC/IM, vent rib. Weight: 7 lbs. Checkered
walnut pistol-gip stock and fluted forearm. Made 1976-80 by
Lanber Arms S. A., Zaldibar (Vizcaya), Spain.

Harrington & Richardson
Model 1212 Field

Harrington & Richardson
Model 1212 Waterfowl

Harrington & Richardson
Golden Squire — Model 159

Harrington & Richardson
Harrich No. 1

MODEL 1212
WATERFOWL GUN. . . . . **NiB $372 Ex $298 Gd $202**
Same as Field Gun except chambered for 12-ga, 3-inch mag. shells, has 30-inch bbls., M/F chokes, stock and recoil pad, weight: 7.5 lbs. Made 1976-1980.

MODEL 1908
SINGLE-SHOT SHOTGUN . . . . **NiB $153 Ex $97 Gd $61**
Takedown. Automatic ejector. Gauges: 12, 16, 24 and 28. Bbls.: 26- to 32-inch, F choke. Weight: 5.25 to 6.5 lbs. depending on ga. and bbl. length. Casehardened receiver. Plain pistol-grip stock. Bead front sight. Made 1908-1934.

MODEL 1908 .410 (12MM)
SINGLE-SHOT SHOTGUN . . . . **NiB $143 Ex $114 Gd $78**
Same general specifications as standard Model 1908 except chambered for .410 or 12mm shot cartridge w/bbl. milled down at receiver to give a more pleasing contour.

MODEL 1915 SINGLE-SHOT SHOTGUN
Takedown. Both non-auto and auto-ejectors available. Gauges: 24, 28, .410, 14mm and 12mm. Bbls.: 26- or 28-inch, F choke. Weight: 4 to 4.75 lbs. depending on ga. and bbl. length. Plain black walnut stock w/semi pistol-grip.
24 ga. . . . . **NiB $210 Ex $168 Gd $114**
28, .410 ga. **NiB $172 Ex $138 Gd $94**

FOLDING GUN . . . . **NiB $172 Ex $138 Gd $94**
Single bbl. hammer shotgun hinged at the front of the frame, the bbl. folds down against the stock. Light Frame model: gauges — 28, 14mm, .410; 22-inch bbl.; weighs about 4.5 lbs. Heavy Frame model: gauges — 12, 16, 20, 28, .410; 26-inch bbl.; weighs from 5.75 to 6.5 lbs. Plain pistol-grip stock and forend. Disc. 1942.

GOLDEN SQUIRE MODEL 159
SINGLE-BARREL
HAMMER SHOTGUN . . . . **NiB $127 Ex $102 Gd $69**
Hammerless. Side lever. Automatic ejection. Gauges: 12, 20. Bbls.: 30-inch in 12 ga., 28-inch in 20 ga., both F choke. Weight: About 6.5 lbs. Straight-grip stock w/recoil pad, forearm w/Schnabel. Made 1964-66.

GOLDEN SQUIRE JR. MODEL 459. . **NiB $147 Ex $117 Gd $80**
Same as Model 159 except gauges 20 and .410, 26-inch bbl., youth stock. Made in 1964.

HARRICH NO. 1 SINGLE-BARREL
TRAP GUN . . . . **NiB $1525 Ex $1220 Gd $829**
Anson & Deeley-type locking system w/Kersten top locks and double underlocking lugs. Sideplates engraved w/hunting scenes. 12 ga. Bbls.: 32-, 34-inch; F choke; high vent rib. Weight: 8.5 lbs. Checkered Monte Carlo stock w/pistol-grip and recoil pad, beavertail forearm, of select walnut. Made in Ferlach, Austria, 1971-75.

Harrington & Richardson
Topper No. 48

Harrington & Richardson
Topper No. 099

Harrington & Richardson
Topper No. 162 — Slug Gun

Harrington & Richardson
Topper Model 198 (098)

Harrington & Richardson
Topper Model 490 — Greenwing

"TOP RIB"
SINGLE-BARREL SHOTGUN . . . . **NiB $212 Ex $176 Gd $131**
Takedown. Auto ejector. Gauges: 12, 16 and 20. Bbls.: 28- to 30-inch, F choke w/full-length matted top rib. Weight: 6.5 to 7 lbs. depending on ga. and bbl. length. Black walnut pistol-grip stock (capped) and forend; both checkered. Flexible rubber buttplate. Made during 1930s.

TOPPER NO. 48 SINGLE-BARREL
HAMMER SHOTGUN . . . . **NiB $166 Ex $134 Gd $91**
Similar to old Model 8 Standard. Takedown. Top lever. Auto ejector. Gauges: 12, 16, 20, .410. Bbls.: plain; 26- to 30-inch; M or F choke. Weight: 5.5 to 6.5 lbs. depending on ga. and bbl. length. Plain pistol-grip stock and forend. Made 1946-57.

TOPPER MODEL 099 DELUXE . . . . . **NiB $134 Ex $107 Gd $72**
Same as Model 158 except has matte nickel finish, semipistol grip walnut-finished American hardwood stock; semibeavertail forearm; 12, 16, 20, and .410 ga. Made 1982-86.

TOPPER MODEL 148 SINGLE-SHOT
HAMMER SHOTGUN . . . . **NiB $141 Ex $112 Gd $76**
Takedown. Side lever. Auto-ejection. Gauges: 12, 16, 20, .410.

(cont'd.) TOPPER MODEL 148
Bbls.: 12 ga.,30-, 32- and 36-inch; 16 ga., 28- and 30-inch; 20 and .410 ga., 28-inch; F choke. Weight: 5 to 6.5 lbs. Plain pistol-grip stock and forend, recoil pad. Made 1958-61.

TOPPER MODEL 158 (058) SINGLE-SHOT
HAMMER SHOTGUN . . . . **NiB $147 Ex $117 Gd $80**
Takedown. Side lever. Automatic ejection. Gauges: 12, 20, .410 (2.75-inch and 3-inch shells); 16 (2.75-inch). bbl. length and choke combinations: 12 ga., 36-inch/F, 32-inch/F, 30-inch/F, 28-inch/F or M; .410, 28-inch/F. Weight: about 5.5 lbs. Plain pistol-grip stock and forend, recoil pad. Made 1962-81. Note: Designation changed to 058 in 1974.

TOPPER MODEL 162 SLUG GUN. . **NiB $193 Ex $154 Gd $105**
Same as Topper Model 158 except has 24-inch bbl., Cyl. bore, w/rifle sights. Made 1968-86.

TOPPER MODEL 176 10 GA.
MAGNUM . . . . **NiB $185 Ex $148 Gd $101**
Similar to Model 158, but has 36-inch heavy bbl. chambered for 3.5-inch 10- ga. Mag. shells, weight: 10 lbs.; stock w/Monte Carlo comb and recoil pad, longer and fuller forearm. Made 1977-86.

Harrington & Richardson
Topper — Classic Youth

Harrington & Richardson
Topper — Deluxe

TOPPER MODEL 188 DELUXE ..... NiB $159 Ex $127 Gd $87
Same as standard Topper Model 148 except has chromed frame, stock and forend in black, red, yellow, blue, green, pink, or purple colored finish. .410 ga. only. Made 1958-61.

TOPPER MODEL 198 (098) DELUXE ...... NiB $166 Ex $133 Gd $90
Same as Model 158 except has chrome-plated frame, black finished stock and forend; 12, 20 and .410 ga. Made 1962-81. Note: Designation changed to 098 in 1974.

TOPPER JR. MODEL 480 .... NiB $153 Ex $97 Gd $71
Similar to No. 48 Topper except has youth-size stock, 26-inch bbl, .410 ga. only. Made 1958-61.

TOPPER NO. 488 DELUXE .... NiB $154 Ex $123 Gd $84
Same as standard No. 48 Topper except chrome-plated frame, black lacquered stock and forend, recoil pad. Disc. 1957.

TOPPER MODEL 490 .... NiB $147 Ex $117 Gd $80
Same as Model 158 except has youth-size stock (3 inches shorter), 26-inch bbl.; 20 and 28 ga. (M choke), .410 (F). Made 1962-86.

TOPPER MODEL 490 GREENWING .... NiB $166 Ex $133 Gd $90
Same as the Model 490 except has a special high-polished finish. Made 1981-86.

TOPPER JR. MODEL 580 .... NiB $127 Ex $102 Gd $69
Same as Model 480 except has colored stocks as on Model 188. Made 1958-61.

TOPPER MODEL 590 .... NiB $134 Ex $107 Gd $72
Same as Model 490 except has chrome-plated frame, black finished stock and forend. Made 1962-63.

The following models are manufactured and distributed by the reorganized company of H&R 1871, Inc.

MODEL 098 TOPPER CLASSIC YOUTH ..... NiB $121 Ex $97 Gd $66
Same as Topper Junior except also available in 28 ga. and has checkered American black walnut stock/forend w/satin finish and recoil pad. Made 1991 to date.

MODEL 098 TOPPER DELUXE ...... NiB $121 Ex $97 Gd $66
Same as Model 098 Single Shot Hammer except in 12 ga., 3-inch chamber only. 28-inch bbl.; Mod. choke tube. Made 1992 to date.

MODEL 098 TOPPER
DELUXE RIFLED SLUG GUN ...... NiB $153 Ex $122 Gd $83
Same as Topper Deluxe Shotgun except has compensated 24-inch rifled slug bbl. Nickel plated receiver and blued bbl. Black finished hardwood stock. Made 1996 to date.

MODEL 098 TOPPER HAMMER
SINGLE-SHOT SHOTGUN .... NiB $102 Ex $82 Gd $55
Side lever. Automatic ejector. Gauges: 12, 20 and .410; 3-inch chamber. Bbls.: 28-inch, (12 ga./M); 26-inch, (20 ga./M); 26-inch (.410/F). Weight: 5 to 6 lbs. Satin nickel receiver, blued bbl. Plain pistol-grip stock and semibeavertail forend w/black finish. Re-Intro. 1992.

MODEL 098 TOPPER JUNIOR ...... NiB $108 Ex $87 Gd $59
Same as Model 098 except has youth-size stock and 22-inch bbl. 20 or .410 ga. only. Made 1991 to date.

MODEL .410 TAMER SHOTGUN .... NiB $121 Ex $97 Gd $66
Takedown. Topper-style single-shot, side lever action w/auto ejector. Gauge: .410; 3-inch chamber. 19.5-inch bbl. 33 inches overall. Weight: 5.75 lbs. Black polymer thumbhole stock designed to hold 4 extra shotshells. Matte nickel finish. Made 1994 to date.

MODEL N. W. T. F. TURKEY MAG
Same as Model 098 Single-Shot Hammer except has 24-inch bbl. chambered 10 or 12 ga. w/3.5-inch chamber w/screw-in choke tube. Weight: 6 lbs. American hardwood stock, Mossy Oak camo finish. Made 1991-96.
NWTF 10 ga. Turkey Mag (Made 1996) .... NiB $143 Ex $114 Gd $78
NWTF 12 ga. Turkey Mag (Made 1991-95).. NiB $126 Ex $101 Gd $68

MODEL N. W. T. F.
YOUTH TURKEY GUN .... NiB $140 Ex $112 Gd $75
Same as Model N.W.T.F. Turkey Mag except has 22-inch bbl. chambered in 20 ga. w/3-inch chamber and fixed full choke. Realtree camo finish. Made 1994-95.

MODEL SB1-920
ULTRA SLUG HUNTER .... NiB $189 Ex $151 Gd $103
Special 12 ga. action w/12 ga. bbl. blank underbored to 20 ga. to form a fully rifled slug bbl. Gauge: 20 w/3 inch chamber. 24-inch bbl. Weight: 8.5 lbs. Satin nickel receiver, blued bbl. Walnut finished hardwood Monte Carlo stock. Made 1996-98.

Heckler & Koch Red Lion Mark II

Heckler & Koch Classic Lion Grade I

MODEL ULTRA SLUG HUNTER $138
12 or 20 ga. w/3-inch chamber. 22- or 24-inch rifled bbl. Weight: 9
lbs. Matte black receiver and bbl. Walnut finished hardwood Monte
Carlo stock. Made 1997 to date.

MODEL ULTRA SLUG HUNTER DELUXE . . . . . NiB $198 Ex $158 Gd $107
Similar to Ultra Slug Hunter model except with compensated bbl.
Made 1997 to date.

HECKLER & KOCH FABARM SHOTGUNS — Oberndorf/Neckar, West Germany, and Sterling, Virginia

CLASSIC LION SIDE-BY-SIDE SHOTGUN
12 ga. only. 28- or 30-inch non-ported Tribor bbl. w/3-inch chamber. 46.5 to 48.5-inches overall. Weight: 7 to 7.2 lbs. Five choke
tubes; C, IC, M, IM, F. Traditional boxlock design. Oil-finished walnut forearms and stocks w/diamond-cut checkering. Imported 1999
to date.
Classic Lion Grade I . . . . NiB $1312 Ex $1050 Gd $714
Classic Lion Grade II . . . . NiB $1990 Ex $1583 Gd $1076

CAMO LION SEMI-AUTO SHOTGUN . . . . NiB $867 Ex $739 Gd $459
12 ga. Only. 24 to 28-inches Tribor bbl. 44.25-48.25-inches overall.
Weight: 7-7.2 lbs. 3 inch chamber w/5 choke tubes - C, IC, M, IM,
F. 2-shot mag. Camo covered walnut stock w/rear front bar sights.
Imp. 1999 to date.

MAX LION O/U SHOTGUN . . . . NiB $1729 Ex $1479 Gd $816
12 or 20 ga. 26- 28- or 30-inch TriBore system bbls. 42.5-47.25-
inches overall. Weight: 6.8-7.8 lbs. 3-inch chamber w/5 choke
tubes - C, IC, M, IM, F. Single selective adj. trigger and auto ejectors. Side plates w/high-grade stock and rubber recoil pad. Made
1999 to date.

RED LION MARK II SEMI-AUTO
SHOTGUN . . . . NiB $759 Ex $607 Gd $413
12 ga. Only. 24- 26- or 28-inch TriBore system bbls. 44.25 to 48.25-
inches overall. Weight: 7 to 7.2 lbs. 3-inch chamber w/five choke
tubes- C, IC, M, IM, F. Two shot magazine. Matte finish w/walnut wood
stock. Rubber vented recoil pad w/leather cover. Made 1999 to date.

SILVER LION O/U SHOTGUN . . . . NiB $1152 Ex $923 Gd $631
12 or 20 ga. 26- 28- or 30-inch TriBore system bbls. 43.25-47.25 inch-
esoverall. 3-inch chamber w/5 choke tubes - C, IC, M, IM, F. Single
selective trig. and auto ejectors. Wal. stock w/rubber recoil pad.
Made 1999 to date.

SPORTING CLAY LION
SEMI-AUTO SHOTGUN . . . . NiB $886 Ex $709 Gd $482
12 ga. only. 28- or 30-inch bbl. w/3-inch chamber and ported
Tribore system barrel. Matte finish w/gold plated trigger and carrier
release button. Made 1999 to date.

HERCULES SHOTGUNS

See Listings under "W" for Montgomery Ward.

HEYM SHOTGUNS — Münnerstadt, Germany

MODEL 22S
"SAFETY" SHOTGUN/
RIFLE COMBINATION . . . . NiB $3264 Ex $2611 Gd $1776
16 and 20 ga. Cal: .22 Mag., .22 Hornet, .222 Rem., .222 Rem.
Mag., 5.6x50R Mag., 6.5x57R, 7x57R, .243 Win. 24-inch bbls. 40
inches overall. Weight: About 5.5 lbs. Single-set trigger. Left-side
bbl. selector. Integral dovetail base for scope mounting. Arabesque
engraving. Walnut stock. Disc. 1993.

MODEL 55 BF SHOTGUN/
RIFLE COMBO . . . . NiB $7086 Ex $5668 Gd $3855
12, 16 and 20 ga. Calibers: 5.6x50R Mag., 6.5x57R, 7x57R, 7x65R,
.243 Win., .308 Win., .30-06. 25-inch bbls. 42-inches overall.
Weight: About 6.75 lbs. Black satin-finished, corrosion-resistant
bbls. of Krupp special steel. Hand-checkered walnut stock w/long
pistol-grip. Hand-engraved leaf scroll. German cheekpiece. Disc.
1988.

J. C. HIGGINS SHOTGUNS

See Sears, Roebuck & Company.

HUGLU HUNTING FIREARMS — Huglu, Turkey, Imported by Turkish Firearms Corp.

MODEL 101 B 12 AT-DT
COMBO O/U TRAP . . . . NiB $2034 Ex $1627 Gd $1107
Over/Under boxlock. 12 ga. w/3-inch chambers. Combination 30-
or 32-inch top single & O/U bbls. w/fixed chokes or choke tubes.
Weight: 8 lbs. Automatic ejectors or extractors. Single selective trig-
ger. Manual safety. Circassian walnut Monte Carlo trap stock
w/palm-swell grip and recoil pad. Silvered frame w/engraving.
Imported 1993-97.

Heym Model 22S
"Safety" Shotgun/Rifle Combination Gun

Heym Model 55
BF Shotgun/Rifle

MODEL 101 B 12 ST O/U TRAP.... NiB $1372 Ex $1098 Gd $746
Same as Model 101 AT-DT except in 32-inch O/U configuration only. Imported 1994-96.

MODEL 103 B 12 ST O/U
Boxlock. Gauges: 12, 16, 20, 28 or .410. 28-inch bbls. w/fixed chokes. Engraved action w/inlaid game scene and dummy sideplates. Double triggers, extractors and manual safety. Weight: 7.5 lbs. Circassian walnut stock. Imported 1995-96.
Model 103B w/extractors .... NiB $1004 Ex $803 Gd $546
28 and .410, add.................................. $100

MODEL 103 C 12 ST O/U
Same general specs as Model 103 B 12 S except w/extractors or ejectors. 12 or 20 ga. w/3-inch chambers. Black receiver w/50% engraving coverage. Imported 1995-97.
Model 103C w/extractors .... NiB $1014 Ex $811 Gd $552
Model 103C w/ejectors......... NiB $1269 Ex 1015 Gd $691

MODEL 103 D 12 ST O/U
Same gen. specs as Mdl. 103 B 12 ST except stand. boxlock. Ext. or eject. 12 or 20 ga. w/3-inch chambers. 80% engraving coverage. Imp. 1995-97.
Model 103D w/extractors .... NiB $988 Ex $790 Gd $538
Model 103D w/ejectors......... NiB $1243 Ex $994 Gd $676

MODEL 103 F 12 ST O/U
Same as Model 103 B except extractors or ejectors. 12 or 20 ga. only. 100% engraving coverage. Imported 1996-97.
Model 103F w/extractors .... NiB $1084 Ex $867 Gd $590
Model 103F w/ejectors........ NiB $1339 Ex $1071 Gd $728

MODEL 104 A 12 ST O/U
Boxlock. Gauges: 12, 20, 28 or .410. 28-inch bbls. w/fixed chokes or choke tubes. Silvered, engraved receiver w/15% engraving coverage. Double triggers, manual safety and extractors or ejectors. Weight: 7.5 lbs. Circassian walnut stock w/field dimensions. Imported 1995-97.
Model 104A w/extractors ......NiB $957 Ex $765 Gd $520
Model 104A w/ejectors........ NiB $1212 Ex $969 Gd $659

(cont'd.) MODEL 104 A 12 ST O/U
28 and .410, add $100
W/Choke Tubes, add $50

MODEL 200 SERIES DOUBLE
Boxlock. Gauges: 12, 20, 28, or .410 w/3-inch chambers. 28-inch bbls. w/fixed chokes. Silvered, engraved receiver. Extractors, manual safety, single selective trigger or double triggers. Weight: 7.5 lbs. Circassian walnut stock. Imported 1995-97.
Model 200 (w/15%
engraving coverage, SST) .... NiB $988 Ex $790 Gd $538
Model 201 (w/30%
engraving coverage, SST)....... NiB $1269 Ex $1015 Gd $690
Model 202 (w/Greener
cross bolt, DT)............... NiB $1052 Ex $841 Gd $572
28 and .410, add...................................$100

HIGH STANDARD SPORTING ARMS — East Hartford, Connecticut, Formerly High Standard Mfg. Corp. of Hamden, Conn.

In 1966, High Standard introduced new series of Flite-King Pumps and Supermatic autoloaders, both readily identifiable by the damascened bolt and restyled checkering. To avoid confusion, these models are designated "Series II" in this text. This is not an official factory designation. Operation of this firm was discontinued in 1984.

FLITE-KING FIELD
PUMP—12 GA.................. NiB $274 Ex $219 Gd $149
Hammerless. Magazine holds 5 shells. Bbls.: 26-inch IC, 28-inch M or F, 30-inch F choke. Weight: 7.25 lbs. Plain pistol-grip stock and slide handle. Made 1960-66.

FLITE-KING BRUSH—12 GA...... NiB $204 Ex $184 Gd $153
Same as Flite-King Field 12 except has 18- or 20-inch bbl. (cylinder bore) w/rifle sights. Made 1962-64.

SHOTGUNS

High Standard Flite-King Brush

High Standard Flite-King Deluxe Rib — 12 Gauge

High Standard Flite-King Deluxe Rib — 12 Gauge (Adjustable Choke)

FLITE-KING BRUSH DELUXE . . . . . NiB $270 Ex $235 Gd $153
Same as Flite-King Brush except has adj. peep rear sight, checkered pistol grip, recoil pad, fluted slide handle, swivels and sling. Not available w/18-inch bbl. Made 1964-66.

FLITE-KING BRUSH (SERIES II). . . . NiB $260 Ex $208 Gd $141
Same as Flite-King Deluxe 12 (II) except has 20-inch bbl., cylinder bore, w/rifle sights. Weight: 7 lbs. Made 1966-75.

FLITE-KING BRUSH DELUXE (II) . . NiB $303 Ex $241 Gd $164
Same as Flite-King Brush (II) except has adj. peep rear sight, swivels and sling. Made 1966-75.

FLITE-KING DELUXE 12 GA. (SERIES II)
Hammerless. 5-shot magazine. 27-inch plain bbls.w/adj. choke. 26-inch IC, 28-inch M or F. 30-inch F choke. Weight: About 7.25 lbs. Checkered pistol-grip stock and forearm, recoil pad. Made 1966-75.
W/adj. choke . . . . NiB $303 Ex $243 Gd $165
W/O adj. choke . . . . NiB $275 Ex $220 Gd $149

FLITE-KING DELUXE
20, 28, .410 GA. (SERIES II) . . . . . . NiB $271 Ex $217 Gd $148
Same as Flite-King Deluxe 12 (II) except chambered for 20 and .410 ga. 3-inch shell, 28 ga. 2.75-inch shell w/20- or 28-inch plain bbl. Weight: About 6 lbs. Made 1966-75.

FLITE-KING DELUXE RIB 12 GA. . . . . . NiB $333 Ex $266 Gd $180
Same as Flite-King Field 12 except vent rib bbl. (28-inch M or F. 30-inch F). Checkered stock and forearm. Made 1961-66.

FLITE-KING DELUXE RIB 12 GA. (II)
Same as Flite-King Deluxe 12 (II) except has vent rib bbl., available in 27-inch w/adj. choke, 28-inch M or F, 30-inch F choke. Made 1966-75.
W/adj. choke . . . . NiB $357 Ex $286 Gd $194
W/O adj. choke. . . . . NiB $333 Ex $266 Gd $181

FLITE-KING DELUXE RIB 20 GA. . . . . NiB $320 EX $256 GD $174
Same as Flite-King Field 20 except vent-rib bbl. (28 inch M or F), checkered stock and slide handle. Made 1962-66.

FLITE-KING DELUXE RIB 20, 28, .410 GA. (SERIES II)
Same as Flite-King Deluxe 20, 28, .410 (II) except 20 ga. available w/27-inch adj. choke, 28-inch M or F choke. Weight: about 6.25 lbs. Made 1966-75.
W/adj. choke. . . . . NiB $376 Ex $301 Gd $205
W/O adj. choke. . . . . NiB $351 Ex $281 Gd $191

FLITE-KING DELUXE SKEET GUN
12 GA. (SERIES II) . . . . NiB $325 Ex $260 Gd $176
Same as Flite-King Deluxe Rib 12 (II) except available only w/26-inch vent rib bbl., SK choke, recoil pad optional. Made 1966-75.

FLITE-KING DELUXE SKEET GUN
20, 28, .410 GA. (SERIES II). . . . . . NIB $376 EX $301 GD $205
Same as Flite-King Deluxe Rib 20, 28, .410 (II) except available only w/26-inch vent-rib bbl., SK choke. Made 1966-75.

FLITE-KING DELUXE
TRAP GUN (II) . . . . NIB $309 EX $247 GD $167
Same as Flite-King Deluxe Rib 12 (II) except available only w/30-inch vent-rib bbl., F choke; trap-style stock. Made 1966-75.

FLITE-KING FIELD PUMP 20 GA. . . . . NIB $249 EX $199 GD $136
Hammerless. Chambered for 3-inch Magnum shells, also handles 2.75-inch. Magazine holds four shells. Bbls.: 26-inch IC, 28-inch M or F choke. Weight: About 6 lbs. Plain pistol-grip stock and slide handle. Made 1961-66.

FLITE-KING PUMP SHOTGUNS 16 GA.
Same general specifications as Flite-King 12 except not available in Brush, Skeet and Trap Models or 30-inch bbl. Values same as for 12-ga. guns. Made 1961-65.

High Standard Flite-King Field
12 Gauge

High Standard Flite-King Field
20 Gauge

High Standard Flite-King Field Trophy
20 Gauge

High Standard Supermatic Deluxe
12 Gauge (II)

High Standard Supermatic Deluxe
12 Gauge (II) (Adjustable Choke)

FLITE-KING PUMP SHOTGUNS (.410 GA.)
Same general specifications as Flite-King 20 except not available in Special and Trophy Models, or w/other than 26-inch choke bbl. Values same as for 20 ga. guns. Made 1962-66.

FLITE-KING SKEET
12 GA. . . . . **NiB $357 Ex $286 Gd $194**
Same as Flite-King Deluxe Rib except 26-inch vent rib bbl., w/SK choke. Made 1962-66.

FLITE-KING SPECIAL 12 GA. . . . . . **NiB $260 Ex $208 Gd $141**
Same as Flite-King Field 12 except has 27-inch bbl. w/adj. choke. Made 1960-66.

FLITE-KING SPECIAL 20 GA. . . . . . **NiB $266 Ex $213 Gd $145**
Same as Flite-King Field 20 except has 27-inch bbl. w/adj. choke. Made 1961-66.

FLITE-KING TRAP 12 GA. . . . . **NiB $357 Ex $286 Gd $194**
Same as Flite-King Deluxe Rib 12 except 30-inch vent rib bbl., F choke, special trap stock w/recoil pad. Made 1962-66.

FLITE-KING TROPHY 12 GA. . . . . . **NiB $333 Ex $266 Gd $181**
Same as Flite-King Deluxe Rib 12 except has 27-inch vent rib bbl. w/adj. choke. Made 1960-66.

FLITE-KING TROPHY
20 GA. . . . . **NiB $357 Ex $286 Gd $194**
Same as Flite-King Deluxe Rib 20 except has 27-inch vent rib bbl. w/adj. choke. Made 1962-66.

SUPERMATIC DEER GUN . . . . **NiB $351 Ex $281 Gd $191**
Same as Supermatic Field 12 except has 22-inch bbl. (cylinder bore) w/rifle sights, checkered stock and forearm, recoil pad. Weight: 7.75 lbs. Made in 1965.

SUPERMATIC DELUXE 12 GA. (SERIES II)
Gas-operated autoloader. Four shot magazine. Bbls.: Plain; 27-inch w/adj. choke (disc. about 1970); 26-inch IC, 28-inch M or F. 30-inch F choke. Weight: About 7.5 lbs. Checkered pistol-grip stock and forearm, recoil pad. Made 1966-75.
W/adj. choke . . . . **NiB $376 Ex $301 Gd $205**
W/O adj. choke . . . . **NiB $305 Ex $250 Gd $180**

SUPERMATIC DELUXE 20 GA. (SERIES II)
Same as Supermatic Deluxe 12 (II) except chambered for 20 ga. Three inch shell; bbls. available in 27-inch w/adj. choke (disc. about 1970), 26-inch IC, 28-inch M or F choke. Weight: About 7 lbs. Made 1966-75.
W/adj. choke . . . . **NiB $274 Ex $219 Gd $149**
W/O adj. choke . . . . **NiB $325 Ex $260 Gd $176**

SUPERMATIC DELUXE DEER GUN (II) NiB $414 Ex $331 Gd $225
Same as Supermatic Deluxe 12 (II) except has 22-inch bbl., cylinder bore, w/rifle sights. Weight: 7.75 lbs. Made 1966-74.

SUPERMATIC DELUXE DUCK
12 GA. MAGNUM (SERIES II) . . . . . **NiB $285 Ex $229 Gd $159**
Same as Supermatic Deluxe 12 (II) except chambered for 3-inch magnum shells, 3-shot magazine, 30-inch plain bbl., F choke. Weight: 8 lbs. Made 1966-74.

High Standard Supermatic Deluxe Deer II

High Standard Supermatic Deluxe Duck Rib

High Standard Supermatic Deluxe Rib

High Standard Supermatic Duck —12 Gauge Magnum

SUPERMATIC DELUXE RIB
12 GA. . . . . NiB $271 Ex $217 Gd $148
Same as Supermatic Field 12 except vent rib bbl. (28-inch M or F, 30-inch F), checkered stock and forearm. Made 1961-66.

SUPERMATIC DELUXE RIB 12 GA. (II)
Same as Supermatic Deluxe 12 (II) except has vent rib bbl.; available in 27-inch w/adj. choke, 28-inch M or F, 30-inch F choke. Made 1966-75.
W/adj. choke . . . . NiB $338 Ex $270 Gd $184
W/O adj. choke . . . . NiB $306 Ex $245 Gd $166

SUPERMATIC DELUXE RIB
20 GA. . . . . NiB $338 Ex $270 Gd $184
Same as Supermatic Field 20 except vent rib bbl. (28-inch M or F), checkered stock and forearm. Made 1963-66.

SUPERMATIC DELUXE RIB 20 GA. (II)
Same as Supermatic Deluxe 20 (II) except has vent rib bbl. Made 1966-75.
W/adj. choke . . . . NiB $309 Ex $247 Gd $167
W/O adj. choke . . . . NiB $285 Ex $227 Gd $155

SUPERMATIC DELUXE
SKEET GUN
12 GA. (SERIES II) . . . . NiB $309 Ex $247 Gd $167
Same as Supermatic Deluxe Rib 12 (II) except available only w/26-inch vent rib bbl., SK choke. Made 1966-75.

SUPERMATIC DELUXE SKEET GUN
20 GA. (SERIES II) . . . . NiB $320 Ex $256 Gd $174
Same as Supermatic Deluxe Rib 20 (II) except available only w/26-inch vent rib bbl., SK choke. Made 1966-75.

SUPERMATIC DELUXE
TRAP GUN (SERIES II) . . . . NiB $333 Ex $266 Gd $181
Same as Supermatic Deluxe Rib 12 (II) except available only w/30-inch vent rib bbl., full choke; trap-style stock. Made 1966-75.

SUPERMATIC DELUXE DUCK RIB
12 GA. MAG. (SERIES II) . . . . NiB $309 Ex $247 Gd $167
Same as Supermatic Deluxe Rib 12 (II) except chambered for 3-inch magnum shells, 3-shot magazine; 30-inch vent rib bbl., F choke. Weight: 8 lbs. Made 1966-75.

SUPERMATIC DUCK 12 GA. MAG. . . . . NiB $309 Ex $247 Gd $167
Same as Supermatic Field 12 except chambered for 3-inch Magnum shell, 30-inch F choke bbl., recoil pad. Made 1961-66.

SUPERMATIC TROPHY 12 GA. . . . . NiB $260 Ex $208 Gd $141
Same as Supermatic Deluxe Rib 12 except has 27-inch vent-rib bbl. w/adj. choke. Made 1961-66.

SUPERMATIC DUCK RIB 12 GA. MAG.. . . . . NiB $333 Ex $266 Gd $181
Same as Supermatic Duck 12 Magnum except has vent rib bbl., checkered stock and forearm. Made 1961-66.

SUPERMATIC FIELD AUTOLOADING
SHOTGUN 12 GA. . . . . NiB $357 Ex $286 Gd $194
Gas-operated. Magazine holds four shells. Bbls.: 26-inch IC, 28-inch M or F choke, 30-inch F choke. Weight: About 7.5 lbs. Plain pistol-grip stock and forearm. Made 1960-66.

SUPERMATIC FIELD AUTOLOADING
SHOTGUN 20 GA.. . . . . NiB $274 Ex $219 Gd $149
Gas-operated. Chambered for 3-inch mag. shells, also handles 2.75-inch. Magazine holds three shells. Bbls.: 26-inch IC, 28-inch M or F choke. Weight: About 7 lbs. Plain pistol-grip stock and forearm. Made 1963-66.

SUPERMATIC SHADOW AUTOMATIC . . . NiB $402 Ex $321 Gd $218
Gas-operated. Ga.: 12, 20, 2.75- or 3-inch chamber in 12 ga., 3-inch in 20 ga. Mag. holds four 2.75-inch shells, three 3-inch. Bbls.: Full-size airflow rib; 26-inch (IC or SK choke), 28-inch (M, IM or F), 30-inch (trap or F choke), 12-ga. 3-inch Mag. available only in 30-inch F choke; 20 ga. not available in 30-inch. Weight: 12 ga., 7 lbs. Checkered walnut stock and forearm. Made 1974-75 by Caspoll Int'l., Inc., Tokyo.

High Standard Supermatic Duck Rib — 12 Gauge

High Standard Supermatic Shadow Automatic

High Standard Supermatic Shadow Indy

High Standard Supermatic Shadow Seven

SUPERMATIC SHADOW
INDY O/U . . . . **NiB 1014 Ex $811 Gd $552**
Boxlock. Fully engraved receiver. Selective auto ejectors. Selective single trigger. 12 ga. 2.75-inch chambers. Bbls.: Full-size airflow rib; 27.5 inch both SK choke, 29.75-inch IM/F or F/F. Weight: W/29.75-inch bbls., 8 lbs. 2 oz. Pistol-grip stock w/recoil pad, ventilated forearm, skip checkering. Made 1974-75 by Caspoll Int'l., Inc., Tokyo.

SUPERMATIC SHADOW SEVEN . . . **NiB $861 Ex $688 Gd $468**
Same general specifications as Shadow Indy except has conventional vent rib, less elaborate engraving, standard checkering forearm is not vented, no recoil pad. 27.5-inch bbls.; also available in IC/M, M/F choke. Made 1974-75.

SUPERMATIC SKEET 12 GA. . . . . . . **NiB $274 Ex $219 Gd $149**
Same as Supermatic Deluxe Rib 12 except 26-inch vent-rib bbl. w/SK choke. Made 1962-66.

SUPERMATIC SKEET 20 GA. . . . . . . **NiB $294 Ex $235 Gd $159**
Same as Supermatic Deluxe Rib 20 except 26-inch vent-rib bbl. w/SK choke. Made 1964-66.

SUPERMATIC SPECIAL 12 GA. . . . . **NiB $243 Ex $194 Gd $132**
Same as Supermatic Field 12 except has 27-inch bbl. w/adj. choke. Made 1960-66.

SUPERMATIC SPECIAL 20 GA. . . . . **NiB $268 Ex $214 Gd $146**
Same as Supermatic Field 20 except has 27-inch bbl. w/adj. choke. Made 1963-66.

SUPERMATIC TRAP 12 GA. . . . . **NiB $274 Ex $219 Gd $149**
Same as Supermatic Deluxe Rib 12 except 30-inch vent rib bbl., F choke, special trap stock w/recoil pad. Made 1962-66.

SUPERMATIC TROPHY 20 GA. . . . . . **NiB $287 Ex $229 Gd $156**
Same as Supermatic Deluxe Rib 20 except has 27-inch vent rib bbl. w/adj. choke. Made 1963-66.

HOLLAND & HOLLAND, LTD. — *London England*

BADMINTON MODEL HAMMERLESS DOUBLE-BARREL SHOTGUN. ORIGINALLY NO. 2 GRADE
General specifications same as Royal Model except without self-opening action. Made as a game gun or pigeon and wildfowl gun. Introduced in 1902. Disc.

W/double triggers	NiB $10,856	Ex $8684	Gd $5905
W/single trigger	NiB $12,416	Ex $9932	Gd $6754
20 ga., add.			25%
28 ga., add.			40%
.410, add			65%

CENTENARY MODEL HAMMERLESS
DOUBLE-BARREL SHOTGUN
Lightweight (5.5 lbs.). 12 ga. game gun designed for 2-inch shell. Made in four grades—Model Deluxe, Royal, Badminton, Dominion — values same as shown for standard guns in those grades. Disc. 1962.

High Standard Supermatic Special

High Standard Supermatic Trophy

Holland & Holland
Royal Model

Holland & Holland Badminton

Holland & Holland Dominion

DOMINION MODEL HAMMERLESS
DOUBLE-BBL. SHOTGUN .... NiB $6408 Ex $5126 Gd $3486
Game Gun. Sidelock. Auto ejectors. Double triggers. Gauges: 12, 16, 20. bbls. 25- to 30-inch, any standard boring. Checkered stock and forend, straight grip standard. Disc. 1967.

MODEL DELUXE HAMMERLESS DOUBLE
Same as Royal Model except has special engraving and exhibition grade stock and forearm. Currently manufactured.
W/double triggers ...... NiB $59,150 Ex $47,320 Gd $32,178
W/single trigger .... NiB $64,675 Ex $51,740 Gd $35,183

NORTHWOOD MODEL HAMMERLESS
DOUBLE-BARREL SHOTGUN.. NiB $6884 Ex $5507 Gd $3745
Anson & Deeley system boxlock. Auto ejectors. Double triggers. Gauges: 12, 16, 20, 28 in Game Model; 28 ga. not offered in Pigeon Model; Wildfowl Model in 12 ga. only (3-inch chambers available). Bbls.: 28-inch standard in Game and Pigeon Models, 30-inch in Wildfowl Model; other lengths, any standard choke combination

(cont'd) NORTHWOOD MODEL
HAMMERLESS DOUBLE-BARREL SHOTGUN
available. Weight: From 5 to 7.75 lbs. depending on ga. and bbls. Checkered straight-grip or pistol-grip stock and forearm. Disc.

RIVIERA MODEL
PIGEON GUN .... NiB $15,014 Ex $12,012 Gd $8168
Same as Badminton Model but supplied w/two sets of bbls., double triggers. Disc. 1967.

ROYAL MODEL HAMMERLESS DOUBLE
Self-opening. Sidelocks hand-detachable. Auto ejectors. Double triggers or single trigger. Gauges: 12, 16, 20, 28 .410. Built to customer's specifications as to bbl. length, chokes, etc. Made as a Game Gun or Pigeon and Wildfowl Gun, the latter having treble-grip action and side clips. Checkered stock and forend, straight grip standard. Made from 1885 to date.
W/double triggers ...... NiB $58,826 Ex $47,060 Gd $32,000
W/single trigger .... NiB $63,376 Ex $50,700 Gd $34,476

Holland & Holland
Royal Double-Barrel Shotgun

IGA Coach Gun

SHOTGUNS

ROYAL MODEL O/U
Sidelocks, hand-detachable. Auto-ejectors. Double triggers or single trigger. 12 ga. Built to customer's specifications as to bbl. length, chokes, etc. Made as a Game Gun or Pigeon and Wildfowl Gun. Checkered stock and forend, straight grip standard. Note: In 1951 Holland & Holland introduced its New Model Under/Over w/an improved, narrower action body. Disc. 1960.

**New model
(double triggers)** . . . . NiB $38,026 Ex $30,420 Gd $20,686
**New model
(single trigger)** . . . . NiB $39,650 Ex $31,720 Gd $21,570
**Old model
(double triggers)** . . . . NiB $32,436 Ex $25,948 Gd $17,645
**Old model
(single trigger)** . . . . NiB $34,450 Ex $27,560 Gd $18,741

SINGLE-SHOT SUPER TRAP GUN
Anson & Deeley system boxlock. Auto-ejector. No safety. 12 ga. Bbls.: Wide vent rib, 30- or 32-inch, w/Extra Full choke. Weight: About 8.75 lbs. Monte Carlo stock w/pistol grip and recoil pad, full beavertail forearm. Models differ in grade of engraving and wood. Disc.

**Standard
grade** . . . . NiB $5526 Ex $4420 Gd $3006
**Deluxe
grade** . . . . NiB $8776 Ex $7020 Gd $4774
**Exhibition
grade** . . . . NiB $10,726 Ex $8580 Gd $5834

SPORTING O/U . . . . NiB $27,950 Ex $22,360 Gd $5,205
Blitz action. Auto ejectors; single selective trigger. Gauges: 12 or 20 w/2.75-inch chambers. Barrels: 28- to 32-inch w/screw-in choke tubes. Hand-checkered European walnut straight-grip or pistol grip stock, forearm. Made 1993 to date.

HOLLAND & HOLLAND SPORTING
O/U DELUXE . . . . NiB $36,336 Ex $29,068 Gd $19,766
Same general specs as Sporting O/U except better engraving and select wood. Made 1993 to date.

HUNTER ARMS COMPANY —
Fulton, New York

HUNFULTON HAMMERLESS DOUBLE-BARREL. SHOTGUN
Boxlock. Plain extractors. Double triggers or non-selective single trigger. Gauges: 12 16, 20. Bbls.: 26- to 32-inch various choke combinations. Weight: about 7 lbs. Checkered pistol-grip stock and forearm. Disc. 1948.

W/double triggers . . . . NiB $393 Ex $314 Gd $213
W/single trigger . . . . NiB $666 Ex $479 Gd $362

SPECIAL HAMMERLESS DOUBLE-BARREL. SHOTGUN
Boxlock. Plain extractors. Double triggers or non-selective single trigger. Gauges: 12,16, 20. Bbls.: 26- to 30-inch various choke combinations. Weight: 6.5 to 7.25 lbs. depending on bbl. length and ga. Checkered full pistol-grip stock and forearm. Disc. 1948.

W/double triggers . . . . NiB $602 Ex $481 Gd $327
W/single trigger . . . . NiB $746 Ex $597 Gd $405

IGA SHOTGUNS — Veranopolis, Brazil
Imported by Stoeger Industries, Inc. Accokeek, Maryland

COACH GUN
Side-by-side double. Gauges: 12, 20 and .410. 20-inch bbls. w/3-inch chambers. Fixed chokes (standard model) or screw-in tubes (deluxe model). Weight: 6.5 lbs. Double triggers. Ejector and automatic safety. Blued or nickel finish. Hand-rubbed oil-finished pistol grip stock and forend w/hand checkering (hardwood on standard model or Brazilian walnut (deluxe). Imported 1983 to date.

Standard Coach Gun (blued finish) . . . . NiB $271 Ex $217 Gd $148
Standard Coach Gun (nickel finish) . . . NiB $333 Ex $266 Gd $181
**Standard Coach Gun
(engraved stock)** . . . . NiB $357 Ex $286 Gd $194
Deluxe Coach Gun (intro. 1997) . . . NiB $393 Ex $314 Gd $217
Choke tubes, add $20

IGA Turkey S/S Shotgun

IGA Condor Turkey O/U Shotgun

IGA Condor Waterfowl O/U Shotgun

CONDOR I O/U SINGLE-TRIGGER SHOTGUN
Gauges: 12 or 20. 26- or 28-inch bbls. of chrome-molybdenum steel. Chokes: Fixed — M/F or IC/M; screw-in choke tubes (12 and 20 ga.). Three inch chambers. Weight: 6.75 to 7 lbs. Sighting rib w/anti-glare surface. Hand-checkered hardwood pistol-grip stock and forend. Imported 1983 to date.
W/fixed chokes . . . . NiB $357 Ex $286 Gd $194
W/screw-in tubes . . . . NiB $406 Ex $324 Gd $220

CONDOR II O/U DOUBLE-TRIGGER
SHOTGUN . . . . NiB $351 Ex $280 Gd $191
Same general specifications as the Condor I O/U except w/double triggers and fixed chokes only; 26-inch bbls., IC/M; 28-inch bbls., M/F.

CONDOR SUPREME . . . . NiB $545 Ex $436 Gd $297
Same general specifications as Condor I except upgraded w/fine-checkered Brazilian walnut buttstock and forend, a matte-laquered finish, and a massive monoblock that joins the bbls. in a solid one-piece assembly at the breech end. Bbls. w/recessed interchangeable choke tubes formulated for use w/steel shot. Automatic ejectors. Imported 1996 to date.

CONDOR TURKEY MODEL
O/U SHOTGUN . . . . NiB $635 Ex $508 Gd $346
12 gauge only. 26-inch vent-rib bbls. w/3-inch chambers fitted w/recessed interchangeable choke tubes. Weight: 8 lbs. Mechanical single trigger. Ejectors and automatic safety. Advantage camouflage on stock and bbls. Made 1997 to date.

CONDOR WATERFOWL MODEL . . . . . NiB $649 Ex $519 Gd $353
Similar to Condor Turkey-Advantage camo model except w/30-inch bbls. Made 1998 to date.

DELUXE HUNTER CLAY SHOTGUN
Same general specifications and values as IGA Condor Supreme. Imported 1997 to date.

ERA 2000 O/U SHOTGUN . . . . NiB $468 Ex $374 Gd $254
Gauge: 12 w/3-inch chambers. 26- or 28-inch bbls. of chrome-molybdenum steel w/screw-in choke tubes. Extractors. Manual safety. (Mechanical triggers.) Weight: 7 lbs. Checkered Brazilian hardwood stock w/oil finish. Imported 1992-95.

REUNA SINGLE-SHOT SHOTGUN
Visible hammer. Under-lever release. Gauges: 12, 20 and .410; 3-inch chambers. 26- or 28-inch bbls. w/fixed chokes or screw-in choke tubes (12 ga. only). Extractors. Weight: 5.25 to 6.5 lbs. Plain Brazilian hardwood stock and semi-beavertail forend. Imported 1992 to date.
W/fixed choke . . . . NiB $108 Ex $87 Gd $59
W/choke tubes . . . . NiB $185 Ex $148 Gd $101

UPLANDER SIDE-BY-SIDE SHOTGUN
Gauges: 12, 20, 28 and .410. 26- or 28-inch bbls. of chrome-molybdenum steel. Various fixed-choke combinations; screw-in choke tubes (12 and 20 ga.). Three inch chambers (2.75-inch in 28 ga.). Weight: 6.25 to 7 lbs. Double triggers. Automatic safety. Matte-finished solid sighting rib. Hand checkered pistol-grip or straight stock and forend w/hand-rubbed, oil-finish. Imported 1983 to date.
Upland w/fixed chokes . . . . NiB $296 Ex $237 Gd $161
Upland w/screw-in tubes . . . . NiB $357 Ex $287 Gd $194
English model (straight grip) . . . . . . NiB $345 Ex $275 Gd $188
Ladies model . . . . NiB $357 Ex $286 Gd $194
Supreme model . . . . NiB $478 Ex $382 Gd $260
Youth model . . . . NiB $320 Ex $256 Gd $174

UPLANDER TURKEY
MODEL S/S DOUBLE . . . . NiB $469 Ex $375 Gd $255
12 gauge only. 24-inch solid rib bbls. w/3-inch chambers choked F&F. Weight: 6.75 lbs. Double triggers. Automatic safety. Advantage camouflage on stock and bbls. Made 1997 to date.

ITHACA GUN COMPANY — King Ferry (formerly Ithaca), New York. Now Ithaca Acquisition Corp./Ithaca Gun Co.

MODEL 37 BICENTENNIAL
COMMEMORATIVE. . . . . NiB $663 Ex $433 Gd $295
Limited to issue of 1976. Similar to Model 37 Supreme except has special Bicentennial design etched on receiver, full-fancy walnut stock and slide handle. Serial numbers U.S.A. 0001 to U.S.A. 1976. Originally issued w/presentation case w/cast-pewter belt buckle. Made in 1976. Best value is for gun in new, unfired condition.

IGA Deluxe Hunter Clay Shotgun

IGA Uplander Side-by-Side Shotgun

Ithaca Model 37 English Ultra

Ithaca Model 37 Featherlight Standard

Ithaca Model 37 Deerslayer Super Deluxe

Ithaca Model 37 Supreme Grade

SHOTGUNS

MODEL 37 DEERSLAYER DELUXE

Formerly "Model 87 Deerslayer Deluxe" reintroduced under the original Model 37 designation w/the same specifications. Available w/smooth bore or rifled bbl. Reintroduced 1996.

Deluxe model (smoothbore) . . . . . . **NiB $448 Ex $358 Gd $244**
Deluxe model (rifled bbl.) . . . . **NiB $502 Ex $401 Gd $272**

MODEL 37 DEERSLAYER II . . . . **NiB $535 Ex $428 Gd $292**

Gauges: 12 or 20 ga. Five shot capacity. 20- or 25-inch rifled bbl. Weight: 7 lbs. Monte Carlo checkered walnut stock and forearm. Receiver drilled and tapped for scope mount. Made 1996 to date.

MODEL 37 DEERSLAYER STANDARD . . . . **NiB $319 Ex $255 Gd $173**

Same as Model 37 Standard except has 20- or 26-inch bbl. bored for rifled slugs, rifle-type open rear sight and ramp front sight. Weight: 5.75 to 6.5 lbs. depending on ga. and bbl. length. Made 1959-86.

MODEL 37 DEERSLAYER
SUPER DELUXE . . . . **NiB $414 Ex $331 Gd $225**

Formerly "Deluxe Deerslayer." Same as Model 37 Standard Deerslayer except has stock and slide handle of fancy walnut. Made from 1962-86.

MODEL 37 ENGLISH ULTRA . . . . . **NiB $475 Ex $379 Gd $258**

Same general specifications as Model 37 Ultralite except straight buttstock, 25-inch Hot Forged vent-rib bbl. Made 1984-87.

MODEL 37 FEATHERLIGHT STANDARD GRADE
SLIDE-ACTION REPEATING SHOTGUN

Adaptation of the earlier Remington Model 17, a Browning design patented in 1915. Hammerless. Takedown. Gauges: 12, 16 (disc. 1973), 20. Four shell magazine. Bbl. lengths: 26-, 28-, 30-inch (the latter in 12 ga. only); standard chokes. Weight: From 5.75 to 7.5 lbs. depending on ga. and bbl. length. Checkered pistol-grip stock and slide handle. Some guns made in the 1950s and 1960s have grooved slide handle; plain or checkered pistol-grip. Made 1937-84.

Standard w/checkered pistol-grip . . **NiB $287 Ex $229 Gd $156**
W/plain stock . . . . **NiB $255 Ex $204 Gd $139**
Mdl 37D Deluxe (1954-77) . . . . **NiB $363 Ex $290 Gd $198**
Mdl 37DV Deluxe vent rib (1962-84) . . . **NiB $414 Ex $331 Gd $225**
Mdl 37R Deluxe
solid rib (1955-61) . . . . **NiB $351 Ex $280 Gd $191**
Mdl 37V Standard
vent rib (1962-84) . . . . **NiB $338 Ex $270 Gd $184**

**Ithaca Model 51
Deluxe Trap**

**MODEL 37 FIELD GRADE
MAG. W/TUBES** . . . . **NiB $335 Ex $267 Gd $182**
Same general specifications as Model 37 Featherlight except 32-inch bbl. and detachable choke tubes. Vent rib bbl. Made 1984-87.

MODEL 37 NEW CLASSIC . . . . **NiB $603 Ex $481 Gd $327**
Ggs: 12 or 20 ga. 20- or 28-inch vent rib bbl. w/choke tubes. Knuckle-cut receiver and orig. style "ring-tail" forend. Lim. prod. 1998 to date.

MODEL 37 THOUSAND DOLLAR GRADE
Custom built, elaborately engraved and inlaid w/gold, hand-finished working parts, stock and forend of select figured walnut. General specifications same as standard Model 37. Note: The same gun was designated the $1000 Grade prior to World War II. Made 1937-67.
$1000 grade . . . . **NiB $6681 Ex $5345 Gd $3634**
$5000 grade . . . . **NiB $6375 Ex $5100 Gd $3468**

MODEL 37 SUPREME GRADE. . . . . **NiB $669 Ex $535 Gd $364**
Available in Skeet or Trap Gun, similar to Model 37T. Made 1967-86 and 1996-97.

MODEL 37 ULTRALITE
Same general specifications as Model 37 Featherlight except streamlined forend, gold trigger, Sid Bell grip cap and vent rib. Weight: 5 to 5.75 lbs. Made 1984-87.
Standard . . . . **NiB $465 Ex $372 Gd $253**
W/choke tubes . . . . **NiB $504 Ex $403 Gd $274**

MODEL 37R SOLID RIB GRADE
Same general specifications as the Model 37 Featherlight except has a raised solid rib, adding about .25 pounds of weight. Made 1937-67.
W/checkered grip
and slide handle . . . . **NiB $382 Ex $306 Gd $208**
W/plain stock . . . . **NiB $376 Ex $403 Gd $205**

MODEL 37S SKEET GRADE. . . . . . . **NiB $542 Ex $433 Gd $295**
Same general specifications as the Model 37 Featherlight except has vent rib and large extension-type forend; weight: About .5 lb. more. Made 1937-55.

MODEL 37T TARGET GRADE . . . . . **NiB $503 Ex $402 Gd $272**
Same general specifications as Model 37 Featherlight except has vent-rib bbl., checkered stock and slide handle of fancy walnut (choice of skeet- or trap-style stock). Note: This model replaced Model 37S Skeet and Model 37T Trap. Made 1955-61.

MODEL 37T TRAP GRADE . . . . **NiB $542 Ex $433 Gd $295**
Same gen. specs. as Mdl. 37S except has straighter trap-style stock of select walnut, recoil pad; weight: About .5 lb. more. Made 1937-55.

MODEL 37 TURKEYSLAYER
Gauges: 12 ga. (Standard) or 20 ga. (youth). Slide action. 22-inch bbl. Extended choke tube. Weight: 7 lbs. Advantage camouflage or Realtree pattern. Made 1996 to date.
Standard model . . . . **NiB $468 Ex $374 Gd $254**
Youth model(intro. 1998) . . . . **NiB $502 Ex $401 Gd $272**

MODEL 37 WATERFOWLER . . . . . . **NiB $488 Ex $391 Gd $265**
12 ga. only w/28-inch bbl. Wetlands camouflage. Made 1998 to date.

MODEL 51 DEERSLAYER. . . . . **NiB $368 Ex $294 Gd $200**
Same as Model 51 Standard except has 24-inch plain bbl. w/slug boring, rifle sights, recoil pad. Weight: About 7.25 lbs. Made 1972-84.

MODEL 51 DELUXE SKEET GRADE . . . **NiB $504 Ex $403 Gd $274**
Same as Model 51 Standard except 26-inch vent-rib bbl. only, SK choke, skeet-style stock, semi-fancy wood. Weight: About 8 lbs. Made 1970-87.

MODEL 51 DELUXE TRAP GRADE
Same as Model 51 Standard except 12 ga. only, 30-inch bbl. w/broad floating rib, F choke, trap-style stock w/straight or Monte Carlo comb, semifancy wood, recoil pad. Weight: About 8 lbs. Made 1970-87.
W/straight stock . . . . **NiB $434 Ex $348 Gd $237**
W/Monte Carlo stock . . . . **NiB $461 Ex $369 Gd $251**

MODEL 51 STANDARD AUTOMATIC SHOTGUN
Gas-operated. Gauges: 12, 20. 3-shot. Bbls.: Plain or vent rib, 30-inch F choke (12 ga. only), 28-inch F or M, 26-inch IC. Weight: 7.25-7.75 lbs. depending on ga. and bbl. Checkered pistol-grip stock, forearm. Made 1970-80. Still avail. in 12 and 20 ga., 28-inch M choke only.
W/plain barrel. . . . . **NiB $294 Ex $235 Gd $159**
W/ventilated rib . . . . **NiB $351 Ex $280 Gd $191**

MODEL 51 STANDARD MAGNUM
Same as Model 51 Standard except has 3-inch chamber, handles Magnum shells only; 30-inch bbl. in 12 ga., 28-inch in 20 ga., F or M choke, stock w/recoil pad. Weight: 7.75-8 lbs. Made 1972 to date.
W/plain bbl. (disc. 1976) . . . . **NiB $285 Ex $227 Gd $155**
W/ventilated rib . . . . **NiB $333 Ex $266 Gd $181**

MODEL 51A TURKEY GUN. . . . . . . **NiB $357 Ex $286 Gd $194**
Same general specifications as standard Model 51 Magnum except 26-inch bbl. and matte finish. Disc. 1986.

MODEL 66 LONG TOM . . . . **NiB $127 Ex $102 Gd $69**
Same as Model 66 Standard except has 36-inch F choke bbl., 12 ga. only, checkered stock and recoil pad standard. Made 1969-74.

MODEL 66 STANDARD SUPER SINGLE LEVER
Single shot. Hand-cocked hammer. Gauges: 12 (disc. 1974), 20, .410, 3-inch chambers. Bbls.: 12 ga., 30-inch F choke, 28-inch F or M; 20 ga., 28-inch F or M; .410, 26-inch F. Weight: About 7 lbs. Plain or checkered straight-grip stock, plain forend. Made 1963-78.
Standard model . . . . **NiB $159 Ex $128 Gd $87**
Vent rib model (20 ga., checkered
stock, recoil pad, 1969-74) . . . . . . **NiB $185 Ex $148 Gd $101**
Youth model (20 & .410 ga., 26-inch bbl.,
shorter stock, recoil pad, 1965-78). . . . . **NiB $159 Ex $127 Gd $87**

MODEL 66RS BUCKBUSTER. . . . . . **NiB $192 Ex $153 Gd $104**
Same as Model 66 Standard except has 22-inch bbl. cylinder bore w/rifle sights, later version has recoil pad. Originally offered in 12 and 20 ga.; the former was disc. in 1970. Made 1967-78.

FEDERAL
PREMIUM
AMMUNITION

For a few weeks each year, the leading cause of high blood pressure isn't cholesterol.

Boil a year's worth of dreaming down to that four-second moment of truth and you'll be no stranger to inner turmoil. There's the adrenaline. The knots in your stomach. That shaking in your knees you hope won't find its way to your trigger finger. When your moment comes, be prepared with new Vital-Shok™ from the world leader in premium ammunition. It's available in the world's finest big game bullets including Nosler, Sierra, Barnes, and the unrivaled Speer Trophy Bonded Bear Claw™ that features 95% bullet retention. Simply put, there's nothing better for taking trophy animals. We know, because at Federal we search the world over for the highest performing components, and load them with a prescription that can relieve a season's worth of blood pressure in a way no diet <u>ever could</u>.

To find your nearest premium ammunition dealer, visit www.federalpremium.com.

Every shot counts™

FEDERAL
PREMIUM®
AMMUNITION

VITAL-SHOK™

20
CENTERFIRE
RIFLE CARTRIDGES
CARTOUCHES

**Ithaca Model
66RS Buckbuster**

Previously issued as the Ithaca Model 37, the Model 87 guns listed below were made available through the Ithaca Acquisition Corp. From 1986-95. Production of the Model 37 resumed under the original logo in 1996.

MODEL 87 DEERSLAYER SHOTGUN
Gauges: 12 or 20, 3-inch chamber. Bbls.: 18.5-, 20- or 25-inch (w/special or rifled bore). Weight: 6 to 6.75 lbs. Ramp blade front sight, adj. rear. Receiver grooved for scope. Checkered American walnut pistol-grip stock and forearm. Made 1988-96.
Basic model . . . . NiB $351 Ex $281 Gd $191
Basic Field Combo (w/extra 28-inch bbl.)
. . . . NiB $402 Ex $321 Gd $218
Deluxe model . . . . NiB $376 Ex $301 Gd $205
Deluxe Combo (w/extra 28-inch bbl.)
. . . . NiB $478 Ex $382 Gd $260
DSPS model (8-shot) . . . . NiB $357 Ex $286 Gd $194
Field model . . . . NiB $306 Ex $245 Gd $163
Monte Carlo model . . . . NiB $325 Ex $260 Gd $176
Ultra model (disc. 1991) . . . . NiB $447 Ex $357 Gd $243

MODEL 87 DEERSLAYER II
RIFLED SHOTGUN . . . . NiB $414 Ex $331 Gd $225
Similar to Standard Deerslayer except w/solid frame construction and 25-inch rifled bbl. Monte Carlo stock. Made 1988-96.

MODEL 87 ULTRALITE
FIELD PUMP SHOTGUN. . . . . NiB $395 Ex $315 Gd $215
Gauges: 12 and 20; 2.75-inch chambers. 25-inch bbl. w/choke tube. Weight: 5 to 6 lbs. Made 1988-90.

MODEL 87 FIELD GRADE
Gauge: 12 or 20.; 3-inch chamber. Five shot magazine. Fixed chokes or screw-in choke tubes (IC, M, F). Bbls.: 18.5-inch (M&P); 20- and 25-inch (Combo); 26-, 28-, 30-inch vent rib. Weight: 5 to 7 lbs. Made from 1988-96.
Basic field model (disc. 1993) . . . . . NiB $370 Ex $296 Gd $201
Camo model . . . . NiB $402 Ex $321 Gd $218
Deluxe model . . . . NiB $433 Ex $347 Gd $236
Deluxe Combo model . . . . NiB $440 Ex $352 Gd $240
English model . . . . NiB $376 Ex $301 Gd $205
Hand grip model
(w/polymer pistol-grip) . . . . NiB $414 Ex $332 Gd $225
M&P model (disc. 1995) . . . . NiB $357 Ex $286 Gd $194
Supreme model . . . . NiB $574 Ex $459 Gd $312
Turkey model. . . . . NiB $376 Ex $301 Gd $205
Ultra Deluxe model (disc. 1992) . . . NiB $465 Ex $372 Gd $253

HAMMERLESS DOUBLE-BARREL SHOTGUNS
Boxlock. Plain extractors, auto ejectors standard on the "E" grades. Double triggers, non-selective or selective single trigger extra. Gauges: Magnum 10, 12; 12, 16, 20, 28, .410. Bbls.: 26- to 32-inch, any standard boring. Weight: 5.75 (.410) to 10.5 lbs. (Magnum 10).

(cont'd.) HAMMERLESS DOUBLE-BARREL SHOTGUNS
Checkered pistol-grip stock and forearm standard. Higher grades differ from Field Grade in quality of workmanship, grade of wood, checkering, engraving, etc.; general specifications are the same. Ithaca doubles made before 1925 (serial number 425,000) the rotary bolt and a stronger frame were adopted. Values shown are for this latter type; earlier models valued about 50% lower. Smaller gauge guns may command up to 75% higher. Disc. 1948.
Field grade. . . . . NiB $870 Ex $696 Gd $473
No. 1 grade . . . . NiB $930 Ex $744 Gd $608
No. 2 grade . . . . NiB $1396 Ex $1117 Gd $760
No. 3 grade . . . . NiB $1779 Ex $1423 Gd $968
No. 4E grade (ejector). . . . . NiB $3181 Ex $2443 Gd $1731
No. 5E grade (ejector). . . . . NiB $7587 Ex $3417 Gd $4127
No. 7E grade (ejector) $12,750
$2000 (pre-war $1000) grade
ejector and selective single trigger standard $9129

Extras:
Magnum 10 or 12 ga.
(in other than the four highest grades), add. 20%
Automatic ejectors (grades No. 1, 2, 3, w/ejectors designated
No. 1E, 2E, 3E), add. $200
Selective single trigger, add $250
Non-selective single trigger, add $175
Beavertail forend (Field No. 1 or 2), add. $150
Beavertail forend (No. 3 or 4), add $175
Beavertail forend (No. 5, 7 or $2000 grade), add $250
Ventilated rib (No. 4, 5, 7 or $2000 grade), add $250
Ventilated rib (lower grades), add $175

LSA-55 TURKEY GUN . . . . NiB $669 Ex $536 Gd $364
Over/under shotgun/rifle combination. Boxlock. Exposed hammer. Plain extractor. Single trigger. 12 ga./222 Rem. 24.5-inch ribbed bbls. (rifle bbl. has muzzle brake). Weight: About 7 lbs. Folding leaf rear sight, bead front sight. Checkered Monte Carlo stock and forearm. Made 1970-77 by Oy Tikkakoski AB, Finland.

MAG-10 AUTOMATIC SHOTGUN
Gas-operated. 10 ga. 3.5-inch Magnum. Three shot. 32-inch plain (Standard Grade only) or vent-rib bbl. F choke. Weight: 11 lbs., plain bbl.; 11.5 lbs., vent rib. Standard grade has plain stock and forearm. Deluxe and Supreme Grades have checkering, semi-fancy and fancy wood respectively, and stud swivel. All have recoil pad. Deluxe and Supreme grades made 1974-1982. Standard Grade intro. in 1977. All grades disc. 1986.
Camo model . . . . NiB $720 Ex $576 Gd $392
Deluxe grade. . . . . NiB $756 Ex $605 Gd $411
Roadblocker . . . . NiB $780 Ex $624 Gd $425
Standard grade, plain barrel . . . . . NiB $635 Ex $508 Gd $346
Standard grade, ventilated rib . . . . NiB $666 Ex $532 Gd $362
Standard grade, w/tubes . . . . NiB $756 Ex $605 Gd $411
Supreme grade. . . . . NiB $877 Ex $702 Gd $477

SHOTGUNS

Ithaca Hammerless
Field Grade

Ithaca Hammerless
No. 2

Ithaca Hammerless
No. 4

SINGLE-SHOT TRAP, FLUES AND KNICK MODELS

Boxlock. Hammerless. Ejector. 12 ga. only. Bbl. lengths: 30-, 32-, 34-inch (32-inch only in Victory grade). Vent rib. Weight: About 8 lbs. Checkered pistol-grip stock and forend. Grades differ only in quality of workmanship, engraving, checkering, wood, etc. Flues Model, serial numbers under 400,000, made 1908-1921. Triple-bolted Knick Model, serial numbers above 400,000, made since 1921. Victory Model disc. in 1938, No. 7-E in 1964, No. 4-E in 1976, No. 5-E in 1986, Dollar Grade in 1991. Values shown are for Knick Model; Flues models about 50% lower.

Victory grade . . . . NiB $1164 Ex $931 Gd $633
No. 4-E. . . . . NiB $2796 Ex $2236 Gd $1520
No. 5-E. . . . . NiB $3244 Ex $2545 Gd $1765
No. 6-E . . . . NiB $15,600+ Ex $12,480+ Gd $8486+
No. 7-E. . . . . NiB $6233 Ex $4987 Gd $3391
$5000 grade
(prewar $1000 grade). . . . . NiB $11,505 Ex $9204 Gd $6259
Sousa grade. . . . . NiB $13,000+ Ex $10,400+ Gd $7072+

NOTE: *The following Ithaca-Perazzi shotguns were manufactured by Manifattura Armi Perazzi, Brescia, Italy. See also separate Perazzi listings.*

PERAZZI COMPETITION I SKEET. . . . . NiB $3446 Ex $2756 Gd $1945
Boxlock. Auto ejectors. Single trigger. 12 ga. 26.75-inch vent-rib bbls. SK choke w/integral muzzle brake. Weight: About 7.75 lbs. Checkered skeet-style pistol-grip buttstock and forearm; recoil pad. Made 1969-74.

PERAZZI COMPETITION TRAP I O/U . . . . NiB $3576 Ex $2756 Gd $1945
Boxlock. Auto ejectors. Single trigger. 12 ga. 30- or 32-inch vent-rib bbls. IM/F choke. Weight: About 8.5 lbs. Checkered pistol-grip stock, forearm; recoil pad. Made 1969-74.

PERAZZI COMPETITION I
TRAP SINGLE BARREL. . . . . NiB $2536 Ex $2028 Gd $1379
Boxlock. Auto ejection. 12 ga. 32- or 34-inch bbl., vent rib, F choke. Weight: 8.5 lbs. Checkered Monte Carlo stock and beavertail forearm, recoil pad. Made 1973-78.

PERAZZI COMPETITION IV
TRAP GUN. . . . . NiB $3114 Ex $2491 Gd $1694
Boxlock. Auto ejection. 12 ga. 32- or 34-inch bbl. With high, wide vent rib, four interchangeable choke tubes (Extra Full, F, IM, M). Weight: About 8.75 lbs. Checkered Monte Carlo stock and beavertail forearm, recoil pad. Fitted case. Made 1977-78.

Ithaca Mag-10
Standard

Ithaca Model 5-E

Ithaca Single-Shot Trap
"Dollar Grade"

Ithaca-Perazzi
Competition I Skeet

Ithaca-Perazzi
Competition I Trap

Ithaca-Perazzi
Light Game

Ithaca-Perazzi
Mirage Trap

PERAZZI LIGHT GAME O/U FIELD
. . . . NiB $3951 Ex $3161 Gd $2150
Boxlock. Auto ejectors. Single trigger. 12 ga. 27.5-inch vent rib bbls., M/F or IC/M choke. Weight: 6.75 lbs. Checkered field-style stock and forearm. Made 1972-74.

PERAZZI MIRAGE LIVE BIRD . . NiB $4437 Ex $3548 Gd $2413
Same as Mirage Trap except has 28-inch bbls., M and Extra Full choke, special stock and forearm for live bird shooting. Weight: About 8 lbs. Made 1973-78.

PERAZZI MIRAGE SKEET . . . . . . NiB $3753 Ex $3002 Gd $2042
Same as Mirage Trap except has 28-inch bbls. w/integral muzzle brakes, SK choke, skeet-stype stock and forearm. Weight: About 8 lbs. Made 1973-78.

PERAZZI MIRAGE TRAP . . . . . . NiB $3890 Ex $3052 Gd $2115
Same general specifications as MX-8 Trap except has tapered rib. Made 1973-78.

PERAZZI MT-6 SKEET . . . . NiB $3890 Ex $3051 Gd $2076
Same as MT-6 Trap except has 28-inch bbls. w/two skeet choke tubes instead of Extra Full and F, skeet-style stock and forearm. Weight: About 8 lbs. Made 1976-78.

PERAZZI MT-6 TRAP COMBO . . . . NiB $4907 Ex $3925 Gd $2670
MT-6 w/extra single under bbl. w/high-rise aluminum vent rib, 32- or 34-inch; seven interchanageable choke tubes (IC through Extra Full). Fitted case. Made 1977-78.

PERAZZI MT-6
TRAP O/U . . . . NiB $3405 Ex $2724 Gd $1852
Boxlock. Auto selective ejectors. Non-selective single trigger. 12 ga. Barrels separated, wide vent rib, 30-or 32-inch, five interchangeable choke tubes (Extra full, F, IM, M, IC). Weight: About 8.5 lbs. Checkered pistol-grip stock/forearm, recoil pad. Fitted case. Made 1976-78.

PERAZZI MX
8 TRAP COMBO . . . . NiB $5391 Ex $4313 Gd $2933
MX-8 w/extra single bbl., vent rib, 32- or 34-inch, F choke, forearm; two trigger groups included. Made 1973-78.

PERAZZI MX-8 TRAP
O/U . . . . NiB $3951 Ex $3160 Gd $2150
Boxlock. Auto selective ejectors. Non-selective single trigger. 12 ga. Bbls.: High vent rib; 30- or 32-inch, IM/F choke. Weight: 8.25 to 8.5 lbs. Checkered Monte Carlo stock and forearm, recoil pad. Made 1969-78.

PERAZZI SINGLE-BARREL
TRAP GUN . . . . NiB $2627 Ex $2101 Gd $1429
Boxlock. Auto ejection. 12 ga. 34-inch vent rib bbl., F choke. Weight: Abaout 8.5 lbs. Checkered pistol-grip stock, forearm; recoil pad. Made 1971-72.

The following Ithaca-SKB shotguns, manufactured by SKB Arms Company, Tokyo, Japan, were distributed in the U.S. by Ithaca Gun Company from 1966-1976. See also listings under SKB.

Ithaca-SKB
Model 100

Ithaca-SKB
Model 280 English

Ithaca-SKB
Model 700 Skeet Grade

Ithaca-SKB
Model 900 Deluxe

SKB MODEL 100 SIDE-BY-SIDE. . . . NiB $524 Ex $419 Gd $285
Boxlock. Plain extractors. Selective single trigger. Auto safety.
Gauges: 12 and 20; 2.75-inch and 3-inch chambers respectively.
Bbls.: 30-inch, F/F (12 ga. only); 28-inch, F/M; 26-inch, IC/M (12 ga.
only); 25-inch, IC/M (20 ga. only). Weight: 12 ga., about 7 lbs.; 20
ga., about 6 lbs. Checkered stock and forend. Made 1966-76.

SKB MODEL 150 FIELD GRADE . . . NiB $555 Ex $444 Gd $302
Same as Model 100 except has fancier scroll engraving, beavertail
forearm. Made 1972-74.

SKB 200E FIELD GRADE S/S . . . . . . NiB $786 Ex $629 Gd $427
Same as Model 100 except auto selective ejectors, engraved and silver-plated frame, gold-plated nameplate and trigger, beavertail forearm. Made 1966-76.

SKB MODEL 200E SKEET GUN . . . . NiB $851 Ex $680 Gd $463
Same as Model 200E Field Grade except 26-inch (12 ga.) and
25-inch (20 ga./2.75-inch chambers) bbls., SK choke; nonautomatic safety and recoil pad. Made 1966-76.

SKB MODEL 280 ENGLISH . . . . NiB $993 Ex $795 Gd $541
Same as Model 200E except has scrolled game scene engraving on
frame, English-style straight-grip stock; 30-inch bbls. not available;
special quail gun in 20 ga. has 25-inch bbls., both bored IC. Made
1971-76.

**SKB MODEL 300 STANDARD
AUTOMATIC SHOTGUN**
Recoil-operated. Gauges: 12, 20 (3-inch). Five shot. Bbls.: plain or
vent rib; 30-inch F choke (12 ga. only), 28-inch F or M, 26-inch IC.
Weight: about 7 lbs. Checkered pistol-grip stock and forearm. Made
1968-72.
W/plain barrel . . . . NiB $306 Ex $244 Gd $166
W/ventilated rib . . . . NiB $344 Ex $276 Gd $187

**SKB MODEL 500
FIELD GRADE O/U . . . . NiB $552 Ex $442 Gd $301**
Boxlock. Auto selective ejectors. Selective single trigger. Non-automatic safety. Gauges: 12 and 20; 2.75-inch and 3-inch chambers
respectively. Vent-rib bbls.: 30-inch M/F (12 ga. only); 28-inch M/F;
26-inch IC/M. Weight: 12 ga., about 7.5 lbs; 20 ga., about 6.5 lbs.
Checkered stock and forearm. Made 1966-76.

SKB MODEL 500 MAGNUM . . . . . . NiB $648 Ex $518 Gd $353
Same as Model 500 Field Grade except chambered for 3-inch 12 ga.
shells, has 30-inch bbls., IM/F choke. Weight: About 8 lbs. Made 1973-76.

SKB MODEL 600 DOUBLES GUN . . . . NiB $760 Ex $608 Gd $414
Same as Model 600 Trap Grade except specially choked for 21-yard
first target, 30-yard second. Made 1973-75.

SKB MODEL 600 FIELD GRADE . . . NiB $716 Ex $573 Gd $389
Same as Model 500 except has silver-plated frame, higher grade
wood. Made 1969-76.

SKB MODEL 600 MAGNUM . . . . . . NiB $744 Ex $595 Gd $405
Same as Model 600 Field Grade except chambered for 3-inch 12 ga.
shells; has 30-inch bbls., IM/F choke. Weight: 8.5 lbs. Made 1969-72.

SKB MODEL 600 SKEET GRADE
Same as Model 500 except also available in 28 and .410 ga., has silver-plated frame, higher grade wood, recoil pad, 26- or 28-inch
bbls. (28-inch only in 28 and .410), SK choke. Weight: 7 to 7.75 lbs.
depending on ga. and bbl. length. Made 1966-76.
12 or 20 ga. NiB $872 Ex $728 Gd $545
28 or .410 ga. . . . . NiB $968 Ex $806 Gd $598

SKB MODEL 600 SKEET SET . . . . NiB $2074 Ex $1659 Gd $1128
Model 600 Skeet Grade w/matched set of 20, 28 and .410 ga. bbls.,
28-inch, fitted case. Made 1970-76.

Ithaca-SKB
Century Trap

Ithaca-SKB
Century II Trap

Ithaca-SKB
Model XL300

SKB MODEL 600
TRAP GRADE O/U . . . . **NiB $697 Ex $557 Gd $379**
Same as Model 500 except 12 ga. only, has silver-plated frame, 30- or 32-inch bbls. choked F/F or F/IM, choice of Monte Carlo or straight stock of higher grade wood, recoil pad. Weight: About 8 lbs. Made 1966-76.

SKB MODEL 680 ENGLISH . . . . . . **NiB $734 Ex $588 Gd $399**
Same as Model 600 Field Grade except has intricate scroll engraving, English-style straight-grip stock and forearm of extra-fine walnut; 30-inch bbls. not available. Made 1973-76.

SKB MODEL 700
SKEET COMBO SET . . . . **NiB $3296 Ex $2636 Gd $1792**
Model 700 Skeet Grade w/matched set of 20, 28 and .410 ga. bbls., 28-inch fitted case. Made 1970-71.

SKB MODEL 700 SKEET GRADE . . . **NiB $954 Ex $744 Gd $433**
Same as Model 600 Skeet Grade except not available in 28 and .410 ga., has more elaborate scroll engraving, extra-wide rib, higher grade wood. Made 1969-75.

SKB MODEL 700 TRAP GRADE . . . . **NiB $917 Ex $734 Gd $499**
Same as Model 600 Trap Grade except has more elaborate scroll engraving, extra-wide rib, higher grade wood. Made 1969-75.

SKB MODEL 700
DOUBLES GUN . . . . **NiB $1058 Ex $846 Gd $575**
Same as Model 700 Trap Grade except choked for 21-yard first target, 30-yard second target. Made 1973-75.

SKB MODEL 900
DELUXE AUTOMATIC . . . . **NiB $410 Ex $328 Gd $223**
Same as Model 30 except has game scene etched and gold-filled on receiver, vent rib standard. Made 1968-72.

SKB MODEL 900 SLUG GUN . . . . . **NiB $370 Ex $296 Gd $202**
Same as Model 900 Deluxe except has 24-inch plain bbl. w/slug boring, rifle sights. Weight: About 6.5 lbs. Made 1970-72.

SKB CENTURY SINGLE-SHOT
TRAP GUN . . . . **NiB $818 Ex $655 Gd $445**
Boxlock. Auto ejector. 12 ga. Bbls.: 32- or 34-inch, vent rib, F choke.

(cont'd) **SKB CENTURY SINGLE-SHOT**
Weight: About 8 lbs. Checkered walnut stock w/pistol grip, straight or Monte Carlo comb, recoil pad, beavertail forearm. Made 1973-74.

SKB CENTURY II . . . . **NiB $748 Ex $598 Gd $407**
Boxlock. Auto ejector. 12 ga. Bbls: 32- or 34-inch, vent rib, F choke. Weight: 8.25 lbs. Improved version of Century. Same general specifications except has higher comb on checkered stock stock, reverse-taper beavertail forearm w/redesigned locking iron. Made 1975-76.

SKB MODEL XL300 STANDARD AUTOMATIC
Gas-operated. Gauges: 12, 20 (3-inch). Five shot. Bbls.: Plain or vent rib; 30-inch F choke (12 ga. only), 28-inch F or M, 26-inch IC. Weight: 6 to 7.5 lbs. depending on ga. and bbl. Checkered pistol-grip stock, forearm. Made 1972-76.
W/plain barrel . . . . **NiB $280 Ex $224 Gd $152**
W/ventilated rib . . . . **NiB $306 Ex $244 Gd $166**

SKB MODEL XL900
DELUXE AUTOMATIC . . . . **NiB $358 Ex $286 Gd $194**
Same as Model XL300 except has game scene finished in silver on receiver, vent rib standard. Made 1972-76. See illustration previous page.

SKB MODEL XL
900 SKEET GRADE . . . . **NiB $436 Ex $348 Gd $237**
Gas-operated. Gauges: 12, 20 (3-inch). Five shot tubular magazine. Same as Model XL900 Deluxe except has scrolled receiver finished in black chrome, 26-inch bbl. only, SK choke, skeet-style stock. Weight: 7 or 7.5 lbs. depending on ga. Made 1972-76.

SKB MODEL XL
900 SLUG GUN . . . . **NiB $384 Ex $307 Gd $209**
Same as Model XL900 Deluxe except has 24-inch plain bbl. w/slug boring, rifle sights. Weight: 6.5 or 7 lbs. depending on ga. Made 1972-76.

SKB MODEL
XL900 TRAP GRADE . . . . **NiB $425 Ex $340 Gd $232**
Same as Model XL900 Deluxe except 12 ga. only, has scrolled receiver finished in black chrome, 30-inch bbl. only, IM or F choke, trap style w/straight or Monte Carlo comb, recoil pad. Weight: About 7.75 lbs. Made 1972-76.

SHOTGUNS

Krieghoff Model 32
Standard Field Gun

Krieghoff Model 32
Single-Shot Trap

IVER JOHNSON ARMS & CYCLE WORKS — Fitchburg, Massachusetts. Currently a division of the American Military Arms Corp., Jacksonville, Arkansas

CHAMPION GRADE SINGLE-SHOT HAMMER SHOTGUN
Auto ejector. Gauges: 12,16, 20, 28 and .410. Bbls.: 26- to 36-inch, F choke. Weight: 5.75 to 7.5 lbs. depending on ga. and bbl.length. Plain pistol-grip stock and forend. Extras include checkered stock and forend, pistol-grip cap and knob forend. Known as Model 36. Also made in a Semi-Octagon Breech, Top Matted and Jacketed Breech (extra heavy) models. Made in Champion Lightweight as Model 39 in gauges 24, 28, 32 and .410, .44 and .45 caliber, 12 and 14mm w/same extras. $200; add $100 in the smaller and obsolete gauges. Made 1909-73.

Standard model . . . . NiB $185 Ex $148 Gd $100
Semi-octagon breech . . . . NiB $302 Ex $242 Gd $164
Top matted rib (disc. 1948) . . . . . . NiB $284 Ex $227 Gd $154

HERCULES GRADE HAMMERLESS DOUBLE
Boxlock. (Some made w/false sideplates.) Plain extractors and auto ejectors. Double or Miller single triggers (both selective or non-selective). Gauges: 12, 16, 20 and .410. Bbl. lengths: 26- to 32-inch, all chokes. Weight: 5.75 to 7.75 lbs. depending on ga. and bbl. length. Checkered stock and forend. Straight grip in .410 ga. w/both 2.5- and 3-inch chambers. Extras include Miller single trigger, Jostam Anti-Flinch recoil pad and Lyman ivory sights at extra cost. Disc. 1946.

W/double triggers, extractors . . . . . NiB $707 Ex $566 Gd $385
W/double triggers, auto. ejectors . . . . . NiB $851 Ex $680 Gd $463
W/non-selective single trigger, add $100
W/selective single trigger, add. $135
.410 ga., add $185

MATTED RIB SINGLE-SHOT HAMMER SHOTGUN
IN SMALLER GAUGES. . . . . NiB $358 Ex $286 Gd $194
Same general specifications as Champion Grade except has solid matted top rib, checkered stock and forend. Weight: 6 to 6.75 lbs. Disc. 1948.

SILVER SHADOW
O/U SHOTGUN
Boxlock. Plain extractors. Double triggers or non-selective single trigger. 12 ga., 3-inch chambers. Bbls.: 26-inch IC/M; 28-inch IC/M, 28-inch M/F; 30-inch both F choke; vent rib. Weight: w/28-inch bbls., 7.5 lbs. Checkered pistol-grip stock/forearm. Made by F. Marocchi, Brescia, Italy 1973-78.

Model 412 w/double triggers . . . . . NiB $488 Ex $390 Gd $265
Model 422 w/single trigger . . . . . . NiB $612 Ex $489 Gd $333

SKEETER MODEL HAMMERLESS DOUBLE
Boxlock. Plain extractors or selective auto ejectors. Double triggers or Miller single trigger (selective or non-selective). Gauges: 12, 16, 20, 28 and .410. 26- or 28-inch bbls., skeet boring standard. Weight: About 7.5 lbs.; less in smaller gauges. Pistol- or straight-grip stock and beavertail forend, both checkered, of select fancy-figured black walnut. Extras include Miller single trigger, selective or non-selective, Jostam Anti-Flinch recoil pad and Lyman ivory rear sight at additional cost. Disc. 1942.

W/double triggers,
plain extractors . . . . NiB $1396 Ex $1117 Gd $759
W/double triggers,
automatic ejectors . . . . NiB $1708 Ex $1367 Gd $930
W/non-selective
single trigger, add $150
W/selective single
trigger, add $200
20 ga., add 25%
28 ga., add 75%
.410 ga., add 90%

SPECIAL TRAP SINGLE-SHOT
HAMMER SHOTGUN . . . . NiB $402 Ex $321 Gd $219
Auto ejector. 12 ga. only. 32-inch bbl. w/vent rib, F choke. Checkered pistol-grip stock and forend. Weight: about 7.5 lbs. Disc. 1942.

SUPER TRAP HAMMERLESS DOUBLE
Boxlock. Plain extractors. Double trigger or Miller single trigger (slective or non-selective), 12 ga. only, F choke 32-inch bbl., vent rib. Weight: 8.5 lbs. Checkered pistol-grip stock and beavertail forend, recoil pad, Disc. 1942.

W/double triggers . . . . NiB $1144 Ex $780 Gd $416
W/non-selective
single trigger, add $100
W/selective single trigger, add. $100

KBI INC. SHOTGUNS

See listings under Armscor, Baikal, Charles Daly, Fias, & Omega

KESSLER ARMS CORP. — Silver Creek, New York

LEVER-MATIC REPEATING SHOTGUN
. . . . NiB $181 Ex $144 Gd $98
Lever action. Takedown. Gauges: 12, 16, 20; three-shot magazine. Bbls.: 26-, 28-, 30-inch; F choke. Plain pistol-grip stock, recoil pad. Weight: 7 to 7.75 lbs. Disc. 1953.

Krieghoff K-80
w/Screw-in Choke Tubes

Krieghoff K-80
Trap Unsingle

THREE SHOT BOLT-ACTION REPEATER . . . NiB $96 Ex $76 Gd $52
Takedown. Gauges: 12, 16, 20. Two-shell detachable box magazine. Bbls.: 28-inch in 12 and 16 ga.; 26-inch in 20 ga.; F choke. Weight: 6.25 to 7.25 lbs. depending on ga. and bbl. length. Plain one-piece pistol-grip stock recoil pad. Made 1951-53.

H. KRIEGHOFF JAGD UND SPORTWAFFEN-FABRIK — Ulm (Donau), West Germany

MODEL 32 FOUR-BARREL SKEET SET
Over/under w/four sets of matched bbls.: 12, 20, 28 and .410 ga., in fitted case. Available in six grades that differ in quality of engraving and wood. Disc. 1979.

Standard grade . . . . NiB $11,524 Ex $9218 Gd $6269
München grade . . . . NiB $12,811 Ex $10,249 Gd $6969
San Remo grade. . . . . NiB $15,772 Ex $12,617 Gd $8580
Monte Carlo grade . . . . . . NiB $20,536 Ex $16,428 Gd $11,171
Crown grade. . . . . NiB $25,428 Ex $20,342 Gd $13,833
Super Crown grade. . . . . . NiB $27,681 Ex $22,145 Gd $15,059
Exhibition grade . . . . NiB $38,561 Ex $30,849 Gd $20,977

MODEL 32 STANDARD GRADE O/U
Similar to prewar Remington Model 23. Boxlock. Auto ejector. Single trigger. Gauges: 12, 20, 28, .410. Bbls.: Vent rib, 26.5- to 32-inch, any chokes. Weight: 12 ga. Field gun w/28-inch bbls., about 7.5 lbs. Checkered pistol-grip stock and forearm of select walnut; available in field, skeet and trap styles. Made 1958-1981.

W/one set of bbls. . . . . NiB $3608 Ex $2886 Gd $1962
Low-rib two-bbl. trap combo . . NiB $4641 Ex $3713 Gd $2524
Vandalia (high-rib) two- bbl. trap combo . . NiB $4886 Ex $3909 Gd $2658

MODEL 32 STANDARD GRADE
SINGLE-SHOT TRAP GUN . . . . . NiB $1796 Ex $1437 Gd $977
Same action as over/under. 12 ga. 32- or 34-inch bbl. w/high vent rib on bbl.; M, IM, or F choke. Checkered Monte Carlo buttstock w/thick cushioned recoil pad, beavertail forearm. Disc. 1979.

MODEL K-80
Refined and enhanced version of the Mdl. 32. Single selective mech. trig., adj. for position; release trigger optional. Fixed chokes or screw-in choke tubes. Interchangeable front bbl. Hangers to adjust point of impact. Quick-removable stock. Color casehardened or satin grey fin. rec.; alum. alloy rec. on lightweight models. Avail. in stand. plus 5 engraved grades. Made 1980 to date. Standard grade shown except where noted.

SKEET MODELS
Skeet International . . . . NiB $6054 Ex $4843 Gd $3293
Skeet Special . . . . NiB $51 Ex $4259 Gd $2896

(cont'd.) MODEL K-80
Skeet standard model . . . . NiB $5086 Ex $4068 Gd $2767
Skeet w/choke tubes . . . . NiB $6116 Ex $4892 Gd $3327
SKEET SETS
Standard grade 2-bbl. set . . . . . NiB $9698 Ex $7758 Gd $5276
Standard grade 4-bbl. set . . NiB $13,279 Ex $10,623 Gd $7224
Bavaria grade 4-bbl. set . . NiB $18,926 Ex $15,141 Gd $10,296
Danube grade 4-bbl. set . . . . NiB $24,643 Ex $19,714 Gd $13,405
Gold Target grade 4-bbl. set . . . . NiB $28,969 Ex $23,175 Gd $15,759
SPORTING MODELS
Pigeon . . . . NiB $6649 Ex $5319 Gd $3617
Sporting Clays . . . . NiB $6692 Ex $5353 Gd $3640
TRAP MODELS
Trap Combo. . . . . NiB $9006 Ex $7205 Gd $4900
Trap Single. . . . . NiB $6374 Ex $5098 Gd $3467
Trap Standard . . . . NiB $5916 Ex $4733 Gd $3219
Trap Unsingle . . . . NiB $6624 Ex $5299 Gd $3604
RT models (removable trigger) add $1385

KRIEGHOFF MODEL KS-5 SINGLE-BARREL TRAP
Boxlock w/no sliding top-latch. Adjustable or optional release trigger. Gauge: 12; 2.75-inch chamber. Bbl.: 32-, 34-inch w/fixed choke or screw-in tubes. Weight: 8.5 lbs. Adjustable or Monte Carlo European walnut stock. Blued or nickel receiver. Made from 1980 to date. Redesigned and streamlined in 1993.

Standard model w/fixed chokes . . . NiB $3284 Ex $2626 Gd $1786
Standard model w/tubes . . . . . . NiB $3856 Ex $3084 Gd $2098
Special model w/adj. rib & stock
. . . . . NiB $4114 Ex $3291 Gd $2238
Special model w/adj. rib
& stock, choke tubes . . . . NiB $4700 Ex $3759 Gd $2556

TRUMPF DRILLING . . . . NiB $9264 Ex $7823 Gd $5979
Boxlock. Steel or Dural receiver. Split extractor or ejector for shotgun bbls. Double triggers. Gauges: 12, 16, 20; latter w/either 2.75- or 3-inch chambers. Calibers: .243, 6.5x57r5, 7x57r5, 7x65r5, .30-06; other calibers available. 25-inch bbls. w/solid rib, folding leaf rear sight, post or bead front sight; rifle bbl. soldered or free floating. Weight: 6.6 to 7.5 lbs. depending on type of receiver, ga. and caliber. Checkered pistol-grip stock w/cheekpiece and forearm of figured walnut, sling swivels. Made 1953 to date.

NEPTUN DRILLING . . . . NiB $12,296 Ex $9836 Gd $6689
Same general specifications as Trumpf model except has sidelocks w/hunting scene engraving. Currently manufactured.

NEPTUN-PRIMUS DRILLING
. . . . . NiB $14,099 Ex $11,278 Gd $7669
Deluxe version of Neptun model; has detachable sidelocks, higher grade engraving and fancier wood. Currently manufactured.

**Krieghoff
Neptun Drilling**

**Krieghoff ULM
Over/Under**

TECK O/U
RIFLE-SHOTGUN . . . . NiB $6889 Ex $5510 Gd $3747
Boxlock. Kersten dble. crossbolt system. Steel or Dural receiver. Split extractor or eject. for shotgun bbl. Single or double triggers. Gauges: 12, 16, 20; latter w/either 2.75- or 3-inch chamber. Cal: .22 Hornet, .222 Rem., .222 Rem. Mag., 7x57r5, 7x64, 7x65r5, .30-30, .300 Win. Mag., .30-06, .308, 9.3x74R. 25-inch bbls. With solid rib, folding leaf rear sight, post or bead front sight; over bbl. is shotgun, under bbl. rifle (later fixed or interchangeable; ext. rifle bbl., $175). Wt: 7.9-9.5 lbs. depending on type of rec. and caliber. Checkered pistol-grip stock w/cheekpiece and semi-beavertail forearm of fig. walnut, sling swivels. Made 1967 to date. Note: This comb. gun is similar in appearance to the same model shotgun.

TECK O/U SHOTGUN . . . . NiB $6444 Ex $5155 Gd $3505
Boxlock. Kersten double crossbolt system. Auto ejector. Single or double triggers. Gauges: 12, 16, 20; latter w/either 2.75- or 3-inch chambers. 28-inch vent-rib bbl., M/F choke. Weight: About 7 lbs. Checkered walnut pistol-grip stock and forearm. Made 1967-89.

ULM O/U
RIFLE-SHOTGUN . . . . NiB $16,416 Ex $14,162 Gd $11,279
Same general specifications as Teck model except has sidelocks w/leaf Arabesque engraving. Made from 1963 to date. Note: This combination gun is similar in appearance to the same model shotgun.

ULM O/U SHOTGUN . . . . . NiB $12,225 Ex $10,192 Gd $7590
Same general specifications as Teck model except has sidelocks w/leaf Arabesque engraving. Made 1958 to date.

ULM-P LIVE PIGEON GUN
Sidelock. Gauge: 12. 28- and 30-inch bbls. Chokes: F/IM. Weight: 8 lbs. Oil-finished, fancy English walnut stock w/semi-beavertail forearm. Light scrollwork engraving. Tapered, vent rib. Made from 1983 to date.
Bavaria . . . . NiB $18,154 Ex $14,935 Gd $10,815
Standard . . . . NiB $14,099 Ex $11,690 Gd $8609

ULM-PRIMUS O/U. . . . . NiB $11,619 Ex $9296 Gd $6321
Deluxe version of Ulm model; detachable sidelocks, higher grade engraving and fancier wood. Made 1958 to date.

ULM-PRIMUS O/U
RIFLE-SHOTGUN . . . . NiB $18,663 Ex $16,269 Gd $13,206
Deluxe version of Ulm model; has detachable sidelocks, higher grade engraving and fancier wood. Made 1963 to date. Note: This combination gun is similar in appearance to the same model shotgun.

ULM-S SKEET GUN
Sidelock. Gauge: 12. Bbl.: 28-inch. Chokes: Skeet/skeet. Other specifications similar to the Model ULM-P. Made 1983-86.
Bavaria . . . . NiB $11,839 Ex $9883 Gd $7380
Standard . . . . NiB $9779 Ex $8235 Gd $6259

ULM-P O/U LIVE TRAP GUN
Over/under sidelock. Gauge: 12. 30-inch bbl. Tapered vent rib. Chokes: IM/F; optional screw-in choke. Custom grade versions command a higher price. Disc. 1986.
Bavaria . . . . NiB $17,832 Ex $14,678 Gd $10,640
Standard . . . . NiB $14,099 Ex $11,690 Gd $8609

ULTRA O/U RIFLE-SHOTGUN
Deluxe Over/Under combination w/25-inch vent-rib bbls. Chambered 12 ga. only and various rifle calibers for lower bbl. Kickspanner design permits cocking w/thumb safety. Satin receiver. Weight: 6 lbs. Made from 1985 to date.
Ultra O/U combination . . . . . . NiB $4886 Ex $4218 Gd $3363
Ultra B w/selective front trigger . . . NiB $5144 Ex $4424 Gd $3502

LANBER SHOTGUNS — Spain

MODEL 82 O/U SHOTGUN . . . . . . NiB $515 Ex $412 Gd $280
Boxlock. Gauge: 12 or 20; 3-inch chambers. 26- or 28-inch vent-rib bbls. w/ejectors and fixed chokes. Weight: 7 lbs., 2 oz. Double or single-selective trigger. Engraved silvered receiver. Checkered European walnut stock and forearm. Imported 1994.

MODEL 87 DELUXE . . . . NiB $804 Ex $644 Gd $438
Over/Under; boxlock. Single selective trigger. 12 or 20 gauge w/3-inch chambers. Barrels: 26- or 28-inch w/choke tubes. Silvered engraved receiver. Imported 1994 only.

MODEL 97 SPORTING CLAYS . . . . NiB $837 Ex $669 Gd $455
Over/Under; boxlock. Single selective trigger. 12 ga. w/2.75-inch chambers. Bbls: 28-inch w/choke tubes. European walnut stock, forend. Engraved receiver. Imported 1994 only.

MODEL 844 MST MAGNUM O/U . . . . NiB $432 Ex $345 Gd $235
Field grade. Gauge: 12. 3-inch Mag. chambers. 30-inch flat vent-rib bbls. Chokes: M/F. Weight: 7 lbs., 7 oz. Single selective trigger. Blued bbls. and engraved receiver. European walnut stock w/hand-checkered pistol grip and forend. Imported 1984-86.

MODEL 2004 LCH O/U . . . . NiB $612 Ex $489 Gd $333
Field grade. Gauge: 12. 2.75-inch chambers. 28-inch flat vent-rib bbls. 5 interchangeable choke tubes: Cyl, IC, M, IM, F. Weight: About 7 lbs. Single selective trigger. Engraved silver receiver w/fine-line scroll. Walnut stock w/checkered pistol-grip and forend. Rubber recoil pad. Imported 1984-86.

MODEL 2004 LCH O/U SKEET . . . . NiB $766 Ex $613 Gd $417
Same as Model 2004 LCH except 28-inch bbls. w/5 interchangeable choke tubes. Imported 1984-86.

Lamber Model
82 Field Grade

Laurona Grand
Trap — GTO

MODEL 2004
LCH O/U TRAP . . . . NiB $753 Ex $602 Gd $410
Gauge: 12. 30-inch vent-rib bbls. Three interchangeable choke
tubes: M, IM, F. Manual safety. Other specifications same as Model
2004 LCH O/U. Imported 1984-86.

CHARLES LANCASTER — London, England

"TWELVE-TWENTY" DOUBLE-BARREL
SHOTGUN . . . . NiB $15,313 Ex $12,250 Gd $8330
Sidelock, self-opener. Gauge: 12. Bbls.: 24 to 30 inches standard.
Weight: About 5.75 lbs. Elaborate metal engraving. Highest quality
English or French walnut buttstock and forearm. Imported by
Stoeger in the 1950s.

JOSEPH LANG & SONS — London, England

HIGHEST QUALITY
O/U SHOTGUN . . . . NiB $27,000 Ex $21,600 Gd $14,688
Sidelock. Gauges: 12, 16, 20, 28 and .410. Bbls.: 25 to 30 inches standard. Highest grade English or French walnut buttstock and
forearm. Selective single trigger. Imported by Stoeger in 1950s.

LAURONA SHOTGUNS — Eibar, Spain

GRAND TRAP COMBO
Same general specifications as Model 300 except supplied w/29-
inch over/under bbls., screw-in choke tubes and 34-inch single bar-
rel. Disc. 1992.
Model GTO (top single) . . . . NiB $2291 Ex $1832 Gd $1246
Model GTU (bottom single) . . . NiB $2427 Ex $1941 Gd $1320
Extra Field O/U bbls.
(12 or 20 ga.), ... NiB $845 Ex $676 Gd $459

SILHOUETTE 300 O/U
Boxlock. Single selective trigger. Selective automatic ejectors. Gauge:
12; 2.75-, 3- or 3.5-inch chambers. 28- or 29-inch vent-rib bbls.
w/flush or knurled choke tubes. Weight: 7.75 to 8 lbs. Checkered pis-
tol-grip European walnut stock and beavertail forend. Engraved
receiver w/silvered finish and black chrome bbls. Made 1988-92.
Model 300 Sporting Clays . . . . . . NiB $1287 Ex $1004 Gd $670
Model 300 Trap . . . . NiB $1287 Ex $1004 Gd $670
Model 300 Trap, single . . . . NiB $1287 Ex $1004 Gd $670
Model 300 Ultra-Magnum . . . . . . NiB $1339 Ex $1056 Gd $670

SUPER MODEL O/U SHOTGUNS
Boxlock. Single selective or twin single triggers. Selective automat-
ic ejectors. Gauges: 12 or 20; 2.75- or 3-inch chambers. 26-, 28- or
29-inch vent-rib bbls. w/fixed chokes or screw-in choke tubes.
Weight: 7 to 7.25 lbs. Checkered pistol-grip European walnut stock.
Engraved receiver w/silvered finish and black chrome bbls. Made
from 1985 to date.
Model 82 Super Game (disc.) . . . . . NiB $671 Ex $537 Gd $365
Model 83 MG Super Game . . . . . . NiB $1026 Ex $821 Gd $558
Model 84 S Super Trap . . . . NiB $1345 Ex $1076 Gd $731
Model 85 MG Super Game . . . . . . NiB $1040 Ex $832 Gd $566
Model 85 MG 2-bbl. set . . . . . . NiB $1912 Ex $1501 Gd $1030
Model 85 MS Special Sporting (disc.). . . NiB $1309 Ex $1048 Gd $712
Model 85 MS Super Trap . . . . NiB $1281 Ex $1054 Gd $719
Model 85 MS Pigeon . . . . NiB $1352 Ex $1025 Gd $697
Model 85 S Super Skeet. . . . . NiB $1352 Ex $1081 Gd $734

LEBEAU-COURALLY SHOTGUNS — Belgium

BOXLOCK SIDE
BY-SIDE SHOTGUNS . . . . . . NiB $17,438 Ex $13,950 Gd $9486
Gauges: 12, 16, 20 and 28. 26- to 30-inch bbls. Weight: 6.5 lbs.
average. Checkered, hand-rubbed, oil-finished, straight-grip stock of
French walnut. Classic forend. Made from 1986 to date.

**Lefever A Grade
Hammerless Double-Barrel Shotgun**

LEFEVER ARMS COMPANY —
Syracuse and Ithaca, N.Y.

Lefever sidelock hammerless double-barrel shotguns were made by Lefever Arms Company of Syracuse, New York from about 1885-1915 (serial numbers 1 to 70,000) when the firm was sold to Ithaca Gun Company of Ithaca, New York. Production of these models was continued at the Ithaca plant until 1919 (serial numbers 70,001 to 72,000). Grades listed are those that appear in the last catalog of the Lefever Gun Company, Syracuse. In 1921, Ithaca introduced the boxlock Lefever Nitro Special double, followed in 1934 by the Lefever Grade A; there also were two single-barrel Lefevers made from 1927-42. Manufacture of Lefever brand shotguns was disc. in 1948. Note: "New Lefever" boxlock shotguns made circa 1904-06 by D. M. Lefever Company, Bowling Green, Ohio, are included in a separate listing.

GRADE HAMMERLESS DOUBLE-BARREL SHOTGUN

Boxlock. Plain extractors or auto ejector. Single or double triggers. Gauges: 12, 16, 20, .410. Bbls.: 26-32 inches, standard chokes. Weight: About 7 lbs. in 12 ga. Checkered pistol-grip stock and forearm. Made 1934-42.

W/plain extractors, double triggers. NiB $1008 Ex $806 Gd $548
W/automatic ejector, add $250
W/single trigger, add $100
W/Beavertail Forearm, add $75
16 ga., add 25%
20 ga., add 45%
.410 ga., add 200%

GRADE SKEET MODEL

Same as A Grade except standard features include auto ejector, single trigger, beavertail forearm; 26-inch bbls., skeet boring. Disc. 1942.

A grade skeet model, 12 ga. . . . . NiB $1212 Ex $967 Gd $658
16 ga., add 45%
20 ga., add 90%
.410 ga., add 200%

HAMMERLESS SINGLE-SHOT

TRAP GUN . . . . NiB $587 Ex $469 Gd $318
Boxlock. Ejector. 12 ga. only. 30- or 32-inch bbl.; vent rib. Weight: About 8 lbs. Checkered pistol-grip stock and forend, recoil pad. Made 1927-42.

LONG RANGE HAMMERLESS
SINGLE-BARREL FIELD GUN . . . . . NiB $358 Ex $286 Gd $194
Boxlock. Plain extractor. Gauges: 12, 16, 20, .410. Bbl. lengths: 26-32 inches. Weight: 5.5 to 7 lbs. depending on ga. and bbl. length. Checkered pistol-grip stock and forend. Made 1927-42.

NITRO SPECIAL HAMMERLESS DOUBLE

Boxlock. Plain extractors. Single or double triggers. Gauges: 12, 16, 20, .410. Bbls.: 26- to 32-inch, standard chokes. Weight: about 7 lbs. in 12 ga. Checkered pistol-grip stock and forend. Made 1921-48.

Nitro Special W/ double triggers . . . . NiB $540 Ex $411 Gd $246
Nitro Special W/ single trigger . . . . NiB $644 Ex $515 Gd $350
16 ga., add 25%
20 ga., add 50%
.410 ga., add 200%

SIDELOCK HAMMERLESS DOUBLES

Plain extractors or auto ejectors. Double triggers or selective single trigger. Gauges: 10, 12, 16, 20. Bbls.: 26-32 inches; standard choke combinations. Weight: 5.75 to 10.5 lbs. depending on ga. and bbl. length. Checkered walnut straight-grip or pistol-grip stock and forearm. Grades differ chiefly in quality of workmanship, engraving, wood, checkering, etc.; general specifications are the same. DS and DSE Grade guns lack the cocking indicators found on all other models. Suffix "E" means model has auto ejector; also standard on A, AA, Optimus, and Thousand Dollar Grade guns.

Grade	NiB	Ex	Gd
H grade	$1886	$1508	$1025
HE grade	$2502	$2002	$1361
G grade	$2204	$1763	$1199
GE grade	$2958	$2366	$1609
F grade	$1971	$1577	$1072
FE grade	$3013	$2410	$1638
E grade	$2866	$2293	$1559
EE grade	$4414	$3531	$2401
D grade	$3542	$2834	$1927
DE grade	$5526	$4420	$3006
DS grade	$1535	$1228	$835
DSE grade	$1904	$1523	$1036
C grade	$4856	$3884	$2641
CE grade	$9094	$7275	$4947
B grade	$5844	$4675	$3179
BE grade	$10,559	$8447	$5744
A grade	$18,339	$16,054	$14,829
AA grade	$27,170	$21,736	$14,780
Optimus grade	$37,050	$29,640	$20,155
Thousand Dollar grade	$55,250	$44,200	$30,056
W/single trigger, add			10%
10 ga., add			15%
16 ga., add			45%
20 ga., add			90%

D. M. LEFEVER COMPANY —
Bowling Green, Ohio

In 1901, D. M. "Uncle Dan" Lefever, founder of the Lefever Arms Company, withdrew from that firm to organize D. M. Lefever, Sons & Company (later D. M. Lefever Company) to manufacture the "New Lefever" boxlock double- and single-barrel shotguns. These were produced at Bowling Green, Ohio, from about 1904-1906, when Dan Lefever died and the factory closed permanently. Grades listed are those that appear in the last catalog of D. M. Lefever Co.

HAMMERLESS DOUBLE-BARREL SHOTGUNS
"New Lefever." Boxlock. Auto ejector standard on all grades except O Excelsior, which was regularly supplied w/plain extractors (auto ejector offered as an extra). Double triggers or selective single trigger (latter standard on Uncle Dan Grade, extra on all others). Gauges: 12, 16, 20. Bbls.: Any length and choke combination. Weight: 5.5 to 8 lbs. depending on ga. and bbl. length. Checkered walnut straight-grip or pistol-grip stock and forearm. Grades differ chiefly in quality of workmanship, engraving, wood, checkering, etc. General specifications are the same.

O Excelsior grade
w/plain extractors . . . . NiB $3316 Ex $2652 Gd $1803
O Excelsior grade
w/automatic ejectors. . . . . NiB $3764 Ex $3011 Gd $2048
No. 9, F grade . . . . NiB $4674 Ex $3739 Gd $2543
No. 8, E grade . . . . NiB $5526 Ex $4420 Gd $3006
No. 7, D grade. . . . . NiB $5948 Ex $4758 Gd $3235
No. 6, C grade. . . . . NiB $6754 Ex $5403 Gd $3674
No. 5, B grade . . . . NiB $8964 Ex $7171 Gd $4877
No. 4, AA grade. . . . . NiB $13,000 Ex $10,400 Gd $7072
Uncle Dan grade . . . . NiB $19,500 Ex $15,600 Gd $10,608
W/single trigger, add 10%
16 ga., add 45%
20 ga., add 15%

D. M. LEFEVER SINGLE-BARREL
TRAP GUN. . . . . NiB $6494 Ex $5195 Gd $3533
Boxlock. Auto ejector. 12 ga. only. Bbls.: 26- to 32 inches, F choke. Weight: 6.5 to 8 lbs. depending on bbl. length. Checkered walnut pistol-grip stock and forearm.

MAGTECH SHOTGUNS — San Antonio, Texas
Mfd. By CBC in Brazil
MODEL 586.2 SLIDE-ACTION SHOTGUN
Gauge: 12; 3-inch chamber. 19-, 26- or 28-inch bbl.; fixed chokes or integral tubes. 46.5 inches overall. Weight: 8.5 lbs. Double-action slide bars. Brazilian hardwood stock. Polished blued finish. Imported 1992 to date.
Model 586.2 F
(28-inch bbl., fixed choke) . . . . NiB $223 Ex $178 Gd $121
Model 586.2 P
(19-inch plain bbl., cyl. bore) . . . . . NiB $223 Ex $178 Gd $121
Model 586.2 S
(24-inch bbl., rifle sights, cyl. bore) . . . NiB $229 Ex $184 Gd $125
Model 586.2 VR
(vent rib w/tubes) . . . . NiB $223 Ex $178 Gd $121

MARLIN FIREARMS CO. — North Haven (formerly New Haven), Conn.

MODEL 16 VISIBLE HAMMER SLIDE-ACTION REPEATER
Takedown. 16 ga. Five shell tubular magazine. Bbls.: 26- or 28-inch, standard chokes. Weight: About 6.25 lbs. Pistol-grip stock, grooved slide handle; checkering on higher grades. Difference among grades is in quality of wood, engraving on Grades C and D. Made 1904-10.
Grade A . . . . NiB $414 Ex $331 Gd $225
Grade B . . . . NiB $574 Ex $459 Gd $312
Grade C . . . . NiB $702 Ex $561 Gd $381
Grade D. . . . . NiB $1434 Ex $1147 Gd $780

Lefever Sidelock AA Grade

Lefever Sidelock DE Grade

Lefever Sidelock Sideplate BE Grade

Lefever Sidelock Sideplate CE Grade

Lefever Sidelock Optimus Grade

SHOTGUNS

Magtech Model 586.2
Slide-Action

Marlin Model 17
Standard

Marlin Model 28B
Hammerless Slide-Action Repeater

Marlin Model 30
Visible Hammer Slide-Action Repeater

Marlin Model 43A
Hammerless Slide-Action Repeater

MODEL 17 BRUSH GUN . . . . NiB $357 Ex $286 Gd $194
Same as Model 17 Standard except has 26-inch bbl., cylinder bore.
Weight: About 7 lbs. Made 1906-08.

MODEL 17 RIOT GUN . . . . NiB $381 Ex $305 Gd $207
Same as Model 17 Standard except has 20-inch bbl., cylinder bore.
Weight: About 6.88 lbs. Made 1906-08.

MODEL 17 STANDARD VISIBLE HAMMER
SLIDE-ACTION REPEATER . . . . NiB $357 Ex $286 Gd $194
Solid frame.12 ga. 5-shot tubular magazine. Bbls.: 30- or 32-inch, F
choke. Weight: About 7.5 lbs. Straight-grip stock, grooved slide handle. Made 1906-08.

MODEL 19 VISIBLE HAMMER SLIDE-ACTION REPEATER
Similar to Model 1898 but improved, lighter weight, w/two extrac-
tors, matted sighting groove on receiver top. Weight: About 7 lbs.
Made 1906-07.
Grade A . . . . NiB $363 Ex $291 Gd $198
Grade B . . . . NiB $629 Ex $503 Gd $343
Grade C . . . . NiB $682 Ex $546 Gd $371
Grade D . . . . NiB $1396 Ex $1117 Gd $760

MODEL 21 TRAP VISIBLE HAMMER
SLIDE-ACTION REPEATER
Similar to Model 19 w/same general specifications except has
straight-grip stock. Made 1907-09.
Grade A . . . . NiB $357 Ex $286 Gd $194
Grade B . . . . NiB $526 Ex $421 Gd $287
Grade C . . . . NiB $666 Ex $532 Gd $362
Grade D . . . . NiB $1339 Ex $1071 Gd $728

MODEL 24 VISIBLE HAMMER SLIDE-ACTION REPEATER
Similar to Model 19 but has improved takedown system and auto
recoil safety lock, solid matted rib on frame. Weight: About 7.5 lbs.
Made 1908-15.
Grade A . . . . NiB $332 Ex $266 Gd $181
Grade B . . . . NiB $551 Ex $441 Gd $299
Grade C . . . . NiB $697 Ex $557 Gd $378
Grade D. . . . . NiB $1447 Ex $1158 Gd $787

MODEL 26
BRUSH GUN . . . . NiB $303 Ex $242 Gd $164
Same as Model 26 Standard except has 26-inch bbl., cylinder bore.
Weight: About 7 lbs. Made 1909-15.

Marlin Model 43T
Hammerless Slide-Action Repeater

Marlin Model 53
Hammerless Slide-Action

Marlin Model 55
Goose Gun

Marlin Model 55
Humter Bolt-Action Repeater

Marlin Model 55
Swap Gun

MODEL 26 RIOT GUN . . . . **NiB $271 Ex $217 Gd $148**
Same as Model 26 Standard except has 20-inch bbl., cylinder bore.
Weight: About 6.88 lbs. Made 1909-15.

**MODEL 26 STANDARD VISIBLE HAMMER
SLIDE-ACTION REPEATER** . . . . **NiB $285 Ex $227 Gd $155**
Similar to Model 24 Grade A except solid frame and straight-grip
stock. 30- or 32-inch full choke bbl. Weight: About 7.13 lbs. Made
from 1909-15.

MODEL 28 HAMMERLESS SLIDE-ACTION REPEATER
Takedown. 12 ga. Five shot tubular magazine. Bbls.: 26-, 28-, 30-,
32-inch, standard chokes; matted-top bbl. except on Model 28D,
which has solid matted rib. Weight: About 8 lbs. Pistol-grip stock,
grooved slide handle; checkering on higher grades. Grades differ in
quality of wood, engraving on Models 28C and 28D. Made 1913-
22; all but Model 28A disc. in 1915. See illustration previous page.
Model 28A . . . . NiB $339 Ex $270 Gd $184
Model 28B . . . . NiB $487 Ex $390 Gd $265
Model 28C . . . . NiB $631 Ex $505 Gd $343
Model 28D . . . . NiB $1326 Ex $1061 Gd $721

MODEL 28T TRAP GUN . . . . **NiB $602 Ex $481 Gd $327**
Same as Model 28 except has 30-inch matted-rib bbl., F choke,
straight-grip stock w/high-fluted comb of fancy walnut, checkered.
Made in 1915.

**MODEL 28TS
TRAP GUN** . . . . **NiB $435 Ex $348 Gd $237**
Same as Model 28T except has matted-top bbl., plainer stock. Made
in 1915.

MODEL 30 FIELD GUN . . . . **NiB $335 Ex $267 Gd $182**
Same as Model 30 Grade B except has 25-inch bbl., M choke,
straight-grip stock. Made 1913-14.

MODEL 30 VISIBLE HAMMER SLIDE-ACTION REPEATER
Similar to Model 16 but w/Model 24 improvements. Made 1910-14.
See illustration previous page.
Grade A . . . . NiB $368 Ex $294 Gd $200
Grade B . . . . NiB $568 Ex $455 Gd $309
Grade C . . . . NiB $729 Ex $583 Gd $397
Grade D . . . . NiB $1562 Ex $1250 Gd $850

MODELS 30A, 30B, 30C, 30D
Same as Model 30; designations were changed in 1915. Also avail-
able in 20 ga. w/25- or 28-inch bbl., matted-top bbl. on all grades.
Suffixes "A," "B," "C" and "D" correspond to former grades. Made
in 1915.
Model 30A . . . . NiB $428 Ex $343 Gd $233
Model 30B . . . . NiB $535 Ex $449 Gd $291
Model 30C . . . . NiB $797 Ex $636 Gd $433
Model 30D . . . . NiB $1371 Ex $1096 Gd $746

Marlin Model 59
Bolt-Action Single

Marlin Model 60
Single Shot

MODEL 31 HAMMERLESS SLIDE-ACTION REPEATER
Similar to Model 28 except scaled down for 16 and 20 ga. Bbls.: 25-inch (20 ga. only), 26-inch (16 ga. only), 28-inch, all w/matted top, standard chokes. Weight: 16 ga., about 6.75 lbs.; 20 ga., about 6 lbs. Pistol-grip stock, grooved slide handle; checkering on higher grades; straight-grip stock optional on Model 31D. Made 1915-17; Model 31A until 1922.

Model 31A	NiB $381	Ex $305	Gd $207
Model 31B	NiB $514	Ex $411	Gd $279
Model 31C	NiB $666	Ex $736	Gd $362
Model 31D	NiB $1453	Ex $1163	Gd $790

MODEL 31F FIELD GUN . . . . NiB $408 Ex $357 Gd $255
Same as Model 31B except has 25-inch bbl., M choke, straight- or pistol-grip stock. Made 1915-17.

MODEL 42A VISIBLE HAMMER
SLIDE-ACTION REPEATER . . . . NiB $255 Ex $229 Gd $153
Similar to pre-World War I Model 24 Grade A w/same general specifications but not as high quality. Made from 1922-34.

MODEL 43 HAMMERLESS SLIDE-ACTION REPEATER
Similar to pre-World War I Models 28A, 28T and 28TS, w/same general specifications but not as high quality. Made 1923-30.

Model 43A	NiB $287	Ex $230	Gd $156
Model 43T	NiB $568	Ex $454	Gd $309
Model 43TS	NiB $602	Ex $481	Gd $327

MODEL 44 HAMMERLESS SLIDE-ACTION REPEATER
Similar to pre-World War I Model 31A w/same general specifications but not as high quality. 20 ga. only. Model 44A is a standard-grade field gun. Model 44S Special Grade has checkered stock and slide handle of fancy walnut. Made 1923-35.

Model 44A	NiB $372	Ex $298	Gd $202
Model 44S	NiB $453	Ex $362	Gd $247

MODEL 49 VISIBLE HAMMER SLIDE-
ACTION REPEATING SHOTGUN . . NiB $454 Ex $363 Gd $247
Economy version of Model 42A, offered as a bonus on the purchase of four shares of Marlin stock. About 3000 were made 1925-28.

MODEL 50DL BOLT
ACTION SHOTGUN . . . . NiB $271 Ex $217 Gd $148
Gauge: 12 w/3-inch chamber. Two shot magazine. 28-inch bbl. w/modified choke. 48.75 inches overall. Weight: 7.5 lbs. Checkered black synthetic stocks w/ventilated rubber recoil pad. Made 1997 to date.

MODEL 53 HAMMERLESS
SLIDE-ACTION REPEATER . . . . NiB $357 Ex $286 Gd $194
Similar to Model 43A w/same general specifications. Made 1929-30.

MODEL 55 GOOSE GUN
Same as Model 55 Hunter except chambered for 12-ga. 3-inch Magnum shell, has 36-inch bbl., F choke, swivels and sling. Weight: About 8 lbs. Walnut stock (standard model) or checkered black synthetic stock w/ventilated rubber recoil pad (GDL model). Made 1962 to date.

Model 55 Goose Gun . . . . NiB $220 Ex $176 Gd $119
Model 55GDL Goose Gun
(intro. 1997) . . . . NiB $327 Ex $262 Gd $178

MODEL 55 HUNTER BOLT-ACTION REPEATER
Takedown. Gauges: 12, 16, 20. Two shot clip magazine. 28-inch bbl. (26-inch in 20 ga.), F or adj. choke. Plain pistol-grip stock; 12 ga. has recoil pad. Weight: About 7.25 lbs.; 20 ga., 6.5 lbs. Made 1954-65.

W/plain bbl. . . . . NiB $83 Ex $66 Gd $45
W/adj. choke . . . . NiB $105 Ex $84 Gd $57

MODEL 55 SWAMP GUN . . . . NiB $108 Ex $87 Gd $59
Same as Model 55 Hunter except chambered for 12-ga. 3-inch Magnum shell, has shorter 20.5-inch bbl. w/adj. choke, sling swivels and slightly better-quality stock. Weight: About 6.5 lbs. Made 1963-65.

MODEL 55S SLUG GUN . . . . NiB $147 Ex $117 Gd $80
Same as Model 55 Goose Gun except has 24-inch bbl., cylinder bore, rifle sights. Weight: About 7.5 lbs. Made 1974-79.

MODEL 59 AUTO-SAFE
BOLT-ACTION SINGLE . . . . NiB $108 Ex $87 Gd $59
Takedown. Auto thumb safety, .410 ga. 24-inch bbl., F choke. Weight: About 5 lbs. Plain pistol-grip stock. Made 1959-61.

MODEL 60 SINGLE-SHOT
SHOTGUN . . . . NiB $201 Ex $160 Gd $109
Visible hammer. Takedown. Boxlock. Automatic ejector. 12 ga. 30- or 32-inch bbl., F choke. Weight: About 6.5 lbs. Pistol-grip stock, beavertail forearm. Note: Only about 600 were produced in 1923.

MODEL 63 HAMMERLESS SLIDE-ACTION REPEATER
Similar to Models 43A and 43T w/same general specifications. Model 63TS Trap Special is same as Model 63T Trap Gun except stock style and dimensions to order. Made 1931-35.

Model 63A . . . . NiB $332 Ex $266 Gd $180
Model 63T or 63TS . . . . NiB $424 Ex $339 Gd $230

Marlin Model 90
Standard Over-and-Under

Marlin Model 120
Magnum Slide-Action Repeater

Marlin Model 410
Lever-Action Repeater

Marlin Model 512
Slugmaster

Marlin Model 55-10
Super Goose 10

Marlin Premier Mark I
Slide-Action Repeater

Marlin Premier Mark IV

Marlin-Glenfield
Model 50 Bolt-Action Repeater

SHOTGUNS

GRADING: **NiB** = New in Box   **Ex** = Excellent or NRA 95%   **Gd** = Good or NRA 68%

Marocchi Conquista
Sporting Clays

MODEL 90 STANDARD O/U SHOTGUN

Hammerless. Boxlock. Double triggers; non-selective single trigger was available as an extra on pre-war guns except .410. Gauges: 12, 16, 20, .410. Bbls.: Plain; 26-, 28- or 30-inch; chokes IC/M or M/F; bbl. design changed in 1949, eliminating full-length rib between bbls. Weight: 12 ga., about 7.5 lbs.; 16 and 20 ga., about 6.25 lbs. Checkered pistol-grip stock and forearm, recoil pad standard on prewar guns. Postwar production: Model 90-DT (double trigger), Model 90-ST (single trigger). Made 1937-58.

W/double triggers .... NiB $478 Ex $382 Gd $260
W/single trigger .... NiB $600 Ex $479 Gd $326
Combination model............. NiB $720 Ex $576 Gd $392
16 ga., deduct 10%
20 ga., add 15%
.410, add 30%

MODEL 120 MAGNUM

SLIDE-ACTION REPEATER........ NiB $300 Ex $240 Gd $163
Hammerless. Takedown. 12 ga. (3-inch). Four shot tubular magazine. Bbls.: 26-inch vent rib, IC; 28-inch vent rib M choke; 30-inch vent rib, F choke; 38-inch plain, F choke; 40-inch plain, F choke; 26-inch slug bbl. w/rifle sights, IC. Weight: About 7.75 lbs. Checkered pistol-grip stock and forearm, recoil pad. Made 1971-85.

MODEL 120 SLUG GUN......... NiB $287 Ex $230 Gd $156

Same general specifications as Model 120 Magnum except w/20-inch bbl. and about .5 lb. lighter in weight. No vent rib. Adj. rear rifle sights; hooded front sight. Disc. 1990.

MODEL 410 LEVER-ACTION REPEATER

Action similar to that of Marlin Model 93 rifle. Visible hammer. Solid frame. .410 ga. (2.5-inch shell). Five shot tubular magazine. 22- or 26-inch bbl., F choke. Weight: About 6 lbs. Plain pistol-grip stock and grooved beavertail forearm. Made 1929-32.

Model 410 w/22-inch bbl....... NiB $1447 Ex $1158 Gd $787
Model 410 w/26-inch bbl....... NiB $2051 Ex $964 Gd $656
Deluxe model, add................................. 30%

MODEL 512 SLUGMASTER SHOTGUN

Bolt-action repeater. Gauge: 12; 3-inch chamber, 2-shot magazine. 21-inch rifled bbl. w/adj. open sight. Weight: 8 lbs. Walnut-finished birch stock (standard model) or checkered black synthetic stock w/ventilated rubber recoil pad (GDL model). Made 1994 to date.

Model 512 Slugmaster........... NiB $301 Ex $241 Gd $163
Model 512DL Slugmaster
(intro. 1998) .... NiB $327 Ex $262 Gd $178
Model 512P Slugmaster
w/ported bbl. (intro. 1999)....... NiB $335 Ex $267 Gd $182

MODEL 1898 VISIBLE HAMMER SLIDE-ACTION REPEATER

Takedown. 12 ga. Five shell tubular magazine. Bbls.: 26-, 28-, 30-, 32-inch; standard chokes. Weight: About 7.25 lbs. Pistol-grip stock, grooved slide handle; checkering on higher grades. Difference among grades is in quality of wood, engraving on Grades C and D. Made 1898-05. Note: This was the first Marlin shotgun.

Grade A (Field) .... NiB $357 Ex $280 Gd $204
Grade B .... NiB $586 Ex $505 Gd $306
Grade C .... NiB $892 Ex $721 Gd $515

(cont'd.) MODEL 1898 VISIBLE HAMMER

Grade D .... NiB $1800 Ex $1550 Gd $721

MODEL 55-10 SUPER GOOSE 10.. NiB $220 Ex $176 Gd $119

Similar to Model 55 Goose Gun except chambered for 10 ga. 3.5-inch Magnum shell, has 34-inch heavy bbl., F choke. Weight: About 10.5 lbs. Made 1976-85. See illustration on page 495.

PREMIER MARK I

SLIDE-ACTION REPEATER........ NiB $210 Ex $168 Gd $114
Hammerless. Takedown. 12 ga. Magazine holds 3 shells. Bbls.: 30-inch F choke, 28-inch M, 26-inch IC or SK choke. Weight: About 6 lbs. Plain pistol-grip stock and forearm. Made in France 1960-63.

PREMIER MARK II AND IV

Same action and mechanism as Premier Mark except engraved receiver (Mark IV is more elaborate), checkered stock and forearm, fancier wood, vent rib and similar refinements. Made 1960-63.

Premier Mark II .... NiB $287 Ex $229 Gd $156
Premier Mark IV (plain barrel) .... NiB $319 Ex $255 Gd $173
Premier Mark IV (vent rib barrel) .... NiB $376 Ex $301 Gd $205

GLENFIELD MODEL 50

BOLT-ACTION REPEATER .... NiB $83 Ex $66 Gd $45
Similar to Model 55 Hunter except chambered for 12-or 20-ga., 3-inch Magnum shell; has 28-inch bbl. in 12 ga., 26-inch in 20 ga., F choke. Made 1966-74.

GLENFIELD 778 SLIDE-ACTION

REPEATER .... NiB $236 Ex $189 Gd $129
Hammerless. 12 ga. 2.75-inch or 3-inch. Four shot tubular magazine. Bbls.: 26-inch IC, 28-inch M, 30-inch F, 38-inch MXR, 20-inch slug bbl. Weight: 7.75 lbs. Checkered pistol-grip. Made from 1979-84.

MAROCCHI SHOTGUNS — Brescia, Italy Imported by Precision Sales International of Westfield, MA

CONQUISTA MODEL O/U SHOTGUN

Boxlock. Gauge: 12; 2.75-inch chambers. 28-, 30- or 32-inch vent rib bbl. Fixed choke or internal tubes. 44.38 to 48 inches overall. Weight: 7.5 to 8.25 lbs. Adj. single-selective trigger. Checkered American walnut stock w/recoil pad. Imported since 1994.

Lady Sport Grade I .... NiB $1917 Ex $1534 Gd $1043
Lady Sport Grade II.......... NiB $2295 Ex $1835 Gd $1248
Lady Sport Grade III .... NiB $4139 Ex $3310 Gd $2252
Skeet Model Grade I .... NiB $1626 Ex $1313 Gd $893
Skeet Model Grade II .... NiB $2054 Ex $1643 Gd $1118
Skeet Model Grade III .... NiB $3312 Ex $2649 Gd $1801
Sporting Clays Grade I .... NiB $1806 Ex $1444 Gd $982
Sporting Clays Grade II....... NiB $2117 Ex $1693 Gd $1152
Sporting Clays Grade III ...... NiB $3250 Ex $2600 Gd $1769
Trap Model Grade I.......... NiB $1876 Ex $1501 Gd $1021
Trap Model Grade II .... NiB $2230 Ex $1784 Gd $1213
Trap Model Grade III........ NiB $3161 Ex $2776 Gd $1887

Maverick Model 60
Autoloading Shotgun

Maverick Model 88
Pump Shotgun (Vent Rib)

Merkel Model
47E Side-by-Side

SHOTGUNS

MAVERICK ARMS, INC. — Eagle Pass, Texas

MODEL 60 AUTOLOADING SHOTGUN
Gauge: 12, 2.75- or 3-inch chamber. Five round capacity. Bbls.: Magnum or non-Magnum; 24- or 28-inch w/fixed choke or screw-in tubes, plain or vent rib; blued. Weight: 7.25 lbs. Black synthetic buttstock and forend. Announced in 1993, but not produced.

Standard model . . . . NiB $356 Ex $285 Gd $194
Combo model
w/extra 18.5 inch bbl. . . . . NiB $398 Ex $318 Gd $216
Turkey/Deer model
(w/ghost ring sights) . . . . NiB $413 Ex $330 Gd $224

MODEL 88 BULLPUP . . . . NiB $287 Ex $229 Gd $156
Gauge: 12; 3-inch chamber. Bbl.: 18.5-inch w/fixed choke, blued. Weight: 9.5 lbs. Dual safeties: Grip style and crossbolt. Fixed sights in carrying handle. High-impact black synthetic stock; trigger-forward bullpup configuration w/twin pistol-grip design. Made 1991-94.

MODEL 88 DEER GUN . . . . NiB $194 Ex $155 Gd $105
Crossbolt safety and dual slide bars. Cylinder bore choke. Gauge: 12 only w/3-inch chamber. Bbl.: 24-inch. Weight: 7 lbs. Synthetic stock and forearm.

MODEL 88 PUMP SHOTGUN
Gauge: 12; 2.75- or 3-inch chamber. Bbl.: 28 inches/M or 30 inches/F w/fixed choke or screw-in integral tubes; plain or vent rib, blued. Weight: 7.25 lbs. Bead front sight. Black synthetic or wood buttstock and forend; forend grooved. Made from 1989 to date.

Synthetic stock
w/plain bbl. . . . . NiB $172 Ex $138 Gd $94
Synthetic stock
w/vent-rib bbl.. . . . . NiB $192 Ex $153 Gd $104
Synthetic Combo
w/18.5 inch bbl.. . . . . NiB $217 Ex $173 Gd $118
Wood stock
w/vent-rib bbl./tubes. . . . . NiB $210 Ex $168 Gd $114
Wood Combo w/vent-rib bbl./tubes . . . . NiB $249 Ex $199 Gd $136

MODEL 88 SECURITY . . . . NiB $181 Ex $144 Gd $98
Crossbolt safety and dual slide bars. Optional heat shield. Cylinder bore choke. Gauge: 12 only w/3-inch chamber. Bbl.: 18.5-inches. Weight: 6 lbs., 8 ozs. Synthetic stock and forearm. Made 1993 to date.

MODEL 91 PUMP SHOTGUN
Same as Model 88, except w/2.75-, 3- or 3.5-inch chamber, 28-inch bbl. W/ACCU-F choke, crossbolt safety and synthetic stock only. Made 1991-95.

Synthetic stock w/plain bbl. . . . . . . NiB $230 Ex $184 Gd $124
Synthetic stock w/vent-rib bbl.. . . . NiB $243 Ex $194 Gd $132

MODEL 95 BOLT-ACTION . . . . NiB $159 Ex $127 Gd $87
Modified, fixed choke. Built-in 2-round magazine. Gauge: 12 only. Bbl.: 25-inch. Weight: 6.75 lbs. Bead sight. Synthetic stock and rubber recoil pad. Made 1995 to date.

GEBRÜDER MERKEL — Suhl, Germany
Mfd. by Suhler Jagd-und Sportwaffen GmbH,
Imported by GSI, Inc., Trussville, AL,
(Previously by Armes de Chasse)

MODEL 8 HAMMERLESS DOUBLE. . . NiB $1204 Ex $963 Gd $654
Anson & Deeley boxlock action w/Greener double-bbl. hook lock. Double triggers. Extractors. Automatic safety. Gauges: 12, 16, 20; 2.75- or 3-inch chambers. 26-or 28-inch bbls. w/fixed standard chokes. Checkered European walnut stock, pistol-grip or English-style w/or w/o cheekpiece. Scroll-engraved receiver w/tinted marble finish.

SIDE-BY-SIDE MODEL 47E . . . . NiB $2360 Ex $2300 Gd $1565
Hammerless boxlock similar to Model 8 except w/automatic ejectors and cocking indicators. Double hook bolting. Single selective or double triggers. 12, 16 or 20 ga. w/2.75-inch chambers. Standard bbl lengths, choke combos. Hand-checkered European walnut stock, forearm; pistol-grip and cheekpiece or straight English style; sling swivels.

Merkel Model 47LSC
Sporting Clay

Merkel Model 47S
Hammerless Sidelock

Merkel Model 247S
Hammerless Sidelock

Merkel Model 347S
Hammerless Sidelock

Merkel Model 122
Hammerless Double

MODEL 47LSC
SPORTING CLAYS S/S . . . . . NiB $2826 Ex $2261 Gd $1538
Anson & Deeley boxlock action w/single-selective adj. trigger, cocking indicators and manual safety. Gauge: 12; 3-inch chambers. 28-inch bbls.w/Briley choke tubes and H&H-style ejectors. Weight: 7.25 lbs. Color case-hardened receiver w/Arabesque engraving. Checkered select-grade walnut stock, beavertail forearm. Imported 1993-94.

MODELS 47SL, 147SL, 247SL, 347SL, 447SL
HAMMERLESS SIDELOCKS
Same general specifications as Model 147E except has sidelocks engraved w/Arabesques, borders, scrolls or game scenes in varying degrees of elaborateness.

Model 47SL . . . . NiB $5091 Ex $4073 Gd $2770
Model 147SL . . . . NiB $5594 Ex $4475 Gd $3043
Model 147SSL. . . . . NiB $6082 Ex $4866 Gd $3309
Model 247SL . . . . NiB $5658 Ex $4526 Gd $3078
Model 347SL . . . . NiB $6019 Ex $4815 Gd $3274
Model 447SL . . . . NiB $6508 Ex $5206 Gd $3540
28 ga. .410, add 20%

NOTE: Merkel over/under guns were often supplied with accessory barrels, interchangeable to convert the gun into an arm of another type; for example, a set might consist of one pair each of shotgun, rifle and combination gun barrels. Each pair of interchangeable barrels has a value of approximately one-third that of the gun with which they are supplied.

MODEL 100 O/U SHOTGUN
Hammerless. Boxlock. Greener crossbolt. Plain extractor. Double triggers. Gauges: 12, 16, 20. Made w/plain or ribbed bbls. in various lengths and chokes. Plain finish, no engraving. Checkered forend and stock w/pistol grip and cheekpiece or English-style. Made prior to WWII.
W/plain bbl. . . . . NiB $1951 Ex $1560 Gd $1061
W/ribbed bbl. . . . . NiB $2018 Ex $1614 Gd $1097

MODELS 101 AND 101E O/U
Same as Model 100 except ribbed bbl. standard, has separate extractors (ejectors on Model 101E), English engraving. Made prior to World War II.
Model 101 . . . . NiB $2073 Ex $1658 Gd $1128
Model 101E . . . . NiB $2231 Ex $1785 Gd $1213

MODEL 122
HAMMERLESS DOUBLE . . . . NiB $3821 Ex $3057 Gd $2079
Similar to the Model 147S except w/nonremovable sidelocks in gauges 12, 16 or 20. Imported since 1993.

MODEL 122E
HAMMERLESS SIDELOCK............**NiB $4243 Ex $3394 Gd $2308**
Similar to the Model 122 except w/removable sidelocks and cocking indicators. Importation disc. 1992.

MODEL 126E
HAMMERLESS SIDELOCK........**NiB $28,969 Ex $23,175 Gd $15,759**
Holland & Holland system, hand-detachable locks. Auto ejectors. Double triggers. 12, 16 or 20 gauge w/standard bbl. lengths and chokes. Checkered forend and pistol-grip stock; available w/cheekpiece or English-style buttstock. Elaborate game scenes and engraving. Made prior to WW II.

MODEL 127E
HAMMERLESS SIDELOCK........**NiB $29,549 Ex $23,639 Gd $16,074**
Similar to the Model 126E except w/elaborate scroll engraving on removable sidelocks w/cocking indicators. Made prior to WW II.

MODEL 128E
HAMMERLESS BOXLOCK DOUBLE...**NiB $12,554 Ex $10,042 Gd $6829**
Scalloped Anson & Deeley action w/hinged floorplate and removable sideplates. Auto-ejectors. Double triggers. Elaborate hunting scene or Arabesque engraving. 12, 16 or 20 gauge w/various bbl. lengths and chokes. Checkered forend and stock w/pistol grip and cheekpiece or English-style. Made prior to WW II.

MODEL 130
HAMMERLESS BOXLOCK DOUBLE...**NiB $12,554 Ex $10,042 Gd $6829**
Similar to Model 128E except w/fixed sideplates. Auto ejectors. Double triggers. Elaborate hunting scene or Arabesque engraving. Made prior to WW II.

MODESL 147 & 147E HAMMERLESS BOXLOCK DOUBLE-BARREL SHOTGUN
Anson & Deeley system w/extractors or auto ejectors. Single selective or double triggers. Gauges: 12, 16, 20 or 28 ga. (Three inch chambers available in 12 and 20 ga.). Bbls.: 26-inch standard, other lengths available w/any standard choke combination. Weight: 6.5 lbs. Checkered straight-grip stock and forearm. Disc. 1998.
Model 147 w/extractors ......**NiB $2569 Ex $2055 Gd $1398**
Model 147E w/ejectors ....**NiB $3026 Ex $2420 Gd $1646**

MODELS 200, 200E, 201, 201E, 202 AND 202E O/U SHOTGUNS
Hammerless. Boxlock. Kersten double crossbolt. Scalloped frame. Sideplates on Models 202 and 202E. Arabesque or hunting engraving supplied on all except Models 200 and 200E. "E" models have ejectors, others have separate extractors, signal pins, double triggers. Gauges: 12, 16, 20, 24, 28, 32 (last three not available in postwar guns). Ribbed bbls. in various lengths and chokes. Weight: 5.75 to 7.5 lbs. depending on bbl. length and gauge. Checkered forend and stock w/pistol grip and cheekpiece or English-style. The 200, 201, and 202 differ in overall quality, engraving, wood, checkering, etc.; aside from the faux sideplates on Models 202 and 202E, general specifications are the same. Models 200, 201, 202, and 202E, all made before WW II, are disc. Models 201E &202E in production w/revised 2000 series nomenclature.

Model			
Model 200	NiB $2291	Ex $1832	Gd $1246
Model 200E	NiB $3213	Ex $2570	Gd $1678
Model 200 ES Skeet...................	NiB $4758	Ex $3806	Gd $2588
Model 200ET Trap	NiB $4571	Ex $3656	Gd $2486
Model 200 SC Sporting Clays	NiB $5144	Ex $4115	Gd $2798
Model 201 (disc.)...................	NiB $2769	Ex $2214	Gd $1506
Model 201E (Pre-WW II)	NiB $3173	Ex $2539	Gd $1726
Model 201E (Post-WW II)..............	NiB $4520	Ex $3615	Gd $2459
Model 201 ES Skeet..................	NiB $7204	Ex $5763	Gd $3919
Model 201 ET Trap...................	NiB $7146	Ex $5717	Gd $3887
Model 202 (disc.)...................	NiB $3663	Ex $2930	Gd $1993
Model 202E (Pre-WW II)	NiB $4314	Ex $3450	Gd $2346
Model 202 E (Post-WW II & 2002EL).....	NiB $6721	Ex $5377	Gd $3656

Merkel Model 147E
Hammerless Boxlock Double-Barrel Shotgun

Merkel Model 200E
O/U Shotgun

Merkel Model 203E
Sidelock O/U Shotgun

SHOTGUNS

Merkel Model 303E O/U Shotgun

MODEL 203E SIDELOCK O/U SHOTGUNS

Hammerless action w/hand-detachable sidelocks. Kersten double cross bolt, auto ejectors and double triggers. Gauges: 12 or 20 (16, 24, 28 and 32 disc.). 26.75- or 28-inch vent rib bbls. Arabesque engraving standard or hunting engraving optional on coin-finished receiver. Checkered English or pistol-grip stock and forend. See illustration previous page.

Model 203E sidelock (disc. 1998) . . NiB $6136 Ex $4908 Gd $3337
Model 203ES skeet
(imported 1993-97) . . . . NiB $8749 Ex $6999 Gd $46759
Model 203ET trap (disc. 1997) . . . . NiB $8800 Ex $7040 Gd $4787

MODEL 204E

O/U SHOTGUN . . . . NiB $7404 Ex $5922 Gd $4027
Similar to Model 203E; has Merkel sidelocks, fine English engraving. Made prior to World War II.

MODEL 210E

SIDE-LOCK O/U SHOTGUN . . . NiB $5980 Ex $4784 Gd $3254
Kersten double cross-bolt, scroll-engraved, casehardened receiver. 12, 16 or 20 ga. Double-triggers; pistol-grip stock w/cheekpiece.

MODEL 211E

SIDE-LOCK O/U SHOTGUN . . . NiB $7236 Ex $5789 Gd $3937
Same specifications as Model 210E except w/engraved hunting scenes on silver-gray receiver.

MODELS 300, 300E, 301, 301E AND 302 O/U

Merkel-Anson system boxlock. Kersten double crossbolt, two underlugs, scalloped frame, sideplates on Model 302. Arabesque or hunting engraving. "E" models and Model 302 have auto ejectors, others have separate extractors. Signal pins. Double triggers. Gauges: 12, 16, 20, 24, 28, 32. Ribbed bbls. in various lengths and chokes. Checkered forend and stock w/pistol grip and cheekpiece or English-style. Grades 300, 301 and 302 differ in overall quality, engraving, wood, checkering, etc.; aside from the dummy sideplates on Model 302, general specifications are the same. Manufactured prior to World War II.

Model 300 . . . . NiB $2684 Ex $2148 Gd $1461
Model 300E . . . . NiB $3284 Ex $2626 Gd $1786
Model 301 . . . . NiB $6946 Ex $5557 Gd $3779
Model 301E . . . . NiB $8305 Ex $6643 Gd $4518
Model 302 . . . . NiB $14,803 Ex $11,842 Gd $8052

MODEL 303EL O/U

SHOTGUN . . . . NiB $17,349 Ex $13,879 Gd $9438
Similar to Model 203E. Has Kersten crossbolt, double underlugs, Holland & Holland-type hand-detachable sidelocks, auto-ejectors. This is a finer gun than Model 203E. Currently manufactured.

MODEL 304E O/U

SHOTGUN . . . . NiB $22,306 Ex $17,752 Gd $12,134
Special version of the Model 303E-type, but higher quality throughout. This is the top grade Merkel over/under. Currently manufactured.

MODELS 400, 400E, 401, 401E O/U

Similar to Model 101 except have Kersten double crossbolt, Arabesque engraving on Models 400 and 400E, hunting engraving on Models 401 and 401E, finer general quality. "E" models have Merkel ejectors, others have separate extractors. Made prior to World War II.

Model 400 . . . . NiB $2195 Ex $1756 Gd $1194
Model 400E . . . . NiB $2796 Ex $2237 Gd $1521
Model 401 . . . . NiB $2337 Ex $1869 Gd $1271
Model 401E . . . . NiB $3858 Ex $3087 Gd $2099

O/U COMBINATION GUNS ("BOCKBÜCHSFLINTEN")

Shotgun bbl. over, rifle bbl. under. Gauges: 12, 16, 20; calibers: 5.6x35 Vierling, 7x57r5, 8x57JR, 8x60R Mag., 9.3x53r5, 9.3x72r5, 9.3x74R and others including domestic calibers from .22 Hornet to .375 H&H. Various bbl. lengths, chokes and weights. Other specifications and values correspond to those of Merkel over/under shotguns listed below. Currently manufactured. Model 210 & 211 series disc. 1992.

Models 410, 410E, 411E
(see shotgun models 400, 400E, 401, 401E)
Models 210, 210E, 211, 211E, 212, 212E
(see shotgun models 200, 200E, 201, 201E, 202, 202E)

MODEL 2000EL O/U SHOTGUNS

Kersten double cross-bolt. Gauges: 12 and 20. 26.75- or 28-inch bbls. Weight: 6.4 to 7.28 lbs. Scroll engraved silver-gray receiver. Automatic ejectors and single selective or double triggers. Checkered forend and stock w/pistol grip and cheekpiece or English-style stock w/luxury grade wood. Imported 1998 to date.

Model 2000EL Standard . . . . . NiB $5027 Ex $4022 Gd $2735
Model 2000EL Sporter . . . . NiB $5232 Ex $4186 Gd $2847

MODEL 2001EL O/U SHOTGUNS

Gauges: 12, 16, 20 and 28; Kersten double cross-bolt lock receiver. 26.75- or 28-inch IC/mod, mod/full bbls. Weight: 6.4 to 7.28 lbs. Three-piece forearm, automatic ejectors and single selective or double triggers. Imported 1993 to date.

Model 2001EL 12 ga. . . . . NiB $5975 Ex $4780 Gd $3251
Model 2001EL 16 ga. (disc. 1997)
. . . . NiB $5975 Ex $4780 Gd $3251
Model 2001EL 20 ga. . . . . NiB $5975 Ex $4780 Gd $3251
Model 2001EL 28 ga.
(made 1995) . . . . NiB $6584 Ex $5266 Gd $3581

MODEL 2002EL . . . . NiB $6721 Ex $5377 Gd $3656
Same specifications as Model 2000EL except hunting scenes w/Arabesque engraving.

ANSON DRILLINGS

Three-bbl. combination guns; usually made w/double shotgun bbls., over rifle bbl., although "Doppelbüchsdrillingen" were made w/two rifle bbls. over and shotgun bbl. under. Hammerless.

Miida Model 612
Field Grade O/U

(cont'd.) ANSON DRILLINGS

Boxlock. Anson & Deeley system. Side clips. Plain extractors. Double triggers. Gauges: 12, 16, 20; rifle calibers: 7X57r5, 8X57JR and 9.3X74R are most common, but other calibers from 5.6mm to 10.75mm available. Bbls.: standard drilling 25.6 inches; short drilling, 21.6 inches. Checkered pistol-grip stock and forend. The three models listed differ chiefly in overall quality, grade of wood, etc.; general specifications are the same. Made prior to WW II.

Model 142 Engraved	NiB $5339	Ex $4271	Gd $2905
Model 142 Standard	NiB $4030	Ex $3224	Gd $2192
Model 145 Field	NiB $3364	Ex $2690	Gd $1829

MIIDA SHOTGUNS — Manufactured for Marubeni America Corp., New York, N.Y., by Olin-Kodensha Co., Tochigi, Japan

MODEL 612 FIELD GRADE O/U . . . NiB $825 Ex $660 Gd $449
Boxlock. Auto ejectors. Selective single trigger. 12 ga. Bbls.: Vent rib; 26-inch, IC/M; 28-inch, M/F choke. Weight: W/26-inch bbl., 6 lbs., 11 oz. Checkered pistol-grip stock and forearm. Made 1972-74.

MODEL 2100 SKEET GUN . . . . NiB $933 Ex $747 Gd $508
Similar to Model 612 except has more elaborate engraving on frame (50 percent coverage), skeet-style stock and forearm of select grade wood; 27-inch vent-rib bbls., SK choke. Weight: 7 lbs., 11 oz. Made 1972-74.

**MODEL 2200T TRAP GUN,
MODEL 2200S SKEET GUN . . . . . . NiB $972 Ex $778 Gd $528**
Similar to Model 612 except more elaborate engraving on frame (60 percent coverage), trap- or skeet-style stock and semi-beavertail forearm of fancy walnut, recoil pad on trap stock. Bbls.: Wide vent rib; 29.75-inch, IM/F choke on Trap Gun; 27-inch, SK choke on Skeet Gun. Weight: Trap, 7 lbs., 14 oz.; Skeet, 7 lbs., 11 oz. Made 1972-74.

**MODEL 2300T TRAP GUN,
MODEL 2300S SKEET GUN . . . . . NiB $1039 Ex $831 Gd $565**
Same as models 2200T and 2200S except more elaborate engraving on frame (70% coverage). Made 1972-74.

**GRANDEE MODEL GRT/IRS
TRAP/SKEET GUN . . . . NiB $2562 Ex $2050 Gd $1394**
Boxlock w/sideplates. Frame, breech ends of bbls., trigger guard and locking lever fully engraved and gold inlaid. Auto ejectors. Selective single trigger. 12 ga. Bbls.: Wide vent rib; 29-inch, F choke on Trap Gun; 27-inch, SK choke on Skeet Gun. Weight: Trap, 7 lbs., 14 oz.; Skeet, 7 lbs., 11 oz. Trap- or skeet-style stock and semi-beavertail forearm of extra fancy wood, recoil pad on trap stock. Made 1972-74.

MITCHELL ARMS — Santa Ana, California

MODEL 9104/9105 PUMP SHOTGUNS
Slide action in Field/Riot configuration. Gauge: 12; 5-shot tubular magazine. 20-inch bbl.; fixed choke or screw-in tubes. Weight: 6.5 lbs. Plain walnut stock. Made 1994 to date.

(cont'd.) MODEL 9104/9105 PUMP SHOTGUNS

Model 9104 (w/plain bbl.)	NiB $236	Ex $189	Gd $127
Model 9105 (w/rifle sight)	NiB $504	Ex $199	Gd $952
W/choke tubes, add			$20

MODEL 9108/9109 PUMP SHOTGUN
Slide action in Military/Police/Riot configuration. Gauge: 12, 7-shot tubular magazine. 20-inch bbl.; fixed choke or screw-in tubes. Weight: 6.5 lbs. Plain walnut stock and grooved slide handle w/brown, green or black finish. Blued metal. Made 1994 to date.

Model 9108 (w/plain bbl.)	NiB $243	Ex $194	Gd $132
Model 9109 (w/rifle sights)	NiB $264	Ex $209	Gd $142
W/choke tubes, add			$20

MODEL 9111/9113 PUMP SHOTGUN
Slide action in Military/Police/Riot configuration. Gauge: 12; 6-shot tubular magazine. 18.5-inch bbl.; fixed choke or screw-in tubes. Weight: 6.5 lbs. Synthetic or plain walnut stock and grooved slide handle w/brown, green or black finish. Blued metal. Made 1994 to date.

Model 9111 (w/plain bbl.)	NiB $236	Ex $189	Gd $129
Model 9113 (w/rifle sights)	NiB $261	Ex $209	Gd $142
W/choke tubes, add			$20

MODEL 9114/9114FS
Slide action in Military/Police/Riot configuration. Gauge: 12; 7-shot tubular magazine. 20-inch bbl.; fixed choke or screw-in tubes. Weight: 6.5-7 lbs. Synthetic pistol-grip or folding stock. Blued metal. Made 1994 to date.

Model 9114	NiB $287	Ex $229	Gd $156
Model 9114FS	NiB $319	Ex $255	Gd $173

**MODEL 9115/9115FS
PUMP SHOTGUN . . . . NiB $319 Ex $255 Gd $173**
Slide action in Military/Police/Riot configuration. Gauge: 12; 6-shot tubular magazine. 18.5-inch bbl. w/heat-shield handguard. Weight: 7 lbs. Gray synthetic stock and slide handle. Parkerized metal. Made 1994 to date.

MONTGOMERY WARD

See shotgun listings under "W"

MORRONE SHOTGUN — Manufactured by Rhode Island Arms Company, Hope Valley, RI

STANDARD MODEL 46 O/U . . . . . NiB $970 Ex $776 Gd $527
Boxlock. Plain extractors. Non-selective single trigger. Gauges: 12, 20. Bbls.: Plain, vent rib; 26-inch IC/M; 28-inch M/F choke. Weight: About 7 lbs., 12 ga.; 6 lbs., 20 ga. Checkered straight- or pistol-grip stock and forearm. Made 1949-53. Note: Less than 500 of these guns were produced, about 50 in 20 ga., a few had vent-rib bbls. Value shown is for 12 ga. w/plain bbls.; the rare 20 ga. and vent-rib types should bring considerably more.

SHOTGUNS

Mossberg Model 83D

Mossberg Model 85D
Bolt-Action Repeating Shotgun

Mossberg Model 183K

Mossberg Model 185K

Mossberg Model 200K
Slide-Action Repeater

Mossberg Model 395K
Bolt-Action Repeater

O. F. MOSSBERG & SONS, INC. —
North Haven, Connecticut,
Formerly New Haven, Conn.

MODEL 83D OR 183D . . . . NiB $134 Ex $108 Gd $73
3-shot. Takedown. .410 ga. only. Two shell fixed top-loading magazine. 23-inch bbl. w/two interchangeable choke tubes (M/F). Later
production had 24-inch bbl. Plain one-piece pistol-grip stock.
Weight: about 5.5 lbs. Originally designated Model 83D, changed
in 1947 to Model 183D. Made 1940-71.

**MODEL 85D OR 185D BOLT-ACTION
REPEATING SHOTGUN** . . . . NiB $114 Ex $92 Gd $61
Takedown. Three-shot. 20 ga. only. Two-shell detachable box mag-
azine. 25-inch bbl., three interchangeable choke tubes (F, M, IC).

(cont'd.) MODEL 85D OR 185D
Later production had 26-inch bbl. w/F/IC choke tubes. Weight:
About 6.25 lbs. Plain one-piece, pistol-grip stock. Originally desig-
nated Model 85D, changed in 1947 to Model 185D. Made 1940-71.

MODEL 183K . . . . NiB $128 Ex $102 Gd $70
Same as Model 183D except has 25-inch bbl. w/variable C-Lect-
Choke instead of interchangeable choke tubes. Made 1953-86.

MODEL 185K . . . . NiB $135 Ex $108 Gd $73
Same as Model 185D except has variable C-Lect-Choke instead of
interchangeable choke tubes. Made 1950-63.

MODEL 190D . . . . NiB $128 Ex $102 Gd $70
Same as Model 185D except in 16 ga. Weight: About 6 lbs. Made
1955-71.

Mossberg Mode 500
Accu-Choke

Mossberg Model 500
Camo Pump

Mossberg Model 500
Bullpup Shotgun

MODEL 190K . . . . **NiB $135 Ex $108 Gd $73**
Same as Model 185K except in 16 ga. Takedown. Three shot; 2-shell magazine. Weight: About 6.75 lbs. Made 1956-63.

MODEL 195D . . . . **NiB $135 Ex $107 Gd $73**
Same as Model 185D except in 12 ga. Takedown. Three shot; 2-shell magazine. Weight: About 6.75 lbs. Made 1955-71.

MODEL 195K . . . . **NiB $135 Ex $107 Gd $73**
Same as Model 185K except in 12 ga. Takedown. Three shot; 2-shell magazine. Weight: About 7.5 lbs. Made 1956-63.

MODEL 200D . . . . **NiB $140 Ex $112 Gd $76**
Same as Model 200K except w/two interchangeable choke tubes instead of C-Lect choke. Made 1955-59.

MODEL 200K
SLIDE-ACTION REPEATER . . . . **NiB $155 Ex $124 Gd $83**
12 ga. 3-shot detachable box magazine. 28-inch bbl. C-Lect choke. Plain pistol-grip stock. Black nylon slide handle. Weight: About 7.5 lbs. Made 1955-59.

MODEL 395K BOLT-ACTION REPEATER . . . . . **NiB $129 Ex $103 Gd $70**
Takedown. Three shot (detachable-clip magazine holds two shells).12 ga. (3-inch chamber). 28-inch bbl. w/C-Lect-Choke. Weight: About 7.5 lbs. Monte Carlo stock w/recoil pad. Made 1963-83.

MODEL 385K . . . . **NiB $129 Ex $103 Gd $70**
Same as Model 395K except 20 ga. (3-inch), 26-inch bbl. w/C-Lect-Choke. Weight: About 6.25 lbs.

Mossberg Model 500
Camper

MODEL 390K . . . . **NiB $140 Ex $112 Gd $76**
Same as Model 395K except 16 ga. (2.75-inch). Made 1963-74.

MODEL 395S SLUGSTER . . . . **NiB $168 Ex $134 Gd $91**
Same as Model 395K except has 24-inch bbl., cylinder bore, rifle sights, swivels and web sling. Weight: About 7 lbs. Made 1968-81.

MODEL 500 ACCU-CHOKE SHOTGUN . . . . . **NiB $274 Ex $219 Gd $149**
Pump-action. Gauge: 12. 24- or 28-inch bbl. Weight: 7.25 lbs. Checkered walnut-finished wood stock w/ventilated recoil pad. Available w/synthetic field or Speed-Feed stocks. Drilled and tapped receivers, swivels and camo sling on camo models. Made from 1987 to date.

Mossberg Model 500
Persuader Law Enforcement

Mossberg Model 500
Mariner

MODEL 500 BANTAM SHOTGUN

Same as Model 500 Sporting Pump except 20 or .410 ga. only. 22-inch w/ACCU-Choke tubes or 24-inch w/F choke; vent rib. Scaled-down checkered hardwood or synthetic stock w/standard or Realtree camo finish. Made from 1990-96 and 1998-99.

Bantam Model (hardwood stock) . . . . NiB $236 Ex $188 Gd $128
Bantam Model (synthetic stock) . . . . NiB $222 Ex $178 Gd $120
Bantam Model (Realtree camo), add. $50

MODEL 500 BULLPUP SHOTGUN . . . . . . NiB $483 Ex $386 Gd $263

Pump. Gauge: 12. 6- or 8-shot capacity. Bbl.: 18.5 to 20 inches. 26.5 and 28.5 inches overall. Weight: About 9.5 lbs. Multiple independent safety systems. Dual pistol grips, rubber recoil pad. Fully enclosed rifle-type sights. Synthetic stock. Ventilated bbl. heat shield. Made 1987-90.

MODEL 500 CAMO PUMP

Same as Model 500 Sporting Pump except 12 ga. only. Receiver drilled and tapped. QD swivels and camo sling. Special camouflage finish.
Standard model . . . . NiB $238 Ex $185 Gd $126
Combo model (w/ext. Slugster bbl.) . . . NiB $306 Ex $237 Gd $161

MODEL 500 CAMPER . . . . NiB $246 Ex $197 Gd $134

Same general specifications as Model 500 Field Grade except .410 bore, 6-shot magazine, 18.5-inch plain cylinder bore bbl. Synthetic pistol grip and camo carrying case. Made 1986-90.

MODEL 500 FIELD GRADE
HAMMERLESS SLIDE-ACTION REPEATER

Pre-1977 type. Takedown. Gauges: 12, 16, 20, .410. Three inch chamber (2.75-inch in 16 ga.). Tubular magazine holds five 2.75-inch shells or four three-inch. Bbls.: Plain- 30-inch regular or heavy Magnum, F choke (12 ga. only); 28-inch, M or F; 26-inch, IC or adj. C-Lect-Choke; 24-inch Slugster, cylinder bore, w/rifle sights. Weight: 5.75 to lbs. Plain pistol-grip stock w/recoil pad, grooved slide handle. After 1973, these guns have checkered stock and slide handles; Models 500AM and 500AS have receivers etched w/game scenes. The latter has swivels and sling. Made 1962-76.

Model 500A, 12 ga., ... NiB $249 Ex $200 Gd $136
Model 500AM, 12 ga., hvy. Mag. bbl. . . . . NiB $257 Ex $206 Gd $140
Model 500AK, 12 ga., C-Lect-Choke . . . . NiB $289 Ex $232 Gd $158
Model 500AS, 12 ga., Slugster . . . . NiB $297 Ex $238 Gd $162
Model 500B 16 ga., ... NiB $249 Ex $200 Gd $136
Model 500BK, 16 ga., C-Lect-Choke . . . . . NiB $303 Ex $242 Gd $165
Model 500BS, 16 ga., Slugster . . . . NiB $289 Ex $232 Gd $158
Model 500C 20 ga., ... NiB $251 Ex $201 Gd $137
Model 500CK, 20 ga., C-Lect-Choke . . . . . NiB $322 Ex $258 Gd $175
Model 500CS, 20 ga., Slugster . . . . NiB $289 Ex $232 Gd $158
Model 500E, .410 ga., ... NiB $315 Ex $252 Gd $172
Model 500EK, .410 ga., C-Lect-Choke . . . . NiB $354 Ex $283 Gd $193

MODEL 500 "L" SERIES

"L" in model designation. Same as pre-1977 Model 500 Field Grade except not available in 16 ga., has receiver etched w/different game scenes; Accu-Choke w/three interchangeable tubes (IC, M, F) standard, restyled stock and

(cont'd.) MODEL 500 "L" SERIES

slide handle. Bbls.: plain or vent rib; 30- or 32-inch, heavy, F choke (12 ga. Magnum and vent rib only); 28-inch, Accu-Choke (12 and 20 ga.); 26-inch F choke (.410 bore only); 18.5-inch (12 ga. only), 24-inch (12 and 20 ga.) Slugster w/rifle sights, cylinder bore. Weight: 6 to 8.5 lbs. Intro. 1977.

Model 500ALD, 12 ga.,
plain bbl. (disc. 1980) . . . . NiB $281 Ex $227 Gd $158
Model 500ALDR, 12 ga., vent rib . . . . NiB $322 Ex $258 Gd $175
Model 500ALMR, 12 ga.,
Heavy Duck Gun (disc. 1980) . . . . NiB $322 Ex $258 Gd $175
Model 500ALS, 12 ga., Slugster (disc. 1981) . . . NiB $258 Ex $206 Gd $140
Model 500CLD, 20 ga.,
plain bbl. (disc. 1980) . . . . NiB $251 Ex $201 Gd $137
Model 500CLDR, 20 ga., vent rib . . . . NiB $289 Ex $232 Gd $158
Model 500CLS, 20 ga.,
Slugster (disc. 1980) . . . . NiB $322 Ex $258 Gd $175
Model 500EL, .410 ga.,
plain bbl. (disc. 1980) . . . . NiB $277 Ex $221 Gd $150
Model 500ELR, .410 ga., vent rib . . . . NiB $322 Ex $258 Gd $175

MODEL 500 MARINER SHOTGUN . . . . . . NiB $412 Ex $309 Gd $154

Slide action. Gauge: 12. 18.5 or 20-inch bbl. Six shot and 8-shot respectively. Weight: 7.25 lbs. High-strength synthetic buttstock and forend. Available in extra round-carrying Speed Feed synthetic butt-stock. All metal treated for protection against saltwater corrosion. Intro. 1987.

MODEL 500 MUZZLE LOADER COMBO . . NiB $336 Ex $269 Gd $182

Same as Model 500 Sporting Pump except w/extra 24-inch rifled .50-caliber muzzleloading bbl. w/ramrod. Made from 1992 to date.

MODEL 500 PERSUADER LAW ENFORCEMENT

Similar to pre-1977 Model 500 Field Grade except 12 ga. only, 6- or 8-shot, has 18.5- or 20-inch plain bbl., cylinder bore, either shotgun or rifle sights, plain pistol-grip stock and grooved slide handle, sling swivels. Special Model 500ATP8-SP has bayonet lug, Parkerized finish. Currently manufactured.

Model 500ATP6, 6-shot, 18.5-inch
bbl., shotgun sights . . . . NiB $249 Ex $200 Gd $136
Model 500ATP6CN, 6-shot,
nickle finish "Cruiser" pistol-grip. . . . . . . NiB $264 Ex $210 Gd $143
Model 500ATP6N, 6-shot, nickel
finish, 2.75- or 3-inch Mag. shells . . . . . . NiB $256 Ex $205 Gd $139
Model 500ATP6S, 6-shot,
18.5-inch bbl., rifle sights . . . . NiB $249 Ex $200 Gd $136
Model 500ATP8, 8-shot,
20-inch bbl., shotgun sights . . . . NiB $276 Ex $221 Gd $149
Model 500ATP8S, 8-shot,
20-inch bbl., rifle sights . . . . NiB $290 Ex $232 Gd $158
Model 500ATP8-SP Spec. Enforcement . . . NiB $338 Ex $270 Gd $183
Model 500 Bullpup . . . . NiB $534 Ex $426 Gd $290
Model 500 Intimidator w/laser sight, blued . . . NiB $492 Ex $394 Gd $268
Model 500 Intimidator w/laser sight,
parkerized . . . . NiB $507 Ex $405 Gd $275
Model 500 Security combo pack . . . . NiB $203 Ex $162 Gd $110

**Mossberg Model 500
Turkey/Deer Combo**

**Mossberg Model 590
Military**

**Mossberg Model 595
Bolt-Action Repeater**

MODEL 500 PIGEON GRADE
Same as Model 500 Super Grade except higher quality w/fancy wood, floating vent rib; field gun hunting dog etching, trap and skeet guns have scroll etching. Bbls.: 30-inch, F choke (12 ga. only); 28-inch, M choke; 26-inch, SK choke or C-Lect-Choke. Made 1971-75.

Model 500APR, 12 ga., field, trap or skeet . . . NiB $451 Ex $360 Gd $245
Model 500APKR, 12 ga.
field gun, C-Lect-Choke . . . . NiB $463 Ex $371 Gd $252
Model 500 APTR, 12 ga.,
Trap gun, Monte Carlo stock . . . . NiB $547 Ex $438 Gd $298
Model 500CPR, 20 ga., field or skeet gun . . . . NiB $470 Ex $376 Gd $255
Model 500EPR, .410 ga.
field or skeet gun . . . . NiB $483 Ex $386 Gd $263

MODEL 500 PUMP COMBO SHOTGUN . . . . NiB $315 Ex $252 Gd $172
Gauges: 12 and 20. 24- and 28-inch bbl. w/adj. rifle sights. Weight: 7 to 7.25 lbs. Available w/blued or camo finish. Drilled and tapped receiver w/sling swivels and camo web sling. Made from 1987 to date.

MODEL 500 PUMP SLUGSTER SHOTGUN
Gauges: 12 or 20 w/3-inch chamber. 24-inch smoothbore or rifled bbl. w/adj. rifle sights or intregral scope mount and optional muzzle break (1997 porting became standard). Weight: 7 to 7.25 lbs. Wood or synthetic stock w/standard or Woodland Camo finish. Blued, matte black or Marinecote metal finish. Drilled and tapped receiver w/camo sling and swivels. Made 1987 to date.

Slugster (w/cyl. bore, rifle sights) . . . . NiB $247 Ex $198 Gd $134
Slugster (w/rifled bore, ported) . . . . NiB $311 Ex $249 Gd $170
Slugster (w/rifled bore, unported) . . . . NiB $276 Ex $220 Gd $150
Slugster (w/rifled bore, ported,
integral scope mount) . . . . NiB $346 Ex $277 Gd $188
Slugster (w/Marinecote and
synthetic stock), add $60
Slugster (w/Truglo fiber optics), add. $30

MODEL 500 REGAL SLIDE-ACTION REPEATER
Similar to regular Model 500 except higher quality workmanship throughout. Gauges: 12 and 20. Bbls.: 26- and 28-inch w/various chokes, or Accu-Choke. Weight: 6.75 to 7.5 lbs. Checkered walnut stock and forearm. Made 1985 to date.

Model 500 w/Accu-Choke . . . . NiB $249 Ex $200 Gd $136
Model 500 w/fixed choke . . . . NiB $230 Ex $183 Gd $125

MODEL 500 SPORTING PUMP
Gauges: 12, 20 or .410, 2.75- or 3-inch chamber. Bbls.: 22 to 28 inches w/fixed choke or screw-in tubes; plain or vent rib. Weight: 6.25 to 7.25 lbs. White bead front sight, brass mid-bead. Checkered hardwood buttstock and forend w/walnut finish.

Standard model . . . . NiB $251 Ex $201 Gd $137
Field combo (w/extra Slugster bbl.) . . . . NiB $315 Ex $252 Gd $172

MODEL 500 SUPER GRADE
Same as pre-1977 Model 500 Field Grade except not made in 16 ga., has vent rib bbl., checkered pistol grip and slide handle. Made 1965-76.

Model 500AR, 12 ga. . . . . NiB $264 Ex $210 Gd $143
Model 500AMR, 12 ga.,
heavy magnum bbl. . . . . NiB $297 Ex $238 Gd $162
Model 500AKR, 12 ga., C-Lect-Choke . . . . . . NiB $304 Ex $243 Gd $165
Model 500CR 20 ga. . . . . NiB $284 Ex $227 Gd $154
Model 500CKk, 20 ga., C-Lect-Choke. . . . . . . NiB $372 Ex $318 Gd $251
Model 500ER, .410 ga. . . . . NiB $256 Ex $205 Gd $139
Model 500EKR, .410 ga., C-Lect-Choke . . . . . NiB $324 Ex $260 Gd $176

MODEL 500 TURKEY/DEER COMBO. . . . . . . NiB $344 Ex $275 Gd $186
Pump (slide action). Gauge: 12. 20- and 24-inch bbls. Weight: 7.25 lbs. Drilled and tapped receiver, camo sling and swivels. Adj. rifle sights and camo finish. Vent rib. Made from 1987 to date.

**Mossberg Model 1000
Junior Autoloading**

**Mossberg Model 5500
Guardian**

MODEL 500 TURKEY GUN . . . . NiB $317 Ex $254 Gd $173
Same as Model 500 Camo Pump except w/24-inch ACCU-Choke bbl.
w/extra full choke tube and ghost ring sights. Made from 1992 to date.

MODEL 500 VIKING PUMP SHOTGUN
Gauges: 12 or 20 w/3-inch chamber. 24-, 26- or 28-inch bbls. available in smoothbore w/Accu-Choke and vent rib or rifled bore w/iron sights and optional muzzle break (1997 porting became standard). Optional optics: Slug Shooting System (SSS). Weight: 6.9 to 7.2 lbs. Moss-green synthetic stock. Matte black metal finish. Made 1996-98.
Mdl. 500 Viking
(w/VR & choke tubes, unported) . . . . NiB $222 Ex $178 Gd $120
Mdl. 500 Viking (w/rifled bore, ported) . . . NiB $276 Ex $211 Gd $143
Mdl. 500 Viking
(w/rifled bore, SSS & ported) . . . . NiB $354 Ex $283 Gd $193
Mdl. 500 Viking
(w/rifled bore, unported) . . . . NiB $251 Ex $201 Gd $140
Mdl. 500 Viking Turkey
(w/VR, tubes, ported) . . . . NiB $226 Ex $180 Gd $123

**MODEL 500
WATERFOWL/DEER COMBO** . . . . NiB $341 Ex $273 Gd $185
Same general specifications as the Turkey/Deer combo except w/either 28- or 30-inch bbl. along w/the 24-inch bbl. Made from 1987 to date.

**MODEL 500 ATR SUPER
GRADE TRAP** . . . . NiB $429 Ex $343 Gd $233
Same as pre-1977 Model 500 Field Grade except 12 ga. only w/vent-rib bbl.; 30-inch F choke, checkered Monte Carlo stock w/recoil pad, beavertail slide handle. Made 1968-71.

**MODEL 500DSPR DUCK STAMP
COMMEMORATIVE** . . . . NiB $689 Ex $551 Gd $375
Limited edition of 1000 to commemorate the Migratory Bird Hunting Stamp program. Same as Model 500DSPR Pigeon Grade 12-Gauge Magnum Heavy Duck Gun w/heavy 30-inch vent-rib bbl., F choke; receiver has special wood duck etching. Gun accompanied by a special wall plaque. Made in 1975.

MODEL 590 BULLPUP . . . . NiB $451 Ex $360 Gd $245
Same general specifications as the Model 500 Bullpup except 20-inch bbl. and 9-shot magazine. Made 1989-90.

MODEL 590 MARINER PUMP
Same general specifications as the Model 590 Military Security except has Marinecote metal finish and field configuration synthetic stock w/pistiol-grip conversion included. Made from 1989 to date.
Model 590 Mariner (w/18.5-inch bbl.) . . . . NiB $318 Ex $254 Gd $172
Model 590 Mariner (w/20-inch bbl.) . . . . NiB $333 Ex $266 Gd $180
Model 590 Mariner (w/grip conversion), add $20
Model 590 Mariner (w/ghost ring sight), add $50

MODEL 590 MILITARY SECURITY . . . . NiB $389 Ex $311 Gd $211
Same general specifications as the Model 590 Military except there is no heat shield and gun has short pistol-grip style instead of buttstock. Weight: About 6.75 lbs. Made from 1987 to date.

MODEL 590 MILITARY SHOTGUN
Slide-action. Gauge: 12. 9-shot capacity. 20-inch bbl. Weight: about 7 lbs. Synthetic or hardwood buttstock and forend. Ventilated bbl. heat shields. Equipped w/bayonet lug. Blued or Parkerized finish. Made from 1987 to date. See illustration Previous Page.
Synthetic model, blued . . . . NiB $341 Ex $273 Gd $185
Synthetic model Parkerized . . . . . . NiB $367 Ex $294 Gd $200
Speedfeed model, blued . . . . NiB $360 Ex $288 Gd $196
Speedfeed model, Parkerized . . . . . NiB $360 Ex $288 Gd $196
Intimidator model
w/laser sight, blued . . . . NiB $470 Ex $376 Gd $255
Intimidator model
w/laser sight, Parkerized . . . . NiB $483 Ex $386 Gd $263
For ghost ring sight, add $75

**MODEL 595/595K
BOLT-ACTION REPEATER** . . . . NiB $182 Ex $145 Gd $99
12 ga. only. Four shot detachable magazine. 18.5-inch bbl. Weight: About 7 lbs. Walnut finished stock w/recoil pad and sling swivels. Made 1985-86.

MODEL 695 BOLT-ACTION SLUGSTER
Gauge: 12 w/3-inch chamber. Two round detachable magazine. 22-inch fully rifled and ported bbl. w/blade front and folding leaf rear sights. Receiver drilled and tapped for Weaver style scope bases. Also available w/1.5x-4.5x scope or fiber optics installed. Weight: 7.5 lbs. Black synthetic stock w/swivel studs and recoil pad. Made 1996 to date.
Model 695 (w/ACCU-choke bbl.) . . NiB $212 Ex $170 Gd $115
Model 695
(w/open sights) . . . . NiB $276 Ex $220 Gd $150
Model 695
(w/1.5x-4.5x Bushnell scope) . . . . . NiB $389 Ex $311 Gd $211
Model 695 (w/Truglo fiber optics) . . . . NiB $304 Ex $243 Gd $165
Model 695 OFM Camo . . . . NiB $262 Ex $209 Gd $142

MODEL 695 BOLT-ACTION TURKEY GUN NiB $264 Ex $210 Gd $143
Similar to 695 Slugster Model except has smoothbore 22-inch bbl. w/extra-full turkey Accu-choke tube. Bead front and U-notch rear sights. Full OFM camo finish. Made 1996 to date.

MODEL 712 AUTOLOADING SHOTGUN
Gas-operated, takedown, hammerless shotgun w/5-shot (4-shot w/3-inch chamber) tubular magazine. 12 ga. Bbls.: 28-inch vent rib or 24-inch plain bbl. Slugster w/rifle sights. Fixed choke or ACCU-choke tube system. Weight: 7.5 lbs. Plain alloy receiver w/top-mounted ambidextrous safety. Checkered

(cont'd.) MODEL 712 AUTOLOADING SHOTGUN
Mdl. 712 w/fixed chokes . . . . NiB $270 Ex $216 Gd $146
Mdl. 712 w/ACCU-Choke tube system . . . . . NiB $304 Ex $243 Gd $165
Mdl. 712 Regal w/ACCU-Choke tube system . NiB $338 Ex $270 Gd $183
Mdl. 712 Regal w/ACCU-Choke II tube sys. . . NiB $372 Ex $297 Gd $202

MODEL 835 FIELD PUMP SHOTGUN
Similar to the Model 9600 Regal except has walnut-stained hardwood stock and one ACCU-Choke tube only.
Standard model . . . . NiB $277 Ex $221 Gd $150
Turkey model . . . . NiB $289 Ex $232 Gd $158
Combo model (24- & 28-inch bbls.) NiB $315 Ex $252 Gd $172

MODEL 835 "NWTF" ULTI-MA SHOTGUN
National Wild Turkey Federation pump-action. Gauge: 12, 3.5-inch chamber. 24-inch vent-rib bbl. w/four ACCU-MAG chokes. Realtree camo finish. QD swivel and post. Made 1989-93.
Limited Edition model . . . . NiB $451 Ex $360 Gd $245
Special Edition model . . . . NiB $380 Ex $304 Gd $207

MODEL 835 REGAL ULTI-MAG PUMP
Gauge: 12, 3.5-inch chamber. Bbls.: 24- or 28-inch vent-rib w/ACCU-Choke screw-in tubes. Weight: 7.75 lbs. White bead front, brass mid-bead. Checkered hardwood or synthetic stock w/camo finish. Made 1991-96.
Special model . . . . NiB $289 Ex $232 Gd $158
Standard model . . . . NiB $360 Ex $288 Gd $196
Camo Synthetic model . . . . NiB $386 Ex $309 Gd $210
Combo model . . . . NiB $418 Ex $335 Gd $228

MODEL 835 VIKING PUMP SHOTGUN
Gauge: 12 w/3-inch chamber. 28-inch smoothbore bbl. w/Accu-Choke, vent rib and optional muzzle brake (in 1997 porting became standard). Weight: 7.7 lbs. Green synthetic stock. Matte black metal finish. Made 1996-98.
Model 835 Viking (w/VR and
choke tubes, ported) . . . . NiB $276 Ex $221 Gd $149
Model 835 Viking (w/VR
and choke tubes, unported) . . . . . . NiB $264 Ex $210 Gd $143

MODEL 1000 AUTOLOADING SHOTGUN
Gas-operated, takedown, hammerless shotgun w/tubular magazine. Gauges: 12, 20; 2.75- or 3-inch chamber. Bbls.: 22- to 30-inch vent rib w/fixed choke or ACCU-Choke tubes; or 22-inch plain bbl, Slugster w/rifle sights. Weight: 6.5 to 7.5 lbs. Scroll-engraved alloy receiver, crossbolt-type safety. Checkered walnut buttstock and forend. Imported from Japan 1986-87.
Junior model, 20 ga., 22-inch bbl. . . NiB $421 Ex $337 Gd $230
Standard model w/fixed choke . . . . NiB $434 Ex $347 Gd $235
Standard model w/choke tubes . . . NiB $458 Ex $367 Gd $249

MODEL 1000 SUPER AUTOLOADING SHOTGUN
Similar to Model 1000, but in 12 ga. only w/3-inch chamber and new gas metering system. Bbls.: 26-, 28- or 30-inch vent rib w/ACCU-Choke tubes.
Standard model w/choke tubes . . . NiB $509 Ex $407 Gd $277
Waterfowler model (Parkerized) . . NiB $547 Ex $438 Gd $298

MODEL 1000S SUPER SKEET . . . . . NiB $606 Ex $484 Gd $330
Similar to Model 1000 in 12 or 20 ga., except w/all-steel receiver and vented jug-type choke for reduced muzzle jump. Bright-point front sight and brass mid-bead. 1 and 2 oz. forend cap weights.

MODEL 5500 AUTOLOADING SHOTGUN
Gas-operated. Takedown. 12 ga. only. Four shot magazine (3-shot w/3-inch shells). Bbls.: 18.5- to 30-inch; various chokes. Checkered walnut finished hardwood. Made 1985-86.
Model 5500 w/ACCU-Choke . . . . . NiB $289 Ex $232 Gd $158
Model 5500 modified junior . . . . . NiB $296 Ex $236 Gd $160

(cont'd.) MODEL 5500 AUTOLOADING SHOTGUN
Model 5500 Slugster . . . . NiB $306 Ex $245 Gd $167
Model 5500 12 ga. . . . . NiB $260 Ex $208 Gd $141
Model 5500 Guardian . . . . NiB $249 Ex $199 Gd $135

MODEL 5500 MKII AUTOLOADING SHOTGUN
Same as Model 5500 except equipped w/two Accu-Choke bbls.: 26-inch ported for non-Magnum 2.75-inch shells; 28-inch for magnum loads. Made 1988-93.
Standard model . . . . NiB $274 Ex $219 Gd $149
Camo model . . . . NiB $306 Ex $244 Gd $166
NWTF Mossy Oak model . . . . NiB $336 Ex $269 Gd $182
USST model (Made 1991-92) . . . . . NiB $287 Ex $230 Gd $157

MODEL 6000 AUTO SHOTGUN. . . NiB $287 Ex $230 Gd $157
Similar to the Model 9200 Regal except has 28-inch vent-rib bbl. w/mod. ACCU-Choke tube only. Made from 1993 to date.

MODEL 9200 CAMO SHOTGUN
Similar to the Model 9200 Regal except has synthetic stock and forend and is completely finished in camouflage pattern (incl. bbl.). Made from 1993 to date.
Standard model (OFM camo) . . . . . NiB $403 Ex $322 Gd $219
Turkey model (Mossy Oak camo) . . . . . NiB $446 Ex $356 Gd $242
Turkey model (Shadow Branch camo) . . . NiB $530 Ex $424 Gd $288
Comb. model (24 & 28-inch bbls.
w/OFM camo) . . . . NiB $495 Ex $397 Gd $269

MODEL 9200 CROWN (REGAL) AUTOLOADER
Gauge: 12; 3-inch chamber. Bbls.: 18.5- to 28-inch w/ACCU-Choke tubes; plain or vent rib. Weight: 7.25 to 7.5 lbs. Checkered hardwood buttstock and forend w/walnut finish. Made from 1992 to date.
Model 9200 Bantam (w/1-inch shorter stock) . . . . NiB $389 Ex $311 Gd $211
Model 9200 w/ACCU-Choke . . . . NiB $403 Ex $322 Gd $219
Model 9200 w/rifled bbl. . . . . NiB $417 Ex $334 Gd $228
Model 9200 Combo (w/extra Slugster bbl.) . . . . NiB $468 Ex $374 Gd $253
Model 9200 SP (w/matte blue finish,
18.5-inch bbl.) . . . . NiB $318 Ex $254 Gd $173

MODEL 9200 PERSUADER . . . . NiB $341 Ex $273 Gd $185
Similar to the Model 9200 Regal except has 18.5-inch plain bbl. w/fixed mod. choke. Parkerized finish. Black synthetic stock w/sling swivels. Made 1996 to date.

MODEL 9200 A1 JUNGLE GUN . . . NiB $618 Ex $515 Gd $232
Similar to the Model 9200 Persuader except has mil-spec heavy wall 18.5-inch plain bbl. w/cyl. bore designed for 00 Buck shot. 12 ga. w/2.75-inch chamber. 5-shot magazine. 38.5 inches overall. Weight: 7 lbs. Black synthetic stock. Parkerized finish. Made 1998 to date.

MODEL 9200 SPECIAL HUNTER . . NiB $403 Ex $322 Gd $219
Similar to the Model 9200 Regal except has 28-inch vent-rib bbl. w/ACCU-Choke tubes. Parkerized finish. Black synthetic stock. Made from 1998 to date.

MODEL 9200 TROPHY
Similar to the Model 9200 Regal except w/24-inch rifled bbl. or 24- or 28-inch vent-rib bbl. w/ACCU-Choke tubes. Checkered walnut stock w/sling swivels. Made from 1992-98.
Trophy (w/vent rib bbl.) $297
Trophy (w/rifled bbl. & cantilever scope mount) $318
Trophy (w/rifled bbl. & rifle sights) $286

MODEL 9200 USST AUTOLOADER $311
Similar to the Model 9200 Regal except has 26-inch vent-rib bbl. w/ACCU-Choke tubes. "United States Shooting Team" engraved on receiver. Made from 1993 to date.

SHOTGUNS

Navy Arms Model 83
Bird Hunter O/U

Navy Arms Model 100
Field Hunter Double-Barrel Shotgun

MODEL 9200
VIKING AUTOLOADER. . . . . **NiB $372 Ex $297 Gd $202**
Gauge: 12 w/3-inch chamber. 28-inch smoothbore bbl. W/Accu-Choke and vent rib. Weight: 7.7 lbs. Green synthetic stock. Matte black metal finish. Made 1996-98.

MODEL HS410
HOME SECURITY PUMP SHOTGUN
Gauge: .410; 3-inch chamber. Bbl.: 18.5-inch w/muzzle brake; blued. Weight: 6.25 lbs. Synthetic stock and pistol-grip slide. Optional laser sight. Made from 1990 to date. A similar version of this gun is marketed by Maverick Arms under the same model designation.
Standard model . . . . **NiB $238 Ex $191 Gd $134**
Laser model . . . . **NiB $418 Ex $335 Gd $228**

LINE LAUNCHER. . . . . **NiB $869 Ex $695 Gd $473**
Gauge: 12 w/blank cartridge. Projectile travels from 250 to 275 feet.

"NEW HAVEN BRAND" SHOTGUNS
Promotional models, similar to their standard guns but plainer in finish, are marketed by Mossberg under the "New Haven" brand name. Values generally are about 20 percent lower than for corresponding standard models.

NAVY ARMS SHOTGUNS —
Ridgefield, New Jersey

MODEL 83/93 BIRD HUNTER O/U
Hammerless. Boxlock, engraved receiver. Gauges: 12 and 20; 3-inch chambers. Bbls.: 28-inch chrome lined w/double vent-rib construction. Checkered European walnut stock and forearm. Gold plated triggers. Imported 1984-90.
Model 83 w/extractors . . . . **NiB $289 Ex $232 Gd $158**
Model 93 w/ejectors . . . . **NiB $341 Ex $273 Gd $185**

MODEL 95/96 O/U SHOTGUN
Same as the Model 83/93 except w/five interchangeable choke tubes. Imported 1984-90.
Model 95 w/extractors . . . . **NiB $380 Ex $304 Gd $207**
Model 96 w/ejectors . . . . **NiB $508 Ex $406 Gd $275**

MODEL 100/150 FIELD HUNTER
DOUBLE-BARREL SHOTGUN
Boxlock. Gauges: 12 and 20. Bbls.: 28-inch chrome lined. Checkered European walnut stock and forearm. Imported 1984-90.
Model 100 . . . . **NiB $357 Ex $286 Gd $194**
Model 150 (auto ejectors) . . . . **NiB $470 Ex $376 Gd $255**

MODEL 100 O/U SHOTGUN . . . . . **NiB $238 Ex $191 Gd $130**
Hammerless, takedown shotgun w/engraved chrome receiver. Single trigger. 12, 20, 28, or .410 ga. w/3-inch chambers. Bbls.: 26-inch (F/F or SK/SK); vent rib. Weight: 6.25 lbs. Checkered European walnut buttstock and forend. Imported 1986-90.

NEW ENGLAND FIREARMS —
Gardner, Massachusetts

In 1987, New England Firearms was established as an independent company producing selected H&R models under the NEF logo after Harrington & Richardson suspended operations on January 24, 1986. In 1991, H&R 1871, Inc. was formed from the residual of the parent H&R company and then took over the New England Firearms facility. H&R 1871 produced firearms under both their logo and the NEF brand name until 1999, when the Marlin Firearms Company acquired the assets of H&R 1871.

NEW ENGLAND FIREARMS NWTF TURKEY SPECIAL
Similar to Turkey and Goose models except 10 or 20 gauge w/22- or 24-inch plain bbl. w/screw-in full-choke tube. Mossy Oak camo finish on entire gun. Made from 1992-96.
Turkey Special 10 ga. . . . . **NiB $194 Ex $165 Gd $149**
Turkey Special 20 ga. . . . . **NiB $113 Ex $93 Gd $62**

NRA FOUNDATION YOUTH . . . . . . **NiB $176 Ex $141 Gd $97**
Smaller scale version of Pardner Model chambered for 20, 28 or .410 w/22- inch plain bbl. High luster blue finish. NRA Foundation logo laser etched on stock. Made 1999 to date.

PARDNER SHOTGUN
Takedown. Side lever. Single bbl. Gauges: 12, 20 and .410 w/3-inch chamber; 16 and 28 w/2.75-inch chamber. 26-, 28- or 32-inch, plain bbl. w/fixed choke. Weight: 5-6 lbs. Bead front sight. Pistol grip-style hardwood stock w/walnut finish. Made from 1988 to date.
Standard model . . . . **NiB $101 Ex $80 Gd $55**
Youth model . . . . **NiB $108 Ex $87 Gd $58**
Youth Turkey model . . . . **NiB $122 Ex $97 Gd $66**
W/32-inch bbl., add $15

PARDNER SPECIAL PURPOSE 10 GA. SHOTGUN
Similar to the standard Pardner model except chambered 10 ga. only w/3.5-inch chamber. 24- or 28-inch, plain bbl. w/full choke tube or fixed choke. Weight: 9.5 lbs. Bead front sight. Pistol-grip-style hardwood stock w/camo or matte black finish. Made from 1989 to date.
Special Purpose model w/fixed choke . . **NiB $128 Ex $102 Gd $70**
W/camo finish, add $15
W/choke tube, add $20
W/24-inch bbl. turkey option, add $30

Noble Model 65

Noble Model 66RCLP
Hammerless Slide-Action Repeating Shotgun

Noble Key Lock Fire Control Mechanism
Supplied with models 66, 166L, and 602

PARDNER SPECIAL PURPOSE
WATERFOWL SINGLE-SHOT . . . . . . **NiB $161 Ex $129 Gd $88**
Similar to Special Purpose 10 Ga. model except w/32-inch bbl.
Mossy Oak camo stock w/swivel and sling. Made 1988 to date.

PARDNER TURKEY GUN
Similar to Pardner model except chambered in 12 ga. w/3.0- or 3.5-
inch chamber. 24-inch plain bbl. W/turkey full-choke tube or fixed
choke. Weight: 9.5 lbs. American hardwood stock w/camo or matte
black finish. Made from 1999 to date.
Standard Turkey model . . . . **NiB $142 Ex $113 Gd $77**
Camo Turkey model . . . . **NiB $155 Ex $124 Gd $84**

SURVIVOR SERIES
Takedown single bbl. shotgun w/side lever release, Automatic ejector and patented transfer-bar safety. Gauges: 12, 20, and .410/.45
ACP w/3-inch chamber. 22-inch bbl. w/modified choke and bead
sight. Weight: 6 lbs. Polymer stock and forend w/hollow cavity for
storage. Made 1992-93 and 1995 to date.
12 or 20 ga.
w/blued finish . . . . **NiB $120 Ex $96 Gd $65**
12 or 20 ga.
w/nickel finish . . . . **NiB $152 Ex $122 Gd $83**
.410/.45 ACP, add . . . . **NiB $38 Ex $30 Gd $20**

TRACKER SLUG GUN
Similar to Pardner model except in 10, 12 or 20 ga. w/24-inch
w/cylinder choke or rifled slug bbl. (Tracker II). Weight: 6 lbs.
American hardwood stock w/walnut or camo finish, Schnabel
forend, sling swivel studs. Made from 1992 to date.
Tracker Slug
(10 ga.) . . . . **NiB $123 Ex $98 Gd $67**
Tracker Slug
(12 or 20 ga.) . . . . **NiB $124 Ex $93 Gd $52**
Tracker II (rifled bore) . . . . **NiB $155 Ex $124 Gd $62**

NIKKO FIREARMS LTD. — Tochigi, Japan

See listings under Golden Eagle Firearms, Inc.

NOBLE MANUFACTURING COMPANY —
Haydenville, Massachusetts

Series 602 and 70 are similar in appearance to the corresponding
Model 66 guns.

MODEL 40 HAMMERLESS SLIDE-ACTION
REPEATING SHOTGUN . . . . **NiB $148 Ex $118 Gd $80**
Solid frame. 12 ga. only. Five shell tubular magazine. 28-inch bbl.
w/ventilated Multi-Choke. Weight: About 7.5 lbs. Plain pistol-grip
stock, grooved slide handle. Made 1950-55.

MODEL 50
SLIDE-ACTION . . . . **NiB $148 Ex $118 Gd $80**
Same as Model 40 except w/o Multi-Choke. M or F choke bbl.
Made 1953-55.

MODEL 60 HAMMERLESS SLIDE-ACTION
REPEATING SHOTGUN . . . . **NiB $209 Ex $167 Gd $113**
Solid frame. 12 and 16 ga. Five shot tubular magazine. 28-inch bbl.
w/adj. choke. Plain pistol-grip stock w/recoil pad, grooved slide
handle. Weight: About 7.5 lbs. Made 1955-66.

MODEL 65 . . . . **NiB $174 Ex $139 Gd $95**
Same as Model 60 except without adj. choke and recoil pad. M or
F choke bbl. Made 1955-66.

MODEL 66CLP . . . . **NiB $161 Ex $129 Gd $88**
Same as Model 66RCLP except has plain bbl. Introduced in 1967. Disc.

MODEL 66RCLP HAMMERLESS SLIDE-ACTION
REPEATING SHOTGUN . . . . **NiB $203 Ex $162 Gd $110**
Solid frame. Key lock fire control mechanism. Gauges: 12, 16. 3-
inch chamber in 12 ga. Five shot tubular magazine. 28-inch bbl.,
vent rib, adj. choke. Weight: About 7.5 lbs. Checkered pistol-grip
stock and slide handle, recoil pad. Made 1967-70.

MODEL 66RLP . . . . **NiB $186 Ex $149 Gd $102**
Same as Model 66RCLP except w/F or M choke. Made 1967-1970.

Noble Model 66XL

Noble Model 80
Autoloading Shotgun

Noble Model 166L
Deer Gun

Noble Model 420
Hammerless Double

MODEL 66XL . . . . **NiB $161 Ex $129 Gd $88**
Same as Model 66RCL except has plain bbl., F or M choke, slide handle only checkered, no recoil pad. Made 1967-70.

MODEL 70CLP HAMMERLESS SLIDE-ACTION
REPEATING SHOTGUN . . . . **NiB $186 Ex $149 Gd $102**
Solid frame. .410 gauge. Magazine holds 5 shells. 26-inch bbl. w/adj. choke. Weight: About 6 lbs. Checkered buttstock and forearm, recoil pad. Made 1958-70.

MODEL 70RCLP . . . . **NiB $194 Ex $154 Gd $105**
Same as Model 70CLP except has vent rib. Made 1967-70.

MODEL 70RLP . . . . **NiB $180 Ex $144 Gd $98**
Same as Model 70CLP except has vent rib and no adj. choke. Made 1967-70.

MODEL 70XL . . . . **NiB $135 Ex $108 Gd $73**
Same as Model 70CLP except without adj. choke and checkering on buttstock. Made 1958-70.

MODEL 80
AUTOLOADING SHOTGUN. . . . . . **NiB $236 Ex $188 Gd $128**
Recoil-operated. .410 ga. Magazine holds three 3-inch shells, four 2.5-inch shells. 26-inch bbl., full choke. Weight: About 6 lbs. Plain pistol-grip stock and fluted forearm. Made 1964-66.

MODEL 166L DEER GUN . . . . **NiB $264 Ex $210 Gd $143**
Solid frame. Key lock fire control mechanism. 12 ga. 2.75-inch chamber. Five shot tubular magazine. 24-inch plain bbl., specially bored for rifled slug. Lyman peep rear sight, post ramp front sight.

(cont'd.) MODEL 166L DEER GUN
Receiver dovetailed for scope mounting. Weight: About 7.25 lbs. Checkered pistol-grip stock and slide handle, swivels and carrying strap. Made 1967-70.

MODEL 420
HAMMERLESS DOUBLE . . . . **NiB $342 Ex $273 Gd $185**
Boxlock. Plain extractors. Double triggers. Gauges: 12 ga. 3-inch mag.; 16 ga.; 20 ga. 3-inch mag.; .410 ga. Bbls.: 28-inch, except .410 in 26-inch, M/F choke. Weight: About 6.75 lbs. Engraved frame. Checkered walnut stock and forearm. Made 1958-70.

MODEL 450E
HAMMERLESS DOUBLE . . . . **NiB $383 Ex $306 Gd $208**
Boxlock. Engraved frame. Selective auto ejectors. Double triggers. Gauges: 12, 16, 20. 3-inch chambers in 12 and 20 ga. 28-inch bbls., M/F choke. Weight: About 6 lbs., 14 oz., 12 ga. Checkered pistol-grip stock and beavertail forearm, recoil pad. Made 1967-70.

MODEL 602CLP . . . . **NiB $200 Ex $160 Gd $108**
Same as Model 602RCLP except has plain bbl. Made 1958-70.

MODEL 602RCLP
HAMMERLESS SLIDE-ACTION
REPEATING SHOTGUN . . . . **NiB $212 Ex $170 Gd $115**
Solid frame. Key lock fire control mechanism. 20 ga. 3-inch chamber. Five shot tubular magazine. 28-inch bbl., vent rib, adj. choke. Weight: About 6.5 lbs. Checkered pistol-grip stock/slide handle, recoil pad. Made 1967-70.

Omega Deluxe Side-by-Side Shotgun

Parker B.H. Grade

Noble Model 450E Hammerless Double

Parker C.H. Grade

MODEL 602RLP . . . . **NiB $194 Ex $154 Gd $105**
Same as Model 602RCLP except without adj. choke, bored F or M choke. Made 1967-70.

MODEL 602XL . . . . **NiB $161 Ex $129 Gd $88**
Same as Model 602RCL except has plain bbl., F or M choke, slide handle only checkered, no recoil pad. Made 1958-70.

MODEL 662 . . . . **NiB $200 Ex $160 Gd $108**
Same as Model 602CLP except has aluminum receiver and bbl. Weight: About 4.5 lbs. Made 1966-70.

OMEGA SHOTGUNS — Brescia, Italy, and Korea

FOLDING OVER/UNDER SHOTGUN, STANDARD
Hammerless Boxlock. Gauges: 12, 20, 28 w/2.75-inch chambers or .410 w/3-inch chambers. Bbls.: 26- or 28-inch vent-rib w/fixed chokes (IC/M, M/F or F/F (.410). Automatic safety. Single trigger. 40.5 inches overall (42.5 inches, 20 ga., 28-inch bbl.). Weight: 6 to 7.5 lbs. Checkered European walnut stock and forearm. Imported 1984-94.
Standard model (12 ga.) . . . . **NiB $438 Ex $340 Gd $206**
Standard model (20 ga.) . . . . **NiB $438 Ex $340 Gd $206**
Standard model (28 ga. & .410) . . . . **NiB $509 Ex $407 Gd $277**

O/U SHOTGUN, DELUXE . . . . **NiB $428 Ex $342 Gd $233**
Gauges: 20, 28 and .410. 26- or 28-inch vent-rib bbls. 40.5 inches overall (42.5 inches, 20 ga., 28-inch bbl.). Chokes: IC/M, M/F or F/F (.410). Weight: About 5.5-6 lbs. Single trigger. Automatic safety. European walnut stock w/checkered pistol grip and tulip forend. Imported from Italy 1984-90.

OMEGA DELUXE
SIDE-BY-SIDE SHOTGUN . . . . **NiB $213 Ex $171 Gd $116**
Same general specifications as the Standard Side-by-Side except has checkered European walnut stock and low bbl. rib. Made in Italy from 1984-89.

STANDARD SIDE-BY-SIDE SHOTGUN, ...NiB $212 Ex $170 Gd $115
Gauge: .410. 26-inch bbl. 40.5 inches overall. Choked F/F. Weight: 5.5 lbs. Double trigger. Manual safety. Checkered beechwood stock and semi-pistol grip. Imported from Italy 1984-89.

DELUXE SINGLE-SHOT SHOTGUN . . . . **NiB $106 Ex $84 Gd $58**
Same general specifications as the Standard single bbl. except has checkered walnut stock, top lever break, fully-blued receiver, vent rib. Imported from Korea 1984-87.

STANDARD SINGLE-SHOT SHOTGUN
Gauges: 12, 16, 20, 28 and .410. Bbl. lengths: 26-,28- or 30-inch. Weight: 5 lbs., 4 oz. to 5 lbs., 11 oz. Indonesian walnut stock. Matte-chromed receiver and top lever break. Imported from Korea 1984-87.
Standard fixed . . . . **NiB $83 Ex $67 Gd $45**
Standard folding . . . . **NiB $161 Ex $129 Gd $88**
Deluxe folding . . . . **NiB $200 Ex $160 Gd $108**

PARKER BROTHERS — Meriden, Connecticut

This firm was taken over by Remington Arms Company in 1934 and its production facilities moved to Remington's Ilion, New York, plant.

HAMMERLESS DOUBLE-BARREL SHOTGUNS
Grades V.H. through A-1 Special. Boxlock. Auto ejectors. Double triggers or selective single trigger. Gauges: 10, 12, 16, 20, 28, .410. Bbls.: 26- to 32-inch, any standard boring. Weight: 6.88-8.5 lbs.,12 ga. Stock and forearm of select walnut, checkered; straight, half-or full-pistol grip. Grades differ only in quality of workmanship, grade of wood, engraving, checkering, etc. General specifications are the same for all. Disc. about 1940.
V.H. grade, 12 or 16 ga. . . . . **NiB $3212 Ex $2570 Gd $1748**
V.H. grade, 20 ga. . . . . **NiB $4700 Ex $3759 Gd $2556**
V.H. grade, 28 ga. . . . . **NiB $7661 Ex $6128 Gd $4167**
V.H. grade, .410 ga. . . . . **NiB $19,249 Ex $15,398 Gd $10,471**
G.H. grade, 12 ga. . . . . **NiB $4371 Ex $3497 Gd $2378**
G.H. grade, 16 ga. . . . . **NiB $4571 Ex $3656 Gd $2486**

SHOTGUNS

Parker A-1 Special Grade

Parker A.H. Grade

Parker S.C. Grade

Parker D.H. Grade

Parker
G.H. Grade

(cont'd.) HAMMERLESS DOUBLE-BARREL SHOTGUNS

G.H. grade, 20 ga. . . . . NiB $6172 Ex $4938 Gd $3358
G.H. grade, 28 ga. . . . . NiB $9656 Ex $7725 Gd $5253
G.H. grade, .410 ga. . . . . NiB $24,463 Ex $19,714 Gd $1405
D.H. grade, 12 or 16 ga. . . . . NiB $7030 Ex $5624 Gd $3823
D.H. grade, 20 ga. . . . . NiB $9038 Ex $7230 Gd $4916
D.H. grade, 28 ga. . . . . NiB $13,588 Ex $10,871 Gd $7392
D.H. grade, .410 ga. . . . . NiB $45,577 Ex $36,462 Gd $24,794
C.H. grade, 12 or 16 ga. . . . . NiB $7802 Ex $6242 Gd $4240
C.H. grade, 20 ga. . . . . NiB $10,189 Ex $8151 Gd $5543
C.H. grade, 28 ga. . . . . NiB $1931 Ex $1545 Gd $1051
B.H. grade, 12 or 16 ga. . . . . NiB $11,665 Ex $9332 Gd $6345
B.H. grade, 20 ga. . . . . NiB $20,471 Ex $16,377 Gd $11,136
B.H. grade, 28 ga. . . . . NiB $38,239 Ex $30,591 Gd $20,802
A.H. grade, 12 or 16 ga. . . . . NiB $27,038 Ex $21,630 Gd $14,708
A.H. grade, 20 ga. . . . . NiB $33,604 Ex $26,883 Gd $18,280
A.H. grade, 28 ga. . . . . NiB $59,482 Ex $47,586 Gd $32,080
A.A.H. grade, 12 or 16 ga. . . . . . . NiB $61,723 Ex $49,378 Gd $33,577
A.A.H. grade, 12 or 16 ga. . . . . . . NiB $51,371 Ex $41,097 Gd $27,946
A.A.H. grade, 20 ga. . . . . NiB $74,932 Ex $59,946 Gd $40,763
A.A.H. grade, 28 ga. . . . . NiB $111,626 Ex $89,301 Gd $60,724
A-1 Special grade, 12 or 16 ga. . . . . . NiB $96,562 Ex $77,250 Gd $52,530
A-1 Special grade, 20 ga. . . . . NiB $142,140 Ex $113,712 Gd $77,324
A-1 Special grade, 28 ga. . . . . . . NiB $190,035 Ex $152,028 Gd $103,379
W/selective-single trigger, add 20%
W/ventilated rib, add 35%
For non-ejector guns, deduct 30%

SINGLE-SHOT TRAP GUNS

Hammerless. Boxlock. Ejector. 12 ga. only. Bbl. lengths: 30-, 32-, 34-inch, any boring, vent rib. Weight: 7.5-8.5 lbs. Stock and fore-arm of select walnut, checkered; straight, half-or full-pistol grip. The five grades differ only in quality of workmanship, grade of wood, checkering, engraving, etc. General specifications same for all. Disc. about 1940.

S.C. grade . . . . NiB $5021 Ex $4017 Gd $2732
S.B. grade . . . . NiB $6141 Ex $4913 Gd $3339
S.A. grade . . . . NiB $6875 Ex $5500 Gd $3740
S.A.A. grade . . . . NiB $8798 Ex $7039 Gd $4786
S.A.1 Special . . . . NiB $27,038 Ex $21,630 Gd $14,708

SKEET GUN

Same as other Parker doubles from Grade V.H.E. up except selective single trigger and beavertail forearm are standard on this model, as are 26-inch bbls., SK choke. Discontinued about 1940. Values are 35 percent higher.

TROJAN HAMMERLESS DOUBLE-BARREL SHOTGUN

Boxlock. Plain extractors. Double trigger or single trigger. Gauges: 12, 16, 20. Bbls.: 30-inch both F choke (12 ga. only), 26- or 28-inch M and F choke. Weight: 6.25-7.75 lbs. Checkered pistol-grip stock and forearm. Disc. 1939.

12 ga. . . . . NiB $2337 Ex $1869 Gd $1271
16 ga. . . . . NiB $3109 Ex $2486 Gd $1691
20 ga. . . . . NiB $4037 Ex $3229 Gd $2195

Parker-Hale Model 545A

Parker-Hale Model 645E

Parker Trojan Hammerless
Double-Barrel Shotgun

PARKER REPRODUCTIONS — Middlesex, New Jersey

HAMMERLESS DOUBLE-BARREL SHOTGUNS

Reproduction of the original Parker boxlock. Single selective trigger or double triggers. Selective automatic ejectors. Automatic safety. Gauges: 12, 16, 20, 28 or .410 w/2.75- or 3-inch chambers. Bbls.: 26- or 28-inch w/fixed or internal screw choke tubes SK/SK, IC/M, M/F. Weight: 5.5-7 lbs. Checkered English-style or pistol-grip American walnut stock w/beavertail or splinter forend and checkered skeleton buttplate. Color casehardened receiver with game scenes and scroll engraving. Produced in Japan by Olin Kodensha 1984-88.

DHE grade, 12 ga.	NiB $3412	Ex $2729	Gd $1856
DHE grade, 12 ga Sporting Clays.	NiB $4281	Ex $3425	Gd $2329
DHE grade, 20 ga.	NiB $2826	Ex $2261	Gd $1538
DHE grade, 28 ga.	NiB $3155	Ex $2523	Gd $1716
DHE grade 2-barrel set (16 & 20 ga.)	NiB $5472	Ex $4377	Gd $2977
DHE grade 2-barrel set (28 & .410)	NiB $6116	Ex $4892	Gd $3327
DHE grade 3-barrel set	NiB $7590	Ex $6072	Gd $4129
B grade Bank Note Lim. Ed., 12 ga.	NiB $5401	Ex $4321	Gd $2939
B grade Bank Note Lim. Ed., 20 ga.	NiB $6760	Ex $5407	Gd $3677
B grade Bank Note Lim. Ed., 28 ga.	NiB $10,551	Ex $8441	Gd $5740
B grade Bank Note Lim. Ed., .410 ga.	NiB $9979	Ex $8600	Gd $5782
A-1 Special grade, 12 ga.	NiB $9779	Ex $7833	Gd $5320
A-1 Special grade, 16 ga.	NiB $11,524	Ex $9218	Gd $6269
A-1 Special grade, 20 ga.	NiB $9393	Ex $7514	Gd $5109
A-1 Special grade, 28 ga.	NiB $14,099	Ex $11,278	Gd $7669
A-1 Special gr. 2-barrel set	NiB $11,009	Ex $8806	Gd $5988
A-1 Special gr. 3-barrel set	NiB $26,394+	Ex $21,115+	Gd $14,358+
A-1 Special gr. custom engraved	NiB $16,094	Ex $12,875	Gd $8955
A-1 Special gr. custom 2-barrel set	NiB $12,296	Ex $9836	Gd $6689
Extra barrel set, add			$250

PARKER-HALE SHOTGUNS — Mfd. by Ignacio Ugartechea, Spain

MODEL 645A (AMERICAN)

SIDE-BY-SIDE SHOTGUN . . . . NiB $1062 Ex $850 Gd $578
Gauges: 12, 16 and 20. Boxlock action. 26- and 28-inch bbls. Chokes: IC/M, M/F. Weight: 6 lbs. average. Single non-selective trigger. Automatic safety. Hand-checkered pistol grip walnut stock w/beavertail forend. Raised matted rib. English scroll-design engraved receiver. Discontinued 1990.

MODEL 645E (ENGLISH) SIDE-BY-SIDE SHOTGUN

Same general specifications as the Model 645A except double triggers, straight grip, splinter forend, checkered butt and concave rib. Disc. 1990.

(cont'd.) **MODEL 645E (ENGLISH) SIDE-BY-SIDE SHOTGUN**
MODEL 645E

12, 16, 20 ga. with 26- or 28-inch bbl.	NiB $1126	Ex $900	Gd $613
28, .410 ga. with 27-inch bbl.	NiB $1530	Ex $1223	Gd $831

MODEL 645E-XXV

12, 16, 20 ga. with 25-inch bbl.	NiB $1062	Ex $874	Gd $578
28, .410 ga. with 25-inch bbl.	NiB $1440	Ex $1152	Gd $784

PEDERSEN CUSTOM GUNS — North Haven, Connecticut, Div. of O. F. Mossberg & Sons, Inc.

MODEL 1000 O/U HUNTING SHOTGUN

Boxlock. Auto ejectors. Selective single trigger. Gauges: 12, 20. 2.75-inch chambers in 12 ga., 3-inch in 20 ga. Bbls.: Vent rib; 30-inch M/F (12 ga. only); 28-inch IC/M (12 ga. only), M/F; 26-inch IC/M. Checkered pistol-grip stock and forearm. Grade I is the higher quality gun with custom stock dimensions, fancier wood, more elaborate engraving, silver inlays. Made 1973-75.

Grade I	NiB $2317	Ex $1854	Gd $1261
Grade II	NiB $1864	Ex $1491	Gd $1015

MODEL 1000 MAGNUM

Same as Model 1000 Hunting Gun except chambered for 12-ga. Magnum 3-inch shells, 30-inch bbls., IM/F choke. Made 1973-75.

Grade I	NiB $2511	Ex $2008	Gd $1366
Grade II	NiB $2054	Ex $1643	Gd $1118

MODEL 1000 SKEET GUN

Same as Model 1000 Hunting Gun except has skeet-style stock; 26- and 28-inch bbls. (12 ga. only), SK choke. Made 1973-75.

Grade I	NiB $2158	Ex $1726	Gd $364
Grade II	NiB $1746	Ex $1397	Gd $950

MODEL 1000 TRAP GUN

Same as Model 1000 Hunting Gun except 12 ga. only, has Monte Carlo trap-style stock, 30- or 32-inch bbls., M/F or IM/F choke. Made 1973-75.

Grade I	NiB $1905	Ex $1524	Gd $1036
Grade II	NiB $1540	Ex $1232	Gd $836

SHOTGUNS

Pedersen Model 1000 Grade I

Pedersen Model 1000 Grade II

MODEL 1500 O/U
HUNTING SHOTGUN . . . . NiB $781 Ex $623 Gd $423
Boxlock. Auto ejectors. Selective single trigger. 12 ga. 2.75- or 3-inch chambers. Bbls.: vent rib; 26-inch IC/M; 28- and 30-inch M/F; Magnum has 30-inch, IM/F choke. Weight: 7-7.5 lbs., depending on bbl. length. Checkered pistol-grip stock and forearm. Made 1973-75.

MODEL 1500 SKEET GUN . . . . NiB $804 Ex $643 Gd $438
Same as Model 1500 Hunting Gun except has skeet-style stock, 27-inch bbls., SK choke. Made 1973-75.

MODEL 1500 TRAP GUN . . . . NiB $666 Ex $532 Gd $362
Same as Model 1500 Hunting Gun except has Monte Carlo trap-style stock, 30- or 32-inch bbls., M/F or IM/F chokes. Made 1973-75.

MODEL 2000 HAMMERLESS DOUBLE
Boxlock. Auto ejectors. Selective single trigger. Gauges: 12, 20. 2.75-inch chambers in 12 ga., 3-inch in 20 ga. Bbls.: Vent rib; 30-inch M/F (12 ga. only); 28-inch M/F, 26-inch IC/M choke. Checkered pistol-grip stock and forearm. Grade I is the higher quality gun w/custom dimensions, fancier wood, more elaborate engraving, silver inlays. Made 1973-74.
Grade I . . . . NiB $2511 Ex $2008 Gd $1366
Grade II . . . . NiB $2311 Ex $1849 Gd $1258

MODEL 2500
HAMMERLESS DOUBLE . . . . NiB $470 Ex $376 Gd $255
Boxlock. Auto ejectors. Selective single trigger. Gauges: 12, 20. 2.75-inch chambers in 12 ga., 3-inch in 20 ga. Bbls.: Vent rib; 28-inch M/F; 26-inch IC/M choke. Checkered pistol-grip stock and forearm. Made 1973-74.

MODEL 4000 HAMMERLESS SLIDE-ACTION
REPEATING SHOTGUN . . . . NiB $483 Ex $386 Gd $263
Custom version of Mossberg Model 500. Full-coverage floral engraving on receiver. Gauges: 12, 20, .410. Three inch chamber. Bbls.: Vent rib; 26-inch IC or SK choke; 28-inch F or M; 30-inch F. Weight: 6-8 lbs. depending on ga. and bbl. Checkered stock and slide handle of select wood. Made in 1975.

MODEL 4000 TRAP GUN . . . . NiB $492 Ex $394 Gd $268
Same as standard Model 4000 except 12 ga. only, has 30-inch F choke bbl., Monte Carlo trap-style stock w/recoil pad. Made in 1975.

MODEL 4500 . . . . NiB $439 Ex $351 Gd $239
Same as Model 4000 except has simpler scroll engraving. Made in 1975.

MODEL 4500 TRAP GUN . . . . NiB $451 Ex $360 Gd $245
Same as Model 4000 Trap Gun except has simpler scroll engraving. Made in 1975.

J. C. PENNEY CO., INC. — Dallas, Texas
MODEL 4011
AUTOLOADING SHOTGUN. . . . . . NiB $223 Ex $178 Gd $121
Hammerless. Five shot magazine. Bbls.: 26-inch IC; 28-inch M or F; 30-inch F choke. Weight: 7.25 lbs. Plain pistol-grip stock and slide handle.

MODEL 6610
SINGLE-SHOT SHOTGUN . . . . NiB $102 Ex $82 Gd $55
Hammerless. Takedown. Auto ejector. Gauges: 12, 16, 20 and .410. Bbl. length: 28-36 inches. Weight: About 6 lbs. Plain pistol-grip stock and forearm.

MODEL 6630
BOLT-ACTION SHOTGUN . . . . NiB $141 Ex $112 Gd $76
Takedown. Gauges: 12, 16, 20. Two shot clip magazine. 26- and 28-inch bbl. lengths; with or without adj. choke. Plain pistol-grip stock. Weight: About 7.25 lbs.

MODEL 6670
SLIDE-ACTION SHOTGUN . . . . NiB $166 Ex $133 Gd $95
Hammerless. Gauges: 12, 16, 20, and .410. Three shot tubular magazine. Bbls.: 26- to 30-inch; various chokes. Weight: 6.25-7.25 lbs. Walnut finished hardwood stock.

MODEL 6870 SLIDE-ACTION
SHOTGUN . . . . NiB $238 Ex $187 Gd $130
Hammerless. Gauges: 12, 16, 20, .410. Four shot magazine. Bbls.: Vent rib; 26- to 30-inch, various chokes. Weight: Average 6.5 lbs. Plain pistol-grip stock.

PERAZZI SHOTGUNS — Manufactured by Manifattura Armi Perazzi, Brescia, Italy

See also listings under Ithaca-Perazzi.

DB81 O/U TRAP . . . . NiB $4924 Ex $3940 Gd $2679
Gauge: 12; 2.75-inch chambers. 29.5- or 31.5-inch bbls. w/wide vent rib; M/F chokes. Weight: 8 lbs., 6 oz. Detachable and interchangeable trigger with flat V-springs. Bead front sight. Interchangeable and custom-made checkered stock; beavertail forend. Imported 1988 to date.

DB81 SINGLE-SHOT TRAP . . . . NiB $4924 Ex $3940 Gd $2679
Same general specifications as the DB81 over/under except in single bbl. version w/32- or 34-inch wide vent-rib bbl., F choke. Imported 1988 to date.

Perazzi — DB81 Over/Under Trap

Perazzi — Mirage Over/Under Shotgun

Perazzi — MX3 Over/Under Shotgun

Perazzi — MX8 Over/Under Shotgun

GRAND AMERICAN 88 SPECIAL SINGLE TRAP
Same general specifications as MX8 Special Single Trap except w/high ramped rib. Fixed choke or screw-in choke tubes.
Model 88 standard . . . . **NiB $4346 Ex $3476 Gd $2364**
**Model 88 w/interchangeable
choke tubes** . . . . **NiB $4629 Ex $3703 Gd $2518**

MIRAGE O/U SHOTGUN
Gauge: 12; 2.75-inch chambers. Bbls.: 27.63-, 29.5- or 31.5-inch vent-rib w/fixed chokes or screw-in choke tubes. Single selective trigger. Weight: 7 to 7.75 lbs. Interchangeable and custom-made checkered buttstock and forend.
**Competition Trap,
Skeet, Pigeon, Sporting** . . . . **NiB $6218 Ex $4975 Gd $3383**
Skeet 4-barrel sets . . . . . . **NiB $13,197 Ex $10,557 Gd $7179**
**Competition Special (w/adj.
4-position trigger) add**. **$350**

MX1 O/U SHOTGUN
Similar to Model MX8 except w/ramp-style, tapered rib and modified stock configuration.
**Competition Trap, Skeet,
Pigeon & Sporting** . . . . **NiB $3244 Ex $2596 Gd $1764**
MX1C (w/choke tubes) . . . . **NiB $3424 Ex $2740 Gd $1862**
MX1B (w/flat low rib) . . . . **NiB $3115 Ex $2493 Gd $1694**

MX2 O/U SHOTGUN
Similar to Model MX8 except w/broad high-ramped competition rib.
**Competition-Trap, Skeet,
Pigeon & Sporting** . . . . **NiB $3927 Ex $3141 Gd $2136**
MX2C (w/choke tubes) . . . . **NiB $4474 Ex $3579 Gd $2434**

MX3 O/U SHOTGUN
Similar to Model MX8 except w/ramp-style, tapered rib and modified stock configuration.

(cont'd.) MX3 O/U SHOTGUN
**Competition Trap, Skeet,
Pigeon & Sporting** . . . . . . **NiB $46,289 Ex $37,032 Gd $25,181**
Competition Special (w/adj. 4-position trigger) add **$300**
Game models . . . . **NiB $4114 Ex $3291 Gd $2238**
Combo O/U plus SB . . . . **NiB $5086 Ex $4068 Gd $2767**
SB Trap 32- or 34-inch . . . . . . **NiB $3470 Ex $2776 Gd $1888**
Skeet 4-bbl. sets . . . . **NiB $11,009 Ex $8806 Gd $5988**
Skeet Special 4-bbl. sets . . . . **NiB $11,233 Ex $8987 Gd $6111**

MX3 SPECIAL PIGEON SHOTGUN. . . **NiB $4924 Ex $3940 Gd $2679**
Gauge: 12; 2.75-inch chambers. 29.5- or 31.5-inch vent rib bbl.; IC/M and extra full chokes. Weight: 8 lbs., 6 oz. Detachable and interchangeable trigger group w/flat V-springs. Bead front sight. Interchangeable and custom-made checkered stock for live pigeon shoots; splinter forend. Imported 1991 to date.

MX4 O/U SHOTGUN
Similar to Model MX3 in appearance and shares the MX8 locking system. Detachable, adj. 4-position trigger standard. Interchangeable choke tubes optional.
Competition Trap, Skeet, Pigeon & Sporting
. . . . **NiB $4700 Ex $3759 Gd $2556**
MX4C (w/choke tubes) . . . . **NiB $5015 Ex $4012 Gd $2728**

MX5 O/U GAME GUN
Similar to Model MX8 except in hunting configuration, chambered in 12 or 20 ga. Non-detachable single selective trigger.
MX5 Standard . . . . **NiB $3213 Ex $2570 Gd $1748**
MX5C (w/choke tubes) . . . . **NiB $3541 Ex $2832 Gd $1926**

MX6 AMER. TRAP SINGLE-BARREL . . **NiB $2961 Ex $2369 Gd $1611**
Single shot. Removable trigger group. 12 ga. Barrels: 32- or 34-inch with fixed or choke tubes. Raised vent rib. Checkered European walnut Monte Carlo stock, beavertail forend. Imported 1995 to date.

GRADING: **NiB** = New in Box   **Ex** = Excellent or NRA 95%   **Gd** = Good or NRA 68%

Perazzi — MX20 Over/Under Game Gun

Perazzi — TMX Single Shot Trap

MX6 SKEET O/U . . . . **NiB $3348 Ex $2678 Gd $1821**
Same general specs as MX6 American Trap single barrel except over/under; boxlock. Barrels: 26.75- or 27.50-inch. Imported 1995 to date.

MX6 SPORTING O/U . . . . **NiB $3514 Ex $2812 Gd $1912**
Same specs as MX6 American Trap single barrel except over/under; boxlock. Single selective trigger; external selector. Barrels: 28.38-, 29.50-, or 31.50-inch. Imported 1995 to date.

MX6 TRAP O/U . . . . **NiB $2951 Ex $2361 Gd $1605**
Same general specs as MX6 American Trap single barrel except over/under; boxlock. Barrels: 29.50-, 30.75-, or 31.50-inch. Imported 1995 to date.

MX7 O/U SHOTGUN . . . . **NiB $4185 Ex $3347 Gd $2276**
Similar to Model MX12 except w/MX3-style receiver and top-mounted trigger selector. Bbls.: 28.73-, 2.5-, 31.5-inch w/vent rib; screw-in choke tubes. Imported 1992 to date.

MX8 O/U SHOTGUN
Gauge: 12, 2.75-inch chambers. Bbls.: 27.63-, 29.5- or 31.5-inch vent-rib w/fixed chokes or screw-in choke tubes. Weight: 7 to 8.5 lbs. Interchangeable and custom-made checkered stock; beavertail forend. Special models have detachable and interchangeable 4-position trigger group w/flat V-springs. Imported 1988 to date.
MX8 Standard . . . . **NiB $3806 Ex $3045 Gd $2070**
MX8 Special (adj. 4-pos. trigger) . . . . . . **NiB $3909 Ex $3127 Gd $2127**
MX8 Special single
(32-or 34-inch bbl.) . . . . **NiB $3703 Ex $2962 Gd $2015**
MX8 Special combo . . . . **NiB $7612 Ex $6089 Gd $4141**

MX8/20 O/U SHOTGUN . . . . . **NiB $3862 Ex $3090 Gd $2101**
Similar to the Model MX8 except w/smaller frame and custom stock. Available in sporting or game configurations with fixed chokes or screw-in tubes. Imported 1993 to date.

MX9 O/U SHOTGUN . . . . **NiB $6946 Ex $5557 Gd $3779**
Gauge: 12; 2.75-inch chambers. Bbls.: 29.5- or 30.5-inch w/choke tubes and vent side rib. Selective trigger. Checkered walnut stock w/adj. cheekpiece. Available in single bbl., combo, O/U trap, skeet, pigeon and sporting models. Imported 1993 to date.

MX10 O/U SHOTGUN . . . . . . **NiB $6793 Ex $5434 Gd $3696**
Similar to the Model MX9 except w/fixed chokes and different rib configuration. Imported 1993 to date.

MX10 PIGEON-ELECTROCIBLES O/U . . . . **NiB $6615 Ex $5291 Gd $3598**
Over/Under; boxlock. Removable trigger group; external selector. 12 gauge. Barrels: 27.50- or 29.50-inch. Checkered European walnut adjustable stock, beavertail forend. Imported 1995 to date.

MX11 AMERICAN TRAP COMBO . . **NiB $5368 Ex $4295 Gd $2920**
Over/Under; boxlock. External selector. Removable trigger group; single selective trigger. 12 ga. Bbls: 29-1/2- to 34-inch with fixed or choke tubes; vent rib. European walnut Monte Carlo adjustable stock, beavertail forend. Imported 1995 to date.

MX11 AMERICAN TRAP
SINGLE BARREL . . . . **NiB $4758 Ex $3806 Gd $2588**
Same general specs as MX11 American Trap combo except 32- or 34-inch single bbl. Imported 1995 to date.

MX11 PIGEON-ELECTROCIBLES O/U . **NiB $4957 Ex $3965 Gd $2697**
Same specs as MX11 American Trap combo except 27.50 O/U bbls. Checkered European walnut pistol grip adjustable stock, beavertail forend. Imported 1995 to date.

MX11 SKEET O/U . . . . **NiB $5015 Ex $4012 Gd $2728**
Same general specs as MX11 American Trap combo except 26.75 or 27.50-inch O/U bbls. Checkered European walnut pistol-grip adjustable stock, beavertail forend. Imported 1995 to date.

MX11 SPORTING O/U . . . . **NiB $5472 Ex $4377 Gd $2977**
Same general specs as MX11 American Trap combo except 28.38, 29.50-, or 31.50-inch O/U bbls. Checkered European walnut pistol-grip adjustable stock, beavertail forend. Imported 1995 to date.

MX11 TRAP O/U . . . . **NiB $4957 Ex $3965 Gd $2697**
Same general specs as MX11 American Trap combo except 29.50,-30.75, or 31.50-inch O/U bbls. Checkered European walnut pistol-grip adjustable stock, beavertail forend. Imported 1995 to date.

MX12 O/U GAME GUN
Gauge: 12, 2.75-inch chambers. Bbls.: 26-, 27.63-, 28.38- or 29.5-inch, vent rib, fixed chokes or screw-in choke tubes. Non-detachable single selective trigger group w/coil springs. Weight: 7.25 lbs. Interchangeable and custom-made checkered stock; Schnabel forend.
MX12 Standard . . . . **NiB $4957 Ex $3965 Gd $2697**
MX12C (w/choke tubes) . . . . . . **NiB $5472 Ex $4377 Gd $2977**

MX14 AMERICAN TRAP
SINGLE-BARREL . . . . **NiB $4165 Ex $3332 Gd $2266**
Single shot. Removable trigger group; unsingle configuration. 12 ga. Bbl: 34-inch with fixed or choke tubes; vent rib. Checkered European walnut Monte Carlo adjustable stock, beavertail forend. Imported 1995 to date.

MX15 AMERICAN TRAP
SINGLE-BARREL . . . . **NiB $4641 Ex $3713 Gd $2525**
Full choke. Detachable trigger group. Gauge: 12 only with 2.75-inch chamber. Bbls: 32 and 34-inch. Weight: 8 lbs., 6 oz. .

Powell No. 7
Aristocrat Grade Double

Piotti
Piuma Boxlock Side-by-Side Shotgun

MX20 O/U GAME GUN
Gauges: 20, 28 and .410; 2.75- or 3-inch chambers. 26-inch vent-rib bbls., M/F chokes or screw-in chokes. Auto selective ejectors. Selective single trigger. Weight: 6 lbs., 6 oz. Non-detachable coil-spring trigger. Bead front sight. Interchangeable and custom-made checkered stock w/Schnabel forend. Imported from 1988 to date.
Standard grade . . . . NiB $4886 Ex $3909 Gd $2658
Standard grade
w/gold outline . . . . NiB $8501 Ex $6800 Gd $4624
MX20C w/choke tubes . . . . . . NiB $5253 Ex $4202 Gd $2857
SC3 grade . . . . NiB $9173 Ex $7339 Gd $4990
SCO grade . . . . NiB $12,660 Ex $10,127 Gd $6887

MX28 O/U GAME GUN . . . NiB $14,098 Ex $11,278 Gd $7669
Similar to the Model MX12 except chambered in 28 ga. w/26-inch bbls. fitted to smaller frame. Imported 1993 to date.

MX410 O/U GAME GUN . . . . . NiB $14,098 Ex $11,278 Gd $7669
Similar to the Model MX12 except in .410 bore w/3-inch chambers, 26-inch bbls. fitted to smaller frame. Imported 1993 to date.

TM1 SPECIAL
SINGLE-SHOT TRAP . . . . NiB $4226 Ex $3380 Gd $2298
Gauge: 12- 2.75-inch chambers. 32- or 34-inch bbl. w/wide vent rib; full choke. Weight: 8 lbs., 6 oz. Detachable and interchangeable trigger group with coil springs. Bead front sight. Interchangeable and custom-made stock w/checkered pistol grip and beavertail forend. Imported 1988 to date.

TMX SPECIAL
SINGLE-SHOT TRAP . . . . NiB $4391 Ex $3512 Gd $2388
Same general specifications as Model TM1 Special except w/ultra-high rib. Interchangeable choke tubes optional.

PIOTTI SHOTGUNS — Italy

BOSS O/U . . . . NiB $34,000 Ex $28,000 Gd $13,000
Over/Under; sidelock. Gauges: 12 or 20. Barrels: 26- to 32-inch. Standard chokes. Best quality walnut. Custom-made to customer's specifications. Imported 1993 to date.

KING NO. 1 SIDELOCK . . . NiB $20,900 Ex $17,000 Gd $7000
Gauges: 10, 12, 16, 20, 28 and .410. 25- to 30-inch bbls. (12 ga.), 25- to 28-inch (other ga.). Weight: About 5 lbs. (.410) to 8 lbs. (12 ga.) Holland & Holland pattern sidelock. Double triggers standard. Coin finish or color casehardened. Level file-cut rib. Full-coverage scroll engraving, gold inlays. Hand-rubbed, oil-finished, straight-grip stock with checkered butt, splinter forend.

KING EXTRA SIDE-BY-SIDE
SHOTGUN . . . . NiB $21,125 Ex $17,000 Gd $10,000
Same general specifications as the Piotti King No. 1 except has choice of engraving, gold inlays, plus stock is of exhibition-grade wood.

LUNIK SIDE-LOCK
SHOTGUN
. . . . NiB $21,438 Ex $17,950 Gd $13,486
Same general specifications as the Monte Carlo model except has level, file-cut rib. Renaissance-style, large scroll engraving in relief, gold crown in top lever, gold name, and gold crest in forearm, finely figured wood.

MONTE CARLO
SIDE-LOCK SHOTGUN . . . . . NiB $10,938 Ex $8750 Gd $5950
Gauges: 10, 12, 16, 20, 28 or .410. Bbls.: 25- to 30-inch. Holland & Holland pattern sidelock. Weight: 5-8 lbs. Automatic ejectors. Double triggers. Hand-rubbed oil-finished straight-grip stock with checkered butt. Choice of Purdey-style scroll and rosette or Holland & Holland-style large scroll engraving.

PIUMA BOXLOCK
SIDE-BY-SIDE SHOTGUN . . . . NiB $10,494 Ex $8395 Gd $5709
Same general specifications as the Monte Carlo model except has Anson & Deeley boxlock action w/demi-bloc bbls., scalloped frame. Standard scroll and rosette engraving. Hand-rubbed, oil-finished straight-grip stock.

WILLIAM POWELL & SON LTD. — Birmingham, England

NO. 1 BEST GRADE
DOUBLE-BARREL
SHOTGUN . . . . NiB $50,112 Ex $39,000 Gd $18,000
Sidelock. Gauges: Made to order with 12, 16 and 20 the most common. Bbls.: Made to order in any length but 28 inches was recommended. Highest grade French walnut buttstock and forearm with fine checkering. Metal elaborately engraved. Imported by Stoeger about 1938-51.

NO. 2 BEST GRADE
DOUBLE-BARREL . . . . . . NiB $27,500 Ex $22,000 Gd $14,960
Same general specifications as the Powell No. 1 except plain finish without engraving. Imported by Stoeger about 1938-51.

NO. 6 CROWN GRADE
DOUBLE-BARREL . . . . NiB $13,750 Ex $11,000 Gd $7480
Boxlock. Gauges: Made to order with 12, 16 and 20 the most common. Bbls.: Made to order, but 28 inches was recommended. Highest grade French walnut buttstock and forearm w/fine checkering. Metal elaborately engraved. Uses Anson & Deeley locks. Imported by Stoeger about 1938-51.

NO. 7 ARISTOCRAT GRADE
DOUBLE-BARREL
SHOTGUN . . . . NiB $6875 Ex $5500 Gd $740
Same general specifications as the Powell No. 6 except w/lower quality wood and metal engraving.

SHOTGUNS

Premier Ambassador
Field Grade

Premier Continental
Field Grade

PRECISION SPORTS SHOTGUNS — Cortland, New York, Manufactured by Ignacio Ugartechea, Spain

600 SERIES AMERICAN HAMMERLESS DOUBLES
Boxlock. Single selective trigger. Selective automatic ejectors. Automatic safety. Gauges: 12, 16, 20, 28, .410; 2.75- or 3-inch chambers. Bbls.: 26-,27- or 28-inch w/raised matte rib; choked IC/M or M/F. Weight: 5.75-7 lbs. Checkered pistol-grip walnut butt-stock with beavertail forend. Engraved silvered receiver with blued bbls. Imported from Spain 1986-94.

640A (12, 16, 20 ga. w/extractors) ...... NiB $871 Ex $697 Gd $474
640A (28, .410 ga. w/extractors) .... NiB $1014 Ex $811 Gd $551
640 Slug Gun (12 ga. w/extractors) ..... NiB $993 Ex $794 Gd $541
645A (12, 16, 20 ga. w/ejectors) .... NiB $939 Ex $751 Gd $511
645A (28, .410 ga. w/ejectors) .... NiB $1149 Ex $919 Gd $624
645A (20/28 ga. two-bbl. set) .... NiB $1345 Ex $1075 Gd $731
650A (12 ga. w/extractors, choke tubes) ... NiB $885 Ex $708 Gd $481
655A (12 ga. w/ejectors, choke tubes) ... NiB $980 Ex $784 Gd $533

600 SERIES ENGLISH HAMMERLESS DOUBLES
Boxlock. Same general specifications as American 600 series except w/double triggers and concave rib. Checkered English-style walnut stock w/splinter forend, straight grip and oil finish.

640E (12, 16, 20 ga. w/extractors) ...... NiB $750 Ex $599 Gd $407
640E (28, .410 ga. w/extractors) .... NiB $845 Ex $676 Gd $459
640 Slug Gun (12 ga. w/extractors) ..... NiB $993 Ex $794 Gd $541
645E (12, 16, 20 ga. w/ejectors) .... NiB $1014 Ex $811 Gd $551
645E (28, .410 ga. w/ejectors) .... NiB $966 Ex $772 Gd $525
645E (20/28 ga. two-bbl. set) .... NiB $1277 Ex $1022 Gd $695
650E (12 ga. w/extractors, choke tubes) .... NiB $879 Ex $702 Gd $478
655E (12 ga. w/ejectors, choke tubes) .... NiB $939 Ex $751 Gd $511

MODEL 640M MAGNUM 10 HAMMERLESS DOUBLE
Similar to Model 640E except in 10 ga. w/3.5-inch Mag. chambers. Bbls.: 26-, 30-, 32-inch choked F/F.

Model 640M Big Ten, Turkey ..... NiB $869 Ex $695 Gd $473
Model 640M Goose Gun........ NiB $895 Ex $716 Gd $487

MODEL 645E-XXV HAMMERLESS DOUBLE
Similar to Model 645E except w/25-inch bbl. and Churchill-style rib.

645E-XXV (12, 16, 20 ga. w/ejectors) ...... NiB $939 Ex $751 Gd $511
645E-XXV (28, .410 ga. w/ejectors) ...... NiB $1074 Ex $859 Gd $585

PREMIER SHOTGUNS

Premier shotguns have been produced by various gunmakers in Europe.

AMBASSADOR MODEL
FIELD GRADE HAMMERLESS
DOUBLE-BARREL SHOTGUN..... NiB $424 Ex $339 Gd $231
Sidelock. Plain extractors. Double triggers. Gauges: 12, 16, 20, .410. 3-inch chambers in 20 and .410 ga., 2.75- inch in 12 and 16 ga. Bbls.: 26-inch in .410 ga., 28 inch in other ga.; choked M/F. Weight: 6 lbs., 3 oz.-7 lbs., 3 oz. depending on gauge. Checkered pistol-grip stock and beavertail forearm. Intro. in 1957; disc.

BRUSH KING .... NiB $301 Ex $242 Gd $164
Same as standard Regent model except chambered for 12 (2.75-inch) and 20 ga. (3-inch) only; has 22-inch bbls., IC/M choke, straight-grip stock. Weight: 6 lbs., 3 oz. in 12 ga.; 5 lbs., 12 oz. in 20 ga. Introduced in 1959; disc.

CONTINENTAL MODEL
FIELD GRADE HAMMER
DOUBLE-BARREL SHOTGUN..... NiB $424 Ex $339 Gd $231
Sidelock. Exposed hammers. Plain extractors. Double triggers. Gauges: 12, 16, 20, .410. Three inch chambers in 20 and .410 ga., 2.75-inch in 12 and 16 ga. Bbls.: 26-inch in .410 ga.; 28-inch in other ga.; choked M/F. Weight: 6 lbs., 3 oz.-7 lbs., 3 oz. depending on gauge. Checkered pistol-grip stock and English-style forearm. Introduced in 1957; disc.

MONARCH SUPREME GRADE HAMMERLESS
DOUBLE-BARREL SHOTGUN..... NiB $454 Ex $363 Gd $249
Boxlock. Auto ejectors. Double triggers. Gauges: 12, 20. 2.75-inch chambers in 12 ga., 3-inch in 20 ga. Bbls.: 28-inch M/F; 26-inch IC/M choke. Weight: 6 lbs., 6 oz., 7 lbs., 2 oz. depending on gauge and bbl. Checkered pistol-grip stock and beavertail forearm of fancy walnut. Introduced in 1959; disc.

PRESENTATION
CUSTOM GRADE .... NiB $1151 Ex $920 Gd $625
Similar to Monarch model but made to order of higher quality with hunting scene engraving, gold and silver inlay, fancier wood. Introduced in 1959; disc.

REGENT 10 GA.
MAGNUM EXPRESS .... NiB $357 Ex $286 Gd $194
Same as standard Regent model except chambered for 10-ga. Magnum 3.5-inch shells, has heavier construction, 32-inch bbls. choked F/F, stock with recoil pad. Weight: 11.25 lbs. Introduced in 1957; disc.

REGENT 12 GA.
MAGNUM EXPRESS .... NiB $320 Ex $256 Gd $174
Same as standard Regent model except chambered for 12-ga. Magnum 3-inch shells, has 30-inch bbls. choked F and F, stock with recoil pad. Weight: 7.25 lbs. Introduced in 1957; disc.

Purdey Hammerless
Double-Barrel Shotgun

Purdey Over and Under

Purdey Single-Shot Trap

REGENT FIELD GRADE HAMMERLESS
DOUBLE-BARREL SHOTGUN..... NiB $287 Ex $230 Gd $156
Boxlock. Plain extractors. Double triggers. Gauges: 12, 16, 20, 28, .410. Three inch chambers in 20 and .410 ga., 2.75-inch in other gauges. Bbls.: 26-inch IC/M, M/F (28 and .410 ga. only); 28-inch M/F; 30-inch M/F (12 ga. only). Weight: 6 lbs., 2 oz.-7 lbs., 4 oz. depending on gauge and bbl. Checkered pistol-grip stock and beavertail forearm. Introduced in 1955; disc.

JAMES PURDEY & SONS, LTD. — London, England

HAMMERLESS DOUBLE-BARREL SHOTGUN
Sidelock. Auto ejectors. Single or double triggers. Gauges: 12, 16, 20. Bbls.: 26-, 27-, 28-, 30-inch (latter in 12 ga. only); any boring, any shape or style of rib. Weight: 5.25-5.5 lbs. depending on model, gauge and bbl length. Checkered stock and forearm, straight grip standard, pistol-grip also available. Purdey guns of this type have been made from about 1880 to date. Models include: Game Gun, Featherweight Game Gun, Two-Inch Gun (chambered for 12 ga. 2-inch shells), Pigeon Gun (w/3rd fastening and side clips), values of all models are the same.
With double triggers..... NiB $40,625 Ex $32,500 Gd $22,100
With single trigger ...... NiB $43,438 Ex $34,750 Gd $23,630

OVER/UNDER SHOTGUN
Sidelock. Auto ejectors. Single or double triggers. Gauges: 12 16, 20. Bbls.: 26-, 27-, 28-, 30-inch (latter in 12 ga. only); any boring, any style rib. Weight: 6-7.5 pounds depending on gauge and bbl. length. Checkered stock and forend, straight or pistol grip. Prior to WW II, the Purdey Over/Under Gun was made with a Purdey action; since the war James Purdey & Sons have acquired the business of James Woodward & Sons and all Purdey over/under guns are now built on the Woodward principle. General specifications of both types are the same.
With Purdey act., double triggers ... NiB $80,000 Ex $50,000 Gd $22,000
With Woodward action,
double triggers .... NiB $55,750 Ex $45,000 Gd $31,240
W/single trigger, add .... NiB $1875 Ex $1500 Gd $1020

Purdey Hammerless
Double-Barrel Shotgun

Purdey Hammerless
Double-Barrel Shotgun
w/Single Trigger

SINGLE-BARREL TRAP GUN . NiB $11,625 Ex $9300 Gd $6324
Sidelock. Mechanical features similar to those of the over/under model with Purdey action. 12 ga. only. Built to customer's specifications. Made prior to World War II.

REMINGTON ARMS CO. — Ilion, New York

Eliphalet Remington Jr. began making long arms with his father in 1816. In 1828 they moved their facility to Ilion, N.Y., where it remained a family-run business for decades. As the family began to diminish, other people bought controlling interests and today, still a successful gunmaking company, it is a subsidiary of the DuPont Corporation.

SHOTGUNS

Remington Model 11-87
Premier Autoloader

MODEL 10A STANDARD GRADE
SLIDE-ACTION REPEATING SHOTGUN . . . . . NiB $372 Ex $297 Gd $202
Hammerless. Takedown. 6-shot. 12 ga. only. Five shell tubular magazine. Bbls.: Plain; 26- to 32-inch; choked F, M or Cyl. Weight: About
7.5 lbs. Plain pistol-grip stock, grooved slide handle. Made 1907-29.

MODEL 11 SPECIAL, TOURNAMENT,
EXPERT AND PREMIER GRADE GUNS
These higher grade models differ from the Model 11A in general
quality, grade of wood, checkering, engraving, etc. General specifi-
cations are the same.
Model 11B Special grade . . . . NiB $574 Ex $459 Gd $312
Model 11D Tournament grade . . . NiB $1149 Ex $919 Gd $624
Model 11E Expert grade . . . . . . NiB $1615 Ex $1292 Gd $879
Model 11F Premier grade . . . . . NiB $2602 Ex $2082 Gd $1415

MODEL 11A STANDARD GRADE AUTOLOADER
Hammerless Browning type. 5-shot. Takedown. Gauges: 12, 16, 20.
Tubular magazine holds four shells. Bbls.: Plain, solid or vent rib,
lengths from 26-32 inches, F, M, IC, Cyl., SK chokes. Weight: About
8 lbs., 12 ga.; 7.5 lbs., 16 ga.; 7.25 lbs., 20 ga. Checkered pistol grip
and forend. Made 1905-49.
With plain barrel . . . . NiB $322 Ex $258 Gd $175
With solid-rib barrel . . . . NiB $418 Ex $335 Gd $228
With ventilated-rib barrel . . . . NiB $470 Ex $376 Gd $255

MODEL 11R RIOT GUN . . . . NiB $372 Ex $297 Gd $202
Same as Model 11A Standard grade except has 20-inch plain bar-
rel, 12 ga. only. Remington Model 11-48. (See Remington
Sportsman-48 Series.)

MODEL 11-87 PREMIER AUTOLOADER
Gas-operated. Hammerless. Gauge: 12; 3-inch chamber. Bbl.: 26-,
28- or 30-inch with REMChoke. Weight: 8.13- 8.38 lbs., depending
on bbl. length. Checkered walnut stock and forend in satin finish.
Made 1987 to date.
Premier Deer Gun . . . . NiB $545 Ex $436 Gd $297
Premier Deer Gun w/cant-
ilever scope mount . . . . NiB $690 Ex $494 Gd $301
Premier Skeet . . . . NiB $559 Ex $447 Gd $304
Premier Sporting Clays . . . . NiB $670 Ex $536 Gd $365
Premier Sporting Clays SCNP (nickel plated) . . . . . . NiB $709 Ex $566 Gd $385
Premier Standard Autoloader . . . . NiB $559 Ex $447 Gd $304
Premier Trap . . . . NiB $658 Ex $526 Gd $357
Left-hand models, add $55

MODEL 11-87 SPECIAL PURPOSE MAGNUM
Same general specifications as Model 11-87 Premier except with
non-reflective wood finish and Parkerized metal. 21-, 26- or 28-inch
vent-rib bbl. with REMChoke tubes. Made 1987-93.
Model 11-87 SP Field Magnum . . . . NiB $656 Ex $525 Gd $356
Model 11-87 SP Deer Gun (w/21-inch bbl.). . . NiB $594 Ex $476 Gd $323
Model 11-87 SP Deer Gun
w/cantilever scope mount . . . . NiB $644 Ex $515 Gd $350

MODEL 11-87 SPS MAGNUM
Same general specifications as Model 11-87 Special Purpose
Magnum except with synthetic buttstock and forend. 21-, 26- or 28-
inch vent-rib bbl. with REMChoke tubes. Matte black or Mossy Oak
camo finish (except NWTF turkey gun). Made 1990 to date.
Model 11-87 SPS Magnum (matte black) . . . . . NiB $587 Ex $470 Gd $319
Model 11-87 SPS Camo (Mossy Oak camo) . . NiB $616 Ex $492 Gd $335
Model 11-87 SPS Deer Gun (w/21 inch bbl.) . . NiB $530 Ex $424 Gd $288
Model 11-87 SPS Deer Gun w/cant. scope mt. . . . . NiB $602 Ex $481 Gd $327
Model 11-87 NWTF Turkey Gun
(Brown Trebark) disc. 1993 . . . . NiB $700 Ex $560 Gd $381
Model 11-87 NWTF Turkey Gun
(Greenleaf) disc. 1996 . . . . NiB $673 Ex $538 Gd $366
Model 11-87 NWTF Turkey
Gun (Mossy Oak) disc. 1996 . . . . NiB $686 Ex $549 Gd $374
Model 11-87 NWTF Turkey Gun
(Mossy Oak Breakup) introduced 1999 . . . . . . NiB $700 Ex $560 Gd $381
Model 11-87 NWTF 20 ga. Turkey Gun
(Mossy Oak Breakup) Produced 1998 only . . . NiB $658 Ex $526 Gd $357
Model 11-87 SPST Turkey Gun (matte bl.) . . . NiB $602 Ex $481 Gd $326

MODEL 11-96 EURO LIGHTWEIGHT
AUTOLOADING SHOTGUN . . . . NiB $654 Ex $523 Gd $355
Lightweight version of Model 11-87 w/reprofiled receiver. 12 ga.
only w/3-inch chamber. 26- or 28-inch bbl. w/6mm vent rib and
REM Choke tubes. Semi-fancy Monte Carlo walnut buttstock and
forearm. Weight: 6.8 lbs. w/26-inch bbl. Made 1996 to date.

MODEL 17A STANDARD GRADE SLIDE-ACTION REPEATING SHOTGUN
Hammerless. Takedown. Five shot. 20 ga. only. Four shell tubular magazine. Bbls.: plain; 26- to 32-inch; choked F, M or Cyl. Weight: About 5.75
lbs. Plain pistol-grip stock, grooved slide handle. Made 1921-33. Note: The
present Ithaca Model 37 is an adaptation of this Browning design.
Plain barrel . . . . NiB $399 Ex $318 Gd $217
Solid rib . . . . NiB $534 Ex $426 Gd $290

MODEL 29A STANDARD GRADE
SLIDE-ACTION REPEATING SHOTGUN . . . . . NiB $429 Ex $342 Gd $233
Hammerless. Takedown. Six shot. 12 ga. only. Five shell tubular magazine. Bbls.: plain- 26- to 32-inch, choked F, M or Cyl. Weight: About
7.5 lbs. Checkered pistol-grip stock and slide handle. Made 1929-33.

MODEL 29T TARGET GRADE . . . . . NiB $492 Ex $394 Gd $268
Same general specifications as Model 29A except has trap-style stock with
straight grip, extension slide handle, vent rib bbl. Disc. 1933.

MODEL 31 AND 31L SKEET GRADE
Same general specifications as Model 31A except has 26-inch bbl. with
raised solid or vent rib, SK choke, checkered pistol-grip stock and
beavertail forend. Weight: About 8 lbs., 12 ga. Made 1932-1939.
Model 31 Standard w/raised solid rib . . . . NiB $764 Ex $612 Gd $416
Model 31 Standard w/ventilated rib . . . . . NiB $919 Ex $735 Gd $501
Model 31L Lightweight w/raised solid rib . . . . . NiB $695 Ex $556 Gd $378
Model 31L Lightweight w/ventilated rib . . NiB $841 Ex $674 Gd $458

Remington Model 11-87 SPS

Remington Model 11-87 SPS Camo

Remington Model 11-87 SP Walnut Stock

Remington Model SP-10 Magnum Camo

MODEL 31 SPECIAL, TOURNAMENT, EXPERT AND PREMIER GRADE GUNS

These higher grade models differ from the Model 31A in general quality, grade of wood, checkering, engraving, etc. General specifications are the same.

Model 31B Special grade . . . . NiB $673 Ex $538 Gd $366
Model 31D Tournament grade . . . . NiB $972 Ex $778 Gd $528
Model 31E Expert grade . . . . NiB $1339 Ex $1071 Gd $728
Model 31F Premier grade . . . . . NiB $2183 Ex $1746 Gd $1188

MODEL 31A SLIDE-ACTION REPEATER

Hammerless. Takedown. 3- or 5-shot. Gauges: 12, 16, 20. Tubular magazine. Bbls.: Plain, solid or vent rib; lengths from 26 -32 inches; F, M, IC, C or SK choke. Weight: About 7.5 lbs., 12 ga.; 6.75 lbs., 16 ga.; 6.5 lbs., 20 ga. Earlier models have checkered pistol-grip stock and slide handle; later models have plain stock and grooved slide handle. Made 1931-49.

Model 31A with plain barrel . . . . . NiB $397 Ex $317 Gd $215
Model 31A with solid rib barrel . . . NiB $483 Ex $386 Gd $263
Model 31A with vent rib barrel . . . NiB $519 Ex $415 Gd $282
Model 31H Hunters' Special
w/sporting-style stock . . . . NiB $483 Ex $386 Gd $263
Model 31R Riot Gun w/20-
inch plain bbl., 12 ga. . . . . NiB $338 Ex $270 Gd $183

MODEL 31S TRAP SPECIAL/31TC TRAP GRADE

Same general specifications as Model 31A except 12 ga. only, has 30- or 32-inch vent-rib bbl., F choke, checkered trap stock with full pistol grip and recoil pad, checkered extension beavertail forend. Weight: About 8 lbs. (Trap Special has solid-rib bbl., half pistol-grip stock with standard walnut forend.)

Model 31S Trap Special . . . . NiB $519 Ex $415 Gd $282
Model 31TC Trap grade . . . . NiB $689 Ex $551 Gd $375

MODEL 32 SKEET GRADE

Same general specifications as Model 32A except 26- or 28-inch bbl., SK choke, beavertail forend, selective single trigger only. Weight: About 7.5 lbs. Made 1932-42.

MODEL 32 TOURNAMENT, EXPERT AND PREMIER GRADE GUNS

These higher-grade models differ from the Model 32A in general quality, grade of wood, checkering, engraving, etc. General specifications are the same. Made 1932-42.

Model 32D Tournament grade . . . . NiB $3856 Ex $3085 Gd $2098
Model 32E Expert grade . . . . . . NiB $4832 Ex $3865 Gd $2628
Model 32F Premier grade . . . . NiB $6566 Ex $5253 Gd $3572

MODEL 32A STANDARD GRADE O/U

Hammerless. Takedown. Auto ejectors. Early model had double triggers, later built with selective single trigger only. 12 ga. only. Bbls.: Plain, raised matted solid or vent rib; 26-, 28-, 30-, 32-inch; F/M choke standard, option of any combination of F, M, IC, C, SK choke. Weight: About 7.75 lbs. Checkered pistol-grip stock and forend. Made 1932-42.

With double triggers . . . . NiB $1996 Ex $1596 Gd $1086
With selective single trigger . . . NiB $2254 Ex $1802 Gd $1226
With raised solid rib, add $200
With ventilated rib, add $300

MODEL 32TC

TARGET (TRAP) GRADE . . . . . . NiB $3123 Ex $2498 Gd $1698
Same general specifications as Model 32A except 30- or 32-inch vent-rib bbl., F choke, trap-style stock with checkered pistol-grip and beavertail forend. Weight: About 8 lbs. Made 1932-42.

MODEL 89 (1889) . . . . NiB $1224 Ex $978 Gd $665
Hammers. Circular action. Gauges: 10, 12, 16, 28- to 32-inch bls.; steel or Damascus twist. Weight 7-10 lbs. Made 1889-1908.

MODEL 90-T SINGLE-SHOT TRAP . . . . . NiB $2055 Ex $1644 Gd $1118
Gauge: 12; 2.75-inch chambers. 30-, 32- or 34-inch vent-rib bbl. with fixed chokes or screw-in REMChokes; ported or non-ported. Weight: 8.25 lbs. Checkered American walnut standard or Monte Carlo stock with low-luster finish. Engraved sideplates and drop-out trigger group optional. Made 1990-97.

GRADING: NiB = New in Box   Ex = Excellent or NRA 95%   Gd = Good or NRA 68%

Remington Model 870
Competition Trap

Remington Model 870
Brushmaster

Remington Model 870
Express Super Magnum

Remington Model 870
Marine Magnum

Remington Model 870
Special Field

MODEL 396 O/U

Boxlock. 12 ga. only w/2.75-inch chamber. 28- and 30-inch blued bbls. w/Rem chokes. Weight: 7.50 lbs. Nitride-grayed, engraved receiver, trigger guard, tang, hinge pins and forend metal. Engraved sideplates. Checkered satin-finished American walnut stock w/target style forend. Made 1996 to date.

396 Sporting

Clays . . . . NiB $1931 Ex $1545 Gd $1051
396 Skeet. . . . . NiB $2000 Ex $1600 Gd $1089

MODEL 870

"ALL AMERICAN" TRAP GUN . . . NiB $1026 Ex $821 Gd $558
Same as Model 870TB except custom grade with engraved receiver, trigger guard and bbl.; Monte Carlo or straight-comb stock and forend of fancy walnut; available only with 30-inch F choke bbl. Made 1972-77.

MODEL 870 COMPETITION TRAP

. . . . NiB $580 Ex $463 Gd $315
Based on standard Model 870 receiver except is single-shot with gas-assisted recoil-reducing system, new choke design, a high step-up vent rib and redesigned stock, forend with cut checkering and satin finish. Weight: 8.5 lbs. Made 1981-87.

MODEL 870 STANDARD . . . . NiB $380 Ex $304 Gd $207

Same as Model 870 Wingmaster Riot Gun except has rifle-type sights.

MODEL 870 BRUSHMASTER DELUXE

Same as Model 870 Standard except available in 20 ga. as well as 12, has cut-checkered, satin-finished American walnut stock and forend, recoil pad.

Right-hand model . . . . NiB $417 Ex $334 Gd $228
Left-hand model . . . . NiB $488 Ex $390 Gd $266

MODEL 870 EXPRESS

Same general specifications Model 870 Wingmaster except has low-luster walnut-finished hardwood stock with pressed checkering and black recoil pad. Gauges: 12, 20 or .410, 3-inch chambers. Bbls.: 26- or 28-inch vent-rib with REMChoke; 25-inch vent-rib with fixed choke (.410 only). Black oxide metal finish. Made 1987 to date.

Model 870 Express (12 or
20 ga., REMChoke) . . . . NiB $251 Ex $201 Gd $137
Model 870 Express
(.410 w/fixed choke) . . . . NiB $284 Ex $227 Gd $155
Express Combo (w/extra
20-inch deer bbl.) . . . . NiB $341 Ex $273 Gd $185

Remington Model 870
Special Purpose Deer Gun

Remington Model 870
Wingmaster Field Gun

MODEL 870 EXPRESS DEER GUN
Same general specifications as Model 870 Express except in 12 ga. only, 20-inch bbl. with fixed IC choke, adj. rifle sights and Monte Carlo stock. Made 1991 to date.
Express Deer Gun
w/standard barrel . . . . NiB $276 Ex $221 Gd $149
Express Deer Gun
w/rifled barrel . . . . NiB $311 Ex $248 Gd $168

MODEL 870 EXPRESS SUPER MAGNUM
Similar to Model 870 Express except chambered for 12 ga. mag. w/3.5-inch chamber. Bbls.: 23-, 26- or 28-inch vent rib w/REM Choke. Checkered low-luster walnut-finished hardwood, black synthetic or camo buttstock and forearm. Matte black oxide metal finish or full camo finish. Made 1998 to date.
Model 870 ESM
(w/hardwood stock) . . . . NiB $262 Ex $209 Gd $142
Model 870 ESM
(w/black synthetic stock) . . . . NiB $276 Ex $220 Gd $150
Model 870 ESM
(w/camo synthetic stock) . . . . NiB $375 Ex $300 Gd $204
Model 870 ESM Synthetic
Turkey (w/synthetic stock) . . . . NiB $276 Ex $220 Gd $150
Model 870 ESM como
Turkey (w/full camo) . . . . NiB $354 Ex $283 Gd $193
Model 870 ESM combo
(w/full camo, extra bbl.) . . . . NiB $417 Ex $334 Gd $228

MODEL 870 EXPRESS
SYNTHETIC HOME DEFENSE . . . . . NiB $249 Ex $200 Gd $136
Slide action, hammerless, takedown. 12 ga. only. 18-inch bbl. w/cylinder choke and bead front sight. Positive checkered synthetic stock and forend with non-reflective black finish. Made 1995 to date.

MODEL 870EXPRESS TURKEY GUN . . . NiB $276 Ex $209 Gd $220
Same general specifications as Model 870 Express except has 21-inch vent-rib bbl. and Turkey Extra-Full REMChoke. Made 1991 to date.

MODEL 870 EXPRESS YOUTH GUN . . NiB $262 Ex $209 Gd $142
Same general specifications as Model 870 Express except has scaled-down stock with 12.5-inch pull and 21-inch vent rib bbl. with REMChoke. Made 1991 to date.

MODEL 870 LIGHTWEIGHT
Same as standard Model 870 but with scaled-down receiver and lightweight mahogany stock; 20 ga. only. 2.75-inch chamber. Bbls.: plain or vent rib; 26-inch, IC; 28-inch, M or F choke. REMChoke available from 1987. Weight 5.75 lbs. w/26-inch plain bbl. American walnut stock and forend with satin or Hi-gloss finish. Made 1972-94.
With plain barrel . . . . NiB $287 Ex $230 Gd $157
With ventilated rib barrel . . . . NiB $317 Ex $254 Gd $173
With REMChoke barrel . . . . NiB $360 Ex $288 Gd $196

MODEL 870 LIGHTWEIGHT MAGNUM
Same as Model 870 Lightweight but chambered for 20 ga. Magnum 3-inch shell; 28-inch bbl., plain or vent rib, F choke. Weight: 6 lbs. with plain bbl. Made 1972-94.
With plain barrel . . . . NiB $348 Ex $278 Gd $190
With ventilated rib barrel . . . . NiB $396 Ex $317 Gd $215

MODEL 870 MAGNUM DUCK GUN
Same as Model 870 Field Gun except has 3-inch chamber 12 and 20 gauge Magnum only. 28- or 30-inch bbl., plain or vent rib, M or F choke, recoil pad. Weight: About 7 or 6.75 lbs. Made 1964 to date.
With plain barrel . . . . NiB $417 Ex $334 Gd $228
With ventilated rib barrel . . . . NiB $459 Ex $368 Gd $250

MODEL 870
MARINE MAGNUM . . . . NiB $437 Ex $349 Gd $259
Same general specifications as Model 870 Wingmaster except with 7-shot magazine, 18-inch plain bbl. with fixed IC choke, bead front sight and nickel finish. Made 1992 to date.

MODEL 870
SA SKEET GUN, SMALLBORE. . . . . NiB $418 Ex $335 Gd $228
Similar to Wingmaster Model 870SA except chambered for 28 and .410 ga. (2.5-inch chamber for latter); 25-inch vent rib bbl., SK choke. Weight: 6 lbs., 28 ga.; 6.5 lbs., .410. Made 1969-82.

MODEL 870 MISSISSIPPI
MAGNUM DUCK GUN . . . . NiB $428 Ex $342 Gd $233
Same as Remington Model 870 Magnum duck gun except has 32-inch bbl. "Ducks Unlimited" engraved receiver, Made in 1983.

MODEL 870
SPECIAL FIELD SHOTGUN . . . . NiB $417 Ex $334 Gd $228
Pump action. Hammerless. Gauge: 12 or 20. 21-inch vent-rib bbl. with REMChoke. 41.5 inches overall. Weight: 6-7 lbs. Straight-grip checkered walnut stock and forend. Made 1987-95.

MODEL 870 SPECIAL PURPOSE DEER GUN
Similar to Special Purpose Magnum except with 20-inch IC choke, rifle sights. Matte black oxide and Parkerized finish. Oil-finished, checkered buttstock and forend with recoil pad. Made 1986 to date.
Model 870 SP Deer Gun . . . . NiB $354 Ex $283 Gd $193
Model 870 SP Deer Gun,
cant. scope mt. . . . . NiB $418 Ex $335 Gd $228

MODEL 870 SPECIAL
PURPOSE MAGNUM . . . . NiB $417 Ex $334 Gd $228
Similar to the 870 Magnum duck gun except with 26-, 28- or 30-inch vent rib REMChoke bbl.12 ga. only; 3-inch chamber. Oil-finished field-grade stock with recoil pad, QD swivels and Cordura sling. Made 1985 to date.

SHOTGUNS

**Remington Model 870TC
Wingmaster Trap**

MODEL 870SPS MAGNUM
Same general specifications Model 870 Special Purpose Magnum except with synthetic stock and forend. 26- or 28-inch vent-rib bbl. with REMChoke tubes. Matte black or Mossy Oak camo finish. Made 1991 to date.
70 SPS Mag. (black syn. stock) .... NiB $400 Ex $319 Gd $217
870 SPS-T Camo (Mossy Oak camo)...... NiB $414 Ex $332 Gd $225

MODEL 870 WINGMASTER FIELD GUN
Same general specifications as Model 870AP except checkered stock and forend. Later models have REMChoke systems in 12 ga. Made 1964 to date.
With plain barrel .... NiB $274 Ex $218 Gd $148
With ventilated rib barrel .... NiB $322 Ex $257 Gd $175

MODEL 870 WINGMASTER FIELD GUN, SMALL BORE
Same as standard Model 870 except w/scaled-down lightweight receivers. Gauges: 28 and .410. Plain or vent rib 25-inch bbl. choked IC, M or F. Weight: 5.5-6.25 lbs. depending on gauge and bbl. Made 1969-94.
With plain barrel .... NiB $518 Ex $414 Gd $281
With ventilated-rib barrel .... NiB $596 Ex $468 Gd $318

MODEL 870 WINGMASTER
MAGNUM DELUXE GRADE ...... NiB $522 Ex $418 Gd $284
Same as Model 870 Magnum standard grade except has checkered stock and extension beavertail forearm, bbl. with matted top surface. Disc. in 1963.

MODEL 870 WINGMASTER
MAGNUM STANDARD GRADE ... NiB $458 Ex $367 Gd $249
Same as Model 870AP except chambered for 12 ga. 3-inch Magnum, 30-inch F choke bbl., recoil pad. Weight: About 8.25 lbs. Made 1955-63.

MODEL 870 WINGMASTER REMCHOKE SERIES
Slide action, hammerless, takedown with blued all-steel receiver. Gauges: 12, 20; 3-inch chamber. Tubular magazine. Bbls.: 21-, 26-, 28-inch vent-rib with REM Choke. Weight: 7.5 lbs. (12 ga.). Satin-finished, checkered walnut buttstock and forend with recoil pad. Right- or left-hand models. Made 1986 to date.
Standard model, 12 ga. .... NiB $342 Ex $273 Gd $185
Standard model, 20 ga. .... NiB $365 Ex $291 Gd $198
Youth model, 21-inch barrel ...... NiB $359 Ex $287 Gd $195

MODEL 870ADL WINGMASTER DELUXE GRADE
Same general specifications as Wingmaster Model 870AP except has pistol-grip stock and extension beavertail forend, both finely checkered; matted top surface or vent-rib bbl. Made 1950-63.
With matted top-surface barrel.... NiB $348 Ex $278 Gd $190
With ventilated-rib barrel .... NiB $391 Ex $313 Gd $213

MODEL 870AP WINGMASTER STANDARD GRADE
Hammerless. Takedown. Gauges: 12, 16, 20. Tubular magazine holds four shells. Bbls.: Plain, matted top surface or vent rib; 26-inch IC, 28-inch M or F choke, 30-inch F choke (12 ga. only). Weight: About 7 lbs., 12 ga.; 6.75 lbs., 16 ga.; 6.5 lbs., 20 ga. Plain pistol-grip stock, grooved forend. Made 1950-63.
With plain barrel .... NiB $257 Ex $206 Gd $140
With matted surface barrel....... NiB $271 Ex $216 Gd $147
With ventilated rib barrel .... NiB $297 Ex $237 Gd $161
Left-hand model .... NiB $309 Ex $247 Gd $168

MODEL 870BDL WINGMASTER DELUXE SPECIAL
Same as Model 870ADL except select American walnut stock and forend. Made 1950-63.
With matted surface barrel .... NiB $372 Ex $297 Gd $202
With ventilated-rib barrel .... NiB $412 Ex $330 Gd $223

REMINGTON MODEL 870D, 870F WINGMASTER TOURNAMENT AND PREMIER GRADE GUNS
These higher-grade models differ from the Model 870AP in general quality, grade of wood, checkering, engraving, etc. General operating specifications are essentially the same. Made 1950 to date.
Model 870D Tournament grade ...... NiB $2542 Ex $2033 Gd $1383
Model 870F Premier grade .... NiB $5594 Ex $4475 Gd $3043
Model 870F Premier gr. w/gold inlay ..... NiB $8877 Ex $7101 Gd $4829

REMINGTON MODEL 870R
WINGMASTER RIOT GUN .... NiB $360 Ex $288 Gd $196
Same as Model 870AP except 20-inch bbl., IC choke, 12 ga. only.

REMINGTON MODEL 870SA WINGMASTER SKEET GUN
Same general specifications as Model 870AP except has 26-inch vent-rib bbl., SK choke, ivory bead front sight, metal bead rear sight, pistol-grip stock and extension beavertail forend. Weight: 6.75 to 7.5 lbs. depending on gauge. Made 1950-82.
Model 870SA Skeet grade (disc. 1982) ...... NiB $372 Ex $297 Gd $202
Model 870SC Skeet Target
grade (disc. 1980) .... NiB $534 Ex $426 Gd $290

REMINGTON MODEL 870TB
WINGMASTER TRAP SPECIAL .... NiB $451 Ex $360 Gd $245
Same general specifications as Model 870AP Wingmaster except has 28- or 30-inch vent rib bbl., F choke, metal bead front sight, no rear sight. "Special" grade trap-style stock and forend, both checkered, recoil pad. Weight: About 8 lbs. Made 1950-81.

REMINGTON MODEL
870TC TRAP GRADE .... NiB $606 Ex $484 Gd $330
Same as Model 870 Wingmaster TC except has tournament-grade walnut in stock and forend w/satin finish. Over-bored 30-inch vent rib bbl. w/ 2.75-inch chamber and RemChoke tubes. Reissued in 1996. See separate listing for earlier model.

REMINGTON MODEL 870TC WINGMASTER TRAP GRADE
Same as Model 870TB except higher-grade walnut in stock and forend, has both front and rear sights. Made 1950-79. Model 870 TC reissued in 1996. See separate listing for later model.
Model 870 TC Trap (Standard).... NiB $612 Ex $489 Gd $333
Model 870 TC Trap (Monte Carlo) .. NiB $638 Ex $510 Gd $347

REMINGTON MODEL
878A AUTOMASTER .... NiB $277 Ex $219 Gd $146
Gas-operated Autoloader. 12 ga., 3-shot magazine. Bbls.: 26-inch IC, 28-inch M choke, 30-inch F choke. Weight: About 7 lbs. Plain pistol-grip stock and forearm. Made 1959-62.

NOTE: *New stock checkering patterns and receiver scroll markings were incorporated on all standard Model 1100 field, magnum, skeet and trap models in 1979.*

Remington Model 1100
Field w/Ventilated Rib

Remington Model 1100
Deer Gun

Remington Model 1100
SA Skeet Gun

MODEL 1100 AUTOMATIC FIELD GUN

Gas-operated. Hammerless. Takedown. Gauges: 12, 16, 20. Bbls.: plain or vent. rib; 30-inch F, 28-inch M or F, 26-inch IC; or REMChoke tubes. Weight: Average 7.25-7.5 lbs. depending on ga. and bbl. length. Checkered walnut pistol-grip stock and forearm in high-gloss finish. Made 1963 to date. 16 ga. discontinued.

With plain barrel . . . . NiB $341 Ex $273 Gd $185
With ventilated-rib barrel . . . . NiB $392 Ex $314 Gd $213
REMChoke model . . . . NiB $432 Ex $345 Gd $235
REMChoke, Left-hand action . . . . . NiB $469 Ex $376 Gd $255

MODEL 1100 DEER GUN . . . . NiB $439 Ex $351 Gd $239

Same as Model 1100 Field Gun except has 22-inch barrel, IC, with rifle-type sights; 12 and 20 ga. only; recoil pad. Weight: About 7.25 lbs. Made 1963-96.

MODEL 1100 DUCKS UNLIMITED
ATLANTIC COMMEMORATIVE. . . . NiB $983 Ex $787 Gd $536

Limited production for one year. Similar specifications to Model 1100 Field except with 32-inch F choke, vent rib bbl. 12-ga. Magnum only. Made in 1982.

MODEL 1100 DUCKS UNLIMITED "THE
CHESAPEAKE" COMMEMORATIVE NiB $709 Ex $568 Gd $396

Limited edition 1 to 2400. Same general specifications as Model 1100 Field except sequentially numbered with markings "The Chesapeake." 12 ga. Magnum with 30-inch F choke, vent rib bbl. Made in 1981.

REMINGTON MODEL 1100 FIELD GRADE, SMALL BORE

Same as standard Model 1100 but scaled down. Gauges: 28, .410. 25-inch bbl., plain or vent rib; IC, M or F choke. Weight: 6.25-7 lbs. depending on gauge and bbl. Made 1969-94.

With plain barrel . . . . NiB $545 Ex $436 Gd $297
With ventilated rib . . . . NiB $644 Ex $515 Gd $349

MODEL 1100 LIGHTWEIGHT

Same as standard Model 1100 but scaled-down receiver and lightweight mahogany stock; 20 ga. only, 2.75-inch chamber. Bbls.: Plain or vent rib; 26-inch IC; 28-inch M and F choke. Weight: 6.25 lbs. Made 1971 to date.

With plain barrel . . . . NiB $473 Ex $378 Gd $256
With ventilated rib . . . . NiB $534 Ex $426 Gd $290

MODEL 1100 LIGHTWEIGHT MAGNUM

Same as Model 1100 Lightweight but chambered for 20 gauge Magnum 3-inch shell; 28-inch bbl., plain or vent rib, F choke. Weight: 6.5 lbs. Made 1971 to date.

With plain barrel . . . . NiB $507 Ex $405 Gd $275
With ventilated rib . . . . NiB $567 Ex $454 Gd $309
With choke tubes . . . . NiB $609 Ex $486 Gd $331

MODEL 1100 LT-20
DUCKS UNLIMITED
SPECIAL COMMEMORATIVE . . . . . NiB $638 Ex $510 Gd $347

Limited edition 1 to 2400. Same general specifications as Model 1100 Field except sequentially numbered with markings, "The Chesapeake." 20 ga. only. 26-inch IC, vent-rib bbl. Made in 1981.

MODEL 1100 LT-20 SERIES

Same as Model 1100 Field Gun except in 20 ga. with shorter 23-inch vent rib bbl., straight-grip stock. REMChoke series has 21-inch vent rib bbl., choke tubes. Weight: 6.25 lbs. Checkered grip and forearm. Made 1983 to date.

Model 1100
LT-20 Special . . . . NiB $520 Ex $416 Gd $283
Model 1100
LT-20 Deer Gun . . . . NiB $492 Ex $394 Gd $268
Model 1100
LT-20 Youth . . . . NiB $507 Ex $406 Gd $275

REMINGTON MODEL
1100 MAGNUM . . . . NiB $451 Ex $360 Gd $245

Limited production. Similar to the Model 1100 Field except with 26-inch F choke, vent rib bbl. and 3-inch chamber. Made in 1981.

MODEL 1100 MAGNUM DUCK GUN

Same as Model 1100 Field Gun except has 3-inch chamber, 12 and 20 ga. Mag. only. 30-inch plain or vent rib bbl. in 12 ga., 28-inch in 20 ga.; M or F choke. Recoil pad. Weight: About 7.75 lbs. Made 1963-88.

With plain barrel . . . . NiB $399 Ex $318 Gd $217
With ventilated
rib barrel . . . . NiB $452 Ex $362 Gd $246

Remington Model 1100
Special Field

Remington Model 1100
Tournament Trap

Remington Model 3200
"One of 1000" Skeet

MODEL 1100
ONE OF 3000 FIELD . . . . **NiB $1216 Ex $973 Gd $662**
Limited edition, numbered 1 to 3000. Similar to Model 1100 Field except with fancy wood and gold-trimmed etched hunting scenes on receiver. 12 gauge with 28-inch Mod., vent rib bbl. Made in 1980.

MODEL 1100 SA SKEET GUN
Same as Model 1100 Field Gun, 12 and 20 ga. except has 26-inch vent-rib bbl., SK choke or with Cutts Compensator. Weight: 7.25-7.5 lbs. Made 1963-94.
With skeet-
choked barrel . . . . **NiB $509 Ex $407 Gd $277**
With Cutts Comp. . . . . **NiB $528 Ex $422 Gd $287**
Left-hand action . . . . **NiB $547 Ex $438 Gd $298**

MODEL 1100 SA
LIGHTWEIGHT SKEET . . . . **NiB $483 Ex $386 Gd $263**
Same as Model 1100 Lightweight except has skeet-style stock and forearm, 26-inch vent-rib bbl., SK choke. Made 1971-97.

MODEL 1100 SA
SKEET SMALL BORE . . . . **NiB $547 Ex $438 Gd $298**
Similar to standard Model 1100SA except chambered for 28 and .410 ga. (2.5-inch chamber for latter); 25-inch vent-rib bbl., SK choke. Weight: 6.75 lbs., 28 ga.; 7.25 lbs., .410. Made 1969 to date.

MODEL 1100 SB
LIGHTWEIGHT SKEET . . . . **NiB $534 Ex $426 Gd $290**
Same as Model 1100SA Lightweight except has select wood. Introduced in 1977.

MODEL 1100
SB SKEET GUN . . . . **NiB $507 Ex $405 Gd $275**
Same specifications as Model 1100SA except has select wood. Made 1963-97.

MODEL 1100
SPECIAL FIELD SHOTGUN . . . . **NiB $534 Ex $426 Gd $290**
Gas-operated. Five shot. Hammerless. Gauges: 12 and 20. 21-inch vent-rib bbl. with REMChoke. Weight: 6.5-7.25 lbs. Straight-grip checkered walnut stock and forend. Made 1987 to date.

MODEL 1100 SP MAGNUM
Same as Model 1100 Field except 12 ga. only with 3-inch chambers. Bbls.: 26- or 30-inch F choke; or 26-inch with REM Choke tubes; vent rib. Non-reflective matte black, Parkerized bbl. and receiver. Satin-finished stock and forend. Made 1981 to date.
With fixed choke . . . . **NiB $418 Ex $335 Gd $228**
With REMChoke . . . . **NiB $470 Ex $376 Gd $255**

MODEL 1100 TOURNAMENT AND PREMIER
These higher grade guns differ from standard models in overall quality, grade of wood, checkering, engraving, gold inlays, etc. General specifications are the same. Made 1963 to date.
Model 1100D
Tournament . . . . **NiB $2678 Ex $1905 Gd $1339**
Model 1100F
Premier . . . . **NiB $5871 Ex $4326 Gd $2840**
Model 1100F Premier
with gold inlay . . . . **NiB $8961 Ex $5098 Gd $3425**

MODEL 1100
TOURNAMENT SKEET . . . . **NiB $642 Ex $573 Gd $349**
Similar to Model 1100 Field except with 26-inch bbl. SK choke. Gauges: 12, LT-20, 28, and .410. Features select walnut stocks and new cut-checkering patterns. Made 1979-89.

MODEL 1100TA TRAP GUN . . . . . . **NiB $452 Ex $351 Gd $239**
Similar to Model 1100TB Trap Gun except with regular-grade stocks. Available in both left- and right-hand versions. Made 1979-86.

MODEL 1100TB TRAP GUN
Same as Model 1100 Field Gun except has special trap stock, straight or Monte Carlo comb, recoil pad; 30-inch vent-rib bbl., F or M trap choke; 12 ga. only. Weight: 8.25 lbs. Made 1963-79.
With straight stock . . . . **NiB $483 Ex $386 Gd $262**
With Monte Carlo stock . . . . **NiB $508 Ex $406 Gd $275**

MODEL 1900
HAMMERLESS DOUBLE . . . . **NiB $1095 Ex $876 Gd $595**
Improved version of Model 1894. Boxlock. Auto ejector. Double triggers. Gauges: 10, 12, 16. Bbls.: 28 to 32 inches. Value shown is for standard grade with ordnance steel bbls. Made 1900-10.

Remington Rider No. 9 Single-Shot Shotgun

Remington Sportsman Autoloader

Remington Sportsman — 48A

MODEL 3200
COMPETITION SKEET GUN . . . . NiB $1680 Ex $1344 Gd $914
Same as Model 3200 Skeet Gun except has gilded scrollwork on frame, engraved forend, latch plate and trigger guard, select fancy wood. Made 1973-84.

MODEL 3200
COMPETITION SKEET SET . . . . NiB $5350 Ex $4281 Gd $2911
Similar specifications to Model 3200 Field. 12-ga. O/U with additional, interchangeable bbls. in 20, 28, and .410 ga. Cased. Made 1980-84.

MODEL 3200
COMPETITION TRAP GUN . . . . NiB $2065 Ex $1652 Gd $1124
Same as Model 3200 Trap Gun except has gilded scrollwork on frame, engraved forend, latch plate and trigger guard, select fancy wood. Made 1973-84.

MODEL 3200
FIELD GRADE MAGNUM . . . . . . NiB $1745 Ex $1396 Gd $950
Same as Model 3200 Field except chambered for 12 ga. mag. 3-inch shells 30-inch bbls., M and F or both F choke. Made 1975-84.

MODEL 3200 FIELD GRADE O/U . . . NiB $1153 Ex $923 Gd $627
Boxlock. Auto ejectors. Selective single trigger. 12 ga. 2.75-inch chambers. Bbls.: Vent rib, 26- and 28-inch M/F; 30-inch IC/M. Weight: About 7.75 lbs. with 26-inch bbls. Checkered pistol-grip stock/forearm. Made 1973-78.

MODEL 3200
"ONE OF 1000" SKEET . . . . NiB $1915 Ex $1532 Gd $1041
Same as Model 3200 "One of 1000" Trap except has 26- or 28-inch bbls., SK choke, skeet-style stock and forearm. Made in 1974.

MODEL 3200
"ONE OF 1000" TRAP . . . . NiB $2080 Ex $1663 Gd $1131
Limited edition numbered 1 to 1000. Same general specifications as Model 3200 Trap Gun but has frame, trigger guard and forend latch elaborately engraved (designation "One of 1,000" on frame side), stock and forearm of high grade walnut. Supplied in carrying case. Made in 1973.

MODEL 3200 SKEET GUN . . . . . NiB $1517 Ex $1213 Gd $825
Same as Model 3200 Field Grade except skeet-style stock and full beavertail forearm, 26- or 28-inch bbls., SK choke. Made 1973-80.

MODEL 3200
SPECIAL TRAP GUN . . . . NiB $1368 Ex $1094 Gd $744
Same as Model 3200 Trap Gun except has select fancy-grade wood and other minor refinements. Made 1973-84.

MODEL 3200 TRAP GUN . . . . . . NiB $1259 Ex $1006 Gd $684
Same as Model 3200 Field Grade except trap-style stock w/Monte Carlo or straight comb, select wood, beavertail forearm, 30- or 32-inch bbls. w/ventilated rib, IM/F or F/F chokes. Made 1973-77.

RIDER NO. 9
SINGLE-SHOT SHOTGUN . . . . NiB $418 Ex $335 Gd $228
Improved version of No. 3 Single Barrel Shotgun made in the late 1800s. Semi-hammerless. Gauges 10, 12, 16, 20, 24, 28. 30- to 32-inch plain bbl. Weight: About 6 lbs. Plain pistol-grip stock and forearm. Auto ejector. Made 1902-10.

SP-10
MAGNUM AUTOLOADER . . . . NiB 1026 Ex $821 Gd $555
Takedown. Gas-operated with stainless steel piston. 10 ga., 3.5-inch chamber. Bbls.: 26- or 30-inch vent-rib with REMChoke screw-in tubes. Weight: 11 to 11.25 lbs. Metal bead front. Checkered walnut stock with satin finish. Made 1989 to date.

SP-10
MAGNUM TURKEY COMBO . . . . NiB $1037 Ex $829 Gd $564
Same general specifications as Model SP-10 Magnum except has extra 22-inch REMChoke bbl. with M, F and Turkey extra-full tubes. Rifle sights. QD swivels and camo sling. Made 1991 to date.

PEERLESS O/U. . . . . NiB $1070 Ex $856 Gd $582
Boxlock action and removable, engraved sideplates. Gauge: 12 only with 3-inch chambers. Barrels: 26-, 28-, or 30-inch with vent rib and REMChoke system. Automatic safety and single selective trigger. Weight: 7.25 lbs. to 7.5 lbs. Blued receiver and bbls. Checkered American walnut stock. Made 1993-98.

SPORTSMAN A STANDARD GRADE
AUTOLOADER
Same general specifications as Model 11A except magazine holds two shells. Also available in "B" Special Grade, "D" Tournament Grade, "E" Expert Grade, "F" Premier Grade. Made 1931-48. Same values as for Model 11A.
48D . . . . NiB $1133 Ex $850 Gd $463

Remington Sportsman 48SC Skeet Target Grade

Remington Sportsman 48A Standard

Remington Sportsman 48A Small Gauge

SPORTSMAN SKEET GUN
Same general specifications as the Sportsman A except has 26-inch bbl. (plain, solid or vent rib), SK choke, beavertail forend. Disc. 1949.

With plain barrel . . . . NiB $397	Ex $214	Gd $215
With solid-rib barrel . . . . NiB $483	Ex $386	Gd $263
With ventilated rib barrel . . . . NiB $531	Ex $425	Gd $289

SPORTSMAN-48A STANDARD GRADE 3-SHOT AUTOLOADER
Streamlined receiver. Hammerless. Takedown. Gauges: 12, 16, 20. Tubular magazine holds two shells. Bbls.: Plain, matted top surface or vent rib; 26-inch IC, 28-inch M or F choke, 30-inch F choke (12 ga. only). Weight: About 7.5 lbs., 12 ga.; 6.25 lbs., 16 ga.; 6.5 lbs., 20 ga. Pistol-grip stock, grooved forend, both checkered. Made 1949-59.

With plain bbl. . . . . NiB $360	Ex $304	Gd $196
With matted top-surface bbl. . . . . NiB $396	Ex $317	Gd $215
With ventilated rib bbl. . . . . NiB $421	Ex $337	Gd $230

SPORTSMAN-48 B, D, F SPECIAL, TOURNAMENT AND PREMIER GRADE GUNS
These higher grade models differ from the Sportsman-48A in general quality, grade of wood, checkering, engraving, etc. General specifications are the same. Made 1949-59.

Sportsman-48B Special grade . . . . . NiB $434	Ex $347	Gd $235
Sportsman-48D Tournament grade . . . NiB $948	Ex $758	Gd $515
Sportsman-48F Premier grade . . . . NiB $2073	Ex $1658	Gd $1128

SPORTSMAN-48SA SKEET GUN
Same general specifications as Sportsman-48A except has 26-inch bbl. with matted top surface or vent rib, SK choke, ivory bead front sight, metal bead rear sight. Made 1949-60.

With matted top-surface barrel . . . NiB $354	Ex $283	Gd $193
With ventilated rib barrel . . . . NiB $430	Ex $335	Gd $228
Sportsman-48SC Skeet		
Target grade . . . . NiB $515	Ex $412	Gd $280
Sportsman-48SD Skeet		
Tournament grade . . . . NiB $927	Ex $742	Gd $505
Sportsman-48SF Skeet		
Premier grade . . . . NiB $2183	Ex $1746	Gd $1188

MODEL 11-48A RIOT GUN . . . . . . NiB $244	Ex $249	Gd $169

Same as Model 11-48A except 20-inch plain barrel and 12 ga. only. Disc. in 1969.

MODEL 11-48A STANDARD GRADE 4-SHOT AUTOLOADER .410 & 28 GAUGE
Same general specifications as Sportsman-48A except gauge, 3-shell magazine, 25-inch bbl. Weight: About 6.25 lbs. 28 ga. introduced 1952, .410 in 1954. Disc. in 1969. Values same as shown for Sportsman-48A.

MODEL 11-48A STANDARD GRADE 5-SHOT AUTOLOADER
Same general specifications as Sportsman-48A except magazine holds four shells, forend not grooved. Also available in Special Grade (11-48B), Tournament Grade (11-48D) and Premier Grade (11-48F). Made 1949-69. Values same as shown for Sportsman-48A.

MODEL 11-48SA
.410 AND 28 GA. SKEET . . . . NiB $397	Ex $317	Gd $215

Same general specifications as Model 11-48A 28 gauge except has 25-inch vent rib bbl., SK choke. 28 ga. introduced 1952, .410 in 1954.

SPORTSMAN-58 SKEET, TARGET, TOURNAMENT AND PREMIER GRADES
These higher grade models differ from the Sportsman-58SA in general quality, grade of wood, checkering, engraving, and other refinements. General operating and physical specifications are the same.

Sportsman-58C Skeet Target . . . . . . NiB $580	Ex $463	Gd $315
Sportsman-58D Skeet Tournament. . . . . NiB $850	Ex $680	Gd $462
Sportsman-58SF Skeet Premier . . NiB $1668	Ex $1334	Gd $907

SPORTSMAN-58 TOURNAMENT AND PREMIER
These higher grade models differ from the Sportsman-58ADL with vent-rib bbl. in general quality, grade of wood, checkering, engraving, etc. General specifications are the same.

Sportsman-58D Tournament . . . . . . NiB $918	Ex $733	Gd $499
Sportsman-58F Premier. . . . . NiB $1706	Ex $1365	Gd $928

SPORTSMAN-58ADL AUTOLOADER
Deluxe grade. Gas-operated. 12 ga. Three shot magazine. Bbls.: plain or vent rib, 26-, 28- or 30-inch; IC, M or F choke, or Remington Special Skeet choke. Weight: About 7 lbs. Checkered pistol-grip stock and forearm. Made 1956-64.

With plain barrel . . . . NiB $342	Ex $273	Gd $185
With ventilated rib barrel . . . . NiB $396	Ex $317	Gd $215

Richland Model 200

Richland Model 202

Richland Model 707 Deluxe

Richland Model 711
Long Range Waterfowl Magnum

SPORTSMAN-58BDL DELUXE SPECIAL GRADE
Same as Model 58ADL except select grade wood.
With plain barrel . . . . NiB $360 Ex $288 Gd $196
With ventilated rib barrel . . . . NiB $422 Ex $337 Gd $230

SPORTSMAN-58SA
SKEET GRADE . . . . NiB $410 Ex $328 Gd $222
Same general specifications as Model 58ADL with vent-rib bbl.
except special skeet stock and forearm.

REVELATION SHOTGUNS
See Western Auto listings.

RICHLAND ARMS COMPANY — Blissfield, Michigan; Manufactured in Italy and Spain

MODEL 200
FIELD GRADE DOUBLE . . . . NiB $326 Ex $291 Gd $178
Hammerless, boxlock, Anson & Deeley-type. Plain extractors.
Double triggers. Gauges: 12, 16, 20, 28, .410 (3-inch chambers in
20 and .410; others have 2.75-inch). Bbls.: 28-inch M/F choke, 26-
inch IC/M; .410 with 26-inch M/F only; 22-inch IC/M in 20 ga. only.
Weight: 6 lbs., 2 oz. to 7 lbs., 4 oz. Checkered walnut stock with
cheekpiece, pistol grip, recoil pad; beavertail forend. Made in Spain
1963 to date.

MODEL 202
ALL PURPOSE FIELD GUN . . . . NiB $312 Ex $250 Gd $170
Hammerless, boxlock, Anson & Deeley-type. Same as Model 200

(cont'd.) MODEL 202 ALL-PURPOSE FIELD GUN
except has two sets of barrels same gauge. 12 ga.: 30-inch bbls. F/F,
3-inch chambers; 26-inch bbls. IC/M, 2.75-inch chambers. 20
gauge: 28-inch bbls. M/F; 22-inch bbls. IC/M, 3-inch chambers.
Made 1963 to date.

MODEL 707
DELUXE FIELD GUN . . . . NiB $344 Ex $275 Gd $187
Hammerless, boxlock, triple bolting system. Plain extractors.
Double triggers. Gauges: 12, 2.75-inch chambers; 20, 3-inch
chambers. Bbls.: 12 ga., 28-inch M/F, 26-inch IC/M; 20 ga., 30-
inch F/F, 28-inch M/F, 26-inch IC/M. Weight: 6 lbs., 4 oz. to 6
lbs., 15 oz. Checkered walnut stock and forend, recoil pad.
Made 1963-72.

MODEL 711 LONG-RANGE WATERFOWL
MAGNUM DOUBLE-BARREL SHOTGUN
Hammerless, boxlock, Anson & Deeley-type, Purdey triple lock.
Plain extractors. Double triggers. Auto safety. Gauges: 10, 3.5-inch
chambers; 12, 3-inch chambers. Bbls.: 10 ga., 32-inch; 12 ga., 30-
inch; F/F. Weight: 10 ga., 11 pounds; 12 ga., 7.75 lbs. Checkered
walnut stock and beavertail forend; recoil pad. Made in Spain
1963 to date.
10 ga. magnum . . . . NiB $414 Ex $331 Gd $225
12 ga. magnum . . . . NiB $351 Ex $280 Gd $191

MODEL 808
O/U SHOTGUN . . . . NiB $417 Ex $334 Gd $227
Boxlock. Plain extractors. Non-selective single trigger. 12 ga. only.
Bbls. (Vickers steel): 30-inch F/F; 28-inch M/F; 26-inch IC/M.
Weight: 6 lbs., 12 oz. to 7 lbs., 3 oz. Checkered walnut
stock/forend. Made in Italy 1963-68.

Richland Model 808
Over/Under

Rossi
Hammerless Double-Barrel Shotgun

Rossi
Overland Hammer Double

Rigby Regal
Side Lock

JOHN RIGBY & COMPANY — London, England

HAMMERLESS BOX LOCK DOUBLE-BARREL SHOTGUNS
Auto ejectors. Double triggers. Made in all gauges, barrel lengths and chokes. Checkered stock and forend, straight grip standard. Made in two grades: Sackville and Chatsworth. These guns differ in general quality, engraving, etc.; specifications are the same.
Sackville grade . . . . NiB $5938 Ex $4750 Gd $3230
Chatsworth grade . . . . NiB $4456 Ex $3564 Gd $2424

HAMMERLESS SIDE LOCK DOUBLE-BARREL SHOTGUNS
Auto ejectors. Double triggers. Made in all gauges, barrel lengths and chokes. Checkered stock and forend, straight grip standard. Made in two grades: Regal (best quality) and Sandringham; these guns differ in general quality, engraving, etc., specifications are the same.
Regal grade . . . . NiB $12,500 Ex $10,000 Gd $6000
Sandringham grade . . . . NiB $9500 Ex $7500 Gd $3775

AMADEO ROSSI, S.A. — Sao Leopoldo, Brazil

HAMMERLESS DOUBLE-
BARREL SHOTGUN. . . . . NiB $338 Ex $270 Gd $184
Boxlock. Plain extractors. Double triggers. 12 ga. Three inch chambers. Bbls.: 26-inch IC/M; 28-inch M/F choke. Weight: 7 to 7.5 lbs. Pistol-grip stock and beavertail forearm, uncheckered. Made 1974 to date. Note: H&R Model 404 (1969-72) is same gun.

OVERLAND

HAMMER DOUBLE . . . . NiB $271 Ex $217 Gd $148
Sidelock. Plain extractors. Double triggers. Gauges: 12, .410; 3-inch chambers. Bbls.: 20-inch, IC/M in 12 g.; 26-inch, F/F choke in .410. Weight: 7 lbs. (12 ga.); 6 lbs. (.410). Pistol-grip stock and beavertail forearm, uncheckered. Note: Because of its resemblance to the short-barreled doubles carried by guards riding shotgun on 19th-century stagecoaches, the 12 ga. version originally was called the "Coach Gun." Made 1968-89.

ROTTWEIL SHOTGUNS — West Germany

MODEL 72 O/U
SHOTGUN. . . . . NiB $1951 Ex $1560 Gd $1061
Hammerless, takedown with engraved receiver. 12 ga.; 2.75-inch chambers. 26.75-inch bbls. with SK/SK chokes. Weight: 7.5 lbs. Interchangeable trigger groups and buttstocks. Checkered French walnut buttstock and forend. Imported from West Germany.

MODEL 650 FIELD
O/U SHOTGUN . . . . NiB $763 Ex $611 Gd $415
Breech action. Gauge: 12. 28-inch bbls. Six screw-in choke tubes. Automatic ejectors. Engraved receiver. Checkered pistol grip stock. Made 1984-86.

AMERICAN SKEET. . . . . NiB $1896 Ex $1516 Gd $1031
Boxlock action. Gauge: 12. 27-inch vent-rib bbls. 44.5 inches overall. SK chokes. Weight: 7.5 lbs. Designed for tube sets. Hand-checkered European walnut stock with modified forend. Made 1984-87.

INTERNATIONAL
TRAP SHOTGUN. . . . . NiB $1951 Ex $1560 Gd $1061
Box lock action. Gauge: 12. 30-inch bbls. 48.5 inches overall. Weight: 8 lbs. Choked IM/F. Selective single trigger. Metal bead front sight. Checkered European walnut stock w/pistol grip. Engraved action. Made 1984-87.

Rottweil American Skeet

Ruger Red Label — 20 Gauge (1982)

Ruger Red Label Over and Under (Stainless)

STURM, RUGER & COMPANY, INC. — Southport, Connecticut

PLAIN GRADE RED LABEL O/U
Boxlock. Auto ejectors. Selective single trigger. 12, 20 or 28 ga. w/2.75- or 3-inch chambers. 26-inch vent-rib bbl., IC/M or SK choke. Single selective trigger. Selective automatic ejectors. Automatic top safety. Standard gold bead front sight. Pistol-grip or English-style American walnut stock and forearm w/hand-cut checkering. The 20 ga. Model was introduced in 1977; 12 ga. version in 1982 and the stainless receiver became standard in 1985. Choke tubes were optional in 1988 and standard in 1990. Weight: 7.0 to 7.5 lbs.

Red Label w/fixed chokes . . . . NiB $837 Ex $669 Gd $455
Red Label w/screw-in tubes . . . . . NiB $1072 Ex $858 Gd $583
Red Label w/grade 1 engraving. . . . NiB $2183 Ex $1746 Gd $1188
Red Label w/grade 2 engraving . . . NiB $2523 Ex $2019 Gd $1372
Red Label w/grade 3 engraving . . . NiB $2879 Ex $2303 Gd $1566

RED LABEL O/U ALL-WEATHER STAINLESS
Gauges: 12 ga. Only. Bbls.: 26- 28- or 30-inch w/various chokes, fixed or screw-in tubes. Stainless receiver and barrel. Checkered black synthetic stock and forearm. Weight: 7.5 lbs. Made 1999 to date.

All-weather stainless model . . . . . NiB $1159 Ex $927 Gd $630
W/30-inch bbl., add $56

RED LABEL "WOODSIDE" O/U
Similar to the Red Label O/U Stainless except in 12 ga. only with wood sideplate extensions. Made 1995 to date.

Standard Woodside . . . . NiB $1517 Ex $1213 Gd $825
Engraved Woodside . . . . NiB $2143 Ex $1715 Gd $1166

RED LABEL SPORTING CLAYS O/U
Similar to the standard Red Label model except chambered 12 or 20 ga. only w/30-inch vent-rib bbls., no side ribs; back-bored w/screw-in choke tubes (not interchangeable w/other Red Label O/U models). Brass front and mid-rib beads. Made 1992 to date.

Standard Sporting Clays. . . . . . . NiB $1327 Ex $1062 Gd $722
Engraved Sporting Clays . . . . . . NiB $2353 Ex $1881 Gd $1279

Sarasqueta Model 3 Hammerless Boxlock

RED LABEL SPECIAL EDITION - WILDLIFE FOREVER
Limited edition commemorating the 50th Wildlife Forever anniversary. Similar to the standard Red Label model except chambered 12 ga. only w/engraved receiver enhanced w/gold mallard and pheasant inlays. 300 produced in 1993.

Special edition. . . . . NiB $1699 Ex $1360 Gd $924
Special edition w/hard case . . . NiB $1849 Ex $1479 Gd $1005

VICTOR SARASQUETA, S. A. — Eibar, Spain

SARASQUETA MODEL 3 HAMMERLESS BOXLOCK DOUBLE-BARREL SHOTGUN
Plain extractors or auto ejectors. Double triggers. Gauges: 12, 16, 20. Made in various bbl. lengths, chokes and weights. Checkered stock and forend, straight grip standard. Imported 1985-87.

Model 3, plain extractors . . . . NiB $457 Ex $366 Gd $249
Model 3E, automatic ejectors . . . . . NiB $574 Ex $458 Gd $312

HAMMERLESS SIDELOCK DOUBLES
Automatic ejectors (except on Models 4 and 203 which have plain extractors). Double triggers. Gauges: 12, 16, 20. Barrel lengths, chokes and weights made to order. Checkered stock and forend, straight grip standard. Models differ chiefly in overall quality, engraving, grade of wood, checkering, etc.; general specifications are the same. Imported 1985-87.

SHOTGUNS

Sarasqueta Models 6E, 11E and 12E

Sauer Model 66 Field Grade III

Sauer Model 66 Field Grade II

(*cont'd.*) **HAMMERLESS SIDELOCK DOUBLES**
Model 4	NiB $638	Ex $510	Gd $346
Model 4E	NiB $689	Ex $551	Gd $375
Model 203	NiB $666	Ex $533	Gd $362
Model 203E	NiB $723	Ex $579	Gd $393
Model 6E	NiB $839	Ex $672	Gd $456
Model 7E	NiB $898	Ex $718	Gd $488

(*cont'd.*) **HAMMERLESS SIDELOCK DOUBLES**
Model 10E	NiB $1643	Ex $1314	Gd $894
Model 11E	NiB $1699	Ex $1360	Gd $924
Model 12E	NiB $1952	Ex $1561	Gd $1064

J. P. SAUER & SOHN — Eckernförde, Germany, Formerly located in Suhl, Germany

MODEL 66 O/U FIELD GUN
Purdey-system action with Holland & Holland-type sidelocks. Selective single trigger. Selective auto ejectors. Automatic safety. Available in three grades of engraving. 12 ga. only. Krupp special steel bbls. w/vent rib 28-inch, M/F choke. Weight: About 7.25 lbs. Checkered walnut stock and forend; recoil pad. Made 1966-75.
Grade I	NiB $2400	Ex $1920	Gd $1306
Grade II	NiB $3184	Ex $2546	Gd $1731
Grade III	NiB $4242	Ex $3393	Gd $2307

MODEL 66 O/U SKEET GUN
Same as Model 66 Field Gun except 26-inch bbls. with wide vent rib, SK choked- skeet-style stock and ventilated beavertail forearm; non-automatic safety. Made 1966-75.
Grade I	NiB $2331	Ex $1865	Gd $1268
Grade II	NiB $3187	Ex $2549	Gd $1733
Grade III	NiB $4525	Ex $3619	Gd $2462

MODEL 66 O/U TRAP GUN
Same as Model 66 Skeet Gun except has 30-inch bbls. choked F/F or M/F; trap-style stock. Values same as for Skeet model. Made 1966-75.

MODEL 3000E DRILLING
Combination rifle and double barrel shotgun. Blitz action with Greener crossbolt, double underlugs, separate rifle cartridge extractor, front set trigger, firing pin indicators, Greener side safety, sear slide selector locks right shotgun bbl. for firing rifle bbl. Gauge/calibers12 ga. (2.75-inch chambers); .222, .243, .30-06, 7x65R. 25-inch Krupp-Special steel bbls.; M/F choke automatic folding leaf rear rifle sight. Weight: 6.5 to 7.25 lbs. depending on rifle caliber. Checkered walnut stock and forend; pistol grip, Monte Carlo comb and cheekpiece, sling swivels. Standard model with Arabesque engraving; Deluxe model with hunting scenes engraved on action. Currently manufactured. Note: Also see listing under Colt.
Standard model	NiB $4394	Ex $3514	Gd $2390
Deluxe model	NiB $5324	Ex $4259	Gd $2896

ARTEMIS DOUBLE-BARREL SHOTGUN
Holland & Holland-type sidelock with Greener crossbolt double underlugs, double sear safeties, selective single trigger, selective auto ejectors. Grade I with fine-line engraving, Grade II with full English Arabesque engraving. 12 ga. (2.75-inch chambers). Krupp special steel bbls., 28-inch, M/F choke. Weight: About 6.5 lbs. Checkered walnut pistol-grip stock and beavertail forend; recoil pad. Made 1966-77.
Grade I . . . . NiB $5658 Ex $4526 Gd $3078
Grade II . . . . NiB $7010 Ex $5608 Gd $3813

BBF 54 O/U COMBINATION RIFLE/SHOTGUN
Blitz action with Kersten lock, front set trigger fires rifle bbl., slide-operated sear safety. Gauge/calibers: 16 ga.; .30-30, .30-06, 7x65R, 25-inch Krupp special steel bbls.; shotgun bbl. F choke, folding-leaf rear sight. Weight: About 6 lbs. Checkered walnut stock and forend; pistol grip, mod. Monte Carlo comb and cheekpiece, sling swivels. Standard model with Arabesque engraving; Deluxe model with hunting scenes engraved on action. Currently manufactured.
Standard model . . . . NiB $2683 Ex $2147 Gd $1460
Deluxe model . . . . NiB $3108 Ex $2486 Gd $1691

ROYAL DOUBLE-BARREL SHOTGUNS
Anson & Deeley action (boxlock) with Greener crossbolt, double underlugs, signal pins, selective single trigger, selective auto ejectors, auto safety. Scalloped frame with Arabesque engraving. Krupp special steel bbls. Gauges: 12, 2.75-inch chambers, 20, 3-inch chambers. Bbls.: 30-inch (12 ga. only) and 28-inch, M/F- 26-inch (20 ga. only), IC/M. Weight: 12 ga., about 6.5 lbs.; 20 ga., 6 lbs. Checkered walnut pistol-grip stock and beavertail forend; recoil pad. Made 1955-77.
Standard model . . . . NiB $1584 Ex $1267 Gd $861
20 ga. . . . . NiB $2080 Ex $1663 Gd $1131

SAVAGE ARMS — Westfield, Massachusetts
Formerly located in Utica, New York

MODEL 24 22-.410
O/U COMBINATION . . . . NiB $166 Ex $133 Gd $90
Same as Stevens No. 22-.410 with walnut stock and forearm. Made 1950-65.

MODEL 24C
CAMPER'S COMPANION . . . . NiB $195 Ex $136 Gd $93
Same as Model 24FG except made in .22 Magnum/20 ga. only; has 20-inch bbls., shotgun tube Cyl. bore. Weight: 5.75 lbs. Trap in butt provides ammunition storage; comes with carrying case. Made 1972-89.

MODEL 24 . . . . NiB $236 Ex $189 Gd $129
Same as Models 24DL and 24MDL except frame has black or case-hardened finish. Game scene decoration of frame eliminated in 1974; forearm uncheckered after 1976. Made 1970-88.

MODEL 24DL . . . . NiB $174 Ex $140 Gd $96
Same general specifications as Model 24S except top-lever opening; satin-chrome-finished frame decorated with game scenes, checkered Monte Carlo stock and forearm. Made 1965-69.

MODEL 24F-12T TURKEY GUN . . . NiB $451 Ex $361 Gd $246
12- or 20-ga. shotgun bbl./.22 Hornet, .223 or .30-30 caliber rifle. 24-inch blued bbls., 3-inch chambers, extra removable F choke tube. Hammer block safety. Color casehardened frame. DuPont Rynite camo stock. Swivel studs. Made 1989 to date.

Sauer Model 3000E Drilling

Sauer BBF 54 Combination Rifle/Shotgun

Sauer Royal Double-Barrel Shotgun

MODEL 24FG FIELD GRADE . . . . . . NiB $166 Ex $134 Gd $91
Same general specifications as Model 24S except top lever opening. Made 1972 to date.

MODEL 24MDL . . . . NiB $178 Ex $143 Gd $97
Same as Model 24DL except rifle bbl. chambered for 22 WMR. Made 1965-69.

MODEL 24MS . . . . NiB $166 Ex $134 Gd $91
Same as Model 24S except rifle bbl. chambered for 22 WMR. Made 1965-71.

Savage Model 24
.22-/.410 O/U Combination

Savage Model 24-VS
Camper/Survival/Centerfire Rifle/Shotgun

MODEL 24S O/U COMBINATION . NiB $185 Ex $148 Gd $101
Boxlock. Visible hammer. Side lever opening. Plain extractors.
Single trigger. 20 ga. or .410 bore shotgun bbl. under 22 LR bbl., 24-
inch. Open rear sight, ramp front, dovetail for scope mounting.
Weight: About 6.75 lbs. Plain pistol-grip stock and forearm. Made
1965-71.

MODEL 24V . . . . NiB $312 Ex $250 Gd $170
Similar to Model 24D except 20 ga. under .222 Rem., .22 Rem.,
.357 Mag., .22 Hornet or .30-30 rifle bbl. Made 1971-89.

MODEL 24-VS CAMPER/SURVIVAL/
CENTERFIRE RIFLE/SHOTGUN. . . . NiB $261 Ex $208 Gd $142
Similar to Model 24V except .357 Rem. Mag. over 20 ga. Nickel finish full-length stock and accessory pistol-grip stock. Overall length:
36 inches with full stock; 26 inches w/pistol grip. Weight: About 6.5
lbs. Made 1983-88.

MODEL 28A STANDARD GRADE
SLIDE-ACTION REPEATING SHOTGUN . . . . NiB $319 Ex $255 Gd $173
Hammerless. Takedown. 12 ga. Five shell tubular magazine. Plain
bbl., lengths: 26-,28-, 30-, 32-inches, choked C/M/F. Weight: About
7.5 lbs. with 30-inch bbl. Plain pistol-grip stock, grooved slide handle. Made 1928-31.

MODEL 28B . . . . NiB $338 Ex $270 Gd $184
Raised matted rib; otherwise the same as Model 28A.

MODEL 28D TRAP GRADE. . . . . . . NiB $363 Ex $291 Gd $198
Same general specifications as Model 28A except has 30-inch F
choke bbl. w/matted rib, trap-style stock w/checkered pistol grip,
checkered slide handle of select walnut.

MODEL 30 SOLID FRAME HAMMERLESS
SLIDE-ACTION SHOTGUN. . . . . . . NiB $229 Ex $184 Gd $124
Gauges: 12, 16, 20, .410. 2.75-inch chamber in 16 ga., 3- inch in
other ga. Magazine holds four 2.75-inch shells or three 3-inch
shells. Bbls.: Vent rib; 26-, 28-, 30-inch; IC, M, F choke. Weight:
Average 6.25 to 6.75 lbs. depending on ga. Plain pistol-grip stock
(checkered on later production), grooved slide handle. Made
1958-70.

MODEL 30 TAKEDOWN SLUG GUN . . NiB $212 Ex $169 Gd $115
Same as Model 30FG except 21-inch cyl. bore bbl. with rifle sights.
Made 1971-79.

MODEL 30AC SOLID FRAME . . . . . NiB $236 Ex $189 Gd $128
Same as Model 30 Solid Frame except has 26-inch bbl. with adj.
choke; 12 ga. only. Made 1959-70.

MODEL 30AC TAKEDOWN. . . . . . . NiB $234 Ex $187 Gd $126
Same as Model 30FG except has 26-inch bbl. with adj. choke; 12
and 20 ga. only. Made 1971-72.

MODEL 30ACL SOLID FRAME . . . . NiB $249 Ex $199 Gd $136
Same as Model 30AC Solid Frame except left-hand model with ejection port and safety on left side; 12 ga. only. Made 1960-64.

MODEL 30D TAKEDOWN. . . . . . . NiB $212 Ex $169 Gd $115
Deluxe Grade. Same as Model 30FG except has receiver engraved
with game scene, vent rib bbl., recoil pad. Made 1971 to date.

MODEL 30FG TAKEDOWN HAMMERLESS
SLIDE-ACTION SHOTGUN. . . . . NiB $174 Ex $140 Gd $96
Field Grade. Gauges: 12, 20, .410. Three inch chamber. Magazine
holds four 2.75-inch shells or three 3-inch shells. Bbls.: plain; 26-
inch F choke (.410 ga. only); 28-inch M/F choke; 30-inch F choke
(12 ga. only). Weight: Average 7 to 7.75 lbs. depending on gauge.
Checkered pistol-grip stock, fluted slide handle. Made 1970-79.

MODEL 30L SOLID FRAME . . . . . . NiB $206 Ex $164 Gd $112
Same as Model 30 Solid Frame except left-handed model with ejection port and safety on left side; 12 ga. only. Made 1959-70.

MODEL 30T SOLID FRAME
TRAP AND DUCK . . . . NiB $236 Ex $189 Gd $129
Same as Model 30 Solid Frame except only in 12 ga. w/30-inch F
choke bbl.; has Monte Carlo stock with recoil pad, weight: About 8
lbs. Made 1963-70.

MODEL 30T TAKE DOWN
TRAP GUN . . . . NiB $212 Ex $169 Gd $115
Same as Model 30D except only in 12 ga. w/30-inch F choke bbl.
Monte Carlo stock with recoil pad. Made 1970-73.

MODEL 69-RXL SLIDE-ACTION
SHOTGUN . . . . NiB $199 Ex $159 Gd $108
Similar to Model 67 (law enforcement configuration). Hammerless,
side ejection top tang safe for left- or right-hand use. 12 ga. chambered for 2.75- and 3-inch magnum shells. 18.25-inch bbl. Tubular
magazine holds 6 rounds (one less for 3-inch mag). Walnut finish
hardwood stock with recoil pad and grooved operating handle.
Weight: About 6.5 lbs. Made 1982-89.

MODEL 210F BOLT-ACTION
SLUG GUN . . . . NiB $351 Ex $281 Gd $191
Built on Savage 110 action. Gauge: 12 w/3-inch chamber. Two
round detachable magazine. 24-inch fully rifled bbl. Receiver
drilled and tapped for scope mounts w/no sights. Weight: 7.5 lbs.
Checkered black synthetic stock w/swivel studs and recoil pad.
Made 1997 to date.

MODEL 210FT BOLT-ACTION SHOTGUN . . . NiB $421 Ex $337 Gd $228
Similar to Model 210F except has smoothbore 24-inch bbl. w/choke
tubes. Bead front and U-notch rear sights. Advantage Camo finish.
Made 1997 to date.

Savage 24-C

Savage 24-D

Savage Model 24-F -12T

Savage Model 24-V

Savage Model 30

Savage Model 30 Slug Gun

Savage Model 30-FG

SHOTGUNS

MODEL 220 SINGLE-BARREL SHOTGUN. . NiB $126 Ex $101 Gd $69
Hammerless. Takedown. Auto ejector. Gauges: 12,16, 20 .410. Single shot. Bbl. lengths: 12 ga., 28- to 36-inch, 16 ga., 28- to 32-inch; 20 ga., 26- to 32-inch; .410 bore, 26-and 28-inch. F choke. Weight: about 6 lbs. Plain pistol-grip stock and wide forearm. Made 1938-65.

MODEL 220AC . . . . NiB $151 Ex $120 Gd $82
Same as Model 220 except has Savage adj. choke.

MODEL 220L. . . . . NiB $108 Ex $87 Gd $59
Same general specifications as Model 220 except has side lever opening instead of top lever. Made 1965-72.

MODEL 220P . . . . NiB $126 Ex $101 Gd $68
Same as Model 220 except has PolyChoke bbl., made in 12 ga. with 30-inch bbl., 16 and 20 ga. with 28-inch bbl., no .410 bore; recoil pad.

Savage Model 69-RXL

Savage Model 220

Savage Model 242

MODEL 242 O/U SHOTGUN . . . . . NiB $363 Ex $294 Gd $198
Similar to Model 24D except both bbls. .410 bore, F choke. Weight: About 7 lbs. Made 1977-80.

MODEL 312 FIELD GRADE O/U . . . NiB $537 Ex $428 Gd $292
Gauge: 12; 2.75- or 3-inch chambers. 26- or 28-inch bbls. w/vent rib; F/M/IC chokes. 43 or 45 inches overall. Weight: 7 lbs. Internal hammers. Top tang safety. American walnut stock with checkered pistol grip and recoil pad. Made 1990-93.

MODEL 312 SPORTING CLAYS O/U . . . . . NiB $568 Ex $455 Gd $309
Same as Model 312 Field Grade except furnished with number 1 and number 2 Skeet tubes and 28-inch bbls. only. Made 1990-93.

MODEL 312 TRAP O/U . . . . NiB $608 Ex $487 Gd $330
Same as Model 312 Field Grade except with 30-inch bbls. only, Monte Carlo buttstock, weight: 7.5 lbs. Made 1990-93.

MODEL 330 O/U SHOTGUN . . . . . NiB $568 Ex $455 Gd $309
Boxlock. Plain extractors. Selective single trigger. Gauges: 12, 20. 2.75-inch chambers in 12 ga., 3-inch in 20 gauge. Bbls.: 26-inch IC/M; 28-inch M/F; 30-inch M/F choke (12 ga. only). Weight: 6.25 to 7.25 lbs., depending on gauge. Checkered pistol-grip stock and forearm. Made 1969-78.

MODEL 333 O/U SHOTGUN
Boxlock. Auto ejectors. Selective single trigger. Gauges: 12, 20. 2.75-inch chambers in 12 ga., 3-inch in 20 ga. Bbls.: vent rib; 26-inch SK choke, IC/M; 28-inch M/F; 30-inch M/F choke (12 ga. only). Weight: Average 6.25 to 7.25 lbs. Checkered pistol-grip stock and forearm. Made 1973-78.
Model 333 12 ga. . . . . NiB $648 Ex $518 Gd $352
Model 333 20 ga. . . . . NiB $787 Ex $629 Gd $427

MODEL 333T TRAP GUN . . . . NiB $574 Ex $459 Gd $312
Similar to Model 330 except only in 12 ga. with 30-inch vent-rib bbls., IM/F choke; Monte Carlo stock w/recoil pad. Weight: 7.75 lbs. Made 1972-79.

MODEL 420
O/U SHOTGUN
Boxlock. Hammerless. Takedown. Automatic safety. Double triggers or non-selective single trigger. Gauges: 12, 16, 20. Bbls.: Plain, 26- to 30-inch (the latter in 12 ga. only); choked M/F, C/IC. Weight with 28-inch bbls.: 12 ga., 7.75 lbs.; 16 ga., 7.5 lbs.; 20 ga., 6.75 lbs. Plain pistol-grip stock and forearm. Made 1938-42.
With double triggers . . . . NiB $427 Ex $342 Gd $233
With single trigger . . . . NiB $487 Ex $390 Gd $265

MODEL 430
Same as Model 420 except has matted top bbl., checkered stock of select walnut with recoil pad, checkered forearm. Made 1938-42.
With double triggers . . . . NiB $488 Ex $390 Gd $265
With single trigger . . . . NiB $537 Ex $428 Gd $292

MODEL 440
O/U SHOTGUN . . . . NiB $514 Ex $411 Gd $312
Boxlock. Plain extractors. Selective single trigger. Gauges: 12, 20. 2.75-inch chambers in 12 ga., 3-inch in 20 ga. Bbls.: Vent rib; 26-inch SK choke, IC/M; 28-inch M/F; 30-inch M/F choke (12 ga. only). Weight: Average 6 to 6.5 lbs. depending on ga. Made 1968-72.

MODEL 440T
TRAP GUN . . . . NiB $532 Ex $426 Gd $290
Similar to Model 440 except only in 12 ga. with 30-inch bbls., extra-wide vent rib, IM/F choke. Trap-style Monte Carlo stock and semibeavertail forearm of select walnut, recoil pad. Weight: 7.5 lbs. Made 1969-72.

MODEL 444 DELUXE
O/U SHOTGUN . . . . NiB $537 Ex $428 Gd $292
Similar to Model 440 except has auto ejectors, select walnut stock and semi-beavertail forearm. Made 1969-72.

Savage Model 312
Field Grade O/U

Savage Model 312
Trap O/U

Savage Model 330

Savage Model 333Y

Savage Model 333
20 Gauge

SHOTGUNS

MODEL 550
HAMMERLESS DOUBLE . . . . **NiB $269 Ex $215 Gd $147**
Boxlock. Auto ejectors. Non-selective single trigger. Gauges: 12, 20. 2.75-inch chamber in 12 ga., 3-inch in 20 ga. Bbls.: Vent rib; 26-inch IC/M; 28-inch M/F; 30-inch M/F choke (12 ga. only). Weight: 7 to 8 lbs. Checkered pistol-grip stock and semi-beavertail forearm. Made 1971-73. See illustration page 516.

MODEL 720 STANDARD GRADE
5 SHOT AUTOLOADING
SHOTGUN . . . . **NiB $271 Ex $173 Gd $148**
Browning type. Takedown. 12 and 16 ga. Four shell tubular magazine. Bbl.: plain; 26- to 32-inch (the latter in 12 ga. only); choked IC, M, F. Weight: About 8.25 lbs., 12 ga. with 30-inch bbl.; 16 ga., about .5 lb. lighter. Checkered pistol-grip stock and forearm. Made 1930-49.

MODEL 726 UPLAND SPORTER GRADE
3-SHOT AUTOLOADING
SHOTGUN . . . . **NiB $275 Ex $220 Gd $149**
Same as Model 720 except has 2-shell magazine capacity. Made 1931-49.

MODEL 740C
SKEET GUN . . . . **NiB $349 Ex $270 Gd $232**
Same as Model 726 except has special skeet stock and full beavertail forearm, equipped with Cutts Compensator. Bbl. length overall with spreader tube is about 24.5 inches. Made 1936-49.

MODEL 745LIGHT-WEIGHT
AUTOLOADER . . . . **NiB $271 Ex $217 Gd $148**
Three- or five-shot models. Same general specifications as Model 720 except has lightweight alloy receiver, 12 ga.only, 28-inch plain bbl. Weight: About 6.75 lbs. Made 1940-49.

MODEL 750
AUTOMATIC SHOTGUN . . . . **NiB $280 Ex $224 Gd $153**
Browning-type autoloader. Takedown. 12 ga. Four shot tubular magazine. Bbls.: 28-inch F or M choke; 26-inch IC. Weight: About 7.25 lbs. Checkered walnut pistol-grip stock and grooved forearm. Made 1960-67.

MODEL 750-AC
. . . . **NiB $315 Ex $252 Gd $171**
Same as Model 750 except has 26-inch bbl. with adj. choke. Made 1964-67.

Savage Model 440

Savage Model 440T

Savage Model 550

Savage Model 750

Savage Model 775

Savage Model 775-SC

MODEL 750-SC . . . . **NiB $287 Ex $229 Gd $156**
Same as Model 750 except has 26-inch bbl. with Savage Super Choke. Made 1962-63.

**MODEL 755 STANDARD
GRADE AUTOLOADER** . . . . **NiB $271 Ex $217 Gd $148**
Streamlined receiver. Takedown.12 and 16 ga. Four shell tubular magazine (a three-shot model with magazine capacity of two shells was also produced until 1951). Bbl.: Plain, 30-inch F choke (12 ga. only), 28-inch F or M, 26-inch IC. Weight: About 8.25 lbs., 12 ga. Checkered pistol-grip stock and forearm. Made 1949-58.

MODEL 755-SC . . . . **NiB $267 Ex $214 Gd $145**
Same as Model 755 except has 26-inch bbl. w/recoil-reducing, adj. Savage Super Choke.

MODEL 775 LIGHTWEIGHT . . . . . . **NiB $274 Ex $219 Gd $149**
Same general specifications as Model 755 except has lightweight alloy receiver, weight: About 6.73 lbs. Made 1950-65.

MODEL 775-SC . . . . **NiB $287 Ex $229 Gd $156**
Same as Model 775 except has 26-inch bbl. with Savage Super Choke.

**MODEL 2400 O/U
COMBINATION** . . . . **NiB $631 Ex $586 Gd $529**
Boxlock action similar to that of Model 330. Plain extractors. Selective single trigger. 12-ga. (2.75-inch chamber) shotgun bbl., F choke over .308 Win. or .222 Rem. rifle bbl.; 23.5-inch; solid matted rib with blade front sight and folding leaf rear, dovetail for scope mounting. Weight: About 7.5 lbs. Monte Carlo stock w/pistol grip and recoil pad, semibeavertail forearm, checkered. Made 1975-79 by Valmet.

Savage Model 2400
O/U Combination Gun

SEARS, ROEBUCK & COMPANY — Chicago, Illinois. (J. C. Higgins and Ted Williams Models)

Although they do not correspond to specific models below, the names Ted Williams and J. C. Higgins have been used to designate various Sears shotguns at various times.

MODEL 18
BOLT-ACTION REPEATER . . . . NiB $108 Ex $87 Gd $59
Takedown. 3-shot top-loading magazine. Gauge: .410 only. Bbl.: 25-inch w/variable choke. Weight: About 5.75 lbs.

MODEL 20 SLIDE-ACTION REPEATER . . NiB $214 Ex $171 Gd $116
Hammerless. 5-shot magazine. Bbls.: 26- to 30-inch w/various chokes. Weight: 7.25 lbs. Plain pistol-grip stock and slide handle.

MODEL 21 SLIDE-ACTION REPEATER . . . . . NiB $236 Ex $189 Gd $129
Same general specifications as the Model 20 except vent rib and adj. choke.

MODEL 30 SLIDE-ACTION REPEATER . . . NiB $223 Ex $178 Gd $121
Hammerless. Gauges: 12, 16, 20 and .410. Four shot magazine. Bbls.: 26- to 30-inch, various chokes. Weight: 6.5 lbs. Plain pistol-grip stock, grooved slide handle.

MODEL 97 SINGLE-SHOT SHOTGUN. . . . . . NiB $82 Ex $66 Gd $45
Takedown. Visible hammer. Automatic ejector. Gauges: 12, 16, 20 and .410. Bbls.: 26- to 36-inch, F choke. Weight: Average 6 lbs. Plain pistol-grip stock and forearm.

MODEL 97-AC SINGLE-SHOT SHOTGUN. . . . . NiB $102 Ex $82 Gd $55
Same general specifications as Model 97 except fancier stock and forearm.

MODEL 101.7 DOUBLE-BARREL
SHOTGUN . . . . NiB $214 Ex $171 Gd $116
Boxlock. Double triggers. Gauges: 12, 16, 20, .410. Bbls.: 26- to 32-inch, choked M and F. Weight: From 6 to 7.5 lbs. Plain stock and forend.

MODEL 101.7C DOUBLE-BARREL
SHOTGUN . . . . NiB $229 Ex $173 Gd $92
Same general specifications as Model 101.7 except checkered stock and forearm.

MODEL 101.25 BOLT-ACTION SHOTGUN . . . . NiB $102 Ex $82 Gd $55
Takedown. .410 gauge. Five shell tubular magazine. 24-inch bbl., F choke. Weight: About 6 lbs. Plain, one-piece pistol-grip stock.

MODEL 101.40 SINGLE-SHOT SHOTGUN . . NiB $87 Ex $69 Gd $47
Takedown. Visible hammer. Automatic ejector. Gauges: 12, 16, 20 and .410. Bbls.: 26- to 36-inch, F choke. Weight: Average 6 lbs. Plain pistol-grip stock and forearm.

MODEL 101.1120 BOLT-ACTION REPEATER . . . . . NiB $102 Ex $82 Gd $55
Takedown. .410 ga. 24-inch bbl., F choke. Weight: About 5 lbs. Plain one-piece pistol-grip stock.

MODEL 101.1380 BOLT-ACTION REPEATER . . . NiB $115 Ex $92 Gd $62
Takedown. Gauges: 12, 16, 20. Two shell detachable box magazine. 26-inch bbl., F choke. Weight: About 7 lbs. Plain one-piece pistol-grip stock.

MODEL 101.1610 DOUBLE-BARREL
SHOTGUN . . . . NiB $314 Ex $251 Gd $171
Boxlock. Double triggers. Plain extractors. Gauges: 12, 16, 20 and .410. Bbls.: 24- to 30-inch. Various chokes, but mostly M and F. Weight: About 7.5 lbs, 12 ga. Checkered pistol-grip stock and forearm.

MODEL 101.1701 DOUBLE-BARREL
SHOTGUN . . . . NiB $312 Ex $250 Gd $170
Same general specifications as Model 101.1610 except satin chrome frame and select walnut stock and forearm.

MODEL 101.5350-D
BOLT-ACTION REPEATER . . . . NiB $97 Ex $78 Gd $52
Takedown. Gauges: 12, 16, 20. 2-shell detachable box magazine. 26-inch bbl., F choke. Weight: About 7.25 lbs. Plain one piece pistol-grip stock.

MODEL 101.5410
BOLT-ACTION REPEATER . . . . NiB $102 Ex $80 Gd $54
Same general specifications as Model 101.5350-D.

SKB ARMS COMPANY — Tokyo, Japan
Imported by G.U. Inc., Omaha, Nebraska

MODEL 385 SIDE-BY-SIDE . . . . . NiB $1668 Ex $1334 Gd $907
Boxlock action w/double locking lugs. Gauges: 12, 20 and 28 w/2.75- and 3-inch chambers. 26- or 28-inch bbls. w/Inter-Choke tube system. Single selective trigger. Selective automatic ejectors and automatic safety. Weight: 6 lbs., 10 oz. Silver nitride receiver w/engraved scroll and game scene. Solid rib w/flat matte finish and metal front bead sight. Checkered American walnut English or pistol-grip stock. Imported 1992 to date.

MODELS 300 AND 400 SIDE-BY-SIDE DOUBLES
Similar to Model 200E except higher grade. Models 300 and 400 differ in that the latter has more elaborate engraving and fancier wood.
Model 300 . . . . NiB $925 Ex $740 Gd $503
Model 400 . . . . NiB $1126 Ex $900 Gd $613

MODEL 400 SKEET . . . . NiB $1062 Ex $850 Gd $578
Similar to Model 200E Skeet except higher grade with more elaborate engraving and full fancy wood.

MODEL 480 ENGLISH . . . . NiB $1382 Ex $1106 Gd $752
Similar to Model 280 English except higher grade with more elaborate engraving and full fancy wood.

SHOTGUNS

SKB Model 585 Field

SKB Model 605 Trap

SKB Model 885 Trap

MODEL 500 SERIES O/U SHOTGUN
Boxlock. Gauges: 12 and 20 w/2.75-or 3-inch chambers. Bbls.: 26-, 28- or 30-inch with vent rib; fixed chokes. Weight: 7.5 to 8.5 lbs. Single selective trigger. Selective automatic ejectors. Manual safety. Checkered walnut stock. Blue finish with scroll engraving. Imported 1967-80.
500 Field, 12 ga. . . . . NiB $541 Ex $433 Gd $294
500 Field, 20 ga. . . . . NiB $642 Ex $513 Gd $349
500 Magnum, 12 ga.
3-inch chambers . . . . NiB $609 Ex $486 Gd $331

MODEL 500 SMALL
GAUGE O/U SHOTGUN . . . . NiB $673 Ex $538 Gd $366
Similar to Model 500 except gauges 28 and .410; has 28-inch vent-rib bbls., M/F chokes. Weight: About 6.5 lbs.

MODEL 505 O/U SHOTGUN
Blued boxlock action. Gauge: 12, 20, 28 and .410. Bbls.: 26-, 28, 30-inch; IC/M, M/F or inner choke tubes. 45.19 inches overall. Weight: 6.6 to 7.4 lbs. Hand checkered walnut stock. Metal bead front sight, ejectors, single selective trigger and ejectors. Introduced 1988.
Standard Field, Skeet or Trap grade. . . . . . . NiB $898 Ex $718 Gd $488
Standard Two-bbl. Field set . . . . . NiB $1368 Ex $1094 Gd $744
Skeet grade, three-bbl. set . . . . NiB $1951 Ex $1560 Gd $1061
Sporting Clays . . . . NiB $959 Ex $767 Gd $522
Trap grade two-bbl. set . . . . NiB $1651 Ex $1320 Gd $898

MODEL 585 DELUXE O/U SHOTGUN
Boxlock. Gauges: 12, 20, 28 and .410; 2.75-or 3-inch chambers. Bbls.: 26-, 28-, 30-, 32- or 34-inch with vent rib; fixed chokes or Inter-choke tubes. Weight: 6.5 to 8.5 lbs. Single selective trigger. Selective automatic ejectors. Manual safety. Checkered walnut stock in standard or Monte Carlo style. Silver nitride finish with engraved game scenes. Made 1987 to date.
Field, Skeet, Trap grades . . . . NiB $1221 Ex $976 Gd $663
Field grade, two-bbl. set . . . . . . NiB $2155 Ex $1724 Gd $1172
Skeet set (20, 28, .410 ga.) . . . . NiB $2618 Ex $2095 Gd $1424
Sporting Clays . . . . NiB $1486 Ex $1190 Gd $809
Trap Combo (two-bbl.) . . . . NiB $2155 Ex $1724 Gd $1172

MODEL 600 SERIES O/U SHOTGUN
Similar to 500 Series except w/silver nitride receiver. Checkered deluxe walnut stock in both Field and Target Grade configurations . Imported 1969-80.
600 Field, 12 ga. . . . . NiB $673 Ex $538 Gd $366
600 Field, 20 ga. . . . . NiB $865 Ex $669 Gd $515
600 Magnum, 12 ga.
3-inch chambers . . . . NiB $742 Ex $515 Gd $335
600 Skeet or Trap grade . . . . NiB $721 Ex $566 Gd $412
600 Trap Doubles Gun. . . . . NiB $673 Ex $538 Gd $366

MODEL 600 SMALL GA. . . . . NiB $876 Ex $772 Gd $468
Same as Model 500 Small Gauge except higher grade with more elaborate engraving and fancier wood.

MODEL 605 SERIES O/U SHOTGUN
Similar to the Model 505 except w/engraved silver nitride receiver and deluxe wood. Introduced 1988.
Field, Skeet, Trap grade . . . . NiB $921 Ex $736 Gd $500
Skeet three-bbl. set . . . . NiB $1998 Ex $1599 Gd $1087
Sporting Clays . . . . NiB $932 Ex $746 Gd $507

MODEL 680 ENGLISH O/U SHOTGUN
Similar to 600 Series except w/English style select walnut stock and fine scroll engraving. Imported 1973-77.
680 English, 12 ga. . . . . NiB $777 Ex $621 Gd $422
680 English, 20 ga. . . . . NiB $886 Ex $787 Gd $482

MODEL 685 DELUXE O/U
Similar to the 585 Deluxe except with semi-fancy American walnut stock. Gold trigger and jeweled barrel block. Silvered receiver with fine engraving.
Field, Skeet, Trap grade . . . . NiB $1267 Ex $1014 Gd $689
Field grade, two-bbl. set . . . . . . NiB $1976 Ex $1580 Gd $1074
Skeet set . . . . NiB $2697 Ex $2157 Gd $1467
Sporting Clays . . . . NiB $1309 Ex $1048 Gd $712
Trap Combo. two bbl. . . . . NiB $1951 Ex $1560 Gd $1061

Sile Field Master II

MODEL 800 SKEET/TRAP O/U
Similar to Model 700 Skeet and Trap except higher grade with more elaborate engraving and fancier wood.
Model 800 Skeet . . . . NiB $352 Ex $1051 Gd $714
Model 800 Trap . . . . NiB $1191 Ex $953 Gd $648

MODEL 880 SKEET/TRAP
Similar to Model 800 Skeet except has sideplates.
Model 880 Skeet . . . . NiB $1439 Ex $1231 Gd $837
Model 880 Trap . . . . NiB $1577 Ex $1262 Gd $858

MODEL 885 DELUXE O/U
Similar to the 685 Deluxe except with engraved sideplates.
Field, Skeet, Trap grade . . . . NiB $1252 Ex $1002 Gd $682
Field grade, two-bbl. set . . . . . . NiB $1976 Ex $1580 Gd $1074
Skeet Set . . . . NiB $3173 Ex $2539 Gd $1726
Sporting Clays . . . . NiB $1614 Ex $1292 Gd $879
Trap Combo. . . . . NiB $2618 Ex $2095 Gd $1424

The following SKB shotguns were distributed by Ithaca Gun Co. from 1966-76. For specific data, see corresponding listings under Ithaca.

CENTURY SINGLE-BARREL TRAP GUN
The SKB catalog does not differentiate between Century and Century II; however, specifications of current Century are those of Ithaca-SKB Century II.
Century (505) . . . . NiB $925 Ex $740 Gd $503
Century II (605) . . . . NiB $1072 Ex $858 Gd $583

GAS-OPERATED AUTOMATIC SHOTGUNS
Model XL300 with plain barrel . . . . NiB $341 Ex $273 Gd $185
Model XL300 with vent rib . . . . NiB $380 Ex $304 Gd $213
Model XL900 . . . . NiB $336 Ex $269 Gd $182
Model XL900 Trap . . . . NiB $399 Ex $319 Gd $217
Model XL900 Skeet . . . . NiB $410 Ex $328 Gd $222
Model XL900 Slug . . . . NiB $360 Ex $288 Gd $1996
Model 1300 Upland, Slug . . . . NiB $458 Ex $367 Gd $249
Model 1900 Field, Trap, Slug . . . . . NiB $515 Ex $412 Gd $280

SKB OVER/UNDER SHOTGUNS
Model 500 Field . . . . NiB $547 Ex $438 Gd $298
Model 500 Magnum . . . . NiB $642 Ex $513 Gd $349
Model 600 Field . . . . NiB $743 Ex $594 Gd $404
Model 600 Magnum . . . . NiB $771 Ex $617 Gd $420
Model 600 Trap . . . . NiB $735 Ex $552 Gd $375
Model 600 Doubles . . . . NiB $715 Ex $572 Gd $389
Model 600 Skeet—12 or 20 ga. . . . . NiB $779 Ex $623 Gd $423
Model 600 Skeet—28 or .410. . . . . . NiB $845 Ex $676 Gd $459
Model 600 Skeet Combo. . . . . NiB $2054 Ex $1643 Gd $1118
Model 600 English . . . . NiB $727 Ex $582 Gd $396
Model 700 Trap. . . . . NiB $908 Ex $727 Gd $494
Model 700 Doubles . . . . NiB $798 Ex $639 Gd $434
Model 700 Skeet. . . . . NiB $869 Ex $695 Gd $473
Model 700 Skeet Combo. . . . . NiB $2260 Ex $1808 Gd $1229

SKB RECOIL-OPERATED AUTOMATIC SHOTGUNS
Model 300—with plain barrel . . . . NiB $303 Ex $242 Gd $165
Model 300—with vent rib . . . . NiB $341 Ex $273 Gd $185
Model 900 . . . . NiB $385 Ex $308 Gd $209
Model 900 Slug . . . . NiB $367 Ex $294 Gd $200

SKB SIDE-BY-SIDE DOUBLE-BARREL SHOTGUNS
Model 100. . . . . NiB $491 Ex $393 Gd $268
Model 150. . . . . NiB $550 Ex $440 Gd $299
Model 200E . . . . NiB $815 Ex $651 Gd $443
Model 200E Skeet . . . . NiB $804 Ex $643 Gd $438
Model 280 English . . . . NiB $1119 Ex $894 Gd $609

SIG SAUER — (SIG) Schweizerische Industrie-Gesellschaft, Neuhausen, Switzerland

MODEL SA3 O/U SHOTGUN
Monobloc boxlock action. Single selective trigger. Automatic ejectors. Gauges: 12 or 20 w/3- inch chambers. 26-, 28- or 30-inch vent rib bbls. w/choke tubes. Weight: 6.8 to 7.1 lbs. Checkered select walnut stock and forearm. Satin nickel-finished receiver w/game scene and blued bbls. Imported 1997-98.
Field model . . . . NiB $1231 Ex $976 Gd $664
Sporting Clays model . . . . NiB $1325 Ex $1060 Gd $721

MODEL SA5 O/U SHOTGUN
Similar to SA3 Model except w/detachable sideplates. Gauges: 12 or 20 w/3- inch chambers. 26.5-, 28- or 30-inch vent rib bbls. w/choke tubes. Imported 1997-99.
Field model . . . . NiB $2257 Ex $1806 Gd $1228
Sporting Clays model . . . . NiB $2443 Ex $1954 Gd $1329

SILE SHOTGUNS — Sile Distributors, New York, NY

FIELD MASTER II O/U SHOTGUN. . . . . NiB $580 Ex $463 Gd $315
Gauge: 12, 3-inch chambers. 28-inch bbl., IC, M, IM, F choke tubes. 45.25 inches overall. Weight: 7.25 lbs. Satin-finished walnut, checkered stock and forend. Introduced 1989.

L. C. SMITH SHOTGUNS — Made 1890-1945 by Hunter Arms Company, Fulton, N.Y.; 1946-51 and 1968-73 by Marlin Firearms Company, New Haven, Conn.

L. C. SMITH DOUBLE-BARREL SHOTGUNS
Values shown are for L. C. Smith doubles made by Hunter. Those of 1946-51 Marlin manufacture generally bring prices about 1/3 lower. Smaller gauge models, especially in the higher grades, command premium prices: Up to 50 percent more for 20 gauge, up to 400 percent for .410 gauge.

SHOTGUNS

L.C. Smith Crown

L.C. Smith Field

(cont'd.) L. C. SMITH DOUBLE-BARREL SHOTGUNS
Crown grade, double triggers,
automatic ejectors . . . . NiB $6347 Ex $5077 Gd $3453
Crown grade, selective single trigger,
automatic ejectors . . . . NiB $7428 Ex $4969 Gd $4041
Deluxe grade, selective single trigger,
automatic ejectors . . . NiB $22,531+ Ex $18,025+ Gd $12,257+
Eagle grade, double triggers,
automatic ejectors . . . . NiB $5170 Ex $4135 Gd $2812
Eagle grade, selective
single trigger . . . . NiB $5516 Ex $4413 Gd $3000
Field grade, double trigger
plain extractors . . . . NiB $1209 Ex $967 Gd $658
Field grade, double triggers,
auto. ej. . . . . NiB $1615 Ex $1292 Gd $879
Field grade, non-selective single trigger,
plain extractors . . . . NiB $1520 Ex $1216 Gd $827
Field grade, selective single trigger,
automatic ejectors . . . . NiB $1615 Ex $1292 Gd $879
Ideal grade, double triggers,
plain extractors . . . . NiB $1690 Ex $1351 Gd $919
Ideal grade, double triggers,
auto. ej. . . . . NiB $2290 Ex $1832 Gd $1246
Ideal grade, selective single trigger,
automatic ejectors . . . . NiB $2636 Ex $2108 Gd $1434
Monogram grade, selective single trigger,
automatic ejectors . . . . NiB $12,971 Ex $10,376 Gd $7057
Olympic grade, selective single trigger,
automatic ejectors . . . . NiB $2419 Ex $1935 Gd $1315
Premier grade, selective single trigger
automatic ejectors . . . NiB $17,703+ Ex $14,162+ Gd $9630+
Skeet Special, non-selective single trigger,
automatic ejectors . . . . NiB $2331 Ex $1865 Gd $1268
Skeet Special, selective single trigger,
auto ejectors . . . . NiB $3042 Ex $2433 Gd $1654
.410 ga. . . . . NiB $13,519 Ex $10,815 Gd $7354
Specialty grade, double triggers,
auto ejectors . . . . NiB $3913 Ex $3130 Gd $2129
Specialty grade, selective single trigger,
automatic ejectors. . . . . NiB $4184 Ex $3346 Gd $2276
Trap grade, sel. single trigger,
auto ej. . . . . NiB $1750 Ex $1400 Gd $953

L C. SMITH HAMMERLESS DOUBLE-BARREL SHOTGUNS
Sidelock. Auto ejectors standard on higher grades, extra on Field
and Ideal Grades. Double triggers or Hunter single trigger (non-
selective or selective). Gauges: 12, 16, 20, .410. Bbls.: 26- to 32-
inch, any standard boring. Weight: 6.5 to 8.25 lbs., 12 ga.
Checkered stock and forend; choice of straight, half or full pistol
grip, beavertail or standard-type forend. Grades differ only in quality of workmanship, wood, checkering, engraving, etc. Same general specifications apply to all. Manufacture of these L. C. Smith guns

(cont'd.) L C. SMITH HAMMERLESS DOUBLE-BARREL SHOTGUNS
was discontinued in 1951. Production of Field Grade 12 ga. was
resumed 1968-73. Note: L. C. Smith Shotguns manufactured by the
Hunter Arms Co. 1890-13 were designated by numerals to indicate
grade with the exception of Pigeon and Monogram.
00 grade . . . . NiB $1517 Ex $1213 Gd $825
0 grade . . . . NiB $1851 Ex $1480 Gd $1006
1 grade . . . . NiB $2054 Ex $1643 Gd $1150
2 grade . . . . NiB $2263 Ex $1810 Gd $1231
3 grade . . . . NiB $3219 Ex $2575 Gd $1751
Pigeon . . . . NiB $4037 Ex $3229 Gd $2195
4 grade . . . . NiB $8497 Ex $6798 Gd $4629
5 grade . . . . NiB $9193 Ex $7354 Gd $5001
Monogram . . . . NiB $11,118 Ex $8894 Gd $5047
A1 . . . . NiB $6759 Ex $3785 Gd $2574
A2. NiB $11,491 Ex $9193 Gd $6251
A3 . . . . NiB $25,750+ Ex $20,600+ Gd $14,008+

L. C. SMITH HAMMERLESS DOUBLE
MODEL 1968 FIELD GRADE. . . . . . NiB $727 Ex $582 Gd $396
Re-creation of the original L. C. Smith double. Sidelock. Plain
extractors. Double triggers. 12 ga. 28-inch vent-rib bbls., M/F
choke. Weight: About 6.75 lbs. Checkered pistol-grip stock and
forearm. Made 1968-73.

L. C. SMITH HAMMERLESS DOUBLE
MODEL 1968 DELUXE . . . . NiB $1048 Ex $837 Gd $569
Same as 1968 Field Grade except has Simmons floating vent rib,
beavertail forearm. Made 1971-73.

L. C. SMITH SINGLE-SHOT TRAP GUNS
Boxlock. Hammerless. Auto ejector.12 gauge only. Bbl. lengths: 32-
or 34-inch. Vent rib. Weight: 8 to 8.25 lbs. Checkered pistol-grip
stock and forend, recoil pad. Grades vary in quality of workman-
ship, wood, engraving, etc.; general specifications are the same.
Disc. 1951. Note: Values shown are for L. C. Smith single-barrel trap
guns made by Hunter. Those of Marlin manufacture generally bring
prices about one-third lower.
Olympic grade. . . . . NiB $1825 Ex $1460 Gd $992
Specialty grade . . . . NiB $2291 Ex $1832 Gd $1246
Crown grade . . . . NiB $3988 Ex $3190 Gd $2169
Monogram grade. . . . . NiB $5941 Ex $4752 Gd $3232
Premier grade . . . . NiB $9186 Ex $7348 Gd $4998
Deluxe grade. . . . . NiB $14,194 Ex $11,356 Gd $7722

SMITH & WESSON SHOTGUNS —
Springfield, Massachusetts, Mfd. by Howa
Machinery, Ltd., Nagoya, Japan
*In 1985, Smith and Wesson sold its shotgun operation to O. F.
Mossberg & Sons, Inc.*

L.C. Smith 1968 Field Grade

L.C. Smith 1968 Deluxe

L.C. Smith Single-Shot Trap Gun

Smith & Wesson Model 1000 Magnum

Smith & Wesson Model 3000 Slide Action

MODEL 916 SLIDE-ACTION REPEATER

Hammerless. Solid frame. Gauges: 12, 16, 20. Three inch chamber in 12 and 20 ga. Five shot tubular magazine. Bbls.: plain or vent rib; 20-inch C (12 ga., plain only); 26-inch IC- 28-inch M or F; 30-inch F choke (12 ga. only). Weight: With 28-inch plain bbl., 7.25 lbs. Plain pistol-grip stock, fluted slide handle. Made 1972-81.

With plain bbl. . . . . NiB $174 Ex $140 Gd $96
With ventilated rib bbl. . . . . NiB $223 Ex $178 Gd $121

MODEL 916T

Same as Model 916 except takedown, 12 ga. only. Not available with 20-inch bbl. Made 1976-81.

With plain bbl. . . . . NiB $189 Ex $151 Gd $102
With ventilated rib bbl. . . . . NiB $223 Ex $178 Gd $121

MODEL 1000 AUTOLOADER . . . . . NiB $330 Ex $265 Gd $180

Gas-operated. Takedown. Gauges: 12, 20. 2.75-inch chamber in 12 ga., 3-inch in 20 ga. Four shot magazine. Bbls.: Vent rib, 26-inch SK choke, IC; 28-inch M or F; 30-inch F choke (12 ga. only). Weight: With 28-inch bbl., 6.5 lbs. in 20 ga.,7.5 lbs. in 12 ga. Checkered pistol-grip stock and forearm. Made 1972 to date.

MODEL 1000 MAGNUM . . . . NiB $406 Ex $324 Gd $220

Same as standard Model 1000 except chambered for 12 ga. magnum, 3-inch shells; 30-inch bbl. only, M or F choke; stock with recoil pad. Weight: About 8 lbs. Introduced in 1977.

MODEL 1000P . . . . NiB $352 Ex $282 Gd $191

Same general specifications as Model C 3000 Slide Action, but an earlier version.

MODEL 3000

SLIDE ACTION . . . . NiB $357 Ex $286 Gd $194
Hammerless. 20-ga. Bbls.: 26-inch IC; 28-inch M or F. Chambered for 3-inch magnum and 2.75-inch loads. American walnut stock and forearm. Checkered pistol grip and forearm. Introduced 1982.

SPRINGFIELD ARMS — Built by Savage Arms Company, Utica, New York

SPRINGFIELD DOUBLE-BARREL

HAMMER SHOTGUN . . . . NiB $414 Ex $331 Gd $225
Gauges: 12 and 16. Bbls.: 28 to 32 inches. In 12 ga., 32-inch model, both bbls. have F choke. All other gauges and barrel lengths are left barrel, Full; right barrel, Mod. Weight: 7.25 to 8.25 lbs., depending on gauge and barrel length. Black walnut checkered buttstock and forend. Disc. 1934.

SQUIRES BINGHAM CO., INC. — Makati, Rizal, Philippines

MODEL 30

PUMP SHOTGUN . . . . NiB $204 Ex $163 Gd $111
Hammerless. 12 ga. Five shot magazine. Bbl.: 20-inch Cyl.; 28-inch M; 30-inch F choke. Weight: About 7 lbs. Pulong Dalaga stock and slide handle. Currently manufactured.

Squires Bingham Model 30 Pump Shotgun

J. STEVENS ARMS COMPANY — Chicopee Falls, Massachusetts, Division of Savage Arms Corporation

NO. 20 "FAVORITE" SHOTGUN . . NiB $335 Ex $267 Gd $182
Calibers: .22 and .32 Shot. Smoothbore bbl. Blade front sight; no rear. Made 1893-1939.

NO. 39 NEW MODEL POCKET SHOTGUN . . . . NiB $645 Ex $515 Gd $351
Gauge: .410. Calibers: .38-40 Shot, .44-40 Shot. Bbls.: 10, 12, 15 or 18 inches, half-octagonal smoothbore. Shotgun sights. Made 1895-1906.

NO. 22-.410 O/U COMBINATION GUN
.22 caliber rifle barrel over .410 ga. shotgun barrel. Visible hammer. Takedown. Single trigger. 24-inch bbls., shotgun bbl. F choke. Weight: About 6 lbs. Open rear sight and ramp front sight of sporting rifle type. Plain pistol-grip stock and forearm; originally supplied with walnut stock and forearm. "Tenite" (plastic) was used in later production. Made 1938-50. Note: This gun is now manufactured as the Savage Model 24.
With wood stock and forearm . . . . NiB $223 Ex $179 Gd $121
With Tenite stock and forearm . . . . . NiB $165 Ex $133 Gd $91

MODEL 51 BOLT-ACTION SHOTGUN . . . . NiB $108 Ex $87 Gd $59
Single shot. Takedown. .410 ga. 24-inch bbl., F choke. Weight: About 4.75 lbs. Plain one-piece pistol-grip stock. checkered on later models. Made 1962-71.

MODEL 58 BOLT-ACTION REPEATER . . . . NiB $134 Ex $107 Gd $72
Takedown. Gauges: 12, 16, 20. Two shell detachable box magazine. 26-inch bbl., F choke. Weight: About 7.25 lbs. Plain one piece pistol-grip stock on early models w/takedown screw on bottom of forend. Made 1933-81. Note: Later production models have 3-inch chamber in 20 ga., checkered stock with recoil pad.

MODEL 58-.410 BOLT-ACTION REPEATER . . . . NiB $126 Ex $101 Gd $69
Takedown. .410 ga. Three shell detachable box magazine. 24-inch bbl., F choke. Weight: About 5.5 lbs. Plain one piece pistol-grip stock, checkered on later production. Made 1937-81.

MODEL 59 BOLT-ACTION REPEATER . . . . NiB $172 Ex $138 Gd $94
Takedown. .410 ga. Five shell tubular magazine. 24-inch bbl., F choke. Weight: About 6 lbs. Plain, one piece pistol-grip stock, checkered on later production. Made 1934-73.

MODEL 67 PUMP SHOTGUN
Hammerless, side-ejection solid-steel receiver. Gauges: 12, 20 and .410, 2.75- or 3-inch shells. Bbls.: 21-, 26-, 28- 30-inch with fixed chokes or interchangeable choke tubes, plain or vent rib. Weight: 6.25 to 7.5 lbs. Optional rifle sights. Walnut-finished hardwood stock with corncob-style forend.

(cont'd.) **MODEL 67 PUMP SHOTGUN**
Standard model, plain bbl. . . . . NiB $223 Ex $178 Gd $121
Standard model, vent rib . . . . NiB $236 Ex $189 Gd $129
Standard model, w/choke tubes . . . NiB $249 Ex $199 Gd $136
Slug model w/rifle sights . . . . NiB $210 Ex $168 Gd $114
Lobo model, matte finish . . . . NiB $274 Ex $219 Gd $149
Youth model, 20 ga. . . . . NiB $236 Ex $189 Gd $129
Camo model. w/choke tubes . . . . . NiB $287 Ex $229 Gd $156

MODEL 67 WATERFOWL SHOTGUN . . . . NiB $261 Ex $208 Gd $142
Hammerless. Gauge: 12. Three shot tubular magazine. Walnut finished hardwood stock. Weight: About 7.5 lbs. Made 1972-89.

MODEL 77 SLIDE-ACTION REPEATER . . . . NiB $201 Ex $160 Gd $109
Solid frame. Gauges: 12, 16, 20. Five shot tubular magazine. Bbls.: 26-inch IC, 28-inch M or F choke. Weight: About 7.5 lbs. Plain pistol-grip stock with recoil pad, grooved slide handle. Made 1954-71.

MODEL 77-AC . . . . NiB $236 Ex $189 Gd $129
Same as Model 77 except has Savage Super Choke.

MODEL 79-VR SUPER VALUE . . . . . NiB $223 Ex $178 Gd $121
Hammerless, side ejection. Bbl.: Chambered for 2.75-inch and 3-inch mag. shells. 12, 20, and .410 ga. vent rib. Walnut finished hardwood stock with checkering on grip. Weight: 6.75-7 lbs. Made 1979-90.

MODEL 94 SINGLE-SHOT SHOTGUN . . . NiB $115 Ex $92 Gd $62
Takedown. Visible hammer. Auto ejector. Gauges: 12, 16, 20, 28, .410. Bbls.: 26-, 28-, 30-, 32-, 36-inch, F choke. Weight: About 6 lbs. depending on gauge and barrel. Plain pistol-grip stock and forearm. Made 1939-61.

MODEL 94C . . . . NiB $159 Ex $127 Gd $87
Same as Model 94 except has checkered stock, fluted forearm on late production. Made 1965-90.

MODEL 94Y YOUTH GUN . . . . NiB $157 Ex $125 Gd $85
Same as Model 94 except made in 20 and .410 ga. only; has 26-inch F choke bbl., 12.5-inch buttstock with recoil pad; checkered pistol grip and fluted forend on late production. Made 1959-90.

MODEL 95 SINGLE-SHOT SHOTGUN . . . NiB $115 Ex $92 Gd $62
Solid frame. Visible hammer. Plain extractor. 12 ga. Three inch chamber. Bbls.: 28-inch M- 30-inch F choke. Weight: About 7.25 lbs. Plain pistol-grip stock, grooved forearm. Made 1965-69.

MODEL 107 SINGLE-SHOT HAMMER SHOTGUN . . . . NiB $108 Ex $87 Gd $59
Takedown. Auto ejector. Gauges: 12, 16, 20, .410. Bbl. lengths: 28- and 30-inch (12 and 16 ga.), 28-inch (20 ga.), 26-inch (.410); F choke only. Weight: About 6 lbs., 12 bore ga. Plain pistol-grip stock and forearm. Made about 1937-53.

MODEL 124 CROSS-BOLTREPEATER . . . NiB $169 Ex $136 Gd $92
Hammerless. Solid frame. 12 ga. only. Two shot tubular magazine. 28-inch bbl.; IC, M or F choke. Weight: About 7 lbs. Tenite stock and forearm. Made 1947-52.

Stevens Model 51

Stevens Model 58

Stevens Model 58-410

Stevens Model 67 Pump Shotgun

Stevens Model 67 Waterfowl Shotgun

Stevens Model 77

Stevens Model 94C

Stevens Model 95

SHOTGUNS

GRADING: **NiB** = New in Box   **Ex** = Excellent or NRA 95%   **Gd** = Good or NRA 68%

Stevens Model
94 Youth

Stevens Model 124
Cross-Bolt Repeater

MODEL 240 O/U SHOTGUN . . . . . NiB $315 Ex $252 Gd $171
Visible hammer. Takedown. Double triggers. .410 ga. 26-inch bbls.,
F choke. Weight: 6 lbs. Tenite (plastic) pistol-grip stock and forearm.
Made 1940-49.

MODEL 258 BOLT-ACTION
REPEATER . . . . NiB $121 Ex $97 Gd $66
Takedown. 20-gauge. Two shell detachable box magazine. 26-inch
barrel, Full choke. Weight: About 6.25 lbs. Plain, one piece pistol-
grip stock. Made 1937-65.

MODEL 311 SPRINGFIELD
HAMMERLESS DOUBLE
Same general specifications as Stevens Model 530 except earlier
production has plain stock and forearm; checkered on current guns.
Originally produced as a "Springfield" gun, this model became a
part of the Stevens line in 1948 when the Springfield brand name
was discontinued. Made 1931-89.
Pre-WW II . . . . NiB $385 Ex $307 Gd $209
Post-WW II . . . . NiB $339 Ex $270 Gd $184

MODEL 311-R
HAMMERLESS DOUBLE . . . . NiB $276 Ex $220 Gd $150
Same general specifications as Stevens Model 311 except compact
design for law enforcement use. Bbls.: 18.25-inch 12 gauge with
solid rib, chambered for 2.75 and 3-inch Mag. shells. Double triggers and auto top tang safety. Walnut finished hardwood stock with
recoil pad and semi-beavertail forend. Weight: About 6.75 lbs.
Made 1982-89.

MODEL 530
HAMMERLESS DOUBLE . . . . NiB $338 Ex $270 Gd $184
Boxlock. Double triggers. Gauges: 12, 16, 20, .410. Bbl. lengths:
26- to 32-inch; choked M/F, C/M, F/F. Weight: 6 to 7.5 pounds
depending on gauge and barrel length. Checkered pistol-grip stock
and forearm; some early models with recoil pad. Made 1936-54.

MODEL 530M . . . . NiB $245 Ex $196 Gd $133
Same as Model 530 except has Tenite (plastic) stock and forearm.
Disc. about 1947.

MODEL 530ST
DOUBLE GUN . . . . NiB $309 Ex $249 Gd $167
Same as Model 530 except has non-selective single trigger. Disc.

MODEL 620 HAMMERLESS
SLIDE-ACTION
REPEATING SHOTGUN . . . . NiB $315 Ex $252 Gd $171
Takedown. Gauges: 12, 16, 20. Five shell tubular magazine. Bbl.
lengths: 26-, 28-, 30-, 32-inch; choked F, M IC, C. Weight: About
7.75 lbs., 12 ga.; 7.25 lbs., 16 ga.- 6 lbs., 20 ga. Checkered pistol-
grip stock and slide handle. Made 1927-53.

MODEL 620-C . . . . NiB $315 Ex $252 Gd $171
Same specifications as Model 620 except equipped with Cutts
Compensator and two choke tubes.

MODEL 620-P . . . . NiB $329 Ex $263 Gd $180
Same specifications as Model 620 equipped with Aero-Dyne
PolyChoke and 27-inch bbl.

MODEL 620-PV . . . . NiB $329 Ex $263 Gd $180
Same specifications as Model 620 except equipped with ventilated
PolyChoke and 27-inch bbl.

MODEL 621 . . . . NiB $386 Ex $308 Gd $209
Same as Model 620 except has raised solid matted-rib barrel. Disc.

MODEL 820 HAMMERLESS
SLIDE-ACTION
REPEATING SHOTGUN . . . . NiB $249 Ex $199 Gd $136
Solid frame. 12 gauge only. Five shell tubular magazine. 28-inch
barrel; IC, M or F choke. Weight: About 7.5 lbs. Plain pistol-grip
stock, grooved slide handle. Early models furnished w/Tenite buttstock and forend. Made 1949-54.

MODEL
820-SC . . . . NiB $274 Ex $219 Gd $149
Same as Model 820 except has Savage Super Choke.

MODEL 940 SINGLE-
SHOT SHOTGUN . . . . NiB $103 Ex $83 Gd $55
Same general specifications as Model 94 except has side lever
opening instead of top lever. Made 1961-70.

MODEL 940Y
YOUTH GUN . . . . NiB $126 Ex $101 Gd $68
Same general specifications as Model 94Y except has side lever
opening instead of top lever. Made 1961-70.

Stevens Model 258

Stevens Model 311

Stevens Model 530

Stevens Model 620

Stevens Model 620-P

Stevens Model 820

MODEL 9478 . . . . **NiB $109 Ex $87 Gd $59**
Takedown. Visible hammer. Automatic ejector. Gauges: 12, 20, .410. Bbls.: 26-, 28-, 30-, 36-inch; Full choke. Weight: Average 6 pounds depending on gauge and barrel. Plain pistol-grip stock and forearm. Made 1978-85.

MODEL 5151 SPRINGFIELD . . . . . . **NiB $393 Ex $314 Gd $213**
Same specifications as the Stevens Model 311 except with checkered grip and forend; equipped with recoil pad and two ivory sights.

STOEGER SHOTGUNS

See IGA and Tikka Shotguns

TAR-HUNT CUSTOM RIFLES, INC. — Bloomsburg, PA

MODEL RSG-12 MATCHLESS
BOLT-ACTION SLUG GUN . . . . . **NiB $1750 Ex $1400 Gd $953**
Similar to Professional model except has McMillan Fibergrain stock and deluxe blue finish. Made 1995 to date.

MODEL RSG-12 PEERLESS
BOLT-ACTION SLUG GUN . . . . . **NiB $1825 Ex $1460 Gd $992**
Similar to Professional model except has McMillan Fibergrain stock and deluxe NP-3 (Nickel/Teflon) metal finish. Made 1995 to date.

MODEL RSG-12 PROFESSIONAL
BOLT-ACTION SLUG GUN
Bolt action 12 ga. w/2.75-inch chamber, 2-round detachable magazine, 21.5-inch fully rifled bbl. w/ or w/o muzzle brake. Receiver drilled and tapped for scope mounts w/no sights. Weight: 7.75 lbs. 41.5 inches overall. Checkered black McMillan fiberglass stock w/swivel studs and Pachmayr Deacelerator pad. Made 1991 to date.
RSG-12 model
W/O muzzle brake (disc. 1993) . . . . NiB $1409 Ex $1127 Gd $766
RSG-12 model
W/muzzle brake . . . . NiB $1550 Ex $1240 Gd $844

MODEL RSG-20 MOUNTAINEER
BOLT ACTION SLUG GUN . . . . . NiB $1267 Ex $1014 Gd $689
Similar to Professional model except 20 ga. w/2.75 inch chamber. Black McMillan synthetic stock w/blind magazine. Weight: 6.5 lbs. Made 1997 to date.

TECNI-MEC SHOTGUNS — Italy, Imported by RAHN Gun Work, Inc., Hastings, MI

MODEL SPL 640
FOLDING SHOTGUN
Gauges: 12, 16, 20, 24, 28, 32 and .410 bore. 26-inch bbl. Chokes: IC/IM. Weight: 6.5 lbs. Checkered walnut pistol-grip stock and forend. Engraved receiver. Available with single or double triggers. Imported 1988-94.
640 w/single trigger . . . . NiB $451 Ex $361 Gd $245
640 w/double trigger. . . . . NiB $509 Ex $407 Gd $277

THOMPSON/CENTER ARMS — Rochester, New Hampshire

CONTENDER
.410 GA. CARBINE . . . . NiB $360 Ex $288 Gd $196
Gauge: .410 smoothbore. 21-inch vent rib bbl. 34.75 inches overall. Weight: About 5.25 lbs. Bead front sight. Rynite stock and forend. Made 1991 to date.

ENCORE
20 GA. SHOTGUN
Gauge: 20 smoothbore w/rifled slug bbl. or 26-inch vent-rib bbl. w/three internal screw choke tubes, 38 to 40.5 inches overall. Weight: About 5.25 to 6 lbs. Bead or fiber optic sights. Walnut stock and forend. Made 2000 to date.
Encore 20 ga.
W/vent rib . . . . NiB $534 Ex $426 Gd $290
Encore 20 ga.
w/rifled slug bbl. . . . . NiB $492 Ex $394 Gd $268
W/extra
bbl., add $262

MODEL '87
HUNTER SHOTGUN. . . . . NiB $470 Ex $376 Gd $255
Single shot. Gauge: 10 or 12, 3.5-inch chamber, 25-inch field bbl. with F choke. Weight: 8 lbs. Bead front sight. American black walnut stock with recoil pad. Made 1987 to 1992.

MODEL '87
HUNTER SLUG . . . . NiB $483 Ex $386 Gd $263
Gauge: 10 (3.5-inch chamber) or 12 (3-inch chamber). Same general specifications as Model '87 Hunter Shotgun except with 22-inch slug (rifled) bbl. and rifle sights. Made 1987 to 1992.

TIKKA SHOTGUNS — Manufactured by: Armi Marocchi, Italy, (formerly by Valmet), Riihimaki, Finland

M 07 SHOTGUN/
RIFLE COMBINATION . . . . NiB $1024 Ex $819 Gd $557
Gauge/caliber: 12/.222 Rem. Shotgun bbl.: About 25 inches; rifled bbl.: About 22.75 inches. 40.66 inches overall. Weight: About 7 lbs. Dovetailed for telescopic sight mounts Single trigger with selector between the bbls. Vent rib. Monte Carlo-style walnut stock with checkered pistol grip and forend. Made 1965-87.

M 77 O/U SHOTGUN. . . . . NiB $123 Ex $98 Gd $67
Gauge: 12. 27-inch vent-rib bbls., approx. 44 inches overall, weight: About 7.25 lbs. Bbl. selector. Ejectors. Monte Carlo-style walnut stock with checkered pistol grip and forend; rollover cheekpiece. Made 1977-87.

M 77K SHOTGUN/ RIFLE
COMBINATION . . . . NiB $1352 Ex $1081 Gd $735
Gauge: 12/70. Calibers: .222 Rem., 5.6x52r5, 6.5x55, 7x57r5, 7x65r5, .308 Win. Vent-rib bbls.: About 25 inches (shotgun); 23 inches (rifle), 42.3 inches overall. Weight: About 7.5 lbs. Double triggers. Monte Carlo-style walnut stock with checkered pistol grip and forend; rollover cheekpiece. Made 1977-86.

412S/512S SHOOTING SYSTEM
Boxlock action with both under lug and sliding top latch locking mechanism designed to accept interchangeable monobloc barrels, including O/U shotgun, combination and double rifle configurations. Blued or satin nickel receiver w/cocking indicators. Selective single trigger design w/barrel selector incorporated into the trigger (double triggers available). Blued barrels assemblies w/extractors or auto ejectors as required. Select American walnut stock with checkered pistol grip and forend. Previously produced in Finland (same as the former Valmet Model 412) but currently manufactured in Italy by joint venture arrangement with Armi Marocchi. From 1990-93, Stoeger Industries imported this model as the 412/S. In 1993 the nomenclature of this shooting system was changed to 512/S and is now imported under that designation. Note: For double rifle values, see Tikka Rifles.

MODEL 412S/512S O/U SHOTGUN
Gauge: 12 w/3-inch chambers. 24-, 26-, 28- or 30-inch chrome-lined bbls. w/blued finish and integral stainless steel choke tubes. Weight: 7.25 to 7.5 lbs. Blue or matte nickel receiver. Select American walnut stock with checkered pistol grip and forend. Imported 1990 to date.
Standard Field model . . . . NiB $804 Ex $644 Gd $438
Standard Trap model . . . . NiB $959 Ex $767 Gd $522
Premium Field model . . . . NiB $869 Ex $695 Gd $473
Premium Trap model . . . . NiB $1153 Ex $922 Gd $627
Sporting Clays model . . . . NiB $972 Ex $778 Gd $528
Standard Trap model . . . . NiB $1153 Ex $922 Gd $627
W/Extra O/U shotgun bbl., add $575
W/Extra O/U combination bbl., add $695
W/Extra O/U rifle bbl., add $995

MODEL 412S/512S OVER/UNDER COMBINATION
Gauge: 12 w/3-inch chamber. Calibers: .222 Rem., .30-06 or .308 Win. Blue or matte nickel receiver, 24-inch chrome-lined bbls. w/extractors and blued finish. Weight: 7.25 to 7.5 lbs. Select American walnut stock with checkered pistol grip and forend. Imported 1990 to date.
Standard Combination model . . . . NiB $966 Ex $772 Gd $525
Premium Combination model . . . . NiB $1024 Ex $819 Gd $557
Extra barrel options. . . . . NiB $1024 Ex $819 Gd $557

TRADITIONS PERFORMANCE FIREARMS — Importers of shotguns produced by Fausti Stefano of Brescia, Italy and ATA Firearms, Turkey.

CLASSIC SERIES, FIELD I O/U
Available in 12, 20, 28 (2 3/4-inch chamber) and .410 gauge, 26- or 28-inch vent rib bbls. W/fixed chokes and extractors. Weight: 6 3/4 to 7 1/4 lbs. Blued finish, silver receiver engraved with game birds. Single, selective trigger. Brass bead front sight. European walnut stock. Overall length 43 to 45 inches. Intro. 2000. ....**$637**

FIELD HUNTER MODEL
Same as Field I except 12 and 20 gauge, 3-inch chambers, screw-in chokes and extractors....................................**$689**

FIELD II MODEL
Same as Field I except with screw-in chokes and automatic ejectors.
....**$813**

FIELD III GOLD MODEL
Same as Field I model except 12 gauge only, high-grade, oil-finish walnut, coin-finish receiver with engraved pheasants and woodcock, deep blue finish on barrels, automatic ejectors and non-slip recoil pad.....................................**$1029**

CLASSIC SERIES O/U SPORTING CLAY III
Available in 12 and 20 gauge, 3-inch chambers, high grade walnut stock, oil-satin finish, palm swell Schnabel forend. 28- and 30-inch bbls. with 3/8-inch top and middle vent rib, red target front bead sight. Automatic ejectors, extended choke tubes. Weight: 8 1/4 lbs. Intro. 2000....................................**$1225**

SPORTING CLAY II MODEL
Same as Sporting Clay III model but with European walnut stocks, cut checkering and extended choke tubes. Overall length: 47 inches. Weight: 7 3/4 lbs......................................**$988**

UPLAND III MODEL
Same as Sporting Clay III model but round pistol grip and Schnabel forend, blued receiver with engraved upland scene, weight: 7 1/2 lbs **$1091**

UPLAND II MODEL
Same as Upland III model except with English walnut straight-grip stock and Schnabel forend, 24- and 26-inch vent rib bbls., floral engraving on blued receiver, automatic ejectors. **$864**

MAG 350 SERIES
TURKEY II O/U
Magnum 3 1/2-inch chambers in 12 gauge only, 24- and 26-inch bbls., screw-in flush fitting chokes: F and XF. Matte finish, engraved receiver, Mossy Oak or Realtree camo. Intro. 2000. ....**$916**

WATERFOWL II MODEL
Same as Turkey II model except with Advantage Wetlands camo stock and barrels, weight: 8 lbs., overall length 45 inches. Waterfowl model has 28-inch bbls. **$916**

MAG HUNTER II
Same as Turkey II model except blued engraved receiver and matte finish walnut stocks, 3 1/2-inch chambers, 28-inch bbls. with screw-in chokes...**$823**

ELITE SERIES DOUBLE-BARREL SHOTGUNS
ELITE FIELD III ST
Checkered English walnut straight stock, splinter forend, fixed chokes. Available in 28 and .410 gauge, 26-inch chrome-lined bbls., Cylinder and Modified chokes. Silver trigger guard and receiver with hand-finished engraving of upland game scenes with gold inlays. Automatic ejectors. Brass front sight bead. Weight: About 6 1/2 lbs. Intro. 2000..............................**$2162**

ELITE HUNTER ST
Same as Elite Field model except 12 and 20 gauge, European walnut stock, beavertail forend, screw-in choke tubes, extractors, three-inch chambers. Blued finish. Vent-rib, tang safety. Weight: 6 1/2 pounds **$1029**

ELITE FIELD I ST
Same as Elite Field III except single trigger, fixed chokes, extractors; European walnut stock. Available in 12, 20, 28 (2 3/4-inch chambers) and .410 gauge; fixed IC/M chokes. Weight: 5 3/4 to 6 1/2 lbs. **$947**

ELITE FIELD I DT
Same as Elite Field I except with double triggers, fixed chokes, extractors. Available in 12, 20, 28 (2 3/4-inch chambers) and .410. Bbls: 26 inches, fixed IC/M chokes. Weight: 5 1/2 to 6 1/4 lbs **$895**

ALS 2100 SEMI-AUTOMATIC SHOTGUNS
FIELD SERIES, WALNUT MODEL
Gas-operated, 12 and 20 gauge, 3-inch chambers, cut-checkered Turkish walnut stock and forend, blued 26- and 28-inch vent rib bbls., multi-choke system, chrome bore lining. Weight: About 6 lbs. Rifled barrel with cantilever mount available Intro. 2001....**$494**

SYNTHETIC STOCK MODEL
Same as the ALS 2100 Walnut model except with synthetic stock, matted finish on receiver and bbl., weight: About 6 lbs **$473**

YOUTH MODEL
Same as ALS 2100 Walnut model except with a shorter walnut stock (length of pull: 13 1/2 inches). Available in 12 or 20 gauge with 24-inch vent rib barrel, weight: 5 1/2 to 6lbs.................**$494**

HUNTER COMBO MODEL
Same as ALS 2100 Walnut model except comes with two bbls. (28-inch vent rib and 24-inch slug), TruGlo adjustable sights and cantilever mount. Available with Turkish walnut or synthetic stock with matte barrel finish. Weight: 6 1/2 lbs.
(Walnut) **$649**
(Synthetic) **$596**

SLUG HUNTER MODEL
Same as ALS 2100 Walnut except with fully-rifled barrel, choice of walnut or synthetic stocks, matte or blue finish; rifle or TruGlo adjustable sights. Weight: About 6 1/4 lbs.................**$565**

TURKEY HUNTER/WATERFOWL MODEL
Same as ALS 2100 Walnut except with synthetic stock, 3-inch chambers, 26-inch vent rib bbl., screw-in chokes, Mossy Oak or Realtree camo stocks.....................................**$535**

HOME SECURITY MODEL
Same as ALS 2100 Walnut but with 20-inch cylinder-bore bbl., synthetic stock, 3-inch chambers, six-shot capacity with 2 3/4-inch shells. Weight: About 6 lbs..............................**$411**

SHOTGUNS

Valmet Model 412 K
O/U Field Shotgun

Ward Western Field Model 50

Ward Western Field Model 52

TRISTAR SPORTING ARMS — North Kansas City, MO

MODEL 1887 LEVER-ACTION REPEATER .... NiB $580 Ex $464 Gd $315
Copy of John Browning's Winchester Model 1887 lever-action shotgun. 12 ga. only. 30-inch bbl. which may be cut down to any desired length of 18 inches or more. Version shown has 20-inch bbl. Imported 1997-98.

MODEL 300 O/U SHOTGUN ..... NiB $418 Ex $335 Gd $228
Similar to the Model 333 except 12 ga. only w/3-inch chambers, 26- or 28-inch vent rib bbls. w/extractors and fixed chokes. Etched receiver w/double triggers and standard walnut stock. Imported 1994-98.

MODEL 311 SIDE-BY-SIDE SHOTGUN
Boxlock action w/underlug and Greener cross bolt. 12 or 20 ga. w/3-inch chambers, 20, 28- or 30-inch bbls. w/choke tubes or fixed chokes (311R). Double triggers. Extractors. Black chrome finish. Checkered Turkish walnut buttstock and forend. Weight: 6.9 to 7.2 lbs. Imported 1994-97.
311 Model (w/extractors and choke tubes) ... NiB $580 Ex $463 Gd $315
311R Model
(w/20-inch bbls. and fixed chokes) .... NiB $418 Ex $335 Gd $228

MODEL 330 O/U SHOTGUN
Similar to the Model 333 except 12 ga. only w/3-inch chambers. 26-, 28- or 30-inch vent rib bbls w/extractors or ejectors and fixed chokes or choke tubes. Etched receiver and standard walnut stock. Imported 1994 to date.
330 model (w/ extractor and fixed chokes) ... NiB $509 Ex $407 Gd $277
330 D model (w/ejectors and choke tubes) ... NiB $676 Ex $541 Gd $368

MODEL 333 O/U SHOTGUN
Boxlock action. 12 or 20 ga. w/3-inch chambers. 26-, 28- or 30-inch vent rib bbls. w/choke tubes. Single selective trigger. Selective automatic ejectors. Engraved receiver w/satin nickel finish. Checkered Turkish fancy walnut buttstock and forend. Weight: 7.5 to 7.75 lbs. Imported 1994 to date..
333 Field model .... NiB $777 Ex $621 Gd $422
333 Sporting Clays model (1994-97) ..... NiB $879 Ex $702 Gd $478
333 TRL Ladies Field model .... NiB $790 Ex $632 Gd $430
333 SCL Ladies Sporting Clays model
(1994-97) .... NiB $898 Ex $719 Gd $488

SHOTGUNS OF ULM — Ulm, West Germany

See listings under Krieghoff.

U.S. REPEATING ARMS CO. — New Haven, Connecticut

See Winchester Shotgun listings.

VALMET OY — Jyväskylä, Finland

NOTE: In 1987, Valmet and Sako merged and the Valmet production facilities were moved to Riihimaki, Finland. In 1989 a joint venture agreement was made with Armi Marocchi, and when production began in Italy, the Valmet name was changed to Tikka (Oy Tikkakoski Ab).

See also Savage Models 330, 333T, 333 and 2400, which were produced by Valmet.

VALMET LION O/U SHOTGUN ... NiB $492 Ex $394 Gd $268
Boxlock. Selective single trigger. Plain extractors. 12 ga. only. Bbls.: 26-inch IC/M; 28-inch M/F, 30-inch M/F, F/F. Weight: About 7 lbs. Checkered pistol-grip stock and forearm. Imported 1947-68.

MODEL 412 K O/U FIELD SHOTGUN .... NiB $830 Ex $664 Gd $452
Hammerless. 12-ga., 3-inch chamber, 36-inch bbl., F/F chokes. American walnut Monte Carlo stock. Made 1982-87.

MODEL 412 K SHOTGUN RIFLE
COMBINATION .... NiB $998 Ex $798 Gd $543
Similar to model 412 K except bottom bbl. chambered for .222 Rem., .223 Rem., .243 Win., .308 Win. or .30-06. 12-ga. shotgun bbl. with IM choke. Monte Carlo American walnut stock, recoil pad.

MODEL 412 KE O/U
FIELD SHOTGUN .... NiB $804 Ex $644 Gd $438
12-ga. chambered for 2.75-inch shells. 26-inch bbl., IC/M chokes; 28-inch bbl., M/F chokes; 12-ga. chambered for 3-inch shells, 30-inch bbl., M/F chokes. 20-ga. (3-inch shells); 26-inch bbl., IC/M chokes; 28-inch bbl., M/ F chokes. American walnut Monte Carlo stock.

Weatherby Model 82
Autoloading Shotgun

MODEL 412 KE SKEET. . . . . NiB $939 Ex $751 Gd $511
Similar to Model 412 K except skeet stock and chokes. 12 and 20 ga. Disc. 1989.

MODEL 412 KE TRAP . . . . NiB $980 Ex $784 Gd $553
Similar to Model 412 K Field except trap stock, recoil pad. 30-inch bbls., IM/F chokes. Disc.1989.

MODEL 412 3-BARREL SET . . . . . . .NiB $2569 EX $2055 GD $1398

MONTGOMERY WARD — Chicago, Illinois
Western Field and Hercules Models

Although they do not correspond to specific models below, the names Western Field and Hercules have been used to designate various Montgomery Ward shotguns at various times.

MODEL 25 SLIDE-ACTION REPEATER . . . . . . NiB $204 Ex $163 Gd $111
Solid frame. 12 ga. only. Two or 5-shot tubular magazine. 28-inch bbl., various chokes. Weight: About 7.5 lbs. Plain pistol-grip stock, grooved slide handle.

MODEL 40 O/U SHOTGUN. . . . . . NiB $702 Ex $562 Gd $381
Hammerless. Boxlock. Double triggers. Gauges: 12, l6, 20, .410. Bbls.: Plain; 26- to 30-inch, various chokes. Checkered pistol-grip stock and forearm.

**MODEL 40N
SLIDE-ACTION REPEATER**. . . . . . . NiB $210 Ex $168 Gd $114
Same general specifications as Model 25.

(WESTERN FIELD) MODEL 50 PUMPGUN . . . NiB $217 Ex $173 Gd $118
Solid frame. Gauges: 12 and 16. Two and 5-shot magazine. 26-, 28- or 30-inch bbl., 48 inches overall w/28-inch bbl. Weight: 7.25 - 7.75 lbs. Metal bead front sight. Walnut stock and grooved forend.

**(WESTERN FIELD) MODEL 52
DOUBLE-BARREL SHOTGUN**. . . . . NiB $247 Ex $198 Gd $135
Hammerless coil-spring action. Gauges: 12, 16, 20 and .410. 26-, 28-, or 30-inch bbls., 42 to 46 inches overall, depending upon bbl. length. Weight: 6 (.410 ga. w/26-inch bbl.) to 7.25 lbs. (12 ga. w/30-inch bbls.), depending upon gauge and bbl. length. Casehardened receiver; blued bbls. Plain buttstock and forend. Made circa 1954.

MODEL 172 BOLT-ACTION SHOTGUN . . . . . . NiB $108 Ex $87 Gd $59
Takedown. Two shot detachable clip magazine.12 ga. 28-inch bbl. with variable choke. Weight: About 7.5 lbs. Monte Carlo stock with recoil pad.

MODEL 550A SLIDE-ACTION REPEATER . . . . NiB $249 Ex $199 Gd $136
Takedown. Gauges: 12, 16, 20, .410. Five shot tubular magazine. Bbls.: Plain, 26- to 30-inch, various chokes. Weight: 6 (.410 ga. w/26-inch bbl.) to 8 lbs. (12 ga. w/30-inch bbls.). Plain pistol-grip stock and grooved slide handle.

**MODEL SB300 DOUBLE-BARREL
SHOTGUN**. . . . . NiB $267 Ex $214 Gd $145
Same general specifications as Model SD52A.

MODEL SB312 DOUBLE-BARREL SHOTGUN. . . NiB $301 Ex $241 Gd $163
Boxlock. Double triggers. Plain extractors. Gauges: 12, 16, 20, .410. Bbls.: 24- to 30-inch. Various chokes. Weight: About 7.5 lbs. in 12 ga.; 6.5 lbs in .410 ga. Checkered pistol-grip stock and forearm.

MODEL SD52A DOUBLE-BARREL SHOTGUN. . . . NiB $223 Ex $178 Gd $121
Boxlock. Double triggers. Plain extractors. Gauges: 12, 16, 20, .410. Bbls.: 26- to 32-inch, various chokes. Plain forend and pistol-grip buttstock. Weight: 6 (.410 ga., 26-inch bbls.) to 7.5 lbs. (12 ga., 32-inch bbls.).

WEATHERBY, INC. — Atascadero, California
(previously South Gate, California)

MODEL 82 AUTOLOADING SHOTGUN
Hammerless, gas-operated. 12 ga. only. Bbls.: 22- to 30-inch, various integral or fixed chokes. Weight: 7.5 lbs. Checkered walnut stock and forearm. Imported 1982-89.
Standard Autoloading Shotgun . . . . NiB $417 Ex $334 Gd $227
**BuckMaster Auto Slug
w/rifle sights (1986-90)** . . . . NiB $424 Ex $339 Gd $231
W/fixed chokes, deduct. $40

MODEL 92 SLIDE-ACTION SHOTGUN
Hammerless, short-stroke action. 12 ga.; 3-inch chamber. Tubular magazine. Bbls.: 22-, 26-, 28-, 30-inch with fixed choke or IMC choke tubes; plain or vent rib with rifle sights. Weight: 7.5 lbs. Engraved, matte black receiver and blued barrel. Checkered high-gloss buttstock and forend. Imported from Japan since 1982.
Standard Model 92 . . . . NiB $333 Ex $266 Gd $180
**BuckMaster Pump Slug
w/rifle sights (intro. 1986)**. . . . . NiB $357 Ex $286 Gd $194
W/fixed chokes, deduct. $25

ATHENA O/U SHOTGUN
Engraved boxlock action with Greener crossbolt and sideplates. Gauges: 12, 20, 28 and .410; 2.75- or 3.5-inch chambers. Bbls.: 26-, 28-, 30- or 32-inch with fixed or IMC Multi-choke tubes. Weight: 6.75 to 7.38 lbs. Single selective trigger. Selective auto ejectors. Top tang safety. Checkered Claro walnut stock and forearm with high-luster finish. Imported 1982 to date.
**Field Model w/IMC multi-choke
(12 or 20 ga.)** . . . . NiB $2155 Ex $1724 Gd $1172
Field Model w/fixed chokes (28 or .410 ga.) . . NiB $2000 Ex $15601 Gd $1089
Skeet Model w/fixed chokes (12 or 20 ga.) . . . . . NiB $1806 Ex $1444 Gd $982
**Skeet Model w/fixed chokes
(28 or .410 ga.)** . . . . NiB $2018 Ex $1614 Gd $1097
Master skeet tube set . . . . NiB $3479 Ex $2783 Gd $1892
Trap Model w/IC tubes . . . . NiB $1846 Ex $1477 Gd $1004
Grade V (1993 to date) . . . . NiB $2259 Ex $1807 Gd $1229

SHOTGUNS

GRADING: **NiB** = New in Box **Ex** = Excellent or NRA 95% **Gd** = Good or NRA 68%

Weatherby Model 92
Slide-Action Shotgun

Weatherby Athena
O/U Shotgun

Weatherby Centurion
Automatic Shotgun

Weatherby Olympian Trap
O/U Shotgun

Weatherby Orion
O/U Shotgun

Weatherby Patrician
Deluxe Grade

Weatherby Regency
Trap Gun

CENTURION AUTOMATIC SHOTGUN
Gas-operated. Takedown. 12 ga. 2.75-inch chamber. Three shot magazine. Bbls.: Vent ribs; 26-inch SK, IC or M 28-inch M or F; 30-inch Full choke. Weight: With 28-inch bbl., 7 lbs. 10.5 oz. Checkered pistol-grip stock and forearm, recoil pad. Made in Japan 1972-81.
Centurion Field grade . . . . NiB $342 Ex $273 Gd $185
Centurion Trap Gun
(30-inch full choke bbl.) . . . . NiB $397 Ex $317 Gd $215
Centurion Deluxe (etched
receiver, fancy wood) . . . . NiB $518 Ex $414 Gd $281

OLYMPIAN O/U SHOTGUN
Gauges: 12 and 20. 2.75- (12 ga.) and 3-inch (20 ga.) chambers. Bbls.: 26-, 28-, 30, and 32-inch. Weight: 6.75 - 8.75 lbs. American walnut stock and forend.
Field
Model . . . . NiB $911 Ex $728 Gd $495
Skeet
Model . . . . NiB $935 Ex $748 Gd $509
Trap
Model . . . . NiB $918 Ex $733 Gd $499

ORION O/U SHOTGUN
Boxlock with Greener crossbolt. Gauges: 12, 20, 28 and .410; 2.75- or 3-inch chambers. Bbls.: 26-, 28, 30-, 32- or 34-inch with fixed or IMC Multi-Choke tubes. Weight: 6.5 to 9 lbs. Single selective trigger. Selective auto ejectors. Top tang safety. Checkered, high-gloss pistol-grip Claro walnut stock and forearm. Finish: Grade I, plain blued receive; Grade II, engraved blued receiver; Grade III, silver gray receiver. Imported 1982 to date.

Orion I Field w/IC (12 or 20 ga.) . . . . NiB $1097 Ex $878 Gd $596
Orion II Field w/IC (12 or 20 ga.) . . . . NiB $1141 Ex $914 Gd $621
Orion II Classic w/IC (12, 20 or 28 ga.) . . . . NiB $1129 Ex $900 Gd $613
Orion II Sporting Clays w/IC (12 ga.) . . . . . . NiB $1313 Ex $1051 Gd $714
Orion III Field w/IC (12 or 20 ga.) . . . . NiB $1182 Ex $946 Gd $643
Orion III Classic w/IC (12 or 20 ga.) . . . . . . NiB $1423 Ex $1139 Gd $775
Orion III English Field w/IC (12 or 20 ga.) . . NiB $1382 Ex $1106 Gd $752
Orion Upland w/IC (12 or 20 ga.) . . . . NiB $1274 Ex $1019 Gd $693
Skeet II w/fixed chokes . . . . NiB $1382 Ex $1106 Gd $752
Super Sporting Clays . . . . NiB $1691 Ex $1353 Gd $921

PATRICIAN SLIDE-ACTION SHOTGUN
Hammerless. Takedown. 12 ga. 2.75-inch chamber. Four shot tubular magazine. Bbls.: Vent rib; 26-inch, SK, IC M; 28-inch, M F; 30-inch, F choke. Weight: With 28-inch bbl., 7 lbs., 7 oz. Checkered pistol-grip stock and slide handle, recoil pad. Made in Japan 1972-82.
Patrician Field grade . . . . NiB $285 Ex $227 Gd $155
Patrician Deluxe (etched receiver,
fancy grade wood) . . . . NiB $333 Ex $266 Gd $181
Patrician Trap Gun (30-inch F choke bbl.) . . . . NiB $303 Ex $242 Gd $164

REGENCY FIELD GRADE O/U SHOTGUN. . . . NiB $1247 Ex $997 Gd $678
Boxlock with sideplates, elaborately engraved. Auto ejectors. Selective single trigger. Gauges: 12, 20. 2.75-inch chamber in 12 ga., 3-inch in 20 ga. Bbls.: Vent rib; 26-inch SK, IC/M, M/F (20 ga. only); 28-inch SK, IC/M, M/F; 30-inch M/F (12 ga only). Weight with 28-inch bbls.: 7 lbs., 6 oz., 12 ga.; 6 lbs., 14 oz., 20 ga. Checkered pistol-grip stock and forearm of fancy walnut. Made in Italy 1965-82.

REGENCY TRAP GUN . . . . NiB $1279 Ex $1023 Gd $696
Similar to Regency Field Grade except has trap-style stock with straight or Monte Carlo comb. Bbls. have vent side ribs and high, wide vent top rib; 30- or 32-inch, M/F, IM/F or F/F chokes. Weight: With 32-inch bbls., 8 lbs. Made in Italy 1965-1982.

WESTERN ARMS CORP. — Ithaca, New York
Division of Ithaca Gun Company

LONG RANGE HAMMERLESS DOUBLE
Boxlock. Plain extractors. Single or double triggers. Gauges: 12, 16, 20, .410. Bbls.: 26- to 32-inch, M/F choke standard. Weight: 7.5 lbs., 12 ga. Plain pistol-grip stock and forend. Made 1929-46.
With double triggers . . . . NiB $315 Ex $252 Gd $171
With single trigger . . . . NiB $402 Ex $321 Gd $218

WESTERN AUTO SHOTGUNS —
Kansas City, Missouri

MODEL 300H SLIDE-ACTION REPEATER . . . . NiB $249 Ex $199 Gd $136
Gauges: 12,16, 20, .410. Four shot tubular magazine. Bbls.: 26- to 30-inch, various chokes. Weight: About 7 lbs. Plain pistol-grip stock, grooved slide handle.

MODEL 310A SLIDE-ACTION REPEATER . . . . NiB $236 Ex $189 Gd $129
Takedown. 12 ga. Five shot tubular magazine. Bbls.: 28- and 30-inch. Weight: About 7.5 lbs. Plain pistol-grip stock.

Westley Richards Deluxe Sidelock

MODEL 310B SLIDE-ACTION REPEATER. . . . NiB $223 Ex $178 Gd $121
Same general specifications as Model 310A except chambered for 16 ga.

MODEL 310C SLIDE-ACTION REPEATER . . . . NiB $249 Ex $199 Gd $136
Same general specifications as Model 310A except chambered for 20 ga.

MODEL 310E SLIDE-ACTION REPEATER. . . . NiB $287 Ex $229 Gd $156
Same general specifications as Model 310A except chambered for .410 bore.

MODEL 325BK BOLT-ACTION REPEATER . . . . . NiB $113 Ex $91 Gd $61
Takedown. Two shot detachable clip magazine. 20 ga. 26-inch bbl. with variable choke. Weight: 6.25 lbs.

WESTERN FIELD SHOTGUNS
See "W" for listings under Montgomery Ward.

WESTLEY RICHARDS & CO., LTD. — Birmingham, England

The Pigeon and Wildfowl gun, available in all of the Westley Richards models except the Ovundo, has the same general specifications as the corresponding standard field gun except has magnum action of extra strength and treble bolting, chambered for 12 gauge only (2.75- or 3-inch); 30-inch full choke barrels standard. Weight: About 8 lbs. The manufacturer warns that 12-gauge magnum shells should not be used in their standard weight double-barrel shotguns.

BEST QUALITY BOXLOCK HAMMERLESS DOUBLE-BARREL SHOTGUN
Boxlock. Hand-detachable locks and hinged cover plate. Selective ejectors. Double triggers or selective single trigger. Gauges: 12, 16, 20. Barrel lengths and boring to order. Weight: 5.5 to 6.25 lbs. depending on ga. and bbl. length. Checkered stock and forend, straight or half-pistol grip. Also supplied in Pigeon and Wildfowl models with same values. Made from 1899 to date.
With double triggers . . . . NiB $21,312 Ex $17,050 Gd $11,594
With selective single trigger . . . . NiB $24,062 Ex $19,250 Gd $13,090

BEST QUALITY SIDELOCK HAMMERLESS DOUBLE-BARREL SHOTGUN
Hand-detachable sidelocks. Selective ejectors. Double triggers or selective single trigger. Gauges: 12, 16, 20, 28, .410. Bbl. lengths and boring to order. Weight: 4.75 to 6.75 lbs., depending on ga. and bbl. length. Checkered stock and forend, straight or half-pistol grip. Also supplied in Pigeon and Wildfowl models with same values. Currently manufactured.
With double triggers. . . . . NiB $25,031 Ex $20,225 Gd $14,073
With selective single trigger . . . . NiB $27,250 Ex $22,000 Gd $15,280

SHOTGUNS

Westley Richards
Best Quality Sidelock

Westley Richards
Deluxe Boxlock

Westley Richards
Model E

Winchester Model 12 Classic
Limited Edition Grade I

Winchester Model 12
Field Gun — 1972 Type

MODEL DELUXE BOX LOCK
HAMMERLESS DOUBLE-BARREL SHOTGUN
Same general specifications as standard Best Quality gun except higher quality throughout. Has Westley Richards top-projection and treble-bite lever-work, hand-detachable locks. Also supplied in Pigeon and Wildfowl models with same values. Currently manufactured.
With double triggers .... NiB $11,188 Ex $8950 Gd $6086
With selective
single trigger .... NiB $30,000 Ex $28,000 Gd $12,000

MODEL DELUXE SIDELOCK
Same as Best Quality Sidelock except higher grade engraving and wood. Currently manufactured.
With double triggers .... NiB $25,000 Ex $20,000 Gd $13,600
With single trigger ...... NiB $30,000 Ex $24,000 Gd $16,320

MODEL E HAMMERLESS DOUBLE
Anson & Deeley-type boxlock action. Selective ejector or non-ejector. Double triggers. Gauges: 12, 16, 20. Barrel lengths and boring to order. Weight: 5.5 to 7.25 lbs. depending on type, ga. and bbl. length. Checkered stock and forend, straight or half-pistol grip. Also supplied in Pigeon and Wildfowl models with same values. Currently manufactured.
Ejector model .... NiB $4744 Ex $3795 Gd $2581
Non-ejector model .... NiB $4125 Ex $3300 Gd $2244

OVUNDO (O/U) .... NiB $18,744 Ex $14,995 Gd $10,197
Hammerless. Boxlock. Hand-detachable locks. Dummy sideplates. Selective ejectors. Selective single trigger. 12 ga. Barrel lengths and boring to order. Checkered stock/forend, straight or half-pistol grip. Mfd. before WW II.

TED WILLIAMS SHOTGUNS

See Sears shotguns.

WINCHESTER SHOTGUNS —
New Haven, Connecticut

Formerly Winchester Repeating Arms Co., now mfd. by Winchester-Western Div., Olin Corp., and by U.S. Repeating Arms Company. In 1999, production rights were acquired by Browning Arms.

MODEL 12 CLASSIC LIMITED EDITION
Gauge: 20; 2.75-inch chamber. Bbl.: 26-inch vent rib; IC. Weight: 7 lbs. Checkered walnut buttstock and forend. Polished blue finish (Grade I) or engraved with gold inlays (Grade IV). Made 1993 to 1995.
Grade I (4000) .... NiB $895 Ex $716 Gd $487
Grade IV (1000) .... NiB $1410 Ex $1128 Gd $767

Winchester Model 12
Pigeon Grade

Winchester Model 12
Standard

Winchester Model 12
Trap w/Monte Carlo Stock

Winchester Model 12
12-4 Engraving

MODEL 12 FEATHERWEIGHT.....NiB $521 Ex $417 Gd $283
Same as Model 12 Standard w/plain barrel except has alloy trigger guard. Modified takedown w/redesigned magazine tube, cap and slide handle. 12 ga. only. Bbls.: 26-inch IC; 28-inch M or F; 30-inch F choke. Serial numbers with "F" prefix. Weight: About 6.75 lbs. Made 1959-62.

MODEL 12 FIELD GUN, 1972 TYPE......NiB $638 Ex $510 Gd $346
Same general specifications as Standard Model 12 but 12 ga. only, 26- 28- or 30-inch vent rib bbl., standard chokes. Engine-turned bolt and carrier. Hand-checkered stock/slide handle of semifancy walnut. Made 1972-75.

MODEL 12 HEAVY DUCK GUN
Same general specifications as Standard Grade except 12 ga. only chambered for 3-inch shells. 30- or 32-inch plain, solid or vent rib bbl. w/full choke only. Three shot magazine. Checkered slide handle and pistol-grip walnut buttstock w/recoil pad. Weight: 8.5 to 8.75 lbs. Made 1935-63.
Heavy Duck Gun, plain bbl. ....NiB $850 Ex $680 Gd $462
Heavy Duck Gun, solid
rib (disc. 1959).........................NiB $1281 Ex $1025 Gd $697
Heavy Duck Gun, vent rib
(Special order only) ....NiB $1668 Ex $1334 Gd $907

MODEL 12 PIGEON GRADE
Deluxe versions of the regular Model 12 Standard or Field Gun, Duck Gun, Skeet Gun and Trap Gun made on special order. This grade has finer finish throughout, hand-smoothed action, engine-

(cont'd.) MODEL 12 PIGEON GRADE
turned breech bolt and carrier, stock and extension slide handle of high grade walnut, fancy checkering, stock dimensions to individual specifications. Engraving and carving available at extra cost ranging from about $135 to over $1000. Disc. 1965.
Field Gun, plain bbl. ....NiB $1771 Ex $1416 Gd $963
Field Gun, vent rib....................NiB $2159 Ex $1727 Gd $1174
Skeet Gun, matted rib ....NiB $1976 Ex $1580 Gd $1074
Skeet Gun, vent rib ....NiB $2478 Ex $1983 Gd $1348
Skeet Gun, Cutts Compensator ....NiB $1451 Ex $1161 Gd $789
Trap Gun, matted rib...................NiB $2116 Ex $1693 Gd $1152
Trap Gun, vent rib ....NiB $2337 Ex $1869 Gd $1271
16 ga. (Field), add 20%
16 ga. (Skeet), add 90%
20 ga. (Field), add 25%
20 ga. (Skeet), add 45%
28 ga. (Skeet), add 350%

MODEL 12 RIOT GUN ....NiB $804 Ex $644 Gd $438
Same general specifications as plain barrel Model 12 Standard except has 20-inch cylinder bore bbl.,12 gauge only. Made 1918-1963.

MODEL 12 SKEET GUN ....NiB $1095 Ex $875 Gd $595
Gauges: 12, 16, 20, 28. Five shot tubular magazine. 26-inch matted rib bbl., SK choke. Weight: About 7.75 lbs., 12 ga.; 6.75 lbs., other gauges. Bradley red or ivory bead front sight. Winchester 94B middle sight. Checkered pistol-grip stock and extension slide handle. Disc. after WWII.

Winchester Model 21
Custom Grade

Winchester Model 21
Pigeon Grade

MODEL 12 SKEET GUN, CUTTS COMPENSATOR .... NiB $918 Ex $733 Gd $498
Same general specifications as standard Model 12 Skeet Gun except has plain bbl. fitted with Cutts Compensator, 26 inches overall. Disc. 1954.

MODEL 12 SKEET GUN, PLAIN-BARREL ..... NiB $850 Ex $680 Gd $462
Same general specifications as standard Model 12 Skeet except w/no rib.

MODEL 12 SKEET GUN, VENT RIB .... NiB $1481 Ex $1184 Gd $805
Same general specifications as standard Model 12 Skeet Gun except has 26-inch bbl. with vent rib, 12 and 20 ga. Disc. in 1965.

MODEL 12 SKEET GUN, 1972 TYPE........ NiB $933 Ex $747 Gd $508
Same gen. specifications as Standard Model 12 but 12 ga. only. 26-inch vent rib bbl., SK choke. Engine-turned bolt and carrier. Hand-checkered skeet-style stock and slide handle of choice walnut, recoil pad. Made 1972-75.

MODEL 12 STANDARD GR., MATTED RIB..... NiB $1174 Ex $939 Gd $656
Same general specifications as plain bbl. Model 12 Standard except has solid raised matted rib. Disc. after World War II.

MODEL 12 STANDARD GR., VENT RIB.... NiB $1327 Ex $1062 Gd $724
Same general specifications as plain barrel Model 12 Standard except has vent rib. 26.75- or 30-inch bbl.,12 ga. only. Disc. after World War II.

MODEL 12 STANDARD SLIDE-ACTION REPEATER
Hammerless. Takedown. Gauges: 12, 16, 20, 28. Six shell tubular magazine. Plain bbl. Lengths: 26- to 32-inches; choked F to Cyl. Weight: About 7.5 lbs., 12 ga. 30-inch, 6.5 lbs. in other ga. with 28-inch bbl. Plain pistol-grip stock, grooved slide handle. Made 1912-64.
12 ga., 28-inch bbl. (full choke) .... NiB $766 Ex $613 Gd $417
16 ga. .... NiB $676 Ex $541 Gd $368
20 ga. .... NiB $895 Ex $716 Gd $487
28 ga. .... NiB $3856 Ex $3085 Gd $2098

MODEL 12 SUPER PIGEON GRADE . NiB $3084 Ex $2467 Gd $1678
Custom version of Model 12 with same general specifications as standard models. 12 ga. only. 26-, 28- or 30-inch vent-rib bbl., any standard choke. Engraved receiver. Hand-smoothed and fitted action. Full fancy walnut stock and forearm made to individual order. Made 1965-72.

MODEL 12 TRAP GUN
Same general specifications as Standard Model 12 except has straighter stock, checkered pistol grip and extension slide handle, recoil pad, 30-inch matted-rib bbl., F choke, 12 ga. only. Disc. after World War II; vent rib model disc. 1965.
Matted rib bbl. .... NiB $985 Ex $788 Gd $536
With straight stock, vent rib ...... NiB $978 Ex $782 Gd $531
With Monte Carlo stock, vent rib .... NiB $1281 Ex $1025 Gd $697

MODEL 12 TRAP GUN, 1972 TYPE .... NiB $895 Ex $716 Gd $487

(cont'd.) MODEL 12 TRAP GUN, 1972 TYPE
Same general specifications as Standard Model 12 but 12 gauge only. 30-inch vent-rib bbl., F choke. Engine-turned bolt and carrier. Hand-checkered trap-style stock (straight or Monte Carlo comb) and slide handle of select walnut, recoil pad. Intro. in 1972. Disc.

MODEL 20 SINGLE-SHOT HAMMER GUN .... NiB $723 Ex $579 Gd $393
Takedown. .410 bore. 2.5-inch chamber. 26-inch bbl., F choke. Checkered pistol-grip stock and forearm. Weight: About 6 lbs. Made 1919-24.

ORIGINAL MODEL 21 DOUBLE-BARREL SHOTGUNS (ORIGINAL PRODUCTION SERIES - 1930 TO 1959)
Hammerless. Boxlock. Automatic safety. Double triggers or selective single trigger, selective or non-selective ejection (all postwar Model 21 shotguns have selective single trigger and selective ejection). Gauges: 12, 16, 20, 28 and .410 bore. Bbls.: Raised matted rib or vent rib; 26-, 28-, 30-, 32-inch, the latter in 12 ga. only; F, IM, M, IC, SK chokes. Weight: 7.5 lbs., 12 ga. w/30-inch bbl.; about 6.5 lbs. 16 or 20 ga. w/28-inch bbl. Checkered pistol- or straight-grip stock, regular or beavertail forend. Made 1930-59.

Standard grade, 12 ga. .... NiB $4886 Ex $3909 Gd $2658
Standard grade, 16 ga. .... NiB $6151 Ex $4920 Gd $3345
Standard grade, 20 ga. .... NiB $6367 Ex $5093 Gd $3464
Tournament grade, 12 ga.
(1933-34)........................ NiB $5144 Ex $4115 Gd $2798
Tournament grade, 16 ga.
(1933-34)........................ NiB $6374 Ex $5098 Gd $3467
Tournament grade, 20 ga.
(1933-34)........................ NiB $7590 Ex $6072 Gd $4129
Trap grade, 12 ga. (1940-59) ..... NiB $4957 Ex $3965 Gd $2697
Trap grade, 16 ga. (1940-59) ..... NiB $5556 Ex $4444 Gd $3022
Trap grade, 20 ga. (1940-59) ..... NiB $6895 Ex $5516 Gd $3750
Skeet grade, 12 ga. (1936-59)..... NiB $4886 Ex $3909 Gd $2658
Skeet grade, 16 ga. (1936-59)..... NiB $5620 Ex $4496 Gd $3057
Skeet grade, 20 ga. (1936-59)..... NiB $6547 Ex $5238 Gd $3561
Duck Gun, 12 ga. 3-inch (1940-52) ... NiB $5401 Ex $4321 Gd $2939
Magnum Gun, 12 ga. 3-inch
(1953-59)........................ NiB $5215 Ex $4171 Gd $2837
Magnum Gun, 20 ga. 3-inch
(1953-59)........................ NiB $6374 Ex $5098 Gd $3467
Cust. built/deluxe gr.,
12 ga.(1933-59)............. NiB $7719 Ex $6175 Gd $4199
Cust. built/deluxe gr.,
16 ga. (1933-59) .... NiB $8949 Ex $7158 Gd $4868
Cust. built/deluxe gr.,
20 ga. (1933-59) .... NiB $9850 Ex $7879 Gd $5358
Custom built/deluxe grade, 28 ga.(1933-59) .... Very Rare*
Custom built/deluxe grade, .410 1933-59) .... Very Rare*
*Fewer than 100 sm. bore models (28 ga. and .410) were built, which precludes accurate pricing, but projected values could exceed $30,000. Such rare specimens should be authenticated by factory letter and/or independent appraisals.

Winchester Model 23

Winchester Model 24

Winchester Model 25

Winchester Model 36

Winchester Model 37

Winchester Model 37A

Winchester Model 37A Youth

SHOTGUNS

(cont'd) **ORIGINAL MODEL 21**

W/vent rib on 12 ga. models, add $650
W/vent rib on 16 ga. models, add $1500
W/vent rib on 20 ga. models, add $1000
W/double triggers ans extractors, deduct 30%
W/double trigger, selective ejection, deduct 20%
For Custom Engraving from this period:
No. 1 Pattern, add 25%
No. 2 Pattern, add 35%
No. 3 Pattern, add 50%
No. 4 Pattern, add 35%
No. 5 Pattern, add 65%

(cont'd) **ORIGINAL MODEL 21**
No. 6 Pattern, add 75%

**MODEL 21 CUSTOM, PIGEON, GRAND AMERICAN
(CUSTOM SHOP SERIES - PRODUCTION 1959 TO 1981)**
Since 1959 the Model 21 has been offered through the Custom Shop in deluxe models. (Custom, Pigeon, Grand American) on special order. General specifications same as for Model 21 standard models except these custom guns have full fancy American walnut stock and forearm with fancy checkering, finely polished and hand-smoothed working parts, etc.; engraving inlays, carved stocks and other extras are available at additional cost. Made 1959-81.

Winchester
Model 40 Skeet

Winchester
Model 41 Deluxe

(cont'd) **MODEL 21 CUSTOM, PIGEON,**
Custom grade, 12 ga.................... NiB $9721 Ex $7776 Gd $5288
Custom grade, 16 ga................ NiB $14,806 Ex $11,845 Gd $8055
Custom grade, 20 ga.............. NiB $13,198 Ex $10,557 Gd $7179
Pigeon grade, 12 ga. .... NiB $15,129 Ex $12,102 Gd $8230
Pigeon grade, 16 ga. .... NiB $21,244 Ex $16,995 Gd $11,557
Pigeon grade, 20 ga. .... NiB $19,635 Ex $15,707 Gd $10,681
Grand American, 12 ga. .... NiB $23,111 Ex $18,488 Gd $12,572
Grand American, 16 ga. .... NiB $36,694 Ex $29,355 Gd $19,961
Grand American, 20 ga. .... NiB $27,360 Ex $29,355 Gd $14,883
Grand American 3-barrel Set .... $23,175 to $39,140
Small Bore Models
(28 ga. And .410) .... Very Rare*
*Fewer than 20 Small Bore models (28 ga. and .410) were built during this period, which precludes accurate pricing, but projected values could exceed $35,000. Such rare specimens should be authenticated by factory letter and/or independent appraisals.
For Custom Shop Engraving from this period:
#1 Pattern, add 10%
#2 Pattern, add 15%
#3 Pattern, add 25%
#4 Pattern, add 35%
#5 Pattern, add 45%
#6 Pattern, add 50%

MODEL 21 - U.S.R.A. CUSTOM-BUILT SERIES (CUSTOM SHOP PRODUCTION 1982 TO DATE)
In 1982, the individual model designations for the Model 21 were changed again when U. S. Repeating Arms Company assumed production. The new model nomenclature for the Custom/Built catagory, includes: Standard Custom, Special Custom and Grand American — all of which are available on special order through the Custom Shop. General specifications remained the same on these consolidated model variations and included the addition of a Small Bore 2-Barrel Set (28/.410) and a 3-Barrel Set (20/28/.410). Made 1982 to date.
Custom Built -
Standard Custom...................... NiB $6245 Ex $4995 Gd $3397
Custom Built -
Special Custom .... NiB $7404 Ex $5922 Gd $4027
Custom Built - Grand American ...... NiB $13,519 Ex $10,815 Gd $7354
Custom Built - Grand
American 2-barrel set............. NiB $44,999 Ex $35,998 Gd $24,479
Custom Built - Grand
American 3-barrel set............. NiB $67,594 Ex $54,075 Gd $36,771
The values shown above represent the basic model in each catagory. Since many customers took advantage of the custom built options, individual gun appointments vary and values will need to be adjusted accordingly. For this reason, individual appraisals should be obtained on all subject firearms.

MODEL 23 SIDE-BY-SIDE SHOTGUN
Boxlock. Single trigger. Automatic safety. Gauges: 12, 20, 28, .410. Bbls.: 25.5-, 26-, 28-inch with fixed chokes or Winchoke tubes. Weight: 5.88 to 7 lbs. Checkered American walnut buttstock and forend. Made in 1979 for Olin at its Olin-Kodensha facility, Japan.
Classic 23 — Gold inlay, engraved .... NiB $1951 Ex $1515 Gd $1030
Custom 23 — Plain receiver,
Winchoke system .... NiB $1153 Ex $922 Gd $627
Heavy Duck 23 — Standard .... NiB $1887 Ex $14514 Gd $1029
Lightweight 23 — Classic .... NiB $1877 Ex $1502 Gd $1020
Light Duck 23 — Standard .... NiB $1777 Ex $1421 Gd $966
Light Duck 23 — 12 ga. Golden Quail ... NiB $2086 Ex $1669 Gd $1134
Light Duck 23 — .410 Golden Quail ..... NiB $3631 Ex $2905 Gd $1975
Custom Set 23 — 20 & 28 ga.......... NiB $5708 Ex $4567 Gd $3105

MODEL 24 HAMMERLESS DOUBLE
Boxlock. Double triggers. Plain extractors. Auto safety. Gauges: 12, 16, 20. Bbls.: 26-inch IC/M; 28-inch M/F (also IC/M in 12 ga. only); 30-inch M and F in 12 ga. only. Weight: About 7.5 lbs., 12 ga. Metal bead front sight. Plain pistol-grip stock, semi-beavertail forearm. Made 1939-57.
Model 24, 12 ga. .... NiB $668 Ex $535 Gd $364
Model 24, 16 ga. .... NiB $744 Ex $594 Gd $404
Model 24, 20 ga. .... NiB $1081 Ex $644 Gd $438

MODEL 25 RIOT GUN ..... NiB $530 Ex $424 Gd $288
Same as Model 25 Standard except has 20-inch cylinder bore bbl., 12 ga. only. Made 1949-55.

MODEL 25 SLIDE-ACTION REPEATER....... NiB $483 Ex $386 Gd $263
Hammerless. Solid frame. 12 ga. only. Four shell tubular magazine. 28-in. Plain bbl.; IC, M or F choke. Weight: About 7.5 lbs. Metal bead front sight. Plain pistol-grip stock, grooved slide handle. Made 1949-55.

MODEL 36 SINGLE-SHOT BOLT ACTION.... NiB $580 Ex $463 Gd $315
Takedown. Uses 9mm Short or Long shot or ball cartridges interchangeably. 18-inch bbl. Plain stock. Weight: About 3 lbs. Made 1920-27.

MODEL 37 SINGLE-SHOT SHOTGUN
Semi-hammerless. Auto ejection. Takedown. Gauges: 12, 16, 20, 28, .410. Bbl. lengths: 28-, 30-, 32-inch in all gauges except .410; 26- or 28-inch in .410; all barrels plain with F choke. Weight: About 6.5 pounds, 12 ga. Made 1937-63.
12 ga................................. NiB $313 Ex $250 Gd $170
16 ga................................. NiB $251 Ex $201 Gd $137
20 ga................................. NiB $360 Ex $288 Gd $196
20 ga. (Youth w/red dot indicator) .... NiB $435 Ex $367 Gd $249
28 ga. (red letter only) .... NiB $1494 Ex $1195 Gd $812
410 ga. .... NiB $428 Ex $342 Gd $233
Other "Red Letter" models, add 20%
W/32-inch bbl., add 15%

Winchester Model 42
Classic Limited Edition

Winchester Model 42
Standard

MODEL 37A SINGLE SHOT SHOTGUN
Similar to Model 370 except has engraved receiver and gold trigger, checkered pistol-grip stock, fluted forearm; 16 ga. available with 30-inch bbl. only. Made 1973-80.

Model 37A, 12, 16, or 20 ga. . . . . . . NiB $161 Ex $129 Gd $88
Model 37A, 28 ga. . . . . NiB $238 Ex $191 Gd $130
Model 37A, .410 ga. . . . . NiB $289 Ex $232 Gd $158
W/32-inch bbl., add $20

MODEL 37A YOUTH. . . . . NiB $174 Ex $139 Gd $95
Similar to Model 370 Youth except has engraved receiver and gold trigger, checkered pistol-grip stock, fluted forearm. Made 1973-80.

MODEL 40 STANDARD AUTOLOADER. . NiB $743 Ex $594 Gd $404
Streamlined receiver. Hammerless. Takedown. 12 ga. only. Four shot tubular magazine. 28- or 30-inch bbl.; M or F choke. Weight: About 8 lbs. Bead sight on ramp. Plain pistol-grip stock, semi-beavertail forearm. Made 1940-41.

MODEL 40 SKEET GUN . . . . NiB $966 Ex $772 Gd $525
Same general specifications as Model 40 Standard except has 24-inch plain bbl. w/Cutts Compensator and screw-in choke tube, checkered forearm and pistol grip, grip cap. Made 1940-1941.

MODEL 41 SINGLE-SHOT BOLT ACTION
Takedown. .410 bore. 2.5-inch chamber (chambered for 3-inch shells after 1932). 24-inch bbl., F choke. Plain straight stock standard. Also made in deluxe version. Made 1920-34.

Standard model . . . . NiB $642 Ex $513 Gd $349
Deluxe model . . . . NiB $772 Ex $618 Gd $420

MODEL 42 CLASSIC LTD. EDITION. NiB $1610 Ex $1287 Gd $875
Gauge: .410 with 2.75-inch chamber. Bbl.: 26-inch vent rib; F choke. Weight: 7 lbs. Checkered walnut buttstock and forend. Engraved blue with gold inlays. Limited production of 850. Made 1993.

MODEL 42 DELUXE . . . . NiB $5767 Ex $4613 Gd $3137
Same general specifications as the Model 42 Trap Grade except available w/vent rib after 1955. Finer finish throughout w/hand-smoothed action, engine-turned breech bolt and carrier, stock and extension slide handle of high grade walnut, fancy checkering, stock dimensions to individual specifications. Engraving and carving were offered at extra cost. Made 1940-63. Note: Exercise caution on VR models not marked "DELUXE" on the bottom of the receiver. A factory letter will insure that the rib was installed during the initial manufacturing process. Unfortunately, factory authentication is not always possible due to missing or destroyed records. To further complicate this matter, not all VR ribs were installed by Winchester. From 1955-63, both Deluxe and Skeet Grade models were available with Simmons style ribs. After-market rib installations are common.

MODEL 42 PIGEON GRADE
This higher-grade designation is similar to the Deluxe grade and is available in all configurations. May be identified by engraved Pigeon located at the base of the magazine tube. Most production occurred in the late 1940's. *NOTE: To determine the value of any Model 42 Pigeon Grade, add 50 % to value listed under the specified Model 42 configuration.*

MODEL 42 SKEET GUN
Same general specifications as Model 42 Standard except has checkered straight or pistol-grip stock and extension slide handle, 26- or 28-inch plain, solid-rib or vent-rib bbl. May be choked F., Mod., Imp. Cyl. or Skeet. Note: Some Model 42 Skeet Guns are chambered for 2.5-inch shells only. Made 1933-63.

Model 42 Skeet
w/plain bbl. . . . . NiB $2440 Ex $1952 Gd $1327
Model 42 Skeet
w/solid rib . . . . NiB $3212 Ex $2570 Gd $1747
Model 42 Skeet
w/vent rib . . . . NiB $4313 Ex $3450 Gd $2346
W/2.5-inch
chamber, add 35%

MODEL 42 TRAP GRADE
This higher grade designation was available in both field and skeet configurations and is fitted w/deluxe wood w/trap grade checkering pattern and marked "TRAP" on bottom of receiver. Made 1934-39. Superseded by the Deluxe model in 1940.

Model 42 Trap grade
w/plain bbl. . . . . NiB $8755 Ex $7210 Gd $3605
Model 42 Trap grade
w/solid rib . . . . NiB $5665 Ex $4635 Gd $2060
Model 42 Trap grain
w/vent rib . . . . NiB $6695 Ex $5150 Gd $2317

MODEL 42 STANDARD GRADE
Hammerless. Takedown. .410 bore (3- or 2.5-inch shell). Tubular magazine holds five 3-inch or six 2.5-inch shells. 26- or 28-inch plain or solid-rib bbl.; cylinder bore, M or F choke. Weight: 5.8 to 6.5 lbs. Plain pistol-grip stock; grooved slide handle. Made 1933-63.

Model 42 Standard w/plain bbl. . NiB $1281 Ex $1025 Gd $697
Model 42 Standard w/solid rib . . . . NiB $2008 Ex $1854 Gd $1442

MODEL 50 FIELD GUN, VENT RIB . . . NiB $509 Ex $407 Gd $277
Same as Model 50 Standard except has vent rib.

MODEL 50 SKEET GUN . . . . NiB $581 Ex $465 Gd $315
Same as Model 50 Standard except has 26-inch vent-rib bbl. with SK choke, skeet-style stock of select walnut.

Winchester Model 50 Skeet

Winchester Model 97 Riot Gun

Winchester Model 101

MODEL 50 STANDARD GRADE . . . NiB $452 Ex $362 Gd $246
Non-recoiling bbl. and independent chamber. Gauges: 12 and 20. Two shot tubular magazine. Bbl.: 12 ga. — 26-, 28-, 30-inch; 20 ga. — 26-, 28-inch; IC, SK, M, F choke. Checkered pistol-grip stock and forearm. Weight: About 7.75 lbs. Made 1954-61.

MODEL 50 TRAP GUN . . . . NiB $772 Ex $592 Gd $360
Same as Model 50 Standard except 12 ga. only, has 30-inch vent-rib bbl. with F choke, Monte Carlo stock of select walnut.

MODEL 59 AUTO-LOADING SHOTGUN . . . NiB $609 Ex $486 Gd $331
Gauge: 12. Magazine holds two shells. Alloy receiver. Win-Lite steel and fiberglass bbl.: 26-inch IC, 28-inch M or F choke, 30-inch F choke; also furnished with 26-inch bbl. with Versalite choke (interchangeable F, M, IC tubes; one supplied with gun). Weight: About 6.5 lbs. Checkered pistol-grip stock and forearm. Made 1959-65.

MODEL 97 BUSH GUN
Takedown or solid frame. Same general specifications as standard Model 97 except w/26-inch cylinder bore bbl. Made 1897-1931.
Model 97 Riot Gun w/solid frame . . . NiB $122 Ex $98 Gd $67
Model 97 Riot Gun takedown . . . . NiB $1062 Ex $850 Gd $578

MODEL 97 RIOT GUN
Takedown or solid frame. Same general specifications as standard Model 97 except 12 ga. only, 20-inch cylinder bore bbl. Made 1898-1935.
Model 97 Riot Gun w/solid frame . . . NiB $1224 Ex $978 Gd $665
Model 97 Riot Gun takedown . . . . NiB $1062 Ex $850 Gd $578

MODEL 97 TRAP, TOURNAMENT AND PIGEON
These higher grade models offer higher overall quality than the standard grade. Made 1897-39.
Standard Trap grade . . . . NiB $1449 Ex $1159 Gd $788
Special Trap grade . . . . NiB $1564 Ex $1313 Gd $893
Tournament grade (Black Diamond) . . . . NiB $2559 Ex $2047 Gd $1392
Pigeon grade . . . . NiB $4957 Ex $3965 Gd $2696

MODEL 97 TRENCH GUN . . . . NiB $2054 Ex $1643 Gd $1118
Solid frame. Same as Model 97 Riot Gun except has handguard and

(cont'd.) MODEL 97 TRENCH GUN
is equipped with a bayonet. World War I government issue, 1917-18.
Model 97 Trench Gun
w/solid frame . . . . NiB $3013 Ex $2410 Gd $1639
Model 97 Trench Gun takedown. . . . NiB $1274 Ex $1020 Gd $693

MODEL 97 SLIDE-ACTION REPEATER
Standard Grade. Takedown or solid frame. Gauges: 12 and 16. 5-shell tubular magazine. Bbl.: Plain; 26 to 32 inches, the latter in 12 ga. only; choked F to Cyl. Weight: About 7.75 lbs. (12 ga. w/28-inch barrel). Plain pistol-grip stock, grooved slide handle. Made 1897-1957.
Model 97, 12 ga. w/solid frame . . . NiB $851 Ex $681 Gd $462
Model 97, 16 ga. w/solid frame . . NiB $1110 Ex $888 Gd $604
Model 97, 12 ga. takedown. . . . . . NiB $881 Ex $705 Gd $479
Model 97, 16 ga. takedown. . . . . . NiB $1147 Ex $918 Gd $624

NOTE: All Winchester Model 101s are mfd. for Olin Corp. at its Olin-Kodensha facility in Tochigi, Japan. Production for Olin Corp. stopped in Nov. 1987. Importation of Model 101s was continued by Classic Doubles under that logo until 1990. See separate heading for additional data.

MODEL 101 DIAMOND
GRADE TARGET . . . . NiB $1706 Ex $1365 Gd $928
Similar to Model 101 Standard except silvered frame and Winchoke interchangeable choke tubes. Made 1981-90.

MODEL 101 FIELD GUN O/U
Boxlock. Engraved receiver. Auto ejectors. Single selective trigger. Combination bbl. selector and safety. Gauges: 12 and 28, 2.75-inch chambers; 20 and .410, 3-inch chambers. Vent rib bbls.: 30-(12 ga. only) and 26.5-inch, IC/M. Weight: 6.25 to 7.75 lbs. depending on gauge and bbl. length. Hand-checkered French walnut and forearm. Made 1963-81. Gauges other than 12 introduced 1966.
12 and 20 ga. . . . . NiB $966 Ex $772 Gd $525
28 and .410 ga. . . . . NiB $1191 Ex $953 Gd $648
12 and 20 ga. mag. . . . . NiB $1024 Ex $819 Gd $557

Winchester Model 370

Winchester Model 1001
Sporting Clays

Winchester Model 1200
Field Gun

Winchester Model 1200
Field Gun w/Vent Rib

MODEL 101 QUAIL SPECIAL O/U
Same specifications as small-frame Model 101 except in 28 and
.410 ga. with 3-inch chambers. 25.5-inch bbls. with choke tubes
(28 ga.) or M/F chokes (.410). Imported from Japan in 1984-87.
12 ga. . . . . **NiB $2156 Ex $1724 Gd $1173**
20 ga. . . . . **NiB $2562 Ex $2049 Gd $1394**
28 ga. . . . . **NiB $3177 Ex $2541 Gd $1778**
.410 ga. . . . . **NiB $2231 Ex $1784 Gd $1213**

MODEL 101 SHOTGUN/RIFLE
COMBINATION GUN . . . . **NiB $2290 Ex $1832 Gd $1246**
12-ga. Winchoke bbl. on top and rifle bbl. chambered for .30-06 on
bottom (over/under). 25-inch bbls. Engraved receiver. Hand checkered walnut stock and forend. Weight: 8.5 lbs. Mfd. for Olin Corp.
in Japan.

MODEL 370
SINGLE-SHOT SHOTGUN . . . . **NiB $121 Ex $97 Gd $66**
Visible hammer. Auto ejector. Takedown. Gauges: 12, 16, 20, 28,
.410. 2.75-inch chambers in 16 and 28 ga., 3-inch in other ga.
Bbls.: 12 ga., 30-, 32- or 36-inch,16 ga; 30- or 32-inch; 20 and 28
ga., 28-inch; .410 bore, 26-inch, all F choke. Weight: 5.5-6.25 lbs.
Plain pistol-grip stock and forearm. Made 1968-73.

MODEL 370 YOUTH
Same as standard Model 370 except has 26-inch bbl. and 12.5-inch
stock with recoil pad; 20 gauge with IM choke, .410 bore with F
choke. Made 1968-73.
Model 370, 12,
16, or 20 ga. . . . . **NiB $140 Ex $112 Gd $75**
Model 37A, 28 ga. . . . . **NiB $201 Ex $160 Gd $109**
Model 37A, .410 ga. . . . . **NiB $166 Ex $134 Gd $91**

MODEL 1001 O/U SHOTGUN
Boxlock. 12 ga., 2.75- or 3-inch chambers. Bbls.: 28- or 30-inch
vent rib; WinPlus choke tubes. Weight: 7-7.75 lbs. Checkered wal-
nut buttstock and forend. Blued finish with scroll engraved receiver.
Made 1993 to date.
Field model
(28-inch bbl., 3-inch) . . . . **NiB $972 Ex $778 Gd $528**
Sporting
Clays . . . . **NiB $1095 Ex $875 Gd $595**
Sporting
Clays Lite . . . . **NiB $1008 Ex $806 Gd $548**

MODEL 1200
DEER GUN . . . . **NiB $251 Ex $201 Gd $1**
Same as standard Model 1200, except has special 22-inch bbl. with
rifle-type sights, for rifled slug or buckshot; 12 ga. only. Weight: 6.5
lbs. Made 1965-74.

MODEL 1200 DEFENDER SERIES
SLIDE-ACTION SECURITY SHOTGUNS
Hammerless. 12 ga. w/3-inch chamber. 18-inch bbl. w/cylin-
der bore and metal front bead or rifle sights. Four or 7-shot
magazine. Weight: 5.5 to 6.75 lbs. 25.6 inches (PG Model) or
38.6 inches overall. Matte blue finish. Synthetic pistol grip or
walnut finished hardwood buttstock w/grooved synthetic or
hardwood slide handle. NOTE: Even though the 1200 series
was introduced in 1964 and was supplanted by the Model
1300 in 1978, the Security series (including the Defender
model) was marketed under 1200 series alpha-numeric product codes (G1200DM2R) until 1989. In 1990, the same
Defender model was marketed under a 4-digit code (7715) and
was then advertised in the 1300 series.

**Winchester Model 1300
Deer Series — Black Shadow
Synthetic Stock**

**Winchester Model 1300
Deer Series — Advantage
Full Camo Pattern**

**Winchester Model 1300
Defender Series — Stainless
Marine Synthetic Stock**

(cont'd) MODEL 1200 DEFENDER SERIES
Defender
w/hardwood stock,bead sight . . . . . NiB $210 Ex $168 Gd $114
Defender
W/hardwood stock, rifle sights . . . . NiB $223 Ex $179 Gd $121
Defender model w/pistol-grip stock . . . NiB $230 Ex $184 Gd $124
Defender Combo model
W/extra 28-inch plain bbl. . . . . NiB $261 Ex $209 Gd $142
Defender Combo model
W/extra 28-inch vent rib bbl. . . . . . NiB $281 Ex $224 Gd $153

MODEL 1200 FIELD GUN — MAGNUM
Same as standard Model 1200 except chambered for 3-inch 12 and 20 ga. magnum shells; plain or vent-rib bbl., 28- or 30-inch, F choke. Weight: 7.38 to 7.88 lbs. Made 1964-83.
With plain bbl. . . . . NiB $242 Ex $184 Gd $124
With vent rib bbl. . . . . NiB $257 Ex $206 Gd $140
Add for Winchester recoil reduction system $65

MODEL 1200 RANGER
SLIDE-ACTION SHOTGUN . . . . NiB $229 Ex $184 Gd $124
Hammerless. 12 and 20 ga.; 3-inch chambers. Walnut finished hardwood stock, ribbed forearm. 28-inch vent-rib bbl.; Winchoke system. Weight: 7.25 lbs. Made 1982 to 1990 by U. S. Repeating Arms.

MODEL 1200 RANGER YOUTH
SLIDE-ACTION SHOTGUN . . . . NiB $223 Ex $179 Gd $121
Same general specifications as standard Ranger Slide-Action except chambered for 20 ga. only, has Four shot magazine, recoil pad on buttstock, weight: 6.5 lbs. Mfd. by U. S. Repeating Arms.

MODEL 1200 SLIDE-ACTION FIELD GUN
Front-locking rotary bolt. Takedown. 4-shot magazine. Gauges: 12, 16, 20 (2.75-inch chamber). Bbl.: Plain or vent rib; 26-, 28-, 30-inch; IC, M, F choke or with Winchoke (interchangeable tubes IC-M-F). Weight: 6.5 to 7.25 lbs. Checkered pistol-grip stock and fore

(cont'd.) MODEL 1200 SLIDE-ACTION FIELD GUN
arm (slide handle), recoil pad; also avail. 1966-70 w/Winchester recoil reduction system (Cycolac stock). Made 1964-83.
With plain bbl. . . . . NiB $223 Ex $179 Gd $121
With vent rib bbl. . . . . NiB $235 Ex $188 Gd $128
Add for Winchester recoil reduction system $65
Add for Winchoke $25

MODEL 1200 STAINLESS
MARINE SERIES SLIDE-ACTION SECURITY SHOTGUN
Similar to Model 1200 Defender except w/6-shot magazine. 18-inch bbl. of ordnance stainless steel w/cylinder bore and rifle sights. Weight: 7 lbs. Bright chrome finish. Synthetic pistol grip or walnut finished hardwood buttstock w/grooved synthetic or hardwood slide handle.Made 1984-90.
Marine model w/hardwood stock . . . NiB $255 Ex $194 Gd $87
Marine model w/pistol-grip stock . . NiB $255 Ex $194 Gd $87

MODEL 1200 STAINLESS POLICE
SERIES SLIDE-ACTION SECURITY SHOTGUN
Similar to Model 1200 Defender except w/6-shot magazine. 18-inch bbl. of ordnance stainless steel w/cylinder bore and rifle sights. Weight: 7 lbs. Matte chrome finish. Synthetic pistol grip or walnut-finished hardwood buttstock w/grooved synthetic or hardwood slide handle.Made 1984-90.
Police model w/hardwood stock . . . NiB $271 Ex $217 Gd $148
Police model w/pistol grip stock . . . NiB $333 Ex $266 Gd $181

MODEL 1200 TRAP GUN
Same as standard Model 1200 except 12 gauge only. Has 2-shot magazine, 30-inch vent-rib bbl., Full choke or 28-inch with Winchoke. Semi-fancy walnut stock, straight Made 1965-73. Also available 1966-70 with Winchester recoil reduction system.
With straight-trap stock . . . . NiB $321 Ex $256 Gd $174
With Monte Carlo stock . . . . NiB $400 Ex $319 Gd $216
Add for Winchester recoil reduction system $75
Add for Winchoke $30

Winchester Model 1300
Lady Defender — Synthetic Full Stock

Winchester Model 1300
Lady Defender — Synthetic Pistol Grip Stock

Winchester Model 1300
Defender 5-Shot Combo

Winchester Model 1300
Turkey Gun

Winchester Model 1300
XTR w/Winchoke

Winchester Model 1300
Magnum Waterfowl

SHOTGUNS

MODEL 1200 RANGER

COMBINATION SHOTGUN . . . . . . **NiB $271 Ex $217 Gd $148**
Same as Ranger Deer combination except has one 28-inch vent-rib bbl. with M choke and one 18-inch Police Cyl. bore bbl. Made 1987-90.

MODEL 1200 SKEET GUN . . . . **NiB $341 Ex $272 Gd $185**
Same as standard Model 1200 except 12 and 20 ga. only; has 2-shot magazine, specially tuned trigger, 26-inch vent-rib bbl. SK choke, semi-fancy walnut stock and forearm. Weight: 7.25 to 7.5 lbs. Made 1965-73. Also avail. 1966-70 with Winchester recoil reduction system (add $50 to value).

MODEL 1300 CAMOPACK . . . . **NiB $381 Ex $305 Gd $207**
Gauge: 12.3-inch Magnum. Four shot magazine. Bbls.: 30-and 22-inch with Winchoke system. Weight: 7 lbs. Laminated stock with Win-Cam camouflage green, cut checkering, recoil pad, swivels and sling. Made 1987-88.

MODEL 1300 DEER SERIES

Similar to standard Model 1300 except 12 or 20 ga. only w/special 22-inch cyl. bore or rifled bbl. and rifle-type sights. Weight: 6.5 lbs. Checkered walnut or synthetic stock w/satin walnut, black or Advantage Full Camo Pattern finish. Matte blue or full-camo metal finish. Made 1994 to date.

Deer model
w/walnut stock (intro. 1994) . . . . . . **NiB $354 Ex $284 Gd $193**
Black Shadow Deer
w/synthetic stock (intro. 1994) . . . . **NiB $241 Ex $193 Gd $131**
Advantage Full Camo
Pattern (1995-98) . . . . **NiB $341 Ex $272 Gd $185**
Deer Combo
w/22- and 28-inch bbls. (1994-98) . . . . **NiB $301 Ex $241 Gd $130**
W/rifled bbl. (intro. 1996), add **$25**

MODEL 1300 DEFENDER SERIES

Gauges: 12 or 20 ga. 18- 24- 28-inch vent rib bbl. w/3-inch chamber. Four 7- or 8- shot magazine. Weight: 5.6 to 7.4 lbs. Blued, chrome or matte stainless finish. Wood or synthetic stock. Made 1985 to date.

Combo model . . . . **NiB $433 Ex $346 Gd $236**
Hardwood stock model . . . . **NiB $247 Ex $198 Gd $135**
Synthetic pistol-grip model . . . . **NiB $274 Ex $219 Gd $148**
Synthetic stock . . . . **NiB $261 Ex $208 Gd $142**
Lady Defender synthetic
Stock (made 1996) . . . . **NiB $281 Ex $234 Gd $152**
Lady Defender synthetic
Pistol-grip (made 1996) . . . . **NiB $249 Ex $199 Gd $136**
Stainless marine synthetic stock . . . **NiB $414 Ex $332 Gd $225**

MODEL 1300 DELUXE SLIDE-ACTION

Gauges: 12 and 20 w/3-inch chamber. Four shot magazine. Bbl.:22, 26 or 28 inch vent rib bbl. w/Winchoke tubes. Weight: 6.5 lbs. Checkered walnut buttstock and forend w/high luster finish. Polished blue metal finish with roll-engraved receiver. Made 1984 to date.

Model 1300 Deluxe
w/high gloss finish. . . . . **NiB $357 Ex $286 Gd $194**
Model 1300 Ladies/Youth
w/22-inch bbl.(disc. 1992) . . . . **NiB $314 Ex $251 Gd $171**

MODEL 1300 FEATHERWEIGHT SLIDE-ACTION SHOTGUN

Hammerless. Takedown. Four shot magazine. Gauges: 12 and 20 (3-inch chambers). Bbls.: 22, 26 or 28 inches w/plain or vent rib w/Winchoke tubes. Weight: 6.38 to 7 lbs. Checkered walnut buttstock, grooved slide handle. Made 1978-94.

Model 1300 FW (plain bbl.) . . . . . . **NiB $281 Ex $224 Gd $152**
Model 1300 FW (vent rib) . . . . **NiB $329 Ex $263 Gd $180**
Model 1300 FW XTR . . . . **NiB $343 Ex $274 Gd $187**

MODEL 1300 RANGER SERIES

Gauges: 12 or 20 ga. w/3-inch chamber. Five shot magazine. 22-(Rifled), 26- or 28-inch vent-rib bbl. w/Winchoke tubes. Weight: 7.25 lbs. Blued finish. Walnut-finished hardwood buttstock and forend. Made 1984 to date.

Standard model . . . . **NiB $287 Ex $230 Gd $156**
Combo model . . . . **NiB $351 Ex $281 Gd $191**
Ranger Deer combo
(D&T w/rings & bases) . . . . **NiB $370 Ex $296 Gd $201**
Ranger Ladies/Youth . . . . **NiB $294 Ex $235 Gd $159**

MODEL 1300 SLIDE-ACTION FIELD GUN

Takedown w/front-locking rotary bolt. Gauges: 12, 20 w/3-inch chamber. Four shot magazine. Bbl.: Vent rib; 26-, 28-, 30-inch w/Win-choke tubes IC-M-F). Weight: 7.25 lbs. Checkered walnut or synthetic stock w/standard, black or Advantage Full Camo Pattern finish. Matte blue or full-camo metal finish. Made 1994 to date.

Model 1300 Standard Field
(w/walnut stock) . . . . **NiB $259 Ex $207 Gd $141**
Model 1300 Black Shadow
(w/black synthetic stock). . . . . **NiB $220 Ex $177 Gd $119**
Model 1300 Advantage Camo . . . . . **NiB $321 Ex $257 Gd $174**

MODEL 1300 SLUG HUNTER SERIES

Similar to standard Model 1300 except chambered 12 ga. only w/special 22-inch smoothbore w/Sabot-rifled choke tube or fully rifled bbl. w/rifle-type sights. Weight: 6.5 lbs. Checkered walnut, hardwood or laminated stock w/satin walnut or WinTuff finish. Matte blue metal finish. Made 1988-94.

Slug Hunter w/hardwood stock . . . **NiB $301 Ex $241 Gd $163**
Slug Hunter w/laminated stock . . . . **NiB $354 Ex $283 Gd $193**
Slug Hunter w/walnut stock . . . . . . **NiB $327 Ex $262 Gd $179**
Whitetails Unlimited
w/beavertail forend . . . . **NiB $335 Ex $267 Gd $182**
W/sabot-rifled choke tubes, add **$15**

MODEL 1300 TURKEY SERIES

Gauges: 12 or 20 ga. 22-inch bbl. w/3-inch chamber. Four shot magazine. 43 inches overall. Weight: 6.4 to 6.75 lbs. Buttstock and magazine cap, sling studs w/Cordura sling. Drilled and tapped to accept scope base. Checkered walnut, synthetic or laminated wood stock w/low luster finish. Matte blue or full camo finish. Made 1985 to date.

Turkey Advantage Full Camo. . . . . **NiB $315 Ex $252 Gd $171**
Turkey Realtree All-Purpose Full Camo. . . . . **NiB $345 Ex $275 Gd $188**
Turkey Realtree Gray
All-Purpose Full Camo . . . . **NiB $357 Ex $286 Gd $194**
Turkey Realtree All-Purpose
Camo (matte metal) . . . . **NiB $301 Ex $241 Gd $163**
Turkey Black Shadow
(black synthetic stock) . . . . **NiB $207 Ex $165 Gd $112**
Turkey Win-Cam (green laminated wood) . . . **NiB $320 Ex $256 Gd $174**
Turkey Win-Cam Combo
(22- and 30-inch bbls.) . . . . **NiB $357 Ex $286 Gd $194**
Turkey Win-Cam NWTF
(22- and 30-inch bbls.) . . . . **NiB $335 Ex $267 Gd $182**
Turkey Win-Cam Youth/
Ladies model (20 ga.) . . . . **NiB $395 Ex $315 Gd $215**
Turkey Win-Tuf (br. laminated wood) . . **NiB $327 Ex $262 Gd $179**

MODEL 1300 WATERFOWL SLIDE-ACTION SHOTGUN

Similar to 1300 Standard model except has 28- or 30-inch vent rib bbl. w/Winchoke tubes. Weight: 7 lbs. Matte blue metal finish. Checkered walnut finished hardwood or brown laminated Win-Tuffwood stock w/camo sling, swivels and recoil pad. Made 1984-92.
Model 1300 Waterfowl w/hardwood stock . . . **NiB $301 Ex $241 Gd $163**
Model 1300 Waterfowl w/laminated stock. . . . . **NiB $327 Ex $262 Gd $179**

Winchester Model 1400 Field

Winchester Model 1500 w/Plain Barrel

Winchester Model 1500
w/Vent Rib Barrel

MODEL 1300 XTR SLIDE-ACTION . NiB $395 Ex $315 Gd $215
Hammerless. Takedown. Four shot magazine. Gauges: 12 and 20 (3-inch chambers). Bbl.: Plain or vent rib; 28-inch bbls.; Winchoke (interchangeable tubes IC-M-F). Weight: About 7 lbs.

MODEL 1400 AUTOMATIC FIELD GUN
Gas-operated. Front-locking rotary bolt. Takedown. Two shot magazine. Gauges: 12, 16, 20 (2.75-inch chamber). Bbl.: Plain or vent rib; 26-, 28-, 30-inch; IC, M, F choke, or with Winchoke (interchangeable tubes IC-M-F). Weight: 6.5 to 7.25 lbs. Checkered pistol-grip stock and forearm, recoil pad, also available with Winchester recoil reduction system (Cycolac stock). Made 1964-68.
With plain bbl. . . . . NiB $303 Ex $242 Gd $164
With vent rib bbl. . . . . NiB $333 Ex $266 Gd $181
Add for Winchester recoil reduction system $100
Add for Winchoke $25

MODEL 1400 DEER GUN . . . . NiB $301 Ex $241 Gd $163
Same as standard Model 1400 except has special 22-inch bbl. with rifle-type sights, for rifle slug or buckshot; 12 ga. only. Weight: 6.25 lbs. Made 1965-68.

MODEL 1400 MARK II DEER GUN. NiB $351 Ex $281 Gd $191
Same general specifications as Model 1400 Deer Gun. Made 1968-73.

MODEL 1400 MARK II FIELD GUN
Same general specifications as Model 1400 Field Gun, except not chambered for 16 gauge; Winchester Recoil Reduction System not available after 1970- only 28-inch barrels w/Winchoke offered after 1973. Made 1968-78.
With plain bbl. . . . . NiB $321 Ex $257 Gd $174
With plain bbl. and Winchoke . . . . . NiB $348 Ex $278 Gd $192
With vent-rib bbl. . . . . NiB $368 Ex $294 Gd $200
With vent-rib bbl. and Winchoke . . NiB $395 Ex $315 Gd $215
Add for Winchester recoil reduction system $100

**MODEL 1400 MARK II
SKEET GUN** . . . . NiB $414 Ex $332 Gd $225
Same general specifications as Model 1400 Skeet Gun. Made 1968-73.

MODEL 1400 MARK II TRAP GUN
Same general specifications as Model 1400 Trap Gun except also

(cont'd) **MODEL 1400 MARK II TRAP GUN**
furnished with 28-inch bbl. and Winchoke. Winchester recoil reduction system not available after 1970. Made 1968-73.
With straight stock . . . . NiB $449 Ex $359 Gd $244
With Monte Carlo stock . . . . NiB $491 Ex $392 Gd $266
With Winchester recoil reduction system, add $100
With Winchoke, add $25

MODEL 1400 MARK II UTILITY SKEET NiB $336 Ex $269 Gd $183
Same general specifications as Model 1400 Mark II Skeet Gun except has stock and forearm of field grade walnut. Made 1970-73.

MODEL 1400 MARK II UTILITY TRAP . NiB $371 Ex $297 Gd $202
Same as Model 1400 Mark II Trap Gun except has Monte Carlo stock/forearm of field grade walnut. Made 1970-73.

**MODEL 1400 RANGER
SEMIAUTOMATIC SHOTGUN** . . . . NiB $261 Ex $208 Gd $142
Gauges: 12, 20. Two shot magazine. 28-inch vent rib bbl. with F choke. Overall length: 48.63 inches. Weight: 7 to 7.25 lbs. Walnut finish, hardwood stock and forearm with cut checkering. Made 1984 to 1990 by U. S. Repeating Arms.

**MODEL 1400 RANGER SEMIAUTOMATIC
DEER SHOTGUN.** . . . . NiB $274 Ex $219 Gd $149
Same general specifications as Ranger Semiautomatic except 24.13-inch plain bbl. with rifle sights. Mfd. by U.S. Repeating Arms.

MODEL 1400 SKEET GUN . . . . NiB $386 Ex $308 Gd $209
Same as standard Model 1400 except 12 and 20 ga. only, 26-inch vent-rib bbl., SK choke, semi-fancy walnut stock and forearm. Weight: 7.25 to 7.5 lbs. Made 1965-68. Also available with Winchester recoil reduction system (add $50 to value).

MODEL 1400 TRAP GUN
Same as standard Model 1400 except 12 ga. only with 30-inch vent-rib bbl., F choke. Semi-fancy walnut stock, straight or Monte Carlo trap style. Also available with Winchester recoil reduction system. Weight: About 8.25 lbs. Made 1965-68.
With straight stock . . . . NiB $434 Ex $348 Gd $237
With Monte Carlo stock . . . . NiB $468 Ex $374 Gd $254
Add for Winchester recoil red. system. $100

SHOTGUNS

Winchester Ranger Deer

Winchester Ranger Slide-Action

Winchester Model 1885
Single-Shot

Winchester Model 1
Field Super-X

Winchester Xpert
96 Field

Winchester Xpert
96 Trap

MODEL 1500 XTR SEMIAUTOMATIC . . NiB $319 Ex $255 Gd $173
Gas-operated. Gauges: 12 and 20 (2.75-inch chambers). Bbl.: Plain or vent rib; 28-inch; WinChoke (interchangeable tubes IC-M-F). American walnut stock and forend; checkered grip and forend. Weight: 7.25 lbs. Made 1978-82.

MODEL 1885
SINGLE-SHOT SHOTGUN . . . . NiB $3819 Ex $3085 Gd $2098
Falling-block action, same as Model 1885 Rifle. Highwall receiver. Solid frame or takedown. 20 ga. 3-inch chamber. 26-inch bbl.; plain, matted or matted rib; Cyl. bore, M or F choke. Weight: About 5.5 lbs. Straight-grip stock and forearm. Made 1914-16.

MODEL 1887 LEVER-ACTION SHOTGUN
First of John Browning's patent shotgun designs produced by Winchester. 10 or 12 ga. on casehardened frame fitted w/20-inch blued, cylinder bore or full choke 30- or 32-inch bbl. Plain or checkered walnut stock and forend. Made 1887 to 1901.
Model 1887 10 or 12 ga. standard . . . . NiB $2399 Ex $1920 Gd $1306
Model 1887 10 or 12 ga. deluxe. . . NiB $5021 Ex $4017 Gd $2732
Model 1887 10 or 12 ga. riot gun . . . . NiB $2285 Ex $1828 Gd $1243

(cont'd.) MODEL 1887 LEVER-ACTION SHOTGUN
W/.70-150 Ratchet rifled bbl.
.70 cal. rifle/87 produced) . . . . NiB $3284 Ex $2625 Gd $1786
W/3 or 4 blade Del. Damascus bbl., add. 20%

MODEL 1901 LEVER-ACTION SHOTGUN
Same general specifications as Model 1887, of which this is a redesigned version. 10 ga. only. Made 1901-20.
Model 1901 Standard. . . . . . . NiB $2000 Ex $1601 Gd $1089
Model 1901 Deluxe . . . . NiB $2549 Ex $2039 Gd $1386

MODEL 1911 AUTO-
LOADING SHOTGUN. . . . . NiB $612 Ex $489 Gd $333
Hammerless. Takedown. 12 gauge only. Four shell tubular magazine. Bbl.: plain, 26- to 32-inch, standard borings. Weight: About 8.5 lbs. Plain or checkered pistol-grip stock and forearm. Made 1911-25.

RANGER DEER COMBINATION . . . NiB $294 Ex $235 Gd $159
Gauge: 12, 3-inch Magnum. Three shot magazine. Bbl.: 24-inch Cyl. bore deer bbl. and 28-inch vent rib bbl. with WinChoke system. Weight: 7.25 lbs. Made 1987-90.

Woodward
Single-Shot Trap

Woodward O/U
Special Trap Grade

SUPER-X MODEL I AUTO FIELD GUN. . . . NiB $483 Ex $386 Gd $262
Gas-operated. Takedown.12 ga. 2.75-inch chamber Four shot magazine. Bbl.: Vent rib 26-inch IC; 28-inch M or F; 30-inch F choke. Weight: About 7 lbs. Checkered pistol-grip stock. Made 1974-84.

SUPER-X MODEL I SKEET GUN . . . NiB $727 Ex $582 Gd $396
Same as Super-X Field Gun except has 26-inch bbl., SK choke, skeet-style stock and forearm of select walnut. Made 1974-84.

SUPER-X MODEL I TRAP GUN
Same as Super-X Field Gun except has 30-inch bbl., IM or F choke, trap-style stock (straight or Monte Carlo comb) and forearm of select walnut, recoil pad. Made 1974-84.
With straight stock . . . . NiB $574 Ex $459 Gd $312
With Monte Carlo stock . . . . NiB $668 Ex $535 Gd $364

XPERT MODEL 96 O/U FIELD GUN . . . . . NiB $913 Ex $729 Gd $495
Boxlock action similar to Model 101. Plain receiver. Auto ejectors. Selective single trigger. Gauges: 12, 20. 3-inch chambers. Bbl.: Vent rib; 26-inch IC/M; 28-inch M/F, 30-inch F/F choke (12 ga. only). Weight: 6.25 to 8.25 lbs. depending on ga. and bbls. Checkered pistol-grip stock and forearm. Made 1976-81 for Olin Corp. at its Olin-Kodensha facility in Japan.

XPERT MODEL 96 SKEET GUN. . . . NiB $966 Ex $772 Gd $525
Same as Xpert Field Gun except has 2.75-inch chambers, 27-inch bbls., SK choke, skeet-style stock and forearm. Made 1976-1981.

XPERT MODEL 96 TRAP GUN
Same as Xpert Field Gun except 12 ga. only, 2.75-inch chambers, has 30-inch bbls., IM/F or F/F choke, trap-style stock (straight or Monte Carlo comb) with recoil pad. Made 1976-81.
With straight stock . . . . NiB $885 Ex $709 Gd $482
With Monte Carlo stock . . . . NiB $910 Ex $728 Gd $495

JAMES WOODWARD & SONS — London, England

James Woodward & Sons was acquired by James Purdey & Sons after World War II.

BEST QUALITY HAMMERLESS DOUBLE
Sidelock. Automatic ejectors. Double triggers or single trigger. Built to order in all standard gauges, bbl. lengths, boring and other specifications. Made as a field gun, pigeon and wildfowl gun, skeet gun or trap gun. Manufactured prior to World War II.
12 ga.
w/double triggers . . . . . . NiB $26,906 Ex $21,525 Gd $14,637
20 ga.
w/double triggers . . . . . . NiB $30,516 Ex $24,412 Gd $16,600

(cont'd.) **BEST QUALITY HAMMERLESS DOUBLE**
28 ga.
w/double triggers . . . . . . NiB $37,731 Ex $30,187 Gd $20,527
.410 ga.
w/double triggers . . . . . . NiB $42,656 Ex $34,125 Gd $23,205
W/selective single trigger, add 5%

BEST QUALITY O/U SHOTGUN
Sidelock. Automatic ejectors. Double triggers or single trigger. Built to order in all standard gauges, bbl. lengths, boring and other specifications, including Special Trap Grade with vent rib. Woodward introduced this type of gun in 1908. Made until World War II.
12 ga.
w/double triggers . . . . . . NiB $29,531 Ex $23,425 Gd $16,065
20 ga.
w/double triggers . . . . . . NiB $39,703 Ex $31,762 Gd $21,598
28 ga.
w/double triggers . . . . . . NiB $52,172 Ex $41,737 Gd $28,381
.410 ga.
w/double triggers . . . . NiB $59,062 Ex $47,250+ Gd $32,130
W/single trigger, add 5%

BEST QUALITY SINGLE-SHOT TRAP. . . . . . . NiB $12,406 Ex $9925 Gd $6749
Sidelock. Mechanical features of the O/U gun. Vent rib bbl. 12 ga. only. Built to customer's specifications and measurements, including type and amount of checkering, carving and engraving. Made prior to World War II.

ZEPHYR SHOTGUNS — Manufactured by Victor Sarasqueta Company, Eibar, Spain

MODEL 1 O/U SHOTGUN . . . . NiB $1191 Ex $953 Gd $648
Same general specifications as Field Model O/U except with more elaborate engraving, finer wood and checkering. Imported by Stoeger 1930s-51.

MODEL 2 O/U SHOTGUN . . . . NiB $1561 Ex $1248 Gd $849
Sidelock. Auto ejectors. Gauges: 12, 16, 20, 28 and .410. Bbls.: 25 to 30 inches most common. Modest scroll engraving on receiver and sideplates. Checkered, straight-grain select walnut buttstock and forend. Imported by Stoeger 1930s-51.

MODEL 3 O/U SHOTGUN. . . . NiB $2155 Ex $1724 Gd $1173
Same general specifications as Zephyr Model 2 O/U except with more elaborate engraving, finer wood and checkering. Imported by Stoeger 1930s-51.

SHOTGUNS

Zephyr Crown, Premier and Royal Grades

MODEL 400E FIELD GRADE DOUBLE-BARREL SHOTGUN

Anson & Deeley boxlock system. Gauges: 12 16, 20, 28 and .410. Bbls.: 25 to 30 inches. Weight: 4.5 lbs. (.410) to 6.25 lbs. (12 ga.). Checkered French walnut buttstock and forearm. Modest scroll engraving on bbls., receiver and trigger guard. Imported by Stoeger 1930s-50s.

12, 16 or 20 ga.	NiB $1407 Ex $1125 Gd $764
28 or .410 ga.	NiB $1584 Ex $1267 Gd $861
W/selective single trigger, add	$200

MODEL 401 E SKEET GRADE DOUBLE-BARREL SHOTGUN

Same general specifications as Field Grade except with beavertail forearm. Bbls.: 25 to 28 inches. Imported by Stoeger 1930s-50s.

12, 16 or 20 ga.	NiB $1680 Ex $1344 Gd $914
28 or .410 ga.	NiB $1848 Ex $1478 Gd $1005
W/selective single trigger, add	$350
W/nonselective single trigger, add	$250

MODEL 402E DELUXE
DOUBLE-BARREL SHOTGUN . . NiB $2140 Ex $1712 Gd $1164

Same general specifications as Model 400E Field Grade except for custom refinements. The action was carefully hand-honed for smoother operation; finer, elaborate engraving throughout, plus higher quality wood in stock and forearm. Imported by Stoeger 1930s-50s.

CROWN GRADE . . . . NiB $1529 Ex $1227 Gd $831

Boxlock. Gauges: 12, 16, 20, 28 and .410. Bbls.: 25 to 30 inches standard but any lengths could be ordered. Weight: 6 lbs., 4 oz. (.410) to 7 lbs., 4 oz. (12 ga.). Checkered Spanish walnut stock and beavertail forearm. Receiver engraved with scroll patterns. Imported by Stoeger 1938-51.

FIELD MODEL
O/U SHOTGUN . . . . NiB $747 Ex $597 Gd $407

Anson & Deeley boxlock. Auto ejectors. Gauges: 12, 16 and 20. Bbls.: 25 to 30 inches standard- full-length matt rib. Double triggers. Checkered buttstock and forend. Light scroll engraving on receiver. Imported by Stoeger 1930s-51.

HONKER SINGLE-SHOT SHOTGUN . . . . . NiB $510 Ex $408 Gd $277

Sidelock. Gauge: 10; 3.5-inch magnum. 36-inch vent rib barrel w/F choke. Weight: 10.5 lbs. Checkered select Spanish walnut buttstock and beavertail forend; recoil pad. Imported by Stoeger 1950s-72.

PINEHURST
DOUBLE-BARREL SHOTGUN . . . . NiB $1095 Ex $876 Gd $595

Boxlock. Gauges: 12, 16, 20, 28 and .410. Bbls.: 25 to 28 inches most common. Checkered, select walnut buttstock and forend. Selective single trigger and auto ejectors. Imported by Stoeger 1950s-72.

PREMIER GRADE
DOUBLE-BARREL SHOTGUN . . . . NiB $2375 Ex $1900 Gd $1292

Sidelock. Gauges: 12, 16, 20, 28 and .410. Bbls.: Any length, but 25 to 30 inches most popular. Weight: 4.5 lbs. (.410) to 7 lbs. (12 ga.). Checkered high-grade French walnut buttstock and forend. Imported by Stoeger 1930s-51.

ROYAL GRADE
DOUBLE-BARREL SHOTGUN . . . . . NiB $3663 Ex $930 Gd $1993

Same general specifications as the Premier Grade except with more elaborate engraving, finer checkering and wood. Imported by Stoeger 1930s-51.

STERLINGWORTH II
DOUBLE-BARREL SHOTGUN . . . . . NiB $921 Ex $736 Gd $501

Genuine sidelocks with color-casehardened sideplates. Gauges: 12, 16, 20 and .410. Bbls.: 25 to 30 inches. Weight: 6 lbs., 4 oz. (.410) to 7 lbs., 4 oz. (12 ga.). Select Spanish walnut buttstock and beavertail forearm. Light scroll engraving on receiver and sideplates. Automatic, sliding-tang safety. Imported by Stoeger 1950s-72.

THUNDERBIRD
DOUBLE-BARREL SHOTGUN . . . . NiB $922 Ex $737 Gd $502

Sidelock. Gauges: 12 and 10 Magnum. Bbls.: 32-inch, both F choke. Weight: 8 lbs., 8 oz. (12 ga.), 12 lbs. (10 ga.). Receiver elaborately engraved with waterfowl scenes. Checkered select Spanish walnut buttstock and beavertail forend. Plain extractors, double triggers. Imported by Stoeger 1950-72.

UPLAND KING
DOUBLE-BARREL SHOTGUN . . . NiB $1071 Ex $857 Gd $583

Sidelock. Gauges: 12, 16, 20, 28 and .410. Bbls.: 25 to 28 inches most popular. Checkered buttstock and forend of select walnut. Selective single trigger and auto ejectors. Imported by Stoeger 1950-72.

UPLANDER 4E
DOUBLE-BARREL SHOTGUN . . . . NiB $869 Ex $695 Gd $473

Same general specifications as the Zephyr Sterlingworth II except with selective auto ejectors and highly polished sideplates. Imported by Stoeger 1951-72.

WOODLANDER II
DOUBLE-BARREL SHOTGUN . . . . NiB $609 Ex $486 Gd $331

Boxlock. Gauges: 12, 20 and .410. Bbls.: 25 to 30 inches. Weight: 6 lbs., 4 oz. (.410) to 7 lbs., 4 oz. (12 ga.). Checkered Spanish walnut stock and beavertail forearm. Engraved receiver. Imported by Stoeger 1950-72.

Angelo Zoli — Patricia Side-by Side

ANGELO ZOLI —
Mississauga, Ontario, Canada
ALLEY CLEANER
S/S SHOTGUN . . . . **NiB $638 Ex $510 Gd $346**
Gauges: 12 and 20. 20-inch bbl. 26.5 inches overall. Weight: 7 lbs. average. Chokes: F/M, F, IM, M, IC, SK. Chrome-lined barrels. Walnut stock and engraved action. Made 1986-87.

APACHE O/U FIELD SHOTGUN
Gauge: 12. Chokes: F/M, F, IM, M, IC and stock fixed or tubes. 20-inch bbl. Short vent rib. Weight: 7.5 lbs. Checkered walnut stock and forearm. Lever action. Pistol grip. Made 1986-88.
Apache w/fixed chokes . . . . **NiB $428 Ex $342 Gd $233**
Apache w/choke tubes . . . . **NiB $519 Ex $415 Gd $282**

DAINO I AND II
FOLDING SINGLE SHOT
Gauges: 12, 20 and .410. 28- or 30-inch bbl. Weight: 6 lbs. average. Choke: Full. Chrome-lined barrel, vent rib. Pistol-grip walnut stock. Engraved action. Made 1986-88.
Daino I w/top lever . . . . **NiB $152 Ex $122 Gd $82**
Daino II w/bottom lever . . . . **NiB $165 Ex $132 Gd $90**

HK 2000 SEMIAUTO-
MATIC SHOTGUN . . . . **NiB $676 Ex $541 Gd $363**
Gauge: 12. Five shot capacity. Bbls.: 24-, 26-, 28- and 30-inch; vent rib. Weight: 6.5 to 7.5 lbs. Checkered walnut stock and forearm. Glossy finish. Pistol grip. Engraved receiver. Made 1988.

PATRICIA
SIDE-BY-SIDE SHOTGUNS . . . . . **NiB $1339 Ex $1071 Gd $728**
Gauge: .410 only. 28-inch bbl. Choke: F/M. Weight: 5.5 lbs. Automatic ejectors; Zoli single selective trigger, box lock. Hand-checkered walnut stock with English straight grip, splinter forearm. Made 1986-88.

SAINT GEORGE
O/U COMPETITION . . . . **NiB $1964 Ex $1571 Gd $1068**
Gauge: 12. 30- and 32-inch vent rib barrels. Weight: 8 lbs. Single selective trigger. Oil-finished, pistol-grip walnut stock. Made 1986-88.

SILVER SNIPE
O/U SHOTGUN . . . . **NiB $603 Ex $482 Gd $328**
Purdey-type box lock with crossbolt. Selective single trigger. Gauges: 12, 20; 3-inch chambers. Bbls.: 26-, 28- or 30-inch with a variety of choke combinations. Weight: 5.75 to 6.75 lbs. Checkered European walnut buttstock and forend. Made in Italy.

Z43 STANDARD
O/U SHOTGUN . . . . **NiB $410 Ex $328 Gd $222**
Gauge: 12 or 20. 26-, 28- or 30-inch bbls. Chokes: F/M, M/IC Weight: 6.75 to 8 lbs. vent lateral ribs, standard extractors, single non-selective trigger. Glossy-finished walnut stock and forearm. Automatic safety. Made 1986-88.

ANTONIO ZOLI, U.S.A., INC. — Fort Wayne, Indiana, Manufactured in Italy
SILVER FALCON
O/U . . . . **NiB $1166 Ex $933 Gd $634**
Gauges: 12 and 20; 3-inch chambers. 26- or 28-inch blued barrels. Weight: 6.25 to 7.25 lbs. Antiqued silver finish on receiver. Pistol-grip stock of Turkish Circassian walnut with polyurethane-type finish. Imported 1989-1990.

UPLANDER
SIDE/SIDE SHOTGUN . . . . **NiB $766 Ex $613 Gd $417**
Gauges: 12 and 20. Casehardened receiver. Checkered oil-finished, hand-rubbed stock of Turkish Circassian walnut; splinter forend. Imported 1989-90.

Index

INDEX

Woodsman Target Model, First Issue, 51
Woodsman Target Model, Second Issue, 51
Woodsman Target Model, Third Issue, 51
World War I 50th Anniversary Commemorative
  Series, 51
World War II 50th Anniversary Commemorative, 51
World War II Commemorative, 51
World War II D-Day Invasion Commemorative, 51
World War II Golden Anniversary V-J Day Tribute, 52
SINGLE-SHOT PISTOLS & DERRINGERS
Camp Perry Model Second Issue, 53
Camp Perry Model Single-Shot Pistol, First Issue, 53
Civil War Centennial, 53
Derringer No. 4 Commemoratives, 53
Derringer No. 4, 53
Lord and Lady Derringers, 53
Rock Island Arsenal Centennial, 53
REVOLVERS
38 DS II, 53
Agent (LW) DA, Second Issue, 53
Agent DA, First Issue, 53
Anaconda DA, 53
Anaconda Titanium DA, 54
Army Special DA, 54
Bankers' Special DA, 54
Bisley Model SA, 54
Buntline Special 45, 54
Cobra DA, Square Butt, 54
Cobra DA, Round Butt, First Issue, 54
Cobra DA, Second Issue, 54
Commando Special DA Revolver, 54
Detective Special DA, First Issue , 54
Detective Special DA, 2nd Issue, 55
Detective Special DA, 3rd Issue , 55
Detective Special DA, 4th Issue, 55
Diamondback DA, 55
DA Army, 55
Frontier Scout, 56
Frontier Scout Commemoratives, 56
1961 Issues:
Kansas Statehood Centennial, 56
Pony Express Centennial, 56
1962 Issues:
Columbus, Ohio, Sesquicentennial, 56
Fort Findlay Cased Pair, 56
Fort Findlay, Ohio, Sesquicentennial, 56
New Mexico Golden Anniversary, 56
West Virginia Statehood Centennial, 56
1963 Issues:
Arizona Territorial Centennial, 56
Battle of Gettysburg Centennial, 56
Carolina Charter Tercentenary, 56
Fort Stephenson, Ohio Sesquicentennial, 56
General John Hunt Morgan Indiana Raid, 56
Idaho Territorial Centennial, 56
1964 Issues:
California Gold Rush, 56
Chamizal Treaty, 56
General Hood Centennial, 56
Montana Territorial Centennial, 56
Nevada "Battle Born", 56
Nevada Statehood Centennial, 56
New Jersey Tercentenary, 56
St. Louis Bicentennial, 56
Wyoming Diamond Jubilee, 56
1965 Issues:
Appomattox Centennial, 56
Forty-Niner Miner, 56
General Meade Campaign, 56
Kansas Cowtown Series—Wichita, 56
Old Fort Des Moines Reconstruction, 56
Oregon Trail, 56
St. Augustine Quadricentennial, 56
1966 Issues:
Colorado Gold Rush, 57
Dakota Territory, 57
Indiana Sesquicentennial, 57
Kansas Cowtown Series—Abilene, 57
Kansas Cowtown Series—Dodge City, 57
Oklahoma Territory, 57
1967 Issues:
Alamo , 57
Kansas Cowtown Series—Coffeyville, 57
Kansas Trail Series—Chisholm Trail, 57
Lawman Series—Bat Masterson, 57
1968 Issues:
Kansas Trail Series—Pawnee Trail, 5
Kansas Trail Series—Santa Fe Trail, 57

Lawman Series—Pat Garrett, 57
Nebraska Centennial, 57
1969 Issues:
Alabama Sesquicentennial, 57
Arkansas Territory Sesquicentennial, 57
California Bicentennial, 57
General Nathan Bedford Forrest, 57
Golden Spike, 57
Kansas Trail Series—Shawnee Trail, 57
Lawman Series—Wild Bill Hickock, 57
1970 Issues:
Kansas Fort Series—Fort Hays, 57
Kansas Fort Series—Fort Larned, 57
Kansas Fort Series—Fort Riley, 57
Lawman Series—Wyatt Earp, 57
Maine Sesquicentennial, 57
Missouri Sesquicentennial, 57
1971 Issues:
Kansas Fort Series—Fort Scott, 57
1972 Issues:
Florida Territory Sesquicentennial, 57
1973 Issues:
Arizona Ranger, 57
King Cobra Revolver, 57
Lawman MK III DA Revolver, 57
Lawman MK V DA Revolver, 58
Magnum Carry DA Revolver, 58
Marine Corps Model (1905) DA Revolver, 58
Metropolitan MK III DA Revolver, 58
New DA Central Fire Revolver, 58
New Frontier Buntline Special, 58
New Frontier SA 22 Revolver, 58
New Frontier SA Army Revolver, 58
New Navy (1889) DA, First Issue , 58
New Navy (1892) DA, Second Issue, 58
New Pocket DA Revolver, 58
New Police DA Revolver, 58
New Police Target DA Revolver, 58
New Service DA Revolver, 59
New Service Target, 59
Officers' Model Match, 59
Officers' Model Special, 59
Officers' Model Target DA Revolver, First Issue, 59
Officers' Model Target, Second Issue, 59
Official Police DA Revolver, 59
Official Police MK III DA Revolver, 60
Peacekeeper DA Revolver, 60
Peacemaker 22 Revolver, 60
Peacemaker 22 2nd Amendment Commemorative, 60
Pocket Positive DA Revolver, 60
Police Positive DA, First Issue, 60
Police Positive DA, Second Issue, 60
Police Positive Special DA Revolver, 60
Police Positive Target DA Revolver, 60
Python DA Revolver, 61
Shooting Master DA Revolver, 61
SA Army — 125th Anniversary, 61 - 63
SA Army — Commemorative, 63
SA Army Commemorative Models
1963 Issues:
Arizona Territorial Centennial, 63
West Virginia Statehood Centennial, 63
1964 Issues:
Chamizal Treaty, 63
Colonel Sam Colt Sesquicentennial, 63
Deluxe Presentation, 63
Montana Territorial Centennial, 63
Nevada "Battle Born", 63
Nevada Statehood Centennial, 63
New Jersey Tercentenary, 63
Pony Express Presentation, 63
St. Louis Bicentennial, 63
Wyatt Earp Buntline, 63
1965 Issues:
Appomattox Centennial, 63
Old Fort Des Moines Reconstruction, 63
1966 Issues:
Abercrombie & Fitch Trailblazer—Chicago, 63
Abercrombie & Fitch Trailblazer—New York, 63
Abercrombie & Fitch Trailblazer—San Francisco, 63
California Gold Rush, 63
General Meade, 63
Pony Express Four Square, 63
1967 Issues:
Alamo, 63
Lawman Series—Bat Masterson, 63
1968 Issues:
Lawman Series—Pat Garrett, 63

1969 Issues:
Lawman Series—Wild Bill Hickok, 63
1970 Issues:
Lawman Series—Wyatt Earp, 63
Missouri Sesquicentennial, 63
Texas Ranger, 63
1971 Issues:
NRA Centennial, 63
1975 Issues:
Peacemaker Centennial, 63
Peacemaker Centennial 44-40, 63
Peacemaker Centennial Cased Pair, 63
1979 Issues:
Ned Buntline 45, 63
1986 Issues:
Colt 150th Anniversary, 63
Colt 150th Anniversay (Engraved), 63
SA Cowboy Revolver, 63
SA Sheriff's Model 45, 63
Three-Fifty-Seven DA Revolver, 63
Trooper DA Revolver, 63
Trooper MK III DA Revolver, 64
Trooper MK V Revolver, 64
U.S. Bicentennial Commemorative Set, 64
Viper DA Revolver, 64
RIFLES
AR-15 A2 Delta Match H-BAR Rifle, 224
AR-15 A2 Government Model, 224
AR-15 A2 Sporter II, 225
AR-15 Compact 9mm Carbine, 225
AR-15 Semiautomatic Sporter, 226
AR-15 Sporter Competition H-BAR Rifle, 226
AR-15 Sporter Competition H-BAR (RS), 226
AR-15 Sporter Match Target, 226
AR-15 Sporter Target Rifle, 226
Lightning Magazine Rifle - Large Frame, 226
Lightning Magazine Rifle - Medium Frame, 227
Lightning Magazine Rifle - Small Frame, 227
Stagecoach 22 Autoloader, 227
1-22 Single-Shot Bolt-Action, 227
22 Autoloader, 227
Custom Sporting Rifle, 227
Deluxe Rifle, 227
Models of 1957 Rifles, 227
Model of 1961, 227
Model of 1961 Standard Rifle, 227
Standard Rifle, 227
Colt-Sauer Drillings-see Colt shotgun listings.
Grand African, 228
Grand Alaskan, 228
Magnum, 228
Short Action, 228
Sporting Rifle, 228
SHOTGUNS
Auto — Magnum, 448
Auto — Magnum Custom, 449
Auto — Ultra Light Custom, 449
Auto — Ultra Light Standard, 449
Custom Hammerless Double, 449
Custom Pump, 449
Sauer Drilling, 449
Standard Pump Shotgun, 449
COMMANDO CARBINES
Mark III Semiautomatic Carbine, 228
Mark 9, 228
Mark 45, 228
CONNECTICUT VALLEY CLASSICS
Classic Field Over/Under, 449
Classic Sporter Over/Under, 449
CONTINENTAL RIFLES
Double Rifle, 228
COONAN ARMS
Model 357 Magnum Cadet Compact, 64
Model 357 Magnum Auto, 64
COOPER ARMS
Model 21, 229
Model 22, 229
Model 22 Pro Varmint, 229
Model 36 TRP-1 Series, 229
Model 36CF Bolt-Action Rifle, 229
Model 36RF Bolt-Action Rifle, 229
Model 38 Single Shot, 229
Model 40 Classic Bolt-Action Rifle, 229
CUMBERLAND MOUNTAIN ARMS
Plateau Rifle, 229
CZ
  PISTOLS
  Model 27, 65

INDEX

INDEX

GRADING:　**NiB** = New in Box　　**Ex** = Excellent or NRA 95%　　**Gd** = Good or NRA 68%

INDEX

INDEX

GRADING: **NiB** = New in Box   **Ex** = Excellent or NRA 95%   **Gd** = Good or NRA 68%

INDEX